Primis Content Center

McGraw-Hill's Primis Online gives you access to the world's be_____ur fingertips. With a few mouse clicks, you can create customized le_____ably. When you adopt a Primis Online text, you decide the best format for _____ **ed black-and-white or electronic books.**

McGraw-Hill's Primis Online includes most all of our market-leading textbooks, as well as, the most extensive case collection available. We feature over 9,000 case studies from prominent case providers such as Harvard Business School Publishing, Ivey, Darden, and Thunderbird. We also offer exclusive McGraw-Hill cases through our Dess/Lumpkin/Eisner and Pinnacle collections. You are free to mix and match text and case content in whatever way best suits your student's needs. Some ideas to consider:

- Combine chapters from more than one McGraw-Hill textbook.
- Delete chapters that you do not cover.
- Include special readings or assignments with textbook chapters.
- Change the order of chapters to perfectly match your syllabus.
- Add your syllabus, lecture notes or PowerPoints to the textbook.
- Combine chapters from the Study Guide to the custom book.

For your convenience we have cross-referenced the cases throughout our collection and organized them both topically and alphabetically. Details on the origins of the cases are found in the source information.

If you are looking for a particular case by name or number, use the search function at the top right of the screen.

Feel free to use the Primis site to do any of these things now at: http://www.primisonline.com or http://www.primisonline.com/dess. Build as many complimentary books as you like. There is no obligation. Printed book will arrive at your door in about a week. Ebooks only take about 24 hours.

If you adopt a printed version, students can purchase the text through your local campus bookstore.

If you adopt and electronic book, students can buy their course materials online from our eBookstore at http://ebooks.primisonline.com.

Custom Printed Books or eBooks

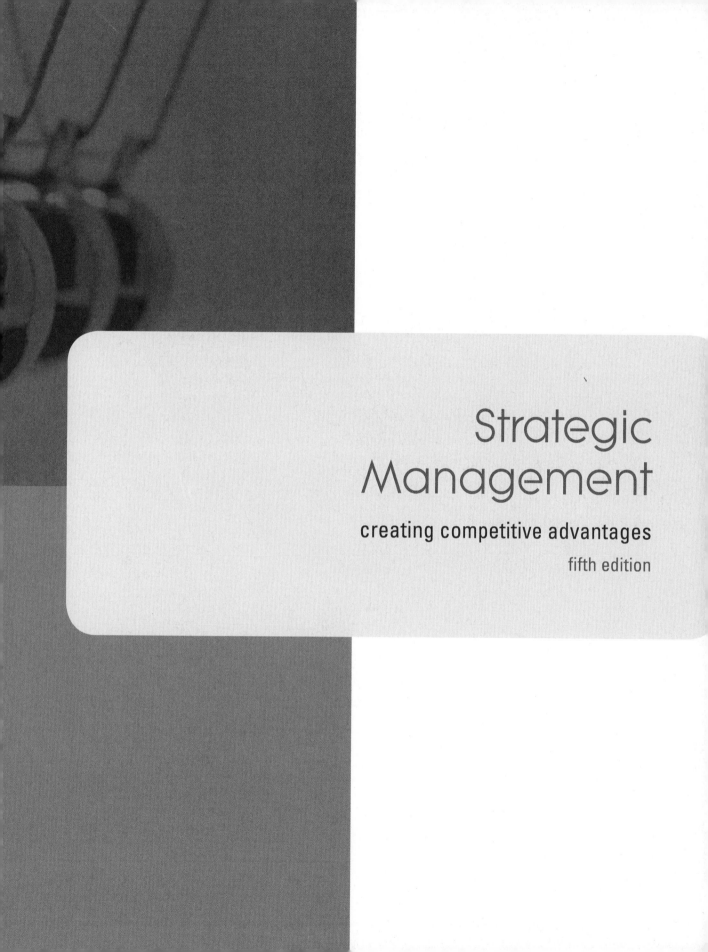

Strategic Management

creating competitive advantages

fifth edition

Gregory G. Dess
University of Texas
at Dallas

G. T. Lumpkin
Syracuse University

Alan B. Eisner
Pace University

Strategic Management

creating competitive advantages

fifth edition

McGraw-Hill Irwin

The McGraw-Hill Companies

McGraw-Hill
Irwin

STRATEGIC MANAGEMENT: CREATING COMPETITIVE ADVANTAGES

Published by McGraw-Hill/Irwin, a business unit of The McGraw-Hill Companies, Inc., 1221 Avenue of the Americas, New York, NY, 10020. Copyright © 2010, 2008, 2007, 2006, 2004 by The McGraw-Hill Companies, Inc. All rights reserved. No part of this publication may be reproduced or distributed in any form or by any means, or stored in a database or retrieval system, without the prior written consent of The McGraw-Hill Companies, Inc., including, but not limited to, in any network or other electronic storage or transmission, or broadcast for distance learning.

Some ancillaries, including electronic and print components, may not be available to customers outside the United States.

This book is printed on acid-free paper.

2 3 4 5 6 7 8 9 0 DOW/DOW 1 0 9 8 7 6 5 4 3 2 1 0

ISBN 978-0-07-724626-6
MHID 0-07-724626-8

Vice president and editor-in-chief: *Brent Gordon*
Publisher: *Paul Ducham*
Executive editor: *Michael Ablassmeir*
Director of development: *Ann Torbert*
Development editor II: *Laura Griffin*
Development editor: *Kelly I. Pekelder*
Vice president and director of marketing: *Robin J. Zwettler*
Senior marketing manager: *Anke Braun Weekes*
Vice president of editing, design and production: *Sesha Bolisetty*
Senior project manager: *Harvey Yep*
Senior production supervisor: *Debra R. Sylvester*
Cover and Interior designer: *Pam Verros*
Senior photo research coordinator: *Jeremy Cheshareck*
Senior media project manager: *Susan Lombardi*
Cover image: © istockphoto
Typeface: *10/12 Times Roman*
Compositor: *Laserwords Private Limited*
Printer: *R. R. Donnelley*

Library of Congress Cataloging-in-Publication Data

Dess, Gregory G.
    Strategic management : creating competitive advantages / Gregory
G. Dess, G. T. Lumpkin, Alan B. Eisner. — 5th ed.
      p. cm.
    Includes index.
    ISBN-13: 978-0-07-724626-6 (alk. paper)
    ISBN-10: 0-07-724626-8 (alk. paper)
    1. Strategic planning. I. Lumpkin, G. T. II. Eisner, Alan B.
III. Title.
HD30.28.D4743 2010
658.4'012—dc22
                            2009026612

www.mhhe.com

Dedication

To my family, Margie and Taylor;
my parents, Bill and Mary Dess;
and Michael O'Brien
–Greg

To my lovely wife, Vicki,
and my students and colleagues
–Tom

To my family, Helaine,
Rachel, and Jacob
–Alan

About the Authors

Gregory G. Dess is the Andrew R. Cecil Endowed Chair in Management at the University of Texas at Dallas. His primary research interests are in strategic management, organization–environment relationships, and knowledge management. He has published numerous articles on these subjects in both academic and practitioner-oriented journals. He also serves on the editorial boards of a wide range of practitioner-oriented and academic journals. In August 2000, he was inducted into the *Academy of Management Journal*'s Hall of Fame as one of its charter members. Professor Dess has conducted executive programs in the United States, Europe, Africa, Hong Kong, and Australia. In December 2009, he will receive an honorary doctorate from the university of Bern (Switzerland). During 1994 he was a Fulbright Scholar in Oporto, Portugal. He received his PhD in Business Administration from the University of Washington (Seattle) and a BIE degree from Georgia Tech.

G. T. (Tom) Lumpkin is the Chris J. Witting Chair and Professor of Entrepreneurship at Syracuse University in New York. Prior to joining the faculty at Syracuse, Tom was the Kent Hance Endowed Chair and Professor of Entrepreneurship at Texas Tech University. His research interests include entrepreneurial orientation, opportunity recognition, strategy-making processes, social entrepreneurship, and innovative forms of organizing work. He has published numerous research articles in journals such as *Strategic Management Journal, Academy of Management Journal, Academy of Management Review, Journal of Business Venturing,* and *Entrepreneurship: Theory and Practice.* He is a member of the editorial review boards of *Strategic Entrepreneurship Journal, Entrepreneurship Theory & Practice,* and the *Journal of Business Venturing.* He received his PhD in management from the University of Texas at Arlington and MBA from the University of Southern California.

Alan B. Eisner is Professor of Management and Graduate Management Program Chair at the Lubin School of Business, Pace University. He received his PhD in management from the Stern School of Business, New York University. His primary research interests are in strategic management, technology management, organizational learning, and managerial decision making. He has published research articles and cases in journals such as *Advances in Strategic Management, International Journal of Electronic Commerce, International Journal of Technology Management, American Business Review, Journal of Behavioral and Applied Management,* and *Journal of the International Academy for Case Studies.* He is the Associate Editor of the Case Association's peer reviewed journal, *The CASE Journal.*

Preface

Welcome to the Fifth Edition of *Strategic Management: Creating Competitive Advantages*! We're very pleased with the positive market response of our previous editions. We are also most appreciative of the extensive and constructive feedback that many strategy professionals have taken the time to give us. We are always striving to improve our work, and many of their ideas have been incorporated into the Fifth Edition as well as previous editions. We are happy to acknowledge these many contributors later in the Preface.

Let's briefly revisit a fundamental question: Why did we write the book in the first place? We would all agree that there have always been some solid strategy books in the market. However, we felt that there was a strong need for a book that students and faculty would think satisfied the three *R*'s that we always kept in mind during our work: relevant, rigorous, and readable. That is, our tagline has become: "Strong enough for the professor, but made for the student," and we have consistently received such feedback from faculty who have used our book. Perhaps Professor Stephen Vitucci (Tarleton State University) said it best:

> I want it to be rigorous but something that they can read and understand. The Dess, Lumpkin, and Eisner text I am currently using is exactly what I like and, more importantly, what my students need and like.

We were also recently contacted by Liz Welch and Sabina Nawaz, former General Manager and Senior Director, respectively, at Microsoft. They are now external consultants who conduct course offerings for Microsoft, several divisions of ITT, and other well-known firms. The author team was very gratified by their strong support of our text which we feel verifies "external validity" and practical relevance of our work:

> As organizational and leadership development consultants, we are always looking for great tools, case studies, and examples to better deliver core strategy concepts to our clients. Not only does DLE's *Strategic Management* provide us with that, it is almost a "one-stop shop" in this regard. The book has a comprehensive conceptual model with timely, relevant, and well-researched examples and cases. We have found it to be of conceptual as well as practical use and highly recommend it to consultants and leaders alike.

To earn such praise, we strive to use an engaging writing style free of unnecessary jargon, cover all the traditional bases, and integrate some central themes—such as globalization, technology, ethics, and entrepreneurship—throughout the book that are vital in understanding strategic management in today's global economy. We draw on short examples from business practices to bring concepts to life and provide 116 Strategy Spotlights (more detailed examples in sidebars) to drive home key points.

Unlike other strategy texts, we provide three separate chapters that address timely topics about which business students should have a solid understanding. These are the role of intellectual assets in value creation (Chapter 4), entrepreneurial strategy and competitive dynamics (Chapter 8), and fostering entrepreneurship in established organizations (Chapter 12). We also provide an excellent set of cases to help students analyze, integrate, and apply strategic management concepts.

In developing *Strategic Management: Creating Competitive Advantages,* we certainly didn't forget the instructors. After all, you have a very challenging (but rewarding) job. We did our best to help you. We provide a variety of supplementary materials that should help you in class preparation and delivery. Our chapter notes, for example, do not simply summarize the material in the chapter. Rather, we always ask ourselves (consistent with the concept of strategy!): "How can we add value?" Thus, for each chapter, we provide numerous questions to pose to guide discussion, at least 12 boxed examples to supplement chapter material, and three "teaching tips" to further engage students. Also, the author team completed the entire test bank ourselves—along with the aforementioned chapter notes. That is, unlike most of our rivals, we didn't farm them out to others. We really believe that our involvement demonstrates our commitment to the entire package and helps enhance consistency and quality.

Let's now address some of the key substantive changes in the Fifth Edition. Then, we'll cover some of the major features that have been consistent throughout our editions.

What's New? Highlights of the Fifth Edition

We've endeavored to add new material to the chapters that reflects both the feedback that we have received from reviewers and the challenges and opportunities that face today's managers. This also included, of course, carefully reviewing a wide variety of books, academic journals, practitioner journals, and the business press. We've worked hard to avoid "chapter creep." That is, when we add new material, we delete others (which includes cutting redundant examples). In addition, we benefitted from the work of Rae Pinkham, a professional editor. She went over all of the chapters line-by-line to tighten our writing. The result is that we were able to update our material and add new content—and at the same time keep the chapter length about the same. We certainly appreciate her fine efforts!

Here are some of the major changes in the Fifth Edition:

- **All of the 12 opening "Learning from Mistakes" that lead off each chapter are totally new.** Unique to this text, these vignettes are all examples of what can go wrong, and they serve as an excellent vehicle for clarifying and reinforcing strategy concepts. After all, what can be learned when one simply admires perfection?
- **We have increased the number of "Strategy Spotlights" (sidebar examples) from 90 to 116.** About half of these are brand new to this edition and many of the others have been carefully updated. We were able to add more and still save some space by focusing on bringing important strategy concepts to life.
- **We have added 14 more exhibits to the text.** This, along with the two four-color pictures in each chapter (a feature that we added with the fourth edition), aids learning and improves visual appeal. To further enhance readability and impact, we work hard to write short paragraphs and provide many indented examples throughout the book.
- **"Crowdsourcing" is a new theme throughout the book.** It originated with the open-source movement, a community of developers working together to create alternatives to Microsoft's products. However, it has expanded in recent years to include many approaches in which a wide range of businesses are enlisting the masses to solve problems, suggest new products, provide feedback, and enhance demand for products and services. After introducing this theme in Chapter 1, we provide seven "Strategy Spotlights" where firms are effectively using this innovative process. For example, in Chapter 2, we discuss how Virgin Mobile USA used it for everything from designing phones to coming up with names for service plans. Chapter 3 mentions how Cookshack, a small producer of ovens for barbecue and smoked foods, used crowdsourcing to, in effect, turn its customers into its customer service department! And, in Chapter 10, we explain how Eli Lilly, the pharmaceutical giant, launched Innocentive—the first online, incentive-based scientific network for the global research and development community.
- **Our discussion of environmental sustainability has been extended throughout the text.** As noted by Daniel Esty and Andrew Winston in their award-winning book *Green to Gold:* "Environmental leaders see their businesses through an environmental lens, finding opportunities to cut costs, reduce risk, and enhance intangible

value. They build deeper connections with customers, employees, and other stakeholders."[*] Given the salience of environmental sustainability in today's global economy, we discuss this issue throughout the text—including eight "Strategy Spotlights." For example, in Chapter 1, we explain how Shaw Industries, an industrial flooring producer, used its recycling efforts to both reduce its costs and eliminate its need for PVC plastic—a potentially toxic substance. Chapter 4 discusses how "going green" helps attract talent, and Chapter 8 explains how "eco-entrepreneurs" have recycled milk jugs, tires, and jars to create playground equipment, garage flooring, and glass awards, respectively! To provide some balance on this topic, we also discuss how some energy companies have been accused of "greenwashing" (that is, making unsubstantiated claims about how environmentally friendly a firm's products are) in their sustainability programs.

Key content changes for the chapters include:

- **Chapter 1 introduces the concept of "crowdsourcing," which, as noted above, becomes a theme throughout the text.** This innovative approach to open sourcing has provided a wide variety of businesses with a new source for products, ideas, and many value-adding activities. We also illustrate the complexities inherent in the stakeholder concept by addressing the many conflicting demands faced by the world's largest retailer—Wal-Mart.
- **Chapter 1 provides a summary of the worldwide financial crisis that intensified in 2008 and 2009.** We address not only some of the root causes but also how it has dramatically affected many industries, such as automobiles, dining, retail, and technology.
- **Chapter 2 addresses some recent insights from Michael Porter on the effective use of the five-forces model of industry profitability.** In our previous editions, we discussed caveats in performing an industry analysis, such as how some firms have prospered in low-profit industries, the detrimental effects of exploiting buyer power, and the salient role of complementors in industry analysis. Now, we include Porter's new perspectives on the importance of understanding the structural underpinnings of profitability, such as an awareness of time horizons and the value of quantitative factors in performing an in-depth analysis.
- **Chapter 3 discusses how businesses can use blogs and social networking sites to enhance their reputation—or how such sites can erode key stakeholders' perceptions.** Comcast, for example, was badly hurt when an angry customer put a video on YouTube of a technician who fell asleep on his couch! However, on the bright side, firms like Southwest Airlines, Whole Foods, and the shoe store Zappos have effectively used social messaging services.
- **Chapter 5 extends our discussion of the industry life cycle concept by explaining why old technologies don't just fade away.** Using examples as diverse as mainframes, carburetors, and coronary bypass surgery, three approaches are suggested: retreating to more defensible ground, using the new to improve the old, and improving the price-performance trade-off.
- **Chapter 6 draws on the stakeholder concept to show how antitakeover measures may benefit stakeholders other than management.** Antitakeover defenses, such as poison pills, typically are viewed as simply measures to entrench and protect management. However, this is not always the case. We discuss how such defenses can also serve to protect employees, the community at large, and customers.

*Esty, D. C. & Winston, A. S. 2009. *Green to gold: How Smart Companies Use Environmental Sustainability to Innovate, Create Value, and Build Competitive Advantage.* Hoboken, NJ: Wiley, 14.

- **Chapter 7 addresses an important rationale for international expansion—taking advantage of arbitrage opportunities.** Simply put, arbitrage involves buying something where it is cheap and selling it where it commands a higher price. It can be applied to almost any factor of production and every stage of the value chain.
- **Chapter 8 (Entrepreneurial Strategy and Competitive Dynamics)** has been reconfigured to include a section on competitive dynamics that addresses the cycle of actions and responses that are initiated when a new player enters a competitive marketplace. This is a hot issue in strategy and has important implications for competitive advantage—the core topic of our book. We address competitive dynamics for such rivals as Facebook and MySpace, as well as AMD and Intel (chip makers). The first part of the chapter draws on materials that were previously part of Chapter 13 on creating new ventures.
- **Chapter 9 extends our discussion of corporate governance in the international context.** Here, we discuss "multilatinas," which have pursued a strategy of regional and international expansion. We address some of the governance and transparency issues that Latin-owned companies need to improve upon in order to ensure access to international capital markets.
- **Chapter 11 introduces the idea of integrative thinking developed in Roger Martin's book *The Opposable Mind*.** Leaders are often faced with decision alternatives that pose difficult dilemmas. The best leaders are those who avoid thinking in terms of either-or trade-offs. Instead, they seek out creative solutions that synthesize opposing perspectives.
- **Chapter 12 draws on Christensen's work on innovation.** We distinguish between *sustaining innovations* that energize markets by, for example, extending sales and *disruptive innovations* that overturn markets by providing new approaches to meeting customer needs. In rapidly changing environments, it is vital to understand how to manage different types of innovative activity.
- **Chapter 13 updates our Appendix: Sources of Company and Industry Information.** We appreciate the contributions of Ruthie Brock and Carol Byrne in providing this comprehensive information. It is organized to cover a range of issues, such as competitive intelligence, annual report collections, company rankings, business websites, and strategic and competitive analysis. It should be invaluable in analyzing companies and industries.

What Remains the Same: Key Features from Earlier Editions

Let's now briefly address some of the exciting features that remain from the earlier editions.

- **Traditional organizing framework with three other chapters on timely topics.** Crisply written chapters cover all of the strategy bases and address contemporary topics. First, the chapters are divided logically into the traditional sequence: strategy analysis, strategy formulation, and strategy implementation. Second, we include three chapters on such timely topics as intellectual capital/knowledge management, entrepreneurial strategy and competitive dynamics, and fostering corporate entrepreneurship and new ventures.
- **"Learning from Mistakes" chapter-opening cases.** To enhance student interest, we begin each chapter with a case that depicts an organization that has suffered a dramatic performance drop, or outright failure, by failing to adhere to sound strategic management concepts and principles. We believe that this feature serves to underpin the value of the concepts in the course and that it is a preferred teaching approach to merely providing examples of outstanding companies that always seem to get it right! After all,

isn't it better (and more challenging) to diagnose problems than admire perfection? As Dartmouth's Sydney Finkelstein, author of *Why Smart Executives Fail,* notes: "We live in a world where success is revered, and failure is quickly pushed to the side. However, some of the greatest opportunities to learn—both for individuals and organizations—come from studying what goes wrong."* We'll see how, for example, Motorola failed to keep up with customer expectations in the Chinese mobile-phone market and saw its market share sharply erode, how Michelin's PAX "run-flat" tire failed because they didn't create a differentiation advantage that justified the premium price, and how Richard Fuld's toxic leadership played a key role in Lehman Brothers' demise. *BusinessWeek* named Fuld one of the worst managers of 2008 and claimed that he "drove his people hard and ignored warning signs, rewarding risk and greed."

- **Consistent chapter format and features to reinforce learning.** We have included several features in each chapter to add value and create an enhanced learning experience. First, each chapter begins with an overview and a set of bullets pointing to key learning objectives. Second, as previously noted, the opening case describes a situation in which a company's performance eroded because of a lack of proper application of strategy concepts. Third, at the end of each chapter there are four different types of questions/exercises that should help students assess their understanding and application of material:

  1. Summary review questions.
  2. Experiential exercises.
  3. Application questions and exercises.
  4. Ethics questions

Given the emergence of the Internet and e-commerce, each chapter contains at least one exercise that involves the use of the Internet.

- **"Reflecting on Career Implications" for each chapter.** This feature—at the end of each chapter—will help instructors drive home the immediate relevance/value of strategy concepts. It focuses on how an understanding of key concepts helps business students early in their careers.
- **Key Terms.** Approximately a dozen key terms for each chapter are identified in the margins of the pages. This addition was made in response to reviewer feedback and improves students' understanding of core strategy concepts.
- **Clear articulation and illustration of key concepts.** Key strategy concepts are introduced in a clear and concise manner and are followed by timely and interesting examples from business practice. Such concepts include value-chain analysis, the resource-based view of the firm, Porter's five-forces model, competitive advantage, boundaryless organizational designs, digital strategies, corporate governance, ethics, and entrepreneurship.
- **Extensive use of sidebars.** We include over 90 sidebars (or about six per chapter) called "Strategy Spotlights." The Strategy Spotlights not only illustrate key points but also increase the readability and excitement of new strategy concepts.
- **Integrative themes.** The text provides a solid grounding in ethics, globalization, and technology. These topics are central themes throughout the book and form the basis for many of the Strategy Spotlights.
- **Implications of concepts for small businesses.** Many of the key concepts are applied to start-up firms and smaller businesses, which is particularly important since many students have professional plans to work in such firms.
- **Not just a textbook but an entire package.** *Strategic Management* features the best chapter teaching notes available today. Rather than merely summarizing the key

*Personal communication, June 20, 2005.

points in each chapter, we focus on value-added material to enhance the teaching (and learning) experience. Each chapter includes dozens of questions to spur discussion, teaching tips, in-class group exercises, and about a dozen detailed examples from business practice to provide further illustrations of key concepts.

Student Support Materials

- **Online Learning Center (OLC)** The following resources are available to students via the publisher's OLC at www.mhhe.com/dess5e:
    - Chapter quizzes students can take to gauge their understanding of material covered in each chapter.
    - A selection of PowerPoint slides for each chapter.
    - Links to strategy simulations the Business Strategy Game & GLO-BUS. Both provide a powerful and constructive way of connecting students to the subject matter of the course with a competition among classmates on campus and around the world.

Instructor Support Materials

- **Instructor's Manual (IM).** Prepared by the textbook authors, the accompanying IM contains summary/objectives, lecture/discussion outlines, discussion questions, extra examples not included in the text, teaching tips, reflecting on career implications, experiential exercises, and more.
- **Test Bank.** Prepared by the authors, the test bank contains more than 1,000 true/false, multiple-choice, and essay questions. It has now been tagged with learning objectives as well as Bloom's Taxonomy and AACSB criteria.

Assurance of Learning Ready. Assurance of Learning is an important element of many accreditation standards. Dess 5e is designed specifically to support your Assurance of Learning initiatives. Each chapter in the book begins with a list of numbered learning objectives that appear throughout the chapter, as well as in the end-of-chapter questions and exercises. Every test bank question is also linked to one of these objectives, in addition to level of difficulty, topic area, Bloom's Taxonomy level, and AACSB skill area. *EZ Test,* McGraw-Hill's easy-to-use test bank software, can search the test bank by these and other categories, providing an engine for targeted Assurance of Learning analysis and assessment.

AACSB Statement. The McGraw-Hill Companies is a proud corporate member of AACSB International. Understanding the importance and value of AACSB accreditation, Dess 5e has sought to recognize the curricula guidelines detailed in the AACSB standards for business accreditation by connecting selected questions in Dess 5e and the test bank to the general knowledge and skill guidelines found in the AACSB standards. The statements contained in Dess 5e are provided only as a guide for the users of this text. The AACSB leaves content coverage and assessment within the purview of individual schools, the mission of the school, and the faculty. While Dess 5e and the teaching package make no claim of any specific AACSB qualification or evaluation, we have labeled selected questions within Dess 5e according to the six general knowledge and skills areas.

Computerized Test Bank Online. A comprehensive bank of test questions is provided within a computerized test bank powered by McGraw-Hill's flexible electronic testing program, *EZ Test Online* (www.eztestonline.com). *EZ Test Online* allows you to create paper and online tests or quizzes in this easy-to-use program! Imagine being able to create and access your test or quiz anywhere, at any time without installing the testing software. Now, with *EZ Test Online,* instructors can select questions from multiple McGraw-Hill test banks or author their own, and then either print the test for paper distribution or give it online.

Test Creation.
- Author/edit questions online using the 14 different question type templates.
- Create printed tests or deliver online to get instant scoring and feedback.
- Create questions pools to offer multiple versions online – great for practice.
- Export your tests for use in *WebCT, Blackboard, PageOut,* and Apple's *iQuiz.*
- Compatible with *EZ Test Desktop* tests you've already created.
- Sharing tests with colleagues, adjuncts, TAs is easy.

Online Test Management.
- Set availability dates and time limits for your quiz or test.
- Control how your test will be presented.
- Assign points by question or question type with drop down menu.
- Provide immediate feedback to students or delay until all finish the test.
- Create practice tests online to enable student mastery.
- Your roster can be uploaded to enable student self-registration.

Online Scoring and Reporting.
- Automated scoring for most of *EZ Test*'s numerous question types.
- Allows manual scoring for essay and other open response questions.
- Manual rescoring and feedback is also available.
- *EZ Test*'s grade book is designed to easily export to your grade book.
- View basic statistical reports.

Support and Help.
- User's guide and built-in page-specific help.
- Flash tutorials for getting started on the support site.
- Support website: www.mhhe.com/eztest.
- Product specialist available at 1-800-331-5094.
- Online Training: http://auth.mhhe.com/mpss/workshops/.

- **PowerPoint Presentation.** Prepared by Brad Cox of Midlands Tech, it consists of more than 400 slides incorporating an outline for the chapters tied to learning objectives. Also included are multiple-choice questions that can be used as Classroom Performance System (CPS) questions as well as additional examples outside of the text to promote class discussion.
- **Instructor's Resource CD-ROM.** All instructor supplements are available in this one-stop multimedia resource, which includes the Instructor's Manual, Test Bank, and PowerPoint Presentations.
- **Online Learning Center (OLC).** The instructor section of www.mhhe.com/dess5e also includes the Instructor's Manual, PowerPoint Presentations, and additional resources.
- **The Business Strategy Game and GLO-BUS Online Simulations.** Both allow teams of students to manage companies in a head-to-head contest for global market leadership. These simulations give students the immediate opportunity to experiment with various strategy options and to gain proficiency in applying the concepts and tools they have been reading about in the chapters. To find out more or to register, please visit www.mmhe.com/thompsonsims.

Additional Resources

- **McGraw-Hill/Primis Custom Publishing.** You can customize this text. McGraw-Hill/Primis Online's digital database offers you the flexibility to customize your course, including material from the largest online collection of textbooks, readings, and cases. Primis leads the way in customized eBooks with hundreds of titles available at prices that save your students over 20 percent off bookstore prices. For more information, please visit www.primisonline.com/dess or call 800-228-0634.

- **Dess in eBook format.** With the CourseSmart eTextbook, students can save up to 45 percent off the cost of a print book, reduce their impact on the environment, and access powerful Web tools for learning. Faculty can review and compare the full text online without having to wait for a print desk copy. CourseSmart is an online eTextbook, which means users access and view their textbook online when connected to the Internet or download to their computer. With an eBook, students can do the following:

  - Search the entire book with the click of a button.
  - Highlight, make notes, and share them with their friends.
  - Print only the pages needed for maximum portability.
  - Try a free chapter to see whether they're right for them.

  eBooks also include tech support in case help is ever needed. Finding your eBook is easy. Visit www.CourseSmart.com and search by title, author, or ISBN.

- *BusinessWeek* **subscription.** Students can subscribe to *BusinessWeek* for a special rate in addition to the price of the text. Students will receive a passcode card shrink-wrapped with their new text. The card directs students to a Web site where they enter the code and then gain access to *BusinessWeek's* registration page to enter their address information and set up their print and online subscription. please ask your McGraw-Hill/Irwin representative for more information.

Acknowledgments

Strategic Management represents far more than just the joint efforts of the three co-authors. Rather, it is the product of the collaborative input of many people. Some of these individuals are academic colleagues, others are the outstanding team of professionals at McGraw-Hill/Irwin, and still others are those who are closest to us—our families. It is time to express our sincere gratitude.

First, we'd like to acknowledge the dedicated instructors who have graciously provided their insights since the inception of the text. Their input has been very helpful in both pointing out errors in the manuscript and suggesting areas that needed further development as additional topics. We sincerely believe that the incorporation of their ideas has been critical to improving the final product. These professionals and their affiliations are:

The Reviewer Hall of Fame

Moses Acquaah, *University of North Carolina–Greensboro*

Todd Alessandri, *Syracuse University*

Larry Alexander, *Virginia Polytechnic Institute*

Brent B. Allred, *College of William & Mary*

Allen C. Amason, *University of Georgia*

Kathy Anders, *Arizona State University*

Peter H. Antoniou, *California State University, San Marcos*

Dave Arnott, *Dallas Baptist University*

Marne L. Arthaud-Day, *Kansas State University*

Jay Azriel, *York University of Pennsylvania*

Jeffrey J. Bailey, *University of Idaho*

Bruce Barringer, *University of Central Florida*

Barbara R. Bartkus, *Old Dominion University*

Barry Bayon, *Bryant University*

Brent D. Beal, *Louisiana State University*

Joyce Beggs, *University of North Carolina–Charlotte*

Michael Behnam, *Suffolk University*

Kristen Bell DeTienne, *Brigham Young University*

Eldon Bernstein, *Lynn University*

Dusty Bodie, *Boise State University*

William Bogner, *Georgia State University*

Jon Bryan, *Bridgewater State College*

Charles M. Byles, *Virginia Commonwealth University*

Mikelle A. Calhoun, *Valparaiso University*

Thomas J. Callahan, *University of Michigan, Dearborn*

Samuel D. Cappel, *Southeastern Louisiana State University*

Gary Carini, *Baylor University*

Shawn M. Carraher, *Texas A&M University, Commerce*

Tim Carroll, *University of South Carolina*

Don Caruth, *Amberton University*

Maureen Casile, *Bowling Green State University*

Gary J. Castrogiovanni, *Florida Atlantic University*

Radha Chaganti, *Rider University*

Theresa Cho, *Rutgers University*

Bruce Clemens, *Western New England College*

Betty S. Coffey, *Appalachian State University*

Wade Coggins, *Webster University, Fort Smith Metro Campus*

Susan Cohen, *University of Pittsburgh*

George S. Cole, *Shippensburg University*

Joseph Coombs, *Texas A & M University*

Christine Cope Pence, *University of California, Riverside*

James J. Cordeiro, *SUNY Brockport*

Jeffrey Covin, *Indiana University*

Keith Credo, *Auburn University*

Deepak Datta, *University of Texas at Arlington*

James Davis, *University of Notre Dame*

David Dawley, *West Virginia University*

Helen Deresky, *State University of New York, Plattsburgh*

Rocki-Lee DeWitt, *University of Vermont*

Jay Dial, *Ohio State University*

Michael E. Dobbs, *Arkansas State University*

Jonathan Doh, *Villanova University*

Tom Douglas, *Clemson University*

Jon Down, *Oregon State University*

Alan E. Ellstrand, *University of Arkansas*

Dean S. Elmuti, *Eastern Illinois University*

Clare Engle, *Concordia University*

Tracy Ethridge, *Tri-County Technical College*

William A. Evans, *Troy State University, Dothan*

Frances H. Fabian, *University of Memphis*

Angelo Fanelli, *Warrington College of Business*

Michael Fathi, *Georgia Southwestern University*

Carolyn J. Fausnaugh, *Florida Institute of Technology*

Tamela D. Ferguson, *University of Louisiana at Lafayette*

David Flanagan, *Western Michigan University*

Isaac Fox, *University of Minnesota*

Deborah Francis, *Brevard College*

Steven A. Frankforter, *Winthrop University*

Vance Fried, *Oklahoma State University*

Naomi A. Gardberg, *CNNY Baruch College*

J. Michael Geringer, *California Polytechnic State University*

Diana L. Gilbertson, *California State University, Fresno*

Matt Gilley, *St. Mary's University*

Debora Gilliard, *Metropolitan State College of Denver*

Yezdi H. Godiwalla, *University of Wisconsin–Whitewater*

Sanjay Goel, *University of Minnesota, Duluth*

Sandy Gough, *Boise State University*

Allen Harmon, *University of Minnesota, Duluth*

Niran Harrison, *University of Oregon*

Paula Harveston, *Berry College*

Donald Hatfield, *Virginia Polytechnic Institute*

Kim Hester, *Arkansas State University*

John Hironaka, *California State University, Sacramento*

Alan Hoffman, *Bentley College*

Gordon Holbein, *University of Kentucky*

Stephen V. Horner, *Arkansas State University*

Jill Hough, *University of Tulsa*

John Humphreys, *Eastern New Mexico University*

James G. Ibe, *Morris College*

Jay J. Janney, *University of Dayton*

Lawrence Jauch, *University of Louisiana–Monroe*

Dana M. Johnson, *Michigan Technical University*

Homer Johnson, *Loyola University, Chicago*

James Katzenstein, *California State University, Dominguez Hills*

Franz Kellermanns, *Mississippi State University*

Craig Kelley, *California State University, Sacramento*

Donna Kelley, *Babson College*

Dave Ketchen, *Auburn University*

John A. Kilpatrick, *Idaho State University*

Helaine J. Korn, *Baruch College,CUNY*

Stan Kowalczyk, *San Francisco State University*

Daniel Kraska, *North Central State College*

Donald E. Kreps, *Kutztown University*

Jim Kroeger, *Cleveland State University*

Subdoh P. Kulkarni, *Howard University*

Ron Lambert, *Faulkner University*

Theresa Lant, *New York University*

Ted Legatski, *Texas Christian University*

David J. Lemak, *Washington State University–Tri-Cities*

Cynthia Lengnick-Hall, *University of Texas at San Antonio*

Donald L. Lester, *Arkansas State University*

Wanda Lester, *North Carolina A&T State University*

Benyamin Lichtenstein, *University of Massachusetts at Boston*

Jun Lin, *SUNY at New Paltz*

Zhiang (John) Lin, *University of Texas at Dallas*

Dan Lockhart, *University of Kentucky*

John Logan, *University of South Carolina*

Kevin Lowe, *University of North Carolina, Greensboro*

Doug Lyon, *Fort Lewis College*

Hao Ma, *Bryant College*

Rickey Madden, *Ph.D., Presbyterian College*

James Maddox, *Friends University*

Ravi Madhavan, *University of Pittsburgh*

Paul Mallette, *Colorado State University*

Santo D. Marabella, *Moravian College*

Catherine Maritan, *Syracuse University*

Daniel Marrone, *Farmingdale State College, SUNY*

Sarah Marsh, *Northern Illinois University*

John R. Massaua, *University of Southern Maine*

Larry McDaniel, *Alabama A&M University*

Abagail McWilliams, *University of Illinois, Chicago*

John E. Merchant, *California State University, Sacramento*

John M. Mezias, *University of Miami*

Michael Michalisin, *Southern Illinois University at Carbondale*

Doug Moesel, *University of Missouri–Columbia*

Fatma Mohamed, *Morehead State University*

Debra Moody, *University of North Carolina, Charlotte*

Gregory A. Moore, *Middle Tennessee State University*

James R. Morgan, *Dominican University and UC Berkeley Extension*

Sara A. Morris, *Old Dominion University*

Carolyn Mu, *Baylor University*

Stephen Mueller, *Northern Kentucky University*

John Mullane, *Middle Tennessee State University*

Gerry Nkombo Muuka, *Murray State University*

Anil Nair, *Old Dominion University*

V.K. Narayanan, *Drexel University*

Maria L. Nathan, *Lynchburg College*

Louise Nemanich, *Arizona State University*

Charles Newman, *University of Maryland, University College*

Stephanie Newport, *Austin Peay State University*

Bill Norton, *University of Louisville*

Yusuf A. Nur, *SUNY Brockport*

Jeffrey R. Nystrom, *University of Colorado*

d.t. ogilvie, *Rutgers University*

Floyd Ormsbee, *Clarkson University*

Karen L. Page, *University of Wyoming*

Jacquelyn W. Palmer, *University of Cincinnati*

Julie Palmer, *University of Missouri, Columbia*

Daewoo Park, *Xavier University*

Gerald Parker, *Saint Louis University*

Ralph Parrish, *University of Central Oklahoma*

Douglas K. Peterson, *Indiana State University*

Edward Petkus, *Mary Baldwin College*

Michael C. Pickett, *National University*

Peter Ping Li, *California State University, Stanislaus*

Michael W. Pitts, *Virginia Commonwealth University*

Laura Poppo, *Virginia Tech*

Steve Porth, *Saint Joseph's University*

Jodi A. Potter, *Robert Morris University*

Scott A. Quatro, *Grand Canyon University*

Nandini Rajagopalan, *University of Southern California*

Annette L. Ranft, *Florida State University*

Abdul Rasheed, *University of Texas at Arlington*

George Redmond, *Franklin University*

Kira Reed, *Syracuse University*

Clint Relyea, *Arkansas State University*

Barbara Ribbens, *Western Illinois University*

Maurice Rice, *University of Washington*

Violina P. Rindova, *University of Maryland, College Park*

Ron Rivas, *Canisius College*

David Robinson, *Indiana State University– Terre Haute*

Kenneth Robinson, *Kennesaw State University*

Simon Rodan, *San Jose State University*

Patrick R. Rogers, *North Carolina A&T State University*

John K. Ross III, *Texas State University, San Marcos*

Robert Rottman, *Kentucky State University*

Matthew R. Rutherford, *Gonzaga University*

Carol M. Sanchez, *Grand Valley State University*

William W. Sannwald, *San Diego State University*

Yolanda Sarason, *Colorado State University*

Marguerite Schneider, *New Jersey Institute of Technology*

Roger R. Schnorbus, *University of Richmond*

Terry Sebora, *University of Nebraska– Lincoln*

John Seeger, *Bentley College*

Jamal Shamsie, *Michigan State University*

Mark Shanley, *University of Illinois at Chicago*

Lois Shelton, *California State University, Northridge*

Herbert Sherman, *Long Island University*

Chris Shook, *Auburn University*

Jeremy Short, *Texas Tech University*

Mark Simon, *Oakland University, Michigan*

Rob Singh, *Morgan State University*

Bruce Skaggs, *University of Kentucky*

Wayne Smeltz, *Rider University*

Anne Smith, *University of Tennessee*

Andrew Spicer, *University of South Carolina*

James D. Spina, *University of Maryland*

John Stanbury, *George Mason University & Inter-University Institute of Macau, SAR China*

Timothy Stearns, *California State University, Fresno*

Elton Stephen, *Austin State University*

Alice Stewart, *Ohio State University*

Ram Subramanian, *Grand Valley State University*

Roy Suddaby, *University of Iowa*

Michael Sullivan, *UC Berkeley Extension*

Marta Szabo White, *Georgia State University*

Justin Tan, *York University, Canada*

Qingju Tao, *Lehigh University*

Linda Teagarden, *Virginia Tech*

Bing-Sheng Teng, *George Washington University*

Alan Theriault, *University of California–Riverside*

Tracy Thompson, *University of Washington, Tacoma*

Karen Torres, *Angelo State University*

Robert Trumble, *Virginia Commonwealth University*

K.J. Tullis, *University of Central Oklahoma*

Craig A. Turner, *Ph.D., East Tennessee State University*

Beverly Tyler, *North Carolina State University*

Rajaram Veliyath, *Kennesaw State University*

S. Stephen Vitucci, *Tarleton State University–Central Texas*

Jay A. Vora, *St. Cloud State University*

Jorge Walter, *Portland State University*

Bruce Walters, *Louisiana Tech University*

Edward Ward, *St. Cloud State University*

N. Wasilewski, *Pepperdine University*

Andrew Watson, *Northeastern University*

Larry Watts, *Stephen F. Austin University*

Paula S. Weber, *St. Cloud State University*

Kenneth E. A. Wendeln, *Indiana University*

Robert R. Wharton, *Western Kentucky University*

Laura Whitcomb, *California State University–Los Angeles*

Scott Williams, *Wright State University*

Diana Wong, *Bowling Green State University*

Beth Woodard, *Belmont University*

John E. Wroblewski, *State University of New York–Fredonia*

Anne York, *Creighton University*

Michael Zhang, *Sacred Heart University*

Monica Zimmerman, *Temple University*

Second, the authors would like to thank several faculty colleagues who were particularly helpful in the review, critique, and development of the book and supplementary materials. Greg's colleagues at the University of Texas at Dallas also have been helpful and supportive. These individuals include Mike Peng, Joe Picken, Kumar Nair, John Lin, Seung-Hyun Lee, Tev Dalgic, and Jane Salk. His administrative assistant, Mary Vice, has been extremely helpful. Former MBA student Naga Damaraju, along with two doctoral students, Brian Pinkham and Erin Pleggenkuhle-Miles, have provided many useful inputs and ideas. He also appreciates the support of his dean and associate dean, Hasan Pirkul and Varghese Jacob, respectively. Tom would like to thank Gerry Hills, Abagail McWilliams, Darold Barnum, Mike Miller, Rod Shrader, James Gillespie, Lou Coco, and other colleagues at the University of Illinois at Chicago, for their continued support. Tom also thanks Kim Boal, Keith Brigham, Will Gunderson, Joe Lee, Alejandra Marin, Todd Moss, Tyge Payne, Jeremy Short, Don Stull, Bill Wan, Abby Wang, Andy Yu, Nikki Bohannon, Bill Gardner, Emily Herrin, Beck Lopez, and Ron Mitchell at Texas Tech University for their support. Special thanks also to Jeff Stambaugh for his vital contribution to new materials prepared for the Fourth Edition. Tom also extends a special thanks to Benyamin Lichtenstein for his support and encouragement. Both Greg and Tom wish to thank a special colleague, Abdul Rasheed at the University of Texas at Arlington, who certainly has been a valued source of friendship and ideas for us for many years. He provided many valuable contributions to the Fifth Edition. Alan thanks his colleagues at Pace University and the Case Association for their support in developing these fine case selections. Special thanks go to Jamal Shamsie at Michigan State University for his support in developing the case selections for this edition. And we appreciate Doug Sanford, at University of Towson for his expertise with one of our new pedagogical features—the key terms in each chapter.

Third, we would like to thank the team at McGraw-Hill/Irwin for their outstanding support throughout the process. This begins with John Biernat, formerly Publisher, who signed us to our original contract. John was always available to provide support and valued input during the entire process. In editorial, executive editor Mike Ablassmeir, development editor Laura Griffin, and editorial coordinator Kelly Pekelder, kept things on track, responded quickly to our never-ending needs and requests, and offered insights and encouragement. Once the manuscript was completed and revised, senior project manager Harvey Yep expertly guided us through the production process. Susan Lombardi did an outstanding job in helping us with the supplementary materials. Jeremy Cheshareck, senior photo research coordinator, and freelance designer Pam Verros provided excellent design photo, and art work. We also appreciate executive marketing manager Anke Weekes and marketing coordinator Annie Ferro for their energetic, competent, and thorough marketing efforts. Last, but certainly not least, we thank MHI's 70 plus outstanding book reps—who serve on the "front lines." Clearly, they deserve a lot of credit for our success.

Finally, we would like to thank our families. For Greg this includes his parents, William and Mary Dess, who have always been there for him. His wife, Margie, and daughter, Taylor, have been a constant source of love and companionship. Greg would also like to recognize Michael O'Brien. He was one of my first mentors—which took place in Seoul, Korea. I was attending high school there while my father served in the U.S. Air Force. Mike didn't have to lecture us on leadership and other management concepts—he led by example. He's a person with *many* friends and no enemies! Tom thanks his wife Vicki for her constant love and companionship. Tom also thanks Lee Hetherington and Thelma Lumpkin for their inspiration, as well as his mom Katy, and his sister Kitty, for a lifetime of support. Alan thanks his family—his wife Helaine and his children Rachel and Jacob—for their love and support. He also thanks his parents, Gail Eisner and the late Marvin Eisner, for their support and encouragement.

guided tour

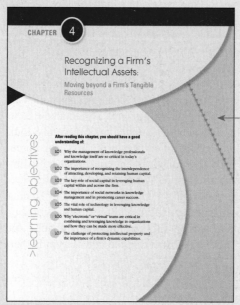

Learning Objectives

Learning Objectives now numbered LO1, LO2, LO3, etc. with corresponding icons in the margins to indicate where learning objectives are covered in the text.

Learning from Mistakes

Learning from Mistakes are examples of where things went wrong. Failures are not only interesting but also sometimes easier to learn from. And students realize strategy is not just about "right or wrong" answers, but requires critical thinking.

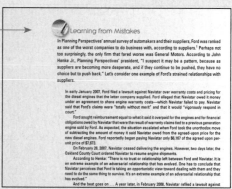

Strategy Spotlight

These boxes weave themes of ethics, globalization, and technology into every chapter of the text, providing students with a thorough grounding necessary for understanding strategic management. Select boxes incorporating crowdsourcing or environmental sustainability theme include the following icons:

Key Terms

Key Terms defined in the margins have been added to improve students' understanding of core strategy concepts.

stakeholder management A firm's strategy for recognizing and responding to the interests of all its salient stakeholders.

Reflecting on Career Implications

This new section before the summary of every chapter consists of examples on how understanding of key concepts helps business students early in their careers.

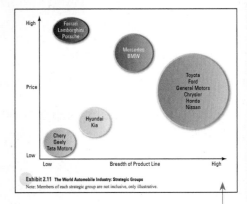

Exhibit 2.11 **The World Automobile Industry: Strategic Groups**
Note: Members of each strategic group are not inclusive, only illustrative.

Exhibits

Both new and improved exhibits in every chapter provide visual presentations of the most complex concepts covered to support student comprehension.

Reflecting on Career Implications . . .

- *Attributes of Strategic Management:* How do your activities and actions contribute to the goals of your organization? Observe the decisions you make on the job. What are the short-term and long-term implications of your decisions and actions? Have you recently made a decision that might yield short-term profits but might negatively impact the long-term goals of the organization (e.g., cutting maintenance expenses to meet a quarterly profit target)?
- *Intended versus Emergent Strategies:* Don't be too inflexible in your career strategies; strive to take advantage of new opportunities as they arise. Many promising career opportunities may "emerge" that were not part of your intended career strategy or your specific job assignment. Take initiative by pursuing opportunities to get additional training (e.g., learn a software or a statistical package), volunteering for a short-term overseas assignment, etc.
- *Ambidexterity:* Avoid defining your role in the organization too narrowly; look for opportunities to leverage your talents and your organization's resources to create value for your organization. This often involves collaborating with people in other departments or with your organization's customers and suppliers.
- *Strategic Coherence:* Focus your efforts on the "big picture" in your organization. In doing this, you should always strive to assure that your efforts are directed toward your organization's vision, mission, and strategic objectives.

support materials

Online Learning Center (OLC)

The website www.mhhe.com/dess5e follows the text chapter-by-chapter. OLC content is ancillary and supplementary germane to the textbook. As students read the book, they can go online to take self-grading quizzes, review material, or work through interactive exercises. It includes chapter quizzes, student PowerPoint slides, and links to strategy simulations The *Business Strategy Game* and GLO-BUS.

The instructor section also includes the Instructor's Manual, PowerPoint Presentations, Case Study Teaching Notes, Interactive Case Grid, Video Guide, and Case Web Links as well as all student resources.

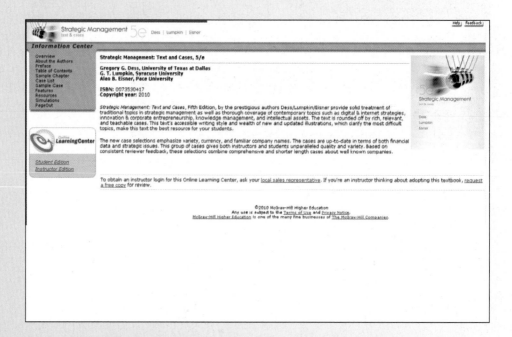

Brief Contents

part 1 Strategic Analysis

1 Strategic Management: Creating Competitive Advantages 2

2 Analyzing the External Environment of the Firm 38

3 Assessing the Internal Environment of the Firm 78

4 Recognizing a Firm's Intellectual Assets: Moving beyond a Firm's Tangible Resources 118

part 2 Strategic Formulation

5 Business-Level Strategy: Creating and Sustaining Competitive Advantages 156

6 Corporate-Level Strategy: Creating Value through Diversification 194

7 International Strategy: Creating Value in Global Markets 232

8 Entrepreneurial Strategy and Competitive Dynamics 270

part 3 Strategic Implementation

9 Strategic Control and Corporate Governance 310

10 Creating Effective Organizational Designs 346

11 Strategic Leadership: Creating a Learning Organization and an Ethical Organization 382

12 Managing Innovation and Fostering Corporate Entrepreneurship 424

part 4 Case Analysis

13 Analyzing Strategic Management Cases 462

Indexes *I-1*

Contents

part 1 Strategic Analysis

Chapter 1
Strategic Management: Creating Competitive Advantages 2

What Is Strategic Management? 9

Defining Strategic Management 9
The Four Key Attributes of Strategic Management 10

The Strategic Management Process 12

Intended versus Realized Strategies 13
Strategy Analysis 13
Strategy Formulation 15
Strategy Implementation 16

**The Role of Corporate Governance
    and Stakeholder Management** 16

Alternative Perspectives of Stakeholder Management . . . 18
*Social Responsibility and Environmental
    Sustainability: Moving beyond the Immediate
    Stakeholders* 21

**The Strategic Management Perspective:
An Imperative throughout the Organization** . . . 24

Ensuring Coherence in Strategic Direction 25

Organizational Vision 26
Mission Statements 28
Strategic Objectives 29
Summary 32

Chapter 2
Analyzing the External Environment of the Firm. 38

**Creating the Environmentally Aware
    Organization** 41

*The Role of Scanning, Monitoring, Competitive
Intelligence, and Forecasting* 41
SWOT Analysis 47

The General Environment 47

The Demographic Segment 49
The Sociocultural Segment 49
The Political/Legal Segment 50
The Technological Segment 51
The Economic Segment 52
The Global Segment 52
*Relationships among Elements of the
    General Environment* 53

The Competitive Environment 56

Porter's Five-Forces Model of Industry Competition 56
*How the Internet and Digital Technologies
    Are Affecting the Five Competitive Forces* 62
Using Industry Analysis: A Few Caveats 67
Strategic Groups within Industries 70
Summary 73

Chapter 3
Assessing the Internal Environment of the Firm. 78

Value-Chain Analysis 82

Primary Activities 83
Support Activities 85
*Interrelationships among Value-Chain Activities
    within and across Organizations* 89
Applying the Value Chain to Service Organizations 90

Resource-Based View of the Firm 91

Types of Firm Resources 93
*Firm Resources and Sustainable
    Competitive Advantages* 94
*The Generation and Distribution of a Firm's Profits:
    Extending the Resource-Based View of the Firm* 99

**Evaluating Firm Performance:
    Two Approaches.** 101

Financial Ratio Analysis 101
*Integrating Financial Analysis and Stakeholder
    Perspectives: The Balanced Scorecard* 104
Summary 108
*Appendix to Chapter 3: How the Internet and Digital
Technologies Add Value* 113

Chapter 4
Recognizing a Firm's Intellectual Assets: Moving beyond a Firm's Tangible Resources. 118

**The Central Role of Knowledge
    in Today's Economy.** 120

**Human Capital: The Foundation
    of Intellectual Capital** 123

Attracting Human Capital 125
Developing Human Capital 126
Retaining Human Capital 129
*Enhancing Human Capital: The Role of Diversity
    in the Workforce* 131

The Vital Role of Social Capital............. 133

*How Social Capital Helps Attract and
   Retain Talent* 134
*Social Networks: Implications for Knowledge
   Management and Career Success* 136
The Potential Downside of Social Capital 140

**Using Technology to Leverage Human
   Capital and Knowledge**.................. 141

Using Networks to Share Information.............. 141
*Electronic Teams: Using Technology
   to Enhance Collaboration*....................... 143
*Codifying Knowledge for Competitive
   Advantage* 144

**Protecting the Intellectual Assets of the
Organization: Intellectual Property
   and Dynamic Capabilities** 147

Intellectual Property Rights 147
Dynamic Capabilities 147
Summary 149

part 2 Strategic Formulation

Chapter 5
Business-Level Strategy: Creating and Sustaining Competitive Advantages..................... 156

**Types of Competitive Advantage
   and Sustainability** 158

Overall Cost Leadership........................... 160
Differentiation................................... 165
Focus.. 170
*Combination Strategies: Integrating Overall
   Low Cost and Differentiation* 172

**How the Internet and Digital Technologies
   Are Affecting the Competitive
   Strategies** 176

Overall Cost Leadership........................... 176
Differentiation................................... 177
Focus.. 178
*Are Combination Strategies the Key
   to E-Business Success?*......................... 179

**Industry Life-Cycle Stages: Strategic
   Implications**.......................... 179

Strategies in the Introduction Stage 182
Strategies in the Growth Stage 182
Strategies in the Maturity Stage 183
Strategies in the Decline Stage 184
Turnaround Strategies............................ 187
Summary 188

Chapter 6
Corporate-Level Strategy: Creating Value through Diversification 194

**Making Diversification Work:
   An Overview**.......................... 198

**Related Diversification: Economies
   of Scope and Revenue Enhancement**....... 199

Leveraging Core Competencies 200
Sharing Activities 201

Related Diversification: Market Power....... 203

Pooled Negotiating Power......................... 203
Vertical Integration 206

**Unrelated Diversification: Financial
   Synergies and Parenting**................ 209

Corporate Parenting and Restructuring 209
Portfolio Management............................ 211
*Caveat: Is Risk Reduction a Viable Goal
   of Diversification?* 214

The Means to Achieve Diversification....... 214

Mergers and Acquisitions 215
Strategic Alliances and Joint Ventures.............. 220
Internal Development 222

**How Managerial Motives Can Erode
   Value Creation**........................ 223

Growth for Growth's Sake......................... 223
Egotism 224
Antitakeover Tactics 225
Summary... 227

Chapter 7
International Strategy: Creating Value in Global Markets 232

The Global Economy: A Brief Overview...... 234

**Factors Affecting a Nation's
   Competitiveness**....................... 235

Factor Endowments............................... 237
Demand Conditions 237
Related and Supporting Industries 237
Firm Strategy, Structure, and Rivalry............... 238
*Concluding Comment on Factors Affecting
   a Nation's Competitiveness* 238

**International Expansion: A Company's
   Motivations and Risks** 238

Motivations for International Expansion 238
Potential Risks of International Expansion.......... 243
*Global Dispersion of Value Chains: Outsourcing
   and Offshoring* 246

Achieving Competitive Advantage in Global Markets 248

Two Opposing Pressures: Reducing Costs and Adapting to Local Markets 248
International Strategy 250
Global Strategy 251
Multidomestic Strategy 253
Transnational Strategy 255
Global or Regional? A Second Look at Globalization 257

Entry Modes of International Expansion 259

Exporting 260
Licensing and Franchising 261
Strategic Alliances and Joint Ventures 261
Wholly Owned Subsidiaries 263
Summary 265

Chapter 8
Entrepreneurial Strategy and Competitive Dynamics 270

Recognizing Entrepreneurial Opportunities 273

Entrepreneurial Opportunities 276
Entrepreneurial Resources 279
Entrepreneurial Leadership 285

Entrepreneurial Strategy 285

Entry Strategies 286
Generic Strategies 290
Combination Strategies 293

Competitive Dynamics 294

New Competitive Action 294
Threat Analysis 295
Motivation and Capability to Respond 297
Types of Competitive Actions 300
Likelihood of Competitive Reaction 301
Choosing Not to React: Forbearance and Co-opetition 302
Summary 304

part 3 Strategic Implementation

Chapter 9
Strategic Control and Corporate Governance 310

Ensuring Informational Control: Responding Effectively to Environmental Change 313

A Traditional Approach to Strategic Control 313
A Contemporary Approach to Strategic Control 314

Attaining Behavioral Control: Balancing Culture, Rewards, and Boundaries 316

Building a Strong and Effective Culture 317
Motivating with Rewards and Incentives 318
Setting Boundaries and Constraints 320
Behavioral Control in Organizations: Situational Factors 323
Evolving from Boundaries to Rewards and Culture 323

The Role of Corporate Governance 324

The Modern Corporation: The Separation of Owners (Shareholders) and Management 326
Governance Mechanisms: Aligning the Interests of Owners and Managers 327
External Governance Control Mechanisms 332
Corporate Governance: An International Perspective 336
Summary 340

Chapter 10
Creating Effective Organizational Designs 346

Traditional Forms of Organizational Structure 349

Patterns of Growth of Large Corporations: Strategy-Structure Relationship 349
Simple Structure 351
Functional Structure 351
Divisional Structure 353
Matrix Structure 356
International Operations: Implications for Organizational Structure 357
Global Start-Ups: A New Phenomenon 358
How an Organization's Structure Can Influence Strategy Formulation 359

Linking Strategic Reward and Evaluation Systems to Business-Level and Corporate-Level Strategies 360

Business-Level Strategy: Reward and Evaluation Systems 361
Corporate-Level Strategy: Reward and Evaluation Systems 362

Boundaryless Organizational Designs 363

The Barrier-Free Organization 364
The Modular Organization 367
The Virtual Organization 370
Boundaryless Organizations: Making Them Work 372

Creating Ambidextrous Organizational Designs 375

Ambidextrous Organizations: Key Design Attributes ... 375
Why Was the Ambidextrous Organization the Most Effective Structure? 376
Summary 376

Chapter 11
Strategic Leadership: Creating a Learning Organization and an Ethical Organization 382

Leadership: Three Interdependent Activities............................ 385

Setting a Direction 386
Designing the Organization 388
Nurturing an Excellent and Ethical Culture.......... 388

Elements of Effective Leadership 390

Integrative Thinking 390
Overcoming Barriers to Change.................... 391
The Effective Use of Power 393

Emotional Intelligence: A Key Leadership Trait 394

Self-Awareness 396
Self-Regulation 397
Motivation.................................... 397
Empathy 397
Social Skill 397
Emotional Intelligence: Some Potential Drawbacks and Cautionary Notes........................ 398

Developing a Learning Organization 400

Inspiring and Motivating People with a Mission or Purpose 401
Empowering Employees at All Levels 401
Accumulating and Sharing Internal Knowledge...... 402
Gathering and Integrating External Information 404
Challenging the Status Quo and Enabling Creativity... 406

Creating an Ethical Organization 407

Individual Ethics versus Organizational Ethics 407
Integrity-Based versus Compliance-Based Approaches to Organizational Ethics 410
Role Models 411
Corporate Credos and Codes of Conduct............ 412
Reward and Evaluation Systems................... 414
Policies and Procedures 415
Summary..................................... 418

Chapter 12
Managing Innovation and Fostering Corporate Entrepreneurship 424

Managing Innovation 427

Types of Innovation............................ 427
Challenges of Innovation 431
Defining the Scope of Innovation 432
Managing the Pace of Innovation................. 432
Staffing to Capture Value from Innovation 433
Collaborating with Innovation Partners............ 434

Corporate Entrepreneurship 435

Focused Approaches to Corporate Entrepreneurship............................. 439
Dispersed Approaches to Corporate Entrepreneurship............................. 440
Measuring the Success of Corporate Entrepreneurship Activities 442

Real Options Analysis: A Useful Tool 444

Applications of Real Options Analysis to Strategic Decisions 444
Potential Pitfalls of Real Options Analysis 445

Entrepreneurial Orientation 447

Autonomy 448
Innovativeness................................. 449
Proactiveness 452
Competitive Aggressiveness 453
Risk Taking 455
Summary..................................... 457

part 4 Case Analysis

Chapter 13
Analyzing Strategic Management Cases 462

Why Analyze Strategic Management Cases?................................ 464

How to Conduct a Case Analysis 465

Become Familiar with the Material 467
Identify Problems 468
Conduct Strategic Analyses...................... 469
Propose Alternative Solutions..................... 471
Make Recommendations 471

How to Get the Most from Case Analysis 473

Using Conflict-Inducing Decision-Making Techniques in Case Analysis.............. 475

Symptoms of Groupthink and How to Prevent It....... 478
Using Conflict to Improve Decision Making.......... 479

Following the Analysis-Decision-Action Cycle in Case Analysis 481

Summary..................................... 485
Appendix 1 to Chapter 13: Financial Ratio Analysis ... 486
Appendix 2 to Chapter 13: Sources of Company and Industry Information 495

Indexes I-1

Company I-1
Name I-5
Subject I-12

Strategic Management

creating competitive advantages

fifth edition

The Strategic Management Process

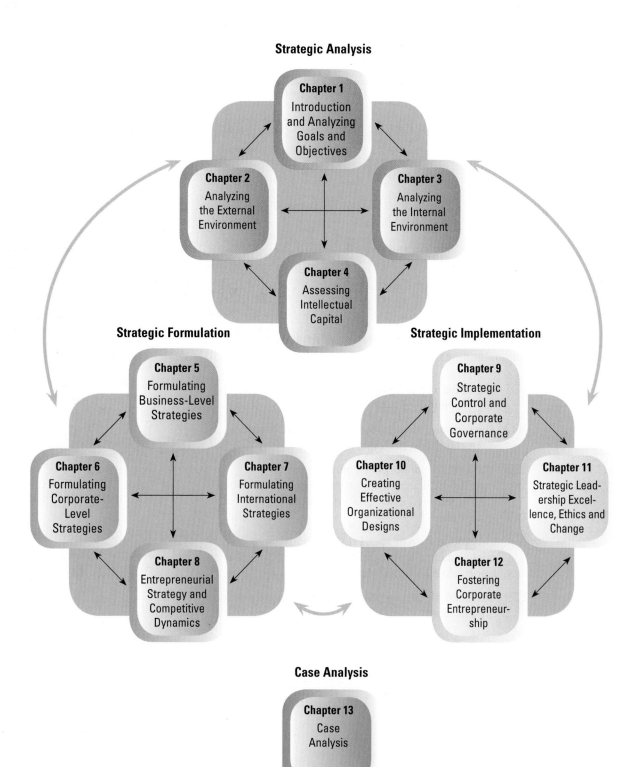

Strategic Analysis

Chapter 1
Introduction and Analyzing Goals and Objectives

Chapter 2
Analyzing the External Environment

Chapter 3
Analyzing the Internal Environment

Chapter 4
Assessing Intellectual Capital

Strategic Formulation

Chapter 5
Formulating Business-Level Strategies

Chapter 6
Formulating Corporate-Level Strategies

Chapter 7
Formulating International Strategies

Chapter 8
Entrepreneurial Strategy and Competitive Dynamics

Strategic Implementation

Chapter 9
Strategic Control and Corporate Governance

Chapter 10
Creating Effective Organizational Designs

Chapter 11
Strategic Leadership Excellence, Ethics and Change

Chapter 12
Fostering Corporate Entrepreneurship

Case Analysis

Chapter 13
Case Analysis

Strategic Management:

Creating Competitive Advantages

>learning objectives

After reading this chapter, you should have a good understanding of:

LO1 The definition of strategic management and its four key attributes.

LO2 The strategic management process and its three interrelated and principal activities.

LO3 The vital role of corporate governance and stakeholder management as well as how "symbiosis" can be achieved among an organization's stakeholders.

LO4 The importance of social responsibility, including environmental sustainability, and how it can enhance a corporation's innovation strategy.

LO5 The need for greater empowerment throughout the organization.

LO6 How an awareness of a hierarchy of strategic goals can help an organization achieve coherence in its strategic direction.

We define strategic management as *consisting of the analyses, decisions, and actions an organization undertakes in order to create and sustain competitive advantages.* At the heart of strategic management is the question: How and why do some firms outperform others? Thus, the challenge to managers is to decide on strategies that provide advantages that can be sustained over time. There are four key attributes of strategic management. It is directed at overall organizational goals, includes multiple stakeholders, incorporates short-term as well as long-term perspectives, and recognizes trade-offs between effectiveness and efficiency. We discuss the above definition and the four key attributes in the first section.

The second section addresses the strategic management process. The three major processes are strategy analysis, strategy formulation, and strategy implementation. These three components parallel the analyses, decisions, and actions in the above definition. We discuss how each of the 12 chapters addresses these three processes and provide examples from each chapter.

The third section discusses two important and interrelated concepts: corporate governance and stakeholder management. Corporate governance addresses the issue of who "governs" the corporation and determines its direction. It consists of three primary participants: stockholders (owners), management (led by the chief executive officer), and the board of directors (elected to monitor management). Stakeholder management recognizes that the interests of various stakeholders, such as owners, customers, and employees, can often conflict and create challenging decision-making dilemmas for managers. However, we discuss how some firms have been able to achieve "symbiosis" among stakeholders wherein their interests are considered interdependent and can be achieved simultaneously. We also discuss the important role of social responsibility, including the need for corporations to incorporate environmental sustainability in their strategic actions.

The fourth section addresses factors in the business environment that have increased the level of unpredictable change for today's leaders. Such factors have also created the need for a greater strategic management perspective and reinforced the role of empowerment throughout the organization.

The final section focuses on the need for organizations to ensure consistency in their vision, mission, and strategic objectives which, collectively, form a hierarchy of goals. While visions may lack specificity, they must evoke powerful and compelling mental images. Strategic objectives are much more specific and are essential for driving toward overall goals.

Learning from Mistakes

What makes the study of strategic management so interesting? One thing is that struggling firms can become stars, while high flyers can become earthbound very rapidly. As colorfully noted by Arthur Martinez, Sears' former chairman: "Today's peacock is tomorrow's feather duster." Consider, for example, the change in membership on the prestigious *Fortune 500* list of the largest U. S. firms:[1]

- Of the 500 companies that appeared on the first list in 1955, only 71 have a place on this list today.
- Nearly 2,000 companies have appeared on the list since its inception, and most are long gone from it. Just making the list guarantees nothing about your ability to endure.
- Some of the most powerful companies on today's list—businesses like Intel, Apple, Google, and Dell—grew from nothing to great on the strength of new technologies, bumping venerable old companies off the list.

Let's take a look at Mitch Caplan's tenure at one firm with which you may be familiar—E*Trade. Perhaps, you have used their financial services (brokerage and banking) or have watched their humorous television commercials with the "talking baby."[2] The business press glowingly wrote about how Mitch Caplan, their CEO, enacted a brilliant turnaround. After he took over in 2003, E*Trade's profits soared to $389 million in 2004—compared to an average *loss* of $75 million the previous three years. And, E*Trade was recognized by *InformationWeek* as one of the 40 top firms in the financial services industry for delivering IT solutions to solve business problems.

We'll briefly summarize how Caplan engineered E*Trade's turnaround. However, since we will be opening each chapter in *Strategic Management* with an example of "Learning from Mistakes," we will then focus on how his E*Trade career abruptly ended on a negative note. In effect, it is a "rags to riches to rags" story.

Key elements of Caplan's successful turnaround included:

- He cut costs by sharply reducing their bloated advertising budget and selling unrelated businesses, such as a national ATM network, kiosks in Target stores, a palatial New York retail branch that sold E*Trade souvenirs, and a TV business-news service. In addition, employee headcount was cut from about 5,000 to 4,000.
- Caplan changed the firm's culture and instilled more discipline. He moved the headquarters from Menlo Park, California, to New York City. In effect, he left behind the propeller beanies, rubber chickens, and geeky props that created a loose work atmosphere. In its place were jackets and ties.
- Besides cutting costs and changing the culture, Caplan also refocused the firm on its core banking operations. Here, it had a clear advantage over rivals such as Charles Schwab Corp. and Ameritrade. By offering banking products such as loans and checking accounts to its brokerage customers, he was able to build the nation's eighth-largest thrift. The new financial services became a huge profit center—accounting for 40 percent of all revenues and 48 percent of total profits. Between 2000 and 2004, E*Trade had nearly quadrupled its number of bank accounts and increased its brokerage accounts from 2.4 million to 2.9 million. And until mid-2006 E*Trade was on a tear—coming off a four-year run in which earnings rose 200 percent to $629 million. It was on track to have its best year since its founding in 1986.

So far so good. But, as we noted earlier, this story does *not* have a happy ending. While E*Trade's main business was online investing, Caplan aggressively expanded the banking operations that made and bought mortgage loans and invested in securities backed by mortgages. *[continued]*

As noted by a *Fortune* writer, "Back in 2003, the firm's banking unit began investing in mortgage-backed securities . . . a whole hodgepodge of bundled loan investments that, as it turned out, no one really understood."* In the beginning, these were great for business and by early 2007 its investments in home-equity and mortgage-based securities were worth billions. These investments threw off so much cash that they made up 58 percent of E*Trade's revenues.

However, the great ride came to a rapid halt in mid-2007. Credit markets seized up and practically overnight E*Trade watched its loan portfolio—and a significant portion of its revenues—evaporate. By November 2007, a Citigroup analyst's report suggested that the company's bad loans could push the firm into bankruptcy and E*Trade's customers withdrew $2.5 billion in assets in one day. The firm lost $1.7 billion in the last three months of 2007, and it saw over $56 billion in customer assets evaporate over a five-month period.

Mitch Caplan resigned on November, 29, 2007. At a meeting of E*Trade's board, lawyers, and bankers on that date, he said: "This company is my life. I will do what you want me to, but I think sweeping changes need to be made." One change quickly became self-evident.

It is a humiliating comedown for E*Trade and Mitch Caplan, who failed to sufficiently anticipate the impact of mortgage failures. The online broker kept moving deeper into mortgage banking and Caplan, described by the *Wall Street Journal* as "an eternally optimistic manager," often spoke of mortgages as the "bedrock asset" of America. But at one point, when E*Trade's mortgage portfolio began to rapidly deteriorate, he stated: "We honestly can't predict where this is going anymore and we just shouldn't even try to peg the bottom anymore." Perhaps that statement concisely summarizes what *really* went wrong.

In some ways E*Trade's tale is universal: Its corporate officers have seen firsthand how quickly and cruelly the market can punish any company with exposure to mortgage-backed securities—*or indeed, any business it doesn't understand.*

Today's leaders, such as those at E*Trade face a large number of complex challenges in the global marketplace. In considering how much credit (or blame) they deserve, two perspectives of leadership come immediately to mind: the "romantic" and "external control" perspectives.[3] First, let's look at the **romantic view of leadership.** Here, the implicit assumption is that the leader is the key force in determining an organization's success—or lack thereof.[4] This view dominates the popular press in business magazines such as *Fortune, BusinessWeek,* and *Forbes,* wherein the CEO is either lauded for his or her firm's success or chided for the organization's demise.[5] Consider, for example, the credit that has been bestowed on leaders such as Jack Welch, Andrew Grove, and Herb Kelleher for the tremendous accomplishments of their firms, General Electric, Intel, and Southwest Airlines, respectively.

romantic view of leadership situations in which the leader is the key force determining the organization's success—or lack thereof.

Similary, Apple's success in the last decade has been attributed almost entirely to Steve Jobs, its CEO.[6] Apple's string of hit products such as iMac computers, iPods, and iPhones are testament to his genius for developing innovative, user-friendly, and aesthetically pleasing products. In addition to being a perfectionist in product design, Jobs also is a master showman with a cult following. On January 14, 2009, he announced that he was taking a medical leave through June. Perhaps not surprisingly, Apple's stock immediately dropped 10 percent—wiping out approximately $8 billion in market value.

Finally, consider how David Maisel really turned around his firm's fortunes. As chairman of Marvel Studios, he convinced the board that film production "however chancy, would pay off big." And it certainly did—with the big hit *Iron Man* starring Robert Downey Jr., about an industrialist who fights terrorists and arms dealers in a red-and-yellow metal suit.

---

* Mortgage-backed securities are securities issued by lending institutions that are backed by mortgage loans. The holder of these securities receives a steady stream of cash from the repayment of principal and interest on the mortgages. Although backed by mortgage loans, the value of these securities can go down if borrowers start defaulting or if the underlying value of the real estate goes below the amount owed to lenders.

Marvel Studios: Maybe Chairman David Maisel Is the Real "Iron Man"

With 2005 revenues of only $391 million from character licensing, toy sales, and comic book publishing, Marvel needed financial heft to run with big Hollywood studios such as Sony and Warner Bros. Enter the chairman, David Maisel. In 2005, he convinced the board of directors to borrow $525 million to set up an innovative film fund to bankroll *Iron Man* and fund other film projects through 2011. To raise such a huge amount of money, Marvel pledged the future film revenues for 12 of its characters (such as Spider-Man, X-Men) as collateral for the bank loans.

To make *Iron Man,* Marvel drew down about $150 million from the film fund and is paying Paramount Pictures 10 percent of net revenues from ticket and video sales on top of its fees for marketing and distribution. The payoff: *Iron Man* could generate over $1 billion in box-office,

home-video, and other sales. (In its first three weeks of release, the film generated more than $222 million in ticket sales and by late-2008 had grossed $574 million worldwide.)

Marvel is riding high. *The Incredible Hulk,* starring Edward Norton, was released in mid-June 2008. Future films will feature *Iron Man 2, Thor,* and *Captain America.* Marvel has also signed an agreement in which Paramount will distribute Marvel's next five self-produced feature films on a worldwide basis. According to Rob Moore, Vice Chairman of Paramount Pictures: "Marvel's iconic brand, its popular characters and its proven ability to create compelling and visually spellbinding films complements Paramount's great history of filmmaking. We look forward to a long and successful run together."

Interestingly, Marvel has had a star-crossed past. It filed for bankruptcy twice in the 1990s during a period in which a speculative bubble among comic book collectors burst, sales plummeted, and lots of comic shops went out of business. But its fortunes have recently soared. During the past two years, Marvel's net profit has nearly tripled and its stock has doubled. As noted by *BusinessWeek:* "For now . . . Maisel's street cred in Hollywood is, well, super."

Sources: Siklos, R. 2008. Spoiler alert: Comic books are alive and kicking. *CNNMoney.com,* October 13: np; Rockenwagner, P. 2008. Marvel Studios enters into new worldwide distribution agreement with Paramount: Projected slate to include *Iron Man 2, Thor, Captain America* and *The Avenger. Global .factiva.com,* September 29: np; Grover, R. 2008. Iron Man spawns a marvel of a movie studio. *Businessweek.com,* April 29: np; and, Grover, R. 2008. A secret identity for Marvel. *BusinessWeek.* May 19: 34.

Many more profitable projects have followed or are in the planning stages. We address these successful initiatives in Strategy Spotlight 1.1.

On the other hand, when things don't go well, much of the failure of an organization can also, rightfully, be attributed to the leader.[7] For example, when Carly Fiorina was fired as CEO of Hewlett Packard, the firm enjoyed an immediate increase in its stock price of 7 percent—hardly a strong endorsement of her leadership! Caplan led E*Trade's foray into mortgage-backed securities. When this created enormous losses in 2008, he abruptly departed the firm.

However, this reflects only part of the picture. Consider another perspective called **external view of leadership.** Here, rather than making the implicit assumption that the leader is the most important factor in determining organizational outcomes, the focus is on external factors that may positively or negatively affect a firm's success. We don't have to look far to support this perspective. For example, E*Trade's decline can be largely attributed to external factors. The sudden decline in real estate values in 2008 sharply eroded the value of its mortgage-backed securities. This, in turn, led to huge write downs in the value of E*Trade's assets. The decline in stock prices caused far fewer people to engage in stock trades as well. The general climate of a lack of confidence in financial institutions also led to huge withdrawals from customer accounts.

external view of leadership
situations in which external forces— where the leader has limited influence— determine the organization's success.

The Financial Crisis: Its Causes and Its Effects on Industries

By early 2009, it became increasingly evident that the U.S. was entering a period of deep and prolonged recession. What seemed like years of limitless expansion had come to a screeching halt by the second half of 2008. Several banks and financial institutions had collapsed, auto companies were crying for a bailout, and the ranks of the unemployed were swelling rapidly. Despite an unprecedented $700 billion infusion into the credit markets and repeated interest rate cuts by the Federal Reserve, it was unclear if the worst was over. How did the nation get into this situation?

- Until recent years, when a bank made a mortgage loan, typically for 30 years, several safeguards were observed to make sure that the bank would be able to recover the loan. These included insisting on a substantial down payment and a thorough verification of the borrower's capacity to repay. Once a loan was made, the bank had to wait 15 or 30 years to recover the loan.

- Starting in the 1990s, banks discovered a new way to make quicker and higher profits from mortgages, called *securitization*. This involved bundling several mortgages together and selling it to an investor either at home or abroad. The investor's income came from the principal and interest payments of the mortgage loan, while the banks made their money from the fees and points collected up front. Instead of waiting 30 years, now they were getting their money back in three months, meaning that they could use the money to make fresh loans.

- Once the banks embraced securitization, the emphasis was on making more and more loans and quickly turning around and selling these mortgage-backed securities to investors. But given that there is not an infinite pool of credit-worthy borrowers who are able to make substantial down payments, banks began to relax the rules for making mortgages. Down payments went down from 20% to 10% to 5% and eventually to 0%. Then came innovations like interest-only loans (where no principal is paid), adjustable rate mortgages (where a borrower gets the benefit of a low interest rate for the first few years), and even loans in which the borrower paid only a part of the interest every month, effectively allowing the loan balance to increase every month! Some banks even began allowing "no verification" loans, wherein a borrower could state an artificially high income and qualify for a loan without any fear that the bank would verify the stated income!

- Why did banks, which are supposed to be prudent, engage in such unwise practices? And why did investors buy these mortgage-backed securities? The answer lies in their expectations about the real estate market. Given that residential real estate prices have risen steadily in the U.S. over the years, the banks felt that there was adequate collateral. Investors bought these securities because rating agencies were giving these securities high ratings. Interestingly, the very fact that anyone could qualify for a loan brought more buyers into the market, causing property prices to rise even faster, effectively causing a housing bubble.

- As more of the subprime borrowers began to default, the housing bubble eventually burst. As more foreclosed homes came into the market, property prices plummeted, and more borrowers walked away from their homes because they saw no point in paying the bank $500,000 for a house now worth only $400,000. This caused a vicious cycle of declining property values and foreclosures. The mortgage-backed securities now had insufficient collateral, forcing the banks to take massive write-offs.

- As the losses of the banks piled up, financial institutions had little money to lend, causing the credit markets to come to a standstill. Suddenly, even people with good credit ratings could not get a loan from the bank to buy a house or a car. In addition to causing real estate prices to further spiral downward, this hurt everyone who depends on credit. The auto companies saw their sales go down 30 percent to 40 percent because potential buyers could not get credit. Small businesses could not get loans from banks and were forced to lay off employees or shut down altogether. As the job losses mounted month after month, the country became mired in the worst recession since the Great Depression.

Let's see the impact the financial meltdown has had on various industries.

- The U.S. auto industry was severely negatively impacted by the financial crisis. U.S. auto sales had hit a peak of 17 million in 2005. 16.1 million cars were sold in 2007. In comparison, the 2008 sales were a dismal 13.2 million. And, according to projections by IHS Global Insight, it may go down to 10.3 million in 2009. J.D. Power Inc. estimates that at least *(continued)*

(continued) half a million customers who wanted to buy were unable to do so because of tighter credit markets in the last quarter of 2008. Such sales declines left the U.S. auto companies with no choice but to plead for bailouts from the government.

- Brinker International Inc. (parent of popular casual dining restaurants such as Chili's, On the Border, and Maggiano's Italian Grill) closed down 47 restaurants in the second half of 2008. In early January 2009, they announced that they would be closing another 35 restaurants. According to Steven Kron, restaurant analyst for Goldman Sachs, as many as 12,000 restaurants will shut down nationally before the end of the recession.

- Retail sales suffered across all segments of the retail industry. In the consumer electronics segment, Circuit City was one of the earliest victims and had to file for bankruptcy. Jewelers Tiffany and Zales experienced sales declines over 20 percent.

- Even high flyers like Micosoft and Intel found that they were not immune to the ripple effects of the financial meltdown. In January 2009 Microsoft announced they would be laying off 5,000 people, the first such layoff in the 34-year history of the company, in response to an 11 percent drop in net income in the previous quarter. Intel's sales dropped 23 percent and its net income declined a massive 90 percent in the fourth quarter of 2008, triggering layoffs of over 5,000 employees.

Sources: Spiers, E. 2008. Putting lipstick on a pig. *Fortune*, September 29: 80; Freeman, S. 2008. Auto sales fall 27% as credit tightens. *Washington Post*, October 2: D01; Robinson-Jacobs, K. 2009. Chili's parent Brinker to close 35 restaurants. *Dallas Morning News*, January 23: D3; Vance, A. 2009. Microsoft slashes jobs as sales fall. *New York Times*, January 2: np; Hamilton, A. 2008. Why Circuit City busted, while Best Buy boomed. *Time Magazine*, November 11; np; Zale drops to all-time low after CFO steps down. 2009. *Associated Press*, January 21: np; When fortune frowned: A special report on the world economy. 2008. *Economist*, October 11: 1–33; and, Blinder, A.S. 2009. Six errors on the path to financial crisis. *New York Times*, January 24: np.

The combined effects of these external factors were huge losses not just at E*Trade but at financial institutions across the country. Of course, what started as a financial industry crisis had negative effects all across the economy through massive layoffs, a sharp decline in consumer demand, and the severe erosion of profitability for firms in virtually all sectors of the economy. Strategy Spotlight 1.2 provides a more detailed look at the global financial crisis of 2008.

Before moving on, it is important to point out that successful executives are often able to navigate around the difficult circumstances that they face. At times it can be refreshing to see the optimistic position they take when they encounter seemingly insurmountable odds. Of course, that's not to say that one should be naïve or Pollyannaish. Consider, for example, how one CEO is handling trying times:[8]

Name a general economic woe, and the chances are that Charles Needham is dealing with it.

- Market turmoil has knocked 80 percent off the shares of South Africa's Metorex, the mining company that he heads.
- The plunge in global commodities is slamming prices for the copper, cobalt, and other minerals Metorex unearths across Africa. The credit crisis makes it harder to raise money.
- And fighting has again broken out in the Democratic Republic of Congo, where Metorex has a mine and several projects in development.

Such problems might send many executives to the window ledge. Yet Needham appears unruffled as he sits down at a conference table in the company's modest offices in a Johannesburg suburb. The combat in northeast Congo, he notes, is far from Metorex's mine. Commodity prices are still high, in historical terms. And Needham is confident he can raise enough capital, drawing on relationships with South African banks. "These are the kinds of things you deal with, doing business in Africa," he says.

What Is Strategic Management?

Given the many challenges and opportunities in the global marketplace, today's managers must do more than set long-term strategies and hope for the best.[9] They must go beyond what some have called "incremental management," whereby they view their job as making a series of small, minor changes to improve the efficiency of their firm's operations.[10] That is fine if your firm is competing in a very stable, simple, and unchanging industry. But there aren't many of those left. The pace of change is accelerating, and the pressure on managers to make both major and minor changes in a firm's strategic direction is increasing.

Rather than seeing their role as merely custodians of the status quo, today's leaders must be proactive, anticipate change, and continually refine and, when necessary, make dramatic changes to their strategies. The strategic management of the organization must become both a process and a way of thinking throughout the organization.

Defining Strategic Management

Strategic management consists of the analyses, decisions, and actions an organization undertakes in order to create and sustain competitive advantages. This definition captures two main elements that go to the heart of the field of strategic management.

First, the strategic management of an organization entails three ongoing processes: *analyses, decisions,* and *actions.* Strategic management is concerned with the *analysis* of strategic goals (vision, mission, and strategic objectives) along with the analysis of the internal and external environment of the organization. Next, leaders must make strategic decisions. These *decisions,* broadly speaking, address two basic questions: What industries should we compete in? How should we compete in those industries? These questions also often involve an organization's domestic and international operations. And last are the *actions* that must be taken. Decisions are of little use, of course, unless they are acted on. Firms must take the necessary actions to implement their **strategies.** This requires leaders to allocate the necessary resources and to design the organization to bring the intended strategies to reality.

Second, the essence of strategic management is the study of why some firms outperform others.[11] Thus, managers need to determine how a firm is to compete so that it can obtain advantages that are sustainable over a lengthy period of time. That means focusing on two fundamental questions:

- *How should we compete in order to create **competitive advantages** in the marketplace?* Managers need to determine if the firm should position itself as the low-cost producer or develop products and services that are unique and will enable the firm to charge premium prices. Or should they do some combination of both?
- *How can we create competitive advantages in the marketplace that are unique, valuable, and difficult for rivals to copy or substitute?* That is, managers need to make such advantages sustainable, instead of temporary.

Rivals almost always copy ideas that work. In the 1980s, American Airlines tried to establish a competitive advantage by introducing the frequent flyer program. Within weeks, all the airlines did the same thing. Overnight, frequent flyer programs became a necessary tool for competitive parity instead of a competitive advantage. The challenge, therefore, is to create competitive advantages that are sustainable.

Sustainable competitive advantage cannot be achieved through operational effectiveness alone.[12] The popular management innovations of the last two decades—total quality, just-in-time, benchmarking, business process reengineering, outsourcing—are all about operational effectiveness. **Operational effectiveness** means performing similar activities better than rivals. Each of these is important, but none lead to sustainable competitive advantage because everyone is doing them. Strategy is all about being different.

strategic management the analyses, decisions, and actions an organization undertakes in order to create and sustain competitive advantages.

>LO1
The definition of strategic management and its four key attributes.

Strategy The ideas, decisions, and actions that enable a firm to succeed.

Competitive advantage A firm's resources and capabilities that enable it to overcome the competitive forces in its industry(ies).

operational effectiveness performing similar activities better than rivals.

Sustainable competitive advantage is possible only by performing different activities from rivals or performing similar activities in different ways. Companies such as Wal-Mart, Southwest Airlines, and IKEA have developed unique, internally consistent, and difficult-to-imitate activity systems that have provided them with sustained competitive advantages. A company with a good strategy must make clear choices about what it wants to accomplish. Trying to do everything that your rivals do eventually leads to mutually destructive price competition, not long-term advantage.

The Four Key Attributes of Strategic Management

Before discussing the strategic management process, let's briefly talk about four attributes of strategic management.[13] It should become clear how this course differs from other courses that you have had in functional areas, such as accounting, marketing, operations, and finance. Exhibit 1.1 provides a definition and the four attributes of strategic management.

First, strategic management is *directed toward overall organizational goals and objectives.* That is, effort must be directed at what is best for the total organization, not just a single functional area. Some authors have referred to this perspective as "organizational versus individual rationality."[14] That is, what might look "rational" or ideal for one functional area, such as operations, may not be in the best interest of the overall firm. For example, operations may decide to schedule long production runs of similar products to lower unit costs. However, the standardized output may be counter to what the marketing department needs to appeal to a demanding target market. Similarly, research and development may "overengineer" the product to develop a far superior offering, but the design may make the product so expensive that market demand is minimal. Therefore, in this course you will look at cases and strategic issues from the perspective of the organization rather than that of the functional area(s) in which you have the strongest background.

Second, strategic management *includes multiple stakeholders in decision making.*[15] **Stakeholders** are those individuals, groups, and organizations who have a "stake" in the success of the organization, including owners (shareholders in a publicly held corporation), employees, customers, suppliers, the community at large, and so on. (We'll discuss this in more detail later in this chapter.) Managers will not be successful if they focus on a single stakeholder. For example, if the overwhelming emphasis is on generating profits for the owners, employees may become alienated, customer service may suffer, and the suppliers may resent demands for pricing concessions. However, many organizations can satisfy multiple stakeholder needs simultaneously. For example, financial performance may increase because employees who are satisfied with their jobs work harder to enhance customer satisfaction—leading to higher profits.

stakeholders
individuals, groups, and organizations who have a stake in the success of the organization, including owners (shareholders in a publicly held corporation), employees, customers, suppliers, and the community at large.

Exhibit 1.1
Strategic Management Concepts

Definition: Strategic management consists of the analyses, decisions, and actions an organization undertakes in order to create and sustain competitive advantages.

Key Attributes of Strategic Management

- Directs the organization toward overall goals and objectives.
- Includes multiple stakeholders in decision making.
- Needs to incorporate short-term and long-term perspectives.
- Recognizes trade-offs between efficiency and effectiveness.

Third, strategic management *requires incorporating both short-term and long-term perspectives.*[16] Peter Senge, a leading strategic management author, has referred to this need as a "creative tension."[17] That is, managers must maintain both a vision for the future of the organization as well as a focus on its present operating needs. However, financial markets can exert significant pressures on executives to meet short-term performance targets. Studies have shown that corporate leaders often take a short-term approach to the detriment of creating long-term shareholder value. Consider the following:

> According to recent studies, only 59 percent of financial executives say they would pursue a positive net present value project if it meant missing the quarter's consensus earnings per-share estimate. Worse, 78 percent say they would sacrifice value—often a great deal of value—to smooth earnings. Similarly, managers are more likely to cut R&D to reverse an earning slide if a significant amount of the company's equity is owned by institutions with high portfolio turnover. Many companies have the same philosophy about long-term investments such as infrastructure and employee training.[18]

Fourth, strategic management *involves the recognition of trade-offs between effectiveness and efficiency.* Some authors have referred to this as the difference between "doing the right thing" (**effectiveness**) and "doing things right" (**efficiency**).[19] While managers must allocate and use resources wisely, they must still direct their efforts toward the attainment of overall organizational objectives. Managers who only focus on meeting short-term budgets and targets may fail to attain the broader goals. Consider the following amusing story told by Norman Augustine, former CEO of defense giant, Martin Marietta (now Lockheed Martin):

> I am reminded of an article I once read in a British newspaper which described a problem with the local bus service between the towns of Bagnall and Greenfields. It seemed that, to the great annoyance of customers, drivers had been passing long queues of would-be passengers with a smile and a wave of the hand. This practice was, however, clarified by a bus company official who explained, "It is impossible for the drivers to keep their timetables if they must stop for passengers."[20]

Clearly, the drivers who were trying to stay on schedule had ignored the overall mission. As Augustine noted, "Impeccable logic but something seems to be missing!"

Successful managers must make many trade-offs. It is central to the practice of strategic management. At times, managers must focus on the short term and efficiency; at other times the emphasis is on the long term and expanding a firm's product-market scope in order to anticipate opportunities in the competitive environment. For example, consider Kevin Sharer's perspective. He is CEO of Amgen, the giant $15 billion biotechnology firm:

> A CEO must always be switching between what I call different altitudes—tasks of different levels of abstraction and specificity. At the highest altitude you're asking the big questions: What are the company's mission and strategy? Do people understand and believe in these aims? Are decisions consistent with them? At the lowest altitude, you're looking at on-the-ground operations: Did we make that sale? What was the yield on that last lot in the factory? How many days of inventory do we have for a particular drug? And then there's everything in between: How many chemists do we need to hire this quarter? What should we pay for a small biotech company that has a promising new drug? Is our production capacity adequate to roll out a product in a new market?[21]

Some authors have developed the concept of **"ambidexterity"** which refers to a manager's challenge to both align resources to take advantage of existing product markets as well as proactively explore new opportunities.[22] Strategy Spotlight 1.3 discusses ambidextrous behaviors that are required for success in today's challenging marketplace.

effectiveness tailoring actions to the needs of an organization rather than wasting effort, or "doing the right thing."

efficiency performing actions at a low cost relative to a benchmark, or "doing things right."

ambidexterity the challenge managers face of both aligning resources to take advantage of existing product markets as well as proactively exploring new opportunities.

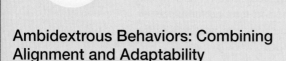

Ambidextrous Behaviors: Combining Alignment and Adaptability

A recent study involving 41 business units in 10 multinational companies identified four ambidextrous behaviors in individuals. Such behaviors are the essence of ambidexterity, and they illustrate how a dual capacity for alignment and adaptability can be woven into the fabric of an organization at the individual level.

They take time and are alert to opportunities beyond the confines of their own jobs. A large computer company's sales manager became aware of a need for a new software module that nobody currently offered. Instead of selling the customer something else, he worked up a business case for the new module. With management's approval, he began working full time on its development.

They are cooperative and seek out opportunities to combine their efforts with others. A marketing manager for Italy was responsible for supporting a newly acquired subsidiary. When frustrated about the limited amount of contact she had with her peers in other countries, she began discussions with them. This led to the creation of a European marketing forum which meets quarterly to discuss issues, share best practices, and collaborate on marketing plans.

They are brokers, always looking to build internal networks. When visiting the head office in St. Louis, a Canadian plant manager heard about plans for a $10 million investment for a new tape manufacturing plant. After inquiring further about the plans and returning to Canada, he contacted a regional manager in Manitoba, who he knew was looking for ways to build his business. With

some generous support from the Manitoba government, the regional manager bid for, and ultimately won, the $10 million investment.

They are multitaskers who are comfortable wearing more than one hat. Although an operations manager for a major coffee and tea distributor was charged with running his plant as efficiently as possible, he took it upon himself to identify value-added services for his clients. By developing a dual role, he was able to manage operations and develop a promising electronic module that automatically reported impending problems inside a coffee vending machine. With corporate funding, he found a subcontractor to develop the software, and he then piloted the module in his own operations. It was so successful that it was eventually adopted by operations managers in several other countries.

A recent *Harvard Business Review* article provides some useful insights on how one can become a more ambidextrous leader. Consider the following questions:

- **Do you meet your numbers?**
- **Do you help others?**
- **What do you do for your peers?** Are you just their in-house competitor?
- **When you manage up, do you bring problems—or problems with possible solutions?**
- **Are you transparent?** Managers who get a reputation for spinning events gradually lose the trust of peers and superiors.
- **Are you developing a group of senior-managers who know you and are willing to back your original ideas with resources?**

Source: Birkinshaw, J. & Gibson, C. 2004. Building ambidexterity into an organization. *MIT Sloan Management Review*, 45 (4): 47–55; and, Bower, J. L. 2007. Solve the succession crisis by growing inside-out leaders. *Harvard Business Review*, 85 (11): 90–99.

>LO2

The strategic management process and its three interrelated and principal activities.

The Strategic Management Process

We've identified three ongoing processes—analyses, decisions, and actions—that are central to strategic management. In practice, these three processes—often referred to as strategy analysis, strategy formulation, and strategy implementation—are highly interdependent and do not take place one after the other in a sequential fashion in most companies.

Intended versus Realized Strategies

Henry Mintzberg, a management scholar at McGill University, argues that viewing the strategic management process as one in which analysis is followed by optimal decisions and their subsequent meticulous implementation neither describes the strategic management process accurately nor prescribes ideal practice.[23] He sees the business environment as far from predictable, thus limiting our ability for analysis. Further, decisions are seldom based on optimal rationality alone, given the political processes that occur in all organizations.[24]

Taking into consideration the limitations discussed above, Mintzberg proposed an alternative model. As depicted in Exhibit 1.2, decisions following from analysis, in this model, constitute the ***intended*** **strategy** of the firm. For a variety of reasons, the intended strategy rarely survives in its original form. Unforeseen environmental developments, unanticipated resource constraints, or changes in managerial preferences may result in at least some parts of the intended strategy remaining *unrealized*. On the other hand, good managers will want to take advantage of a new opportunity presented by the environment, even if it was not part of the original set of intentions. For example, consider the wind energy industry.[25]

> In October 2008, the United States Congress extended a key wind tax credit and many states have mandates requiring utilities to tap renewable energy. Such legislation, combined with falling clean energy costs and wildly cyclical prices for coal, oil, and gas, has created a surge in demand for companies such as GE Wind Energy, which makes large turbines and fan blades. Not surprisingly, such businesses have increased hiring and research and development, as well as profit and revenue forecasts.[25]

Thus, the final **realized strategy** of any firm is a combination of deliberate and emergent strategies.

Next, we will address each of the three key strategic management processes: strategy analysis, strategy formulation, and strategy implementation and provide a brief overview of the chapters.

Exhibit 1.3 depicts the strategic management process and indicates how it ties into the chapters in the book. Consistent with our discussion above, we use two-way arrows to convey the interactive nature of the processes.

Strategy Analysis

Strategy analysis may be looked upon as the starting point of the strategic management process. It consists of the "advance work" that must be done in order to effectively formulate and implement strategies. Many strategies fail because managers may want to formulate

intended strategy strategy in which organizational decisions are determined only by analysis.

realized strategy strategy in which organizational decisions are determined by both analysis and unforeseen environmental developments, unanticipated resource constraints, and/or changes in managerial preferences.

Exhibit 1.2 **Realized Strategy and Intended Strategy: Usually Not the Same**

Source: From Mintzberg, H. & Waters, J. A., "Of Strategies: Deliberate and Emergent," *Strategic Management Journal,* Vol. 6, 1985, pp. 257–272. Copyright © John Wiley & Sons Limited. Reproduced with permission.

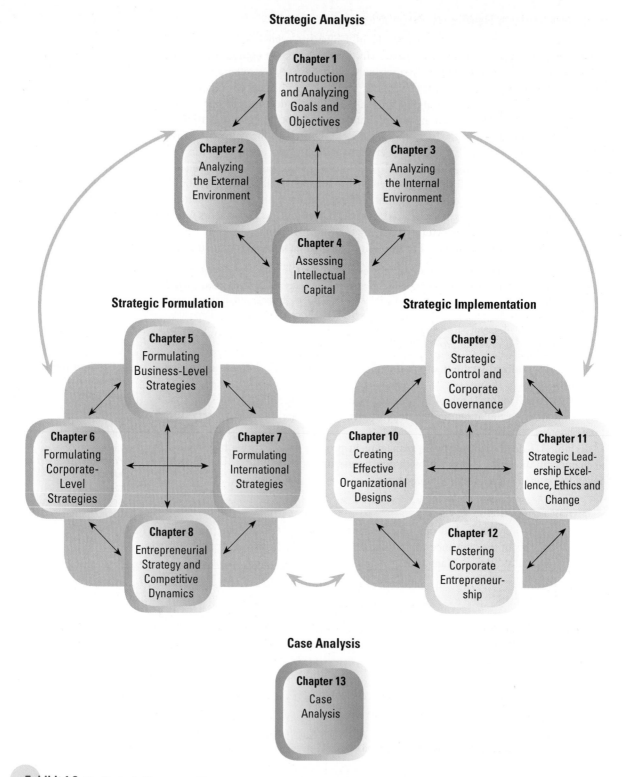

Strategic Analysis

Chapter 1
Introduction and Analyzing Goals and Objectives

Chapter 2
Analyzing the External Environment

Chapter 3
Analyzing the Internal Environment

Chapter 4
Assessing Intellectual Capital

Strategic Formulation

Chapter 5
Formulating Business-Level Strategies

Chapter 6
Formulating Corporate-Level Strategies

Chapter 7
Formulating International Strategies

Chapter 8
Entrepreneurial Strategy and Competitive Dynamics

Strategic Implementation

Chapter 9
Strategic Control and Corporate Governance

Chapter 10
Creating Effective Organizational Designs

Chapter 11
Strategic Leadership Excellence, Ethics and Change

Chapter 12
Fostering Corporate Entrepreneurship

Case Analysis

Chapter 13
Case Analysis

Exhibit 1.3 The Strategic Management Process

and implement strategies without a careful analysis of the overarching goals of the organization and without a thorough analysis of its external and internal environment.

Analyzing Organizational Goals and Objectives (Chapter 1) A firm's vision, mission, and strategic objectives form a hierarchy of goals that range from broad statements of intent and bases for competitive advantage to specific, measurable strategic objectives.

Analyzing the External Environment of the Firm (Chapter 2) Managers must monitor and scan the environment as well as analyze competitors. Two frameworks of the external environment are provided: (1) the general environment consists of several elements, such as demographic, technological, and economic segments, and (2) the industry environment consists of competitors and other organizations that may threaten the success of a firm's products and services.

Assessing the Internal Environment of the Firm (Chapter 3) Analyzing the strengths and relationships among the activities that constitute a firm's value chain (e.g., operations, marketing and sales, and human resource management) can be a means of uncovering potential sources of competitive advantage for the firm.[26]

Assessing a Firm's Intellectual Assets (Chapter 4) The knowledge worker and a firm's other intellectual assets (e.g., patents, trademarks) are becoming increasingly important as the drivers of competitive advantages and wealth creation. We also assess how well the organization creates networks and relationships as well as how technology can enhance collaboration among employees and provide a means of accumulating and storing knowledge.[27]

Strategy Formulation

A firm's strategy formulation is developed at several levels. First, business-level strategy addresses the issue of how to compete in a given business to attain competitive advantage. Second, corporate-level strategy focuses on two issues: (a) what businesses to compete in and (b) how businesses can be managed to achieve synergy; that is, they create more value by working together than if they operate as stand-alone businesses. Third, a firm must determine the best method to develop international strategies as it ventures beyond its national boundaries. Fourth, managers must formulate effective entrepreneurial initiatives.

Formulating Business-Level Strategy (Chapter 5) The question of how firms compete and outperform their rivals and how they achieve and sustain competitive advantages goes to the heart of strategic management. Successful firms strive to develop bases for competitive advantage, which can be achieved through cost leadership and/or differentiation as well as by focusing on a narrow or industrywide market segment.[28]

Formulating Corporate-Level Strategy (Chapter 6) Corporate-level strategy addresses a firm's portfolio (or group) of businesses. It asks (1) What business (or businesses) should we compete in? and (2) How can we manage this portfolio of businesses to create synergies among the businesses?

Formulating International Strategy (Chapter 7) When firms enter foreign markets, they face both opportunities and pitfalls.[29] Managers must decide not only on the most appropriate entry strategy but also how they will go about attaining competitive advantages in international markets.

Entrepreneurial Strategy and Competitive Dynamics (Chapter 8) Entrepreneurial activity aimed at new value creation is a major engine for economic growth. For entrepreneurial initiatives to succeed viable opportunities must be recognized and effective strategies must be formulated.

Strategy Implementation

Clearly, sound strategies are of no value if they are not properly implemented.[30] Strategy implementation involves ensuring proper strategic controls and organizational designs, which includes establishing effective means to coordinate and integrate activities within the firm as well as with its suppliers, customers, and alliance partners.[31] Leadership plays a central role, including ensuring that the organization is committed to excellence and ethical behavior. It also promotes learning and continuous improvement and acts entrepreneurially in creating and taking advantage of new opportunities.

Strategic Control and Corporate Governance (Chapter 9) Firms must exercise two types of strategic control. First, informational control requires that organizations continually monitor and scan the environment and respond to threats and opportunities. Second, behavioral control involves the proper balance of rewards and incentives as well as cultures and boundaries (or constraints). Further, successful firms (those that are incorporated) practice effective corporate governance.

Creating Effective Organizational Designs (Chapter 10) To succeed, firms must have organizational structures and designs that are consistent with their strategy. And, in today's rapidly changing competitive environments, firms must ensure that their organizational boundaries—those internal to the firm and external—are more flexible and permeable.[32] Often, organizations develop strategic alliances to capitalize on the capabilities of other organizations.

Creating a Learning Organization and an Ethical Organization (Chapter 11) Effective leaders set a direction, design the organization, and develop an organization that is committed to excellence and ethical behavior. In addition, given rapid and unpredictable change, leaders must create a "learning organization" to ensure that the entire organization can benefit from individual and collective talents.

Fostering Corporate Entrepreneurship (Chapter 12) With rapid and unpredictable change in the global marketplace, firms must continually improve and grow as well as find new ways to renew their organizations. Corporate entrepreneurship and innovation provide firms with new opportunities, and strategies should be formulated that enhance a firm's innovative capacity.

Chapter 13, "Analyzing Strategic Management Cases," provides guidelines and suggestions on how to evaluate cases in this course. Thus, the concepts and techniques discussed in these 12 chapters can be applied to real-world organizations.

Let's now address two concepts—corporate governance and stakeholder management—that are critical to the strategic management process.

>LO3

The vital role of corporate governance and stakeholder management as well as how "symbiosis" can be achieved among an organization's stakeholders.

The Role of Corporate Governance and Stakeholder Management

Most business enterprises that employ more than a few dozen people are organized as corporations. As you recall from your finance classes, the overall purpose of a corporation is to maximize the long-term return to the owners (shareholders). Thus, we may ask: Who is really responsible for fulfilling this purpose? Robert Monks and Neil Minow provide a useful definition of **corporate governance** as "the relationship among various participants in determining the direction and performance of corporations. The primary participants are (1) the shareholders, (2) the management (led by the chief executive officer), and (3) the board of directors."[33] This relationship is illustrated in Exhibit 1.4.

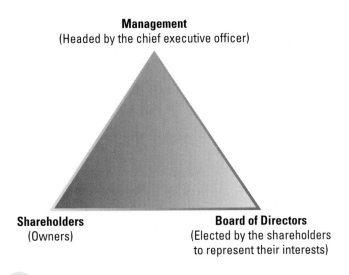

Management
(Headed by the chief executive officer)

Shareholders
(Owners)

Board of Directors
(Elected by the shareholders
to represent their interests)

Exhibit 1.4   **The Key Elements of Corporate Governance**

corporate governance the relationship among various participants in determining the direction and performance of corporations. The primary participants are (1) the shareholders, (2) the management (led by the chief executive officer), and (3) the board of directors.

The board of directors (BOD) are the elected representatives of the shareholders charged with ensuring that the interests and motives of management are aligned with those of the owners (i.e., shareholders). In many cases, the BOD is diligent in fulfilling its purpose. For example, Intel Corporation, the giant $38 billion maker of microprocessor chips, is widely recognized as an excellent example of sound governance practices. Its BOD follows guidelines to ensure that its members are independent (i.e., not members of the executive management team and do not have close personal ties to top executives) so that they can provide proper oversight, it has explicit guidelines on the selection of director candidates (to avoid "cronyism"), and it provides detailed procedures for formal evaluations of directors and the firm's top officers.[34] Such guidelines serve to ensure that management is acting in the best interests of shareholders.[35]

Recently, there has been much criticism as well as cynicism by both citizens and the business press about the poor job that management and the BODs of large corporations are doing. We only have to look at the scandals at firms such as Arthur Andersen, WorldCom, Enron, Tyco, and ImClone Systems.[36] Such malfeasance has led to an erosion of the public's trust in the governance of corporations. For example, a recent Gallup poll found that 90 percent of Americans felt that people leading corporations could not be trusted to look after the interests of their employees, and only 18 percent thought that corporations looked after their shareholders. Forty-three percent, in fact, believed that senior executives were in it only for themselves. In Britain, that figure, according to another poll, was an astonishing 95 percent.[37] Perhaps worst of all, in another study, 60 percent of directors (the very people who decide how much executives should earn) felt that executives were "dramatically overpaid"![38]

It is now clear that much of the bonus pay awarded to executives on Wall Street in the past few years was richly undeserved.[39] In the three years that led up to the recent collapse of seven big financial institutions, the chief executives of those firms collected a total of $80 million in performance bonuses and raked in $210 million in severance pay and earnings from stock sales. Let's take a closer look at a few of these payouts (the amounts below represent bonus pay, severance, and gains from stock sales from 2005 to late 2008):

- Richard Fuld, Lehman Brothers ($172 million)
- Kerry Killinger, Washington Mutual ($37 million)
- Martin Sullivan, American International Group ($36 million)

- Michael Perry, Indymac, Federal Bank ($20 million)
- Kenneth Thompson, Wachovia Corporation ($14 million)

Clearly, there is a strong need for improved corporate governance, and we will address this topic in Chapter 9.[40] We focus on three important mechanisms to ensure effective corporate governance: an effective and engaged board of directors, shareholder activism, and proper managerial rewards and incentives.[41] In addition to these internal controls, a key role is played by various external control mechanisms.[42] These include the auditors, banks, analysts, an active financial press, and the threat of hostile takeovers.

Alternative Perspectives of Stakeholder Management

Stakeholder management A firm's strategy for recognizing and responding to the interests of all its salient stakeholders.

Generating long-term returns for the shareholders is the primary goal of a publicly held corporation.[43] As noted by former Chrysler vice chairman Robert Lutz, "We are here to serve the shareholder and create shareholder value. I insist that the only person who owns the company is the person who paid good money for it."[44]

Despite the primacy of generating shareholder value, managers who focus solely on the interests of the owners of the business will often make poor decisions that lead to negative, unanticipated outcomes.[45] For example, decisions such as mass layoffs to increase profits, ignoring issues related to conservation of the natural environment to save money, and exerting excessive pressure on suppliers to lower prices can certainly harm the firm in the long run. Such actions would likely lead to negative outcomes such as alienated employees, increased governmental oversight and fines, and disloyal suppliers.

Clearly, in addition to *shareholders,* there are other *stakeholders* (e.g. suppliers, customers) who must be explicitly taken into account in the strategic management process.[46] A stakeholder can be defined as an individual or group, inside or outside the company, that has a stake in and can influence an organization's performance. Each stakeholder group makes various claims on the company. Exhibit 1.5 provides a list of major stakeholder groups and the nature of their claims on the company.

Zero Sum or Symbiosis?   There are two opposing ways of looking at the role of stakeholder management in the strategic management process.[47] The first one can be termed "zero sum." In this view, the role of management is to look upon the various stakeholders as competing for the organization's resources. In essence, the gain of one individual or group is the loss of another individual or group. For example, employees want higher wages (which drive down profits), suppliers want higher prices for their inputs and slower, more flexible delivery times (which drive up costs), customers want fast deliveries and higher quality (which drive up costs), the community at large wants charitable contributions (which take money from company goals), and so on. This zero-sum thinking is

Exhibit 1.5
An Organization's Key Stakeholders and the Nature of Their Claims

Stakeholder Group	Nature of Claim
Stockholders	Dividends, capital appreciation
Employees	Wages, benefits, safe working environment, job security
Suppliers	Payment on time, assurance of continued relationship
Creditors	Payment of interest, repayment of principal
Customers	Value, warranties
Government	Taxes, compliance with regulations
Communities	Good citizenship behavior such as charities, employment, not polluting the environment

rooted, in part, in the traditional conflict between workers and management, leading to the formation of unions and sometimes ending in adversarial union–management negotiations and long, bitter strikes.

Consider, for example, the many stakeholder challenges facing Wal-Mart, the world's largest retailer. We address these in Strategy Spotlight 1.4.

There will always be some conflicting demands. However, organizations can achieve mutual benefit through *stakeholder symbiosis,* which recognizes that stakeholders are dependent upon each other for their success and well-being.[48] Consider Outback Steakhouse:[49]

> Outback Steakhouse asked their employees to identify on a six-point scale how strongly they agreed or disagreed that Outback's principles and beliefs (P&Bs) were practiced in their particular restaurants. The turnover rate of the hourly employees in the group most strongly agreeing that the P&Bs were their stores' guiding ethos was half what it was in the group most strongly disagreeing. Five times as many customers in the strongly agreeing group indicated that they were likely to return. Further, at the strongly agreeing group's restaurants, revenues were 8.9 percent higher, cash flow was 27 percent higher, and pretax profit was 48 percent higher. Not surprisingly, it is now mandatory that Outback managers conduct this survey.

Crowdsourcing: Stakeholders Can Fulfill Multiple Roles   Thus far, we have implicitly assumed that stakeholders' roles are fixed. That is, a stakeholder is . . . pick one: a customer, supplier, employee, competitor, and so fourth. However, in practice, that is certainly not the case. Consider Shaw Industries, a vertically integrated carpet producer (which we discuss in Chapter 6). It acquired Amoco's polypropylene fiber manufacturing facilities, which provide carpet fibers for both internal use and sale to other manufacturers. Thus, some of Shaw's competitors are also its customers. Similarly, a retailer may share space on tractor trailers that it uses to ship products to its stores. This helps to decrease everyone's logistics costs—hence rivals become customers (or collaborators). And rivals can become key allies (within the boundaries of the same firm) when a firm acquires competitors to consolidate an industry—as has been the case in a myriad of industries such as finance, defense, and funeral homes.

To show how stakeholder roles are becoming more fluid, we'd like to introduce a concept that will be a theme through the text: **crowdsourcing.**[50] When and where did the term originate? In January 2006, open sourcing was, for most businesspeople, little more than an online curiosity. At that time, Jeff Howe of *Wired* magazine started to write an article about the phenomenon. However, he soon discovered a far more important story to be told: Large—as well as small—companies in a wide variety of industries had begun farming out serious tasks to individuals and groups on the Internet. Together with his editor, Mark Robinson, they coined a new term to describe the phenomenon. In June 2006, the article appeared in which *crowdsourcing* was defined as the tapping of the "latent talent of the (online) crowd." It has become the term of choice for a process that is infiltrating many aspects of business life.

crowdsourcing
practice wherein the Internet is used to tap a broad range of individuals and groups to generate ideas and solve problems.

Clearly, *crowdsourcing* has claimed some well-known successes, particularly on the product development front: Consider:

- The Linux operating system, created as an open-source alternative to Windows and UNIX, can be downloaded free and altered to suit any user's needs. And, with all the firepower brought to bear by the online open-source community, bugs in the system get fixed in a matter of hours.
- One of Amazon's smartest moves was to invite their customers to write online reviews. The customers are neither paid nor controlled by the company, but the content that they create adds enormous value to other customers and, therefore, to Amazon.

Wal-Mart: Some Challenging Stakeholder Issues

With 2008 revenues exceeding $400 billion, Wal-Mart is the world's largest retailer. Name practically any product category, from groceries to photo processing, and there's a good chance Wal-Mart is the No. 1 player in that space. Its buyer power is immense. For example, Wal-Mart isn't just Procter & Gamble's biggest customer—Wal-Mart is bigger than P&G's next nine customers *combined*. And, as one would expect, Wal-Mart faces a lot of challenges in managing demands/expectations from various stakeholders.

● Wal-Mart, the world's largest retailer, always faces many challenging issues which affect many stakeholders.

Wal-Mart strives to ramp up growth while many stakeholders are watching nervously: employees and trade unions; shareholders, investors, and creditors; suppliers

and joint venture partners; the governments of the U.S. and other nations where the retailer operates; and customers. In addition, many nongovernmental organizations, particularly in countries where the retailer buys its products, are closely monitoring Wal-Mart. Wal-Mart's stakeholders have different interests, and not all of them share the firm's goals. Each group has the ability, in various degrees, to influence the firm's choices and results. Clearly, this wasn't the case when Sam Walton built his first store in Rogers, Arkansas, in 1962.

Wal-Mart's slowing growth in the U.S. has many causes: a saturated home market, its customers' limited disposable incomes, and intense competition from rivals such as Costco and Target. The company has been subjected to negative publicity because of its strong dependence on imports, criticism about the wages and benefits it offers its roughly 1.3 million employees, and charges that illegal aliens work in its stores. Such factors have generated unfavorable publicity and intensified people's opposition to Wal-Mart's opening stores in urban areas.

Compounding Wal-Mart's challenges are that some of its strengths have turned into disadvantages. For example, its large market share in some product categories makes it difficult to grow same-store sales. Its low-cost sourcing practices have rendered it vulnerable to many health, safety, and environmental concerns that surround products manufactured in China. Further, its supply chain expertise does not help in the case of fashion and organic products, and its low-price image erodes its ability to sell upscale products (which, of course, offer better profit margins). Moreover, Wal-Mart's deep roots in rural America are of little use in overseas markets.

With regard to environment sustainability, Wal-Mart is determined to use its clout for good. It's pushing to create "zero waste" stores and sell more green products, with its sales of 145 million energy-saving light bulbs already dampening U.S. electricity consumption. In October 2005, it set ambitious environmental and sustainability goals, such as cutting total packaging 5 percent by 2013 and doubling the gas mileage of its trucking fleet by 2015.

On the global front, it's forcing Chinese manufacturers to clean up their ways. In November 2008, it told big mainland suppliers that they must become 20 percent more energy-efficient within three years to stay on contract, and they must disclose more. With Wal-Mart's pressure on China, the impact could be profound. As sustainability consultant Andrew Winston argues: "Only Wal-Mart is big enough to daunt China's worst practices. Even those who blame it for other practices recognize Wal-Mart's power in going green."

Sources: McGregor, J. 2008. The world's most influential companies. *BusinessWeek,* December 22: 43–53; Camillus, J. 2008. Strategy as a wicked problem. *Harvard Business Review,* 86 (5): 100–101; Sacks, D. 2007. Working with the enemy. *Fast Company,* September: 74–81; and, Fishman, C. 2006. The Wal-Mart effect and a decent society: Who knew shopping was so important. *Academy of Management Perspectives,* 20 (3): 6–25.

strategy spotlight

Crowdsourcing: How Customers Also Became Suppliers at Intuit

Intuit, the financial software powerhouse, began operations in 1984. Its first product was Quicken, which has now been purchased by more people than all other personal finance products combined. About two decades later, Intuit decided to test the idea of customer-support forums. However, it wanted to avoid the hassles of building and managing them. Thus, it turned to LiveWorld, a specialist in creating, operating, and moderating social networks and online communities.

The Quicken forums are organized according to products and computer type—PC or Mac. Other customers quickly answer Quicken queries, typically in helpful detail. In fact, volunteers answer 70 percent of all support questions—taking an enormous load off Quicken's customer service staff. For example, when a 10-year customer complained that some of his mutual fund data wasn't showing in a Quicken capital gains report, several other customers began a dialogue. Some wrote long, detailed explanations of the entire capital-gains process.

As one would expect, LiveWorld and its rivals charge for their services. Whether a company wants to take that route to get customers to serve themselves depends on its culture, finances, and technical savvy. However, it is an option that several companies such as America Online, Campbell Soup, Dove, and MINI Cooper, have embraced.

Source: Libert, B. & Spector, J. 2008. *We are smarter than me.* Philadelphia: Wharton School Publishing.

crowdsourcing

- Roughly five million users per month swear by Wikipedia, the free online encyclopedia created and updated by Internet volunteers to the tune of roughly two million articles and counting.

Throughout the book, we will introduce examples of *crowdsourcing* to show its relevance to key strategy concepts. For example, in Chapter 2, we'll discuss how Virgin Mobile USA has used it for everything from designing phones to coming up with names for service plans. Chapter 5 discusses Netflix, which has offered a $1 million prize to anyone who can build a system that is 10 percent better than Cinematch—its in-house system to personalize movie recommendations. And, in Chapter 10, we discuss how Eli Lilly, the pharmaceutical giant launched Innocentive, the first online, incentive-based scientific network created specifically for the global research and development community.

Strategy Spotlight 1.5 provides an example of how customers also became valued suppliers—and, in the process, help save money in its customer service operation.

Social Responsibility and Environmental Sustainability: Moving beyond the Immediate Stakeholders

Organizations cannot ignore the interests and demands of stakeholders such as citizens and society in general that are beyond its immediate constituencies—customers, owners, suppliers, and employees. That is, they must consider the needs of the broader community at large and act in a socially responsible manner.[51]

Social responsibility is the expectation that businesses or individuals will strive to improve the overall welfare of society.[52] From the perspective of a business, this means that managers must take active steps to make society better by virtue of the business being in existence.[53] Similar to norms and values, actions that constitute socially responsible behavior tend to change over time. In the 1970s affirmative action was a high priority and during the 1990s and up to the present time, the public has been concerned about environmental

social responsibility the expectation that businesses or individuals will strive to improve the overall welfare of society.

quality. Many firms have responded to this by engaging in recycling and reducing waste. And in the wake of terrorist attacks on New York City and the Pentagon, as well as the continuing threat from terrorists worldwide, a new kind of priority has arisen: the need to be vigilant concerning public safety.

>LO4
The importance of social responsibility, including environmental sustainability, and how it can enhance a corporation's innovation strategy.

Today, demands for greater corporate responsibility have accelerated.[54] These include corporate critics, social investors, activists, and, increasingly, customers who claim to assess corporate responsibility when making purchasing decisions. Such demands go well beyond product and service quality.[55] They include a focus on issues such as labor standards, environmental sustainability, financial and accounting reporting, procurement, and environmental practices.[56] At times, a firm's reputation can be tarnished by exceedingly poor judgment on the part of one of its managers.

> In 2006, Judith Regan, a publisher at HarperCollins, was set to publish a book by O. J. Simpson called *If I Did It,* detailing how he would have committed the 1995 murder of his ex-wife Nicole Brown Simpson and her friend, Ron Goldman. The book was characterized by Regan as O. J.'s "confession," and it earned the world's outrage as an "evil sweeps stunt" that will likely be remembered as a low point in American culture. Regan's boss, News Corporation Chairman Rupert Murdoch cancelled the book and the TV special that was also planned. But this was not before pre-orders for *If I Did It* cracked the Top 20 on Amazon.com. Not surprisingly, Judith Regan was fired.[57]

A key stakeholder group that appears to be particularly susceptible to corporate social responsibility (CSR) initiatives is customers.[58] Surveys indicate a strong positive relationship between CSR behaviors and consumers' reactions to a firm's products and services.[59] For example:

- Corporate Citizenship's poll conducted by Cone Communications found that "84 percent of Americans say they would be likely to switch brands to one associated with a good cause, if price and quality are similar."[60]
- Hill & Knowlton/Harris's Interactive poll reveals that "79 percent of Americans take corporate citizenship into account when deciding whether to buy a particular company's product and 37 percent consider corporate citizenship an important factor when making purchasing decisions."[61]

Such findings are consistent with a large body of research that confirms the positive influence of CSR on consumers' company evaluations and product purchase intentions across a broad range of product categories.

The Triple Bottom Line: Incorporating Financial as well as Environmental and Social Costs

Triple bottom line Assessment of a firm's financial, social, and environmental performance.

Many companies are now measuring what has been called a **"triple bottom line."** This involves assessing financial, social, and environmental performance. Shell, NEC, Procter & Gamble, and others have recognized that failing to account for the environmental and social costs of doing business poses risks to the company and its community.[62]

The environmental revolution has been almost four decades in the making.[63] In the 1960s and 1970s, companies were in a state of denial regarding their firms' impact on the natural environment. However, a series of visible ecological problems created a groundswell for strict governmental regulation. In the U.S., Lake Erie was "dead," and in Japan, people died of mercury poisoning. Clearly, the effects of global warming are being felt throughout the world. Some other examples include the following:

- Ice roads are melting, so Canadian diamond miners must airlift equipment at great cost instead of trucking it in.
- More severe storms and rising seas mean oil companies must build stronger rigs, and cities must build higher seawalls.

- The loss of permafrost and protective sea ice may force villages like Alaska's Shismaref to relocate.
- Yukon River salmon and fisheries are threatened by a surge of parasites associated with a jump in water temperature.
- Later winters have let beetles spread in British Columbia killing 22 million acres of pine forests, an area the size of Maine.
- In Mali, Africa, crops are threatened. The rainy season is now too short for rice, and the dry season is too hot for potatoes.[64]

Stuart Hart, writing in the *Harvard Business Review,* addresses the magnitude of problems and challenges associated with the natural environment:

> The challenge is to develop a *sustainable global economy:* an economy that the planet is capable of supporting indefinitely. Although we may be approaching ecological recovery in the developed world, the planet as a whole remains on an unsustainable course. Increasingly, the scourges of the late twentieth century—depleted farmland, fisheries, and forests; choking urban pollution; poverty; infectious disease; and migration—are spilling over geopolitical borders. The simple fact is this: in meeting our needs, we are destroying the ability of future generations to meet theirs ... corporations are the only organizations with the resources, the technology, the global reach, and, ultimately, the motivation to achieve sustainability.[65]

● These parabolic mirrors in a California desert focus solar energy. Solar power is a more sustainable, environmentally friendly option than nuclear power plants or coal- and oil-fired power plants.

Environmental sustainability is now a value embraced by the most competitive and successful multinational companies.[66] The McKinsey Corporation's survey of more than 400 senior executives of companies around the world found that 92 percent agreed with former Sony President Akio Morita's contention that the environmental challenge will be one of the central issues in the 21st century.[67] Virtually all executives acknowledged their firm's responsibility to control pollution, and 83 percent agreed that corporations have an environmental responsibility for their products even after they are sold.

For many successful firms, environmental values are now becoming a central part of their cultures and management processes. And, as noted earlier, environmental impacts are being audited and accounted for as the "third bottom line." According to one 2004 corporate report, "If we aren't good corporate citizens as reflected in a Triple Bottom Line that takes into account social and environmental responsibilities along with financial ones—eventually our stock price, our profits, and our entire business could suffer."[68] And, according to a KPMG study of 350 firms: "More big multinational firms are seeing the benefits of improving their environmental performance. . . . Firms are saving money and boosting share performance by taking a close look at how their operations impact the environment . . . Companies see that they can make money as well." Strategy Spotlight 1.6 discusses how Shaw Industries benefits financially from its environmental initiatives.

Shaw Industries: It Pays to Go Green

Shaw Industries, a Berkshire Hathaway company, produces carpet tile—industrial flooring that is installed in office buildings around the world. In 1999, Shaw was confronted by growing environmental concern over carpet waste (more than 95 percent of old carpet is ripped up and dumped in landfills) and the specter of higher raw-materials costs. Its response: embark on a major initiative to rethink its business and create what it calls "the carpet of the twenty-first century."

Carpet tile like Shaw's consists of the backing, which holds the carpet flat, and the face fiber, which creates the soft walking surface. Prior to 1995 Shaw produced a branded backing made from PVC plastic—a potentially toxic substance that is difficult to recycle. So, at substantial expense, the firm searched for a more sustainable solution.

Based on an intuitive understanding of sustainability, Shaw recognized the need for a simple palette of nontoxic materials for its product. It also made virtuous recycling a goal. Its choice of Nylon 6 face fiber, branded Eco Solution Q, and a polyolefin backing, called EcoWorx, gave Shaw materials that could be cycled from high-value application to high-value application without ever losing performance or functionality.

The company developed an integrated production system that could take carpet at the end of its useful life, separate the backing, grind it up, and put it right back into the manufacturing process. Coming out at the other end was brand-new carpet tile. The Environmental Protection Agency (EPA) recognized EcoWorx with its Presidential Green Chemistry Challenge Award in 2003. The next year, Shaw exited from PVC carpet backing not only because of environmental sustainability issues but also because 70 percent of their customers selected the new technology. As of 2008, Shaw had 500 million square feet of EcoWorx installed around the world. According to Randy Merritt, Executive Vice President of Marketing:

> EcoWorx meets customer demand for a PVC alternative product and provides a sustainable flooring solution that makes good economic, functional and environmental sense for all stakeholders.

Another key benefit was that Shaw's sustainable product platform also helped free the company from the vagaries of the raw-materials markets that plague the industry. Petroleum is the primary input for both the backing and the fiber used in most products, and when Shaw began its efforts oil was at $19 a barrel. Given that oil has typically traded at several times that figure in recent years, Shaw seems like a savvy visionary. In essence, Shaw can look to a future when the skyscrapers of the world's cities, rather than the wellheads of Saudi Arabia, will supply its raw materials!

Source: Unruh, G. C. 2008. The biosphere rules. *Harvard Business Review,* 86 (2): 111–117; www.shawgreenedge.com; and, Allmond, K. 2004. Shaw ceases production of polyvinyl chloride, replacement carpet tile backing recognized by the EPA. Shaw Industries Press Release, June 14.

environmental sustainability

>LO5
The need for greater empowerment throughout the organization.

The Strategic Management Perspective: An Imperative throughout the Organization

Strategic management requires managers to take an integrative view of the organization and assess how all of the functional areas and activities fit together to help an organization achieve its goals and objectives. This cannot be accomplished if only the top managers in the organization take an integrative, strategic perspective of issues facing the firm and everyone else "fends for themselves" in their independent, isolated functional areas. Instead, people throughout the organization must strive toward overall goals.

The need for such a perspective is accelerating in today's increasingly complex, interconnected, ever-changing, global economy. As noted by Peter Senge of MIT, the days when Henry Ford, Alfred Sloan, and Tom Watson (top executives at Ford, General Motors, and IBM, respectively) "learned for the organization are gone." He goes on to say:

> In an increasingly dynamic, interdependent, and unpredictable world, it is simply no longer possible for anyone to "figure it all out at the top." The old model, "the top thinks and the

local acts," must now give way to integrating thinking and acting at all levels. While the challenge is great, so is the potential payoff. "The person who figures out how to harness the collective genius of the people in his or her organization," according to former Citibank CEO Walter Wriston, "is going to blow the competition away."[69]

To develop and mobilize people and other assets, leaders are needed throughout the organization.[70] No longer can organizations be effective if the top "does the thinking" and the rest of the organization "does the work." Everyone must be involved in the strategic management process. There is a critical need for three types of leaders:

- *Local line leaders* who have significant profit-and-loss responsibility.
- *Executive leaders* who champion and guide ideas, create a learning infrastructure, and establish a domain for taking action.
- *Internal networkers* who, although they have little positional power and formal authority, generate their power through the conviction and clarity of their ideas.[71]

Sally Helgesen, author of *The Web of Inclusion: A New Architecture for Building Great Organizations,* also expressed the need for leaders throughout the organization. She asserted that many organizations "fall prey to the heroes-and-drones syndrome, exalting the value of those in powerful positions while implicitly demeaning the contributions of those who fail to achieve top rank."[72] Culture and processes in which leaders emerge at all levels, both up and down as well as across the organization, typify today's high-performing firms.[73]

Top-level executives are key in setting the tone for the empowerment of employees. Consider Richard Branson, founder of the Virgin Group, whose core businesses include retail operations, hotels, communications, and an airline. He is well known for creating a culture and an informal structure where anybody in the organization can be involved in generating and acting upon new business ideas. In an interview, he stated,

> [S]peed is something that we are better at than most companies. We don't have formal board meetings, committees, etc. If someone has an idea, they can pick up the phone and talk to me. I can vote "done, let's do it." Or, better still, they can just go ahead and do it. They know that they are not going to get a mouthful from me if they make a mistake. Rules and regulations are not our forte. Analyzing things to death is not our kind of thing. We very rarely sit back and analyze what we do.[74]

To inculcate a strategic management perspective throughout the organization, managers must often make a major effort to effect transformational change. This involves extensive communication, incentives, training, and development. For example, under the direction of Nancy Snyder, a corporate vice president, Whirlpool, the world's largest producer of household appliances, brought about a significant shift in the firm's reputation as an innovator.[75] This five-year initiative included both financial investments in capital spending as well as a series of changes in management processes, including training innovation mentors, making innovation a significant portion of leadership development programs, enrolling all salaried employees in online courses in business innovation, and providing employees with an innovation portal that allows them access to multiple innovation tools and data. We discuss Whirlpool's initiatives in more detail in Chapter 11.

We'd like to close with our favorite example of how inexperience can be a virtue. It further reinforces the benefits of having broad involvement throughout the organization in the strategic management process (see Strategy Spotlight 1.7).

Ensuring Coherence in Strategic Direction

Employees and managers throughout the organization must strive toward common goals and objectives. By specifying desired results, it becomes much easier to move forward. Otherwise, when no one knows what the firm is striving to accomplish, they have no idea of what to work toward.

>LO6
How an awareness of a hierarchy of strategic goals can help an organization achieve coherence in its strategic direction.

Strategy and the Value of Inexperience

Peter Gruber, chairman of Mandalay Entertainment, explained how his firm benefited from the creative insights of an inexperienced intern.

Sometimes life is all about solving problems. In the movie business, at least, there seems to be one around every corner. One of the most effective lessons I've learned about tackling problems is to start by asking not "How to?" but rather "What if?" I learned that lesson from a young woman who was interning on a film I was producing. She actually saved the movie from being shelved by the studio.

The movie, *Gorillas in the Mist,* had turned into a logistical nightmare. We wanted to film at an altitude of 11,000 feet, in the middle of the jungle, in Rwanda—then on the verge of a revolution—and to use more than 200 animals. Warner Brothers, the studio financing the movie, worried that we would exceed our budget. But our biggest problem was that the screenplay required the gorillas to do what we wrote—in other words, to "act." If they couldn't or wouldn't, we'd have to fall back on a formula that the studio had seen fail before: using dwarfs in gorilla suits on a soundstage.

Source: Gruber, P. 1998. My greatest lesson. *Fast Company* 15: 88, 90.

We called an emergency meeting to solve these problems. In the middle of it, a young intern asked, "What if you let the gorillas write the story?" Everyone laughed and wondered what she was doing in the meeting with experienced filmmakers. Hours later, someone casually asked her what she had meant. She said, "What if you sent a really good cinematographer into the jungle with a ton of film to shoot the gorillas. Then you could write a story around what the gorillas did on film." It was a brilliant idea. And we did exactly what she suggested: We sent Alan Root, an Academy Award–nominated cinematographer, into the jungle for three weeks. He came back with phenomenal footage that practically wrote the story for us. We shot the film for $20 million—half of the original budget!

This woman's inexperience enabled her to see opportunities where we saw only boundaries. This experience taught me three things. First, ask high-quality questions, like "What if?" Second, find people who add new perspectives and create new conversations. As experienced filmmakers, we believed that our way was the only way—and that the intern lacked the experience to have an opinion. Third, pay attention to those with new voices. If you want unlimited options for solving a problem, engage the what if before you lock onto the how to. You'll be surprised by what you discover.

---

hierarchy of goals organizational goals ranging from, at the top, those that are less specific yet able to evoke powerful and compelling mental images, to, at the bottom, those that are more specific and measurable.

vision organizational goal(s) that evoke(s) powerful and compelling mental images.

Organizations express priorities best through stated goals and objectives that form a **hierarchy of goals,** which includes its vision, mission, and strategic objectives.[76] What visions may lack in specificity, they make up for in their ability to evoke powerful and compelling mental images. On the other hand, strategic objectives tend to be more specific and provide a more direct means of determining if the organization is moving toward broader, overall goals.[77] Visions, as one would expect, also have longer time horizons than either mission statements or strategic objectives. Exhibit 1.6 depicts the hierarchy of goals and its relationship to two attributes: general versus specific and time horizon.

Organizational Vision

A **vision** is a goal that is "massively inspiring, overarching, and long term."[78] It represents a destination that is driven by and evokes passion. A vision may or may not succeed; it depends on whether everything else happens according to a firm's strategy. As Mark Hurd, Hewlett-Packard's CEO, humorously pointed out, "Without execution, vision is just another word for hallucination."[79]

Leaders must develop and implement a vision. In a survey of executives from 20 different countries, respondents were asked what they believed were a leader's key traits.[80]

Exhibit 1.6 A Hierarchy of Goals

Ninety-eight percent responded that "a strong sense of vision" was the most important. Similarly, when asked about the critical knowledge skills, the leaders cited "strategy formulation to achieve a vision" as the most important skill. In other words, managers need to have not only a vision but also a plan to implement it. Regretfully, 90 percent reported a lack of confidence in their own skills and ability to conceive a vision. For example, T. J. Rogers, CEO of Cypress Semiconductor, an electronic chipmaker that faced some difficulties in 1992, lamented that his own shortsightedness caused the danger, "I did not have the 50,000-foot view, and got caught."[81]

One of the most famous examples of a vision is Disneyland's: "To be the happiest place on earth." Other examples are:

- "Restoring patients to full life." (Medtronic)
- "We want to satisfy all of our customers' financial needs and help them succeed financially." (Wells Fargo)
- "Our vision is to be the world's best quick service restaurant." (McDonald's)
- "To organize the world's information and make it universally accessible and useful." (Google)

Although such visions cannot be accurately measured by a specific indicator of how well they are being achieved, they do provide a fundamental statement of an organization's values, aspirations, and goals. Such visions go well beyond narrow financial objectives, of course, and strive to capture both the minds and hearts of employees.

The vision statement may also contain a slogan, diagram, or picture—whatever grabs attention.[82] The aim is to capture the essence of the more formal parts of the vision in a few words that are easily remembered, yet that evoke the spirit of the entire vision statement. In its 20-year battle with Xerox, Canon's slogan, or battle cry, was "Beat Xerox." Motorola's slogan is "Total Customer Satisfaction." Outboard Marine Corporation's slogan is "To Take the World Boating."

Clearly, vision statements are not a cure-all. Sometimes they backfire and erode a company's credibility. Visions fail for many reasons, including the following:[83]

The Walk Doesn't Match the Talk   An idealistic vision can arouse employee enthusiasm. However, that same enthusiasm can be quickly dashed if employees find that senior management's behavior is not consistent with the vision. Often, vision is a sloganeering campaign of new buzzwords and empty platitudes like "devotion to the customer," "teamwork," or "total quality" that aren't consistently backed by management's action.

Irrelevance   Visions created in a vacuum—unrelated to environmental threats or opportunities or an organization's resources and capabilities—often ignore the needs of those who are expected to buy into them. Employees reject visions that are not anchored in reality.

Not the Holy Grail   Managers often search continually for the one elusive solution that will solve their firm's problems—that is, the next "holy grail" of management. They may have tried other management fads only to find that they fell short of their expectations. However, they remain convinced that one exists. A vision simply cannot be viewed as a magic cure for an organization's illness.

Too Much Focus Leads to Missed Opportunities   The downside of too much focus is that in directing people and resources toward a grandiose vision, losses can be devastating. Consider, Samsung's ambitious venture into automobile manufacturing:

> In 1992, Kun-Hee Lee, chairman of South Korea's Samsung Group, created a bold strategy to become one of the 10 largest car makers by 2010. Seduced by the clarity of the vision, Samsung bypassed staged entry through a joint venture or initial supply contract. Instead, Samsung borrowed heavily to build a state-of-the-art research and design facility and erect a greenfield factory, complete with cutting-edge robotics. Samsung Auto suffered operating losses and crushing interest charges from the beginning. And within a few years the business was divested for a fraction of the initial investment.[84]

An Ideal Future Irreconciled with the Present   Although visions are not designed to mirror reality, they must be anchored somehow in it. People have difficulty identifying with a vision that paints a rosy picture of the future but does not account for the often hostile environment in which the firm competes or that ignores some of the firm's weaknesses.

Mission Statements

mission statement
a set of organizational goals that include both the purpose of the organization, its scope of operations, and the basis of its competitive advantage.

A company's **mission statement** differs from its vision in that it encompasses both the purpose of the company as well as the basis of competition and competitive advantage.

Exhibit 1.7 contains the vision statement and mission statement of WellPoint Health Network, a giant $61 billion managed health care organization. Note that while the vision statement is broad based, the mission statement is more specific and focused on the means by which the firm will compete.

Effective mission statements incorporate the concept of stakeholder management, suggesting that organizations must respond to multiple constituencies. Customers, employees, suppliers, and owners are the primary stakeholders, but others may also play an important role.

Exhibit 1.7
Comparing WellPoint Health Network's Vision and Mission

Vision
WellPoint *will redefine our industry:*
Through a new generation of consumer-friendly products that put individuals back in control of their future.

Mission
The WellPoint companies provide health *security* by offering a *choice* of quality branded health and related financial services *designed* to meet the *changing* expectations of individuals, families, and their sponsors throughout a *lifelong* relationship.

Source: WellPoint Health Network company records.

Mission statements also have the greatest impact when they reflect an organization's enduring, overarching strategic priorities and competitive positioning. Mission statements also can vary in length and specificity. The two mission statements below illustrate these issues.

- To produce superior financial returns for our shareholders as we serve our customers with the highest quality transportation, logistics, and e-commerce. (Federal Express)
- To be the very best in the business. Our game plan is status go . . . we are constantly looking ahead, building on our strengths, and reaching for new goals. In our quest of these goals, we look at the three stars of the Brinker logo and are reminded of the basic values that are the strength of this company . . . People, Quality and Profitability. Everything we do at Brinker must support these core values. We also look at the eight golden flames depicted in our logo, and are reminded of the fire that ignites our mission and makes up the heart and soul of this incredible company. These flames are: Customers, Food, Team, Concepts, Culture, Partners, Community, and Shareholders. As keeper of these flames, we will continue to build on our strengths and work together to be the best in the business. (Brinker International, whose restaurant chains include Chili's and On the Border)[85]

Few mission statements identify profit or any other financial indicator as the sole purpose of the firm. Indeed, many do not even mention profit or shareholder return.[86] Employees of organizations or departments are usually the mission's most important audience. For them, the mission should help to build a common understanding of purpose and commitment to nurture.

A good mission statement, by addressing each principal theme, must communicate why an organization is special and different. Two studies that linked corporate values and mission statements with financial performance found that the most successful firms mentioned values other than profits. The less successful firms focused almost entirely on profitability.[87] In essence, profit is the metaphorical equivalent of oxygen, food, and water that the body requires. They are not the point of life, but without them, there is no life.

Although vision statements tend to be quite enduring and seldom change, a firm's mission can and should change when competitive conditions dramatically change or the firm is faced with new threats or opportunities. Strategy Spotlight 1.8 provides an example of a firm, NextJet, that changed its mission in order to realize new opportunities.

Strategic Objectives

Strategic objectives are used to operationalize the mission statement.[88] That is, they help to provide guidance on how the organization can fulfill or move toward the "higher goals" in the goal hierarchy—the mission and vision. Thus, they are more specific and cover a more well-defined time frame. Setting objectives demands a yardstick to measure the fulfillment of the objectives.[89]

Exhibit 1.8 lists several firms' strategic objectives—both financial and nonfinancial. While most of them are directed toward generating greater profits and returns for the owners of the business, others are directed at customers or society at large.

For objectives to be meaningful, they need to satisfy several criteria. They must be:

- *Measurable.* There must be at least one indicator (or yardstick) that measures progress against fulfilling the objective.
- *Specific.* This provides a clear message as to what needs to be accomplished.
- *Appropriate.* It must be consistent with the organization's vision and mission.
- *Realistic.* It must be an achievable target given the organization's capabilities and opportunities in the environment. In essence, it must be challenging but doable.
- *Timely.* There must be a time frame for achieving the objective. As the economist John Maynard Keynes once said, "In the long run, we are all dead!"

strategic objectives
A set of organizational goals that are used to operationalize the mission statement and that are specific and cover a well-defined time frame.

strategy spotlight

1.8

NextJet's Change of Mission

The dot-com crash was only the first blow to NextJet, Inc., a Dallas-based business launched in 1999 to ship packages overnight. The bigger blow came with the September 11 terrorist attacks, when passenger airlines were forced to add security and reduce flights. One of NextJet's strengths was its nationwide network of local courier services that got packages to and from airports, all coordinated through their proprietary software that could determine the optimal routing. However, the company's business model fell apart when it could not rely on the airlines to get packages between cities quickly enough to make the added cost for same-day delivery worthwhile.

Rather than give up, NextJet reinvented the business around the idea that its most important asset was the software itself. The company's new mission received almost

immediate validation when its software was deployed successfully at United Parcel Service (UPS). NextJet's software provides Atlanta-based UPS with tools for setting online rates and tracking packages. While a lot of same-day business did evaporate when corporations tightened the reins on spending, some things can't wait overnight to be shipped. For example, makers of hospital equipment may need to ship critical parts within a few hours. NextJet's software can help shippers make important decisions in less than a second, finding the fastest and most economical route among air, truck, and courier operations. In addition to UPS, its customers include FedEx, Greyhound, and Menlo Worldwide.

NextJet serves a very large industry segment—Service Parts & Logistics (SPL). The annual expenditures for spare parts in the United States are estimated to be $500 billion. And managers have increased their focus on the importance of effective logistics operations, given its potential impact on a firm's income. After all, whether or not a production line is running can often depend on the quick and effective installation of relatively inexpensive spare parts.

Sources: Goldstein, A. 2002. NextJet is hoping that its software can deliver. *Dallas Morning News,* December 4: 1–3; Nelson, M. G. 2001. NextJet network adds wireless. *Information Week,* April 30: 34; Anonymous. 2004. Who's who in e-logistics. www.americanshipper.com, September; and Hudspeth, B., & Jones, J. 2004. Service parts and logistics: Should you in-source or outsource? *3pl line,* www.inboundlogistics.com, October.

Exhibit 1.8
Strategic Objectives

Strategic Objectives (Financial)

- Increase sales growth 6 percent to 8 percent and accelerate core net earnings growth from 13 percent to 15 percent per share in each of the next 5 years. (Procter & Gamble)
- Generate Internet-related revenue of $1.5 billion. (AutoNation)
- Increase the contribution of Banking Group earnings from investments, brokerage, and insurance from 16 percent to 25 percent. (Wells Fargo)
- Cut corporate overhead costs by $30 million per year. (Fortune Brands)

Strategic Objectives (Nonfinancial)

- We want a majority of our customers, when surveyed, to say they consider Wells Fargo the best financial institution in the community. (Wells Fargo)
- We want to operate 6,000 stores by 2010—up from 3,000 in the year 2000. (Walgreen's)
- We want to be the top-ranked supplier to our customers. (PPG)
- Reduce greenhouse gases by 10 percent (from a 1990 base) by 2010. (BP Amoco)

Sources: Company documents and annual reports.

When objectives satisfy the above criteria, there are many benefits. First, they help to channel all employees' efforts toward common goals. This helps the organization concentrate and conserve valuable resources and work collectively in a timely manner.

Second, challenging objectives can help to motivate and inspire employees to higher levels of commitment and effort. Much research has supported the notion that people work harder when they are striving toward specific goals instead of being asked simply to "do their best."

Third, as we noted earlier in the chapter, there is always the potential for different parts of an organization to pursue their own goals rather than overall company goals. Although well intentioned, these may work at cross-purposes to the organization as a whole. Meaningful objectives thus help to resolve conflicts when they arise.

Finally, proper objectives provide a yardstick for rewards and incentives. They will ensure a greater sense of equity or fairness when rewards are allocated.

In summary, an organization must take care to ensure consistency throughout in how it implements strategic objectives. Consider how Textron, a $13 billion conglomerate, ensures that its corporate goals are effectively implemented:

> At Textron, each business unit identifies "improvement priorities" that it must act upon to realize the performance outlined in the firm's overall strategic plan. Each improvement priority is translated into action items with clearly defined accountabilities, timetables, and key performance indicators (KPIs) that enable executives to tell how a unit is delivering on a priority. Improvement priorities and action items cascade to every level at the firm—from the management committee (consisting of Textron's top five executives) down to the lowest levels in each of the company's 10 business units. Says Lewis Campbell, Textron's CEO, "Everyone needs to know: 'If I have only one hour to work, here's what I'm going to focus on.' Our goal deployment process makes each individual's accountabilities and priorities clear."[90]

As indicated in this example, organizations have lower-level objectives that are more specific than strategic objectives. These are often referred to as short-term objectives—essential components of a firm's "action plan" that are critical in implementing the firm's chosen strategy. We discuss these issues in detail in Chapter 9.

Reflecting on Career Implications . . .

- *Attributes of Strategic Management:* How do your activities and actions contribute to the goals of your organization? Observe the decisions you make on the job. What are the short-term and long-term implications of your decisions and actions? Have you recently made a decision that might yield short-term profits but might negatively impact the long-term goals of the organization (e.g., cutting maintenance expenses to meet a quarterly profit target)?
- *Intended versus Emergent Strategies:* Don't be too inflexible in your career strategies; strive to take advantage of new opportunities as they arise. Many promising career opportunities may "emerge" that were not part of your intended career strategy or your specific job assignment. Take initiative by pursuing opportunities to get additional training (e.g., learn a software or a statistical package), volunteering for a short-term overseas assignment, etc.
- *Ambidexterity:* Avoid defining your role in the organization too narrowly; look for opportunities to leverage your talents and your organization's resources to create value for your organization. This often involves collaborating with people in other departments or with your organization's customers and suppliers.
- *Strategic Coherence:* Focus your efforts on the "big picture" in your organization. In doing this, you should always strive to assure that your efforts are directed toward your organization's vision, mission, and strategic objectives.

Summary

We began this introductory chapter by defining strategic management and articulating some of its key attributes. Strategic management is defined as "consisting of the analyses, decisions, and actions an organization undertakes to create and sustain competitive advantages." The issue of how and why some firms outperform others in the marketplace is central to the study of strategic management. Strategic management has four key attributes: It is directed at overall organizational goals, includes multiple stakeholders, incorporates both short-term and long-term perspectives, and incorporates trade-offs between efficiency and effectiveness.

The second section discussed the strategic management process. Here, we paralleled the above definition of strategic management and focused on three core activities in the strategic management process—strategy analysis, strategy formulation, and strategy implementation. We noted how each of these activities is highly interrelated to and interdependent on the others. We also discussed how each of the 12 chapters in this text fits into the three core activities.

Next, we introduced two important concepts—corporate governance and stakeholder management—which must be taken into account throughout the strategic management process. Governance mechanisms can be broadly divided into two groups: internal and external. Internal governance mechanisms include shareholders (owners), management (led by the chief executive officer), and the board of directors. External control is exercised by auditors, banks, analysts, and an active business press as well as the threat of takeovers. We identified five key stakeholders in all organizations: owners, customers, suppliers, employees, and society at large. Successful firms go beyond an overriding focus on satisfying solely the interests of owners. Rather, they recognize the inherent conflicts that arise among the demands of the various stakeholders as well as the need to endeavor to attain "symbiosis"—that is, interdependence and mutual benefit—among the various stakeholder groups. The emerging practice of crowdsourcing, wherein the Internet is used to generate ideas and solve problems, is leading to an evolution in stakeholder roles. Managers must also recognize the need to act in a socially responsible manner which, if done effectively, can enhance a firm's innovativeness. They also should recognize and incorporate issues related to environmental sustainability in their strategic actions.

In the fourth section, we discussed factors that have accelerated the rate of unpredictable change that managers face today. Such factors, and the combination of them, have increased the need for managers and employees throughout the organization to have a strategic management perspective and to become more empowered.

The final section addressed the need for consistency among a firm's vision, mission, and strategic objectives. Collectively, they form an organization's hierarchy of goals. Visions should evoke powerful and compelling mental images. However, they are not very specific. Strategic objectives, on the other hand, are much more specific and are vital to ensuring that the organization is striving toward fulfilling its vision and mission.

Summary Review Questions

1. How is "strategic management" defined in the text, and what are its four key attributes?

2. Briefly discuss the three key activities in the strategic management process. Why is it important for managers to recognize the interdependent nature of these activities?

3. Explain the concept of "stakeholder management." Why shouldn't managers be solely interested in stockholder management, that is, maximizing the returns for owners of the firm—its shareholders?

4. What is "corporate governance"? What are its three key elements and how can it be improved?

5. How can "symbiosis" (interdependence, mutual benefit) be achieved among a firm's stakeholders?

6. Why do firms need to have a greater strategic management perspective and empowerment in the strategic management process throughout the organization?

7. What is meant by a "hierarchy of goals"? What are the main components of it, and why must consistency be achieved among them?

Key Terms

romantic view of leadership, 5
external view of leadership, 6
strategic management, 9
strategy 9
competitive advantage 9
operational effectiveness, 9
stakeholders, 10
effectiveness, 11
efficiency, 11
ambidexterity, 11
intended strategy, 13
realized strategy, 13
corporate governance, 17
stakeholder management 18
crowdsourcing, 19
social responsibility, 21
triple bottom line, 22
hierarchy of goals, 26
vision, 26
mission statement, 28
strategic objectives, 29

Experiential Exercise

Using the Internet or library sources, select four organizations—two in the private sector and two in the public sector. Find their mission statements. Complete the following exhibit by identifying the stakeholders that are mentioned. Evaluate the differences between firms in the private sector and those in the public sector.

Name			
Mission Statement			
Stakeholders (✓ = mentioned)			
1. Customers			
2. Suppliers			
3. Managers/employees			
4. Community-at-large			
5. Owners			
6. Others?			
7. Others?			

Application Questions Exercises

1. Go to the Internet and look up one of these company sites: www.walmart.com, www.ge.com, or www.fordmotor.com. What are some of the key events that would represent the "romantic" perspective of leadership? What are some of the key events that depict the "external control" perspective of leadership?

2. Select a company that competes in an industry in which you are interested. What are some of the recent demands that stakeholders have placed on this company? Can you find examples of how the company is trying to develop "symbiosis" (interdependence and mutual benefit) among its stakeholders? (Use the Internet and library resources.)

3. Provide examples of companies that are actively trying to increase the amount of empowerment in the strategic management process throughout the organization. Do these companies seem to be having positive outcomes? Why? Why not?

4. Look up the vision statements and/or mission statements for a few companies. Do you feel that they are constructive and useful as a means of motivating employees and providing a strong strategic direction? Why? Why not? (*Note:* Annual reports, along with the Internet, may be good sources of information.)

Ethics Questions

1. A company focuses solely on short-term profits to provide the greatest return to the owners of the business (i.e., the shareholders in a publicly held firm). What ethical issues could this raise?

2. A firm has spent some time—with input from managers at all levels—in developing a vision statement and a mission statement. Over time, however, the behavior of some executives is contrary to these statements. Could this raise some ethical issues?

References

1. Collins, J. 2008. The secret of enduring greatness. *Fortune,* May 5: 74. It is interesting to note that a 2008 article in the *Academy of Management Perspectives* (Resnick, B. G. & Smut, T. J. From good to great. 22 [4]: 6–12) found that only 1 of the 11 companies that Collins identified as "great" in his best-selling book *Good to Great* continued to exhibit superior stock market performance according to Collins' own measure. This provides further evidence regarding the difficulty in sustaining excellence in today's global marketplace.

2. Brooker, K. 2008. The day $2 billion walked out the door. *Fortune,* April 14: 99–106; Craig, S., Zuckerman, G., & Karnitschnig, M. 2007. Why Citadel pounced on wounded E*Trade. *The Wall Street Journal,* November 30: A1, A12; Craig, S. 2007. E*Trade to get help from Citadel. *The Wall Street Journal,* November 29: A3; Craig, S. 2007. E*Trade plunges 59% on analyst's warnings; bank unit goes awry. *The Wall Street Journal,* November 13: A1; A21; Weber, J. E*Trade rises from the ashes. *BusinessWeek,* January 17: 58–59; and, Schmerken, I. 2004. Innovation in motion. *Wall Street & Technology,* October 22–26: np. We'd like to note that in Chapter 5 of our previous edition of *Strategic Management,* we—like the business press—wrote about Caplan's remarkable turnaround.

3. For a discussion of the "romantic" versus "external control" perspective, refer to Meindl, J. R. 1987. The romance of leadership and the evaluation of organizational performance. *Academy of Management Journal* 30: 92–109; and Pfeffer, J. & Salancik, G. R. 1978. *The external control of organizations: A resource dependence perspective.* New York: Harper & Row.

4. A recent perspective on the "romantic view" of leadership is provided by Mintzberg, H. 2004. Leadership and management development: An afterword. *Academy of Management Executive,* 18(3): 140–142.

5. For a discussion of the best and worst managers for 2008, read: Anonymous. 2009. The best managers. *BusinessWeeek,* January 19: 40–41; and, The worst managers. On page 42 in the same issue.

6. Burrows, P. 2009. Apple without its core? *BusinessWeek.* January 26/February 2: 31.

7. For a study on the effects of CEOs on firm performance, refer to: Kor, Y. Y. & Misangyi, V. F. 2008. *Strategic Management Journal,* 29 (11): 1357–1368.

8. Ewing, J. 2008. South Africa emerges from the shadows. *BusinessWeek.* December 15: 52–56.

9. For an interesting perspective on the need for strategists to maintain a global mind-set, refer to Begley, T. M. & Boyd, D. P. 2003. The need for a global mind-set. *MIT Sloan Management Review* 44(2): 25–32.

10. Porter, M. E. 1996. What is strategy? *Harvard Business Review* 74(6): 61–78.

11. See, for example, Barney, J. B. & Arikan, A. M. 2001. The resource-based view: Origins and implications. In Hitt, M. A., Freeman, R. E., & Harrison, J. S. (Eds.), *Handbook of strategic management:* 124–189. Malden, MA: Blackwell.

12. Porter, M. E. 1996. What is strategy? *Harvard Business Review,* 74(6): 61–78; and Hammonds, K. H. 2001. Michael Porter's big ideas. *Fast Company,* March: 55–56.

13. This section draws upon Dess, G. G. & Miller, A. 1993. *Strategic management.* New York: McGraw-Hill.

14. See, for example, Hrebiniak, L. G. & Joyce, W. F. 1986. The strategic importance of managing myopia. *Sloan Management Review,* 28(1): 5–14.

15. For an insightful discussion on how to manage diverse stakeholder groups, refer to Rondinelli, D. A. & London, T. 2003. How corporations and environmental groups cooperate: Assessing cross-sector alliances and collaborations. *Academy of Management Executive,* 17(1): 61–76.

16. Some dangers of a short-term perspective are addressed in: Van Buren, M. E. & Safferstone, T. 2009. The quick wins paradox. *Harvard Business Review,* 67(1): 54–61.

17. Senge, P. 1996. Leading learning organizations: The bold, the powerful, and the invisible. In Hesselbein, F., Goldsmith, M., & Beckhard, R. (Eds.), *The leader of the future:* 41–58. San Francisco: Jossey-Bass.

18. Samuelson, J. 2006. A critical mass for the long term. *Harvard Business Review,* 84(2): 62, 64; and, Anonymous. 2007. Power play. *The Economist,* January 20: 10–12.

19. Loeb, M. 1994. Where leaders come from. *Fortune,* September 19: 241 (quoting Warren Bennis).

20. Address by Norman R. Augustine at the Crummer Business School, Rollins College, Winter Park, FL, October 20, 1989.

21. Hemp, P. 2004. An Interview with CEO Kevin Sharer. *Harvard Business Review,* 82(7/8): 66–74.

22. New perspectives on "management models" are addressed in: Birkinshaw, J. & Goddard, J. 2009. What is your management model? *MIT Sloan Management Review,* 50 (2): 81–90.

23. Mintzberg, H. 1985. Of strategies: Deliberate and emergent. *Strategic Management Journal,* 6: 257–272.

24. Some interesting insights on decision-making processes are found in: Nutt, P. C. 2008. Investigating the success of decision making processes. *Journal of Management Studies,* 45(2): 425–455.

25. Aston, A. 2009. How to bet on cleantech. *BusinessWeek,* January 5: 70–71.

26. A study investigating the sustainability of competitive advantage is: Newbert, S. L. 2008. Value, rareness, competitive advantages, and performance: A conceptual-level empirical investigation of the resource-based view of the firm. *Strategic Management Journal,* 29(7): 745–768.

27. Good insights on mentoring are addressed in: DeLong, T. J., Gabarro, J. J., & Lees, R. J. 2008. Why mentoring matters in a hypercompetitive world. *Harvard Business Review*, 66(1): 115–121.

28. A unique perspective on differentiation strategies is: Austin, R. D. 2008. High margins and the quest for aesthetic coherence. *Harvard Business Review*, 86(1): 18–19.

29. Some insights on partnering in the global area are discussed in: MacCormack, A. & Forbath, T. 2008. *Harvard Business Review*, 66(1): 24, 26.

30. An interesting discussion of the challenges of strategy implementation is: Neilson, G. L., Martin, K. L., & Powers, E. 2008. The secrets of strategy execution. *Harvard Business Review*, 86(6): 61–70.

31. Interesting perspectives on strategy execution involving the link between strategy and operations are addressed in: Kaplan, R. S. & Norton, D.P. 2008. Mastering the management system. *Harvard Business Review*, 66(1): 62–77.

32. An innovative perspective on organizational design is found in: Garvin, D. A. & Levesque, L. C. 2008. The multiunit enterprise. *Harvard Business Review*, 86(6): 106–117.

33. Monks, R. & Minow, N. 2001. *Corporate governance* (2nd ed.). Malden, MA: Blackwell.

34. Intel Corp. 2007. *Intel corporation board of directors guidelines on significant corporate governance issues.* www.intel.com

35. Jones, T. J., Felps, W., & Bigley, G. A. 2007. Ethical theory and stakeholder-related decisions: The role of stakeholder culture. *Academy of Management Review*, 32(1): 137–155.

36. For example, see The best (& worst) managers of the year, 2003. *BusinessWeek,* January 13: 58–92; and Lavelle, M. 2003. Rogues of the year. *Time,* January 6: 33–45.

37. Handy, C. 2002. What's a business for? *Harvard Business Review,* 80(12): 49–55.

38. Anonymous, 2007. In the money. *Economist,* January 20: 3–6.

39. Hessel, E. & Woolley, S. 2008. Your money or your life. *Forbes,* October 27: 52.

40. Some interesting insights on the role of activist investors can be found in: Greenwood, R. & Schol, M. 2008. When (not) to listen to activist investors. *Harvard Business Review,* 66(1): 23–24.

41. For an interesting perspective on the changing role of boards of directors, refer to Lawler, E. & Finegold, D. 2005. Rethinking governance. *MIT Sloan Management Review,* 46(2): 67–70.

42. Benz, M. & Frey, B. S. 2007. Corporate governance: What can we learn from public governance? *Academy of Management Review,* 32(1): 92–104.

43. The salience of shareholder value is addressed in: Carrott, G. T. & Jackson, S. E. 2009. Shareholder value must top the CEO's agenda. *Harvard Business Review,* 67(1): 22–24.

44. Stakeholder symbiosis. 1998. *Fortune,* March 30: S2.

45. An excellent review of stakeholder management theory can be found in: Laplume, A. O., Sonpar, K., & Litz, R. A. 2008. Stakeholder theory: Reviewing a theory that moves us. *Journal of Management,* 34(6): 1152–1189.

46. For a definitive, recent discussion of the stakeholder concept, refer to Freeman, R. E. & McVae, J. 2001. A stakeholder approach to strategic management. In Hitt, M. A., Freeman, R. E., & Harrison, J. S. (Eds.). *Handbook of strategic management:* 189–207. Malden, MA: Blackwell.

47. For an insightful discussion on the role of business in society, refer to Handy, op. cit.

48. Stakeholder symbiosis. op. cit., p. S3.

49. Sullivan, C. T. 2005. A stake in the business. *Harvard Business Review,* 83(9): 57–67.

50. Our discussion of crowdsourcing draws on the first two books that have addressed this concept: Libert, B. & Spector, J. 2008. *We are smarter than me.* Philadelphia: Wharton Publishing; and, Howe, J. 2008. *Crowdsourcing.* New York: Crown Business. Eric von Hippel has addressed similar ideas in his earlier book (2005. *Democratizing innovation.* Cambridge, MA: MIT Press).

51. An excellent theoretical discussion on stakeholder activity is Rowley, T. J. & Moldoveanu, M. 2003. When will stakeholder groups act? An interest- and identity-based model of stakeholder group mobilization. *Academy of Management Review,* 28(2): 204–219.

52. Thomas, J. G. 2000. Macroenvironmetal forces. In Helms, M. M. (Ed.), *Encyclopedia of management.* (4th ed.): 516–520. Farmington Hills, MI: Gale Group.

53. For a strong advocacy position on the need for corporate values and social responsibility, read Hollender, J. 2004. What matters most: Corporate values and social responsibility. *California Management Review,* 46(4): 111–119.

54. Waddock, S. & Bodwell, C. 2004. Managing responsibility: What can be learned from the quality movement. *California Management Review,* 47(1): 25–37.

55. For a discussion of the role of alliances and collaboration on corporate social responsibility initiatives, refer to Pearce, J. A. II. & Doh, J. P. 2005. The high impact of collaborative social initiatives. *MIT Sloan Management Review,* 46(3): 30–40.

56. Insights on ethical behavior and performance are addressed in: Trudel, R. & Cotte, J. 2009. *MIT Sloan Management Review,* 50(2): 61–68.

57. Anonymous, 2006. If I did it. *BusinessWeek.* December 18: 108.

58. Bhattacharya, C. B. & Sen, S. 2004, Doing better at doing good: When, why, and how consumers respond to corporate social initiatives. *California Management Review,* 47(1): 9–24.

59. For some findings on the relationship between corporate social responsibility and firm performance, see: Margolis, J. D. & Elfenbein, H. A. 2008. *Harvard Business Review,* 86(1): 19–20.

60. Cone Corporate Citizenship Study, 2002, www.coneinc.com.

61. Refer to www.bsr.org.

62. An insightful discussion of the risks and opportunities associated with global warming, refer to: Lash, J. & Wellington, F. 2007. Competitive advantage on a warming planet. *Harvard Business Review,* 85(3): 94–102.

63. This section draws on Hart, S. L. 1997. Beyond greening: Strategies for a sustainable world. *Harvard Business Review,* 75(1): 66–76, and Berry, M. A. & Rondinelli, D. A. 1998. Proactive corporate environmental management: A new industrial revolution. *Academy of Management Executive,* 12(2): 38–50.

64. Carey, J. 2006. Business on a warmer planet. *BusinessWeek,* July 17: 26–29.

65. Hart, op. cit., p. 67.

66. For a creative perspective on environmental sustainability and competitive advantage as well as ethical implications, read Ehrenfeld, J. R. 2005. The roots of sustainability. *MIT Sloan Management Review,* 46(2): 23–25.

67. McKinsey & Company. 1991. *The corporate response to the environmental challenge.* Summary Report, Amsterdam: McKinsey & Company.

68. Vogel, D. J. 2005. Is there a market for virtue? The business case for corporate social responsibility. *California Management Review,* 47(4): 19–36.

69. Senge, P. M. 1990. The leader's new work: Building learning organizations. *Sloan Management Review,* 32(1): 7–23.

70. For an interesting perspective on the role of middle managers in the strategic management process, refer to Huy, Q. H. 2001. In praise of middle managers. *Harvard Business Review,* 79(8): 72–81.

71. Senge, 1996, op. cit., pp. 41–58.

72. Helgesen, S. 1996. Leading from the grass roots. In Hesselbein, F., Goldsmith, M., & Beckhard, R. (Eds.), *The leader of the future:* 19–24. San Francisco: Jossey-Bass.

73. Wetlaufer, S. 1999. Organizing for empowerment: An interview with AES's Roger Sant and Dennis Blake. *Harvard Business Review,* 77(1): 110–126.

74. Kets de Vries, M. F. R. 1998. Charisma in action: The transformational abilities of Virgin's Richard Branson and ABB's Percy Barnevik. *Organizational Dynamics,* 26(3): 7–21.

75. Hamel, G. 2006. The why, what, and how of management innovation. *Harvard Business Review,* 84(2): 72–84.

76. An insightful discussion about the role of vision, mission, and strategic objectives can be found in: Collis, D. J. & Rukstad, M. G. 2008. Can you say what your strategy is? *Harvard Business Review,* 66(4): 82–90.

77. Our discussion draws on a variety of sources. These include Lipton, M. 1996. Demystifying the development of an organizational vision. *Sloan Management Review,* 37(4): 83–92; Bart, C. K. 2000. Lasting inspiration. *CA Magazine,* May: 49–50; and Quigley, J. V. 1994. Vision: How leaders develop it, share it, and sustain it. *Business Horizons,* September–October: 37–40.

78. Lipton, op. cit.

79. Hardy, Q. 2007. The uncarly. *Forbes,* March 12: 82–90.

80. Some interesting perspective on gender differences in organizational vision are discussed in: Ibarra, H. & Obodaru, O. 2009. Women and the vision thing. *Harvard Business Review,* 67(1): 62–70.

81. Quigley, op. cit.

82. Ibid.

83. Lipton, op. cit. Additional pitfalls are addressed in this article.

84. Sull, D. N. 2005. Strategy as active waiting. *Harvard Business Review,* 83(9): 120–130.

85. Company records.

86. Lipton, op. cit.

87. Sexton, D. A. & Van Aukun, P. M. 1985. A longitudinal study of small business strategic planning. *Journal of Small Business Management,* January: 8–15, cited in Lipton, op. cit.

88. For an insightful perspective on the use of strategic objectives, refer to Chatterjee, S. 2005. Core objectives: Clarity in designing strategy. *California Management Review,* 47(2): 33–49.

89. Ibid.

90. Mankins, M. M. & Steele, R. 2005. Turning great strategy into great performance. *Harvard Business Review,* 83(5): 66–73.

Analyzing the External Environment of the Firm

After reading this chapter, you should have a good understanding of:

LO1 The importance of developing forecasts of the business environment.

LO2 Why environmental scanning, environmental monitoring, and collecting competitive intelligence are critical inputs to forecasting.

LO3 Why scenario planning is a useful technique for firms competing in industries characterized by unpredictability and change.

LO4 The impact of the general environment on a firm's strategies and performance.

LO5 How forces in the competitive environment can affect profitability, and how a firm can improve its competitive position by increasing its power vis-à-vis these forces.

LO6 How the Internet and digitally based capabilities are affecting the five competitive forces and industry profitability.

LO7 The concept of strategic groups and their strategy and performance implications.

Strategies are not and should not be developed in a vacuum. They must be responsive to the external business environment. Otherwise, your firm could become, in effect, the most efficient producer of buggy whips, leisure suits, or slide rules. To avoid such strategic mistakes, firms must become knowledgeable about the business environment. One tool for analyzing trends is forecasting. In the development of forecasts, environmental scanning and environmental monitoring are important in detecting key trends and events. Managers also must aggressively collect and disseminate competitor intelligence. The information gleaned from these three activities is invaluable in developing forecasts and scenarios to minimize present and future threats as well as to exploit opportunities. We address these issues in the first part of this chapter. We also introduce a basic tool of strategy analysis—the concept of SWOT analysis (strengths, weaknesses, opportunities, and threats).

In the second part of the chapter, we present two frameworks for analyzing the external environment—the general environment and the competitive environment. The general environment consists of six segments—demographic, sociocultural, political/legal, technological, economic, and global. Trends and events in these segments can have a dramatic impact on your firm.

The competitive environment is closer to home. It consists of five industry-related factors that can dramatically affect the average level of industry profitability. An awareness of these factors is critical in making decisions such as which industries to enter and how to improve your firm's current position within an industry. This is helpful in neutralizing competitive threats and increasing power over customers and suppliers. We also address how industry and competitive practices are being affected by the capabilities provided by Internet technologies. In the final part of this section, we place firms within an industry into strategic groups based on similarities in resources and strategies. As we will see, the concept of strategic groups has important implications for the intensity of rivalry and how the effects of a given environmental trend or event differ across groups.

Learning from Mistakes

Until 2004, Motorola was No. 1 or No. 2 in the China mobile-phone market.[1] But in recent years, its share has plummeted from 21 percent in 2006 to about 8 percent in 2008. In contrast, Nokia's share has soared to 38 percent and Samsung has grown to 16 percent—leaving Motorola a distant third. Let's take a look at what went wrong.

In China, coming out with new models is important because big-city consumers replace their phones frequently and put a priority on models that are cool-looking and reasonably priced. According to an analyst: "They haven't come up with the next-generation product that replaces the Razr. The guys that replaced it were Nokia, Samsung, and even LG."

Unfortunately, when rivals came out with similar models, Motorola's entries were pricey multimedia phones that didn't attract consumers. And while Motorola developed a smart phone for China, the Ming, the touch screen device did little to boost Motorola's overall position.

The result: Chinese consumers have soured on the Motorola brand. Chen Xin, a 37-year-old Beijing resident who works for a local info-tech company, once bought five Motorola phones over a four-year span. But now he prefers Nokia and Sony Ericsson models, calling Motorola phones "ugly and not very easy to operate."

Such a steep decline is costly for Motorola. With 583 million cell phones in use, China is the world's largest mobile market. The Chinese bought 176 million handsets in 2007 and about 200 million in 2008. These figures compare to sales of 186 million units in the U.S. and Canada. And before its recent slide, Motorola was narrowing its overall gap with archrival Nokia.

As one would expect, Motorola's dwindling fortunes in China reflect its overall erosion in market share. For 2008's third quarter, unit sales dropped 32 percent, to 25.4 million units from a year earlier, and the company's market share dropped to 8.4 percent globally—down from 9.5 percent in the second quarter and 22.4 percent in 2006—when its Razr handset was all the rage. Motorola recently announced plans to cut about 3,000 jobs—two-thirds of them in the handset division. As one would expect, its share price has tumbled: from $21 at the end of 2006 to around $5 in early 2009.

Successful managers must recognize opportunities and threats in their firm's external environment. They must be aware of what's going on outside their company. If they focus exclusively on the efficiency of internal operations, the firm may degenerate into the world's most efficient producer of buggy whips or carbon paper. But if they miscalculate the market, opportunities will be lost—hardly an enviable position for their firm.

In *Competing for the Future,* Gary Hamel and C. K. Prahalad suggest that "every manager carries around in his or her head a set of biases, assumptions, and presuppositions about the structure of the relevant 'industry,' about how one makes money in the industry, about who the competition is and isn't, about who the customers are and aren't, and so on."[2] Environmental analysis requires you to continually question such assumptions. Peter Drucker labeled these interrelated sets of assumptions the "theory of the business."[3] The sudden reversal in Motorola's fortunes clearly illustrates that if a company does not keep pace with changes in the external environment, it becomes difficult to sustain competitive advantages and deliver strong financial results.

A firm's strategy may be good at one point in time, but it may go astray when management's frame of reference gets out of touch with the realities of the actual business situation. This results when management's assumptions, premises, or beliefs are incorrect or when internal inconsistencies among them render the overall "theory of the business" invalid. As Warren Buffett, investor extraordinaire, colorfully notes, "Beware of past performance 'proofs.' If history books were the key to riches, the Forbes 400 would consist of librarians."

In the business world, many once successful firms have fallen. Consider the high-tech company Novell, which went head-to-head with Microsoft. Novell bought market-share loser WordPerfect to compete with Microsoft Word. The result? A $1.3 billion loss when Novell sold WordPerfect to Corel. And today we may wonder who will be the next Circuit City or *Encyclopaedia Britannica.*

Creating the Environmentally Aware Organization

So how do managers become environmentally aware?[4] We will now address three important processes—scanning, monitoring, and gathering competitive intelligence—used to develop forecasts.[5] Exhibit 2.1 illustrates relationships among these important activities. We also discuss the importance of scenario planning in anticipating major future changes in the external environment and the role of SWOT analysis.[6]

The Role of Scanning, Monitoring, Competitive Intelligence, and Forecasting

Environmental Scanning **Environmental scanning** involves surveillance of a firm's external environment to predict environmental changes and detect changes already under way.[7,8] This alerts the organization to critical trends and events before changes develop a discernible pattern and before competitors recognize them.[9] Otherwise, the firm may be forced into a reactive mode.[10]

Experts agree that spotting key trends requires a combination of knowing your business and your customer as well as keeping an eye on what's happening around you. Such a big-picture/small-picture view enables you to better identify the emerging trends that will affect your business. We suggest a few tips in Exhibit 2.2.

At times, your company may benefit from studies conducted by outside experts in a particular industry. A. T. Kearney, a large international consulting company, identified several key issues in the automobile industry, including.[11]

- **Globalization.** This is not a new trend but it has intensified, with enormous opportunities opening up in Asia, central and eastern Europe, and Latin America.[12]
- **Time to Market.** Despite recent improvements, there's still a gap between product development cycles in the United States and Europe compared to Japan. This gap may be widening as Japanese companies continue to make improvements.

>LO1
The importance of developing forecasts of the business environment.

>LO2
Why environmental scanning, environmental monitoring, and collecting competitive intelligence are critical inputs to forecasting.

environmental scanning surveillance of a firm's external environment to predict environmental changes and detect changes already under way.

Globalization the dual trends of a) increasing international exchange of goods, money, information, people, and ideas; and b) increasing similarity among countries of laws, rules, norms, values, and income levels.

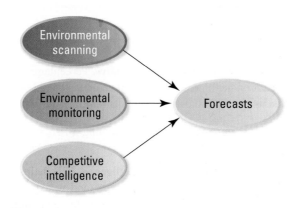

Exhibit 2.1 **Inputs to Forecasting**

Exhibit 2.2
Some Suggestions on How to Spot Hot Trends

- **Listen.** Ask your customers questions about your products and services. Ask what they are looking for next. Find out what media they're watching and what they think of current events.

- **Pay attention.** Read trade publications related to your industry to identify key issues. Watch industries that are always on the cutting edge, such as technology, music, and fashion, in order to discover emerging trends that may affect your business.

- **Follow trends online.** Trend-hunting websites such as trendhunter.com and jwtintelligence.com offer up the trends du jour. Add them to your regular Web-surfing itinerary.

- **Go old school.** Ask your customers what they think. Organize online or in-person focus groups to find out what people are thinking. You can also launch social media groups or chat rooms to gather feedback from your audience.

Source: Moran, G. 2008. Be your own trendspotter. *Entrepreneur,* December: 17.

- ***Shifting Roles and Responsibilities.*** Design responsibility, purchasing, and even project management and systems engineering are shifting from original equipment manufacturers to integrators/suppliers.

Consider how disadvantaged you would be as an executive in the global automobile industry if you were unaware of such trends.

Strategy Spotlight 2.1 addresses how Virgin Mobile USA uses crowdsourcing to help it keep abreast of trends and promising opportunities.

environmental monitoring a firm's analysis of the external environment that tracks the evolution of environmental trends, sequences of events, or streams of activities.

Environmental Monitoring **Environmental monitoring** tracks the evolution of environmental trends, sequences of events, or streams of activities. They may be trends that the firm came across by accident or ones that were brought to its attention from outside the organization. Monitoring enables firms to evaluate how dramatically environmental trends are changing the competitive landscape.

One of the authors of this text has conducted on-site interviews with executives from several industries to identify indicators that firms monitor as inputs to their strategy process. Examples of such indicators included:

- ***A Motel 6 executive.*** The number of rooms in the budget segment of the industry in the United States and the difference between the average daily room rate and the consumer price index (CPI).
- ***A Pier 1 Imports executive.*** Net disposable income (NDI), consumer confidence index, and housing starts.
- ***A Johnson & Johnson medical products executive.*** Percentage of gross domestic product (GDP) spent on health care, number of active hospital beds, and the size and power of purchasing agents (indicates the concentration of buyers).

Such indices are critical for managers in determining a firm's strategic direction and resource allocation.

competitive intelligence a firm's activities of collecting and interpreting data on competitors, defining and understanding the industry, and identifying competitors' strengths and weaknesses.

Competitive Intelligence **Competitive intelligence** (CI) helps firms define and understand their industry and identify rivals' strengths and weaknesses.[13] This includes the intelligence gathering associated with collecting data on competitors and interpreting such data. Done properly, competitive intelligence helps a company avoid surprises by anticipating competitors' moves and decreasing response time.[14]

Crowdsourcing: How Virgin Mobile USA Enhances Its Environmental Awareness

Virgin Mobile USA—a joint venture of Richard Branson's Virgin Group and Sprint Nextel—relies on 2,000 carefully selected online customers, referred to as "Insiders" by Virgin, to keep it aware of trends and promising opportunities. Considered a "team of elite, young, and active customers," Virgin rewards them with free calling minutes and phone upgrades. The Insider community—a very hip focus group—provides input on everything from designing phones to coming up with names for service plans. As one executive puts it: "Ultimately, we want to put young consumers backstage, that is, in influential positions."

However, being accepted as part of the in-crowd is not the only way to be heard and earn rewards at Virgin Mobile USA. Its pay-as-you-go, no-contract service has attracted 4.6 million phone users and offers all of its mostly young "Chatty Cathys" and "Texter Thomases" the chance to earn free phone minutes merely by paying attention and providing feedback on a corporate sponsor's advertisement. Any Virgin Mobile customer who watches 30-second commercials on his or her computer screen, reads text messages on a cell phone, or fills out brand survey questionnaires can earn up to 75 minutes a month of free airtime. Called Sugar Mama, the program provides a notoriously talkative group the chance to stay one step ahead of a dead cell phone by voicing their opinions. Virgin Mobile claims that about 1,000 subscribers have signed up for the program each day since it was initiated in mid-2006. And the firm awarded around 9 million minutes. However, not everyone is a fan. According to one website post: "This may sound like a good way to get some extra minutes of air time, but the air time you earn doesn't really make it worthwhile. Why watch a 30-second commercial just for a single minute of air time? If you need the airtime that bad, you might as well throw your phone away."

Sugar Mama enables sponsoring partners to tap into the thoughts and opinions of a coveted marketing segment. And they are happy to pay for the privilege. As one corporate media executive pointed out, knowing that these young consumers don't get paid unless they watch an ad and answer questions helps assure advertisers that they are receiving honest feedback. Consider Virgin Mobile's enticing promotion directed at advertisers:

Virgin Mobile Users Are:

- First at trying new things and convincing others to do the same.
- Passionate about the brands and music they connect with.
- Not afraid to be different.
- Ambitious and career-oriented.
- Active social thought leaders

Source: Libert, B. & Spector, J. 2008. *We are smarter than me.* Philadelphia: Wharton School Publishing; www.ultramercial.com. Undated, np.; and, mobilevirgin.instantspot.com. Posted April 28, 2007.

crowdsourcing

Examples of competitive analysis are evident in daily newspapers and periodicals such as *The Wall Street Journal, BusinessWeek,* and *Fortune.* For example, banks continually track home loan, auto loan, and certificate of deposit (CD) interest rates charged by rivals. Major airlines change hundreds of fares daily in response to competitors' tactics. Car manufacturers are keenly aware of announced cuts or increases in rivals' production volume, sales, and sales incentives (e.g., rebates and low interest rates on financing). This information is used in their marketing, pricing, and production strategies.

The Internet has dramatically accelerated the speed at which firms can find competitive intelligence. Leonard Fuld, founder of the Cambridge, Massachusetts, training and consulting firm Fuld & Co., specializes in competitive intelligence.[15] His firm often profiles top company and business group managers and considers these issues: What is their background? What is their style? Are they marketers? Are they cost cutters? Fuld has found that the more articles he collects and the more biographies he downloads, the better he can develop profiles.

strategy spotlight

2.2

Ethical Guidelines on Competitive Intelligence: United Technologies

United Technologies (UT) is a $28 billion global conglomerate composed of world-leading businesses with rich histories of technological pioneering, such as Otis Elevator, Carrier Air Conditioning, and Sikorsky (helicopters). It was founded in 1853 and has an impressive history of technological accomplishments. UT built the first working helicopter, developed the first commercially available hydrogen cells, and designed complete life support systems for space shuttles. UT believes strongly in a robust code of ethics. In the last decade, they have clearly articulated their principles governing business conduct. These include an antitrust guide, an ethics guide when contracting with the U.S. government and foreign governments, a policy on accepting gifts from suppliers, and guidelines for proper usage of e-mail. One such document is the Code of Ethics Guide on Competitive Intelligence. This encourages managers and workers to ask themselves these five questions whenever they have ethical concerns.

Sources: Nelson, B. 2003. The thinker. *Forbes*, March 3: 62–64; and The Fuld war room—Survival kit 010. Code of ethics (printed 2/26/01).

1. Have I done anything that coerced somebody to share this information? Have I, for example, threatened a supplier by indicating that future business opportunities will be influenced by the receipt of information with respect to a competitor?

2. Am I in a place where I should not be? If, for example, I am a field representative with privileges to move around in a customer's facility, have I gone outside the areas permitted? Have I misled anybody in order to gain access?

3. Is the contemplated technique for gathering information evasive, such as sifting through trash or setting up an electronic "snooping" device directed at a competitor's facility from across the street?

4. Have I misled somebody in a way that the person believed sharing information with me was required or would be protected by a confidentiality agreement? Have I, for example, called and misrepresented myself as a government official who was seeking some information for some official purpose?

5. Have I done something to evade or circumvent a system intended to secure or protect information?

One of Fuld & Co.'s clients asked it to determine the size, strength, and technical capabilities of a privately held company. Initially, it was difficult to get detailed information. Then one analyst used Deja News (www.dejanews.com), now part of Google, to tap into some online discussion groups. The analyst's research determined that the company had posted 14 job openings on one Usenet group. That posting was a road map to the competitor's development strategy.

At times, a firm's aggressive efforts to gather competitive intelligence may lead to unethical or illegal behaviors.[16] Strategy Spotlight 2.2 provides an example of a company, United Technologies, that has set clear guidelines to help prevent unethical behavior.

A word of caution: Executives must be careful to avoid spending so much time and effort tracking the actions of traditional competitors that they ignore new competitors. Further, broad environmental changes and events may have a dramatic impact on a firm's viability. Peter Drucker, considered the father of modern management, wrote:

> Increasingly, a winning strategy will require information about events and conditions outside the institution: noncustomers, technologies other than those currently used by the company and its present competitors, markets not currently served, and so on.[17]

Consider the fall of the once-mighty *Encyclopaedia Britannica*.[18] Its demise was not caused by a traditional competitor in the encyclopedia industry. It was caused by new technology. CD-ROMs came out of nowhere and devastated the printed encyclopedia industry. Why? A full set of the *Encyclopaedia Britannica* sells for about $2,000, but an encyclopedia on CD-ROM, such as Microsoft *Encarta,* sells for about $50. To make matters worse, many people receive *Encarta* free with their personal computers.

Environmental Forecasting Environmental scanning, monitoring, and competitive intelligence are important inputs for analyzing the external environment. **Environmental forecasting** involves the development of plausible projections about the direction, scope, speed, and intensity of environmental change.[19] Its purpose is to predict change.[20] It asks: How long will it take a new technology to reach the marketplace? Will the present social concern about an issue result in new legislation? Are current lifestyle trends likely to continue?

environmental forecasting the development of plausible projections about the direction, scope, speed, and intensity of environmental change.

Some forecasting issues are much more specific to a particular firm and the industry in which it competes. Consider how important it is for Motel 6 to predict future indicators, such as the number of rooms, in the budget segment of the industry. If its predictions are low, it will build too many units, creating a surplus of room capacity that would drive down room rates.

A danger of forecasting is that managers may view uncertainty as black and white and ignore important gray areas.[21] The problem is that underestimating uncertainty can lead to strategies that neither defend against threats nor take advantage of opportunities.

>LO3

Why scenario planning is a useful technique for firms competing in industries characterized by unpredictability and change.

In 1977 one of the colossal underestimations in business history occurred when Kenneth H. Olsen, president of Digital Equipment Corp., announced, "There is no reason for individuals to have a computer in their home." The explosion in the personal computer market was not easy to detect in 1977, but it was clearly within the range of possibilities at the time. And, historically, there have been underestimates of the growth potential of new telecommunication services. The electric telegraph was derided by Ralph Waldo Emerson, and the telephone had its skeptics. More recently, an "infamous" McKinsey study in the early 1980s predicted fewer than 1 million cellular users in the United States by 2000. Actually, there were nearly 100 million.[22]

Obviously, poor predictions never go out of vogue. Consider some of the "gems" associated with the global financial crisis that began in 2008.[23]

- "Freddie Mac and Fannie Mae are fundamentally sound. . . . I think they are in good shape going forward."—Barney Frank (D-Mass.), House Financial Services Committee Chairman, July 14, 2008. (*Two months later, the government forced the mortgage giants into conservatorships.*)
- "Existing home sales to trend up in 2008"—Headline of a National Association of Realtors press release, December 9, 2007. (*On December 23, 2007, the group said November sales were down 11 percent from a year earlier in the worst housing slump since the Great Depression.*)
- "I think you'll see $150 a barrel [of oil] by the end of the year."—T. Boone Pickens, June 20, 2008. (*Oil was then around $135 a barrel. By late December it was around $40.*)
- "I expect there will be some failures. . . . I don't anticipate any serious problems of that sort among the large internationally active banks."—Ben Bernanke, Federal Reserve Chairman, February 28, 2008. (*In September, Washington Mutual became the largest financial institution in U.S. history to fail. Citigroup needed an even bigger rescue in November.*)
- "In today's regulatory environment, it's virtually impossible to violate rules."— Bernard Madoff, money manager, October 20, 2007. (*On December 11, 2008, Madoff was arrested for allegedly running a Ponzi scheme that may have lost investors $50 billion.*)

Scenario analysis is a more in-depth approach to forecasting. It draws on a range of disciplines and interests, among them economics, psychology, sociology, and demographics. It usually begins with a discussion of participants' thoughts on ways in which societal

scenario analysis an in-depth approach to environmental forecasting that involves experts' detailed assessments of societal trends, economics, politics, technology, or other dimensions of the external environment.

Scenario Planning at Shell Oil Company

Preparing to cope with uncertainty is one of the biggest strategic challenges faced by most businesses. There are few tools for coping with strategic uncertainty, especially over medium- to long-term horizons. One technique that has proved its usefulness is scenario planning.

Scenario planning is different from other tools for strategic planning such as trend analysis or high and low forecasts. The origins of scenario planning lie with the military, which used it to cope effectively with multiple challenges and limited resources.

In the 1960s and 1970s, Shell combined analytical tools with information to create scenarios of possible outcomes. The result of the 1973 oil embargo was a sharp increase in crude oil prices, short supplies of gasoline for consumers, and a depressed world economy. However, Shell's strategic planning, including the use of scenarios, had strongly suggested that a more unstable environment was coming, with a shift of power from oil companies to oil producers. As a result of the precautionary actions it took, Shell was in a better position than most oil companies when the 1973 embargo occurred. Shell also uses scenario planning to plan major new oil field investments because elements of risk can be identified and explored over a considerable period of time.

Sources: Martin, R. 2002. The oracles of oil. *Business 2.0,* January: 35–39; www.touchstonerenard.co.uk/Expertise/Strategy/Scenario_Planning/scenario_planning.htm; and Epstein, J. 1998. Scenario planning: An introduction. *The Futurist,* September: 50–52.

The Shell process of scenario planning involves the following stages:

1. Interviews with people both inside and outside the business, using an open-ended questioning technique to encourage full and frank answers.
2. Analysis of interviews by issue in order to build a "natural agenda" for further processing.
3. Synthesis of each agenda to draw out underlying areas of uncertainty/dispute and possible interrelationships among issues.
4. A small number of workshops to explore key issues to improve understanding and identify gaps for further research. These generate a wide range of strategy options.
5. A workshop to identify and build a small number of scenarios that may occur in the next 10 to 15 years or even later.
6. A testing of strategy options against the scenarios in order to assess robustness (i.e., whether or not a given strategy is effective under more than one scenario).

Other practitioners of scenario planning include Levi Strauss, which uses scenario planning to consider potential impacts of everything from cotton deregulation to the total disappearance of cotton from this planet. Also, a German insurance company anticipated the fall of the Berlin wall and made plans to expand in central Europe. And in 1990 when Nelson Mandela was released from a South African prison, he met with a panel that helped him create scenarios to chart out the country's future. Scenario planning helps by considering not just trends or forecasts but also how they could be upset by events and the outcomes that may result.

trends, economics, politics, and technology may affect an issue.[24] For example, consider Lego. The popular Danish toy manufacturer has a strong position in the construction toys market. But what would happen if this broadly defined market should change dramatically? After all, Lego is competing not only with producers of similar products but also on a much broader canvas for a share of children's playtime. In this market, Lego has a host of competitors, many of them computer based; still others have not yet been invented. Lego may end up with an increasing share of a narrow, shrinking market (much like IBM in the declining days of the mainframe computer). To avoid such a fate, managers must consider a wider context than their narrow, traditional markets, by laying down guidelines for at least 10 years in the future to anticipate rapid change. Strategy Spotlight 2.3 provides an example of scenario planning at Shell Oil Company.

SWOT Analysis

To understand the business environment of a particular firm, you need to analyze both the general environment and the firm's industry and competitive environment. Generally, firms compete with other firms in the same industry. An industry is composed of a set of firms that produce similar products or services, sell to similar customers, and use similar methods of production. Gathering industry information and understanding competitive dynamics among the different companies in your industry is key to successful strategic management.

One of the most basic techniques for analyzing firm and industry conditions is **SWOT analysis**. SWOT stands for strengths, weaknesses, opportunities, and threats. It provides "raw material"—a basic listing of conditions both inside and surrounding your company.

The <u>S</u>trengths and <u>W</u>eaknesses refer to the internal conditions of the firm—where your firm excels (strengths) and where it may be lacking relative to competitors (weaknesses). <u>O</u>pportunities and <u>T</u>hreats are environmental conditions external to the firm. These could be factors either in the general or competitive environment. In the general environment, one might experience developments that are beneficial for most companies such as improving economic conditions, that lower borrowing costs or trends that benefit some companies and harm others. An example is the heightened concern with fitness, which is a threat to some companies (e.g., tobacco) and an opportunity to others (e.g., health clubs). Opportunities and threats are also present in the competitive environment among firms competing for the same customers.

The general idea of SWOT analysis is that a firm's strategy must:

* build on its strengths,
* remedy the weaknesses or work around them,
* take advantage of the opportunities presented by the environment, and,
* protect the firm from the threats.

Despite its apparent simplicity, the SWOT approach has been very popular. First, it forces managers to consider both internal and external factors simultaneously. Second, its emphasis on identifying opportunities and threats makes firms act proactively rather than reactively. Third, it raises awareness about the role of strategy in creating a match between the environmental conditions and the firm's internal strengths and weaknesses. Finally, its conceptual simplicity is achieved without sacrificing analytical rigor. (We will also address some of the limitations of SWOT analysis in Chapter 3.)

SWOT analysis
a framework for analyzing a company's internal and external environment and that stands for strengths, weaknesses, opportunities, and threats.

The General Environment

The **general environment** is composed of factors that can have dramatic effects on firm strategy.[25] Typically, a firm has little ability to predict trends and events in the general environment and even less ability to control them. When listening to CNBC, for example, you can hear many experts espouse different perspectives on what action the Federal Reserve Board may take on short-term interest rates—an action that can have huge effects on the valuation of entire economic sectors. Also, it's difficult to predict future political events such as the ongoing Middle East peace negotiations and tensions on the Korean peninsula. Dramatic innovations in information technology (e.g., the Internet) have helped keep inflation in check by lowering the cost of doing business in the United States at the beginning of the 21st century.[26]

We divide the general environment into six segments: demographic, sociocultural, political/legal, technological, economic, and global. Exhibit 2.3 provides examples of key trends and events in each of the six segments of the general environment.

general environment
factors external to an industry, and usually beyond a firm's control, that affect a firm's strategy.

>LO4
The impact of the general environment on a firm's strategies and performance.

Exhibit 2.3
General Environment:
Key Trends and Events

Demographic

- Aging population
- Rising affluence
- Changes in ethnic composition
- Geographic distribution of population
- Greater disparities in income levels

Sociocultural

- More women in the workforce
- Increase in temporary workers
- Greater concern for fitness
- Greater concern for environment
- Postponement of family formation

Political/Legal

- Tort reform
- Americans with Disabilities Act (ADA) of 1990
- Repeal of Glass-Steagall Act in 1999 (banks may now offer brokerage services)
- Deregulation of utility and other industries
- Increases in federally mandated minimum wages
- Taxation at local, state, federal levels
- Legislation on corporate governance reforms in bookkeeping, stock options, etc. (Sarbanes-Oxley Act of 2002)

Technological

- Genetic engineering
- Emergence of Internet technology
- Computer-aided design/computer-aided manufacturing systems (CAD/CAM)
- Research in synthetic and exotic materials
- Pollution/global warming
- Miniaturization of computing technologies
- Wireless communications
- Nanotechnology

Economic

- Interest rates
- Unemployment rates
- Consumer Price Index
- Trends in GDP
- Changes in stock market valuations

Global

- Increasing global trade
- Currency exchange rates
- Emergence of the Indian and Chinese economies
- Trade agreements among regional blocs (e.g., NAFTA, EU, ASEAN)
- Creation of WTO (leading to decreasing tariffs/free trade in services)

The Demographic Segment

Demographics are the most easily understood and quantifiable elements of the general environment. They are at the root of many changes in society. Demographics include elements such as the aging population,[27] rising or declining affluence, changes in ethnic composition, geographic distribution of the population, and disparities in income level.

The impact of a demographic trend, like all segments of the general environment, varies across industries. Rising levels of affluence in many developed countries bode well for brokerage services as well as for upscale pets and supplies. However, this trend may adversely affect fast-food restaurants because people can afford to dine at higher-priced restaurants. Fast-food restaurants depend on minimum-wage employees to operate efficiently, but the competition for labor intensifies as more attractive employment opportunities become prevalent, thus threatening the employment base for restaurants. Let's look at the details of one of these trends.

The aging population in the United States and other developed countries has important implications. The U.S. Bureau of Statistics states that only 14 percent of American workers were 55 and older in 2002.[28] However, by 2012 that figure will increase to 20 percent, or one in five, of all U.S. workers. At the same time, the United States is expected to experience a significant drop in younger workers aged 25 to 44, making it increasingly important for employers to recruit and retain older workers. Similarly, the National Association of Manufacturing estimates that as baby boomers continue retiring, the United States will have 7 million more jobs than workers by 2010.

Strategy Spotlight 2.4 addresses an attractive market for financial advisors—America's 77 million baby boomers who are nearing retirement. And as we will see, not all of their motives are noble.

Demographic segment of the general environment genetic and observable characteristics of a population including the levels and growth of age, density, sex, race, ethnicity, education, geographic region, and income.

The Sociocultural Segment

Sociocultural forces influence the values, beliefs, and lifestyles of a society. Examples include a higher percentage of women in the workforce, dual-income families, increases in the number of temporary workers, greater concern for healthy diets and physical fitness, greater interest in the environment, and postponement of having children. Such forces enhance sales of products and services in many industries but depress sales in others. The increased number of women in the workforce has increased the need for business clothing merchandise but decreased the demand for baking product staples (since people would have less time to cook from scratch). This health and fitness trend has helped industries that manufacture exercise equipment and healthful foods but harmed industries that produce unhealthful foods.

Increased educational attainment by women in the workplace has led to more women in upper management positions.[29] Given such educational attainment, it is hardly surprising that companies owned by women have been one of the driving forces of the U.S. economy; these companies (now more than 9 million in number) account for 40 percent of all U.S. businesses and have generated more than $3.6 trillion in annual revenue. In addition, women have a tremendous impact on consumer spending decisions. Not surprisingly, many companies have focused their advertising and promotion efforts on female consumers. Consider, for example, Lowe's efforts to attract female shoppers:

Sociocultural segment of the general environment the values, beliefs, and lifestyles of a society.

> Lowe's has found that women prefer to do larger home-improvement projects with a man— be it a boyfriend, husband, or neighbor.[30] As a result, in addition to its "recipe card classes" (that explain various projects that take only one weekend), Lowe's offers co-ed store clinics for projects like sink installation. "Women like to feel they're given the same attention as a male customer," states Lowe's spokespersons Julie Valeant-Yenichek, who points out that most seminar attendees, whether male or female, are inexperienced.

Home Depot recently spent millions of dollars to add softer lighting and brighter signs in 300 stores. Why? It is an effort to match rival Lowe's appeal to women.

Baby Boomers' 401-k Plans: An Easy Mark?

Over the next 20 years, a record $17 trillion will move from pension funds and 401-k accounts into the hands of freshly minted retirees, according to the trade group Investment Company Institute. This reflects America's 77 million baby boomers. By 2030, nearly one in five U.S. residents is expected to be 65 and older. And looking ahead, by 2050, this group is expected to increase to 88.5 million—more than doubling the 38.7 million in 2008. What's more, the 85 and older population is expected to more than triple, from 5.4 million to 19 million between 2008 and 2050.

As one would expect, the pot of money associated with this demographic group—and the hefty asset management fees that it will generate—has financial services firms very excited. And, of course, not all of these professionals have their clients' interests at heart. Many brokers, for example, are promising early retirement, fat investment returns, and big annual cash withdrawals. Often they are succeeding in seducing investors to turn over their retirement accounts—and then putting them in high-fee and often inappropriate investments. Claims the CEO of the securities industry's private oversight group: "This is an emerging problem. The issue has intensified for the next generation of retirees—the largest we've ever seen."

Source: Der Hovanesian, M. 2008. Ruined by 401(k) predators. *BusinessWeek*, July 14 & 21: 60–66; and, Desmond, M. 2008. Cities where your nest egg goes farthest. Forbes.com. October 24: np.

Many seminars by financial advisors—both on a company's premises and off-site—can be breeding grounds for fraud. In 2007, federal and state regulators examined 110 securities firms and branch offices that offer so-called free-lunch sessions. They found most to be little more than thinly veiled sales presentations, with some suggesting unrealistic scenarios such as "How to receive a 13.3% return" and "How $100K can pay $1 million to your heirs." Under federal regulations, brokers can't guarantee specific rates of return or promise investors they'll outlive their money. The regulators' study also found that 10 percent of the seminars appeared to be downright fraudulent, prompting investigations. Below are a few examples of illegal tactics used and the associated compensation paid to injured parties:

- Regulators ordered a unit of Citigroup to pay a $3 million fine and $12.2 million to 200 ex-BellSouth employees who were told by brokers that they could earn 12 percent on their accounts.

- Four Kansas City Southern employees were awarded $2.1 million after InterSecurities brokers said that they could safely withdraw from their accounts amounts equal to their salaries.

- Thirty-two former ExxonMobil employees received $13.8 million after Securities America advisors told them they could retire at 55 and that 14 percent returns were a "no-brainer."

The Political/Legal Segment

Political/legal segment of the general environment how a society creates and exercises power, including rules, laws, and taxation policies.

Political processes and legislation influence environmental regulations with which industries must comply.[31,32] Some important elements of the political/legal arena include tort reform, the Americans with Disabilities Act (ADA) of 1990, the repeal of the Glass-Steagall Act in 1999 (banks may now offer brokerage services), deregulation of utilities and other industries, and increases in the federally mandated minimum wage.[33]

Government legislation can also have a significant impact on the governance of corporations. The U.S. Congress passed the Sarbanes-Oxley Act in 2002, which greatly increases the accountability of auditors, executives, and corporate lawyers. This act responded to the widespread perception that existing governance mechanisms failed to protect the interests of shareholders, employees, and creditors. Clearly, Sarbanes-Oxley has also created a tremendous demand for professional accounting services.

Legislation can also affect firms in the high-tech sector of the economy by expanding the number of temporary visas available for highly skilled foreign professionals.[34] For example, a bill passed by the U.S. Congress in October 2000 allowed 195,000 H-1B visas for each of the following three years—up from a cap of 115,000. However, beginning in 2006 and continuing through 2008, the annual cap on H-1B visas has shrunk to only 65,000—with an

How Microsoft "Gets Around" H-1B Visa Restrictions

In March 2008, Microsoft Chairman Bill Gates took one of his company's most problematic issues to the U.S. Senate. During his testimony, he criticized U.S. immigration policy that limits the H-1B visas issued to skilled workers from foreign countries—workers that Microsoft would urgently like to hire. Gates told the lawmakers: "It makes no sense to tell well-trained, highly skilled individuals—many of whom are educated at top universities—that the U.S. does not welcome or value them" and that the U.S. "will find it far more difficult to maintain its competitive edge over the next 50 years if it excludes those who are able

and willing to help us compete." Gates also claimed that Microsoft hires four Americans in supporting roles for every high-skilled H-1B visa holder it hires. Despite his efforts, the senators ignored his pleas and the visa policy went unchanged.

What to do? Six months later, Microsoft opened an office in Richmond, British Columbia, a suburb of Vancouver. Here, it hopes to place hundreds of workers unable to obtain visas a few miles south in the U.S. Placing workers in the same time zone will help them to collaborate—given that the facility is located just 130 miles north of Microsoft's Redmond, Washington, campus. And it is just a 2 ½ hour drive on Interstate 5 if one needs face time. It certainly doesn't hurt that Canada does not place limits on visas for skilled workers. An unusually pointed press release by Microsoft stated: "The Vancouver area is a global gateway with a diverse population, is close to Microsoft's offices in Redmond, and allows the company to recruit and retain highly skilled people affected by immigration issues in the U.S."

Sources: MacDonald, I. 2008. Finesse the visa crisis with a worker-mobility plan. *Harvard Business Review*, 86(11): 28–29; Greene, J. 2008. Case study: Microsoft's Canadian solution. *BusinessWeek*, January 28: 51; MacDonald, I. 2008. Tech firms get creative in employing foreigners. *Dallas Morning News*, November 16: 5D; and, Anonymous. 2007. Microsoft to open Canada center in response to U.S. immigration. www.workpermit.com, July 10: np.

additional 20,000 visas available for foreigners with a Master's or higher degree from a U.S. institution. Many of the visas are for professionals from India with computer and software expertise. As one would expect, this is a political "hot potato" for industry executives as well as U.S. labor and workers' right groups. The key arguments against increases in H-1B visas are that H-1B workers drive down wages and take jobs from Americans.

Strategy Spotlight 2.5 discusses one of the proactive steps that Microsoft has taken to address this issue.

The Technological Segment

Developments in technology lead to new products and services and improve how they are produced and delivered to the end user. Innovations can create entirely new industries and alter the boundaries of existing industries.[35] Technological developments and trends include genetic engineering, Internet technology, computer-aided design/computer-aided manufacturing (CAD/CAM), research in artificial and exotic materials, and, on the downside, pollution and global warming.[36] Petroleum and primary metals industries spend significantly to reduce their pollution. Engineering and consulting firms that work with polluting industries derive financial benefits from solving such problems.

Nanotechnology is becoming a very promising area of research with many potentially useful applications.[37] Nanotechnology takes place at industry's tiniest stage: one billionth of a meter. Remarkably, this is the size of 10 hydrogen atoms in a row. Matter at such a tiny scale behaves very differently. Familiar materials—from gold to carbon soot—display startling and useful new properties. Some transmit light or electricity. Others become harder than diamonds or turn into potent chemical catalysts. What's more, researchers have found that a tiny dose of nanoparticles can transform the chemistry and nature of far bigger things. Exhibit 2.4 lists a few of the potential ways in which nanotechnology could revolutionize industries.

technological segment of the general environment innovation and state of knowledge in industrial arts, engineering, applied sciences, and pure science; and their interaction with society.

Exhibit 2.4 How Nanotechnology Might Revolutionize Various Industries

- **To fight cancer,** sensors will be able to detect a single cancer cell and will help guide nanoparticles that can burn tumors from the inside out, leaving healthy cells alone.

- **To transform energy,** nano-enhanced solar panels will feed cheap electricity onto superconducting power lines made of carbon nanotubes.

- **To replace silicon,** carbon nanotubes will take over when silicon peters out, leading to far faster chips that need less power than today's chips.

- **For space travel,** podlike crawlers will carry cargo thousands of miles up a carbon-nanotube cable to a space station for billions less than rocket launches.

Source: Baker, S. & Aston, A. 2004. Universe in a grain of sand. *BusinessWeek*, October 11: 139–140.

There are downsides to technology. In addition to ethical issues in biotechnology, there are threats to our environment associated with the emission of greenhouse gases. Some firms have taken a proactive approach. BP Amoco plans to decrease its greenhouse gas emissions by giving each of its 150 business units a quota of emission permits and encouraging the units to trade them. If a unit cuts emissions and has leftover permits, it can sell them to other units that are having difficulty meeting their goals.[38]

The Economic Segment

Economic segment of the general environment characteristics of the economy including national income and monetary conditions.

The economy affects all industries, from suppliers of raw materials to manufacturers of finished goods and services, as well as all organizations in the service, wholesale, retail, government, and nonprofit sectors.[39] Key economic indicators include interest rates, unemployment rates, the Consumer Price Index, the gross domestic product, and net disposable income. Interest-rate increases have a negative impact on the residential home construction industry but a negligible (or neutral) effect on industries that produce consumer necessities such as prescription drugs or common grocery items.

Other economic indicators are associated with equity markets. Perhaps the most watched is the Dow Jones Industrial Average (DJIA), which is composed of 30 large industrial firms. When stock market indexes increase, consumers' discretionary income rises and there is often an increased demand for luxury items such as jewelry and automobiles. But when stock valuations decrease, demand for these items shrinks. Strategy Spotlight 2.6 provides some examples of how the recession that intensified throughout 2008 affected the purchase of luxury goods.

The Global Segment

Global segment of the general environment influences from foreign countries including foreign market opportunities, foreign-based competition, and expanded capital markets.

More firms are expanding their operations and market reach beyond the borders of their "home" country. Globalization provides both opportunities to access larger potential markets and a broad base of production factors such as raw materials, labor, skilled managers, and technical professionals. However, such endeavors also carry many political, social, and economic risks.[40]

Examples of key elements include currency exchange rates, increasing global trade, the economic emergence of China, trade agreements among regional blocs (e.g., North American Free Trade Agreement, European Union), and the General Agreement on Tariffs and Trade (GATT) (lowering of tariffs).[41] Increases in trade across national boundaries also provide benefits to air cargo and shipping industries but have a minimal impact on service industries such as bookkeeping and routine medical services. The emergence of China as an economic power has benefited many industries, such as construction, soft drinks, and computers. However, it has had a negative impact on the defense industry in the United States as diplomatic relations between the two nations improve.

strategy spotlight

The Recession's Impact on Luxury Goods

With financial markets in distress, extensive Wall Street layoffs, and consumer confidence sliding to its lowest point in several years, marketers of high-end goods and services—often insulated from economic slowdowns—are beginning to experience a sharp decline. Below are some examples from businesses polled by *Fortune* magazine:

- Bookings at the hotel chain, Leading Hotels of the World, declined 10 percent in 2008. With corporate clients representing 25 percent of their business, Senior Vice President Dan Neumann expects things to get worse.

- Allen Brothers, a high-end cataloger and supplier of beef to premier steakhouses such as Del Frisco's, says that restaurant customers are exchanging prime cuts for lower-grade meats.

- Fort Lauderdale–based broker Anchor Yachts says that yacht sales in the $200,000 to $800,000 range are down 50 percent. Sellers have cut prices 20 percent.

- At Pilates on Fifth in Midtown Manhattan, co-owner Katherine Corp states that many of her clients are trading down—exchanging $90 private lessons for cheaper group classes.

Sources: Helm, B. 2008. How to sell luxury to penny-pinchers. *Business-Week,* November 10: 60; and, Boyle, M. 2008. The luxury recession. *Fortune,* April 14: 30.

● Almost every industry has been adversely affected by the recession that began in 2008—including expensive yachts.

In the automobile industry, several discount players have entered the luxury game. For example, Hyundai is selling entry-level luxury in the worst possible selling environment in memory. Their strategy: depict more snooty rivals as overpriced. In its ads, Hyundai notes that its new Genesis sedan ($33,000) has the same sound system as a Rolls-Royce Phantom ($300,000-plus). Their ad says: "If you'd rather have money than a hood ornament" the Genesis may "look even better than a Rolls-Royce."

Also, consider the cost of terrorism. A recent survey indicates that for S&P 500 firms, the threat has caused direct and indirect costs of $107 billion a year. This figure includes extra spending (on insurance and redundant capacity, for instance) as well as lost revenues (from fearful consumers' decreased activity).[42]

Relationships among Elements of the General Environment

In our discussion of the general environment, we see many relationships among the various elements.[43] For example, a demographic trend in the United States, the aging of the population, has important implications for the economic segment (in terms of tax policies to provide benefits to increasing numbers of older citizens). Another example is the emergence of information technology as a means to increase the rate of productivity gains in the United States and other developed countries. Such use of IT results in lower inflation (an important element of the economic segment) and helps offset costs associated with higher labor rates.

The effects of a trend or event in the general environment vary across industries. Governmental legislation (political/legal) to permit the importation of prescription drugs from foreign countries is a very positive development for drugstores but a very negative event for U.S. drug manufacturers. Exhibit 2.5 provides other examples of how the impact of trends or events in the general environment can vary across industries.

Before moving on, let's consider the Internet. The Internet has been a leading and highly visible component of a broader technological phenomenon—the emergence of digital technology. These technologies are altering the way business is conducted and having an impact on nearly every business domain. Strategy Spotlight 2.7 addresses the impact of the Internet and digital technologies on the business environment.

Exhibit 2.5
The Impact of General Environmental Trends on Various Industries

Segment/Trends and Events	Industry	Positive	Neutral	Negative
Demographic				
Aging population	Health care	✓		
	Baby products			✓
Rising affluence	Brokerage services	✓		
	Fast foods			✓
	Upscale pets and supplies	✓		
Sociocultural				
More women in the workforce	Clothing	✓		
	Baking products (staples)			✓
Greater concern for health and fitness	Home exercise equipment	✓		
	Meat products			✓
Political/legal				
Tort reform	Legal services			✓
	Auto manufacturing	✓		
Americans with Disabilities Act (ADA)	Retail			✓
	Manufacturers of elevators, escalators, and ramps	✓		
Technological				
Genetic engineering	Pharmaceutical	✓		
	Publishing		✓	
Pollution/global warming	Engineering services	✓		
	Petroleum			✓
Economic				
Interest rate increases	Residential construction			✓
	Most common grocery products		✓	
Global				
Increasing global trade	Shipping	✓		
	Personal service		✓	
Emergence of China as an economic power	Soft drinks	✓		
	Defense			✓

strategy spotlight

The Internet and Digital Technologies: Affecting Many Environmental Segments

The Internet has dramatically changed the way business is conducted in every corner of the globe. According to digital economy visionary Don Tapscott:

> The Net is much more than just another technology development; the Net represents something qualitatively new—an unprecedented, powerful, universal communications medium. Far surpassing radio and television, this medium is digital, infinitely richer, and interactive.... Mobile computing devices, broadband access, wireless networks, and computing power embedded in everything from refrigerators to automobiles are converging into a global network that will enable people to use the Net just about anywhere and anytime.

The Internet provides a platform or staging area for the application of numerous technologies, rapid advances in knowledge, and unprecedented levels of global communication and commerce. Even technologies that don't require the Internet to function, such as wireless phones and GPS, rely on the Internet for data transfer and communications.

Growth in Internet usage has surged in recent years both among individual users as well as businesses.

Sources: Anonymous. 2005. SMBs believe in the Web. eMarketer.com, www.emarketer.com, May 16. Downes, L. & Mui, C. 1998. *Unleashing the killer app*. Boston: Harvard Business School Press. Green, H. 2003. Wi-Fi means business. *BusinessWeek*, April 28: 86–92; McGann, R. 2005. Broadband: High speed, high spend. *ClickZ Network*, www.clickz.com, January 24; Tapscott, D. 2001. Rethinking strategy in a Networked World. *Strategy and Business*, Third Quarter: 34–41; and, Yang, C. 2003. Beyond wi-fi: A new wireless age. *BusinessWeek*, December 15: 84–88.

Exhibit 2.6 illustrates (2000–2008) worldwide growth trends in Internet use. Business use of the Internet has become nearly ubiquitous throughout the economy. Major corporations all have a Web presence, and many companies use the Internet to interact with key stakeholders. For example, some companies have direct links with suppliers through online procurement systems that automatically reorder inventories and supplies. Companies such as Cisco Systems even interact with their own employees using the Internet to update employment records, such as health care information and benefits.

Small and medium-sized enterprises (SMEs) are also relying on the Internet more than ever. A recent study found that 87 percent of SMEs are receiving monthly revenue from their Web site, and 42 percent derive more than a quarter of their monthly revenue from their Internet presence. According to Joel Kocher, CEO of Interland, "We are getting to the point in most small-business categories where it will soon be safe to say that if you're not online, you're not really serious about being in business."

Despite these advances, the Internet and digital technologies still face numerous challenges. For example, international standards for digital and wireless communications are still in flux. As a result, cell phones and other devices that work in the United States are often useless in many parts of Europe and Asia. And, unlike analog systems, electronic bits of data that are zooming through space can be more easily lost, stolen, or manipulated. However, even with these problems, Internet and digital technologies will continue to be a growing global phenomenon. As Andy Grove, former chairman of Intel, stated, "The world now runs on Internet time."

Geographic Regions	Internet Users, 2000	Internet Users, 2008	%Population (Penetration)	Usage Growth, 2000–2008
Africa	4,514,400	51,065,630	5.3%	1,031%
Asia	114,304,000	578,538,257	15.3%	406%
Europe	105,096,093	384,633,765	48.1%	266%
Middle East	3,284,800	41,939,200	21.3%	1,176%
North America	108,096,800	248,241,969	73.6%	129%
Latin America/ Caribbean	18,068,919	139,009,209	24.1%	669%
Oceania/Australia	7,620,480	20,204,331	59.5%	165%
World Total	360,985,492	1,463,632,361	21.9%	305%

Source: www.internetworldstats.com

Exhibit 2.6 Growth in Internet Activity

The Competitive Environment

Managers must consider the competitive environment (also sometimes referred to as the task or industry environment). The nature of competition in an industry, as well as the profitability of a firm, is often more directly influenced by developments in the competitive environment.

The **competitive environment** consists of many factors that are particularly relevant to a firm's strategy. These include competitors (existing or potential), customers, and suppliers. Potential competitors may include a supplier considering forward integration, such as an automobile manufacturer acquiring a rental car company, or a firm in an entirely new industry introducing a similar product that uses a more efficient technology.

Next, we will discuss key concepts and analytical techniques that managers should use to assess their competitive environments. First, we examine Michael Porter's five-forces model that illustrates how these forces can be used to explain an industry's profitability.[44] Second, we discuss how the five forces are being affected by the capabilities provided by Internet technologies. Third, we address some of the limitations, or "caveats," that managers should be familiar with when conducting industry analysis. Finally, we address the concept of strategic groups, because even within an industry it is often useful to group firms on the basis of similarities of their strategies. As we will see, competition tends to be more intense among firms *within* a strategic group than between strategic groups.

competitive environment
factors that pertain to an industry and affect a firm's strategies.

Porter's Five-Forces Model of Industry Competition

The "five-forces" model developed by Michael E. Porter has been the most commonly used analytical tool for examining the competitive environment. It describes the competitive environment in terms of five basic competitive forces.[45]

1. The threat of new entrants.
2. The bargaining power of buyers.
3. The bargaining power of suppliers.
4. The threat of substitute products and services.
5. The intensity of rivalry among competitors in an industry.

Each of these forces affects a firm's ability to compete in a given market. Together, they determine the profit potential for a particular industry. The model is shown in Exhibit 2.7. A manager should be familiar with the five-forces model for several reasons. It helps you decide whether your firm should remain in or exit an industry. It provides the rationale for increasing or decreasing resource commitments. The model helps you assess how to improve your firm's competitive position with regard to each of the five forces.[46] For example, you can use insights provided by the five-forces model to create higher entry barriers that discourage new rivals from competing with you.[47] Or you may develop strong relationships with your distribution channels. You may decide to find suppliers who satisfy the price/performance criteria needed to make your product or service a top performer.

Threat of new entrants the possibility that the profits of established firms in the industry may be eroded by new competitors.

The Threat of New Entrants   The threat of new entrants refers to the possibility that the profits of established firms in the industry may be eroded by new competitors.[48] The extent of the threat depends on existing barriers to entry and the combined reactions from existing competitors.[49] If entry barriers are high and/or the newcomer can anticipate a sharp retaliation from established competitors, the threat of entry is low. These circumstances discourage new competitors. There are six major sources of entry barriers.

Exhibit 2.7 **Porter's Five-Forces Model of Industry Competition**

Source: Reprinted with permission of The Free Press, a division of Simon & Schuster Adult Publishing Group, from *Competitive Strategy: Techniques for Analyzing Industries and Competitors* by Michael E. Porter. Copyright © 1980, 1998 by The Free Press. All rights reserved.

Economies of Scale Economies of scale refers to spreading the costs of production over the number of units produced. The cost of a product per unit declines as the absolute volume per period increases. This deters entry by forcing the entrant to come in at a large scale and risk strong reaction from existing firms or come in at a small scale and accept a cost disadvantage. Both are undesirable options.

Product Differentiation When existing competitors have strong brand identification and customer loyalty, differentiation creates a barrier to entry by forcing entrants to spend heavily to overcome existing customer loyalties.

Capital Requirements The need to invest large financial resources to compete creates a barrier to entry, especially if the capital is required for risky or unrecoverable up-front advertising or research and development (R&D).

Switching Costs A barrier to entry is created by the existence of one-time costs that the buyer faces when switching from one supplier's product or service to another.

Access to Distribution Channels The new entrant's need to secure distribution for its product can create a barrier to entry.

Cost Disadvantages Independent of Scale Some existing competitors may have advantages that are independent of size or economies of scale. These derive from:

• Proprietary products
• Favorable access to raw materials
• Government subsidies
• Favorable government policies

In an environment where few, if any, of these entry barriers are present, the threat of new entry is high. For example, if a new firm can launch its business with a low capital investment and operate efficiently despite its small scale of operation, it is likely to be a threat. One company that failed because of low entry barriers in an industry is ProCD.[50] You probably never heard of this company. It didn't last very long. ProCD provides an example of a firm that failed because it entered an industry with very low entry barriers.

The story begins in 1986 when Nynex (a former Baby Bell company) issued the first electronic phone book, a compact disk containing all listings for the New York City area. It charged $10,000 per copy and sold the CDs to the FBI, IRS, and other large commercial and government organizations. James Bryant, the Nynex executive in charge of the project, smelled a fantastic business opportunity. He quit Nynex and set up his own firm, ProCD, with the ambitious goal of producing an electronic directory covering the entire United States.

The telephone companies, fearing an attack on their highly profitable Yellow Pages business, refused to license digital copies of their listings. Bryant was not deterred. He hired Chinese workers at $3.50 a day to type every listing from every U.S. telephone book into a database. The result contained more than 70 million phone numbers and was used to create a master disk that enabled ProCD to make hundreds of thousands of copies. Each CD sold for hundreds of dollars and cost less than a dollar each to produce.

It was a profitable business indeed! However, success was fleeting. Competitors such as Digital Directory Assistance and American Business Information quickly launched competing products with the same information. Since customers couldn't tell one product from the next, the players were forced to compete on price alone. Prices for the CD soon plummeted to a few dollars each. A high-priced, high-margin product just months earlier, the CD phone book became little more than a cheap commodity.

Bargaining power of buyers the threat that buyers may force down prices, bargain for higher quality or more services, and play competitors against each other.

The Bargaining Power of Buyers   Buyers threaten an industry by forcing down prices, bargaining for higher quality or more services, and playing competitors against each other. These actions erode industry profitability.[51] The power of each large buyer group depends on attributes of the market situation and the importance of purchases from that group compared with the industry's overall business. A buyer group is powerful when:

- *It is concentrated or purchases large volumes relative to seller sales.* If a large percentage of a supplier's sales are purchased by a single buyer, the importance of the buyer's business to the supplier increases. Large-volume buyers also are powerful in industries with high fixed costs (e.g., steel manufacturing).
- *The products it purchases from the industry are standard or undifferentiated.* Confident they can always find alternative suppliers, buyers play one company against the other, as in commodity grain products.
- *The buyer faces few switching costs.* Switching costs lock the buyer to particular sellers. Conversely, the buyer's power is enhanced if the seller faces high switching costs.
- *It earns low profits.* Low profits create incentives to lower purchasing costs. On the other hand, highly profitable buyers are generally less price sensitive.
- *The buyers pose a credible threat of backward integration.* If buyers are either partially integrated or pose a credible threat of backward integration, they are typically able to secure bargaining concessions.
- *The industry's product is unimportant to the quality of the buyer's products or services.* When the quality of the buyer's products is not affected by the industry's product, the buyer is more price sensitive.

At times, a firm or set of firms in an industry may increase its buyer power by using the services of a third party. FreeMarkets Online is one such third party.[52] Pittsburgh-based FreeMarkets has developed software enabling large industrial buyers to organize online auctions for qualified suppliers of semistandard parts such as fabricated components,

Playing "Hard Ball" with Job Applicants: Buy Now, Pay Later?

Companies will likely "buy now, pay later" if they play hard ball with job applicants as the economy sours and unemployment rates rise. According to researchers at Vanderbilt University, employees who felt they were mistreated during the recruiting process feel less committed—for years. Approximately 100 MBA graduates were surveyed about how they were hired by their employers. Those who felt that they were treated unfairly were twice as likely to be looking for opportunities outside their company—even after five years!

What were some common "interactional injustices" during the hiring process? Slow responses from employers, offers that were withdrawn if not accepted immediately, and a company whose attitude is "You need us." A valuable message for businesses positioning themselves to succeed in the economic recovery: "Don't abuse the momentary power you have as an employer. It'll come back to bite you."

Source: Hof, R. D. 2008 Hired, with hard feelings. *BusinessWeek*, November 6: 15.

packaging materials, metal stampings, and services. By aggregating buyers, FreeMarkets increases the buyers' bargaining power. The results are impressive. In its first 48 auctions, most participating companies saved over 15 percent; some saved as much as 50 percent.

Although a firm may be tempted to take advantage of its suppliers because of high buyer power, it must be aware of the potential long-term backlash from such actions. Strategy Spotlight 2.8 discusses how newly hired employees may feel resentful and become demotivated if they believe that they were treated unfairly during the recruitment process—a time when their bargaining power may have been rather low relative to the company.

The Bargaining Power of Suppliers   Suppliers can exert bargaining power by threatening to raise prices or reduce the quality of purchased goods and services. Powerful suppliers can squeeze the profitability of firms so far that they can't recover the costs of raw material inputs.[53] The factors that make suppliers powerful tend to mirror those that make buyers powerful. A supplier group will be powerful when:

> **Bargaining power of suppliers** the threat that suppliers may raise prices or reduce the quality of purchased goods and services.

- *The supplier group is dominated by a few companies and is more concentrated (few firms dominate the industry) than the industry it sells to.* Suppliers selling to fragmented industries influence prices, quality, and terms.
- *The supplier group is not obliged to contend with substitute products for sale to the industry.* The power of even large, powerful suppliers can be checked if they compete with substitutes.
- *The industry is not an important customer of the supplier group.* When suppliers sell to several industries and a particular industry does not represent a significant fraction of its sales, suppliers are more prone to exert power.
- *The supplier's product is an important input to the buyer's business.* When such inputs are important to the success of the buyer's manufacturing process or product quality, the bargaining power of suppliers is high.
- *The supplier group's products are differentiated or it has built up switching costs for the buyer.* Differentiation or switching costs facing the buyers cut off their options to play one supplier against another.
- *The supplier group poses a credible threat of forward integration.* This provides a check against the industry's ability to improve the terms by which it purchases.

Strategy Spotlight 2.9 discusses how catfish farmers enhanced their bargaining power vis-à-vis their customers—large agribusiness firms—by forming a cooperative.

strategy spotlight

Enhancing Supplier Power: The Creation of Delta Pride Catfish

The formation of Delta Pride Catfish in 1981 is an example of the power that a group of suppliers can attain if they exercise the threat of forward integration. Catfish farmers in Mississippi had historically supplied their harvest to processing plants run by large agribusiness firms such as ConAgra and Farm Fresh. When the farmers increased their production of catfish in response to growing demand in the early 1970s, they found, much to their chagrin, that processors were holding back on their plans to increase their processing capabilities in hopes of higher retail prices for catfish.

Source: Cargile, D. 2005. Personal communication. (Vice President of Sales, Delta Pride Catfish, Inc.), February 2; Anonymous. 2003. Delta Pride Catfish names Steve Osso President and CEO. www.deltabusiness.journal.com, February; and Fritz, M. 1988. Agribusiness: Catfish story. *Forbes,* December 12: 37.

What action did the farmers take? They responded by forming a cooperative, raising $4.5 million, and constructing their own processing plant, which they supplied themselves. Within two years, ConAgra's market share had dropped from 35 percent to 11 percent, and Farm Fresh's market share fell by over 20 percent.

By the late 1980s, Delta Pride controlled over 40 percent of the 280-million-pound-per-year U.S. catfish market. It has continued to grow by including value-added products such as breaded and marinated catfish products. One such product is Country Crisp Catfish Strips, a bakeable, breaded product with country-style seasoning. By 2005, Delta Pride had more than 500 employees. Its approximately 100 shareholders are mostly catfish farmers who own more than 60,000 acres of catfish production ponds and produce more than 200 million pounds of live catfish each year.

Threat of substitute products and services the threat of limiting the potential returns of an industry by placing a ceiling on the prices that firms in that industry can profitably charge without losing too many customers to substitute products.

The Threat of Substitute Products and Services   All firms within an industry compete with industries producing substitute products and services.[54] Substitutes limit the potential returns of an industry by placing a ceiling on the prices that firms in that industry can profitably charge. The more attractive the price/performance ratio of substitute products, the tighter the lid on an industry's profits.

Identifying substitute products involves searching for other products or services that can perform the same function as the industry's offerings. This may lead a manager into businesses seemingly far removed from the industry. For example, the airline industry might not consider video cameras much of a threat. But as digital technology has improved and wireless and other forms of telecommunication have become more efficient, teleconferencing has become a viable substitute for business travel. That is, the rate of improvement in the price–performance relationship of the substitute product (or service) is high.

Teleconferencing can save both time and money, as IBM found out with its "Manager Jam" idea.[55] With 319,000 employees scattered around six continents, it is one of the world's largest businesses (including 32,000 managers) and can be a pretty confusing place. The shift to an increasingly mobile workplace means many managers supervise employees they rarely see face-to-face. To enhance coordination, Samuel Palmisano, IBM's new CEO, launched one of his first big initiatives: a two-year program exploring the role of the manager in the 21st century. "Manager Jam," as the project was nicknamed, was a 48-hour real-time Web event in which managers from 50 different countries swapped ideas and strategies for dealing with problems shared by all of them, regardless of geography. Some 8,100 managers logged on to the company's intranet to participate in the discussion forums.

Renewable energy resources are also a promising substitute product and are rapidly becoming more economically competitive with fossil fuels. Strategy Spotlight 2.10 addresses this critical issue.

The Growing Viability of Renewable Resources as Substitutes for Fossil Fuels

Renewable resources currently provide just over 6 percent of total U.S. energy. However, that figure could increase rapidly in the years ahead, according to a joint report issued in September 2006 by the Worldwatch Institute and the Center for Progress, entitled "American Energy: The Renewable Path to Energy Security."

The report indicates that many of the new technologies that harness renewables are, or soon will be, economically competitive with fossil fuels. Dynamic growth rates are driving down costs and spurring rapid advances in technologies. And, since 2000, global wind energy generation has more than tripled, solar cell production has risen six-fold, production of fuel ethanol from crops has more than doubled, and biodiesel production has expanded nearly four-fold. Annual global investment in "new" renewable energy has risen almost six-fold since 1995, with cumulative investment over the period nearly $180 billion.

A November 2006 study by the RAND Corporation is consistent with the aforementioned report. It asserts that the economy of the United States would likely benefit, rather than be slowed, if the nation attained the goal of supplying 25 percent of its energy needs from renewable sources by 2025. Such developments would also reduce U.S. dependence on oil, which would mean a substantial start on capping greenhouse gas emissions, which most scientists link to global warming.

Deep Patel, founder of Los Angeles–based online clean-energy technologies retailer GoGreenSolar.com, provides some practical insights:

- *Clean energy is regional:* Think solar in sunny climates like California, geothermal in Nevada, and wind in blustery states such as Oklahoma.

- *Big corporations tend to hire established, renewable energy companies.* "But no one's paying as much attention to smaller businesses and homeowners that want to go solar. For entrepreneurs, that represents the biggest untapped market."

- *Consumers need help* "taking a staged approach to going solar." At GoGreenSolar, a "Plug N Play Solar Power Kit" starts consumers off with two solar panels that they can add to later. Patel's prediction: more such modular solutions will become available.

Sources: Anonymous. 2008. Clean Energy. *Entrepreneur,* December: 59; Clayton, M. 2006. Greener, cleaner . . . and competitive. www.csmonitor.com. December 4; and, Anonymous. 2006. Renewables becoming cost-competitive with fossil fuels in the U.S. www.worldwatch.org. September 18.

 environmental sustainability

The Intensity of Rivalry among Competitors in an Industry   Firms use tactics like price competition, advertising battles, product introductions, and increased customer service or warranties. Rivalry occurs when competitors sense the pressure or act on an opportunity to improve their position.[56]

Some forms of competition, such as price competition, are typically highly destabilizing and are likely to erode the average level of profitability in an industry.[57] Rivals easily match price cuts, an action that lowers profits for all firms. On the other hand, advertising battles expand overall demand or enhance the level of product differentiation for the benefit of all firms in the industry. Rivalry, of course, differs across industries. In some instances it is characterized as warlike, bitter, or cutthroat, whereas in other industries it is referred to as polite and gentlemanly. Intense rivalry is the result of several interacting factors, including the following:

- ***Numerous or equally balanced competitors.*** When there are many firms in an industry, the likelihood of mavericks is great. Some firms believe they can make moves without being noticed. Even when there are relatively few firms, and they are nearly equal in size and resources, instability results from fighting among companies having the resources for sustained and vigorous retaliation.

Intensity of rivalry among competitors in an industry the threat that customers will switch their business to competitors within the industry.

- *Slow industry growth.* Slow industry growth turns competition into a fight for market share, since firms seek to expand their sales.
- *High fixed or storage costs.* High fixed costs create strong pressures for all firms to increase capacity. Excess capacity often leads to escalating price cutting.
- *Lack of differentiation or switching costs.* Where the product or service is perceived as a commodity or near commodity, the buyer's choice is typically based on price and service, resulting in pressures for intense price and service competition. Lack of switching costs, described earlier, has the same effect.
- *Capacity augmented in large increments.* Where economies of scale require that capacity must be added in large increments, capacity additions can be very disruptive to the industry supply/demand balance.
- *High exit barriers.* Exit barriers are economic, strategic, and emotional factors that keep firms competing even though they may be earning low or negative returns on their investments. Some exit barriers are specialized assets, fixed costs of exit, strategic interrelationships (e.g., relationships between the business units and others within a company in terms of image, marketing, shared facilities, and so on), emotional barriers, and government and social pressures (e.g., governmental discouragement of exit out of concern for job loss).

Rivalry between firms is often based solely on price, but it can involve other factors. Take Pfizer's market position in the impotence treatment market. Pfizer was the first pharmaceutical firm to develop Viagra, a highly successful drug that treats impotence.

In several countries, the United Kingdom among them, Pfizer faced a lawsuit by Eli Lilly & Co. and Icos Corp. challenging its patent protection. These two pharmaceutical firms recently entered into a joint venture to market Cialis, a drug to compete with Viagra. The U.K. courts agreed and lifted the patent.

This opened the door for Eli Lilly and Icos to proceed with challenging Pfizer's market position. Because Cialis has fewer side effects than Viagra, the drug has the potential to rapidly decrease Pfizer's market share in the United Kingdom if physicians switch prescriptions from Viagra to Cialis. If future patent challenges are successful, Pfizer may see its sales of Viagra erode rapidly.[58] But Pfizer is hardly standing still. It recently doubled its advertising expenditures on Viagra.

Exhibit 2.8 summarizes our discussion of industry five-forces analysis. It points out how various factors such as economies of scale and capital requirements affect each "force."

How the Internet and Digital Technologies Are Affecting the Five Competitive Forces

>LO6

How the Internet and digitally based capabilities are affecting the five competitive forces and industry profitability.

The Internet and other digital technologies are having a significant impact on nearly every industry. These technologies have fundamentally changed the ways businesses interact with each other and with consumers. In most cases, these changes have affected industry forces in ways that have created many new strategic challenges. In this section, we will evaluate Michael Porter's five-forces model in terms of the actual use of the Internet and the new technological capabilities that it makes possible.

The Threat of New Entrants In most industries, the threat of new entrants has increased because digital and Internet-based technologies lower barriers to entry. For example, businesses that reach customers primarily through the Internet may enjoy savings on other traditional expenses such as office rent, sales-force salaries, printing, and postage. This may encourage more entrants who, because of the lower start-up expenses, see an opportunity to capture market share by offering a product or performing a service more efficiently than existing competitors. Thus, a new cyber entrant can use the savings provided by the Internet to charge lower prices and compete on price despite the incumbent's scale advantages.

Threat of New Entrants Is High When:	High	Low
Economies of scale are		X
Product differentiation is		X
Capital requirements are		X
Switching costs are		X
Incumbent's control of distribution channels is		X
Incumbent's proprietary knowledge is		X
Incumbent's access to raw materials is		X
Incumbent's access to government subsidies is		X

Power of Buyers Is High When:	High	Low
Concentration of buyers relative to suppliers is	X	
Switching costs are		X
Product differentiation of suppliers is		X
Threat of backward integration by buyers is	X	
Extent of buyer's profits is		X
Importance of the supplier's input to quality of buyer's final product is		X

Power of Suppliers Is High When:	High	Low
Concentration relative to buyer industry is	X	
Availability of substitute products is		X
Importance of customer to the supplier is		X
Differentiation of the supplier's products and services is	X	
Switching costs of the buyer are	X	
Threat of forward integration by the supplier is	X	

Threat of Substitute Products Is High When:	High	Low
The differentiation of the substitute product is	X	
Rate of improvement in price–performance relationship of substitute product is	X	

Intensity of Competitive Rivalry Is High When:	High	Low
Number of competitors is	X	
Industry growth rate is		X
Fixed costs are	X	
Storage costs are	X	
Product differentiation is		X
Switching costs are		X
Exit barriers are	X	
Strategic stakes are	X	

Exhibit 2.8 Competitive Analysis Checklist

Alternatively, because digital technologies often make it possible for young firms to provide services that are equivalent or superior to an incumbent, a new entrant may be able to serve a market more effectively, with more personalized services and greater attention to product details. A new firm may be able to build a reputation in its niche and charge premium prices. By so doing, it can capture part of an incumbent's business and erode profitability. Consider Voice Over Internet Protocol (VOIP), a fast growing alternative to traditional phone service, which is expected to reach 25 million U.S. households by 2012.[59] Savings of 20 to 30 percent are common for VOIP consumers. This is driving prices down and lowering telecom industry profits. More importantly it threatens the value of the phone line infrastructure that the major carriers have invested in so heavily.

Another potential benefit of Web-based business is access to distribution channels. Manufacturers or distributors that can reach potential outlets for their products more efficiently by means of the Internet may enter markets that were previously closed to them. Access is not guaranteed, however, because strong barriers to entry exist in certain industries.[60]

The Bargaining Power of Buyers   The Internet and wireless technologies may increase buyer power by providing consumers with more information to make buying decisions and by lowering switching costs. But these technologies may also suppress the power of traditional buyer channels that have concentrated buying power in the hands of a few, giving buyers new ways to access sellers. To sort out these differences, let's first distinguish between two types of buyers: end users and buyer channel intermediaries.

End users are the final customers in a distribution channel. Internet sales activity that is labeled "B2C"—that is, business-to-consumer—is concerned with end users. The Internet is likely to increase the power of these buyers for several reasons. First, the Internet provides large amounts of consumer information. This gives end users the information they need to shop for quality merchandise and bargain for price concessions. The automobile industry provides an excellent example. For a small fee, agencies such as Consumers Union (publishers of *Consumer Reports*) will provide customers with detailed information about actual automobile manufacturer costs.[61] This information, available online, can be used to bid down dealers' profits. Second, an end user's switching costs are also potentially much lower because of the Internet. Switching may involve only a few clicks of the mouse to find and view a competing product or service online.

In contrast, the bargaining power of distribution channel buyers may decrease because of the Internet. *Buyer channel intermediaries* are the wholesalers, distributors, and retailers who serve as intermediaries between manufacturers and end users. In some industries, they are dominated by powerful players that control who gains access to the latest goods or the best merchandise. The Internet and wireless communications, however, make it much easier and less expensive for businesses to reach customers directly. Thus, the Internet may increase the power of incumbent firms relative to that of traditional buyer channels. Strategy Spotlight 2.11 illustrates some of the changes brought on by the Internet that have affected the industry's two types of buyers.

The Bargaining Power of Suppliers   Use of the Internet and digital technologies to speed up and streamline the process of acquiring supplies is already benefiting many sectors of the economy. But the net effect of the Internet on supplier power will depend on the nature of competition in a given industry. As with buyer power, the extent to which the Internet is a benefit or a detriment also hinges on the supplier's position along the supply chain.

The role of suppliers involves providing products or services to other businesses. The term "B2B"—that is, business-to-business—often refers to businesses that supply or sell to other businesses. The effect of the Internet on the bargaining power of suppliers is a double-edged sword. On the one hand, suppliers may find it difficult to hold onto customers because buyers can do comparative shopping and price negotiations so much faster on

Buyer Power in the Book Industry: The Role of the Internet

The $25 billion book publishing industry illustrates some of the changes brought on by the Internet that have affected buying power among two types of buyers—end users and buyer channel intermediaries. Prior to the Internet, book publishers worked primarily through large distributors. These intermediaries such as Tennessee-based Ingram, one of the largest and most powerful distributors, exercised strong control over the movement of books from publishers to bookstores. This power was especially strong relative to small, independent publishers who often found it difficult to get their books into bookstores and in front of potential customers.

Sources: Healy, M. 2008. Book Industry Trends 2008 shows publishers' net revenues rose 4.4 percent in 2007 to reach $37.26 billion. www.bisg.org. May 31: np; Books "most popular online buy." 2008. newsvote.bbc.co.uk. January 29: np. Hoynes, M. 2002. Is it the same for book sales? BookWeb.org, www.bookweb.org, March 20; www.parapublishing.com; Teague, D. 2005. U.S. book production reaches new high of 195,000 titles in 2004; Fiction soars. Bowker.com, www.bowker.com, May 24; and Teicher, C. M. 2007. March of the small presses. *Publishers Weekly*, www.publishersweekly.com, March 26.

The Internet has significantly changed these relationships. Publishers can now negotiate distribution agreements directly with online retailers such as Amazon and Books-A-Million. Such online bookstores now account for about $4 billion in annual sales. And small publishers can use the Internet to sell directly to end users and publicize new titles, without depending on buyer channel intermediaries to handle their books. By using the Internet to appeal to niche markets, 63,000 small publishers with revenues of less than $50 million each generated $14.2 billion in sales in 2005—over half of the industry's total sales.

Future trends for the industry look favorable. The Book Industry Study Group (BISG) released figures in May 2008 which estimated that publishers' revenues in 2007 reached $37.3 billion, up 4.4 percent from 2006's total. BISG expects revenues to increase to $43.5 billion by the end of 2012. There is also good news for online book sellers: According to results from a 2008 worldwide survey by Nielsen Online, 41 percent of users had bought books online—up from 34 percent just two years earlier.

the Internet. This is especially damaging to supply-chain intermediaries, such as product distributors, who cannot stop suppliers from directly accessing other potential business customers. In addition, the Internet inhibits the ability of suppliers to offer highly differentiated products or unique services. Most procurement technologies can be imitated by competing suppliers, and the technologies that make it possible to design and customize new products rapidly are being used by all competitors.

On the other hand, several factors may also contribute to stronger supplier power. First, the growth of new Web-based business may create more downstream outlets for suppliers to sell to. Second, suppliers may be able to create Web-based purchasing arrangements that make purchasing easier and discourage their customers from switching. Online procurement systems directly link suppliers and customers, reducing transaction costs and paperwork.[62] Third, the use of proprietary software that links buyers to a supplier's website may create a rapid, low-cost ordering capability that discourages the buyer from seeking other sources of supply. Amazon.com, for example, created and patented One-Click purchasing technology that speeds up the ordering process for customers who enroll in the service.[63]

Finally, suppliers will have greater power to the extent that they can reach end users directly without intermediaries. Previously, suppliers often had to work through intermediaries who brought their products or services to market for a fee. But a process known as *disintermediation* is removing the organizations or business process layers responsible for intermediary steps in the value chain of many industries.[64] Just as the Internet is eliminating some business functions, it is creating an opening for new functions. These new activities are entering the value chain by a process known as *reintermediation*—the introduction of new types of intermediaries. Many of these new functions are affecting traditional supply chains. For example, delivery services are enjoying a boom because of the Internet. Many more consumers are choosing to have products delivered to their door rather than going out to pick them up.

The Threat of Substitutes   Along with traditional marketplaces, the Internet has created a new marketplace and a new channel. In general, therefore, the threat of substitutes is heightened because the Internet introduces new ways to accomplish the same tasks.

Consumers will generally choose to use a product or service until a substitute that meets the same need becomes available at a lower cost. The economies created by Internet technologies have led to the development of numerous substitutes for traditional ways of doing business. For example, a company called Conferenza is offering an alternative way to participate in conferences for people who don't want to spend the time and money to attend. Conferenza's website provides summaries of many conference events, quality ratings using an "event intelligence" score, and schedules of upcoming events.[65]

Another example of substitution is in the realm of electronic storage. With expanded desktop computing, the need to store information electronically has increased dramatically. Until recently, the trend has been to create increasingly larger desktop storage capabilities and techniques for compressing information that create storage efficiencies. But a viable substitute has recently emerged: storing information digitally on the Internet. Companies such as My Docs Online Inc. are providing Web-based storage that firms can access simply by leasing space online. Since these storage places are virtual, they can be accessed anywhere the Web can be accessed. Travelers can access important documents and files without transporting them physically from place to place. Cyberstorage is not free, but it is cheaper and more convenient than purchasing and carrying disk storage.[66]

The Intensity of Competitive Rivalry   Because the Internet creates more tools and means for competing, rivalry among competitors is likely to be more intense. Only those competitors that can use digital technologies and the Web to give themselves a distinct image, create unique product offerings, or provide "faster, smarter, cheaper" services are likely to capture greater profitability with the new technology. Such gains are hard to sustain, however, because in most cases the new technology can be imitated quickly. Thus, the Internet tends to increase rivalry by making it difficult for firms to differentiate themselves and by shifting customer attention to issues of price.

Rivalry is more intense when switching costs are low and product or service differentiation is minimized. Because the Internet makes it possible to shop around, it has "commoditized" products that might previously have been regarded as rare or unique. Since the Internet reduces the importance of location, products that previously had to be sought out in geographically distant outlets are now readily available online. This makes competitors in cyberspace seem more equally balanced, thus intensifying rivalry.

The problem is made worse for marketers by the presence of shopping robots ("bots") and infomediaries that search the Web for the best possible prices. Consumer websites like mySimon and PriceSCAN seek out all the Web locations that sell similar products and provide price comparisons.[67] Obviously, this focuses the consumer exclusively on price. Some shopping infomediaries, such as BizRate and CNET, not only search for the lowest prices on many different products but also rank the customer service quality of different sites that sell similarly priced items.[68] Such infomediary services are good for consumers because they give them the chance to compare services as well as price. For businesses, however, they increase rivalry by consolidating the marketing message that consumers use to make a purchase decision into a few key pieces of information over which the selling company has little control.

Exhibit 2.9 summarizes many of the ways the Internet is affecting industry structure. These influences will also change how companies develop and deploy strategies to generate above-average profits and sustainable competitive advantage.

Exhibit 2.9 How the Internet and Digital Technologies Influence Industry

	Benefits to Industry (+)	Disadvantages to Industry (−)
Threat of New Entrants		• Lower barriers to entry increases number of new entrants.
		• Many Internet-based capabilities can be easily imitated.
Bargaining Power of Buyers	• Reduces the power of buyer intermediaries in many distribution channels.	• Switching costs decrease. • Information availability online empowers end users.
Bargaining Power of Suppliers	• Online procurement methods can increase bargaining power over suppliers.	• The Internet gives suppliers access to more customers and makes it easier to reach end users. • Online procurement practices deter competition and reduce differentiating features.
Threat of Substitutes	• Internet-based increases in overall efficiency can expand industry sales.	• Internet-based capabilities create more opportunities for substitution.
Intensity of Rivalry		• Since location is less important, the number of competitors increases. • Differences among competitors are harder to perceive online. • Rivalry tends to focus on price and differentiating features are minimized.

Sources: Bodily, S. & Venkataraman, S. 2004. Not walls, windows: Capturing value in the digital age. *Journal of Business Strategy,* 25(3): 15–25; Lumpkin, G. T., Droege, S. B., & Dess, G. G. 2002. E-commerce strategies: Achieving sustainable competitive advantage and avoiding pitfalls. *Organizational Dynamics,* 30 (Spring): 1–17.

Using Industry Analysis: A Few Caveats

For industry analysis to be valuable, a company must collect and evaluate a wide variety of information. As the trend toward globalization accelerates, information on foreign markets as well as on a wider variety of competitors, suppliers, customers, substitutes, and potential new entrants becomes more critical. Industry analysis helps a firm not only to evaluate the profit potential of an industry but also consider various ways to strengthen its position vis-à-vis the five forces. However, we'd like to address a few caveats.

First, *managers must not always avoid low profit industries (or low profit segments in profitable industries).*[69] Such industries can still yield high returns for some players who pursue sound strategies. As examples, consider Paychex, a payroll-processing company, and WellPoint Health Network, a huge health care insurer:[70]

Paychex, with $2 billion in revenues, became successful by serving small businesses. Existing firms had ignored them because they assumed that such businesses could not afford the service. When Paychex's founder, Tom Golisano, failed to convince his bosses at Electronic Accounting Systems that they were missing a great opportunity, he launched the firm. It now serves nearly 600,000 clients in the United States and Germany. Paychex's after-tax-return on sales is a stunning 28 percent.

In 1986, WellPoint Health Network (when it was known as Blue Cross of California) suffered a loss of $160 million. That year, Leonard Schaeffer became CEO and challenged the conventional wisdom that individuals and small firms were money losers. (This was certainly "heresy" at the time—the firm was losing $5 million a year insuring 65,000 individuals!) However, by the early 1990s, the health insurer was leading the industry in profitability. The firm has continued to grow and outperform its rivals even during economic downturns. By 2008, its revenues and profits were $61 billion and $3.4 billion, respectively—each figure representing an *annual* increase of over 36 percent for the most recent two-year period.

Second, five-forces analysis implicitly *assumes a zero-sum game, determining how a firm can enhance its position relative to the forces.* Yet such an approach can often be short-sighted; that is, it can overlook the many potential benefits of developing constructive win–win relationships with suppliers and customers. Establishing long-term mutually beneficial relationships with suppliers improves a firm's ability to implement just-in-time (JIT) inventory systems, which let it manage inventories better and respond quickly to market demands. A recent study found that if a company exploits its powerful position against a supplier, that action may come back to haunt the company.[71] Consider, for example, General Motors' heavy-handed dealings with its suppliers:[72]

> GM has a reputation for particularly aggressive tactics. Although it is striving to crack down on the most egregious of these, it continues to rank dead last in the annual supplier satisfaction survey. "It's a brutal process," says David E. Cole, who is head of the Center for Automotive Research in Ann Arbor. "There are bodies lying by the side of the road."
>
> Suppliers point to one particularly nasty tactic: shopping their technology out the back door to see if rivals can make it cheaper. In one case, a GM purchasing manager showed a supplier's new brake design to Delphi Corporation. He was fired. However, in a recent survey, parts executives said they tend to bring hot new technology to other carmakers first. This is yet another reason GM finds it hard to compete in an intensely competitive industry.

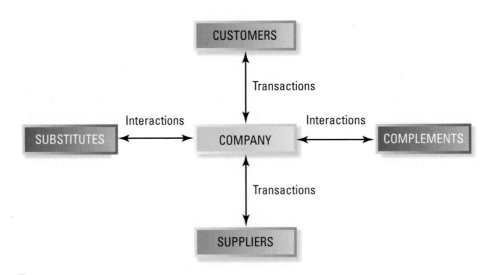

Exhibit 2.10 **The Value Net**

Source: Adapted and reprinted by permission of *Harvard Business Review.* Exhibit from "The Right Game: Use Game Theory to Shape Strategy," by A. Brandenburger and B. J. Nalebuff, July–August 1995. Copyright © 1995 by the Harvard Business School Publishing Corporation. All rights reserved.

Third, the five-forces analysis also has been criticized for *being essentially a static analysis*. External forces as well as strategies of individual firms are continually changing the structure of all industries. The search for a dynamic theory of strategy has led to greater use of game theory in industrial organization economics research and strategy research.

Based on game-theoretic considerations, Brandenburger and Nalebuff recently introduced the concept of the value net,[73] which in many ways is an extension of the five-forces analysis. It is illustrated in Exhibit 2.10. The value net represents all the players in the game and analyzes how their interactions affect a firm's ability to generate and appropriate value. The vertical dimension of the net includes suppliers and customers. The firm has direct transactions with them. On the horizontal dimension are substitutes and complements, players with whom a firm interacts but may not necessarily transact. The concept of complementors is perhaps the single most important contribution of value net analysis and is explained in more detail below.

Complements typically are products or services that have a potential impact on the value of a firm's own products or services. Those who produce complements are usually referred to as complementors.[74] Powerful hardware is of no value to a user unless there is software that runs on it. Similarly, new and better software is possible only if the hardware on which it can be run is available. This is equally true in the video game industry, where the sales of game consoles and video games complement each other. Nintendo's success in the early 1990s was a result of their ability to manage their relationship with their complementors. They built a security chip into the hardware and then licensed the right to develop games to outside firms. These firms paid a royalty to Nintendo for each copy of the game sold. The royalty revenue enabled Nintendo to sell game consoles at close to their cost, thereby increasing their market share, which, in turn, caused more games to be sold and more royalties to be generated.[75]

Despite efforts to create win–win scenarios, conflict among complementors is inevitable.[76] After all, it is naive to expect that even the closest of partners will do you the favor of abandoning their own interests. And even the most successful partnerships are seldom trouble free. Power is a factor that comes into play as we see in Strategy Spotlight 2.12 with the example of Apple's iPod—an enormously successful product.

We would like to close this section with some recent insights from Michael Porter, the originator of the five-forces analysis.[77] He addresses two critical issues in conducting a good industry analysis, which will yield an improved understanding of the root causes of profitability: (1) choosing the appropriate time frame and (2) a rigorous quantification of the five forces.

- *Good industry analysis looks rigorously at the structural underpinnings of profitability. A first step is to understand the time horizon.* One of the essential tasks in industry analysis is to distinguish short-term fluctuations from structural changes. A good guideline for the appropriate time horizon is the full business cycle for the particular industry. For most industries, a three- to five-year horizon is appropriate. However, for some industries with long lead times, such as mining, the appropriate horizon may be a decade or more. It is average profitability over this period, not profitability in any particular year, which should be the focus of analysis.
- *The point of industry analysis is not to declare the industry attractive or unattractive but to understand the underpinnings of competition and the root causes of profitability.* As much as possible, analysts should look at industry structure quantitatively, rather than be satisfied with lists of qualitative factors. Many elements of five forces can be quantified: the percentage of the buyer's total cost accounted for by the industry's product (to understand buyer price sensitivity); the percentage of industry sales required to fill a plant or operate a logistical network to efficient scale (to help assess barriers to entry); and the buyer's switching cost (determining the inducement an entrant or rival must offer customers).

complements
products or services that have an impact on the value of a firm's products or services.

>LO7
The concept of strategic groups and their strategy and performance implications.

Apple's iPod: Relationships with Its Complementors

In 2002, Steve Jobs began his campaign to cajole the major music companies into selling tracks to iPod users through the iTunes Music Store, an online retail site. Most industry executives, after being burned by illegal file-sharing services like Napster and Kazaa, just wanted digital music to disappear. However, Jobs's passionate vision persuaded them to climb on board. He promised to reduce the risks that they faced by offering safeguards against piracy, as well as a hip product (iPod) that would drive sales.

However, Apple had a much stronger bargaining position when its contracts with the music companies came up for renewal in April 2005. By then, iTunes had captured 80 percent of the market for legal downloads. The music companies, which were receiving between 60 and 70 cents per download, wanted more. Their reasoning: If the iTunes Music Store would only charge $1.50 or $2.00 per track, they could double or triple their revenues and profits. Since Jobs knew that he could sell more iPods if the music was cheap, he was determined to keep the price of a download at 99 cents and to maintain Apple's margins. Given iTunes' dominant position, the music companies had little choice but to relent.

Apple's foray into music has been tremendously successful. Between 2006 and 2008, iPod sales increased from $7.7 billion to $9.2 billion—a 19 percent increase. And, other music related products and services soared

from $1.9 billion to $3.3 billion over the same period—an impressive 74 percent increase. Despite tough competition, Apple still dominates the music player business with 70 percent of the U.S. market.

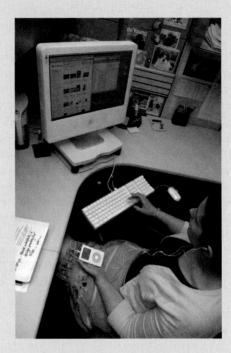

● A female employee sits at her desk equipped with both an iMac and an iPod. She works on a spreadsheet, uses iTunes, and listens to an iPod.

Source: Hesseldahl, A. 2008. Now that we all have iPods. *BusinessWeek,* December 15: 36; Apple Computer Inc. 10-K, 2008; and, Yoffie, D. B. & Kwak, M. 2006. With friends like these: The art of managing complementors. *Harvard Business Review,* 84(9): 88–98.

Strategic Groups within Industries

In an industry analysis, two assumptions are unassailable: (1) No two firms are totally different, and (2) no two firms are exactly the same. The issue becomes one of identifying groups of firms that are more similar to each other than firms that are not, otherwise known as **strategic groups**.[78] This is important because rivalry tends to be greater among firms that are alike. Strategic groups are clusters of firms that share similar strategies. After all, is Kmart more concerned about Nordstrom or Wal-Mart? Is Mercedes more concerned about Hyundai or BMW? The answers are straightforward.[79]

These examples are not meant to trivialize the strategic groups concept.[80] Classifying an industry into strategic groups involves judgment. If it is useful as an analytical tool, we must exercise caution in deciding what dimensions to use to map these firms. Dimensions include breadth of product and geographic scope, price/quality, degree of vertical

strategic groups
clusters of firms that share similar strategies.

integration, type of distribution (e.g., dealers, mass merchandisers, private label), and so on. Dimensions should also be selected to reflect the variety of strategic combinations in an industry. For example, if all firms in an industry have roughly the same level of product differentiation (or R&D intensity), this would not be a good dimension to select.

What value is the strategic groups concept as an analytical tool? *First, strategic groupings help a firm identify barriers to mobility that protect a group from attacks by other groups.*[81] Mobility barriers are factors that deter the movement of firms from one strategic position to another. For example, in the chainsaw industry, the major barriers protecting the high-quality/dealer-oriented group are technology, brand image, and an established network of servicing dealers.

The second value of strategic grouping is that it *helps a firm identify groups whose competitive position may be marginal or tenuous.* We may anticipate that these competitors may exit the industry or try to move into another group. In recent years in the retail department store industry, firms such as JCPenney and Sears have experienced extremely difficult times because they were stuck in the middle, neither an aggressive discount player like Wal-Mart nor a prestigious upscale player like Neiman Marcus.

Third, strategic groupings *help chart the future directions of firms' strategies.* Arrows emanating from each strategic group can represent the direction in which the group (or a firm within the group) seems to be moving. If all strategic groups are moving in a similar direction, this could indicate a high degree of future volatility and intensity of competition. In the automobile industry, for example, the competition in the minivan and sport utility segments has intensified in recent years as many firms have entered those product segments.

Fourth, strategic groups are *helpful in thinking through the implications of each industry trend for the strategic group as a whole.* Is the trend decreasing the viability of a group? If so, in what direction should the strategic group move? Is the trend increasing or decreasing entry barriers? Will the trend decrease the ability of one group to separate itself from other groups? Such analysis can help in making predictions about industry evolution. A sharp increase in interest rates, for example, tends to have less impact on providers of higher-priced goods (e.g., Porsches) than on providers of lower-priced goods (e.g., Chevrolet Cobalt) whose customer base is much more price sensitive.

Exhibit 2.11 provides a strategic grouping of the worldwide automobile industry.[82] The firms in each group are representative; not all firms are included in the mapping. We have identified four strategic groups. In the top left-hand corner are high-end luxury automakers who focus on a very narrow product market. Most of the cars produced by the members of this group cost well over $100,000. Some cost many times that amount. The 2008 Ferrari F430 costs $187,000 and the Lamborghini Gallardo $208,000[83] (in case you were wondering how to spend your employment signing bonus). Players in this market have a very exclusive clientele and face little rivalry from other strategic groups. At the other extreme, in the lower left-hand corner is a strategic group that has low-price/quality attributes and targets a narrow market. These players, Hyundai and Kia, limit competition from other strategic groups by pricing their products very low. The third group (near the middle) consists of firms high in product pricing/quality and average in their product-line breadth. The final group (at the far right) consists of firms with a broad range of products and multiple price points. These firms have entries that compete at both the lower end of the market (e.g., the Ford Focus) and the higher end (e.g., Chevrolet Corvette).

The auto market has been very dynamic and competition has intensified in recent years.[84] Many firms in different strategic groups compete in the same product markets, such as minivans and sport utility vehicles. In the late 1990s Mercedes entered the fray with its M series, and Porsche has a recent entry as well with its Cayenne, a 2004 model.

Some players are also going more upscale with their product offerings. Recently, Hyundai introduced its Genesis, starting at $33,000. This brings Hyundai into direct competition with entries from other strategic groups such as Toyota's Camry and Honda's Accord.

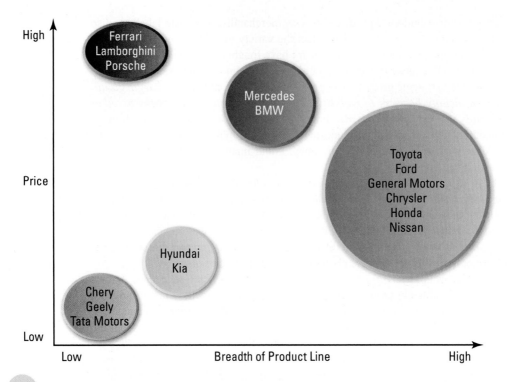

Exhibit 2.11 The World Automobile Industry: Strategic Groups

Note: Members of each strategic group are not inclusive, only illustrative.

Hyundai is offering an extensive warranty (10 years, 100,000 miles) in an effort to offset customer perceptions of their lower quality. To further intensify competition, some key automakers are providing offerings in lower-priced segments. BMW, with their 1-series, is a well-known example. Such cars, priced in the low $30,000s, compete more directly with products from broad-line manufacturers like Ford, General Motors, and Toyota.

Such models are competing in an industry that has experienced relatively flat unit sales in the first half of this decade. However, things have turned increasingly sour. U.S. automobile sales dropped to 13.2 million units in 2008—compared to 16.7 million units in 2007. Consulting firm IHS Global Insight expects 2009 U.S. sales to drop to only 10.3 million units—nearly a 40 percent decline from two years earlier.[85] Needless to say, one should expect incentive-laden offerings to appear at dealer lots for some time to come.

Our discussion would not be complete, of course, without paying some attention to recent entries in the automobile industry that will likely lead to the formation of a new strategic group—placed at the bottom left corner of the grid in Exhibit 2.11. Three firms—China's Zhejiang Geely Holding Company, China's Chery Automobile Company, and India's Tata Motors—have introduced models that bring new meaning to the term "sub-compact."[86] Let's take a look at these econoboxes.

> Chery's QQ model sells for between $4,000 and $7,000 in the Chinese market and sports horsepower in the range of 51 to 74. Geely's best-selling four-door sedan, the Free Cruiser, retails from $6,300 and $6,900. The firm is planning to go more upscale with the Geely KingKong ($7,500–$10,000), a four-door 1.5- to 1.8-liter sedan, and the Vision ($9,700–$15,300), a 1.8-liter four-door sedan. But, for price-points, India's Tata Motors has everyone beat. In January 2008, it unveiled the Nano with an astonishing retail price of only $2,500. It is a four-door, five-seat hatchback that gets 54 miles per gallon. But before you order one—keep in mind that it only comes with a 30 horsepower engine.

Reflecting on Career Implications . . .

- *Creating the Environmentally Aware Organization:* In your career, what are some ways in which you can engage in scanning, monitoring, and intelligence gathering for future job opportunities? Consider, for example, subscribing to your field's professional publications and becoming actively involved in relevant professional organizations.
- *SWOT Analysis:* From a career standpoint, periodically evaluate your strengths and weaknesses as well as potential opportunities and threats to your career. In addition, strive to seek input from trusted peers and superiors.
- *General Environment:* Carefully evaluate the elements of the general environment facing your firm. Identify factors (e.g., rapid technological change) that can provide promising career opportunities as well as possibilities for you to add value for your organization. In doing this, don't focus solely on "internal factors" of your organization.
- *Five-Forces Analysis:* Consider the five-forces affecting the industry within which your organization competes. If the "forces" are unfavorable, the long-term profit potential of the industry may be unattractive. And, there will likely be fewer resources available and—all other things being equal—fewer career opportunities.

Summary

Managers must analyze the external environment to minimize or eliminate threats and exploit opportunities. This involves a continuous process of environmental scanning and monitoring as well as obtaining competitive intelligence on present and potential rivals. These activities provide valuable inputs for developing forecasts. In addition, many firms use scenario planning to anticipate and respond to volatile and disruptive environmental changes.

We identified two types of environments: the general environment and the competitive environment. The six segments of the general environment are demographic, sociocultural, political/legal, technological, economic, and global. Trends and events occurring in these segments, such as the aging of the population, higher percentages of women in the workplace, governmental legislation, and increasing (or decreasing) interest rates, can have a dramatic effect on a firm. A given trend or event may have a positive impact on some industries and a negative, neutral, or no impact at all on others.

The competitive environment consists of industry-related factors and has a more direct impact than the general environment. Porter's five-forces model of industry analysis includes the threat of new entrants, buyer power, supplier power, threat of substitutes, and rivalry among competitors. The intensity of these factors determines,

in large part, the average expected level of profitability in an industry. A sound awareness of such factors, both individually and in combination, is beneficial not only for deciding what industries to enter but also for assessing how a firm can improve its competitive position. We discuss how many of the changes brought about by the digital economy can be understood in the context of five-forces analysis. The limitations of five-forces analysis include its static nature and its inability to acknowledge the role of complementors. Although we addressed the general environment and competitive environment in separate sections, they are quite interdependent. A given environmental trend or event, such as changes in the ethnic composition of a population or a technological innovation, typically has a much greater impact on some industries than on others.

The concept of strategic groups is also important to the external environment of a firm. No two organizations are completely different nor are they exactly the same. The question is how to group firms in an industry on the basis of similarities in their resources and strategies. The strategic groups concept is valuable for determining mobility barriers across groups, identifying groups with marginal competitive positions, charting the future directions of firm strategies, and assessing the implications of industry trends for the strategic group as a whole.

Summary Review Questions

1. Why must managers be aware of a firm's external environment?

2. What is gathering and analyzing competitive intelligence and why is it important for firms to engage in it?

3. Discuss and describe the six elements of the external environment.

4. Select one of these elements and describe some changes relating to it in an industry that interests you.

5. Describe how the five forces can be used to determine the average expected profitability in an industry.

6. What are some of the limitations (or caveats) in using five-forces analysis?

7. Explain how the general environment and industry environment are highly related. How can such interrelationships affect the profitability of a firm or industry?

8. Explain the concept of strategic groups. What are the performance implications?

Experiential Exercise

Select one of the following industries: personal computers, airlines, or automobiles. For this industry, evaluate the strength of each of Porter's five forces as well as complementors.

Key Terms

environmental scanning, 41
globalization 41
environmental monitoring, 42
competitive intelligence, 42
environmental forecasting, 45
scenario analysis, 45
SWOT analysis, 47
general environment, 47
demographic segment of the general environment 49
sociocultural segment of the general environment 49
political/legal segment of the general environment 50
technological segment of the general environment 51
economic segment of the general environment 52
global segment of the general environment 52
competitive environment, 56
threat of new entrants 56
bargaining power of buyers 58
bargaining power of suppliers 59
threat of substitute products and services 60
intensity of rivalry among competitors in an industry 61
complements, 69
strategic groups, 70

Industry Force	High? Medium? Low?	Why?
1. Threat of new entrants		
2. Power of buyers		
3. Power of suppliers		
4. Power of substitutes		
5. Rivalry among competitors		
6. Complementors		

Application Questions Exercises

1. Imagine yourself as the CEO of a large firm in an industry in which you are interested. Please (1) identify major trends in the general environment, (2) analyze their impact on the firm, and (3) identify major sources of information to monitor these trends. (Use Internet and library resources.)

2. Analyze movements across the strategic groups in the U.S. retail industry. How do these movements within this industry change the nature of competition?

3. What are the major trends in the general environment that have impacted the U.S. pharmaceutical industry?

4. Go to the Internet and look up www.kroger.com. What are some of the five forces driving industry competition that are affecting the profitability of this firm?

Ethics Questions

1. What are some of the legal and ethical issues involved in collecting competitor intelligence in the following situations?

   a. Hotel A sends an employee posing as a potential client to Hotel B to find out who Hotel B's major corporate customers are.

   b. A firm hires an MBA student to collect information directly from a competitor while claiming the information is for a course project.

   c. A firm advertises a nonexistent position and interviews a rival's employees with the intention of obtaining competitor information.

2. What are some of the ethical implications that arise when a firm tries to exploit its power over a supplier?

References

1. Einhorn, B. & Crockett, R. O. 2008. Motorola: Fading in China. *Business-Week,* September 8: 56; Kharif, O. & Crockett, R. O. 2008. Motorola's turn-around plans meet with skepticism. Businessweek.com, October 31: np; and, Moritz, S. 2008. Motorola delays breakup, cuts jobs. CNNMoney.com, October 30: np.

2. Hamel, G. & Prahalad, C. K. 1994. *Competing for the future.* Boston: Harvard Business School Press.

3. Drucker, P. F. 1994. Theory of the business. *Harvard Business Review,* 72: 95–104.

4. For an insightful discussion on managers' assessment of the external environment, refer to Sutcliffe, K. M. & Weber, K. 2003. The high cost of accurate knowledge. *Harvard Business Review,* 81(5): 74–86.

5. For insights on recognizing and acting on environmental opportunities, refer to: Alvarez, S. A. & Barney, J. B. 2008. Opportunities, organizations, and entrepreneurship: Theory and debate. *Strategic Entrepreneurship Journal,* 2(3): entire issue.

6. Charitou, C. D. & Markides, C. C. 2003. Responses to disruptive strategic innovation. *MIT Sloan Management Review,* 44(2): 55–64.

7. Our discussion of scanning, monitoring, competitive intelligence, and forecasting concepts draws on several sources. These include Fahey, L. & Narayanan, V. K. 1983. *Macroenvironmental analysis for strategic management.* St. Paul, MN: West; Lorange, P., Scott, F. S., & Ghoshal, S. 1986. *Strategic control.* St. Paul, MN: West;

Ansoff, H. I. 1984. *Implementing strategic management.* Englewood Cliffs, NJ: Prentice Hall; and Schreyogg, G. & Stienmann, H. 1987. Strategic control: A new perspective. *Academy of Management Review,* 12: 91–103.

8. An insightful discussion on how leaders can develop "peripheral vision" in environmental scanning is found in: Day, G. S. & Schoemaker, P. J. H. 2008. Are you a "vigilant leader"? *MIT Sloan Management Review,* 49 (3): 43–51.

9. Elenkov, D. S. 1997. Strategic uncertainty and environmental scanning: The case for institutional influences on scanning behavior. *Strategic Management Journal,* 18: 287–302.

10. For an interesting perspective on environmental scanning in emerging economies see May, R. C., Stewart, W. H., & Sweo, R. 2000. Environmental scanning behavior in a transitional economy: Evidence from Russia. *Academy of Management Journal,* 43(3): 403–27.

11. Bowles, J. 1997. Key issues for the automotive industry CEOs. *Fortune,* August 18: S3.

12. An interesting perspective on China's emergence as a global power is in: Fuller, J. 2008. The beneficent dragon. *MIT Sloan Management Review,* Spring: 88.

13. Walters, B. A. & Priem, R. L. 1999. Business strategy and CEO intelligence acquisition. *Competitive Intelligence Review,* 10(2): 15–22.

14. Prior, V. 1999. The language of competitive intelligence, Part 4. *Competitive Intelligence Review,* 10(1): 84–87.

15. Zahra, S. A. & Charples, S. S. 1993. Blind spots in competitive analysis. *Academy of Management Executive* 7(2): 7–27.

16. Wolfenson, J. 1999. The world in 1999: A battle for corporate honesty. *The Economist* 38: 13–30.

17. Drucker, P. F. 1997. The future that has already happened. *Harvard Business Review,* 75(6): 22.

18. Evans, P. B. & Wurster, T. S. 1997. Strategy and the new economics of information. *Harvard Business Review,* 75(5): 71–82.

19. Fahey & Narayanan, op. cit., p. 41.

20. Insights on how to improve predictions can be found in: Cross, R., Thomas, R. J., & Light, D. A. 2009. The prediction lover's handbook. *MIT Sloan Management Review,* 50 (2): 32–34.

21. Courtney, H., Kirkland, J., & Viguerie, P. 1997. Strategy under uncertainty. *Harvard Business Review,* 75(6): 66–79.

22. Odlyzko, A. 2003. False hopes. *Red Herring,* March: 31.

23. Coy, P. 2009. Worst predictions about 2008. *BusinessWeek,* January 12: 15–16.

24. For an interesting perspective on how Accenture practices and has developed its approach to scenario planning, refer to Ferguson, G., Mathur, S., & Shah, B. 2005. Evolving from information to insight. *MIT Sloan Management Review,* 46(2): 51–58.

25. Dean, T. J., Brown, R. L., & Bamford, C. E. 1998. Differences in large and small firm responses to environmental context: Strategic implications

from a comparative analysis of business formations. *Strategic Management Journal,* 19: 709–728.

26. Some insights on management during economic downturns are in: Colvin, G. 2009. How to manage your business in a recession. *Fortune,* January 19: 88–93.

27. Colvin, G. 1997. How to beat the boomer rush. *Fortune,* August 18: 59–63.

28. Guntner, T. 2006. Still working and loving it. *BusinessWeek,* October 16: 108; Warner, M. 2004. Home Depot goes old school. *Business 2.0,* June: 74; and, O'Brien, S. 2005. Over 50 and looking for work? www.seniorliving.about.com.

29. Challenger, J. 2000. Women's corporate rise has reduced relocations. *Lexington (KY) Herald-Leader,* October 29: D1.

30. Tsao, A. 2005. Retooling home improvement, Businesssweek.com, February, 14; and, Grow, B. 2004. Who wears the wallet in the family? *BusinessWeek,* August 16:10.

31. Watkins, M. D. 2003. Government games. *MIT Sloan Management Review* 44(2): 91–95.

32. A discussion of the political issues surrounding caloric content on meals is in: Orey, M. 2008. A food fight over calorie counts. *BusinessWeek,* February 11: 36.

33. For a discussion of the linkage between copyright law and innovation, read: Guterman, J. 2009. Does copyright law hinder innovation? *MIT Sloan Management Review,* 50(2): 14–15.

34. Davies, A. 2000. The welcome mat is out for nerds. *BusinessWeek,* May 21: 17; Broache, A. 2007. Annual H-1B visa cap met—already.*news.cnet.com,* April 3: np; and, Anonymous. Undated. Cap count for H-1B and H-2B workers for fiscal year 2009. www.uscis.gov: np.

35. Anonymous. Business ready for Internet revolution. 1999. *Financial Times,* May 21: 17.

36. A discussion of an alternate energy—marine energy—is the topic of: Boyle, M. 2008. Scottish power. *Fortune.* March 17: 28.

37. Baker, S. & Aston, A. 2005. The business of nanotech. *BusinessWeek,* February 14: 64–71.

38. Ginsburg, J. 2000. Letting the free market clear the air. *BusinessWeek,* November 6: 200, 204.

39. For an insightful discussion of the causes of the global financial crisis, read: Johnson, S. 2009. The global financial crisis—What really precipitated it? *MIT Sloan Management Review.* 50(2): 16–18.

40. A interesting and balanced discussion on the merits of multinationals to the U.S. economy is found in: Mandel, M. 2008. Multinationals: Are they good for America? *BusinessWeek,* March 10: 41–64.

41. Insights on risk perception across countries are addressed in: Purda, L. D. 2008. Risk perception and the financial system. *Journal of International Business Studies,* 39(7): 1178–1196.

42. Byrnes, N. 2006. The high cost of fear. *BusinessWeek,* November 6: 16.

43. Goll, I. & Rasheed, M. A. 1997. Rational decision-making and firm performance: The moderating role of environment. *Strategic Management Journal,* 18: 583–591.

44. This discussion draws heavily on Porter, M. E. 1980. *Competitive strategy:* Chapter 1. New York: Free Press.

45. Ibid.

46. Rivalry in the airline industry is discussed in: Foust, D. 2009. Which airlines will disappear in 2009? *BusinessWeek,* January 19: 46–47.

47. Fryer, B. 2001. Leading through rough times: An interview with Novell's Eric Schmidt. *Harvard Business Review,* 78(5): 117–123.

48. For a discussion on the importance of barriers to entry within industries, read Greenwald, B. & Kahn, J. 2005. *Competition demystified: A radically simplified approach to business strategy.* East Rutherford, NJ: Portfolio.

49. A discussion of how the medical industry has erected entry barriers that have resulted in lawsuits is found in: Whelan, D. 2008. Bad medicine. *BusinessWeek,* March 10: 86–98.

50. The ProCD example draws heavily upon Shapiro, C. & Varian, H. R. 2000. Versioning: The smart way to sell information. *Harvard Business Review,* 78(1): 106–114.

51. Wise, R. & Baumgarter, P. 1999. Go downstream: The new profit imperative in manufacturing. *Harvard Business Review,* 77(5): 133–141.

52. Salman, W. A. 2000. The new economy is stronger than you think. *Harvard Business Review,* 77(6): 99–106.

53. Mudambi, R. & Helper, S. 1998. The "close but adversarial" model of supplier relations in the U.S. auto industry. *Strategic Management Journal,* 19: 775–792.

54. Trends in the solar industry are discussed in: Carey, J. 2009. Solar: The sun will come out tomorrow. *BusinessWeek,* January 12: 51.

55. Tischler, L. 2002. IBM: Manager jam. *Fast Company,* October: 48.

56. An interesting analysis of self-regulation in an industry (chemical) is in: Barnett, M. L. & King, A. A. 2008. Good fences make good neighbors: A longitudinal analysis of an industry self-regulatory institution. *Academy of Management Journal,* 51(6): 1053–1078.

57. For an interesting perspective on the intensity of competition in the supermarket industry, refer to Anonymous. 2005. Warfare in the aisles. *The Economist,* April 2: 6–8.

58. Marcial, G. 2000. Giving Viagra a run for its money. *BusinessWeek,* October 23: 173.

59. McGann, R. 2005. VOIP poised to take flight? *ClickZ.com,* February 23, www.clickz.com.

60. For an interesting perspective on changing features of firm boundaries, refer to Afuah, A. 2003. Redefining firm boundaries in the face of Internet: Are firms really shrinking? *Academy of Management Review,* 28(1): 34–53.

61. www.consumerreports.org.

62. Time to rebuild. 2001. *Economist,* May 19: 55–56.

63. www.amazon.com.

64. For more on the role of the Internet as an electronic intermediary, refer to Carr, N. G. 2000. Hypermediation: Commerce as clickstream. *Harvard Business Review,* 78(1): 46–48.

65. Olofson, C. 2001. The next best thing to being there. *Fast Company,* April: 175; and www.conferenza.com.

66. Lelii, S. R. 2001. Free online storage a thing of the past ? *eWEEK,* April 22.

67. www.mysimon.com; and www.pricescan.com.

68. www.cnet.com; and www.bizrate.com.

69. For insights into strategies in a low-profit industry, refer to: Hopkins, M. S. 2008. The management lessons of a beleaguered industry. *MIT Sloan Management Review,* 50(1): 25–31.

70. Foust, D. 2007. The best performers. *BusinessWeek,* March 26: 58–95; Rosenblum, D., Tomlinson, D., & Scott, L. 2003. Bottom-feeding for blockbuster businesses. *Harvard Business Review,* 81(3): 52–59; Paychex 2006 Annual Report; and, WellPoint Health Network 2005 Annual Report.

71. Kumar, N. 1996. The power of trust in manufacturer-retailer relationship. *Harvard Business Review,* 74(6): 92–110.

72. Welch, D. 2006. Renault-Nissan: Say hello to Bo. *BusinessWeek,* July 31: 56–57.

73. Brandenburger, A. & Nalebuff, B. J. 1995. The right game: Use game theory to shape strategy. *Harvard Business Review,* 73(4): 57–71.

74. For a scholarly discussion of complementary assets and their relationship to competitive advantage, refer to Stieglitz, N. & Heine, K. 2007. Innovations and the role of complementarities in a strategic theory of the firm. *Strategic Management Journal,* 28(1): 1–15.

75. A useful framework for the analysis of industry evolution has been proposed by Professor Anita McGahan of Boston University. Her analysis is based on the identification of the core activities and the core assets of an industry and the threats they face. She suggests that an industry may follow one of four possible evolutionary trajectories—radical change, creative change, intermediating change, or progressive change—based on these two types of threats of obsolescence. Refer to: McGahan, A. M. 2004. How industries change. *Harvard Business Review,* 82(10): 87–94.

76. Yoffie, D. B. & Kwak, M. 2006. With friends like these: The art of managing complementors. *Harvard Business Review,* 84(9): 88–98.

77. Porter, M. I. 2008. The five competitive forces that shape strategy. *Harvard Business Review,* 86 (1): 79–93.

78. Peteraf, M. & Shanley, M. 1997. Getting to know you: A theory of strategic group identity. *Strategic Management Journal,* 18 (Special Issue): 165–186.

79. An interesting scholarly perspective on strategic groups may be found in Dranove, D., Perteraf, M., & Shanley, M. 1998. Do strategic groups exist? An economic framework for analysis. *Strategic Management Journal,* 19(11): 1029–1044.

80. For an empirical study on strategic groups and predictors of performance, refer to Short, J. C., Ketchen, D. J., Jr., Palmer, T. B., & Hult, T. M. 2007. Firm, strategic group, and industry influences on performance. *Strategic Management Journal,* 28(2): 147–167.

81. This section draws on several sources, including Kerwin, K. R. & Haughton, K. 1997. Can Detroit make cars that baby boomers like? *BusinessWeek,* December 1: 134–148; and Taylor, A., III. 1994. The new golden age of autos. *Fortune,* April 4: 50–66.

82. Csere, C. 2001. Supercar supermarket. *Car and Driver,* January: 118–127.

83. Healey, J. R. 1999. Groomed so as not to marry. *USA Today,* August 6: B1; and, Edmunds.com.

84. For a discussion of the extent of over-capacity in the worldwide automobile industry, read: Roberts, D., Matlack, C., Busyh, J., & Rowley, I. 2009. A hundred factories too many. *BusinessWeek,* January 19: 42–43.

85. '08 ends bleakly for car makers. 2009. *Dallas Morning News,* January 6: 1D, 5D.

86. This discussion draws on: Wojdyla, B. 2008. The $2500 Tata Nano, unveiled in India. jalopnik.com, January 10: np; Roberts, D. 2008. China's Geely has global auto ambitions. businessweek .com, July 27: np; and, Fairclough, G. 2007. In China, Chery Automobile drives an industry shift. *The Wall Street Journal,* December 4: A1, A17.

Assessing the Internal Environment of the Firm

>learning objectives

After reading this chapter, you should have a good understanding of:

LO1 The benefits and limitations of SWOT analysis in conducting an internal analysis of the firm.

LO2 The primary and support activities of a firm's value chain.

LO3 How value-chain analysis can help managers create value by investigating relationships among activities within the firm and between the firm and its customers and suppliers.

LO4 The resource-based view of the firm and the different types of tangible and intangible resources, as well as organizational capabilities.

LO5 The four criteria that a firm's resources must possess to maintain a sustainable advantage and how value created can be appropriated by employees and managers.

LO6 The usefulness of financial ratio analysis, its inherent limitations, and how to make meaningful comparisons of performance across firms.

LO7 The value of the "balanced scorecard" in recognizing how the interests of a variety of stakeholders can be interrelated.

LO8 How firms are using Internet technologies to add value and achieve unique advantages. (Appendix)

Two firms compete in the same industry and both have many strengths in a variety of functional areas: marketing, operations, logistics, and so on. However, one of these firms outperforms the other by a wide margin over a long period of time. How can this be so? This chapter endeavors to answer that question.

We begin with two sections that include frameworks for gaining key insights into a firm's internal environment: value-chain analysis and the resource-based view of the firm. In value-chain analysis, we divide a firm's activities into a series of value-creating steps. We then explore how individual activities within the firm add value, and also how *interrelationships* among activities within the firm, and between the firm and its suppliers and customers, create value.

In the resource-based view of the firm, we analyze the firm as a collection of tangible and intangible resources as well as organizational capabilities. Advantages that tend to be sustainable over time typically arise from creating *bundles* of resources and capabilities that satisfy four criteria: they are valuable, rare, difficult to imitate, and difficult to substitute. Not all of the value created by a firm will necessarily be kept (or appropriated) by the owners. We discuss the four key factors that determine how profits will be distributed between owners as well as employees and managers.

In the closing sections, we discuss how to evaluate a firm's performance and make comparisons across firms. We emphasize both the inclusion of financial resources and the interests of multiple stakeholders. Central to our discussion is the concept of the balanced scorecard, which recognizes that the interests of different stakeholders can be interrelated. We also consider how a firm's performance evolves over time and how it compares with industry norms and key competitors.

In an appendix to this chapter, we explore how Internet-based businesses and incumbent firms are using digital technologies to add value. We consider four activities—search, evaluation, problem solving, and transaction—as well as three types of content—customer feedback, expertise, and entertainment programming. Such technology-enhanced capabilities are providing new means with which firms can achieve competitive advantages.

Learning from Mistakes

In Planning Perspectives' annual survey of automakers and their suppliers, Ford was ranked as one of the worst companies to do business with, according to suppliers.[1] Perhaps not too surprisingly, the only firm that fared worse was General Motors. According to John Henke Jr., Planning Perspectives' president, "I suspect it may be a pattern, because as suppliers are becoming more desperate, and if they continue to be pushed, they have no choice but to push back." Let's consider one example of Ford's strained relationships with suppliers.

In early January 2007, Ford filed a lawsuit against Navistar over warranty costs and pricing for the diesel engines that the latter company supplied. Ford alleged that Navistar owed it money under an agreement to share engine warranty costs—which Navistar failed to pay. Navistar said that Ford's claims were "totally without merit" and that it would "vigorously respond in court."

Ford sought reimbursement equal to what it said it overpaid for the engines and for financial obligations owed by Navistar that were the result of warranty claims tied to a previous generation engine sold by Ford. As expected, the situation escalated when Ford took the unorthodox move of subtracting the amount of money it said Navistar owed from the agreed-upon price for the new diesel engines. Ford reportedly began paying Navistar only $6,167 of the agreed upon per-unit price of $7,673.

On February 26, 2007, Navistar ceased delivering the engines. However, two days later, the Oakland County Court ordered Navistar to resume engine shipments.

According to Henke: "There is no trust or relationship left between Ford and Navistar. It is an extreme example of an adversarial relationship that has evolved. One has to conclude that Navistar perceives that Ford is taking an opportunistic view toward dealing with them and they need to do the same thing to survive. It's an extreme example of an adversarial relationship that has evolved."

And the beat goes on . . . A year later, in February 2008, Navistar refiled a lawsuit against Ford for violating a diesel engine contract in which Ford had promised that Navistar would be Ford's primary manufacturer and supplier of V-6 and V-8 diesel engines in North America. The suit sought "at least hundreds of millions of dollars." According to the lawsuit, Ford will introduce a 4.4-liter diesel engine for production in North America by late 2009 or 2010. Ford intends to produce the engine itself for use in the F-150 pickup—and possibly other vehicles. The lawsuit claims that Ford cannot manufacture the engine without violating its contract with Navistar.

In this chapter we will place heavy emphasis on the value-chain concept. That is, we focus on the key value-creating activities (e.g., operations, marketing and sales, and procurement) that a firm must effectively manage and integrate in order to attain competitive advantages in the marketplace. However, firms must not only pay close attention to their own value-creating activities but must also maintain close and effective relationships with key organizations outside the firm boundaries such as suppliers, customers, and alliance partners. Clearly, Ford's adversarial relationship with Navistar is a good example of bad practice!

>LO1

The benefits and limitations of SWOT analysis in conducting an internal analysis of the firm.

Before moving to value-chain analysis, let's briefly revisit the benefits and limitations of SWOT analysis. As discussed in Chapter 2, a SWOT analysis consists of a careful listing of a firm's strengths, weaknesses, opportunities, and threats. While we believe SWOT analysis is very helpful as a starting point, it should not form the primary basis for evaluating a firm's internal strengths and weaknesses or the opportunities and threats in the environment. Strategy Spotlight 3.1 elaborates on the limitations of the traditional SWOT approach.

The Limitations of SWOT Analysis

SWOT analysis is a tried-and-true tool of strategic analysis. SWOT (strengths, weaknesses, opportunities, threats) analysis is used regularly in business to initially evaluate the opportunities and threats in the business environment as well as the strengths and weaknesses of a firm's internal environment. Top managers rely on SWOT to stimulate self-reflection and group discussions about how to improve their firm and position it for success.

But SWOT has its limitations. It is just a starting point for discussion. By listing the firm's attributes, managers have the raw material needed to perform more in-depth strategic analysis. However, SWOT cannot show them how to achieve a competitive advantage. They must not make SWOT analysis an end in itself, temporarily raising awareness about important issues but failing to lead to the kind of action steps necessary to enact strategic change.

Consider the ProCD example from Chapter 2, page 58. A brief SWOT analysis might include the following:

Strengths	Opportunities
First-mover advantage	Demand for electronic phone books
Low labor cost	Sudden growth in use of digital technology

Weaknesses	Threats
Inexperienced new company	Easily duplicated product
No proprietary information	Market power of incumbent firms

The combination of low production costs and an early-mover advantage in an environment where demand for CD-based phone books was growing rapidly seems to indicate that ProCD founder James Bryant had a golden opportunity. But the SWOT analysis did not reveal how to turn those strengths into a competitive advantage, nor did it highlight how rapidly the environment would change, allowing imitators to come into the market and erode his first-mover advantage. Let's look at some of the limitations of SWOT analysis.

Strengths May Not Lead to an Advantage

A firm's strengths and capabilities, no matter how unique or impressive, may not enable it to achieve a competitive advantage in the marketplace. It is akin to recruiting a concert pianist to join a gang of thugs—even though such an ability is rare and valuable, it hardly helps the organization attain its goals and objectives! Similarly, the skills of a highly creative product designer would offer little competitive advantage to a firm that produces low-cost commodity products. Indeed, the additional expense of hiring such an individual could erode the firm's cost advantages. If a firm builds its strategy on a capability that cannot, by itself, create or sustain competitive advantage, it is essentially a wasted use of resources. ProCD had several key strengths, but it did not translate them into lasting advantages in the marketplace.

SWOT's Focus on the External Environment Is Too Narrow

Strategists who rely on traditional definitions of their industry and competitive environment often focus their sights too narrowly on current customers, technologies, and competitors. Hence they fail to notice important changes on the periphery of their environment that may trigger the need to redefine industry boundaries and identify a whole new set of competitive relationships. Reconsider the example from Chapter 2 of *Encyclopaedia Britannica*, whose competitive position was severely eroded by a "nontraditional" competitor—CD-based encyclopedias (e.g., Microsoft *Encarta*) that could be used on home computers.

SWOT Gives a One-Shot View of a Moving Target

A key weakness of SWOT is that it is primarily a static assessment. It focuses too much of a firm's attention on one moment in time. Essentially, this is like studying a single frame of a motion picture. You may be able to identify the principal actors and learn something about the setting, but it doesn't tell you much about the plot. Competition among organizations is played out over time. As circumstances, capabilities, and strategies change, static analysis techniques do not reveal the dynamics of the competitive environment. Clearly, ProCD was unaware that its competitiveness was being eroded so quickly.

SWOT Overemphasizes a Single Dimension of Strategy

Sometimes firms become preoccupied with a single strength or a key feature of the product or service they are offering and ignore other factors needed for competitive success. For example, Food Lion, a large grocery retailer, paid a heavy price for its excessive emphasis on cost control. The resulting problems with labor and the negative publicity led to its eventual withdrawal from several markets.

SWOT analysis has much to offer, but only as a starting point. By itself, it rarely helps a firm develop competitive advantages that it can sustain over time.

Sources: Shapiro, C. & Varian, H. R. 2000. Versioning: The Smart Way to Sell Information. *Harvard Business Review*, 78(1): 99–106; and Picken, J. C. & Dess, G. G. 1997. *Mission Critical.* Burr Ridge, IL: Irwin Professional Publishing.

We will now turn to value-chain analysis. As you will see, it provides greater insights into analyzing a firm's competitive position than SWOT analysis does by itself.

Value-Chain Analysis

value-chain analysis
a strategic analysis of an organization that uses value-creating activities.

Value-chain analysis views the organization as a sequential process of value-creating activities. The approach is useful for understanding the building blocks of competitive advantage and was described in Michael Porter's seminal book *Competitive Advantage*.[2] Value is the amount that buyers are willing to pay for what a firm provides them and is measured by total revenue, a reflection of the price a firm's product commands and the quantity it can sell. A firm is profitable when the value it receives exceeds the total costs involved in creating its product or service. Creating value for buyers that exceeds the costs of production (i.e., margin) is a key concept used in analyzing a firm's competitive position.

primary activities
sequential activities of the value chain that refer to the physical creation of the product or service, its sale and transfer to the buyer, and its service after sale, including inbound logistics, operations, outbound logistics, marketing and sales, and service.

Porter described two different categories of activities. First, five **primary activities**— inbound logistics, operations, outbound logistics, marketing and sales, and service— contribute to the physical creation of the product or service, its sale and transfer to the buyer, and its service after the sale. Second, **support activities**—procurement, technology development, human resource management, and general administration—either add value by themselves or add value through important relationships with both primary activities and other support activities. Exhibit 3.1 illustrates Porter's value chain.

To get the most out of value-chain analysis, view the concept in its broadest context, without regard to the boundaries of your own organization. That is, place your organization within a more encompassing value chain that includes your firm's suppliers, customers, and alliance partners. Thus, in addition to thoroughly understanding how value is created within the organization, be aware of how value is created for other organizations in the overall supply chain or distribution channel.[3]

>LO2
The primary and support activities of a firm's value chain.

Next, we'll describe and provide examples of each of the primary and support activities. Then, we'll provide examples of how companies add value by means of relationships among activities within the organization as well as activities outside the organization, such as those activities associated with customers and suppliers.[4]

support activities activities of the value chain that either add value by themselves or add value through important relationships with both primary activities and other support activities; including procurement, technology development, human resource management, and general administration.

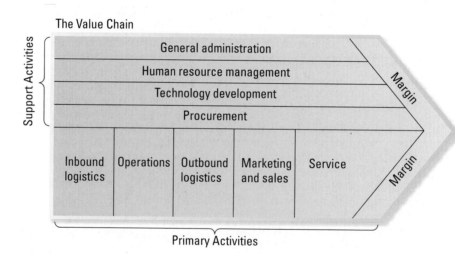

Exhibit 3.1 **The Value Chain: Primary and Support Activities**

Source: Adapted with the permission of The Free Press, a division of Simon & Schuster Adult Publishing Group, from *Competitive Advantage: Creating and Sustaining Superior Performance* by Michael E. Porter. Copyright © 1985, 1998 by Michael E. Porter. All rights reserved.

Primary Activities

Five generic categories of primary activities are involved in competing in any industry, as shown in Exhibit 3.2. Each category is divisible into a number of distinct activities that depend on the particular industry and the firm's strategy.[5]

Inbound Logistics   Inbound logistics is primarily associated with receiving, storing, and distributing inputs to the product. It includes material handling, warehousing, inventory control, vehicle scheduling, and returns to suppliers.

Just-in-time (JIT) inventory systems, for example, were designed to achieve efficient inbound logistics. In essence, Toyota epitomizes JIT inventory systems, in which parts deliveries arrive at the assembly plants only hours before they are needed. JIT systems will play a vital role in fulfilling Toyota's commitment to fill a buyer's new car order in just five days.[6] This standard is in sharp contrast to most competitors that require approximately 30 days' notice to build vehicles. Toyota's standard is three times faster than even Honda Motors, considered to be the industry's most efficient in order follow-through. The five days represent the time from the company's receipt of an order to the time the car leaves the assembly plant. Actual delivery may take longer, depending on where a customer lives. How can Toyota achieve such fast turnaround?

- Its 360 key suppliers are now linked to the company by way of computer on a virtual assembly line.
- Suppliers load parts onto trucks in the order in which they will be installed.
- Parts are stacked on trucks in the same place each time to help workers unload them quickly.
- Deliveries are required to meet a rigid schedule with as many as 12 trucks a day and no more than four hours between trucks.

Exhibit 3.2
The Value Chain: Some Factors to Consider in Assessing a Firm's Primary Activities

Inbound Logistics

- Location of distribution facilities to minimize shipping times.
- Warehouse layout and designs to increase efficiency of operations for incoming materials.

Operations

- Efficient plant operations to minimize costs.
- Efficient plant layout and workflow design.
- Incorporation of appropriate process technology.

Outbound Logistics

- Effective shipping processes to provide quick delivery and minimize damages.
- Shipping of goods in large lot sizes to minimize transportation costs.

Marketing and Sales

- Innovative approaches to promotion and advertising.
- Proper identification of customer segments and needs.

Service

- Quick response to customer needs and emergencies.
- Quality of service personnel and ongoing training.

Source: Adapted from Porter, M.E. 1985. *Competitive Advantage: Creating and Sustaining Superior Performance*. New York: Free Press.

Operations   Operations include all activities associated with transforming inputs into the final product form, such as machining, packaging, assembly, testing, printing, and facility operations.

Creating environmentally friendly manufacturing is one way to use operations to achieve competitive advantage. Shaw Industries (now part of Berkshire Hathaway), a world-class competitor in the floor-covering industry, is well known for its concern for the environment.[7] It has been successful in reducing the expenses associated with the disposal of dangerous chemicals and other waste products from its manufacturing operations. Its environmental endeavors have multiple payoffs. Shaw has received many awards for its recycling efforts—awards that enhance its reputation.

Outbound Logistics   Outbound logistics is associated with collecting, storing, and distributing the product or service to buyers. These activities include finished goods, warehousing, material handling, delivery vehicle operation, order processing, and scheduling.

Campbell Soup uses an electronic network to facilitate its continuous-replenishment program with its most progressive retailers.[8] Each morning, retailers electronically inform Campbell of their product needs and of the level of inventories in their distribution centers. Campbell uses that information to forecast future demand and to determine which products require replenishment (based on the inventory limits previously established with each retailer). Trucks leave Campbell's shipping plant that afternoon and arrive at the retailers' distribution centers the same day. The program cuts the inventories of participating retailers from about a four- to a two-weeks' supply. Campbell Soup achieved this improvement because it slashed delivery time and because it knows the inventories of key retailers and can deploy supplies when they are most needed.

The Campbell Soup example also illustrates the win–win benefits of exemplary value-chain activities. Both the supplier (Campbell) and its buyers (retailers) come out ahead. Since the retailer makes more money on Campbell products delivered through continuous replenishment, it has an incentive to carry a broader line and give the company greater shelf space. After Campbell introduced the program, sales of its products grew twice as fast through participating retailers as through all other retailers. Not surprisingly, supermarket chains love such programs.

Marketing and Sales   These activities are associated with purchases of products and services by end users and the inducements used to get them to make purchases.[9] They include advertising, promotion, sales force, quoting, channel selection, channel relations, and pricing.[10, 11]

It is not always enough to have a great product.[12] The key is to convince your channel partners that it is in their best interests not only to carry your product but also to market it in a way that is consistent with your strategy.[13] Consider Monsanto's efforts at educating distributors to improve the value proposition of its line of Saflex® windows.[14] The products had a superior attribute: The window design permitted laminators to form an exceptional type of glass by sandwiching a plastic sheet interlayer between two pieces of glass. This product is not only stronger and offers better ultraviolet protection than regular glass, but also when cracked, it adheres to the plastic sheet—an excellent safety feature for both cars and homes.

Despite these benefits, Monsanto had a hard time convincing laminators and window manufacturers to carry these products. According to Melissa Toledo, brand manager at Monsanto, "Saflex was priced at a 30 percent premium above traditional glass, and the various stages in the value chain (distributors and retailers) didn't think there would be a demand for such an expensive glass product." What did Monsanto do? It reintroduced Saflex as KeepSafe® and worked to coordinate the product's value propositions. By analyzing the experiences of all of the players in the supply chain, it was able to create marketing programs that helped each build a business aimed at selling its products. Said Toledo, "We want to know how they go about selling those types of products, what challenges they face, and what they think they need to sell our products. This helps us a lot when we try to provide them with these needs."[15]

At times, a firm's marketing initiatives may become overly aggressive and lead to actions that are both unethical and illegal.[16] For example:

- **Burdines.** This department store chain is under investigation for allegedly adding club memberships to its customers' credit cards without prior approval.
- **Fleet Mortgage.** This company has been accused of adding insurance fees for dental coverage and home insurance to its customers' mortgage loans without the customers' knowledge.
- **HCI Direct.** Eleven states have accused this direct-mail firm with charging for panty hose samples that customers did not order.
- **Juno Online Services.** The Federal Trade Commission brought charges against this Internet service provider for failing to provide customers with a telephone number to cancel service.

Strategy Spotlight 3.2 addresses a key element of marketing—marketing research. We discuss how Kraft Foods Inc. was able to reinvent their iconic cookie in the U.S. market—the Oreo—to succeed in the Chinese market.

Service   This primary activity includes all actions associated with providing service to enhance or maintain the value of the product, such as installation, repair, training, parts supply, and product adjustment.

Let's see how two retailers are providing exemplary customer service. At Sephora.com, a customer service representative taking a phone call from a repeat customer has instant access to what shade of lipstick she likes best. This will help the rep cross-sell by suggesting a matching shade of lip gloss. CEO Jim Wiggett expects such personalization to build loyalty and boost sales per customer. Nordstrom, the Seattle-based department store chain, goes even a step further. It offers a cyber-assist: A service rep can take control of a customer's Web browser and literally lead her to just the silk scarf that she is looking for. CEO Dan Nordstrom believes that such a capability will close enough additional purchases to pay for the $1 million investment in software.

Strategy Spotlight 3.3 provides an example of how a firm—Cookshack—was able to use crowdsourcing to, in effect, turn its customers into a customer service department!

Support Activities

Support activities in the value chain can be divided into four generic categories, as shown in Exhibit 3.3. Each category of the support activity is divisible into a number of distinct value activities that are specific to a particular industry. For example, technology development's discrete activities may include component design, feature design, field testing, process engineering, and technology selection. Similarly, procurement may include qualifying new suppliers, purchasing different groups of inputs, and monitoring supplier performance.

Procurement   Procurement refers to the function of purchasing inputs used in the firm's value chain, not to the purchased inputs themselves.[17] Purchased inputs include raw materials, supplies, and other consumable items as well as assets such as machinery, laboratory equipment, office equipment, and buildings.[18, 19]

Microsoft has improved its procurement process (and the quality of its suppliers) by providing formal reviews of its suppliers. One of Microsoft's divisions has extended the review process used for employees to its outside suppliers.[20] The employee services group,

Adapting Oreos to the Chinese Market

Although the Oreo has long been the top-selling cookie in the U.S. market, Kraft Foods Inc. had to reinvent it to make it sell well in the world's most populous nation. Chinese Oreo sales represent a tiny fraction of Kraft's $37.2 billion in annual revenues. However, the cookie's journey in China exemplifies the kind of entrepreneurial transformation that CEO Irene Rosenfeld is trying to spread throughout the food giant. She has been putting more power in the hands of Kraft's various business units around the world—telling employees that decisions about Kraft products should not all be made by people at the Northfield, Illinois, headquarters.

Oreos were first introduced to the U.S. market in 1912. However, it wasn't until 1996 that Kraft sold them in China. Nine years later, Shawn Warren, a 37-year-old Kraft veteran—who had spent years marketing the company's cookies and crackers around the world—arrived on the scene. He noticed that Oreo's China sales had been flat for the previous five years. The problem: Kraft kept selling the U.S. version of Oreos in China. According to Warren, Albert Einstein's definition of insanity characterized Kraft: doing the same thing over and over and expecting different results.

Mr. Warren assigned his team to a lengthy research project that yielded some interesting findings. For one thing, Kraft learned that traditional Oreos were too sweet for Chinese tastes. Also, the packages of 14 Oreos priced at 72 cents were too expensive.

The company developed 20 prototypes of reduced-sugar Oreos and tested them with Chinese consumers

Source: Jargon, J. 2008. Kraft Reformulates Oreo, Scores in China. online.wsj.com, May 1: np.

● Kraft Foods Inc. has been very successful in adapting Oreos to the Chinese market.

before arriving at a formula that tasted right. Kraft also introduced packages containing fewer Oreos for only 29 cents.

Still, Kraft realized that it needed to do more than just tweak its recipe to capture a larger share of the Chinese market. After more experimentation, it remade the Oreo in 2006—it consisted of four layers of crispy wafer filled with vanilla and chocolate cream, coated in chocolate. The firm also developed a proprietary handling process to ensure that the product could be shipped across the country, withstanding the cold climate in the north and the hot, humid weather in the south—and still be ready to melt in the mouth.

The efforts have paid off—over the past two years, Kraft has doubled its Oreo revenue in China. And, with the help of those sales, worldwide sales of Oreos topped $1 billion for the first time.

which is responsible for everything from travel to 401(k) programs to the on-site library, outsources more than 60 percent of the services it provides. Unfortunately, the employee services group was not providing them with enough feedback. This was feedback that the suppliers wanted to get and that Microsoft wanted to give.

The evaluation system that Microsoft developed helped clarify its expectations to suppliers. An executive noted: "We had one supplier—this was before the new system—that would have scored a 1.2 out of 5. After we started giving this feedback, and the supplier understood our expectations, its performance improved dramatically. Within six months, it scored a 4. If you'd asked me before we began the feedback system, I would have said that was impossible."

3.3

Crowdsourcing: How Cookshack Gets "Free" Customer Service!

For more than 40 years, Cookshack has been producing outdoor ovens for home and commercial use in a 21,000 square foot factory in Ponca City, Oklahoma. Their major claim: its machines make barbecue and smoked foods "without a lot of fuss." That's because the food is wood-cooked at low temperature under static conditions with no through movement of air (which tends to dry meat) and no need for water pans (moisture stays in the oven).

Cookshack has 25 employees and actively encourages its customers to contact the company—its toll-free number is prominently shown on every page of its website. Its forums are a key adjunct to its live customer service and are meant to provide a body of knowledge that can't be transmitted in a phone call. The forums provide assistance 24 hours a day, seven days a week, and they are clearly popular. A recent visit to the "open forum" section revealed 1,640 topics and 13,000 posts!

Hour by hour, and day by day, hundreds of online Cookshack customers sign on to its various forums to ask and answer questions about barbeque sauce (another product line), smoker and barbeque ovens, and cooking techniques for everything from sausage, turkey, and ribs—to deer, salmon, and dog bones. The last one was from "Lucy" on behalf of her dog, Carole, and received 12 responses.

Cookshack has succeeded in creating a folksy, friendly site and designing forums and archives tailored to all tastes. The end result: it has sold its customers on providing their own customer support.

environmental
sustainability

Source: Libert, B. & Spector, J. 2008. *We Are Smarter Than Me.* Philadelphia: Wharton School Publishing; and forum.cookshack.com.

Exhibit 3.3   The Value Chain: Some Factors to Consider in Assessing a Firm's Support Activities

General Administration

- Effective planning systems to attain overall goals and objectives.
- Excellent relationships with diverse stakeholder groups.
- Effective information technology to integrate value-creating activities.

Human Resource Management

- Effective recruiting, development, and retention mechanisms for employees.
- Quality relations with trade unions.
- Reward and incentive programs to motivate all employees.

Technology Development

- Effective R&D activities for process and product initiatives.
- Positive collaborative relationships between R&D and other departments.
- Excellent professional qualifications of personnel.

Procurement

- Procurement of raw material inputs to optimize quality and speed and to minimize the associated costs.
- Development of collaborative win-win relationships with suppliers.
- Analysis and selection of alternative sources of inputs to minimize dependence on one supplier.

Source: Adapted from Porter, M.E. 1985. *Competitive Advantage: Creating and Sustaining Superior Performance.* New York: Free Press.

Technology Development   Every value activity embodies technology.[21] The array of technologies employed in most firms is very broad, ranging from technologies used to prepare documents and transport goods to those embodied in processes and equipment or the product itself.[22] Technology development related to the product and its features supports the entire value chain, while other technology development is associated with particular primary or support activities.

The Allied Signal and Honeywell merger brought together roughly 13,000 scientists and an $870 million R&D budget that should lead to some innovative products and services in two major areas: performance materials and control systems. Some of the possible innovations include:

- *Performance materials.* The development of uniquely shaped fibers with very high absorption capability. When employed in the company's Fram oil filters, they capture 50 percent more particles than ordinary filters. This means that cars can travel further with fewer oil changes.
- *Control systems.* Working with six leading oil companies, Honeywell developed software using "self-learning" algorithms that predict when something might go wrong in an oil refinery before it actually does. Examples include a faulty gas valve or hazardous spillage.[23]

Human Resource Management   Human resource management consists of activities involved in the recruiting, hiring, training, development, and compensation of all types of personnel.[24] It supports both individual primary and support activities (e.g., hiring of engineers and scientists) and the entire value chain (e.g., negotiations with labor unions).[25]

Like all great service companies, JetBlue Airways Corporation is obsessed with hiring superior employees.[26] But they found it difficult to attract college graduates to commit to careers as flight attendants. JetBlue developed a highly innovative recruitment program for flight attendants—a one-year contract that gives them a chance to travel, meet lots of people, and then decide what else they might like to do. They also introduced the idea of training a friend and employee together so that they could share a job. With such employee-friendly initiatives, JetBlue has been very successful in attracting talent.

Jeffrey Immelt, GE's chairman, addresses the importance of effective human resource management:[27]

> Human resources has to be more than a department. GE recognized early on—50 or 60 years ago—that in a multibusiness company, the common denominators are people and culture. From an employee's first day at GE, she discovers that she's in the people-development business as much as anything else. You'll find that most good companies have the same basic HR processes that we have, but they're discrete. HR at GE is not an agenda item; it is the agenda.

Strategy Spotlight 3.4 discusses a rather unique approach to individual performance evaluations: eliminate the metrics!

General Administration   General administration consists of a number of activities, including general management, planning, finance, accounting, legal and government affairs, quality management, and information systems. Administration (unlike the other support activities) typically supports the entire value chain and not individual activities.[28]

Although general administration is sometimes viewed only as overhead, it can be a powerful source of competitive advantage. In a telephone operating company, for example, negotiating and maintaining ongoing relations with regulatory bodies can be among the most important activities for competitive advantage. Also, in some industries top management plays a vital role in dealing with important buyers.[29]

Removing Individual Metrics in Performance Evaluations

ITT China President William Taylor wanted to know why employee turnover was so high in the Shanghai sales office. The local manager knew the answer: If the sales manager gave workers an average "3" on the 1-5 performance scale, they'd stop talking to him and, in some cases, quit shortly thereafter. The manager lamented: "They're losing face in the organization. It would be great if we could do something about the scores."

Comments like that popped up around the world. For example, in southern Europe, the focus on individual performance didn't sit well with the region's more "collec-

tive ethos," claims James Duncan, director of ITT's talent development. And in Scandinavia, where there's more of "a sense of equality between bosses and workers," says Duncan, some workers asked, "What gives you the right to rate me a 3?" That led ITT to make the radical decision to ditch performance ratings altogether.

Most employees, who still require a detailed evaluation, cheered the changes. In one of the ITT plants in Shenyang, China, the new system has helped to cut the plant's attrition rate in half. The change isn't as popular in the U.S., where some metrics-loving engineers in the defense business remain attached to the old rankings. Still, most people have come around. Says Duncan, "It's not just Asia and Europe." No matter what culture you are from, everyone "likes the fact that they're treated like an adult in this discussion."

Source: McGregor, J. 2008. Case study: To Adapt, ITT Lets Go of Unpopular Ratings. *BusinessWeek*, January 28: 46.

The strong and effective leadership of top executives can also make a significant contribution to an organization's success. As we discussed in Chapter 1, chief executive officers (CEOs) such as Herb Kelleher, Andrew Grove, and Jack Welch have been credited with playing critical roles in the success of Southwest Airlines, Intel, and General Electric.

Information systems can also play a key role in increasing operating efficiencies and enhancing a firm's performance.[30] Consider Walgreen Co.'s introduction of Intercom Plus, a computer-based prescription management system. Linked by computer to both doctors' offices and third-party payment plans, the system automates telephone refills, store-to-store prescription transfers, and drug reordering. It also provides information on drug interactions and, coupled with revised workflows, frees up pharmacists from administrative tasks to devote more time to patient counseling.[31]

> **>LO3**
> How value-chain analysis can help managers create value by investigating relationships among activities within the firm and between the firm and its customers and suppliers.

Interrelationships among Value-Chain Activities within and across Organizations

We have defined each of the value-chain activities separately for clarity of presentation. Managers must not ignore, however, the importance of relationships among value-chain activities.[32] There are two levels: (1) **interrelationships** among activities within the firm and (2) relationships among activities within the firm and with other organizations (e.g., customers and suppliers) that are part of the firm's expanded value chain.[33]

With regard to the first level, recall AT&T's innovative Resource Link program wherein employees who have reached their plateau may apply for temporary positions in other parts of the organization. Clearly, this program has the potential to benefit all activities within the firm's value chain because it creates opportunities for top employees to lend their expertise to all of the organization's value-creating activities.

With regard to the second level, Campbell Soup's use of electronic networks enabled it to improve the efficiency of outbound logistics.[34] However, it also helped Campbell manage the ordering of raw materials more effectively, improve its production scheduling, and help its customers better manage their inbound logistics operations.

> **interrelationships** collaborative and strategic exchange relationships between value-chain activities either a) within firms or b) between firms. Strategic exchange relationships involve exchange of resources such as information, people, technology, or money that contribute to the success of the firm.

Environmental Sustainability via an Energy-Efficient Supply Chain

Given the increasing concerns about fuel prices, long-term energy availability, and climate change, many firms are paying increased attention to one of the most pervasive places where energy can be conserved: the industrial supply chain. The supply chain is the production and distribution network that encompasses the sourcing, manufacturing, transportation, commercialization, distribution, consumption, and disposal of goods.

For example, in 2006 the Carbon Trust, a United Kingdom–based research and advisory group, discovered a "perverse incentive" in the sourcing of raw potatoes for the manufacture of snack foods. Charged with studying the carbon footprint of potato chips, the Trust's researchers discovered that since prices were set by weight, farmers typically control humidification to produce moister and, hence, heavier potatoes. Even within the strictly limited specifications of moisture content set by the food manufacturers, the extra grams of water are significant. The extra cooking needed to burn them off accounted for an unexpectedly high percentage of the chips' energy consumption. In effect, production-related greenhouse gases dwarfed the emissions from transportation.

The solution, wrote the Carbon Trust, was to change the procurement contract—to provide farmers with an incentive to produce potatoes with less moisture. Thus, the manufacturers would be in a better position to take advantage of carbon trading credits and other regulations for greenhouse gas reduction. And it would serve to set a precedent for further collaboration between food producers and their agricultural suppliers.

environmental sustainability

Source: Parry, P., Martha, J., & Grenon, G. 2007. The Energy-Efficient Supply Chain. *Strategy + Business*, August 7: np.

Strategy Spotlight 3.5 discusses how attention to an energy-efficient supply chain can not only enhance environmental sustainability, but also improve production efficiency.

Applying the Value Chain to Service Organizations

The concepts of inbound logistics, operations, and outbound logistics suggest managing the raw materials that might be manufactured into finished products and delivered to customers. However, these three steps do not apply only to manufacturing. They correspond to any transformation process in which inputs are converted through a work process into outputs that add value. For example, accounting is a sort of transformation process that converts daily records of individual transactions into monthly financial reports. In this example, the transaction records are the inputs, accounting is the operation that adds value, and financial statements are the outputs.

What are the "operations," or transformation processes, of service organizations? At times, the difference between manufacturing and service is in providing a customized solution rather than mass production as is common in manufacturing. For example, a travel agent adds value by creating an itinerary that includes transportation, accommodations, and activities that are customized to your budget and travel dates. A law firm renders services that are specific to a client's needs and circumstances. In both cases, the work process (operation) involves the application of specialized knowledge based on the specifics of a situation (inputs) and the outcome that the client desires (outputs).

The application of the value chain to service organizations suggests that the value-adding process may be configured differently depending on the type of business a firm is engaged in. As the preceding discussion on support activities suggests, activities such as procurement and legal services are critical for adding value. Indeed, the activities that may only provide support to one company may be critical to the primary value-adding activity of another firm.

Exhibit 3.4 provides two models of how the value chain might look in service industries. In the retail industry, there are no manufacturing operations. A firm, such as Best

Retail: Primary Value-Chain Activities

| Partnering with vendors | Purchasing goods | Managing and distributing inventory | Operating stores | Marketing and selling |

Engineering Services: Primary Value-Chain Activities

| Research and development | Engineering | Designs and solutions | Marketing and sales | Service |

Exhibit 3.4 **Some Examples of Value Chains in Service Industries**

Buy, adds value by developing expertise in the procurement of finished goods and by displaying them in their stores in a way that enhances sales. Thus, the value chain makes procurement activities (i.e., partnering with vendors and purchasing goods) a primary rather than a support activity. Operations refer to the task of operating Best Buy's stores.

For an engineering services firm, research and development provides inputs, the transformation process is the engineering itself, and innovative designs and practical solutions are the outputs. Arthur D. Little, for example, is a large consulting firm with offices in 20 countries. In its technology and innovation management practice, A. D. Little strives to make the best use of the science, technology and knowledge resources available to create value for a wide range of industries and client sectors. This involves activities associated with research and development, engineering, and creating solutions as well as downstream activities such as marketing, sales, and service. How the primary and support activities of a given firm are configured and deployed will often depend on industry conditions and whether the company is service and/or manufacturing oriented.

Resource-Based View of the Firm

The **resource-based view (RBV) of the firm** combines two perspectives: (1) the internal analysis of phenomena within a company and (2) an external analysis of the industry and its competitive environment.[35] It goes beyond the traditional SWOT (strengths, weaknesses, opportunities, threats) analysis by integrating internal and external perspectives. The ability of a firm's resources to confer competitive advantage(s) cannot be determined without taking into consideration the broader competitive context. A firm's resources must be evaluated in terms of how valuable, rare, and hard they are for competitors to duplicate. Otherwise, the firm attains only competitive parity.

As noted earlier (in Strategy Spotlight 3.1), a firm's strengths and capabilities—no matter how unique or impressive—do not necessarily lead to competitive advantages in the marketplace. The criteria for whether advantages are created and whether or not they can be sustained over time will be addressed later in this section. Thus, the RBV is a very useful framework for gaining insights as to why some competitors are more profitable than

resource-based view of the firm perspective that firms' competitive advantages are due to their endowment of strategic resources that are valuable, rare, costly to imitate, and costly to substitute.

>LO4

The resource-based view of the firm and the different types of tangible and intangible resources, as well as organizational capabilities.

others. As we will see later in the book, the RBV is also helpful in developing strategies for individual businesses and diversified firms by revealing how core competencies embedded in a firm can help it exploit new product and market opportunities.

In the two sections that follow, we will discuss the three key types of resources that firms possess (summarized in Exhibit 3.5): tangible resources, intangible resources, and

Exhibit 3.5
The Resource-Based View of the Firm: Resources and Capabilities

Tangible Resources	
Financial	• Firm's cash account and cash equivalents.
	• Firm's capacity to raise equity.
	• Firm's borrowing capacity.
Physical	• Modern plant and facilities.
	• Favorable manufacturing locations.
	• State-of-the-art machinery and equipment.
Technological	• Trade secrets.
	• Innovative production processes.
	• Patents, copyrights, trademarks.
Organizational	• Effective strategic planning processes.
	• Excellent evaluation and control systems.

Intangible Resources	
Human	• Experience and capabilities of employees.
	• Trust.
	• Managerial skills.
	• Firm-specific practices and procedures.
Innovation and creativity	• Technical and scientific skills.
	• Innovation capacities.
Reputation	• Brand name.
	• Reputation with customers for quality and reliability.
	• Reputation with suppliers for fairness, non–zero-sum relationships.

Organizational Capabilities

• Firm competencies or skills the firm employs to transfer inputs to outputs.

• Capacity to combine tangible and intangible resources, using organizational processes to attain desired end.

EXAMPLES:

• Outstanding customer service.

• Excellent product development capabilities.

• Innovativeness of products and services.

• Ability to hire, motivate, and retain human capital.

Source: Adapted from Barney, J. B. 1991. Firm Resources and Sustained Competitive Advantage. *Journal of Management:* 17: 101; Grant, R. M. 1991. *Contemporary Strategy Analysis:* 100–102. Cambridge England: Blackwell Business and Hitt, M. A., Ireland, R. D., & Hoskisson, R. E. 2001. *Strategic Management: Competitiveness and Globalization* (4th ed.). Cincinnati: South-Western College Publishing.

organizational capabilities. Then we will address the conditions under which such assets and capabilities can enable a firm to attain a sustainable competitive advantage.[36]

It is important to note that resources by themselves typically do not yield a competitive advantage. Even if a basketball team recruited an all-star center, there would be little chance of victory if the other members of the team were continually outplayed by their opponents or if the coach's attitude was so negative that everyone, including the center, became unwilling to put forth their best efforts.

In a business context, a firm's excellent value-creating activities (e.g., logistics) would not be a source of competitive advantage if those activities were not integrated with other important value-creating activities such as marketing and sales. Thus, a central theme of the resource-based view of the firm is that competitive advantages are created (and sustained) through the bundling of several resources in unique combinations.[37]

Types of Firm Resources

Firm resources are all assets, capabilities, organizational processes, information, knowledge, and so forth, controlled by a firm that enable it to develop and implement value-creating strategies.

Tangible Resources   These are assets that are relatively easy to identify. They include the physical and financial assets that an organization uses to create value for its customers. Among them are financial resources (e.g., a firm's cash, accounts receivables, and its ability to borrow funds); physical resources (e.g., the company's plant, equipment, and machinery as well as its proximity to customers and suppliers); organizational resources (e.g., the company's strategic planning process and its employee development, evaluation, and reward systems); and technological resources (e.g., trade secrets, patents, and copyrights).

Many firms are finding that high-tech, computerized training has dual benefits: It develops more effective employees and reduces costs at the same time. Employees at FedEx take computer-based job competency tests every 6 to 12 months.[38] The 90-minute computer-based tests identify areas of individual weakness and provide input to a computer database of employee skills—information the firm uses in promotion decisions.

Intangible Resources   Much more difficult for competitors (and, for that matter, a firm's own managers) to account for or imitate are **intangible resources,** which are typically embedded in unique routines and practices that have evolved and accumulated over time. These include human resources (e.g., experience and capability of employees, trust, effectiveness of work teams, managerial skills), innovation resources (e.g., technical and scientific expertise, ideas), and reputation resources (e.g., brand name, reputation with suppliers for fairness and with customers for reliability and product quality). A firm's culture may also be a resource that provides competitive advantage.[39]

For example, you might not think that motorcycles, clothes, toys, and restaurants have much in common. Yet Harley-Davidson has entered all of these product and service markets by capitalizing on its strong brand image—a valuable intangible resource.[40] It has used that image to sell accessories, clothing, and toys, and it has licensed the Harley-Davidson Café in New York City to provide further exposure for its brand name and products.

Strategy Spotlight 3.6 discusses how various social networking sites have the potential to play havoc with a firm's reputation.

Organizational Capabilities   **Organizational capabilities** are not specific tangible or intangible assets, but rather the competencies or skills that a firm employs to transform inputs into outputs.[41] In short, they refer to an organization's capacity to deploy tangible and intangible resources over time and generally in combination, and to leverage those capabilities to bring about a desired end.[42] Examples of organizational capabilities are outstanding customer service, excellent product development capabilities, superb innovation processes, and flexibility in manufacturing processes.[43]

tangible resources organizational assets that are relatively easy to identify, including physical assets, financial resources, organizational resources, and technological resources.

intangible resources organizational assets that are difficult to identify and account for and are typically embedded in unique routines and practices, including human resources, innovation resources, and reputation resources.

organizational capabilities the competencies and skills that a firm employs to transform inputs into outputs.

strategy spotlight

Blogs, Social Networking Sites, and Corporate Reputations: A Lethal Combination?

Customers are now connecting with and drawing power from one another. The mechanism: online social technologies such as blogs, social networking sites like MySpace, user-generated content sites like YouTube, and countless communities across the Web. They are defining their own perspective on companies and brands—a perspective that is often at odds with the image a company wants to project. This groundswell of people using technologies to get the things they need from one another, rather than from the companies, has tilted the balance of power from company to customer.

Let's look at an example: Brian Finkelstein, a law student, had trouble with the cable modem in his home. A Comcast Cable repairman arrived to fix the problem. However, when the technician had to call the home office for a key piece of information, he was put on hold for so long that he fell asleep on Finkelstein's couch. Outraged, Finkelstein made a video of the sleeping technician and posted it on YouTube. The clip became a hit—with more than a million viewings. And, to this day, it continues to undermine Comcast's efforts to improve its reputation for customer service.

Source: Bernoff, J. & Li, C. 2008. Harnessing the Power of the Oh-So-Social Web. *MIT Sloan Management Review*, 49 (3): 36–42; and, Stelter, B. 2008. Griping Online? Comcast Hears and Talks Back. nytimes.com, July 25: np.

But Comcast is working hard to improve its reputation. It has a lot of work to do—after all, the company was ranked at the bottom of the most recent American Customer Satisfaction Index, which tracks consumer opinions of more than 200 companies. And hundreds of customers have filed grievances on a site called comcastmustdie.com.

One of Comcast's initiatives to try to turn things around is headed by Frank Eliason, its digital care manager. He uses readily available online tools to monitor public comments on blogs, message boards, and social networks for any mention of Comcast. When Eliason sees a complaint, he contacts the source and tries to defuse the problem. "When you're having a two-way conversation, you really get to clear the air," says Eliason.

Comcast says the online outreach is part of a larger effort to revamp its customer service. In just five months, Eliason, whose job redefines customer service, has reached out to well over 1,000 customers online.

Comcast is not the only company trying to reach out to customers online. Using the social messaging service Twitter, Southwest Airlines answers customer questions about ticket prices and flight delays, Whole Foods Market posts details about discounts, and the chief executive of the online shoe store Zappos shares details of his life with 7,200 "followers." Many other companies also monitor online discussion groups. But given its track record, Comcast felt they needed to take the extra step: contacting customers who are discussing the company online.

Gillette's capability to combine several technologies has been one of the keys to its unparalleled success in the wet-shaving industry. Key technologies include its expertise concerning the physiology of facial hair and skin, the metallurgy of blade strength and sharpness, the dynamics of a cartridge moving across skin, and the physics of a razor blade severing the hair—highly specialized areas for which Gillette has unique capabilities. Combining these technologies has helped the company to develop innovative products such as the Excel, Sensor Excel, MACH 3, and Fusion shaving systems.[44]

Firm Resources and Sustainable Competitive Advantages

>LO5

The four criteria that a firm's resources must possess to maintain a sustainable advantage and how value created can be appropriated by employees and managers.

As we have mentioned, resources alone are not a basis for competitive advantages, nor are advantages sustainable over time.[45] In some cases, a resource or capability helps a firm to increase its revenues or to lower costs but the firm derives only a temporary advantage because competitors quickly imitate or substitute for it. Many e-commerce businesses in the early 2000s saw their profits seriously eroded because new (or existing) competitors easily duplicated their business model. For example, Priceline.com, expanded its offerings from enabling customers to place bids online for airline tickets to a wide variety of other products. However, it was easy for competitors (e.g., a consortium of major airlines) to duplicate Priceline's products and services. Ultimately, its market capitalization had plummeted roughly 98 percent from its all-time high.

For a resource to provide a firm with the potential for a sustainable competitive advantage, it must have four attributes.[46] First, the resource must be valuable in the sense that it exploits opportunities and/or neutralizes threats in the firm's environment. Second, it must be rare among the firm's current and potential competitors. Third, the resource must be difficult for competitors to imitate. Fourth, the resource must have no strategically equivalent substitutes. These criteria are summarized in Exhibit 3.6. We will now discuss each of these criteria. Then, we will examine how Dell's competitive advantage, which seemed secure just a few years ago, has eroded.

Is the Resource Valuable?   Organizational resources can be a source of competitive advantage only when they are valuable. Resources are valuable when they enable a firm to formulate and implement strategies that improve its efficiency or effectiveness. The SWOT framework suggests that firms improve their performance only when they exploit opportunities or neutralize (or minimize) threats.

The fact that firm attributes must be valuable in order to be considered resources (as well as potential sources of competitive advantage) reveals an important complementary relationship among environmental models (e.g., SWOT and five-forces analyses) and the resource-based model. Environmental models isolate those firm attributes that exploit opportunities and/or neutralize threats. Thus, they specify what firm attributes may be considered as resources. The resource-based model then suggests what additional characteristics these resources must possess if they are to develop a sustained competitive advantage.

Is the Resource Rare?   If competitors or potential competitors also possess the same valuable resource, it is not a source of a competitive advantage because all of these firms have the capability to exploit that resource in the same way. Common strategies based on such a resource would give no one firm an advantage. For a resource to provide competitive advantages, it must be uncommon, that is, rare relative to other competitors.

This argument can apply to bundles of valuable firm resources that are used to formulate and develop strategies. Some strategies require a mix of multiple types of resources—tangible assets, intangible assets, and organizational capabilities. If a particular bundle of firm resources is not rare, then relatively large numbers of firms will be able to conceive of and implement the strategies in question. Thus, such strategies will not be a source of competitive advantage, even if the resource in question is valuable.

Can the Resource Be Imitated Easily?   Inimitability (difficulty in imitating) is a key to value creation because it constrains competition.[47] If a resource is inimitable, then any profits generated are more likely to be sustainable.[48] Having a resource that competitors can easily copy generates only temporary value. This has important implications. Since managers

Is the resource or capability . . .	Implications
Valuable?	• Neutralize threats and exploit opportunities
Rare?	• Not many firms possess
Difficult to imitate?	• Physically unique
	• Path dependency (how accumulated over time)
	• Causal ambiguity (difficult to disentangle what it is or how it could be re-created)
	• Social complexity (trust, interpersonal relationships, culture, reputation)
Difficult to substitute?	• No equivalent strategic resources or capabilities

Exhibit 3.6
Four Criteria for Assessing Sustainability of Resources and Capabilities

often fail to apply this test, they tend to base long-term strategies on resources that are imitable. IBP (Iowa Beef Processors) became the first meatpacking company in the United States to modernize by building a set of assets (automated plants located in cattle-producing states) and capabilities (low-cost "disassembly" of carcasses) that earned returns on assets of 1.3 percent in the 1970s. By the late 1980s, however, ConAgra and Cargill had imitated these resources, and IBP's profitability fell by nearly 70 percent, to 0.4 percent.

Monster.com entered the executive recruiting market by providing, in essence, a substitute for traditional bricks-and-mortar headhunting firms. Although Monster.com's resources are rare and valuable, they are subject to imitation by new rivals—other dot-com firms. Why? There are very low entry barriers for firms wanting to try their hand at recruitment. For example, many job search dot-coms have emerged in recent years, including jobsearch.com, headhunter.com, nationjob.com, and hotjobs.com. In all, there are approximately 30,000 online job boards available to job seekers. It would be most difficult for a firm to attain a sustainable advantage in this industry.

Clearly, an advantage based on inimitability won't last forever. Competitors will eventually discover a way to copy most valuable resources. However, managers can forestall them and sustain profits for a while by developing strategies around resources that have at least one of the following four characteristics.[49]

Physical Uniqueness The first source of inimitability is physical uniqueness, which by definition is inherently difficult to copy. A beautiful resort location, mineral rights, or Pfizer's pharmaceutical patents simply cannot be imitated. Many managers believe that several of their resources may fall into this category, but on close inspection, few do.

path dependency
a characteristic of resources that is developed and/or accumulated through a unique series of events.

Path Dependency A greater number of resources cannot be imitated because of what economists refer to as **path dependency.** This simply means that resources are unique and therefore scarce because of all that has happened along the path followed in their development and/or accumulation. Competitors cannot go out and buy these resources quickly and easily; they must be built up over time in ways that are difficult to accelerate.

The Gerber Products Co. brand name for baby food is an example of a resource that is potentially inimitable. Re-creating Gerber's brand loyalty would be a time-consuming process that competitors could not expedite, even with expensive marketing campaigns. Similarly, the loyalty and trust that Southwest Airlines employees feel toward their firm and its cofounder, Herb Kelleher, are resources that have been built up over a long period of time. Also, a crash R&D program generally cannot replicate a successful technology when research findings cumulate. Clearly, these path-dependent conditions build protection for the original resource. The benefits from experience and learning through trial and error cannot be duplicated overnight.

causal ambiguity
a characteristic of a firm's resources that is costly to imitate because a competitor cannot determine what the resource is and/or how it can be re-created.

Causal Ambiguity The third source of inimitability is termed **causal ambiguity.** This means that would-be competitors may be thwarted because it is impossible to disentangle the causes (or possible explanations) of either what the valuable resource is or how it can be re-created. What is the root of 3M's innovation process? You can study it and draw up a list of possible factors. But it is a complex, unfolding (or folding) process that is hard to understand and would be hard to imitate.

Often, causally ambiguous resources are organizational capabilities, involving a complex web of social interactions that may even depend on particular individuals. When Continental and United tried to mimic the successful low-cost strategy of Southwest Airlines, the planes, routes, and fast gate turnarounds were not the most difficult aspects for them to copy. Those were all rather easy to observe and, at least in principle, easy to duplicate. However, they could not replicate Southwest's culture of fun, family, frugality, and focus since no one can clearly specify exactly what that culture is or how it came to be.

social complexity
a characteristic of a firm's resources that is costly to imitate because the social engineering required is beyond the capability of competitors, including interpersonal relations among managers, organizational culture, and reputation with suppliers and customers.

Social Complexity A firm's resources may be imperfectly inimitable because they reflect a high level of **social complexity.** Such phenomena are typically beyond the ability of firms to systematically manage or influence. When competitive advantages are based on social complexity, it is difficult for other firms to imitate them.

A wide variety of firm resources may be considered socially complex. Examples include interpersonal relations among the managers in a firm, its culture, and its reputation with its suppliers and customers. In many of these cases, it is easy to specify how these socially complex resources add value to a firm. Hence, there is little or no causal ambiguity surrounding the link between them and competitive advantage. But an understanding that certain firm attributes, such as quality relations among managers, can improve a firm's efficiency does not necessarily lead to systematic efforts to imitate them. Such social engineering efforts are beyond the capabilities of most firms.

Although complex physical technology is not included in this category of sources of imperfect inimitability, the exploitation of physical technology in a firm typically involves the use of socially complex resources. That is, several firms may possess the same physical technology, but only one of them may have the social relations, culture, group norms, and so on to fully exploit the technology in implementing its strategies. If such complex social resources are not subject to imitation (and assuming they are valuable and rare and no substitutes exist), this firm may obtain a sustained competitive advantage from exploiting its physical technology more effectively than other firms.

Are Substitutes Readily Available?   The fourth requirement for a firm resource to be a source of sustainable competitive advantage is that there must be no strategically equivalent valuable resources that are themselves not rare or inimitable. Two valuable firm resources (or two bundles of resources) are strategically equivalent when each one can be exploited separately to implement the same strategies.

Substitutability may take at least two forms. First, though it may be impossible for a firm to imitate exactly another firm's resource, it may be able to substitute a similar resource that enables it to develop and implement the same strategy. Clearly, a firm seeking to imitate another firm's high-quality top management team would be unable to copy the team exactly. However, it might be able to develop its own unique management team. Though these two teams would have different ages, functional backgrounds, experience, and so on, they could be strategically equivalent and thus substitutes for one another.

Second, very different firm resources can become strategic substitutes. For example, Internet booksellers such as Amazon.com compete as substitutes for bricks-and-mortar booksellers such as B. Dalton. The result is that resources such as premier retail locations become less valuable. In a similar vein, several pharmaceutical firms have seen the value of patent protection erode in the face of new drugs that are based on different production processes and act in different ways, but can be used in similar treatment regimes. The coming years will likely see even more radical change in the pharmaceutical industry as the substitution of genetic therapies eliminates certain uses of chemotherapy.[50]

To recap this section, recall that resources and capabilities must be rare and valuable as well as difficult to imitate or substitute in order for a firm to attain competitive advantages that are sustainable over time.[51] Exhibit 3.7 illustrates the relationship among the four criteria of sustainability and shows the competitive implications.

In firms represented by the first row of Exhibit 3.7, managers are in a difficult situation. When their resources and capabilities do not meet any of the four criteria, it would be difficult to develop any type of competitive advantage, in the short or long term. The resources and capabilities they possess enable the firm neither to exploit environmental opportunities nor neutralize environmental threats. In the second and third rows, firms have resources and capabilities that are valuable as well as rare, respectively. However, in both cases the resources and capabilities are not difficult for competitors to imitate or substitute. Here, the firms could attain some level of competitive parity. They could perform on par with equally endowed rivals or attain a temporary competitive advantage. But their advantages would be easy for competitors to match. It is only in the fourth row, where all

Is a resource or capability . . .				
Valuable?	Rare?	Difficult to Imitate?	Without Substitutes?	Implications for Competitiveness?
No	No	No	No	Competitive disadvantage
Yes	No	No	No	Competitive parity
Yes	Yes	No	No	Temporary competitive advantage
Yes	Yes	Yes	Yes	Sustainable competitive advantage

Source: Adapted from Barney, J. B. 1991. Firm Resources and Sustained Competitive Advantage. *Journal of Management,* 17: 99–120.

four criteria are satisfied, that competitive advantages can be sustained over time. Next, let's look at Dell and see how its competitive advantage, which seemed to be sustainable for a rather long period of time, has eroded.

Dell's Eroding (Sustainable?) Competitive Advantage   In 1984, Michael Dell started Dell Inc. in a University of Texas dorm room with an investment of $1,000.[52] By 2006, Dell had attained annual revenues of $56 billion and a net income of $3.6 billion—making Michael Dell one of the richest people in the world. Dell achieved this meteoric growth by differentiating itself through the direct sales approach that it pioneered. Its user-configurable products met the diverse needs of its corporate and institutional customer base. Exhibit 3.8 summarizes how Dell achieved its remarkable success by integrating its tangible resources, intangible resources, and organizational capabilities.

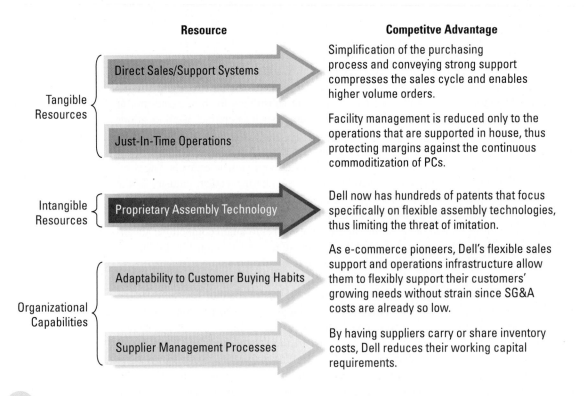

Exhibit 3.8 Dell's Tangible Resources, Intangible Resources, and Organizational Capabilities

Dell continued to maintain this competitive advantage by strengthening its value-chain activities and interrelationships that are critical to satisfying the largest market opportunities. It achieved this by (1) implementing e-commerce direct sales and support processes that accounted for the sophisticated buying habits of the largest markets and (2) matching its inventory management to its extensive supplier network. Dell also sustained these advantages by investing in intangible resources, such as proprietary assembly methods and packaging configurations, that helped to protect against the threat of imitation.

Dell recognized that the PC is a complex product with components sourced from several different technologies and manufacturers. Thus, in working backward from the customer's purchasing habits, Dell saw that the company could build valuable solutions by organizing its resources and capabilities around build-to-specification tastes, making both the sales and integration processes flexible, and passing on overhead expenses to its suppliers. Even as the PC industry became further commoditized, Dell was one of the few competitors that was able to retain solid margins. It accomplished this by adapting its manufacturing and assembly capabilities to match the PC market's trend toward user compatibility.

For many years, it looked as if Dell's competitive advantage over its rivals would be sustainable for a very long period of time. However, by early 2007, Dell was falling behind its rivals in market share. This led to a significant decline in its stock price—followed by a complete shake-up of the top management team. But what led to Dell's competitive decline in the first place?[53]

- Dell had become so focused on cost that it failed to pay attention to the design of the brand. Customers increasingly began to see the product as a commodity.
- Much of the growth in the PC industry today is in laptops. Customers demand a sleeker, better-designed machine instead of just the cheapest laptop. Also, they often want to see the laptop before they buy it.
- When Dell outsourced its customer service function to foreign locations, it led to a decline in customer support. This eroded Dell's brand value.
- Dell's efforts to replicate its made-to-order, no middleman strategy to other products such as printers and storage devices proved to be a failure. This is because customers saw little need for customization of these products.
- Rivals such as HP have been improving their product design and reducing their costs.[54] Thus, they now have cost parity with Dell, while enjoying a better brand image and the support of an extensive dealer network.

● Dell's competitive position in personal computers—including desktops and laptops—has eroded in recent years.

The Generation and Distribution of a Firm's Profits: Extending the Resource-Based View of the Firm

The resource-based view of the firm has been useful in determining when firms will create competitive advantages and enjoy high levels of profitability. However, it has not been developed to address how a firm's profits (often referred to as "rents" by economists) will be distributed to a firm's management and employees.[55] This becomes an important issue because firms may be successful in creating competitive advantages that can be sustainable for a period of time but much of the profits can be retained (or "appropriated") by its employees and managers instead of flowing to the owners of the firm (i.e., the stockholders).*

Consider Viewpoint DataLabs International, a Salt Lake City–based company that makes sophisticated three-dimensional models and textures for film production houses, video games, and car manufacturers. This example will help to show how employees are often able to obtain (or "appropriate") a high proportion of a firm's profits:

> Walter Noot, head of production, was having trouble keeping his highly skilled Generation X employees happy with their compensation. Each time one of them was lured away for more money, everyone would want a raise. "We were having to give out raises every six months—30 to 40 percent—then six months later they'd expect the same. It was a big struggle to keep people happy."[56]

At Viewpoint DataLabs, much of the profits are being generated by the highly skilled professionals working together. They are able to exercise their power by successfully demanding more financial compensation. In part, management has responded favorably because they are united in their demands, and their work involves a certain amount of social complexity and causal ambiguity—given the complex, coordinated efforts that their work entails.

Four factors help explain the extent to which employees and managers will be able to obtain a proportionately high level of the profits that they generate:[57]

- *Employee Bargaining Power.* If employees are vital to forming a firm's unique capability, they will earn disproportionately high wages. For example, marketing professionals may have access to valuable information that helps them to understand the intricacies of customer demands and expectations, or engineers may understand unique technical aspects of the products or services. Additionally, in some industries such as consulting, advertising, and tax preparation, clients tend to be very loyal to individual professionals employed by the firm, instead of to the firm itself. This enables them to "take the clients with them" if they leave. This enhances their bargaining power.
- *Employee Replacement Cost.* If employees' skills are idiosyncratic and rare (a source of resource-based advantages), they should have high bargaining power based on the high cost required by the firm to replace them. For example, Raymond Ozzie, the software designer who was critical in the development of Lotus Notes, was able to dictate the terms under which IBM acquired Lotus.
- *Employee Exit Costs.* This factor may tend to reduce an employee's bargaining power. An individual may face high personal costs when leaving the organization. Thus, that individual's threat of leaving may not be credible. In addition, an employee's expertise may be firm-specific and of limited value to other firms. Causal ambiguity may make it difficult for the employee to explain his or her specific contribution to a given project. Thus, a rival firm might be less likely to pay a high wage premium since it would be unsure of the employee's unique contribution.
- *Manager Bargaining Power.* Managers' power is based on how well they create resource-based advantages. They are generally charged with creating value through the process of organizing, coordinating, and leveraging employees as well as other forms of capital such as plant, equipment, and financial capital (addressed further in Chapter 4). Such activities provide managers with sources of information that may not be readily available to others. Thus, although managers may not know as much about the specific nature of customers and technologies, they are in a position to have a more thorough, integrated understanding of the total operation.

---

* Economists define rents as profits (or prices) in excess of what is required to provide a normal return.

Chapter 9 addresses the conditions under which top-level managers (such as CEOs) of large corporations have been, at times, able to obtain levels of total compensation that would appear to be significantly disproportionate to their contributions to wealth generation as well as to top executives in peer organizations. Here, corporate governance becomes a critical control mechanism. For example, William Esrey and Ronald T. LeMay (the former two top executives at Sprint Corporation) earned more than $130 million in stock options because of "cozy" relationships with members of their board of directors, who tended to approve with little debate huge compensation packages.[58]

Such diversion of profits from the owners of the business to top management is far less likely when the board members are truly independent outsiders (i.e., they do not have close ties to management). In general, given the external market for top talent, the level of compensation that executives receive is based on factors similar to the ones just discussed that determine the level of their bargaining power.[59]

Evaluating Firm Performance: Two Approaches

This section addresses two approaches to use when evaluating a firm's performance. The first is financial ratio analysis, which, generally speaking, identifies how a firm is performing according to its balance sheet, income statement, and market valuation. As we will discuss, when performing a financial ratio analysis, you must take into account the firm's performance from a historical perspective (not just at one point in time) as well as how it compares with both industry norms and key competitors.[60]

The second perspective takes a broader stakeholder view. Firms must satisfy a broad range of stakeholders, including employees, customers, and owners, to ensure their long-term viability. Central to our discussion will be a well-known approach—the balanced scorecard—that has been popularized by Robert Kaplan and David Norton.[61]

Financial Ratio Analysis

The beginning point in analyzing the financial position of a firm is to compute and analyze five different types of financial ratios:

- Short-term solvency or liquidity
- Long-term solvency measures
- Asset management (or turnover)
- Profitability
- Market value

financial ratio analysis a technique for measuring the performance of a firm according to its balance sheet, income statement, and market valuation.

Exhibit 3.9 summarizes each of these five ratios.

Appendix 1 to Chapter 13 (the Case Analysis chapter) provides detailed definitions for and discussions of each of these types of ratios as well as examples of how each is calculated. Refer to pages 486 to 494.

A meaningful ratio analysis must go beyond the calculation and interpretation of financial ratios.[62] It must include how ratios change over time as well as how they are interrelated. For example, a firm that takes on too much long-term debt to finance operations will see an immediate impact on its indicators of long-term financial leverage. The additional debt will negatively affect the firm's short-term liquidity ratio (i.e., current and quick ratios) since the firm must pay interest and principal on the additional debt each year until it is retired. Additionally, the interest expenses deducted from revenues reduce the firm's profitability.

A firm's financial position should not be analyzed in isolation. Important reference points are needed. We will address some issues that must be taken into account to make financial analysis more meaningful: historical comparisons, comparisons with industry norms, and comparisons with key competitors.

>LO6

The usefulness of financial ratio analysis, its inherent limitations, and how to make meaningful comparisons of performance across firms.

Exhibit 3.9   A Summary of Five Types of Financial Ratios

I. Short-term solvency, or liquidity, ratios

$$\text{Current ratio} = \frac{\text{Current assets}}{\text{Current liabilities}}$$

$$\text{Quick ratio} = \frac{\text{Current assets} - \text{Inventory}}{\text{Current liabilities}}$$

$$\text{Cash ratio} = \frac{\text{Cash}}{\text{Current liabilities}}$$

II. Long-term solvency, or financial leverage, ratios

$$\text{Total debt ratio} = \frac{\text{Total assets} - \text{Total equity}}{\text{Total assets}}$$

$$\text{Debt-equity ratio} = \text{Total debt/Total equity}$$

$$\text{Equity multiplier} = \text{Total assets/Total equity}$$

$$\text{Times interest earned ratio} = \frac{\text{EBIT}}{\text{Interest}}$$

$$\text{Cash coverage ratio} = \frac{\text{EBIT} + \text{Depreciation}}{\text{Interest}}$$

III. Asset utilization, or turnover, ratios

$$\text{Inventory turnover} = \frac{\text{Cost of goods sold}}{\text{Inventory}}$$

$$\text{Days' sales in inventory} = \frac{365 \text{ days}}{\text{Inventory turnover}}$$

$$\text{Receivables turnover} = \frac{\text{Sales}}{\text{Accounts receivable}}$$

$$\text{Days' sales in receivables} = \frac{365 \text{ days}}{\text{Receivables turnover}}$$

$$\text{Total asset turnover} = \frac{\text{Sales}}{\text{Total assets}}$$

$$\text{Capital intensity} = \frac{\text{Total assets}}{\text{Sales}}$$

IV. Profitability ratios

$$\text{Profit margin} = \frac{\text{Net income}}{\text{Sales}}$$

$$\text{Return on assets (ROA)} = \frac{\text{Net income}}{\text{Total assets}}$$

$$\text{Return on equity (ROE)} = \frac{\text{Net income}}{\text{Total equity}}$$

$$\text{ROE} = \frac{\text{Net income}}{\text{Sales}} \times \frac{\text{Sales}}{\text{Assets}} \times \frac{\text{Assets}}{\text{Equity}}$$

V. Market value ratios

$$\text{Price-earnings ratio} = \frac{\text{Price per share}}{\text{Earnings per share}}$$

$$\text{Market-to-book ratio} = \frac{\text{Market value per share}}{\text{Book value per share}}$$

Historical Comparisons   When you evaluate a firm's financial performance, it is very useful to compare its financial position over time. This provides a means of evaluating trends. For example, Microsoft reported revenues of $60 billion and net income of $17.7 billion in 2008. Almost all firms—except a few of the largest and most profitable companies in the world—would be very happy with such financial success. These figures reflect an annual growth in revenue and net income of 36 percent and 40 percent, respectively, for the 2004 to 2006 time period. Had Microsoft's revenues and net income in 2008 been $40 billion and $10 billion, respectively, it would still be a very large and highly profitable enterprise. However, such performance significantly damaged Microsoft's market valuation and reputation as well as the careers of many of its executives.

Exhibit 3.10 illustrates a 10-year period of return on sales (ROS) for a hypothetical company. As indicated by the dotted trend lines, the rate of growth (or decline) differs substantially over time periods.

Comparison with Industry Norms   When you are evaluating a firm's financial performance, remember also to compare it with industry norms. A firm's current ratio or profitability may appear impressive at first glance. However, it may pale when compared with industry standards or norms.

Comparing your firm with all other firms in your industry assesses relative performance. Banks often use such comparisons when evaluating a firm's creditworthiness. Exhibit 3.11

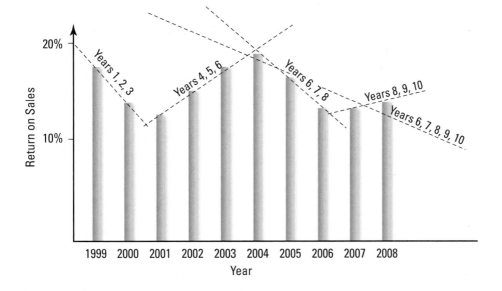

Exhibit 3.10 Historical Trends: Return on Sales (ROS) for a Hypothetical Company

includes a variety of financial ratios for three industries: semiconductors, grocery stores, and skilled-nursing facilities. Why is there such variation among the financial ratios for these three industries? There are several reasons. With regard to the collection period, grocery stores operate mostly on a cash basis, hence a very short collection period. Semiconductor manufacturers sell their output to other manufacturers (e.g., computer makers) on terms such as 2/15 net 45, which means they give a 2 percent discount on bills paid within 15 days and start charging interest after 45 days. Skilled-nursing facilities also have a longer collection period than grocery stores because they rely on payments from insurance companies.

The industry norms for return on sales also highlight differences among these industries. Grocers, with very slim margins, have a lower return on sales than either skilled-nursing facilities or semiconductor manufacturers. But how might we explain the differences between skilled-nursing facilities and semiconductor manufacturers? Health care facilities, in general, are limited in their pricing structures by Medicare/Medicaid regulations and by insurance reimbursement limits, but semiconductor producers have pricing structures determined by the market. If their products have superior performance, semiconductor manufacturers can charge premium prices.

Exhibit 3.11
How Financial Ratios Differ across Industries

Financial Ratio	Semiconductors	Grocery Stores	Skilled-Nursing Facilities
Quick ratio (times)	1.9	0.6	1.2
Current ratio (times)	3.9	1.9	1.6
Total liabilities to net worth (%)	30.2	71.4	156.9
Collection period (days)	49.0	2.6	30.3
Assets to sales (%)	147.3	19.5	113.9
Return on sales (%)	24	1.1	2.4

Source: Dun & Bradstreet. *Industry Norms and Key Business Ratios, 2007–2008*. One Year Edition, SIC #3600–3699 (Semiconductors); SIC #5400–5499 (Grocery Stores); SIC #8000–8099 (Skilled-Nursing Facilities). New York: Dun & Bradstreet Credit Services.

Exhibit 3.12
Comparison of Procter
& Gamble's and Key
Competitors' Drug
Revenues and R&D
Expenditures

Company (or division)	Sales* ($ billions)	R&D Budget ($ billions)
P&G Drug Division	$ 0.8	$0.38
Bristol-Myers Squibb	20.2	1.80
Pfizer	27.4	4.00
Merck	32.7	2.10

Source: Berner, R. 2000. Procter & Gamble: Just Say No to Drugs. *BusinessWeek*, October 9: 128; data courtesy of Lehman Brothers and Procter & Gamble.

*Data: Lehman Brothers, Procter & Gamble Co.

Comparison with Key Competitors   Recall from Chapter 2 that firms with similar strategies are members of a strategic group in an industry. Furthermore, competition is more intense among competitors within groups than across groups. Thus, you can gain valuable insights into a firm's financial and competitive position if you make comparisons between a firm and its most direct rivals. Consider Procter & Gamble's ill-fated efforts to enter the highly profitable pharmaceutical industry. Although P&G is a giant in consumer products, its efforts over two decades produced nominal profits. In 1999 P&G spent $380 million on R&D in drugs—22 percent of its total corporate R&D budget. Its drug unit produced only 2 percent of the company's $40 billion sales. Why? While $380 million is a large sum, its key competitors dwarf P&G. Consider the drug revenues and R&D budgets of P&G compared to its main rivals as shown in Exhibit 3.12. *BusinessWeek*'s take on P&G's chances in an article entitled "Just Say No to Drugs" was this: "Don't bet on it. P&G may be a giant in detergent and toothpaste, but the consumer-products maker is simply outclassed by the competition."[63]

Integrating Financial Analysis and Stakeholder Perspectives: The Balanced Scorecard

>LO7
The value of
the "balanced
scorecard" in
recognizing how the
interests of a variety
of stakeholders can
be interrelated.

It is useful to see how a firm is performing over time in terms of several ratios. However, such traditional approaches to performance assessments can be a double-edged sword.[64] Many important transactions that managers make—investments in research and development, employee training and development, and, advertising and promotion of key brands—may greatly expand a firm's market potential and create significant long-term shareholder value. But such critical investments are not reflected positively in short-term financial reports. Financial reports typically measure expenses, not the value created. Thus, managers may be penalized for spending money in the short term to improve their firm's long-term competitive viability!

Now consider the other side of the coin. A manager may destroy the firm's future value by dissatisfying customers, depleting the firm's stock of good products coming out of R&D, or damaging the morale of valued employees. Such budget cuts, however, may lead to very good short-term financials. The manager may look good in the short run and even receive credit for improving the firm's performance. In essence, such a manager has mastered "denominator management," whereby decreasing investments makes the return on investment (ROI) ratio larger, even though the actual return remains constant or shrinks.

**balanced score-
card** a method of
evaluating a firm's
performance using
performance mea-
sures from the
customers', internal,
innovation and learn-
ing, and financial
perspectives.

The Balanced Scorecard: Description and Benefits   To provide a meaningful integration of the many issues that come into evaluating a firm's performance, Kaplan and Norton developed a **"balanced scorecard."**[65] This provides top managers with a fast but comprehensive view of the business. In a nutshell, it includes financial measures that reflect the results of actions already taken, but it complements these indicators with measures of

Exhibit 3.13
The Balanced Scorecard's Four Perspectives

- How do customers see us? (customer perspective)
- What must we excel at? (internal business perspective)
- Can we continue to improve and create value? (innovation and learning perspective)
- How do we look to shareholders? (financial perspective)

customer satisfaction, internal processes, and the organization's innovation and improvement activities—operational measures that drive future financial performance.

The balanced scorecard enables managers to consider their business from four key perspectives: customer, internal, innovation and learning, and financial. These are briefly described in Exhibit 3.13.

Customer Perspective Clearly, how a company is performing from its customers' perspective is a top priority for management. The balanced scorecard requires that managers translate their general mission statements on customer service into specific measures that reflect the factors that really matter to customers. For the balanced scorecard to work, managers must articulate goals for four key categories of customer concerns: time, quality, performance and service, and cost. For example, lead time may be measured as the time from the company's receipt of an order to the time it actually delivers the product or service to the customer.

Internal Business Perspective Customer-based measures are important. However, they must be translated into indicators of what the firm must do internally to meet customers' expectations. Excellent customer performance results from processes, decisions, and actions that occur throughout organizations in a coordinated fashion, and managers must focus on those critical internal operations that enable them to satisfy customer needs. The internal measures should reflect business processes that have the greatest impact on customer satisfaction. These include factors that affect cycle time, quality, employee skills, and productivity. Firms also must identify and measure the key resources and capabilities they need for continued success.

Innovation and Learning Perspective Given the rapid rate of markets, technologies, and global competition, the criteria for success are constantly changing. To survive and prosper, managers must make frequent changes to existing products and services as well as introduce entirely new products with expanded capabilities. A firm's ability to improve, innovate, and learn is tied directly to its value. Simply put, only by developing new products and services, creating greater value for customers, and increasing operating efficiencies can a company penetrate new markets, increase revenues and margins, and enhance shareholder value. A firm's ability to do well from an innovation and learning perspective is more dependent on its intangible than tangible assets. Three categories of intangible assets are critically important: human capital (skills, talent, and knowledge), information capital (information systems, networks), and organization capital (culture, leadership).

Financial Perspective Measures of financial performance indicate whether the company's strategy, implementation, and execution are indeed contributing to bottom-line improvement. Typical financial goals include profitability, growth, and shareholder value. Periodic financial statements remind managers that improved quality, response time, productivity, and innovative products benefit the firm only when they result in improved sales, increased market share, reduced operating expenses, or higher asset turnover.[66]

Consider how Sears, the huge retailer, found a strong causal relationship between employee attitudes, customer attitudes, and financial outcomes.[67] Through an ongoing study, Sears developed (and continues to refine) what it calls its total performance indicators, or TPI—a set of indicators for assessing their performance with customers, employees, and investors. Sears's quantitative model has shown that a 5.0 percent improvement in employee attitudes leads to a 1.3 percent improvement in customer satisfaction, which in turn drives a 0.5 percent improvement in revenue. Thus, if a single store improved its employee attitude by 5.0 percent. Sears could predict with confidence that if the revenue growth in the district as a whole were 5.0 percent, the revenue growth in this particular store would be 5.5 percent. Interestingly, Sears's managers consider such numbers as rigorous as any others that they work with every year. The company's accounting firm audits management as closely as it audits the financial statements.

A key implication is that managers do not need to look at their job as balancing stakeholder demands. They must avoid the following mind-set: "How many units in employee satisfaction do I have to give up to get some additional units of customer satisfaction or profits?" Instead, the balanced scorecard provides a win–win approach—increasing satisfaction among a wide variety of organizational stakeholders, including employees (at all levels), customers, and stockholders.

Limitations and Potential Downsides of the Balanced Scorecard   There is general agreement that there is nothing inherently wrong with the concept of the balanced scorecard.[68] The key limitation is that some executives may view it as a "quick fix" that can be easily installed. However, implementing a balanced metrics system is an evolutionary process. It is not a one-time task that can be quickly checked off as "completed." If managers do not recognize this from the beginning and fail to commit to it long term, the organization will be disappointed. Poor execution becomes the cause of such performance outcomes. And organizational scorecards must be aligned with individuals' scorecards to turn the balanced scorecards into a powerful tool for sustained performance.*

In a recent study of 50 Canadian medium-size and large organizations, the number of users expressing skepticism about scorecard performance was much greater than the number claiming positive results. However, the overwhelming perspective was that balanced scorecards can be worthwhile in clarifying an organization's strategy, and if this can be accomplished, better results will follow. A few companies stated categorically that scorecards have improved their firm's financial results. For example, one respondent claimed that "We did not meet our financial goals previously, but since implementing our balanced scorecard, we have now met our goals three years running."

On the other hand, a greater number of respondents agreed with the statement "Balanced scorecards don't really work." Some representative comments included: "It became just a number-crunching exercise by accountants after the first year," "It is just the latest management fad and is already dropping lower on management's list of priorities as all fads eventually do," and "If scorecards are supposed to be a measurement tool, why is it so hard to measure their results?" There is much work to do before scorecards can become a viable framework to measure sustained strategic performance.

Problems often occur in the balanced scorecard implementation efforts when there is an insufficient commitment to learning and the inclusion of employees' personal ambitions. Without a set of rules for employees that address continuous process improvement and the personal improvement of individual employees, there will be limited employee buy-in and insufficient cultural change. Thus, many improvements may be temporary and superficial. Often, scorecards that failed to attain alignment and improvements dissipated very quickly. And, in many cases, management's efforts to improve performance were seen

---

* Building on the concepts that are the foundation of the balanced scorecard approach, Kaplan and Norton have recently developed a useful tool called the strategy map. Strategy maps show the cause and effect links by which specific improvements in different areas lead to a desired outcome. Strategy maps also help employees see how their jobs are related to the overall objectives of the organization. They also help us understand how an organization can convert its assets—both tangible and intangible—into tangible outcomes. Refer to Kaplan, R. S. & Norton, D. P. 2000. Having Trouble with Your Strategy? Then Map It. *Harvard Business Review,* 78(10): 167–176.

Exhibit 3.14
Potential Limitations of the Balanced Scorecard

Most agree that the balanced scorecard concept is a useful and an appropriate management tool. However, there are many design and implementation issues that may short circuit its value, including the following:

- **Lack of a Clear Strategy.** A scorecard can be developed without the aid of a strategy. However, it then becomes a key performance indicator or stakeholder system, lacking in many of the attributes offered from a true balanced scorecard.
- **Limited or Ineffective Executive Sponsorship.** Although training and education is important, without tenacious leadership and support of a scorecard project, the effort is most likely doomed.
- **Too Much Emphasis on Financial Measures Rather than Nonfinancial Measures.** This leads to measures that do not connect to the drivers of the business and are not relevant to performance improvement.
- **Poor Data on Actual Performance.** This can negate most of the effort invested in defining performance measures because a company can't monitor actual changes in results from changes in behavior.
- **Inappropriate Links of Scorecard Measures to Compensation.** Although this can focus managerial and employee attention, exercising it too soon can produce many unintended side effects such as dysfunctional decision making by managers looking to cash in.
- **Inconsistent or Inappropriate Terminology.** Everyone must speak the same language if measurement is to be used to guide change within an organization. Translating strategy into measures becomes even more difficult if everyone cannot agree on (or understand) the same language and terminology.

Sources: Angel, R. & Rampersad, H. 2005. Do Scorecards Add Up? Camagazine.com. May: np; and Niven, P. 2002. *Balanced Scorecard Step by Step: Maximizing Performance and Maintaining Results.* New York: John Wiley & Sons.

as divisive and were viewed by employees as aimed at benefiting senior management compensation. This fostered a "what's in it for me?" attitude. Exhibit 3.14 summarizes some of the potential downsides of the balanced scorecard.

Reflecting on Career Implications . . .

- *The Value Chain:* Carefully analyze where you can add value in your firm's value chain. How might your firm's support activities (e.g., information technology, human resource practices) help you accomplish your assigned tasks more effectively?
- *The Value Chain:* Consider important relationships among activities both within your firm as well as between your firm and its suppliers, customers, and alliance partners.
- *Resource-Based View of the Firm:* Are your skills and talents rare, valuable, difficult to imitate, and have few substitutes? If so, you are in a better position to add value for your firm—and earn rewards and incentives. How can your skills and talents be enhanced to help satisfy these criteria to a greater extent? More training? Change positions within the firm? Consider career options at other organizations?
- *Balanced Scorecard:* In your decision making, strive to "balance" the four perspectives: customer, internal business, innovation and learning, and financial. Do not focus too much on short-term profits. Do your personal career goals provide opportunities to develop your skills in all four directions?

Summary

In the traditional approaches to assessing a firm's internal environment, the primary goal of managers would be to determine their firm's relative strengths and weaknesses. Such is the role of SWOT analysis, wherein managers analyze their firm's strengths and weaknesses as well as the opportunities and threats in the external environment. In this chapter, we discussed why this may be a good starting point but hardly the best approach to take in performing a sound analysis. There are many limitations to SWOT analysis, including its static perspective, its potential to overemphasize a single dimension of a firm's strategy, and the likelihood that a firm's strengths do not necessarily help the firm create value or competitive advantages.

We identified two frameworks that serve to complement SWOT analysis in assessing a firm's internal environment: value-chain analysis and the resource-based view of the firm. In conducting a value-chain analysis, first divide the firm into a series of value-creating activities. These include primary activities such as inbound logistics, operations, and service as well as support activities such as procurement and human resources management. Then analyze how each activity adds value as well as how *interrelationships* among value activities in the firm and among the firm and its customers and suppliers add value. Thus, instead of merely determining a firm's strengths and weaknesses per se, you analyze them in the overall context of the firm and its relationships with customers and suppliers—the value system.

The resource-based view of the firm considers the firm as a bundle of resources: tangible resources, intangible resources, and organizational capabilities. Competitive advantages that are sustainable over time generally arise from the creation of bundles of resources and capabilities. For advantages to be sustainable, four criteria must be satisfied: value, rarity, difficulty in imitation, and difficulty in substitution. Such an evaluation requires a sound knowledge of the competitive context in which the firm exists. The owners of a business may not capture all of the value created by the firm. The appropriation of value created by a firm between the owners and employees is determined by four factors: employee bargaining power, replacement cost, employee exit costs, and manager bargaining power.

An internal analysis of the firm would not be complete unless you evaluate its performance and make the appropriate comparisons. Determining a firm's performance requires an analysis of its financial situation as well as a review of how well it is satisfying a broad range of stakeholders, including customers, employees, and stockholders. We discussed the concept of the balanced scorecard, in which four perspectives must be addressed: customer, internal business, innovation and learning, and financial. Central to this concept is the idea that the interests of various stakeholders can be interrelated. We provide examples of how indicators of employee satisfaction lead to higher levels of customer satisfaction, which in turn lead to higher levels of financial performance. Thus, improving a firm's performance does not need to involve making trade-offs among different stakeholders. Assessing the firm's performance is also more useful if it is evaluated in terms of how it changes over time, compares with industry norms, and compares with key competitors.

In the Appendix to Chapter 3, we discuss how Internet and digital technologies have created new opportunities for firms to add value. Four value-adding activities that have been enhanced by Internet capabilities are search, evaluation, problem solving, and transaction. These four activities are supported by three different types of content that Internet businesses often use—customer feedback, expertise, and entertainment programming. Seven business models have been identified that are proving successful for use by Internet firms. These include commission, advertising, markup, production, referral, subscription, and fee-for-service–based models. Firms also are finding that combinations of these business models can contribute to greater success.

Summary Review Questions

1. SWOT analysis is a technique to analyze the internal and external environment of a firm. What are its advantages and disadvantages?

2. Briefly describe the primary and support activities in a firm's value chain.

3. How can managers create value by establishing important relationships among the value-chain activities both within their firm and between the firm and its customers and suppliers?

4. Briefly explain the four criteria for sustainability of competitive advantages.

5. Under what conditions are employees and managers able to appropriate some of the value created by their firm?

6. What are the advantages and disadvantages of conducting a financial ratio analysis of a firm?

7. Summarize the concept of the balanced scorecard. What are its main advantages?

Key Terms

value-chain analysis, 82
primary activities, 82
support activities, 82
interrelationships 89
resource-based view
  of the firm, 91
tangible resources, 93
intangible resources, 93
organizational
  capabilities, 93
path dependency, 96
causal ambiguity, 96

social complexity, 96
financial ratio
  analysis, 101
balanced scorecard, 104
search activities, 114
evaluation activities, 114
problem-solving
  activities, 114
transaction
  activities, 115
business model, 116

Experiential Exercise

Dell Computer is a leading firm in the personal computer industry, with annual revenues of $61 billion during its 2008 fiscal year. Dell had created a very strong competitive position via its "direct model," whereby it manufactures its personal computers to detailed customer specifications. However, its advantage has been eroded recently by strong rivals such as HP.

Below we address several questions that focus on Dell's value-chain activities and interrelationships among them as well as whether they are able to attain sustainable competitive advantage(s). (We discuss Dell in this chapter on pages 98–99.)

1. Where in Dell's value chain are they creating value for their customer?

Value-Chain Activity	Yes/No	How Does Dell Create Value for the Customer?
Primary:		
Inbound logistics		
Operations		
Outbound logistics		
Marketing and sales		
Service		
Support:		
Procurement		
Technology development		
Human resource management		
General administration		

2. What are the important relationships among Dell's value-chain activities? What are the important interdependencies? For each activity, identify the relationships and interdependencies.

	Inbound logistics	Operations	Outbound logistics	Marketing and sales	Service	Procurement	Technology development	Human resource management	General administration
Inbound logistics									
Operations									
Outbound logistics									
Marketing and sales									
Service									
Procurement									
Technology development									
Human resource management									
General administration									

3. What resources, activities, and relationships enable Dell to achieve a sustainable competitive advantage?

Resource/Activity	Is It Valuable?	Is It Rare?	Are There Few Substitutes?	Is It Difficult to Make?
Inbound logistics				
Operations				
Outbound logistics				
Marketing and sales				
Service				
Procurement				
Technology development				
Human resource management				
General administration				

Application Questions Exercises

1. Using published reports, select two CEOs who have recently made public statements regarding a major change in their firm's strategy. Discuss how the successful implementation of such strategies requires changes in the firm's primary and support activities.

2. Select a firm that competes in an industry in which you are interested. Drawing upon published financial reports, complete a financial ratio analysis. Based on changes over time and a comparison with industry norms, evaluate the firm's strengths and weaknesses in terms of its financial position.

3. How might exemplary human resource practices enhance and strengthen a firm's value-chain activities?

4. Using the Internet, look up your university or college. What are some of its key value-creating activities that provide competitive advantages? Why?

Ethics Questions

1. What are some of the ethical issues that arise when a firm becomes overly zealous in advertising its products?

2. What are some of the ethical issues that may arise from a firm's procurement activities? Are you aware of any of these issues from your personal experience or businesses you are familiar with?

References

1. Wiley, R. 2008. Navistar re-files lawsuit against Ford Motor Company. reuters.com, February 28: np.; Pope, B. 2007. Ford, Navistar working toward compromise. wardsauto.com, March 8: np.; Anonymous. 2007. Navistar files another lawsuit against Ford. uk.reuters.com, np.; and, Hoffman, B. G. 2007. Ford-Navistar showdown could threaten truck production. detnews.com, February 27: np.

2. Our discussion of the value chain will draw on Porter, M. E. 1985. Competitive advantage: chap. 2. New York: Free Press.

3. Dyer, J. H. 1996. Specialized supplier networks as a source of competitive advantage: Evidence from the auto industry. Strategic Management Journal, 17: 271–291.

4. For an insightful perspective on value-chain analysis, refer to Stabell, C. B. & Fjeldstad, O. D. 1998. Configuring value for competitive advantage: On chains, shops, and networks. Strategic Management Journal, 19: 413–437. The authors develop concepts of value chains, value shops, and value networks to extend the value-creation logic across a broad range of industries. Their work builds on the seminal contributions of Porter, 1985, op. cit., and others who have addressed how firms create value through key interrelationships among value-creating activities.

5. Ibid.

6. Maynard, M. 1999. Toyota promises custom order in 5 days. USA Today, August 6: B1.

7. Shaw Industries. 1999. Annual report: 14–15.

8. Fisher, M. L. 1997. What is the right supply chain for your product? Harvard Business Review, 75(2): 105–116.

9. Jackson. M. 2001. Bringing a dying brand back to life. Harvard Business Review, 79(5): 53–61.

10. Anderson, J. C. & Nmarus, J. A. 2003. Selectively pursuing more of your customer's business. MIT Sloan Management Review, 44(3): 42–50.

11. Insights on advertising are addressed in: Rayport, J. F. 2008. Where is advertising? Into 'stitials. Harvard Business Review, 66(5): 18–20.

12. An insightful discussion of the role of identity marketing—that is, the myriad labels that people use to express who they are—in successful marketing activities is found in Reed, A., II & Bolton, L. E. 2005. The complexity of identity. MIT Sloan Management Review, 46(3): 18–22.

13. Insights on the usefulness of off-line ads are the focus of: Abraham, M. 2008. The off-line impact of online ads. Harvard Business Review, 66(4): 28.

14. Berggren, E. & Nacher, T. 2000. Why good ideas go bust. Management Review, February: 32–36.

15. For an insightful perspective on creating effective brand portfolios, refer to Hill, S., Ettenson, R., & Tyson, D. 2005. Achieving the ideal brand portfolio. MIT Sloan Management Review, 46(2): 85–90.

16. Haddad, C. & Grow, B. 2001. Wait a second—I didn't order that! BusinessWeek, July 16: 45.

17. For a scholarly discussion on the procurement of technology components, read Hoetker, G. 2005. How much you know versus how well I know you: Selecting a supplier for a technically innovative component. Strategic Management Journal, 26(1): 75–96.

18. For a discussion on criteria to use when screening suppliers for back-office functions, read Feeny, D., Lacity, M., & Willcocks, L. P. 2005. Taking the measure of outsourcing providers. MIT Sloan Management Review, 46(3): 41–48.

19. For a study investigating sourcing practices, refer to: Safizadeh, M. H., Field, J. M., & Ritzman, L. P. 2008. Sourcing practices and boundaries of the firm in the financial services industry. Strategic Management Journal, 29(1): 79–92.

20. Imperato, G. 1998. How to give good feedback. Fast Company, September: 144–156.

21. Bensaou, B. M. & Earl, M. 1998. The right mindset for managing information technology. Harvard Business Review, 96(5): 118–128.

22. A discussion of R&D in the pharmaceutical industry is in: Garnier, J-P.

2008. Rebuilding the R&D engine in big pharma. *Harvard Business Review,* 66(5): 68–76.

23. Donlon, J. P. 2000. Bonsignore's bid for the big time. *Chief Executive,* March: 28–37.

24. Ulrich, D. 1998. A new mandate for human resources. *Harvard Business Review,* 96(1): 124–134.

25. A study of human resource management in China is: Li, J., Lam, K., Sun, J. J. M., & Liu, S. X. Y. 2008. Strategic resource management, institutionalization, and employment modes: An empirical study in China. *Strategic Management Journal,* 29(3): 337–342.

26. Wood, J. 2003. Sharing jobs and working from home: The new face of the airline industry. AviationCareer.net, February 21.

27. Green, S., Hasan, F., Immelt, J. Marks, M., & Meiland, D. 2003. In search of global leaders. *Harvard Business Review,* 81(8): 38–45.

28. For insights on the role of information systems integration in fostering innovation refer to: Cash, J. I. Jr., Earl, M. J., & Morison, R. 2008. Teaming up to crack innovation and enterprise integration. *Harvard Business Review,* 66(11): 90–100.

29. For a cautionary note on the use of IT, refer to McAfee, A. 2003. When too much IT knowledge is a dangerous thing. *MIT Sloan Management Review,* 44(2): 83–90.

30. Walgreen Co. 1996. *Information technology and Walgreens: Opportunities for employment,* January; and Dess, G. G. & Picken, J. C. 1997. *Beyond productivity.* New York: AMACOM.

31. The important role in IT for a Japanese bank is addressed in: Upton, D. M. & Staats, B. R. 2008. Radically simple IT. *Harvard Business Review,* 66(3): 118–124.

32. For an interesting perspective on some of the potential downsides of close customer and supplier relationships, refer to Anderson, E. & Jap, S. D. 2005. The dark side of close relationships. *MIT Sloan Management Review,* 46(3): 75–82.

33. Day, G. S. 2003. Creating a superior customer-relating capability. *MIT Sloan Management Review,* 44(3): 77–82.

34. To gain insights on the role of electronic technologies in enhancing a firm's connections to outside suppliers and customers, refer to Lawrence, T. B., Morse, E. A., & Fowler, S. W. 2005. Managing your portfolio of connections. *MIT Sloan Management Review,* 46(2): 59–66.

35. Collis, D. J. & Montgomery, C. A. 1995. Competing on resources: Strategy in the 1990's. *Harvard Business Review,* 73(4): 119–128; and Barney, J. 1991. Firm resources and sustained competitive advantage. *Journal of Management,* 17(1): 99–120.

36. For recent critiques of the resource-based view of the firm, refer to: Sirmon, D. G., Hitt, M. A., & Ireland, R. D. 2007. Managing firm resources in dynamic environments to create value: Looking inside the black box. *Academy of Management Review,* 32(1): 273–292; and Newbert, S. L. Empirical research on the resource-based view of the firm: An assessment and suggestions for future research. *Strategic Management Journal,* 28(2): 121–146.

37. For insights into research findings on the linkage between resources and performance, refer to: Crook, T. R., Ketchen, D. J., Jr., Combs, J. G., & Todd, S. Y. 2008. Strategic resources and performance: A meta-analysis. *Strategic Management Journal,* 29(11): 1141–1154.

38. Henkoff, R. 1993. Companies that train the best. *Fortune,* March 22: 83; and Dess & Picken, *Beyond productivity,* p. 98.

39. Barney, J. B. 1986. Types of competition and the theory of strategy: Towards an integrative framework. *Academy of Management Review,* 11(4): 791–800.

40. Harley-Davidson. 1993. Annual report.

41. For a rigorous, academic treatment of the origin of capabilities, refer to Ethiraj, S. K., Kale, P., Krishnan, M. S., & Singh, J. V. 2005. Where do capabilities come from and how do they matter? A study of the software services industry. *Strategic Management Journal,* 26(1): 25–46.

42. For an academic discussion on methods associated with organizational capabilities, refer to Dutta, S., Narasimhan, O., & Rajiv, S. 2005. Conceptualizing and measuring capabilities: Methodology and empirical application. *Strategic Management Journal,* 26(3): 277–286.

43. Lorenzoni, G. & Lipparini, A. 1999. The leveraging of interfirm relationships as a distinctive organizational capability: A longitudinal study. *Strategic Management Journal,* 20: 317–338.

44. A discussion of organizational capabilities and entry timing is in: Lee, G. K. 2008. Relevance of organizational capabilities and dynamics: What to learn from entrants' product portfolios about the determinants of entry timing. *Strategic Management Journal,* 29 (12): 1257–1280.

45. A study investigating the sustainability of competitive advantage is: Newbert, S. L. 2008. Value, rareness, competitive advantages, and performance: A conceptual-level empirical investigation of the resource-based view of the firm. *Strategic Management Journal,* 29(7): 745–768.

46. Barney, J. 1991. Firm resources and sustained competitive advantage. *Journal of Management,* 17(1): 99–120.

47. Barney, 1986, op. cit. Our discussion of inimitability and substitution draws upon this source.

48. A study that investigates the performance implications of imitation is: Ethiraj, S. K. & Zhu, D. H. 2008. Performance effects of imitative entry. *Strategic Management Journal,* 29(8): 797–818.

49. Deephouse, D. L. 1999. To be different, or to be the same? It's a question (and theory) of strategic balance. *Strategic Management Journal,* 20: 147–166.

50. Yeoh, P. L. & Roth, K. 1999. An empirical analysis of sustained advantage in the U.S. pharmaceutical industry: Impact of firm resources and capabilities. *Strategic Management Journal,* 20: 637–653.

51. Robins, J. A. & Wiersema, M. F. 2000. Strategies for unstructured competitive

environments: Using scarce resources to create new markets. In Bresser, R. F., et al., (Eds.), *Winning strategies in a deconstructing world:* 201–220. New York: John Wiley.

52. For an insightful case on how Dell was able to build its seemingly sustainable competitive advantage in the marketplace, refer to "Matching Dell" by Jan W. Rivkin and Michael E. Porter, Harvard Business School Case 9-799-158 (June 6, 1999).

53. Byrnes, N. & Burrows, P. 2007. Where Dell went wrong. *BusinessWeek*, February 18: 62–63; and Smith, A. D. 2007. Dell's moves create buzz. *Dallas Morning News*. Februrary 21: D1.

54. For an insightful perspective on how HP has increased its market share and profitability in the personal computer market, refer to: Edwards, C. 2008. How HP got the wow! back. *BusinessWeek*, December 22: 60–61. HP surpassed Dell in fall 2006 to become the world's largest PC manufacturer, and it increased its market share from 14.5 percent to 18.8 percent between June 2005 and September 2008.

55. Amit, R. & Schoemaker, J. H. 1993. Strategic assets and organizational rent. *Strategic Management Journal*, 14(1): 33–46; Collis, D. J. & Montgomery, C. A. 1995. Competing on resources: Strategy in the 1990's. *Harvard Business Review*, 73(4): 118–128; Coff, R. W. 1999. When competitive advantage doesn't lead to performance: The resource-based view and stakeholder bargaining power. *Organization Science*, 10(2): 119–133; and Blyler, M. & Coff, R. W. 2003. Dynamic capabilities, social capital, and rent appropriation: Ties that split pies. *Strategic Management Journal*, 24: 677–686.

56. Munk, N. 1998. The new organization man. *Fortune*, March 16: 62–74.

57. Coff, op. cit.

58. Lavelle, L. 2003. Sprint's board needs a good sweeping, too. *BusinessWeek*, February 24: 40; Anonymous. 2003. Another nail in the coffin. *The Economist*, February 15: 69–70; and Byrnes, N., Dwyer, P., & McNamee, M. 2003. Hacking away at tax shelters, *BusinessWeek*, February 24: 41.

59. We have focused our discussion on how internal stakeholders (e.g., employees, managers, and top executives) may appropriate a firm's profits (or rents). For an interesting discussion of how a firm's innovations may be appropriated by external stakeholders (e.g., customers, suppliers) as well as competitors, refer to Grant, R. M. 2002. *Contemporary strategy analysis* (4th ed.): 335–340. Malden, MA: Blackwell.

60. Luehrman, T. A. 1997. What's it worth? A general manager's guide to valuation. *Harvard Business Review*, 45(3): 132–142.

61. See, for example, Kaplan, R. S. & Norton, D. P. 1992. The balanced scorecard: Measures that drive performance. *Harvard Business Review*, 69(1): 71–79.

62. Hitt, M. A., Ireland, R. D., & Stadter, G. 1982. Functional importance of company performance: Moderating effects of grand strategy and industry type. *Strategic Management Journal*, 3: 315–330.

63. Berner, R. 2000. Procter & Gamble: Just say no to drugs. *BusinessWeek*, October 9: 128.

64. Kaplan & Norton, op. cit.

65. Ibid.

66. For a discussion of the relative value of growth versus increasing margins, read Mass, N. J. 2005. The relative value of growth. *Harvard Business Review*, 83(4): 102–112.

67. Rucci, A. J., Kirn, S. P., & Quinn, R. T. 1998. The employee-customer-profit chain at Sears. *Harvard Business Review*, 76(1): 82–97.

68. Our discussion draws upon: Angel, R. & Rampersad, H. 2005. Do scorecards add up? camagazine.com. May: np.; and Niven, P. 2002. *Balanced scorecard step by step: Maximizing performance and maintaining results*. New York: John Wiley & Sons.

APPENDIX TO CHAPTER 3

How the Internet and Digital Technologies Add Value

The Internet has changed the way business is conducted. By providing new ways to interact with customers and using digital technologies to streamline operations, the Internet is helping companies create new value propositions. Let's take a look at several ways these changes have added new value. Exhibit 3A.1 illustrates four related activities that are being revolutionized by the Internet—search, evaluation, problem solving, and transactions.[1]

> **>LO8**
>
> How firms are using Internet technologies to add value and achieve unique advantages. (Appendix)

Search Activities

Search refers to the process of gathering information and identifying purchase options. The Internet has enhanced both the speed of information gathering and the breadth of information that can be accessed. This enhanced search capability is one of the key reasons the Internet has lowered switching costs—by decreasing the cost of search. These efficiency gains have greatly benefited buyers.

[1]The ideas in this section draw on several sources, including Zeng, M. & Reinartz, W. 2003. Beyond Online Search: The Road to Profitability. *California Management Review*, Winter: 107–130; and Stabell, C. B. & Fjeldstad, O. D. 1998. Configuring Value for Competitive Advantage: On Chains, Shops, and Networks. *Strategic Management Journal*, 19: 413–437.

Exhibit 3A.1 Internet Activities that Add Value

Sources: Adapted from Zeng, M., & Reinartz, W. 2003. Beyond online search: The road to profitability. *California Management Review.* Winter: 107–130; and Stabell, C. B., & Fjeldstad, O. D. 1998. Configuring value for competitive advantage: On chains, shops, and networks. *Strategic Management Journal,* 19: 413–437.

Suppliers also have benefited. Small suppliers that had difficulty getting noticed can be found more easily, and large suppliers can publish thousands of pages of information for a fraction of the cost that hard-copy catalogs once required. Additionally, online search engines have accelerated the search process to incredible speeds. Consider the example of Google:

> Google, a search engine developed as a project by two graduate students, became the number one search service in just four years. Why? Because it is capable of incredible things. Using over 10,000 networked computers, it searches 3 billion Web pages in an average of 500 milliseconds. To do the same search manually, by thumbing through 3 billion pages at the rate of one minute per page, would take 5,707 years. This ability has made Google an essential tool for many businesses. As a result, Google has built a powerful advertising business. Mark Kini, who runs a small limousine service in Boston, spends 80 percent of his advertising budget on Google and other search engines. "It's how we survive," says Kini.[2]

Evaluation Activities

Evaluation refers to the process of considering alternatives and comparing the costs and benefits of various options. Online services that facilitate comparative shopping, provide product reviews, and catalog customer evaluations of performance have made the Internet a valuable resource.[3] For example, BizRate.com offers extensive product ratings that can help evaluate products. Sites such as CNET that provide comparative pricing have helped lower prices even for quality products that have traditionally maintained premium prices. Opinion-based sites such as ePinions.com and PlanetFeedback.com provide reports of consumer experiences with various vendors.

Many Internet businesses, according to digital business experts Ming Zeng and Werner Reinartz, could improve their performance by making a stronger effort to help buyers evaluate purchases.[4] Even so, only certain types of products can be evaluated online. Products such as CDs that appeal primarily to the sense of sound sell well on the Internet. But products that appeal to multiple senses are harder to evaluate online. This explains why products such as furniture and fashion have never been strong online sellers. It's one thing to look at a leather sofa, but to be able to sit on it, touch, and smell the leather online are impossible.

Problem-Solving Activities

Problem solving refers to the process of identifying problems or needs and generating ideas and action plans to address those needs. Whereas evaluation is primarily product-related, problem solving is typically used in the context of services. Customers usually have unique problems that are handled one at a time. For example, online travel services such as Travelocity help customers select from many options

search activities a way that digital technologies and the Internet have added value to firms' operations by enhancing the gathering of information and identifying purchase options.

evaluation activities a way that digital technologies and the Internet have added value to firms' operations by facilitating the comparison of the costs and benefits of various options.

problem-solving activities a way that digital technologies and the Internet have added value to firms' operations by identifying problems or needs and generating ideas and action plans to address those needs.

[2]Hardy, Q. 2003. All Eyes on Google. *Forbes,* May 26, www.forbes.com.
[3]For an interesting discussion of how successful Internet-based companies are using evaluation to add value see Weiss, L. M., Capozzi, M. M., & Prusak, L. 2004. Learning from the Internet Giants. *Sloan Management Review,* 45(4): 79–84.
[4]Zeng & Reinartz, *op.cit.*

to form a unique travel package. Furthermore, problem solving often involves providing answers immediately (compared to the creation of a new product). Firms in industries such as medicine, law, and engineering are using the Internet and digital technologies to deliver many new solutions.

Many products involve both a service and a product component; therefore, both problem solving and evaluation may be needed. Dell Computer's website is an example of a site that has combined the benefits of both. By creating a website that allows for customization of individual computers, they address the unique concerns of customers "one computer at a time." But the site also features a strong evaluative component because it allows users to compare the costs and features of various options. Shoppers can even compare their customized selection to refurbished Dell computers that are available at a substantially lower cost.

Transaction Activities

Transaction refers to the process of completing the sale, including negotiating and agreeing contractually, making payments, and taking delivery. Numerous types of Internet-enabled activities have contributed to lowering this aspect of overall transaction costs. Auctions of various sorts, from raw materials used in manufacturing to collectibles sold on eBay, facilitate the process of arriving at mutually agreed-on prices. Services such as PayPal provide a third-party intermediary that facilitates transactions between parties who never have (and probably never will) meet. Amazon.com's One-Click technology allows for very rapid purchases, and Amazon's overall superiority in managing order fulfillment has made its transactions process rapid and reliable. Amazon's success today can be attributed to a large extent to its having sold this transaction capability to other companies such as Target, Toys "R" Us and even Borders (another bookseller!).[5]

transaction activities a way that digital technologies and the Internet have added value to firms' operations by completing sales efficiently, including negotiating and agreeing contractually, making payments, and taking delivery.

Other Sources of Competitive Advantage

There are other factors that can be important sources of competitive advantage. One of the most important of these is content. The Internet makes it possible to capture vast amounts of content at a very low cost. Three types of content can improve the value proposition of a website—customer feedback, expertise, and entertainment programming.

- *Customer Feedback.* Buyers often trust what other buyers say more than a company's promises. One type of content that can enhance a website is customer testimonials. Remember the leather sofa online? The testimonials of other buyers can build confidence and add to the chances that the purchaser will buy online sight unseen. This is one way that content can be a source of competitive advantage. Being able to interact with like-minded customers by reading their experiences or hearing how they have responded to a new product offering builds a sense of belonging that is otherwise hard to create.
- *Expertise.* The Internet has emerged as a tremendously important learning tool. Fifty-one percent of users compare the Internet to a library.[6] The prime reason many users go to the Web is to gain expertise. Websites that provide new knowledge or unbiased information are highly valuable. Additionally the problem-solving function often involves educating consumers regarding options and implications of various choices. For example, LendingTree.com, the online loan company, provides a help center that includes extensive information and resources about obtaining loans, maintaining good credit, and so forth. Further, the expertise function is not limited to consumer sites. In the case of B2B businesses, websites that facilitate sharing expert knowledge help build a sense of community in industry or professional groups.
- *Entertainment Programming.* The Internet is being used by more and more people as an entertainment medium. With technologies such as streaming media, which allows the Internet to send televisionlike images and sound, computers can provide everything from breaking news to video games to online movies. A study by the Pew Internet and American Life Project indicates that among people using high-speed broadband service, TV viewing is down and online activity has increased. One reason is that the technology is interactive, which means that viewers don't just passively watch, but they use the Web to create art or play online games. Businesses have noticed this trend, of course, and are creating Web content that is not just informative but entertaining.

[5]Bayers, C. 2002. The Last Laugh. *Business 2.0,* September: 86–93.
[6]Greenspan, R. 2003. Internet Not for Everyone. *CyberAtlas,* April 16, www.cyberatlas.com.

These three types of content—customer feedback, expertise, and entertainment programming—are potential sources of competitive advantage. That is, they create advantages by making the value creation process even stronger. Or, if they are handled poorly, they diminish performance.

Business Models

business model
a method and a set of assumptions that explain how a business creates value and earns profits in a competitive environment.

The Internet provides a unique platform or staging area for business activity, which has become, in some ways, like a new marketplace. How do firms conduct business in this new arena? One way of addressing this question is by describing various Internet business models. A business model is a method and a set of assumptions that explain how a business creates value and earns profits in a competitive environment. Some of these models are quite simple and traditional even when applied in an Internet context. Others have features that are unique to the digitally networked, online environment. In this section, we discuss seven Internet business models that account for the vast majority of business conducted online.[7]

- *Commission-Based* **Models** are used by businesses that provide services for a fee. The business is usually a third-party intermediary, and the commission charged is often based on the size of the transaction. The most common type is a brokerage service, such as a stock-broker (e.g., Schwab.com), real estate broker (e.g., Remax.com), or transaction broker (e.g., PayPal .com). This category also includes auction companies such as eBay. In exchange for putting buyers and sellers together, eBay earns a commission.
- *Advertising-Based* **Models** are used by companies that provide content and/or services to visitors and sell advertising to businesses that want to reach those visitors. It is similar to the broadcast television model, in which viewers watch shows produced with advertising dollars. A key difference is that online visitors can interact with both the ads and the content. Large portals such as Yahoo.com are in this category as well as specialty portals such as iNest.com, which provides services for buyers of newly constructed homes. Epinions.com, a recommender system, is just one example of the many types of content that are often available.
- *Markup-Based* **Models** are used by businesses that add value in marketing and sales (rather than production) by acquiring products, marking up the price, and reselling them at a profit. Also known as the merchant model, it applies to both wholesalers and retailers. Amazon.com is the best-known example in this category. It also includes bricks-and-mortar companies such as Wal-Mart, which has a very successful online operation, and vendors whose products are purely digital such as Fonts.com, which sells downloadable fonts and photographs.
- *Production-Based* **Models** are used by companies that add value in the production process by converting raw materials into value-added products. Thus, it is also referred to as the manufacturing model. The Internet adds value to this model in two key ways. First, it lowers marketing costs by enabling direct contact with end users. Second, such direct contact facilitates customization and problem solving. Dell's online ordering system is supported by a state-of-the-art customized manufacturing process. Travelocity uses its rich database of travel options and customer profiles to identify, produce, and deliver unique solutions.
- *Referral-Based* **Models** are used by firms that steer customers to another company for a fee. One type is the affiliate model, in which a vendor pays an affiliate a fee each time a visitor clicks through the affiliate's website and makes a purchase from the vendor. Many name-brand companies use affiliate programs. For example, WeddingChannel.com, which provides a bridal registry where wedding guests can buy gifts from companies such as Tiffany's, Macy's, or Crate & Barrel, receives a fee each time a sale is made through its website. Another referral-based example is Yesmail.com, which generates leads using e-mail marketing.
- *Subscription-Based* **Models** are used by businesses that charge a flat fee for providing either a service or proprietary content. Internet service providers are one example of this model. Companies such as America Online and Earthlink supply Internet connections for fees that are charged whether buyers use the service or not. Subscription-based models are also used by content creators such as the *Economist* or the *New York Times*. Although

---

[7]Afuah, A. & Tucci, C.L. 2003. *Internet Business Models and Strategies* (2nd ed). New York: McGraw-Hill; and, Timmers, P. 1999. *Electronic Commerce*. New York: Wiley.

these recognizable brands often provide free content, only a small portion is available free. The *Economist,* for example, advertises that 70 percent of its content is available only to subscribers.

- *Fee-for-Service–Based* **Models** are used by companies that provide ongoing services similar to a utility company. Unlike the commission-based model, the fee-for-service model involves a pay-as-you-go system. That is, activities are metered and companies pay only for the amount of service used. Application service providers fall in this category. For example, eProject. com provides virtual work space where people in different physical locations can collaborate online. Users essentially rent Internet space, and a host of tools that make it easy to interact, for a fee based on their usage.

Exhibit 3A.2 summarizes the key feature of each Internet business model, suggests what role content may play in the model, and addresses how the four value-adding activities—search, evaluation, problem solving, and transaction—can be sources of competitive advantage.

Exhibit 3A.2
Internet Business Models

Type	Features and Content	Sources of Competitive Advantage
Commission-Based	Charges commissions for brokerage or intermediary services. Adds value by providing expertise and/or access to a wide network of alternatives.	Search Evaluation Problem solving Transaction
Advertising-Based	Web content paid for by advertisers. Adds value by providing free or low-cost content—including customer feedback, expertise, and entertainment programming—to audiences that range from very broad (general content) to highly targeted (specialized content).	Search Evaluation
Markup-Based	Resells marked-up merchandise. Adds value through selection, through distribution efficiencies, and by leveraging brand image and reputation. May use entertainment programming to enhance sales.	Search Transaction
Production-Based	Sells manufactured goods and custom services. Adds value by increasing production efficiencies, capturing customer preferences, and improving customer service.	Search Problem solving
Referral-Based	Charges fees for referring customers. Adds value by enhancing a company's product or service offering, tracking referrals electronically, and generating demographic data. Expertise and customer feedback often included with referral information.	Search Problem solving Transaction
Subscription-Based	Charges fees for unlimited use of service or content. Adds value by leveraging strong brand name, providing high-quality information to specialized markets, or providing access to essential services. May consist entirely of entertainment programming.	Evaluation Problem solving
Fee-for-Service–Based	Charges fees for metered services. Adds value by providing service efficiencies, expertise, and practical outsourcing solutions.	Problem solving Transaction

Sources: Afuah, A. & Tucci, C. L. 2003. *Internet Business Models and Strategies* (2nd ed). New York: McGraw-Hill; Rappa, M. 2005. *Business Models on the Web,* digitalenterprise.org/models/models.html; and Timmers, P. 1999. *Electronic Commerce.* New York: Wiley.

Recognizing a Firm's Intellectual Assets:

Moving beyond a Firm's Tangible Resources

After reading this chapter, you should have a good understanding of:

LO1 Why the management of knowledge professionals and knowledge itself are so critical in today's organizations.

LO2 The importance of recognizing the interdependence of attracting, developing, and retaining human capital.

LO3 The key role of social capital in leveraging human capital within and across the firm.

LO4 The importance of social networks in knowledge management and in promoting career success.

LO5 The vital role of technology in leveraging knowledge and human capital.

LO6 Why "electronic" or "virtual" teams are critical in combining and leveraging knowledge in organizations and how they can be made more effective.

LO7 The challenge of protecting intellectual property and the importance of a firm's dynamic capabilities.

One of the most important trends that managers must consider is the significance of the knowledge worker in today's economy. Managers must both recognize the importance of top talent and provide mechanisms to leverage human capital to innovate and, in the end, develop products and services that create value.

The first section addresses the increasing role of knowledge as the primary means of wealth generation in today's economy. A company's value is not derived solely from its physical assets, such as plant, equipment, and machinery. Rather, it is based on knowledge, know-how, and intellectual assets—all embedded in people.

The second section discusses the key resource itself, human capital, which is the foundation of intellectual capital. We explore ways in which the organization can attract, develop, and retain top talent—three important, interdependent activities. With regard to attracting human capital, we address issues such as "hiring for attitude, training for skill." One of the issues regarding developing human capital is encouraging widespread involvement throughout the organization. Our discussion on retaining human capital addresses issues such as the importance of having employees identify with an organization's mission and values. We also address the value of a diverse workforce.

The attraction, development, and retention of human capital are necessary but not sufficient conditions for organizational success. In the third section we address social capital—networks of relationships among a firm's members. This is especially important where collaboration and sharing information are critical. We address why social capital can be particularly important in attracting human capital and making teams effective. We also address the vital role of social networks—both in improving knowledge management and in promoting career success.

The fourth section addresses the role of technology in leveraging human capital. Examples range from e-mail and the use of networks to facilitate collaboration among individuals to more complex forms of technologies, such as sophisticated knowledge management systems. We discuss how electronic teams can be effectively managed. We also address how technology can help to retain knowledge.

The last section discusses the differences between protection of physical property and intellectual property. We suggest that the development of dynamic capabilities may be one of the best ways that a firm can protect its intellectual property.

Learning from Mistakes

Consider two of the most iconoclastic artists of modern times: Vincent van Gogh and Pablo Picasso.[1] Paintings by both have fetched over $100 million. And both of them were responsible for some of the most iconic images in the art world: Van Gogh's *Self-Portrait* (the one sans the earlobe) and *Starry Night* and Picasso's *The Old Guitarist* and *Guernica*. However, there is an important difference between van Gogh and Picasso. Van Gogh died penniless. Picasso's estate was estimated at $750 million when he died in 1973. Although both were iconoclasts, it was Picasso who was the successful one—at least during his lifetime. What was the difference?

Van Gogh's primary connection to the art world was through his brother. Unfortunately, this connection did not feed directly into the money that could have turned him into a living success. In contrast, Picasso's myriad connections provided him with access to commercial riches. As noted by Gregory Berns in his new book *Iconoclast: A Neuroscientist Reveals How to Think Differently*, "Picasso's wide ranging social network, which included artists, writers, and politicians, meant that he was never more than a few people away from anyone of importance in the world."

In effect, van Gogh was a loner, and the charismatic Picasso was an active member of multiple social circles. In social networking terms, van Gogh was a solitary "node" who had few connections. Picasso, on the other hand, was a "hub" who embedded himself in a vast network that stretched across various social lines. Where Picasso smoothly navigated multiple social circles, van Gogh had to struggle just to maintain connections with even those closest to him. van Gogh inhabited an alien world; whereas, Picasso was a social magnet. And because he knew so many people, the world was at his fingertips. From his perspective, the world was smaller.

Without doubt, there were many reasons why van Gogh died penniless. His mental illness was certainly a factor (which likely contributed to his being a loner). But the broader point for corporations is the following: How do you connect talented loners to networks so that their creativity and ideas can be captured and leveraged? And how do you ensure that your talent is less like van Gogh and more like Picasso?

Managers are always looking for stellar professionals who can take their organizations to the next level. However, attracting talent is a necessary but *not* sufficient condition for success. In today's knowledge economy, it does not matter how big your stock of resources is—whether it be top talent, physical resources, or financial capital. Rather, the question becomes: How good is the organization at attracting top talent and leveraging that talent to produce a stream of products and services valued by the marketplace?

The Central Role of Knowledge in Today's Economy

>LO1

Why the management of knowledge professionals and knowledge itself are so critical in today's organizations.

Central to our discussion is an enormous change that has accelerated over the past few decades and its implications for the strategic management of organizations.[2] For most of the 20th century, managers focused on tangible resources such as land, equipment, and money as well as intangibles such as brands, image, and customer loyalty. Efforts were directed more toward the efficient allocation of labor and capital—the two traditional factors of production.

How times have changed. Today, more than 50 percent of the gross domestic product (GDP) in developed economies is knowledge-based; it is based on intellectual assets and intangible people skills.[3] In the U.S., intellectual and information processes create most of the value for firms in large service industries (e.g., software, medical care, communications, and education), which make up 76 percent of the U.S. GDP. In the manufacturing sector, intellectual activities like R&D, process design, product design, logistics, marketing, and technological innovation produce the preponderance of value added.[4] To drive home the point, Gary Hamel and C. K. Prahalad, two leading writers in strategic management state:

> The machine age was a physical world. It consisted of things. Companies made and distributed things (physical products). Management allocated things (capital budgets); management invested in things (plant and equipment).
>
> In the machine age, people were ancillary, and things were central. In the information age, things are ancillary, knowledge is central. A company's value derives not from things, but from knowledge, know-how, intellectual assets, competencies—all embedded in people.[5]

In the **knowledge economy,** wealth is increasingly created by effective management of knowledge workers instead of by the efficient control of physical and financial assets. The growing importance of knowledge, coupled with the move by labor markets to reward knowledge work, tells us that investing in a company is, in essence, buying a set of talents, capabilities, skills, and ideas—intellectual capital—not physical and financial resources.[6]

Let's provide a few examples. People don't buy Microsoft's stock because of its software factories; it doesn't own any. Rather, the value of Microsoft is bid up because it sets standards for personal-computing software, exploits the value of its name, and forges alliances with other companies. Similarly, Merck didn't become the "Most Admired" company, for seven consecutive years in *Fortune*'s annual survey, because it can manufacture pills, but because its scientists can discover medicines. P. Roy Vagelos, who was CEO of Merck, the $24 billion pharmaceutical giant, during its long run atop the "Most Admired" survey, said, "A low-value product can be made by anyone anywhere. When you have knowledge no one else has access to—that's dynamite. We guard our research even more carefully than our financial assets."[7]

To apply some numbers to our arguments, let's ask, What's a company worth?[8] Start with the "big three" financial statements: income statement, balance sheet, and statement of cash flow. If these statements tell a story that investors find useful, then a company's market value* should roughly (but not precisely, because the market looks forward and the books look backward) be the same as the value that accountants ascribe to it—the book value of the firm. However, this is not the case. A study compared the market value with the book value of 3,500 U.S. companies over a period of two decades. In 1978 the two were similar: Book value was 95 percent of market value. However, market values and book values have diverged significantly. By late 2008, the S&P industrials were—on average—trading at 2.2 times book value.[9] Robert A. Howell, an expert on the changing role of finance and accounting, muses that "The big three financial statements . . . are about as useful as an 80-year-old Los Angeles road map."

The gap between a firm's market value and book value is far greater for knowledge-intensive corporations than for firms with strategies based primarily on tangible assets.[10] Exhibit 4.1 shows the ratio of market-to-book value for some well-known companies. In firms where knowledge and the management of knowledge workers are relatively important contributors to developing products and services—and physical resources are less critical—the ratio of market-to-book value tends to be much higher. Many writers have defined **intellectual capital** as the difference between a firm's market value and book value—that is, a measure of the value of a firm's intangible assets.[11] This broad definition

knowledge economy an economy where wealth is created through the effective management of knowledge workers instead of by the efficient control of physical and financial assets.

intellectual capital the difference between the market value of the firm and the book value of the firm, including assets such as reputation, employee loyalty and commitment, customer relationships, company values, brand names, and the experience and skills of employees.

---

* The market value of a firm is equal to the value of a share of its common stock times the number of shares outstanding. The book value of a firm is primarily a measure of the value of its tangible assets. It can be calculated by the formula: total assets − total liabilities.

Exhibit 4.1

Ratio of Market Value to Book Value for Selected Companies

Company	Annual Sales ($ billions)	Market Value ($ billions)	Book Value ($ billions)	Ratio of Market to Book Value
Genentech	11.7	85.8	11.9	7.2
Google	16.6	101.9	22.7	4.5
Oracle	22.4	85.6	23.1	3.7
Nucor	16.6	11.8	5.1	2.3
Union Pacific (Railroad)	16.2	21.6	15.6	1.4
International Paper	21.9	4.6	8.6	.5

Note: The data on market valuations are as of January 26, 2009. All other financial data are based on the most recently available balance sheets and income statements.

human capital
the individual capabilities, knowledge, skills, and experience of a company's employees and managers.

social capital
the network of friendships and working relationships between talented people both inside and outside the organization.

explicit knowledge
knowledge that is codified, documented, easily reproduced, and widely distributed.

tacit knowledge
knowledge that is in the minds of employees and is based on their experiences and backgrounds.

includes assets such as reputation, employee loyalty and commitment, customer relationships, company values, brand names, and the experience and skills of employees.[12] Thus, simplifying, we have:

$$\text{Intellectual captial} = \text{Market value of firm} - \text{Book value of the firm}$$

How do companies create value in the knowledge-intensive economy? The general answer is to attract and leverage human capital effectively through mechanisms that create products and services of value over time.

First, **human capital** is the "*individual* capabilities, knowledge, skills, and experience of the company's employees and managers."[13] This knowledge is relevant to the task at hand, as well as the capacity to add to this reservoir of knowledge, skills, and experience through learning.[14]

Second, **social capital** is "the network of relationships that individuals have throughout the organization." Relationships are critical in sharing and leveraging knowledge and in acquiring resources.[15] Social capital can extend beyond the organizational boundaries to include relationships between the firm and its suppliers, customers, and alliance partners.[16]

Third is the concept of "knowledge," which comes in two different forms. First, there is **explicit knowledge** that is codified, documented, easily reproduced, and widely distributed, such as engineering drawings, software code, and patents.[17] The other type of knowledge is **tacit knowledge.** That is in the minds of employees and is based on their experiences and backgrounds.[18] Tacit knowledge is shared only with the consent and participation of the individual.

New knowledge is constantly created through the continual interaction of explicit and tacit knowledge. Consider, two software engineers working together on a computer code. The computer code is the explicit knowledge. By sharing ideas based on each individual's experience—that is, their tacit knowledge—they create new knowledge when they modify the code. Another important issue is the role of "socially complex processes," which include leadership, culture, and trust.[19] These processes play a central role in the creation of knowledge.[20] They represent the "glue" that holds the organization together and helps to create a working environment where individuals are more willing to share their ideas, work in teams, and, in the end, create products and services of value.[21]

Numerous books have been written on the subject of knowledge management and the central role that it has played in creating wealth in organizations and countries throughout the developed world.[22] Here, we focus on some of the key issues that organizations must address to compete through knowledge.

We will now turn our discussion to the central resource itself—human capital—and some guidelines on how it can be attracted/selected, developed, and retained. Tom Stewart, editor of the *Harvard Business Review,* noted that organizations must also undergo significant efforts to protect their human capital. A firm may "diversify the ownership of vital knowledge by emphasizing teamwork, guard against obsolescence by developing learning programs, and shackle key people with golden handcuffs."[23] In addition, people are less likely to leave an organization if there are effective structures to promote teamwork and information sharing, strong leadership that encourages innovation, and cultures that demand excellence and ethical behavior. Such issues are central to this chapter. Although we touch on these issues throughout this chapter, we provide more detail in later chapters. We discuss organizational controls (culture, rewards, and boundaries) in Chapter 9, organization structure and design in Chapter 10, and a variety of leadership and entrepreneurship topics in Chapters 11 and 12.

Human Capital: The Foundation of Intellectual Capital

Organizations must recruit talented people—employees at all levels with the proper sets of skills and capabilities coupled with the right values and attitudes. Such skills and attitudes must be continually developed, strengthened, and reinforced, and each employee must be motivated and her efforts focused on the organization's goals and objectives.[24]

The rise to prominence of knowledge workers as a vital source of competitive advantage is changing the balance of power in today's organization. Knowledge workers place professional development and personal enrichment (financial and otherwise) above company loyalty. Attracting, recruiting, and hiring the "best and the brightest," is a critical first step in the process of building intellectual capital. At a symposium for CEOs, Bill Gates said, "The thing that is holding Microsoft back . . . is simply how [hard] we find it to go out and recruit the kind of people we want to grow our research team."[25]

>LO2
The importance of recognizing the interdependence of attracting, developing, and retaining human capital.

Hiring is only the first of three processes in which all successful organizations must engage to build and leverage their human capital. Firms must also *develop* employees to fulfill their full potential to maximize their joint contributions.[26] Finally, the first two processes are for naught if firms can't provide the working environment and intrinsic and extrinsic rewards to *retain* their best and brightest.[27]

These activities are highly interrelated. We would like to suggest the imagery of a three-legged stool (see Exhibit 4.2).[28]If one leg is weak or broken, the stool collapses.

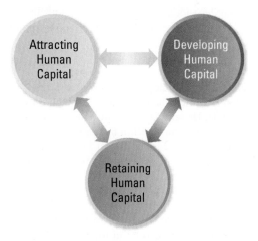

Exhibit 4.2 **Human Capital: Three Interdependent Activities**

Going "Green" Helps Attract Talent

When companies go "green," they often find that the benefits extend beyond the environment. Eco-friendly strategies can also help attract young talent and reduce costs. According to Lindsey Pollack, author of *Getting from College to Career:*

> Students are looking to work for companies that care about the environment. They are almost expecting greenness like they expect work-life balance, ethnic diversity, and globalization.

A recent poll on green employment by MonsterTRAK .com, a job website geared toward students and entry-level hires, found that 80 percent of young professionals are interested in securing a job that has a positive impact on the environment, and 92 percent would be more inclined to work for a company that is environmentally friendly. And, in another survey, 68 percent of Millennials said they would refuse to work for an employer that is not socially responsible.

In response, paper maker NewPage Corp. distributes a brochure that highlights the firm's commitment to environmental responsibility when it recruits on campuses. It showcases the company's new corporate headquarters, in Miamisburg, Ohio, that uses 28 percent to 39 percent less energy than a standard office building and is furnished with environmentally friendly materials. Says NewPage CEO Mark Sunwyn, "At the end of the day, we are competing with everyone else for the best talent, and this is a generation that is very concerned with the environment."

To meet the growing demand for students interested in working for green companies, MonsterTRAK, a unit of the giant employment firm Monster.com, launched GreenCareers. It was the first online recruitment service that focuses on green employment. EcoAmerica and the Environmental Defense Fund, two environmental nonprofits, are adding their expertise in partnership with MonsterTRAK. "EcoAmerica approached MonsterTRAK to create GreenCareers because there is an urgent need to reach and educate environmentally 'agnostic' audiences, in this case college students, about the ways they can address climate change and other serious environmental problems," claims Mark Charnock, vice president and general manager at MonsterTRAK.

Sources: Luhby, T. 2008. How to Lure Gen Y Workers? CNNMoney.com, August 17: np; Mattioli. 2007. How Going Green Draws Talent, Cut Costs. *Wall Street Journal,* November 13: B10; and, Odell, A. M. 2007. Working for the Earth: Green Companies and Green Jobs Attract Employees. www.socialfunds .com, October 9: np.

environmental sustainability

To illustrate such interdependence, poor hiring impedes the effectiveness of development and retention processes. In a similar vein, ineffective retention efforts place additional burdens on hiring and development. Consider the following anecdote, provided by Jeffrey Pfeffer of the Stanford University Business School:

> Not long ago, I went to a large, fancy San Francisco law firm—where they treat their associates like dog doo and where the turnover is very high. I asked the managing partner about the turnover rate. He said, "A few years ago, it was 25 percent, and now we're up to 30 percent." I asked him how the firm had responded to that trend. He said, "We increased our recruiting." So I asked him, "What kind of doctor would you be if your patient was bleeding faster and faster, and your only response was to increase the speed of the transfusion?"[29]

Clearly, stepped-up recruiting is a poor substitute for weak retention. Although there are no simple, easy-to-apply answers, we can learn from what leading-edge firms are doing to attract, develop, and retain human capital in today's highly competitive marketplace.[30] Before moving on, Strategy Spotlight 4.1 addresses the importance of a firm's "green" or environmental sustainability strategy in attracting young talent.

Attracting Human Capital

All we can do is bet on the people we pick. So my whole job is picking the right people.

Jack Welch, former chairman, General Electric Company[31]

The first step in the process of building superior human capital is input control: attracting and selecting the right person. Human resource professionals often approach employee selection from a "lock and key" mentality—that is, fit a key (a job candidate) into a lock (the job). Such an approach involves a thorough analysis of the person and the job. Only then can the right decision be made as to how well the two will fit together. How can you fail, the theory goes, if you get a precise match of knowledge, ability, and skill profiles? Frequently, however, the precise matching approach places its emphasis on task-specific skills (e.g., motor skills, specific information processing capabilities, and communication skills) and puts less emphasis on the broad general knowledge and experience, social skills, values, beliefs, and attitudes of employees.

Many have questioned the precise matching approach. They argue that firms can identify top performers by focusing on key employee mind-sets, attitudes, social skills, and general orientations. If they get these elements right, the task-specific skills can be learned quickly. (This does not imply, however, that task-specific skills are unimportant; rather, it suggests that the requisite skill sets must be viewed as a necessary but not sufficient condition.) This leads us to a popular phrase today and serves as the title of the next section.

"Hire for Attitude, Train for Skill" Organizations are increasingly emphasizing general knowledge and experience, social skills, values, beliefs, and attitudes of employees.[32] Consider Southwest Airlines' hiring practices, which focus on employee values and attitudes. Given its strong team orientation, Southwest uses an "indirect" approach. For example, the interviewing team asks a group of employees to prepare a five-minute presentation about themselves. During the presentations, interviewers observe which candidates enthusiastically support their peers and which candidates focus on polishing their own presentations while the others are presenting.[33] The former are, of course, favored.

Alan Cooper, president of Cooper Software, Inc., in Palo Alto, California, goes further. He cleverly *uses technology* to hone in on the problem-solving ability of his applicants and their attitudes before an interview even takes place. He has devised a "Bozo Filter," an online test that can be applied to any industry. Before you spend time on whether job candidates will work out satisfactorily, find out how their minds work. Cooper advised, "Hiring was a black hole. I don't talk to bozos anymore, because 90 percent of them turn away when they see our test. It's a self-administering bozo filter."[34] How does it work?

> The online test asks questions designed to see how prospective employees approach problem-solving tasks. For example, one key question asks software engineer applicants to design a table-creation software program for Microsoft Word. Candidates provide pencil sketches and a description of the new user interface. Another question used for design communicators asks them to develop a marketing strategy for a new touch-tone phone—directed at consumers in the year 1850. Candidates e-mail their answers back to the company, and the answers are circulated around the firm to solicit feedback. Only candidates with the highest marks get interviews.

Sound Recruiting Approaches and Networking Companies that take hiring seriously must also take recruiting seriously. The number of jobs that successful knowledge-intensive companies must fill is astonishing. Ironically, many companies still have no shortage of applicants. For example, Google, ranked fourth on *Fortune*'s 2009 "100 Best Companies to Work For," still attracts 777,000 applicants a year—even though hiring has slowed.[35] The challenge becomes having the right job candidates, not the greatest number of them.

GE Medical Systems, which builds CT scanners and magnetic resonance imaging (MRI) systems, relies extensively on networking. They have found that current employees are the best source for new ones. Recently, Steven Patscot, head of staffing and leadership development, made a few simple changes to double the number of referrals. First, he simplified the process—no complex forms, no bureaucracy, and so on. Second, he increased incentives. Everyone referring a qualified candidate received a gift certificate from Sears. For referrals who were hired, the "bounty" increases to $2,000. Although this may sound like a lot of money, it is "peanuts" compared to the $15,000 to $20,000 fees that GE typically pays to headhunters for each person hired.[36] Also, when someone refers a former colleague or friend for a job, his or her credibility is on the line. Thus, employees will be careful in recommending people for employment unless they are reasonably confident that these people are good candidates. This provides a good "screen" for the firm in deciding whom to hire. Hiring the right people makes things a lot easier: fewer rules and regulations, less need for monitoring and hierarchy, and greater internalization of organizational norms and objectives.

Consider some of the approaches that companies are currently using to recruit and retain young talent. As baby boomers retire, people in this demographic group are becoming more and more important in today's workforce. We also provide some "tips" on how to get hired. We address these issues in Exhibit 4.3.

Developing Human Capital

It is not enough to hire top-level talent and expect that the skills and capabilities of those employees remain current throughout the duration of their employment. Rather, training and development must take place at all levels of the organization.[37] For example, Solectron assembles printed circuit boards and other components for its Silicon Valley clients.[38] Its employees receive an average of 95 hours of company-provided training each year. Chairman Winston Chen observed, "Technology changes so fast that we estimate 20 percent of an engineer's knowledge becomes obsolete each year. Training is an obligation we owe to our employees. If you want high growth and high quality, then training is a big part of the equation." Although the financial returns on training may be hard to calculate, most experts believe it is essential. One company that has calculated the benefit from training is Motorola. Every dollar spent on training returns $30 in productivity gains over the following three years.

In addition to training and developing human capital, firms must encourage widespread involvement, monitor and track employee development, and evaluate human capital.[39]

Encouraging Widespread Involvement   Developing human capital requires the active involvement of leaders at all levels. It won't be successful if it is viewed only as the responsibility of the human resources department. Each year at General Electric, 200 facilitators, 30 officers, 30 human resource executives, and many young managers actively participate in GE's orientation program at Crotonville, its training center outside New York City. Topics include global competition, winning on the global playing field, and personal examination of the new employee's core values vis-à-vis GE's values. As a senior manager once commented, "There is nothing like teaching Sunday school to force you to confront your own values."

Transferring Knowledge   Often in our lives, we need to either transfer our knowledge to someone else (a child, a junior colleague, a peer) or access accumulated bits of wisdom—someone else's tacit knowledge.[40] This is a vital aspect of developing human capital.[41] However, before we can even begin to plan such a transfer, we need to understand how our brains process incoming information. According to Dorothy A. Leonard of Harvard University:

> Our existing tacit knowledge determines how we assimilate new experiences. Without receptors—hooks on which to hang new information—we may not be able to perceive and process the information. It is like being sent boxes of documents but having no idea how they could or should be organized.

Here are some "best practices" that companies are using to help recruit and retain today's high-maintenance Millennials. This generation has also been termed "Generation Y" or "Echo Boom" and includes people born after 1982:

- ***Don't fudge the sales pitch.*** High-tech presentations and one-on-one attention may be attractive to undergrads, but the pitch had better match the experience. Today's ultraconnected students can get the lowdown on a company by spending five minutes on a social networking site.

- ***Let them have a life.*** Wary of their parents' 80-hour workweeks, Millennials strive for more balance, so liberal vacations are a must. They also want assurances they'll be able to use it. At KPMG, 80 percent of employees used 40 hours of paid time off in the six months through May 2006.

- ***No time clocks, please.*** Recent grads don't mind long hours if they can work them on their own time. Lockheed Martin and its comptroller of the currency allow employees to work nine-hour days and take every other Friday off.

- ***Give them responsibility.*** A chance to work on fulfilling projects and develop ones of their own is important to Millennials. Google urges entry-level employees to spend 20 percent of their time developing new ideas. PepsiCo allows promising young employees to manage small teams in six months.

- ***Feedback and more feedback.*** Career planning advice and frequent performance appraisals are keys to holding on to young hires. Lehman Brothers provides new hires with two mentors—a slightly older peer to help them get settled and a senior employee to give long-term guidance.

- ***Giving back matters.*** Today's altruistic young graduates expect to have opportunities for community service. Wells Fargo encourages its employees to teach financial literacy classes in the community. Accenture and Bain allow employees to consult for nonprofits.

Some advice on how to get hired (based on Fortune's "100 Best Companies to Work For"):

- **It helps to know someone.** Almost all of the "Best Companies" rely extensively on employee referrals. Principal Financial Group and many others get about 40 percent of new hires this way.

- **Play up volunteer work on your resume.** Companies are enthusiastic about community outreach, and they prefer to hire people who are too.

- **Unleash your inner storyteller.** By far the most popular interview style is what's known as behavioral, meaning that you will be asked to describe troublesome situations in past jobs and tell exactly how you handled them.

- **No lone rangers need apply.** By and large, team players are wanted. "I actually count the number of times a candidates says 'I' in an interview," says Adobe's recruiting director, Jeff Vijungco. "We'd rather hear 'we.'"

- **Be open to learning new things.** Showing passion is a must, and most of the "100 Best" pride themselves on creating "learning environments." Thus, talk about the skills you'd like to acquire or polish. Declaring that you're already the best at what you do is a turnoff.

Source: Fisher, A. 2008. How to Get Hired by a "Best" Company. *Fortune,* February 4: 96; and Gerdes, L. 2006. The Top 50 Employers for New College Grads. *BusinessWeek,* September 18: 64–81.

Effective Mentoring: Insights from Two Executives

Two successful executives share their insights by responding to the question: How important is finding—and being—a mentor?

Michelle Coleman Mayes, Senior Vice President and Chief Legal Officer, Allstate Corporation:

It's plural, it isn't dessert—you need more than one. I've found that the people who really get to know you well see things in you that you cannot see in yourself. And, if you think you're perfect, you probably just haven't met the right person to tell you the truth.

You need to think of an image where your hands are stretched both ways. I don't care how old you are,

you're always looking for someone when you need help, and there is always somebody that's been there before you. And you'd better pay it forward, meaning you reach back and you help somebody else.

Sheryl Sandberg, Vice President of Global Online Sales and Operations, Google Inc.

You need different kinds of mentors for different parts of your life—professional and personal. I think the best mentor-mentee relationships are based on really knowing the person in some mutual interest. So at work, the best way for me to develop people is to engage with them substantively on an issue. A better question than "Can you help me?" is "I have this problem and I'd love your views on this." Mentors aren't stamps; you can't collect them indiscriminately. You have to really develop those relationships.

Source: Hymowitz, C. 2007. View from the Top. *Wall Street Journal,* November 19: R6.

This cognitive limitation also applies to the organizational level. When GE Healthcare sets up or transfers operations, it appoints an experienced manager as the "pitcher" and a team in the receiving plant as the "catcher." These two teams work together, often over a period of years—first at the pitcher's location and then at the catcher's. To ensure a smooth transition, the pitching team needs to be sensitive to the catching team's level of experience and familiarity with GE Healthcare procedures.

Strategy Spotlight 4.2 discusses the perspective of two senior executives on how to make mentoring more effective.

Monitoring Progress and Tracking Development Whether a firm uses on-site formal training, off-site training (e.g., universities), or on-the-job training, tracking individual progress—and sharing this knowledge with both the employee and key managers—becomes essential. Like many leading-edge firms, GlaxoSmithKline (GSK) places strong emphasis on broader experiences over longer time periods. Dan Phelan, senior vice president and director of human resources, explained, "We ideally follow a two-plus-two-plus-two formula in developing people for top management positions." This reflects the belief that GSK's best people should gain experience in two business units, two functional units (such as finance and marketing), and in two countries.

Evaluating Human Capital In today's competitive environment, collaboration and interdependence are vital to organizational success. Individuals must share their knowledge and work constructively to achieve collective, not just individual, goals. However, traditional systems evaluate performance from a single perspective (i.e., "top down") and generally don't address the "softer" dimensions of communications and social skills, values, beliefs, and attitudes.[42]

To address the limitations of the traditional approach, many organizations use 360-degree evaluation and feedback systems.[43] Here, superiors, direct reports, colleagues,

Exhibit 4.4
An Excerpt from General Electric's 360-Degree Leadership Assessment Chart

Vision	• Has developed and communicated a clear, simple, customer-focused vision/direction for the organization.
	• Forward-thinking, stretches horizons, challenges imaginations.
	• Inspires and energizes others to commit to Vision. Captures minds. Leads by example.
	• As appropriate, updates Vision to reflect constant and accelerating change affecting the business.

Customer/Quality Focus

Integrity

Accountability/Commitment

Communication/Influence

Shared Ownership/Boundaryless

Team Builder/Empowerment

Knowledge/Expertise/Intellect

Initiative/Speed

Global Mind-Set

Source: Adapted from Slater, R. 1994. *Get Better or Get Beaten:* 152–155. Burr Ridge, IL: Irwin Professional Publishing.

Note: This evaluation system consists of 10 "characteristics"—Vision, Customer/Quality Focus, Integrity, and so on. Each of these characteristics has four "performance criteria." For illustrative purposes, the four performance criteria of "Vision" are included.

and even internal and external customers rate a person's performance.[44] Managers rate themselves to have a personal benchmark. The 360-degree feedback system complements teamwork, employee involvement, and organizational flattening. As organizations continue to push responsibility downward, traditional top-down appraisal systems become insufficient.[45] For example, a manager who previously managed the performance of 3 supervisors might now be responsible for 10 and is less likely to have the in-depth knowledge needed to appraise and develop them adequately. Exhibit 4.4 provides a portion of GE's 360-degree system.

Evaluation systems must also ensure that a manager's success does not come at the cost of compromising the organization's core values. Such behavior generally leads to only short-term wins for both the manager and the organization. The organization typically suffers long-term losses in terms of morale, turnover, productivity, and so on. Accordingly, Merck's former chairman, Ray Gilmartin, told his employees, "If someone is achieving results but not demonstrating the core values of the company, at the expense of our people, that manager does not have much of a career here."

Retaining Human Capital

It has been said that talented employees are like "frogs in a wheelbarrow."[46] They can jump out at any time! By analogy, the organization can either try to force employees to stay in the firm or try to keep them from jumping out by creating incentives.[47] In other words, today's leaders can either provide the work environment and incentives to keep productive employees and management from wanting to bail out, or they can use legal means such as employment contracts and noncompete clauses.[48] Firms must prevent the transfer of valuable and sensitive information outside the organization. Failure to do so would be the neglect of a leader's fiduciary responsibility to shareholders. However, greater efforts should be directed at the former (e.g., good work environment and incentives), but, as we all know, the latter (e.g., employment contracts and noncompete clauses) have their place.[49]

Identifying with an Organization's Mission and Values   People who identify with and are more committed to the core mission and values of the organization are less likely to stray or bolt to the competition. For example, take the perspective of Steve Jobs, Apple's widely admired CEO:[50]

> When I hire somebody really senior, competence is the ante. They have to be really smart. But the real issue for me is: Are they going to fall in love with Apple? Because if they fall in love with Apple, everything else will take care of itself. They'll want to do what's best for Apple, not what's best for them, what's best for Steve, or anyone else.

"Tribal loyalty" is another key factor that links people to the organization.[51] A tribe is not the organization as a whole (unless it is very small). Rather, it is teams, communities of practice, and other groups within an organization or occupation.

Brian Hall, CEO of Values Technology in Santa Cruz, California, documented a shift in people's emotional expectations from work. From the 1950s on, a "task first" relationship—"tell me what the job is, and let's get on with it"—dominated employee attitudes. Emotions and personal life were checked at the door. In the past few years, a "relationship-first" set of values has challenged the task orientation. Hall believes that it will become dominant. Employees want to share attitudes and beliefs as well as workspace.

Challenging Work and a Stimulating Environment   Arthur Schawlow, winner of the 1981 Nobel Prize in physics, was asked what made the difference between highly creative and less creative scientists. His reply: "The labor of love aspect is very important. The most successful scientists often are not the most talented.[52] But they are the ones impelled by curiosity. They've got to know what the answer is."[53] Such insights highlight the importance of intrinsic motivation: the motivation to work on something because it is exciting, satisfying, or personally challenging.[54]

One way firms keep highly mobile employees motivated and challenged is through opportunities that lower barriers to an employee's mobility within a company. For example, Shell Oil Company has created an "open sourcing" model for talent. Jobs are listed on Shell's intranet, and, with a two-month notice, employees can go to work on anything that interests them. Monsanto[55] has developed a similar approach. According to one executive:

> Because we don't have a lot of structure, people will flow toward where success and innovation are taking place. We have a free-market system where people can move, so you have an outflow of people in areas where not much progress is being made. Before, the HR function ran processes like management development and performance evaluation. Now it also facilitates this movement of people.

Exhibit 4.5 lists the best practices that leading-edge organizations are using to create a challenging and stimulating work environment to help attract and retain top young talent.

Financial and Nonfinancial Rewards and Incentives   Financial rewards are a vital organizational control mechanism (as we will discuss in Chapter 9). Money—whether in the form of salary, bonus, stock options, and so forth—can mean many different things to people. It might mean security, recognition, or a sense of freedom and independence.

Paying people more is seldom the most important factor in attracting and retaining human capital.[56] Most surveys show that money is not the most important reason why people take or leave jobs, and that money, in some surveys, is not even in the top 10. Consistent with these findings, Tandem Computers (now part of Hewlett-Packard) typically doesn't tell people being recruited what their salaries would be. People who asked were told that their salaries were competitive. If they persisted along this line of questioning,

Exhibit 4.5
Creating a Challenging and Stimulating Workplace

Company (Industry)	Comments
Lockheed Martin (Defense)	Offers leadership programs in communications, engineering, finance, human resources, information systems, and operations.
Enterprise Rent-a-Car (Transportation)	Management training program amounts to an MBA crash course for executive wannabes. New hires get to run their own business.
Verizon Wireless (Telecommunications)	Verizon Wireless recently launched a retail training program where participants work in as many as three locations over two years.
National Instruments (Technology)	NI puts its money where its mouth is, spending over $30,000 a year to train each participant in its engineering leadership program.
L'Oreal (Consumer Goods)	Rising entry-level marketing stars are put through a fast-paced training program that lasts between 18 months and two years.
Vanguard (Financial Services)	Four extensive rotational training and development programs range from 12 to 24 months in length with three to six rotations.
Adobe Systems (Software)	A culture of openness pervades the firm: The CEO answers e-mails within 24 hours, and employee councils feed management with ideas.
Recreational Equipment (REI) (Outdoor Gear/Equipment)	Winners of challenge grants get up to $300 of gear to tackle an outdoor goal; also offers generous sabbaticals.

Source: O'Brien, J. M. 2008. The Best 100 Companies to Work For. *Fortune,* February 4: 61–94; and Gerdes, L. 2006. The Top 50 Employers for New College Grads. *BusinessWeek,* September 18: 64–81.

they would not be offered a position. Why? Tandem realized a rather simple idea: People who come for money will leave for money.

Another nonfinancial reward is accommodating working families with children. Balancing demands of family and work is a problem at some point for virtually all employees.

Strategy Spotlight 4.3 discusses some of the challenges (and solutions) with the use of flextime. With this popular employment practice, flextime allows employees greater flexibility in when and where they do their work.

Enhancing Human Capital: The Role of Diversity in the Workforce

A combination of demographic trends and accelerating globalization of business has made the management of cultural differences a critical issue.[57] Workforces, which reflect demographic changes in the overall population, will be increasingly heterogeneous along dimensions such as gender, race, ethnicity, and nationality. Demographic trends in the United States indicate a growth in Hispanic Americans from 6.9 million in 1960 to over 35 million in 2000, an expected increase to over 55 million by 2020. Similarly, the Asian-American population should grow to 20 million in 2020 from 12 million in 2000 and only 1.5 million in 1970. And the African-American population is becoming more ethnically heterogeneous. Census estimates project that by 2010 as many as 10 percent of Americans of African descent will be immigrants from Africa or the Caribbean.[58]

strategy spotlight

Solving the Challenges of Flexible Work Arrangements

A recent study by Hewitt Associates, a human resources consulting firm, found that 75 percent of companies offered some kind of flexible work arrangement. However, these policies have earned mixed results. Working remotely can leave employees feeling isolated and managers feeling they lack control. Further, flextimers often find themselves squeezed into policies that are anything but flexible. "The work–life movement has always had a heavy layer of one-size-fits-all-ism," says Stewart D. Friedman, head of the Work/Life Integration Project at the Wharton School at the University of Pennsylvania.

How are companies addressing these challenges? Let's look at two examples:

- Hewlett-Packard offers a personality test so workers can determine whether they are suited to, in effect, toiling in their pajamas. Among other things, the test assesses whether workers can handle limited supervision.

Source: Conlin, M. 2008. Out of Sight, Yes. Out of Mind, No. *Business Week*, February 18: 60; and Conlin, M. 2006. Smashing the Clock. *BusinessWeek*, December 11: 60–68.

- Studies at IBM found that if teams went more than three days without meeting, their happiness and productivity declined. Now managers are required to bring teams together at least once every three days—physically or virtually—for reasons that have nothing to do with completing an assignment.

Below are some suggested best practices or tips for making flextime programs work:

- **Measure.** Before unplugging workers, metrics are key to ensuring that productivity, engagement, and turnover improve.

- **Tailor.** Imposing new work rules rarely pays because managers and workers need to tailor schedules to their needs.

- **Trust.** Inevitably, some untethered workers will slack off. Managers need to trust, then rely on data to assess performance.

- **Educate.** Location-agnostic work is a hard concept to grasp. Thus, refresher courses are a must for managers and workers.

- **Gather.** When workers are nomads, regular gatherings, in person or by videoconference, help retain a team dynamic.

Such demographic changes have implications not only for the labor pool but also for customer bases, which are also becoming more diverse. This creates important organizational challenges and opportunities.

The effective management of diversity can enhance the social responsibility goals of an organization.[59] However, there are many other benefits as well. Six other areas where sound management of diverse workforces can improve an organization's effectiveness and competitive advantages are: (1) cost, (2) resource acquisition, (3) marketing, (4) creativity, (5) problem-solving, and (6) organizational flexibility.

- *Cost Argument.* As organizations become more diverse, firms effective in managing diversity will have a cost advantage over those that are not.
- *Resource Acquisition Argument.* Firms with excellent reputations as prospective employers for women and ethnic minorities will have an advantage in the competition for top talent. As labor pools shrink and change in composition, such advantages will become even more important.
- *Marketing Argument.* For multinational firms, the insight and cultural sensitivity that members with roots in other countries bring to marketing efforts will be very useful. A similar rationale applies to subpopulations within domestic operations.
- *Creativity Argument.* Less emphasis on conformity to norms of the past and a diversity of perspectives will improve the level of creativity.

- **Problem-Solving Argument.** Heterogeniety in decision-making and problem-solving groups typically produces better decisions because of a wider range of perspectives as well as more thorough analysis. Jim Schiro, CEO of PriceWaterhouseCoopers, explains, "When you make a genuine commitment to diversity, you bring a greater diversity of ideas, approaches, and experiences and abilities that can be applied to client problems. After all, six people with different perspectives have a better shot at solving complex problems than sixty people who all think alike."[60]
- **Organizational Flexibility Argument.** With effective programs to enhance workplace diversity, systems become less determinant, less standardized, and therefore more fluid. Such fluidity should lead to greater flexibility to react to environmental changes. Reactions should be faster and less costly.

In the past, a diversity officer ensured compliance with EEOC (Equal Employment Opportunity Commission) requirements or, at best, made minimal efforts to produce the appearance of diversity. Today organizations realize that the role of a Chief Diversity Officer (CDO) can add real value. Strategy Spotlight 4.4 discusses how the role of the CDO at MTV Networks (part of Viacom) has evolved and how its business has benefited from a diverse workforce.

● Workforces are becoming more heterogeneous along dimensions such as gender, race, ethnicity, and nationality.

The Vital Role of Social Capital

>LO3
The key role of social capital in leveraging human capital within and across the firm.

Successful firms are well aware that the attraction, development, and retention of talent *is a necessary but not sufficient condition* for creating competitive advantages.[61] In the knowledge economy, it is not the stock of human capital that is important, but the extent to which it is combined and leveraged. In a sense, developing and retaining human capital becomes less important as key players (talented professionals, in particular) take the role of "free agents" and bring with them the requisite skill in many cases. Rather, the development of social capital (that is, the friendships and working relationships among talented individuals) gains importance, because it helps tie knowledge workers to a given firm.[62] Knowledge workers often exhibit greater loyalties to their colleagues and their profession than their employing organization, which may be "an amorphous, distant, and sometimes threatening entity."[63] Thus, a firm must find ways to create "ties" among its knowledge workers.

Let's look at a hypothetical example. Two pharmaceutical firms are fortunate enough to hire Nobel Prize–winning scientists.[64] In one case, the scientist is offered a very attractive salary, outstanding facilities and equipment, and told to "go to it!" In the second case, the scientist is offered approximately the same salary, facilities, and equipment plus one additional ingredient: working in a laboratory with 10 highly skilled and enthusiastic scientists. Part of the job is to collaborate with these peers and jointly develop promising drug compounds. There is little doubt as to which scenario will lead to a higher probability of retaining the scientist. The interaction, sharing, and collaboration will create a situation in which the scientist will develop firm-specific ties and be less likely to "bolt" for a higher salary offer. Such ties are critical because knowledge-based resources tend to be more tacit in nature, as we mentioned early in this chapter. Therefore, they are much more difficult to

strategy spotlight

MTV: Benefiting from a Diverse Workforce

Managers know that heterogeneous workforces are rich seedbeds for ideas. However, companies seldom tap employees for insights and experiences specific to their cultures. Further, barriers of language, geography, and association often prevent diverse employees from collaborating on innovation efforts.

Chief Diversity Officers (CDOs) are probably more familiar with the cultural breadth and variety of their companies' talent than anyone. Consequently, they are in an excellent position to bring together different groups to produce innovation.

On October 28, 2006, MTV Networks, a unit of Viacom International Inc. announced that Billy Dexter was appointed the firm's first Executive Vice President and Chief Diversity Officer. He will lead MTV's global initiatives to foster the highest levels of diversity throughout every aspect of the business.

Source: Johansson, F . 2005. Masters of the Multicultural. *Harvard Business Review,* 83(10): 18–19; and Anonymous. 2006. MTV Networks Names Billy Dexter as Chief Diversity Officer. *PRNewswire.* October 28. np.

Judy McGrath, Chairman and CEO of MTV Networks states:

> We are completely committed to diversity and inclusion, because it's the most creative and vibrant thing we can do for our future. The audience for our content is increasingly global, diverse in thought, demographic, and lifestyle. Over the years, no other initiative has so enriched MTV Networks, or made us more relevant and successful.

How has MTV Networks benefited from their diversity?

One cross-cultural group discovered marketing opportunities in the similarities between North American country music and Latin American music, which use many of the same instruments, feature singers with similar vocal styles, and—in the U.S. Sunbelt—appeal to much the same audience. Other groups have influenced the multicultural content of Nickelodeon's children's programming. Says Tom Freston, MTV's former CEO, "Those teams are diverse by design to generate innovation. The probability that you will get a good, original, innovative idea with that type of chemistry is simply much higher."

protect against loss (i.e., the individual quitting the organization) than other types of capital, such as equipment, machinery, and land.

Another way to view this situation is in terms of the resource-based view of the firm that we discussed in Chapter 3. That is, competitive advantages tend to be harder for competitors to copy if they are based on "unique bundles" of resources.[65] So, if employees are working effectively in teams and sharing their knowledge and learning from each other, not only will they be more likely to add value to the firm, but they also will be less likely to leave the organization, because of the loyalties and social ties that they develop over time.

How Social Capital Helps Attract and Retain Talent

The importance of social ties among talented professionals creates a significant challenge (and opportunity) for organizations. In *The Wall Street Journal*, Bernard Wysocki described the increase in a type of "Pied Piper Effect," in which teams or networks of people are leaving one company for another.[66] The trend is to recruit job candidates at the crux of social relationships in organizations, particularly if they are seen as having the potential to bring with them valuable colleagues.[67] This is a process that is referred to as "hiring via personal networks." Let's look at one instance of this practice.

> Gerald Eickhoff, founder of an electronic commerce company called Third Millennium Communications, tried for 15 years to hire Michael Reene. Why? Mr. Eickhoff says that he has "these Pied Piper skills." Mr. Reene was a star at Andersen Consulting in the 1980s

Alumni Programs: A Great Way to Stay in Touch

Michael Jacobson had worked in securities practices at Cooley Godward, a Palo Alto, California law firm, for a dozen years. Nobody was happy when he gave notice in 1998. Everyone felt that it would be difficult to get along without him.

However, a few months later, Cooley Godward's managers couldn't have been happier. Why? Jacobson's new job was as general counsel at a little-known online auction site called eBay! When the site needed outside counsel, Jacobsen tapped his former employer. A few months later, Cooley Godward was lead counsel for eBay's record-breaking $1.3 billion initial public offering. "It's a great relationship," says Mark Pitchford, partner and chief operating officer of the firm.

With such a "lucky break," Cooley Godward no longer leaves such matters to chance. In January 2004, it launched an alumni program to help the firm stay in touch

with its former attorneys. Such programs are not particularly new to corporate America. Firms such as McKinsey & Company, Ernst & Young, and Procter & Gamble have had them in place for years. However, as partners at Cooley Godward have found, smaller firms can also benefit from alumni initiatives. "Former employees are a resource," says John Izzo, president of Izzo Consulting, a firm based in Vancouver, Washington. The firm advises small businesses on employee training and retention issues.

Despite the potential benefits of maintaining active contact with former employees, many employers treat them as just another name in the Rolodex—or even worse, as a competitive threat. Izzo warns that this can be a big mistake. Often, he claims, former staffers can act as goodwill ambassadors for their former employers, helping to refer new talent and clients. They may even return at a later point and will require little training. And with the job market now showing signs of improvement and many employees more likely to move on, alumni programs could become very important, especially at firms that have a hard time recruiting and retaining qualified professionals.

Source: Rich, L. 2005. Don't Be a Stranger. *Inc.,* January: 32–33.

---

and at IBM in the 1990s. He built his businesses and kept turning down overtures from Mr. Eickhoff.

However, in early 2000, he joined Third Millennium as chief executive officer, with a salary of just $120,000 but with a 20 percent stake in the firm. Since then, he has brought in a raft of former IBM colleagues and Andersen subordinates. One protégé from his time at Andersen, Mary Goode, was brought on board as executive vice president. She promptly tapped her own network and brought along former colleagues.

Wysocki considers the Pied Piper effect one of the underappreciated factors in the war for talent today. This is because one of the myths of the New Economy is rampant individualism, wherein individuals find jobs on the Internet career sites and go to work for complete strangers. Perhaps, instead of Me Inc., the truth is closer to We Inc.[68]

Another example of social relationships causing human capital mobility is the emigration of talent from an organization to form start-up ventures. Microsoft is perhaps the best-known example of this phenomenon.[69] Professionals frequently leave Microsoft en masse to form venture capital and technology start-ups, called "Baby Bills," built around teams of software developers. For example, Ignition Corporation, of Bellevue, Washington, was formed by Brad Silverberg, a former Microsoft senior vice president. Eight former Microsoft executives, among others, founded the company.

Social relationships can provide an important mechanism for obtaining both resources and information from individuals and organizations outside the boundary of a firm.[70] Strategy Spotlight 4.5 touts the benefits of firms' alumni programs. It describes how eBay's general counsel became an excellent source of business for his prior employer.

Social Networks: Implications for Knowledge Management and Career Success

>LO4

The importance of social networks in knowledge management and in promoting career success.

Managers face many challenges driven by such factors as rapid changes in globalization and technology. Leading a successful company is more than a one-person job. As Tom Malone recently put it in *The Future of Work,* "As managers, we need to shift our thinking from command and control to coordinate and cultivate—the best way to gain power is sometimes to give it away."[71] The move away from top-down bureaucratic control to more open, decentralized network models makes it more difficult for managers to understand how work is actually getting done, who is interacting with whom both within and outside the organization, and the consequences of these interactions for the long-term health of the organization. In short, coordination, cultivation, and collaboration are increasingly becoming the mode of work at every level.[72]

social network analysis analysis of the pattern of social interactions among individuals.

But how can this be done? **Social network analysis** depicts the pattern of interactions among individuals and helps to diagnose effective and ineffective patterns.[73] It helps identify groups or clusters of individuals that comprise the network, individuals who link the clusters, and other network members. It helps diagnose communication patterns and, consequently, communication effectiveness.[74] Such analysis of communication patterns is helpful because the configuration of group members' social ties within and outside the group affects the extent to which members connect to individuals who:

- convey needed resources,
- have the opportunity to exchange information and support,
- have the motivation to treat each other in positive ways, and,
- have the time to develop trusting relationships that might improve the groups' effectiveness.

However, such relationships don't "just happen."[75] Developing social capital requires interdependence among group members. Social capital erodes when people in the network become independent. And increased interactions between members aid in the development and maintenance of mutual obligations in a social network.[76]

Let's take a brief look at a simplified network analysis to get a grasp of the key ideas. In Exhibit 4.6, the links are used to depict informal relationships among individuals involving communication flows, personal support, and advice networks. There may be

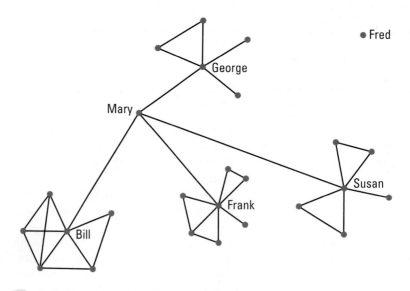

Exhibit 4.6 A Simplified Social Network

some individuals with literally no linkages, such as Fred. These individuals are typically labeled "isolates." However, most people do have some linkages with others.

To simplify, there are two primary types of mechanisms through which social capital will flow: *closure relationships* (depicted by Bill, Frank, George, and Susan) and *bridging relationships* (depicted by Mary). As we can see, in the former relationships one member is central to the communication flows in a group. In contrast, in the latter relationship, one person "bridges" or brings together groups that would have been otherwise unconnected.

Both closure and bridging relationships have important implications for the effective flow of information in organizations and for the management of knowledge. We will now briefly discuss each of these types of relationships. We will also address some of the implications that understanding social networks has for one's career success.

Closure   With **closure,** many members have relationships (or ties) with other members. As indicated in Exhibit 4.6, Bill's group would have a higher level of closure than Frank, Susan, or George's groups because more group members are connected to each other. Through closure, group members develop strong relationships with each other, high levels of trust, and greater solidarity. High levels of trust help to ensure that informal norms in the group are easily enforced and there is less "free riding." Social pressure will prevent people from withholding effort or shirking their responsibilities. In addition, people in the network are more willing to extend favors and "go the extra mile" on a colleague's behalf because they are confident that their efforts will be reciprocated by another member in their group. Another benefit of a network with closure is the high level of emotional support. This becomes particularly valuable when setbacks occur that may destroy morale or an unexpected tragedy happens that might cause the group to lose its focus. Social support helps the group to rebound from misfortune and get back on track.

But high levels of closure often come with a price. Groups that become too closed can become insular. They cut themselves off from the rest of the organization and fail to share what they are learning from people outside their group. Research shows that while managers need to encourage closure up to a point, if there is too much closure, they need to encourage people to open up their groups and infuse new ideas through bridging relationships.[77]

closure the degree to which all members of a social network have relationships (or ties) with other group members.

Bridging Relationships   The closure perspective rests on an assumption that there is a high level of similarity among group members. However, members can be quite heterogeneous with regard to their positions in either the formal or informal structures of the group or the organization. Such heterogeneity exists because of, for example, vertical boundaries (different levels in the hierarchy) and horizontal boundaries (different functional areas).

Bridging relationships, in contrast to closure, stresses the importance of ties connecting people. Employees who bridge disconnected people tend to receive timely, diverse information because of their access to a wide range of heterogeneous information flows. Such bridging relationships span a number of different types of boundaries.

The University of Chicago's Ron Burt originally coined the term **"structural holes"** to refer to the social gap between two groups. Structural holes are common in organizations. When they occur in business, managers typically refer to them as "silos" or "stovepipes." Sales and engineering are a classic example of two groups whose members traditionally interact with their peers rather than across groups.

A study that Burt conducted at Raytheon, a $21 billion U.S. electronics company and military contractor, provides further insight into the benefits of bridging.[78]

bridging relationships relationships in a social network that connect otherwise disconnected people.

structural holes social gaps between groups in a social network where there are few relationships bridging the groups.

> Burt studied several hundred managers within Raytheon's supply chain group and asked each manager to write down ideas to improve the company's supply chain management. Then he asked two Raytheon executives to rate the ideas. The conclusion: *The best suggestions consistently came from managers who discussed ideas outside their regular work group.*

The Value (and Limitations) of Informal Friendships in Organizations

Rope courses and Outward Bound-type activities help white-collar workers develop corporate collegiality through socializing, sweating and sharing stressful situations. People go in as co-workers and come out as friends. However, wholesale congeniality can actually make teams *less* effective.

Recently, Joe Labianca (now at the University of Kentucky) and two colleagues studied 60 teams in 11 companies representing a wide variety of industries. In the most effective teams, about half of the relationships among members were close enough to be considered friendships. However, in teams where the number of friendships approached 100 percent, performance dropped dramatically. Why? Such groups suffered because they were insular, impermeable to outside influences, and unhealthily self-reliant. Members may have developed a high level of trust and commitment with each other but they were too dependent on their own members for new insights and initiatives. At times, those problems can be avoided by brainstorming or by assigning someone in the group to be a devil's advocate. But where friendships are especially close, even those techniques are unlikely to produce dramatically differing perspectives.

Sources: Labianca, J . 2004. The Ties That Bind. *Harvard Business Review,* 82(10): 19; Oh, H. Chung, M., & Labianca, G . 2004. Group Social Capital and Group Effectiveness: The Role of Informal Socializing Ties. *Academy of Management Journal,* 47(6): 860–875; and Labianca, J . 2007. Personal communication. February 28.

The friendships that benefit teams most are formed *outside the group.* Business-centered relationships with people in other parts of the company are important for transmitting simple work flow information. But even more important are relationships that extend into the social sphere—to lunches and dinners and after-work drinks. Such interactions are especially valuable sources of social capital. Team members who socialize in this way, particularly with top managers and with leaders of other teams play a key role in bridging groups and individuals who otherwise would be unconnected to their own group. This enables them to bring back to their groups strategic information, task-related advice, and political and social support.

Higher-level managers can't require employees to befriend people outside their own domains. However, they can encourage it. Team leaders should be told that developing a broad social network is part of their job. Managers should set aside funds for cross-functional social activities and create opportunities for employees to bond around common hobbies or pursuits. When composing teams, leaders should consider whom—as well as what—potential members know. And mentoring programs should aim to place company fledglings beneath the wings of veterans from other departments rather than with people they work with every day.

To sum up, there is nothing wrong with Outward Bound activities. However, instead of braving the wilderness, teams should venture into the far corners of their own organization!

Burt found that Raytheon managers were good at thinking of ideas but bad at developing them. Too often, Burt said, the managers discussed their ideas with colleagues already in their informal discussion network. Instead, he said, they should have had discussions outside their typical contacts, particularly with an informal boss, or someone with enough power to be an ally but not an actual supervisor.

Strategy Spotlight 4.6 addresses the value of informal friendships as an effective source of social capital. Interestingly, it also discusses the downside of insular, self-reliant groups.

Before we address the implications of social network theory for managers' career success, one might ask: Which is the more valuable mechanism to develop and nurture social capital—closure or bridging relationships? As with many aspects of strategic management, the answer becomes: "It all depends." So let's consider a few contingent issues.[79]

First, consider firms in competitive environments characterized by rapidly changing technologies and markets. Such firms should bridge relationships across networks because they need a wide variety of timely sources of information. Also, innovation is facilitated if there are multiple, interdisciplinary perspectives. On the other hand, firms competing in a stable environment would typically face a rather small amount of unpredictability.

Thus, the cohesive ties associated with network closure would help to ensure the timely and effective implementation of strategies.

A second contingent factor would be the type of business strategies that a firm may choose to follow (a topic that we address next in Chapter 5). Managers with social networks characterized by closure would be in a preferred position if their firm is following an overall low cost strategy.[80] Here, there is a need for control and coordination to implement strategies that are rather constrained by pressures to reduce costs. Alternatively, the uncertainties generally associated with differentiation strategies (i.e., creating products that are perceived by customers as unique and highly valued) would require a broad range of information sources and inputs. Social networks characterized by bridging relationships across groups would access the diverse informational sources needed to deal with more complex, multifaceted strategies.

A caveat: In both contingencies that we have discussed—competitive environment and business strategy—closure and bridging relationships across groups are necessary. Our purpose is to address where one type should be more dominant.

Implications for Career Success Effective social networks provide many advantages.[81] They can also play a key role in an individual's career advancement and success. From an individual's perspective, social networks deliver three unique advantages: private information, access to diverse skill sets, and power.[82] Managers see these advantages at work every day but might not consider how their networks regulate them.

Private Information We make judgments, using both public and private information. Today, public information is available from many sources, including the Internet. However, since it is so accessible, public information offers less competitive advantage than it used to.

In contrast, private information from personal contacts can offer something not found in publicly available sources, such as the release date of a new product or knowledge about what a particular interviewer looks for in candidates. Private information can give managers an edge, though it is more subjective than public information since it cannot be easily verified by independent sources, such as Dunn & Bradstreet. Consequently the value of your private information to others—and the value of others' private information to you—depends on how much trust exists in the network of relationships.

Access to Diverse Skill Sets Linus Pauling, one of only two people to win a Nobel Prize in two different areas and considered one of the towering geniuses of the 20th century, attributed his creative success not to his immense brainpower or luck but to his diverse contacts. He said, "The best way to have a good idea is to have a lot of ideas."

While expertise has become more specialized during the past 15 years, organizational, product, and marketing issues have become more interdisciplinary. This means that success is tied to the ability to transcend natural skill limitations through others. Highly diverse network relationships, therefore, can help you develop more complete, creative, and unbiased perspectives on issues. Trading information or skills with people whose experiences differ from your own, provides you with unique, exceptionally valuable resources. It is common for people in relationships to share their problems. If you know enough people, you will begin to see how the problems that another person is struggling with can be solved by the solutions being developed by others. If you can bring together problems and solutions, it will greatly benefit your career.

Power Traditionally, a manager's power was embedded in a firm's hierarchy. But, when corporate organizations became flatter, more like pancakes than pyramids, that power was repositioned in the network's brokers (people who bridged multiple networks), who could adapt to changes in the organization, develop clients, and synthesize opposing points of view. Such brokers weren't necessarily at the top of the hierarchy or experts in their fields, but they linked specialists in the firm with trustworthy and informative relationships.[83]

Developing Social Capital: Do Women and Men Differ?

Several years ago, Boris Groysberg conducted a study in which he warned managers about the risks associated with hiring star performers away from companies. His research investigated more than 1,000 star stock analysts, and he found that when one of them switches companies, not only does the star's performance plunge, but also the market value of the star's new company declines. In addition, the players don't tend to stay with their new firms very long—despite the generous pay packages that lured them in the first place. So everyone loses out.

However, when Groysberg further analyzed the data, he gained some new insights. One group of analysts maintained their stardom after changing employers: women. Unlike their male counterparts, female stars who switched firms performed just as well, in aggregate, as those who stayed put.

Why the gender discrepancy? There were two explanations. *First, the best female analysts appear to have built their franchises on portable, external relationships with clients and companies they covered—rather than on rela-tionships within their firms.* In contrast, male analysts built up greater firm- and team-specific human capital. That is, they invested more in internal networks and unique capabilities and resources of the firms where they worked.

Second, women took greater care when assessing a prospective employer. They evaluated their options more carefully and analyzed a wider range of factors than men did before deciding to uproot themselves from a firm where they had been successful. Female star analysts, it seems, take their work environment more seriously yet rely on it less than male stars do. And they tend to look for a firm that will allow them to keep building their successful franchise their own way.

There is a clear explanation as to why the female analysts spent more time developing their external networks. Most salespeople, traders, and investment bankers are men. And men tend to spend more time with other men. Not surprisingly, the star women in the study were generally thwarted in their efforts to integrate themselves into the existing power structure. Thus, they went to greater lengths to cultivate relationships with clients and contacts at the companies they covered. Their decision to maintain such an external focus rested on four main factors: uneasy in-house relationships, poor mentorships, neglect by colleagues, and a vulnerable position in the labor market.

Source: Groysberg, B . 2008. How Star Women Build Portable Skills. *Harvard Business Review*, 86 (2): 74–81.

Most personal networks are highly clustered; that is, an individual's friends are likely to be friends with one another as well. Most corporate networks are made up of several clusters that have few links between them. Brokers are especially powerful because they connect separate clusters, thus stimulating collaboration among otherwise independent specialists.

Before moving on, Strategy Spotlight 4.7 discusses an interesting research study. It points out how women may differ from men in how they develop their social networks.

The Potential Downside of Social Capital

We'd like to close our discussion of social capital by addressing some of its limitations. First, some firms have been adversely affected by very high levels of social capital because it may breed **"groupthink"**—a tendency not to question shared beliefs.[84] Such thinking may occur in networks with high levels of closure where there is little input from people outside of the network. In effect, too many warm and fuzzy feelings among group members prevent people from rigorously challenging each other. People are discouraged from engaging in the "creative abrasion" that Dorothy Leonard of Harvard University describes as a key source of innovation.[85] Two firms that were well known for their collegiality, strong sense of employee membership, and humane treatment—Digital Equipment (now part of Hewlett-Packard) and Polaroid—suffered greatly from market misjudgments and strategic errors. The aforementioned aspects of their culture contributed to their problems.

groupthink
a tendency in an organization for individuals not to question shared beliefs.

Second, if there are deep-rooted mindsets, there would be a tendency to develop dysfunctional human resource practices. That is, the organization (or group) would continue to hire, reward, and promote like-minded people who tend to further intensify organizational inertia and erode innovation. Such homogeneity would increase over time and decrease the effectiveness of decision-making processes.

Third, the socialization processes (orientation, training, etc.) can be expensive in terms of both financial resources and managerial commitment. Such investments can represent a significant opportunity cost that should be evaluated in terms of the intended benefits. If such expenses become excessive, profitability would be adversely affected.

Finally, individuals may use the contacts they develop to pursue their own interests and agendas that may be inconsistent with the organization's goals and objectives. Thus, they may distort or selectively use information to favor their preferred courses of action or withhold information in their own self-interest to enhance their power to the detriment of the common good. Drawing on our discussion of social networks, this is particularly true in an organization that has too many bridging relationships but not enough closure relationships. In high closure groups, it is easier to watch each other to ensure that illegal or unethical acts don't occur. By contrast, bridging relationships make it easier for a person to play one group or individual off on another, with no one being the wiser.[86] We will discuss some behavioral control mechanisms in Chapter 9 (rewards, control, boundaries) that reduce such dysfunctional behaviors and actions.[87]

Using Technology to Leverage Human Capital and Knowledge

>LO5
The vital role of technology in leveraging knowledge and human capital.

Sharing knowledge and information throughout the organization can be a means of conserving resources, developing products and services, and creating new opportunities. In this section we will discuss how technology can be used to leverage human capital and knowledge within organizations as well as with customers and suppliers beyond their boundaries.

Using Networks to Share Information

As we all know, e-mail is an effective means of communicating a wide variety of information. It is quick, easy, and almost costless. Of course, it can become a problem when employees use it extensively for personal reasons. And we all know how fast jokes or rumors can spread within and across organizations!

Below is an example of how a CEO curbed what he felt was excessive e-mail use in his firm.[88]

> Scott Dockter, CEO of PBD Worldwide Fulfillment Services in Alpharetta, Georgia, launched "no e-mail Friday." Why? He suspected that overdependence on e-mail at PBD, which offers services such as call center management and distribution, was hurting productivity and, perhaps, sales. Accordingly, he instructed his 275 employees to pick up the phone or meet in person each Friday, and reduce e-mail use the rest of the time.
>
> That was tough to digest, especially for the younger staffers. "We discovered a lot of introverts . . . who had drifted into a pattern of communicating by e-mail," says Dockter. "However, in less than four months, the simple directive resulted in quicker problem-solving, better teamwork, and, best of all, happier customers." "Our relationship with PBD is much stronger," says Cynthia Fitzpatrick of Crown Financial Ministries. "You can't get to know someone through e-mail."

E-mail can also cause embarrassment—if one is not careful. Consider the plights of Countrywide Financial Corp's embattled (and recently deposed) CEO and a potential CEO of another firm. The message certainly has a cautionary tone (Strategy Spotlight 4.8)

Email Faux Pas: How Countrywide's CEO and a "Potential CEO" Blew It

Countrywide Financial's CEO

The chairman of beleaguered Countrywide Financial Corporation raised eyebrows and tempers with his caustic reply to an e-mail plea from a man about to lose his home. "Disgusting," Angelo Mozilo wrote in his inadvertent reply to Daniel Bailey Jr., who had requested a modification in his adjustable-rate mortgage. He contended that he didn't fully understand the terms, was wrongly told he could refinance after a year, and was on the verge of losing his home of 16 years because of the steep payments. Bailey sent his e-mail to 20 Countrywide addresses. He used language from a form letter on the website LoanSafe.org, which offers advice to borrowers in trouble.

Countrywide said that such mass e-mails had flooded its inboxes and disrupted operations. Mozilo wrote: "This is unbelievable. Most of these letters now have the same wording. Obviously they are being counseled by some person or by the Internet. Disgusting." Unfortunately, Mozilo clicked "Reply" instead of "Forward"—sending his comments back to Bailey.

Bailey posted the response on a LoanSafe forum—touching off a furor on housing websites. Countrywide issued a statement saying the company and Mozilo "regret any misunderstanding caused by his inadvertent response to an e-mail by Mr. Bailey. Countrywide is actively working to help borrowers like Mr. Bailey keep their homes."

Sources: Anonymous. 2008. Countrywide CEO Mozilo Criticizes e-Mail. biz .yahoo.com, May 21: np; Angelo Mozilo, en.wikipedia.org, np; Barr, A. & Goldstein, S. 2008. Bank of America to Buy Countrywide. www.marketwatch .com, January 11: np; and Goldsmith, M . 2009. How Not to Lose the Top Job. *Harvard Business Review,* 87(1): 72–80.

Countrywide lost $1.2 billion in the third quarter of 2007 and another $222 million in the fourth quarter as the subprime mortgage crisis hit. And the firm's stock dropped 80 percent between February and the end of the 2007. During the same period, Mozilo received a $1.7 million salary and $20 million in performance-based stock awards and sold $121 million in stock. He was forced out of Countrywide on July 1, 2008, at which time his firm was acquired by Bank of America. As a footnote, Henry G. Cisneros, a former HUD chairman and member of the Countrywide board of directors, described Mozilo as "sick with stress—the final chapter of his life is the infamy that's been brought on him, or that he brought on himself." CNN named Mozilo as one of the "Ten Most Wanted: Culprits" of the 2008 financial collapse in the United States.

The Derailed "CEO Candidate"

Marshall Goldsmith, one of the world's best-known executive coaches, relates an example of how an executive derailed his successful career at a firm by carelessly sending a "toxic" email:

> I witnessed a series of e-mails between a potential CEO and a friend inside the company. The first e-mail to the friend provided an elaborate description of "why the current CEO is an idiot." The friend sent a reply. Several rounds of e-mails followed. Then the friend sent an e-mail containing a funny joke. The potential CEO decided that the current CEO would love this joke and forwarded it to him. You can guess what happened next. The CEO scrolled down the e-mail chain and found the "idiot" message. The heir apparent was gone in a week.

E-mail can, however, be a means for top executives to communicate information efficiently. For example, Martin Sorrell, chairman of WPP Group PLC, a $2.4 billion advertising and public relations firm, is a strong believer in the use of e-mail.[89] He e-mails all of his employees once a month to discuss how the company is doing, address specific issues, and offer his perspectives on hot issues, such as new business models for the Internet. He believes that it keeps people abreast of what he is working on.

Technology can also enable much more sophisticated forms of communication in addition to knowledge sharing. Buckman Laboratories is a $464 million specialty chemicals company based in Memphis, Tennessee, with approximately 1,450 employees in over 100 countries. Buckman has successfully used its global knowledge sharing network—known as K'Netix—to enhance its competitive advantages:[90]

> Here's an example of how the network can be applied. One of Buckman's paper customers in Michigan realized that the peroxide it was adding to remove ink from old magazines was

no longer working. A Buckman sales manager presented this problem to the knowledge network. Within two days, salespeople from Belgium and Finland identified a likely cause: Bacteria in the paper slurry was producing an enzyme that broke down the peroxide. The sales manager recommended a chemical to control the bacteria, solving the problem. You can imagine how positive the customer felt about Buckman. And with the company and the customer co-creating knowledge, a new level of trust and value can emerge.

Electronic Teams: Using Technology to Enhance Collaboration

Technology enables professionals to work as part of electronic, or virtual, teams to enhance the speed and effectiveness with which products are developed. For example, Microsoft has concentrated much of its development on **electronic teams** (or e-teams) that are networked together.[91] This helps to accelerate design and testing of new software modules that use the Windows-based framework as their central architecture. Microsoft is able to foster specialized technical expertise while sharing knowledge rapidly throughout the firm. This helps the firm learn how its new technologies can be applied rapidly to new business ventures such as cable television, broadcasting, travel services, and financial services.

What are electronic teams (or e-teams)? There are two key differences between e-teams and more traditional teams:[92]

- E-team members either work in geographically separated work places or they may work in the same space but at different times. E-teams may have members working in different spaces and time zones, as is the case with many multinational teams.
- Most of the interactions among members of e-teams occur through electronic communication channels such as fax machines and groupware tools such as e-mail, bulletin boards, chat, and videoconferencing.

E-teams have expanded exponentially in recent years.[93] Organizations face increasingly high levels of complex and dynamic change. E-teams are also effective in helping businesses cope with global challenges. Most e-teams perform very complex tasks and most knowledge-based teams are charged with developing new products, improving organizational processes, and satisfying challenging customer problems. For example, Eastman Kodak's e-teams design new products, Hewlett Packard's e-teams solve clients' computing problems, and Sun Microsystems' e-teams generate new business models.

Advantages   There are multiple advantages of e-teams.[94] In addition to the rather obvious use of technology to facilitate communications, the potential benefits parallel the other two major sections in this chapter—human capital and social capital.

First, e-teams are less restricted by the geographic constraints that are placed on face-to-face teams. Thus, e-teams have the potential to acquire a broader range of "human capital" or the skills and capacities that are necessary to complete complex assignments. So, e-team leaders can draw upon a greater pool of talent to address a wider range of problems since they are not constrained by geographic space. Once formed, e-teams can be more flexible in responding to unanticipated work challenges and opportunities because team members can be rotated out of projects when demands and contingencies alter the team's objectives.

Second, e-teams can be very effective in generating "social capital"—the quality of relationships and networks that leaders and team members form. Such capital is a key lubricant in work transactions and operations. Given the broader boundaries associated with e-teams, members and leaders generally have access to a wider range of social contacts than would be typically available in more traditional face-to-face teams. Such contacts are often connected to a broader scope of clients, customers, constituents, and other key stakeholders.

>LO6
Why "electronic" or "virtual" teams are critical in combining and leveraging knowledge in organizations and how they can be made more effective.

electronic teams
a team of individuals that completes tasks primarily through e-mail communication.

Challenges However, there are challenges associated with making e-teams effective. Successful action by both traditional teams and e-teams requires that:

- Members *identify* who among them can provide the most appropriate knowledge and resources, and,
- E-team leaders and key members know how to *combine* individual contributions in the most effective manner for a coordinated and appropriate response.

Group psychologists have termed such activities "identification and combination" activities and teams that fail to perform them face a "process loss."[95] Process losses prevent teams from reaching high levels of performance because of inefficient interaction dynamics among team members. Such poor dynamics require that some collective energy, time, and effort be devoted to dealing with team inefficiencies, thus diverting the team away from its objectives. For example, if a team member fails to communicate important information at critical phases of a project, other members may waste time and energy. This can lead to conflict and resentment as well as to decreased motivation to work hard to complete tasks.

The potential for process losses tends to be more prevalent in e-teams than in traditional teams because the geographical dispersion of members increases the complexity of establishing effective interaction and exchanges. Generally, teams suffer process loss because of low cohesion, low trust among members, a lack of appropriate norms or standard operating procedures, or a lack of shared understanding among team members about their tasks. With e-teams, members are more geographically or temporally dispersed, and the team becomes more susceptible to the risk factors that can create process loss. Such problems can be exacerbated when team members have less than ideal competencies and social skills. This can erode problem-solving capabilities as well as the effective functioning of the group as a social unit.

Codifying Knowledge for Competitive Advantage

There are two different kinds of knowledge. Tacit knowledge is embedded in personal experience and shared only with the consent and participation of the individual. Explicit (or codified) knowledge, on the other hand, is knowledge that can be documented, widely distributed, and easily replicated. One of the challenges of knowledge-intensive organizations is to capture and codify the knowledge and experience that, in effect, resides in the heads of its employees. Otherwise, they will have to constantly "reinvent the wheel," which is both expensive and inefficient. Also, the "new wheel" may not necessarily be superior to the "old wheel."[96]

Once a knowledge asset (e.g., a software code or processes) is developed and paid for, it can be reused many times at very low cost, assuming that it doesn't have to be substantially modified each time. Let's take the case of a consulting company, such as Accenture (formerly Andersen Consulting).[97] Since the knowledge of its consultants has been codified and stored in electronic repositories, it can be employed in many jobs by a huge number of consultants. Additionally, since the work has a high level of standardization (i.e., there are strong similarities across the numerous client engagements), there is a rather high ratio of consultants to partners. For example, the ratio of consultants to partners is roughly 30, which is quite high. As one might expect, there must be extensive training of the newly hired consultants for such an approach to work. The recruits are trained at Accenture's Center for Professional Education, a 150-acre campus in St. Charles, Illinois. Using the center's knowledge-management respository, the consultants work through many scenarios designed to improve business processes. In effect, the information technologies enable the consultants to be "implementers, not inventors."

Access Health, a call-in medical center, also uses technology to capture and share knowledge. When someone calls the center, a registered nurse uses the company's "clinical

How 3M Retains Knowledge

As the issue of retiring employees becomes more critical at 3M, retaining employee knowledge has become a high priority. 3M applies what it calls high-tech, low-tech, and no-tech methods to a gamut of knowledge-retention measures.

"No-tech tools like storytelling work best for getting to that deep, tactical knowledge. Searchable knowledge bases are the best tools for knowledge that can be written down," according to Barry Dayton, head of 3M's knowledge-management program.

The company's searchable knowledge base, called Maven, makes the job information gleaned from 2,000 technical-service engineers across the globe accessible to all 3M employees. That's a huge business advantage in an industry where about 30 percent of U.S.-based technical-service engineers are set to retire soon, says Dayton.

Maven is a high-tech extension of a database system already in place at 3M's call centers. Historically, if call center representatives couldn't find an answer to a technical question, they'd call a technical-service

engineer. "The rep called a favorite tech engineer and that person emailed them a file or PDF," Dayton says. "With this new process, that information goes into a corporate knowledge base that the whole company can search."

Another tool in the 3M knowledge retention arsenal is storytelling—considerably less formal than Maven. How does it work? A 3M department will identify business scenarios that, though they don't crop up often, happen often enough to merit consideration. And when they do come up, they can throw a wrench into day-to-day plant operations. Examples include a switchover to a new machine or a repair to production equipment that takes it offline.

After situations are identified, Dayton's department creates groups of experts—including production, maintenance, and engineering employees who previously encountered similar situations. They sit in a conference room and have facilitators ask them questions. Software is used to map out their diagnosis of what happened and what they did as a result. "We polish that up a little bit and publish it on their plant portal so that operators, in their spare time or when something happens, can do a quick search," says Dayton.

Source: Thilmany, J . 2008. Passing on Know-How: Knowledge Retention Strategies Can Keep Employees' Workplace-Acquired Wisdom from Walking Out the Door When They Retire. *HR Magazine*, June: np.

decision architecture" to assess the caller's symptoms, rule out possible conditions, and recommend a home remedy, doctor's visit, or trip to the emergency room. The company's knowledge repository contains algorithms of the symptoms of more than 500 illnesses. According to CEO Joseph Tallman, "We are not inventing a new way to cure disease. We are taking available knowledge and inventing processes to put it to better use." The software algorithms were very expensive to develop, but the investment has been repaid many times over. The first 300 algorithms that Access Health developed have each been used an average of 8,000 times a year. Further, the company's paying customers—insurance companies and provider groups—save money because many callers would have made expensive trips to the emergency room or the doctor's office had they not been diagnosed over the phone.

The large number of baby boomers retiring over the next several years creates many key challenges for organizations. Strategy Spotlight 4.9 discusses what 3M is doing to help retain key knowledge that might otherwise be lost when boomers leave the firm.

We close this section with a series of questions managers should consider in determining (1) how effective their organization is in attracting, developing, and retaining human capital and (2) how effective they are in leveraging human capital through social capital and technology. These questions, included in Exhibit 4.7, summarize some of the key issues addressed in this chapter.

Human Capital

Recruiting "Top-Notch" Human Capital

- Does the organization assess attitude and "general makeup" instead of focusing primarily on skills and background in selecting employees at all levels?
- How important are creativity and problem-solving ability? Are they properly considered in hiring decisions?
- Do people throughout the organization engage in effective networking activities to obtain a broad pool of worthy potential employees? Is the organization creative in such endeavors?

Enhancing Human Capital through Employee Development

- Does the development and training process inculcate an "organizationwide" perspective?
- Is there widespread involvement, including top executives, in the preparation and delivery of training and development programs?
- Is the development of human capital effectively tracked and monitored?
- Are there effective programs for succession at all levels of the organization, especially at the top-most levels?
- Does the firm effectively evaluate its human capital? Is a 360-degree evaluation used? Why? Why not?
- Are mechanisms in place to assure that a manager's success does not come at the cost of compromising the organization's core values?

Retaining the Best Employees

- Are there appropriate financial rewards to motivate employees at all levels?
- Do people throughout the organization strongly identify with the organization's mission?
- Are employees provided with a stimulating and challenging work environment that fosters professional growth?
- Are valued amenities provided (e.g., flex time, child-care facilities, telecommuting) that are appropriate given the organization's mission, strategy, and how work is accomplished?
- Is the organization continually devising strategies and mechanisms to retain top performers?

Social Capital

- Are there positive personal and professional relationships among employees?
- Is the organization benefiting (or being penalized) by hiring (or by voluntary turnover) en masse?
- Does an environment of caring and encouragement rather than competition enhance team performance?
- Do the social networks within the organization have the appropriate levels of closure and bridging relationships?
- Does the organization minimize the adverse effects of excessive social capital, such as excessive costs and "groupthink"?

Technology

- Has the organization used technologies such as e-mail and networks to develop products and services?
- Does the organization effectively use technology to transfer best practices across the organization?
- Does the organization use technology to leverage human capital and knowledge both within the boundaries of the organization and among its suppliers and customers?
- Has the organization effectively used technology to codify knowledge for competitive advantage?
- Does the organization try to retain some of the knowledge of employees when they decide to leave the firm?

Source: Adapted from Dess, G. G., & Picken, J. C. 1999. *Beyond Productivity:* 63–64. New York: AMACON.

Protecting the Intellectual Assets of the Organization: Intellectual Property and Dynamic Capabilities

In today's dynamic and turbulent world, unpredictability and fast change dominate the business environment. Firms can use technology, attract human capital, or tap into research and design networks to get access to pretty much the same information as their competitors. So what would give firms a sustainable competitive advantage?[98] Protecting a firm's intellectual property requires a concerted effort on the part of the company. After all, employees become disgruntled and patents expire. The management of intellectual property (IP) involves, besides patents, contracts with confidentiality and noncompete clauses, copyrights, and the development of trademarks. Moreover, developing dynamic capabilities is the only avenue providing firms with the ability to reconfigure their knowledge and activities to achieve a sustainable competitive advantage.

>LO7
The challenge of protecting intellectual property and the importance of a firm's dynamic capabilities.

Intellectual Property Rights

Intellectual property rights are more difficult to define and protect than property rights for physical assets (e.g., plant, equipment, and land). However, if intellectual property rights are not reliably protected by the state, there will be no incentive to develop new products and services. Property rights have been enshrined in constitutions and rules of law in many countries. In the information era, though, adjustments need to be made to accommodate the new realities of knowledge. Knowledge and information are fundamentally different assets from the physical ones that property rights have been designed to protect.

The protection of intellectual rights raises unique issues, compared to physical property rights. IP is characterized by significant development costs and very low marginal costs. Indeed, it may take a substantial investment to develop a software program, an idea, or a digital music tune. Once developed, though, their reproduction and distribution cost may be almost zero, especially if the Internet is used. Effective protection of intellectual property is necessary before any investor will finance such an undertaking. Appropriation of their returns is harder to police since possession and deployment are not as readily observable. Unlike physical assets, intellectual property can be stolen by simply broadcasting it. Recall Napster and MP3 as well as the debates about counterfeit software, music CDs, and DVDs coming from developing countries such as China. Part of the problem is that using an idea does not prevent others from simultaneously using it for their own benefit, which is typically impossible with physical assets. Moreover, new ideas are frequently built on old ideas and are not easily traceable.

Strategy Spotlight 4.10 describes the many legal battles fought by a Canadian firm, Research in Motion of Waterloo, the developer of the popular BlackBerry. This example illustrates the high stakes that ride on intellectual property rights.

Countries are attempting to pass new legislation to cope with developments in new pharmaceutical compounds, stem cell research, and biotechnology. However, a firm that is faced with this challenge today cannot wait for the legislation to catch up. New technological developments, software solutions, electronic games, online services, and other products and services contribute to our economic prosperity and the creation of wealth for those entrepreneurs who have the idea first and risk bringing it to the market.

Dynamic Capabilities

Dynamic capabilities entail the capacity to build and protect a competitive advantage. This rests on knowledge, assets, competencies, and complementary assets and technologies as well as the ability to sense and seize new opportunities, generate new knowledge, and reconfigure existing assets and capabilities.[99] According to David Teece, an economist at the University of California at Berkeley, dynamic capabilities are related to the entrepreneurial side

dynamic capabilities
a firm's capacity to build and protect a competitive advantage, which rests on knowledge, assets, competencies, complementary assets, and technologies. Dynamic capabilities include the ability to sense and seize new opportunities, generate new knowledge, and reconfigure existing assets and capabilities.

strategy spotlight

4.10

Research in Motion, Maker of the BlackBerry, Loses an Intellectual Property Lawsuit

Research in Motion (RIM) is a Waterloo, Ontario–based company that is best known for developing the Black-Berry, a wireless device that integrates the functionalities of a cell phone with the ability to receive e-mail messages. During its brief history, it has become one of the fastest growing companies in North America. Founded by Mike Lazaridis, a former University of Waterloo student in 1984, Research in Motion was a competent but obscure technology firm until 1999 when the first BlackBerry was released. Through the development of integrated hardware, software, and services that support multiple wireless network standards, the BlackBerry has enabled RIM to grow from less than $50 million in sales revenue in 1999 to $6 billion by 2008. Even more impressive, by 2009 the company can boast a market capitalization in excess of $30 billion. RIM's commitment to their slogan "always on, always connected" has won them a legion of dedicated followers around the globe.

Interestingly, legal challenges have been the biggest obstacles that Research in Motion has faced in the eight years since the introduction of the first BlackBerry. In 2000, NTP, a pure patent-holding company, filed suit against RIM for violation of five of its patents and petitioned the court for an injunction on the sale and support of BlackBerry devices. The case dragged on for years, and RIM felt relatively secure that no injunction would be issued. On February 24, 2006, things dramatically changed. U.S. District Court Judge James Spencer indicated that he was inclined to grant the injunction and that his ruling was imminent. Faced with the acute risk of an unfavorable decision,

RIM settled only one week later for $612.5 million. It wound up paying a fortune for rights that were dubious at best—given that all five NTP patents had already been preliminarily invalidated by the U.S. Patent and Trademark Office and that two of them then received a final rejection.

● Research in Motion (RIM) has faced litigation over its highly successful BlackBerry.

Sources: Henkel, J. & Reitzig, M. 2008. Patent Sharks. *Harvard Business Review,* 86(6): 129–133; Hesseldahl, A. 2006. RIM's Latest Patent Problem. *BusinessWeek Online,* May 2: np; Anonymous. 2006. Settlement Reached in BlackBerry Patent Case. (The Associated Press) MSNBC .Com. March 3: np; and Wolk, M . 2006. RIM Pays Up, Taking "One for the Team." MSNBC.Com. March 3.

of the firm and are built within a firm through its environmental and technological "sensing" apparatus, its choices of organizational form, and its collective ability to strategize. Dynamic capabilities are about the ability of an organization to challenge the conventional wisdom within its industry and market, learn and innovate, adapt to the changing world, and continuously adopt new ways to serve the evolving needs of the market.[100]

Examples of dynamic capabilities include product development, strategic decision making, alliances, and acquisitions.[101] Some firms have clearly developed internal processes and routines that make them superior in such activities. For example, 3M and Apple are ahead of their competitors in product development. Cisco Systems has made numerous acquisitions over the years. They seem to have developed the capability to identify and evaluate potential acquisition candidates and seamlessly integrate them once the acquisition is completed. Other organizations can try to copy Cisco's practices. However, Cisco's combination of the resources of the acquired companies and their reconfiguration that Cisco has already achieved places them well ahead of their competitors. As markets become increasingly dynamic, traditional sources of long-term competitive advantage become less relevant. In such markets, all that a firm can strive for are a series of temporary advantages. Dynamic capabilities allow a firm to create this series of temporary advantages through new resource configurations.[102]

Reflecting on Career Implications . . .

- **Human Capital:** Does your organization effectively attract, develop, and retain talent? If not, you may have fewer career opportunities to enhance your human capital at your organization. Take advantage of your organization's human resource programs such as tuition reimbursement, mentoring, etc.
- **Human Capital:** Does your organization value diversity? What kinds of diversity seem to be encouraged (e.g., age-based or ethnicity-based)? If not, there may be limited perspectives on strategic and operational issues and a career at this organization may be less attractive to you.
- **Social Capital:** Does your organization have effective programs to build and develop social capital such that professionals develop strong "ties" to the organization? Alternatively, is social capital so strong that you see effects occur such as "groupthink"? From your perspective, how might you better leverage social capital towards pursuing other career opportunities?
- **Technology:** Does your organization provide and effectively use technology (e.g., groupware, knowledge management systems) to help you leverage your talents and expand your knowledge base?

Summary

Firms throughout the industrial world are recognizing that the knowledge worker is the key to success in the marketplace. However, we also recognize that human capital, although vital, is still only a necessary, but not a sufficient, condition for creating value. We began the first section of the chapter by addressing the importance of human capital and how it can be attracted, developed, and retained. Then we discussed the role of social capital and technology in leveraging human capital for competitive success. We pointed out that intellectual capital—the difference between a firm's market value and its book value—has increased significantly over the past few decades. This is particularly true for firms in knowledge-intensive industries, especially where there are relatively few tangible assets, such as software development.

The second section of the chapter addressed the attraction, development, and retention of human capital. We viewed these three activities as a "three-legged stool"—that is, it is difficult for firms to be successful if they ignore or are unsuccessful in any one of these activities. Among the issues we discussed in *attracting* human capital were "hiring for attitude, training for skill" and the value of using social networks to attract human capital. In particular, it is important to attract employees who can collaborate with others, given the importance of collective efforts such as teams and task forces.

With regard to *developing* human capital, we discussed the need to encourage widespread involvement throughout the organization, monitor progress and track the development of human capital, and evaluate human capital. Among the issues that are widely practiced in evaluating human capital is the 360-degree evaluation system. Employees are evaluated by their superiors, peers, direct reports, and even internal and external customers. We also addressed the value of maintaining a diverse workforce. Finally, some mechanisms for retaining human capital are employees' identification with the organization's mission and values, providing challenging work and a stimulating environment, the importance of financial and nonfinancial rewards and incentives, and providing flexibility and amenities. A key issue here is that a firm should not overemphasize financial rewards. After all, if individuals join an organization for money, they also are likely to leave for money. With money as the primary motivator, there is little chance that employees will develop firm-specific ties to keep them with the organization.

The third section of the chapter discussed the importance of social capital in leveraging human capital. Social capital refers to the network of relationships that individuals have throughout the organization as well as with customers and suppliers. Such ties can be critical in obtaining both information and resources. With regard to recruiting, for example, we saw how some firms are able to hire en masse groups of individuals who are part of social networks. Social relationships can also be very important in the effective functioning of groups. Finally, we discussed some of the potential downsides of social capital. These include the expenses that firms may bear when promoting social and working relationships among individuals as well as the potential for "groupthink," wherein individuals are reluctant to express divergent (or opposing) views on an issue because of social pressures to conform. We also introduced the concept of social networks. The relative advantages of being central in a network versus bridging multiple networks was discussed. We addressed the key role that social networks can play in both improving knowledge management and promoting career success.

The fourth section addressed the role of technology in leveraging human capital. We discussed relatively simple means of using technology, such as e-mail and networks where individuals can collaborate by way of personal computers. We provided suggestions and guidelines on how electronic teams can be effectively managed. We also addressed more sophisticated uses of technology, such as sophisticated management systems. Here knowledge can be codified and reused at very low cost, as we saw in the examples of firms in the consulting, health care, and high-technology industries.

In the last section we discussed the increasing importance of protecting a firm's intellectual property. Although traditional approaches such as patents, copyrights, and trademarks are important, the development of dynamic capabilities may be the best protection in the long run.

Summary Review Questions

1. Explain the role of knowledge in today's competitive environment.
2. Why is it important for managers to recognize the interdependence in the attraction, development, and retention of talented professionals?
3. What are some of the potential downsides for firms that engage in a "war for talent"?
4. Discuss the need for managers to use social capital in leveraging their human capital both within and across their firm.
5. Discuss the key role of technology in leveraging knowledge and human capital.

Key Terms

knowledge economy, 121
intellectual capital, 121
human capital, 122
social capital, 122
explicit knowledge, 122
tacit knowledge, 122
social network
  analysis, 136
closure, 137
bridging
  relationships, 137
structural holes, 137
groupthink, 140
electronic teams, 143
dynamic
  capabilities, 147

Experiential Exercise

Johnson & Johnson, a leading health care firm with $64 billion in revenues, is often rated as one of *Fortune*'s "Most Admired Firms." It is also considered an excellent place to work and has generated high return to shareholders. Clearly, they value their human capital. Using the Internet and/or library resources, identify some of the actions/strategies Johnson & Johnson has taken to attract, develop, and retain human capital. What are their implications?

Activity	Actions/Strategies	Implications
Attracting human capital		
Developing human capital		
Retaining human capital		

Application Questions Exercises

1. Look up successful firms in a high-technology industry as well as two successful firms in more traditional industries such as automobile manufacturing and retailing. Compare their market values and book values. What are some implications of these differences?

2. Select a firm for which you believe its social capital—both within the firm and among its suppliers and customers—is vital to its competitive advantage. Support your arguments.

3. Choose a company with which you are familiar. What are some of the ways in which it uses technology to leverage its human capital?

4. Using the Internet, look up a company with which you are familiar. What are some of the policies and procedures that it uses to enhance the firm's human and social capital?

Ethics Questions

1. Recall an example of a firm that recently faced an ethical crisis. How do you feel the crisis and management's handling of it affected the firm's human capital and social capital?

2. Based on your experiences or what you have learned in your previous classes, are you familiar with any companies that used unethical practices to attract talented professionals? What do you feel were the short-term and long-term consequences of such practices?

References

1. Hayashi, A. M. 2008. Why Picasso out earned van Gogh. *MIT Sloan Management Review,* Fall: 11–12; and, Berns, G. 2008. *A neuroscientist reveals how to think differently.* Harvard Business Press: Boston.

2. Parts of this chapter draw upon some of the ideas and examples from Dess, G. G. & Picken, J. C. 1999. *Beyond Productivity.* New York: AMACOM.

3. An acknowledged trend: The world economic survey. 1996. *The Economist,* September 2(8): 25–28.

4. Quinn, J. B., Anderson, P., & Finkelstein, S. 1996. Leveraging intellect. *Academy of Management Executive,* 10(3): 7–27.

5. Hamel, G. & Prahalad, C. K. 1996. Competing in the new economy: Managing out of bounds. *Strategic Management Journal,* 17: 238.

6. Stewart, T. A. 1997. *Intellectual capital: The new wealth of organizations.* New York: Doubleday/Currency.

7. Leif Edvisson and Michael S. Malone have a similar, more detailed definition of *intellectual capital:* "the combined knowledge, skill, innovativeness, and ability to meet the task at hand." They consider intellectual capital to equal human capital plus structural capital. *Structural capital* is defined as "the hardware, software, databases, organization structure, patents, trademarks, and everything else of organizational capability that supports those employees' productivity—in a word, everything left at the office when the employees go home."

Edvisson, L. & Malone, M. S. 1997. *Intellectual capital: Realizing your company's true value by finding its hidden brainpower:* 10–14. New York: HarperBusiness.

8. Stewart, T. A. 2001. Accounting gets radical. *Fortune,* April 16: 184–194.

9. Adams, S. & Kichen, S. 2008. Ben Graham then and now. *Forbes,* November 10: 56.

10. An interesting discussion of Steve Jobs's impact on Apple's valuation is in: Lashinsky, A. 2009. Steve's leave—what does it really mean? *Fortune,* February 2: 96–102.

11. Thomas Stewart has suggested this formula in his book *Intellectual Capital.* He provides an insightful discussion on pages 224–225, including some of the limitations of this approach to measuring intellectual capital. We recognize, of course, that during the late 1990s and in early 2000, there were some excessive market valuations of high-technology and Internet firms. For an interesting discussion of the extraordinary market valuation of Yahoo!, an Internet company, refer to Perkins, A. B. 2001. The Internet bubble encapsulated: Yahoo! *Red Herring,* April 15: 17–18.

12. Roberts, P. W. & Dowling, G. R. 2002. Corporate reputation and sustained superior financial performance. *Strategic Management Journal,* 23(12): 1077–1095.

13. For a recent study on the relationships between human capital, learning, and sustainable competitive advantage, read Hatch, N. W. & Dyer, J. H. 2005. Human capital and learning as a source of sustainable competitive advantage. *Strategic Management Journal,* 25: 1155–1178.

14. One of the seminal contributions on knowledge management is Becker, G. S. 1993. *Human capital: A theoretical and empirical analysis with special reference to education* (3rd ed.). Chicago: University of Chicago Press.

15. For an excellent overview of the topic of social capital, read Baron, R. A. 2005. Social capital. In Hitt, M. A. & Ireland, R. D. (Eds.), *The Blackwell encyclopedia of management* (2nd ed.): 224–226. Malden, MA: Blackwell.

16. For an excellent discussion of social capital and its impact on organizational performance, refer to Nahapiet, J. & Ghoshal, S. 1998. Social capital, intellectual capital, and the organizational advantage. *Academy of Management Review,* 23: 242–266.

17. An interesting discussion of how knowledge management (patents) can enhance organizational performance can be found in Bogner, W. C. & Bansal, P. 2007. Knowledge management as the basis of sustained high performance. *Journal of Management Studies,* 44(1): 165–188.

18. Polanyi, M. 1967. *The tacit dimension.* Garden City, NY: Anchor Publishing.

19. Barney, J. B. 1991. Firm resources and sustained competitive advantage. *Journal of Management,* 17: 99–120.

20. For an interesting perspective of empirical research on how knowledge can adversely affect performance, read Haas, M. R. & Hansen, M. T. 2005. When using knowledge can hurt performance: The value of organizational capabilities in a management consulting company. *Strategic Management Journal,* 26(1): 1–24.

21. New insights on managing talent are provided in: Cappelli, P. 2008. Talent management for the twenty-first century. *Harvard Business Review,* 66(3): 74–81.

22. Some of the notable books on this topic include Edvisson & Malone, op. cit.; Stewart, op. cit.; and Nonaka, I. & Takeuchi, I. 1995. *The knowledge creating company.* New York: Oxford University Press.

23. Stewart, T. A. 2000. Taking risk to the marketplace. *Fortune,* March 6: 424.

24. Insights on the Generation X's perspective on the workplace are in: Erickson, T. J. 2008. Task, not time: Profile of a Gen Y job. *Harvard Business Review,* 86(2): 19.

25. Dutton, G. 1997. Are you technologically competent? *Management Review,* November: 54–58.

26. Some workplace implications for the aging workforce are addressed in: Strack, R., Baier, J., & Fahlander, A. 2008. Managing demographic risk. *Harvard Business Review,* 66(2): 119–128.

27. For a discussion of attracting, developing, and retaining top talent, refer to Goffee, R. & Jones, G. 2007. Leading clever people. *Harvard Business Review,* 85(3): 72–89.

28. Dess & Picken, op. cit.: 34.

29. Webber, A. M. 1998. Danger: Toxic company. *Fast Company,* November: 152–161.

30. Some interesting insights on why home-grown American talent is going abroad is found in: Saffo, P. 2009. A looming American diaspora. *Harvard Business Review,* 87(2): 27.

31. Morris, B. 1997. Key to success: People, people, people. *Fortune,* October 27: 232.

32. For insights on management development and firm performance in several countries, refer to: Mabey, C. 2008. Management development and firm performance in Germany, Norway, Spain, and the UK. *Journal of International Business Studies,* 39(8): 1327–1342.

33. Martin, J. 1998. So, you want to work for the best. . . . *Fortune,* January 12: 77.

34. Cardin, R. 1997. Make your own Bozo Filter. *Fast Company,* October–November: 56.

35. Levering, R. & Moskowitz, M. 2009. And the winners are . . . *Fortune.* February 2: 67–78.

36. Martin, op. cit.; Henkoff, R. 1993. Companies that train best. *Fortune,* March 22: 53–60.

37. An interesting perspective on developing new talent rapidly when they join an organization can be found in Rollag, K., Parise, S., & Cross, R. 2005. Getting new hires up to speed quickly. *MIT Sloan Management Review,* 46(2): 35–41.

38. Stewart, T. A. 1998. Gray flannel suit? moi? *Fortune,* March 18: 80–82.

39. An interesting perspective on how Cisco Systems develops its talent can be found in Chatman, J., O'Reilly, C., & Chang, V. 2005. Cisco Systems: Developing a human capital strategy. *California Management Review,* 47(2): 137–166.

40. This section is based on Leonard, D. A. & Swap, W. 2004. Deep smarts. *Harvard Business Review,* 82(9): 88–97.

41. Useful insights on coaching can be found in: Coutu, D. & Kauffman, C. 2009. What coaches can do for you? *Harvard Business Review,* 67(1): 91–97.

42. For an innovative perspective on the appropriateness of alternate approaches to evaluation and rewards, refer to Seijts, G. H. & Lathan, G. P. 2005. Learning versus performance goals: When should each be used? *Academy of Management Executive,* 19(1): 124–132.

43. The discussion of the 360-degree feedback system draws on the article UPS. 1997. 360-degree feedback: Coming from all sides. *Vision* (a UPS Corporation internal company publication), March: 3; Slater, R. 1994. *Get better or get beaten: Thirty-one leadership secrets from Jack Welch.* Burr Ridge, IL: Irwin; Nexon, M. 1997. General Electric: The secrets of the finest company in the world. *L'Expansion,* July 23: 18–30; and Smith, D. 1996. Bold new directions for human resources. *Merck World* (internal company publication), October: 8.

44. Interesting insights on 360-degree evaluation systems are discussed in: Barwise, P. & Meehan, Sean. 2008. So you think you're a good listener. *Harvard Business Review,* 66(4): 22–23.

45. Insights into the use of 360-degree evaluation are in: Kaplan, R. E. & Kaiser, R.B. 2009. Stop overdoing your strengths. *Harvard Business Review,* 87(2): 100–103.

46. Kets de Vries, M. F. R. 1998. Charisma in action: The transformational abilities of Virgin's Richard Branson and ABB's Percy Barnevik. *Organizational Dynamics,* Winter: 20.

47. For an interesting discussion on how organizational culture has helped Zappos become number one in *Fortune*'s 2009 survey of the best companies to work for, see: O'Brien, J. M. 2009. Zappos knows how to kick it. *Fortune,* February 2: 54–58.

48. We have only to consider the most celebrated case of industrial espionage in recent years, wherein José Ignacio Lopez was indicted in a German court for stealing sensitive product planning documents from his former employer, General Motors, and sharing them with his executive colleagues at Volkswagen. The lawsuit was dismissed by the German courts, but Lopez and his colleagues were investigated by the U.S. Justice Department. Also consider the recent litigation involving noncompete employment contracts and confidentiality clauses of *International Paper v. Louisiana-Pacific, Campbell Soup v. H. J. Heinz Co.,* and *PepsiCo v. Quaker Oats's Gatorade.* In addition to retaining valuable human resources and often their valuable network of customers, firms must also protect proprietary information and knowledge. For interesting insights, refer to Carley, W. M. 1998. CEO gets hard lesson in how not to keep his lieutenants. *The Wall Street Journal,* February 11: A1, A10; and Lenzner, R. & Shook, C. 1998. Whose Rolodex is it, anyway? *Forbes,* February 23: 100–103.

49. For an insightful discussion of retention of knowledge workers in today's economy, read Davenport, T. H. 2005. *The care and feeding of the knowledge worker.* Boston, MA: Harvard Business School Press.

50. Fisher, A. 2008. America's most admired companies. *Fortune,* March 17: 74.

51. Stewart, T. A. 2001. *The wealth of knowledge.* New York: Currency.

52. For insights on fulfilling one's potential, refer to: Kaplan, R. S. 2008. Reaching your potential. *Harvard Business Review,* 66(7/8): 45–57.

53. Amabile, T. M. 1997. Motivating creativity in organizations: On doing what you love and loving what you do. *California Management Review,* Fall: 39–58.

54. For an insightful perspective on alternate types of employee–employer relationships, read Erickson, T. J. & Gratton, L. 2007. What it means to work here. *Harvard Business Review,* 85(3): 104–112.

55. Monsanto has been part of Pharmacia since 2002. *Hoover's Handbook of Am. Bus.* 2004: 562.

56. Pfeffer, J. 2001. Fighting the war for talent is hazardous to your organization's health. *Organizational Dynamics,* 29(4): 248–259.

57. Cox, T. L. 1991. The multinational organization. *Academy of Management Executive,* 5(2): 34–47. Without doubt, a great deal has been written on the topic of creating and maintaining an effective diverse workforce. Some excellent, recent books include: Harvey, C. P. & Allard, M. J. 2005. *Understanding and managing diversity: Readings, cases, and exercises.* (3rd ed.). Upper Saddle River, NJ: Pearson Prentice-Hall; Miller, F. A. & Katz, J. H. 2002. *The inclusion breakthrough: Unleashing the real power of diversity.* San Francisco: Berrett Koehler; and Williams, M. A. 2001. *The 10 lenses: Your guide to living and working in a multicultural world.* Sterling, VA: Capital Books.

58. www.rand.org/publications/RB/RB/5050.

59. This section, including the six potential benefits of a diverse workforce, draws on Cox, T. H. & Blake, S. 1991. Managing cultural diversity: Implications for organizational competitiveness. *Academy of Management Executive,* 5(3): 45–56.

60. www.pwcglobal.com/us/eng/careers/diversity/index.html.

61. This discussion draws on Dess, G. G. & Lumpkin, G. T. 2001. Emerging issues in strategy process research. In Hitt, M. A., Freeman, R. E. & Harrison, J. S. (Eds.). *Handbook of strategic management:* 3–34. Malden, MA: Blackwell.

62. Adler, P. S. & Kwon, S. W. 2002. Social capital: Prospects for a new concept. *Academy of Management Review,* 27(1): 17–40.

63. Capelli, P. 2000. A market-driven approach to retaining talent. *Harvard Business Review,* 78(1): 103–113.

64. This hypothetical example draws on Peteraf, M. 1993. The cornerstones of competitive advantage. *Strategic Management Journal,* 14: 179–191.

65. Wernerfelt, B. 1984. A resource-based view of the firm. *Strategic Management Journal,* 5: 171–180.

66. Wysocki, B., Jr. 2000. Yet another hazard of the new economy: The Pied Piper Effect. *The Wall Street Journal,* March 20: A1–A16.

67. Ideas on how managers can more effectively use their social network are addressed in: McGrath, C. & Zell, D. 2009. Profiles of trust: Who to turn to, and for what. *MIT Sloan Management Review,* 50(2): 75–80.

68. Ibid.

69. Buckman, R. C. 2000. Tech defectors from Microsoft resettle together. *The Wall Street Journal,* October: B1–B6.

70. An insightful discussion of the interorganizational aspects of social capital can be found in Dyer, J. H. & Singh, H. 1998. The relational view: Cooperative strategy and sources of interorganizational competitive advantage. *Academy of Management Review,* 23: 66–79.

71. A study of the relationship between social networks and performance in China is found in: Li, J. J., Poppo, L., & Zhou, K. Z. 2008. Do managerial ties in China always produce value? Competition, uncertainty, and domestic vs. foreign firms. *Strategic Management Journal,* 29(4): 383–400.

72. Hoppe, B. 2005. Structural holes, Part one. connectedness.blogspot.com. January 18: np.

73. There has been a tremendous amount of theory building and empirical research in recent years in the area of social network analysis. Unquestionably, two of the major contributors to this domain have been Ronald Burt and J. S. Coleman. For excellent background discussions, refer to: Burt, R. S. 1992. *Structural holes: The social structure of competition.* Cambridge, MA: Harvard University Press; Coleman, J. S. 1990. *Foundations of social theory.* Cambridge, MA: Harvard University Press; and Coleman, J. S. 1988. Social capital in the creation of human capital. *American Journal of Sociology.* 94: S95–S120. For a more recent review and integration of current thought on social network theory, consider: Burt, R. S. 2005. *Brokerage & closure: An introduction to social capital.* Oxford Press: New York.

74. Our discussion draws on the concepts developed by Burt, 1992, op. cit.; Coleman, 1990, op. cit.; Coleman, 1988, op. cit.; and Oh, H., Chung, M. & Labianca, G. 2004. Group social capital and group effectiveness: The role of informal socializing ties. *Academy of Management Journal,* 47(6): 860–875. We would like to thank Joe Labianca (University of Kentucky) for his helpful feedback and ideas in our discussion of social networks.

75. Arregle, J. L., Hitt, M. A., Sirmon, D. G., & Very, P. 2007. The development of organizational social capital: Attributes of family firms. *Journal of Management Studies,* 44(1): 73–95.

76. A novel perspective on social networks is in: Pentland, A. 2009. How social networks network best. *Harvard Business Review,* 87(2): 37.

77. Oh et al., op. cit.

78. Hoppe, op. cit.

79. The discussion of these two contingent factors draws on Dess, G. G. & Shaw, J. D. 2001. Voluntary turnover, social capital, and organizational performance. *Academy of Management Review,* 26(3): 446–456.

80. The business-level strategies of overall low cost and differentiation draws upon Michael E. Porter's classic work and will be discussed in more detail in Chapter 5. Source: Porter, M. E. 1985. *Competitive advantage.* Free Press: New York.

81. Perspectives on how to use and develop decision networks are discussed in: Cross, R., Thomas, R. J., & Light, D. A. 2009. How "who you know" affects what you decide. *MIT Sloan Management Review,* 50(2): 35–42.

82. Our discussion of the three advantages of social networks draws on Uzzi, B. & Dunlap. S. 2005. How to build your network. *Harvard Business Review,* 83(12): 53–60. For a recent, excellent review on the research exploring the relationship between social capital and managerial performance, read Moran, P. 2005. Structural vs. relational embeddedness: Social capital and managerial performance. *Strategic Management Journal,* 26(12): 1129–1151.

83. A perspective on personal influence is in: Christakis, N. A. 2009. The dynamics of personal influence. *Harvard Business Review,* 87(2): 31.

84. Prusak, L. & Cohen, D. 2001. How to invest in social capital. *Harvard Business Review,* 79(6): 86–93.

85. Leonard, D. & Straus, S. 1997. Putting your company's whole brain to work. *Harvard Business Review,* 75(4): 110–122.

86. For an excellent discussion of public (i.e., the organization) versus private (i.e., the individual manager) benefits of social capital, refer to Leana, C. R. & Van Buren, H. J. 1999. Organizational social capital and employment practices. *Academy of Management Review,* 24(3): 538–555.

87. The authors would like to thank Joe Labianca, University of Kentucky, and John Lin, University of Texas at Dallas, for their very helpful input in our discussion of social network theory and its practical implications.

88. Brady, D. 2006. *!#?@ the e-mail. Can we talk?. *BusinessWeek,* December 4: 109.

89. Taylor, W. C. 1999. Whatever happened to globalization? *Fast Company,* December: 228–236.

90. Prahalad, C. K. & Ramaswamy, V. 2004. *The future of competition: Co-creating value with customers.* Boston: Harvard Business School Press.

91. Lei, D., Slocum, J., & Pitts, R. A. 1999. Designing organizations for competitive advantage: The power of unlearning and learning. *Organizational Dynamics,* Winter: 24–38.

92. This section draws upon Zaccaro, S. J. & Bader, P. 2002. E-Leadership and the challenges of leading e-teams: Minimizing the bad and maximizing the good. *Organizational Dynamics,* 31(4): 377–387.

93. Kirkman, B. L., Rosen, B., Tesluk, P. E., & Gibson, C. B. 2004. The impact of team empowerment on virtual team performance: The moderating role of face-to-face interaction. *Academy of Management Journal,* 47(2): 175–192.

94. The discussion of the advantages and challenges associated with e-teams draws on Zacarro & Bader, op. cit.

95. For a recent study exploring the relationship between team empowerment, face-to-face interaction, and performance in virtual teams, read Kirkman, Rosen, Tesluk, & Gibson, op. cit.

96. For an innovative study on how firms share knowledge with competitors and the performance implications, read Spencer, J. W. 2003. Firms' knowledge sharing strategies in the global innovation system: Empirical evidence from the flat panel display industry. *Strategic Management Journal,* 24(3): 217–235.

97. The examples of Andersen Consulting and Access Health draw upon Hansen, M. T., Nohria, N., & Tierney, T. 1999. What's your strategy for managing knowledge? *Harvard Business Review,* 77(2): 106–118.

98. This discussion draws on Conley, J. G. 2005. Intellectual capital management, Kellogg School of Management and Schulich School of Business, York University, Toronto, KS 2003; Conley, J. G. & Szobocsan, J. 2001. Snow White shows the way. *Managing Intellectual Property,* June: 15–25; Greenspan, A. 2004. Intellectual property rights, The Federal Reserve Board, Remarks by the chairman, February 27; and Teece, D. J. 1998. Capturing value from knowledge assets, *California Management Review,* 40(3): 54–79. The authors would like to thank Professor Theo Peridis, York University, for his contribution to this section.

99. A study of the relationship between dynamic capabilities and related diversification is: Doving, E. & Gooderham, P. N. 2008. *Strategic Management Journal,* 29(8): 841–858.

100. A perspective on strategy in turbulent markets is in: Sull, D. 2009. How to thrive in turbulent markets. *Harvard Business Review,* 87 (2): 78–88.

101. Lee, G. K. 2008. Relevance of organizational capabilities and its dynamics: What to learn from entrants' product portfolios about the determinants of entry timing. *Strategic Management Journal,* 29(12): 1257–1280.

102. Eisenhardt, K. M. & Martin, J. E. 2000. Dynamic capabilities: What are they? *Strategic Management Journal,* 21: 1105–1121.

Business-Level Strategy:

Creating and Sustaining Competitive Advantages

After reading this chapter, you should have a good understanding of:

LO1 The central role of competitive advantage in the study of strategic management.

LO2 The three generic strategies: overall cost leadership, differentiation, and focus.

LO3 How the successful attainment of generic strategies can improve a firm's relative power vis-à-vis the five forces that determine an industry's average profitability.

LO4 The pitfalls managers must avoid in striving to attain generic strategies.

LO5 How firms can effectively combine the generic strategies of overall cost leadership and differentiation.

LO6 How Internet-enabled business models are being used to improve strategic positioning.

LO7 The importance of considering the industry life cycle to determine a firm's business-level strategy and its relative emphasis on functional area strategies and value-creating activities.

LO8 The need for turnaround strategies that enable a firm to reposition its competitive position in an industry.

How firms compete with each other and how they attain and sustain competitive advantages go to the heart of strategic management. In short, the key issue becomes: Why do some firms outperform others and enjoy such advantages over time? This subject, business-level strategy, is the focus of Chapter 5.

The first part of the chapter draws on Michael Porter's framework of generic strategies. He identifies three strategies—overall cost leadership, differentiation, and focus—that firms may apply to outperform their rivals in an industry. We begin by describing each of these strategies and providing examples of firms that have successfully attained them as a means of outperforming competitors in their industry. Next, we address how these strategies help a firm develop a favorable position vis-à-vis the "five forces" (Chapter 2). We then suggest some of the pitfalls that managers must avoid if they are to successfully pursue these generic strategies and discuss the conditions under which firms may effectively combine generic strategies to outperform rivals. We close this section by addressing how competitive strategies should be revised and redeployed in light of the shifts in industry and competitive forces caused by Internet and digital strategies. Here, combination strategies are the most solid because they integrate the new capabilities with sound principles.

The second part of Chapter 5 discusses a vital consideration in the effective use of business-level strategies: industry life cycles. The four stages of the industry life cycle—introduction, growth, maturity, and decline—are indicative of an evolving management process that affects factors such as the market growth rate and the intensity of competition. Accordingly, the stages of an industry's life cycle are an important contingency that managers should take into account when making decisions concerning the optimal overall business-level strategies and the relative emphasis to place on functional capabilities and value-creating activities. At times, firms are faced with performance declines and must find ways to revitalize their competitive positions. The actions followed to do so are referred to as turnaround strategies, which may be needed at any stage of the industry life cycle. However, they occur more frequently during the maturity and decline stages.

Learning from Mistakes

About a half-century ago, Groupe Michelin sparked a revolution in the tire industry when it introduced the steel-belted radial.[1] In 2004, it hoped for another coup with the new PAX run-flat tire, which can keep rolling smoothly for up to 120 miles even if completely deflated by a puncture.

It was the French tire maker's biggest new product push since the radial. The appeal of a run-flat is certainly attractive to any driver who has changed a tire on the shoulder of a busy highway or wished the spare didn't take up so much room in the trunk. Michelin predicted that the PAX would one day dominate the $70 billion-a-year tire market—much as radials now do, commanding nearly 100 percent of the market in the industrialized world. Claimed Chairman Edouard Michelin: "Like the radial, the PAX system is a groundbreaking innovation." However, things didn't turn out as planned. Let's take a closer look.

On April 20, 2008, the *New York Times* carried the sad headline "Michelin Giving Up on PAX Run-Flat Tire." So much for an innovation that was supposed to revolutionize the tire industry. Clearly, this was a big bet innovation, intended to overturn the industry.

While it is easy to be an "armchair quarterback" and retrospectively criticize Michelin's innovation, there were some trouble signs early on. For example, a *BusinessWeek* article appearing about four months after PAX's introduction noted that the PAX tires didn't fit into conventionally designed vehicles. To use them, cars had to be equipped with a specially designed chassis and wheels; hence, a PAX-friendly car can't take regular tires. Thus, to get the tires replaced, a customer had to find an authorized PAX service center to repair or replace the tires. Such a lack of compatibility with preexisting infrastructure proved to be a contributor to the product's undoing. In fact, the PAX's design (with an inner ring to provide more strength) was much more difficult to repair—requiring special equipment to mount and dismount the tire. That equipment was only available at Michelin stores or Honda dealers. This led to several lawsuits, and on some websites, consumers complained about the difficulty of finding shops and equipment to work on PAX. They also cited excessive tire wear and replacement costs as high as $1,600 for a set of four tires. Perhaps not too surprisingly, about two years after PAX's introduction, it only held about 5 percent of the total market for run-flat tires.

Although Michelin enjoyed some success, such as having the PAX tires as standard equipment on the 2005–2007 Honda Odyssey Touring minivan, other firms failed to adopt. As it turned out, the PAX was not a huge advance over other run-flat technologies. And it required specialized equipment and systemic changes. Thus, it was a far cry from the promise of a tire that would revolutionize driving habits and totally change an industry.

Ultimately, the goal of all competitive strategies is to create value for the customer. Michelin was seeking to create a differentiation advantage and charge a premium price. However, customers did not perceive sufficient value in the PAX technology to cover the cost of creating the product.

Types of Competitive Advantage and Sustainability

>LO1

The central role of competitive advantage in the study of strategic management.

Michael Porter presented three generic strategies that a firm can use to overcome the five forces and achieve competitive advantage.[2] Each of Porter's generic strategies has the potential to allow a firm to outperform rivals in their industry. The first, *overall cost leadership,* is based on creating a low-cost-position. Here, a firm must manage the relationships throughout the value chain and lower costs throughout the entire chain. Second, *differentiation* requires a firm to create products and/or services that are unique and valued. Here, the primary emphasis is on "nonprice" attributes for which customers will

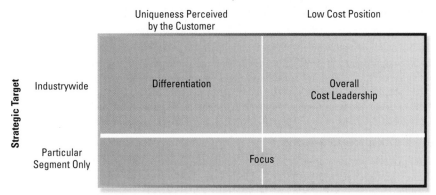

Competitive Advantage

	Uniqueness Perceived by the Customer	Low Cost Position
Industrywide	Differentiation	Overall Cost Leadership
Particular Segment Only	Focus	

Strategic Target

Exhibit 5.1 **Three Generic Strategies**

Source: Adapted with the permission of The Free Press, a division of Simon & Schuster Adult Publishing Group, from *Competitive Strategy: Techniques for Analyzing Industries and Competitors* by Michael E. Porter. Copyright © 1980, 1998 by The Free Press. All rights reserved.

gladly pay a premium.[3] Third, a *focus* strategy directs attention (or "focus") toward narrow product lines, buyer segments, or targeted geographic markets and they must attain advantages either through differentiation or cost leadership.[4] Whereas the overall cost leadership and differentiation strategies strive to attain advantages industrywide, focusers have a narrow target market in mind. Exhibit 5.1 illustrates these three strategies on two dimensions: competitive advantage and strategic target.

Both casual observation and research support the notion that firms that identify with one or more of the forms of competitive advantage outperform those that do not.[5] There has been a rich history of strategic management research addressing this topic. One study analyzed 1,789 strategic business units and found that businesses combining multiple forms of competitive advantage (differentiation and overall cost leadership) outperformed businesses that used only a single form. The lowest performers were those that did not identify with any type of advantage. They were classified as "stuck in the middle." Results of this study are presented in Exhibit 5.2.[6]

For an example of the dangers of being "stuck in the middle," consider Coach and Tiffany—two brands in the "affordable luxury" category.[7] Such brands target

>LO2

The three generic strategies: overall cost leadership, differentiation, and focus.

Exhibit 5.2 **Competitive Advantage and Business Performance**

	Competitive Advantage					
	Differentiation and Cost	**Differentiation**	**Cost**	**Differentiation and Focus**	**Cost and Focus**	**Stuck in the Middle**
Performance						
Return on investment (%)	35.5	32.9	30.2	17.0	23.7	17.8
Sales growth (%)	15.1	13.5	13.5	16.4	17.5	12.2
Gain in market share (%)	5.3	5.3	5.5	6.1	6.3	4.4
Sample size	123	160	100	141	86	105

middle-class customers for whom a $300 bag is a splurge. After sales and stock declines, they are migrating away from the middle—and going either higher or lower:

> In early 2008, Coach said that it would turn 40 of its nearly 300 stores into a more upscale format that will offer higher-end bags and concierge services. Tiffany, on the other hand, took the opposite tack. A new store opening in California will not sell any of its $148,000 diamond necklaces and instead focus on less expensive products like its $200-and-under silver jewelry. Claims Pat Conroy, head of Deloitte & Touche's consumer products sector: "Being in the middle is not a good place to be. You get assaulted from everyone."

Overall Cost Leadership

overall cost leadership a firm's generic strategy based on appeal to the industrywide market using a competitive advantage based on low cost.

The first generic strategy is overall cost leadership. Overall cost leadership requires a tight set of interrelated tactics that include:

- Aggressive construction of efficient-scale facilities.
- Vigorous pursuit of cost reductions from experience.
- Tight cost and overhead control.
- Avoidance of marginal customer accounts.
- Cost minimization in all activities in the firm's value chain, such as R&D, service, sales force, and advertising.

Exhibit 5.3 draws on the value-chain concept (see Chapter 3) to provide examples of how a firm can attain an overall cost leadership strategy in its primary and support activities.

experience curve the decline in unit costs of production as cumulative output increases.

Key to an overall cost leadership strategy is the **experience curve**, which refers to how business "learns" to lower costs as it gains experience with production processes. With experience, unit costs of production decline as output increases in most industries. The experience curve concept is discussed in Strategy Spotlight 5.1 and Exhibit 5.4.

To generate above-average performance, a firm following an overall cost leadership position must attain **competitive parity** on the basis of differentiation relative to competitors.[8] In other words, a firm achieving parity is similar to its competitors, or "on par," with respect to differentiated products.[9] Competitive parity on the basis of differentiation permits a cost leader to translate cost advantages directly into higher profits than competitors. Thus, the cost leader earns above-average returns.[10]

competitive parity a firm's achievement of similarity, or being "on par," with competitors with respect to low cost, differentiation, or other strategic product characteristic.

The failure to attain parity on the basis of differentiation can be illustrated with an example from the automobile industry—the ill-fated Yugo. Below is an excerpt from a speech by J. W. Marriott, Jr., Chairman of the Marriott Corporation:[11]

> . . . money is a big thing. But it's not the only thing. In the 1980s, a new automobile reached North America from behind the Iron Curtain. It was called the Yugo, and its main attraction was price. About $3,000 each. But the only way they caught on was as the butt of jokes. Remember the guy who told his mechanic, "I want a gas cap for my Yugo." "OK," the mechanic replied, "that sounds like a fair trade."

Yugo was offering a lousy value proposition. The cars literally fell apart before your eyes. And the lesson was simple. Price is just one component of value. No matter how good the price, the most cost-sensitive consumer won't buy a bad product.

Next, we discuss some examples of how firms enhance cost leadership position.

While other managed care providers were having a string of weak years, WellPoint, based in Thousand Oaks, California, has had a number of banner years and recently enjoyed an annual profit growth of over 35 percent to $3.3 billion over the past three years.[12] Chairman Leonard Schaeffer credits the company's focus on innovation for both expanding revenues and cutting costs. For example, WellPoint asked the Food and Drug Administration (FDA) to make the allergy drug Claritin available over the counter. Surprisingly, this may be the first time that an insurer has approached the FDA with such a request. Schaeffer claimed, "They were kind of stunned," but the FDA agreed to consider it. It was a smart

Exhibit 5.3
**Value-Chain Activities:
Examples of Overall
Cost Leadership**

Support Activities

Firm Infrastructure

- Few management layers to reduce overhead costs.
- Standardized accounting practices to minimize personnel required.

Human Resource Management

- Minimize costs associated with employee turnover through effective policies.
- Effective orientation and training programs to maximize employee productivity.

Technology Development

- Effective use of automated technology to reduce scrappage rates.
- Expertise in process engineering to reduce manufacturing costs.

Procurement

- Effective policy guidelines to ensure low-cost raw materials (with acceptable quality levels).
- Shared purchasing operations with other business units.

Primary Activities

Inbound Logistics

- Effective layout of receiving dock operations.

Operations

- Effective use of quality control inspectors to minimize rework.

Outbound Logistics

- Effective utilization of delivery fleets

Marketing and Sales

- Purchase of media in large blocks.
- Sales force utilization is maximized by territory management.

Service

- Thorough service repair guidelines to minimize repeat maintenance calls.
- Use of single type of vehicle to minimize repair costs.

Source: Adapted from: Porter, M.E. 1985. *Competitive Advantage: Creating and Sustaining Superior Performance.* New York: Free Press.

move for WellPoint. If approved as an over-the-counter drug, Claritin would reduce patient visits to the doctor and eliminate the need for prescriptions—two reimbursable expenses for which WellPoint would otherwise be responsible.

Stephen Sanger, CEO of General Mills, recently came up with an idea that helped his firm cut costs.[13] To improve productivity, he sent technicians to watch pit crews during a

The Experience Curve

The experience curve, developed by the Boston Consulting Group in 1968, is a way of looking at efficiencies developed through a firm's cumulative experience. In its basic form, the experience curve relates production costs to production output. As output doubles, costs decline by 10 percent to 30 percent. For example, if it costs $1 per unit to produce 100 units, the per unit cost will decline to between 70 to 90 cents as output increases to 200 units.

What factors account for this increased efficiency? First, the success of an experience curve strategy depends on the industry life cycle for the product. Early stages of a product's life cycle are typically characterized by rapid gains in technological advances in production efficiency. Most experience curve gains come early in the product life cycle.

Second, the inherent technology of the product offers opportunities for enhancement through gained experience. High-tech products give the best opportunity for gains in production efficiencies. As technology is developed, "value engineering" of innovative production processes is implemented, driving down the per unit costs of production.

Third, a product's sensitivity to price strongly affects a firm's ability to exploit the experience curve. Cutting the price of a product with high demand elasticity—where demand increases when price decreases—rapidly creates consumer purchases of the new product. By cutting prices, a firm can increase demand for its product. The increased demand in turn increases product manufacture, thus increasing the firm's experience in the manufacturing process. So by decreasing price and increasing demand, a firm gains manufacturing experience in that particular product, which drives down per unit production costs.

Fourth, the competitive landscape factors into whether or not a firm might benefit from an experience curve strategy. If other competitors are well positioned in

the market, have strong capital resources, and are known to promote their product lines aggressively to gain market share, an experience curve strategy may lead to nothing more than a price war between two or more strong competitors. But if a company is the first to market with the product and has good financial backing, an experience curve strategy may be successful.

In an article in the *Harvard Business Review,* Pankaj Ghemawat recommended answering several questions when considering an experience curve strategy.

- Does my industry exhibit a significant experience curve?
- Have I defined the industry broadly enough to take into account interrelated experience?
- What is the precise source of cost reduction?
- Can my company keep cost reductions proprietary?
- Is demand sufficiently stable to justify using the experience curve?
- Is cumulated output doubling fast enough for the experience curve to provide much strategic leverage?
- Do the returns from an experience curve strategy warrant the risks of technological obsolescence?
- Is demand price-sensitive?
- Are there well-financed competitors who are already following an experience curve strategy or are likely to adopt one if my company does?

Michael Porter suggested, however, that the experience curve is not useful in all situations. Whether or not to base strategy on the experience curve depends on what specifically causes the decline in costs. For example, if costs drop from efficient production facilities and not necessarily from experience, the experience curve is not helpful. But as Sharon Oster pointed out in her book on competitive analysis, the experience curve can help managers analyze costs when efficient learning, rather than efficient machinery, is the source of cost savings.

Sources: Ghemawat, P. 1985. Building Strategy on the Experience Curve. *Harvard Business Review,* March–April: 143–149; Porter, M. E. 1996. *On Competition.* Boston: Harvard Business Review Press; and Oster, S. M. 1994. *Modern Competitive Analysis* (2nd ed.). New York: Oxford University Press.

NASCAR race. That experience inspired the techies to figure out how to reduce the time it takes to switch a plant line from five hours to 20 minutes. This provided an important lesson: Many interesting benchmarking examples can take place far outside of an industry. Often, process improvements involve identifying the best practices in other industries and adapting them for implementation in your own firm. After all, when firms benchmark competitors in their own industry, the end result is often copying and playing catch-up.[14]

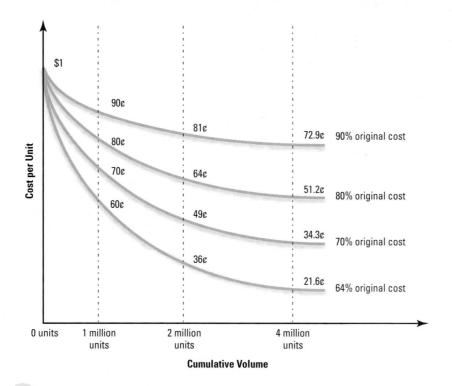

Exhibit 5.4 Comparing Experience Curve Effects

A business that strives for a low-cost advantage must attain an absolute cost advantage relative to its rivals.[15] This is typically accomplished by offering a no-frills product or service to a broad target market using standardization to derive the greatest benefits from economies of scale and experience. However, such a strategy may fail if a firm is unable to attain parity on important dimensions of differentiation such as quick responses to customer requests for services or design changes. Strategy Spotlight 5.2 discusses Ryanair—a firm that has developed a very unique overall cost leadership strategy. One might say that it "one upped" Southwest Airlines!

Overall Cost Leadership: Improving Competitive Position vis-à-vis the Five Forces An overall low-cost position enables a firm to achieve above-average returns despite strong competition. It protects a firm against rivalry from competitors, because lower costs allow a firm to earn returns even if its competitors eroded their profits through intense rivalry. A low-cost position also protects firms against powerful buyers. Buyers can exert power to drive down prices only to the level of the next most efficient producer. Also, a low-cost position provides more flexibility to cope with demands from powerful suppliers for input cost increases. The factors that lead to a low-cost position also provide substantial entry barriers from economies of scale and cost advantages. Finally, a low-cost position puts the firm in a favorable position with respect to substitute products introduced by new and existing competitors.

A few examples will illustrate these points. Ryanair's close attention to costs helps to protect them from buyer power and intense rivalry from competitors. Thus, they are able to drive down costs and enjoy relatively high power over their customers. By increasing productivity and lowering unit costs, General Mills (and its competitors in that industry) enjoy greater scale economies and erect higher entry barriers for others. Finally, as competitors

>LO3
How the successful attainment of generic strategies can improve a firm's relative power vis-à-vis the five forces that determine an industry's average profitability.

strategy spotlight

Ryanair: A Highly Effective Overall Cost Leadership Strategy

Michael O'Leary, CEO of Ryanair Holdings PLC, makes no apologies for his penny-pinching. Want to check luggage? You'll pay up to $9.50 per bag for the privilege. Expecting free drinks and snacks? You'll be disappointed. Even a bottle of water will cost you $3.40. And it is not just the passengers who are affected. Flight crews buy their own uniforms, and staff at Ryanair's Spartan Dublin Airport headquarters must supply their own pens. After a customer sued Ryanair for charging $34 for the use of a wheelchair, the company added a 63 cent "wheelchair levy" to every ticket!

Low-fare U.S. carriers have taken the opposite approach of Ryanair by adding perks such as leather seats, live television, and business class. "All of the low-cost carriers' costs have gotten a little out of control," says Tim Sieber, general manager of The Boyd Group, an Evergreen (Colorado) aviation consultant. Clearly Ryanair hasn't followed its industry peers.

Ryanair has been extremely successful. For 2006, its revenues were $2.1 billion—only one-seventh the size of British Airways (BA). However, its operating margins are 22.7 percent—three times as large as BA's. By 2008,

Ryanair's revenues had increased to $3.5 billion—a 66% increase over 2006.

What is O'Leary's secret? He thinks like a retailer and charges for every little thing. Imagine the seat as a cell phone: It comes free, or nearly free, but its owner winds up spending money on all sorts of services.

However, what O'Leary loses in seat revenue he more than makes up by turning both his planes and the Ryanair Web site into stores brimming with irresistible goodies, even as he charges for such "perks" as priority boarding and assigned seating.

Sounds outrageous? Probably so, but the strategy is clearly working. Although its average fare is $53, compared with $92 for Southwest Airlines, Ryanair's net margins are, at 18 percent—more than double the 7 percent achieved by Southwest. Says Nick van den Brul, an aviation analyst: "Ryanair is Wal-Mart with wings." As O'Leary says, "You want luxury? Go somewhere else."

A few other Ryanair practices include:

- Flight attendants sell digital cameras ($137.50) and iPocket MP3 players ($165).

- The seats don't recline, seat-back pockets have been removed to cut cleaning time and speed turn-around of the planes, there's no entertainment, and seat-back trays will soon carry ads.

- Ryanair sells more than 98 percent of its tickets online. Its Web site offers insurance, hotels, car rentals, and more—even online bingo.

Sources: Ryanair Annual Report, 2008; Capell, K. 2006. Wal-Mart with Wings. *BusinessWeek.* November 27: 44–45; Kumar, N. 2006. Strategies to Fight Low-Cost Rivals. *Harvard Business Review,* 84(12): 104–113; and *Ryanair Annual Report,* 2006.

such as WellPoint lower costs through means such as petitioning the FDA to make certain drugs available over the counter, they become less vulnerable to substitutes such as Internet-based competitors.

Potential Pitfalls of Overall Cost Leadership Strategies Potential pitfalls of overall cost leadership strategy include:

>LO4

The pitfalls managers must avoid in striving to attain generic strategies.

- ***Too much focus on one or a few value-chain activities.*** Would you consider a person to be astute if he cancelled his newspaper subscription and quit eating out to save money, but then "maxed out" several credit cards, requiring him to pay hundreds of dollars a month in interest charges? Of course not. Similarly, firms need to pay attention to all activities in the value chain. Too often managers make big cuts in operating expenses, but don't question year-to-year spending on capital projects. Or managers may decide to cut selling and marketing expenses but ignore manufacturing expenses. Managers should explore *all* value-chain activities, including relationships among them, as candidates for cost reductions.

- **All rivals share a common input or raw material.** Here, firms are vulnerable to price increases in the factors of production. Since they're competing on costs, they are less able to pass on price increases, because customers can take their business to rivals who have lower prices. Consider the hardship experienced by fertilizer producers when energy prices spiked.[16] A quadrupling of prices to $10 per thousand cubic feet of natural gas forced firms to shut down nearly half of their production capacity. Why? Natural gas accounts for over 70 percent of the fertilizer's cost. According to Betty-Ann Hegge, senior vice president of Potash Corporation of Saskatchewan, Inc., North America's second largest producer, "Many companies are not even covering their cash costs at these prices."

- **The strategy is imitated too easily.** One of the common pitfalls of a cost-leadership strategy is that a firm's strategy may consist of value-creating activities that are easy to imitate.[17] Such was the case with online brokers in recent years.[18] As of early 2001, there were about 140 online brokers, hardly symbolic of an industry where imitation is extremely difficult. But according to Henry McVey, financial services analyst at Morgan Stanley, "We think you need five to ten" online brokers.

  What are some of the dynamics? First, although online brokers were geared up to handle 1.2 million trades a day, volume had shrunk to about 834,000—a 30 percent drop. Thus, competition for business intensified. Second, when the stock market is down, many investors trust their instincts less and seek professional guidance from brokerages that offer differentiated services. Eric Rajendra of A. T. Kearney, an international consulting company, claimed, "The current (online broker) model is inadequate for the pressures the industry is facing now."

- **A lack of parity on differentiation.** As noted earlier, firms striving to attain cost leadership advantages must obtain a level of parity on differentiation. Firms providing online degree programs may offer low prices. However, they may not be successful unless they can offer instruction that is perceived as comparable to traditional providers. For them, parity can be achieved on differentiation dimensions such as reputation and quality and through signaling mechanisms such as accreditation agencies.

- **Erosion of cost advantages when the pricing information available to customers increases.** This is becoming a more significant challenge as the Internet dramatically increases both the quantity and volume of information available to consumers about pricing and cost structures. Life insurance firms offering whole life insurance provide an interesting example.[19] One study found that for each 10 percent increase in consumer use of the Internet, there is a corresponding reduction in insurance prices to consumers of 3 to 5 percent. Recently, the nationwide savings (or, alternatively, reduced revenues to providers) was between $115 and $125 million annually.

Differentiation

As the name implies, a **differentiation strategy** consists of creating differences in the firm's product or service offering by creating something that is perceived *industrywide* as unique and valued by customers.[20] Differentiation can take many forms:

- Prestige or brand image (Adam's Mark hotels, BMW automobiles).[21]
- Technology (Martin guitars, Marantz stereo components, North Face camping equipment).
- Innovation (Medtronic medical equipment, Nokia cellular phones).
- Features (Cannondale mountain bikes, Honda Goldwing motorcycles).
- Customer service (Nordstrom department stores, Sears lawn equipment retailing).
- Dealer network (Lexus automobiles, Caterpillar earthmoving equipment).

Exhibit 5.5 draws on the concept of the value chain as an example of how firms may differentiate themselves in primary and support activities.

differentiation strategy
a firm's generic strategy based on creating differences in the firm's product or service offering by creating something that is perceived *industrywide* as unique and valued by customers.

Exhibit 5.5

Value-Chain
Activities: Examples of
Differentiation

Support Activities

Firm Infrastructure

- Superior MIS—To integrate value-creating activities to improve quality.
- Facilities that promote firm image.
- Widely respected CEO enhances firm reputation.

Human Resource Management

- Programs to attract talented engineers and scientists.
- Provide training and incentives to ensure a strong customer service orientation.

Technology Development

- Superior material handling and sorting technology.
- Excellent applications engineering support.

Procurement

- Purchase of high-quality components to enhance product image.
- Use of most prestigious outlets.

Primary Activities

Inbound Logistics

- Superior material handling operations to minimize damage.
- Quick transfer of inputs to manufacturing process.

Operations

- Flexibility and speed in responding to changes in manufacturing specifications.
- Low defect rates to improve quality.

Outbound Logistics

- Accurate and responsive order processing.
- Effective product replenishment to reduce customer inventory.

Marketing and Sales

- Creative and innovative advertising programs.
- Fostering of personal relationship with key customers.

Service

- Rapid response to customer service requests.
- Complete inventory of replacement parts and supplies.

Source: Adapted from Porter, M.E. 1985. *Competitive Advantage: Creating and Sustaining Superior Performance.* New York: Free Press.

Firms may differentiate themselves along several different dimensions at once.[22] For example, BMW is known for its high prestige, superior engineering, and high-quality automobiles. And, Harley-Davidson differentiates on image and dealer services.[23]

Firms achieve and sustain differentiation advantages and attain above-average performance when their price premiums exceed the extra costs incurred in being unique.[24] For example, both BMW and Harley-Davidson must increase consumer costs to offset added marketing expenses. Thus, a differentiator will always seek out ways of distinguishing itself from similar competitors to justify price premiums greater than the costs incurred by differentiating. The role of design in achieving differentiation is addressed in: Brown, T. 2008. Design thinking. *Harvard Business Review*. 86(6): 84–92. Clearly, a differentiator cannot ignore costs. After all, its premium prices would be eroded by a markedly inferior cost position. Therefore, it must attain a level of cost *parity* relative to competitors. Differentiators can do this by reducing costs in all areas that do not affect differentiation. Porsche, for example, invests heavily in engine design—an area in which its customers demand excellence—but it is less concerned and spends fewer resources in the design of the instrument panel or the arrangement of switches on the radio.[25]

Many companies successfully follow a differentiation strategy.[26] For example, FedEx's CEO and founder, Fred Smith, claims that the key to his firm's success is innovation.[27] He contends his management team didn't understand their real goal when they started the firm in 1971: "We thought that we were selling the transportation of goods; in fact, we were selling peace of mind." They now provide drivers with a handheld computer and a transmitting device so that customers can track their packages from their desktop PCs.

Lexus, a division of Toyota, provides an example of how a firm can strengthen its differentiation strategy by *achieving integration at multiple points along the value chain.*[28] Although the luxury car line was not introduced until the late 1980s, by the early 1990s the cars had already soared to the top of J. D. Power & Associates's customer satisfaction ratings.

> In the spirit of benchmarking, one of Lexus's competitors hired Custom Research Inc. (CRI), a marketing research firm, to find out why Lexus owners were so satisfied. CRI conducted a series of focus groups in which Lexus drivers eagerly offered anecdotes about the special care they experienced from their dealers. It became clear that, although Lexus was manufacturing cars with few mechanical defects, it was the extra care shown by the sales and service staff that resulted in satisfied customers. Such pampering is reflected in the feedback from one customer who claimed she never had a problem with her Lexus. However, upon further probing, she said, "Well, I suppose you could call the four times they had to replace the windshield a 'problem.' But frankly, they took care of it so well and always gave me a loaner car, so I never really considered it a problem until you mentioned it now." An insight gained in CRI's research is that perceptions of product quality (design, engineering, and manufacturing) can be strongly influenced by downstream activities in the value chain (marketing and sales, service).

Strategy Spotlight 5.3 addresses how Netflix, the successful Internet movie rental company, uses crowdsourcing to enhance its differentiation.

Differentiation: Improving Competitive Position vis-à-vis the Five Forces

Differentiation provides protection against rivalry since brand loyalty lowers customer sensitivity to price and raises customer switching costs.[29] By increasing a firm's margins, differentiation also avoids the need for a low-cost position. Higher entry barriers result because of customer loyalty and the firm's ability to provide uniqueness in its products or services.[30] Differentiation also provides higher margins that enable a firm to deal with supplier power. And it reduces buyer power, because buyers lack comparable alternatives and are therefore less price sensitive.[31] Supplier power is also decreased because there is

strategy spotlight

Crowdsourcing: How Netflix Boosts Its Differentiation

Netflix is well-known for its inviting online presentation and efficient distribution system. However, this highly successful movie-rental company prides itself on its capability to offer subscribers a compact list of films that they are likely to enjoy watching. And it must be working: Netflix sends 35,000 titles a day to its 7.5 million subscribers.

"Imagine that our Website was a brick-and-mortar store," says Netflix vice president, James Bennett. "When people walk through the door, they see DVDs rearrange themselves. The movies that might interest them fly onto the shelves, and all the rest go to the back room."

The movies, of course, don't do the rearranging—that is done by the customers themselves, with an assist from a computer program called Cinematch, which Netflix developed in 2000. Customers are invited to rate each film they watch on a 1 to 5 scale. Cinematch analyzes these ratings, searches through 80,000 titles in inventory, and determines the list of films tailored to the taste of each of the firm's subscribers. By enticing them to rate films, Netflix achieves the latest in business innovation—getting customers to serve themselves.

Netflix is not unique in their use of so-called recommenders. Consider other online retailers such as Amazon,

Apple, eBay, and Overstock. All of these rely on their customers for a helping hand in predicting what products the customers will prefer—whether the product is bedding, books, CDs, or DVDs. Customer ratings are used to rank corporate service providers as well.

For all these companies, the recommender system provides more than a chance to create an extra service. It helps them to establish a stronger connection with their customers. And studies have shown that it can substantially increase online sales.

The extent of Netflix's commitment to personalized movie recommendations was made clear in 2006 when it offered a $1 million prize to anyone who could build a system that is at least 10 percent better than Cinematch. The competition is to end in 2011. Thus far, Netflix has received 169 submissions, several of which were an improvement over Cinematch. The best coders quickly managed to improve on the existing system by 5 percent. But, so far, the top contestant—a team of coders from AT&T—had still only improved on Cinematch by 8.43 percent. So close, yet so far . . .

Netflix has also developed another crowdsourcing feature called Friends. Here, subscribers see each other's list of films watched and compare the ratings they have awarded the films—in exchange for suggestions on other films to watch.

Sources: Libert, B. & Spector, J. 2008. *We Are Smarter Than Me.* Philadelphia: Wharton Publishing; and Howe, J. 2008. *Crowdsourcing.* New York: Crown Business.

crowdsourcing

a certain amount of prestige associated with being the supplier to a producer of highly differentiated products and services. Last, differentiation enhances customer loyalty, thus reducing the threat from substitutes.

Our examples illustrate these points. Lexus has enjoyed enhanced power over buyers because its top J. D. Power ranking makes buyers more willing to pay a premium price. This lessens rivalry, since buyers become less price-sensitive. The prestige associated with its brand name also lowers supplier power since margins are high. Suppliers would probably desire to be associated with prestige brands, thus lessening their incentives to drive up prices. Finally, the loyalty and "peace of mind" associated with a service provider such as FedEx makes such firms less vulnerable to rivalry or substitute products and services.

Potential Pitfalls of Differentiation Strategies   Potential pitfalls of a differentiation strategy include:

- *Uniqueness that is not valuable.* A differentiation strategy must provide unique bundles of products and/or services that customers value highly. It's not enough just to be "different." An example is Gibson's Dobro bass guitar. Gibson came up with a

168 Part 2:: Strategic Formulation

unique idea: Design and build an acoustic bass guitar with sufficient sound volume so that amplification wasn't necessary. The problem with other acoustic bass guitars was that they did not project enough volume because of the low-frequency bass notes. By adding a resonator plate on the body of the traditional acoustic bass, Gibson increased the sound volume. Gibson believed this product would serve a particular niche market—bluegrass and folk artists who played in small group "jams" with other acoustic musicians. Unfortunately, Gibson soon discovered that its targeted market was content with their existing options: an upright bass amplified with a microphone or an acoustic electric guitar. Thus, Gibson developed a unique product, but it was not perceived as valuable by its potential customers.[32]

- **Too much differentiation.** Firms may strive for quality or service that is higher than customers desire. Thus, they become vulnerable to competitors who provide an appropriate level of quality at a lower price. For example, consider the expensive Mercedes-Benz S-Class, which ranges in price between $75,000 and $125,000.[33] *Consumer Reports* described it as "sumptuous," "quiet and luxurious," and a "delight to drive." The magazine also considered it to be the least reliable sedan available in the United States. According to David Champion, who runs their testing program, the problems are electronic. "The engineers have gone a little wild," he says. "They've put every bell and whistle that they think of, and sometimes they don't have the attention to detail to make these systems work." Some features include: a computer-driven suspension that reduces body roll as the vehicle whips around a corner; cruise control that automatically slows the car down if it gets too close to another car; and seats that are adjustable 14 ways and that are ventilated by a system that uses eight fans.

- **Too high a price premium.** This pitfall is quite similar to too much differentiation. Customers may desire the product, but they are repelled by the price premium. For example, Duracell (a division of Gillette) recently charged too much for batteries.[34] The firm tried to sell consumers on its superior quality products, but the mass market wasn't convinced. Why? The price differential was simply too high. At a CVS drugstore just one block from Gillette's headquarters, a four-pack of Energizer AA batteries was on sale at $2.99 compared with a Duracell four-pack at $4.59. Duracell's market share dropped 2 percent in a recent two-year period, and its profits declined over 30 percent. Clearly, the price/performance proposition Duracell offered customers was not accepted.

- **Differentiation that is easily imitated.** As we noted in Chapter 3, resources that are easily imitated cannot lead to sustainable advantages. Similarly, firms may strive for, and even attain, a differentiation strategy that is successful for a time. However, the advantages are eroded through imitation. Consider Cereality's innovative differentiation strategy of stores which offer a wide variety of cereals and toppings for around $4.00.[35] As one would expect, once their idea proved successful, competitors entered the market because much of the initial risk had already been taken. Rivals include an Iowa City restaurant named the Cereal Cabinet, the Cereal Bowl in Miami, and Bowls: A Cereal Joint in Gainesville, Florida. Says David Roth, one of Cereality's founders: "With any good business idea, you're faced with people who see you've cracked the code and who try to cash in on it."

- **Dilution of brand identification through product-line extensions.** Firms may erode their quality brand image by adding products or services with lower prices and less quality. Although this can increase short-term revenues, it may be detrimental in the long run. Consider Gucci.[36] In the 1980s Gucci wanted to capitalize on its prestigious brand name by launching an aggressive strategy of revenue growth. It added a set of lower-priced canvas goods to its product line. It also pushed goods heavily into department stores and duty-free channels and allowed its name to appear on a host of licensed items such as watches, eyeglasses, and perfumes. In the short term, this

Exhibit 5.6
Potential Pitfalls of
Overall Cost Leadership
and Differentiation
Strategies

Overall Cost Leadership:

- Too much focus on one or a few value-chain activities.
- All rivals share a common input or raw material.
- The strategy is imitated too easily.
- A lack of parity on differentiation.
- Erosion of cost advantages when the pricing information available to customers increases.

Differentiation:

- Uniqueness that is not valuable.
- Too much differentiation.
- The price premium is too high.
- Differentiation that is easily imitated.
- Dilution of brand identification through product-line extensions.
- Perceptions of differentiation may vary between buyers and sellers.

strategy worked. Sales soared. However, the strategy carried a high price. Gucci's indiscriminate approach to expanding its products and channels tarnished its sterling brand. Sales of its high-end goods (with higher profit margins) fell, causing profits to decline.

- ***Perceptions of differentiation may vary between buyers and sellers.*** The issue here is that "beauty is in the eye of the beholder." Companies must realize that although they may perceive their products and services as differentiated, their customers may view them as commodities. Indeed, in today's marketplace, many products and services have been reduced to commodities.[37] Thus, a firm could overprice its offerings and lose margins altogether if it has to lower prices to reflect market realities.

Exhibit 5.6 summarizes the pitfalls of overall cost leadership and differentiation strategies. In addressing the pitfalls associated with these two generic strategies there is one common, underlying theme. Managers must be aware of the dangers associated with concentrating so much on one strategy that they fail to attain parity on the other.

Focus

focus strategy a firm's generic strategy based on appeal to a narrow market segment within an industry.

A **focus strategy** is based on the choice of a narrow competitive scope within an industry. A firm following this strategy selects a segment or group of segments and tailors its strategy to serve them. The essence of focus is the exploitation of a particular market niche. As you might expect, narrow focus itself (like merely "being different" as a differentiator) is simply not sufficient for above-average performance.

The focus strategy, as indicated in Exhibit 5.1, has two variants. In a cost focus, a firm strives to create a cost advantage in its target segment. In a differentiation focus, a firm seeks to differentiate in its target market. Both variants of the focus strategy rely on providing better service than broad-based competitors who are trying to serve the focuser's target segment. Cost focus exploits differences in cost behavior in some segments, while differentiation focus exploits the special needs of buyers in other segments.

Let's look at examples of two firms that have successfully implemented focus strategies. Network Appliance (NA) has developed a more cost-effective way to store and distribute computer files.[38] Its larger rival, EMC, makes mainframe-style products priced over

Paccar: 'Trucking along. . .' with a Successful Focus Strategy

Paccar, a $15 billion Bellevue, Washington–based heavy-truck maker with about 20 percent of the North American market, has chosen to focus on one group of customers: owner-operators. These are the drivers who own their trucks and contract directly with shippers or serve as subcontractors to larger trucking companies. Such operators have limited clout as truck buyers. They are also less price sensitive because of their strong emotional ties to and economic dependence on the product. They take great pride in their trucks, in which they spend most of their time.

Paccar has invested heavily to develop a variety of features with owner-operators in mind: luxurious sleeper cabins, plush leather seats, noise-insulated cabins, sleek exterior styling, and so forth. At Paccar's extensive network of dealers, prospective buyers use software to select among thousands of options to put their personal signature on their trucks. These customized trucks are built to order, not to stock, and are delivered in six to eight weeks. Paccar's trucks also have aerodynamic designs that reduce fuel consumption, and they maintain their resale value better than other trucks. Paccar's roadside assistance program and

● Paccar's Kenworth and Peterbilt brands of semi tractors have become status symbols at truck stops.

IT-supported system for distributing spare parts reduce the time a truck is out of service. All these are crucial considerations for an owner-operator. Customers pay Paccar a 10 percent premium, and its Kenworth and Peterbilt brands are considered status symbols at truck stops.

Source: Porter, M. E. 2008. The Five Competitive Forces That Shape Strategy. *Harvard Business Review*, 86(1): 78–97.

$1 million that store files and accommodate Internet traffic. NA makes devices that cost under $200,000 for particular storage jobs such as caching (temporary storage) of Internet content. Focusing on such narrow segments has certainly paid off for NA; it has posted a remarkable 20 straight quarters of revenue growth.

Bessemer Trust competes in the private banking industry.[39] A differentiation focuser, it targets families with a minimum of $5 million in assets, who desire both capital preservation and wealth accumulation. In other words, these are not people who want to put all their "eggs in a dot-com basket." Bessemer configures its activities for highly personalized service by assigning one account officer for every 14 families. Meetings are more likely to be held at a client's ranch or yacht than in Bessemer's office. Bessemer offers a wide range of customized services, such as investment management, estate administration, oversight of oil and gas investments, and accounting for race horses and aircraft. Despite the industry's most generous compensation of account officers and the highest personnel cost as a percentage of operating expenses, Bessemer's focused differentiation strategy is estimated to yield the highest return on equity in the industry.

Strategy Spotlight 5.4 discusses Paccar, a highly successful heavy-truck manufacturer that has created a successful focus strategy.

Focus: Improving Competitive Position vis-à-vis the Five Forces   Focus requires that a firm either have a low-cost position with its strategic target, high differentiation, or both. As we discussed with regard to cost and differentiation strategies, these positions provide defenses against each competitive force. Focus is also used to select niches that are least vulnerable to substitutes or where competitors are weakest.

Let's look at our examples to illustrate some of these points. First, Bessemer Trust experienced lower rivalry and greater bargaining power by providing products and services to a targeted market segment that was less price-sensitive. New rivals had difficulty attracting customers away from Bessemer based only on lower prices. Similarly, the brand image and quality that this brand evoked heightened rivals' entry barriers. Additionally, we could reasonably speculate that Bessemer Trust enjoyed some protection against substitute products and services because of their relatively high reputation, brand image, and customer loyalty. With regard to the strategy of cost focus, Network Appliances, the successful rival to EMC in the computer storage industry, was better able to absorb pricing increases from suppliers as a result of its lower cost structure, reducing supplier power.

Potential Pitfalls of Focus Strategies   Potential pitfalls of focus strategies include:

- *Erosion of cost advantages within the narrow segment.* The advantages of a cost focus strategy may be fleeting if the cost advantages are eroded over time. For example, Dell's pioneering direct selling model in the personal computer industry has been eroded by rivals such as Hewlett Packard as they gain experience with Dell's distribution method. Similarly, other firms have seen their profit margins drop as competitors enter their product segment.

- *Even product and service offerings that are highly focused are subject to competition from new entrants and from imitation.* Some firms adopting a focus strategy may enjoy temporary advantages because they select a small niche with few rivals. However, their advantages may be short-lived. A notable example is the multitude of dot-com firms that specialize in very narrow segments such as pet supplies, ethnic foods, and vintage automobile accessories. The entry barriers tend to be low, there is little buyer loyalty, and competition becomes intense. And since the marketing strategies and technologies employed by most rivals are largely nonproprietary, imitation is easy. Over time, revenues fall, profits margins are squeezed, and only the strongest players survive the shakeout.

- *Focusers can become too focused to satisfy buyer needs.* Some firms attempting to attain advantages through a focus strategy may have too narrow a product or service. Consider many retail firms. Hardware chains such as Ace and True Value are losing market share to rivals such as Lowe's and Home Depot that offer a full line of home and garden equipment and accessories. And given the enormous purchasing power of the national chains, it would be difficult for such specialty retailers to attain parity on costs.

Combination Strategies: Integrating Overall Low Cost and Differentiation

>LO5

How firms can effectively combine the generic strategies of overall cost leadership and differentiation.

Perhaps the primary benefit to firms that integrate low-cost and differentiation strategies is the difficulty for rivals to duplicate or imitate.[40] This strategy enables a firm to provide two types of value to customers: differentiated attributes (e.g., high quality, brand identification, reputation) and lower prices (because of the firm's lower costs in value-creating activities). The goal is thus to provide unique value to customers in an efficient manner.[41] Some firms are able to attain both types of advantages simultaneously. For example, superior quality can lead to lower costs because of less need for rework in manufacturing, fewer warranty claims, a reduced need for customer service personnel to resolve customer complaints, and so forth. Thus, the benefits of combining advantages can be additive, instead of merely involving trade-offs. Next, we consider three approaches to combining overall low cost and differentiation.

combination strategies firms' integrations of various strategies to provide multiple types of value to customers.

Automated and Flexible Manufacturing Systems   Given the advances in manufacturing technologies such as CAD/CAM (computer aided design and computer aided manufacturing) as well as information technologies, many firms have been able to manufacture unique products in relatively small quantities at lower costs—a concept known as **mass customization.**[42]

Let's consider Andersen Windows of Bayport, Minnesota—a $1 billion manufacturer of windows for the building industry.[43] Until about 20 years ago, Andersen was a mass producer, in small batches, of a variety of standard windows. However, to meet changing customer needs, Andersen kept adding to its product line. The result was catalogs of ever-increasing size and a bewildering set of choices for both homeowners and contractors. Over a 6-year period, the number of products tripled, price quotes took several hours, and the error rate increased. This not only damaged the company's reputation, but also added to its manufacturing expenses.

mass customization a firm's ability to manufacture unique products in small quantities at low cost.

To bring about a major change, Andersen developed an interactive computer version of its paper catalogs that it sold to distributors and retailers. Salespersons can now customize each window to meet the customer's needs, check the design for structural soundness, and provide a price quote. The system is virtually error free, customers get exactly what they want, and the time to develop the design and furnish a quotation has been cut by 75 percent. Each showroom computer is connected to the factory, and customers are assigned a code number that permits them to track the order. The manufacturing system has been developed to use some common finished parts, but it also allows considerable variation in the final products. Despite its huge investment, Andersen has been able to lower costs, enhance quality and variety, and improve its response time to customers.

Exhibit 5.7 provides other examples of how flexible production systems have enabled firms to successfully engage in mass customization for their customers:[44]

Exploiting the Profit Pool Concept for Competitive Advantage   A profit pool is defined as the total profits in an industry at all points along the industry's value chain.[45] Although the concept is relatively straightforward, the structure of the profit pool can be complex.[46] The potential pool of profits will be deeper in some segments of the value chain than in others, and the depths will vary within an individual segment. Segment profitability

Exhibit 5.7
Effective Uses of Flexible Production Systems

- At Nikeid.com, customers can design an athletic or casual shoe to their specifications online, selecting almost every element of the shoe from the material of the sole to the color of the shoelace.

- Eleuria sells custom perfumes. Each product is created in response to a user profile constructed from responses to a survey about habits and preferences. Eleuria then provides a sample at modest cost to verify fit.

- Lands' End offers customized shirts and pants. Consumers specify style parameters, measurements, and fabrics through the firm's website. These settings are saved so that returning users can easily order a duplicate item.

- Cannondale permits consumers to specify the parameters that define a road bike frame, including custom colors and inscriptions. The user specifies the parameters on the firm's website and then arranges for delivery through a dealer.

Source: Randall, T., Terwiesch, C. & Ulrich, K. T. 2005. Principles for User Design of Custom Products. *California Management Review,* 47 (4): 68–85.

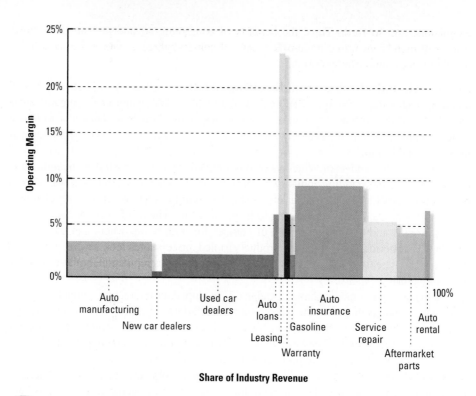

Exhibit 5.8 The U.S. Automobile Industry's Profit Pool

Source: Adapted and reprinted by permission of *Harvard Business Review,* Exhibit from "Profit Pools: A Fresh Look at Strategy," by O. Gadiesh and J. L. Gilbert, May–June 1998. Copyright © 1999 by the Harvard Business School Publishing Corporation; all rights reserved.

may vary widely by customer group, product category, geographic market, or distribution channel. Additionally, the pattern of profit concentration in an industry is very often different from the pattern of revenue generation.

Consider the automobile industry profit pool in Exhibit 5.8. Here we see little relationship between the generation of revenues and capturing of profits. While manufacturing generates most of the revenue, this value activity is far smaller profitwise than other value activities such as financing and extended warranty operations. So while a car manufacturer may be under tremendous pressure to produce cars efficiently, much of the profit (at least proportionately) can be captured in the aforementioned downstream operations. Thus, a carmaker would be ill-advised to focus solely on manufacturing and leave downstream operations to others through outsourcing.

Coordinating the "Extended" Value Chain by Way of Information Technology

Many firms have achieved success by integrating activities throughout the "extended value chain" by using information technology to link their own value chain with the value chains of their customers and suppliers. As noted in Chapter 3, this approach enables a firm to add value not only through its own value-creating activities, but also for its customers and suppliers.

Such a strategy often necessitates redefining the industry's value chain. A number of years ago, Wal-Mart took a close look at its industry's value chain and decided to reframe the competitive challenge.[47] Although its competitors were primarily focused on retailing—merchandising and promotion—Wal-Mart determined that it was not so much in the retailing industry as in the transportation logistics and communications industries.

Here, linkages in the extended value chain became central. That became Wal-Mart's chosen battleground. By redefining the rules of competition that played to its strengths, Wal-Mart has attained competitive advantages and dominates its industry.

Integrated Overall Low-Cost and Differentiation Strategies: Improving Competitive Position vis-à-vis the Five Forces   Firms that successfully integrate both differentiation and cost advantages create an enviable position. For example, Wal-Mart's integration of information systems, logistics, and transportation helps it to drive down costs and provide outstanding product selection. This dominant competitive position, serves to erect high entry barriers to potential competitors that have neither the financial nor physical resources to compete head-to-head. Wal-Mart's size—over $400 billion in 2008 sales— provides the chain with enormous bargaining power over suppliers. Its low pricing and wide selection reduce the power of buyers (its customers), because there are relatively few competitors that can provide a comparable cost/value proposition. This reduces the possibility of intense head-to-head rivalry, such as protracted price wars. Finally, Wal-Mart's overall value proposition makes potential substitute products (e.g., Internet competitors) a less viable threat.

Pitfalls of Integrated Overall Cost Leadership and Differentiation Strategies
The pitfalls of integrated overall cost leadership and differentiation include:

- *Firms that fail to attain both strategies may end up with neither and become "stuck in the middle."* A key issue in strategic management is the creation of competitive advantages that enable a firm to enjoy above-average returns. Some firms may become "stuck in the middle" if they try to attain both cost and differentiation advantages. An example that we are all familiar with would be the Big 3 U.S. automobile makers. They are plagued by expensive "legacy costs" associated with pension and health care obligations—a central issue in 2008 federal bailout legislation. And, they suffer from long-term customer perceptions of mediocre quality—inferior to their European and Japanese rivals. The troubling quality perceptions persist despite the fact that the Big 3 has attained approximate parity with their Japanese and European competitors in recent J. D. Power surveys.
- *Underestimating the challenges and expenses associated with coordinating value-creating activities in the extended value chain.* Integrating activities across a firm's value chain with the value chain of suppliers and customers involves a significant investment in financial and human resources. Firms must consider the expenses linked to technology investment, managerial time and commitment, and the involvement and investment required by the firm's customers and suppliers. The firm must be confident that it can generate a sufficient scale of operations and revenues to justify all associated expenses.
- *Miscalculating sources of revenue and profit pools in the firm's industry.* Firms may fail to accurately assess sources of revenue and profits in their value chain. This can occur for several reasons. For example, a manager may be biased due to his or her functional area background, work experiences, and educational background. If the manager's background is in engineering, he or she might perceive that proportionately greater revenue and margins were being created in manufacturing, product, and process design than a person whose background is in a "downstream" value-chain activity such as marketing and sales. Or politics could make managers "fudge" the numbers to favor their area of operations. This would make them responsible for a greater proportion of the firm's profits, thus improving their bargaining position.

A related problem is directing an overwhelming amount of managerial time, attention, and resources to value-creating activities that produce the greatest margins—to the detriment of other important, albeit less profitable, activities. For example, a car manufacturer may focus too much on downstream activities, such as warranty fulfillment and financing operations, to the detriment of differentiation and cost of the cars themselves.

How the Internet and Digital Technologies Are Affecting the Competitive Strategies

>LO6

How Internet-enabled business models are being used to improve strategic positioning.

Internet and digital technologies have swept across the economy and now have an impact on how nearly every company conducts its business. These changes have created new cost efficiencies and avenues for differentiation. However, the presence of these technologies is so widespread that it is questionable how any one firm can use them effectively in ways that genuinely set them apart from rivals. Thus, to stay competitive, firms must update their strategies to reflect the new possibilities and constraints that these phenomena represent. In this section, we address both the opportunities and the pitfalls that Internet and digital technologies offer to companies using overall cost leadership, differentiation, and focus strategies. We also briefly consider two major impacts that the Internet is having on business: lowering transaction costs and enabling mass customization.

Overall Cost Leadership

The Internet and digital technologies are creating new opportunities for firms to achieve low-cost advantages by enabling them to manage costs and achieve greater efficiencies. Managing costs, and even changing the cost structures of certain industries, is a key feature of the new digital economy. Most analysts agree that the Internet's ability to lower transaction costs is transforming business. Broadly speaking, *transaction costs* refer to all the various expenses associated with conducting business. It applies not just to buy/sell transactions but to the costs of interacting with every part of a firm's value chain, within and outside the firm. Think about it. Hiring new employees, meeting with customers, ordering supplies, addressing government regulations—all of these exchanges have some costs associated with them. Because business can be conducted differently on the Internet, new ways of saving money are changing the competitive landscape.

Other factors also help to lower transaction costs. The process of disintermediation (in Chapter 2) has a similar effect. Each time intermediaries are used in a transaction, additional costs are added. Removing intermediaries lowers transaction costs. The Internet reduces the costs to search for a product or service, whether it is a retail outlet (as in the case of consumers) or a trade show (as in the case of business-to-business shoppers). Not only is the need for travel eliminated but so is the need to maintain a physical address, whether it's a permanent retail location or a temporary presence at a trade show.

Exhibit 5.9 identifies several types of cost leadership strategies that are made possible by Internet and digital technologies. These cost savings are available throughout a firm's value chain, in both primary and support activities.

Exhibit 5.9

Internet-Enabled Low-Cost Leader Strategies

- Online bidding and order processing are eliminating the need for sales calls and are minimizing sales force expenses.
- Online purchase orders are making many transactions paperless, thus reducing the costs of procurement and paper.
- Direct access to progress reports and the ability for customers to periodically check work in progress is minimizing rework.
- Collaborative design efforts using Internet technologies that link designers, materials suppliers, and manufacturers are reducing the costs and speeding the process of new product development.

Potential Internet-Related Pitfalls for Low-Cost Leaders   One of the biggest threats to low-cost leaders is imitation. This problem is intensified for business done on the Internet. Most of the advantages associated with contacting customers directly, and even capabilities that are software driven (e.g., customized ordering systems or real-time access to the status of work in progress), can be duplicated quickly and without threat of infringement on proprietary information. Another pitfall relates to companies that become overly enamored with using the Internet for cost-cutting. Companies that do so may suffer if they place too much attention on one business activity and ignore others. They may jeopardize customer relations or neglect other cost centers, such as providing services or controlling turnover and recruiting expenses, which then dig into their cost advantages.

Differentiation

For many companies, Internet and digital technologies have enhanced their ability to build brand, offer quality products and services, and achieve other differentiation advantages. Among the most striking trends are new ways to interact with consumers. In particular, the Internet is creating new ways of differentiating by enabling *mass customization,* which improves the response to customer wishes. Mass customization has been growing for years as flexible manufacturing systems have made manufacturing more adaptable and electronic data interchange has made communications more direct. But the Internet has generated a giant leap forward in the amount of control customers can have in influencing the process. Such capabilities are changing the way companies develop unique product and service offerings, build their reputation, and preserve their brand image.

Methods like mass customization are changing how companies go to market and are challenging some of the tried-and-true techniques of differentiation. Traditionally, companies reached customers using high-end catalogs, the showroom floor, personal sales calls and products using prestige packaging, celebrity endorsements, and charity sponsorships. All of these avenues are still available and may still be effective, depending on a firm's competitive environment. But many customers now judge the quality and uniqueness of a product or service by their ability to be involved in its planning and design, combined with speed of delivery and reliable results. Internet and digitally based capabilities are thus changing the way differentiators make exceptional products and achieve superior service. Such improvements are being made at a reasonable cost, allowing firms to achieve parity on the basis of overall cost leadership.

Exhibit 5.10 identifies differentiation activities that are made possible by Internet and digital technologies. Opportunities to differentiate are available in all parts of a company's value chain—both primary and support activities.

Exhibit 5.10
Internet-Enabled Differentiation Strategies

- Personalized online access provides customers with their own "site within a site" in which their prior orders, status of current orders, and requests for future orders are processed directly on the supplier's website.
- Online access to real-time sales and service information is being used to empower the sales force and continually update R&D and technology development efforts.
- Internet-based knowledge management systems that link all parts of the organization are shortening response times and accelerating organization learning.
- Quick online responses to service requests and rapid feedback to customer surveys and product promotions are enhancing marketing efforts.

Potential Internet-Related Pitfalls for Differentiators   Traditional differentiation strategies such as building strong brand identity and prestige pricing have been undermined by Internet-enabled capabilities such as the ability to compare product features side-by-side or bid online for competing services. The sustainability of Internet-based gains from differentiation will deteriorate if companies offer differentiating features that customers don't want or create a sense of uniqueness that customers don't value. The result can be a failed value proposition—the value companies thought they were offering, does not translate into sales.

Focus

A focus strategy targets a narrow market segment with customized products and/or services. With focus strategies, the Internet offers new avenues in which to compete because they can access markets less expensively (low cost) and provide more services and features (differentiation). Some claim that the Internet has opened up a new world of opportunities for niche players who seek to access small markets in a highly specialized fashion.[48] Niche businesses are among the most active users of digital technologies and e-business solutions. According to the ClickZ.com division of Jupitermedia Corporation, 77 percent of small businesses agree that a website is essential for small business success. Small businesses also report that the Internet has helped them grow (58 percent), made them more profitable (51 percent), and helped reduce transaction costs (49 percent).[49] Clearly niche players and small businesses are using the Internet and digital technologies to create more viable focus strategies.

Many aspects of the Internet economy favor focus strategies because niche players and small firms have been able to extend their reach and effectively compete with larger competitors. For example, niche firms have been quicker than Fortune 1000 firms to adopt blogging as a way to create a community and gather customer feedback.[50] Effective use of blogs is an example of how focusers are using the new technology to provide the kinds of advantages that have been the hallmark of a focus strategy in the past—specialized knowledge, rapid response, and strong customer service. Thus, the Internet has provided many firms that pursue focus strategies with new tools for creating competitive advantages.

Exhibit 5.11 outlines several approaches to strategic focusing that are made possible by Internet and digital technologies. Both primary and support activities can be enhanced using the kind of singlemindedness that is characteristic of a focus strategy.

Potential Internet-Related Pitfalls for Focusers   A key danger for focusers using the Internet relates to correctly assessing the size of the online marketplace. Focusers can misread the scope and interests of their target markets. This can cause them to focus on segments that are too narrow to be profitable or to lose their uniqueness in overly broad niches, making them vulnerable to imitators or new entrants.

Exhibit 5.11

Internet-Enabled Focus Strategies

> - Permission marketing techniques are focusing sales efforts on specific customers who opt to receive advertising notices.
> - Niche portals that target specific groups are providing advertisers with access to viewers with specialized interests.
> - Virtual organizing and online "officing" are being used to minimize firm infrastructure requirements.
> - Procurement technologies that use Internet software to match buyers and sellers are highlighting specialized buyers and drawing attention to smaller suppliers.

What happens when an e-business focuser tries to overextend its niche? Efforts to appeal to a broader audience by carrying additional inventory, developing additional content, or offering additional services can cause it to lose the cost advantages associated with a limited product or service offering. Conversely, when focus strategies become too narrow, the e-business may have trouble generating enough activity to justify the expense of operating the website.

Are Combination Strategies the Key to E-Business Success?

Because of the changing dynamics presented by digital and Internet-based technologies, new strategic combinations that make the best use of the competitive strategies may hold the greatest promise.[51] Many experts agree that the net effect of the digital economy is *fewer* rather than more opportunities for sustainable advantages.[52] This means strategic thinking becomes more important.

More specifically, the Internet has provided all companies with greater tools for managing costs. So it may be that cost management and control will become more important management tools. In general, this may be good if it leads to an economy that makes more efficient use of its scarce resources. However, for individual companies, it may shave critical percentage points off profit margins and create a climate that makes it impossible to survive, much less achieve sustainable above-average profits.

Many differentiation advantages are also diminished by the Internet. The ability to comparison shop—to check product reviews and inspect different choices with a few clicks of the mouse—is depriving some companies, such as auto dealers, of the unique advantages that were the hallmark of their prior success. Differentiating is still an important strategy, of course. But how firms achieve it may change, and the best approach may be to combine differentiation with other competitive strategies.

Perhaps the greatest beneficiaries are the focusers who can use the Internet to capture a niche that previously may have been inaccessible. However, because the same factors that make it possible for a small niche player to be a contender may make that same niche attractive to a big company. That is, an incumbent firm that previously thought a niche market was not worth the effort may use Internet technologies to enter that segment for a lower cost than in the past. The larger firm can then bring its market power and resources to bear in a way that a smaller competitor cannot match.

A combination strategy challenges a company to carefully blend alternative strategic approaches and remain mindful of the impact of different decisions on the firm's value-creating processes and its extended value-chain activities. Strong leadership is needed to maintain a bird's-eye perspective on a company's overall approach and to coordinate the multiple dimensions of a combination strategy.

Strategy Spotlight 5.5 describes the efforts of Liberty Mutual, a company that used Internet and digital technologies to successfully combine both differentiation and overall low-cost advantages.

Industry Life Cycle Stages: Strategic Implications

The **industry life cycle** refers to the stages of introduction, growth, maturity, and decline that occur over the life of an industry. In considering the industry life cycle, it is useful to think in terms of broad product lines such as personal computers, photocopiers, or long-distance telephone service. Yet the industry life cycle concept can be explored from several levels, from the life cycle of an entire industry to the life cycle of a single variation or model of a specific product or service.

Why are industry life cycles important?[53] The emphasis on various generic strategies, functional areas, value-creating activities, and overall objectives varies over the course of an industry life cycle. Managers must become even more aware of their firm's strengths

industry life cycle
the stages of introduction, growth, maturity, and decline that typically occur over the life of an industry.

Liberty Mutual's Electronic Invoice System: Combining Low Cost and Differentiation Advantages

Boston-based Liberty Mutual Group is a leading global insurer and the sixth largest property and casualty insurer in the United States. Its largest line of business is personal automobile insurance. Liberty Mutual has $85.5 billion in assets and $23.5 billion in annual revenues—ranking the firm 102nd on the Fortune 500 list of the largest corporations.

In 2000, Liberty Mutual became one of the first companies to experiment with electronic invoices. It set up a pilot program with a few law firms to submit its bills through a secured website. These firms, for the most part, handle claims litigation for Liberty, defending its policyholders in lawsuits. Its success with this program convinced Liberty that it could achieve significant cost savings and also pass along differentiating features to its customers and strategic partners. Liberty now processes nearly 400,000 electronic legal-services invoices a year—70 percent of the total invoices that the firm receives.

As expected, the initial transition was quite expensive. The company invested nearly $1 million in the first four years. However, Liberty estimates that the electronic invoice program saves the company $750,000 a year in direct costs by streamlining the distribution, payment, storage, and retrieval of invoices. E-invoices enable Liberty to move from intake to payment with half the staff that it had taken to process paper invoices. The firm has also created new efficiencies by cutting costs resulting from data entry errors, late payments, and overpayments. As a relatively minor issue, Liberty saves more than $20,000 per year on postage, photocopying, archiving, and retrieval costs.

The legal invoices are organized by litigation phase or task—for example, taking a deposition or reporting a witness statement. Work is diced into tiny increments of

six minutes or less. A single invoice that covers a month of complex litigation, for example, can include well over 1,000 lines. However, by building and mining a database of law firm billing practices, Liberty is able to generate a highly granular report card about law firm activities and performance. The new knowledge generated by this system not only increases internal effectiveness but also allows Liberty to provide detailed feedback to clients and other external stakeholders.

Online invoicing has also helped speed up both processing and response time. Liberty can instantaneously see how firms deploy and bill for partners, paralegals, and other staff, how they compare with each other on rates, hours, and case outcomes; and whether, how, and how often they send duplicate invoices or charge for inappropriate services. The system also allows Liberty to instantly review all of the time billed for a particular attorney across many cases, enabling the firm to reconstruct the total time billed to Liberty during a single day. More than once they have found that attorneys have billed more than 24 hours in a day. Liberty is also able to easily expose prohibited formula billing patterns (wherein, for example, they are billed a set amount for a service instead of actual time spent). In two cases in which formula billing was used, Liberty found that there were more than $28,000 in suspected overcharges.

Liberty Mutual is in the process of developing a large database of law firms' billing practices on different types of cases. The database should eventually enable Liberty to evaluate a law firm's billing activities and compare them to the norms of all of its partner firms. With such intelligence, it will be a rather straightforward matter to rate each firm's cost effectiveness in handling certain types of cases and match firms with cases accordingly.

Liberty's decision to use electronic invoices was initially based on the potential for cost savings. But the differentiating advantages it has achieved in terms of rapid feedback, decreased response time, and a knowledge trove in databases that can be electronically mined has provided the company with a fruitful combination of Internet-based strategic advantages.

Sources: Coyle, M., & Angevine, R. 2007. Liberty Mutual Group reports fourth quarter 2006 results. February 26, www.libertymutual.com; and Smunt, T. L., & Sutcliffe, C. L., 2004. There's Gold in Them Bills. *Harvard Business Review*, 82(9): 24–25.

and weaknesses in many areas to attain competitive advantages. For example, firms depend on their research and development (R&D) activities in the introductory stage. R&D is the source of new products and features that everyone hopes will appeal to customers. Firms develop products and services to stimulate consumer demand. Later, during the maturity phase, the functions of the product have been defined, more competitors have entered the market, and competition is intense. Managers then place greater emphasis on production efficiencies and process (as opposed to the product) engineering in order to lower manufacturing costs. This helps to protect the firm's market position and to extend the product life cycle because the firm's lower costs can be passed on to consumers in the form of lower prices, and price-sensitive customers will find the product more appealing.

Exhibit 5.12 illustrates the four stages of the industry life cycle and how factors such as generic strategies, market growth rate, intensity of competition, and overall objectives change over time. Managers must strive to emphasize the key functional areas during each

>LO7

The importance of considering the industry life cycle to determine a firm's business-level strategy and its relative emphasis on functional area strategies and value-creating activities.

Stage / Factor	Introduction	Growth	Maturity	Decline
Generic strategies	Differentiation	Differentiation	Differentiation Overall cost leadership	Overall cost leadership Focus
Market growth rate	Low	Very large	Low to moderate	Negative
Number of segments	Very few	Some	Many	Few
Intensity of competition	Low	Increasing	Very intense	Changing
Emphasis on product design	Very high	High	Low to moderate	Low
Emphasis on process design	Low	Low to moderate	High	Low
Major functional area(s) of concern	Research and development	Sales and marketing	Production	General management and finance
Overall objective	Increase market awareness	Create consumer demand	Defend market share and extend product life cycles	Consolidate, maintain, harvest, or exit

Exhibit 5.12 Stages of the Industry Life Cycle

of the four stages and to attain a level of parity in all functional areas and value-creating activities. For example, although controlling production costs may be a primary concern during the maturity stage, managers should not totally ignore other functions such as marketing and R&D. If they do, they can become so focused on lowering costs that they miss market trends or fail to incorporate important product or process designs. Thus, the firm may attain low-cost products that have limited market appeal.

It is important to point out a caveat. While the life cycle idea is analogous to a living organism (i.e., birth, growth, maturity, and death), the comparison has limitations.[54] Products and services go through many cycles of innovation and renewal. Typically, only fad products have a single life cycle. Maturity stages of an industry can be "transformed" or followed by a stage of rapid growth if consumer tastes change, technological innovations take place, or new developments occur. The cereal industry is a good example. When medical research indicated that oat consumption reduced a person's cholesterol, sales of Quaker Oats increased dramatically.[55]

Strategies in the Introduction Stage

introduction stage the first stage of the industry life cycle characterized by (1) new products that are not known to customers, (2) poorly defined market segments, (3) unspecified product features, (4) low sales growth, (5) rapid technological change, (6) operating losses, and (7) a need for financial support.

In the **introduction stage,** products are unfamiliar to consumers.[56] Market segments are not well defined, and product features are not clearly specified. The early development of an industry typically involves low sales growth, rapid technological change, operating losses, and the need for strong sources of cash to finance operations. Since there are few players and not much growth, competition tends to be limited.

Success requires an emphasis on research and development and marketing activities to enhance awareness. The challenge becomes one of (1) developing the product and finding a way to get users to try it, and (2) generating enough exposure so the product emerges as the "standard" by which all other rivals' products are evaluated.

There's an advantage to being the "first mover" in a market.[57] It led to Coca-Cola's success in becoming the first soft-drink company to build a recognizable global brand and enabled Caterpillar to get a lock on overseas sales channels and service capabilities.

However, there can also be a benefit to being a "late mover." Target carefully considered its decision to delay its Internet strategy. Compared to its competitors Wal-Mart and Kmart, Target was definitely an industry laggard. But things certainly turned out well:[58]

> By waiting, Target gained a late mover advantage. The store was able to use competitors' mistakes as its own learning curve. This saved money, and customers didn't seem to mind the wait: When Target finally opened its website, it quickly captured market share from both Kmart and Wal-Mart Internet shoppers. Forrester Research Internet analyst Stephen Zrike commented, "There's no question, in our mind, that Target has a far better understanding of how consumers buy online."

Examples of products currently in the introductory stages of the industry life cycle include electric vehicles, solar panels, and high-definition television (HDTV).

Strategies in the Growth Stage

growth stage the second stage of the product life cycle characterized by (1) strong increases in sales; (2) growing competition; (3) developing brand recognition; and (4) a need for financing complementary value-chain activities such as marketing, sales, customer service, and research and development.

The **growth stage** is characterized by strong increases in sales. Such potential attracts other rivals. In the growth stage, the primary key to success is to build consumer preferences for specific brands. This requires strong brand recognition, differentiated products, and the financial resources to support a variety of value-chain activities such as marketing and sales, and research and development. Whereas marketing and sales initiatives were mainly directed at spurring *aggregate* demand—that is, demand for all such products in the introduction stage—efforts in the growth stage are directed toward stimulating *selective* demand, in which a firm's product offerings are chosen instead of a rival's.

Revenues increase at an accelerating rate because (1) new consumers are trying the product and (2) a growing proportion of satisfied consumers are making repeat purchases.[59]

In general, as a product moves through its life cycle, the proportion of repeat buyers to new purchasers increases. Conversely, new products and services often fail if there are relatively few repeat purchases. For example, Alberto-Culver introduced Mr. Culver's Sparklers, which were solid air fresheners that looked like stained glass. Although the product quickly went from the introductory to the growth stage, sales collapsed. Why? Unfortunately, there were few repeat purchasers because buyers treated them as inexpensive window decorations, left them there, and felt little need to purchase new ones. Examples of products currently in the growth stage include Internet servers and personal digital assistants (e.g., Palm Pilots).

Strategies in the Maturity Stage

In the **maturity stage** aggregate industry demand softens. As markets become saturated, there are few new adopters. It's no longer possible to "grow around" the competition, so direct competition becomes predominant.[60] With few attractive prospects, marginal competitors exit the market. At the same time, rivalry among existing rivals intensifies because of fierce price competition at the same time that expenses associated with attracting new buyers are rising. Advantages based on efficient manufacturing operations and process engineering become more important for keeping costs low as customers become more price sensitive. It also becomes more difficult for firms to differentiate their offerings, because users have a greater understanding of products and services.

An article in *Fortune* magazine that addressed the intensity of rivalry in mature markets was aptly titled "A Game of Inches." It stated, "Battling for market share in a slowing industry can be a mighty dirty business. Just ask laundry soap archrivals Unilever and Procter & Gamble."[61] These two firms have been locked in a battle for market share since 1965. Why is the competition so intense? There is not much territory to gain and industry sales were flat. An analyst noted, "People aren't getting any dirtier." Thus, the only way to win is to take market share from the competition. To increase its share, Procter & Gamble (P&G) spends $100 million a year promoting its Tide brand on television, billboards, buses, magazines, and the Internet. But Unilever isn't standing still. Armed with an $80 million budget, it launched a soap tablet product named Wisk Dual Action Tablets. For example, it delivered samples of this product to 24 million U.S. homes in Sunday newspapers, followed by a series of TV ads. P&G launched a counteroffensive with Tide Rapid Action Tablets ads showed in side-by-side comparisons of the two products dropped into beakers of water. In the promotion, P&G claimed that its product is superior because it dissolves faster than Unilever's product.

Although this is only one example, many product classes and industries, including consumer products such as beer, automobiles, and televisions, are in maturity.

Firms do not need to be "held hostage" to the life-cycle curve. By positioning or repositioning their products in unexpected ways, firms can change how customers mentally categorize them. Thus, firms are able to rescue products floundering in the maturity phase of their life cycles and return them to the growth phase.

Two positioning strategies that managers can use to affect consumers' mental shifts are **reverse positioning,** which strips away "sacred" product attributes while adding new ones, and **breakaway positioning,** which associates the product with a radically different category.[62] We discuss each of these positioning strategies below and then provide an example of each in Strategy Spotlight 5.6.

Reverse Positioning   This assumes that although customers may desire more than the baseline product, they don't necessarily want an endless list of features. Such companies make the creative decision to step off the augmentation treadmill and shed product attributes that the rest of the industry considers sacred. Then, once a product is returned to its baseline state, the stripped-down product adds one or more carefully selected attributes that

maturity stage
the third stage of the product life cycle characterized by (1) slowing demand growth, (2) saturated markets, (3) direct competition, (4) price competition, and (5) strategic emphasis on efficient operations.

reverse positioning
a break in industry tendency to continuously augment products, characteristic of the product life cycle, by offering products with fewer product attributes and lower prices.

breakaway positioning a break in industry tendency to incrementally improve products along specific dimensions, characteristic of the product life cycle, by offering products that are still in the industry but that are perceived by customers as being different.

would usually be found only in a highly augmented product. Such an unconventional combination of attributes allows the product to assume a new competitive position within the category and move backward from maturity into a growth position on the life cycle curve.

Breakaway Positioning   As noted above, with reverse positioning, a product establishes a unique position in its category but retains a clear category membership. However, with breakaway positioning, a product escapes its category by deliberately associating with a different one. Thus, managers leverage the new category's conventions to change both how products are consumed and with whom they compete. Instead of merely seeing the breakaway product as simply an alternative to others in its category, consumers perceive it as altogether different.

When a breakaway product is successful in leaving its category and joining a new one, it is able to redefine its competition. Similar to reverse positioning, this strategy permits the product to shift backward on the life-cycle curve, moving from the rather dismal maturity phase to a thriving growth opportunity.

Strategy Spotlight 5.6 provides examples of reverse and breakaway positioning.

Strategies in the Decline Stage

Although all decisions in the phases of an industry life cycle are important, they become particularly difficult in the **decline stage.** Firms must face up to the fundamental strategic choices of either exiting or staying and attempting to consolidate their position in the industry.[63]

decline stage the fourth stage of the product life cycle characterized by (1) falling sales and profits, (2) increasing price competition, and (3) industry consolidation.

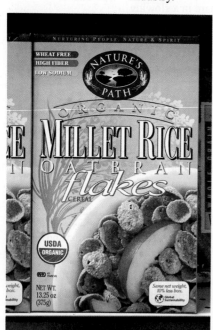

● Many consumer food products such as cereal are in the mature stage of the product life cycle. However, some organic products are enjoying high rates of growth.

The decline stage occurs when industry sales and profits begin to fall. Typically, changes in the business environment are at the root of an industry or product group entering this stage.[64] Changes in consumer tastes or a technological innovation can push a product into decline. Typewriters have entered into the decline stage because of the word processing capabilities of personal computers. Compact disks have forced cassette tapes into decline in the prerecorded music industry, and digital video disks (DVDs) are replacing compact disks. About 30 years earlier, of course, cassette tapes had led to the demise of long-playing records (LPs).

Products in the decline stage often consume a large share of management time and financial resources relative to their potential worth. Sales and profits decline. Also, competitors may start drastically cutting their prices to raise cash and remain solvent. The situation is further aggravated by the liquidation of assets, including inventory, of some of the competitors that have failed. This further intensifies price competition.

In the decline stage, a firm's strategic options become dependent on the actions of rivals. If many competitors leave the market, sales and profit opportunities increase. On the other hand, prospects are limited if all competitors remain.[65] If some competitors merge, their increased market power may erode the opportunities for the remaining players. Managers must carefully monitor the actions and intentions of competitors before deciding on a course of action.

Four basic strategies are available in the decline phase: *maintaining, harvesting, exiting,* or *consolidating.*[66]

* ***Maintaining*** refers to keeping a product going without significantly reducing marketing support, technological development, or other investments, in the hope that competitors will eventually exit the market. Many offices, for example, still use typewriters for filling out forms and other purposes that cannot be completed on a PC. In some rural

Reverse and Breakaway Positioning: How to Avoid Being Held Hostage to the Life-Cycle Curve

When firms adopt a reverse or breakaway positioning strategy, there is typically no pretense about what they are trying to accomplish. In essence, they subvert convention through unconventional promotions, prices, and attributes. That becomes a large part of their appeal—a cleverly positioned product offering. Next we discuss Commerce Bank's reverse positioning and Swatch's breakaway positioning.

Commerce Bank

While most banks offer dozens of checking and savings accounts and compete by trying to offer the highest interest rates, Commerce Bank takes a totally different approach. It pays among the lowest rates in its market. Further, it offers a very limited product line—just four checking accounts, for example. One would think that such a stingy approach would seem to scare off customers. However, Commerce Bank has been very successful. Between 1999 and 2005, it expanded from 120 to 373 branches and its total assets have soared from $5.6 billion to $39 billion.

How has it been so successful? It has stripped away all of what customers expect—lots of choices and peak interest rates and it has *reverse positioned* itself as "the most convenient bank in America." It's open seven days a week, including evenings until 8 p.m. You can get a debit card while you wait. And, when it rains, an escort with an umbrella will escort you to your car. Further, the bank offers free coffee, newspapers, and most of the branches

have free coin-counting machines that customers love (in one recent week, customers fed the machines a total of $28 million in loose change). Not too surprisingly, despite the inferior rates and few choices, new customers are flocking to the bank.

Swatch

Interestingly, the name "Swatch" is often misconstrued as a contraction of the words *Swiss watch*. However, Nicholas Hayek, Chairman, affirms that the original contraction was "Second Watch"—the new watch was introduced as a new concept of watches as casual, fun, and relatively disposable accessories. And therein lies Swatch's *breakaway positioning*.

When Swatch was launched in 1983, Swiss watches were marketed as a form of jewelry. They were serious, expensive, enduring, and discreetly promoted. Once a customer purchased one, it lasted a lifetime. Swatch changed all of that by defining its watches as playful fashion accessories which were showily promoted. They inspired impulse buying—customers would often purchase half a dozen in different designs. Their price—$40 when the brand was introduced—expanded Swatch's reach beyond its default category (watches as high-end jewelry) and moved it into the fashion accessory category, where it has different customers and competitors. Swatch was the official timekeeper of the 1996, 2000, and 2004 Summer Olympics.

Today, The Swatch Group is the largest watch company in the world. It has acquired many brands over the years including Omega, Longines, Calvin Klein, and Hamilton. Revenues have grown to $3.6 billion in 2005 and net income has increased to $500 million. And it remains on a roll. As of February 2007, its stock had soared 42 percent over the prior 52-week period.

Sources: Moon, Y. 2005. Break Free from the Product Life Cycle. *Harvard Business Review,* 83(5): 87–94; Commerce Bancorp, Inc. www.hoovers.com; Swatch. en.wikipedia.org; and www.commercebank.com.

areas, rotary (or dial) telephones persist because of the older technology used in central switching offices. Thus, there may still be the potential for revenues and profits.

- *Harvesting* involves obtaining as much profit as possible and requires that costs be reduced quickly. Managers should consider the firm's value-creating activities and cut associated budgets. Value-chain activities to consider are primary (e.g., operations, sales and marketing) and support (e.g., procurement, technology development). The objective is to wring out as much profit as possible.

- *Exiting the market* involves dropping the product from a firm's portfolio. Since a residual core of consumers exist, eliminating it should be carefully considered. If the firm's exit involves product markets that affect important relationships with other product markets in the corporation's overall portfolio, an exit could have repercussions for the whole corporation. For example, it may involve the loss of valuable brand names or human capital with a broad variety of expertise in many value-creating activities such as marketing, technology, and operations.

consolidation strategy a firm's acquiring or merging with other firms in an industry in order to enhance market power and gain valuable assets.

- *Consolidation* involves one firm acquiring at a reasonable price the best of the surviving firms in an industry. This enables firms to enhance market power and acquire valuable assets. One example of a consolidation strategy took place in the defense industry in the early 1990s. As the cliché suggests, "peace broke out" at the end of the Cold War and overall U.S. defense spending levels plummeted.[67] Many companies that make up the defense industry saw more than 50 percent of their market disappear. Only one-quarter of the 120,000 companies that once supplied the Department of Defense still serve in that capacity; the others have shut down their defense business or dissolved altogether. But one key player, Lockheed Martin, became a dominant rival by pursuing an aggressive strategy of consolidation. During the 1990s, it purchased 17 independent entities, including General Dynamics' tactical aircraft and space systems divisions, GE Aerospace, Goodyear Aerospace, and Honeywell ElectroOptics. These combinations enabled Lockheed Martin to emerge as the top provider to three governmental customers: the Department of Defense, the Department of Energy, and NASA.

Examples of products currently in the decline stage of the industry life cycle include automotive spark plugs (replaced by electronic fuel ignition), videocassette recorders (replaced by digital video disk recorders), and personal computer zip drives (replaced by compact disk read-write drives). And, as we mentioned previously, compact disks are being replaced by digital video disks (DVDs).

The introduction of new technologies and associated products does not always mean that old technologies quickly fade away. Research shows that in a number of cases, old technologies actually enjoy a very profitable "last gasp."[68] Examples include mainframe computers (versus minicomputers and PCs), coronary artery bypass graft surgery (versus angioplasty), and CISC (Complex Instruction Set Computing) architecture in computer processors versus RISC (Reduced Instruction Set Computing). In each case, the advent of new technology prompted predictions of the demise of the older technology, but each of these has proved to be resilient survivors. What accounts for their continued profitability and survival?

Retreating to more defensible ground is one strategy that firms specializing in technologies threatened with rapid obsolescence have followed. For example, while angioplasty may be appropriate for relatively healthier patients with blocked arteries, sicker, higher-risk patients seem to benefit more from coronary artery bypass graft surgery. This enabled the surgeons to concentrate on the more difficult cases and improve the technology itself. The advent of television unseated the radio as the major source of entertainment from American homes. However, the radio has survived and even thrived in venues where people are also engaged in other activities, such as driving.

Using the new to improve the old is a second approach. Carburetor manufacturers have improved the fuel efficiency of their product by incorporating electronic controls that were originally developed for electronic fuel injection systems. Similarly, CISC computer chip manufacturers have adopted many features from RISC chips.

Improving the price-performance trade-off is a third approach. IBM continues to make money selling mainframes long after their obituary was written. It retooled the technology using low-cost microprocessors and cut their prices drastically. Further, it invested and updated the software, enabling them to offer clients such as banks better performance and lower costs.

Clearly, "last gasps" may not necessarily translate into longer term gains, as the experience of the integrated steel mills suggests. When the first mini-mills appeared, integrated steel mills shifted to higher margin steel, but eventually mini-mills entered even the last strongholds of the integrated steel mills.

Turnaround Strategies

A **turnaround strategy** involves reversing performance decline and reinvigorating growth toward profitability. A need for turnaround may occur at any stage in the life cycle but is more likely to occur during maturity or decline.

Most turnarounds require a firm to carefully analyze the external and internal environments.[69] The external analysis leads to identification of market segments or customer groups that may still find the product attractive.[70] Internal analysis results in actions aimed at reduced costs and higher efficiency. A firm needs to undertake a mix of both internally and externally oriented actions to effect a turnaround.[71] In effect, the cliché "you can't shrink yourself to greatness" applies.

A study of 260 mature businesses in need of a turnaround identified three strategies used by successful companies.[72]

- *Asset and cost surgery.* Very often, mature firms tend to have assets that do not produce any returns. These include real estate, buildings, etc. Outright sales or sale and leaseback free up considerable cash and improve returns. Investment in new plants and equipment can be deferred. Firms in turnaround situations try to aggressively cut administrative expenses and inventories and speed up collection of receivables. Costs also can be reduced by outsourcing production of various inputs for which market prices may be cheaper than in-house production costs.
- *Selective product and market pruning.* Most mature or declining firms have many product lines that are losing money or are only marginally profitable. One strategy is to discontinue such product lines and focus all resources on a few core profitable areas. For example, in the early 1980s, faced with possible bankruptcy, Chrysler Corporation sold off all its nonautomotive businesses as well as all its production facilities abroad. Focus on the North American market and identification of a profitable niche—namely, minivans—were keys to their eventual successful turnaround.
- *Piecemeal productivity improvements.* There are many ways in which a firm can eliminate costs and improve productivity. Although individually these are small gains, they cumulate over a period of time to substantial gains. Improving business processes by reengineering them, benchmarking specific activities against industry leaders, encouraging employee input to identify excess costs, increasing capacity utilization, and improving employee productivity lead to a significant overall gain.

Software maker Intuit is a case of a quick but well-implemented turnaround strategy. After stagnating and stumbling during the dot-com boom, Intuit, which is known for its Quickbook and Turbotax software, hired Stephen M. Bennett, a 22-year GE veteran, in 1999. He immediately discontinued Intuit's online finance, insurance, and bill-paying operations that were losing money. Instead, he focused on software for small businesses that employ less than 250 people. He also instituted a performance-based reward system that greatly improved employee productivity. Within a few years, Intuit was once again making substantial profits and its stock was up 42 percent.[73]

Even when an industry is in overall decline, pockets of profitability remain. These are segments with customers who are relatively price insensitive. For example, the replacement demand for vacuum tubes affords its manufacturers an opportunity to earn above normal returns although the product itself is technologically obsolete. Surprisingly, within declining industries, there may still be segments that are either stable or growing. Although fountain pens ceased to be the writing instrument of choice a long time ago, the fountain pen industry has successfully reconceptualized the product as a high margin luxury item that signals accomplishment and success. In the final analysis, every business has the potential for rejuvenation. But it takes creativity, persistence, and most of all a clear strategy to translate that potential into reality.

turnaround strategy a strategy that reverses a firm's decline in performance and returns it to growth and profitability.

>LO8
The need for turnaround strategies that enable a firm to reposition its competitive position in an industry.

Reflecting on Career Implications . . .

- *Types of Competitive Advantage:* Always be aware of your organization's business-level strategy. What do you do to help your firm either increase differentiation or lower costs? What are some ways that your role in the firm can help realize these outcomes?
- *Combining Sources of Competitive Advantage:* Are you engaged in activities that simultaneously help your organization increase differentiation and lower costs?
- *Industry Life Cycle:* If your firm is in the mature stage of the industry life cycle, can you think of ways to enhance your firm's level of differentiation in order to make customers less price sensitive to your organization's goods and services?
- *Industry Life Cycle:* If you sense that your career is maturing (or in the decline phase!), what actions can you take to restore career growth and momentum (e.g., training, mentoring, professional networking)? Should you actively consider professional opportunities in other industries?

Summary

How and why firms outperform each other goes to the heart of strategic management. In this chapter, we identified three generic strategies and discussed how firms are able not only to attain advantages over competitors, but also to sustain such advantages over time. Why do some advantages become long-lasting while others are quickly imitated by competitors?

The three generic strategies—overall cost leadership, differentiation, and focus—form the core of this chapter. We began by providing a brief description of each generic strategy (or competitive advantage) and furnished examples of firms that have successfully implemented these strategies. Successful generic strategies invariably enhance a firm's position vis-à-vis the five forces of that industry—a point that we stressed and illustrated with examples. However, as we pointed out, there are pitfalls to each of the generic strategies. Thus, the sustainability of a firm's advantage is always challenged because of imitation or substitution by new or existing rivals. Such competitor moves erode a firm's advantage over time.

We also discussed the viability of combining (or integrating) overall cost leadership and generic differentiation strategies. If successful, such integration can enable a firm to enjoy superior performance and improve its competitive position. However, this is challenging, and managers must be aware of the potential downside risks associated with such an initiative.

The way companies formulate and deploy strategies is changing because of the impact of the Internet and digital technologies in many industries. Further, Internet technologies are enabling the mass customization capabilities of greater numbers of competitors. Focus strategies are likely to increase in importance because the Internet provides highly targeted and lower-cost access to narrow or specialized markets. These strategies are not without their pitfalls, however, and firms need to understand the dangers as well as the potential benefits of Internet-based approaches.

The concept of the industry life cycle is a critical contingency that managers must take into account in striving to create and sustain competitive advantages. We identified the four stages of the industry life cycle—introduction, growth, maturity, and decline—and suggested how these stages can play a role in decisions that managers must make at the business level. These include overall strategies as well as the relative emphasis on functional areas and value-creating activities.

When a firm's performance severely erodes, turnaround strategies are needed to reverse its situation and enhance its competitive position. We have discussed three approaches—asset cost surgery, selective product and market pruning, and piecemeal productivity improvements.

Summary Review Questions

1. Explain why the concept of competitive advantage is central to the study of strategic management.
2. Briefly describe the three generic strategies—overall cost leadership, differentiation, and focus.
3. Explain the relationship between the three generic strategies and the five forces that determine the average profitability within an industry.
4. What are some of the ways in which a firm can attain a successful turnaround strategy?
5. Describe some of the pitfalls associated with each of the three generic strategies.
6. Can firms combine the generic strategies of overall cost leadership and differentiation? Why or why not?
7. Explain why the industry life cycle concept is an important factor in determining a firm's business-level strategy.

Key Terms

overall cost leadership, 160
experience curve, 160
competitive parity, 160
differentiation strategy, 165
focus strategy, 170
combination strategies, 173
mass customization, 173
industry life cycle, 179
introduction stage, 182
growth stage, 182
maturity stage, 183
reverse positioning, 183
breakaway positioning, 183
decline stage, 184
consolidation strategy, 186
turnaround strategy, 187

Experiential Exercise

What are some examples of primary and support activities that enable Nucor, a $23 billion steel manufacturer, to achieve a low-cost strategy? (Fill in table below.)

Application Questions Exercises

1. Go to the Internet and look up www.walmart.com. How has this firm been able to combine overall cost leadership and differentiation strategies?
2. Choose a firm with which you are familiar in your local business community. Is the firm successful in following one (or more) generic strategies? Why or why not? What do you think are some of the challenges it faces in implementing these strategies in an effective manner?
3. Think of a firm that has attained a differentiation focus or cost focus strategy. Are their advantages sustainable? Why? Why not? (*Hint:* Consider its position vis-à-vis Porter's five forces.)
4. Think of a firm that successfully achieved a combination overall cost leadership and differentiation strategy. What can be learned from this example? Are these advantages sustainable? Why? Why not? (*Hint:* Consider its competitive position vis-à-vis Porter's five forces.)

Value-Chain Activity	Yes/No	How Does Nucor Create Value for the Customer?
Primary:		
Inbound logistics		
Operations		
Outbound logistics		
Marketing and sales		
Service		
Support:		
Procurement		
Technology development		
Human resource management		
General administration		

Ethics Questions

1. Can you think of a company that suffered ethical consequences as a result of an overemphasis on a cost leadership strategy? What do you think were the financial and nonfinancial implications?

2. In the introductory stage of the product life cycle, what are some of the unethical practices that managers could engage in to enhance their firm's market position? What could be some of the long-term implications of such actions?

References

1. Jensen, C. 2008. Michelin giving up on PAX run-flat tires. nytimes.com, April 20: np; McGrath, R. 2008. Michelin PAX run-flat: A stillborn revolution. Ritamcgrath.com; Matlack, C. 2004. Michelin: New rubber hits the road. Businessweek.com, August 16: np; and Michelin says no to PAX run-flats. 2007. notchconsulting.wordpress.com, November 20: np.
2. For a recent perspective by Porter on competitive strategy, refer to Porter, M. E. 1996. What is strategy? *Harvard Business Review*, 74(6): 61–78.
3. For insights into how a start-up is using solar technology, see: Gimbel, B. 2009. Plastic power. *Fortune*, February 2: 34.
4. Useful insights on strategy in an economic downturn are in: Rhodes, D. & Stelter, D. 2009. Seize advantage in a downturn. *Harvard Business Review*, 87(2): 50–58.
5. Some useful ideas on maintaining competitive advantages can be found in Ma, H. & Karri, R. 2005. Leaders beware: Some sure ways to lose your competitive advantage. *Organizational Dynamics*, 343(1): 63–76.
6. Miller, A. & Dess, G. G. 1993. Assessing Porter's model in terms of its generalizability, accuracy, and simplicity. *Journal of Management Studies*, 30(4): 553–585.
7. Cendrowski, S. 2008. Extreme retailing. *Fortune*, March 31: 14.
8. For insights on how discounting can erode a firm's performance, read: Stibel, J. M. & Delgrosso, P. 2008. Discounts can be dangerous. *Harvard Business Review*, 66(12): 31.
9. For a scholarly discussion and analysis of the concept of competitive parity, refer to Powell, T. C. 2003. Varieties of competitive parity. *Strategic Management Journal*, 24(1): 61–86.
10. Rao, A. R., Bergen, M. E., & Davis, S. 2000. How to fight a price war. *Harvard Business Review*, 78(2): 107–120.
11. Marriot, J. W. Jr. Our competitive strength: Human capital. A speech given to the Detroit Economic Club on October 2, 2000.
12. Whalen, C. J., Pascual, A. M., Lowery, T., & Muller, J. 2001. The top 25 managers. *BusinessWeek*, January 8: 63.
13. Ibid.
14. For an interesting perspective on the need for creative strategies, refer to Hamel, G. & Prahalad, C. K. 1994. *Competing for the Future*. Boston: Harvard Business School Press.
15. Interesting insights on Wal-Mart's effective cost leadership strategy are found in: Palmeri, C. 2008. Wal-Mart is up for this downturn. *BusinessWeek*, November 6: 34.
16. Symonds, W. C., Arndt, M., Palmer, A. T., Weintraub, A., & Holmes, S. 2001. Trying to break the choke hold. *BusinessWeek*, January 22: 38–39.
17. For a perspective on the sustainability of competitive advantages, refer to Barney, J. 1995. Looking inside for competitive advantage. *Academy of Management Executive*, 9(4): 49–61.
18. Thornton, E., 2001, Why e-brokers are broker and broker. *BusinessWeek*, January 22: 94.
19. Koretz, G. 2001. E-commerce: The buyer wins. *BusinessWeek*, January 8: 30.
20. For an "ultimate" in differentiated services, consider time shares in exotic automobiles such as Lamborghinis and Bentleys. Refer to: Stead, D. 2008. My Lamborghini—today, anyway. *BusinessWeek*, January 18:17.
21. For an interesting perspective on the value of corporate brands and how they may be leveraged, refer to Aaker, D. A. 2004, *California Management Review*, 46(3): 6–18.
22. A unique perspective on differentiation strategies is: Austin, R. D. 2008. High margins and the quest for aesthetic coherence. *Harvard Business Review*, 86(1): 18–19.
23. MacMillan, I. & McGrath, R. 1997. Discovering new points of differentiation. *Harvard Business Review*, 75(4): 133–145; Wise, R. & Baumgarter, P. 1999. Beating the clock: Corporate responses to rapid change in the PC industry. *California Management Review*, 42(1): 8–36.
24. For a discussion on quality in terms of a company's software and information systems, refer to Prahalad, C. K. & Krishnan, M. S. 1999. The new meaning of quality in the information age. *Harvard Business Review*, 77(5): 109–118.
25. Taylor, A., III. 2001. Can you believe Porsche is putting its badge on this car? *Fortune*, February 19: 168–172.
26. Ward, S., Light, L., & Goldstine, J. 1999. What high-tech managers need to know about brands. *Harvard Business Review*, 77(4): 85–95.
27. Rosenfeld, J. 2000. Unit of one. *Fast Company*, April: 98.
28. Markides, C. 1997. Strategic innovation. *Sloan Management Review*, 38(3): 9–23.
29. Bonnabeau, E., Bodick, N., & Armstrong, R. W. 2008. A more rational approach to new-product development. *Harvard Business Review*. 66(3): 96–102.

30. Insights on Google's innovation are in: Iyer, B. & Davenport, T. H. 2008. Reverse engineering Google's innovation machine. *Harvard Business Review.* 66(4): 58–68.

31. A discussion of how a firm used technology to create product differentiation is in: Mehta, S. N. 2009. Under Armor reboots. *Fortune.* February 2: 29–33. (5)

32. The authors would like to thank Scott Droege, a faculty member at Western Kentucky University, for providing this example.

33. Flint, J. 2004. Stop the nerds. *Forbes,* July 5: 80; and, Fahey, E. 2004. Over-engineering 101. *Forbes,* December 13: 62.

34. Symonds, W. C. 2000. Can Gillette regain its voltage? *BusinessWeek,* October 16: 102–104.

35. Caplan, J. 2006. In a real crunch. *Inside Business,* July: A37–A38.

36. Gadiesh, O. & Gilbert, J. L. 1998. Profit pools: A fresh look at strategy. *Harvard Business Review,* 76(3): 139–158.

37. Colvin, G. 2000. Beware: You could soon be selling soybeans. *Fortune,* November 13: 80.

38. Whalen et al., op. cit.: 63.

39. Porter, M. E. 1996. What is strategy? *Harvard Business Review,* 74(6): 61–78.

40. Hall, W. K. 1980. Survival strategies in a hostile environment, *Harvard Business Review,* 58: 75–87; on the paint and allied products industry, see Dess, G. G. & Davis, P. S. 1984. Porter's (1980) generic strategies as determinants of strategic group membership and organizational performance. *Academy of Management Journal,* 27: 467–488; for the Korean electronics industry, see Kim, L. & Lim, Y. 1988. Environment, generic strategies, and performance in a rapidly developing country: A taxonomic approach. *Academy of Management Journal,* 31: 802–827; Wright, P., Hotard, D., Kroll, M., Chan, P., & Tanner, J. 1990. Performance and multiple strategies in a firm: Evidence from the apparel industry. In Dean, B. V. & Cassidy, J. C. (Eds.). *Strategic management: Methods and studies:* 93–110. Amsterdam: Elsevier-North Holland; and Wright, P., Kroll, M., Tu, H., & Helms, M. 1991. Generic strategies and business performance: An empirical study of the screw machine products industry. *British Journal of Management,* 2: 1–9.

41. Gilmore, J. H. & Pine, B. J., II. 1997. The four faces of customization. *Harvard Business Review,* 75(1): 91–101.

42. Ibid. For interesting insights on mass customization, refer to Cattani, K., Dahan, E., & Schmidt, G. 2005. Off-shoring versus "spackling." *MIT Sloan Management Review,* 46(3): 6–7.

43. Goodstein, L. D. & Butz, H. E. 1998. Customer value: The linchpin of organizational change. *Organizational Dynamics,* Summer: 21–34.

44. Randall, T., Terwiesch, C., & Ulrich, K. T. 2005. Principles for user design of customized products. *California Management Review,* 47(4): 68–85.

45. Gadiesh & Gilbert, op. cit.: 139–158.

46. Insights on the profit pool concept are addressed in: Reinartz, W. & Ulaga, W. 2008. How to sell services more profitably. *Harvard Business Review,* 66(5): 90–96.

47. This example draws on Dess & Picken. 1997. op. cit.

48. Seybold, P. 2000. Niches bring riches. *Business 2.0,* June 13: 135.

49. Greenspan, R. 2004. Net drives profits to small biz. ClickZ.com, March 25, www.clickz.com. Greenspan, R. 2002. Small biz benefits from Internet tools. ClickZ.com, March 28, www.clickz.com.

50. Burns, E. 2006. Executives slow to see value of corporate blogging. ClickZ.com, May 9, www.clickz .com.

51. Empirical support for the use of combination strategies in an e-business context can be found in Kim, E., Nam, D., & Stimpert, J. L. 2004. The applicability of Porter's generic strategies in the Digital Age: Assumptions, conjectures, and suggestions. *Journal of Management,* 30(5): 569–589.

52. Porter, M. E. 2001. Strategy and the Internet. *Harvard Business Review,* 79: 63–78.

53. For an interesting perspective on the influence of the product life cycle and rate of technological change on competitive strategy, refer to Lei, D. & Slocum, J. W. Jr. 2005. Strategic and organizational requirements for competitive advantage. *Academy of Management Executive,* 19(1): 31–45.

54. Dickson, P. R. 1994. *Marketing Management:* 293. Fort Worth, TX: Dryden Press; Day, G. S. 1981. The product life cycle: Analysis and application. *Journal of Marketing Research,* 45: 60–67.

55. Bearden, W. O., Ingram, T. N., & LaForge, R. W. 1995. *Marketing principles and practices.* Burr Ridge, IL: Irwin.

56. MacMillan, I. C. 1985. Preemptive strategies. In Guth, W. D. (Ed.). *Handbook of Business Strategy:* 9-1–9-22. Boston: Warren, Gorham & Lamont; Pearce, J. A. & Robinson, R. B. 2000. *Strategic management* (7th ed.). New York: McGraw-Hill; Dickson, op. cit.: 295–296.

57. Bartlett, C. A. & Ghoshal, S. 2000. Going global: Lessons for late movers. *Harvard Business Review,* 78(2): 132–142.

58. Neuborne, E. 2000. E-tailers hit the relaunch key. *BusinessWeek,* October 17: 62.

59. Berkowitz, E. N., Kerin, R. A., & Hartley, S. W. 2000. *Marketing* (6th ed.). New York: McGraw-Hill.

60. MacMillan, op. cit.

61. Brooker, K. 2001. A game of inches. *Fortune,* February 5: 98–100.

62. Our discussion of reverse and breakaway positioning draws on Moon, Y. 2005. Break free from the product life cycle. *Harvard Business Review,* 83(5): 87–94. This article also discusses stealth positioning as a means of overcoming consumer resistance and advancing a product from the introduction to the growth phase.

63. MacMillan, op. cit

64. Berkowitz et al., op. cit.

65. Bearden et al., op. cit.

66. The discussion of these four strategies draws on MacMillan, op. cit.; Berkowitz et al., op. cit.; and Bearden et al., op. cit.

67. Augustine, N. R. 1997. Reshaping an industry: Lockheed Martin's survival story. *Harvard Business Review,* 75(3): 83–94.

68. Snow, D. C. 2008. Beware of old technologies' last gasps. *Harvard Business Review,* January: 17–18. Lohr, S. 2008. Why old technologies are still kicking. *New York Times,* March 23: np; and McGrath, R. G. 2008. Innovation and the last gaps of dying technologies. ritamcgrath.com, March 18: np.

69. A study that draws on the resource-based view of the firm to investigate successful turnaround strategies is: Morrow, J. S., Sirmon, D. G., Hitt, M. A., & Holcomb, T. R. 2007. *Strategic Management Journal,* 28(3): 271–284.

70. For a study investigating the relationship between organizational restructuring and acquisition performance, refer to: Barkema, H. G. & Schijven, M. Toward unlocking the full potential of acquisitions: The role of organizational restructuring. *Academy of Management Journal,* 51(4): 696–722.

71. For some useful ideas on effective turnarounds and handling downsizings, refer to Marks, M. S. & De Meuse, K. P. 2005. Resizing the organization: Maximizing the gain while minimizing the pain of layoffs, divestitures and closings. *Organizational Dynamics,* 34(1): 19–36.

72. Hambrick, D. C. & Schecter, S. M. 1983. Turnaround strategies for mature industrial product business units. *Academy of Management Journal,* 26(2): 231–248.

73. Mullaney, T. J. 2002. The wizard of Intuit. *BusinessWeek,* October 28: 60–63.

Corporate-Level Strategy:

Creating Value through Diversification

After reading this chapter, you should have a good understanding of:

LO1 The reasons for the failure of many diversification efforts.

LO2 How managers can create value through diversification initiatives.

LO3 How corporations can use related diversification to achieve synergistic benefits through economies of scope and market power.

LO4 How corporations can use unrelated diversification to attain synergistic benefits through corporate restructuring, parenting, and portfolio analysis.

LO5 The various means of engaging in diversification— mergers and acquisitions, joint ventures/strategic alliances, and internal development.

LO6 Managerial behaviors that can erode the creation of value.

Corporate-level strategy addresses two related issues: (1) what businesses should a corporation compete in, and (2) how can these businesses be managed so they create "synergy"—that is, more value by working together than if they were freestanding units? As we will see, these questions present a key challenge for today's managers. Many diversification efforts fail or, in many cases, provide only marginal returns to shareholders. Thus, determining how to create value through entering new markets, introducing new products, or developing new technologies is a vital issue in strategic management.

We begin by discussing why diversification initiatives, in general, have not yielded the anticipated benefits. Then, in the next three sections of the chapter, we explore the two key alternative approaches: related and unrelated diversification. With related diversification, corporations strive to enter product markets that share some resources and capabilities with their existing business units or increase their market power. Here we suggest four means of creating value: leveraging core competencies, sharing activities, pooled negotiating power, and vertical integration. With unrelated diversification, there are few similarities in the resources and capabilities among the firm's business units, but value can be created in multiple ways. These include restructuring, corporate parenting, and portfolio analysis approaches. Whereas the synergies to be realized with related diversification come from *horizontal relationships* among the business units, the synergies from unrelated diversification are derived from *hierarchical relationships* between the corporate office and the business units.

The last two sections address (1) the various means that corporations can use to achieve diversification and (2) managerial behaviors (e.g., self-interest) that serve to erode shareholder value. We address merger and acquisitions (M&A), divestitures, joint ventures/strategic alliances, and internal development. Each of these involves the evaluation of important trade-offs. Detrimental managerial behaviors, often guided by a manager's self-interest, are "growth for growth's sake," egotism, and antitakeover tactics. Some of these behaviors raise ethical issues because managers, in some cases, are not acting in the best interests of a firm's shareholders.

Learning from Mistakes

Normally investors will make decisions based on careful evaluation of the fundamentals underlying a company.[1] But, not always. Consider the case of SPACs, or special-purpose acquisition corporations. These are popular Wall Street vehicles whose organizers raise money to spend on yet-to-be determined targets and investors buy solely based on the pedigree of the founders. So, in a way, it is like betting on the jockey—not the horse. Let's look at a case in which, one could say, the horse came up lame.

Investors were eager to pony up $173 for Acquicor, a SPAC formed in 2005 by a group of Apple alumni: co-founder Steve Wozniak, former CEO Gil Amelio, and ex-senior executive Ellen Hancock. Unfortunately, the trio turned that cash into a highly indebted company whose market value has plummeted.

What caused their downfall was the purchase in early 2007 of a southern California chip company called Jazz Semiconductor for $253 million. The timing was terrible. Jazz sells to wireless companies, who had been in a nasty downturn. Shares of Acquicor—renamed Jazz Technologies—cratered from their IPO price of $6 to 71 cents by the end of March 2008.

The three founders had a tough decade even before this recent exploit. Amelio ended his brief reign at Apple in 1997 when Steve Jobs returned. An investment firm that he headed, AmTech, declared bankruptcy in 2003. A similar fate met Exodus Communications, the web-hosting firm that Hancock ran. As for Wozniak, long gone from Apple, a wireless company that he founded called Wheels of Zeus shut down in 2006. One *USA Today* writer humorously claimed: "This is sort of the computing equivalent of Alice Cooper, Grace Slick, and Smokey Robinson announcing they have formed a new band. Legends, yes. The outcome, less certain."

Things became rather lonely at Jazz. Hancock resigned as president in June 2007, followed by Wozniak, who had been an unpaid "chief visionary officer," in February. Amelio hung on, and in February 2008, he told investors that he had succeeded in taking Jazz "from a two-fiddle orchestra to a ten-fiddle orchestra" and that he was "laying the foundation for a much better future." Unfortunately, his optimism was not well placed. About six months later, Israel's Tower Semiconductor acquired Jazz Technologies for $40 million—a far cry from the $253 million invested about 18 months earlier!

If it is any comfort to the trio who started Acquicor, negative returns have been the norm with SPACs. According to Raj Nandiwada, a SPAC analyst: "SPACs that have completed acquisitions have fared far worse than the S&P index." He contends that such poor SPAC returns are primarily due to low-quality sponsors and overpaying for acquisitions.

>LO1

The reasons for the failure of many diversification efforts.

Acquicor's experience with acquisitions is more the rule than the exception. Research shows that the vast majority of acquisitions result in value destruction rather than value creation. Many large multinational firms have also failed to effectively integrate their acquisitions, paid too high a premium for the target's common stock, or were unable to understand how the acquired firm's assets would fit with their own lines of business.[2] And, at times, top executives may not have acted in the best interests of shareholders. That is, the motive for the acquisition may have been to enhance the executives' power and prestige rather than to improve shareholder returns. At times, the only other people who may have benefited were the shareholders of the *acquired* firms—or the investment bankers who advise the acquiring firm, because they collect huge fees upfront regardless of what happens afterward![3]

Consider, for example, Pfizer's announcement on January 26, 2009, that it was acquiring Wyeth for $68 billion in cash and stock—which represented a 15 percent premium.[4] How did the market react? In rather typical fashion, Wyeth's stock went up 2 percent; Pfizer's went down 9 percent. And, interestingly, the shares of Crucell, a Dutch biotech company, sank 10 percent after Wyeth pulled out of talks to buy it.

There have been several studies that were conducted over a variety of time periods that show how disappointing acquisitions have typically turned out. For example:

- A study evaluated the stock market reaction of 600 acquisitions over the period between 1975 and 1991. The results indicated that the acquiring firms suffered an average 4 percent drop in market value (after adjusting for market movements) in the three months following the acquisitions announcement.[5]
- In a study by Solomon Smith Barney of U.S. companies acquired since 1997 in deals for $15 billion or more, the stocks of the acquiring firms have, on average, underperformed the S&P stock index by 14 percentage points and underperformed their peer group by 4 percentage points after the deals were announced.[6]
- A study investigated 270 mergers that took place between 2000 and 2003 in multiple countries and regions. It found that after a merger, sales growth decreased by 6 percent, earnings growth dropped 9.4 percent, and market valuations declined 2.5 percent (figures are adjusted for industry trends and refer to three years pre- or postmerger).[7]

Exhibit 6.1 lists some well-known examples of failed acquisitions and mergers. Recently there have been several acquisitions—often at fire sale prices—by financial services firms during the global financial crisis in 2008. For example, Bank of America bought Merrill Lynch, Wells Fargo purchased Wachovia, and JPMorgan acquired Washington Mutual. Only time will tell how well these turn out over the next few years.

Many acquisitions ultimately result in divestiture—an admission that things didn't work out as planned. In fact, some years ago, a writer for *Fortune* magazine lamented, "Studies show that 33 percent to 50 percent of acquisitions are later divested, giving corporate marriages a divorce rate roughly comparable to that of men and women."[8]

Admittedly, we have been rather pessimistic so far.[9] Clearly, many diversification efforts have worked out very well—whether through mergers and acquisitions, strategic alliances and joint ventures, or internal development. We will discuss many success stories throughout this chapter. Next, we will discuss the primary rationales for diversification.

Exhibit 6.1
Some Well-Known M&A Blunders

Here are examples of some very expensive blunders:

- AOL paid $114 billion to acquire Time Warner in 2001. Over the next two years, AOL Time Warner lost $150 billion in market valuation.
- Conseco paid $5.8 billion to buy Green Tree, a mobile home mortgage lender, in 1998 though the company's net worth was not even $1 billion. In the next two years, Conseco lost 90 percent of its market value!
- Daimler Benz paid $36 billion to acquire Chrysler in 1998. After years of losses, it sold 80.1 percent of the unit to Cerberus Capital Management for $7.4 billion in 2007. And, as of 2009, Cerberus was trying to unload the unit.
- Quaker Oats' acquisition of the once high-flying Snapple for $1.8 billion in 1994 was followed by its divestment for $300 million three years later.
- AT&T bought computer equipment maker NCR for $7.4 billion in 1991, only to spin it off for $3.4 billion six years later.
- Sony acquired Columbia Pictures in 1989 for $4.8 billion although it had no competencies in movie production. Five years later, Sony was forced to take a $2.7 billion write-off on the acquisition.

Source: Gupta, P. 2008. Daimler May Sell Remaining Chrysler Stake. www.reuters.com, September 24: np; and Tully, S. 2006. The (Second) Worst Deal Ever. *Fortune*, October 16: 102–119.

Making Diversification Work: An Overview

Clearly, not all diversification moves, including those involving mergers and acquisitions, erode performance. For example, acquisitions in the oil industry, such as British Petroleum's purchases of Amoco and Arco, are performing well as is the Exxon-Mobil merger. In the automobile industry, the Renault-Nissan alliance, under CEO Carlos Ghosn's leadership, has led to a quadrupling of its collective market capitalization—from $20.4 billion to $84.9 billion—by the end of 2006.[10] Many leading high-tech firms such as Microsoft, Cisco Systems, and Intel have dramatically enhanced their revenues, profits, and market values through a wide variety of diversification initiatives, including acquisitions, strategic alliances, and joint ventures, as well as internal development.*

>LO2
How managers can create value through diversification initiatives.

So the question becomes: Why do some diversification efforts pay off and others produce poor results? This chapter addresses two related issues: (1) What businesses should a corporation compete in? and (2) How should these businesses be managed to jointly create more value than if they were freestanding units?

Diversification initiatives—whether through mergers and acquisitions, strategic alliances and joint ventures, or internal development—must be justified by the creation of value for shareholders.[11] But this is not always the case. Acquiring firms typically pay high premiums when they acquire a target firm. For example, in 2006 Freeport-McMoran paid a 30 percent premium to acquire Phelps Dodge in order to create the largest metals and mining concern in the U.S. In contrast, you and I, as private investors, can diversify our portfolio of stocks very cheaply. With an intensely competitive online brokerage industry, we can acquire hundreds (or thousands) of shares for a transaction fee of as little as $10.00 or less—a far cry from the 30 to 40 percent (or higher) premiums that corporations typically must pay to acquire companies.

diversification
the process of firms expanding their operations by entering new businesses.

Given the seemingly high inherent downside risks and uncertainties, one might ask: Why should companies even bother with diversification initiatives? The answer, in a word, is *synergy,* derived from the Greek word *synergos,* which means "working together." This can have two different, but not mutually exclusive, meanings.

First, a firm may diversify into *related* businesses. Here, the primary potential benefits to be derived come from *horizontal relationships;* that is, businesses sharing intangible resources (e.g., core competencies such as marketing) and tangible resources (e.g., production facilities, distribution channels). Firms can also enhance their market power via pooled negotiating power and vertical integration. For example, Procter & Gamble enjoys many synergies from having businesses that share distribution resources.

Second, a corporation may diversify into *unrelated* businesses.[12] Here, the primary potential benefits are derived largely from *hierarchical relationships;* that is, value creation derived from the corporate office. Examples of the latter would include leveraging some of the support activities in the value chain that we discussed in Chapter 3, such as information systems or human resource practices. Cooper Industries has followed a successful strategy of unrelated diversification. There are few similarities in the products it makes or the industries in which it competes. However, the corporate office adds value through such activities as superb human resource practices and budgeting systems.

Please note that such benefits derived from horizontal (related diversification) and hierarchical (unrelated diversification) relationships are not mutually exclusive. Many

---

* Many high-tech firms, such as Motorola, IBM, Qualcomm, and Intel have also diversified through company-owned venture capital arms. Intel Capital, for example, has invested $4 billion in 1,000 companies over 15 years. Some 160 of those companies have been sold to other firms, while another 150 of them have been publicly listed. In 2006, Intel Capital's investments added $214 million to the parent company's net income. For an insightful discussion of how Apple might benefit from a venture capital initiative, refer to Hesseldahl, A. 2007. What to Do with Apple's Cash. *BusinessWeek,* March 19: 80.

firms that diversify into related areas benefit from information technology expertise in the corporate office. Similarly, unrelated diversifiers often benefit from the "best practices" of sister businesses even though their products, markets, and technologies may differ dramatically.

Exhibit 6.2 provides an overview of how we will address the various means by which firms create value through both related and unrelated diversification and also include a summary of some examples that we will address in this chapter.[13]

Related Diversification: Economies of Scope and Revenue Enhancement

Related diversification enables a firm to benefit from horizontal relationships across different businesses in the diversified corporation by leveraging core competencies and sharing activities (e.g., production and distribution facilities). This enables a corporation to benefit from economies of scope. **Economies of scope** refers to cost savings from leveraging core competencies or sharing related activities among businesses in the corporation. A firm can also enjoy greater revenues if two businesses attain higher levels of sales growth combined than either company could attain independently.

related diversification a firm entering a different business in which it can benefit from leveraging core competencies, sharing activities, or building market power.

economies of scope cost savings from leveraging core competencies or sharing related activities among businesses in a corporation.

Exhibit 6.2
Creating Value through Related and Unrelated Diversification

Related Diversification: Economies of Scope

Leveraging core competencies

- 3M leverages its competencies in adhesives technologies to many industries, including automotive, construction, and telecommunications.

Sharing activities

- McKesson, a large distribution company, sells many product lines, such as pharmaceuticals and liquor, through its superwarehouses.

Related Diversification: Market Power

Pooled negotiating power

- The Times Mirror Company increases its power over customers by providing "one-stop shopping" for advertisers to reach customers through multiple media— television and newspapers—in several huge markets such as New York and Chicago.

Vertical integration

- Shaw Industries, a giant carpet manufacturer, increases its control over raw materials by producing much of its own polypropylene fiber, a key input to its manufacturing process.

Unrelated Diversification: Parenting, Restructuring, and Financial Synergies

Corporate restructuring and parenting

- The corporate office of Cooper Industries adds value to its acquired businesses by performing such activities as auditing their manufacturing operations, improving their accounting activities, and centralizing union negotiations.

Portfolio management

- Novartis, formerly Ciba-Geigy, uses portfolio management to improve many key activities, including resource allocation and reward and evaluation systems.

>LO3

How corporations can use related diversification to achieve synergistic benefits through economies of scope and market power.

For example, a sporting goods store with one or several locations may acquire retail stores carrying other product lines. This enables it to leverage, or reuse, many of its key resources—favorable reputation, expert staff and management skills, efficient purchasing operations—the basis of its competitive advantage(s), over a larger number of stores.[14]

Leveraging Core Competencies

The concept of core competencies can be illustrated by the imagery of the diversified corporation as a tree.[15] The trunk and major limbs represent core products; the smaller branches are business units; and the leaves, flowers, and fruit are end products. The core competencies are represented by the root system, which provides nourishment, sustenance, and stability. Managers often misread the strength of competitors by looking only at their end products, just as we can fail to appreciate the strength of a tree by looking only at its leaves. Core competencies may also be viewed as the "glue" that binds existing businesses together or as the engine that fuels new business growth.

core competencies
a firm's strategic resources that reflect the collective learning in the organization.

Core competencies reflect the collective learning in organizations—how to coordinate diverse production skills, integrate multiple streams of technologies, and market diverse products and services. The knowledge necessary to put a radio on a chip does not in itself assure a company of the skill needed to produce a miniature radio approximately the size of a business card. To accomplish this, Casio, a giant electronic products producer, must synthesize know-how in miniaturization, microprocessor design, material science, and ultrathin precision castings. These are the same skills that it applies in its miniature card calculators, pocket TVs, and digital watches.

For a core competence to create value and provide a viable basis for synergy among the businesses in a corporation, it must meet three criteria.[16]

- ***The core competence must enhance competitive advantage(s) by creating superior customer value.*** Every value-chain activity has the potential to provide a viable basis for building on a core competence.[17] At Gillette, for example, scientists developed the Fusion and Mach 3 after the introduction of the tremendously successful Sensor System because of a thorough understanding of several phenomena that underlie shaving. These include the physiology of facial hair and skin, the metallurgy of blade strength and sharpness, the dynamics of a cartridge moving across skin, and the physics of a razor blade severing hair. Such innovations are possible only with an understanding of such phenomena and the ability to combine such technologies into innovative products. Customers are willing to pay more for such technologically differentiated products.
- ***Different businesses in the corporation must be similar in at least one important way related to the core competence.*** It is not essential that the products or services themselves be similar. Rather, at least one element in the value chain must require similar skills in creating competitive advantage if the corporation is to capitalize on its core competence. At first glance you might think that cars and houses have little in common. However, Strategy Spotlight 6.1 discusses how Toyota creates synergies in a business—manufactured homes—that has little to do with its core business—automobiles.
- ***The core competencies must be difficult for competitors to imitate or find substitutes for.*** As we discussed in Chapter 5, competitive advantages will not be sustainable if the competition can easily imitate or substitute them. Similarly, if the skills associated with a firm's core competencies are easily imitated or replicated, they are not a sound basis for sustainable advantages. Consider Sharp Corporation, a consumer electronics giant with 2008 revenues of $34 billion.[18] It has a set of specialized core competencies in optoelectronics technologies that are difficult to replicate and contribute to its competitive advantages in its core businesses.

Toyota's Diversification into Home Manufacturing

Looking for the biggest Toyota on the market? It's not the Tundra pickups and Sequoia SUVs down at your local dealer. Instead, you'll have to travel to the Toyota factory in Kasugai, a city of 300,000 about three hours west of Tokyo. There you won't see much in the way of horsepower or acceleration. But they are very roomy—as in multiple bedrooms, a living room, kitchen, bath, and patio.

At Kasugai, Toyota's houses are 85 percent completed at the plant before being transported by road and built in just six hours. To improve efficiency, Toyota borrows know-how from its fabled Toyota Production System with its principles of just-in-time delivery and *kaizen,* or continuous improvement. Using methods adopted from car production, anticorrosive paint is applied evenly to the houses' steel frames. Just as in all of Toyota's Japan automobile factories, a banner proclaiming "good thinking, good products" hangs from the roof. "We follow the Toyota way in housing," says Senta Morioka, a managing officer at Toyota.

Toyota sells about 5,000 homes a year and the operation is profitable. Toyota Homes are built from six or more

● Toyota is a world-class automobile producer. Above is a Scion, one of its popular products. Toyota has also diversified into many areas, including manufactured homes.

modules in less than 45 days. A conservative two-story home with 1,000 square feet sells for $200,000. A more expensive, custom-built 2,600 square foot home sells for about $800,000. Toyota Homes are strong and guaranteed for about 60 years—twice the average lifespan of a home in Japan. Although the unit accounts for only .5 percent of total corporate sales (or about $1.4 billion), Toyota is working hard to ramp up that number.

Source: Koerner, P. 2008. Toyota Looking to Expand Stylish Prefab Homes Unit. www.jetsongreen.com. July 3: np; and Rowley, I. 2006. Way, Way, Off-Road. *BusinessWeek,* July 17: 36–37.

Its most successful technology has been liquid crystal displays (LCDs) that are critical components in nearly all of Sharp's products. Its expertise in this technology enabled Sharp to succeed in videocassette recorders (VCRs) with its innovative LCD viewfinder and led to the creation of its Wizard, a personal electronic organizer.

Strategy Spotlight 6.2 provides Steve Jobs' insights on the importance of a firm's core competence. The Apple CEO is widely considered one of America's most respected CEOs.

Sharing Activities

As we saw above, leveraging core competencies involves transferring accumulated skills and expertise across business units in a corporation. Corporations also can achieve synergy by **sharing activities** across their business units. These include value-creating activities such as common manufacturing facilities, distribution channels, and sales forces. As we will see, sharing activities can potentially provide two primary payoffs: cost savings and revenue enhancements.

sharing activities
having activities of two or more businesses' value chains done by one of the businesses.

Steve Jobs Discusses Apple's Core Competence

"One of our biggest insights (years ago) was that we didn't want to get into any business where we didn't own or control the primary technology, because you'll get your head handed to you. We realized that for almost all future consumer electronics, the primary technology was going to be software. And we were pretty good at software. We could do the operating system software. We could write applications like iTunes on the Mac or even PC. We could write the software in the device, like you might put in an iPod or an iPhone. And we could write the back-end software that runs on a cloud, like iTunes. So we could write all these different kinds of software and tweed it all together and make it work seamlessly. And you ask yourself: What other companies can do that? It's a pretty short list."

Source: Fisher, A. 2008. America's Most Admired Companies. *Fortune*, March 17: 74.

Deriving Cost Savings   Typically, this is the most common type of synergy and the easiest to estimate. Peter Shaw, head of mergers and acquisitions at the British chemical and pharmaceutical company ICI, refers to cost savings as "hard synergies" and contends that the level of certainty of their achievement is quite high. Cost savings come from many sources, including elimination of jobs, facilities, and related expenses that are no longer needed when functions are consolidated, or from economies of scale in purchasing. Cost savings are generally highest when one company acquires another from the same industry in the same country. Shaw Industries, recently acquired by Berkshire Hathaway, is the nation's largest carpet producer. Over the years, it has dominated the competition through a strategy of acquisition which has enabled Shaw, among other things, to consolidate its manufacturing operations in a few, highly efficient plants and to lower costs through higher capacity utilization.

Sharing activities inevitably involve costs that the benefits must outweigh such as the greater coordination required to manage a shared activity. Even more important is the need to compromise on the design or performance of an activity so that it can be shared. For example, a salesperson handling the products of two business units must operate in a way that is usually not what either unit would choose if it were independent. If the compromise erodes the unit's effectiveness, then sharing may reduce rather than enhance competitive advantage.

Enhancing Revenue and Differentiation   Often an acquiring firm and its target may achieve a higher level of sales growth together than either company could on its own. Shortly after Gillette acquired Duracell, it confirmed its expectation that selling Duracell batteries through Gillette's existing channels for personal care products would increase sales, particularly internationally. Gillette sold Duracell products in 25 new markets in the first year after the acquisition and substantially increased sales in established international markets. Also, a target company's distribution channel can be used to escalate the sales of the acquiring company's product. Such was the case when Gillette acquired Parker Pen. Gillette estimated that it could gain an additional $25 million in sales of its own Waterman pens by taking advantage of Parker's distribution channels.

Firms also can enhance the effectiveness of their differentiation strategies by means of sharing activities among business units. A shared order-processing system, for example, may permit new features and services that a buyer will value. Also, sharing can reduce the cost of differentiation. For instance, a shared service network may make more advanced, remote service technology economically feasible. To illustrate the potential for enhanced differentiation through sharing, consider $7 billion VF Corporation—producer of such well-known brands as Lee, Wrangler, Vanity Fair, and Jantzen.

> VF's acquisition of Nutmeg Industries and H. H. Cutler provided it with several large customers that it didn't have before, increasing its plant utilization and productivity. But more importantly, Nutmeg designs and makes licensed apparel for sports teams and organizations, while Cutler manufactures licensed brand-name children's apparel, including Walt Disney kids' wear. Such brand labeling enhances the differentiation of VF's apparel products. According to VF President Mackey McDonald, "What we're doing is looking at value-added knitwear, taking our basic fleece from Basset-Walker [one of its divisions], embellishing it through Cutler and Nutmeg, and selling it as a value-added product." Additionally, Cutler's advanced high-speed printing technologies will enable VF to be more proactive in anticipating trends in the fashion-driven fleece market. Claims McDonald, "Rather than printing first and then trying to guess what the customer wants, we can see what's happening in the marketplace and then print it up."[19]

As a cautionary note, managers must keep in mind that sharing activities among businesses in a corporation can have a negative effect on a given business's differentiation. For example, with the merger of Chrysler and Daimler-Benz, many consumers may lower their perceptions of Mercedes's quality and prestige because they felt that common production components and processes were being used across the two divisions. And Ford's Jaguar division was adversely affected as consumers came to understand that it shared many components with its sister divisions at Ford, including Lincoln. Perhaps, it is not too surprising that both Chrysler and Jaguar were divested by their parent corporations.

Strategy Spotlight 6.3 discusses how Freemantle Media leverages its hit television show *American Idol* through its core competencies and shared activities to create multiple revenue streams.

Related Diversification: Market Power

We now discuss how companies achieve related diversification through **market power**. We also address the two principal means by which firms achieve synergy through market power: *pooled negotiating power* and *vertical integration*. Managers do, however, have limits on their ability to use market power for diversification, because government regulations can sometimes restrict the ability of a business to gain very large shares of a particular market. Consider GE's attempt to acquire Honeywell:

> When General Electric announced a $41 billion bid for Honeywell, the European Union stepped in. GE's market clout would have expanded significantly with the deal: GE would supply over one-half the parts needed to build several aircraft engines. The commission's concern, causing them to reject the acquisition, was that GE could use its increased market power to dominate the aircraft engine parts market and crowd out rivals.[20] Thus, while managers need to be aware of the strategic advantages of market power, they must at the same time be aware of regulations and legislation.

market power firms' abilities to profit through restricting or controlling supply to a market or coordinating with other firms to reduce investment.

Pooled Negotiating Power

Similar businesses working together or the affiliation of a business with a strong parent can strengthen an organization's bargaining position relative to suppliers and customers and enhance its position vis-à-vis competitors. Compare, for example, the position of an independent food manufacturer with the same business within Nestlé. Being part of Nestlé provides the business with significant clout—greater bargaining power with suppliers and customers—since it is part of a firm that makes large purchases from suppliers and provides a wide variety of products. Access to the parent's deep pockets increases the business's strength, and the Nestlé unit enjoys greater protection from substitutes and new

pooled negotiating power the improvement in bargaining position relative to suppliers and customers.

American Idol: Far More than Just a Television Show

American Idol is one of several of FremantleMedia's (FM) hit television shows. FM is a division of German media giant Bertlesmann, which has approximately $26 billion in revenues. Some of FM's other well-known television shows are *The Apprentice, The Swan,* and at a ripe old age of 48—*The Price Is Right.*

First shown in the United States in June 2002, *American Idol* became a tremendous overnight success. Although the show may be crass and occasionally cruel, it is undeniably brilliant. It's become the ultimate testament to a singular business achievement: FM has become extremely successful at creating truly global programming. In part, that is due to the creative minds at Fremantle. It has some of the best professionals in the business who have a talent for developing shows that appeal to huge populations with different backgrounds and circumstances.

Amazingly, FM, which created *Pop Idol* in Britain in 2001, is now rolling out the show in its 30th country. There's *Belgium Idool, Portugal Idolos, Deutschland Sucht den SuperStar* (Germany), *SuperStar KZ* (Kazakhstan), and of course, the largest and best-known show, *American Idol,* in the United States. *American Idol* is the primary reason that Fremantle's revenue is up 9 percent to more than $1 billion since the show was launched. According to Fremantle's CEO Tony Cohen, "*Idol* has become a national institution in lots of countries." To illustrate, fans cast more than 65 million votes for the *American Idol* finale in May, 2004—that is two-thirds as many people as voted in the 2004 U.S. presidential election.

The real key to Fremantle's success is not just adapting its television hits to other countries, but systematically leveraging its core product—television shows—to create multiple revenue streams. In essence, the "Fremantle Way" holds lessons not just for show business but for all business. It enables a company to use its core competence of making products of mass appeal and then to customize them for places with widely varying languages, cultures, and mores. It then milks the hits for every penny through tie-ins, spinoffs, innovative uses of technology, and marketing masterstrokes.

The *Idol* franchise has created a wide variety of new revenue streams for Fremantle's German parent, Bertelsmann. Here's how much *American Idol* generated in its first two years since its June 2002 launch:

- *Products ($50 million).* Brand extensions range from videogames and fragrances to a planned microphone-shaped soap-on-a-rope. Fremantle receives a licensing fee from manufacturers.
- *TV Licensing ($75 million).* For its rights fee, Fox gets to broadcast the show and, in turn, sell ads and lucrative sponsorships.
- *Compact Discs (CDs) ($130 million).* The most successful performers on the *Idols* shows have sold millions of CDs; more than one-third of the revenue goes to BMG, which, like Fremantle, is an affiliate of Bertelsmann. In fact, in a *60 Minutes* interview in March 2007, Simon Cowell said that his "only interest in *Idol* was as a vehicle to launch records." Cowell, the show's notoriously brutal judge, works at BMG, which requires every contestant to sign a recording contract.
- *Concerts ($35 million).* Although artists and their management get the bulk of the take, concerts sell records and merchandise and promote the next *Idol* show.

In addition, Fremantle Licensing Worldwide signed Warner Brothers Publications to produce and distribute *Idol* audition books with CDs for the United States, Canada, United Kingdom, and Australia. The new books/CDs—*Pop Idol* (UK), *Australian Idol,* and *Canadian Idol*—join the *American Idol* book/CD.

Sources: Howe, J. 2008 *Crowdsourcing.* New York: Crown Business; Sloan, P. 2004. The Reality Factory. *Business 2.0,* August: 74–82; Cooney, J. 2004. In the News. *License!,* March: 48; and, Anonymous. 2005. Fox on Top in Feb; NBC Languishing at the Bottom. www.indiantelevision.com, March 2.

entrants. Not only would rivals perceive the unit as a more formidable opponent, but the unit's association with Nestlé would also provide greater visibility and improved image.

Consolidating an industry can also increase a firm's market power.[21] This is clearly an emerging trend in the multimedia industry.[22] All of these mergers and acquisitions have a common goal: to control and leverage as many news and entertainment channels as possible.

How 3M's Efforts to Increase Its Market Power Backfired

In the spring and summer of 2006, 3M found itself in court facing three class-action lawsuits launched by consumers and retailers of transparent and invisible adhesive tape (often generically known as "Scotch tape"). The suits all alleged that 3M had unlawfully bullied its way into a monopoly position in the tape market and that, as a result, consumers had been deprived of their rightful amount of choice and often paid up to 40 percent too much for their tape.

One rival that is particularly interested in these cases is LaPage's Inc. of North York, Ontario—3M's only significant competitor in the home and office adhesive tape market. LaPage's has everything to gain from court penalties against 3M's selling practices. This includes greater access to the lucrative North American market. The Canadian company started 3M's legal travails in the first place: all of the current class-action suits were initiated by LePage's.

Back in 1997, LePage's (then based in Pittsburgh) filed a complaint in the Pennsylvania District Court against 3M's practice of selling its various tape products using what was called "bundled rebates." LePage's argued that

it violated the Sherman Act, the century-old U.S. legislation that limited monopoly power. 3M's bundled rebate program offered significant rebates—sometimes in the millions of dollars—to retailers as a reward for selling targeted amounts of six product lines. LePage's claimed that such selling targets were so large that retailers could only meet them by excluding competing products—in this case LePage's tape—from store shelves. For example, LePage's argued that Kmart, which had constituted 10% of LePage's sales dropped the account when 3M started offering the discount chain $1 million in rebates in return for selling more than $15 million worth of 3M products each year. Further, LePage's offered its own conspiracy theory: 3M introduced rebates not simply to grow its sales, but to eliminate LePage's—its only significant competitor.

A jury awarded LePage's $68.5 million in damages (the amount after trebling)—almost 15 percent of the 3M Consumer and Office Business unit's operating income in 2000. The Court of Appeals for the Third Circuit rejected 3M's appeal and upheld the judgment. It concluded that rebate bundling, even if above cost, may exclude equally efficient competitors from offering product (in this case, tape). In the ruling, Judge Dolores K. Sloviter wrote that "they may foreclose portions of the market to a potential competitor who does not manufacture an equally diverse group of products and who therefore cannot make a comparable offer." Therefore, the bundled rebates were judged to be an exploitation of 3M's monopoly power.

Sources: Bush, D. & Gelb, B. D. 2005. When Marketing Practices Raise Antitrust Concerns. *MIT Sloan Management Review,* 46(4): 73–81; Campbell, C. 2006. Tale of the Tape. *Canadian Business.* April 24: 39–40; and Bergstrom, B. 2003. $68M Jury Award Upheld against 3M in Antitrust Case. *The Associated Press:* March 26.

When acquiring related businesses, a firm's potential for pooled negotiating power vis-à-vis its customers and suppliers can be very enticing. However, managers must carefully evaluate how the combined businesses may affect relationships with actual and potential customers, suppliers, and competitors. For example, when PepsiCo diversified into the fast-food industry with its acquisitions of Kentucky Fried Chicken, Taco Bell, and Pizza Hut (now part of Yum! Brands), it clearly benefited from its position over these units that served as a captive market for its soft-drink products. However, many competitors, such as McDonald's, have refused to consider PepsiCo as a supplier of its own soft-drink needs because of competition with Pepsi's divisions in the fast-food industry. Simply put, McDonald's did not want to subsidize the enemy! Thus, although acquiring related businesses can enhance a corporation's bargaining power, it must be aware of the potential for retaliation.

Strategy Spotlight 6.4 discusses how 3M's actions to increase its market power led to a lawsuit (which 3M lost) by a competitor.

Vertical Integration

vertical integration
an expansion or
extension of the firm
by integrating pre-
ceding or successive
production
processes.

Vertical integration occurs when a firm becomes its own supplier or distributor. That is, it represents an expansion or extension of the firm by integrating preceding or successive production processes.[23] The firm incorporates more processes toward the original source of raw materials (backward integration) or toward the ultimate consumer (forward integration). For example, a car manufacturer might supply its own parts or make its own engines to secure sources of supply or control its own system of dealerships to ensure retail outlets for its products. Similarly, an oil refinery might secure land leases and develop its own drilling capacity to ensure a constant supply of crude oil. Or it could expand into retail operations by owning or licensing gasoline stations to guarantee customers for its petroleum products.

Clearly, vertical integration can be a viable strategy for many firms. Strategy Spotlight 6.5 discusses Shaw Industries, a carpet manufacturer that has attained a dominant position in the industry via a strategy of vertical integration. Shaw has successfully implemented strategies of both forward and backward integration. Exhibit 6.3 depicts the stages of Shaw's vertical integration.

Benefits and Risks of Vertical Integration   Vertical integration is a means for an organization to reduce its dependence on suppliers or its channels of distribution to end users. However, the benefits associated with vertical integration—backward or forward—must be carefully weighed against the risks.[24]

The *benefits* of vertical integration include (1) a secure supply of raw materials or distribution channels that cannot be "held hostage" to external markets where costs can fluctuate over time, (2) protection and control over assets and services required to produce and deliver valuable products and services, (3) access to new business opportunities and new forms of technologies, and (4) simplified procurement and administrative procedures since key activities are brought inside the firm, eliminating the need to deal with a wide variety of suppliers and distributors.

Winnebago, the leader in the market for drivable recreational vehicles with a 19.3 percent market share, illustrates some of vertical integration's benefits.[25] The word *Winnebago* means "big RV" to most Americans. And the firm has a sterling reputation for great quality. The firm's huge northern Iowa factories do everything from extruding aluminum for body parts to molding plastics for water and holding tanks to dashboards. Such vertical integration at the factory may appear to be outdated and expensive, but it guarantees excellent quality. The Recreational Vehicle Dealer Association started giving a quality award in 1996, and Winnebago has won it every year.

The *risks* of vertical integration include (1) the costs and expenses associated with increased overhead and capital expenditures to provide facilities, raw material inputs, and distribution channels inside the organization; (2) a loss of flexibility resulting from the inability to respond quickly to changes in the external environment because of the huge

Exhibit 6.3 Simplified Stages of Vertical Integration: Shaw Industries

strategy spotlight

Vertical Integration at Shaw Industries

Shaw Industries (now part of Berkshire Hathaway) is an example of a firm that has followed a very successful strategy of vertical integration. By relentlessly pursuing both backward and forward integration, Shaw has become the dominant manufacturer of carpeting products in the United States. According to CEO Robert Shaw, "We want to be involved with as much of the process of

making and selling carpets as practical. That way, we're in charge of costs." For example, Shaw acquired Amoco's polypropylene fiber manufacturing facilities in Alabama and Georgia. These new plants provide carpet fibers for internal use and for sale to other manufacturers. With this backward integration, fully one-quarter of Shaw's carpet fiber needs are now met in-house. In early 1996 Shaw began to integrate forward, acquiring seven floor-covering retailers in a move that suggested a strategy to consolidate the fragmented industry and increase its influence over retail pricing. Exhibit 6.3 provides a simplified depiction of the stages of vertical integration for Shaw Industries.

Sources: White, J. 2003. Shaw to home in on more with Georgia Tufters deal. *HFN: The Weekly Newspaper for the Home Furnishing Network,* May 5: 32; Shaw Industries. 1993, 2000. Annual reports; and Server, A. 1994. How to escape a price war. *Fortune,* June 13: 88.

investments in vertical integration activities that generally cannot be easily deployed elsewhere; (3) problems associated with unbalanced capacities or unfilled demand along the value chain; and (4) additional administrative costs associated with managing a more complex set of activities. Exhibit 6.4 summarizes the benefits and risks of vertical integration. In making vertical integration decisions, five issues should be considered.[26]

1. *Is the company satisfied with the quality of the value that its present suppliers and distributors are providing?* If the performance of organizations in the vertical chain—both suppliers and distributors—is satisfactory, it may not, in general, be appropriate for a company to perform these activities themselves. Nike and Reebok have outsourced the manufacture of their shoes to countries such as China and Indonesia where labor costs are low. Since the strengths of these companies are typically in design and marketing, it would be advisable to continue to outsource production operations and continue to focus on where they can add the most value.

Exhibit 6.4
Benefits and Risks of Vertical Integration

Benefits
• A secure source of raw materials or distribution channels.
• Protection of and control over valuable assets.
• Access to new business opportunities.
• Simplified procurement and administrative procedures.

Risks
• Costs and expenses associated with increased overhead and capital expenditures.
• Loss of flexibility resulting from large investments.
• Problems associated with unbalanced capacities along the value chain.
• Additional administrative costs associated with managing a more complex set of activities.

2. *Are there activities in the industry value chain presently being outsourced or performed independently by others that are a viable source of future profits?* Even if a firm is outsourcing value-chain activities to companies that are doing a credible job, it may be missing out on substantial profit opportunities. To illustrate, consider the automobile industry's profit pool. As you may recall from Chapter 5, there is much more potential profit in many downstream activities (e.g., leasing, warranty, insurance, and service) than in the manufacture of automobiles. Not surprisingly, carmakers such as Toyota and Honda are undertaking forward integration strategies to become bigger players in these high-profit activities.

3. *Is there a high level of stability in the demand for the organization's products?* High demand or sales volatility are not conducive to vertical integration. With the high level of fixed costs in plant and equipment as well as operating costs that accompany endeavors toward vertical integration, widely fluctuating sales demand can either strain resources (in times of high demand) or result in unused capacity (in times of low demand). The cycles of "boom and bust" in the automobile industry are a key reason why the manufacturers have increased the amount of outsourced inputs.

4. *Does the company have the necessary competencies to execute the vertical integration strategies?* As many companies would attest, successfully executing strategies of vertical integration can be very difficult. For example, Unocal, a major petroleum refiner, which once owned retail gas stations, was slow to capture the potential grocery and merchandise side of the business that might have resulted from customer traffic to its service stations. Unocal lacked the competencies to develop a separate retail organization and culture. The company eventually sold the assets and brand.

5. *Will the vertical integration initiative have potential negative impacts on the firm's stakeholders?* Managers must carefully consider the impact that vertical integration may have on existing and future customers, suppliers, and competitors. After Lockheed Martin, a dominant defense contractor, acquired Loral Corporation, an electronics supplier, for $9.1 billion, it had an unpleasant and unanticipated surprise. Loral, as a captive supplier of Lockheed, is now viewed as a rival by many of its previous customers. Thus, before Lockheed Martin can realize any net synergies from this acquisition, it must make up for the substantial business that it has lost.

Analyzing Vertical Integration: The Transaction Cost Perspective   Another approach that has proved very useful in understanding vertical integration is the **transaction cost perspective**.[27] According to this perspective, every market transaction involves some *transaction costs*. First, a decision to purchase an input from an outside source leads to *search* costs (i.e., the cost to find where it is available, the level of quality, etc.). Second, there are costs associated with *negotiating*. Third, a *contract* needs to be written spelling out future possible contingencies. Fourth, parties in a contract have to *monitor* each other. Finally, if a party does not comply with the terms of the contract, there are *enforcement* costs. Transaction costs are thus the sum of search costs, negotiation costs, contracting costs, monitoring costs, and enforcement costs. These transaction costs can be avoided by internalizing the activity, in other words, by producing the input in-house.

A related problem with purchasing a specialized input from outside is the issue of *transaction-specific investments*. For example, when an automobile company needs an input specifically designed for a particular car model, the supplier may be unwilling to make the investments in plant and machinery necessary to produce that component

transaction cost perspective a perspective that the choice of a transaction's governance structure, such as vertical integration or market transaction, is influenced by transaction costs, including search, negotiating, contracting, monitoring, and enforcement costs, associated with each choice.

for two reasons. First, the investment may take many years to recover but there is no guarantee the automobile company will continue to buy from them after the contract expires, typically in one year. Second, once the investment is made, the supplier has no bargaining power. That is, the buyer knows that the supplier has no option but to supply at ever-lower prices because the investments were so specific that they cannot be used to produce alternative products. In such circumstances, again, vertical integration may be the only option.

Vertical integration, however, gives rise to a different set of costs. These costs are referred to as *administrative costs.* Coordinating different stages of the value chain now internalized within the firm causes administrative costs to go up. Decisions about vertical integration are, therefore, based on a comparison of transaction costs and administrative costs. If transaction costs are lower than administrative costs, it is best to resort to market transactions and avoid vertical integration. For example, McDonald's may be the world's biggest buyer of beef, but they do not raise cattle. The market for beef has low transaction costs and requires no transaction-specific investments. On the other hand, if transaction costs are higher than administrative costs, vertical integration becomes an attractive strategy. Most automobile manufacturers produce their own engines because the market for engines involves high transaction costs and transaction-specific investments.

Unrelated Diversification: Financial Synergies and Parenting

>LO4
How corporations can use unrelated diversification to attain synergistic benefits through corporate restructuring, parenting, and portfolio analysis.

With unrelated diversification, unlike related diversification, few benefits are derived from *horizontal relationships*—that is, the leveraging of core competencies or the sharing of activities across business units within a corporation. Instead, potential benefits can be gained from *vertical (or hierarchical) relationships*—the creation of synergies from the interaction of the corporate office with the individual business units. There are two main sources of such synergies. First, the corporate office can contribute to "parenting" and restructuring of (often acquired) businesses. Second, the corporate office can add value by viewing the entire corporation as a family or "portfolio" of businesses and allocating resources to optimize corporate goals of profitability, cash flow, and growth. Additionally, the corporate office enhances value by establishing appropriate human resource practices and financial controls for each of its business units.

unrelated diversification
a firm entering a different business that has little horizontal interaction with other businesses of a firm.

Corporate Parenting and Restructuring

We have discussed how firms can add value through related diversification by exploring sources of synergy *across* business units. Now, we discuss how value can be created *within* business units as a result of the expertise and support provided by the corporate office.

Parenting The positive contributions of the corporate office are called the **"parenting advantage."**[28] Many firms have successfully diversified their holdings without strong evidence of the more traditional sources of synergy (i.e., horizontally across business units). Diversified public corporations such as BTR, Emerson Electric, and Hanson and leveraged buyout firms such as Kohlberg, Kravis, Roberts & Company, and Clayton, Dublilier & Rice are a few examples.[29] These parent companies create value through management expertise. How? They improve plans and budgets and provide especially competent central functions such as legal, financial, human resource management, procurement, and the like. They also help subsidiaries make wise choices in their own acquisitions, divestitures, and new internal development decisions. Such contributions often help business units to substantially increase their revenues and profits. Consider Texas-based Cooper Industries' acquisition of Champion International, the spark plug company, as an example of corporate parenting:[30]

parenting advantage
the positive contributions of the corporate office to a new business as a result of expertise and support provided and not as a result of substantial changes in assets, capital structure, or management.

Cooper applies a distinctive parenting approach designed to help its businesses improve their manufacturing performance. New acquisitions are "Cooperized"—Cooper audits their manufacturing operations; improves their cost accounting systems; makes their planning, budgeting, and human resource systems conform with its systems; and centralizes union negotiations. Excess cash is squeezed out through tighter controls and reinvested in productivity enhancements, which improve overall operating efficiency. As one manager observed, "When you get acquired by Cooper, one of the first things that happens is a truckload of policy manuals arrives at your door." Such active parenting has been effective in enhancing the competitive advantages of many kinds of manufacturing businesses.

restructuring the intervention of the corporate office in a new business that substantially changes the assets, capital structure, and/or management, including selling off parts of the business, changing the management, reducing payroll and unnecessary sources of expenses, changing strategies, and infusing the new business with new technologies, processes, and reward systems.

Restructuring **Restructuring** is another means by which the corporate office can add value to a business.[31] The central idea can be captured in the real estate phrase "buy low and sell high." Here, the corporate office tries to find either poorly performing firms with unrealized potential or firms in industries on the threshold of significant, positive change. The parent intervenes, often selling off parts of the business; changing the management; reducing payroll and unnecessary sources of expenses; changing strategies; and infusing the company with new technologies, processes, reward systems, and so forth. When the restructuring is complete, the firm can either "sell high" and capture the added value or keep the business and enjoy financial and competitive benefits.[32]

Loews Corporation, a conglomerate with $18 billion in revenues competes in such industries as oil and gas, tobacco, watches, insurance, and hotels. It provides an exemplary example of how firms can successfully "buy low and sell high" as part of their corporate strategy.[33]

Energy accounts for 33 percent of Loews' $30 billion in total assets. In the 1980s it bought six oil tankers for only $5 million each during a sharp slide in oil prices. The downside was limited. After all these huge hulks could easily have been sold as scrap steel. However, that didn't have to happen. Eight years after Loews purchased the tankers, they sold them for $50 million each.

Loews was also extremely successful with its next energy play—drilling equipment. Although wildcatting for oil is very risky, selling services to wildcatters is not, especially if the assets are bought during a down cycle. Loews did just that. It purchased 10 offshore drilling rigs for $50 million in 1989 and formed Diamond Offshore Drilling. In 1995 Loews received $338 million after taking a 30 percent piece of this operation public!

For the restructuring strategy to work, the corporate management must have both the insight to detect undervalued companies (otherwise the cost of acquisition would be too high) or businesses competing in industries with a high potential for transformation.[34] Additionally, of course, they must have the requisite skills and resources to turn the businesses around, even if they may be in new and unfamiliar industries.

Restructuring can involve changes in assets, capital structure, or management.

- *Asset restructuring* involves the sale of unproductive assets, or even whole lines of businesses, that are peripheral. In some cases, it may even involve acquisitions that strengthen the core business.
- *Capital restructuring* involves changing the debt-equity mix, or the mix between different classes of debt or equity. Although the substitution of equity with debt is more common in buyout situations, occasionally the parent may provide additional equity capital.
- *Management restructuring* typically involves changes in the composition of the top management team, organizational structure, and reporting relationships. Tight financial control, rewards based strictly on meeting short- to medium-term performance goals, and reduction in the number of middle-level managers are common steps in management restructuring. In some cases, parental intervention may even result in changes in strategy as well as infusion of new technologies and processes.

Hanson, plc, a British conglomerate, made numerous such acquisitions in the United States in the 1980s, often selling these firms at significant profits after a few years of successful restructuring efforts. Hanson's acquisition and subsequent restructuring of the SCM group is a classic example of the restructuring strategy. Hanson acquired SCM, a diversified manufacturer of industrial and consumer products (including Smith-Corona typewriters, Glidden paints, and Durkee Famous Foods), for $930 million in 1986 after a bitter takeover battle. In the next few months, Hanson sold SCM's paper and pulp operations for $160 million, the chemical division for $30 million, Glidden paints for $580 million, and Durkee Famous Foods for $120 million, virtually recovering the entire original investment. In addition, Hanson also sold the SCM headquarters in New York for $36 million and reduced the headquarters staff by 250. They still retained several profitable divisions, including the titanium dioxide operations and managed them with tight financial controls that led to increased returns.[35]

Exhibit 6.5 summarizes the three primary types of restructuring activities.

Portfolio Management

During the 1970s and early 1980s, several leading consulting firms developed the concept of **portfolio management** to achieve a better understanding of the competitive position of an overall portfolio (or family) of businesses, to suggest strategic alternatives for each of the businesses, and to identify priorities for the allocation of resources. Several studies have reported widespread use of these techniques among American firms.[36]

Description and Potential Benefits   The key purpose of portfolio models is to assist a firm in achieving a balanced portfolio of businesses.[37] This consists of businesses whose profitability, growth, and cash flow characteristics complements each other and adds up to a satisfactory overall corporate performance. Imbalance, for example, could be caused either by excessive cash generation with too few growth opportunities or by insufficient cash generation to fund the growth requirements in the portfolio. Monsanto, for example, used portfolio planning to restructure its portfolio, divesting low-growth commodity chemicals businesses and acquiring businesses in higher-growth industries such as biotechnology.

The Boston Consulting Group's (BCG) growth/share matrix is among the best known of these approaches.[38] In the BCG approach, each of the firm's strategic business units (SBUs) is plotted on a two-dimensional grid in which the axes are relative market share and industry growth rate. The grid is broken into four quadrants. Exhibit 6.6 depicts the BCG matrix. Following are a few clarifications:

1. Each circle represents one of the corporation's business units. The size of the circle represents the relative size of the business unit in terms of revenues.
2. Relative market share, measured by the ratio of the business unit's size to that of its largest competitor, is plotted along the horizontal axis.
3. Market share is central to the BCG matrix. This is because high relative market share leads to unit cost reduction due to experience and learning curve effects and, consequently, superior competitive position.

portfolio management a method of (a) assessing the competitive position of a portfolio of businesses within a corporation, (b) suggesting strategic alternatives for each business, and (c) to identifying priorities for the allocation of resources across the businesses.

Asset Restructuring: The sale of unproductive assets, or even whole lines of businesses, that are peripheral.

Capital Restructuring: Changing the debt-equity mix, or the mix between different classes of debt or equity.

Management Restructuring: Changes in the composition of the top management team, organization structure, and reporting relationships.

Exhibit 6.5
The Three Primary Types of Restructuring Activities

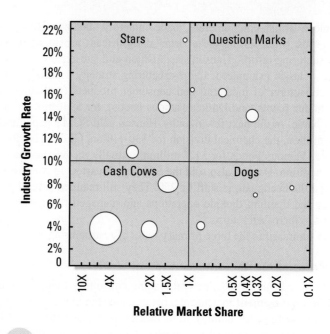

Exhibit 6.6 The Boston Consulting Group (BCG) Portfolio Matrix

Each of the four quadrants of the grid has different implications for the SBUs that fall into the category:

- **Stars** are SBUs competing in high-growth industries with relatively high market shares. These firms have long-term growth potential and should continue to receive substantial investment funding.
- **Question Marks** are SBUs competing in high-growth industries but having relatively weak market shares. Resources should be invested in them to enhance their competitive positions.
- **Cash Cows** are SBUs with high market shares in low-growth industries. These units have limited long-run potential but represent a source of current cash flows to fund investments in "stars" and "question marks."
- **Dogs** are SBUs with weak market shares in low-growth industries. Because they have weak positions and limited potential, most analysts recommend that they be divested.

In using portfolio strategy approaches, a corporation tries to create shareholder value in a number of ways.[39] First, portfolio analysis provides a snapshot of the businesses in a corporation's portfolio. Therefore, the corporation is in a better position to allocate resources among the business units according to prescribed criteria (e.g., use cash flows from the "cash cows" to fund promising "stars"). Second, the expertise and analytical resources in the corporate office provide guidance in determining what firms may be attractive (or unattractive) acquisitions. Third, the corporate office is able to provide financial resources to the business units on favorable terms that reflect the corporation's overall ability to raise funds. Fourth, the corporate office can provide high-quality review and coaching for the individual businesses. Fifth, portfolio analysis provides a basis for developing strategic goals and reward/evaluation systems for business managers. For example, managers of cash cows would have lower targets for revenue growth than managers of stars, but the former would have higher threshold levels of profit targets on proposed projects than the managers of star businesses. Compensation systems would also reflect such realities. Cash cows understandably would be rewarded more on the basis of cash that their businesses generate than would managers of star businesses. Similarly, managers of star businesses would be held to higher standards for revenue growth than managers of cash cow businesses.

To see how companies can benefit from portfolio approaches, consider Ciba-Geigy.

In 1994 Ciba-Geigy adopted portfolio planning approaches to help it manage its business units, which competed in a wide variety of industries, including chemicals, dyes, pharmaceuticals, crop protection, and animal health.[40] It placed each business unit in a category corresponding to the BCG matrix. The business unit's goals, compensation programs, personnel selection, and resource allocation were strongly associated with the category within which the business was placed. For example, business units classified as "cash cows" had much higher hurdles for obtaining financial resources (from the corporate office) for expansion than "question marks" since the latter were businesses for which Ciba-Geigy had high hopes for accelerated future growth and profitability. Additionally, the compensation of a business unit manager in a cash cow would be strongly associated with its success in generating cash to fund other businesses, whereas a manager of a question mark business would be rewarded on his or her ability to increase revenue growth and market share. The portfolio planning approaches appear to be working. In 2006, Ciba-Geigy's (now Novartis) revenues and net income stood at $26 billion and $8 billion, respectively. This represents a 22 percent increase in revenues and a most impressive 40 percent growth in net income over a two-year period.

Limitations   Despite the potential benefits of portfolio models, there are also some notable downsides. First, they compare SBUs on only two dimensions, making the implicit but erroneous assumption that (1) those are the only factors that really matter and (2) every unit can be accurately compared on that basis. Second, the approach views each SBU as a stand-alone entity, ignoring common core business practices and value-creating activities that may hold promise for synergies across business units. Third, unless care is exercised, the process becomes largely mechanical, substituting an oversimplified graphical model for the important contributions of the CEO's (and other corporate managers') experience and judgment. Fourth, the reliance on "strict rules" regarding resource allocation across SBUs can be detrimental to a firm's long-term viability. For example, according to one study, over one-half of all the businesses that should have been cash users (based on the BCG matrix) were instead cash providers.[41] Finally, while colorful and easy to comprehend, the imagery of the BCG matrix can lead to some troublesome and overly simplistic prescriptions. According to one author:

The dairying analogy is appropriate (for some cash cows), so long as we resist the urge to oversimplify it. On the farm, even the best-producing cows eventually begin to dry up. The farmer's solution to this is euphemistically called "freshening" the cow: The farmer arranges a date for the cow with a bull, she has a calf, the milk begins flowing again. Cloistering the cow—isolating her from everything but the feed trough and the milking machines—assures that she will go dry.[42]

To see what can go wrong, consider Cabot Corporation.

Cabot Corporation supplies carbon black for the rubber, electronics, and plastics industries. Following the BCG matrix, Cabot moved away from its cash cow, carbon black, and diversified into stars such as ceramics and semiconductors in a seemingly overaggressive effort to create more revenue growth for the corporation. Predictably, Cabot's return on assets declined as the firm shifted away from its core competence to unrelated areas. The portfolio model failed by pointing the company in the wrong direction in an effort to spur growth—away from their core business. Recognizing its mistake, Cabot Corporation returned to its mainstay carbon black manufacturing and divested unrelated businesses. Today the company is a leader in its field with $3.2 billion in 2008 revenues.[43]

Exhibit 6.7 summarizes the limitations of portfolio model analysis.

Exhibit 6.7
Limitations of Portfolio Models

- They are overly simplistic, consisting of only two dimensions (growth and market share).

- They view each business as separate, ignoring potential synergies across businesses.

- The process may become overly largely mechanical, minimizing the potential value of managers' judgment and experience.

- The reliance on strict rules for resource allocation across SBUs can be detrimental to a firm's long-term viability.

- The imagery (e.g., cash cows, dogs) while colorful, may lead to troublesome and overly simplistic prescriptions.

Caveat: Is Risk Reduction a Viable Goal of Diversification?

One of the purposes of diversification is to reduce the risk that is inherent in a firm's variability in revenues and profits over time. That is, if a firm enters new products or markets that are affected differently by seasonal or economic cycles, its performance over time will be more stable. For example, a firm manufacturing lawn mowers may diversify into snow blowers to even out its annual sales. Or a firm manufacturing a luxury line of household furniture may introduce a lower-priced line since affluent and lower-income customers are affected differently by economic cycles.

At first glance the above reasoning may make sense, but there are some problems with it. First, a firm's stockholders can diversify their portfolios at a much lower cost than a corporation, and they don't have to worry about integrating the acquisition into their portfolio. Second, economic cycles as well as their impact on a given industry (or firm) are difficult to predict with any degree of accuracy.

Notwithstanding the above, some firms have benefited from diversification by lowering the variability (or risk) in their performance over time. Consider Emerson Electronic.[44]

> Emerson Electronic is a $25 billion manufacturer that produces a wide variety of products, including measurement devices for heavy industry, temperature controls for heating and ventilation systems, and power tools sold at Home Depot. Recently, many analysts questioned Emerson's purchase of companies that sell power systems to the volatile telecommunications industry. Why? This industry is expected to experience, at best, minimal growth. However, CEO David Farr maintained that such assets could be acquired inexpensively because of the aggregate decline in demand in this industry. Additionally, he argued that the other business units, such as the sales of valves and regulators to the now-booming oil and natural gas companies, were able to pick up the slack. Therefore, while net profits in the electrical equipment sector (Emerson's core business) sharply decreased, Emerson's overall corporate profits increased 1.7 percent.

Risk reduction in and of itself is rarely viable as a means to create shareholder value. It must be undertaken with a view of a firm's overall diversification strategy.

The Means to Achieve Diversification

We have addressed the types of diversification (e.g., related and unrelated) that a firm may undertake to achieve synergies and create value for its shareholders. Now, we address the means by which a firm can go about achieving these desired benefits.

There are three basic means. First, through acquisitions or mergers, corporations can directly acquire a firm's assets and competencies. Although the terms *mergers* and *acquisitions* are used quite interchangeably, there are some key differences. With

acquisitions, one firm buys another either through a stock purchase, cash, or the issuance of debt.[45] **Mergers,** on the other hand, entail a combination or consolidation of two firms to form a new legal entity. Mergers are relatively rare and entail a transaction among two firms on a relatively equal basis. Despite such differences, we consider both mergers and acquisitions to be quite similar in terms of their implications for a firm's corporate-level strategy.[46]

Second, corporations may agree to pool the resources of other companies with their resource base, commonly known as a joint venture or strategic alliance. Although these two forms of partnerships are similar in many ways, there is an important difference. Joint ventures involve the formation of a third-party legal entity where the two (or more) firms each contribute equity, whereas strategic alliances do not.

Third, corporations may diversify into new products, markets, and technologies through internal development. Called corporate entrepreneurship, it involves the leveraging and combining of a firm's own resources and competencies to create synergies and enhance shareholder value. We address this subject in greater length in Chapter 12.

acquisitions the incorporation of one firm into another through purchase.

mergers the combining of two or more firms into one new legal entity.

Mergers and Acquisitions

The rate of mergers and acquisitions (M&A) had dropped off beginning in 2001. This trend was largely a result of a recession, corporate scandals, and a declining stock market. However, the situation has changed dramatically. Over the past several years, several large mergers and acquisitions were announced. These include:[47]

- Pfizer's acquisition of Wyeth for $68 billion.
- Mittal Steel's acquisition of Arcelor for $33 billion.
- BellSouth's acquisition of AT&T for $86.0 billion.
- Sprint's merger with Nextel for $39 billion.
- Boston Scientific's $27 billion acquisition of medical device maker Guidant.
- Procter & Gamble's purchase of Gillette for $54 billion.
- Kmart Holding Corp.'s acquisition of Sears, Roebuck & Co. for $11 billion.

Exhibit 6.8 illustrates the dramatic increase in worldwide M&A activity in the U.S. up until 2008, when the global recession began. Several factors help to explain the rapid rise between 2002 and 2007. First, there was the robust economy and the increasing corporate profits that had boosted stock prices and cash. For example, the S&P 500 stock index companies, including financial companies, had a record of over $2 trillion in cash and other short-term assets.

Second, the weak U.S. dollar made U.S. assets less expensive relative to other countries. That is, from the perspective of a foreign acquirer, compared to any other period in recent memory, U.S. companies were "cheap." For example, a Euro, which was worth only 80 cents in 1999, was worth $1.35 by mid-2007. This made U.S. companies a relative bargain for a European acquirer.

Third, stricter governance standards were requiring poorly performing CEOs and boards of directors to consider unsolicited offers. In essence, top executives and board members were less likely to be protected by antitakeover mechanisms such as greenmail, poison pills, and golden parachutes (discussed at the end of the chapter).

Motives and Benefits   Growth through mergers and acquisitions has played a critical role in the success of many corporations in a wide variety of high-technology and knowledge-intensive industries. Here, market and technology changes can occur very quickly and unpredictably.[48] Speed—speed to market, speed to positioning, and speed to becoming a viable company—is critical in such industries. For example, Alex Mandl, then AT&T's president, was responsible for the acquisition of McCaw Cellular. Although many industry experts felt the price was too steep, he believed that cellular technology was a

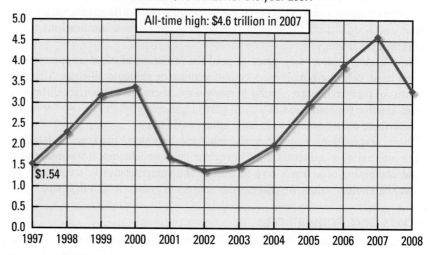

Global Value of Mergers and Acquisitions

Global mergers and acquisitions soared past their previous record and hit $4.6 trillion for the year 2007.

All-time high: $4.6 trillion in 2007

$1.54

Exhibit 6.8 Global Value of Mergers and Acquisitions

Source: Bloomberg; Dealogic; and personal communication with Meredith Leonard at Dealogic on January 27, 2009.

critical asset for the telecommunications business. Mandl claimed, "The plain fact is that acquiring is much faster than building."[49]

Mergers and acquisitions also can be a means of *obtaining valuable resources that can help an organization expand its product offerings and services.* For example, Cisco Systems, a dominant player in networking equipment, acquired more than 70 companies over a recent seven-year period.[50] This provides Cisco with access to the latest in networking equipment. Then it uses its excellent sales force to market the new technology to its corporate customers. Cisco also provides strong incentives to the staff of acquired companies to stay on. To realize the greatest value from its acquisitions, Cisco also has learned to integrate acquired companies efficiently and effectively.[51]

Mergers and acquisitions also can *provide the opportunity for firms to attain the three bases of synergy—leveraging core competencies, sharing activities, and building market power.* Consider Procter & Gamble's $57 billion acquisition of Gillette.[52] First, it helps Procter & Gamble to leverage its core competencies in marketing and product positioning in the area of grooming and personal care brands. For example, P&G has experience in repositioning brands such as Old Spice in this market (which recently passed Gillette's Right Guard brand to become No. 1 in the deodorant market). Gillette has very strong brands in razors and blades. Thus, P&G's marketing expertise enhances its market position. Second, there are opportunities to share value-creating activities. Gillette will benefit from P&G's stronger distribution network in developing countries where the potential growth rate for the industry's products remains higher than in the United States, Europe, or Japan. Consider the insight of A. F. Lafley, P&G's CEO:

> When I was in Asia in the 90s, we had already gone beyond the top 500 cities in China. Today, we're way down into the rural areas. So we add three, four, five Gillette brands, and we don't even have to add a salesperson.

Third, the addition of Gillette increases P&G's market power. In recent years, the growth of powerful global retailers such as Wal-Mart, Carrefour, and Costco has eroded much of the consumer goods industry's pricing power. A central part of P&G's recent strategy has been to focus its resources on enhancing its core brands. Today, 16 of its brands (each with revenues of over $1 billion) account for $30 billion of the firm's $51.4 billion in total revenues. Gillette, with $10.5 billion in total revenues, adds five brands which also have revenues of over $1 billion. P&G anticipates that its growing stable of "superbrands" will help it to weather the industry's tough pricing environment and enhance its power relative to large, powerful retailers such as Wal-Mart and Target.

Merger and acquisition activity also can *lead to consolidation within an industry and can force other players to merge.*[53] In the pharmaceutical industry, the patents for many top-selling drugs are expiring and M&A activity is expected to heat up.[54] For example, a few years ago SG Cowen Securities predicted that between 2000 and 2005, U.S. patents would expire on pharmaceutical products with annual domestic sales of approximately $34.6 billion. Clearly, this is an example of how the political—legal segment of the general environment (discussed in Chapter 2) can affect a corporation's strategy and performance. Although health care providers and patients are happy about the lower-cost generics that will arrive, drug firms are being pressed to make up for lost revenues. Combining top firms such as Glaxo Wellcome and SmithKline Beecham has many potential long-term benefits. They not only promise significant postmerger cost savings, but also the increased size of the combined companies brings greater research and development possibilities.

Corporations can also *enter new market segments by way of acquisitions.* Although Charles Schwab & Co. is best known for providing discount trading services for middle America, it clearly is interested in other target markets.[55] In late 2000 Schwab surprised its rivals by paying $2.7 billion to acquire (divested in 2006) U.S. Trust Corporation, a 147-year-old financial services institution that is a top estate planner for the wealthy. However, Schwab is not ignoring its core market. The firm also purchased Cybercorp Inc., a Texas brokerage company, for $488 million. That firm offers active online traders sophisticated quotes and stock-screening tools. Exhibit 6.9 summarizes the benefits of mergers and acquisitions.

Potential Limitations   As noted in the previous section, mergers and acquisitions provide a firm with many potential benefits. However, at the same time, there are many potential drawbacks or limitations to such corporate activity.[56]

First, *the takeover premium that is paid for an acquisition typically is very high.* Two times out of three, the stock price of the acquiring company falls once the deal is made public. Since the acquiring firm often pays a 30 percent or higher premium for the target company, the acquirer must create synergies and scale economies that result in sales and market gains exceeding the premium price. Firms paying higher premiums set the performance hurdle even higher. For example, Household International paid an 82 percent premium to buy Beneficial, and Conseco paid an 83 percent premium to acquire Green Tree Financial. Historically, paying a high premium over the stock price has been a poor strategy.

Exhibit 6.9
Benefits of Mergers and Acquisitions

- Obtain valuable resources that can help an organization expand its product offerings.
- Provide the opportunity for firms to attain three bases of synergy: leveraging core competencies, sharing activities, and building market power.
- Lead to consolidation within an industry and force other players to merge.
- Enter new market segments.

Second, *competing firms often can imitate any advantages realized or copy synergies that result from the M&A.*[57] Thus, a firm can often see its advantages quickly erode. Unless the advantages are sustainable and difficult to copy, investors will not be willing to pay a high premium for the stock. Similarly, the time value of money must be factored into the stock price. M&A costs are paid up front. Conversely, firms pay for R&D, ongoing marketing, and capacity expansion over time. This stretches out the payments needed to gain new competencies. The M&A argument is that a large initial investment is worthwhile because it creates long-term advantages. However, stock analysts want to see immediate results from such a large cash outlay. If the acquired firm does not produce results quickly, investors often divest the stock, driving the price down.

Third, *managers' credibility and ego can sometimes get in the way of sound business decisions.* If the M&A does not perform as planned, managers who pushed for the deal find their reputation tarnished. This can lead them to protect their credibility by funneling more money, or escalating their commitment, into an inevitably doomed operation. Further, when a merger fails and a firm tries to unload the acquisition, they often must sell at a huge discount. These problems further compound the costs and erode the stock price.

Fourth, *there can be many cultural issues that may doom the intended benefits from M&A endeavors.* Consider, the insights of Joanne Lawrence, who played an important role in the merger between SmithKline and the Beecham Group.[58]

> The key to a strategic merger is to create a new culture. This was a mammoth challenge during the SmithKline Beecham merger. We were working at so many different cultural levels, it was dizzying. We had two national cultures to blend—American and British—that compounded the challenge of selling the merger in two different markets with two different shareholder bases. There were also two different business cultures: One was very strong, scientific, and academic; the other was much more commercially oriented. And then we had to consider within both companies the individual businesses, each of which has its own little culture.

Exhibit 6.10 summarizes the limitations of mergers and acquisitions.

Divestment: The Other Side of the "M&A Coin"   When firms acquire other businesses, it typically generates quite a bit of "press" in business publications such as *The Wall Street Journal, BusinessWeek,* and *Fortune.* It makes for exciting news, and one thing is for sure—large acquiring firms automatically improve their standing in the Fortune 500 rankings (since it is based solely on total revenues). However, managers must also carefully consider the strategic implications of exiting businesses.

divestment the exit of a business from a firm's portfolio.

Divestments, the exit of a business from a firm's portfolio, are quite common. One study found that large, prestigious U.S. companies divested more acquisitions than they had kept.[59] Well-known divestitures in business history include (1) Novell's purchase of WordPerfect for stock valued at $1.4 billion and later sold to Corel for $124 million, and (2) Quaker Oats' unloading of the Snapple Beverage Company to Triarc for only $300 million in 1997—three years after it had bought it for $1.8 billion!

Exhibit 6.10
Limitations of Mergers and Acquisitions

- Takeover premiums paid for acquisitions are typically very high.
- Competing firms often can imitate any advantages or copy synergies that result from the merger or acquisition.
- Managers' egos sometimes get in the way of sound business decisions.
- Cultural issues may doom the intended benefits from M&A endeavors.

Campbell Soup Divests Godiva to Focus on Its Core Business

In August 2007, Campbell Soup decided it would sell Godiva, its superpremium chocolate business— which had been a very profitable brand for them. Campbell didn't base the decision on financial considerations. Rather, Godiva was not consistent with Campbell's values, competencies, and aspirations of nutrition and simplicity. According to Doug Conant, Campbell's CEO: "Although the premium chocolate category is experiencing strong growth and Godiva is well positioned for the future, the premium chocolate business does not fit Campbell's focus on simple meals."

The firm reached an agreement to sell Godiva to Yildiz Holding (which owns the Turkish company Ulker Group) for $850 million in December 2007. By relying on its identity, rather than on financial projections, Campbell made the decision to sell the unit quickly and painlessly.

Source: Camillus, J. 2008. Strategy as a Wicked Problem. *Harvard Business Review,* 86 (5): 98–108.

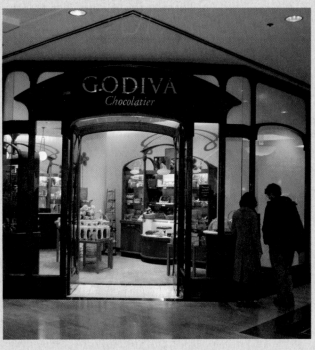

● Campbell Soup divested Godiva. Even though the chocolatier had a very strong market position, Godiva did not fit Campbell's "focus on simple meals."

Divesting a business can accomplish many different objectives.* As the examples above demonstrate, it can be used to help a firm reverse an earlier acquisition that didn't work out as planned. Often, this is simply to help "cut their losses." Other objectives include: (1) enabling managers to focus their efforts more directly on the firm's core businesses,[60] (2) providing the firm with more resources to spend on more attractive alternatives; and (3) raising cash to help fund existing businesses. Strategy Spotlight 6.6 discusses why Campbell Soup divested Godiva—to concentrate on its core business.

---

* Firms can divest their businesses in a number of ways. Sell-offs, spin-offs, equity carve-outs, asset sales/dissolution, and split-ups are some such modes of divestment. In a sell-off, the divesting firm privately negotiates with a third party to divest a unit/subsidiary for cash/stock. In a spin-off, a parent company distributes shares of the unit/subsidiary being divested pro-rata to its existing shareholders and a new company is formed. Equity carve-outs are similar to spin-offs except that shares in the unit/subsidiary being divested are offered to new shareholders. Dissolution involves sale of redundant assets, not necessarily as an entire unit/subsidiary as in sell-offs but a few bits at a time. A split-up, on the other hand, is an instance of divestiture where the parent company is split into two or more new companies and the parent ceases to exist. Shares in the parent company are exchanged for shares in new companies and the exact distribution varies case by case.

Divesting can enhance a firm's competitive position only to the extent that it reduces its tangible (e.g., maintenance, investments, etc.) or intangible (e.g., opportunity costs, managerial attention) costs without sacrificing a current competitive advantage or the seeds of future advantages.[61] To be effective, divesting requires a thorough understanding of a business unit's current ability and future potential to contribute to a firm's value creation. However, since such decisions involve a great deal of uncertainty, it is very difficult to make such evaluations. In addition, because of managerial self-interests and organizational inertia, firms often delay divestments of underperforming businesses.

Successful divestment involves establishing objective criteria for determining divestment candidates.[62] Clearly, firms should not panic and sell for a song in bad times. Private equity firms and conglomerates naturally place great emphasis on value when it comes to assessing which business units to keep. In identifying which assets to sell, the management committee of $13 billion Textron, for example, applies three tests of value to the firm's diverse portfolio—which is composed of some 12 divisions and 72 strategic business units (SBUs). For Textron to retain a business unit:

- The unit's long-term fundamentals must be sound. The team gauges this by assessing the attractiveness of each SBU's market and the unit's competitive strength within that market.
- Textron must be able to grow the unit's intrinsic value by 15 percent or more annually. The team applies this screen by carefully analyzing each SBU's business plan each year and challenging its divisional management teams to assess the value-growth potential of each business objectively.
- The unit's revenues must reach a certain threshold. Textron seeks to hold a portfolio of relevant businesses, each with at least $1 billion in revenue. Businesses that are not generating $1 billion or more in sales—and are not likely to reach this watershed within the foreseeable future—are targets for divestiture.

Strategic Alliances and Joint Ventures

strategic alliance a cooperative relationship between two or more firms.

A **strategic alliance** is a cooperative relationship between two (or more) firms.[63] Alliances may be either informal or formal—that is, involving a written contract. **Joint ventures** represent a special case of alliances, wherein two (or more) firms contribute equity to form a new legal entity.

Strategic alliances and joint ventures are assuming an increasingly prominent role in the strategy of leading firms, both large and small.[64] Such cooperative relationships have many potential advantages.[65] Among these are entering new markets, reducing manufacturing (or other) costs in the value chain, and developing and diffusing new technologies.[66]

joint ventures new entities formed within a strategic alliance in which two or more firms, the parents, contribute equity to form the new legal entity.

Entering New Markets   Often a company that has a successful product or service wants to introduce it into a new market. However, it may not have the financial resources or the requisite marketing expertise because it does not understand customer needs, know how to promote the product, or have access to the proper distribution channels.[67]

The partnerships formed between Time-Warner, Inc., and three African American–owned cable companies in New York City are examples of joint ventures created to serve a domestic market. Time-Warner built a 185,000-home cable system in the city and asked the three cable companies to operate it. Time-Warner supplied the product, and the cable companies supplied the knowledge of the community and the know-how to market the cable system. Joining with the local companies enabled Time-Warner to win the acceptance of the cable customers and to benefit from an improved image in the black community.

Crowdsourcing: Kraft's Strategic Alliance with a Bagel Maker

In 2006, Kraft Foods launched a program on its website that actively seeks out small businesses and inventors as partners for product development. "The world has gotten much smaller, and innovation is happening at small businesses," asserts Steve Goers, vice president for open innovation and investment. Entrepreneurs and inventors submit an average of 40 to 50 ideas each month through www.innovatewithkraft.com. Dozens of ideas, which may also be submitted in writing or by phone, have become new products or enhancements of existing products.

Gary Schwartzberg pitched his product, a cream-filled bagel, as an "all-in-one, portable breakfast for the on-the-go crowd." He was interested in the brand strength of Kraft's Philadelphia Cream Cheese and mailed Kraft a proposal, along with a box of Bagelers, his cream-filled bagels. Says Schwartzberg: "Bagelers are the perfect meal for busy families looking for a quick and convenient meal that tastes great. The secret is in the family recipe we have been using since 1931 coupled with our patented production technology. As we like to say, Bagelers are a whole new way to eat bagels and cream cheese."

Fortunately, Kraft had been working on something similar, in an effort to market its cream cheese in the growing portable-breakfast category. But the firm didn't have bagel-making expertise and hadn't been able to get the product just right. Schwartzberg, on the other hand, had patented a process for "encapsulating" the cream cheese in the center of the bagel without the cream cheese escaping during the baking process. After Kraft executives tasted the product, they flew to Florida to meet with Schwartzberg. They formed an internal team to evaluate the marketability of the product and looked into the production process to make sure the bagels could be produced on a national scale.

Satisfied, the two sides signed a deal in which details are unavailable because of a confidentiality agreement, which is standard practice in such situations. Schwartzberg says it is structured as a strategic alliance and he "has skin in the game." The products are now known as Bagel-Fuls, and they are available in supermarkets throughout the U.S. Branded by Kraft Foods, they are filled with Philadelphia Cream Cheese—the best-selling brand in the U.S.

Sources: Covel, S. 2008. My Brain, Your Brawn. WSJ.com, October 13: np.; and Filled Bagel Industries Announces Launch of Bagelers Cream Cheese–Filled Product. 2003. FoodserviceCentral.com, October 28: np.

crowdsourcing

Strategy Spotlight 6.7 discusses how Kraft Foods, the $37 billion consumer giant, used a strategic alliance with a small bagel producer to generate profits for both firms.

Reducing Manufacturing (or Other) Costs in the Value Chain   Strategic alliances (or joint ventures) often enable firms to pool capital, value-creating activities, or facilities in order to reduce costs. For example, Molson Companies and Carling O'Keefe Breweries in Canada formed a joint venture to merge their brewing operations. Although Molson had a modern and efficient brewery in Montreal, Carling's was outdated. However, Carling had the better facilities in Toronto. In addition, Molson's Toronto brewery was located on the waterfront and had substantial real estate value. Overall, the synergies gained by using their combined facilities more efficiently added $150 million of pretax earnings during the initial year of the venture. Economies of scale were realized and facilities were better utilized.

Developing and Diffusing New Technologies   Strategic alliances also may be used to build jointly on the technological expertise of two or more companies in order to develop products technologically beyond the capability of the companies acting independently.

STMicroelectronics (ST) is a high-tech company based in Geneva, Switzerland, that has thrived—largely due to the success of its strategic alliances.[68] The firm develops and manufactures computer chips for a variety of applications such as mobile phones, set-top boxes, smart cards, and flash memories. In 1995 it teamed up with Hewlett-Packard to develop powerful new processors for various digital applications that are now nearing completion. Another example was its strategic alliance with Nokia to develop a chip that would give Nokia's phones a longer battery life. Here, ST produced a chip that tripled standby time to 60 hours—a breakthough that gave Nokia a huge advantage in the marketplace.

The firm's CEO, Pasquale Pistorio, was among the first in the industry to form R&D alliances with other companies. Now ST's top 12 customers, including HP, Nokia, and Nortel, account for 45 percent of revenues. According to Pistorio, "Alliances are in our DNA." Such relationships help ST keep better-than-average growth rates, even in difficult times. That's because close partners are less likely to defect to other suppliers.

Potential Downsides Despite their promise, many alliances and joint ventures fail to meet expectations for a variety of reasons.[69] First, without the proper partner, a firm should never consider undertaking an alliance, even for the best of reasons.[70] Each partner should bring the desired complementary strengths to the partnership. Ideally, the strengths contributed by the partners are unique; thus synergies created can be more easily sustained and defended over the longer term. The goal must be to develop synergies between the contributions of the partners, resulting in a win–win situation. Moreover, the partners must be compatible and willing to trust each other. Unfortunately, often little attention is given to nurturing the close working relationships and interpersonal connections that bring together the partnering organizations.

Internal Development

Firms can also diversify by means of corporate entrepreneurship and new venture development. **In today's economy, internal development is such an important means by which companies expand their businesses that we have devoted a whole chapter to it (see Chapter 12).** Sony and the Minnesota Mining & Manufacturing Co. (3M), for example, are known for their dedication to innovation, R&D, and cutting-edge technologies. For example, 3M has developed its entire corporate culture to support its ongoing policy of generating at least 25 percent of total sales from products created within the most recent four-year period. During the 1990s, 3M exceeded this goal by achieving about 30 percent of sales per year from new internally developed products.

The luxury hotel chain Ritz-Carlton has long been recognized for its exemplary service. In fact, it is the only service company ever to win two Malcolm Baldrige National Quality Awards. It has built on this capability by developing a highly successful internal venture to offer leadership development programs—both to its employees as well as to outside companies. We address this internal venture in Strategy Spotlight 6.8.

Compared to mergers and acquisitions, firms that engage in internal development capture the value created by their own innovative activities without having to "share the wealth" with alliance partners or face the difficulties associated with combining activities across the value chains of several firms or merging corporate cultures. Also, firms can often develop new products or services at a relatively lower cost and thus rely on their own resources rather than turning to external funding.

There are also potential disadvantages. It may be time consuming; thus, firms may forfeit the benefits of speed that growth through mergers or acquisitions can provide. This may be especially important among high-tech or knowledge-based organizations in fast-paced environments where being an early mover is critical. Thus, firms that choose to diversify through internal development must develop capabilities that allow them to move quickly from initial opportunity recognition to market introduction.

The Ritz-Carlton Leadership Center: A Successful Internal Venture

Companies worldwide often strive to be the "Ritz-Carlton" of their industries. Ritz-Carlton, the large luxury hotel chain, is the only service company to have won the prestigious Malcolm Baldrige National Quality Award twice—in 1992 and 1999 (one year after being acquired by Marriott). It also has placed first in guest satisfaction among luxury hotels in the most recent J.D. Power & Associates hotel survey.

Until a few years ago, being "Ritz-Carlton-like" was just a motivational simile. However, in 2000, the company launched the Ritz-Carlton Leadership Center, where it offers 12 leadership development programs for its employees and seven benchmarking seminars and workshops to outside companies. It also conducts 35 off-site presentations on such topics as "Creating a Dynamic Employee Orientation," and "The Key to Retaining and Selecting Talented Employees." (Incidentally, Ritz-Carlton's annual turnover rate among nonmanagement employees is 25 percent—roughly half the average rate for U.S. luxury hotels.)

Within its first four years of operation, 800 different companies from such industries as health care, banking and finance, hospitality, and the automotive industries have participated in the Leadership Center's programs. And to date it has generated over $2 million in revenues. Says Diana Oreck, Vice President of RCLL: "At Ritz-Carlton we have a credo, motto, and three steps of service that are critical. You can adapt these elements to the vision of what your company culture should be."

To give a few specifics on one of the Leadership Center's programs, consider its "Legendary Service I" course. The topics that are covered include empowerment, using customer recognition to boost loyalty, and Ritz-Carlton's approach to quality. The course lasts two days and costs $2,000 per attendee. Well-known companies that have participated include Microsoft, Morgan Stanley, and Starbucks.

Sources: Jankowski, W. 2008. Ten Minutes with Diana Oreck. www.remodeling.hw.net, August 26: np; corporate.ritzcarlton.com. McDonald, D. 2004. Roll Out the Blue Carpet. *Business 2.0*, May: 53; and Johnson, G. 2003. Nine Tactics to Take Your Corporate University from Good to GREAT. *Training*, July/August: 38–41.

How Managerial Motives Can Erode Value Creation

> **>LO6**
> Managerial behaviors that can erode the creation of value.

Thus far in the chapter we have implicitly assumed that CEOs and top executives are "rational beings"; that is, they act in the best interests of shareholders to maximize long-term shareholder value. In the real world, however, they may often act in their own self-interest. We now address some managerial motives that can serve to erode, rather than enhance, value creation. These include "growth for growth's sake," excessive egotism, and the creation of a wide variety of antitake-over tactics.

Growth for Growth's Sake

managerial motives managers acting in their own self-interest rather than in maximizing long-term shareholder value.

There are huge incentives for executives to increase the size of their firm. And these are not consistent with increasing shareholder wealth. Top managers, including the CEO, of larger firms typically enjoy more prestige, higher rankings for their firms on the Fortune 500 list (based on revenues, *not* profits), greater incomes, more job security, and so on. There is also the excitement and associated recognition of making a major acquisition. As noted by Harvard's Michael Porter, "There's a tremendous allure to mergers and acquisitions. It's the big play, the dramatic gesture. With one stroke of the pen you can add billions to size, get a front-page story, and create excitement in markets."[71]

In recent years many high-tech firms have suffered from the negative impact of their uncontrolled growth. Consider, for example, Priceline.com's ill-fated venture into an online service to offer groceries and gasoline.[72] A myriad of problems—perhaps most

Cornelius Vanderbilt: Going to Great Lengths to Correct a Wrong!

Cornelius Vanderbilt's legendary ruthlessness set a bar for many titans to come. Back in 1853, the Commodore took his first vacation, an extended voyage to Europe aboard his yacht. He was in for a big surprise when he returned. Two of his associates had taken the power of attorney

that he had left them and sold his interest in his steamship concern, Accessory Transit Company, to themselves.

"Gentlemen," he wrote, in a classic battle cry, "you have undertaken to cheat me. I won't sue you, for the law is too slow. I'll ruin you." He converted his yacht to a passenger ship to compete with them and added other vessels. He started a new line, appropriately named *Opposition*. Before long, he bought his way back in and regained control of the company.

Source: McGregor, J. 2007. Sweet Revenge. *BusinessWeek*, January 22: 64–70.

importantly, a lack of participation by manufacturers—caused the firm to lose more than $5 million a *week* prior to abandoning these ventures. Such initiatives are often little more than desperate moves by top managers to satisfy investor demands for accelerating revenues. Unfortunately, the increased revenues often fail to materialize into a corresponding hike in earnings.

At times, executives' overemphasis on growth can result in a plethora of ethical lapses, which can have disastrous outcomes for their companies. A good example (of bad practice) is Joseph Bernardino's leadership at Andersen Worldwide. Bernardino had a chance early on to take a hard line on ethics and quality in the wake of earlier scandals at clients such as Waste Management and Sunbeam. Instead, according to former executives, he put too much emphasis on revenue growth. Consequently, the firm's reputation quickly eroded when it audited and signed off on the highly flawed financial statements of such infamous firms as Enron, Global Crossing, and WorldCom. Bernardino ultimately resigned in disgrace in March 2002, and his firm was dissolved later that year.[73]

Egotism

A healthy ego helps make a leader confident, clearheaded, and able to cope with change. CEOs, by their very nature, are intensely competitive people in the office as well as on the tennis court or golf course. But, sometimes when pride is at stake, individuals will go to great lengths to win. Such behavior, of course, is not a new phenomenon. We discuss the case of Cornelius Vanderbilt, one of the original American moguls, in Strategy Spotlight 6.9.

Egos can get in the way of a "synergistic" corporate marriage. Few executives (or lower-level managers) are exempt from the potential downside of excessive egos. Consider, for example, the reflections of General Electric's former CEO Jack Welch, considered by many to be the world's most admired executive. He admitted to a regrettable decision: "My hubris got in the way in the Kidder Peabody deal. [He was referring to GE's buyout of the soon-to-be-troubled Wall Street firm.] I got wise advice from Walter Wriston and other directors who said, 'Jack, don't do this.' But I was bully enough and on a run to do it. And I got whacked right in the head."[74] In addition to poor financial results, Kidder Peabody was wracked by a widely publicized trading scandal that tarnished the reputations of both GE and Kidder Peabody. Welch ended up selling Kidder in 1994.

The business press has included many stories of how egotism and greed have infiltrated organizations. Some incidents are considered rather astonishing, such as Tyco's former (and now convicted) CEO Dennis Kozlowski's well-chronicled purchase of a $6,000 shower curtain and vodka-spewing, full-size replica of Michaelangelo's David.[75] Other well-known examples of power grabs and extraordinary consumption of compensation and perks include executives at Enron, the Rigas family who were convicted of defrauding Adelphia of roughly $1 billion, former CEO Bernie Ebbers's $408 million loan from WorldCom, and so on.

A more recent example of excess and greed was exhibited by John Thain.[76] On January 22, 2009, he was ousted as head of Merrill Lynch by Bank of America's CEO, Ken Lewis:

> Thain embarrassingly doled out $4 billion in discretionary year-end bonuses to favored employees just before Bank of America's rescue purchase of failing Merrill. The bonuses amounted to about 10 percent of Merrill's 2008 losses.
>
> Obviously, John Thain believed that he was entitled. When he took over ailing Merrill in early 2008, he began planning major cuts, but he also ordered that his office be redecorated. He spent $1.22 million of company funds to make it "livable," which, in part, included $87,000 for a rug, $87,000 for a pair of guest chairs, $68,000 for a 19th-century credenza, and (what really got the attention of the press) $35,000 for a "commode with legs."
>
> He later agreed to repay the decorating costs. However, one might still ask: What kind of person treats other people's money like this? And who needs a commode that costs as much as a new Lexus? Finally, a comment by Bob O'Brien, stock editor at Barrons.com clearly applies: "The sense of entitlement that's been engendered in this group of people has clearly not been beaten out of them by the brutal performance of the financial sector over the course of the last year."

Antitakeover Tactics

Unfriendly or hostile takeovers can occur when a company's stock becomes undervalued. A competing organization can buy the outstanding stock of a takeover candidate in sufficient quantity to become a large shareholder. Then it makes a tender offer to gain full control of the company. If the shareholders accept the offer, the hostile firm buys the target company and either fires the target firm's management team or strips them of their power. Thus, antitakeover tactics are common, including greenmail, golden parachutes, and poison pills.[77]

The first, **greenmail,** is an effort by the target firm to prevent an impending takeover. When a hostile firm buys a large block of outstanding target company stock and the target firm's management feels that a tender offer is impending, they offer to buy the stock back from the hostile company at a higher price than the unfriendly company paid for it. Although this often prevents a hostile takeover, the same price is not offered to preexisting shareholders. However, it protects the jobs of the target firm's management.

Second, a **golden parachute** is a prearranged contract with managers specifying that, in the event of a hostile takeover, the target firm's managers will be paid a significant severance package. Although top managers lose their jobs, the golden parachute provisions protect their income.

Third, **poison pills** are used by a company to give shareholders certain rights in the event of a takeover by another firm. They are also known as shareholder rights plans.

Clearly, antitakeover tactics can often raise some interesting ethical—and legal—issues. Strategy Spotlight 6.10 addresses how antitakeover measures can benefit multiple stakeholders—not just management.

greenmail a payment by a firm to a hostile party for the firm's stock at a premium, made when the firm's management feels that the hostile party is about to make a tender offer.

golden parachute a prearranged contract with managers specifying that, in the event of a hostile takeover, the target firm's managers will be paid a significant severance package.

poison pill used by a company to give shareholders certain rights in the event of takeover by another firm.

How Antitakeover Measures May Benefit Multiple Stakeholders, Not Just Management

Antitakeover defenses represent a gray area, because management can often legitimately argue that such actions are not there solely to benefit themselves. Rather, they can benefit other stakeholders, such as employees, customers, and the community.

In the late 1980s, takeovers were very popular. The Dayton Hudson Corporation (now Target) even appealed to the Minnesota legislature to pass an antitakeover bill to help Dayton Hudson in its struggle with Hafts—the former owners of Dart, a drug store chain on the East Coast. History had shown that the Dayton Hudson management in place at the time was much better able to manage Dayton Hudson in the long run. In addition to Minnesota, many states now have laws that allow firms to take the interests of all stakeholders into account when considering a takeover bid.

In the summer of 2003, Oracle launched a hostile bid for PeopleSoft. Many charged that the tactics of Oracle CEO Larry Ellison had been unfair, and many of People-

Soft's customers took its side, indicating that Oracle ownership would not be of benefit to them. PeopleSoft was concerned that Oracle was merely seeking to buy PeopleSoft for its lucrative base of application software and was not interested in supporting the company's products. Oracle, on the other hand, sued PeopleSoft in an attempt to have the latter's so-called poison pill takeover defense removed.

In December 2004, Oracle struck a deal to buy PeopleSoft—ending a bitter 18-month hostile takeover battle. Oracle's $10.3 billion acquisition valued the firm at $26.50 a share—an increase of 66 percent over its initial offer of $16 a share. Noted analyst John DiFucci: "This is a financial acquisition primarily. Oracle is buying PeopleSoft for its maintenance stream." And, worth noting, PeopleSoft executives, including CEO and company founder David Duffield, did not join Oracle during the conference call announcing the acquisition. Oracle dropped its suit against PeopleSoft in which the former charged that PeopleSoft's "poison pill" takeover defense should be dismissed.

On moral grounds, some antitakeover defenses are not undertaken to entrench and protect management, but often they are. When such defenses are used simply to keep management in power, they are wrong. However, when they are used to defend the long-term financial health of the company and to protect broader stakeholder interests, they will be morally permissible.

Sources: Bowie, N. E. & Werhane, P. H. 2005. *Management Ethics*. Malden, MA: Blackwell Publishing; and La Monica, P. R. 2004. Finally, Oracle to Buy PeopleSoft. CNNMoney.com, December 13: np.

Reflecting on Career Implications . . .

- *Corporate-Level Strategy:* Be aware of your firm's corporate-level strategy. Can you come up with an initiative that will create value both within and across business units?
- *Core Competencies:* What do you see as your core competencies? How can you leverage them both within your business unit as well as across other business units?
- *Sharing Infrastructures:* What infrastructure activities and resources (e.g., information systems, legal) are available in the corporate office that would help you add value for your business unit—or other business units?
- *Diversification:* From your career perspective, what actions can you take to diversify your employment risk (e.g., coursework at a local university, obtain professional certification such as a C.P.A., networking through professional affiliation, etc.)? For example, in periods of retrenchment, such actions will provide you with a greater number of career options.

Summary

A key challenge for today's managers is to create "synergy" when engaging in diversification activities. As we discussed in this chapter, corporate managers do not, in general, have a very good track record in creating value in such endeavors when it comes to mergers and acquisitions. Among the factors that serve to erode shareholder values are paying an excessive premium for the target firm, failing to integrate the activities of the newly acquired businesses into the corporate family, and undertaking diversification initiatives that are too easily imitated by the competition.

We addressed two major types of corporate-level strategy: related and unrelated diversification. With *related diversification* the corporation strives to enter into areas in which key resources and capabilities of the corporation can be shared or leveraged. Synergies come from horizontal relationships between business units. Cost savings and enhanced revenues can be derived from two major sources. First, economies of scope can be achieved from the leveraging of core competencies and the sharing of activities. Second, market power can be attained from greater, or pooled, negotiating power and from vertical integration.

When firms undergo *unrelated diversification* they enter product markets that are dissimilar to their present businesses. Thus, there is generally little opportunity to either leverage core competencies or share activities across business units. Here, synergies are created from vertical relationships between the corporate office and the individual business units. With unrelated diversification, the primary ways to create value are corporate restructuring and parenting, as well as the use of portfolio analysis techniques.

Corporations have three primary means of diversifying their product markets—mergers and acquisitions, joint ventures/strategic alliances, and internal development. There are key trade-offs associated with each of these. For example, mergers and acquisitions are typically the quickest means to enter new markets and provide the corporation with a high level of control over the acquired business. However, with the expensive premiums that often need to be paid to the shareholders of the target firm and the challenges associated with integrating acquisitions, they can also be quite expensive. Not surprisingly, many poorly performing acquisitions are subsequently divested. At times, however, divestitures can help firms refocus their efforts and generate resources. Strategic alliances and joint ventures between two or more firms, on the other hand, may be a means of reducing risk since they involve the sharing and combining of resources. But

such joint initiatives also provide a firm with less control (than it would have with an acquisition) since governance is shared between two independent entities. Also, there is a limit to the potential upside for each partner because returns must be shared as well. Finally, with internal development, a firm is able to capture all of the value from its initiatives (as opposed to sharing it with a merger or alliance partner). However, diversification by means of internal development can be very time-consuming—a disadvantage that becomes even more important in fast-paced competitive environments.

Finally, some managerial behaviors may serve to erode shareholder returns. Among these are "growth for growth's sake," egotism, and antitakeover tactics. As we discussed, some of these issues—particularly antitakeover tactics—raise ethical considerations because the managers of the firm are not acting in the best interests of the shareholders.

Summary Review Questions

1. Discuss how managers can create value for their firm through diversification efforts.

2. What are some of the reasons that many diversification efforts fail to achieve desired outcomes?

3. How can companies benefit from related diversification? Unrelated diversification? What are some of the key concepts that can explain such success?

4. What are some of the important ways in which a firm can restructure a business?

5. Discuss some of the various means that firms can use to diversify. What are the pros and cons associated with each of these?

6. Discuss some of the actions that managers may engage in to erode shareholder value.

Key Terms

diversification 198
related
  diversification, 199
economies
  of scope, 199
core competencies, 200
sharing activities, 201
market power, 203
pooled negotiating
  power 203
vertical integration, 206

transaction cost
  perspective, 208
unrelated
  diversification 209
parenting advantage, 209
restructuring, 210
portfolio
  management, 211
acquisitions, 215
mergers, 215
divestment, 218

strategic alliance, 220 greenmail 225

joint ventures, 220 golden parachute 225

managerial motives 223 poison pill 225

Application Questions Exercises

1. What were some of the largest mergers and acquisitions over the last two years? What was the rationale for these actions? Do you think they will be successful? Explain.

2. Discuss some examples from business practice in which an executive's actions appear to be in his or her self-interest rather than the corporation's well-being.

3. Discuss some of the challenges that managers must overcome in making strategic alliances successful. What are some strategic alliances with which you are familiar? Were they successful or not? Explain.

4. Use the Internet and select a company that has recently undertaken diversification into new product markets. What do you feel were some of the reasons for this diversification (e.g., leveraging core competencies, sharing infrastructures)?

Ethics Questions

1. In recent years there has been a rash of corporate downsizing and layoffs. Do you feel that such actions raise ethical considerations? Why or why not?

2. What are some of the ethical issues that arise when managers act in a manner that is counter to their firm's best interests? What are the long-term implications for both the firms and the managers themselves?

Experiential Exercise

Time Warner (formerly AOL Time Warner) is a firm that follows a strategy of related diversification. Evaluate its success (or lack thereof) with regard to how well it has: (1) built on core competencies, (2) shared infrastructures, and (3) increased market power. (Fill answers in table below.)

Rationale for Related Diversification	Successful/Unsuccessful?	Why?
1. Build on core competencies		
2. Share infrastructures		
3. Increase market power		

References

1. Lashinsky, A. 2008. A SPAC that went splat. *Fortune,* March 31: 20; 2008 pivotal year for SPAC market. 2008. www.reuters.com: np; 2008. Tower completes Jazz acquisition. www. semiconductor-today.com: np; and Maney, K. 2006. Old buddies reunite in hopes of taking the tech world by storm . . . again. www.usatoday.com, October 18: np.

2. Insights on measuring M&A performance are addressed in: Zollo, M. & Meier, D. 2008. What is M&A performance? *BusinessWeek,* 22(3): 55–77.

3. Insights on how and why firms may overpay for acquisitions are addressed in: Malhotra, D., Ku, G., & Murnighan, J. K. 2008. When winning is everything. *Harvard Business Review,* 66(5); 78–86.

4. Pfizer deal helps lift stocks. 2009. online.wsy.com, January 26: np.

5. Dr. G. William Schwert, University of Rochester study cited in Pare, T. P. 1994. The new merger boom. *Fortune.* November 28: 96.

6. Lipin, S. & Deogun, N. 2000. Big mergers of the 1990's prove disappointing to shareholders. *The Wall Street Journal.* October 30: C1.

7. Rothenbuecher, J. & Schrottke, J. 2008. To get value from a merger, grow sales. *Harvard Business Review,* 86 (5): 24–25; and Rothenbuecher, J. 2008. Personal communication, October 1.

8. Pare, T. P. 1994. The new merger boom. *Fortune,* November 28: 96.

9. A discussion of the effects of director experience and acquisition performance is in: McDonald, M. L. & Westphal, J. D. 2008. What do they know? The effects of outside director acquisition experience on firm acquisition performance. *Strategic Management Journal,* 29(11): 1155–1177.

10. Ghosn, C. 2006. Inside the alliance: The win–win nature of a unique business mode. *Address to the Detroit Economic Club,* November 16.

11. For a study that investigates several predictors of corporate diversification, read: Wiersema, M. F. & Bowen, H. P. 2008. Corporate diversification: The impact of foreign competition, industry globalization, and product diversification. *Strategic Management Journal,* 29(2): 114–132.

12. A discussion of Tyco's unrelated diversification strategy is in: Hindo, B. 2008. Solving Tyco's identity crisis. *BusinessWeek,* February 18: 62.

13. Our framework draws upon a variety of sources, including Goold, M. & Campbell, A. 1998. Desperately seeking synergy. *Harvard Business Review,* 76(5): 131–143; Porter, M. E. 1987. From advantage to corporate strategy. *Harvard Business Review,* 65(3): 43–59; and Hitt, M. A., Ireland, R. D., & Hoskisson, R. E. 2001. *Strategic management: competitiveness and globalization* (4th ed.). Cincinnati, OH: South-Western.

14. Collis, D. J. & Montgomery, C. A. 1987. *Corporate strategy: Resources and the scope of the firm.* New York: McGraw-Hill.

15. This imagery of the corporation as a tree and related discussion draws on Prahalad, C. K. & Hamel, G. 1990. The core competence of the corporation. *Harvard Business Review,* 68(3): 79–91. Parts of this section also draw on Picken, J. C. & Dess, G. G. 1997. *Mission critical:* chap. 5. Burr Ridge, IL: Irwin Professional Publishing.

16. This section draws on Prahalad & Hamel, op. cit.; and Porter, op. cit.

17. A recent study that investigates the relationship between a firm's technology resources, diversification, and performance can be found in Miller, D. J. 2004. Firms' technological resources and the performance effects of diversification. A longitudinal study. *Strategic Management Journal,* 25: 1097–1119.

18. Collis & Montgomery, op. cit.

19. Henricks, M. 1994. VF seeks global brand dominance. *Apparel Industry Magazine,* August: 21–40; VF Corporation. 1993. First quarter corporate summary report. *1993 VF Annual Report.*

20. Hill, A. & Hargreaves, D. 2001. Turbulent times for GE-Honeywell deal. *Financial Times,* February 28: 26.

21. An interesting discussion of a merger in the Russian mining industry is in: Bush, J. 2008. Welding a new metals giant. *BusinessWeek,* July 14 & 21: 56.

22. Lowry, T. 2001. Media. *BusinessWeek,* January 8: 100–101.

23. This section draws on Hrebiniak, L. G. & Joyce, W. F. 1984. *Implementing strategy.* New York: MacMillan; and Oster, S. M. 1994. *Modern competitive analysis.* New York: Oxford University Press.

24. The discussion of the benefits and costs of vertical integration draws on Hax, A. C. & Majluf, N. S. 1991. *The strategy concept and process: A pragmatic approach:* 139. Englewood Cliffs, NJ: Prentice Hall.

25. Fahey, J. 2005. Gray winds. *Forbes.* January 10: 143.

26. This discussion draws on Oster, op. cit.; and Harrigan, K. 1986. Matching vertical integration strategies to competitive conditions. *Strategic Management Journal,* 7(6): 535–556.

27. For a scholarly explanation on how transaction costs determine the boundaries of a firm, see Oliver E. Williamson's pioneering books *Markets and Hierarchies: Analysis and Antitrust Implications* (New York: Free Press, 1975) and *The Economic Institutions of Capitalism* (New York: Free Press, 1985).

28. Campbell, A., Goold, M., & Alexander, M. 1995. Corporate strategy: The quest for parenting advantage. *Harvard Business Review,* 73(2): 120–132; and Picken & Dess, op. cit.

29. Anslinger, P. A. & Copeland, T. E. 1996. Growth through acquisition: A fresh look. *Harvard Business Review,* 74(1): 126–135.

30. Campbell et al., op. cit.

31. This section draws on Porter, op. cit.; and Hambrick, D. C. 1985. Turnaround strategies. In Guth, W. D. (Ed.). *Handbook of business strategy:* 10-1–10-32. Boston: Warren, Gorham & Lamont.

32. There is an important delineation between companies that are operated for a long-term profit and those that are bought and sold for short-term gains. The latter are sometimes referred to as "holding companies" and are generally more concerned about financial issues than strategic issues.

33. Lenzner, R. 2007. High on Loews. *Forbes,* February 26: 98–102.

34. Casico. W. F. 2002. Strategies for responsible restructuring. *Academy of Management Executive,* 16(3): 80–91; and Singh, H. 1993. Challenges in researching corporate restructuring. *Journal of Management Studies,* 30(1): 147–172.

35. Cusack, M. 1987. *Hanson Trust: A review of the company and its prospects.* London: Hoare Govett.

36. Hax & Majluf, op. cit. By 1979, 45 percent of Fortune 500 companies employed some form of portfolio analysis, according to Haspelagh, P. 1982. Portfolio planning: Uses and limits. *Harvard Busines Review,* 60: 58–73. A later study conducted in 1993 found that over 40 percent of the respondents used portfolio analysis techniques, but the level of usage was expected to increase to more than 60 percent in the near future: Rigby, D. K. 1994. Managing the management tools. *Planning Review,* September–October: 20–24.

37. Goold, M. & Luchs, K. 1993. Why diversify? Four decades of management thinking. *Academy of Management Executive,* 7(3): 7–25.

38. Other approaches include the industry attractiveness–business strength matrix developed jointly by General Electric and McKinsey and Company, the life-cycle matrix developed

by Arthur D. Little, and the profitability matrix proposed by Marakon. For an extensive review, refer to Hax & Majluf, op. cit.: 182–194.

39. Porter, op. cit.: 49–52.

40. Collis, D. J. 1995. Portfolio planning at Ciba-Geigy and the Newport investment proposal. Harvard Business School Case No. 9-795-040. Novartis AG was created in 1996 by the merger of Ciba-Geigy and Sandoz.

41. Buzzell, R. D. & Gale, B. T. 1987. *The PIMS principles: Linking strategy to performance.* New York: Free Press; and Miller, A. & Dess, G. G. 1996. *Strategic management,* (2nd ed.). New York: McGraw-Hill.

42. Seeger, J. 1984. Reversing the images of BCG's growth share matrix. *Strategic Management Journal,* 5(1): 93–97.

43. Picken & Dess, op. cit.; Cabot Corporation. 2001. 10-Q filing, Securities and Exchange Commission, May 14.

44. Koudsi, S. 2001. Remedies for an economic hangover. *Fortune,* June 25: 130–139.

45. Insights on the performance of serial acquirers is found in: Laamanen, T. & Keil, T. 2008. Performance of serial acquirers: Toward an acquisition program perspective. *Strategic Management Journal,* 29(6): 663–672.

46. Some insights from Lazard's CEO on mergers and acquisitions are addressed in: Stewart, T. A. & Morse, G. 2008. Giving great advice. *Harvard Business Review,* 66(1): 106–113.

47. Coy, P., Thornton, E., Arndt, M., & Grow, B. 2005. Shake, rattle, and merge. *BusinessWeek,* January 10: 32–35; and Anonymous. 2005. Love is in the air. *Economist,* February 5: 9.

48. For an interesting study of the relationship between mergers and a firm's product-market strategies, refer to Krisnan, R. A., Joshi, S., & Krishnan, H. 2004. The influence of mergers on firms' product-mix strategies. *Strategic Management Journal,* 25: 587–611.

49. Carey, D., moderator. 2000. A CEO roundtable on making mergers succeed. *Harvard Business Review,* 78(3): 146.

50. Shinal, J. 2001. Can Mike Volpi make Cisco sizzle again? *BusinessWeek,* February 26: 102–104; Kambil, A., Eselius, E. D., & Monteiro, K. A. 2000. Fast venturing: The quick way to start Web businesses. *Sloan Management Review,* 41(4): 55–67; and Elstrom, P. 2001. Sorry, Cisco: The old answers won't work. *BusinessWeek,* April 30: 39.

51. Like many high-tech firms during the economic slump that began in mid-2000, Cisco Systems has experienced declining performance. On April 16, 2001, it announced that its revenues for the quarter closing April 30 would drop 5 percent from a year earlier—and a stunning 30 percent from the previous three months—to about $4.7 billion. Furthermore, Cisco announced that it would lay off 8,500 employees and take an enormous $2.5 billion charge to write down inventory. By late October 2002, its stock was trading at around $10, down significantly from its 52-week high of $70. Elstrom, op. cit.: 39.

52. Coy, P., Thornton, E., Arndt, M., & Grow, B. 2005, Shake, rattle, and merge. *BusinessWeek,* January 10: 32–35; and, Anonymous. 2005. The rise of the superbrands. *Economist.* February 5: 63–65; and, Sellers, P. 2005. It was a no-brainer. *Fortune,* February 21: 96–102.

53. For a discussion of the trend toward consolidation of the steel industry and how Lakshmi Mittal is becoming a dominant player, read Reed, S. & Arndt, M. 2004. The Raja of steel. *BusinessWeek,* December 20: 50–52.

54. Barrett, A. 2001. Drugs. *BusinessWeek,* January 8: 112–113.

55. Whalen, C. J., Pascual, A. M., Lowery, T., & Muller, J. 2001. The top 25 managers. *BusinessWeek,* January 8: 63.

56. This discussion draws upon Rappaport, A. & Sirower, M. L. 1999. Stock or cash? The trade-offs for buyers and sellers in mergers and acquisitions. *Harvard Business Review,* 77(6): 147–158; and Lipin, S. & Deogun, N. 2000. Big mergers of 90s prove disappointing to shareholders. *The Wall Street Journal,* October 30: C1.

57. The downside of mergers in the airline industry is found in: Gimbel, B.

2008. Why airline mergers don't fly. *Business Week,* March 17: 26.

58. Mouio, A. (Ed.). 1998. Unit of one. *Fast Company,* September: 82.

59. Porter, M. E. 1987. From competitive advantage to corporate strategy. *Harvard Business Review,* 65(3): 43.

60. The divestiture of a business which is undertaken in order to enable managers to better focus on its core business has been termed "downscoping." Refer to Hitt, M. A., Harrison, J. S., & Ireland, R. D. 2001. *Mergers and acquisitions: A guide to creating value for stakeholders.* Oxford Press: New York.

61. Sirmon, D. G., Hitt, M. A., & Ireland, R. D. 2007. Managing firm resources in dynamic environments to create value: Looking inside the black box. *Academy of Management Review,* 32(1): 273–292.

62. This discussion draws on: Mankins, M. C., Harding, D., & Weddigne, R-M. 2008. How the best divest. *Harvard Business Review,* 86 (1): 92–99.

63. A study that investigates alliance performance is: Lunnan, R. & Haugland, S. A. 2008. Predicting and measuring alliance performance: A multidimensional analysis. *Strategic Management Journal,* 29(5): 545–556.

64. For scholarly perspectives on the role of learning in creating value in strategic alliances, refer to Anard, B. N. & Khanna, T. 2000. Do firms learn to create value? *Strategic Management Journal,* 12(3): 295–317; and Vermeulen, F. & Barkema, H. P. 2001. Learning through acquisitions. *Academy of Management Journal,* 44(3): 457–476.

65. For a detailed discussion of transaction cost economics in strategic alliances, read Reuer, J. J. & Arno, A. 2007. Strategic alliance contracts: Dimensions and determinants of contractual complexity. *Strategic Management Journal,* 28(3): 313–330.

66. This section draws on Hutt, M. D., Stafford, E. R., Walker, B. A., & Reingen, P. H. 2000. Case study: Defining the strategic alliance. *Sloan Management Review,* 41(2): 51–62; and Walters, B. A., Peters, S., & Dess, G. G. 1994. Strategic alliances and joint ventures: Making them work. *Business Horizons,* 4: 5–10.

67. A study that investigates strategic alliances and networks is: Tiwana, A. 2008. Do bridging ties complement strong ties? An empirical examination of alliance ambidexterity. *Strategic Management Journal,* 29 (3): 251–272.

68. Edmondson, G. & Reinhardt, A. 2001. From niche player to Goliath. *BusinessWeek,* March 12: 94–96.

69. For an institutional theory perspective on strategic alliances, read: Dacin, M. T., Oliver, C., & Roy, J. P. 2007. The legitimacy of strategic alliances: An institutional perspective. *Strategic Management Journal,* 28(2): 169–187.

70. A study investigating factors that determine partner selection in strategic alliances is found in: Shah, R. H. & Swaminathan, V. 2008. *Strategic Management Journal,* 29(5): 471–494.

71. Porter, op. cit.: 43–59.

72. Angwin, J. S. & Wingfield, N. 2000. How Jay Walker built WebHouse on a theory that he couldn't prove. *The Wall Street Journal,* October 16: A1, A8.

73. The fallen. 2003. *BusinessWeek,* January 13: 80–82.

74. The Jack Welch example draws upon Sellers, P. 2001. Get over yourself. *Fortune,* April 30: 76–88.

75. Polek, D. 2002. The rise and fall of Dennis Kozlowski. *BusinessWeek,* December 23: 64–77.

76. John Thain and his golden commode. 2009. Editorial. Dallasnews .com, January 26: np; Task, A. 2009. Wall Street's $18.4B bonus: The sense of entitlement has not been beaten out. finance.yahoo.com, January 29: np; and Exit Thain. 2009. Newsfinancialcareers.com, January 22: np.

77. This section draws on Weston, J. F., Besley, S., & Brigham, E. F. 1996. *Essentials of managerial finance* (11th ed.): 18–20. Fort Worth, TX: Dryden Press, Harcourt Brace.

International Strategy:

Creating Value in Global Markets

>learning objectives

After reading this chapter, you should have a good understanding of:

LO1 The importance of international expansion as a viable diversification strategy.

LO2 The sources of national advantage; that is, why an industry in a given country is more (or less) successful than the same industry in another country.

LO3 The motivations (or benefits) and the risks associated with international expansion, including the emerging trend for greater offshoring and outsourcing activity.

LO4 The two opposing forces—cost reduction and adaptation to local markets—that firms face when entering international markets.

LO5 The advantages and disadvantages associated with each of the four basic strategies: international, global, multidomestic, and transnational.

LO6 The difference between regional companies and truly global companies.

LO7 The four basic types of entry strategies and the relative benefits and risks associated with each of them.

The global marketplace provides many opportunities for firms to increase their revenue base and their profitability. Furthermore, in today's knowledge-intensive economy, there is the potential to create advantages by leveraging firm knowledge when crossing national boundaries to do business. At the same time, however, there are pitfalls and risks that firms must avoid in order to be successful. In this chapter we will provide insights on how to be successful and create value when diversifying into global markets.

After some introductory comments on the global economy, we address the question: What explains the level of success of a given industry in a given country? To provide a framework for analysis, we draw on Michael Porter's "diamond of national advantage," in which he identified four factors that help to explain performance differences.

In the second section of the chapter, we shift our focus to the level of the firm and discuss some of the major motivations and risks associated with international expansion. Recognizing such potential benefits and risks enables managers to better assess the growth and profit potential in a given country. We also address important issues associated with a topic of growing interest in the international marketplace—offshoring and outsourcing.

Next, in the third section—the largest in this chapter—we address how firms can attain competitive advantages in the global marketplace. We discuss two opposing forces firms face when entering foreign markets: cost reduction and local adaptation. Depending on the intensity of each of these forces, they should select among four basic strategies: international, global, multidomestic, and transnational. We discuss both the strengths and limitations of each of these strategies. We also present a recent perspective which posits that even the largest multinational firms are more regional than global even today.

The final section addresses the four categories of entry strategies that firms may choose in entering foreign markets. These strategies vary along a continuum from low investment, low control (exporting) to high investment, high control (wholly owned subsidiaries and greenfield ventures). We discuss the pros and cons associated with each.

Learning from Mistakes

By 2010, Ford Motor will be introducing a new version of its highly successful small car, the Fiesta, around the world.[1] And in a decision viewed with a bit of trepidation by some executives and announced on February 14, 2008, the vehicle will have the same name in markets across Europe, Asia, South Africa, Australia, and North America. Now, no matter the market, it will be a Fiesta. But that wasn't always the case.

At Ford, as well as other car companies, the name game used to be all about adapting to local tastes. Ford's marketing teams in different countries were left alone to come up with suitable names. Sometimes that can create problems. For example, Ford ended up selling two entirely different vehicles in America and Europe that are both called Fusion. This wouldn't have been much of a problem if information wasn't so readily available online. But these days it definitely is. For example, pictures of the vehicles—one is a sedan, the other a sports-utility vehicle—get mixed up on websites, where 80 percent of car buyers begin their search. Reviews are sometimes interchanged, and consumers can easily get confused.

Finding the right name can be challenging, however. The wrong ones can convey unwanted images, or simply be hard to pronounce. Volkswagen has pushed a global naming strategy for decades and at times has come up with controversial names as a result. Consider the Bora—which is also the wind that blows north by northeast across the Adriatic Sea. After complaints from dealers that Bora sounded "boring," VW eventually renamed the car the Jetta (as in jet stream) in the U.S. More recently, the automaker came out with the Touareg, which is a nomadic African tribe in the Sahara that used to follow a certain wind pattern. A few critics have since pointed out that the tribe owned slaves and were known for their blue-dyed bodies and their talent for torture. Also, the Touareg name is odd and is something that Americans cannot spell or pronounce easily. But the slow-selling SUV is still on the market.

In this chapter we discuss how firms create value and achieve competitive advantage in the global marketplace. Multinational firms are constantly faced with the dilemma of choosing between local adaptation—in product characteristics, names, advertising, and pricing—and global integration. We discuss how firms can avoid pitfalls such as those experienced by Ford Motor and Volkswagen. In addition, we address factors that can influence a nation's success in a particular industry. In our view, this is an important context in determining how well firms might eventually do when they compete beyond their nation's boundaries.

The Global Economy: A Brief Overview

>LO1

The importance of international expansion as a viable diversification strategy.

Managers face many opportunities and risks when they diversify abroad.[2] The trade among nations has increased dramatically in recent years and it is estimated that by 2015, the trade *across* nations will exceed the trade within nations. In a variety of industries such as semiconductors, automobiles, commercial aircraft, telecommunications, computers, and consumer electronics, it is almost impossible to survive unless firms scan the world for competitors, customers, human resources, suppliers, and technology.[3]

GE's wind energy business benefits by tapping into talent around the world. The firm has built research centers in China, Germany, India, and the U.S. "We did it," says CEO Jeffrey Immelt, "to access the best brains everywhere in the world." All four centers have played a key role in GE's development of huge 92-ton turbines:[4]

- Chinese researchers in Shanghai designed the microprocessors that control the pitch of the blade.
- Mechanical engineers from India (Bangladore) devised mathematical models to maximize the efficiency of materials in the turbine.

- Power-systems experts in the U.S. (Niskayuna, New York), which has researchers from 55 countries, do the design work.
- Technicians in Munich, Germany have created a "smart" turbine that can calculate wind speeds and signal sensors in other turbines to produce maximum electricity.

The rise of **globalization**—meaning the rise of market capitalism around the world—has undeniably contributed to the economic boom in America's New Economy, where knowledge is the key source of competitive advantage and value creation.[5] It is estimated that it has brought phone service to about 300 million households in developing nations and a transfer of nearly $2 trillion from rich countries to poor countries through equity, bond investments, and commercial loans.[6]

There have been extremes in the effect of global capitalism on national economies and poverty levels around the world.[7] The economies of East Asia have attained rapid growth, but there has been comparatively little progress in other areas of the world. For example, income in Latin America grew by only 6 percent in the past two decades when the continent was opening up to global capitalism. Average incomes in sub-Saharan Africa and the old Eastern European bloc have actually declined. The World Bank estimates that the number of people living on $1 per day has *increased* to 1.3 billion over the past decade.

Such disparities in wealth among nations raise an important question: Why do some countries and their citizens enjoy the fruits of global capitalism while others are mired in poverty? Or why do some governments make the best use of inflows of foreign investment and know-how and others do not? There are many explanations. Among these are the need of governments to have track records of business-friendly policies to attract multinationals and local entrepreneurs to train workers, invest in modern technology, and nurture local suppliers and managers. Also, it means carefully managing the broader economic factors in an economy, such as interest rates, inflation, and unemployment, as well as a good legal system that protects property rights, strong educational systems, and a society where prosperity is widely shared.

The above policies are the type that East Asia—in locations such as Hong Kong, Taiwan, South Korea, and Singapore—has employed to evolve from the sweatshop economies of the 1960s and 1970s to industrial powers today. On the other hand, many countries have moved in the other direction. For example, in Guatemala only 52.0 percent of males complete fifth grade and an astonishing 39.8 percent of the population subsists on less than $1 per day.[8] (By comparison, the corresponding numbers for South Korea are 98 percent and less than 2 percent, respectively.)

Strategy Spotlight 7.1 provides an interesting perspective on global trade—marketing to the "bottom of the pyramid."[9] This refers to the practice of a multinational firm targeting its goods and services to the nearly 5 billion poor people in the world who inhabit developing countries. Collectively, this represents a very large market with $14 trillion in purchasing power.

Next, we will address in more detail the question of why some nations and their industries are more competitive.[10] This establishes an important context or setting for the remainder of the chapter. After we discuss why some *nations and their industries* outperform others, we will be better able to address the various strategies that *firms* can take to create competitive advantage when they expand internationally.

globalization has two meanings. One is the increase in international exchange, including trade in goods and services as well as exchange of money, ideas, and information. Two is the growing similarity of laws, rules, norms, values, and ideas across countries.

Factors Affecting a Nation's Competitiveness

Michael Porter of Harvard University conducted a four-year study in which he and a team of 30 researchers looked at the patterns of competitive success in 10 leading trading nations. He concluded that there are four broad attributes of nations that individually, and

strategy spotlight

Marketing to the "Bottom of the Pyramid"

Many executives wrongly believe that profitable opportunities to sell consumer goods exist only in countries where income levels are high. Even when they expand internationally, they often tend to limit their marketing to only the affluent segments within the developing countries. Such narrow conceptualizations of the market cause them to ignore the vast opportunities that exist at "the bottom of the pyramid," according to University of Michigan professor C. K. Prahalad. The *bottom of the pyramid* refers to the nearly 5 billion poor people who inhabit the developing countries. Surprisingly, they represent $14 trillion in purchasing power! And they are looking for products and services that can improve the quality of their lives such as clean energy, personal-care products, lighting, and medicines. Multinationals are missing out on growth opportunities if they ignore this vast segment of the market.

Other innovative firms have found creative ways to serve the poor and still make a profit. Grameen Bank in Bangladesh is very different from the money center banks of London or New York. Pioneers of the concept of microcredit, Grameen Bank (whose founder, Muhammad Yunus, won the 2006 Nobel Peace Prize) extends small loans—sometimes as small as $20—to thousands of struggling micro-entrepreneurs who have no collateral to offer. The value of microcredit loans has soared from $4 million to $1.3 billion between 1996 and 2006. Not only are their loan recovery rates comparable to big banks, but they are also changing the lives of thousands of people while making a profit as well. Casas Bahias, the Brazilian retailer, has built a $2.5 billion-a-year chain selling to the poor who live in the *favelas,* the illegal shanty towns. Another amazing example is Aravind Eye Care, an Indian hospital that specializes in cataract surgeries. Today, they are the largest eye care facility in the world, performing more than 200,000 surgeries per year. The secret of their volume: The surgeries cost only about $25! A comparable surgery in the West costs $3,000. And best of all, Aravind has a return on equity of more than 75 percent!

Unilever, the Anglo-Dutch maker of such brands as Dove, Lipton, and Vaseline, built a following among the world's poorest consumers by upending some of the basic rules of marketing. Instead of focusing on value for money, it shrunk packages to set a price even consumers living on $2 a day could afford. It helped people make money to buy its products. "It's not about doing good," but about tapping new markets, says Chief Executive Patrick Cescau.

The strategy was forged about 25 years ago when Indian subsidiary Hindustan Lever (HL) found its products out of reach for millions of Indians. HL came up with a strategy to lower the price while making a profit: single-use packets for everything from shampoo to laundry detergent, costing pennies a pack. A bargain? Maybe not. But it put marquee brands within reach.

It has trained rural women to sell products to their neighbors. "What Unilever does well is get inside these communities, understand their needs, and adapt its business model accordingly," notes a professor at Barcelona's IESE Business School.

No one is helped by viewing the poor as the wretched of the earth. Instead, they are the latest frontier of opportunity for those who can meet their needs. A vast market that is barely tapped, the bottom of the pyramid offers enormous opportunities.

Sources: McGregor, J. 2008. The World's Most Influential Companies. *Business-Week,* December 22: 43–53; Miller, C. C. 2006. Easy Money. *Forbes,* November 27: 134–138; Prahalad, C. K. 2004. Why Selling to the Poor Makes for Good Business. *Fortune,* 150(9): 32–33; Overholt, A. 2005. A New Path to Profit. *Fast Company,* January: 25–26; and Prahalad, C. K. 2005. *The Fortune at the Bottom of the Pyramid: Eradicating Poverty through Profits.* Philadelphia: Wharton School Publishing.

factor endowments (national advantage) a nation's position in factors of production.

demand conditions (national advantage) the nature of home-market demand for the industry's product or service.

as a system, constitute what is termed "the diamond of national advantage." In effect, these attributes jointly determine the playing field that each nation establishes and operates for its industries. These factors are:

- *Factor endowments.* The nation's position in factors of production, such as skilled labor or infrastructure, necessary to compete in a given industry.
- *Demand conditions.* The nature of home-market demand for the industry's product or service.
- *Related and supporting industries.* The presence or absence in the nation of supplier industries and other related industries that are internationally competitive.
- *Firm strategy, structure, and rivalry.* The conditions in the nation governing how companies are created, organized, and managed, as well as the nature of domestic rivalry.

Factor Endowments[11,12]

>LO2
The sources of national advantage; that is, why an industry in a given country is more (or less) successful than the same industry in another country.

Classical economics suggests that factors of production such as land, labor, and capital are the building blocks that create usable consumer goods and services.[13] However, companies in advanced nations seeking competitive advantage over firms in other nations *create* many of the factors of production. For example, a country or industry dependent on scientific innovation must have a skilled human resource pool to draw upon. This resource pool is not inherited; it is created through investment in industry-specific knowledge and talent. The supporting infrastructure of a country—that is, its transportation and communication systems as well as its banking system—are also critical.

Factors of production must be developed that are industry and firm specific. In addition, the pool of resources is less important than the speed and efficiency with which these resources are deployed. Thus, firm-specific knowledge and skills created within a country that are rare, valuable, difficult to imitate, and rapidly and efficiently deployed are the factors of production that ultimately lead to a nation's competitive advantage.

For example, the island nation of Japan has little land mass, making the warehouse space needed to store inventory prohibitively expensive. But by pioneering just-in-time inventory management, Japanese companies managed to create a resource from which they gained advantage over companies in other nations that spent large sums to warehouse inventory.

Demand Conditions

Demand conditions refer to the demands that consumers place on an industry for goods and services. Consumers who demand highly specific, sophisticated products and services force firms to create innovative, advanced products and services to meet the demand. This consumer pressure presents challenges to a country's industries. But in response to these challenges, improvements to existing goods and services often result, creating conditions necessary for competitive advantage over firms in other countries.

Countries with demanding consumers drive firms in that country to meet high standards, upgrade existing products and services, and create innovative products and services. The conditions of consumer demand influence how firms view a market. This, in turn, helps a nation's industries to better anticipate future global demand conditions and proactively respond to product and service requirements.

Denmark, for instance, is known for its environmental awareness. Demand from consumers for environmentally safe products has spurred Danish manufacturers to become leaders in water pollution control equipment—products it successfully exported.

Related and Supporting Industries

Related and supporting industries enable firms to manage inputs more effectively. For example, countries with a strong supplier base benefit by adding efficiency to downstream activities. A competitive supplier base helps a firm obtain inputs using cost-effective, timely methods, thus reducing manufacturing costs. Also, close working relationships with suppliers provide the potential to develop competitive advantages through joint research and development and the ongoing exchange of knowledge.

related and supporting industries (national advantage) the presence, absence, and quality in the nation of supplier industries and other related industries that supply services, support, or technology to firms in the industry value chain.

Related industries offer similar opportunities through joint efforts among firms. In addition, related industries create the probability that new companies will enter the market, increasing competition and forcing existing firms to become more competitive through efforts such as cost control, product innovation, and novel approaches to distribution. Combined, these give the home country's industries a source of competitive advantage.

In the Italian footwear industry the supporting industries enhance national competitive advantage. In Italy, shoe manufacturers are geographically located near their suppliers. The manufacturers have ongoing interactions with leather suppliers and learn about new textures, colors, and manufacturing techniques while a shoe is still in the prototype stage. The manufacturers are able to project future demand and gear their factories for new products long before companies in other nations become aware of the new styles.

Firm Strategy, Structure, and Rivalry

firm strategy, structure, and rivalry (national advantage) the conditions in the nation governing how companies are created, organized, and managed, as well as the nature of domestic rivalry.

Rivalry is particularly intense in nations with conditions of strong consumer demand, strong supplier bases, and high new entrant potential from related industries. This competitive rivalry in turn increases the efficiency with which firms develop, market, and distribute products and services within the home country. Domestic rivalry thus provides a strong impetus for firms to innovate and find new sources of competitive advantage.

This intense rivalry forces firms to look outside their national boundaries for new markets, setting up the conditions necessary for global competitiveness. Among all the points on Porter's diamond of national advantage, domestic rivalry is perhaps the strongest indicator of global competitive success. Firms that have experienced intense domestic competition are more likely to have designed strategies and structures that allow them to successfully compete in world markets.

In the U.S., for example, intense rivalry has spurred companies such as Dell Computer to find innovative ways to produce and distribute its products. This is largely a result of competition from IBM and Hewlett-Packard.

Strategy Spotlight 7.2 discusses India's software industry. It provides an integrative example of how Porter's "diamond" can help to explain the relative degree of success of an industry in a given country. Exhibit 7.1 illustrates India's "software diamond."

Concluding Comment on Factors Affecting a Nation's Competitiveness

Porter drew his conclusions based on case histories of firms in more than 100 industries. Despite the differences in strategies employed by successful global competitors, a common theme emerged: Firms that succeeded in global markets had first succeeded in intensely competitive home markets. We can conclude that competitive advantage for global firms typically grows out of relentless, continuing improvement, and innovation.[14]

>LO3
The motivations (or benefits) and the risks associated with international expansion, including the emerging trend for greater offshoring and outsourcing activity.

International Expansion: A Company's Motivations and Risks

Motivations for International Expansion

There are many motivations for a company to pursue international expansion. The most obvious one is to *increase the size of potential markets* for a firm's products and services.[15] By early 2009, the world's population exceeded 6.7 billion, with the U.S. representing less than 5 percent. Exhibit 7.2 lists the population of the U.S. compared to other major markets abroad.

Many multinational firms are intensifying their efforts to market their products and services to countries such as India and China as the ranks of their middle class have increased over the past decade. These include Procter & Gamble's success in achieving a 50 percent share in China's shampoo market as well as PepsiCo's impressive inroads in the Indian soft-drink market.[16] Let's take a brief look at China's emerging middle class:[17]

- China's middle class has finally attained a critical mass—between 35 million and 200 million people, depending on what definition is used. The larger number is preferred by Fan Gong, director of China's National Economic Research Institute, who fixes the lower boundary of "middle" as a family income of $10,000.
- The central government's emphasis on science and technology has boosted the rapid development of higher education, which is the incubator of the middle class.

strategy spotlight

7.2

India and the Diamond of National Advantage

Consider the following facts:

- SAP, the German software company, has developed new applications for notebook PCs at its 500-engineer Bangladore facility.

- General Electric plans to invest $100 million and hire 2,600 scientists to create the world's largest research and development lab in Bangalore, India.

- Microsoft plans to invest $400 million in new research partnerships in India.

Sources: Ghemawat, P. & Hout, T. 2008. Tomorrow's Global Giants. *Harvard Business Review*, 86(11): 80–88; Mathur, S. K. 2007. Indian IT Industry: A Performance Analysis and a Model for Possible Adoption. ideas.repec.org, January 1: np; Kripalani, M. 2002. Calling Bangalore: Multinationals Are Making It a Hub for High-Tech Research *BusinessWeek*, November 25: 52–54; Kapur, D. & Ramamurti, R. 2001. India's Emerging Competitive Advantage in Services. 2001. *Academy of Management Executive*, 15(2): 20–33; World Bank. *World Development Report*: 6. New York: Oxford University Press. Reuters. 2001. Oracle in India Push, Taps Software Talent. *Washington Post Online*, July 3.

- Over one-fifth of Fortune 1000 companies outsource their software requirements to firms in India.

- Indian software exports have soared from $5.9 billion in 2000 to $23.6 billion in 2005 to a predicted $60 billion by 2010.

- For the past decade, the Indian software industry has grown at a 25 percent annual rate.

- More than 800 firms in India are involved in software services as their primary activity.

- Software and information technology firms in India are projected to employ 2.3 million people by 2010.

- The information technology industry is expected to account for 7 percent of India's Gross Domestic Product (GDP) in 2010—up from only 4.8 percent in 2007.

What is causing such global interest in India's software services industry? Porter's diamond of national advantage helps clarify this question. See Exhibit 7.1.

First, *factor endowments* are conducive to the rise of India's software industry. Through investment **(continued)**

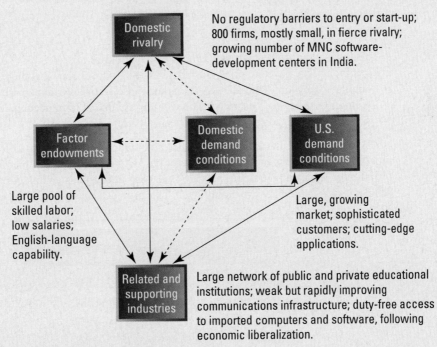

Note: Dashed lines represent weaker interactions.

Exhibit 7.1 India's Diamond in Software

Source: From Kampur D. and Ramamurti R., "India's Emerging Competition Advantage in Services," *Academy of Management Executive: The Thinking Manager's Source.* Copyright © 2001 by Academy of Management. Reproduced with permission of Academy of Management via Copyright Clearance Center.

(continued) in human resource development with a focus on industry-specific knowledge, India's universities and software firms have literally created this essential factor of production. For example, India produces the second largest annual output of scientists and engineers in the world, behind only the United States. In a knowledge-intensive industry such as software, development of human resources is fundamental to both domestic and global success.

Second, *demand conditions* require that software firms stay on the cutting edge of technological innovation. India has already moved toward globalization of its software industry; consumer demand conditions in developed nations such as Germany, Denmark, parts of Southeast Asia, and the United States created the consumer demand necessary to propel India's software makers toward sophisticated software solutions.*

Third, India has the *supplier base as well as the related industries* needed to drive competitive rivalry and enhance competitiveness. In particular, information technology (IT) hardware prices declined rapidly in the 1990s.

* Although India's success cannot be explained in terms of its home market demand (according to Porter's model), the nature of the industry enables software to be transferred among different locations simultaneously by way of communications links. Thus, competitiveness of markets outside India can be enhanced without a physical presence in those markets.

Furthermore, rapid technological change in IT hardware meant that latecomers like India were not locked into older-generation technologies. Thus, both the IT hardware and software industries could "leapfrog" older technologies. In addition, relationships among knowledge workers in these IT hardware and software industries offer the social structure for ongoing knowledge exchange, promoting further enhancement of existing products. Further infrastructure improvements are occurring rapidly.

Fourth, with over 800 firms in the software services industry in India, *intense rivalry forces firms to develop competitive strategies and structures*. Although firms like TCS, Infosys, and Wipro have become large, they were quite small only five years ago. And dozens of small and midsized companies are aspiring to catch up. This intense rivalry is one of the primary factors driving Indian software firms to develop overseas distribution channels, as predicted by Porter's diamond of national advantage.

It is interesting to note that the cost advantage of Indian firms may be eroding. For example, TCS's engineers' compensation has soared 15 percent a year between 2005 and 2008, other Asian companies are trying to steal its customers, and it is working hard to better understand overseas customers. Further, IBM and Accenture are aggressively building up their Indian operations, hiring tens of thousands of sought-after Indians by paying them more, thereby lowering their costs while raising those of TCS.

- China may be viewed as a new example of economies of scale. Many American companies already have factories in China exporting goods. Now that there is a domestic market to go along with the export market, those factories can increase their output with little additional cost. That is one reason why many foreign companies' profits in China have been so strong in recent years.

Expanding a firm's global presence also automatically increases its scale of operations, providing it with a larger revenue and asset base. As we noted in Chapter 5 in discussing overall cost leadership strategies, such an increase in revenues and asset base potentially enables a firm to *attain economies of scale*. This provides multiple benefits. One advantage

Exhibit 7.2
Populations of Selected Nations and the World

Country	June 2009 (in est. millions)
China	1,337
India	1,164
United States	306
Japan	127
Germany	82
World Total	6,778

Source: www.geohive.com/global/pop_data2.php.

How Wal-Mart Profits from Arbitrage

With sales of over $400 billion and net income of $14 billion, Wal-Mart is considered one of the most successful companies in the world. In recent years, Wal-Mart has embarked upon an ambitious international expansion agenda, opening stores in countries such as Mexico, China, Japan, and England. Wal-Mart today has 3,120 stores outside the U.S. Together they account for $90 billion in sales and $4.7 billion in operating income.

Wal-Mart's above average industry profitability has been attributed to various factors, such as their superior logistics, strict control over overhead costs, and effective use of information systems. What is often lost sight of is that their "everyday low pricing" strategy cannot work successfully unless they are able to procure the thousands of items they carry in each of their stores at the lowest possible prices. This is where their expertise in arbitraging plays a critical role. In 2004, Wal-Mart bought $18 billion worth of goods directly from China. By 2006, this had grown to $26.7 billion. If one considers indirect imports through their other suppliers as well, Wal-Mart's total imports from China could be anywhere between $50 billion and $70 billion each year. At a conservative estimate, this represents cost savings of approximately $16 billion to $23 billion! Clearly, the core of Wal-Mart's international strategy is not their international store expansion strategy but their pursuit of worldwide arbitrage opportunities.

Sources: Ghemawat, P. 2007. *Redefining Global Strategy.* Boston: Harvard Business School Press; Scott, R.E. 2007. The Wal-Mart Effect. epi.org, June 26: np; and Basker, E. & Pham, V.H. 2008. Wal-Mart as Catalyst to U.S.-China Trade. ssrn.com; np.

is the spreading of fixed costs such as R&D over a larger volume of production. Examples include the sale of Boeing's commercial aircraft and Microsoft's operating systems in many foreign countries.

Taking advantage of arbitrage opportunities is a second advantage of international expansion. In its simplest form, arbitrage involves buying something from where it is cheap and selling it somewhere where it commands a higher price. A big part of Wal-Mart's success can be attributed to the company's expertise in arbitrage (see Strategy Spotlight 7.3). The possibilities for arbitrage are not necessarily confined to simple trading opportunities. It can be applied to virtually any factor of production and every stage of the value chain. For example, a firm may locate its call centers in India, its manufacturing plants in China, and its R&D in Europe, where the specific types of talented personnel may be available at the lowest possible price. In today's integrated global financial markets, a firm can borrow anywhere in the world where capital is cheap and use it to fund a project in a country where capital is expensive. Such arbitrage opportunities are even more attractive to global corporations because their larger size enables them to buy in huge volume, thus increasing their bargaining power with suppliers.

Extending the life cycle of a product that is in its maturity stage in a firm's home country but that has greater demand potential elsewhere is another benefit of international expansion. As we noted in Chapter 5, products (and industries) generally go through a four-stage life cycle of introduction, growth, maturity, and decline. In recent decades, U.S. soft-drink producers such as Coca-Cola and PepsiCo have aggressively pursued international markets to attain levels of growth that simply would not be available in the United States. Similarly, personal computer manufacturers such as Dell and Hewlett-Packard have sought out foreign markets to offset the growing saturation in the U.S. market.

Finally, *optimizing the physical location for every activity in its value chain* is another benefit. Recall from our discussions in Chapters 3 and 5 that the value chain represents the various activities in which all firms must engage to produce products and services. They include primary activities, such as inbound logistics, operations, and marketing, as well as support activities, such as procurement, R&D, and human resource management. All firms have to make

How Deere & Co. Learned from Its Indian Operations

Companies are increasingly discovering that their international operations are coming up with ideas that resonate far beyond local markets. Case in point: Deere & Co. is pursuing a new market in the U.S.—recreational farmers. And they have innovations developed at their research facility in Pune, India, to thank.

Deere, based in Moline, Illinois, opened the Pune center in 2001 as a way to enter the Indian market. The move was quite unexpected. After all, Deere is known for its heavy-duty farm equipment and big construction gear, and many of India's farmers still use oxen-pulled plows. However, Deere saw potential, and its engineers in Pune responded with four no-frills models. While they didn't include GPS or air conditioning, they were sturdy enough to handle the rigors of commercial farming.

The tractors cost between $8,400 and $11,600 in India and were so basic that Deere never considered selling them in the U.S. But then Indian tractor maker Mahin-dra & Mahindra started selling its no-frill tractors in the U.S., targeting a market that Deere had largely ignored—hobbyists as well as bargain hunters. Such buyers didn't need many advanced features. And it turned out that they coveted the same qualities as Indian farmers: affordability and maneuverability.

Deere, taking a cue from its rival, transplanted a slightly modified version (with softer seats and higher horsepower) of the Indian line of tractors. Called the 5003 model, it sold for $14,400 in the United States. And by 2008, half of the tractors Deere produces in India were making their way overseas. "These tractors are like Swiss Army knives. They get used for anything: mowing, transporting bales of hay, pushing dirt, and removing manure," claims Mike Alvin, a product manager at Deere.

Deere doesn't disclose margins for specific products. However, it certainly sees financial benefits from transplanting Indian innovations to the U.S. Raj Kalathus, the managing director of Deere's Indian division, says the 5003 tractors were born out of "frugal engineering." Because many of Deere's Indian employees witness poverty daily, they took great care to minimize costs. Such innovation isn't just global—it's good business.

Sources: Mero, J. 2008. John Deere's Farm Team. *Fortune*, April 14: 119–124; and. No-Frills Indian Tractors Find Favor with US Farmers. 2008. www.thaindian.com, April 29: np.

critical decisions as to where each activity will take place.[18] Optimizing the location for every activity in the value chain can yield one or more of three strategic advantages: performance enhancement, cost reduction, and risk reduction. We will now discuss each of these.

Performance Enhancement Microsoft's decision to establish a corporate research laboratory in Cambridge, England, is an example of a location decision that was guided mainly by the goal of building and sustaining world-class excellence in selected value-creating activities.[19] This strategic decision provided Microsoft with access to outstanding technical and professional talent. Location decisions can affect the quality with which any activity is performed in terms of the availability of needed talent, speed of learning, and the quality of external and internal coordination.

In Strategy Spotlight 7.4, Deere & Co., the $28 billion construction and farm equipment manufacturer, developed a new tractor at its new research facility in Pune, India, for the local market. Later, the tractor was quickly modified to create a viable alternative to a competitor's offering in the United States.

Cost Reduction Two location decisions founded largely on cost-reduction considerations are (1) Nike's decision to source the manufacture of athletic shoes from Asian countries such as China, Vietnam, and Indonesia, and (2) the decision of many multinational companies to set up production operations just south of the U.S.–Mexico border to access lower-cost labor. These operations are called *maquiladoras*. Such location decisions can affect the cost structure in terms of local manpower and other resources, transportation and logistics, and government incentives and the local tax structure.

Performance enhancement and cost-reduction benefits parallel the business-level strategies (discussed in Chapter 5) of differentiation and overall cost leadership. They can at times be attained simultaneously. Consider our example in the previous section on the Indian software industry. When Oracle set up a development operation in that country, the company benefited both from lower labor costs and operational expenses as well as from performance enhancements realized through the hiring of superbly talented professionals.

Risk Reduction   Given the erratic swings in the exchange ratios between the U.S. dollar and the Japanese yen (in relation to each other and to other major currencies), an important basis for cost competition between Ford and Toyota has been their relative ingenuity at managing currency risks. One way for such rivals to manage currency risks has been to spread the high-cost elements of their manufacturing operations across a few select and carefully chosen locations around the world. Location decisions such as these can affect the overall risk profile of the firm with respect to currency, economic, and political risks.[20]

Potential Risks of International Expansion

When a company expands its international operations, it does so to increase its profits or revenues. As with any other investment, however, there are also potential risks.[21] To help companies assess the risk of entering foreign markets, rating systems have been developed to evaluate political, economic, as well as financial and credit risks.[22] *Euromoney* magazine publishes a semiannual "Country Risk Rating" that evaluates political, economic, and other risks that entrants potentially face.[23] Exhibit 7.3 depicts a sample of country risk ratings, published by the World Bank, from the 178 countries that *Euromoney* evaluates. Note that the lower the score, the higher the country's expected level of risk.[24]

Next we will discuss the four main types of risk: political risk, economic risk, currency risk, and management risk.

Political and Economic Risk   Generally speaking, the business climate in the United States is very favorable. However, some countries around the globe may be hazardous to the health of corporate initiatives because of **political risk.**[25] Forces such as social unrest,

political risk
potential threat to a firm's operations in a country due to ineffectiveness of the domestic political system.

Exhibit 7.3   **A Sample of International Country Risk Rankings**

Rank	Country	Total Risk Assessment	Economic Performance	Political Risk	Total of Debt Indicators	Total of Credit and Access to Finance Indicators
1	Luxembourg	99.51	25.00	24.51	20.00	30.00
2	Switzerland	98.84	23.84	25.00	20.00	30.00
3	United States	98.37	23.96	24.41	20.00	30.00
40	China	71.27	18.93	16.87	19.73	15.74
55	Poland	57.12	18.56	13.97	9.36	15.23
63	Vietnam	52.04	14.80	11.91	18.51	6.82
86	Russia	42.62	11.47	8.33	17.99	4.83
114	Albania	34.23	8.48	5.04	19.62	1.09
161	Mozambique	21.71	3.28	2.75	13.85	1.83
178	Afghanistan	3.92	0.00	3.04	0.00	0.88

Source: Adapted from worldbank.org/html/prddr/trans/so96/art7.htm.

strategy spotlight

Piracy: A Key Threat to World Trade

Counterfeiting has grown up and has become a major threat to multinational corporations. "We've seen a massive increase in the last five years, and there is a risk that it will spiral out of control," claims Anthony Simon, marketing chief of Unilever Bestfoods. "It is no longer a cottage industry."

The figures are astounding. The World Customs Organization estimates that counterfeiting accounts for about 5 percent to 7 percent of global merchandise trade—equivalent to as much as $512 billion. Seizures of fakes by United States customs jumped 46 percent last year as counterfeiters boosted exports to Western markets. Unilever Groups says that knockoffs of its shampoos, soaps, and teas are growing at a rate of 30 percent annually.

Such counterfeiting can also have health and safety implications as well. The World Health Organization says up to 10 percent of medicines worldwide are counterfeit—a deadly hazard that could be costing the pharmaceutical industry $46 billion a year. "You won't die from purchasing a pair of counterfeit blue jeans or a counterfeit golf club. You can die from taking counterfeit pharmaceutical products. And there's no doubt that people have died in China from bad medicine," says John Theirault, head of global security for American pharmaceutical giant, Pfizer. And, sadly, cases like the one in China, where fake baby formula recently killed 60 infants, have investigators stepping up enforcement at U.S. ports. Injuries from overheating counterfeit cell phone batteries purchased right on Verizon store shelves sparked a recall. According to Hal Stratton, of the Consumer Product Safety Commission, "We know of at least one apartment fire that's occurred. We know of at least one burn situation of someone's face that's occurred." And bogus car parts are a $12 billion market worldwide. "Counterfeiting has gone from a local nuisance to a global threat," says Hanns Glatz, DaimlerChrysler's point man on intellectual property.

China is the key to any solution. Given the country's economic power, its counterfeiting is turning into quite the problem itself, accounting for nearly two-thirds of all fake and pirated goods worldwide. Dan Chow, a law professor at Ohio State University who specializes in Chinese counterfeiting provides some perspective: "We have never seen a problem of this size and magnitude in world history. There's more counterfeiting going on in China now than we've ever seen anywhere. We know that 15 to 20 percent of all goods in China are counterfeit."

Source: Engardio, P. & Yang, C. 2006. The Runaway Trade Giant. *BusinessWeek.* April 24: 30–32; Letzing, J. 2007. Antipiracy Group Make's List of Worst-Offendor Nations. www.marketwatch. February 12: np. Balfour, F. 2005. Fake! *BusinessWeek,* February 7: 54–64; Editorial. 2005. *BusinessWeek,* February 7: 96; and Simon, B. 2004. The World's Greatest Fakes. www.cbsnews.com, August 8.

military turmoil, demonstrations, and even violent conflict and terrorism can pose serious threats.[26] Consider, for example, the ongoing tension and violence in the Middle East between Israelis and Palestinians, and the social and political unrest in Indonesia.[27] Such conditions increase the likelihood of destruction of property and disruption of operations as well as nonpayment for goods and services. Thus, countries that are viewed as high risk are less attractive for most types of business.[28]

economic risk
potential threat to a firm's operations in a country due to economic policies and conditions, including property rights laws and enforcement of those laws.

The laws, and the enforcement of laws, associated with the protection of intellectual property rights can be a major potential **economic risk** in entering new countries.[29] Microsoft, for example, has lost billions of dollars in potential revenue through piracy of its software products in many countries, including China. Other areas of the globe, such as the former Soviet Union and some eastern European nations, have piracy problems as well.[30] Firms rich in intellectual property have encountered financial losses as imitations of their products have grown due to a lack of law enforcement of intellectual property rights.[31]

Strategy Spotlight 7.5 discusses a problem that is a severe threat to global trade— piracy. Estimates are that counterfeiting accounts for between 5 to 7 percent of global merchandise trade—the equivalent of as much as $512 billion a year. And the potential corrosive effects include health and safety, not just economic, damage.[32]

Currency Risks Currency fluctuations can pose substantial risks. A company with operations in several countries must constantly monitor the exchange rate between its own

Israel's Strong Shekel Forces Companies to Reevaluate Their Strategies

For years O.R.T. Technologies resisted moving any operations outside of Israel. However, when faced with a sharp rise in the value of the shekel, the maker of specialized software for managing gas stations froze all local hiring and decided to transfer some developmental work to Eastern Europe. Laments CEO Alex Milner: "I never thought I'd

see the day when we would have to move R&D outside of Israel, but the strong shekel has forced us to do so."

For decades, Israelis have viewed the U.S. dollar as a bedrock of financial stability. Apartment prices and salaries are often indexed to it as a hedge against inflation. However, during 2006–2007, the shekel surged 31 percent against the dollar. That also hurts the likes of software shop Flash Networks, where the bulk of the expenses are in shekels, but most sales are in U.S. dollars. Says Flash CEO Liam Galin, "We're only a month into the new year and there's already around a $1 million shortfall in our budget."

Source: Sandler, N. 2008. Israel: Attack of the Super-Shekel. *BusinessWeek*, February 25: 38.

---

currency and that of the host country to minimize **currency risks.** Even a small change in the exchange rate can result in a significant difference in the cost of production or net profit when doing business overseas. When the U.S. dollar appreciates against other currencies, for example, U.S. goods can be more expensive to consumers in foreign countries. At the same time, however, appreciation of the U.S. dollar can have negative implications for American companies that have branch operations overseas. The reason for this is that profits from abroad must be exchanged for dollars at a more expensive rate of exchange, reducing the amount of profit when measured in dollars. For example, consider an American firm doing business in Italy. If this firm had a 20 percent profit in euros at its Italian center of operations, this profit would be totally wiped out when converted into U.S. dollars if the euro had depreciated 20 percent against the U.S. dollar. (U.S. multinationals typically engage in sophisticated "hedging strategies" to minimize currency risk. The discussion of this is beyond the scope of this section.)

> **currency risk**
> potential threat to a firm's operations in a country due to fluctuations in the local currency's exchange rate.

It is important to note that even when government intervention is well intended, the macroeconomic effects of such action can be very negative for multinational corporations. Such was the case in 1997 when Thailand suddenly chose to devalue its currency, the baht, after months of trying to support it at an artificially high level. This, in effect, made the baht worthless compared to other currencies. And in 1998 Russia not only devalued its ruble but also elected not to honor its foreign debt obligations. Strategy Spotlight 7.6 discusses how Israel's strong currency—the shekel—forced two firms to reevaluate their strategies.

Management Risks   **Management risks** may be considered the challenges and risks that managers face when they must respond to the inevitable differences that they encounter in foreign markets. These take a variety of forms: culture, customs, language, income levels, customer preferences, distribution systems, and so on.[33] As we will note later in the chapter, even in the case of apparently standard products, some degree of local adaptation will become necessary.[34]

> **management risk**
> potential threat to a firm's operations in a country due to the problems that managers have making decisions in the context of foreign markets.

Differences in cultures across countries can also pose unique challenges for managers.[35] Cultural symbols can evoke deep feelings.[36] For example, in a series of advertisements aimed at Italian vacationers, Coca-Cola executives turned the Eiffel Tower, Empire State Building, and the Tower of Pisa into the familiar Coke bottle. So far, so good.

How a Local Custom Can Affect a Manufacturing Plant's Operations

At times, a lack of understanding and awareness of local customs can provide some frustrating and embarrassing situations. Such customs can raise issues that must be taken into account in order to make good decisions.

For example, consider the unique problem that Larry Henderson, plant manager, and John Lichthental, manager

Source: Harvey, M. & Buckley, M. R. 2002. Assessing the "Conventional Wisdoms" of Management for the 21st Century Organization. *Organizational Dynamics*, 30(4): 368–378.

of human resources, were faced with when they were assigned by Celanese Chemical Corp. to build a new plant in Singapore. The $125 million plant was completed in July, but according to local custom, a plant should only be christened on "lucky" days. Unfortunately, the next "lucky" day was not until September 3.

Henderson and Lichthental had to convince executives at Celanese's Dallas headquarters to delay the plant opening. It wasn't easy. But after many heated telephone conversations and flaming e-mails, the president agreed to open the new plant on the "lucky" day—September 3.

However, when the white marble columns of the Parthenon that crowns the Acropolis in Athens were turned into Coke bottles, the Greeks became outraged. Why? Greeks refer to the Acropolis as the "holy rock," and a government official said the Parthenon is an "international symbol of excellence" and that "whoever insults the Parthenon insults international culture." Coca-Cola apologized. Below are a few examples of how culture varies across nations.[37]

- ***Ecuador.*** Dinners at Ecuadorian homes last for many hours. Expect drinks and appetizers around 8:00 p.m., with dinner not served until 11:00 p.m. or midnight. You will dismay your hosts if you leave as early as 1:00 a.m. A party at an Ecuadorian home will begin late and end around 4:00 a.m. or 5:00 a.m. Late guests may sometimes be served breakfast before they leave.
- ***France.*** Words in French and English may have the same roots but different meanings or connotations. For example, a French person might "demand" something because *demander* in French means "to ask."
- ***Hong Kong.*** Negotiations occur over cups of tea. Always accept an offer of tea whether you want it or not. When you are served, wait for the host to drink first.
- ***Singapore.*** Singaporeans associate all of the following with funerals, so do not give them as gifts: straw sandals, clocks, a stork or crane, handkerchiefs, or gifts or wrapping paper where the predominant color is white, black, or blue.

Strategy Spotlight 7.7 addresses a rather humorous example of how a local custom can affect operations at a manufacturing plant.

Global Dispersion of Value Chains: Outsourcing and Offshoring

A major recent trend has been the dispersion of the value chains of multinational corporations across different countries; that is, the various activities that constitute the value chain of a firm are now spread across several countries and continents. Such dispersion of value occurs mainly through increasing offshoring and outsourcing.

A report issued by the World Trade Organization describes the production of a particular U.S. car as follows: "30 percent of the car's value goes to Korea for assembly,

17.5 percent to Japan for components and advanced technology, 7.5 percent to Germany for design, 4 percent to Taiwan and Singapore for minor parts, 2.5 percent to U.K. for advertising and marketing services, and 1.5 percent to Ireland and Barbados for data processing. This means that only 37 percent of the production value is generated in the U.S."[38] In today's economy, we are increasingly witnessing two interrelated trends: outsourcing and offshoring.

Outsourcing occurs when a firm decides to utilize other firms to perform value-creating activities that were previously performed in-house.[39] It may be a new activity that the firm is perfectly capable of doing but chooses to have someone else perform for cost or quality reasons. Outsourcing can be to either a domestic or foreign firm.

Offshoring takes place when a firm decides to shift an activity that they were performing in a domestic location to a foreign location.[40] For example, both Microsoft and Intel now have R&D facilities in India, employing a large number of Indian scientists and engineers. Often, offshoring and outsourcing go together; that is, a firm may outsource an activity to a foreign supplier, thereby causing the work to be offshored as well.[41] Spending on offshore information technology will nearly triple between 2004 and 2010 to $60 billion, according to research firm Gartner.[42]

The recent explosion in the volume of outsourcing and offshoring is due to a variety of factors. Up until the 1960s, for most companies, the entire value chain was in one location. Further, the production took place close to where the customers were in order to keep transportation costs under control. In the case of service industries, it was generally believed that offshoring was not possible because the producer and consumer had to be present at the same place at the same time. After all, a haircut could not be performed if the barber and the client were separated!

For manufacturing industries, the rapid decline in transportation and coordination costs has enabled firms to disperse their value chains over different locations. For example, Nike's R&D takes place in the U.S., raw materials are procured from a multitude of countries, actual manufacturing takes place in China or Indonesia, advertising is produced in the U.S., and sales and service take place in practically all the countries. Each value-creating activity is performed in the location where the cost is the lowest or the quality is the best. Without finding optimal locations for each activity, Nike could not have attained its position as the world's largest shoe company.

The experience of the manufacturing sector was also repeated in the service sector by the mid-1990s. A trend that began with the outsourcing of low-level programming and data entry work to countries such as India and Ireland suddenly grew manyfold, encompassing a variety of white collar and professional activities ranging from call-centers to R&D. The cost of a long distance call from the U.S. to India has decreased from about $3 to $0.03 in the last 20 years, thereby making it possible to have call centers located in countries like India, where a combination of low labor costs and English proficiency presents an ideal mix of factor conditions.

Bangalore, India, in recent years, has emerged as a location where more and more U.S. tax returns are prepared. In India, U.S.–trained and licensed radiologists interpret chest X-rays and CT scans from U.S. hospitals for half the cost. The advantages from offshoring go beyond mere cost savings today. In many specialized occupations in science and engineering, there is a shortage of qualified professionals in developed countries, whereas countries, like India, China, and Singapore have what seems like an inexhaustible supply.[43]

For most of the 20th century, domestic companies catered to the needs of local populations. However, with the increasing homogenization of customer needs around the world and the institutionalization of free trade and investment as a global ideology (especially after the creation of the WTO), competition has become truly global. Each company has to

outsourcing using other firms to perform value-creating activities that were previously performed in-house.

offshoring shifting a value-creating activity from a domestic location to a foreign location.

Misiu Systems: Outsourcing Is Not for Everyone

When Todd Hodgen, CEO of Misiu Systems, a Bothell, Washington–based manufacturer of alarm systems, learned that he could save 65 percent of his design costs by outsourcing it to a Taiwanese firm, he was really excited. In addition to cost savings, an added bonus was that the Taiwanese engineers would be working after Misiu's engineers had gone home because of the time differences. This meant that the product development cycle could be greatly accelerated. For a start-up financed mostly with loans from friends and family, the

Source: Wahlgren, E. 2004. The Outsourcing Dilemma. *Inc.*, April: 41–43.

twin advantages of cost savings and reduced cycle time were too much to resist.

After several months of discussions with the contractor and a visit to Taiwan, Hodgen signed the outsourcing agreement. However, things did not quite work out as he had expected. His feedback to the design team in Taiwan often went unheeded. The design was eventually delivered eight months late and the quality fell well short of expectations. Why? The Taiwanese engineers who were supposed to be working solely for him were also working for other clients. Business from a small firm like Misiu was not given the same priority that was given to bigger clients. Eventually Hodgen ended up terminating the agreement with the Taiwanese firm and hiring a U.S. firm to finish the project!

keep its costs low in order to survive.[44] They also must find the best suppliers and the most skilled workers as well as locate each stage of the value chain in places where factor conditions are most conducive. Thus, outsourcing and offshoring are no longer mere options to consider, but an imperative for competitive survival.

While there is a compelling logic for companies to engage in offshoring, there can be many pitfalls. Strategy Spotlight 7.8 discusses the experience of Misiu Systems, a U.S. alarm systems manufacturer that found out the hard way that offshoring is not for everyone.

Achieving Competitive Advantage in Global Markets

We now discuss the two opposing forces that firms face when they expand into global markets: cost reduction and adaptation to local markets. Then we address the four basic types of international strategies that they may pursue: international, global, multidomestic, and transnational. The selection of one of these four types of strategies is largely dependent on a firm's relative pressure to address each of the two forces.

Two Opposing Pressures: Reducing Costs and Adapting to Local Markets

>LO4

The two opposing forces—cost reduction and adaptation to local markets—that firms face when entering international markets.

Many years ago, the famed marketing strategist Theodore Levitt advocated strategies that favored global products and brands. He suggested that firms should standardize all of their products and services for all of their worldwide markets. Such an approach would help a firm lower its overall costs by spreading its investments over as large a market as possible. Levitt's approach rested on three key assumptions:

1. Customer needs and interests are becoming increasingly homogeneous worldwide.
2. People around the world are willing to sacrifice preferences in product features, functions, design, and the like for lower prices at high quality.
3. Substantial economies of scale in production and marketing can be achieved through supplying global markets.[45]

However, there is ample evidence to refute these assumptions.[46] Regarding the first assumption—the increasing worldwide homogeneity of customer needs and interests—consider the number of product markets, ranging from watches and handbags to soft drinks and fast foods. Companies have identified global customer segments and developed global products and brands targeted to those segments. Also, many other companies adapt lines to idiosyncratic country preferences and develop local brands targeted to local market segments. For example, Nestlé's line of pizzas marketed in the United Kingdom includes cheese with ham and pineapple topping on a French bread crust. Similarly, Coca-Cola in Japan markets Georgia (a tonic drink) as well as Classic Coke and Hi-C.

Consider the second assumption—the sacrifice of product attributes for lower prices. While there is invariably a price-sensitive segment in many product markets, there is no indication that this is increasing. In contrast, in many product and service markets—ranging from watches, personal computers, and household appliances, to banking and insurance—there is a growing interest in multiple product features, product quality, and service.

Finally, the third assumption is that significant economies of scale in production and marketing could be achieved for global products and services. Although standardization may lower manufacturing costs, such a perspective does not consider three critical and interrelated points. First, as we discussed in Chapter 5, technological developments in flexible factory automation enable economies of scale to be attained at lower levels of output and do not require production of a single standardized product. Second, the cost of production is only one component, and often not the critical one, in determining the total cost of a product. Third, a firm's strategy should not be product-driven. It should also consider other activities in the firm's value chain, such as marketing, sales, and distribution.

Based on the above, we would have a hard time arguing that it is wise to develop the same product or service for all markets throughout the world. While there are some exceptions, such as Harley-Davidson motorcycles and some of Coca-Cola's soft-drink products, managers must also strive to tailor their products to the culture of the country in which they are attempting to do business. Few would argue that "one size fits all" generally applies.

The opposing pressures that managers face place conflicting demands on firms as they strive to be competitive.[47] On the one hand, competitive pressures require that firms do what they can to *lower unit costs* so that consumers will not perceive their product and service offerings as too expensive. This may lead them to consider locating manufacturing facilities where labor costs are low and developing products that are highly standardized across multiple countries.

In addition to responding to pressures to lower costs, managers also must strive to be *responsive to local pressures* in order to tailor their products to the demand of the local market in which they do business. This requires differentiating their offerings and strategies from country to country to reflect consumer tastes and preferences and making changes to reflect differences in distribution channels, human resource practices, and governmental regulations. However, since the strategies and tactics to differentiate products and services to local markets can involve additional expenses, a firm's costs will tend to rise.

The two opposing pressures result in four different basic strategies that companies can use to compete in the global marketplace: international, global, multidomestic, and transnational. The strategy that a firm selects depends on the degree of pressure that it is facing for cost reductions and the importance of adapting to local markets. Exhibit 7.4 shows the conditions under which each of these strategies would be most appropriate.

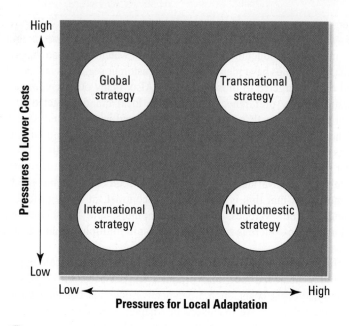

High

Pressures to Lower Costs

Low

Low ← Pressures for Local Adaptation → High

Global strategy

Transnational strategy

International strategy

Multidomestic strategy

Exhibit 7.4 Opposing Pressures and Four Strategies

>LO5
The advantages and disadvantages associated with each of the four basic strategies: international, global, multidomestic, and transnational.

international strategy a strategy based on firms' diffusion and adaptation of the parent companies' knowledge and expertise to foreign markets, used in industries where the pressures for both local adaptation and lowering costs are low.

It is important to note that we consider these four strategies to be "basic" or "pure"; that is, in practice, all firms will tend to have some elements of each strategy.

International Strategy

There are a small number of industries in which pressures for both local adaptation and lowering costs are rather low. An extreme example of such an industry is the "orphan" drug industry. These are medicines for diseases that are severe but affect only a small number of people. Diseases such as the Gaucher disease and Fabry disease fit into this category. Companies such as Genzyme and Oxford GlycoSciences are active in this segment of the drug industry. There is virtually no need to adapt their products to the local markets. And the pressures to reduce costs are low; even though only a few thousand patients are affected, the revenues and margins are significant, because patients are charged up to $100,000 per year. Legislation has made this industry even more attractive. The 1983 Orphan Drug Act provides various tax credits and exclusive marketing rights for any drug developed to treat a disease that afflicts fewer than 200,000 patients. Since 1983, more than 280 orphan drugs have been licensed and used to treat 14 million patients.[48]

An international strategy is based on diffusion and adaptation of the parent company's knowledge and expertise to foreign markets. Country units are allowed to make some minor adaptations to products and ideas coming from the head office, but they have far less independence and autonomy compared to multidomestic companies. The primary goal of the strategy is worldwide exploitation of the parent firm's knowledge and capabilities. All sources of core competencies are centralized.

The majority of large U.S. multinationals pursued the international strategy in the decades following World War II. These companies centralized R&D and product development but established manufacturing facilities as well as marketing organizations abroad. Companies such as McDonald's and Kellogg are examples of firms

Exhibit 7.5
**Strengths and
Limitations of
International
Strategies in the
Global Marketplace**

Strengths	Limitations
• Leverage and diffusion of a parent firm's knowledge and core competencies. • Lower costs because of less need to tailor products and services.	• Limited ability to adapt to local markets • Inability to take advantage of new ideas and innovations occurring in local markets.

following such a strategy. Although these companies do make some local adaptations, they are of a very limited nature. With increasing pressures to reduce costs due to global competition, especially from low-cost countries, opportunities to successfully employ international strategy are becoming more limited. This strategy is most suitable in situations where a firm has distinctive competencies that local companies in foreign markets lack.

Risks and Challenges   Below, are some of the risks and challenges associated with an international strategy.

* Different activities in the value chain typically have different optimal locations. That is, R&D may be optimally located in a country with an abundant supply of scientists and engineers, whereas assembly may be better conducted in a low-cost location. Nike, for example, designs its shoes in the United States, but all the manufacturing is done in countries like China or Thailand. The international strategy, with its tendency to concentrate most of its activities in one location, fails to take advantage of the benefits of an optimally distributed value chain.
* The lack of local responsiveness may result in the alienation of local customers. Worse still, the firm's inability to be receptive to new ideas and innovation from its foreign subsidiaries may lead to missed opportunities.

Exhibit 7.5 summarizes the strengths and weaknesses of international strategies in the global marketplace.

Global Strategy

As indicated in Exhibit 7.4, a firm whose emphasis is on lowering costs tends to follow a global strategy. Competitive strategy is centralized and controlled to a large extent by the corporate office. Since the primary emphasis is on controlling costs, the corporate office strives to achieve a strong level of coordination and integration across the various businesses.[49] Firms following a global strategy strive to offer standardized products and services as well as to locate manufacturing, R&D, and marketing activities in only a few locations.[50]

A global strategy emphasizes economies of scale due to the standardization of products and services, and the centralization of operations in a few locations. As such, one advantage may be that innovations that come about through efforts of either a business unit or the corporate office can be transferred more easily to other locations. Although costs may be lower, the firm following a global strategy may, in general, have to forgo opportunities for revenue growth since it does not invest extensive resources in adapting product offerings from one market to another.

A global strategy is most appropriate when there are strong pressures for reducing costs and comparatively weak pressures for adaptation to local markets. Economies of

global strategy a strategy based on firms' centralization and control by the corporate office, with the primary emphasis on controlling costs, and used in industries where the pressure for local adaptation is low and the pressure for lowering costs is high.

scale becomes an important consideration.[51] Advantages to increased volume may come from larger production plants or runs as well as from more efficient logistics and distribution networks. Worldwide volume is also especially important in supporting high levels of investment in research and development. As we would expect, many industries requiring high levels of R&D, such as pharmaceuticals, semiconductors, and jet aircraft, follow global strategies.

Another advantage of a global strategy is that it can enable a firm to create a standard level of quality throughout the world. Let's look at what Tom Siebel, chairman of Siebel Systems (now part of Oracle), the $2 billion developer of e-business application software, has to say about global standardization.

Our customers—global companies like IBM, Zurich Financial Services, and Citicorp—expect the same high level of service and quality, and the same licensing policies, no matter where we do business with them around the world. Our human resources and legal departments help us create policies that respect local cultures and requirements worldwide, while at the same time maintaining the highest standards. We have one brand, one image, one set of corporate colors, and one set of messages, across every place on the planet. An organization needs central quality control to avoid surprises.[52]

Risks and Challenges   There are, of course, some risks associated with a global strategy.[53]

● Boeing has followed a global strategy, which requires worldwide volume to support its high level of R&D. The picture above shows Boeing 767–200 airplanes being assembled in a factory hangar.

- A firm can enjoy scale economies only by concentrating scale-sensitive resources and activities in one or few locations. Such concentration, however, becomes a "double-edged sword." For example, if a firm has only one manufacturing facility, it must export its output (e.g., components, subsystems, or finished products) to other markets, some of which may be a great distance from the operation. Thus, decisions about locating facilities must weigh the potential benefits from concentrating operations in a single location against the higher transportation and tariff costs that result from such concentration.
- The geographic concentration of any activity may also tend to isolate that activity from the targeted markets. Such isolation may be risky since it may hamper the facility's ability to quickly respond to changes in market conditions and needs.
- Concentrating an activity in a single location also makes the rest of the firm dependent on that location. Such dependency implies that, unless the location has world-class competencies, the firm's competitive position can be eroded if problems arise. A European Ford executive, reflecting on the firm's concentration of activities during a global integration program in the mid-1990s, lamented, "Now if you misjudge the market, you are wrong in 15 countries rather than only one."

Exhibit 7.6 summarizes the strengths and weaknesses of global strategies.

Strengths	Limitations
• Strong integration across various businesses.	• Limited ability to adapt to local markets.
• Standardization leads to higher economies of scale, which lowers costs.	• Concentration of activities may increase dependence on a single facility.
• Helps create uniform standards of quality throughout the world.	• Single locations may lead to higher tariffs and transportation costs.

Exhibit 7.6
Strengths and Limitations of Global Strategies

Multidomestic Strategy

According to Exhibit 7.4, a firm whose emphasis is on differentiating its product and service offerings to adapt to local markets follows a multidomestic strategy.[54] Decisions evolving from a multidomestic strategy tend to be decentralized to permit the firm to tailor its products and respond rapidly to changes in demand. This enables a firm to expand its market and to charge different prices in different markets. For firms following this strategy, differences in language, culture, income levels, customer preferences, and distribution systems are only a few of the many factors that must be considered. Even in the case of relatively standardized products, at least some level of local adaptation is often necessary. Consider, for example, Honda motorcycles.

> While Honda uses a common basic technology, it must develop different types of motorcycles for different regions of the world. For example, North Americans primarily use motorcycles for leisure and sports; thus aggressive looks and high horsepower are key. Southeast Asians provide a counterpoint. Here, motorcycles are a basic means of transportation. Thus, they require low cost and ease of maintenance. And, in Australia and New Zealand, shepherds use motorcycles to herd sheep. Therefore, they demand low-speed torque, rather than high speed and maintenance.[55]

In addition to the products themselves, how they are packaged must sometimes be adapted to local market conditions. Some consumers in developing countries are likely to have packaging preferences very different from Western consumers. For example, single-serve packets, or sachets, are very popular in India.[56] They permit consumers to purchase only what they need, experiment with new products, and conserve cash. Products as varied as detergents, shampoos, pickles, and cough syrup are sold in sachets in India. It is estimated that they make up 20 to 30 percent of the total sold in their categories. In China, sachets are spreading as a marketing device for such items as shampoos. This reminds us of the importance of considering all activities in a firm's value chain (discussed in Chapters 3 and 5) in determining where local adaptations may be required.

Cultural differences may also require a firm to adapt its personnel practices when it expands internationally.[57] For example, some facets of Wal-Mart stores have been easily "exported" to foreign operations, while others have required some modifications.[58] When the retailer entered the German market in 1997, it took along the company "cheer"—Give me a W! Give me an A! Give me an L! Who's Number One? The Customer!—which suited German employees. However, Wal-Mart's 10-Foot Rule, which requires employees to greet any customer within a 10-foot radius, was not so well received in Germany, where employees and shoppers alike weren't comfortable with the custom.

Strategy Spotlight 7.9 describes how U.S. multinationals have adapted to the problem of bribery in various countries while adhering to strict federal laws on corrupt practices abroad.

multidomestic strategy a strategy based on firms' differentiating their products and services to adapt to local markets, used in industries where the pressure for local adaptation is high and the pressure for lowering costs is low.

Dealing with Bribery Abroad

Most multinational firms experience difficult dilemmas when it comes to the question of adapting rules and guidelines, both formal and informal, while operating in foreign countries. A case in point is the Foreign Corrupt Practices Act of 1977, which makes it illegal for U.S. companies to bribe foreign officials to gain business or facilitate approvals and permissions. Unfortunately, in many parts of the world, bribery is a way of life, with large payoffs to government officials and politicians the norm to win government contracts. At a lower level, goods won't clear customs unless routine illegal, but well-accepted, payments, are made to officials. What is an American company to do in such situations?

Intel follows a strict rule-based definition of bribery as "a thing of value given to someone with the intent of obtaining favorable treatment from the recipient." The company strictly prohibits payments to expedite a shipment through customs if the payment did not "follow applicable rules and regulations, and if the agent gives money or payment in kind to a government official for personal benefit." Texas Instruments, on the other hand, follows a middle approach. They require employees to "exercise good judgment" in questionable circumstances "by avoiding activities that could create even the appearance that our decisions could be compromised." And Analog Devices has set up a policy manager as a consultant to overseas operations. The policy manager does not make decisions for country managers. Instead, the policy manager helps country managers think through the issues and provides information on how the corporate office has handled similar situations in the past.

Source: Begley, T. M., & Boyd, D. P. 2003. The Need for a Corporate Global Mind-Set. *MIT Sloan Management Review*, Winter: 25–32.

Risks and Challenges   As you might expect, there are some risks associated with a multidomestic strategy. Among these are the following:

- Typically, local adaptation of products and services will increase a company's cost structure. In many industries, competition is so intense that most firms can ill afford any competitive disadvantages on the dimension of cost. A key challenge of managers is to determine the trade-off between local adaptation and its cost structure. For example, cost considerations led Procter & Gamble to standardize its diaper design across all European markets. This was done despite research data indicating that Italian mothers, unlike those in other countries, preferred diapers that covered the baby's navel. Later, however, P&G recognized that this feature was critical to these mothers, so the company decided to incorporate this feature for the Italian market despite its adverse cost implications.

- At times, local adaptations, even when well intentioned, may backfire. When the American restaurant chain TGI Fridays entered the South Korean market, it purposely incorporated many local dishes, such as kimchi (hot, spicy cabbage), in its menu. This responsiveness, however, was not well received. Company analysis of the weak market acceptance indicated that Korean customers anticipated a visit to TGI Fridays as a visit to America. Thus, finding Korean dishes was inconsistent with their expectations.

- The optimal degree of local adaptation evolves over time. In many industry segments, a variety of factors, such as the influence of global media, greater international travel, and declining income disparities across countries, may lead to increasing global standardization. On the other hand, in other industry segments, especially where the product or service can be delivered over the Internet (such as music), the need for even greater customization and local adaptation may increase

Why Some Films and TV Programs Travel Well across Cultures and National Boundaries—and Others Don't

Remember *The Alamo*—not the nineteenth-century battle between Mexican forces and Texas rebels—but the 2004 movie? The film definitely met the big-budget criterion—it cost Disney nearly $100 million. It did not generate strong box office receipts in English. But what was surprising was Disney's attempt to create crossover appeal to Latinos. These efforts included a more balanced treatment of Anglos versus Mexicans, prominently featuring Tejano folk heroes in the film, and running a separate Spanish-language marketing effort. But such efforts were doomed to fail. Why? According to one authority, because the Alamo is "such an open wound among American Hispanics."

Source: Ghemawat, P. 2007. *Redefining Global Strategy.* Boston: Harvard Business School Press.

There are, however, some TV programs that successfully cross borders. Discovery Networks, which focuses on factual programs, particularly documentaries, provides an excellent example. Founder John Hendricks commented: "Nature and science documentaries are one of the few programs that can be run in almost any country because there's no cultural or political bias to these programs." Further, dubbing or subtitling requirements are minimal, especially for nature documentaries. That is not to say that no variation is required: tastes do differ. Even in documentaries, East Asians are reported to have a predilection for "bloody animal shows" and Australians for forensics. As a result, about 20 percent of Discovery's programming is local. But compared with other kinds of TV programming, these are relatively minor problems. This is why Discovery and its affiliated networks (including the Learning Channel, Travel Channel, and Animal Planet) report reaching a total of 1.4 billion subscribers worldwide.

over time. Firms must recalibrate the need for local adaptation on an ongoing basis; excessive adaptation extracts a price as surely as underadaptation.

Strategy Spotlight 7.10 discusses how some films and TV programs may cross country boundaries rather successfully, while others are less successful. Exhibit 7.7 summarizes the strengths and limitations of multidomestic strategies.

Transnational Strategy

A *transnational strategy* strives to optimize the trade-offs associated with efficiency, local adaptation, and learning.[59] It seeks efficiency not for its own sake, but as a means to achieve global competitiveness.[60] It recognizes the importance of local responsiveness but as a tool for flexibility in international operations.[61] Innovations are regarded as an outcome of a larger process of organizational learning that includes the contributions of everyone in the firm.[62] Also, a core tenet of the transnational model is that a firm's assets and capabilities are dispersed according to the most beneficial location for each activity.

transnational strategy a strategy based on firms' optimizing the trade-offs associated with efficiency, local adaptation, and learning, used in industries where the pressures for both local adaptation and lowering costs are high.

Strengths	Limitations
• Ability to adapt products and services to local market conditions.	• Decreased ability to realize cost savings through scale economies.
• Ability to detect potential opportunities for attractive niches in a given market, enhancing revenue.	• Greater difficulty in transferring knowledge across countries.
	• May lead to "overadaptation" as conditions change.

Exhibit 7.7
Strengths and Limitations of Multidomestic Strategies

Thus, managers avoid the tendency to either concentrate activities in a central location (a global strategy) or disperse them across many locations to enhance adaptation (a multi-domestic strategy). Peter Brabeck, CEO of Nestlé, the giant food company, provides such a perspective.

> We believe strongly that there isn't a so-called global consumer, at least not when it comes to food and beverages. People have local tastes based on their unique cultures and traditions—a good candy bar in Brazil is not the same as a good candy bar in China. Therefore, decision making needs to be pushed down as low as possible in the organization, out close to the markets. Otherwise, how can you make good brand decisions? That said, decentralization has its limits. If you are too decentralized, you can become too complicated—you get too much complexity in your production system. The closer we come to the consumer, in branding, pricing, communication, and product adaptation, the more we decentralize. The more we are dealing with production, logistics, and supply-chain management, the more centralized decision making becomes. After all, we want to leverage Nestlé's size, not be hampered by it.[63]

The Nestlé example illustrates a common approach in determining whether or not to centralize or decentralize a value-chain activity. Typically, primary activities that are "downstream" (e.g., marketing and sales, and service), or closer to the customer, tend to require more decentralization in order to adapt to local market conditions. On the other hand, primary activities that are "upstream" (e.g., logistics and operations), or further away from the customer, tend to be centralized. This is because there is less need for adapting these activities to local markets and the firm can benefit from economies of scale. Additionally, many support activities, such as information systems and procurement, tend to be centralized in order to increase the potential for economies of scale.

A central philosophy of the transnational organization is enhanced adaptation to all competitive situations as well as flexibility by capitalizing on communication and knowledge flows throughout the organization.[64] A principal characteristic is the integration of unique contributions of all units into worldwide operations. Thus, a joint innovation by headquarters and by one of the overseas units can lead potentially to the development of relatively standardized and yet flexible products and services that are suitable for multiple markets.

Asea Brown Boveri (ABB) is a firm that successfully follows a transnational strategy. ABB, with its home bases in Sweden and Switzerland, illustrates the trend toward cross-national mergers that lead firms to consider multiple headquarters in the future. It is managed as a flexible network of units, and one of management's main functions is the facilitation of information and knowledge flows between units. ABB's subsidiaries have complete responsibility for product categories on a worldwide basis. Such a transnational strategy enables ABB to benefit from access to new markets and the opportunity to utilize and develop resources wherever they may be located.

Risks and Challenges   As with the other strategies, there are some unique risks and challenges associated with a transnational strategy.

- *The choice of a seemingly optimal location cannot guarantee that the quality and cost of factor inputs (i.e., labor, materials) will be optimal.* Managers must ensure that the relative advantage of a location is actually realized, not squandered because of weaknesses in productivity and the quality of internal operations. Ford Motor Co., for example, has benefited from having some of its manufacturing operations in Mexico. While some have argued that the benefits of lower wage rates will be partly offset by lower productivity, this does not always have to be the case. Since unemployment in Mexico is higher than in the United States, Ford can be more selective in its hiring practices for its Mexican operations. And, given the lower turnover among its Mexican employees, Ford can justify a high level of investment in training and

Exhibit 7.8
Strengths and
Limitations of
Transnational
Strategies

Strengths	Limitations
• Ability to attain economies of scale.	• Unique challenges in determining optimal locations of activities to ensure cost and quality.
• Ability to adapt to local markets.	
• Ability to locate activities in optimal locations.	• Unique managerial challenges in fostering knowledge transfer.
• Ability to increase knowledge flows and learning.	

development. Thus, the net result can be not only lower wage rates but also higher productivity than in the United States.

• *Although knowledge transfer can be a key source of competitive advantage, it does not take place "automatically."* For knowledge transfer to take place from one subsidiary to another, it is important for the source of the knowledge, the target units, and the corporate headquarters to recognize the potential value of such unique know-how. Given that there can be significant geographic, linguistic, and cultural distances that typically separate subsidiaries, the potential for knowledge transfer can become very difficult to realize. Firms must create mechanisms to systematically and routinely uncover the opportunities for knowledge transfer.

Exhibit 7.8 summarizes the relative advantages and disadvantages of transnational strategies.

Global or Regional? A Second Look at Globalization

>LO6
The difference between regional companies and truly global companies.

Thus far, we have suggested four possible strategies from which a firm must choose once it has decided to compete in the global marketplace. In recent years, many writers have asserted that the process of globalization has caused national borders to become increasingly irrelevant. However, some scholars have recently questioned this perspective, and they have argued that it is unwise for companies to rush into full scale globalization.[65]

Before answering questions about the extent of firms' globalization, let's try to clarify what "globalization" means. Traditionally, a firm's globalization is measured in terms of its foreign sales as a percentage of total sales. However, this measure can be misleading. For example, consider a U.S. firm that has expanded its activities into Canada. Clearly, this initiative is qualitatively different from achieving the same sales volume in a distant country such as China. Similarly, if a Malaysian firm expands into Singapore or a German firm starts selling its products in Austria, this would represent an expansion into a geographically adjacent country. Such nearby countries would often share many common characteristics in terms of language, culture, infrastructure, and customer preferences. In other words, this is more a case of regionalization than globalization.

Extensive analysis of the distribution data of sales across different countries and regions led Alan Rugman and Alain Verbeke to conclude that there is a stronger case to be made in favor of regionalization than globalization. According to their study, a company would have to have at least 20 percent of its sales in each of the three major economic regions—North America, Europe, and Asia—to be considered a global firm. However, they found that only nine of the world's 500 largest firms met this standard! Even when they relaxed the criterion to 20 percent of sales each in at least two of the three regions, the number only increased to 25. *Thus, most companies are regional or, at best, biregional— not global—even today.* Exhibit 7.9 provides a listing of the large firms that met each of these two criteria.

In a world of instant communication, rapid transportation, and governments that are increasingly willing to open up their markets to trade and investment, why are so few

Firms with at least 20 percent sales in Asia, Europe, and North America each but with less than 50 percent sales in any one region:

IBM	Nokia	Coca-Cola
Sony	Intel	Flextronics
Philips	Canon	LVMH

Firms with at least 20 percent sales in at least two of the three regions (Asia, Europe, North America) but with less than 50 percent sales in any one region:

BP Amoco	Alstom	Michelin
Toyota	Aventis	Kodak
Nissan	Daigeo	Electrolux
Unilever	Sun Microsystems	BAE
Motorola	Bridgestone	Alcan
GlaxoSmithKline	Roche	L'Oreal
EADS	3M	Lafarge
Bayer	Skanska	
Ericsson	McDonald's	

Sources: Peng, M.W. 2006. *Global Strategy:* 387. Mason, OH: Thomson Southwestern; and Rugman, A.M., & Verbeke, A. 2004. A Perspective on Regional and Global Strategies of Multinational Enterprises. *Journal of International Business Studies,* 35: 3–18.

firms "global"? The most obvious answer is that distance still matters. After all, it is easier to do business in a neighboring country than in a far away country, all else being equal. Distance, in the final analysis, may be viewed as a concept with many dimensions, not just a measure of geographical distance. For example, both Canada and Mexico are the same distance from the U.S. However, U.S. companies find it easier to expand operations into Canada than into Mexico. Why? Canada and the U.S. share many commonalities in terms of language, culture, economic development, legal and political systems, and infrastructure development. Thus, if we view distance as having many dimensions, the U.S. and Canada are very close, whereas there is greater distance between the U.S. and Mexico. Similarly, when we look at what we might call the "true" distance between the U.S. and China, the effects of geographic distance are multiplied by distance in terms of culture, language, religion, and legal and political systems between the two countries. On the other hand, although U.S. and Australia are geographically distant, the "true" distance is somewhat less when one considers distance along the other dimensions.

Another reason for regional expansion is the rise of the trading blocs. The European Union originally started in the 1950s as a regional trading bloc. However, recently it has achieved a large degree of economic and political integration in terms of common currency and common standards that many thought infeasible, if not impossible, only 20 years ago. The resulting economic benefits have led other regions also to consider similar moves. For example, the North American Free Trade Agreement (NAFTA) has the eventual abolition of all barriers to the free movement of goods and services among Canada, the U.S., and Mexico as its goal. Other regional trading blocks include MERCOSUR (consisting of Argentina, Brazil, Paraguay, and Uruguay) and the Association of Southeast Asian Nations (ASEAN) (consisting of about a dozen Southeast Asian countries).

Regional economic integration has progressed at a faster pace than global economic integration and the trade and investment patterns of the largest companies reflect this reality. After all, regions represent the outcomes of centuries of political and cultural history that results not only in commonalities but also mutual affinity. For example, stretching from Algeria and Morocco in the West to Oman and Yemen in the East, more than 30 countries share the Arabic language and the Muslim religion, making these countries a natural regional bloc. Similarly, the countries of South and Central America share the Spanish language (except Brazil), Catholic religion, and a shared history of Spanish colonialism. No wonder firms find it easier and less risky to expand within their region than to other regions.

Entry Modes of International Expansion

>LO7

The four basic types of entry strategies and the relative benefits and risks associated with each of them.

A firm has many options available to it when it decides to expand into international markets. Given the challenges associated with such entry, many firms first start on a small scale and then increase their level of investment and risk as they gain greater experience with the overseas market in question.[66]

Exhibit 7.10 illustrates a wide variety of modes of foreign entry, including exporting, licensing, franchising, joint ventures, strategic alliances, and wholly owned subsidiaries.[67] As the exhibit indicates, the various types of entry form a continuum ranging from exporting (low investment and risk, low control) to a wholly owned subsidiary (high investment and risk, high control).[68]

There can be frustrations and setbacks as a firm evolves its international entry strategy from exporting to more expensive types, including wholly owned subsidiaries. For example, according to the CEO of a large U.S. specialty chemical company:

> In the end, we always do a better job with our own subsidiaries; sales improve, and we have greater control over the business. But we still need local distributors for entry, and we are still searching for strategies to get us through the transitions without battles over control and performance.[69]

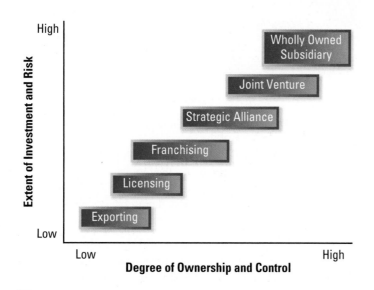

Exhibit 7.10 Entry Modes for International Expansion

Exporting

exporting producing goods in one country to sell to residents of another country.

Exporting consists of producing goods in one country to sell in another.[70] This entry strategy enables a firm to invest the least amount of resources in terms of its product, its organization, and its overall corporate strategy. Many host countries dislike this entry strategy because it provides less local employment than other modes of entry.[71]

Multinationals often stumble onto a stepwise strategy for penetrating markets, beginning with the exporting of products. This often results in a series of unplanned actions to increase sales revenues. As the pattern recurs with entries into subsequent markets, this approach, named a "beachhead strategy," often becomes official policy.

Benefits Such an approach definitely has its advantages. After all, firms start from scratch in sales and distribution when they enter new markets. Because many foreign markets are nationally regulated and dominated by networks of local intermediaries, firms need to partner with local distributors to benefit from their valuable expertise and knowledge of their own markets. Multinationals, after all, recognize that they cannot master local business practices, meet regulatory requirements, hire and manage local personnel, or gain access to potential customers without some form of local partnership.

● Australia is geographically distant from the United States. However, it is much closer when other dimensions are considered, such as income levels, language, culture, and political/legal systems.

Multinationals also want to minimize their own risk. They do this by hiring local distributors and investing very little in the undertaking. In essence, the firm gives up control of strategic marketing decisions to the local partners—much more control than they would be willing to give up in their home market.

Risks and Limitations Exporting is a relatively inexpensive way to enter foreign markets. However, it can still have significant downsides. In a study of 250 instances in which multinational firms used local distributors to implement their exporting entry strategy, the results were dismal. In the vast majority of the cases, the distributors were bought (to increase control) by the multinational firm or fired. In contrast, successful distributors shared two common characteristics:

- They carried product lines that complemented, rather than competed with, the multinational's products.
- They behaved as if they were business partners with the multinationals. They shared market information with the corporations, they initiated projects with distributors in neighboring countries, and they suggested initiatives in their own or nearby markets. Additionally, these distributors took on risk themselves by investing in areas such as training, information systems, and advertising and promotion in order to increase the business of their multinational partners.

The key point is the importance of developing collaborative, win–win relationships.

To ensure more control over operations without incurring significant risks, many firms have used licensing and franchising as a mode of entry. Let's now discuss these and their relative advantages and disadvantages.

Licensing and Franchising

Licensing and franchising are both forms of contractual arrangements. **Licensing** enables a company to receive a royalty or fee in exchange for the right to use its trademark, patent, trade secret, or other valuable item of intellectual property.[72]

Franchising contracts generally include a broader range of factors in an operation and have a longer time period during which the agreement is in effect. Franchising remains a primary form of American business. According to a recent survey, more than 400 U.S. franchisers have international exposure.[73] This is greater than the combined totals of the next four largest franchiser home countries—France, the United Kingdom, Mexico, and Austria.

Benefits   In international markets, an advantage of licensing is that the firm granting a license incurs little risk, since it does not have to invest any significant resources into the country itself. In turn, the licensee (the firm receiving the license) gains access to the trademark, patent, and so on, and is able to potentially create competitive advantages. In many cases, the country also benefits from the product being manufactured locally. For example, Yoplait yogurt is licensed by General Mills from Sodima, a French cooperative, for sale in the United States. The logos of college and professional athletic teams in the United States are another source of trademarks that generate significant royalty income domestically and internationally.

Franchising has the advantage of limiting the risk exposure that a firm has in overseas markets. At the same time, the firm is able to expand the revenue base of the company.

Risks and Limitations   The licensor gives up control of its product and forgoes potential revenues and profits. Furthermore, the licensee may eventually become so familiar with the patent and trade secrets that it may become a competitor; that is, the licensee may make some modifications to the product and manufacture and sell it independently of the licensor without having to pay a royalty fee. This potential situation is aggravated in countries that have relatively weak laws to protect intellectual property. Additionally, if the licensee selected by the multinational firm turns out to be a poor choice, the brand name and reputation of the product may be tarnished.[74]

With franchising, the multinational firm receives only a portion of the revenues, in the form of franchise fees. Had the firm set up the operation itself (e.g., a restaurant through direct investment), it would have had the entire revenue to itself.

Companies often desire a closer collaboration with other firms in order to increase revenue, reduce costs, and enhance their learning—often through the diffusion of technology. To achieve such objectives, they enter into strategic alliances or joint ventures, two entry modes we will discuss next.

Strategic Alliances and Joint Ventures

Joint ventures and strategic alliances have recently become increasingly popular.[75] These two forms of partnership differ in that joint ventures entail the creation of a third-party legal entity, whereas strategic alliances do not. In addition, strategic alliances generally focus on initiatives that are smaller in scope than joint ventures.[76]

Benefits   As we discussed in Chapter 6, these strategies have been effective in helping firms increase revenues and reduce costs as well as enhance learning and diffuse technologies. These partnerships enable firms to share the risks as well as the potential revenues and profits. Also, by gaining exposure to new sources of knowledge and technologies, such partnerships can help firms develop core competencies that can lead to competitive advantages in the marketplace.[77] Finally, entering into partnerships with host country firms can provide very useful information on local market tastes, competitive conditions, legal matters, and cultural nuances.[78]

licensing a contractual arrangement in which a company receives a royalty or fee in exchange for the right to use its trademark, patent, trade secret, or other valuable intellectual property.

franchising a contractual arrangement in which a company receives a royalty or fee in exchange for the right to use its intellectual property; it usually involves a longer time period than licensing and includes other factors, such as monitoring of operations, training, and advertising.

A Joint Venture with Partners from Three Countries

A joint venture has been formed with partners from China, India, and the United States. In December 2006, Tata Consulting Services (TCS), India's largest information technology outsourcing company, joined forces with three Chinese state-owned companies and Microsoft to form a new software development center based in Beijing, China.

The development has been hailed as one of the most striking steps forward in bilateral IT relations between India and China, which for many years have been marred by mutual suspicions. Political leaders, especially in India, have traditionally been skeptical about the export of technology skills from India to China. Why? India had concerns about assisting an economic rival.

One sign of the complexities in establishing such a partnership in China is the time that it has taken to set up TCS China: The parties had signed the initial agreement

to go ahead with the project 17 months earlier in June 2005. Under the agreement, TCS will hold 65 percent of the venture while the three Chinese partners will hold 25 percent. Microsoft will hold the remaining 10 percent. The three Chinese partners are organized under the National Development and Reform Commission, the powerful central government planning agency.

The joint venture will leverage the complementary strengths of the investing parties in technology, software development management, and talent training. Of particular value will be TCS's best processes and practices as well as its experience in handling large and industrial-scale projects. It will also benefit from the resources of the Chinese partners, which run the national software development parks.

Microsoft should also benefit. According to Jonathan Spira, chief analyst of Basex, an IT research firm: "Microsoft is a global company so it makes sense for them to invest and participate in global partnerships, especially in markets as large as China's. China is a region where Microsoft does not have anything close to resembling a foothold."

Sources: Leahy, J. 2006. Asian partnership takes off. www.ft.com, December 5: 3; Anonymous. 2005. TCS and Microsoft intend to establish joint venture with Chinese firms. Microsoft Press Release. June 30, np.; and Anonymous. 2005. Microsoft sets up JV with Tata. www.basex.com. July 1, np.

Joint ventures can often include more than two different parties. Strategy Spotlight 7.11 discusses a joint venture that involved companies from the United States, China, and India.

Risks and Limitations   Managers must be aware of the risks associated with strategic alliances and joint ventures and how they can be minimized.[79] First, there needs to be a clearly defined strategy that is strongly supported by the organizations that are party to the partnership. Otherwise, the firms may work at cross-purposes and not achieve any of their goals. Second, and closely allied to the first issue, there must be a clear understanding of capabilities and resources that will be central to the partnership. Without such clarification, there will be fewer opportunities for learning and developing competencies that could lead to competitive advantages. Third, trust is a vital element. Phasing in the relationship between alliance partners permits them to get to know each other better and develop trust. Without trust, one party may take advantage of the other by, for example, withholding its fair share of resources and gaining access to privileged information through unethical (or illegal) means. Fourth, cultural issues that can potentially lead to conflict and dysfunctional behaviors need to be addressed. An organization's culture is the set of values, beliefs, and attitudes that influence the behavior and goals of its employees.[80] Thus, recognizing cultural differences as well as striving to develop elements of a "common culture" for the partnership is vital. Without a unifying culture, it will become difficult to combine and leverage resources that are increasingly important in knowledge-intensive organizations (discussed in Chapter 4).[81]

Finally, the success of a firm's alliance should not be left to chance.[82] To improve their odds of success, many companies have carefully documented alliance-management knowledge by creating guidelines and manuals to help them manage specific aspects of the entire alliance life cycle (e.g., partner selection and alliance negotiation and contracting). For example, Lotus Corp. (part of IBM) created what it calls its "35 rules of thumb" to manage each phase of an alliance from formation to termination. Hewlett-Packard developed 60 different tools and templates, which it placed in a 300-page manual for guiding decision making. The manual included such tools as a template for making the business case for an alliance, a partner evaluation form, a negotiation template outlining the roles and responsibilities of different departments, a list of the ways to measure alliance performance, and an alliance termination checklist.

When a firm desires the highest level of control, it develops wholly owned subsidiaries. Although wholly owned subsidiaries can generate the greatest returns, they also have the highest levels of investment and risk. We will now discuss them.

Wholly Owned Subsidiaries

A **wholly owned subsidiary** is a business in which a multinational company owns 100 percent of the stock. Two ways a firm can establish a wholly owned subsidiary are to (1) acquire an existing company in the home country or (2) develop a totally new operation (often referred to as a "greenfield venture").

wholly owned subsidiary a business in which a multinational company owns 100 percent of the stock.

Benefits   Establishing a wholly owned subsidiary is the most expensive and risky of the various entry modes. However, it can also yield the highest returns. In addition, it provides the multinational company with the greatest degree of control of all activities, including manufacturing, marketing, distribution, and technology development.[83]

Wholly owned subsidiaries are most appropriate where a firm already has the appropriate knowledge and capabilities that it can leverage rather easily through multiple locations. Examples range from restaurants to semiconductor manufacturers. To lower costs, for example, Intel Corporation builds semiconductor plants throughout the world—all of which use virtually the same blueprint. Knowledge can be further leveraged by hiring managers and professionals from the firm's home country, often through hiring talent from competitors.

Risks and Limitations   As noted, wholly owned subsidiaries are typically the most expensive and risky entry mode. With franchising, joint ventures, or strategic alliances, the risk is shared with the firm's partners. With wholly owned subsidiaries, the entire risk is assumed by the parent company. The risks associated with doing business in a new country (e.g., political, cultural, and legal) can be lessened by hiring local talent.

For example, Wendy's avoided committing two blunders in Germany by hiring locals to its advertising staff.[84] In one case, the firm wanted to promote its "old-fashioned" qualities. However, a literal translation would have resulted in the company promoting itself as "outdated." In another situation, Wendy's wanted to emphasize that its hamburgers could be prepared 256 ways. The problem? The German word that Wendy's wanted to use for "ways" usually meant "highways" or "roads." Although such errors may sometimes be entertaining to the public, it is certainly preferable to catch these mistakes before they confuse the consumer or embarrass the company.

We have addressed entry strategies as a progression from exporting through the creation of wholly owned subsidiaries. However, we must point out that many firms do not follow such an evolutionary approach. Instead, such firms follow rather unique entry strategies; see our discussion of Caterpillar's unconventional entry in China in Strategy Spotlight 7.12.

strategy spotlight

7.12

Caterpillar's Long March to China

Ever since it opened its doors to foreign investment a quarter century ago, China has attracted an enormous amount of foreign direct investment, currently averaging upward of $50 billion a year. However, the Chinese government has been reluctant to allow foreign companies to acquire local firms, especially in sectors that the government considers vital. For example, the attempt by Carlyle Group, a U.S. private equity firm, to buy a majority stake in Xugong Group Construction Machinery (China's leading company in this sector, with sales of $6 billion) was blocked by the Chinese government. Instead, China wants to build its own national champions in such industries.

Given this background, Caterpillar's recent acquisition of Shandong SEM Machinery, a fast-growing Chinese earth-moving-equipment manufacturer, is truly impressive. How did Caterpillar overcome China's reluctance to allow foreign companies to acquire leading Chinese companies? Investing in relationships, long-term thinking, patience, demonstrating commitment, and a creative approach to engaging the Chinese were all keys to Caterpillar's success.

Jim Owens, CEO of Caterpillar, has made numerous visits to China since he went there to negotiate a technology transfer agreement in 1983. Caterpillar started by selling designs for its equipment to several Chinese manufacturers. This not only gave Caterpillar a foothold in China in the late '80s, but it also earned them the gratitude of a nation that was embarking on one of history's biggest construction booms. During the height of the SARS crisis in 2003, Owens sent a deputy to China, thereby demonstrating Caterpillar's solidarity with China in a time of crisis. By 2005, Caterpillar was given permission to acquire a minority stake in SEM. And immediately after the Beijing Olympics of 2008, Caterpillar won the biggest prize of all: full ownership of SEM.

Currently, Caterpillar has 16 manufacturing plants in China, with sales of $2 billion. It plans to invest another $100 million in SEM to triple its output. Given China's infrastructure needs in the coming years, Caterpillar sees double-digit growth ahead for years to come. The lesson for other foreign firms on the lookout for acquisition candidates in China: Deep pockets and an open checkbook will not buy you much in China.

Source: Roberts, D. 2008. Behind Caterpillar's Big Scoop in China. *Business-Week*, December 22: 58; and www.cat.com/cda/components.

Reflecting on Career Implications . . .

- *International Strategy:* Be aware of your organization's international strategy. What percentage of the total firm activity is international? What skills are needed to enhance your company's international efforts? How can you get more involved in your organization's international strategy? For your career, what conditions in your home country might cause you to seek careers abroad?
- *Outsourcing and Offshoring:* What activities in your organization can/should be outsourced or offshored? Be aware that you are competing in the global marketplace for employment and professional advancement. Continually take inventory of your talents, skills, and competencies.
- *International Career Opportunities:* Work assignments in other countries can often provide a career boost. Be proactive in pursuing promising career opportunities in other countries. Anticipate how such opportunities will advance your short- and long-term career aspirations.
- *Management Risks:* Develop cultural sensitivity. This applies, of course, to individuals from different cultures in your home-based organization as well as in your overseas experience.

Summary

We live in a highly interconnected global community where many of the best opportunities for growth and profitability lie beyond the boundaries of a company's home country. Along with the opportunities, of course, there are many risks associated with diversification into global markets.

The first section of the chapter addressed the factors that determine a nation's competitiveness in a particular industry. The framework was developed by Professor Michael Porter of Harvard University and was based on a four-year study that explored the competitive success of 10 leading trading nations. The four factors, collectively termed the "diamond of national advantage," were factor conditions, demand characteristics, related and supporting industries, and firm strategy, structure, and rivalry.

The discussion of Porter's "diamond" helped, in essence, to set the broader context for exploring competitive advantage at the firm level. In the second section, we discussed the primary motivations and the potential risks associated with international expansion. The primary motivations included increasing the size of the potential market for the firm's products and services, achieving economies of scale, extending the life cycle of the firm's products, and optimizing the location for every activity in the value chain. On the other hand, the key risks included political and economic risks, currency risks, and management risks. Management risks are the challenges associated with responding to the inevitable differences that exist across countries such as customs, culture, language, customer preferences, and distribution systems. We also addressed some of the managerial challenges and opportunities associated with offshoring and outsourcing.

Next, we addressed how firms can go about attaining competitive advantage in global markets. We began by discussing the two opposing forces—cost reduction and adaptation to local markets—that managers must contend with when entering global markets. The relative importance of these two factors plays a major part in determining which of the four basic types of strategies to select: international, global, multidomestic, or transnational. The chapter covered the benefits and risks associated with each type of strategy. We also presented a recent perspective by Alan Rugman who argues that despite all the talk of globalization, most of the large multinationals are regional or at best biregional (in terms of geographical diversification of sales) rather than global.

The final section discussed the four types of entry strategies that managers may undertake when entering international markets. The key trade-off in each of these strategies is the level of investment or risk versus the level of control. In order of their progressively greater investment/risk and control, the strategies range from exporting to licensing and franchising, to strategic alliances and joint ventures, to wholly owned subsidiaries. The relative benefits and risks associated with each of these strategies were addressed.

Summary Review Questions

1. What are some of the advantages and disadvantages associated with a firm's expansion into international markets?

2. What are the four factors described in Porter's diamond of national advantage? How do the four factors explain why some industries in a given country are more successful than others?

3. Explain the two opposing forces—cost reduction and adaptation to local markets—that firms must deal with when they go global.

4. There are four basic strategies—international, global, multidomestic, and transnational. What are the advantages and disadvantages associated with each?

5. What is the basis of Alan Rugman's argument that most multinationals are still more regional than global? What factors inhibit firms from becoming truly global?

6. Describe the basic entry strategies that firms have available when they enter international markets. What are the relative advantages and disadvantages of each?

Key Terms

globalization, 235
factor endowments (national advantage), 236
demand conditions (national advantage), 236
related and supporting industries (national advantage), 237
firm strategy, structure, and rivalry (national advantage), 237
political risk, 243
economic risk, 244
currency risk, 245
management risk, 245
outsourcing, 247
offshoring, 247
international strategy, 250
global strategy, 251
multidomestic strategy, 253
transnational strategy, 255
exporting, 260
licensing, 261
franchising, 261
wholly owned subsidiary, 263

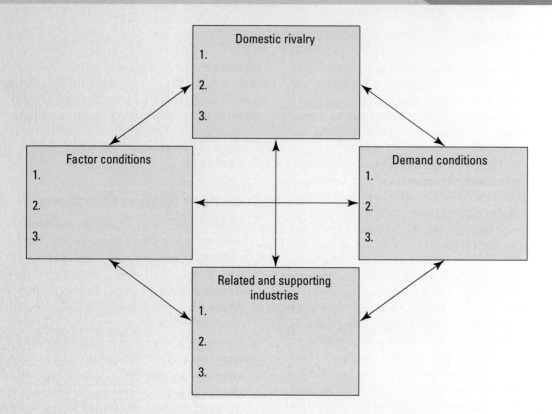

Experiential Exercise

The United States is considered a world leader in the motion picture industry. Using Porter's diamond framework for national competitiveness, explain the success of this industry.

Application Questions Exercises

1. Data on the "competitiveness of nations" can be found at www.imd.ch/wcy/ranking/. This website provides a ranking on a variety of criteria for 49 countries. How might Porter's diamond of national advantage help to explain the rankings for some of these countries for certain industries that interest you?

2. The Internet has lowered the entry barriers for smaller firms that wish to diversify into international markets. Why is this so? Provide an example.

3. Many firms fail when they enter into strategic alliances with firms that link up with companies based in other countries. What are some reasons for this failure? Provide an example.

4. Many large U.S.–based management consulting companies such as McKinsey and Company and the BCG Group have been very successful in the international marketplace. How can Porter's diamond explain their success?

Ethics Questions

1. Over the past few decades, many American firms have relocated most or all of their operations from the United States to countries such as Mexico and China that pay lower wages. What are some of the ethical issues that such actions may raise?

2. Business practices and customs vary throughout the world. What are some of the ethical issues concerning payments that must be made in a foreign country to obtain business opportunities?

References

1. Kiley, D. 2008. One world, one car, one name. *BusinessWeek,* March 24: 63; The name game Touareg? Murano? Where do they get those new car names. 2003. *Chicago Sun Times,* January 30: np; Abuelsamid, S. 2008. Geneva 2008: 2009 Ford Fiesta, a new car with Verve but an old name. autobloggreen.com, February 14: np; and Dolan, M. 2008. Ford speeds to tailor European cars for U.S. crowd: Push for smaller autos is "about our survival": Bumpers are big hurdle. *The Wall Street Journal,* September 8: B3.

2. For a recent discussion on globalization by one of international business's most respected authors, read Ohmae, K. 2005. *The next global stage: Challenges and opportunities in our borderless world.* Philadelphia: Wharton School Publishing.

3. Our discussion of globalization draws upon Engardio, P. & Belton, C. 2000. Global capitalism: Can it be made to work better? *BusinessWeek,* November 6: 72–98.

4. Sellers, P. 2005. Blowing in the wind. *Fortune,* July 25: 63.

5. An interesting and balanced discussion on the merits of multinationals to the U.S. economy is found in: Mandel, M. 2008. Multinationals: Are they good for America? *BusinessWeek,* March 10: 41–64.

6. Engardio & Belton, op. cit.

7. For insightful perspectives on strategy in emerging economies, refer to the article entitled: Strategy research in emerging economies: Challenging the conventional wisdom in the January 2005 issue of *Journal of Management Studies,* 42(1).

8. The above discussion draws on Clifford, M. L., Engardio, P., Malkin, E., Roberts, D., & Echikson, W. 2000. Up the ladder. *BusinessWeek,* November 6: 78–84.

9. A recent discussion of the "bottom of the pyramid" is: Akula, V. 2008. Business basics at the bottom of the pyramid. *Harvard Business Review,* 86(6): 53–59.

10. Some insights into how winners are evolving in emerging markets are addressed in: Ghemawat, P. & Hout, T. 2008. Tomorrow's global giants: Not the usual suspects. *Harvard Business Review,* 66(11): 80–88.

11. For another interesting discussion on a country perspective, refer to Makino, S. 1999. MITI Minister Kaora Yosano on reviving Japan's competitive advantages. *Academy of Management Executive,* 13(4): 8–28.

12. The following discussion draws heavily upon Porter, M. E. 1990. The competitive advantage of nations. *Harvard Business Review,* March–April: 73–93.

13. Landes, D. S. 1998. *The wealth and poverty of nations.* New York: W. W. Norton.

14. A recent study that investigates the relationship between international diversification and firm performance is Lu, J. W. & Beamish, P. W. 2004. International diversification and firm performance: The s-curve hypothesis. *Academy of Management Journal,* 47(4): 598–609.

15. Part of our discussion of the motivations and risks of international expansion draws upon Gregg, F. M. 1999. International strategy. In Helms, M. M. (Ed.). *Encyclopedia of management:* 434–438. Detroit: Gale Group.

16. These two examples are discussed, respectively, in Dawar, N. & Frost, T. 1999. Competing with giants: Survival strategies for local companies in emerging markets. *Harvard Business Review,* 77(2): 119–129; and Prahalad, C. K. & Lieberthal, K. 1998. The end of corporate imperialism. *Harvard Business Review,* 76(4): 68–79.

17. Meredith, R. 2004. Middle kingdom, middle class. *Forbes,* November 15: 188–192; and Anonymous. 2004. Middle class becomes rising power in China. www.Chinadaily.com. November 6.

18. This discussion draws upon Gupta, A. K. & Govindarajan, V. 2001. Converting global presence into global competitive advantage. *Academy of Management Executive,* 15(2): 45–56.

19. Stross, R. E. 1997. Mr. Gates builds his brain trust. *Fortune,* December 8: 84–98.

20. For a good summary of the benefits and risks of international expansion, refer to Bartlett, C. A. & Ghoshal, S. 1987. Managing across borders: New strategic responses. *Sloan Management Review,* 28(5): 45–53; and Brown, R. H. 1994. *Competing to win in a global economy.* Washington, DC: U.S. Department of Commerce.

21. For an interesting insight into rivalry in global markets, refer to MacMillan, I. C., van Putten, A. B., & McGrath, R. G. 2003. Global gamesmanship. *Harvard Business Review,* 81(5): 62–73.

22. It is important for firms to spread their foreign operations and outsourcing relationships with a broad, well-balanced mix of regions and countries to reduce risk and increase potential reward. For example, refer to Vestring, T., Rouse, T., & Reinert, U. 2005. Hedge your offshoring bets. *MIT Sloan Management Review,* 46(3): 27–29.

23. An interesting discussion of risks faced by Lukoil, Russia's largest oil firm is in: Gimbel, B. 2009. Russia's king of crude. *Fortune,* February 2: 88–92.

24. Some insights on how Africa has improved as a potential source of investment is in: Collier, P. & Warnholz, J-L. 2009. Now's the time to invest in Africa. *Harvard Business Review,* 87(2): 23.

25. For a discussion of some of the challenges associated with government corruption regarding entry strategies in foreign markets, read Rodriguez, P.,

Uhlenbruck, K., & Eden, L. 2005. Government corruption and entry strategies of multinationals. *Academy of Management Review*, 30(2): 383–396.

26. For a discussion of the political risks in China for United States companies, refer to Garten, J. E. 1998. Opening the doors for business in China. *Harvard Business Review*, 76(3): 167–175.

27. Shari, M. 2001. Is a holy war brewing in Indonesia? *BusinessWeek*, October 15: 62.

28. Insights on how forensic economics can be used to investigate crimes and wrongdoing are in: Fisman, R. 2009. The rise of forensic economics. *Harvard Business Review*, 87(2): 26.

29. For an interesting perspective on the relationship between diversification and the development of a nation's institutional environment, read Chakrabarti, A., Singh, K., & Mahmood, I. 2007. Diversification and performance: Evidence from East Asian firms. *Strategic Management Journal*, 28(2): 101–120.

30. A study looking into corruption and foreign direct investment is: Brouthers, L. E., Gao, Y., & McNicol, J. P. 2008. *Strategic Management Journal*, 29(6): 673–680.

31. Gikkas, N. S. 1996. International licensing of intellectual property: The promise and the peril. *Journal of Technology Law & Policy*, 1(1): 1–26.

32. Insights into bribery in the international context are addressed in: Martin, K. D., Cullen, J. B., Johnson, J. L., & Parboteeah, P. 2008. Deciding to bribe: A cross-level analysis of firm and home country influences on bribery activity. *Academy of Management Journal*, 50(6): 1401–1422.

33. For an excellent theoretical discussion of how cultural factors can affect knowledge transfer across national boundaries, refer to Bhagat, R. S., Kedia, B. L., Harveston, P. D., & Triandis, H. C. 2002. Cultural variations in the cross-border transfer of organizational knowledge: An integrative framework. *Academy of Management Review*, 27(2): 204–221.

34. An interesting discussion on how local companies compete effectively with large multinationals is in: Bhatacharya, A. K. & Michael, D. C. 2008. *Harvard Business Review*, 66(3): 84–95.

35. To gain insights on the role of national and regional cultures on knowledge management models and frameworks, read Pauleen, D. J. & Murphy, P. 2005. In praise of cultural bias. *MIT Sloan Management Review*, 46(2): 21–22.

36. Berkowitz, E. N. 2000. *Marketing* (6th ed.). New York: McGraw-Hill.

37. Morrison, T., Conaway, W., & Borden, G. 1994. *Kiss, bow, or shake hands*. Avon, MA: Adams Media; and www.executiveplanet.com/business-culture.

38. World Trade Organization. *Annual Report 1998*. Geneva: World Trade Organization.

39. Lei, D. 2005. Outsourcing. In Hitt, M. A. & Ireland, R. D. (Eds.). *The Blackwell encyclopedia of management*. Entrepreneurship: 196–199. Malden, MA: Blackwell.

40. Future trends in offshoring are addressed in: Manning, S., Massini, S., & Lewin, A. Y. 2008. A dynamic perspective on next-generation offshoring: The global sourcing of science and engineering talent. *Academy of Management Perspectives*, 22(3): 35–54.

41. An interesting perspective on the controversial issue regarding the offshoring of airplane maintenance is in: Smith, G. & Bachman, J. 2008. Flying in for a tune-up overseas. *Business Week*. April 21: 26–27.

42. Dolan, K.A. 2006. Offshoring the offshorers. *Forbes*. April 17: 74–78.

43. The discussion above draws from Colvin, J. 2004. Think your job can't be sent to India? Just watch. *Fortune*, December 13: 80; Schwartz, N. D. 2004. Down and out in white collar America. *Fortune*, June 23: 321–325; Hagel, J. 2004. Outsourcing is not just about cost cutting. *The Wall Street Journal*, March 18: A3.

44. Insightful perspectives on the outsourcing of decision making are addressed in: Davenport, T. H. & Iyer, B. 2009. Should you outsource your brain? *Harvard Business Review*. 87 (2): 38. (7)

45. Levitt, T. 1983. The globalization of markets. *Harvard Business Review*, 61(3): 92–102.

46. Our discussion of these assumptions draws upon Douglas, S. P. & Wind, Y. 1987. The myth of globalization. *Columbia Journal of World Business*, Winter: 19–29.

47. Ghoshal, S. 1987. Global strategy: An organizing framework. *Strategic Management Journal*, 8: 425–440.

48. Huber, P. 2009. Who pays for a cancer drug? *Forbes*, January 12: 72.

49. For insights on global branding, refer to Aaker, D. A. & Joachimsthaler, E. 1999. The lure of global branding. *Harvard Business Review*, 77(6): 137–146.

50. For an interesting perspective on how small firms can compete in their home markets, refer to Dawar & Frost, op. cit.: 119–129.

51. Hout, T., Porter, M. E., & Rudden, E. 1982. How global companies win out. *Harvard Business Review*, 60(5): 98–107.

52. Fryer, B. 2001. Tom Siebel of Siebel Systems: High tech the old-fashioned way. *Harvard Business Review*, 79(3): 118–130.

53. The risks that are discussed for the global, multidomestic, and transnational strategies draw upon Gupta & Govindarajan, op. cit.

54. A discussion on how McDonald's adapts its products to overseas markets is in: Gumbel, P. 2008. Big Mac's local flavor. *Fortune*, May 5: 115–121.

55. Sigiura, H. 1990. How Honda localizes its global strategy. *Sloan Management Review*, 31: 77–82.

56. Prahalad & Lieberthal, op. cit.: 68–79. Their article also discusses how firms may have to reconsider their brand management, costs of market building, product design, and approaches to capital efficiency when entering foreign markets.

57. Hofstede, G. 1980. *Culture's consequences: International differences in work-related values*. Beverly Hills, CA: Sage; Hofstede, G. 1993. Cultural

constraints in management theories. *Academy of Management Executive,* 7(1): 81–94; Kogut, B. & Singh, H. 1988. The effect of national culture on the choice of entry mode. *Journal of International Business Studies,* 19: 411–432; and Usinier, J. C. 1996. *Marketing across cultures.* London: Prentice Hall.

58. McCune, J. C. 1999. Exporting corporate culture. *Management Review,* December: 53–56.

59. Prahalad, C. K. & Doz, Y. L. 1987. *The multinational mission: Balancing local demands and global vision.* New York: Free Press.

60. For an insightful discussion on knowledge flows in multinational corporations, refer to: Yang, Q., Mudambi, R., & Meyer, K. E. 2008. Conventional and reverse knowledge flows in multinational corporations. *Journal of Management,* 34(5): 882–902.

61. Kidd, J. B. & Teramoto, Y. 1995. The learning organization: The case of Japanese RHQs in Europe. *Management international review,* 35 (Special Issue): 39–56.

62. Gupta, A. K. & Govindarajan, V. 2000. Knowledge flows within multinational corporations. *Strategic Management Journal,* 21(4): 473–496.

63. Wetlaufer, S. 2001. The business case against revolution: An interview with Nestlé's Peter Brabeck. *Harvard Business Review,* 79(2): 112–121.

64. Nobel, R. & Birkinshaw, J. 1998. Innovation in multinational corporations: Control and communication patterns in international R&D operations. *Strategic Management Journal,* 19(5): 461–478.

65. This section draws upon Ghemawat, P. 2005. Regional strategies for global leadership. *Harvard Business Review.* 84(12): 98–108; Ghemawat, P. 2006. Apocalypse now? *Harvard Business Review.* 84(12): 32; Ghemawat, P. 2001. Distance still matters: The hard reality of global expansion. *Harvard Business Review,* 79(8): 137–147; Peng, M.W. 2006. *Global strategy:* 387. Mason, OH: Thomson Southwestern; and

Rugman, A. M. & Verbeke, A. 2004. A perspective on regional and global strategies of multinational enterprises. *Journal of International Business Studies.* 35: 3–18.

66. For a rigorous analysis of performance implications of entry strategies, refer to Zahra, S. A., Ireland, R. D., & Hitt, M. A. 2000. International expansion by new venture firms: International diversity, modes of entry, technological learning, and performance. *Academy of Management Journal,* 43(6): 925–950.

67. Li, J. T. 1995. Foreign entry and survival: The effects of strategic choices on performance in international markets. *Strategic Management Journal,* 16: 333–351.

68. For a discussion of how home-country environments can affect diversification strategies, refer to Wan, W. P. & Hoskisson, R. E. 2003. Home country environments, corporate diversification strategies, and firm performance. *Academy of Management Journal,* 46(1): 27–45.

69. Arnold, D. 2000. Seven rules of international distribution. *Harvard Business Review,* 78(6): 131–137.

70. Sharma, A. 1998. Mode of entry and ex-post performance. *Strategic Management Journal,* 19(9): 879–900.

71. This section draws upon Arnold, op. cit.: 131–137; and Berkowitz, op. cit.

72. Kline, D. 2003. Strategic licensing. *MIT Sloan Management Review,* 44(3): 89–93.

73. Martin, J. 1999. Franchising in the Middle East. *Management Review.* June: 38–42.

74. Arnold, op. cit.; and Berkowitz, op. cit.

75. An in-depth case study of alliance dynamics is found in: Faems, D., Janssens, M., Madhok, A., & Van Looy, B. 2008. Toward an integrative perspective on alliance governance: Connecting contract design, trust dynamics, and contract application. *Academy of Management Journal,* 51(6): 1053–1078.

76. Knowledge transfer in international joint ventures is addressed in: Inkpen,

A. 2008. Knowledge transfer and international joint ventures. *Strategic Management Journal,* 29(4): 447–453.

77. Manufacturer–supplier relationships can be very effective in global industries such as automobile manufacturing. Refer to Kotabe, M., Martin, X., & Domoto, H. 2003. Gaining from vertical partnerships: Knowledge transfer, relationship duration, and supplier performance improvement in the U.S. and Japanese automotive industries. *Strategic Management Journal,* 24(4): 293–316.

78. For a good discussion, refer to Merchant, H. & Schendel, D. 2000. How do international joint ventures create shareholder value? *Strategic Management Journal,* 21(7): 723–738.

79. This discussion draws upon Walters, B. A., Peters, S., & Dess, G. G. 1994. Strategic alliances and joint ventures: Making them work. *Business Horizons,* 37(4): 5–11.

80. Some insights on partnering in the global area are discussed in: MacCormack, A. & Forbath, T. 2008. *Harvard Business Review,* 66(1): 24, 26.

81. For a rigorous discussion of the importance of information access in international joint ventures, refer to Reuer, J. J. & Koza, M. P. 2000. Asymmetric information and joint venture performance: Theory and evidence for domestic and international joint ventures. *Strategic Management Journal,* 21(1): 81–88.

82. Dyer, J. H., Kale, P., & Singh, H. 2001. How to make strategic alliances work. *MIT Sloan Management Review,* 42(4): 37–43.

83. For a discussion of some of the challenges in managing subsidiaries, refer to O'Donnell, S. W. 2000. Managing foreign subsidiaries: Agents of headquarters, or an independent network? *Strategic Management Journal,* 21(5): 525–548.

84. Ricks, D. 2006. *Blunders in international business* (4th ed.). Malden, MA: Blackwell Publishing.

Entrepreneurial Strategy and Competitive Dynamics

>learning objectives

After reading this chapter, you should have a good understanding of:

LO1 The role of new ventures and small businesses in the U.S. economy.

LO2 The role of opportunities, resources, and entrepreneurs in successfully pursuing new ventures.

LO3 Three types of entry strategies—pioneering, imitative, and adaptive—commonly used to launch a new venture.

LO4 How the generic strategies of overall cost leadership, differentiation, and focus are used by new ventures and small businesses.

LO5 How competitive actions, such as the entry of new competitors into a marketplace, may launch a cycle of actions and reactions among close competitors.

LO6 The components of competitive dynamics analysis—new competitive action, threat analysis, motivation and capability to respond, types of competitive actions, and likelihood of competitive reaction.

N ew technologies, shifting social and demographic trends, and sudden changes in the business environment create opportunities for entrepreneurship. New ventures, which often emerge under such conditions, face unique strategic challenges if they are going to survive and grow. Young and small businesses, which are a major engine of growth in the U.S. economy because of their role in job creation and innovation, must rely on sound strategic principles to be successful.

This chapter addresses how new ventures and entrepreneurial firms can achieve competitive advantages. It also examines how entrepreneurial activity influences a firm's strategic priorities and intensifies the rivalry among an industry's close competitors.

In the first section, we discuss the role of opportunity recognition in the process of new venture creation. Three factors that are important in determining whether a value-creating opportunity should be pursued are highlighted—the nature of the opportunity, the resources available to undertake it, and the characteristics of the entrepreneur(s) pursuing it.

The second section addresses three different types of new entry strategies—pioneering, imitative, and adaptive. Then, the generic strategies (discussed in Chapter 5) as well as combination strategies are addressed in terms of how they apply to new ventures and entrepreneurial firms. Additionally, some of the pitfalls associated with each of these strategic approaches are presented.

In section three, we explain how new entrants and other competitors often set off a series of actions and reactions that affect the competitive dynamics of an industry. In determining how to react to a competitive action, firms must analyze whether they are seriously threatened by the action, how important it is for them to respond, and what resources they can muster to mount a response. They must also determine what type of action is appropriate—strategic or tactical— and whether their close competitors are likely to counterattack. Taken together, these actions often have a strong impact on the strategic choices and overall profitability of an industry.

Learning from Mistakes

The success of an entrepreneurial venture—whether it is undertaken by a small start-up or a major corporation—depends on many factors. The right combination of resources, know-how, and strategic action can lead to above-average profitability and value-creating advantages. However, many things can go wrong. To see how a firm's efforts to launch an entrepreneurial new entry can turn sour, consider the example of Amp'd Mobile.

Mobile technology has turned cell phones into much more than just phones. Not only are they mini-workstations capable of handling online transactions and multiple types of communication, but they can also deliver a wide array of content—music, games, news, videos, and more. Several businesses have been launched to take advantage of these capabilities, including Amp'd Mobile, a 2003 start-up created to provide entertainment content to a unique target audience—18–25 year old males.[1]

The Amp'd business model involved supplying original programming that could be sent directly to users' handsets. The company contracted with Verizon Wireless to operate over Verizon's broadband network and turned its attention to providing edgy content—online gaming, comedy and reality shows, sports programming, and music. The company outfitted itself with an in-house studio for recording live concerts and mobile outdoor broadcasting trucks that could simulcast extreme sports events such as super-cross racing and Ultimate Fighting Championship (UFC). Amp'd also licensed content from MTV Networks and Playboy Enterprises.

The Amp'd management team, which had been successful with an earlier start-up aimed at multicultural youth, based the launch on a key assumption: 18–25 year olds were already savvy users of digital devices. By creating a service that promised "a more relevant, personal experience to the wireless lifestyle," they believed that their target audience would generate significantly more revenue per user than the typical digital phone customer. That business model helped Amp'd become a favorite among venture capitalists. It raised $360 million in equity investments and another $31 million in debt financing.

In early 2007, Amp'd reported it had well over 100,000 users paying in excess of $30 per month for content and data. Because the industry average was just $6.80 per user, its plan seemed to be working. Content alone accounted for nearly 60 percent of its revenues, compared to the average for other carriers of 25 percent. But later the same year, Amp'd Mobile filed for Chapter 11 bankruptcy protection.

What went wrong? Three things plagued this promising start-up. First, Amp'd had a serious collections problem with its 18–25-year-old target audience. According to an affidavit filed by Amp'd president Bill Stone, by May 2007 "nonpaying customers approached 80,000" out of an estimated 175,000 total customers, leading to a serious liquidity crisis. Amp'd had signed 90 percent of its customers on 18-month service contracts, but many simply stopped paying. "Youth is the least loyal [customer] in the whole wireless world," according to Alex Besen, founder of the Besen Group, a wireless industry consultancy.

Amp'd likely did not foresee its collections problem, but its other failures could well have been prevented. Amp'd executives burned through the company's $360 million of investor capital with lavish and uncontrolled spending. It hired executives from all over the U.S and flew or helicoptered them to its Southern California headquarters as needed. It spent millions on marketing, including sponsoring the MTV Video Music Awards and rapper Snoop Dogg's youth football league. It was also known for cosponsoring big bashes, including pool parties at the MTV awards and the 2006 Coachella Music Festival in Palm Springs, California.

One of the biggest problems, however, had to do with the commitment and savvy of its key executives. Insiders reported that the advertising spending problem was made worse because Amp'd executives did not bargain for volume discounts but often paid full price for its ads. And operations were especially weak. Amp'd hired former T-Mobile executive Sue Swenson to bring operations depth. But because of a noncompete clause, she was unable to start **(continued)**

(continued) working for a year. Meanwhile, the operations job fell to President Stone, whose background was marketing, not operations. When customer complaints about service started mounting, Stone added customer service reps rather than investigate the reasons for the complaints.

Eventually the company ceased operations and abandoned its efforts to emerge out of bankruptcy. At the time, it had $164 million in liabilities against $46.6 million in assets. The unpaid bill to Verizon alone was $33 million.

By offering differentiated content to a gadget-loving niche audience, Amp'd Mobile seemed to have identified an attractive opportunity. But the start-up's failure shows what can go wrong when—even though a good opportunity, sufficient resources, and an experienced entrepreneurial team are brought together—that team falls short in their planning and execution efforts. Other independently run mobile virtual network operators (MVNOs), including start-ups Jitterbug and Sonopia, are thriving despite the extra cost of leasing broadband services. IT consultancy Gartner estimates that by 2014, 25 percent of U.S. subscribers will obtain services from this type of niche provider, up from less than 10 percent today. But without a clear strategy and disciplined implementation, such businesses are fighting an uphill battle. Indeed, Amp'd Mobile joins a host of players in the mobile communications space, including sports giant ESPN, who failed to operate profitable business models and were forced to shut down.

The Amp'd Mobile case illustrates how important it is for new entrepreneurial entrants—whether they are start-ups or incumbents—to think and act strategically. Even with a strong resource base and good track record, an ill-conceived strategy and strong competitive forces may prevent what seems like a good idea from taking off.

In this chapter we address entrepreneurial strategies. The previous three chapters have focused primarily on the business-level, corporate-level, and international strategies of incumbent firms. Here we ask: What about the strategies of those entering into a market or industry for the first time? Whether it's a small, young start-up such as Amp'd Mobile or an existing company seeking growth opportunities, new entrants need effective strategies.

Companies wishing to launch new ventures must also be aware that, consistent with the five forces model in Chapter 2, new entrants are a threat to existing firms in an industry. Entry into a new market arena is intensely competitive from the perspective of incumbents in that arena. Therefore, new entrants can nearly always expect a competitive response from other companies in the industry it is entering. Knowledge of the competitive dynamics that are at work in the business environment is an aspect of entrepreneurial new entry that will be addressed later in this chapter.

Before moving on, it is important to highlight the role that entrepreneurial start-ups and small business play in entrepreneurial value creation. Young and small firms are responsible for more innovations and more new job creation than any other type of business.[2] Strategy Spotlight 8.1 addresses some of the reasons why small business and entrepreneurship are viewed favorably in the United States.

>LO1
The role of new ventures and small businesses in the U.S. economy.

Recognizing Entrepreneurial Opportunities

Defined broadly, **entrepreneurship** refers to new value creation. Even though entrepreneurial activity is usually associated with start-up companies, new value can be created in many different contexts including:

- Start-up ventures
- Major corporations
- Family-owned businesses
- Non-profit organizations
- Established institutions

entrepreneurship the creation of new value by an existing organization or new venture that involves the assumption of risk.

strategy spotlight

The Contribution of Small Businesses to the U.S. Economy

In the late 1970s, MIT professor David Birch launched a study to explore the sources of business growth. "I wasn't really looking for anything in particular," says Birch. But the findings surprised him: Small businesses create the most jobs. Since then, Birch and others have shown that it's not just big companies that power the economy. Small business and entrepreneurship have become a major component of new job creation.

Sources: Small Business Administration. 2007. *The Small Business Economy.* Washington, DC: U.S. Government Printing Office; Small Business Administration. 2006. Small Business by the Numbers. *SBA Office of Advocacy,* June, www.sba.gov/advo/; *Inc.* 2001. Small Business 2001: Where We Are Now? May 29: 18–19; Minniti, M., & Bygrave, W. D. 2004. *Global Entrepreneurship Monitor—National Entrepreneurship Assessment: United States of America 2004, Executive Report.* Kansas City, MO: Kauffman Center for Entrepreneurial Leadership; and *Fortune.* 2001. The Heroes: A Portfolio. October 4: 74.

Here are the facts:

- In the United States, there are approximately 5.6 million companies with fewer than 100 employees. Another 100,000 companies have 100 to 500 employees. In addition, approximately 17.0 million individuals are nonemployer sole proprietors.

- Small businesses create the majority of new jobs. According to recent data, small business created three-quarters of U.S. net new jobs in a recent period (2.5 million of the 3.4 million total). A small percentage of the fastest growing entrepreneurial firms (5 to 15 percent) account for a majority of the new jobs created.

- Small businesses (fewer than 500 employees) employ more than half of the private sector workforce (56 million in 2002) and account for more than 50 percent of nonfarm private gross domestic product (GDP). *(continued)*

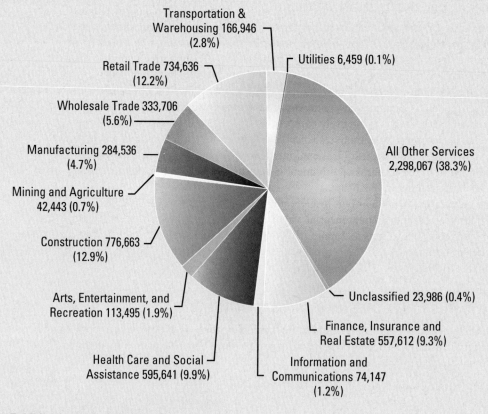

Exhibit 8.1 **All U.S. Small Companies by Industry***

Businesses with 500 or fewer employees in 2005.

Source: Small Business Administration's Office of Advocacy, based on data provided by the U.S. Census Bureau, statistics of U.S. businesses.

(continued)

- Small firms produce 13 to 14 times more patents per employee than large patenting firms and employ 39 percent of high-tech workers (such as scientists and engineers). In addition, smaller entrepreneurial firms account for 55 percent of all innovations.
- Small businesses make up 97 percent of all U.S. exporters and accounted for 29 percent of known U.S. export value in 2001.

Exhibit 8.1 shows the number of small businesses in the United States and how they are distributed through different sectors of the economy.

There are also many types of small businesses. Exhibit 8.2 identifies three major categories that are often small and generally considered to be entrepreneurial—franchises, family businesses, and home-based businesses.

Type	Characteristics
Family Businesses	*Definition:* A family business, broadly defined, is a privately held firm in which family members have some degree of control over the strategic direction of the firm and intend for the business to remain within the family. *Scope:* According to the Family Firm Institute (FFI), family-owned businesses that meet the broad definition above comprise 80 to 90 percent of all business enterprises in the U.S., including 30 to 35 percent of the Fortune 500 companies. Further, 64 percent of the U.S. Gross Domestic Product (GDP) is generated by family-owned businesses.
Franchises	*Definition:* A franchise exists when a company that already has a successful product or service (franchisor) contracts with another business to be a dealer (franchisee) by using the franchisor's name, trademark and business system in exchange for a fee. The most common type is the Business Format Franchise in which the franchisor provides a complete plan, or format, for managing the business. *Scope:* According to the International Franchise Association (IFA), franchises were the cause of $2.31 trillion in annual output in the U.S. in 2005. There are over 900,000 franchise establishments employing more than 11 million people.
Home-Based Businesses	*Definition:* A home-based business, also referred to as SOHO (Small Office/Home Office) consists of companies with 20 or fewer employees, including the self-employed, freelancers, telecommuters, or other independent professionals working from a home-based setting. *Scope:* According to the National Association of Home-Based Businesses (NAHBB), approximately 20 million businesses are home-based. The U.S. Commerce Department estimates that more than half of all small businesses are home-based.

Sources: www.ffi.org; www.franchise.org; and www.workingsolo.com.

Exhibit 8.2   **Types of Entrepreneurial Ventures**

>LO2

The role of opportunities, resources, and entrepreneurs in successfully pursuing new ventures.

For an entrepreneurial venture to create new value, three factors must be present—an entrepreneurial opportunity, the resources to pursue the opportunity, and an entrepreneur or entrepreneurial team willing and able to undertake the opportunity.[3] The entrepreneurial strategy that an organization uses will depend on these three factors. Thus, beyond merely identifying a venture concept, the opportunity recognition process also involves organizing the key people and resources that are needed to go forward. Exhibit 8.3 depicts the three factors that are needed to successfully proceed—opportunity, resources, and entrepreneur(s). In the sections that follow, we address each of these factors.

Entrepreneurial Opportunities

The starting point for any new venture is the presence of an entrepreneurial opportunity. Where do opportunities come from? For new business start-ups, opportunities come from many sources—current or past work experiences, hobbies that grow into businesses or lead to inventions, suggestions by friends or family, or a chance event that makes an entrepreneur aware of an unmet need. For established firms, new business opportunities come from the needs of existing customers, suggestions by suppliers, or technological developments that lead to new advances.[4] For all firms, there is a major, overarching factor behind all viable opportunities that emerge in the business landscape: change. Change creates opportunities. Entrepreneurial firms make the most of changes brought about by new technology, sociocultural trends, and shifts in consumer demand.

How do changes in the external environment lead to new business creation? They spark creative new ideas and innovation. Businesspeople often have ideas for entrepreneurial ventures. However, not all such ideas are good ideas—that is, viable business opportunities. To determine which ideas are strong enough to become new ventures, entrepreneurs must go through a process of identifying, selecting, and developing potential opportunities. This is the process of **opportunity recognition.**[5]

Opportunity recognition refers to more than just the "Eureka!" feeling that people sometimes experience at the moment they identify a new idea. Although such insights are often very important, the opportunity recognition process involves two phases of activity—discovery and evaluation—that lead to viable new venture opportunities.[6]

opportunity recognition the process of discovering and evaluating changes in the business environment, such as a new technology, sociocultural trends, or shifts in consumer demand, that can be exploited.

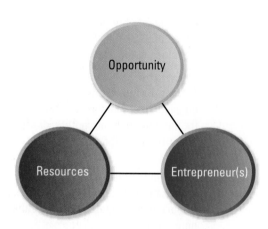

Exhibit 8.3 **Opportunity Analysis Framework**

Sources: Based on Timmons, J. A. & Spinelli, S. 2004. *New Venture Creation* (6th ed.). New York: McGraw-Hill/Irwin; and Bygrave, W. D. 1997. The Entrepreneurial Process. In W. D. Bygrave (Ed.), *The Portable MBA in Entrepreneurship* (2nd ed.). New York: Wiley.

The discovery phase refers to the process of becoming aware of a new business concept.[7] Many entrepreneurs report that their idea for a new venture occurred to them in an instant, as a sort of "Aha!" experience—that is, they had some insight or epiphany, often based on their prior knowledge, that gave them an idea for a new business. The discovery of new opportunities is often spontaneous and unexpected. For example, Howard Schultz, CEO of Starbucks, was in Milan, Italy, when he suddenly realized that the coffee-and-conversation café model that was common in Europe would work in the U.S. as well. According to Schultz, he didn't need to do research to find out if Americans would pay $3 for a cup of coffee—he just *knew.* Starbucks was just a small business at the time but Schultz began literally shaking with excitement about growing it into a bigger business.[8] Strategy Spotlight 8.2 tells how three Internet pioneers identified their business opportunities and grew them into billion-dollar successes.

Opportunity discovery also may occur as the result of a deliberate search for new venture opportunities or creative solutions to business problems. Viable opportunities often emerge only after a concerted effort. It is very similar to a creative process, which may be unstructured and "chaotic" at first but eventually leads to a practical solution or business innovation. To stimulate the discovery of new opportunities, companies often encourage creativity, out-of-the-box thinking, and brainstorming.

Opportunity evaluation, which occurs after an opportunity has been identified, involves analyzing an opportunity to determine whether it is viable and strong enough to be developed into a full-fledged new venture. Ideas developed by new-product groups or in brainstorming sessions are tested by various methods, including talking to potential target customers and discussing operational requirements with production or logistics managers. A technique known as feasibility analysis is used to evaluate these and other critical success factors. This type of analysis often leads to the decision that a new venture project should be discontinued. If the venture concept continues to seem viable, a more formal business plan may be developed.[9]

Among the most important factors to evaluate is the market potential for the product or service. Established firms tend to operate in established markets. They have to adjust to market trends and to shifts in consumer demand, of course, but they usually have a customer base for which they are already filling a marketplace need. New ventures, in contrast, must first determine whether a market exists for the product or service they are contemplating. Thus, a critical element of opportunity recognition is assessing to what extent the opportunity is viable *in the marketplace.*

For an opportunity to be viable, it needs to have four qualities.[10]

- *Attractive.* The opportunity must be attractive in the marketplace; that is, there must be market demand for the new product or service.
- *Achievable.* The opportunity must be practical and physically possible.
- *Durable.* The opportunity must be attractive long enough for the development and deployment to be successful; that is, the window of opportunity must be open long enough for it to be worthwhile.
- *Value creating.* The opportunity must be potentially profitable; that is, the benefits must surpass the cost of development by a significant margin.

If a new business concept meets these criteria, two other factors must be considered before the opportunity is launched as a business: the resources available to undertake it, and the characteristics of the entrepreneur(s) pursuing it. In the next section, we address the issue of entrepreneurial resources; following that, we address the importance of entrepreneurial leaders and teams. But first, consider the opportunities that have been created by the recent surge in interest in environmental sustainability. Strategy Spotlight 8.3 discusses how several eco-entrepreneurs built businesses by creating products from recycled waste.

From Pioneers to Billionaires: Internet Entrepreneurs Who Recognized Winning Opportunities

When founding a business, there is always a moment when the opportunity is first recognized. The recognition may unfold in tiny steps over time or appear suddenly as an Aha! experience. When pioneering entrepreneurs act on such realizations, they change the world for the rest of us. Here are three examples of pioneers who recognized how to use the transforming technology of the Internet to create new competitive advantages and make themselves billionaires (net worth figures as of September 2008).

Pierre Omidyar, Founder of eBay.com (Net Worth: $7.7 Billion)

Most everyone has heard of eBay—it is an icon of the Internet era. The online auction model it championed made it possible for hobbyists, collectors, and seekers of highly specialized products to participate 24/7 in an enormous global "flea market." It is one of the best examples of a business that just was not possible before the Web made it so. As well-known as eBay is, its origins are a bit more murky. Legend has it that founder Pierre Omidyar launched the auction site to help his fiancée sell and find pieces for her Pez-dispenser collection. These humble beginnings, however, were contrived by a public relations manager to attract media attention. In fact, the first thing sold on eBay was a broken laser pointer for $14.83. Omidyar, incredulous, asked the winning buyer if he knew it was broken. The email reply, "I collect broken laser pointers," helped Omidyar recognize he had tapped into a gold mine of business potential. By 2008, eBay had over 15,000 employees and annual revenues of $84.6 billion.

Mark Zuckerberg, Founder of Facebook.com (Net Worth: $1.7 Billion)

It's not clear that Mark Zuckerberg knew what he was onto when he and two friends launched Facebook in a Harvard dorm room in February 2004. But they found out pretty quickly: by the end of the month, over half of Harvard's undergraduates had registered on the service. In April, the site was opened up to another 30 universities, and by June, Zuckerberg had quit Harvard and moved to Palo Alto, California, where venture capitalist Peter Thiel recognized the potential and gave him $500,000 to take Facebook to the next level. It's been anything but level since then. Facebook took off and now has over 140 million users, making it the largest social networking website. In 2007, as investors were clamoring to get in on the action, Microsoft paid $246 million for a 1.6% stake. Facebook was still not profitable by the end of 2008, but Zuckerberg is worth a lot—at 24, he became the youngest person ever to make the Forbes billionaire list.

Marc Benioff, Founder of Salesforce.com (Net Worth: $1.2 Billion)

Managing customer relationships is important for all businesses, large and small. As information technology made it possible to automate thousands of customer accounts electronically, however, customer relationship management (CRM) systems became so complex that only very large companies could afford them. The typical corporate system included customized software, costly installations, and ongoing maintenance fees that shut out most small businesses. Benioff, who had worked for *(continued)*

Sources: Farrell, A. 2008. The Web Billionaires. www.forbes.com, September 8, np.; www.ebay.com; www.facebook.com; www.salesforce.com; and www.wikipedia.com.

● Mark Zuckerberg founded Facebook.com—and became a billionaire at the age of 24!

(continued) Oracle, a major supplier of CRM systems, realized he could use the Internet to provide a simpler and substantially cheaper product online. The earliest customers for Salesforce.com, founded in 1999, were small businesses that paid as little as $50 per month. His early successes made it possible for Benioff to improve his online capabilities, and eventually he landed big customers such as Cisco and Staples. When the company went public in 2004, it was already a market leader in CRM and claimed "CRM" as its New York Stock Exchange stock symbol.

Entrepreneurial Resources

As Exhibit 8.3 indicates, resources are an essential component of a successful entrepreneurial launch. For start-ups, the most important resource is usually money because a new firm typically has to expend substantial sums just to start the business. However, financial resources are not the only kind of resource a new venture needs. Human capital and social capital are also important. Many firms also rely on government resources to help them thrive.[11]

Financial Resources   Hand-in-hand with the importance of markets (and marketing) to new-venture creation, entrepreneurial firms must also have financing. In fact, the level of available financing is often a strong determinant of how the business is launched and its eventual success. Cash finances are, of course, highly important. But access to capital, such as a line of credit or favorable payment terms with a supplier, can also help a new venture succeed.

The types of financial resources that may be needed depend on two factors: the stage of venture development and the scale of the venture.[12] Entrepreneurial firms that are starting from scratch—start-ups—are at the earliest stage of development. Most start-ups also begin on a relatively small scale. The funding available to young and small firms tends to be quite limited. In fact, the majority of new firms are low-budget start-ups launched with personal savings and the contributions of family and friends.[13] Among firms included in the *Entrepreneur* list of the 100 fastest-growing new businesses in a recent year, 61 percent reported that their start-up funds came from personal savings.[14]

Although bank financing, public financing, and venture capital are important sources of small business finance, these types of financial support are typically available only after a company has started to conduct business and generate sales. Even "angel" investors—private individuals who provide equity investments for seed capital during the early stages of a new venture—favor companies that already have a winning business model and dominance in a market niche.[15] According to Cal Simmons, coauthor of *Every Business Needs an Angel,* "I would much rather talk to an entrepreneur who has already put his money and his effort into proving the concept."[16] Strategy Spotlight 8.4 describes one of the newest forms of financing for young and small businesses—an Internet-based phenomenon known as peer-to-peer lending.

Once a venture has established itself as a going concern, other sources of financing become readily available. Banks, for example, are more likely to provide later-stage financing to companies with a track record of sales or other cash-generating activity. Start-ups that involve large capital investments or extensive development costs—such as manufacturing or engineering firms trying to commercialize an innovative product—may have high cash requirements soon after they are founded. Others need financing only when they are on the brink of rapid growth. To obtain such funding, entrepreneurial firms often seek venture capital.

Venture capital is a form of private equity financing through which entrepreneurs raise money by selling shares in the new venture. In contrast to angel investors, who invest their own money, venture capital companies are organized to place the funds of private investors into lucrative business opportunities. Venture capitalists nearly always have high performance expectations from the companies they invest in, but they also provide important managerial advice, and links to key contacts in an industry.[17]

Eco-Entrepreneurs: Creating New Profits from Recycled Products

The "Go Green" movement is rich with business opportunities. One of the most appealing venture ideas is making new products from recycled or waste materials. Ever wonder what happens to the cans, paper, and plastic that goes into your recycling bins? Those and other waste materials are being used to create hundreds of products by eco-entrepreneurs (or "ecopreneurs") intent on making a profit as well as contributing to a more environmentally sustainable planet. Exhibit 8.4 includes examples of several such companies.

All of the companies listed in Exhibit 8.4 are approved by the U.S. Environmental Protection Agency (EPA) to supply recycled-content products. The Resource Conservation and Recovery Act requires federal and federally funded

state and local agencies to use recycled products. To enact this law, the EPA created the Affirmative Procurement Program to designate products—everything from office supplies to roofing materials to engine coolants—made out of materials recovered from waste. Most of the suppliers of these products are entrepreneurial businesses, including minority- and women-owned businesses.

Small businesses are not the only ones launching recycling initiatives. Virgin Atlantic, a member of Virgin Group, recently donated used fabric left over from retrofitting aircraft to Worn Again, a London-based design firm that makes accessories from recycled materials. Safety belts and seat covers have been turned into handbags, carryalls, and toiletry cases that sell from $40 to $105. According to Lysette Gauna, Virgin Atlantic's Creative Director, "Virgin Atlantic is committed to taking practical steps to make its business as sustainable as possible." The Worn Again accessories are "a fun and creative way to recycle our waste," says Gauna, "as well as giving people the chance to own a little piece of Virgin Atlantic history."

Sources: 2008. Virgin Atlantic Launch Worn Again Recycled Airline Seat Bags. www.terracurve.com, September 2; np.; Capell, K. 2008. The Movies and Oxygen Cost Extra. *BusinessWeek,* November 6: 15; Rechelbacher, H. 2008. *Minding Your Business: Profits That Restore the Planet.* San Rafael, CA: Earth Aware Editions; Schaper, M. 2005. *Making ecopreneurs: Developing sustainable entrepreneurship.* Surrey, UK: Ashgate Publishing; and www.epa.gov.

environmental sustainability

Company Name	What They Recycle	What They Make from It
BigToys Inc.	Milk jugs	Playground equipment
Future Solutions, Inc.	Blue jeans and old U.S. currency	Pencils
Rubber Flooring, Inc.	Tires	Kitchen mats and garage flooring
Weisenbach Specialty Printing & Manufacturing	Jars and old windows	Glass awards and vases

Sources: www.bigtoys.com; www.epa.gov; www.futuresolutionsinc.com; www.recycledproducts.com; and www.rubberflooringinc.com.

Exhibit 8.4   Eco-Entrepreneurs Approved by the U. S. Environmental Protection Agency

Despite the importance of venture capital to many fast-growing firms, the majority of external funding for young and small firms comes from informal sources such as family and friends. Exhibit 8.5, based on the *Global Entrepreneurship Monitor* survey of entrepreneurial firms, demonstrates this dramatic difference. A closer look reveals an interesting fact: Firms that obtain venture capital receive funding of about $2.6 million each. In contrast, companies that obtain funding from informal sources typically receive only about $10,000 each. Although relatively few companies receive venture funding, they are attractive to venture capitalists because their profit potential and impact on innovation, job growth, and wealth creation tends to be much greater. Clearly, financial resources are essential for entrepreneurial ventures.[18]

Peer-to-Peer Lending Boosts Entrepreneurs Chances

For start-up entrepreneurs, sometimes only a very small amount of money is needed to launch their ventures. Still, entrepreneurs who lack personal resources or access to funding often find it difficult to get their enterprises started. A new Internet phenomenon has recently emerged that is helping to change that: peer-to-peer lending. Also referred to as social lending, peer-to-peer (P2P) lending is seen as part of the social networking phenomenon that has been enabled by the Web 2.0 technologies that make it possible to interact directly, person to person.

Entrepreneurs who lack collateral but have viable business plans are increasingly turning to P2P solutions. For example, when Lyn Townshend, inventor of the Strock™, a sock-strap combination designed to keep pets from licking and chewing on wounded paws, won the endorsement of a veterinary hospital that is part of a 600-member chain, she needed a loan to ramp-up production. She had quit her job at IBM to start the business and had no income, so the local banks turned her down. Instead, she posted her loan request online and within a few weeks she landed a loan of $9,500 at a 12.75 percent interest rate. She used the funds to trademark her product, buy office equipment, and arrange for production at a nearby factory.

Although each P2P website uses a slightly different approach (see examples below), the basic model for P2P lending is as follows: Borrowers seeking loans post descriptions of their business concepts including the amounts they are attempting to borrow and personal information, including their credit rating. The other participants are lenders—individuals who are looking for opportunities to invest their money for a reasonable return. Lenders review various business proposals and evaluate the borrowers' backgrounds. If interested, they participate in an auctionlike process; the lenders who agree to the lowest interest rates "win" the borrower's loan. The various websites serve as the intermediaries by processing the loans and making payment arrangements. Because the loans are unsecured and the websites make no guarantees, lenders are encouraged to spread their funds around. "We tell people to buy little pieces of a lot of loans," says Ben Decio, president of GlobeFunder.com. Israel Gross, a 24-year-old Wrigley Field beer vendor and University of Chicago graduate student, says, "I have 89 loans out right now. It's small amounts to a lot of people. It's a positive way to make money."

The following Web-based enterprises offer peer-to-peer lending:

- **Lending Club**—A P2P lender that emphasizes borrower-lender interaction and community participation, it helps multiple lenders find opportunities to fund specific borrowers by issuing promissary notes that correspond to specific borrower loans.

- **Zopa**—A UK-based company that calls itself "the world's first social financing company," Zopa has positioned itself as the "anti-bank." Unlike most other P2P lenders, however, it offers CDs and savings accounts.

- **Kiva.org**—One of the first P2P lenders, it operates internationally and focuses on microlending to entrepreneurs in developing countries.

- **Fynanz**—Rather than focusing on start-ups, Fynanz is dedicated solely to student loans. Student borrowers post not only their credit ratings online but also their academic accomplishments and background.

Despite its growing popularity, Gartner bank analyst Avivah Litan is skeptical of P2P lending, in part because it is so new. Although she agrees that it is promising, Litan says, "I think it's too risky. There's no underwriting and no guarantees. It's all based on trust." But trust is part of what makes the social networking aspect of the system work. "That's when the community comes into play," says Rice University Associate Professor Paul Dholakia, an expert in online community participation. "The lenders are basically the policemen and women of the website. They have a lot of discussions. Borrowers have to spend a lot of time and effort in convincing the lenders and creating trust. . . . The community must substitute for the reputation mechanism."

Although P2P lending faces a number of challenges before it becomes a widespread practice, it is indicative of the type of opportunities that social networking has created for credit-strapped small businesses and aspiring entrepreneurs.

Sources: Bandyk, M. 2008. Is Peer-to-Peer Lending a Solution for Start-Ups? Q&A with Paul Dholakia of Rice University. www.usnews.com, July 8: np.; Benderoff, E. 2007. Financing Tool Follows Social Networking: Peer-to-Peer Lending Catching on with Investors, Borrowers. www.chicagotribune.com, October 5, np.; Lee-St. John, J. 2008. Hey, Buddy, Can You Spare $10,000? www.time.com, February 29, np.; www.fynanz.com; www.kiva.org; www.lendingclub.com; www.wikipedia.org; and www.zopa.com.

crowdsourcing

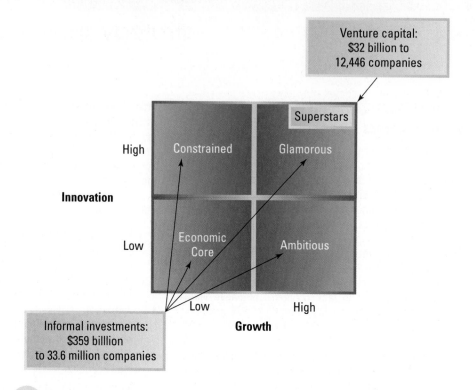

Venture capital:
$32 billion to
12,446 companies

Superstars

High | Constrained | Glamorous

Innovation

Low | Economic Core | Ambitious

Low | High

Growth

Informal investments:
$359 billlion
to 33.6 million companies

Exhibit 8.5 How Different Types of New Ventures Are Financed: Informal Investment versus Venture Capital

Source: Reynolds, P. D., Bygrave, W. D., & Autio, E. 2004. *Global Entrepreneurship Monitor: 2003 Executive Report.* Babson College, London Business School, and the Kauffman Foundation. The classification of the company system used by GEM is based on Kirchhoff, B. 1994. *Entrepreneurship and Dynamic Capitalism.* London: Praeger.

Human Capital   Bankers, venture capitalists, and angel investors agree that the most important asset an entrepreneurial firm can have is strong and skilled management. According to Stephen Gaal, founding member of Walnut Venture Associates, venture investors do not invest in businesses; instead "We invest in people . . . very smart people with very high integrity." Managers need to have a strong base of experience and extensive domain knowledge, as well as an ability to make rapid decisions and change direction as shifting circumstances may require. In the case of start-ups, more is better. New ventures that are started by teams of three, four, or five entrepreneurs are more likely to succeed in the long run than are ventures launched by "lone wolf" entrepreneurs.[19]

Developing a strong team can be a challenge for early-stage entrepreneurial ventures. Cash-strapped founders may find it difficult to find and afford the kind of talent needed to make their start-ups successful. Strategy Spotlight 8.5 describes one source of human capital that not only can provide qualified executives but can also save young ventures' money.

Social Capital   New ventures founded by entrepreneurs who have extensive social contacts are more likely to succeed than are ventures started without the support of a social network.[20] Even though a venture may be new, if the founders have contacts who will vouch for them, they gain exposure and build legitimacy faster.[21] This support can come from several sources: prior jobs, industry organizations, and local business groups such as the chamber of commerce. These contacts can all contribute to a growing network that provides support for the entrepreneurial firm. Janina Pawlowski,

Mommy SWAT Teams

For many entrepreneurial start-ups, experienced and professional help is often hard to find and even harder to afford. Bootstrapping founders are sometimes advised to forget about hiring the best talent and go for the available and affordable instead. But sometimes that solution just won't work—the success of a fledgling start-up may depend on having skilled decision makers involved at critical stages in the venture's development. What's an entrepreneur to do?

Enter Mommy SWAT teams, that is, "smart women with available time." Highly educated and experienced women who have elected to stay home with children can be a valuable resource. It's a win–win situation: employers get top talent at a bargain price and the women get

a chance to update their skills and enjoy a professional challenge.

Consider the example of TangentWorks, a three-employee Web project-integration start-up that needed a business plan. Through informal networking, it was able to identify two highly qualified stay-at-home moms and hire them for a tenth of their former salaries. For TangentWorks, "it was like having a C-level team"—chief financial and marketing officers—"without the salaries," according to CEO Zaina Ajakie.

Bootstrappers may not be the only employers that benefit from this trend. According to Mary Naylor, CEO of VIP Desk, a customer service company that hires stay-at-home moms to provide virtual call center and concierge services, "The work-at-home industry, fueled by well-educated, hard-working stay-at-home moms, is poised to boom given the current economic trends, where companies need flexible, cost-effective employee solutions."

Sources: Shellenbarger, S. 2008. How Stay-at-Home Moms Are Filling an Executive Niche. www.wsj.com, April 30: np.; and Steiner, L. M. 2008. SWAT Moms. voices.washingtonpost.com, May 7: np.

co-founder of the online lending company E-Loan, attributes part of her success to the strong advisors she persuaded to serve on her board of directors, including Tim Koogle, former CEO of Yahoo![22]

Strategic alliances represent a type of social capital that can be especially important to young and small firms.[23] Strategy Spotlight 8.6 presents a few examples of alliances and some potential pitfalls of using alliances.[24]

Government Resources In the U.S., the federal government provides support for entrepreneurial firms in two key arenas—financing and government contracting. The Small Business Administration (SBA) has several loan guarantee programs designed to support the growth and development of entrepreneurial firms. The government itself does not typically lend money but underwrites loans made by banks to small businesses, thus reducing the risk associated with lending to firms with unproven records. The SBA also offers training, counseling, and support services through its local offices and Small Business Development Centers.[25] State and local governments also have hundreds of programs to provide funding, contracts, and other support for new ventures and small businesses.

Another key area of support is in government contracting. Programs sponsored by the SBA and other government agencies ensure that small businesses have the opportunity to bid on contracts to provide goods and services to the government. For example, several of the entrepreneurial firms identified in Strategy Spotlight 8.3 were approved by the Environmental Protection Agency to help government agencies meet federally mandated requirements to use products made from recycled materials. Although working with the government sometimes has its drawbacks in terms of issues of regulation and time-consuming decision making, programs to support small businesses and entrepreneurial activity constitute an important resource for entrepreneurial firms.

Strategic Alliances: A Key Entrepreneurial Resource

Strategic alliances provide a key avenue for growth by entrepreneurial firms. By partnering with other companies, young or small firms can expand or give the appearance of entering numerous markets and/or handling a range of operations. Here are several types of alliances that have been used to extend or strengthen entrepreneurial firms:

Technology Alliances

Tech-savvy entrepreneurial firms often benefit from forming alliances with older incumbents. The alliance allows the larger firm to enhance its technological capabilities and expands the revenue and reach of the smaller firm.

Manufacturing Alliances

The use of outsourcing and other manufacturing alliances by small firms has grown dramatically in recent years. Internet-enabled capabilities such as collaborating online

Sources: Copeland, M. V. & Tilin, A. 2005. Get Someone to Build It. *Business 2.0*, 6(5): 88–90 Misner, I. 2008. Use Small Actions to Get Big Results. *Entrepreneur*. www.entrepreneur.com, December 3. Monahan, J. 2005. All Systems Grow. *Entrepreneur*, March: 78–82; Prince, C. J. 2005. Foreign Affairs. *Entrepreneur*, March: 56; and, Weaver, K. M. & Dickson, P. 2004. Strategic Alliances. In W. J. Dennis, Jr. (Ed.), *NFIB National Small Business Poll*. Washington, DC: National Federation of Independent Business.

about delivery and design specifications has greatly simplified doing business, even with foreign manufacturers.

Retail Alliances

Licensing agreements allow one company to sell the products and services of another in different markets, including overseas. Specialty products—the types sometimes made by entrepreneurial firms—often seem more exotic when sold in another country.

According to the National Federation of Independent Business (NFIB), nearly two-thirds of small businesses currently hold or have held some type of alliance. Strategic alliances among entrepreneurial firms can take many different forms. Exhibit 8.6 shows the different types of partnering that small businesses and small manufacturers in the NFIB study often use.

Although such alliances often sound good, there are also potential pitfalls. Lack of oversight and control is one danger of partnering with foreign firms. Problems with product quality, timely delivery, and receiving payments can also sour an alliance relationship if it is not carefully managed. With technology alliances, there is a risk that big firms may take advantage of the technological know-how of their entrepreneurial partners. However, even with these potential problems, strategic alliances provide a good means for entrepreneurial firms to develop and grow.

Type of Alliance and/or Long-Term Agreement*	Small Manufacturers	Small Businesses
Licensing	20.0%	32.5%
Export/Import	14.4%	7.3%
Franchise	5.0%	5.3%
Marketing	18.0%	25.2%
Distribution	20.1%	20.5%
Production	26.5%	11.3%
Product/Services R&D	12.2%	12.6%
Process R&D	6.7%	5.3%
Purchaser/Supplier	23.5%	13.9%
Outside Contracting	23.2%	28.5%

Source: From Weaver, K. M. & Dickson, P. 2004. Strategic Alliances. In W. J. Dennis, Jr. (Ed.), *NFIB National Small Business Poll*. Washington, DC: National Federation of Independent Business. Reprinted with permission.

*Columns add to over 100 percent because firms may use multiple alliances.

Exhibit 8.6   Use of Strategic Alliances by Small Businesses and Small Manufacturers

Entrepreneurial Leadership

Whether a venture is launched by an individual entrepreneur or an entrepreneurial team, effective leadership is needed. Launching a new venture requires a special kind of leadership. It involves courage, belief in one's convictions, and the energy to work hard even in difficult circumstances. Yet these are the very challenges that motivate most business owners. Entrepreneurs put themselves to the test and get their satisfaction from acting independently, overcoming obstacles, and thriving financially. To do so, they must embody three characteristics of leadership—vision, dedication and drive, and commitment to excellence—and pass these on to all those who work with them:

- *Vision.* This may be an entrepreneur's most important asset. Entrepreneurs envision realities that do not yet exist. But without a vision, most entrepreneurs would never even get their venture off the ground. With vision, entrepreneurs are able to exercise a kind of transformational leadership that creates something new and, in some way, changes the world. Just having a vision, however, is not enough. To develop support, get financial backing, and attract employees, entrepreneurial leaders must share their vision with others.
- *Dedication and drive.* Dedication and drive are reflected in hard work. Drive involves internal motivation; dedication calls for an intellectual commitment that keeps an entrepreneur going even in the face of bad news or poor luck. They both require patience, stamina, and a willingness to work long hours. However, a business built on the heroic efforts of one person may suffer in the long run. That's why the dedicated entrepreneur's enthusiasm is also important—like a magnet, it attracts others to the business to help with the work.[26]
- *Commitment to excellence.* Excellence requires entrepreneurs to commit to knowing the customer, providing quality goods and services, paying attention to details, and continuously learning. Entrepreneurs who achieve excellence are sensitive to how these factors work together. However, entrepreneurs may flounder if they think they are the only ones who can create excellent results. The most successful, by contrast, often report that they owe their success to hiring people smarter than themselves.

In his book *Good to Great,* Jim Collins makes another important point about entrepreneurial leadership: Ventures built on the charisma of a single person may have trouble growing "from good to great" once that person leaves.[27] Thus, the leadership that is needed to build a great organization is usually exercised by a team of dedicated people working together rather than a single leader. Another aspect of this team approach is attracting team members who fit with the company's culture, goals, and work ethic. "Those people who do not share the company's core values," Collins says, "find themselves surrounded by corporate antibodies and ejected like a virus."[28] Thus, for a venture's leadership to be a valuable resource and not a liability it must be cohesive in its vision, drive and dedication, and commitment to excellence.

Once an opportunity has been recognized, and an entrepreneurial team and resources have been assembled, a new venture must craft a strategy. Prior chapters have addressed the strategies of incumbent firms. In the next section, we highlight the types of strategies and strategic considerations faced by new entrants.

Entrepreneurial Strategy

Successfully creating new ventures requires several ingredients. As indicated in Exhibit 8.2, three factors are necessary—a viable opportunity, sufficient resources, and a skilled and dedicated entrepreneur or entrepreneurial team. Once these elements are in place, the new venture needs a strategy. In this section, we consider several different strategic factors that are unique to new ventures and also how the generic strategies introduced in Chapter 5 can

entrepreneurial strategy a strategy that enables a skilled and dedicated entrepreneur, with a viable opportunity and access to sufficient resources, to successfully launch a new venture.

be applied to entrepreneurial firms. We also indicate how combination strategies might benefit entrepreneurial firms and address the potential pitfalls associated with launching new venture strategies.

To be successful, new ventures must evaluate industry conditions, the competitive environment, and market opportunities in order to position themselves strategically. However, a traditional strategic analysis may have to be altered somewhat to fit the entrepreneurial situation. For example, five-forces analysis (as discussed in Chapter 2) is typically used by established firms. It can also be applied to the analysis of new ventures to assess the impact of industry and competitive forces. But you may ask: How does a new entrant evaluate the threat of other new entrants?

First, the new entrant needs to examine barriers to entry. If the barriers are too high, the potential entrant may decide not to enter or to gather more resources before attempting to do so. Compared to an older firm with an established reputation and available resources, the barriers to entry may be insurmountable for an entrepreneurial start-up. Therefore, understanding the force of these barriers is critical in making a decision to launch.

A second factor that may be especially important to a young venture is the threat of retaliation by incumbents. In many cases, entrepreneurial ventures *are* the new entrants that pose a threat to incumbent firms. Therefore, in applying the five-forces model to new ventures, the threat of retaliation by established firms needs to be considered.

Part of any decision about what opportunity to pursue is a consideration of how a new entrant will actually enter a new market. The concept of entry strategies provides a useful means of addressing the types of choices that new ventures have.

Entry Strategies

>LO3

Three types of entry strategies— pioneering, imitative, and adaptive— commonly used to launch a new venture.

One of the most challenging aspects of launching a new venture is finding a way to begin doing business that quickly generates cash flow, builds credibility, attracts good employees, and overcomes the liability of newness. The idea of an entry strategy or "entry wedge" describes several approaches that firms may take to get a foothold in a market.[29] Several factors will affect this decision.

- Is the product/service high-tech or low-tech?
- What resources are available for the initial launch?
- What are the industry and competitive conditions?
- What is the overall market potential?
- Does the venture founder prefer to control the business or to grow it?

In some respects, any type of entry into a market for the first time may be considered entrepreneurial. But the entry strategy will vary depending on how risky and innovative the new business concept is.[30] New-entry strategies typically fall into one of three categories— pioneering new entry, imitative new entry, or adaptive new entry.

Pioneering New Entry   New entrants with a radical new product or highly innovative service may change the way business is conducted in an industry. This kind of breakthrough—creating new ways to solve old problems or meeting customers' needs in a unique new way—is referred to as a **pioneering new entry.** If the product or service is unique enough, a pioneering new entrant may actually have little direct competition. The first personal computer was a pioneering product; there had never been anything quite like it and it revolutionized computing. The first Internet browser provided a type of pioneering service. These breakthroughs created whole new industries and changed the competitive landscape. And breakthrough innovations continue to inspire pioneering entrepreneurial efforts. Strategy Spotlight 8.7 discusses SkyTower Telecommunications, an entrepreneurial venture with a pioneering solution to the problem of overcrowding on wireless transmission towers.

pioneering new entry a firm's entry into an industry with a radical new product or highly innovative service that changes the way business is conducted.

SkyTower Telecommunications' Pioneering Technology

With current technology, wireless communications systems have only three ways to get to your cell phone or computer—radio towers that are often not tall enough and are increasingly overcrowded, satellites that cost $50 to $400 million to launch, and short-range Wi-Fi transmitters. SkyTower proposes a fourth alternative: unmanned, solar-powered airplanes that look like flying wings and send out Internet, mobile phone, and high-definition TV signals.

The planes have already been successfully tested over Hawaii. They are able to fly at an altitude of 12 miles in a tight 2,000-foot-wide circle for six months at a time without landing. Designed as private communication systems for both businesses and consumers, they are able to deliver Internet service for about a third of the cost of DSL or cable.

SkyTower has already received the backing of NASA and $80 million in investment capital. Its target customers are major Internet Service Providers (ISPs). The plan is not without problems, however. For one thing, the Federal Aviation Administration (FAA) currently prohibits the launch of unpiloted planes. Even so, SkyTower's flying wing satellite is a breakthrough technology that is hoping to take wireless communications to new heights and addresses the increasing demand for cost-effective wireless systems.

Sources: Frauenfelder, M. 2002. Look! Up in the Sky! It's a Flying Cell Phone Tower! *Business 2.0*, November: 108–112; and www.avinc.com.

The pitfalls associated with a pioneering new entry are numerous. For one thing, there is a strong risk that the product or service will not be accepted by consumers. The history of entrepreneurship is littered with new ideas that never got off the launching pad. Take, for example, Smell-O-Vision, an invention designed to pump odors into movie theatres from the projection room at preestablished moments in a film. It was tried only once (for the film *Scent of a Mystery*) before it was declared a major flop. Innovative? Definitely. But hardly a good idea at the time.[31]

A pioneering new entry is disruptive to the status quo of an industry. It is likely based on a technological breakthrough such as the one proposed by SkyTower. If it is successful, other competitors will rush in to copy it. This can create issues of sustainability for an entrepreneurial firm, especially if a larger company with greater resources introduces a similar product. For a new entrant to sustain its pioneering advantage, it may be necessary to protect its intellectual property, advertise heavily to build brand recognition, form alliances with businesses that will adopt its products or services, and offer exceptional customer service.

Imitative New Entry Whereas pioneers are often inventors or tinkerers with new technology, imitators usually have a strong marketing orientation. They look for opportunities to capitalize on proven market successes. An **imitative new entry** strategy is used by entrepreneurs who see products or business concepts that have been successful in one market niche or physical locale and introduce the same basic product or service in another segment of the market.

Sometimes the key to success with an imitative strategy is to fill a market space where the need had previously been filled inadequately. Entrepreneurs are also prompted to be imitators when they realize that they have the resources or skills to do a job better than an existing competitor. This can actually be a serious problem for entrepreneurial start-ups if the imitator is an established company. Consider the example of Hugger Mugger Yoga Products, a Salt Lake City producer of yoga apparel and equipment such as yoga mats for practitioners of the ancient exercise art, with annual sales of $7.5 million in a recent year.

imitative new entry a firm's entry into an industry with products or services that capitalize on proven market successes and that usually has a strong marketing orientation.

When founder Sara Chambers started the business in the mid-1980s, there was little competition. But once yoga went mainstream and became the subject of celebrity cover stories, other competitors saw an opportunity to imitate. Then Nike and Reebok jumped into the business with their own mats, clothes, and props. Hugger Mugger was a leading provider and had enjoyed 50 percent annual growth. But even after introducing a mass market line for department stores and hiring 50 independent sales reps, its growth rate has leveled off. Then, in 2005, it sued Gaiam, Inc., another maker of yoga gear, for using Hugger Mugger's trademark on search engines to mislead customers by diverting them to the Gaiam website.[32]

● Yoga's rising popularity has increased demand for related apparel and equipment. Both small players as well as multinational giants such as Nike and Reebok have entered the market.

Recall from Chapter 3 that the quality "difficult to imitate" was viewed as one of the keys to building sustainable advantages.[33] A strategy that can be imitated, therefore, seems like a poor way to build a business. In essence, this is true. But consider the example of a franchise. Clearly, franchising is built on the idea of copying what another business has already done. If a business format is so easy to imitate, can it possibly have any competitive advantages? In the minds of many consumers of franchise products and services, the advantage is *because of* imitation. That is, consumers have confidence in franchises because they are familiar with them. "As time has gone by, the public has come to embrace franchising because they're familiar with the successful franchises and brand," claims Tony DeSio, founder of Mail Boxes Etc. "They know that, from one location to another, they can rely on product consistency." Thus, imitation is one of the central reasons why franchises are successful.

Adaptive New Entry   Most new entrants use a strategy somewhere between "pure" imitation and "pure" pioneering. That is, they offer a product or service that is somewhat new and sufficiently different to create new value for customers and capture market share. Such firms are adaptive in the sense that they are aware of marketplace conditions and conceive entry strategies to capitalize on current trends.

According to business creativity coach Tom Monahan, "Every new idea is merely a spin of an old idea. [Knowing that] takes the pressure off from thinking [you] have to be totally creative. You don't. Sometimes it's one slight twist to an old idea that makes all the difference."[34] An **adaptive new entry** approach does not involve "reinventing the wheel," nor is it merely imitative either. It involves taking an existing idea and adapting it to a particular situation. Exhibit 8.7 presents examples of four young companies that successfully modified or adapted existing products to create new value.

adaptive new entry a firm's entry into an industry by offering a product or service that is somewhat new and sufficiently different to create value for customers by capitalizing on current market trends.

There are several pitfalls that might limit the success of an adaptive new entrant. First, the value proposition must be perceived as unique. Unless potential customers believe a new product or service does a superior job of meeting their needs, they will have little motivation to try it. Second, there is nothing to prevent a close competitor from mimicking the new firm's adaptation as a way to hold on to its customers. Third, once an adaptive entrant achieves initial success, the challenge is to keep the idea fresh. If the attractive features of the new business are copied, the entrepreneurial firm must find ways to adapt and improve the product or service offering.

Exhibit 8.7 **Examples of Adaptive New Entrants**

Company Name	Product	Adaptation	Result
Under Armour, Inc. Founded in 1995	Undershirts and other athletic gear	Used moisture-wicking fabric to create better gear for sweaty sports.	Under Armour has 1,400 employees and 2008 sales in excess of $700 million.
Mint.com Founded in 2005	Comprehensive online money management	Created software that tells users what they are spending by aggregating financial information from online bank and credit card accounts.	Mint has over 600,000 users and is tracking $50 billion in assets.
Plum Organics Founded in 2005	Organic frozen baby food	Made convenient line of frozen baby food using organic ingredients.	Added to Whole Foods product offering in 2006, Plum made $1 million in 2007.
Spanx Founded in 2000	Footless pantyhose and other undergarments for women	Combined nylon and Lycra® to create a new type of undergarment that is comfortable and eliminates panty lines.	5.4 million Spanx products have been sold since 2000.

Sources: Bryan, M. 2007. Spanx Me, Baby! www.observer.com, December 10, np.; Carey, J. 2006. Perspiration Inspiration. *Business Week,* June 5: 64; Palanjian, A. 2008. A Planner Plumbs for a Niche. www.wsj.com, September 30, np.; Worrell, D. 2008. Making Mint. *Entrepreneur,* September: 55; www.mint.com; www.spanx.com; and www.underarmour.com.

Considering these choices, an entrepreneur or entrepreneurial team might ask, Which new entry strategy is best? The choice depends on many competitive, financial, and marketplace considerations. Nevertheless, research indicates that the greatest opportunities may stem from being willing to enter new markets rather than seeking growth only in existing markets. A recent study found that companies that ventured into arenas that were new to the world or new to the company earned total profits of 61 percent. In contrast, companies that made only incremental improvements, such as extending an existing product line, grew total profits by only 39 percent.[35]

These findings led W. Chan Kim and Renee Mauborgne in their new book *Blue Ocean Strategy* to conclude that companies that are willing to venture into market spaces where there is little or no competition—labeled "blue oceans"—will outperform those firms that limit growth to incremental improvements in competitively crowded industries—labeled "red oceans." Companies that identify and pursue blue ocean strategies follow somewhat different rules than those that are "bloodied" by the competitive practices in red oceans. Consider the following elements of a blue ocean strategy:

- *Create uncontested market space.* By seeking opportunities where they are not threatened by existing competitors, blue ocean firms can focus on customers rather than on competition.
- *Make the competition irrelevant.* Rather than using the competition as a benchmark, blue ocean firms cross industry boundaries to offer new and different products and services.
- *Create and capture new demand.* Rather than fighting over existing demand, blue ocean companies seek opportunities in uncharted territory.

- **Break the value/cost trade-off.** Blue ocean firms reject the idea that a trade-off between value and cost is inevitable and instead seek opportunities in areas that benefit both their cost structure and their value proposition to customers.
- **Pursue differentiation and low cost simultaneously.** By integrating the range of a firm's utility, price, and cost activities, blue ocean companies align their whole system to create sustainable strategies.

The essence of blue ocean strategy is not just to find an uncontested market, but to create one. Some blue oceans arise because new technologies create new possibilities, such as eBay's online auction business. Yet technological innovation is not a defining feature of a blue ocean strategy. Most blue oceans are created from within red oceans by companies that push beyond the existing industry boundaries. Any of the new entry strategies described earlier could be used to pursue a blue ocean strategy. Consider the example of Cirque du Soleil, which created a new market for circus entertainment by making traditional circus acts more like theatrical productions:

> By altering the industry boundaries that traditionally defined the circus concept, Cirque du Soleil created a new type of circus experience. Since the days of Ringling Bros. and Barnum & Bailey, the circus had consisted of animal acts, star performers, and Bozo-like clowns. Cirque questioned this formula and researched what audiences really wanted. It found that interest in animal acts was declining, in part because of public concerns over the treatment of circus animals. Because managing animals—and the celebrity trainers who performed with them—was costly, Cirque eliminated them.
>
> Instead, Cirque focused on three elements of the traditional circus tent event that still captivated audiences: acrobatic acts, clowns, and the tent itself. Elegant acrobatics became a central feature of its performances, and clown humor became more sophisticated and less slapstick. Cirque also preserved the image of the tent by creating exotic facades that captured the symbolic elements of the traditional tent. Finally, rather than displaying three different acts simultaneously, as in the classic three-ring circus, Cirque offers multiple productions with theatrical story lines, giving audiences a reason to go to the circus more often. Each production has a different theme and its own original musical score.
>
> Cirque's efforts to redefine the circus concept have paid off. Since 1984, Cirque's productions have been seen by over 90 million people in some 200 cities around the world.[36]

Once created, a blue ocean strategy is difficult to imitate. If customers flock to blue ocean creators, firms rapidly achieve economies of scale, learning advantages, and synergies across their organizational systems. Body Shop, for example chartered new territory by refusing to focus solely on beauty products. Traditional competitors such as Estee Lauder and L'Oreal, whose brands are based on promises of eternal youth and beauty, found it difficult to imitate this approach without repudiating their current images.

These factors suggest that blue ocean strategies provide an avenue by which firms can pursue an entrepreneurial new entry. Such strategies are not without risks, however. A new entrant must decide not only the best way to enter into business but also what type of strategic positioning will work best as the business goes forward. Those strategic choices can be informed by the guidelines suggested for the generic strategies. We turn to that subject next.

Generic Strategies

>LO4

How the generic strategies of overall cost leadership, differentiation, and focus are used by new ventures and small businesses.

Typically, a new entrant begins with a single business model that is equivalent in scope to a business-level strategy (Chapter 5). In this section we address how overall low cost, differentiation, and focus strategies can be used to achieve competitive advantages.

Overall Cost Leadership   One of the ways entrepreneurial firms achieve success is by doing more with less. By holding down costs or making more efficient use of resources than larger competitors, new ventures are often able to offer lower prices and still be profitable. Thus, under the right circumstances, a low-cost leader strategy is a viable alternative for some new ventures. The way most companies achieve low-cost leadership, however, is typically different for young or small firms.

Recall from Chapter 5 that three of the features of a low-cost approach included operating at a large enough scale to spread costs over many units of production (economies of scale), making substantial capital investments in order to increase scale economies, and using knowledge gained from experience to make cost-saving improvements. These elements of a cost-leadership strategy may be unavailable to new ventures. Because new ventures are typically small, they usually don't have high economies of scale relative to competitors. Because they are usually cash strapped, they can't make large capital investments to increase their scale advantages. And because many are young, they often don't have a wealth of accumulated experience to draw on to achieve cost reductions.

Given these constraints, how can new ventures successfully deploy cost-leader strategies? Compared to large firms, new ventures often have simple organizational structures that make decision making both easier and faster. The smaller size also helps young firms change more quickly when upgrades in technology or feedback from the marketplace indicate that improvements are needed. They are also able to make decisions at the time they are founded that help them deal with the issue of controlling costs. For example, they may source materials from a supplier that provides them more cheaply or set up manufacturing facilities in another country where labor costs are especially low. Thus, new firms have several avenues for achieving low cost leadership. Strategy Spotlight 8.8 highlights the success of Vizio, Inc., a new entrant with an overall cost leadership strategy. Whatever methods young firms use to achieve a low-cost advantage, this has always been a way that entrepreneurial firms take business away from incumbents—by offering a comparable product or service at a lower price.

Differentiation   Both pioneering and adaptive entry strategies involve some degree of differentiation. That is, the new entry is based on being able to offer a differentiated value proposition. In the case of pioneers, the new venture is attempting to do something strikingly different, either by using a new technology or deploying resources in a way that radically alters the way business is conducted. Often, entrepreneurs do both.

Amazon founder Jeff Bezos set out to use Internet technology to revolutionize the way books are sold. He garnered the ire of other booksellers and the attention of the public by making bold claims about being the "earth's largest bookseller." As a bookseller, Bezos was not doing anything that had not been done before. But two key differentiating features—doing it on the Internet and offering extraordinary customer service—have made Amazon a differentiated success.

There are several factors that make it more difficult for new ventures to be successful as differentiators. For one thing, the strategy is generally thought to be expensive to enact. Differentiation is often associated with strong brand identity, and establishing a brand is usually considered to be expensive because of the cost of advertising and promotion, paid endorsements, exceptional customer service, etc. Differentiation successes are sometimes built on superior innovation or use of technology. These are also factors where it may be challenging for young firms to excel relative to established competitors.

Nevertheless all of these areas—innovation, technology, customer service, distinctive branding—are also arenas where new ventures have sometimes made a name for themselves even though they must operate with limited resources and experience. To be successful, according to Garry Ridge, CEO of the WD-40 Company, "You need to have a great product, make the end user aware of it, and make it easy to buy."[37] It sounds simple, but it is a difficult challenge for new ventures with differentiation strategies.

Low-Cost Imitator Vizio, Inc., Takes Off

The popularity of flat-panel TVs has grown rapidly since they were first introduced in the late 1990s—today, 34 percent of U.S households have one. When first introduced, major manufacturers such as Samsung, Sony, and Matsushita (maker of Panasonic) made heavy investments in R&D in a competition for technological leadership. As a result, the early flat-panel TVs were expensive. Even as technological advances drove prices down, the TVs were growing larger and flatter, and they continued to command premium prices. By 2002, 50-inch plasma TVs were still selling for $8,000–$10,000. But by then, panel technology had also become somewhat commoditized. That's when William Wang, a former marketer of computer monitors, realized he could use existing technologies to create a high quality TV. Wang discovered he could keep operations lean and outsource everything from tech support to R&D, so he founded Vizio, Inc.

In January 2003, Wang pitched Costco Wholesale Corp. on a 46-inch flat-panel plasma TV for $3,800—half

Sources: Lawton, C., Kane, Y.I., & Dean, J. 2008. U.S. Upstart Takes on TV Giants in Price War. www.wsj.com, April 15, np.; Taub, E. A. 2008. Flat-Panel TV Prices Plummet. www.nytimes.com, December 2, np.; Wilson, S. 2008. Picture It. *Entrepreneur*, July: 43; and www.wikipedia.com.

the price of the competition. Although Costco executives laughed when Wang said he wanted to become the next Sony, they decided to give him a chance. By March 2003, the TVs were being offered in over 300 of Costco's U.S. warehouse stores. Today, Vizio is one of Costco's largest suppliers of TVs.

Vizio's success is due not only to enlightened imitation and low-cost operations, but also to Wang's unique approach to financing growth. Although he initially mortgaged his home and borrowed from family and friends, when he needed additional funding, he targeted the manufacturing partners who were supplying him parts. In 2004, Taiwan-based contract manufacturer AmTran Technology Co. purchased an 8 percent stake in Vizio for $1 million; today, AmTran owns 23 percent of Vizio and supplies over 80 percent of its TVs. "Unlike many PC companies who try to make their money by squeezing the vendor," says Wang, "we try to work with our vendor."

Although Vizio has a long way to go to be the next Sony, it has made remarkable progress. Vizio shipped 12.4 percent of LCD TVs in North America in the last quarter of 2007. Sony's share was just 12.5 percent. Vizio expects year-end sales of $2.6 billion in 2008—not bad for a six-year-old company!

Focus Focus strategies are often associated with small businesses because there is a natural fit between the narrow scope of the strategy and the small size of the firm. A focus strategy may include elements of differentiation and overall cost leadership, as well as combinations of these approaches. But to be successful within a market niche, the key strategic requirement is to stay focused. Here's why:

Despite all the attention given to fast-growing new industries, most start-ups enter industries that are mature.[38] In mature industries, growth in demand tends to be slow and there are often many competitors. Therefore, if a start-up wants to get a piece of the action, it often has to take business away from an existing competitor. If a start-up enters a market with a broad or aggressive strategy, it is likely to evoke retaliation from a more powerful competitor. Young firms can often succeed best by finding a market niche where they can get a foothold and make small advances that erode the position of existing competitors.[39] From this position, they can build a name for themselves and grow.

Consider, for example, the "Miniature Editions" line of books launched by Running Press, a small Philadelphia publisher. The books are palm-sized minibooks positioned at bookstore cash registers as point-of-sale impulse items costing about $4.95. Beginning with just 10 titles in 1993, Running Press grew rapidly and within 10 years had sold over 20 million copies. Even though these books represent just a tiny fraction of total sales in the $23 billion publishing industry, they have been a mainstay for Running Press.[40]

Paradise 4 Paws: A Focused Differentiator

Pampering pets is big business—a $3 billion a year industry according to the American Pet Products Manufacturing Association. So it's no surprise that niche providers of differentiated services would continue to find opportunities in this arena. One such business grew out of an entrepreneurship class at Northwestern's Kellogg School of Management. Paradise 4 Paws operates an upscale 24/7 pet hotel with a dog-bone shaped swimming pool and webcams that allow owners to view their pets remotely.

Sources: Yu, R. 2008. Fancy New Airport Hotels Are Just for Fido and Fluffy. www.usatoday.com, March 11, np.; and Zhou, J. 2008. The Lap of Luxury. *BusinessWeek*, February 4: 18.

What makes this provider of luxury accommodations for cats and dogs different? It's located at Chicago's O'Hare International Airport so that busy travelers can drop their pets off on their way out of town rather than making an extra stop at a kennel. Paradise 4 Paws, which charges $75 per night for dogs and $35 for cats, provides a 22-spot parking lot from which its customers can take a shuttle directly to the terminal. The business is also good for O'Hare, which generates nonaviation revenues from the arrangement. "Given that more people have pets, it's just a natural progression of services that airports should offer," says P4P founder Saq Nadeem. With his backers, who include Kellogg's professors, Nadeem is making plans to open 10 more P4P locations.

As the Running Press example indicates, many new ventures are very successful even though their share of the market is quite small. Giant companies such as Procter & Gamble and Ford are often described in terms of their market share—that is, their share of sales in a whole market. But many of the industries that small firms participate in have thousands of participants that are not direct competitors. For example, auto repair shops in California don't compete with those in Michigan or Georgia. These industries are considered "fragmented" because no single company is strong enough to have power over other competitors. Small firms focus on the market share only in their trade area. This may be defined as a geographical area or a small segment of a larger product group.

Combination Strategies

One of the best ways for young and small businesses to achieve success is by pursuing combination strategies. By combining the best features of low-cost, differentiation, and focus strategies, new ventures can often achieve something truly distinctive.

Entrepreneurial firms are often in a strong position to offer a combination strategy because they have the flexibility to approach situations uniquely. For example, holding down expenses can be difficult for big firms because each layer of bureaucracy adds to the cost of doing business across the boundaries of a large organization.[41]

A similar argument could be made about entrepreneurial firms that differentiate. Large firms often find it difficult to offer highly specialized products or superior customer services. Entrepreneurial firms, by contrast, can often create high-value products and services through their unique differentiating efforts. Strategy Spotlight 8.9 shows how a group of entrepreneurship students took a specialized idea and built it into a differentiated success.

For nearly all new entrants, one of the major dangers is that a large firm with more resources will copy what they are doing. Well-established incumbents that observe the success of a new entrant's product or service will copy it and use their market power to overwhelm the smaller firm. The threat may be lessened for firms that use combination strategies. Because of the flexibility of entrepreneurial firms, they can often enact combination strategies in ways that the large firms cannot copy. This makes the new entrant's strategies much more sustainable.

>LO5

How competitive actions, such as the entry of new competitors into a marketplace, may launch a cycle of actions and reactions among close competitors.

competitive dynamics intense rivalry, involving actions and responses, among similar competitors vying for the same customers in a marketplace.

>LO6

The components of competitive dynamics analysis—new competitive action, threat analysis, motivation and capability to respond, types of competitive actions, and likelihood of competitive reaction.

Perhaps more threatening than large competitors are close competitors, because they have similar structural features that help them adjust quickly and be flexible in decision making. Here again, a carefully crafted and executed combination strategy may be the best way for an entrepreneurial firm to thrive in a competitive environment. Nevertheless, competition among rivals is a key determinant of new venture success. To address this, we turn next to the topic of competitive dynamics.

Competitive Dynamics

New entry into markets, whether by start-ups or by incumbent firms, nearly always threatens existing competitors. This is true in part because, except in very new markets, nearly every market need is already being met, either directly or indirectly, by existing firms. As a result, the competitive actions of a new entrant are very likely to provoke a competitive response from companies that feel threatened. This, in turn, is likely to evoke a reaction to the response. As a result, a competitive dynamic—action and response—begins among the firms competing for the same customers in a given marketplace.

Competitive dynamics—intense rivalry among similar competitors—has the potential to alter a company's strategy. New entrants, may be forced to change their strategies or develop new ones to survive competitive challenges by incumbent rivals. New entry is among the most common reasons why a cycle of competitive actions and reactions gets started. It might also occur because of threatening actions among existing competitors, such as aggressive cost cutting. Thus, studying competitive dynamics helps explain why strategies evolve and reveals how, why, and when to respond to the actions of close competitors. Exhibit 8.8 identifies the factors that competitors need to consider when determining how to respond to a competitive act.

New Competitive Action

Entry into a market by a new competitor is a good starting point to begin describing the cycle of actions and responses characteristic of a competitive dynamic process.[42] However, new entry is only one type of competitive action. Price cutting, imitating successful products, or expanding production capacity are other examples of competitive acts that might provoke competitors to react.

Exhibit 8.8 **Model of Competitive Dynamics**

Sources: Adapted from Chen, M. J. 1996. Competitor Analysis and Interfirm Rivalry: Toward a Theoretical Integration. *Academy of Management Review,* 21(1): 100–134; Ketchen, D. J., Snow, C. C., & Hoover, V. L. 2004. Research on competitive dynamics: Recent Accomplishments and Future Challenges. *Journal of Management,* 30(6): 779–804; and Smith, K. G., Ferrier, W. J., & Grimm, C. M. 2001. King of the Hill: Dethroning the Industry Leader. *Academy of Management Executive,* 15(2): 59–70.

Why do companies launch new competitive actions? There are several reasons:

- Improve market position
- Capitalize on growing demand
- Expand production capacity
- Provide an innovative new solution
- Obtain first mover advantages

new competitive action acts that might provoke competitors to react, such as new market entry, price cutting, imitating successful products, and expanding production capacity.

Underlying all of these reasons is a desire to strengthen financial outcomes, capture some of the extraordinary profits that industry leaders enjoy, and grow the business. Some companies are also motivated to launch competitive challenges because they want to build their reputation for innovativeness or efficiency. For example, Southwest Airlines, once an upstart airline with only a few routes, has become phenomenally successful and an industry leader. For years it went virtually unchallenged. But Southwest's costs have crept up, and now start-up airlines such as JetBlue are challenging the industry leader with their own low-cost strategies.[43] This is indicative of the competitive dynamic cycle. As former Intel Chairman Andy Grove stated, "Business success contains the seeds of its own destruction. The more successful you are, the more people want a chunk of your business and then another chunk and then another until there is nothing left."[44]

When a company enters into a market for the first time, it is like an attack on existing competitors. As indicated earlier in the chapter, any of the entry strategies can be used to take competitive action. But competitive attacks come from many sources besides new entrants. Some of the most intense competition is among incumbent rivals intent on gaining strategic advantages. "Winners in business play rough and don't apologize for it," according to Boston Consulting Group authors George Stalk, Jr. and Rob Lachenauer in their book *Hardball: Are You Playing to Play or Playing to Win*.[45] Exhibit 8.9 outlines their five strategies.

The likelihood that a competitor will launch an attack depends on many factors. In the remaining sections, we discuss factors such as competitor analysis, market conditions, types of strategic actions, and the resource endowments and capabilities companies need to take competitive action.

Threat Analysis

Prior to actually observing a competitive action, companies may need to become aware of potential competitive threats. That is, companies need to have a keen sense of who their closest competitors are and the kinds of competitive actions they might be planning.[46] This may require some environmental scanning and monitoring of the sort described in Chapter 2. Awareness of the threats posed by industry rivals allows a firm to understand what type of competitive response, if any, may be necessary.

threat analysis a firm's awareness of its closest competitors and the kinds of competitive actions they might be planning.

For example, Netflix founder and CEO Reed Hastings has faced numerous competitive threats since launching the online movie rental company in 1997. According to Hastings, however, not all potential threats need to be taken seriously:

> We have to recognize that now there are tens and maybe hundreds of start-ups who think that they are going to eat Netflix's lunch. The challenge for a management team is to figure out which are real threats and which aren't. . . . It's conventional to say, "only the paranoid survive" but that's not true. The paranoid die because the paranoid take all threats as serious and get very distracted.
>
> There are markets that aren't going to get very big, and then there are markets that are going to get big, but they're not directly in our path. In the first camp we have small companies like Movielink—a well-run company but not an attractive model for consumers, sort of a $4-download to watch a movie. We correctly guessed when it launched four years ago that this was not a threat and didn't react to it.

Exhibit 8.9 Five "Hardball" Strategies

Strategy	Description	Examples
Devastate rivals' profit sanctuaries	Not all business segments generate the same level of profits for a company. Through focused attacks on a rival's most profitable segments, a company can generate maximum leverage with relatively smaller-scale attacks. Recognize, however, that companies closely guard the information needed to determine just what their profit sanctuaries are.	In 2005, Wal-Mart began offering low-priced extended warranties on home electronics after learning that its rivals such as Best Buy derived most of their profits from extended warranties.
Plagiarize with pride	Just because a close competitor comes up with an idea first does not mean it cannot be successfully imitated. Second movers, in fact, can see how customers respond, make improvements, and launch a better version without all the market development costs. Successful imitation is harder than it may appear and requires the imitating firm to keep its ego in check.	Blockbuster copied the online DVD rental strategy of its rival Netflix. Not only does Blockbuster continue to struggle even after this imitation, but also Netflix sued Blockbuster for patent violations.
Deceive the competition	A good gambit sends the competition off in the wrong direction. This may cause the rivals to miss strategic shifts, spend money pursuing dead ends, or slow their responses. Any of these outcomes support the deceiving firms' competitive advantage. Companies must be sure not to cross ethical lines during these actions.	Boeing spent several years touting its plans for a new high-speed airliner. After it became clear the customer valued efficiency over speed, Boeing quietly shifted its focus. When Boeing announced its new 7e7 (now 787) Dreamliner, its competitor, Airbus Industries, was surprised and caught without an adequate response, which helped the 787 set new sales records.
Unleash massive and overwhelming force	While many hardball strategies are subtle and indirect, this one is not. This is a full-frontal attack where a firm commits significant resources to a major campaign to weaken rivals' positions in certain markets. Firms must be sure they have the mass and stamina required to win before they declare war against a rival.	Southwest Airlines took on US Airways in Baltimore and drove US Airways' market share from over 50 percent to 10 percent. Southwest recently began flying to Philadelphia and Pittsburgh as well—additional key markets for US Airways.
Raise competitors' costs	If a company has superior insight into the complex cost and profit structure of the industry, it can compete in a way that steers its rivals into relatively higher cost/lower profit arenas. This strategy uses deception to make the rivals think they are winning, when in fact they are not. Again, companies using this strategy must be confident that they understand the industry better than their rivals.	Ecolab, a company that sells cleaning supplies to businesses, encouraged a leading competitor, Diversity, to adopt a strategy to go after the low-volume, high-margin customers. What Ecolab knew that Diversity didn't is that the high servicing costs involved with this segment make the segment unprofitable—a situation Ecolab assured by bidding high enough to lose the contracts to Diversity but low enough to ensure the business lost money for Diversity.

Sources: Berner, R. 2005. Watch Out, Best Buy and Circuit City. *BusinessWeek,* November 10; Halkias, M. 2006. Blockbuster Strikes Back at Netflix Suit. *Dallas Morning News,* June 14; McCartney, S. 2007. Southwest Makes Inroads at Hubs. *The Wall Street Journal,* May 1, page D3; Stalk, G. Jr. 2006. Curveball Strategies to Fool the Competition. *Harvard Business Review,* 84(9): 114–121; and Stalk, Jr., G. & Lachenauer, R. 2004. *Hardball: Are You Playing to Play or Playing to Win?* Cambridge, MA: Harvard Business School Press. Reprinted by permission of Harvard Business School Press from G. Stalk, Jr. and R. Lachenauer. Copyright 2004 by the Harvard Business School Publishing Corporation; all rights reserved.

"The other case I brought up is markets that are going to be very large markets, but we're just not the natural leader. Advertising supported online video, whether that's at CBS.com or You Tube—great market, kind of next door to us. But we don't do advertising-supported video, we do subscription, so it would be a huge competence expansion for us. And it's not a threat to movies."

Being aware of competitors and cognizant of whatever threats they might pose is the first step in assessing the level of competitive threat. Once a new competitive action becomes apparent, companies must determine how threatening it is to their business. Competitive dynamics are likely to be most intense among companies that are competing for the same customers or who have highly similar sets of resources.[47] Two factors are used to assess whether or not companies are close competitors:

- **Market commonality**—Whether or not competitors are vying for the same customers and how many markets they share in common. For example, aircraft manufacturers Boeing and Airbus have a high degree of market commonality because they make very similar products and have many buyers in common.
- **Resource similarity**—The degree to which rivals draw on the same types of resources to compete. For example, the home pages of Google and Yahoo! may look very different, but behind the scenes, they both rely on the talent pool of high-caliber software engineers to create the cutting-edge innovations that help them compete.

When any two firms have both a high degree of market commonality and highly similar resource bases, a stronger competitive threat is present. Such a threat, however, may not lead to competitive action. On the one hand, a market rival may be hesitant to attack a company that it shares a high degree of market commonality with because it could lead to an intense battle. On the other hand, once attacked, rivals with high market commonality will be much more motivated to launch a competitive response. This is especially true in cases where the shared market is an important part of a company's overall business.

How strong a response an attacked rival can mount will be determined by their strategic resource endowments. In general, the same set of conditions holds true with regard to resource similarity. Companies that have highly similar resource bases will be hesitant to launch an initial attack but pose a serious threat if required to mount a competitive response.[48] Greater strategic resources increase a firm's capability to respond. Strategy Spotlight 8.10 addresses how the dynamics of market commonality and resource similarity have shaped the battle between chipmakers Intel and AMD and intensified their competitive rivalry.

Motivation and Capability to Respond

Once attacked, competitors are faced with deciding how to respond. Before deciding, however, they need to evaluate not only how they will respond, but also their reasons for responding and their capability to respond. Companies need to be clear about what problems a competitive response is expected to address and what types of problems it might create.[49] There are several factors to consider.

First, how serious is the impact of the competitive attack to which they are responding? For example, a large company with a strong reputation that is challenged by a small or unknown company may elect to simply keep an eye on the new competitor rather than quickly react or overreact. Part of the story of online retailer Amazon's early success is attributed to Barnes & Noble's over-reaction to Amazon's claim that it was "earth's biggest bookstore." Because Barnes & Noble was already using the phrase "world's largest bookstore," it sued Amazon, but lost. The confrontation made it to the front pages of *The Wall Street Journal* and Amazon was on its way to becoming a household name.[50]

market commonality the extent to which competitors are vying for the same customers in the same markets.

resource similarity the extent to which rivals draw from the same types of strategic resources.

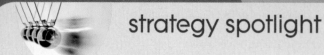

AMD and Intel: Related Rivals

Few business battles are as intensely reported as the one between chipmakers Intel and Advanced Micro Devices (AMD). For years, Intel aggressively advertised its brand by pushing its "Intel Inside" logo to average consumers. In an effort to develop a stronger presence among consumers, AMD launched a successful initiative labeled internally, "War in the Store" to promote sales of AMD-based computers in retailers such as Best Buy. The effort prompted a retaliation by Intel that lowered the cost of chips enough to decrease PC prices $200. Meanwhile, AMD won a recent round when Dell announced it would start using AMD chips in its servers.

Why is the battle between the two companies so intense? Because they are so much alike. Both companies were founded in the late 1960s in Silicon Valley and were partners during their early history. But in 1986, Intel cancelled a key licensing agreement with AMD to manufacture microprocessors and refused to turn over technical details. AMD sued and, after years of litigation, the Supreme Court of California forced Intel to pay AMD over $1 billion in compensation for violations of the contract. The two companies have been battling ever since.

Consider how comparable the two companies are in terms of markets and resources.

Market Commonality

A key issue facing the two chipmakers is that to continue growing, they have had to enter each other's market space.

Sources: Edwards, C. 2006. AMD: Chipping Away at Intel's Lead. *BusinessWeek*, June 12: 72–73; Edwards, C. 2006. Intel Sharpens Its Offensive Game. *BusinessWeek*, July 31: 60. Gonsalves, A. 2007. AMD Pays the Price in Awakening Intel Goliath. *InformationWeek*, www.informationweek.com, April 9; Gaudin, S. 2006. AMD Cracks Top 10 Chip Ranking, Intel Sales Slump. *InformationWeek*, www.informationweek.com, December 5; and www.wikipedia.org.

This is a major reason why the competition has become so heated. For example, Intel dominated that high-end server business in 2003. Now AMD holds 26 percent of the U.S. server chip business and supplies a 48 percent share of the multicore processors (which feature two or more chips on one slice of silicon). To maintain its status as the number one supplier, Intel launched a new family of processors called Core 2 Duo in 2007 that combines the performance of the Pentium 4 with the energy saving features of its notebook computer processors. "We intend to energetically compete for every single microprocessor opportunity," said Intel Executive Vice President Sean M. Maloney.

Resource Similarity

Intel is the world's number one supplier of semiconductors and is expected to have five manufacturing plants by the end of 2007. Because of new manufacturing techniques at three of its plants, it can squeeze more transistors onto a chip and its processors cost less to make than AMD's. By contrast, AMD has just two manufacturing plants but it has moved aggressively to match Intel's muscle. In 2005, it paid $5.4 billion to acquire graphics chipmaker ATI Technologies and has outsourced more manufacturing to Chartered Semiconductors. One result has been that AMD, now the number two maker of processors and graphic cards, increased semiconductor sales by 90 percent in 2006.

The battle between the two companies has been costly in recent years. When Intel retaliated for AMD's rapid gains, the result was slower sales for AMD and first quarter 2006 revenues of $1.23 billion rather than the $1.55 billion analysts expected. Meanwhile, Intel was hurt when Dell decided to begin installing AMD chips in its servers after years of using Intel exclusively. "The competitive dynamics have been more intense than we expected," commented Kevin B. Rollins, Dell's former CEO.

Companies planning to respond to a competitive challenge must also understand their motivation for responding. What is the intent of the competitive response? Is it merely to blunt the attack of the competitor or is it an opportunity to enhance its competitive position? Sometimes the most a company can hope for is to minimize the damage caused by a competitive action.

A company that seeks to improve its competitive advantage may be motivated to launch an attack rather than merely respond to one. For example, Wal-Mart is known for its aggressive efforts to live up to its "everyday low prices" corporate motto. Strategy Spotlight 8.11 describes the retailer's recent assault on rivals Circuit City and Best Buy. A company must also assess its capability to respond. What strategic resources can be deployed to fend off a competitive attack? Does the company have an array of internal strengths it can draw on, or is it operating from a position of weakness?

Wal-Mart's Cutthroat Pricing Schemes

Wal-Mart has a reputation as a relentless competitor in its pursuit of an overall cost leader strategy. Most of that reputation has come from its efforts to drive down costs in its dealings with suppliers. Wal-Mart sometimes goes on the offensive with rivals as well by driving down prices.

Recently, the retail giant took on Circuit City and Best Buy whom it competes with head-on in the consumer electronics market. First Wal-Mart made big improvements in the electronics departments of 1,300 of its 3,100 U.S. stores by spiffing-up displays and adding high-end products such as Apple iPods, Toshiba laptops, and Sony liquid-crystal-display televisions. Then it delivered the two rivals a proverbial one-two punch—offering low-cost extended warranties and slashing prices on flat-panel TVs.

- **Extended warranties.** These are the multiyear protection plans that salespeople offer at the close of a sale on items such as TVs and computers. For both Circuit City and Best Buy, they are one of the most profitable segments of their business, accounting for at least a third of their operating profits. In late 2005, Wal-Mart launched its own extended warranty program at prices nearly 50 percent lower than Best Buy and Circuit City.

- **Flat-panel TVs.** This includes both liquid crystal display and big-screen plasma models that, until the 2006 holiday season, had never sold below $1,000. Wal-Mart broke that barrier by offering a 42-inch flat-panel TV for $998. The cuts were not limited to lesser-known brands such as Viore TV. Wal-Mart also lowered the 42-inch Panasonic high-definition TV by $500 to $1,294. The response was immediate. Circuit City lowered the price on the same Panasonic TV to $1,299 and Best Buy began offering a 42-inch Westinghouse LCD for $999.

Circuit City was among the hardest hit by this cutthroat competition. After several attempts to cut costs and bolster revenues, it filed for bankruptcy in 2008 and was liquidated in 2009. Best Buy, the largest electronic retailer, did a better job of absorbing the shock. Still, its stock fell 9 percent during the first quarter of 2007. Other retailers were also hit hard by the audacious pricing that has been labeled the "Wal-Mart effect" including CompUSA, which is shuttering 126 of its 229 stores, and Tweeter's, which is closing 49 of its 153 stores and laying off 650 workers.

Sources: Boyle, M. & McConnon, A. 2008. Circuit City Files for Bankruptcy. www.businessweek.com, November 10: np. Berner, R. 2005. Watch Out, Best Buy and Circuit City. *BusinessWeek Online*, www.businessweek.com, November 10; and Gogoi, P. 2007. How Wal-Mart's TV Prices Crushed Rivals. *BusinessWeek*, www.businessweek.com, April 27.

Consider, the role of firm age and size in calculating a company's ability to respond. Most entrepreneurial new ventures start out small. The smaller size makes them more nimble compared to large firms so they can respond quickly to competitive attacks. Because they are not well-known, start-ups also have the advantage of the element of surprise in how and when they attack. Innovative uses of technology, for example, allow small firms to deploy resources in unique ways.

Because they are young, however, start-ups may not have the financial resources needed to follow through with a competitive response. In contrast, older and larger firms may have more resources and a repertoire of competitive techniques they can use in a counterattack. Large firms, however, tend to be slower to respond. Older firms tend to be predictable in their responses because they often lose touch with the competitive environment and rely on strategies and actions that have worked in the past.

Other resources may also play a role in whether a company is equipped to retaliate. For example, one avenue of counterattack may be launching product enhancements or new product/service innovations. For that approach to be successful, it requires a company to have both the intellectual capital to put forward viable innovations and the teamwork skills to prepare a new product or service and get it to market. Resources such as cross-functional teams and the social capital that makes teamwork production effective and efficient represent the type of human capital resources that enhance a company's capability to respond.

Exhibit 8.10   Strategic and Tactical Competitive Actions

	Actions	Examples
Strategic Actions	• Entering new markets	• Make geographical expansions • Expand into neglected markets • Target rivals' markets • Target new demographics
	• New product introductions	• Imitate rivals' products • Address gaps in quality • Leverage new technologies • Leverage brand name with related products • Protect innovation with patents
	• Changing production capacity	• Create overcapacity • Tie up raw materials sources • Tie up preferred suppliers and distributors • Stimulate demand by limiting capacity
	• Mergers/Alliances	• Acquire/partner with competitors to reduce competition • Tie up key suppliers through alliances • Obtain new technology/intellectual property • Facilitate new market entry
Tactical Actions	• Price cutting (or increases)	• Maintain low price dominance • Offer discounts and rebates • Offer incentives (e.g., frequent flyer miles) • Enhance offering to move upscale
	• Product/service enhancements	• Address gaps in service • Expand warranties • Make incremetal product improvements
	• Increased marketing efforts	• Use guerilla marketing • Conduct selective attacks • Change product packaging • Use new marketing channels
	• New distribution channels	• Access suppliers directly • Access customers directly • Develop multiple points of contact with customers • Expand Internet presence

Sources: Chen, M. J. & Hambrick, D. 1995. Speed, Stealth, and Selective Attack: How Small Firms Differ from Large Firms in Competitive Behavior. *Academy of Management Journal,* 38: 453–482; Davies, M. 1992. Sales Promotions as a Competitive Strategy. *Management Decision,* 30(7): 5–10; Ferrier, W., Smith, K., & Grimm, C. 1999. The Role of Competitive Action in Market Share Erosion and Industry Dethronement: A Study of Industry Leaders and Challengers. *Academy of Management Journal,* 42(4): 372–388; and Garda, R. A. 1991. Use Tactical Pricing to Uncover Hidden Profits. *Journal of Business Strategy,* 12(5): 17–23.

Types of Competitive Actions

Once an organization determines whether it is willing and able to launch a competitive action, it must determine what type of action is appropriate. The actions taken will be determined by both its resource capabilities and its motivation for responding. There are also marketplace considerations. What types of actions are likely to be most effective given a company's internal strengths and weaknesses as well as market conditions?

Two broadly defined types of competitive action include strategic actions and tactical actions. **Strategic actions** represent major commitments of distinctive and specific resources. Examples include launching a breakthrough innovation, building a new production facility, or merging with another company. Such actions require significant planning and resources and, once initiated, are difficult to reverse.

Tactical actions include refinements or extensions of strategies. Examples of tactical actions include cutting prices, improving gaps in service, or strengthening marketing efforts. Such actions typically draw on general resources and can be implemented quickly. Exhibit 8.10 identifies several types of strategic and tactical competitive actions.

Some competitive actions take the form of frontal assaults, that is, actions aimed directly at taking business from another company or capitalizing on industry weaknesses. This can be especially effective when firms use a low-cost strategy. The airline industry provides a good example of this head-on approach. When Southwest Airlines began its no-frills, no-meals, strategy in the late-1960s, it represented a direct assault on the major carriers of the day. In Europe, Ryanair has directly challenged the traditional carriers with an overall cost leadership strategy. Founded in 1985, Ryanair is one-seventh the size of British Airways in terms of revenues, but in 2006, due to cost-cutting measures that significantly improved operating margins, it had a higher market capitalization of $7.6 billion compared to BA's $7.3 billion.[51]

Guerilla offensives and selective attacks provide an alternative for firms with fewer resources.[52] These draw attention to products or services by creating buzz or generating enough shock value to get some free publicity. The open source software movement, which has been gaining momentum as major corporations become aware of its potential, still lacks the market power and omnipresence that software giant Microsoft enjoys.[53] Loyal users of open source software such as Linux stay connected and share software through online blogs. They also pull the occasional publicity stunt. Recently, users of Firefox, the open source browser developed by the Mozilla Corporation created a crop circle in Oregon based on the Firefox logo. The effort made the local news and garnered thousands of mentions on open source blogs and Internet news organizations.

Some companies limit their competitive response to defensive actions. Such actions rarely improve a company's competitive advantage, but a credible defensive action can lower the risk of being attacked and deter new entry. This may be especially effective during periods such as an industry shake-up, when pricing levels or future demand for a product line become highly uncertain. At such times, tactics such as lowering prices on products that are easily duplicated, buying up the available supply of goods or raw materials, or negotiating exclusive agreements with buyers and/or suppliers can insulate a company from a more serious attack.

Several of the factors discussed earlier in the chapter, such as types of entry strategies and the use of cost leadership versus differentiation strategies, can guide the decision about what types of competitive actions to take. Before launching a given strategy, however, assessing the likely response of competitors is a vital step.[54]

Likelihood of Competitive Reaction

The final step before initiating a competitive response is to evaluate what a competitor's reaction is likely to be. The logic of competitive dynamics suggests that once competitive actions are initiated, it is likely they will be met with competitive responses.[55] The last step before mounting an attack is to evaluate how competitors are likely to respond. Evaluating potential competitive reactions helps companies plan for future counterattacks. It may

strategic actions
major commitments of distinctive and specific resources to strategic initiatives.

tactical actions
refinements or extensions of strategies usually involving minor resource commitments.

also lead to a decision to hold off—that is, not to take any competitive action at all because of the possibility that a misguided or poorly planned response will generate a devastating competitive reaction.

How a competitor is likely to respond will depend on three factors: market dependence, competitor's resources, and the reputation of the firm that initiates the action (actor's reputation). The implications of each of these is described briefly in the following sections.

Market Dependence   If a company has a high concentration of its business in a particular industry, it has more at stake because it must depend on that industry's market for its sales. Single-industry businesses or those where one industry dominates are more likely to mount a competitive response. Young and small firms with a high degree of market dependence may be limited in how they respond due to resource constraints. JetBlue, itself an aggressive competitor, is unable to match some of the perks its bigger rivals can offer, such as first-class seats or international travel benefits.

Competitor's Resources   Previously, we examined the internal resource endowments that a company must evaluate when assessing its capability to respond. Here, it is the competitor's resources that need to be considered. For example, a small firm may be unable to mount a serious attack due to lack of resources. As a result, it is more likely to react to tactical actions such as incentive pricing or enhanced service offerings because they are less costly to attack than large-scale strategic actions. In contrast, a firm with financial "deep pockets" may be able to mount and sustain a costly counterattack. As a way to combat these differences in market power, young firms can strengthen their resource positions by forming strategic alliances. Yahoo!, for example, pressed hard by its young but powerful rival Google, allied itself with a group of seven newspaper chains that publish a total of 176 U.S. daily papers in a content sharing arrangement. Both Yahoo! and the newspaper chains are trying to stay ahead of Google now that it is moving aggressively beyond ads on its search pages.

Actor's Reputation   Whether a company should respond to a competitive challenge will also depend on who launched the attack against it. In previous examples, we have noted that companies such as Wal-Mart and Intel are capable of bold offenses. These competitive actors also have the ability and motivation to mount overwhelming counterattacks. Compared to relatively smaller firms with less market power, competitors are more likely to respond to competitive moves by market leaders. Another consideration is how successful prior attacks have been. For example, price-cutting by the big automakers usually has the desired result—increased sales to price-sensitive buyers—at least in the short run. Given that history, when GM offers discounts or incentives, rivals Ford and Chrysler cannot afford to ignore the challenge and quickly follow suit.

Choosing Not to React: Forbearance and Co-opetition

forbearance a firm's choice of not reacting to a rival's new competitive action.

The above discussion suggests that there may be many circumstances in which the best reaction is no reaction at all. This is known as **forbearance**—refraining from reacting at all as well as holding back from initiating an attack. For example, none of the Japanese automakers attempted to match the employee discount pricing war that cost the big U.S. automakers heavily in terms of lower profits and lost jobs. Yet, during the same period, Honda, Toyota and Nissan enjoyed substantial sales increases over the previous year. Strategy Spotlight 8.12 highlights another recent rivalry—the one between Facebook and MySpace.

co-opetition a firm's strategy of both cooperating and competing with rival firms.

Related to forbearance is the concept of **co-opetition.** This is a term that was coined by network software company Novell's founder and former CEO Raymond Noorda to suggest that companies often benefit most from a combination of competing and cooperating.[56] Close competitors that differentiate themselves in the eyes of consumers may work together behind the scenes to achieve industrywide efficiencies.[57] For example, breweries in Sweden cooperate in recycling used bottles but still compete for customers on the basis of

Facebook versus MySpace

Social networking is not just a fad anymore. It's a big business that has spawned dozens of entrepreneurial launches and captured millions of advertising dollars. Nothing illustrates this better than Rubert Murdoch's decision to pay $580 million to purchase MySpace and make it part of his News Corporation business empire (which includes Fox News and *The Wall Street Journal*). The success of MySpace, whose 2008 revenues are estimated to exceed $600 million, has attracted a host of new entrants angling to get in the social networking game. Among the most successful is Facebook, a comparable service whose number of users recently surpassed MySpace (see Exhibit 8.11).

Facebook and MySpace have a lot in common. They are both interactive, user-submitted networks of friends featuring profile pages, blogs, groups, photos, videos, and links for teenagers and adults. Both have an international following. There are also clear differences—for example, MySpace encourages users to customize their profiles, whereas Facebook allows only plain text; the entertainment-oriented MySpace is headquartered in Beverly Hills, whereas the tech-oriented Facebook is in Silicon Valley. Even so, 65 percent of Facebook users also have a MySpace account according to comScore, an Internet marketing research company. As such, the two companies are in a heated competition for the main thing that makes their business models work—advertising dollars.

Consider the actions and counter-actions the two companies have engaged in during their short histories:

- News Corp. signs a $900 million search and advertising deal with Google, enough to cover the purchase price of MySpace; Microsoft pays $246 million for a 1.6 percent stake in Facebook and assigns 400 salespeople to sell Facebook display ads.

- Facebook opens its platform to third-party developers and within a few months matches and then surpasses the features available on MySpace. A year later, MySpace opens its platform to third-party developers in an attempt to regain the edge.

- MySpace counters its entertainment-only image by opening an office in Silicon Valley with plans to hire hundreds of engineers; Facebook develops virtual gifts and interactive "engagement ads" to make the Facebook experience more entertaining.

Sources: Ante, S. E. 2008. Facebook's Land Grab in the Face of a Downturn. www.businessweek.com, November 20, np.; Kirkpatrick, D. 2007. As Facebook Takes Off, MySpace Strikes Back. www.fortune.com, September 19, np; and, Lacy, S. 2007. What MySpace-Facebook Rivalry? www.businessweek.com, October 19, np.; www.facebook.com; and www.myspace.com.

USERS VS. REVENUES

MySpace has more than twice the revenue of Facebook, but Facebook has surpassed its rival in number of users and is widening its lead

THOUSANDS OF GLOBAL USERS

- FACEBOOK
- MYSPACE

JAN. 07   SEPT. 08

Data: ComScore

Exhibit 8.11 **Competition between Rivals MySpace and Facebook**

Source: Ante, S. E. 2008. Facebook's Land Grab in the Face of a Downturn. www.businessweek.com, November 20, np.

- Facebook creates versions of its website in multiple languages, including Xhosa, Tagalog, and French Canadian to attract niche audiences around the world; MySpace launches a music service with free streaming music as well as downloads, ringtones, and concert tickets to boost growth in customers.

The two companies currently have different strategies—Facebook is dedicated to growing the number of users, while MySpace is concentrating on increasing profits. But both are keenly aware of the high-stakes game they are playing. Although Facebook is expected to have revenues of $300 million in 2008, it is not yet showing a profit. That's not a problem in the short run, according to Peter Thiel, a Facebook investor and board member. "If we stopped growing, we could make money," says Thiel, "but it makes no sense for us to stop growing. We still think it's a land grab where we have to try to get to scale first."

In contrast, MySpace is limiting its efforts to grow users and concentrating instead on profitability. Even so, the company clearly regards Facebook's recent growth surge a threat. According to MySpace president Tom Anderson, Facebook is a formidable rival. "It's the first time I feel like we have a real competitor," says Anderson. "It's a good thing overall, because if there was any complacency within the company, now there's someone you can look at and say, 'Hey, we've got to be better.'"

taste and variety. As long as the benefits of cooperating are enjoyed by all participants in a co-opetition system, the practice can aid companies in avoiding intense and damaging competition.[58]

Despite the potential benefits of co-opetition, companies need to guard against cooperating to such a great extent that their actions are perceived as collusion, a practice that has legal ramifications in the United States. Satellite radio competitors XM and Sirius, after years of intense rivalry, faced several challenges recently related to their efforts to merge their operations.

Once a company has evaluated a competitor's likelihood of responding to a competitive challenge, it can decide what type of action is most appropriate. Competitive actions can take many forms: the entry of a start-up into a market for the first time, an attack by a lower-ranked incumbent on an industry leader, or the launch of a breakthrough innovation that disrupts the industry structure. Such actions forever change the competitive dynamics of a marketplace. Thus, the cycle of actions and reactions that occur in business every day is a vital aspect of entrepreneurial strategy that leads to continual new value creation and the ongoing advancement of economic well-being.

Reflecting on Career Implications . . .

- *Opportunity Recognition:* What ideas for new business activities are actively discussed in your work environment? Could you apply the four characteristics of an opportunity to determine whether they are viable opportunities?
- *Entrepreneurial New Entry:* Are there opportunities to launch new products or services that might add value to the organization? What are the best ways for you to bring these opportunities to the attention of key managers? Or, might this provide an opportunity for you to launch your own entrepreneurial venture?
- *Entrepreneurial Strategy:* Does your organization face competition from new ventures? If so, how are those young firms competing: Low cost? Differentiation? Focus? What could you do to help your company to address those competitive challenges?
- *Competitive Dynamics:* Is your organization "on the offense" with its close competitors or "playing defense"? What types of strategic and/or tactical actions have been taken by your close rivals recently to gain competitive advantages?

Summary

New ventures and entrepreneurial firms that capitalize on marketplace opportunities make an important contribution to the U.S. economy. They are leaders in terms of implementing new technologies and introducing innovative products and services. Yet entrepreneurial firms face unique challenges if they are going to survive and grow.

To successfully launch new ventures or implement new technologies, three factors must be present: an entrepreneurial opportunity, the resources to pursue the opportunity, and an entrepreneur or entrepreneurial team willing and able to undertake the venture. Firms must develop a strong ability to recognize viable opportunities. Opportunity recognition is a process of determining which venture ideas are, in fact, promising business opportunities.

In addition to strong opportunities, entrepreneurial firms need resources and entrepreneurial leadership to thrive. The resources that start-ups need include finan-cial resources as well as human and social capital. Many firms also benefit from government programs that sup-port new venture development and growth. New ventures thrive best when they are led by founders or owners who have vision, drive and dedication, and a commitment to excellence.

Once the necessary opportunities, resources, and entrepreneur skills are in place, new ventures still face numerous strategic challenges. Decisions about the strategic positioning of new entrants can benefit from conducting strategic analyses and evaluating the require-ments of niche markets. Entry strategies used by new ventures take several forms, including pioneering new entry, imitative new entry, and adaptive new entry. Entrepreneurial firms can benefit from using overall low cost, differentiation, and focus strategies although each of these approaches has pitfalls that are unique to young and small firms. Entrepreneurial firms are also in a strong position to benefit from combination strategies.

The entry of a new company into a competitive arena is like a competitive attack on incumbents in that arena. Such actions often provoke a competitive response, which may, in turn, trigger a reaction to the response. As a result, a competitive dynamic—action and response—begins among close competitors. In deciding whether to attack or counterattack, companies must analyze the seri-ousness of the competitive threat, their ability to mount a competitive response, and the type of action—strategic or tactical—that the situation requires. At times, competitors find it is better not to respond at all or to find avenues to cooperate with, rather than challenge, close competitors.

Applications Questions and Answers

1. E-Loan and Lending Tree are two entrepreneurial firms that offer lending services over the Internet.

Summary Review Questions

1. Explain how the combination of opportunities, resources, and entrepreneurs helps determine the char-acter and strategic direction of an entrepreneurial firm.

2. What is the difference between discovery and evalu-ation in the process of opportunity recognition? Give an example of each.

3. Describe the three characteristics of entrepreneurial leadership: vision, dedication and drive, and commit-ment to excellence.

4. Briefly describe the three types of entrepreneurial entry strategies: pioneering, imitative, and adaptive.

5. Explain why entrepreneurial firms are often in a strong position to use combination strategies.

6. What does the term *competitive dynamics* mean?

7. Explain the difference between strategic actions and tactical actions and provide examples of each.

Key Terms

entrepreneurship, 273
opportunity
  recognition, 276
entrepreneurial
  strategy 285
pioneering new entry, 286
imitative new entry, 287
adaptive new entry, 288
competitive
  dynamics, 294

new competitive
  action 295
threat analysis 295
market
  commonality, 297
resource similarity, 297
strategic actions, 301
tactical actions, 301
forbearance 302
co-opetition 302

Evaluate the features of these two companies and, for each company:

a. Evaluate their characteristics and assess the extent to which they are comparable in terms of market commonality and resource similarity.

Company	Market Commonality	Resource Similarity
E-Loan		
Lending Tree		

b. Based on your analysis, what strategic and/or tactical actions might these companies take to improve their competitive position? Could E-Loan and Lending Tree improve their performance more through co-opetition rather than competition? Explain your rationale.

Company	Strategic Actions	Tactical Actions
E-Loan		
Lending Tree		

2. Using the Internet, research the Small Business Administration's website (www.sba.gov). What different types of financing are available to small firms? Besides financing, what other programs are available to support the growth and development of small businesses?

3. Think of an entrepreneurial firm that has been successfully launched in the last 10 years. What kind of entry strategy did it use—pioneering, imitative, or adaptive? Since the firm's initial entry, how has it used or combined overall low-cost, differentiation and/or focus strategies?

4. Select an entrepreneurial firm you are familiar with in your local community. Research the company and discuss how it has positioned itself relative to its close competitors. Does it have a unique strategic advantage? Disadvantage? Explain.

Ethics Questions

1. Imitation strategies are based on the idea of copying another firm's idea and using it for your own purposes. Is this unethical or simply a smart business practice? Discuss the ethical implications of this practice (if any).

2. Intense competition such as price wars are an accepted practice in the United States, but cooperation between companies has legal ramifications because of antitrust laws. Should price wars that drive small businesses or new entrants out of business be illegal? What ethical considerations are raised (if any)?

References

1. The Amp'd Mobile example is based on Kharif, O. 2007. Amp'd Mobile runs out of juice. BusinessWeek.com, June 5: np; and Rosenthal, J. 2007. Mobile meltdown. *Fast Company,* September: 49–53.

2. Small Business Administration. 2004. *The small business economy* Washington, D.C.: U.S. Government Printing Office.

3. Timmons, J. A. & Spinelli, S. 2004. *New venture creation* (6th ed.). New York: McGraw-Hill/Irwin; and Bygrave, W. D. 1997. The entrepreneurial process. In W. D. Bygrave (Ed.), *The portable MBA in entrepreneurship* (2nd ed.). New York: Wiley.

4. Fromartz, S. 1998. How to get your first great idea. *Inc. Magazine,* April 1: 91–94; and, Vesper, K. H. 1990. *New venture strategies,* 2nd ed. Englewood Cliffs, NJ: Prentice-Hall.

5. For an interesting perspective on the nature of the opportunity recognition process, see Baron, R. A. 2006. Opportunity recognition as pattern recognition: How entrepreneurs 'connect the dots' to identify new business opportunities. *Academy of Management Perspectives,* February: 104–119.

6. Gaglio, C. M. 1997. Opportunity identification: Review, critique and suggested research directions. In J. A. Katz, ed. *Advances in entrepreneurship, firm emergence and growth,* vol. 3. Greenwich, CT: JAI Press: 139–202; Lumpkin, G. T., Hills, G. E., & Shrader, R. C. 2004. Opportunity recognition. In Harold L. Welsch, (Ed.), *Entrepreneurship: The Road Ahead,* pp. 73–90. London: Routledge; and, Long, W. & McMullan, W. E. 1984. Mapping the new venture opportunity identification process. *Frontiers of entrepreneurship research, 1984.*

Wellesley, MA: Babson College: 567–90.

7. For an interesting discussion of different aspects of opportunity discovery, see Shepherd, D. A. & De Tienne, D. R. 2005. Prior knowledge, potential financial reward, and opportunity identification. *Entrepreneurship theory & practice*, 29(1): 91–112; and Gaglio, C. M. 2004. The role of mental simulations and counterfactual thinking in the opportunity identification process. *Entrepreneurship theory & practice*, 28(6): 533–552.

8. Stewart, T. A. 2002. How to think with your gut. *Business 2.0*, November: 99–104.

9. For more on the opportunity recognition process, see Smith, B. R., Matthews, C. H., & Schenkel, M. T. 2009. Differences in entrepreneurial opportunities: The role of tacitness and codification in opportunity identification. *Journal of Small Business Management*, 47(1): 38–57.

10. Timmons, J. A. 1997. Opportunity recognition. In W. D. Bygrave, ed. *The portable MBA in entrepreneurship*, 2nd ed. New York: John Wiley: 26–54.

11. Social networking is also proving to be an increasingly important type of entrepreneurial resource. For an interesting discussion, see Aldrich, H. E. & Kim, P. H. 2007. Small worlds, infinite possibilities? How social networks affect entrepreneurial team formation and search. *Strategic Entrepreneurship Journal*, 1(1): 147–166.

12. Bhide, A. V. 2000. *The origin and evolution of new businesses*. New York: Oxford University Press.

13. Small Business 2001: Where are we now? 2001. *Inc. Magazine*, May 29: 18–19; and Zacharakis, A. L., Bygrave, W. D., & Shepherd, D.A. 2000. *Global entrepreneurship monitor—National entrepreneurship assessment: United States of America 2000 Executive Report*. Kansas City, MO: Kauffman Center for Entrepreneurial Leadership.

14. Cooper, S. 2003. Cash cows. *Entrepreneur*, June: 36.

15. Seglin, J. L. 1998. What angels want. *Inc. Magazine*, 20 (7): 43–44.

16. Torres, N.L. 2002. Playing an angel. *Entrepreneur*, May: 130–138.

17. For an interesting discussion of how venture capital practices vary across different sectors of the economy, see Gaba, V. & Meyer, A. D. 2008. Crossing the organizational species barrier: How venture capital practices infiltrated the information technology sector. *Academy of Management Journal*, 51(5): 391–412.

18. For more on how different forms of organizing entrepreneurial firms as well as different stages of new firm growth and development affect financing, see Cassar, G. 2004. The financing of business start-ups. *Journal of Business Venturing*, 19(2): 261–283.

19. Eisenhardt, K. M. & Schoonhoven, C. B. 1990. Organizational growth: Linking founding team, strategy, environment, and growth among U.S. semiconductor ventures, 1978–1988. *Administrative Science Quarterly*, 35: 504–529.

20. Dubini, P. & Aldrich, H. 1991. Personal and extended networks are central to the entrepreneurship process. *Journal of Business Venturing*, 6(5): 305–333.

21. For more on the role of social contacts in helping young firms build legitimacy, see Chrisman, J. J. & McMullan, W. E. 2004. Outside assistance as a knowledge resource for new venture survival. *Journal of Small Business Management*, 42(3): 229–244.

22. Vogel, C. 2000. Janina Pawlowski. *Working woman*, June: 70

23. For a recent perspective on entrepreneurship and strategic alliances, see Rothaermel, F. T. & Deeds, D. L. 2006. Alliance types, alliance experience and alliance management capability in high-technology ventures. *Journal of Business Venturing*, 21(4): 429–460; and Lu, J. W. & Beamish, P. W. 2006. Partnering strategies and performance of SMEs' international joint ventures. *Journal of Business Venturing*, 21(4): 461–486.

24. For more on the role of alliances in creating competitive advantages, see Wiklund, J. & Shepherd, D. A. 2009. The effectiveness of alliances and acquisitions: The role of resource combination activities. *Entrepreneurship Theory & Practice*, 33(1): 193–212.

25. For more information, go to the Small Business Administration website at www.sba.gov.

26. For an interesting study of the role of passion in entrepreneurial success, see Chen, X-P., Yao, X., & Kotha, S. 2009 Entrepreneur passion and preparedness in business plan presentations: A persuasion analysis of venture capitalists' funding decisions. *Academy of Management Journal*, 52 (1): 101–120.

27. Collins, J. 2001. *Good to great*. New York: HarperCollins.

28. Collins, op. cit.

29. The idea of entry wedges was discussed by Vesper, K. 1990. *New venture strategies* (2nd ed.). Englewood Cliffs, NJ: Prentice-Hall; and, Drucker, P. F. 1985. *Innovation and entrepreneurship*. New York: HarperBusiness.

30. See Dowell, G. & Swaminathan, A. 2006. Entry timing, exploration, and firm survival in the early U.S. bicycle industry. *Strategic Management Journal*, 27: 1159–1182, for a recent study of the timing of entrepreneurial new entry.

31. Maiello, M. 2002. They almost changed the world. *Forbes*, December 22: 217–220.

32. Gull, N. 2003. Just say om. *Inc. Magazine*, July: 42–44; Hugger Mugger Yoga Products sues Gaiam, Inc. in federal court for Internet trademark infringement. 2005. www.businesswire.com, March 17: np.

33. More on the role of imitation strategies is addressed in a recent article: Lieberman, M. B. & Asaba, S. 2006. Why do firms imitate each other? *Academy of Management Review*, 31(2): 366–385.

34. Williams, G. 2002. Looks like rain. *Entrepreneur*, September: 104–111.

35. Pedroza, G. M. 2002. Tech tutors. *Entrepreneur*, September: 120.

36. Kim, W. C., and Mauborgne, R. 2004. Blue ocean strategy. *Harvard Business Review*, October: 76–84; and www.cirquedusoleil.com.

37. Romanelli, E. 1989. Environments and strategies of organization start-up: Effects on early survival.

Administrative Science Quarterly, 34(3): 369–87.

38. Wallace, B. 2000. Brothers. *Philadelphia Magazine,* April: 66–75.

39. Buchanan, L. 2003. The innovation factor: A field guide to innovation. *Forbes,* April 21, www.forbes.com.

40. Kim, W. C. & Mauborgne, R. 2005. *Blue ocean strategy.* Boston: Harvard Business School Press.

41. For more on how unique organizational combinations can contribute to competitive advantages of entrepreneurial firms, see Steffens, P., Davidsson, P., & Fitzsimmons, J. Performance configurations over times: Implications for growth- and profit-oriented strategies. *Entrepreneurship Theory & Practice,* 33(1): 125–148.

42. Smith, K. G., Ferrier, W. J., & Grimm, C. M. 2001. King of the hill: Dethroning the industry leader. *Academy of Management Executive,* 15(2): 59–70.

43. Kumar, N. 2006. Strategies to fight low-cost rivals. *Harvard Business Review,* December: 104–112.

44. Grove, A. 1999. *Only the paranoid survive: How to exploit the crises points that challenge every company.* New York: Random House.

45. Stalk, Jr., G. & Lachenauer, R. 2004. *Hardball: Are you playing to play or playing to win?* Cambridge, MA: Harvard Business School Press.

46. Peteraf, M. A. & Bergen, M. A. 2003. Scanning competitive landscapes: A market-based and resource-based framework. *Strategic Management Journal,* 24: 1027–1045.

47. Chen, M. J. 1996. Competitor analysis and interfirm rivalry: Toward a theoretical integration. *Academy of Management Review,* 21(1): 100–134.

48. Chen, 1996, op.cit.

49. Chen, M. J., Su, K. H, & Tsai, W. 2007. Competitive tension: The awareness-motivation-capability perspective. *Academy of Management Journal,* 50(1): 101–118.

50. St. John, W. 1999. Barnes & Noble's Epiphany. *Wired,* www.wired.com, June.

51. Kumar 2006, op. cit.

52. Chen, M. J. & Hambrick, D. 1995. Speed, stealth, and selective attack: How small firms differ from large firms in competitive behavior. *Academy of Management Journal,* 38: 453–482.

53. Lyons, D. 2006. The cheap revolution. *Forbes,* September 18: 102–111.

54. For a discussion of how the strategic actions of Apple Computer contribute to changes in the competitive dynamics in both the cellular phone and music industries, see Burgelman, R. A. & Grove, A. S. 2008. Cross-boundary disruptors: Powerful interindustry entrepreneurial change agents. *Strategic Entrepreneurship Journal,* 1(1): 315–327,

55. Smith, K. G., Ferrier, W. J., & Ndofor, H. 2001. Competitive dynamics research: Critique and future directions. In M. A. Hitt, R. E. Freeman, & J. S. Harrison (Eds.), *The Blackwell handbook of strategic management,* pp. 315–361. Oxford, UK: Blackwell.

56. Gee, P. 2000. Co-opetition: The new market milieu. *Journal of Healthcare Management,* 45: 359–363.

57. Ketchen, D. J., Snow, C. C., & Hoover, V. L. 2004. Research on competitive dynamics: Recent accomplishments and future challenges. *Journal of Management,* 30(6): 779–804.

58. Khanna, T., Gulati, R., & Nohria, N. 2000. The economic modeling of strategy process: Clean models and dirty hands. *Strategic Management Journal,* 21: 781–790.

Strategic Control and Corporate Governance

>learning objectives

After reading this chapter, you should have a good understanding of:

LO1 The value of effective strategic control systems in strategy implementation.

LO2 The key difference between "traditional" and "contemporary" control systems.

LO3 The imperative for "contemporary" control systems in today's complex and rapidly changing competitive and general environments.

LO4 The benefits of having the proper balance among the three levers of behavioral control: culture; rewards and incentives; and, boundaries.

LO5 The three key participants in corporate governance: shareholders, management (led by the CEO), and the board of directors.

LO6 The role of corporate governance mechanisms in ensuring that the interests of managers are aligned with those of shareholders from both the United States and international perspectives.

Organizations must have effective strategic controls if they are to successfully implement their strategies. This includes systems that exercise both informational control and behavioral control. Controls must be consistent with the strategy that the firm is following. In addition, a firm must promote sound corporate governance to ensure that the interests of managers and shareholders are aligned.

In the first section, we address the need to have effective informational control, contrasting two approaches to informational control. The first approach, which we call "traditional," is highly sequential. Goals and objectives are set, then implemented, and after a set period of time, performance is compared to the desired standards. In contrast, the second approach, termed "contemporary," is much more interactive. Here, the internal and external environments are continually monitored, and managers determine whether the strategy itself needs to be modified. Today the contemporary approach is required, given the rapidly changing conditions in virtually all industries.

Next, we discuss behavioral control. Here the firm must strive to maintain a proper balance between culture, rewards, and boundaries. We also argue that organizations that have strong, positive cultures and reward systems can rely less on boundaries, such as rules, regulations, and procedures. When individuals in the firm internalize goals and strategies, there is less need for monitoring behavior, and efforts are focused more on important organizational goals and objectives.

The third section addresses the role of corporate governance in ensuring that managerial and shareholder interests are aligned. We provide examples of both effective and ineffective corporate governance practices. We discuss three governance mechanisms for aligning managerial and shareholder interests: a committed and involved board of directors, shareholder activism, and effective managerial rewards and incentives. Public companies are also subject to external control. We discuss several external control mechanisms, such as the market for corporate control, auditors, banks and analysts, the media, and public activists. We close with a discussion of corporate governance from an international perspective.

Learning from Mistakes

Customer service call centers offer companies the opportunity to communicate with customers and build a positive client relationship. However, after the merger of Sprint and Nextel in 2005, "unhappy customers defected in droves, and profits evaporated." Sprint Nextel has ranked last in customer service among wireless carriers every year since the merger in J.D. Power & Associates surveys. The downturn in business started before Daniel Hesse became CEO of Sprint in late 2007 and has yet to truly turn around.

Prior to the merger, Nextel had taken pride in the firm's strong customer service and low customer turnover rate, or churn (customers moving to another wireless carrier). On the other hand, Sprint had been very good at managing costs. The merged company adopted most of Sprint's quantitative measurement approach to control. Pressure was put on customer service representatives to shorten the amount of time it took to complete a customer call. Gayle R. Romero, who worked in Sprint Nextel call centers for six years, recalled the pressure to end calls quickly in a manager's remarks to her group: "If you don't think you can handle this, I hear McDonald's is hiring." As they feared for their jobs, employees ended calls quickly, whether or not they had really satisfied the customer inquiry. The result was a dramatic increase in customer churn, as unhappy customers moved their business elsewhere.

What went wrong? Too much behavior control can lead to too much focus on measurement of employee actions rather than measurement of outcomes and organizational goals. This leads employees to do only the things that get measured in their jobs. Employees learn to follow the rules and receive the rewards as set forth by management. Managers sometimes focus on increasing efficiency of tasks. If this comes at the expense of monitoring the effectiveness of the tasks they are measuring toward reaching organizational goals, then a perversion of incentives for employees may occur.

The problems for Sprint only increased in 2006 as the firm came under financial pressure related to losing subscribers. Customer service representatives were given sales and renewal targets and cash bonuses for increasing retention. This led to practices that drew lawsuits from customers who felt tricked into extending their subscription contracts. Some customers complained that each call to Sprint automatically increased the length of their subscription contract without their approval. By 2007, Sprint managers had even cracked down on freebies: free phones, service credits, or extra minutes that customer service representatives were allowed to give customers to keep them happy. Employee morale was so low that some workers called Sprint headquarters "Shawshank" after the Maine prison in the 1994 film *The Shawshank Redemption.* The customer base continued to shrink from 53.9 million at the beginning of 2008 to 50.5 million users by the third quarter, well behind rivals AT&T and Verizon Wireless, which had 74.9 million and 70.8 million subscribers, respectively.

New CEO Daniel Hesse changed the tune of Sprint's customer service culture and measurement systems starting in 2008. While his managers are not abandoning quantitative measurement altogether, they are focusing on measuring things that make customers happy to stay on as subscribers. Now, Sprint has eliminated the measure of the amount of time a customer call takes to complete. Instead, Sprint managers measure how frequently representatives resolve customers' problems on the first call and how long customers have to wait to have their call answered by a representative. Bob Johnson, Sprint's new chief service officer, said, "incentives and policies are now driven around improving the [customer] experience."[1]

strategic control
the process of monitoring and correcting a firm's strategy and performance.

We first explore two central aspects of **strategic control:**[2] (1) *informational control,* which is the ability to respond effectively to environmental change, and (2) *behavioral control,* which is the appropriate balance and alignment among a firm's culture, rewards, and boundaries. In the final section of this chapter, we focus on strategic control from a much broader perspective—what is referred to as *corporate governance.* Here, we direct our attention to the need for a firm's shareholders (the owners) and their elected representatives (the board of directors) to ensure that the firm's executives (the management team) strive to fulfill their fiduciary duty of maximizing long-term shareholder value.

Ensuring Informational Control: Responding Effectively to Environmental Change

>LO1
The value of effective strategic control systems in strategy implementation.

We discuss two broad types of control systems: "traditional" and "contemporary." As both general and competitive environments become more unpredictable and complex, the need for contemporary systems increases.

A Traditional Approach to Strategic Control

The **traditional** approach to **strategic control** is sequential: (1) strategies are formulated and top management sets goals, (2) strategies are implemented, and (3) performance is measured against the predetermined goal set, as illustrated in Exhibit 9.1.

Control is based on a feedback loop from performance measurement to strategy formulation. This process typically involves lengthy time lags, often tied to a firm's annual planning cycle. Such traditional control systems, termed "single-loop" learning by Harvard's Chris Argyris simply compare actual performance to a predetermined goal.[3] They are most appropriate when the environment is stable and relatively simple, goals and objectives can be measured with a high level of certainty, and there is little need for complex measures of performance. Sales quotas, operating budgets, production schedules, and similar quantitative control mechanisms are typical. The appropriateness of the business strategy or standards of performance is seldom questioned.[4]

James Brian Quinn of Dartmouth College has argued that grand designs with precise and carefully integrated plans seldom work.[5] Rather, most strategic change proceeds incrementally—one step at a time. Leaders should introduce some sense of direction, some logic in incremental steps.[6] Similarly, McGill University's Henry Mintzberg has written about leaders "crafting" a strategy.[7] Drawing on the parallel between the potter at her wheel and the strategist, Mintzberg pointed out that the potter begins work with some general idea of the artifact she wishes to create, but the details of design—even possibilities for a different design— emerge as the work progresses. For businesses facing complex and turbulent business environments, the craftsperson's method helps us deal with the uncertainty about how a design will work out in practice and allows for a creative element.

Mintzberg's argument, like Quinn's, questions the value of rigid planning and goal-setting processes. Fixed strategic goals also become dysfunctional for firms competing in highly unpredictable competitive environments. Strategies need to change frequently and opportunistically. An inflexible commitment to predetermined goals and milestones can prevent the very adaptability that is required of a good strategy.

Even organizations that have been extremely successful in the past can become complacent or fail to adapt their goals and strategies to the new conditions. An example of such a firm is American International Group (AIG), once one of the largest and most

traditional approach to strategic control a sequential method of organizational control in which (1) strategies are formulated and top management sets goals, (2) strategies are implemented, and (3) performance is measured against the predetermined goal set.

>LO2
The key difference between "traditional" and "contemporary" control systems.

Exhibit 9.1 Traditional Approach to Strategic Control

What Did American International Group Do Wrong?

We can learn some lessons from fallen stars. American International Group (AIG) was one of the largest and most sophisticated insurance firms in the world with $110 billion in annual sales and over $1 trillion in assets. This once invincible stock came crashing down from a 2008 high of $70 a share to $1.25 a share on September 16, 2008. A government funded bailout of $85 billion gave taxpayers warrants for an 80 percent stake in the company.

Problems stemmed from AIG's use of complex derivatives and swaps that transferred and insured credit risks.

Sources: Byrnes, N. 2008. Where AIG Went Wrong. *BusinessWeek,* September 29: 40–42; Chung, J., Daneshkhu, S., Felsted, A., and Guerrera, F. 2008. AIG's Complexity Blamed for Fall. *Financial Times,* October 7: 19; Loomis, C. J. & Burke, D. 2009. AIG: The Company That Came to Dinner. *Fortune,* January 19, 159(1): 70–78.

AIG's solid credit rating from its insurance business helped it "to monetize [its] crediting rating and rent it" for derivatives trades to earn large fees. AIG's problems stemmed from losses in its mortgage insurance business from defaults related to subprime lending and rapidly falling U.S. home prices.

Ratings agencies began to downgrade AIG's credit rating on September 15, 2008, triggering terms of its derivatives contracts and requiring it to put forth $14.5 billion in capital that it did not have. AIG was caught in a crisis of capital and was unable to raise money from Wall Street, so government intervention was required.

As an insurance underwriter, AIG's job was to spread risk around. However, rather than spreading risk, AIG concentrated risk, making bold bets on rising home prices and leaving its whole business exposed to catastrophic losses.

sophisticated insurance firms in the world with $110 billion in annual sales. AIG's stock came crashing down from an early 2008 high of $70 a share to $1.25 by the end of the year on the heels of a combination of bad bets on the direction of U.S. housing prices and margin calls on related derivative trades. AIG had failed to minimize the potential for over-concentration of risk by poor use of its information control systems. We discuss this firm in more detail in Strategy Spotlight 9.1.

>LO3

The imperative for "contemporary" control systems in today's complex and rapidly changing competitive and general environments.

A Contemporary Approach to Strategic Control

Adapting to and anticipating both internal and external environmental change is an integral part of strategic control. The relationships between strategy formulation, implementation, and control are highly interactive, as suggested by Exhibit 9.2. It also illustrates

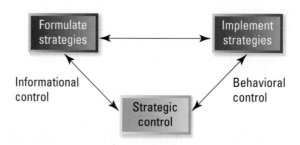

Exhibit 9.2 **Contemporary Approach to Strategic Control**

two different types of strategic control: informational control and behavioral control. **Informational control** is primarily concerned with whether or not the organization is "doing the right things." **Behavioral control,** on the other hand, asks if the organization is "doing things right" in the implementation of its strategy. Both the informational and behavioral components of strategic control are necessary, but not sufficient, conditions for success. What good is a well-conceived strategy that cannot be implemented? Or what use is an energetic and committed workforce if it is focused on the wrong strategic target?

John Weston is the former CEO of ADP Corporation, the largest payroll and tax-filing processor in the world. He captures the essence of contemporary control systems.

> At ADP, 39 plus 1 adds up to more than 40 plus 0. The 40-plus-0 employee is the harried worker who at 40 hours a week just tries to keep up with what's in the "in" basket. . . . Because he works with his head down, he takes zero hours to think about what he's doing, why he's doing it, and how he's doing it. . . . On the other hand, the 39-plus-1 employee takes at least 1 of those 40 hours to think about what he's doing and why he's doing it. That's why the other 39 hours are far more productive.[8]

Informational control deals with the internal environment as well as the external strategic context. It addresses the assumptions and premises that provide the foundation for an organization's strategy. Do the organization's goals and strategies still "fit" within the context of the current strategic environment? Depending on the type of business, such assumptions may relate to changes in technology, customer tastes, government regulation, and industry competition.

This involves two key issues. First, managers must scan and monitor the external environment, as we discussed in Chapter 2. Also, conditions can change in the internal environment of the firm, as we discussed in Chapter 3, requiring changes in the strategic direction of the firm. These may include, for example, the resignation of key executives or delays in the completion of major production facilities.

In the contemporary approach, information control is part of an ongoing process of organizational learning that continuously updates and challenges the assumptions that underlie the organization's strategy. In such "double-loop" learning, the organization's assumptions, premises, goals, and strategies are continuously monitored, tested, and reviewed. The benefits of continuous monitoring are evident—time lags are dramatically shortened, changes in the competitive environment are detected earlier, and the organization's ability to respond with speed and flexibility is enhanced.

Contemporary control systems must have four characteristics to be effective.[9]

1. Focus on constantly changing information that has potential strategic importance.
2. The information is important enough to demand frequent and regular attention from all levels of the organization.
3. The data and information generated are best interpreted and discussed in face-to-face meetings.
4. The control system is a key catalyst for an ongoing debate about underlying data, assumptions, and action plans.

An executive's decision to use the control system interactively—in other words, to invest the time and attention to review and evaluate new information—sends a clear signal to the organization about what is important. The dialogue and debate that emerge from such an interactive process can often lead to new strategies and innovations. Strategy Spotlight 9.2 discusses how executives at Google use an interactive control process.

informational control a method of organizational control in which a firm gathers and analyzes information from the internal and external environment in order to obtain the best fit between the organization's goals and strategies and the strategic environment.

behavioral control a method of organizational control in which a firm influences the actions of employees through culture, rewards, and boundaries.

Google's Interactive Control System

Google has tried typical hierarchical control systems typically found in large firms. However, the firm reverted to its interactive control system within weeks. All of Google's roughly 5,000 product developers work in teams of three engineers. Larger projects simply assemble several teams of three workers. Within teams, there is a rotating "über-tech leader" depending on the project. Engineers tend to work in more than one team and do not need permission to switch teams. According to Shona Brown, VP for operations, "If at all possible, we want people to commit to things rather than be assigned to things." At Google "employees don't need a lot of signoffs to try something new, but they won't get much in the way of resources until they've accumulated some positive user feedback."

Google's executives regularly review projects with project leaders and analyze data about projects. Google uses some of its own webpage ranking technology in the review of software and other business projects. Using their own employees as mini test markets, managers often solicit employee opinions and analyze usage patterns of new product features and technologies. This interactive control of corporate information allows Google to make faster decisions about its business, including:

- Compare performance of customer usage and feedback among all components of the Google business in real time.

- Quickly discover shortfalls before major problems arise.

Sources: Hamel, G. 2007. Break Free. *Fortune*, October 1, 156(7): 119–126; Iyer, B. and Davenport, T. 2008. Reverse Engineering Google's Innovation Machine. *Harvard Business Review*, April: 59–68; Pham, A. 2008. Google to End Virtual World, Lively, Launched by the Internet Giant Less Than Five Months Ago. *Los Angeles Times*, November 21: C3; and Helft, M. 2009. Google Ends Sale of Ads in Papers after 2 Years. *New York Times*, January 21: B3.

- Become aware of unexpected successes that have often led to innovations.

- Discontinue failing products and services in a timely manner to save the company money.

These manager meetings return significant rewards for Google. Innovations that have been implemented as a result of high information control include:

- Gmail, an email system that utilizes Google's core search features to help users organize and find email messages easily.

- Google News, a computer-generated news site that aggregates headlines from more than 4,500 English-language news sources worldwide, groups similar stories together, and displays them according to each reader's personalized interests.

- Google AdSense, a service that matches ads to a website's content and audience and operates on a revenue-sharing business model.

Google managers are able to quickly analyze user feedback and revenue data to discontinue projects that are not working out as originally intended. This information control allows managers to reallocate resources to more promising projects in a timely manner.

- Google Lively, a virtual world simulation, was launched and shut down after five months in 2008 after management determined that the service was not competitive.

- Google Print Ads, Google's automated method of selling ads through auctions to the newspaper industry, was terminated in early 2009 when managers analyzed the data and determined that the revenue stream was negligible compared to the costs of the program.

>LO4

The benefits of having the proper balance among the three levers of behavioral control: culture, rewards and incentives, and boundaries.

Attaining Behavioral Control: Balancing Culture, Rewards, and Boundaries

Behavioral control is focused on implementation—doing things right. Effectively implementing strategy requires manipulating three key control "levers": culture, rewards, and boundaries (see Exhibit 9.3). There are two compelling reasons for an increased emphasis on culture and rewards in a system of behavioral controls.

First, the competitive environment is increasingly complex and unpredictable, demanding both flexibility and quick response to its challenges. As firms simultaneously downsize and

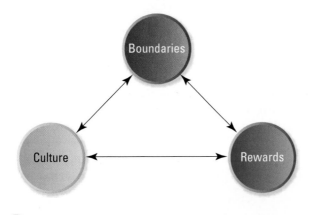

Exhibit 9.3 **Essential Elements of Behavioral Control**

face the need for increased coordination across organizational boundaries, a control system based primarily on rigid strategies, rules, and regulations is dysfunctional. The use of rewards and culture to align individual and organizational goals becomes increasingly important.

Second, the implicit long-term contract between the organization and its key employees has been eroded.[10] Today's younger managers have been conditioned to see themselves as "free agents" and view a career as a series of opportunistic challenges. As managers are advised to "specialize, market yourself, and have work, if not a job," the importance of culture and rewards in building organizational loyalty claims greater importance.

Each of the three levers—culture, rewards, and boundaries—must work in a balanced and consistent manner. Let's consider the role of each.

Building a Strong and Effective Culture

Organizational culture is a system of shared values (what is important) and beliefs (how things work) that shape a company's people, organizational structures, and control systems to produce behavioral norms (the way we do things around here).[11] How important is culture? Very. Over the years, numerous best sellers, such as *Theory Z, Corporate Cultures, In Search of Excellence,* and *Good to Great,* [12] have emphasized the powerful influence of culture on what goes on within organizations and how they perform.

Collins and Porras argued in *Built to Last* that the key factor in sustained exceptional performance is a cultlike culture.[13] You can't touch it or write it down, but it's there in every organization; its influence is pervasive; it can work for you or against you.[14] Effective leaders understand its importance and strive to shape and use it as one of their important levers of strategic control.[15]

> **organizational culture** a system of shared values and beliefs that shape a company's people, organizational structures, and control systems to produce behavioral norms.

The Role of Culture   Culture wears many different hats, each woven from the fabric of those values that sustain the organization's primary source of competitive advantage. Some examples are:

- Federal Express and Southwest Airlines focus on customer service.
- Lexus (a division of Toyota) and Hewlett-Packard emphasize product quality.
- Newell Rubbermaid and 3M place a high value on innovation.
- Nucor (steel) and Emerson Electric are concerned, above all, with operational efficiency.

Culture sets implicit boundaries—unwritten standards of acceptable behavior—in dress, ethical matters, and the way an organization conducts its business.[16] By creating a framework of shared values, culture encourages individual identification with the organization and its objectives. Culture acts as a means of reducing monitoring costs.[17]

Sustaining an Effective Culture   Powerful organizational cultures just don't happen overnight, and they don't remain in place without a strong commitment—both in terms of words and deeds—by leaders throughout the organization.[18] A viable and productive organizational culture can be strengthened and sustained. However, it cannot be "built" or "assembled"; instead, it must be cultivated, encouraged, and "fertilized."[19]

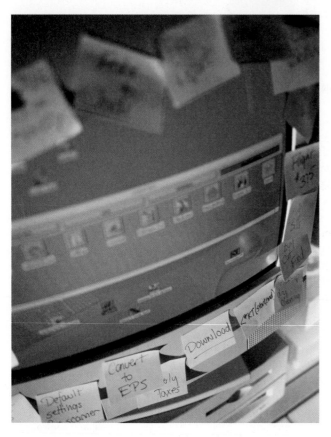

● 3M is well known for its innovative culture. The picture above shows Post-it Notes attached to a computer monitor.

Storytelling is one way effective cultures are maintained. Many are familiar with the story of how Art Fry's failure to develop a strong adhesive led to 3M's enormously successful Post-it Notes. Perhaps less familiar is the story of Francis G. Okie.[20] In 1922 Okie came up with the idea of selling sandpaper to men as a replacement for razor blades. The idea obviously didn't pan out, but Okie was allowed to remain at 3M. Interestingly, the technology developed by Okie led 3M to develop its first blockbuster product: a waterproof sandpaper that became a staple of the automobile industry. Such stories foster the importance of risk taking, experimentation, freedom to fail, and innovation—all vital elements of 3M's culture.

Rallies or "pep talks" by top executives also serve to reinforce a firm's culture. The late Sam Walton was known for his pep rallies at local Wal-Mart stores. Four times a year, the founders of Home Depot—former CEO Bernard Marcus and Arthur Blank—used to don orange aprons and stage Breakfast with Bernie and Arthur, a 6:30 a.m. pep rally, broadcast live over the firm's closed-circuit TV network to most of its 45,000 employees.[21]

Southwest Airlines' "Culture Committee" is a unique vehicle designed to perpetuate the company's highly successful culture. The following excerpt from an internal company publication describes its objectives:

The goal of the Committee is simple—to ensure that our unique Corporate Culture stays alive. . . . Culture Committee members represent all regions and departments across our system and they are selected based upon their exemplary display of the "Positively Outrageous Service" that won us the first-ever Triple Crown; their continual exhibition of the "Southwest Spirit" to our Customers and to their fellow workers; and their high energy level, boundless enthusiasm, unique creativity, and constant demonstration of teamwork and love for their fellow workers.[22]

Motivating with Rewards and Incentives

Reward and incentive systems represent a powerful means of influencing an organization's culture, focusing efforts on high-priority tasks, and motivating individual and collective task performance.[23] Just as culture deals with influencing beliefs, behaviors, and attitudes of people within an organization, the **reward system**—by specifying who gets rewarded and why—is an effective motivator and control mechanism.[24] Consider how John

reward system
policies that specify who gets rewarded and why.

Thompson, CEO of $11 billion software security firm Symantec, distributes financial rewards based on contribution:[25]

> When Thompson arrived at Symantec, any executive who was promoted to vice president automatically received a BMW. Senior management's bonuses were paid quarterly and were heavily skewed toward cash, not stock. Thompson says: "So if the stock didn't do well, they didn't care. We now have a stock option plan that is broad based but not universal. One of the things we recognized early on was that if we were going to grow at the rate that we were growing, we have to be more selective in who we gave options to so as not to dilute the value of our stock. And, the first thing we did was identify a range of employees who were valuable to the company but didn't need equity to come to work, and we focused their compensation around cash bonuses. Then we increased the equity we gave to the engineers and other people that were critical to our long-term success." By paying the two groups of people in a different manner, the new compensation scheme recognizes their distinctive importance.

The Potential Downside   Generally speaking, people in organizations act rationally, each motivated by their personal best interest.[26] However, the collective sum of individual behaviors of an organization's employees does not always result in what is best for the organization; individual rationality is no guarantee of organizational rationality.

As corporations grow and evolve, they often develop different business units with multiple reward systems. They may differ based on industry contexts, business situations, stage of product life cycles, and so on. Subcultures within organizations may reflect differences among functional areas, products, services, and divisions. To the extent that reward systems reinforce such behavioral norms, attitudes, and belief systems, cohesiveness is reduced; important information is hoarded rather than shared, individuals begin working at cross-purposes, and they lose sight of overall goals.

Such conflicts are commonplace in many organizations. For example, sales and marketing personnel promise unrealistically quick delivery times to bring in business, much to the dismay of operations and logistics; overengineering by R&D creates headaches for manufacturing; and so on. Conflicts also arise across divisions when divisional profits become a key compensation criterion. As ill will and anger escalate, personal relationships and performance may suffer.

Creating Effective Reward and Incentive Programs   To be effective, incentive and reward systems need to reinforce basic core values, enhance cohesion and commitment to goals and objectives, and meet with the organization's overall mission and purpose.[27]

At General Mills, to ensure a manager's interest in the overall performance of his or her unit, half of a manager's annual bonus is linked to business-unit results and half to individual performance.[28] For example, if a manager simply matches a rival manufacturer's performance, his or her salary is roughly 5 percent lower. However, if a manager's product ranks in the industry's top 10 percent in earnings growth and return on capital, the manager's total pay can rise to nearly 30 percent beyond the industry norm.

Effective reward and incentive systems share a number of common characteristics. (see Exhibit 9.4). The perception that a plan is "fair and equitable" is critically important. The firm must have the flexibility to respond to changing requirements as its direction and objectives change. In recent years many companies have begun to place more emphasis on growth. Emerson Electric has shifted its emphasis from cost cutting to growth. To ensure that changes take hold, the management compensation formula has been changed from a largely bottom-line focus to one that emphasizes growth, new products, acquisitions, and international expansion. Discussions about profits are handled separately, and a culture of risk taking is encouraged.[29]

Exhibit 9.4
Characteristics of
Effective Reward and
Evaluation Systems

- Objectives are clear, well understood, and broadly accepted.
- Rewards are clearly linked to performance and desired behaviors.
- Performance measures are clear and highly visible.
- Feedback is prompt, clear, and unambiguous.
- The compensation "system" is perceived as fair and equitable.
- The structure is flexible; it can adapt to changing circumstances.

Setting Boundaries and Constraints

In an ideal world, a strong culture and effective rewards should be sufficient to ensure that all individuals and subunits work toward the common goals and objectives of the whole organization.[30] However, this is not usually the case. Counterproductive behavior can arise because of motivated self-interest, lack of a clear understanding of goals and objectives, or outright malfeasance. **Boundaries and constraints** can serve many useful purposes for organizations, including:

boundaries and constraints
rules that specify behaviors that are acceptable and unacceptable.

- Focusing individual efforts on strategic priorities.
- Providing short-term objectives and action plans to channel efforts.
- Improving efficiency and effectiveness.
- Minimizing improper and unethical conduct.

Focusing Efforts on Strategic Priorities   Boundaries and constraints play a valuable role in focusing a company's strategic priorities. A well-known example of a strategic boundary is Jack Welch's (former CEO of General Electric) demand that any business in the corporate portfolio be ranked first or second in its industry. Similarly, Eli Lilly has reduced its research efforts to five broad areas of disease, down from eight or nine a decade ago.[31] This concentration of effort and resources provides the firm with greater strategic focus and the potential for stronger competitive advantages in the remaining areas.

Norman Augustine, Lockheed Martin's former chairman, provided four criteria for selecting candidates for diversification into "closely related" businesses.[32] They must (1) be high tech, (2) be systems-oriented, (3) deal with large customers (either corporations or government) as opposed to consumers, and (4) be in growth businesses. Augustine said, "We have found that if we can meet most of those standards, then we can move into adjacent markets and grow."

Boundaries also have a place in the nonprofit sector. For example, a British relief organization uses a system to monitor strategic boundaries by maintaining a list of companies whose contributions it will neither solicit nor accept. Such boundaries are essential for maintaining legitimacy with existing and potential benefactors.

Providing Short-Term Objectives and Action Plans   In Chapter 1 we discussed the importance of a firm having a vision, mission, and strategic objectives that are internally consistent and that provide strategic direction. In addition, short-term objectives and action plans provide similar benefits. That is, they represent boundaries that help to allocate resources in an optimal manner and to channel the efforts of employees at all levels throughout the organization.[33] To be effective, short-term objectives must have several attributes. They should:

- Be specific and measurable.
- Include a specific time horizon for their attainment.
- Be achievable, yet challenging enough to motivate managers who must strive to accomplish them.

Research has found that performance is enhanced when individuals are encouraged to attain specific, difficult, yet achievable, goals (as opposed to vague "do your best" goals).[34]

Short-term objectives must provide proper direction and also provide enough flexibility for the firm to keep pace with and anticipate changes in the external environment, new government regulations, a competitor introducing a substitute product, or changes in consumer taste. Unexpected events within a firm may require a firm to make important adjustments in both strategic and short-term objectives. The emergence of new industries can have a drastic effect on the demand for products and services in more traditional industries.

Action plans are critical to the implementation of chosen strategies. Unless action plans are specific, there may be little assurance that managers have thought through all of the resource requirements for implementing their strategies. In addition, unless plans are specific, managers may not understand what needs to be implemented or have a clear time frame for completion. This is essential for the scheduling of key activities that must be implemented. Finally, individual managers must be held accountable for the implementation. This helps to provide the necessary motivation and "sense of ownership" to implement action plans on a timely basis. Strategy Spotlight 9.3 illustrates how action plans fit into the mission statement and objectives of a small manufacturer of aircraft interior components. Exhibit 9.5 provides details of an action plan to fulfill one of the firm's objectives.

Improving Operational Efficiency and Effectiveness   Rule-based controls are most appropriate in organizations with the following characteristics:

- Environments are stable and predictable.
- Employees are largely unskilled and interchangeable.
- Consistency in product and service is critical.
- The risk of malfeasance is extremely high (e.g., in banking or casino operations).[35]

McDonald's Corp. has extensive rules and regulations that regulate the operation of its franchises.[36] Its policy manual states, "Cooks must turn, never flip, hamburgers. If they haven't been purchased, Big Macs must be discarded in 10 minutes after being cooked and French fries in 7 minutes. Cashiers must make eye contact with and smile at every customer."

Guidelines can also be effective in setting spending limits and the range of discretion for employees and managers, such as the $2,500 limit that hotelier Ritz-Carlton uses to empower employees to placate dissatisfied customers. Regulations also can be initiated to improve the use of an employee's time at work.[37] Computer Associates restricts the use of e-mail during the hours of 10 a.m. to noon and 2 p.m. to 4 p.m. each day.[38]

Minimizing Improper and Unethical Conduct   Guidelines can be useful in specifying proper relationships with a company's customers and suppliers.[39] Many companies have explicit rules regarding commercial practices, including the prohibition of any form of payment, bribe, or kickback. Cadbury Schweppes has followed a simple but effective step in controlling the use of bribes by specifying that all payments, no matter how unusual, are recorded on the company's books. Its former chairman, Sir Adrian Cadbury, contended that such a practice causes managers to pause and consider whether a payment is simply a bribe or a necessary and standard cost of doing business.[40]

● McDonald's relies on extensive rules and regulations to maintain efficient operations at its restaurants.

Developing Meaningful Action Plans: Aircraft Interior Products, Inc.

MSA Aircraft Interior Products, Inc., is a manufacturing firm based in San Antonio, Texas, that was founded in 1983 by Mike Spraggins and Robert Plenge. The firm fulfills a small but highly profitable niche in the aviation industry with two key products. The Accordia line consists of patented, lightweight, self-contained window-shade assemblies. MSA's interior cabin shells are state-of-the-art assemblies that include window panels, side panels, headliners, and suspension system structures. MSA's products have been installed on a variety of aircraft, such as the Gulfstream series; the Cessna Citation; and Boeing's 727, 737, 757, and 707.

Much of MSA's success can be attributed to carefully articulated action plans consistent with the firm's mission and objectives. During the past five years, MSA has increased its sales at an annual rate of 15 to 18 percent. It has also succeeded in adding many prestigious companies to its customer base. Below are excerpts from MSA's mission statement and objectives as well as the action plans to achieve a 20 percent annual increase in sales.

Mission Statement

- Be recognized as an innovative and reliable supplier of quality interior products for the high-end, personalized transportation segments of the aviation, marine, and automotive industries.

- Design, develop, and manufacture interior fixtures and components that provide exceptional value to

Source: For purposes of confidentiality, some of the information presented in this spotlight has been disguised. We would like to thank company management and Joseph Picken, consultant, for providing us with the information used in this application.

the customer through the development of innovative designs in a manner that permits decorative design flexibility while retaining the superior functionality, reliability, and maintainability of well-engineered, factory-produced products.

- Grow, be profitable, and provide a fair return, commensurate with the degree of risk, for owners and stockholders.

Objectives

1. Achieve sustained and profitable growth over the next three years:
   - 20 percent annual growth in revenues
   - 12 percent pretax profit margins
   - 18 percent return on shareholder's equity

2. Expand the company's revenues through the development and introduction of two or more new products capable of generating revenues in excess of $8 million a year by 2012.

3. Continue to aggressively expand market opportunities and applications for the Accordia line of window-shade assemblies, with the objective of sustaining or exceeding a 20 percent annual growth rate for at least the next three years.

Exhibit 9.5 details an "Action Plan" for Objective 3.

MSA's action plans are supported by detailed month-by-month budgets and strong financial incentives for its executives. Budgets are prepared by each individual department and include all revenue and cost items. Managers are motivated by their participation in a profit-sharing program, and the firm's two founders each receive a bonus equal to three percent of total sales.

Description	Primary Responsibility	Target Date
1. Develop and implement 2008 marketing plan, including specific plans for addressing Falcon 20 retrofit programs and expanded sales of cabin shells.	R. H. Plenge (V.P. Marketing)	December 15, 2009
2. Negotiate new supplier agreement with Gulfstream Aerospace.	M. Spraggins (President)	March 1, 2010
3. Continue and complete the development of the UltraSlim window and have a fully tested and documented design ready for production at a manufacturing cost of less than $900 per unit.	D. R. Pearson (V.P. Operations)	June 15, 2010
4. Develop a window design suitable for L-1011 and similar wide-body aircraft and have a fully tested and documented design ready for production at a manufacturing cost comparable to the current Boeing window.	D. R. Pearson (V.P. Operations)	September 15, 2010

Exhibit 9.5 **Action Plan for Objective Number 3**

Regulations backed up with strong sanctions can also help an organization avoid conducting business in an unethical manner. After the passing of the Sarbanes-Oxley Act (which provides for stiffer penalties for financial reporting misdeeds), many chief financial officers (CFOs) have taken steps to ensure ethical behavior in the preparation of financial statements. For example, Home Depot's CFO, Carol B. Tome, strengthened the firm's code of ethics and developed stricter guidelines. Now all 25 of her subordinates must sign personal statements that all of their financial statements are correct—just as she and her CEO, have to do now.[41]

Behavioral Control in Organizations: Situational Factors

Here, the focus is on ensuring that the behavior of individuals at all levels of an organization is directed toward achieving organizational goals and objectives. The three fundamental types of control are culture, rewards and incentives, and boundaries and constraints. An organization may pursue one or a combination of them on the basis of a variety of internal and external factors.

Not all organizations place the same emphasis on each type of control.[42] In high-technology firms engaged in basic research, members may work under high levels of autonomy. An individual's performance is generally quite difficult to measure accurately because of the long lead times involved in R&D activities. Thus, internalized norms and values become very important.

When the measurement of an individual's output or performance is quite straightforward, control depends primarily on granting or withholding rewards. Frequently, a sales manager's compensation is in the form of a commission and bonus tied directly to his or her sales volume, which is relatively easy to determine. Here, behavior is influenced more strongly by the attractiveness of the compensation than by the norms and values implicit in the organization's culture. The measurability of output precludes the need for an elaborate system of rules to control behavior.

Control in bureaucratic organizations is dependent on members following a highly formalized set of rules and regulations. Most activities are routine and the desired behavior can be specified in a detailed manner because there is generally little need for innovative or creative activity. Managing an assembly plant requires strict adherence to many rules as well as exacting sequences of assembly operations. In the public sector, the Department of Motor Vehicles in most states must follow clearly prescribed procedures when issuing or renewing driver licenses.

Exhibit 9.6 provides alternate approaches to behavioral control and some of the situational factors associated with them.

Evolving from Boundaries to Rewards and Culture

In most environments, organizations should strive to provide a system of rewards and incentives, coupled with a culture strong enough that boundaries become internalized. This reduces the need for external controls such as rules and regulations.

First, hire the right people—individuals who already identify with the organization's dominant values and have attributes consistent with them. We addressed this issue in Chapter 4; recall the "Bozo Filter" developed by Cooper Software. Microsoft's David Pritchard is well aware of the consequences of failing to hire properly.

> If I hire a bunch of bozos, it will hurt us, because it takes time to get rid of them. They start infiltrating the organization and then they themselves start hiring people of lower quality. At Microsoft, we are always looking for people who are better than we are.

Second, training plays a key role. For example, in elite military units such as the Green Berets and Navy SEALs, the training regimen so thoroughly internalizes the culture that individuals, in effect, lose their identity. The group becomes the overriding concern and focal point of their energies. At firms such as FedEx, training not only builds skills, but also plays a significant role in building a strong culture on the foundation of each organization's dominant values.

Exhibit 9.6
Organizational Control:
Alternative Approaches

Approach	Some Situational Factors
Culture: A system of unwritten rules that forms an internalized influence over behavior.	• Often found in professional organizations. • Associated with high autonomy. • Norms are the basis for behavior.
Rules: Written and explicit guidelines that provide external constraints on behavior.	• Associated with standardized output. • Tasks are generally repetitive and routine. • Little need for innovation or creative activity.
Rewards: The use of performance-based incentive systems to motivate.	• Measurement of output and performance is rather straightforward. • Most appropriate in organizations pursuing unrelated diversification strategies. • Rewards may be used to reinforce other means of control.

Third, managerial role models are vital. Andy Grove, former CEO and co-founder of Intel, didn't need (or want) a large number of bureaucratic rules to determine who is responsible for what, who is supposed to talk to whom, and who gets to fly first class (no one does). He encouraged openness by not having many of the trappings of success—he worked in a cubicle like all the other professionals. Can you imagine any new manager asking whether or not he can fly first class? Grove's personal example eliminated such a need.

Fourth, reward systems must be clearly aligned with the organizational goals and objectives. Where do you think rules and regulations are more important in controlling behavior—Home Depot, with its generous bonus and stock option plan, or Wal-Mart, which does not provide the same level of rewards and incentives?

The Role of Corporate Governance

> **>LO5**
> The three key participants in corporate governance: shareholders, management (led by the CEO), and the board of directors.

We now address the issue of strategic control in a broader perspective, typically referred to as "corporate governance." Here we focus on the need for both shareholders (the owners of the corporation) and their elected representatives, the board of directors, to actively ensure that management fulfills its overriding purpose of increasing long-term shareholder value.[43]

> **corporate governance** the relationship among various participants in determining the direction and performance of corporations. The primary participants are (1) the shareholders, (2) the management, and (3) the board of directors.

Robert Monks and Nell Minow, two leading scholars in **corporate governance,** define it as "the relationship among various participants in determining the direction and performance of corporations. The primary participants are (1) the shareholders, (2) the management (led by the CEO), and (3) the board of directors."[*] Our discussion will center on how corporations can succeed (or fail) in aligning managerial motives with the interests of the shareholders and their elected representatives, the board of directors.[44] As you will recall from Chapter 1, we discussed the important role of boards of directors and provided some examples of effective and ineffective boards.[45]

---

* Management cannot ignore the demands of other important firm stakeholders such as creditors, suppliers, customers, employees, and government regulators. At times of financial duress, powerful creditors can exert strong and legitimate pressures on managerial decisions. In general, however, the attention to stakeholders other than the owners of the corporation must be addressed in a manner that is still consistent with maximizing long-term shareholder returns. For a seminal discussion on stakeholder management, refer to Freeman, R. E. 1984. *Strategic Management: A Stakeholder Approach.* Boston: Pitman.

Good Corporate Governance and Performance: Research Evidence

Several studies found a positive relationship between the extent to which a firm practices good corporate governance and its performance outcomes. The results of two of these studies are summarized below.

Sources: Gill, A. 2001. Credit Lyonnais Securities (Asia). *Corporate Governance in Emerging Markets: Saints and Sinners,* April; and Low, C. K. 2002. *Corporate Governance: An Asia-Pacific Critique.* Hong Kong: Sweet & Maxwell Asia; Yu, L. 2008. Does Corporate Governance Matter? *MIT Sloan Management Review,* January 1: 49(2): 10; Abdullah, M., Shah, S., & Hassan, A. 2008. Impact of Corporate Governance on Financial Performance of Firms: Evidence from Pakistan. *Business Review, Cambridge,* December 1: 11(2): 282–289; Jermias, J. 2007. The Effects of Corporate Governance on the Relationship between Innovative Efforts and Performance. *European Accounting Review,* 16(4): 827–854.

1. *A strong correlation between corporate governance and price performance of large companies.* Over a recent three-year period, the average return of large capitalized firms with the best governance practices was more than five times higher than the performance of firms in the bottom corporate governance quartile.

2. *Across emerging markets.* In 10 of the 11 Asian and Latin American markets, companies in the top corporate governance quartile for their respective regions had a significantly higher (averaging 10 percentage points) return on capital employed (ROCE) than their market sample. In 12 of the emerging markets analyzed, companies in the lowest corporate governance quartile had a lower ROCE than the market average.

Good corporate governance plays an important role in the investment decisions of major institutions, and a premium is often reflected in the price of securities of companies that practice it. The corporate governance premium is larger for firms in countries with sound corporate governance practices compared to countries with weaker corporate governance standards.[46] There is a strong correlation between strong corporate governance and superior financial performance (see Strategy Spotlight 9.4).

At the same time, few topics in the business press are generating as much interest (and disdain!) as corporate governance.

Some recent notable examples of flawed corporate governance include:[47]

- Satyam Computer Services, a leading Indian outsourcing company that serves more than a third of the Fortune 500 companies, significantly inflated its earnings and assets for years. The chairman, Ramalinga Raju, resigned and admitted he had cooked the books. Mr. Raju said he had overstated cash on hand by $1 billion and inflated profits and revenues in the September 2008 quarter. Satyam shares sank 78 percent, and the benchmark Sensex index lost 7.3 percent that day (January 7, 2009).

- Former Brocade CEO Gregory Reyes was sentenced to 21 months in prison and fined $15 million for his involvement in backdating stock option grants. Mr. Reyes was the first executive to go on trial and be convicted over the improper dating of stock-option awards, which dozens of companies have acknowledged since the practice came to light (January 17, 2008).

- Hewlett-Packard admitted that outside investigators, led by Chairman Patricia Dunn, used a potentially illegal tactic in which they impersonated directors, journalists, and two employees to obtain personal phone records. Dunn resigned (September 12, 2006).

- Walter Forbes, former chairman of Cendant Corp. (now known as Avis Budget Group, Inc.), was sentenced to 12 years in prison and ordered to pay $3.3 billion in one of America's biggest accounting scandals. He oversaw a decade-long accounting scheme that overstated income. He was convicted on one count of conspiracy and two counts of false reporting (January 17, 2006).

- Board members of Nortel Networks meet with governance-minded investors to discuss possible changes to the board. This is after 10 executives and accounting officials are fired for artificially boosting the company's 2003 financial results (September 30, 2004).

Because of the many lapses in corporate governance, we can see the benefits associated with effective practices.[48] However, corporate managers may behave in their own self-interest, often to the detriment of shareholders. Next we address the implications of the separation of ownership and management in the modern corporation, and some mechanisms that can be used to ensure consistency (or alignment) between the interests of shareholders and those of the managers to minimize potential conflicts.

The Modern Corporation: The Separation of Owners (Shareholders) and Management

Some of the proposed definitions for a *corporation* include:

- "The business corporation is an instrument through which capital is assembled for the activities of producing and distributing goods and services and making investments. Accordingly, a basic premise of corporation law is that a business corporation should have as its objective the conduct of such activities with a view to enhancing the corporation's profit and the gains of the corporation's owners, that is, the shareholders." (Melvin Aron Eisenberg, *The Structure of Corporation Law*)
- "A body of persons granted a charter legally recognizing them as a separate entity having its own rights, privileges, and liabilities distinct from those of its members." (*American Heritage Dictionary*)
- "An ingenious device for obtaining individual profit without individual responsibility." (Ambrose Bierce, *The Devil's Dictionary*)[49]

All of these definitions have some validity and each one reflects a key feature of the corporate form of business organization— its ability to draw resources from a variety of groups and establish and maintain its own persona that is separate from all of them. As Henry Ford once said, "A great business is really too big to be human."

Simply put, a **corporation** is a mechanism created to allow different parties to contribute capital, expertise, and labor for the maximum benefit of each party.[50] The shareholders (investors) are able to participate in the profits of the enterprise without taking direct responsibility for the operations. The management can run the company without the responsibility of personally providing the funds. The shareholders have limited liability as well as rather limited involvement in the company's affairs. However, they reserve the right to elect directors who have the fiduciary obligation to protect their interests.

Over 70 years ago, Columbia University professors Adolf Berle and Gardiner C. Means addressed the divergence of the interests of the owners of the corporation from the professional managers who are hired to run it. They warned that widely dispersed ownership "released management from the overriding requirement that it serve stockholders." The separation of ownership from management has given rise to a set of ideas called "agency theory." Central to agency theory is the relationship between two primary players—the *principals* who are the owners of the firm (stockholders) and the *agents,* who are the people paid by principals to perform a job on their behalf (management). The stockholders elect and are represented by a board of directors that has a fiduciary responsibility to ensure that management acts in the best interests of stockholders to ensure long-term financial returns for the firm.

Agency theory is concerned with resolving two problems that can occur in agency relationships.[51] *The first is the agency problem that arises (1) when the goals of the principals and agents conflict, and (2) when it is difficult or expensive for the principal to*

corporation a mechanism created to allow different parties to contribute capital, expertise, and labor for the maximum benefit of each party.

agency theory a theory of the relationship between principals and their agents, with emphasis on two problems: (1) the conflicting goals of principals and agents, along with the difficulty of principals to monitor the agents, and (2) the different attitudes and preferences towards risk of principals and agents.

verify what the agent is actually doing. The board of directors would be unable to confirm that the managers were actually acting in the shareholders' interests because managers are "insiders" with regard to the businesses they operate and thus are better informed than the principals. Thus, managers may act "opportunistically" in pursuing their own interests—to the detriment of the corporation.[52] Managers may spend corporate funds on expensive perquisites (e.g., company jets and expensive art), devote time and resources to pet projects (initiatives in which they have a personal interest but that have limited market potential), engage in power struggles (where they may fight over resources for their own betterment and to the detriment of the firm), and negate (or sabotage) attractive merger offers because they may result in increased employment risk.[53]

The second issue is the problem of risk sharing. This arises when the principal and the agent have different attitudes and preferences toward risk. The executives in a firm may favor additional diversification initiatives because, by their very nature, they increase the size of the firm and thus the level of executive compensation.[54] At the same time, such diversification initiatives may erode shareholder value because they fail to achieve some synergies that we discussed in Chapter 6 (e.g., building on core competencies, sharing activities, or enhancing market power). Agents (executives) may have a stronger preference toward diversification than shareholders because it reduces their personal level of risk from potential loss of employment. Executives who have large holdings of stock in their firms were more likely to have diversification strategies that were more consistent with shareholder interests—increasing long-term returns.[55] At times, top-level managers engage in actions that reflect their self-interest rather than the interests of shareholders (see Strategy Spotlight 9.5).

Governance Mechanisms: Aligning the Interests of Owners and Managers

>LO6

The role of corporate governance mechanisms in ensuring that the interests of managers are aligned with those of shareholders from both the United States and international perspectives.

As noted above, a key characteristic of the modern corporation is the separation of ownership from control. To minimize the potential for managers to act in their own self-interest, or "opportunistically," the owners can implement some governance mechanisms.[56] First, there are two primary means of monitoring the behavior of managers. These include (1) a committed and involved *board of directors* that acts in the best interests of the shareholders to create long-term value and (2) *shareholder activism*, wherein the owners view themselves as share*owners* instead of share*holders* and become actively engaged in the governance of the corporation. Finally, there are managerial incentives, sometimes called "contract-based outcomes," which consist of *reward and compensation agreements*. Here the goal is to carefully craft managerial incentive packages to align the interests of management with those of the stockholders.[57]

A Committed and Involved Board of Directors   The **board of directors** acts as a fulcrum between the owners and controllers of a corporation. They are the intermediaries who provide a balance between a small group of key managers in the firm based at the corporate headquarters and a sometimes vast group of shareholders. In the United States, the law imposes on the board a strict and absolute fiduciary duty to ensure that a company is run consistent with the long-term interests of the owners—the shareholders. The reality, as we have seen, is somewhat more ambiguous.[58]

The Business Roundtable, representing the largest U.S. corporations, describes the duties of the board as follows:

1. Select, regularly evaluate, and, if necessary, replace the CEO. Determine management compensation. Review succession planning.
2. Review and, where appropriate, approve the financial objectives, major strategies, and plans of the corporation.

board of directors
a group that has a fiduciary duty to ensure that the company is run consistently with the long-term interests of the owners, or shareholders, of a corporation and that acts as an intermediary between the shareholders and management.

Crony Capitalism: Several Examples

When President George W. Bush signed the Sarbanes-Oxley Act into law on July 30, 2002, one of its goals was to prevent the kind of self-dealing and other conflicts of interest that had brought down Enron, WorldCom, Adelphia, and other corporate giants. Among other things, the Sarbanes-Oxley Act bans company loans to executives and prohibits extending the terms of existing loans.

Many companies, however, acted quickly *before* the bill was signed. For example, *one day* before the bill was signed, Crescent Real Estate Equities of Fort Worth, Texas, extended the payback deadline by 10 years on a loan of $26 million to its chief executive, John Goff. And Electronic Arts gave a $4 million loan to Warren Johnson, its chief financial officer, admitting in a filing that it was doing so a month prior to the "prohibition on loans to executive officers."

Despite legislation such as Sarbanes-Oxley and pressures from shareholders, related-party deals are quite common. According to the Corporate Library, a research group in Portland, Maine, 75 percent of 2,000 companies that were studied still engage in them. In essence, that means that companies must make embarrassing disclosures in their proxy statements about nepotism, property leased from top managers, corporate-owned apartments, and other forms of "insiderism."

Consider some examples:

- Two hundred companies have leased or bought airplanes from insiders. For example, Pilgrim's Pride of Pittsburgh, Texas, a chicken processor with $2.6 billion in annual sales has leased an airplane from its chief executive and founder Lonnie Pilgrim since 1985. Mr. Pilgrim made $656,000 in fiscal 2003 from this deal to go along with his $1.7 million in compensation. The company defends the pact as cost-efficient since its headquarters is located in a small town. Pilgrim also provides some bookkeeping services for his personal businesses, but he won't provide details.

- Micky M. Arison is chief executive of Carnival, the big cruise line. He is also chief executive and owner of the Miami Heat of the National Basketball Association. Carnival paid the Heat $675,000 in fiscal 2002 and 2003 for sponsorship and advertising as well as season tickets. Although that may be a rather small sum, given Carnival's $2.2 billion in net income for the period, we could still ask if the money would have been spent on something else if Arison didn't own the team.

- Alliance Semiconductor CEO N. Damodar Reddy has committed $20 million to Solar Ventures, a venture capital company run by his brother C. N. Reddy. Other unnamed insiders purchased undisclosed stakes in Solar. However, Alliance won't disclose whether its CEO is one of them. To date it has invested $12.5 million in Solar. Beth Young, senior research associate of the Corporate Library poses an interesting question: "Is Reddy using shareholder capital just to keep afloat his brother's fund and the insiders' investment?"

Source: MacDonald, E. 2004. Crony Capitalism. *Forbes*, June 21: 140–146.

3. Provide advice and counsel to top management.
4. Select and recommend to shareholders for election an appropriate slate of candidates for the board of directors; evaluate board processes and performance.
5. Review the adequacy of the systems to comply with all applicable laws/regulations.[59]

Given these principles, what makes for a good board of directors?[60] According to the Business Roundtable, the most important quality is a board of directors who are active, critical participants in determining a company's strategies.[61] That does not mean board members should micromanage or circumvent the CEO. Rather, they should provide strong oversight going beyond simply approving the CEO's plans. A board's primary responsibilities are to ensure that strategic plans undergo rigorous scrutiny, evaluate managers against high performance standards, and take control of the succession process.

Although boards in the past were often dismissed as CEO's rubber stamps, increasingly they are playing a more active role by forcing out CEOs who cannot deliver on performance.[62] According to the consulting firm Booz Allen Hamilton, the rate of CEO departures for performance reasons has more than tripled, from 1.3 percent to 4.2 percent, between 1995 and 2002.[63] In 2006, turnover among CEOs increased 30 percent over the previous year.[64] Well-known CEOs like Gerald M. Levin of AOL Time Warner and Jack M. Greenberg of McDonald's paid the price for poor financial performance by being forced to leave. Others, such as Bernard Ebbers of WorldCom, Inc., and Dennis Kozlowski of Tyco International, lost their jobs due to scandals. "Deliver or depart" is clearly the new message from the boards.

Another key component of top-ranked boards is director independence.[65] Governance experts believe that a majority of directors should be free of all ties to either the CEO or the company.[66] That means a minimum of "insiders" (past or present members of the management team) should serve on the board, and that directors and their firms should be barred from doing consulting, legal, or other work for the company.[67] Interlocking directorships—in which CEOs and other top managers serve on each other's boards—are not desirable. But perhaps the best guarantee that directors act in the best interests of shareholders is the simplest: Most good companies now insist that directors own significant stock in the company they oversee.[68]

Such guidelines are not always followed. At times, the practices of the boards of directors are the antithesis of such guidelines. Consider the Walt Disney Co. Over a five-year period, former CEO Michael Eisner pocketed an astonishing $531 million. He likely had very little resistance from his board of directors:

> Many investors view the Disney board as an anachronism. Among Disney's 16 directors is Eisner's personal attorney—who for several years was chairman of the company's compensation committee! There was also the architect who designed Eisner's Aspen home and his parents' apartment. Joining them are the principal of an elementary school once attended by his children and the president of a university to which Eisner donated $1 million. The board also includes the actor Sidney Poitier, seven current and former Disney executives, and an attorney who does business with Disney. Moreover, most of the outside directors own little or no Disney stock. "It is an egregiously bad board—a train wreck waiting to happen," warns Michael L. Useem, a management professor at the University of Pennsylvania's Wharton School.[69]

This example also shows that "outside directors" are only beneficial to strong corporate governance if they are vigilant in carrying out their responsibilities.[70] As humorously suggested by Warren Buffett, founder and chairman of Berkshire Hathaway: "The ratcheting up of compensation has been obscene. . . . There is a tendency to put cocker spaniels on compensation committees, not Doberman pinschers."[71]

Many firms do have exemplary board practices. Below we list some of the excellent practices at Intel Corp., the world's largest semiconductor chip manufacturer, with $35 billion in revenues:[72]

- *Mix of inside and outside directors.* The board believes that there should be a majority of independent directors on the board. However, the board is willing to have members of management, in addition to the CEO, as directors.
- *Board presentations and access to employees.* The board encourages management to schedule managers to be present at meetings who: (1) can provide additional insight into the items being discussed because of personal involvement in these areas, or (2) have future potential that management believes should be given exposure to the board.
- *Formal evaluation of officers.* The Compensation Committee conducts, and reviews with the outside directors, an annual evaluation to help determine the salary and executive bonus of all officers, including the chief executive officer.

Exhibit 9.7 shows how boards of directors can improve their practices.

Exhibit 9.7

Best Practice Ideas: The
New Rules for Directors

Issue	Suggestion
Pay	**Know the Math**
Companies will disclose full details of CEO payouts. Activist investors are already drawing up hit lists of companies where CEO paychecks are out of line with performance.	Before okaying any financial package, directors must make sure they can explain the numbers. They need to adopt the mindset of an activist investor and ask: What's the harshest criticism someone could make about this package?
Strategy	**Make It a Priority**
Boards have been so focused on compliance that duties like strategy and leadership oversight too often get ignored. Only 59 percent of directors in a recent study rated their board favorably on setting strategy	To avoid spending too much time on compliance issues, move strategy up to the beginning of the meeting. Annual one-, two- or three-day offsite meetings on strategy alone are becoming standard for good boards.
Financials	**Put in the Time**
Although 95 percent of directors in the recent study said they were doing a good job of monitoring financials, the number of earnings restatements hit a new high in 2006, after breaking records in 2004 and 2005.	Even nonfinancial board members need to monitor the numbers and keep a close eye on cash flows. Audit committee members should prepare to spend 300 hours a year on committee responsibilities.
Crisis Management	**Dig in**
Some 120 companies are under scrutiny for options backdating, and the 100 largest companies have replaced 56 CEOs in the past five years—nearly double the terminations in the prior five years.	The increased scrutiny on boards means that a perfunctory review will not suffice if a scandal strikes. Directors can no longer afford to defer to management in a crisis. They must roll up their sleeves and move into watchdog mode.

Source: Byrnes, N. & Sassen, J. 2007. Board of Hard Knocks. *BusinessWeek.* January 22: 36–39.

Shareholder Activism   As a practical matter, there are so many owners of the largest American corporations that it makes little sense to refer to them as "owners" in the sense of individuals becoming informed and involved in corporate affairs.[73] However, even an individual shareholder has several rights, including (1) the right to sell the stock, (2) the right to vote the proxy (which includes the election of board members), (3) the right to bring suit for damages if the corporation's directors or managers fail to meet their obligations, (4) the right to certain information from the company, and (5) certain residual rights following the company's liquidation (or its filing for reorganization under bankruptcy laws), once creditors and other claimants are paid off.[74]

Collectively, shareholders have the power to direct the course of corporations.[75] This may involve acts such as being party to shareholder action suits and demanding that key issues be brought up for proxy votes at annual board meetings.[76] The power of shareholders has intensified in recent years because of the increasing influence of large institutional investors such as mutual funds (e.g., T. Rowe Price and Fidelity Investments) and retirement systems such as TIAA-CREF (for university faculty members and school administrative staff).[77] Institutional investors hold approximately 50 percent of all listed corporate stock in the United States.[78]

Shareholder activism refers to actions by large shareholders, both institutions and individuals, to protect their interests when they feel that managerial actions diverge from shareholder value maximization.

shareholder activism actions by large shareholders to protect their interests when they feel that managerial actions of a corporation diverge from shareholder value maximization.

Many institutional investors are aggressive in protecting and enhancing their investments. They are shifting from traders to owners. They are assuming the role of permanent shareholders and rigorously analyzing issues of corporate governance. In the process they are reinventing systems of corporate monitoring and accountability.[79]

Consider the proactive behavior of CalPERS, the California Public Employees' Retirement System, which manages over $200 billion in assets and is the third largest pension fund in the world. Every year CalPERS reviews the performance of U.S. companies in its stock portfolio and identifies those that are among the lowest long-term relative performers and have governance structures that do not ensure full accountability to company owners. This generates a long list of companies, each of which may potentially be publicly identified as a CalPERS "Focus Company"—corporations to which CalPERS directs specific suggested governance reforms. CalPERS meets with the directors of each of these companies to discuss performance and governance issues. The CalPERS Focus List contains those companies that continue to merit public and market attention at the end of the process.

The CalPERS 2008 Focus List singled out four U.S. companies for poor financial and corporate governance.[80] Firms on the list were: *Cheesecake Factory Incorporated* of Calabasas Hills, California; *Hilb Rogal & Hobbs Company* of Glen Allen, Virginia; *Invacare Corporation* of Elyria, Ohio; *La-Z-Boy* of Monroe, Michigan; and *Standard Pacific Corporation* of Irvine, California. A few of CalPERS's concerns:

- Cheesecake Factory, an operator of upscale, full-service, casual dining restaurants, suffers from declining same-store performance and a lack of board accountability to shareholders. The board would not agree to seek shareholder approval to remove the company's 80 percent supermajority voting requirements to amend its corporate bylaws. It has performed well below its peer group for the past five years.
- La-Z-Boy, a manufacturer and marketer of upholstered furniture, has severely underperformed relative to both market indices and its peer group for the past five years. It also lacks board accountability in refusing to remove its classified or "staggered" board structure.

While appearing punitive to company management, such aggressive activism has paid significant returns for CalPERS (and other stockholders of the "Focused" companies). A Wilshire Associates study of the "CalPERS Effect" of corporate governance examined the performance of 62 targets over a five-year period: while the stock of these companies trailed the Standard & Poor's Index by 89 percent in the five-year period before CalPERS acted, the same stocks outperformed the index by 23 percent in the following five years, adding approximately $150 million annually in additional returns to the fund.

Perhaps no discussion of shareholder activism would be complete without mention of Carl Icahn, a famed activist with a personal net worth of about $13 billion:

> The bogeyman I am now chasing is the structure of American corporations, which permit managements and boards to rule arbitrarily and too often receive egregious compensation even after doing a subpar job. Yet they remain accountable to no one.[81]

Managerial Rewards and Incentives   As we discussed earlier in the chapter, incentive systems must be designed to help a company achieve its goals.[82] From the perspective of governance, one of the most critical roles of the board of directors is to create incentives that align the interests of the CEO and top executives with the interests of owners of the corporation—long-term shareholder returns.[83] Shareholders rely on CEOs to adopt policies and strategies that maximize the value of their shares.[84] A combination of three basic policies may create the right monetary incentives for CEOs to maximize the value of their companies:[85]

1. Boards can require that the CEOs become substantial owners of company stock.
2. Salaries, bonuses, and stock options can be structured so as to provide rewards for superior performance and penalties for poor performance.
3. Threat of dismissal for poor performance can be a realistic outcome.

In recent years the granting of stock options has enabled top executives of publicly held corporations to earn enormous levels of compensation. In 2007, the average CEO in the Standard & Poor's 500 stock index took home 433 times the pay of the average worker—up from 40 times the average in 1980. The counterargument, that the ratio is down from the 514 multiple in 2000, doesn't get much traction.[86] It has been estimated that there could be as many as 50 or more companies with CEO pay packages over $150 million.[87]

Many boards have awarded huge option grants despite poor executive performance, and others have made performance goals easier to reach. In 2002 nearly 200 companies swapped or repriced options—all to enrich wealthy executives who are already among the country's richest people. However, stock options can be a valuable governance mechanism to align the CEO's interests with those of the shareholders. The extraordinarily high level of compensation can, at times, be grounded in sound governance principles.[88] For example, Howard Solomon, CEO of Forest Laboratories, received total compensation of $148.5 million in 2001.[89] This represented $823,000 in salary, $400,000 in bonus, and $147.3 million in stock options that were exercised. However, shareholders also did well, receiving gains of 40 percent. The firm has enjoyed spectacular growth over the past ten years, and Solomon has been CEO since 1977. Thus, huge income is attributed largely to gains that have built up over many years. As stated by compensation committee member Dan Goldwasser, "If a CEO is delivering substantial increases in shareholder value, . . . it's only appropriate that he be rewarded for it."

However, the "pay for performance" principle doesn't always hold.[90] In addition to the granting of stock options, boards of directors are often failing to fulfill their fiduciary responsibilities to shareholders when they lower the performance targets that executives need to meet in order to receive millions of dollars. At Ford, for example, its "profit" goal for 2007 was to *lose* $4.9 billion. Ford beat the target, however, and lost *only* $3.9 billion. CEO Alan Mulally was rewarded $12 million in compensation, including a $7 million bonus for exceeding the profit goal. Ford's stock price fell 10 percent in 2007.

TIAA-CREF has provided several principles of corporate governance with regard to executive compensation (see Exhibit 9.8).[91] These include the importance of aligning the rewards of all employees—rank and file as well as executives—to the long-term performance of the corporation; general guidelines on the role of cash compensation, stock, and "fringe benefits"; and the mission of a corporation's compensation committee.[92]

External Governance Control Mechanisms

external governance control mechanisms
methods that ensure that managerial actions lead to shareholder value maximization and do not harm other stakeholder groups and that are outside the control of the corporate governance system.

Thus far, we've discussed internal governance mechanisms. Internal controls, however, are not always enough to ensure good governance. The separation of ownership and control that we discussed earlier requires multiple control mechanisms, some internal and some external, to ensure that managerial actions lead to shareholder value maximization. Further, society-at-large wants some assurance that this goal is met without harming other stakeholder groups. Now we discuss several **external governance control mechanisms** that have developed in most modern economies. These include the market for corporate control, auditors, governmental regulatory bodies, banks and analysts, media, and public activists.

Exhibit 9.8
TIAA-CREF's Principles on the Role of Stock in Executive Compensation

Stock-based compensation plans are a critical element of most compensation programs and can provide opportunities for managers whose efforts contribute to the creation of shareholder wealth. In evaluating the suitability of these plans, considerations of reasonableness, scale, linkage to performance, and fairness to shareholders and all employees also apply. TIAA-CREF, the largest pension system in the world, has set forth the following guidelines for stock-based compensation. Proper stock-based plans should:

- Allow for creation of executive wealth that is reasonable in view of the creation of shareholder wealth. Management should not prosper through stock while shareholders suffer.

- Have measurable and predictable outcomes that are directly linked to the company's performance.

- Be market oriented, within levels of comparability for similar positions in companies of similar size and business focus.

- Be straightforward and clearly described so that investors and employees can understand them.

- Be fully disclosed to the investing public and be approved by shareholders.

Source: www.tiaa-cref.org/pubs.

The Market for Corporate Control   Let us assume for a moment that internal control mechanisms in a company are failing. This means that the board is ineffective in monitoring managers and is not exercising the oversight required of them and that shareholders are passive and are not taking any actions to monitor or discipline managers. Under these circumstances managers may behave opportunistically.[93] Opportunistic behavior can take many forms. First, they can *shirk* their responsibilities. Shirking means that managers fail to exert themselves fully, as is required of them. Second, they can engage in *on the job consumption.* Examples of on the job consumption include private jets, club memberships, expensive artwork in the offices, and so on. Each of these represents consumption by managers that does not in any way increase shareholder value. Instead, they actually diminish shareholder value. Third, managers may engage in *excessive product-market diversification.*[94] As we discussed in Chapter 6, such diversification serves to reduce only the employment risk of the managers rather than the financial risk of the shareholders, who can more cheaply diversify their risk by owning a portfolio of investments. Is there any external mechanism to stop managers from shirking, consumption on the job, and excessive diversification?

The **market for corporate control** is one external mechanism that provides at least some partial solution to the problems described. If internal control mechanisms fail and the management is behaving opportunistically, the likely response of most shareholders will be to sell their stock rather than engage in activism.[95] As more stockholders vote with their feet, the value of the stock begins to decline. As the decline continues, at some point the market value of the firm becomes less than the book value. A corporate raider can take over the company for a price less than the book value of the assets of the company. The first thing that the raider may do on assuming control over the company will be to fire the underperforming management. The risk of being acquired by a hostile raider is often referred to as the **takeover constraint.** The takeover constraint deters management from engaging in opportunistic behavior.[96]

Although in theory the takeover constraint is supposed to limit managerial opportunism, in recent years its effectiveness has become diluted as a result of a number of

market for corporate control an external control mechanism in which shareholders dissatisfied with a firm's management sell their shares.

takeover constraint the risk to management of the firm being acquired by a hostile raider.

defense tactics adopted by incumbent management (see Chapter 6). Foremost among them are poison pills, greenmail, and golden parachutes. Poison pills are provisions adopted by the company to reduce its worth to the acquirer. An example would be payment of a huge one-time dividend, typically financed by debt. Greenmail involves buying back the stock from the acquirer, usually at an attractive premium. Golden parachutes are employment contracts that cause the company to pay lucrative severance packages to top managers fired as a result of a takeover, often running to several million dollars.

Auditors   Even when there are stringent disclosure requirements, there is no guarantee that the information disclosed will be accurate. Managers may deliberately disclose false information or withhold negative financial information as well as use accounting methods that distort results based on highly subjective interpretations. Therefore, all accounting statements are required to be audited and certified to be accurate by external auditors. These auditing firms are independent organizations staffed by certified professionals who verify the firm's books of accounts. Audits can unearth financial irregularities and ensure that financial reporting by the firm conforms to standard accounting practices.

Recent developments leading to the bankruptcy of firms such as Enron and World-Com and a spate of earnings restatements raise questions about the failure of the auditing firms to act as effective external control mechanisms. Why did an auditing firm like Arthur Andersen, with decades of good reputation in the auditing profession at stake, fail to raise red flags about accounting irregularities? First, auditors are appointed by the firm being audited. The desire to continue that business relationship sometimes makes them overlook financial irregularities. Second, most auditing firms also do consulting work and often have lucrative consulting contracts with the firms that they audit. Understandably, some of them tend not to ask too many difficult questions, because they fear jeopardizing the consulting business, which is often more profitable than the auditing work.

The recent restatement of earnings by Xerox is an example of the lack of independence of auditing firms. The SEC filed a lawsuit against KPMG, the world's third largest accounting firm, in January 2003 for allowing Xerox to inflate its revenues by $3 billion between 1997 and 2000. Of the $82 million that Xerox paid KPMG during those four years, only $26 million was for auditing. The rest was for consulting services. When one of the auditors objected to Xerox's practice of booking revenues for equipment leases earlier than it should have, Xerox asked KPMG to replace him. It did.[97]

Banks and Analysts   Commercial and investment banks have lent money to corporations and therefore have to ensure that the borrowing firm's finances are in order and that the loan covenants are being followed. Stock analysts conduct ongoing in-depth studies of the firms that they follow and make recommendations to their clients to buy, hold, or sell. Their rewards and reputation depend on the quality of these recommendations. Their access to information, knowledge of the industry and the firm, and the insights they gain from interactions with the management of the company enable them to alert the investing community of both positive and negative developments relating to a company.

It is generally observed that analyst recommendations are often more optimistic than warranted by facts. "Sell" recommendations tend to be exceptions rather than the norm. Many analysts failed to grasp the gravity of the problems surrounding failed companies such as Enron and Global Crossing till the very end. Part of the explanation may lie in the fact that most analysts work for firms that also have investment banking relationships with the companies they follow. Negative recommendations by analysts can displease the management, who may decide to take their investment banking business to a rival firm. Otherwise independent and competent analysts may be pressured to overlook negative information or tone down their criticism. A recent settlement between the Securities and Exchange Commission and the New York State Attorney General with 10 banks requires them to pay $1.4 billion in penalties and to fund independent research for investors.[98]

Regulatory Bodies   The extent of government regulation is often a function of the type of industry. Banks, utilities, and pharmaceuticals are subject to more regulatory oversight because of their importance to society. Public corporations are subject to more regulatory requirements than private corporations.[99]

All public corporations are required to disclose a substantial amount of financial information by bodies such as the Securities and Exchange Commission. These include quarterly and annual filings of financial performance, stock trading by insiders, and details of executive compensation packages. There are two primary reasons behind such requirements. First, markets can operate efficiently only when the investing public has faith in the market system. In the absence of disclosure requirements, the average investor suffers from a lack of reliable information and therefore may completely stay away from the capital market. This will negatively impact an economy's ability to grow. Second, disclosure of information such as insider trading protects the small investor to some extent from the negative consequences of information asymmetry. The insiders and large investors typically have more information than the small investor and can therefore use that information to buy or sell before the information becomes public knowledge.

The failure of a variety of external control mechanisms led the U.S. Congress to pass the Sarbanes-Oxley Act in 2002. This act calls for many stringent measures that would ensure better governance of U.S. corporations. Some of these measures include:[100]

- *Auditors* are barred from certain types of nonaudit work. They are not allowed to destroy records for five years. Lead partners auditing a client should be changed at least every five years.
- *CEOs* and *CFOs* must fully reveal off-balance-sheet finances and vouch for the accuracy of the information revealed.
- *Executives* must promptly reveal the sale of shares in firms they manage and are not allowed to sell when other employees cannot.
- *Corporate lawyers* must report to senior managers any violations of securities law lower down.

Strategy Spotlight 9.6 discusses some of the expenses that companies have incurred in complying with the Sarbanes-Oxley Act.

Media and Public Activists   The press is not usually recognized as an external control mechanism in the literature on corporate governance. There is no denying that in all developed capitalist economies, the financial press and media play an important indirect role in monitoring the management of public corporations. In the United States, business magazines such as *BusinessWeek* and *Fortune,* financial newspapers such as *The Wall Street Journal* and *Investors Business Daily,* as well as television networks like Financial News Network and CNBC are constantly reporting on companies. Public perceptions about a company's financial prospects and the quality of its management are greatly influenced by the media. Food Lion's reputation was sullied when ABC's *Prime Time Live* in 1992 charged the company with employee exploitation, false package dating, and unsanitary meat handling practices. Bethany McLean of *Fortune* magazine is often credited as the first to raise questions about Enron's long-term financial viability.[101]

Similarly, consumer groups and activist individuals often take a crusading role in exposing corporate malfeasance. Well-known examples include Ralph Nader and Erin Brockovich, who played important roles in bringing to light the safety issues related to GM's Corvair and environmental pollution issues concerning Pacific Gas and Electric Company, respectively. Ralph Nader has created over 30 watchdog groups including:[102]

- *Aviation Consumer Action Project.* Works to propose new rules to prevent flight delays, impose penalties for deceiving passengers about problems, and push for higher compensation for lost luggage.

Governance Reform: The Costs Add Up

In the aftermath of Enron and WorldCom and a spate of corporate scandals early in the decade, the U.S. Congress passed the Sarbanes-Oxley Act in 2002. It was an effort to restore investor confidence in the governance of corporations in general and financial reporting in particular. Three years later, a backlash seems to be developing among executives about the high compliance costs and some of the more draconian requirements.

The major source of resentment is the issue of cost. It is estimated that large corporations with revenues over $4 billion have to spend an average of $35 million a year to implement Sarbanes-Oxley. Medium-sized companies spend $3.1 million a year on average. Smaller companies find the cost of compliance particularly burdensome because they have a smaller revenue base. Some critics go to the extent of arguing that this amounts to a form of regressive taxation against small businesses. Many are even considering delisting to avoid compliance costs.

Costs are not the only problem that companies face. Meeting the requirements of Sarbanes-Oxley is very time consuming as well. For example, the law requires that financial numbers such as value of inventory and receivables are cross-checked. But it requires an army

of additional people and significant additional costs to ensure this. Yellow Roadway Corporation, the nation's largest trucking firm, had to use 200 employees and $9 million to accomplish this in 2004. This was three percent of their total profits. And just think of the lost productivity!

Nasdaq officials say the Sarbanes-Oxley burden is heaviest on the smallest companies, and firms with less than $100 million in revenues make up half of Nasdaq's 3,000 listings. The regulatory costs average two percent of revenue at firms with revenue under $100 million, while they are only 0.1 percent for the biggest companies. Theodore Stebbins, chairman of investment banking at Canaccord Adams says, "Clearly, the low end of the Nasdaq is broken. We can no longer in good conscience recommend to our small clients that they go public on Nasdaq."

How much has Sarbanes-Oxley succeeded in improving governance and ensuring the accuracy and reliability of financial reporting? While it is too early to assess the impact, there is at least some anecdotal evidence that it is having some impact. Visteon Corp., an auto-parts supplier, reported that they uncovered problems with their accounts receivable while complying with the requirements of the act. Similarly, SunTrust Banks Inc. fired three officers after discovering errors in the calculation of loan allowances in their portfolios. Tough but fair regulations can improve governance, but the costs of compliance cannot be ignored.

Source: Brown, E. 2006. London Calling. *Forbes*, May 8: 51–52; and Henry, D. 2005. Death, Taxes & Sarbanes-Oxley? *BusinessWeek*, January 17: 28–31.

- *Center for Auto Safety.* Helps consumers find plaintiff lawyers and agitate for vehicle recalls, increased highway safety standards, and lemon laws.
- *Center for Study of Responsive Law.* This is Nader's headquarters. Home of a consumer project on technology, this group sponsored seminars on Microsoft remedies and pushed for tougher Internet privacy rules. It also took on the drug industry over costs.
- *Pension Rights Center.* This center helped employees of IBM, General Electric, and other companies to organize themselves against cash-balance pension plans.

Corporate Governance: An International Perspective

The topic of corporate governance has long been dominated by agency theory and based on the explicit assumption of the separation of ownership and control.[103] The central conflicts are principal–agent conflicts between shareholders and management. However, such an underlying assumption seldom applies outside of the United States and the United Kingdom. This is particularly true in emerging economies and continental Europe. Here, there is often concentrated ownership, along with extensive family ownership and control, business group structures, and weak legal protection for minority shareholders. Serious conflicts tend to exist between two classes of principals: controlling shareholders and minority shareholders. Such conflicts can be called **principal–principal (PP) conflicts,** as opposed to *principal–agent* conflicts (see Exhibits 9.9 and 9.10).

Strong family control is one of the leading indicators of concentrated ownership. In East Asia (excluding China), approximately 57 percent of the corporations have board chairmen and CEOs from the controlling families. In continental Europe, this number is 68 percent. A very common practice is the appointment of family members as board chairman, CEOs, and other top executives. This happens because the families are controlling (not necessarily majority) shareholders. In 2003, 30-year-old James Murdoch was appointed CEO of British Sky Broadcasting (BSkyB), Europe's largest satellite broadcaster. There was very vocal resistance by minority shareholders. Why was he appointed in the first place? James's father just happened to be Rupert Murdoch, who controlled 35 percent of BSkyB and chaired the board. Clearly, this is a case of a PP conflict.

In general, three conditions must be met for PP conflicts to occur:

- A dominant owner or group of owners who have interests that are distinct from minority shareholders.
- Motivation for the controlling shareholders to exercise their dominant positions to their advantage.
- Few formal (such as legislation or regulatory bodies) or informal constraints that would discourage or prevent the controlling shareholders from exploiting their advantageous positions.

> **principal–principal conflicts** conflicts between two classes of principals—controlling shareholders and minority shareholders—within the context of a corporate governance system.

	Principal–Agent Conflicts	Principal–Principal Conflicts
Goal Incongruence	Between shareholders and professional managers who own a relatively small portion of the firm's equity.	Between controlling shareholders and minority shareholders.
Ownership Pattern	Dispersed—5%–20% is considered "concentrated ownership."	Concentrated—Often greater than 50% of equity is controlled by controlling shareholders.
Manifestations	Strategies that benefit entrenched managers at the expense of shareholders in general (e.g., shirking, pet projects, excessive compensation, and empire building).	Strategies that benefit controlling shareholders at the expense of minority shareholders (e.g., minority shareholder expropriation, nepotism, and cronyism).
Institutional Protection of Minority Shareholders	Formal constraints (e.g., judicial reviews and courts) set an upper boundary on potential expropriation by majority shareholders. Informal norms generally adhere to shareholder wealth maximization.	Formal institutional protection is often lacking, corrupted, or un-enforced. Informal norms are typically in favor of the interests of controlling shareholders ahead of those of minority investors.

Source: Adapted from Young, M., Peng, M. W., Ahlstrom, D., & Bruton, G. 2002. Governing the Corporation in Emerging Economies: A Principal–Principal Perspective. *Academy of Management Best Papers Proceedings,* Denver.

Exhibit 9.9 **Traditional Principal–Agent Conflicts versus Principal–Principal Conflicts: How They Differ along Dimensions**

Exhibit 9.10 Principal–Agent Conflicts and Principal–Principal Conflicts: A Diagram

Source: Young, M. N., Peng, M. W., Ahlstrom, D., Bruton, G. D., & Jiang, 2008. Principal–Principal Conflicts in Corporate Governance. *Journal of Management Studies* 45(1):196–220; and Peng, M. V. 2006. *Global Strategy.* Cincinnati: Thomson South-Western. We are very appreciative of the helpful comments of Mike Young of Hong Kong Baptist University and Mike Peng of the University of Texas at Dallas.

expropriation of minority shareholders activities that enrich the controlling shareholders at the expense of the minority shareholders.

business groups a set of firms that, though legally independent, are bound together by a constellation of formal and informal ties and are accustomed to taking coordinated action.

The result is often that family managers, who represent (or actually are) the controlling shareholders, engage in **expropriation of minority shareholders**, which is defined as activities that enrich the controlling shareholders at the expense of minority shareholders. What is their motive? After all, controlling shareholders have incentives to maintain firm value. But controlling shareholders may take actions that decrease aggregate firm performance if their personal gains from expropriation exceed their personal losses from their firm's lowered performance.

Another ubiquitous feature of corporate life outside of the United States and United Kingdom are *business groups* such as the keiretsus of Japan and the chaebols of South Korea. This is particularly dominant in emerging economies. A **business group** is "a set of firms that, though legally independent, are bound together by a constellation of formal and informal ties and are accustomed to taking coordinated action."[104] Business groups are especially common in emerging economies, and they differ from other organizational forms in that they are communities of firms without clear boundaries.

Business groups have many advantages that can enhance the value of a firm. They often facilitate technology transfer or intergroup capital allocation that otherwise might be impossible because of inadequate institutional infrastructure such as excellent financial services firms. On the other hand, informal ties—such as cross-holdings, board interlocks, and coordinated actions—can often result in intragroup activities and transactions, often at very favorable terms to member firms. Expropriation can be legally done through *related transactions,* which can occur when controlling owners sell firm assets to another firm they own at below market prices or spin off the most profitable part of a public firm and merge it with another of their private firms.

Strategy Spotlight 9.7 provides examples from Latin America of effective corporate governance.

strategy spotlight

Effective and Ineffective Corporate Governance among "Multilatinas"

Latin-owned companies, such as Mexico's Cemex, Argentina's Arcor, and Brazil's Embraer, have been successful in their home markets against U.S. and European competitors. Several of these companies have become "multilatinas," pursuing a strategy of regional and international expansion. Recently, 82 percent of merger and acquisition deals in Latin America were originated by Latin companies. However, while the rise of these Latin firms is promising, it is not enough to ensure they will be competitive globally against large industrialized multinational firms. Access to international capital markets necessary for the "multilatinas" to grow has created a need for a new openness in corporate governance and transparency for these firms.

There are three components emerging-market multinational firms need to implement to succeed:

Sources: Pigorini, P., Ramos, A., & de Souza, I. 2008. Pitting Latin Multinationals against Established Giants. *Strategy+Business*, November 4: www.strategy-business.com/media/file/leading_ideas-20081104.pdf; Martinez, J., Esperanca, J., & de la Torre, J. 2005. Organizational Change among Emerging Latin American Firms: From "Multilatinas" to Multinationals. *Management Research*, 3(3): 173–188; Krauss, C. 2007. Latin American Companies Make Big U.S. Gains. *New York Times*, May 2: www.nytimes.com/2007/05/02/business/worldbusiness/02latin.html.

- **Shareholder rights.** Minority shareholders must be protected through clear and fair dividend distribution and fair valuation in the event of mergers and acquisitions.

- **Compliance.** The audit committee of the board must be empowered to evaluate the financial statements of the firm and interact with both internal and external auditors.

- **Board and management composition.** Because many multilatinas are still in the process of building effective governance systems, it is important that the board members and top managers have credible professional backgrounds and experience.

These firms need to set up the right board and manager dynamics both to improve access to capital and to implement international management. Many multilatinas were or still are family-owned firms. Boards of these firms tend to be filled with members who have a strong loyalty to the controlling family, but not necessarily exposure to global strategic initiatives and strategies. Many of these firms still use centralized information control systems. In order to grow, some firms may have to consider giving local country managers more authority to make decisions.

Reflecting on Career Implications . . .

- *Behavioral Control:* What sources of behavioral control does your organization employ? In general, too much emphasis on rules and regulations may stifle initiative and be detrimental to your career opportunities.
- *Rewards and Incentives:* Is your organization's reward structure fair and equitable? Does it effectively reward outstanding performance? If not, there may be a long-term erosion of morale which may have long-term adverse career implications for you.
- *Culture:* Consider the type of organization culture that would provide the best work environment for your career goals. How does your organization's culture deviate from this concept? Does your organization have a strong and effective culture? If so, professionals are more likely to develop strong "firm specific" ties, which further enhances collaboration.
- *Corporate Governance:* Does your organization practice effective corporate governance? Such practices will enhance a firm's culture and it will be easier to attract top talent. Operating within governance guidelines is usually a strong indicator of organizational citizenship which, in turn, should be good for your career prospects.

Summary

For firms to be successful, they must practice effective strategic control and corporate governance. Without such controls, the firm will not be able to achieve competitive advantages and outperform rivals in the marketplace.

We began the chapter with the key role of informational control. We contrasted two types of control systems: what we termed "traditional" and "contemporary" information control systems. Whereas traditional control systems may have their place in placid, simple competitive environments, there are fewer of those in today's economy. Instead, we advocated the contemporary approach wherein the internal and external environment are constantly monitored so that when surprises emerge, the firm can modify its strategies, goals, and objectives.

Behavioral controls are also a vital part of effective control systems. We argued that firms must develop the proper balance between culture, rewards and incentives, and boundaries and constraints. Where there are strong and positive cultures and rewards, employees tend to internalize the organization's strategies and objectives. This permits a firm to spend fewer resources on monitoring behavior, and assures the firm that the efforts and initiatives of employees are more consistent with the overall objectives of the organization.

In the final section of this chapter, we addressed corporate governance, which can be defined as the relationship between various participants in determining the direction and performance of the corporation. The primary participants include shareholders, management (led by the chief executive officer), and the board of directors. We reviewed studies that indicated a consistent relationship between effective corporate governance and financial performance. There are also several internal and external control mechanisms that can serve to align managerial interests and shareholder interests. The internal mechanisms include a committed and involved board of directors, shareholder activism, and effective managerial incentives and rewards. The external mechanisms include the market for corporate control, banks and analysts, regulators, the media, and public activists. We also addressed corporate governance from both a United States and an international perspective.

Summary Review Questions

1. Why are effective strategic control systems so important in today's economy?

2. What are the main advantages of "contemporary" control systems over "traditional" control systems? What are the main differences between these two systems?

3. Why is it important to have a balance between the three elements of behavioral control—culture; rewards and incentives; and, boundaries?

4. Discuss the relationship between types of organizations and their primary means of behavioral control.

5. Boundaries become less important as a firm develops a strong culture and reward system. Explain.

6. Why is it important to avoid a "one best way" mentality concerning control systems? What are the consequences of applying the same type of control system to all types of environments?

7. What is the role of effective corporate governance in improving a firm's performance? What are some of the key governance mechanisms that are used to ensure that managerial and shareholder interests are aligned?

8. Define principal–principal (PP) conflicts. What are the implications for corporate governance?

Key Terms

strategic control 312
traditional approach to strategic control, 313
informational control, 315
behavioral control, 315
organizational culture, 317
reward system 318
boundaries and constraints 320
corporate governance, 324
corporation, 326
agency theory, 326
board of directors, 327
shareholder activism, 331
external governance control mechanisms, 332
market for corporate control, 333
takeover constraint, 333
principal–principal conflicts, 337
expropriation of minority shareholders 338
business groups, 338

Experiential Exercise

McDonald's Corporation, the world's largest fast-food restaurant chain, with 2008 revenues of $24 billion, has recently been on a "roll." Its shareholder value has more than tripled between April 2003 and April 2009. Using the Internet or library sources, evaluate the quality of the corporation in terms of management, the board of directors, and shareholder activism. Are the issues you list favorable or unfavorable for sound corporate governance?

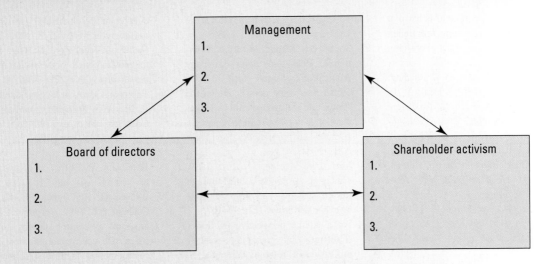

Management
1.
2.
3.

Board of directors
1.
2.
3.

Shareholder activism
1.
2.
3.

Application Questions Exercises

1. The problems of many firms may be attributed to a "traditional" control system that failed to continuously monitor the environment and make necessary changes in their strategy and objectives. What companies are you familiar with that responded appropriately (or inappropriately) to environmental change?

2. How can a strong, positive culture enhance a firm's competitive advantage? How can a weak, negative culture erode competitive advantages? Explain and provide examples.

3. Use the Internet to research a firm that has an excellent culture and/or reward and incentive system. What are this firm's main financial and nonfinancial benefits?

4. Using the Internet, go to the website of a large, publicly held corporation in which you are interested. What evidence do you see of effective (or ineffective) corporate governance?

Ethics Questions

1. Strong cultures can have powerful effects on employee behavior. How does this create inadvertent control mechanisms? That is, are strong cultures an ethical way to control behavior?

2. Rules and regulations can help reduce unethical behavior in organizations. To be effective, however, what other systems, mechanisms, and processes are necessary?

References

1. Ante, S. E. 2008. Sprint's wake-up call. *BusinessWeek,* March 3: 54–57; Holson, L. 2008. Bedeviled by the churn, Sprint tries to win back disgruntled customers. *New York Times,* July 8, Technology: http://www.nytimes.com/2008/07/08/technology/08sprint.html; and Cheng, R. & Sharma, A. 2008. Sprint squeezed as customers flee; Wireless carrier sees drop of 1.3 million subscribers; negotiates new credit agreement. *The Wall Street Journal,* November 8: B5.

2. This chapter draws upon Picken, J. C. & Dess, G. G. 1997. *Mission critical.* Burr Ridge, IL: Irwin Professional Publishing.

3. Argyris, C. 1977. Double-loop learning in organizations. *Harvard Business Review,* 55: 115–125.

4. Simons, R. 1995. Control in an age of empowerment. *Harvard Business Review,* 73: 80–88. This chapter draws on this source in the discussion of informational control.

5. Goold, M. & Quinn, J. B. 1990. The paradox of strategic controls. *Strategic Management Journal,* 11: 43–57.

6. Quinn, J. B. 1980. *Strategies for change.* Homewood, IL: Richard D. Irwin.

7. Mintzberg, H. 1987. Crafting strategy. *Harvard Business Review,* 65: 66–75.

8. Weston, J. S. 1992. Soft stuff matters. *Financial Executive,* July–August: 52–53.

9. This discussion of control systems draws upon Simons, op. cit.

10. For an interesting perspective on this issue and how a downturn in the economy can reduce the tendency toward "free agency" by managers and professionals, refer to Morris, B. 2001. White collar blues. *Fortune,* July 23: 98–110.

11. For a colorful example of behavioral control in an organization, see: Beller, P. C. 2009. Activision's unlikely hero. *Forbes.* February 2: 52–58.

12. Ouchi, W. 1981. *Theory Z.* Reading, MA: Addison-Wesley; Deal, T. E. & Kennedy, A. A. 1982. *Corporate cultures.* Reading, MA: Addison-Wesley; Peters, T. J. & Waterman, R. H. 1982. *In search of excellence.* New York: Random House; Collins, J. 2001. *Good to great.* New York: HarperCollins.

13. Collins, J. C. & Porras, J. I. 1994. *Built to last: Successful habits of visionary companies.* New York: Harper Business.

14. Lee, J. & Miller, D. 1999. People matter: Commitment to employees, strategy, and performance in Korean firms. *Strategic Management Journal,* 6: 579–594.

15. For an insightful discussion of IKEA's unique culture, see Kling, K. & Goteman, I. 2003. IKEA CEO Anders Dahlvig on international growth and IKEA's unique corporate culture and brand identity. *Academy of Management Executive,* 17(1): 31–37.

16. For a discussion of how professionals inculcate values, refer to Uhl-Bien, M. & Graen, G. B. 1998. Individual self-management: Analysis of professionals' self-managing activities in functional and cross-functional work teams. *Academy of Management Journal,* 41(3): 340–350.

17. A perspective on how antisocial behavior can erode a firm's culture can be found in Robinson, S. L. & O'Leary-Kelly, A. M. 1998. Monkey see, monkey do: The influence of work groups on the antisocial behavior of employees. *Academy of Management Journal,* 41(6): 658–672.

18. An interesting perspective on organization culture is in: Mehta, S. N. 2009. UnderArmour reboots. *Fortune,* February 2: 29–33.

19. For insights on social pressure as a means for control, refer to: Goldstein, N. J. 2009. Harnessing social pressure. *Harvard Business Review,* 87(2): 25.

20. Mitchell, R. 1989. Masters of innovation. *BusinessWeek,* April 10: 58–63.

21. Sellers, P. 1993. Companies that serve you best. *Fortune,* May 31: 88.

22. Southwest Airlines Culture Committee. 1993. *Luv Lines* (company publication), March–April: 17–18; for an interesting perspective on the "downside" of strong "cultlike" organizational cultures, refer to Arnott, D. A. 2000. *Corporate cults.* New York: AMACOM.

23. Kerr, J. & Slocum, J. W., Jr. 1987. Managing corporate culture through reward systems. *Academy of Management Executive,* 1(2): 99–107.

24. For a unique perspective on leader challenges in managing wealthy professionals, refer to Wetlaufer, S. 2000. Who wants to manage a millionaire? *Harvard Business Review,* 78(4): 53–60.

25. Neilson, G. L., Pasternack, B. A., & Van Nuys, K. E. 2005. The passive-aggressive organization. *Harvard Business Review,* 83(10): 82–95.

26. These next two subsections draw upon Dess, G. G. & Picken, J. C. 1997. *Beyond productivity.* New York: AMACOM.

27. For a discussion of the benefits of stock options as executive compensation, refer to Hall, B. J. 2000. What you need to know about stock options. *Harvard Business Review,* 78(2): 121–129.

28. Tully, S. 1993. Your paycheck gets exciting. *Fortune,* November 13: 89.

29. Zellner, W., Hof, R. D., Brandt, R., Baker, S., & Greising, D. 1995. Go-go goliaths. *BusinessWeek,* February 13: 64–70.

30. This section draws on Dess & Picken, op. cit.: chap. 5.

31. Simons, op. cit.

32. Davis, E. 1997. Interview: Norman Augustine. *Management Review,* November: 11.

33. This section draws upon Dess, G. G. & Miller, A. 1993. *Strategic management.* New York: McGraw-Hill.

34. For a good review of the goal-setting literature, refer to Locke, E. A. & Latham, G. P. 1990. *A theory of goal setting and task performance.* Englewood Cliffs, NJ: Prentice Hall.

35. For an interesting perspective on the use of rules and regulations that is counter to this industry's (software) norms, refer to Fryer, B. 2001. Tom Siebel of Siebel Systems: High tech the old fashioned way. *Harvard Business Review,* 79(3): 118–130.

36. Thompson, A. A. Jr. & Strickland, A. J., III. 1998. *Strategic management: Concepts and cases* (10th ed.): 313. New York: McGraw-Hill.

37. Ibid.

38. Teitelbaum, R. 1997. Tough guys finish first. *Fortune,* July 21: 82–84.

39. Weaver, G. R., Trevino, L. K., & Cochran, P. L. 1999. Corporate ethics programs as control systems: Influences of executive commitment and environmental factors. *Academy of Management Journal,* 42(1): 41–57.

40. Cadbury, S. A. 1987. Ethical managers make their own rules. *Harvard Business Review,* 65: 3, 69–73.

41. Weber, J. 2003. CFOs on the hot seat. *BusinessWeek,* March 17: 66–70.

42. William Ouchi has written extensively about the use of clan control (which is viewed as an alternate to bureaucratic or market control). Here, a powerful culture results in people aligning their individual interests with those of the firm. Refer to Ouchi, op. cit. This section also draws on Hall, R. H. 2002. *Organizations: Structures, processes, and outcomes* (8th ed.). Upper Saddle River, NJ: Prentice Hall.

43. Interesting insights on corporate governance are in: Kroll, M., Walters, B. A., & Wright, P. 2008. Board vigilance, director experience, and corporate outcomes. *Strategic Management Journal,* 29(4): 363–382.

44. For a brief review of some central issues in corporate governance research, see: Hambrick, D. C., Werder, A. V., & Zajac, E. J. 2008. New directions in corporate governance research. *Organization Science,* 19(3): 381–385.

45. Monks, R. & Minow, N. 2001. *Corporate governance* (2nd ed.). Malden, MA: Blackwell.

46. Pound, J. 1995. The promise of the governed corporation. *Harvard Business Review,* 73(2): 89–98.

47. Maurer, H. & Linblad, C. 2009. Scandal at Satyam. *BusinessWeek,* January 19: 8; Scheck, J. & Stecklow, S. 2008.

Brocade ex-CEO gets 21 months in prison. *The Wall Street Journal*, January 17: A3; Heinzl, M. 2004. Nortel's directors and investors discuss changes to the board. *The Wall Street Journal*, September 30: B4; Editorial. 2003. Pulling Boeing out of a tailspin. *BusinessWeek*, December 15: 136; and Zimmerman, A., Ball, D., & Veen, M. 2003. A global journal report: Supermarket giant Ahoud ousts CEO in big accounting scandal. *The Wall Street Journal*, February 25: A1; Ibid; and Maurer, H. 2006. Is this "the HP way"? *BusinessWeek*, September 25: 34.

48. Corporate governance and social networks are discussed in: McDonald, M.L., Khanna, P., & Westphal, J.D. 2008. *Academy of Management Journal*. 51(3): 453-475.

49. This discussion draws upon Monks & Minow, op. cit.

50. For an interesting perspective on the politicization of the corporation, read: Palazzo, G. & Scherer, A. G. 2008. Corporate social responsibility, democracy, and the politicization of the corporation. *Academy of Management Review*, 33(3): 773–774.

51. Eisenhardt, K. M. 1989. Agency theory: An assessment and review. *Academy of Management Review*, 14(1): 57–74. Some of the seminal contributions to agency theory include Jensen, M. & Meckling, W. 1976. Theory of the firm: Managerial behavior, agency costs, and ownership structure. *Journal of Financial Economics*, 3: 305–360; Fama, E. & Jensen, M. 1983. Separation of ownership and control. *Journal of Law and Economics*, 26: 301, 325; and Fama, E. 1980. Agency problems and the theory of the firm. *Journal of Political Economy*, 88: 288–307.

52. Managers may also engage in "shirking"—that is, reducing or withholding their efforts. See, for example, Kidwell, R. E., Jr. & Bennett, N. 1993. Employee propensity to withhold effort: A conceptual model to intersect three avenues of research. *Academy of Management Review*, 18(3): 429–456.

53. For an interesting perspective on agency and clarification of many related concepts and terms, visit the following website: www.encycogov.com.

54. The relationship between corporate ownership structure and export intensity in Chinese firms is discussed in: Filatotchev, I., Stephan, J., & Jindra, B. 2008. Ownership structure, strategic controls and export intensity of foreign-invested firms in transition economies. *Journal of International Business*, 39(7): 1133–1148.

55. Argawal, A. & Mandelker, G. 1987. Managerial incentives and corporate investment and financing decisions. *Journal of Finance*, 42: 823–837.

56. For an insightful, recent discussion of the academic research on corporate governance, and in particular the role of boards of directors, refer to Chatterjee, S. & Harrison, J. S. 2001. Corporate governance. In Hitt, M. A., Freeman, R. E., & Harrison, J. S. (Eds.). *Handbook of strategic management*: 543–563. Malden, MA: Blackwell.

57. For an interesting theoretical discussion on corporate governance in Russia, see: McCarthy, D. J. & Puffer, S. M. 2008. Interpreting the ethicality of corporate governance decisions in Russia: Utilizing integrative social contracts theory to evaluate the relevance of agency theory norms. *Academy of Management Review*, 33(1): 11–31.

58. This opening discussion draws on Monks & Minow, op. cit. 164, 169; see also Pound, op. cit.

59. Business Roundtable. 1990. *Corporate governance and American competitiveness*, March: 7.

60. The director role in acquisition performance is addressed in: Westphal, J. D. & Graebner, M. E. 2008. What do they know? The effects of outside director acquisition experience on firm acquisition performance. *Strategic Management Journal*, 29(11): 1155–1178.

61. Byrne, J. A., Grover, R., & Melcher, R. A. 1997. The best and worst boards. *BusinessWeek*, November 26: 35–47. The three key roles of boards of directors are monitoring the actions of executives, providing advice, and providing links to the external environment to provide resources. See Johnson, J. L., Daily, C. M., & Ellstrand, A. E. 1996. Boards of directors: A review and research agenda. *Academy of Management Review*, 37: 409–438.

62. The role of outside directors is discussed in: Lester, R. H., Hillman, A., Zardkoohi, A., & Cannella, A. A. Jr. 2008. Former government officials as outside directors: The role of human and social capital. *Academy of Management Journal*, 51(5): 999–1013.

63. McGeehan, P. 2003. More chief executives shown the door, study says. *New York Times*, May 12: C2.

64. Gerdes, L. 2007. Hello, goodbye. *BusinessWeek*, January 22: 16.

65. For an analysis of the effects of outside directors' compensation on acquisition decisions, refer to Deutsch, T., Keil, T., & Laamanen, T. 2007. Decision making in acquisitions: The effect of outside directors' compensation on acquisition patterns. *Journal of Management*, 33(1): 30–56.

66. Director interlocks are addressed in: Kang, E. 2008. Director interlocks and spillover effects of reputational penalties from financial reporting fraud. *Academy of Management Journal*, 51 (3): 537–556.

67. There are benefits, of course, to having some insiders on the board of directors. Inside directors would be more aware of the firm's strategies. Additionally, outsiders may rely too often on financial performance indicators because of information asymmetries. For an interesting discussion, see Baysinger, B. D. & Hoskisson, R. E. 1990. The composition of boards of directors and strategic control: Effects on corporate strategy. *Academy of Management Review*, 15: 72–87.

68. Hambrick, D. C. & Jackson, E. M. 2000. Outside directors with a stake: The linchpin in improving governance. *California Management Review*, 42(4): 108–127.

69. Ibid.

70. Disney has begun to make many changes to improve its corporate governance, such as assigning only

independent directors to important board committees, restricting directors from serving on more than three boards, and appointing a lead director who can convene the board without approval by the CEO. In recent years, the Disney Co. has shown up on some "best" board lists. In addition Eisner has recently relinquished the chairman position.

71. Talk show. 2002. *BusinessWeek,* September 30: 14.

72. Ward, R. D. 2000. *Improving corporate boards.* New York: Wiley.

73. A discussion on the shareholder approval process in executive compensation is presented in: Brandes, P., Goranova, M., & Hall, S. 2008. Navigating shareholder influence: Compensation plans and the shareholder approval process. *Academy of Management Perspectives,* 22(1): 41–57.

74. Monks and Minow, op. cit.: 93.

75. A discussion of the factors that lead to shareholder activism is found in Ryan, L. V. & Schneider, M. 2002. The antecedents of institutional investor activism. *Academy of Management Review,* 27(4): 554–573.

76. For an insightful discussion of investor activism, refer to David, P., Bloom, M., & Hillman, A. 2007. Investor activism, managerial responsiveness, and corporate social performance. *Strategic Management Journal,* 28(1): 91–100.

77. There is strong research support for the idea that the presence of large block shareholders is associated with value-maximizing decisions. For example, refer to Johnson, R. A., Hoskisson, R. E., & Hitt, M. A. 1993. Board of director involvement in restructuring: The effects of board versus managerial controls and characteristics. *Strategic Management Journal,* 14: 33–50.

78. For a discussion of institutional activism and its link to CEO compensation, refer to: Chowdhury, S. D. & Wang, E. Z. 2009. Institutional activism types and CEO compensation. *Journal of Management,* 35(1): 5–36.

79. For an interesting perspective on the impact of institutional ownership on a firm's innovation strategies, see

Hoskisson, R. E., Hitt, M. A., Johnson, R. A., & Grossman, W. 2002. *Academy of Management Journal,* 45(4): 697–716.

80. www.calpers.ca.gov/index.jsp

81. Icahn, C. 2007. Icahn: On activist investors and private equity run wild. *BusinessWeek,* March 12: 21–22. For an interesting perspective on Carl Icahn's transition (?) from corporate raider to shareholder activist, read Grover, R. 2007. Just don't call him a raider. *BusinessWeek,* March 5: 68–69. The quote in the text is part of Icahn's response to the article by R. Grover.

82. For a study of the relationship between ownership and diversification, refer to Goranova, M., Alessandri, T. M., Brandes, P., & Dharwadkar, R. 2007. Managerial ownership and corporate diversification: A longitudinal view, *Strategic Management Journal,* 28(3): 211–226.

83. Jensen, M. C. & Murphy, K. J. 1990. CEO incentives—It's not how much you pay, but how. *Harvard Business Review,* 68(3): 138–149.

84. For a perspective on the relative advantages and disadvantages of "duality"—that is, one individual serving as both Chief Executive Office and Chairman of the Board, see Lorsch, J. W. & Zelleke, A. 2005. Should the CEO be the chairman? *MIT Sloan Management Review,* 46(2): 71–74.

85. A discussion of knowledge sharing is addressed in: Fey, C. F. & Furu, P. 2008. Top management incentive compensation and knowledge sharing in multinational corporations. *Strategic Management Journal,* 29(12): 1301–1324.

86. Sasseen, J. 2007. A better look at the boss's pay. *BusinessWeek,* February 26: 44–45; and Weinberg, N., Maiello, M., & Randall, D. 2008. Paying for failure. *Forbes,* May 19: 114, 116.

87. Byrnes, N. & Sasseen, J. 2007. Board of hard knocks. *BusinessWeek,* January 22: 36–39.

88. Research has found that executive compensation is more closely aligned with firm performance in companies with compensation committees and

boards dominated by outside directors. See, for example, Conyon, M. J. & Peck, S. I. 1998. Board control, remuneration committees, and top management compensation. *Academy of Management Journal,* 41: 146–157.

89. Lavelle, L., Jespersen, F. F., & Arndt, M. 2002. Executive pay. *BusinessWeek,* April 15: 66–72.

90. A perspective on whether or not CEOs are overpaid is provided in: Kaplan, S. N. 2008. Are U.S. CEOs overpaid: A response to Bogle and Walsh, J. P. *Academy of Management Perspectives.* 22(3): 28–34.

91. www.tiaa-cref.org/pubs.

92. Some insights on CEO compensation —and the importance of ethics—are addressed in: Heineman, B. W. Jr. 2008. The fatal flaw in pay for performance. *Harvard Business Review.* 86(6): 31, 34.

93. Such opportunistic behavior is common in all principal-agent relationships. For a description of agency problems, especially in the context of the relationship between shareholders and managers, see Jensen, M. C. & Meckling, W. H. 1976. Theory of the firm: Managerial behavior, agency costs, and ownership structure. *Journal of Financial Economics,* 3: 305–360.

94. Hoskisson, R. E. & Turk, T. A. 1990. Corporate restructuring: Governance and control limits of the internal market. *Academy of Management Review,* 15: 459–477.

95. For an insightful perspective on the market for corporate control and how it is influenced by knowledge intensity, see Coff, R. 2003. Bidding wars over R&D-intensive firms: Knowledge, opportunism, and the market for corporate control. *Academy of Management Journal,* 46(1): 74–85.

96. Walsh, J. P. & Kosnik, R. D. 1993. Corporate raiders and their disciplinary role in the market for corporate control. *Academy of Management Journal,* 36: 671–700.

97. Gunning for KPMG. 2003. *Economist,* February 1: 63.

98. Timmons, H. 2003. Investment banks: Who will foot their bill? *BusinessWeek,* March 3: 116.

99. The role of regulatory bodies in the banking industry is addressed in: Bhide, A. 2009. Why bankers got so reckless. *BusinessWeek,* February 9: 30–31.

100. Wishy-washy: The SEC pulls its punches on corporate-governance rules. 2003. *Economist,* February 1: 60.

101. McLean, B. 2001. Is Enron overpriced? *Fortune,* March 5: 122–125.

102. Bernstein, A. 2000. Too much corporate power. *BusinessWeek,* September 11: 35–37.

103. This section draws upon Young, M. N., Peng, M. W., Ahlstrom, D., Bruton, G. D., & Jiang, Y. 2005. Principal–principal conflicts in corporate governance (un-published manuscript); and, Peng, M. W. 2006. *Globalstrategy.* Cincinnati: Thomson South-Western. We are very appreciative of the helpful comments of Mike Young of Hong Kong Baptist University and Mike Peng of the University of Texas at Dallas.

104. Khanna, T. & Rivkin, J. 2001. Estimating the performance effects of business groups in emerging markets. *Strategic Management Journal,* 22: 45–74.

Creating Effective Organizational Designs

>learning objectives

After reading this chapter, you should have a good understanding of:

LO1 The growth patterns of major corporations and the relationship between a firm's strategy and its structure.

LO2 Each of the traditional types of organizational structure: simple, functional, divisional, and matrix.

LO3 The implications of a firm's international operations for organizational structure.

LO4 Why there is no "one best way" to design strategic reward and evaluation systems, and the important contingent roles of business- and corporate-level strategies.

LO5 The different types of boundaryless organizations—barrier-free, modular, and virtual—and their relative advantages and disadvantages.

LO6 The need for creating ambidextrous organizational designs that enable firms to explore new opportunities and effectively integrate existing operations.

To implement strategies successfully, firms must have appropriate organizational designs. These include the processes and integrating mechanisms necessary to ensure that boundaries among internal activities and external parties, such as suppliers, customers, and alliance partners, are flexible and permeable. A firm's performance will suffer if its managers don't carefully consider both of these organizational design attributes.

In the first section, we begin by discussing the growth patterns of large corporations to address the important relationships between the strategy that a firm follows and its corresponding structure. For example, as firms diversify into related product-market areas, they change their structure from functional to divisional. We then address the different types of traditional structures—simple, functional, divisional, and matrix—and their relative advantages and disadvantages. We close with a discussion of the implications of a firm's international operations for the structure of its organization.

The second section takes the perspective that there is no "one best way" to design an organization's strategic reward and evaluation system. Here we address two important contingencies: business- and corporate-level strategy. For example, when strategies require a great deal of collaboration, as well as resource and information sharing, there must be incentives and cultures that encourage and reward such initiatives.

The third section discusses the concept of the "boundaryless" organization. We do *not* argue that organizations should have no internal and external boundaries. Instead, we suggest that in rapidly changing and unpredictable environments, organizations must strive to make their internal and external boundaries both flexible and permeable. We suggest three different types of boundaryless organizations: barrier-free, modular, and virtual.

The fourth section focuses on the need for managers to recognize that they typically face two opposing challenges: (1) being proactive in taking advantage of new opportunities and (2) ensuring the effective coordination and integration of existing operations. This suggests the need for ambidextrous organizations; that is, firms that can both be efficient in how they manage existing assets and competencies and take advantage of opportunities in rapidly changing and unpredictable environments—conditions that are becoming more pronounced in today's global markets.

Learning from Mistakes

Carl Pope, Executive Director of the Sierra Club, claimed he was "bemused" as he rang the opening bell of the New York Stock Exchange on the Monday before Earth Day 2008 along with Donald Knauss, the CEO of Clorox. But Pope said, "Environmentalists and capitalism have an uneasy relationship, and for many of the companies listed on the Big Board, their most memorable experience with the Sierra Club came in the form of papers served for environmental lawsuits we've brought. [However,] companies are an essential part of the solution if we're going to reshape our economy along sustainable lines."

The Sierra Club has long been associated with the protection of nature. From its inception in 1892, John Muir and other supporters formed the Sierra Club "to make the mountains glad." John Muir was the club's first president, an office he held until his death in 1914. Muir's Sierra Club has gone on to help establish a series of new national parks and a National Wilderness Preservation System. However, Muir would never have imagined that this clean-living organization would partner with a chemical company in 2009.

Clorox introduced its "Green Works" line of products carrying a Sierra Club Logo. It looked like a good deal for both organizations. Clorox should have been pleased that Green Works products were selling well. The Sierra Club, in exchange for its endorsement, received large payments that could be used to help further its environmental conservation work. It seems like this partnership should have been a "clean solution" for the environment.[1]

What Went Wrong? Unfortunately, several key members of the Sierra Club were a little less than bemused with the deal Carl Pope had struck. Pope did not practice "boundaryless" organization coordination by communicating with other parts of the organization in executing the Clorox endorsement. Pope mentioned publicly that the Sierra Club's due diligence included the "toughest scrutiny" of the Clorox products being endorsed. Pope told Sierra Club leaders that "we consulted with the executive committee of the board of directors, the corporate relations committee, the toxics committee, the energy committee, and the environmental quality committee. None of these entities found fault with the Green Works as a product line."

However, others in the organization did not see the same picture of agreement painted by Mr. Pope. Jessica Frohman, the co-chair of the toxics committee, said that her panel never voted on the Clorox products. She said that, while her committee did review Environmental Protection Agency data on the products, its members did not test the products themselves. Furthermore, Frohman said that her committee members were not trained chemists and were not really in a position to guarantee anything about the products. The club's committee on corporate relations did take a vote on the Clorox endorsement deal and rejected it. However, Pope and the executive board "rejected the rejection" by the corporate relations committee and signed the Clorox agreement anyway.

Inside and outside the Sierra Club, tensions ran high and there were unhappy voices. One Clorox advisor, Adviser Makower, said of the deal the Sierra Club struck: "To be tied directly to sales and not reveal [the details], and to be endorsing the products, is, in any world, borderline unethical. . . . It soils the living room for everybody." A former Sierra Club director said that the current club leaders were "destroying the club's credibility. They should all be ashamed of themselves."

While Pope and the Sierra Club have lost loyal members over this controversy, they may have found a silver lining. Millions of shoppers, many of whom had never heard of the Sierra Club, are now being introduced to the club every day as they see the club logo on their bottles of Clorox Green Works cleaning products.

One of the central concepts in this chapter is the importance of boundaryless organizations. Successful organizations create permeable boundaries among the internal activities as well as between the organization and its external customers, suppliers, and alliance partners. We introduced this idea in Chapter 3 in our discussion of the value-chain concept, which consisted of several primary (e.g., inbound logistics, marketing and sales) and support activities (e.g., procurement, human resource management). The underlying cause of the Sierra Club's problem was its inability to establish close and effective working relationships between its various committees and volunteers. Frequently, managers were seemingly more focused on the financial health of the club than on the interests of the club's members.

Today's managers are faced with two ongoing and vital activities in structuring and designing their organizations. First, they must decide on the most appropriate type of organizational structure. Second, they need to assess what mechanisms, processes, and techniques are most helpful in enhancing the permeability of both internal and external boundaries.

Traditional Forms of Organizational Structure

Organizational structure refers to the formalized patterns of interactions that link a firm's tasks, technologies, and people.[2] Structures help to ensure that resources are used effectively in accomplishing an organization's mission. Structure provides a means of balancing two conflicting forces: a need for the division of tasks into meaningful groupings and the need to integrate such groupings in order to ensure efficiency and effectiveness. Structure identifies the executive, managerial, and administrative organization of a firm and indicates responsibilities and hierarchical relationships. It also influences the flow of information as well as the context and nature of human interactions.[3]

organizational structure the formalized patterns of interactions that link a firm's tasks, technologies, and people.

Most organizations begin very small and either die or remain small. Those that survive and prosper embark on strategies designed to increase the overall scope of operations and enable them to enter new product-market domains. Such growth places additional pressure on executives to control and coordinate the firm's increasing size and diversity. The most appropriate type of structure depends on the nature and magnitude of growth.

Patterns of Growth of Large Corporations: Strategy-Structure Relationships

A firm's strategy and structure change as it increases in size, diversifies into new product markets, and expands its geographic scope.[4] Exhibit 10.1 illustrates common growth patterns of firms.

>LO1

The growth patterns of major corporations and the relationship between a firm's strategy and its structure.

A new firm with a *simple structure* typically increases its sales revenue and volume of outputs over time. It may also engage in some vertical integration to secure sources of supply (backward integration) as well as channels of distribution (forward integration). The simple-structure firm then implements a *functional structure* to concentrate efforts on both increasing efficiency and enhancing its operations and products. This structure enables the firm to group its operations into either functions, departments, or geographic areas. As its initial markets mature, a firm looks beyond its present products and markets for possible expansion.

A strategy of related diversification requires a need to reorganize around product lines or geographic markets. This leads to a *divisional structure.* As the business expands in terms of sales revenues, and domestic growth opportunities become somewhat limited, a firm may seek opportunities in international markets. A firm has a wide variety of structures to choose from. These include *international division, geographic area, worldwide product division, worldwide functional,* and *worldwide matrix.* Deciding upon the most appropriate structure when a firm has international operations depends on three primary factors: the extent of international expansion, type of strategy (global, multidomestic, or transnational), and the degree of product diversity.[5]

Some firms may find it advantageous to diversify into several product lines rather than focus their efforts on strengthening distributor and supplier relationships through vertical integration. They would organize themselves according to product lines by implementing a divisional structure. Also, some firms may choose to move into unrelated product areas,

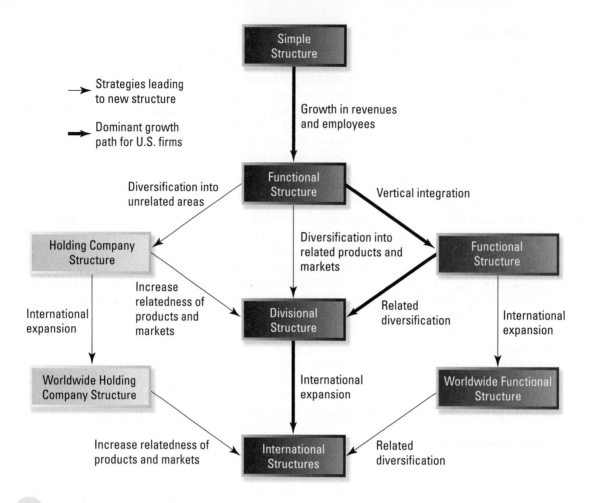

Exhibit 10.1 Dominant Growth Patterns of Large Corporations

Source: Adapted from J. R. Galbraith and R. K. Kazanjian. *Strategy Implementation: Structure, Systems and Process,* 2nd ed. Copyright © 1986.

typically by acquiring existing businesses. Frequently, their rationale is that acquiring assets and competencies is more economical or expedient than developing them internally. Such an unrelated, or conglomerate, strategy requires relatively little integration across businesses and sharing of resources. Thus, a *holding company structure* becomes appropriate. There are many other growth patterns, but these are the most common.*

Now we will discuss some of the most common types of organizational structures—simple, functional, divisional (including two variants: *strategic business unit* and *holding company*), and matrix and their advantages and disadvantages. We will close the section with a discussion of the structural implications when a firm expands its operations into international markets.[6]

---

* The lowering of transaction costs and globalization have led to some changes in the common historical patterns that we have discussed. Some firms are, in effect, bypassing the vertical integration stage. Instead, they focus on core competencies and outsource other value-creation activities. Also, even relatively young firms are going global early in their history because of lower communication and transportation costs. For an interesting perspective on global start-ups, see McDougall, P. P. & Oviatt, B. M. 1996. New Venture Internationalization, Strategic Change and Performance: A Follow-Up Study. *Journal of Business Venturing,* 11: 23–40; and McDougall, P. P. & Oviatt, B. M. (Eds.). 2000. The Special Research Forum on International Entrepreneurship. *Academy of Management Journal,* October: 902–1003.

Simple Structure

The **simple organizational structure** is the oldest, and most common, organizational form. Most organizations are very small and have a single or very narrow product line in which the owner-manager (or top executive) makes most of the decisions. The owner-manager controls all activities, and the staff serves as an extension of the top executive.

Advantages   The simple structure is highly informal and the coordination of tasks is accomplished by direct supervision. Decision making is highly centralized, there is little specialization of tasks, few rules and regulations, and an informal evaluation and reward system. Although the owner-manager is intimately involved in almost all phases of the business, a manager is often employed to oversee day-to-day operations.

Disadvantages   A simple structure may foster creativity and individualism since there are generally few rules and regulations. However, such "informality" may lead to problems. Employees may not clearly understand their responsibilities, which can lead to conflict and confusion. Employees may take advantage of the lack of regulations, act in their own self-interest, which can erode motivation and satisfaction and lead to the possible misuse of organizational resources. Small organizations have flat structures that limit opportunities for upward mobility. Without the potential for future advancement, recruiting and retaining talent may become very difficult.

Functional Structure

When an organization is small (15 employees or less), it is not necessary to have a variety of formal arrangements and groupings of activities. However, as firms grow, excessive demands may be placed on the owner-manager in order to obtain and process all of the information necessary to run the business. Chances are the owner will not be skilled in all specialties (e.g., accounting, engineering, production, marketing). Thus, he or she will need to hire specialists in the various functional areas. Such growth in the overall scope and complexity of the business necessitates a **functional organizational structure** wherein the major functions of the firm are grouped internally. The coordination and integration of the functional areas becomes one of the most important responsibilities of the chief executive of the firm (see Exhibit 10.2).

Functional structures are generally found in organizations in which there is a single or closely related product or service, high production volume, and some vertical integration. Initially, firms tend to expand the overall scope of their operations by penetrating existing markets, introducing similar products in additional markets, or increasing the level of vertical integration. Such expansion activities clearly increase the scope and complexity of the operations. The functional structure provides for a high level of centralization that helps to ensure integration and control over the related product-market activities or multiple primary activities (from inbound logistics to operations to marketing, sales, and service) in the value chain (addressed in Chapters 3 and 4). Strategy Spotlight 10.1 provides an example of an effective functional organization structure—Parkdale Mills.

>LO2
Each of the traditional types of organizational structure: simple, functional, divisional, and matrix.

simple organizational structure an organizational form in which the owner-manager makes most of the decisions and controls activities, and the staff serves as an extension of the top executive.

functional organizational structure an organizational form in which the major functions of the firm, such as production, marketing, R&D, and accounting, are grouped internally.

Exhibit 10.2
Functional Organizational Structure

Parkdale Mills: A Successful Functional Organizational Structure

For more than 80 years, Parkdale Mills, with approximately $1 billion in revenues, has been the industry leader in the production of cotton and cotton blend yarns. Their expertise comes by concentrating on a single product line, perfecting processes, and welcoming innovation. According to CEO Andy Warlick, "I think we've probably spent more than any

two competitors combined on new equipment and robotics. We do this because we have to compete in a global market where a lot of the competition has a lower wage structure and gets subsidies that we don't receive, so we really have to focus on consistency and cost control." Yarn making is generally considered to be a commodity business, and Parkdale is the industry's low-cost producer.

Tasks are highly standardized and authority is centralized with Duke Kimbrell, founder and chairman, and CEO Andy Warlick. The firm operates a bare-bones staff with a small staff of top executives. Kimbrell and Warlick are considered shrewd about the cotton market, technology, customer loyalty, and incentive pay.

Sources: Stewart, C. 2003. The Perfect Yarn. The Manufacturer.com, July 31; www.parkdalemills.com; Berman, P. 1987. The Fast Track Isn't Always the Best Track. *Forbes*, November 2: 60–64; and personal communication with Duke Kimbrell, March 11, 2005.

Advantages   By bringing together specialists into functional departments, a firm is able to enhance its coordination and control within each of the functional areas. Decision making in the firm will be centralized at the top of the organization. This enhances the organizational-level (as opposed to functional area) perspective across the various functions in the organization. In addition, the functional structure provides for a more efficient use of managerial and technical talent since functional area expertise is pooled in a single department (e.g., marketing) instead of being spread across a variety of product-market areas. Finally, career paths and professional development in specialized areas are facilitated.

Disadvantages   The differences in values and orientations among functional areas may impede communication and coordination. Edgar Schein of MIT has argued that shared assumptions, often based on similar backgrounds and experiences of members, form around functional units in an organization. This leads to what are often called "stove pipes" or "silos," in which departments view themselves as isolated, self-contained units with little need for interaction and coordination with other departments. This erodes communication because functional groups may have not only different goals but also differing meanings of words and concepts. According to Schein:

> The word "marketing" will mean product development to the engineer, studying customers through market research to the product manager, merchandising to the salesperson, and constant change in design to the manufacturing manager. When they try to work together, they will often attribute disagreements to personalities and fail to notice the deeper, shared assumptions that color how each function thinks.[7]

Such narrow functional orientations also may lead to short-term thinking based largely upon what is best for the functional area, not the entire organization. In a manufacturing firm, sales may want to offer a wide range of customized products to appeal to the firm's customers; R&D may overdesign products and components to achieve technical elegance; and manufacturing may favor no-frills products that can be produced at low cost by means of long production runs. Functional structures may overburden the top executives in the firm because conflicts have a tendency to be "pushed up" to the top of the organization since there are no managers who are responsible for the specific product lines. Functional structures make it difficult to establish uniform performance standards across the entire organization. It may be relatively easy to evaluate production managers on the basis of production volume and cost control, but establishing performance measures for engineering, R&D, and accounting become more problematic.

Divisional Structure

The **divisional organizational structure** (sometimes called the multidivisional structure or M-Form) is organized around products, projects, or markets. Each of the divisions, in turn, includes its own functional specialists who are typically organized into departments.[8] A divisional structure encompasses a set of relatively autonomous units governed by a central corporate office. The operating divisions are relatively independent and consist of products and services that are different from those of the other divisions. Operational decision making in a large business places excessive demands on the firm's top management. In order to attend to broader, longer-term organizational issues, top-level managers must delegate decision making to lower-level managers. Divisional executives play a key role: they help to determine the product-market and financial objectives for the division as well as their division's contribution to overall corporate performance.[9] The rewards are based largely on measures of financial performance such as net income and revenue. Exhibit 10.3 illustrates a divisional structure.

> **divisional organizational structure** an organizational form in which products, projects, or product markets are grouped internally.

General Motors was among the earliest firms to adopt the divisional organizational structure.[10] In the 1920s the company formed five major product divisions (Cadillac, Buick, Oldsmobile, Pontiac, and Chevrolet) as well as several industrial divisions. Since then, many firms have discovered that as they diversified into new product-market activities, functional structures—with their emphasis on single functional departments—were unable to manage the increased complexity of the entire business.

Advantages   By creating separate divisions to manage individual product markets, there is a separation of strategic and operating control. Divisional managers can focus their efforts on improving operations in the product markets for which they are responsible, and corporate officers can devote their time to overall strategic issues for the entire corporation. The focus on a division's products and markets—by the divisional executives—provides the corporation with an enhanced ability to respond quickly to important changes. Since there

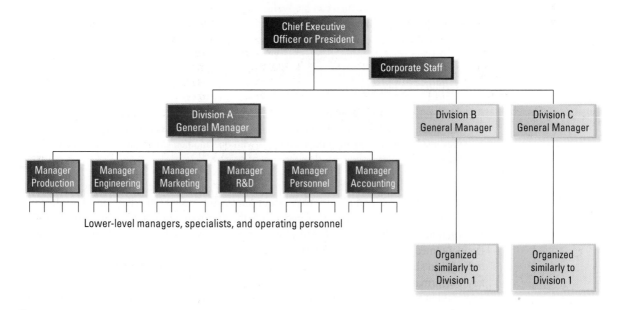

Exhibit 10.3 Divisional Organizational Structure

Brinker International Changes to a Divisional Organizational Structure

Although Brinker International had a traditional functional structure, changes in its competitive outlook forced management to take a closer look at the organizational design of the firm. The firm controls a variety of restaurant chains and bakeries, including Wildfire, Big Bowl, and Chili's.

With all these interests under one corporate roof, management of these disparate entities became difficult. The fragmented $330 billion restaurant and bakery industry caters to highly focused market niches. The original

Source: CEO interview: Ronald A. McDougall, Brinker International. 1999. *Wall Street Transcript,* January 20: 1–4.

functional design of the Brinker chain had some disadvantages as the company grew. With areas separated by function, it became hard to focus efforts on a single restaurant chain. The diverse markets served by the bakeries and restaurants began to lose their focus.

As a result, Brinker International changed to a divisional structure. This allowed the company to consolidate individuals who worked with a single restaurant or bakery chain into a separate division. Brinker referred to these as concept teams, with each concept team responsible for the operation of a single line of business. This focused effort streamlined the company's ability to concentrate on the market niche served by each of its restaurants and bakeries.

---

are functional departments within each division of the corporation, the problems associated with sharing resources across functional departments are minimized. Because there are multiple levels of general managers (executives responsible for integrating and coordinating all functional areas), the development of general management talent is enhanced. Strategy Spotlight 10.2 discusses the rationale behind Brinker Corporation's change in structure from functional to divisional.

Disadvantages It can be very expensive; there can be increased costs due to the duplication of personnel, operations, and investment since each division must staff multiple functional departments. There also can be dysfunctional competition among divisions since each division tends to become concerned solely about its own operations. Divisional managers are often evaluated on common measures such as return on assets and sales growth. If goals are conflicting, there can be a sense of a "zero-sum" game that would discourage sharing ideas and resources among the divisions for the common good of the corporation. Ghoshal and Bartlett, two leading strategy scholars, note:

> As their label clearly warns, divisions divide. The divisional model fragmented companies' resources; it created vertical communication channels that insulated business units and prevented them from sharing their strengths with one another. Consequently, the whole of the corporation was often less than the sum of its parts.[11]

With many divisions providing different products and services, there is the chance that differences in image and quality may occur across divisions. One division may offer no-frills products of lower quality that may erode the brand reputation of another division that has top quality, highly differentiated offerings. Since each division is evaluated in terms of financial measures such as return on investment and revenue growth, there is often an urge to focus on short-term performance. If corporate management uses quarterly profits as the key performance indicator, divisional management may tend to put significant emphasis on "making the numbers" and minimizing activities, such as advertising, maintenance, and capital investments, which would detract from short-term performance measures.

We'll discuss two variations of the divisional form: the strategic business unit (SBU) and holding company structures.

Strategic Business Unit (SBU) Structure   Highly diversified corporations such as ConAgra, a $12 billion food producer, may consist of dozens of different divisions.[12] If ConAgra were to use a purely divisional structure, it would be nearly impossible for the corporate office to plan and coordinate activities because the span of control would be too large. To attain synergies, ConAgra has put its diverse businesses into three primary SBUs: food service (restaurants), retail (grocery stores), and agricultural products.

With an **SBU structure,** divisions with similar products, markets, and/or technologies are grouped into homogeneous units to achieve some synergies. These include those discussed in Chapter 6 for related diversification, such as leveraging core competencies, sharing infrastructures, and market power. Generally the more related businesses are within a corporation, the fewer SBUs will be required. Each of the SBUs in the corporation operates as a profit center.

Advantages The SBU structure makes the task of planning and control by the corporate office more manageable. Also, with greater decentralization of authority, individual businesses can react more quickly to important changes in the environment than if all divisions had to report directly to the corporate office.

Disadvantages   Since the divisions are grouped into SBUs, it may become difficult to achieve synergies across SBUs. If divisions in different SBUs have potential sources of synergy, it may become difficult for them to be realized. The additional level of management increases the number of personnel and overhead expenses, while the additional hierarchical level removes the corporate office further from the individual divisions. The corporate office may become unaware of key developments that could have a major impact on the corporation.

Holding Company Structure   The **holding company structure** (sometimes referred to as a *conglomerate*) is also a variation of the divisional structure. Whereas the SBU structure is often used when similarities exist between the individual businesses (or divisions), the holding company structure is appropriate when the businesses in a corporation's portfolio do not have much in common. Thus, the potential for synergies is limited.

Holding company structures are most appropriate for firms with a strategy of unrelated diversification. Companies such as Hanson Trust, ITT, and the CP group of Thailand have used holding company structure to implement their unrelated diversification strategies. Since there are few similarities across the businesses, the corporate offices in these companies provide a great deal of autonomy to operating divisions and rely on financial controls and incentive programs to obtain high levels of performance from the individual businesses. Corporate staffs at these firms tend to be small because of their limited involvement in the overall operation of their various businesses.[13]

Advantages   The holding company structure has the cost savings associated with fewer personnel and the lower overhead resulting from a small corporate office and fewer hierarchical levels. The autonomy of the holding company structure increases the motivational level of divisional executives and enables them to respond quickly to market opportunities and threats.

Disadvantages   There is an inherent lack of control and dependence that corporate-level executives have on divisional executives. Major problems could arise if key divisional executives leave the firm, because the corporate office has very little "bench strength"— additional managerial talent ready to quickly fill key positions. If problems arise in a division, it may become very difficult to turn around individual businesses because of limited staff support in the corporate office.

strategic business unit (SBU) structure an organizational form in which products, projects, or product market divisions are grouped into homogeneous units.

holding company structure an organizational form that is a variation of the divisional organizational structure in which the divisions have a high degree of autonomy both from other divisions and from corporate headquarters.

Matrix Structure

matrix organizational structure
an organizational form in which there are multiple lines of authority and some individuals report to at least two managers.

One approach that tries to overcome the inadequacies inherent in the other structures is the **matrix organizational structure.** It is a combination of the functional and divisional structures. Most commonly, functional departments are combined with product groups on a project basis. For example, a product group may want to develop a new addition to its line; for this project, it obtains personnel from functional departments such as marketing, production, and engineering. These personnel work under the manager of the product group for the duration of the project, which can vary from a few weeks to an open-ended period of time. The individuals who work in a matrix organization become responsible to two managers: the project manager and the manager of their functional area. Exhibit 10.4 illustrates a matrix structure.

Some large multinational corporations rely on a matrix structure to combine product groups and geographical units. Product managers have global responsibility for the development, manufacturing, and distribution of their own line, while managers of geographical regions have responsibility for the profitability of the businesses in their regions. In the mid-1990s, Caterpillar, Inc., implemented this type of structure.

Dell Computer relies on the matrix concept, with its dual reporting responsibility, to enhance accountability as well as develop general managers. According to former CEO Kevin Rollins:[14]

> We're organized in a matrix of sales regions and product groups. Then we break each of those groups down to a pretty fine level of sub-products and sales sub-segments. Dell has more P&L managers, and smaller business units, than most companies its size. This not only increases accountability to the customer, it helps train general managers by moving them from smaller to larger businesses as their skills develop.
>
> Our matrix organization has a third level—our business councils. For example, we have a small-business sales group in each country, along with product development people who become very familiar with what small-business customers buy. In addition, we have our worldwide small-business council made up of all our small-business GMs and product managers. Everyone in these councils sees everyone else's P&L, so it provides another set of checks and balances.

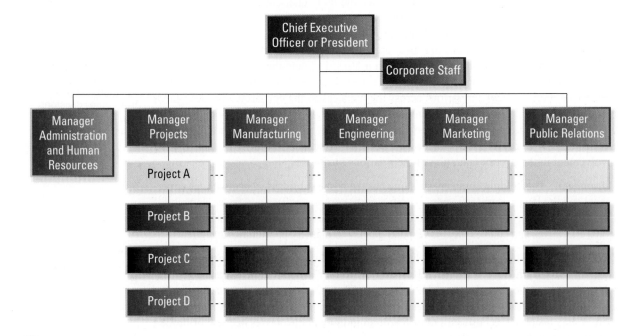

Exhibit 10.4 Matrix Organizational Structure

Advantages   The matrix structure facilitates the use of specialized personnel, equipment, and facilities. Instead of duplicating functions, as would be the case in a divisional structure based on products, the resources are shared. Individuals with high expertise can divide their time among multiple projects. Such resource sharing and collaboration enable a firm to use resources more efficiently and to respond more quickly and effectively to changes in the competitive environment. The flexibility inherent in a matrix structure provides professionals with a broader range of responsibility. Such experience enables them to develop their skills and competencies.

Disadvantages   The dual-reporting structures can result in uncertainty and lead to intense power struggles and conflict over the allocation of personnel and other resources. Working relationships become more complicated. This may result in excessive reliance on group processes and teamwork, along with a diffusion of responsibility, which in turn may erode timely decision making. Exhibit 10.5 briefly summarizes the advantages and disadvantages of the functional, divisional, and matrix organizational structures.

International Operations: Implications for Organizational Structure

Today's managers must maintain an international outlook on their firm's businesses and competitive strategies. In the global marketplace, managers must ensure consistency between their strategies (at the business, corporate, and international levels) and the structure of their organization. As firms expand into foreign markets, they generally follow a pattern of change in structure that parallels the changes in their strategies. Three major contingencies that influence the chosen structure are (1) the type of strategy that is driving a firm's foreign operations, (2) product diversity, and (3) the extent to which a firm is dependent on foreign sales.[15]

As international operations become an important part of a firm's overall operations, managers must make changes that are consistent with their firm's structure. The primary types of structures used to manage a firm's international operations are:[16]

- International division
- Geographic-area division
- Worldwide functional
- Worldwide product division
- Worldwide matrix

Multidomestic strategies are driven by political and cultural imperatives requiring managers within each country to respond to local conditions. The structures consistent with such a strategic orientation are the **international division** and **geographic-area division structures.** Here local managers are provided with a high level of autonomy to manage their operations within the constraints and demands of their geographic market. As a firm's foreign sales increase as a percentage of its total sales, it will likely change from an international division to a geographic-area division structure. And, as a firm's product and/or market diversity becomes large, it is likely to benefit from a **worldwide matrix structure.**

Global strategies are driven by economic pressures that require managers to view operations in different geographic areas to be managed for overall efficiency. The structures consistent with the efficiency perspective are the *worldwide functional* and *worldwide product division* structures. Here, division managers view the marketplace as homogeneous and devote relatively little attention to local market, political, and economic factors. The choice between these two types of structures is guided largely by the extent of product diversity. Firms with relatively low levels of product diversity may opt for a worldwide product division structure. However, if significant product–market diversity results from highly unrelated international acquisitions, a worldwide holding company structure should

>LO3
The implications of a firm's international operations for organizational structure.

international division structure an organizational form in which international operations are in a separate, autonomous division. Most domestic operations are kept in other parts of the organization.

geographic-area division structure a type of divisional organizational structure in which operations in geographical regions are grouped internally.

worldwide matrix structure a type of matrix organizational structure that has one line of authority for geographic-area divisions and another line of authority for worldwide product divisions.

Exhibit 10.5 Functional, Divisional, and Matrix Organizational Structures: Advantages and Disadvantages

Functional Structure

Advantages	Disadvantages
• Pooling of specialists enhances coordination and control.	• Differences in functional area orientation impede communication and coordination.
• Centralized decision making enhances an organizational perspective across functions.	• Tendency for specialists to develop short-term perspective and narrow functional orientation.
• Efficient use of managerial and technical talent.	• Functional area conflicts may overburden top-level decision makers.
• Facilitates career paths and professional development in specialized areas.	• Difficult to establish uniform performance standards.

Divisional Structure

Advantages	Disadvantages
• Increases strategic and operational control, permitting corporate-level executives to address strategic issues.	• Increased costs incurred through duplication of personnel, operations, and investment.
• Quick response to environmental changes.	• Dysfunctional competition among divisions may detract from overall corporate performance.
• Increases focus on products and markets.	• Difficult to maintain uniform corporate image.
• Minimizes problems associated with sharing resources across functional areas.	• Overemphasis on short-term performance.
• Facilitates development of general managers.	

Matrix Structure

Advantages	Disadvantages
• Increases market responsiveness through collaboration and synergies among professional colleagues.	• Dual-reporting relationships can result in uncertainty regarding accountability.
• Allows more efficient utilization of resources.	• Intense power struggles may lead to increased levels of conflict.
• Improves flexibility, coordination, and communication.	• Working relationships may be more complicated and human resources duplicated.
• Increases professional development through a broader range of responsibility.	• Excessive reliance on group processes and teamwork may impede timely decision making.

be implemented. Such firms have very little commonality among products, markets, or technologies, and have little need for integration.

Global Start-Ups: A New Phenomenon

International expansion occurs rather late for most corporations, typically after possibilities of domestic growth are exhausted. Increasingly, we are seeing two interrelated phenomena. First, many firms now expand internationally relatively early in their history. Second, some firms are "born global"—that is, from the very beginning, many start-ups are global in their activities. For example, Logitech Inc., a leading producer of personal computer accessories, was global from day one. Founded in 1982 by a Swiss national and two Italians, the company was headquartered both in California and Switzerland. R&D and manufacturing were also conducted in both locations and, subsequently, in Taiwan and Ireland.[17]

The success of companies such as Logitech challenges the conventional wisdom that a company must first build up assets, internal processes, and experience before venturing into faraway lands. It also raises a number of questions: What exactly is a global start-up? Under what conditions should a company start out as a global start-up? What does it take to succeed as a global start-up?

A **global start-up** has been defined as a business organization that, from inception, seeks to derive significant competitive advantage from the use of resources and the sale of outputs in multiple countries. Right from the beginning, it uses in-puts from around the world and sells its products and services to customers around the world. Geographical boundaries of nation-states are irrelevant for a global start-up.

There is no reason for every start-up to be global. Being global necessarily involves higher communication, coordination, and transportation costs. Therefore, it is important to identify the circumstances under which going global from the beginning is advantageous.[18] First, if the required human resources are globally dispersed, going global may be the best way to access those resources. For example, Italians are masters in fine leather and Europeans in ergonomics. Second, in many cases foreign financing may be easier to obtain and more suitable. Traditionally, U.S. venture capitalists have shown greater willingness to bear risk, but they have shorter time horizons in their expectations for return. If a U.S. start-up is looking for patient capital, it may be better off looking overseas. Third, the target customers in many specialized industries are located in other parts of the world. Fourth, in many industries a gradual move from domestic markets to foreign markets is no longer possible because, if a product is successful, foreign competitors may immediately imitate it. Therefore, preemptive entry into foreign markets may be the only option. Finally, because of high up-front development costs, a global market is often necessary to recover the costs. This is particularly true for start-ups from smaller nations that do not have access to large domestic markets.

Successful management of a global start-up presents many challenges. Communication and coordination across time zones and cultures are always problematic. Since most global start-ups have far less resources than well-established corporations, one key for success is to internalize few activities and outsource the rest. Managers of such firms must have considerable prior international experience so that they can successfully handle the inevitable communication problems and cultural conflicts. Another key for success is to keep the communication and coordination costs low. The only way to achieve this is by creating less costly administrative mechanisms. The boundaryless organizational designs that we discuss in the next section are particularly suitable for global start-ups because of their flexibility and low cost.

Strategy Spotlight 10.3 discusses three global start-ups.

global start-up
a business organization that, from inception, seeks to derive significant advantage from the use of resources and the sale of outputs in multiple countries.

How an Organization's Structure Can Influence Strategy Formulation

Discussions of the relationship between strategy and structure usually strongly imply that structure follows strategy. The strategy that a firm chooses (e.g., related diversification) dictates such structural elements as the division of tasks, the need for integration of activities, and authority relationships within the organization. However, an existing structure can influence strategy formulation. Once a firm's structure is in place, it is very difficult and expensive to change.[19] Executives may not be able to modify their duties and responsibilities greatly, or may not welcome the disruption associated with a transfer to a new location. There are costs associated with hiring, training, and replacing executive, managerial, and operating personnel. Strategy cannot be formulated without considering structural elements.

An organization's structure can also have an important influence on how it competes in the marketplace. It can also strongly influence a firm's strategy, day-to-day operations, and performance.[20] We discussed Brinker International's move to a divisional structure in

Global on Day One

Conventional wisdom would suggest that a firm "get it right" in its home market before venturing abroad. Once established in the home market, a firm could consider the relatively risky move of selling in other countries. However, many new firms are turning conventional wisdom on its head.

More and more start-ups are being born global for two basic reasons. One reason is defensive: to be competitive, many new businesses need to globalize some parts of their business to control costs, access customers, or tap employees from day one. While this might seem an obviously logical choice, until recently many venture capital firms required companies to build locally first, gain a track record, and then branch out. The other reason firms are born global is offensive; many entrepreneurs find that new business opportunities span multiple countries. Going after opportunities in several countries simultaneously from the start can sometimes give firms the operating scope they need to thrive.

Going global is not without significant challenges. Coping with distance in terms of physical, time zone, and cultural dimensions is perhaps a larger hurdle for smaller organizations to tackle. However, start-ups that can articulate a global purpose tend to do better than those with weaker goal orientation toward a global strategy. The following three examples are of start-ups that thought global from day one:

- In 2008, Actavis Pharmaceuticals' revenues were over $2 billion. Robert Wessman took control of this

Sources: Isenberg, D. J. 2008. The Global Entrepreneur. *Harvard Business Review,* December: 107–111; Copeland, M. V. 2004. The Start-Up Oasis. *Business 2.0,* August: 46–48.; Brown, E. 2004. Global Start-Up. *Forbes,* November 29: 150–161.

small generic pharmaceutical maker in his native Iceland in 1999. Within weeks of taking over, he realized that to succeed in the generics market, a player had to globalize its core functions, including manufacturing and R&D. Actavis has since entered 60 countries to gain scale and develop a larger portfolio of drugs. By 2009 the company had 650 products on the market and 400 more in development.

- Baradok Pridor, 38, and Yonatan Aumann, 42, Israeli founders of ClearForest, developed an innovative software product—a program that can analyze unstructured electronic data, such as a webpage or a video clip, as if it were already in a spreadsheet or database. Instead of waiting for customers to show up, right from the beginning, they started sending their engineers to make presentations to potential clients around the world. Today, the company's customers include Dow Chemical, Thomson Financial, and the FBI! They have raised $33 million so far in three rounds of venture financing. Interestingly, the headquarters of the 83-person company is in Boston!

- HyperRoll, an Israeli company that makes software for analyzing massive databases, has raised $28 million in venture funding. Referring to the firm's hiring practices, Yossi Matias, founder of HyperRoll, says, "We build the strongest team possible, unconstrained by locality, affinity, or culture. It requires every employee to accept and support a multicultural environment." Although the firm is essentially an Israeli start-up, he even banned the use of Hebrew in the office to facilitate greater integration between the American and Israeli employees.

order to organize its restaurant groups into different units to focus on market niches. This new structure should enable the firm to adapt to change more rapidly and innovate more effectively with the various restaurant brands. Brinker's management did not feel that they were as effective with their previous functional organizational structure.

> **>LO4**
>
> Why there is no "one best way" to design strategic reward and evaluation systems, and the important contingent roles of business- and corporate-level strategies.

Linking Strategic Reward and Evaluation Systems to Business-Level and Corporate-Level Strategies

The effective use of reward and evaluation systems can play a critical role in motivating managers to conform to organizational strategies, achieve performance targets, and reduce the gap between organizational and individual goals. In contrast, reward systems, if improperly designed, can lead to behaviors that either are detrimental to organizational performance or can lower morale and cause employee dissatisfaction.

As we will see in this section, there is no "one best way" to design reward and evaluation systems. Instead, it is contingent on many factors. Two of the most important factors are a firm's business-level strategy (see Chapter 5) and its corporate-level strategy (see Chapter 6).

Business-Level Strategy: Reward and Evaluation Systems

In Chapter 5 we discussed two approaches that firms may take to secure competitive advantages: overall cost leadership and differentiation.[21] As we might expect, implementing these strategies requires fundamentally different organizational arrangements, approaches to control, and reward and incentive systems.

Overall Cost Leadership   This strategy requires that product lines remain rather stable and that innovations deal mostly with production processes. Given the emphasis on efficiency, costly changes even in production processes tend to be rare. Since products are quite standardized and change rather infrequently, procedures can be developed to divide work into its basic components—those that are routine, standardized, and ideal for semiskilled and unskilled employees. As such, firms competing on the basis of cost must implement tight cost controls, frequent and comprehensive reports to monitor the costs associated with outputs, and highly structured tasks and responsibilities. Incentives tend to be based on explicit financial targets since innovation and creativity are expensive and might tend to erode competitive advantages.

Nucor a highly successful steel producer with $23 billion in revenues, competes primarily on the basis of cost and has a reward and incentive system that is largely based on financial outputs and financial measures.[22] Nucor uses four incentive compensation systems that correspond to the levels of management.

1. *Production incentive program.* Groups of 20 to 40 people are paid a weekly bonus based on either anticipated product time or tonnage produced. Each shift and production line is in a separate bonus group.
2. *Department managers.* Bonuses are based on divisional performance, primarily measured by return on assets.
3. *Employees not directly involved in production.* These include engineers, accountants, secretaries, receptionists, and others. Bonuses are based on two factors: divisional and corporate return on assets.
4. *Senior incentive programs.* Salaries are lower than comparable companies, but a significant portion of total compensation is based on return on stockholder equity. A portion of pretax earnings is placed in a pool and divided among officers as bonuses that are part cash and part stock.

The culture at Nucor reflects its reward and incentive system. Since incentive compensation can account for more than half of their paychecks, employees become nearly obsessed with productivity and apply a lot of pressure on each other. Ken Iverson, a former CEO, recalled an instance in which one employee arrived at work in sunglasses instead of safety glasses, preventing the team from doing any work. Furious, the other workers chased him around the plant with a piece of angle iron!

Differentiation   This strategy involves the development of innovative products and services that require experts who can identify the crucial elements of intricate, creative designs and marketing decisions. Highly trained professionals such as scientists and engineers are essential for devising, assessing, implementing and continually changing complex product designs. This also requires extensive collaboration and cooperation among specialists and functional managers from different areas within a firm. They must evaluate and implement a new design, constantly bearing in mind marketing, financial, production, and engineering considerations.

Given the need for cooperation and coordination in many functional areas, it becomes difficult to evaluate individuals using set quantitative criteria. It also is difficult to measure specific outcomes of such efforts and attribute outcomes to specific individuals. More behavioral measures (how effectively employees collaborate and share information) and intangible incentives and rewards become necessary to support a strong culture and to motivate employees. Consider 3M, a highly innovative company whose core value is innovation.

> Rewards are tied closely to risk-taking and innovation-oriented behavior. Managers are not penalized for product failures. Instead, those same people are encouraged to work on another project that borrows from their shared experience and insight. A culture of creativity and "thinking out of the box" is reinforced by their well-known "15 percent rule," which permits employees to set aside 15 percent of their work time to pursue personal research interests. And a familiar 3M homily, "Thou shall not kill new ideas for products," is known as the 11th commandment. It is the source of countless stories, including one that tells how L. D. DeSimone (3M's former CEO) tried five times (and failed) to kill the project that yielded the 3M blockbuster product, Thinsulate.[23]

Corporate-Level Strategy: Reward and Evaluation Systems

In Chapter 6 we discussed two broad types of diversification strategies: related and unrelated. The type of diversification strategy that a firm follows has important implications for the type of reward and evaluation systems that it should use.

Sharp Corporation, a $36 billion Japanese consumer electronics giant follows a strategy of *related* diversification.[24] Its most successful technology has been liquid crystal displays (LCDs) that are critical components in nearly all of the firm's products. With their expertise in this area, they are moving into high-end displays for cellular telephones, handheld computers, and digital computers.[25]

Given the need to leverage such technologies across multiple product lines, Sharp needs reward and evaluation systems that foster coordination and sharing. It must focus more on individuals' behavior rather than on short-term financial outcomes. Promotion is a powerful incentive, and it is generally based on seniority and subtle skills exhibited over time, such as teamwork and communication. It helps to ensure that the company's reward system will not reward short-term self-interested orientations.

Like many Japanese companies, Sharp's culture reinforces the view that the firm is a family whose members should cooperate for the greater good. With the policy of lifetime employment, turnover is low. This encourages employees to pursue what is best for the entire company. Such an outlook lessens the inevitable conflict over sharing important resources such as R&D knowledge.

In contrast to Sharp, Hanson PLC (a British conglomerate) followed a strategy of unrelated diversification for most of its history. At one time it owned as many as 150 operating companies in areas such as tobacco, footwear, building products, brewing, and food. There were limited product similarities across businesses and therefore little need for sharing of resources and knowledge across divisional boundaries. James Hanson and Gordon White, founders of the company, actually did not permit any sharing of resources between operating companies even if it was feasible!

Their reward and evaluation system placed such heavy emphasis on individual accountability that they viewed resource sharing, with its potential for mutual blaming, unacceptable. The operating managers had more than 60 percent of their compensation tied to annual financial performance of their subsidiaries. All decision making was decentralized so that subsidiary managers could be held responsible for the return on capital they employed. However, there was one area in which they had to obtain approval from the corporate office. No subsidiary manager was allowed to incur a capital expenditure greater than $3,000 without permission from the corporate office. Hanson managed to be successful with a very small corporate office because of its decentralized structure, tight financial controls, and an

Exhibit 10.6
Summary of
Relationships
between Reward and
Evaluation Systems
and Business-Level
and Corporate-Level
Strategies

Level of Strategy	Types of Strategy	Need for Interdependence	Primary Type of Reward and Evaluation System
Business-level	Overall cost leadership	Low	Financial
Business-level	Differentiation	High	Behavioral
Corporate-level	Related diversification	High	Behavioral
Corporate-level	Unrelated diversification	Low	Financial

incentive system that motivated managers to meet financial goals. Gordon White was proud of claiming that he had never visited any of the operating companies that were part of the Hanson empire.[26]

The key issue becomes the need for *in*dependence versus *inter*dependence. With cost leadership strategies and unrelated diversification, there tends to be less need for interdependence. The reward and evaluation systems focus more on the use of financial indicators because unit costs, profits, and revenues can be rather easily attributed to a given business unit or division.

In contrast, firms that follow related diversification strategies have intense needs for tight interdependencies among the functional areas and business units. Sharing of resources, including raw materials, R&D knowledge, marketing information, and so on, is critical to organizational success. It is more important to achieve synergies with value-creating activities and business units than with cost leadership or unrelated strategies. Reward and evaluation systems tend to incorporate more behavioral indicators.

Although Exhibit 10.6 suggests guidelines on how an organization should match its strategies to its evaluation and reward systems, all organizations must have combinations of both financial and behavioral rewards. Both overall cost leadership and unrelated diversification strategies require a need for collaboration and the sharing of best practices across both value-creating activities and business units. General Electric has developed many integrating mechanisms to enhance sharing "best practices" across what would appear to be rather unrelated businesses such as jet engines, appliances, and network television. For both differentiation and related diversification strategies, financial indicators such as revenue growth and profitability should not be overlooked at both the business-unit and corporate levels.

> **>LO5**
> The different types of boundaryless organizations— barrier-free, modular, and virtual—and their relative advantages and disadvantages.

Boundaryless Organizational Designs

The term *boundaryless* may bring to mind a chaotic organizational reality in which "anything goes." This is not the case. As Jack Welch, GE's former CEO, has suggested, boundaryless does not imply that all internal and external boundaries vanish completely, but that they become more open and permeable.[27] Strategy Spotlight 10.4 discusses four types of boundaries.

We are not suggesting that **boundaryless organizational designs** replace the traditional forms of organizational structure, but they should complement them. Sharp Corp. has implemented a functional structure to attain economies of scale with its applied research and manufacturing skills. However, to bring about this key objective, Sharp has relied on several integrating mechanisms and processes:

> To prevent functional groups from becoming vertical chimneys that obstruct product development, Sharp's product managers have responsibility—but not authority—for coordinating the entire set of value-chain activities. And the company convenes enormous numbers of cross-unit and corporate committees to ensure that shared activities, including the corporate R&D unit and sales forces, are optimally configured and allocated among the different product lines. Sharp invests in such time-intensive coordination to minimize the inevitable conflicts that arise when units share important activities.[28]

> **boundaryless organizational designs** organizations in which the boundaries, including vertical, horizontal, external, and geographic boundaries, are permeable.

Boundary Types

There are primarily four types of boundaries that place limits on organizations. In today's dynamic business environment, different types of boundaries are needed to foster high degrees of interaction with outside influences and varying levels of permeability.

1. *Vertical boundaries between levels in the organization's hierarchy.* SmithKline Beecham asks employees at different hierarchical levels to brainstorm ideas for managing clinical trial data. The ideas are incorporated into action plans that significantly cut the new product approval time of its pharmaceuticals. This would not have been possible if the barriers between levels of individuals in the organization had been too high.

2. *Horizontal boundaries between functional areas.* Fidelity Investments makes the functional barriers

Source: Ashkenas, R. 1997. The Organization's New Clothes. In Hesselbein, F., Goldsmith, M., and Beckhard, R. (Eds.). *The Organization of the Future:* 104–106. San Francisco: Jossey Bass.

more porous and flexible among divisions, such as marketing, operations, and customer service, in order to offer customers a more integrated experience when conducting business with the company. Customers can take their questions to one person, reducing the chance that customers will "get the runaround" from employees who feel customer service is not their responsibility. At Fidelity, customer service is everyone's business, regardless of functional area.

3. *External boundaries between the firm and its customers, suppliers, and regulators.* GE Lighting, by working closely with retailers, functions throughout the value chain as a single operation. This allows GE to track point-of-sale purchases, giving it better control over inventory management.

4. *Geographic boundaries between locations, cultures, and markets.* The global nature of today's business environment spurred PricewaterhouseCoopers to use a global groupware system. This allows the company to instantly connect to its 26 worldwide offices.

We will discuss three approaches to making boundaries more permeable, that help to facilitate the widespread sharing of knowledge and information across both the internal and external boundaries of the organization. The *barrier-free* type involves making all organizational boundaries—internal and external—more permeable. Teams are a central building block for implementing the boundaryless organization. The *modular* and *virtual* types of organizations focus on the need to create seamless relationships with external organizations such as customers or suppliers. While the modular type emphasizes the outsourcing of noncore activities, the virtual (or network) organization focuses on alliances among independent entities formed to exploit specific market opportunities.

The Barrier-Free Organization

The "boundary" mind-set is ingrained deeply into bureaucracies. It is evidenced by such clichés as "That's not my job," "I'm here from corporate to help," or endless battles over transfer pricing. In the traditional company, boundaries are clearly delineated in the design of an organization's structure. Their basic advantage is that the roles of managers and employees are simple, clear, well-defined, and long-lived. A major shortcoming was pointed out to the authors during an interview with a high-tech executive: "Structure tends to be divisive; it leads to territorial fights."

Such structures are being replaced by fluid, ambiguous, and deliberately ill-defined tasks and roles. Just because work roles are no longer clearly defined, however, does not mean that differences in skills, authority, and talent disappear. A **barrier-free organization** enables a firm to bridge real differences in culture, function, and goals to find common ground that facilitates information sharing and other forms of cooperative behavior. Eliminating the multiple boundaries that stifle productivity and innovation can enhance the

barrier-free organization an organizational design in which firms bridge real differences in culture, function, and goals to find common ground that facilitates information sharing and other forms of cooperative behavior.

364 Part 3:: Strategic Implementation

United Technologies Corporation's PureCycle: An Effective Use of the Boundaryless Concept

United Technologies Corporation is a giant manufacturing conglomerate that has been on a roll. Revenues and profits for 2006 were $48 billion and $3.7 billion, respectively, which represents an annual increase of over 15 percent over the most recent four-year period.

Like many diversified firms, UTC faced a challenge in developing synergies across business units. UTC's wide variety of products include Carrier heating and air conditioning, Hamilton Sundstrand aerospace systems and industrial products, Otis elevators and escalators, Pratt & Whitney aircraft engines, Sikorsky helicopters, UTC Fire & Security systems, and UTC Power fuel cells. Overall, UTC spends a huge amount of money on research—about 3.5 percent of total revenues.

Historically, UTC's culture placed a high value on decentralized decision making, with each unit operating almost entirely independently of the others. Such an approach may have motivational benefits and helps each unit focus their efforts. However, it leads to "silo business units" and prevents the corporation from generating innovations in the white spaces between business units.

This approach to business troubled UTC senior vice president John Cassidy and Carl Nett, director of the firm's corporate research center, UTRC. The center is staffed with nearly 500 scientists, engineers, and staff who are charged with "bringing future technologies to the point of product insertion." They both believed that tremendous potential for growth existed in the junctures between the business units. However, such collaboration was not consistent with the

history, work practices, and cultural norms at UTC. In fact, Cassidy felt that integrating expertise and talent across business units was an "unnatural act."

What did they do? In 2002, the two executives invited top technical talent from each unit to several brainstorming sessions. The goal was to bring together a diverse set of talented professionals to create and service new markets.

Early on, a potential winner emerged from the intersection of cooling, heating, and power. Engineers from Carrier, Pratt & Whitney, and UTRC recognized that using cooling and heating equipment could transform an innovative power generation concept into a revolutionary product. Called PureCycle, the product contained virtually no new components. However, it offered a breakthrough value proposition: Customers could convert waste heat to electricity at rates substantially below those of utilities. The product held great promise because U.S. industrial plants emit roughly as much waste heat as a 50-gigawatt power plant generates (enough to run most major U.S. cities). Such an innovation certainly helps to conserve natural resources.

In retrospect, engineers involved in the PureCycle project find it hard to believe that nobody had previously thought of the idea. Thierry Jomard, a former Carrier engineer who transferred to UTRC to head the effort explains, "Carrier people are trained to think in terms of using heat exchange to produce cold air—that's the output that counts: the compressor is just there to move the fluid. Pratt & Whitney engineers, on the other hand, are power people. The outcome they are about is power, and they use turbines to get it." It wasn't until they began their collaboration that anyone recognized the opportunities before them.

Sources: www.utc.com; 2005 *UTC Annual Report;* Davidson, A. 2007. Conglomerates: United Technologies. *Forbes,* January 8: 96; and Cross, R., Liedtka, J., & Weiss, L. 2005. A Practical Guide to Social Networks. *Harvard Business Review,* 83(3): 92–101.

environmental sustainability

---

potential of the entire organization. Strategy Spotlight 10.5 describes how United Technologies Corporation used the boundaryless concept.

Creating Permeable Internal Boundaries   For barrier-free organizations to work effectively, the level of trust and shared interests among all parts of the organization must be raised. The organization needs to develop among its employees the skill level needed to work in a more democratic organization. Barrier-free organizations also require a shift in the organization's philosophy from executive to organizational development, and from investments in high-potential individuals to investments in leveraging the talents of all individuals.

Teams can be an important aspect of barrier-free structures.[29] Jeffrey Pfeffer, author of several insightful books, including *The Human Equation,* suggests that teams have three primary advantages.[30] First, teams substitute peer-based control for hierarchical control of work activities. Employees control themselves, reducing the time and energy management needs to devote to control. Second, teams frequently develop more creative solutions to problems because they encourage the sharing of the tacit knowledge held by individuals.[31] Brainstorming, or group problem solving, involves the pooling of ideas and expertise to enhance the chances that at least one group member will think of a way to solve the problems at hand. Third, by substituting peer control for hierarchical control, teams permit the removal of layers of hierarchy and absorption of administrative tasks previously performed by specialists. This avoids the costs of having people whose sole job is to watch the people who watch other people do the work.

● Teams frequently develop more creative solutions to problems because they can share each individual's knowledge.

Effective barrier-free organizations must go beyond achieving close integration and coordination within divisions in a corporation. Research on multidivisional organizations has stressed the importance of interdivisional coordination and resource sharing.[32] This requires interdivisional task forces and committees, reward and incentive systems that emphasize interdivisional cooperation, and common training programs.

Frank Carruba (former head of Hewlett-Packard's labs) found that the difference between mediocre teams and good teams was generally varying levels of motivation and talent.[33] But what explained the difference between good teams and truly superior teams? The key difference—and this explained a 40 percent overall difference in performance—was the way members treated each other: the degree to which they believed in one another and created an atmosphere of encouragement rather than competition. Vision, talent, and motivation could carry a team only so far. What clearly stood out in the "super" teams were higher levels of authenticity and caring, which allowed the full synergy of their individual talents, motivation, and vision.

Developing Effective Relationships with External Constituencies

In barrier-free organizations, managers must also create flexible, porous organizational boundaries and establish communication flows and mutually beneficial relationships with internal (e.g., employees) and external (e.g., customers) constituencies.[34] Michael Dell, founder and CEO of Dell Computer, is a strong believer in fostering close relationships with his customers:

> We're not going to be just your PC vendor anymore. We're going to be your IT department for PCs. Boeing, for example, has 100,000 Dell PCs, and we have 30 people that live at Boeing, and if you look at the things we're doing for them or for other customers, we don't look like a supplier, we look more like Boeing's PC department. We become intimately involved in planning their PC needs and the configuration of their network.
>
> It's not that we make these decisions by ourselves. They're certainly using their own people to get the best answer for the company. But the people working on PCs together, from both Dell and Boeing, understand the needs in a very intimate way. They're right there living it and breathing it, as opposed to the typical vendor who says, "Here are your computers. See you later."[35]

Barrier-free organizations create successful relationships between both internal and external constituencies, but there is one additional constituency—competitors—with whom some organizations have benefited as they developed cooperative relationships. After years of seeing its empty trucks return from warehouses back to production facilities after deliveries, General Mills teamed up with 16 of its competitors. They formed an e-commerce business to help the firms find carriers with empty cargo trailers to piggyback freight loads to distributors near the production facilities.[36] This increases revenue for all network members and reduces fuel costs.

Risks, Challenges, and Potential Downsides   Many firms find that creating and managing a barrier-free organization can be frustrating.[37] Puritan-Bennett Corporation, a manufacturer of respiratory equipment, found that its product development time more than doubled after it adopted team management. Roger J. Dolida, director of R&D, attributed this failure to a lack of top management commitment, high turnover among team members, and infrequent meetings. Often, managers trained in rigid hierarchies find it difficult to make the transition to the more democratic, participative style that teamwork requires.

Christopher Barnes, a consultant with PricewaterhouseCoopers, previously worked as an industrial engineer for Challenger Electrical Distribution (a subsidiary of Westinghouse, now part of CBS) at a plant which produced circuit-breaker boxes. His assignment was to lead a team of workers from the plant's troubled final-assembly operation with the mission: "Make things better." That vague notion set the team up for failure. After a year of futility, the team was disbanded. In retrospect, Barnes identified several reasons for the debacle: (1) limited personal credibility—he was viewed as an "outsider"; (2) a lack of commitment to the team—everyone involved was forced to be on the team; (3) poor communications—nobody was told why the team was important; (4) limited autonomy—line managers refused to give up control over team members; and (5) misaligned incentives—the culture rewarded individual performance over team performance. Barnes's experience has implications for all types of teams, whether they are composed of managerial, professional, clerical, or production personnel.[38] The pros and cons of barrier-free structures are summarized in Exhibit 10.7.

The Modular Organization

As Charles Handy, author of *The Age of Unreason,* has noted:

> While it may be convenient to have everyone around all the time, having all of your workforce's time at your command is an extravagant way of marshaling the necessary resources. It is cheaper to keep them outside the organization . . . and to buy their services when you need them.[39]

The **modular organization** outsources nonvital functions, tapping into the knowledge and expertise of "best in class" suppliers, but retains strategic control. Outsiders

modular organization an organization in which nonvital functions are outsourced, which uses the knowledge and expertise of outside suppliers while retaining strategic control.

Exhibit 10.7
Pros and Cons of Barrier-Free Structures

Pros	Cons
• Leverages the talents of all employees.	• Difficult to overcome political and authority boundaries inside and outside the organization.
• Enhances cooperation, coordination, and information sharing among functions, divisions, SBUs, and external constituencies.	• Lacks strong leadership and common vision, which can lead to coordination problems.
• Enables a quicker response to market changes through a single-goal focus.	• Time-consuming and difficult-to-manage democratic processes.
• Can lead to coordinated win–win initiatives with key suppliers, customers, and alliance partners.	• Lacks high levels of trust, which can impede performance.

● Adidas is one of many athletic shoe companies that has outsourced most of its production to low-cost labor countries such as China and Vietnam.

may be used to manufacture parts, handle logistics, or perform accounting activities.[40] The value chain can be used to identify the key primary and support activities performed by a firm to create value: Which activities do we keep "in-house" and which activities do we outsource to suppliers?[41] The organization becomes a central hub surrounded by networks of outside suppliers and specialists and parts can be added or taken away. Both manufacturing and service units may be modular.[42]

Apparel is an industry in which the modular type has been widely adopted. Nike and Reebok, for example, concentrate on their strengths: designing and marketing high-tech, fashionable footwear. Nike has few production facilities and Reebok owns no plants. These two companies contract virtually all their footwear production to suppliers in China, Vietnam, and other countries with low-cost labor. Avoiding large investments in fixed assets helps them derive large profits on minor sales increases. Nike and Reebok can keep pace with changing tastes in the marketplace because their suppliers have become expert at rapidly retooling to produce new products.[43]

In a modular company, outsourcing the noncore functions offers three advantages.

1. A firm can decrease overall costs, stimulate new product development by hiring suppliers with superior talent to that of in-house personnel, avoid idle capacity, reduce inventories, and avoid being locked into a particular technology.

2. A company can focus scarce resources on the areas where it holds a competitive advantage. These benefits can translate into more funding for R&D hiring the best engineers, and providing continuous training for sales and service staff.

3. An organization can tap into the knowledge and expertise of its specialized supply-chain partners, adding critical skills and accelerating organizational learning.[44]

The modular type enables a company to leverage relatively small amounts of capital and a small management team to achieve seemingly unattainable strategic objectives.[45] Certain preconditions are necessary before the modular approach can be successful. First, the company must work closely with suppliers to ensure that the interests of each party are being fulfilled. Companies need to find loyal, reliable vendors who can be trusted with trade secrets. They also need assurances that suppliers will dedicate their financial, physical, and human resources to satisfy strategic objectives such as lowering costs or being first to market.

Second, the modular company must be sure that it selects the proper competencies to keep in-house. For Nike and Reebok, the core competencies are design and marketing, not shoe manufacturing; for Honda, the core competence is engine technology. An organization must avoid outsourcing components that may compromise its long-term competitive advantages.

Strategic Risks of Outsourcing The main strategic concerns are (1) loss of critical skills or developing the wrong skills, (2) loss of cross-functional skills, and (3) loss of control over a supplier.[46]

Too much outsourcing can result in a firm "giving away" too much skill and control. Outsourcing relieves companies of the requirement to maintain skill levels needed to manufacture essential components.[47] At one time, semiconductor chips seemed like a simple

Outsourcing for Talent: How Sony Develops Video Games

The convergence of Hollywood and Silicon Valley has led to the explosive growth of the worldwide video game industry, with revenues of $66.5 billion in 2008. Recently, it has overtaken the movie industry's box office receipts. While broadcast TV audiences dwindle and movie going stagnates, gaming is emerging as the newest and perhaps strongest pillar in the media world. So it's no surprise that film studios, media giants, game makers, and Japanese electronics companies are all battling to win the "Game Wars." "This is a huge shift we're seeing, and nobody wants to be left behind," says Sony Entertainment Chairman, Michael Lynton.

Sony sells hardware with its PlayStation 3 (PS3) consoles, and it has developed its handheld PlayStation Portable (PSP) product. It also develops games, such as the popular *Gran Turismo* racing and *EverQuest* online. And it owns Sony Pictures and MGM movie studios, whose Spider-Man and James Bond franchises have been mega hit games for Activision and EA. The real payoff for Sony comes in game software sales. While Sony and other console makers sell their hardware for a loss, they typically make $5 to $10 in royalties for every game sold on their platform. PS3 had more than 300 software titles by early 2009.

Starting in 2002 with the previous generation game console, the PS2, Sony has used outside developers to produce most of its games. It has even reached out to gamers themselves. "We didn't want outside developers to be peripheral to our business model," says Andrew House, an early PlayStation team member and executive vice president of Sony Computer Entertainment America. "We knew that the widest variety of content possible was the best way to build the largest consumer base possible." Sony has searched high and low for talent. In 1997, it launched a developer kit aimed at hobbyists. "We sent it to budding college developers who wanted to try their hands," House says. Ideas from those amateurs made their way into commercial games in Japan. Meanwhile, externally developed titles, like *Final Fantasy* and *Madden NFL Football*, helped put Sony's PS2 at the top of the heap in 2001. Sony also launched a Linux developer kit for just $199 in 2002. "It's our way of feeding the market for the future. Some of the first great games were developed by people at home in their garages," says House. "If we're not getting people involved and looking for opportunities very early on, we really are missing out."

Sources: www.sony.com, 2009; Euromonitor International, 2009, Consumer Electronics Report, Global Market Information Database; House, A. 2004. Sony. *Fast Company*, April: 65; and Grover, R., Edwards, C., Rowley, I., & Moon, I. 2005. Game Wars. *BusinessWeek*, February 28: 35–40.

technology to outsource, but they have now become a critical component of a wide variety of products. Companies that have outsourced the manufacture of these chips run the risk of losing the ability to manufacture them as the technology escalates. They become more dependent upon their suppliers.

Cross-functional skills refer to the skills acquired through the interaction of individuals in various departments within a company.[48] Such interaction assists a department in solving problems as employees interface with others across functional units. However, if a firm outsources key functional responsibilities, such as manufacturing, communication across departments can become more difficult. A firm and its employees must now integrate their activities with a new, outside supplier.

The outsourced products may give suppliers too much power over the manufacturer. Suppliers that are key to a manufacturer's success can, in essence, hold the manufacturer "hostage." Nike manages this potential problem by sending full-time "product expatriates" to work at the plants of its suppliers. Also, Nike often brings top members of supplier management and technical teams to its headquarters. This way, Nike keeps close tabs on the pulse of new developments, builds rapport and trust with suppliers, and develops long-term relationships with suppliers to prevent hostage situations.

Strategy Spotlight 10.6 discusses how Sony outsources for talent to develop games for its highly successful video game business. Exhibit 10.8 summarizes the pros and cons of modular structures.[49]

Exhibit 10.8

Pros and Cons of
Modular Structures

Pros	Cons
• Directs a firm's managerial and technical talent to the most critical activities.	• Inhibits common vision through reliance on outsiders.
• Maintains full strategic control over most critical activities—core competencies.	• Diminishes future competitive advantages if critical technologies or other competencies are outsourced.
• Achieves "best in class" performance at each link in the value chain.	• Increases the difficulty of bringing back into the firm activities that now add value due to market shifts.
• Leverages core competencies by outsourcing with smaller capital commitment.	• Leads to an erosion of cross-functional skills.
• Encourages information sharing and accelerates organizational learning.	• Decreases operational control and potential loss of control over a supplier.

The Virtual Organization

In contrast to the "self-reliant" thinking that guided traditional organizational designs, the strategic challenge today has become doing more with less and looking outside the firm for opportunities and solutions to problems. The virtual organization provides a new means of leveraging resources and exploiting opportunities.[50]

virtual organization a continually evolving network of independent companies that are linked together to share skills, costs, and access to one another's markets.

The **virtual organization** can be viewed as a continually evolving network of independent companies—suppliers, customers, even competitors—linked together to share skills, costs, and access to one another's markets.[51] The members of a virtual organization, by pooling and sharing the knowledge and expertise of each of the component organizations, simultaneously "know" more and can "do" more than any one member of the group could do alone. By working closely together, each gains in the long run from individual and organizational learning.[52] The term *virtual*, meaning "being in effect but not actually so," is commonly used in the computer industry. A computer's ability to appear to have more storage capacity than it really possesses is called virtual memory. Similarly, by assembling resources from a variety of entities, a virtual organization may seem to have more capabilities than it really possesses.[53]

The virtual organization is a grouping of units from different organizations that have joined in an alliance to exploit complementary skills in pursuing common strategic objectives. A case in point is Lockheed Martin's use of specialized coalitions between and among three entities—the company, academia, and government—to enhance competitiveness. According to former CEO Norman Augustine:

> The underlying beauty of this approach is that it forces us to reach outward. No matter what your size, you have to look broadly for new ideas, new approaches, new products. Lockheed Martin used this approach in a surprising manner when it set out during the height of the Cold War to make stealth aircraft and missiles. The technical idea came from research done at the Institute of Radio Engineering in Moscow in the 1960s that was published, and publicized, quite openly in the academic media.
>
> Despite the great contrasts among government, academia and private business, we have found ways to work together that have produced very positive results, not the least of which is our ability to compete on a global scale.[54]

Virtual organizations need not be permanent and participating firms may be involved in multiple alliances. Virtual organizations may involve different firms performing complementary value activities, or different firms involved jointly in the same value activities,

strategy spotlight

10.7

How Eli Lilly Used the Collaborative Power of Internet-Based Collaboration to Foster Innovation

The e.Lilly division of pharmaceutical giant Eli Lilly was among the first to harness the collaborative power of the Internet when it launched Innocentive in 2001. Innocentive is the first online, incentive-based scientific network created specifically for the global research and development community. Innocentive's online platform enabled world-class scientists and R&D-based companies to collaborate to attain innovative solutions to complex challenges.

Innocentive offers "seeker companies" the opportunity to increase their R&D potential by posting challenges without violating their confidentiality and intellectual property interests. Seeker companies might be looking for a chemical to be used in art restoration, for example, or the efficient synthesis of butane tetracarboxylic acid. David Bradin, a patent attorney from Seattle, was recently paid

$4,000 for his tetracarboxylic acid formula. And Proctor & Gamble claims that Innocentive has increased its share of its new products originating outside the company from 20 to 35 percent.

Often individuals outside of the seeker company find the best solutions to the company's problem. By using Innocentive to post their problems, companies do not have to admit publicly that they need help, yet they get access to a much broader range of ideas than can be generated inside the firm. Within firms, even those firms hiring the best and brightest scientists and engineers, ideas are tossed around by the same few people over and over. This situation can create a narrowing of the possible solutions to a problem (i.e., groupthink can occur) rather than searching over the broadest range of ideas. Anne Goldberg, technical knowledge manager at Solvay Pharmaceuticals, said, "The benefits [of Innocentive] are mainly in the simultaneous access to a lot of different scientific backgrounds that could bring new perspectives on sometimes old problems."

Sources: Libert, B. & Spector, J. 2008. *We Are Smarter Than Me.* Wharton School Publishing, Philadelphia; Lakhani, K. & Jeppesen, L. 2007. Getting Unusual Suspects to Solve R&D Puzzles. *Harvard Business Review,* 85(5): 30–32; Caldwell, T. 2007. R&D Finds Answers in the Crowd. *Information World Review,* 236: 8.

crowdsourcing

such as production, R&D, and distribution. The percentage of activities that are jointly performed with partners may vary significantly from alliance to alliance.[55]

How does the virtual type of structure differ from the modular type? Unlike the modular type, in which the focal firm maintains full strategic control, the virtual organization is characterized by participating firms that give up part of their control and accept interdependent destinies. Participating firms pursue a collective strategy that enables them to cope with uncertainty through cooperative efforts. The benefit is that, just as virtual memory increases storage capacity, the virtual organizations enhance the capacity or competitive advantage of participating firms. Strategy Spotlight 10.7 addresses the variety of collaborative relationships in the biotechnology industry.

Each company that links up with others to create a virtual organization contributes only what it considers its core competencies. It will mix and match what it does best with the best of other firms by identifying its critical capabilities and the necessary links to other capabilities.[56]

Challenges and Risks Such alliances often fail to meet expectations: The alliance between IBM and Microsoft soured in early 1991 when Microsoft began shipping Windows in direct competition to OS/2, which they jointly developed. The runaway success of Windows frustrated IBM's ability to set an industry standard. In retaliation, IBM entered into an alliance with Microsoft's archrival, Novell, to develop network software to compete with Microsoft's LAN Manager.

The virtual organization demands that managers build relationships with other companies, negotiate win–win deals for all parties find the right partners with compatible goals and values, and provide the right balance of freedom and control. Information systems must be designed and integrated to facilitate communication with current and potential partners.

Managers must be clear about the strategic objectives while forming alliances. Some objectives are time bound, and those alliances need to be dissolved once the objective is fulfilled. Some alliances may have relatively long-term objectives and will need to be clearly monitored and nurtured to produce mutual commitment and avoid bitter fights for control. The highly dynamic personal computer industry is characterized by multiple temporary alliances among hardware, operating systems, and software producers.[57] But alliances in the more stable automobile industry, such as those involving Nissan and Volkswagen have long-term objectives and tend to be relatively stable.

The virtual organization is a logical culmination of joint-venture strategies of the past. Shared risks, costs, and rewards are the facts of life in a virtual organization.[58] When virtual organizations are formed, they involve tremendous challenges for strategic planning. As with the modular corporation, it is essential to identify core competencies. However, for virtual structures to be successful, a strategic plan is also needed to determine the effectiveness of combining core competencies.

The strategic plan must address the diminished operational control and overwhelming need for trust and common vision among the partners. This new structure may be appropriate for firms whose strategies require merging technologies (e.g., computing and communication) or for firms exploiting shrinking product life cycles that require simultaneous entry into multiple geographical markets. It may be effective for firms that desire to be quick to the market with a new product or service. The recent profusion of alliances among airlines was primarily motivated by the need to provide seamless travel demanded by the full-fare paying business traveler. Exhibit 10.9 summarizes the advantages and disadvantages.

Boundaryless Organizations: Making Them Work

Designing an organization that simultaneously supports the requirements of an organization's strategy, is consistent with the demands of the environment, and can be effectively implemented by the people around the manager is a tall order for any manager.[59] The most effective solution is usually a combination of organizational types. That is, a firm may

Exhibit 10.9
Pros and Cons of Virtual Structures

Pros	Cons
• Enables the sharing of costs and skills.	• Harder to determine where one company ends and another begins, due to close interdependencies among players.
• Enhances access to global markets.	
• Increases market responsiveness.	• Leads to potential loss of operational control among partners.
• Creates a "best of everything" organization since each partner brings core competencies to the alliance.	• Results in loss of strategic control over emerging technology.
• Encourages both individual and organizational knowledge sharing and accelerates organizational learning.	• Requires new and difficult-to-acquire managerial skills.

Source: Miles, R. E., & Snow, C. C. 1986. Organizations: New Concepts for New Forms. *California Management Review,* Spring: 62–73; Miles & Snow. 1999. Causes of Failure in Network Organizations. *California Management Review,* Summer: 53–72; and Bahrami, H. 1991. The Emerging Flexible Organization: Perspectives from Silicon Valley. *California Management Review,* Summer: 33–52.

Technical Computer Graphics' Boundaryless Organization

The Technical Computer Graphics (TCG) group manufactures items such as handheld bar code readers and scanning software. The company uses 13 "alliances," or small project teams, employing a total of 200 employees. Each team is responsible for either specific customers or specific products. Alliance teams share a common infrastructure, but they can develop new business opportunities without approval from upper management. Projects often emerge from listening to what customers need.

TCG uses a "triangulation approach"—alliances that include customers, suppliers, and other alliances. Suppliers and customers who provide funding are involved at the outset of the project. The alliances recognize that attaining the initial customer funding is crucial; it stimulates them to focus on what customers have to say. With an emphasis on speed, new products come to market quickly, providing

the firm and its partners with tangible benefits. Sometimes another alliance acts as either the customer or the supplier and provides funding.

While each alliance is independent, it shares financial concern for other alliance teams. When a new business opportunity is discovered, an alliance draws on technical expertise from the other alliances. The purpose is not only to acquire additional knowledge, but also to share accumulated learning. There's no benefit to hoarding information: Learning gained from one software project might prove especially valuable to one under way in another alliance. This technological diffusion of information produces products that quickly reach the market.

TCG's formal structure is designed to ensure that such knowledge diffusion occurs. The company's culture is structured to encourage this as well. The TCG culture attracts both the entrepreneur and the team-oriented person at the same time. Working with multiple stakeholders through TCG's triangulation model forces employees to listen to the customers and respond quickly. Because the customer matters more than the functional title, teams lend expertise to each other in return for sharing the gains realized from supplying value to the customer.

Source: Snow, C. 1997. Twenty-First Century Organizations: Implications for a New Marketing Paradigm. *Journal of the Academy of Marketing Science,* Winter: 72–74; Allred, B., Snow, C., & Miles, R. 1996. Characteristics of Managerial Careers of the 21st Century. *Academy of Management Executive,* November: 17–27; Herzog, V. L. 2001. Trust Building on Corporate Collaborative Teams. *Project Management Journal,* March: 28–41.

outsource many parts of its value chain to reduce costs and increase quality, engage simultaneously in multiple alliances to take advantage of technological developments or penetrate new markets, and break down barriers within the organization to enhance flexibility. In Strategy Spotlight 10.8, we see how Technical Computer Graphics combines both barrier-free and virtual organizational forms.

When an organization faces external pressures, resource scarcity, and declining performance, it tends to become more internally focused, rather than directing its efforts toward managing and enhancing relationships with existing and potential external stakeholders. This may be the most opportune time for managers to carefully analyze their value-chain activities and evaluate the potential for adopting elements of modular, virtual, and barrier-free organizational types.

Achieving the coordination and integration necessary to maximize the potential of an organization's human capital involves much more than just creating a new structure. Techniques and processes to ensure the coordination and integration of an organization's key value-chain activities are critical. Teams are key building blocks of the new organizational forms, and teamwork requires new and flexible approaches to coordination and integration.

Managers trained in rigid hierarchies may find it difficult to make the transition to the more democratic, participative style that teamwork requires. As Douglas K. Smith, co-author of *The Wisdom of Teams,* pointed out, "A completely diverse group must agree on a goal, put the notion of individual accountability aside and figure out how to work with each other. Most of all, they must learn that if the team fails, it's everyone's fault."[60]

Within the framework of an appropriate organizational design, managers must select a mix and balance of tools and techniques to facilitate the effective coordination and integration of key activities. Some of the factors that must be considered include:

- Common culture and shared values.
- Horizontal organizational structures.
- Horizontal systems and processes.
- Communications and information technologies.
- Human resource practices.

Common Culture and Shared Values   Shared goals, mutual objectives, and a high degree of trust are essential to the success of boundaryless organizations. In the fluid and flexible environments of the new organizational architectures, common cultures, shared values, and carefully aligned incentives are often less expensive to implement and are often a more effective means of strategic control than rules, boundaries, and formal procedures.

horizontal organizational structures
organizational forms that group similar or related business units under common management control, facilitate sharing resources and infrastructures to exploit synergies among operating units and help to create a sense of common purpose.

Horizontal Organizational Structures   These structures, which group similar or related business units under common management control, facilitate sharing resources and infrastructures to exploit synergies among operating units and help to create a sense of common purpose. Consistency in training and the development of similar structures across business units facilitates job rotation and cross training and enhances understanding of common problems and opportunities. Cross-functional teams and inter-divisional committees and task groups represent important opportunities to improve understanding and foster cooperation among operating units.

Horizontal Systems and Processes   Organizational systems, policies, and procedures are the traditional mechanisms for achieving integration among functional units. Existing policies and procedures often do little more than institutionalize the barriers that exist from years of managing within the framework of the traditional model. Beginning with an understanding of basic business processes in the context of "a collection of activities that takes one or more kinds of input and creates an output that is of value to the customer," Michael Hammer and James Champy's 1993 best-selling *Reengineering the Corporation* outlined a methodology for redesigning internal systems and procedures that has been embraced by many organizations.[61] Successful reengineering lowers costs, reduces inventories and cycle times, improves quality, speeds response times, and enhances organizational flexibility. Others advocate similar benefits through the reduction of cycle times, total quality management, and the like.

Communications and Information Technologies (IT)   The effective use of IT can play an important role in bridging gaps and breaking down barriers between organizations. Electronic mail and videoconferencing can improve lateral communications across long distances and multiple time zones and circumvent many of the barriers of the traditional model. IT can be a powerful ally in the redesign and streamlining of internal business processes and in improving coordination and integration between suppliers and customers. Internet technologies have eliminated the paperwork in many buyer–supplier relationships, enabling cooperating organizations to reduce inventories, shorten delivery cycles, and reduce operating costs. IT must be viewed more as a prime component of an organization's overall strategy than simply in terms of administrative support.

Human Resource Practices   Change always involves and affects the human dimension of organizations. The attraction, development, and retention of human capital are vital to value creation. As boundaryless structures are implemented, processes are reengineered, and organizations become increasingly dependent on sophisticated ITs, the skills of workers and managers alike must be upgraded to realize the full benefits.

Creating Ambidextrous Organizational Designs

>LO6
The need for creating ambidextrous organizational designs that enable firms to explore new opportunities and effectively integrate existing operations.

In Chapter 1, we introduced the concept of "ambidexterity," which incorporates two contradictory challenges faced by today's managers.[62] First, managers must explore new opportunities and adjust to volatile markets in order to avoid complacency. They must ensure that they maintain *adaptability* and remain proactive in expanding and/or modifying their product–market scope to anticipate and satisfy market conditions. Such competencies are especially challenging when change is rapid and unpredictable.

Second, managers must also effectively exploit the value of their existing assets and competencies. They need to have *alignment*, which is a clear sense of how value is being created in the short term and how activities are integrated and properly coordinated. Firms that achieve both adaptability and alignment are considered *ambidextrous organizations*—aligned and efficient in how they manage today's business but flexible enough to changes in the environment so that they will prosper tomorrow.

Handling such opposing demands is difficult because there will always be some degree of conflict. Firms often suffer when they place too strong a priority on either adaptability or alignment. If it places too much focus on adaptability, the firm will suffer low profitability in the short term. If managers direct their efforts primarily at alignment, they will likely miss out on promising business opportunities.

Ambidextrous Organizations: Key Design Attributes

A recent study by Charles O'Reilly and Michael Tushman[63] provides some insights into how some firms were able to create successful **ambidextrous organizational designs.** They investigated companies that attempted to simultaneously pursue modest, incremental innovations as well as more dramatic, breakthrough innovations. The team investigated 35 attempts to launch breakthrough innovations undertaken by 15 business units in nine different industries. They studied the organizational designs and the processes, systems, and cultures associated with the breakthrough projects as well as their impact on the operations and performance of the traditional businesses.

ambidextrous organizational designs organization designs that attempt to simultaneously pursue modest, incremental innovations as well as more dramatic, breakthrough innovations.

Companies structured their breakthrough projects in one of four primary ways:

- Seven were carried out within existing *functional organizational structures.* The projects were completely integrated into the regular organizational and management structure.
- Nine were organized as *cross-functional teams.* The groups operated within the established organization but outside of the existing management structure.
- Four were organized as *unsupported teams.* Here, they became independent units set up outside the established organization and management hierarchy.
- Fifteen were conducted within *ambidextrous organizations.* Here, the breakthrough efforts were organized within structurally independent units, each having its own processes, structures, and cultures. However, they were integrated into the existing senior management structure.

The performance results of the 35 initiatives were tracked along two dimensions:

- Their success in creating desired innovations was measured by either the actual commercial results of the new product or the application of practical market or technical learning.
- The performance of the existing business was evaluated.

The study found that the organizational structure and management practices employed had a direct and significant impact on the performance of both the breakthrough initiative and the traditional business. The ambidextrous organizational designs were more effective than the other three designs on both dimensions: launching breakthrough products or services (i.e., adaptation) and improving the performance of the existing business (i.e., alignment).

Why Was the Ambidextrous Organization the Most Effective Structure?

The study found that there were many factors. A clear and compelling vision, consistently communicated by the company's senior management team was critical in building the ambidextrous designs. The structure enabled cross-fertilization while avoiding cross-contamination. The tight coordination and integration at the managerial levels enabled the newer units to share important resources from the traditional units such as cash, talent, and expertise. Such sharing was encouraged and facilitated by effective reward systems that emphasized overall company goals. The organizational separation ensured that the new units' distinctive processes, structures, and cultures were not overwhelmed by the forces of "business as usual." The established units were shielded from the distractions of launching new businesses, and they continued to focus all of their attention and energy on refining their operations, enhancing their products, and serving their customers.

Reflecting on Career Implications . . .

- *Strategy–Structure:* Is there an effective "fit" between your organization's strategy and its structure? If not, there may be inconsistencies in how you are evaluated which often leads to role ambiguity and confusion. A poor fit could also affect communication among departments as well as across the organization's hierarchy.
- *Matrix Structure:* If your organization employs elements of a matrix structure (e.g., dual reporting relationships), are there effective structural supporting elements (e.g., culture and rewards)? If not, there could be a high level of dysfunctional conflict among managers.
- *The "Fit" between Rewards and Incentives and "Levels of Strategy" (Business- and Corporate-Level):* What metrics are used to evaluate the performance of your work unit? Are there strictly financial measures of success or are you also rewarded for achieving competitive advantages (through effective innovation, organizational learning, or other activities that increase knowledge but may be costly in the short run)?
- *Boundaryless Organizational Designs:* Does your firm have structural mechanisms (e.g., culture, human resource practices) that facilitate sharing of information across boundaries? If so, you should be better able to enhance your human capital by leveraging your talents and competencies.

Summary

Successful organizations must ensure that they have the proper type of organizational structure. Furthermore, they must ensure that their firms incorporate the necessary integration and processes so that the internal and external boundaries of their firms are flexible and permeable. Such a need is increasingly important as the environments of firms become more complex, rapidly changing, and unpredictable.

In the first section of the chapter, we discussed the growth patterns of large corporations. Although most organizations remain small or die, some firms continue to grow in terms of revenues, vertical integration, and diversity of products and services. In addition, their geographical scope may increase to include international operations. We traced the dominant pattern of growth, which evolves from a simple structure to a functional structure as a firm grows in terms of size and increases its level of vertical integration. After a firm expands into related products and services, its structure changes from a functional to a divisional form of organization.

Finally, when the firm enters international markets, its structure again changes to accommodate the change in strategy.

We also addressed the different types of organizational structure—simple, functional, divisional (including two variations—strategic business unit and holding company), and matrix—as well as their relative advantages and disadvantages. We closed the section with a discussion of the implications for structure when a firm enters international markets. The three primary factors to take into account when determining the appropriate structure are type of international strategy, product diversity, and the extent to which a firm is dependent on foreign sales.

In the second section, we took a contingency approach to the design of reward and evaluation systems. That is, we argued that there is no one best way to design such systems; rather, it is dependent on a variety of factors. The two that we discussed are business- and corporate-level strategies. With an overall cost leadership strategy and unrelated diversification, it is appropriate to rely primarily on cultures and reward systems that emphasize the production outcomes of the organization, because it is rather easy to quantify such indicators. In contrast, differentiation strategies and related diversification require cultures and incentive systems that encourage and reward creativity initiatives as well as the cooperation among professionals in many different functional areas. Here it becomes more difficult to measure accurately each individual's contribution, and more subjective indicators become essential.

The third section of the chapter introduced the concept of the boundaryless organization. We did not suggest that the concept of the boundaryless organization replaces the traditional forms of organizational structure. Rather, it should complement them. This is necessary to cope with the increasing complexity and change in the competitive environment. We addressed three types of boundaryless organizations. The barrier-free type focuses on the need for the internal and external boundaries of a firm to be more flexible and permeable. The modular type emphasizes the strategic outsourcing of noncore activities. The virtual type centers on the strategic benefits of alliances and the forming of network organizations. We discussed both the advantages and disadvantages of each type of boundaryless organization as well as suggested some techniques and processes that are necessary to successfully implement them. These are common culture and values, horizontal organizational structures, horizontal systems and processes, communications and information technologies, and human resource practices.

The final section addresses the need for managers to develop ambidextrous organizations. In today's rapidly changing global environment, managers must be responsive and proactive in order to take advantage of new opportunities. At the same time, they must effectively integrate and coordinate existing operations. Such requirements call for organizational designs that establish project teams that are structurally independent units, with each having its own processes, structures, and cultures. But, at the same time, each unit needs to be effectively integrated into the existing management hierarchy.

Summary Review Questions

1. Why is it important for managers to carefully consider the type of organizational structure that they use to implement their strategies?

2. Briefly trace the dominant growth pattern of major corporations from simple structure to functional structure to divisional structure. Discuss the relationship between a firm's strategy and its structure.

3. What are the relative advantages and disadvantages of the types of organizational structure—simple, functional, divisional, matrix—discussed in the chapter?

4. When a firm expands its operations into foreign markets, what are the three most important factors to take into account in deciding what type of structure is most appropriate? What are the types of international structures discussed in the text and what are the relationships between strategy and structure?

5. Briefly describe the three different types of boundaryless organizations: barrier-free, modular, and virtual.

6. What are some of the key attributes of effective groups? Ineffective groups?

7. What are the advantages and disadvantages of the three types of boundaryless organizations: barrier-free, modular, and virtual?

8. When are ambidextrous organizational designs necessary? What are some of their key attributes?

Key Terms

organizational structure 349

simple organizational structure, 351

functional organizational structure, 351

divisional organizational structure, 353

strategic business unit (SBU) structure, 355

holding company structure, 355

matrix organizational structure, 356

international division structure 357

geographic-area division structure 357

worldwide matrix structure 357

global start-up, 359

boundaryless organizational
designs, 363

barrier-free
organization, 364

modular
organization, 367

virtual organization, 370

horizontal organizational
structures 374

ambidextrous organizational
designs, 375

Experiential Exercise

Many firms have recently moved toward a modular structure. For example, they have increasingly outsourced many of their information technology (IT) activities. Identify three such organizations. Using secondary sources, evaluate (1) the firm's rationale for IT outsourcing and (2) the implications for performance.

Firm	Rationale	Implication(s) for Performance
1.		
2.		
3.		

Application Questions Exercises

1. Select an organization that competes in an industry in which you are particularly interested. Go on the Internet and determine what type of organizational structure this organization has. In your view, is it consistent with the strategy that it has chosen to implement? Why? Why not?

2. Choose an article from *BusinessWeek, Fortune, Forbes, Fast Company,* or any other well-known publication that deals with a corporation that has undergone a significant change in its strategic direction. What are the implications for the structure of this organization?

3. Go on the Internet and look up some of the public statements or speeches of an executive in a major corporation about a significant initiative such as entering into a joint venture or launching a new product line. What do you feel are the implications for making the internal and external barriers of the firm more flexible and permeable? Does the executive discuss processes, procedures, integrating mechanisms, or cultural issues that should serve this purpose? Or are other issues discussed that enable a firm to become more boundaryless?

4. Look up a recent article in the publications listed in question 2 above that addresses a firm's involvement in outsourcing (modular organization) or in strategic alliance or network organizations (virtual organization). Was the firm successful or unsuccessful in this endeavor? Why? Why not?

Ethics Questions

1. If a firm has a divisional structure and places extreme pressures on its divisional executives to meet short-term profitability goals (e.g., quarterly income), could this raise some ethical considerations? Why? Why not?

2. If a firm enters into a strategic alliance but does not exercise appropriate behavioral control of its employees (in terms of culture, rewards and incentives, and boundaries—as discussed in Chapter 9) that are involved in the alliance, what ethical issues could arise? What could be the potential long-term and short-term downside for the firm?

References

1. Pope, Carl. 2008. *Taking the initiative.* Sierra Club executive blog, http://sierraclub.typepad.com/carlpope/2008/04/wall-street-a-1.html; www.sierraclub.org; Kamenetz, A. 2008. Cleaning solutions. *Fast Company,* September: 121–125; and Being green and in the black. 2008. *Retailing Today,* April 28: 47(5): 10, 16.

2. This introductory discussion draws upon Hall, R. H. 2002. *Organizations: Structures, processes, and outcomes* (8th ed.). Upper Saddle River, NJ: Prentice Hall; and Duncan, R. E. 1979. What is the right organization structure? Decision-tree analysis provides the right answer. *Organizational Dynamics,* 7(3): 59–80. For an insightful discussion of strategy-structure relationships in the organization theory and strategic management literatures, refer to Keats, B. & O'Neill, H. M. 2001. Organization structure: Looking through a strategy lens. In Hitt, M. A., Freeman, R. E., & Harrison, J. S. 2001. *The Blackwell handbook of strategic management:* 520–542. Malden, MA: Blackwell.

3. An interesting discussion on the role of organizational design in strategy execution is in: Neilson, G. L., Martin, K. L., & Powers, E. 2009. The secrets to successful strategy execution. *Harvard Business Review,* 87(2): 60–70.

4. This discussion draws upon Chandler, A. D. 1962. *Strategy and structure.* Cambridge, MA: MIT Press; Galbraith J. R. & Kazanjian, R. K. 1986. *Strategy implementation: The role of structure and process.* St. Paul, MN: West Publishing; and Scott, B. R. 1971. Stages of corporate development. Intercollegiate Case Clearing House, 9-371-294, BP 998. Harvard Business School.

5. Our discussion of the different types of organizational structures draws on a variety of sources, including Galbraith & Kazanjian, op. cit.; Hrebiniak, L. G. & Joyce, W. F. 1984. *Implementing strategy.* New York: Macmillan; Distelzweig, H. 2000. Organizational structure. In Helms, M. M. (Ed.). *Encyclopedia of management:* 692–699. Farmington Hills, MI: Gale; and Dess, G. G. & Miller, A. 1993. *Strategic management.* New York: McGraw-Hill.

6. A discussion of an innovative organizational design is in: Garvin, D. A. & Levesque, L. C. 2009. The multiunit enterprise. *Harvard Business Review,* 87(2): 106–117.

7. Schein, E. H. 1996. Three cultures of management: The key to organizational learning. *Sloan Management Review,* 38(1): 9–20.

8. Insights on governance implications for multidivisional forms are in: Verbeke, A. & Kenworthy, T. P. 2008. Multidivisional vs. metanational governance. *Journal of International Business,* 39(6): 940–956.

9. For a discussion of performance implications, refer to Hoskisson, R. E. 1987. Multidivisional structure and performance: The contingency of diversification strategy. *Academy of Management Journal,* 29: 625–644.

10. For a thorough and seminal discussion of the evolution toward the divisional form of organizational structure in the United States, refer to Chandler, op. cit. A rigorous empirical study of the strategy and structure relationship is found in Rumelt, R. P. 1974. *Strategy, structure, and economic performance.* Cambridge, MA: Harvard Business School Press.

11. Ghoshal S. & Bartlett, C. A. 1995. Changing the role of management: Beyond structure to processes. *Harvard Business Review,* 73(1): 88.

12. Koppel, B. 2000. Synergy in ketchup? *Forbes,* February 7: 68–69; and Hitt, M. A., Ireland, R. D., & Hoskisson, R. E. 2001. *Strategic management: Competitiveness and globalization* (4th ed.). Cincinnati, OH: Southwestern Publishing.

13. Pitts, R. A. 1977. Strategies and structures for diversification. *Academy of Management Journal,* 20(2): 197–208.

14. Dell, M. & Rollins, K. 2005. Execution without excuses. *Harvard Business Review,* 83(3): 102–111.

15. Daniels, J. D., Pitts, R. A., & Tretter, M. J. 1984. Strategy and structure of U.S. multinationals: An exploratory study. *Academy of Management Journal,* 27(2): 292–307.

16. Habib, M. M. & Victor, B. 1991. Strategy, structure, and performance of U.S. manufacturing and service MNCs: A comparative analysis. *Strategic Management Journal,* 12(8): 589–606.

17. Our discussion of global start-ups draws from Oviatt, B. M. & McDougall, P. P. 2005. The internationalization of entrepreneurship. *Journal of International Business Studies,* 36(1): 2–8; Oviatt, B. M. & McDougall, P. P. 1994. Toward a theory of international new ventures. *Journal of International Business Studies,* 25(1): 45–64; and Oviatt, B. M. & McDougall, P. P. 1995. Global start-ups: Entrepreneurs on a worldwide stage. *Academy of Management Executive,* 9(2): 30–43.

18. Some useful guidelines for global start-ups are provided in Kuemmerle, W. 2005. The entrepreneur's path for global expansion. *MIT Sloan Management Review,* 46(2): 42–50.

19. See, for example, Miller, D. & Friesen, P. H. 1980. Momentum and revolution in organizational structure. *Administrative Science Quarterly,* 13: 65–91.

20. Many authors have argued that a firm's structure can influence its strategy and performance. These include Amburgey, T. L. & Dacin, T. 1995. As the left foot follows the right? The dynamics of strategic and structural change. *Academy of Management Journal,* 37: 1427–1452; Dawn, K. & Amburgey, T. L. 1991.

Organizational inertia and momentum: A dynamic model of strategic change. *Academy of Management Journal,* 34: 591–612; Fredrickson, J. W. 1986. The strategic decision process and organization structure. *Academy of Management Review,* 11: 280–297; Hall, D. J. & Saias, M. A. 1980. Strategy follows structure! *Strategic Management Journal,* 1: 149–164; and Burgelman, R. A. 1983. A model of the interaction of strategic behavior, corporate context, and the concept of strategy. *Academy of Management Review,* 8: 61–70.

21. This discussion of generic strategies and their relationship to organizational control draws upon Porter, M. E. 1980. *Competitive strategy.* New York: Free Press; and Miller, D. 1988. Relating Porter's business strategies to environment and structure: Analysis and performance implications. *Academy of Management Journal,* 31(2): 280–308.

22. Rodengen, J. L. 1997. *The legend of Nucor Corporation.* Fort Lauderdale, FL: Write Stuff Enterprises.

23. The 3M example draws upon *Blueprints for service quality.* 1994. New York: American Management Association; personal communication with Katerine Hagmeier, program manager, external communications, 3M Corporation, March 26, 1998; Lei, D., Slocum, J. W., & Pitts, R. A. 1999. Designing organizations for competitive advantage: The power of unlearning and learning. *Organizational Dynamics,* 27(3): 24–38; and Graham, A. B. & Pizzo, V. G. 1996. A question of balance: Case studies in strategic knowledge management. *European Management Journal,* 14(4): 338–346.

24. The Sharp Corporation and Hanson plc examples are based on Collis, D. J. & Montgomery, C. A. 1998. Creating corporate advantage. *Harvard Business Review,* 76(3): 70–83.

25. Kunii, I. 2002. Japanese companies' survival skills. *BusinessWeek,* November 18: 18.

26. White, G. 1988. How I turned $3,000 into $10 billion. *Fortune,* November 7: 80–89. After the death of the founders, the Hanson plc conglomerate was found to be too unwieldy and was broken up into several separate, publicly traded corporations. For more on its more limited current scope of operations, see www.hansonplc.com.

27. An interesting discussion on how the Internet has affected the boundaries of firms can be found in Afuah, A. 2003. Redefining firm boundaries in the face of the Internet: Are firms really shrinking? *Academy of Management Review,* 28(1): 34–53.

28. Collis & Montgomery, op. cit.

29. For a discussion of the role of coaching on developing high performance teams, refer to Kets de Vries, M. F. R. 2005. Leadership group coaching in action: The zen of creating high performance teams. *Academy of Management Executive,* 19(1): 77–89.

30. Pfeffer, J. 1998. *The human equation: Building profits by putting people first.* Cambridge, MA: Harvard Business School Press.

31. For a discussion on how functional area diversity affects performance, see Bunderson, J. S. & Sutcliffe, K. M. 2002. *Academy of Management Journal,* 45(5): 875–893.

32. See, for example, Hoskisson, R. E., Hill, C. W. L., & Kim, H. 1993. The multidivisional structure: Organizational fossil or source of value? *Journal of Management,* 19(2): 269–298.

33. Pottruck, D. A. 1997. Speech delivered by the co-CEO of Charles Schwab Co., Inc., to the Retail Leadership Meeting, San Francisco, CA, January 30; and Miller, W. 1999. Building the ultimate resource. *Management Review,* January: 42–45.

34. Public-private partnerships are addressed in: Engardio, P. 2009. State capitalism. *BusinessWeek,* February 9: 38–43.

35. Magretta, J. 1998. The power of virtual integration: An interview with Dell Computer's Michael Dell. *Harvard Business Review,* 76(2): 75.

36. Forster, J. 2001. Networking for cash. *BusinessWeek,* January 8: 129.

37. Dess, G. G., Rasheed, A. M. A., McLaughlin, K. J., & Priem, R. 1995. The new corporate architecture. *Academy of Management Executive,* 9(3): 7–20.

38. Barnes, C. 1998. A fatal case. *Fast Company,* February–March: 173.

39. Handy, C. 1989. *The age of unreason.* Boston: Harvard Business School Press; Ramstead, E. 1997. APC maker's low-tech formula: Start with the box. *The Wall Street Journal,* December 29: B1; Mussberg, W. 1997. Thin screen PCs are looking good but still fall flat. *The Wall Street Journal,* January 2: 9; Brown, E. 1997. Monorail: Low cost PCs. *Fortune,* July 7: 106–108; and Young, M. 1996. Ex-Compaq executives start new company. *Computer Reseller News,* November 11: 181.

40. An original discussion on how opensourcing could help the Big 3 automobile companies is in: Jarvis, J. 2009. How the Google model could help Detroit. *BusinessWeek,* February 9: 32–36.

41. For a discussion of some of the downsides of outsourcing, refer to Rossetti, C. & Choi, T. Y. 2005. On the dark side of strategic sourcing: Experiences from the aerospace industry. *Academy of Management Executive,* 19(1): 46–60.

42. Tully, S. 1993. The modular corporation. *Fortune,* February 8: 196.

43. Offshoring in manufacturing firms is addressed in: Coucke, K. & Sleuwaegen, L. 2008. Offshoring as a survival strategy: Evidence from manufacturing firms in Belgium. *Journal of International Business Studies,* 39(8): 1261–1277.

44. Quinn, J. B. 1992. *Intelligent enterprise: A knowledge and service based paradigm for industry.* New York: Free Press.

45. For an insightful perspective on outsourcing and its role in developing capabilities, read Gottfredson, M., Puryear, R., & Phillips, C. 2005. Strategic sourcing: From periphery to the core. *Harvard Business Review,* 83(4): 132–139.

46. This discussion draws upon Quinn, J. B. & Hilmer, F. C. 1994. Strategic outsourcing. *Sloan Management Review,* 35(4): 43–55.

47. Insights on outsourcing and private branding can be found in: Cehn, S-F. S. 2009. A transaction cost rationale for private branding and its implications for the choice of domestic vs. offshore outsourcing. *Journal of*

International Business Strategy, 40(1): 156–175.

48. For an insightful perspective on the use of outsourcing for decision analysis, read: Davenport, T. H. & Iyer, B. 2009. Should you outsource your brain? *Harvard Business Review,* 87(2): 38.

49. See also Stuckey, J. & White, D. 1993. When and when not to vertically integrate. *Sloan Management Review,* Spring: 71–81; Harrar, G. 1993. Outsource tales. *Forbes ASAP,* June 7: 37–39, 42; and Davis, E. W. 1992. Global outsourcing: Have U.S. managers thrown the baby out with the bath water? *Business Horizons,* July–August: 58–64.

50. For a discussion of knowledge creation through alliances, refer to Inkpen, A. C. 1996. Creating knowledge through collaboration. *California Management Review,* 39(1): 123–140; and Mowery, D. C., Oxley, J. E., & Silverman, B. S. 1996. Strategic alliances and interfirm knowledge transfer. *Strategic Management Journal,* 17 (Special Issue, Winter): 77–92.

51. Doz, Y. & Hamel, G. 1998. *Alliance advantage: The art of creating value through partnering.* Boston: Harvard Business School Press.

52. DeSanctis, G., Glass, J. T., & Ensing, I. M. 2002. Organizational designs for R&D. *Academy of Management Executive,* 16(3): 55–66.

53. Barringer, B. R. & Harrison, J. S. 2000. Walking a tightrope: Creating value through interorganizational alliances. *Journal of Management,* 26: 367–403.

54. Davis, E. 1997. Interview: Norman Augustine. *Management Review,* November: 14.

55. One contemporary example of virtual organizations is R&D consortia. For an insightful discussion, refer to Sakaibara, M. 2002. Formation of R&D consortia: Industry and company effects. *Strategic Management Journal,* 23(11): 1033–1050.

56. Bartness, A. & Cerny, K. 1993. Building competitive advantage through a global network of capabilities. *California Management Review,* Winter: 78–103. For an insightful historical discussion of the usefulness of alliances in the computer industry, see Moore, J. F. 1993. Predators and prey: A new ecology of competition. *Harvard Business Review,* 71(3): 75–86.

57. See Lorange, P. & Roos, J. 1991. Why some strategic alliances succeed and others fail. *Journal of Business Strategy,* January–February: 25–30; and Slowinski, G. 1992. The human touch in strategic alliances. *Mergers and Acquisitions,* July–August: 44–47. A compelling argument for strategic alliances is provided by Ohmae, K. 1989. The global logic of strategic alliances. *Harvard Business Review,* 67(2): 143–154.

58. Some of the downsides of alliances are discussed in Das, T. K. & Teng, B. S. 2000. Instabilities of strategic alliances: An internal tensions perspective. *Organization Science,* 11: 77–106.

59. This section draws upon Dess, G. G. & Picken, J. C. 1997. *Mission critical.* Burr Ridge, IL: Irwin Professional Publishing.

60. Katzenbach, J. R. & Smith, D. K. 1994. *The wisdom of teams: Creating the high performance organization.* New York: HarperBusiness.

61. Hammer, M. & Champy, J. 1993. *Reengineering the corporation: A manifesto for business revolution.* New York: HarperCollins.

62. This section draws on Birkinshaw, J. & Gibson, C. 2004. Building ambidexterity into an organization. *MIT Sloan Management Review,* 45(4): 47–55; and Gibson, C. B. & Birkinshaw, J. 2004. The antecedents, consequences, and mediating role of organizational ambidexterity. *Academy of Management Journal,* 47(2): 209–226. Robert Duncan is generally credited with being the first to coin the term "ambidextrous organizations" in his article entitled: Designing dual structures for innovation. In Kilmann, R. H., Pondy, L. R., & Slevin, D. (Eds.). 1976. *The management of organizations,* vol. 1: 167–188. For a seminal academic discussion of the concept of exploration and exploitation, which parallels adaptation and alignment, refer to: March, J. G. 1991. Exploration and exploitation in organizational learning. *Organization Science,* 2: 71–86.

63. This section is based on O'Reilly, C. A. & Tushman, M. L. 2004. The ambidextrous organization. *Harvard Business Review,* 82(4): 74–81.

Strategic Leadership:

Creating a Learning Organization and an Ethical Organization

>learning objectives

After reading this chapter, you should have a good understanding of:

LO1 The three key interdependent activities in which all successful leaders must be continually engaged.

LO2 Three elements of effective leadership: integrative thinking, overcoming barriers to change, and the effective use of power.

LO3 The crucial role of emotional intelligence (EI) in successful leadership as well as its potential drawbacks.

LO4 The value of creating and maintaining a learning organization in today's global marketplace.

LO5 The leader's role in establishing an ethical organization.

LO6 The difference between integrity-based and compliance-based approaches to organizational ethics.

LO7 Several key elements that organizations must have to become an ethical organization.

To compete in the global marketplace, organizations need to have strong and effective leadership. This involves the active process of both creating and implementing proper strategies. In this chapter we address key activities in which leaders throughout the organization must be involved to be successful in creating and sustaining competitive advantages.

In the first section, we provide a brief overview of the three key leadership activities. These are (1) setting a direction, (2) designing the organization, and (3) nurturing a culture committed to excellence and ethical behavior. Each of these activities is "necessary but not sufficient"; that is, to be effective, leaders must give proper attention to each of them.

Section two addresses practices and capabilities that enable executives to be effective as leaders. To be successful in a complex business environment, leaders must perform a variety of functions and exhibit key strengths. We focus on three capabilities that effective leaders often exhibit—integrative thinking, overcoming barriers to change, and the effective use of power.

The third section discusses the vital role of emotional intelligence (EI) in effective strategic leadership. EI refers to an individual's capacity for recognizing his or her emotions and those of others. It consists of five components: self-awareness, self-regulation, motivation, empathy, and social skills. We also address potential downsides or drawbacks that may result from the ineffective use of EI.

Next we address the important role of a leader in creating a learning organization. Here, leaders must strive to harness the individual and collective talents of individuals throughout the entire organization. Creating a learning organization is particularly important in today's competitive environment, which is increasingly unpredictable, dynamic, and interdependent. The key elements of a learning organization are inspiring and motivating people with a mission or purpose, empowering employees at all levels, accumulating and sharing internal and external information, and challenging the status quo to enable creativity.

The final section discusses a leader's challenge in creating and maintaining an ethical organization. There are many benefits of having an ethical organization. It can provide financial benefits, enhance human capital, and help to ensure positive relationships with suppliers, customers, society at large, and governmental agencies. By contrast failure to operate ethically leading to an ethical crisis can be very costly for many reasons. We address four key elements of an ethical organization: role models, corporate credos and codes of conduct, reward and evaluation systems, and policies and procedures.

Learning from Mistakes

The financial crisis that struck U.S. markets in the fall of 2008 dealt a devastating blow to many companies. Few were hit as hard as Lehman Brothers, the global financial services company that went under in the largest bankruptcy in U.S. history. During a crucial period when stock markets around the world were spiraling downward because of heavy investments in overvalued assets such as subprime mortgages, Lehman was in the center of the storm. It was unable to obtain a government bailout or a buyer, either of which might have saved it from being wiped out. According to some, at least one reason Lehman could not seem to get help and failed when other troubled companies were being salvaged was due to the leadership of the man at the helm—Chairman and CEO Richard S. Fuld, Jr.[1]

Although many would agree that bad luck and bad timing contributed to Lehman's downfall, Fuld was clearly part of the problem. A 30-year veteran of the company, Fuld started as a commercial paper trader and moved through the ranks of Lehman as it expanded into a host of financial services, including investment banking, equity and fixed income sales, research and trading, investment management, and private banking. Fuld was considered a supreme trader by many and, according to a senior partner, "a very smart guy, tough as nails." He was also highly respected for providing strong leadership during some of Lehman's most difficult periods, such as the Asian debt crisis of 1998.

What went wrong? Fuld exhibited traits that may have shaped the culture of Lehman or merely reflected it. Lehman had a reputation for being aggressive; so did Fuld, who was known for his combative nature. Because he was a good trader, he was given a leadership role. But his skills as a manager of people were lacking. He had an intimidating presence and a reputation for speaking to people in monosyllables. He was also said to have an especially bad temper, one that earned him the nickname "Gorilla." Among its worst managers of 2008, *BusinessWeek* reported that Fuld "drove his people hard and ignored warning signs, rewarding risk and greed."

Fuld also seemed to lack a certain sensitivity that good leaders often display. When most Wall Street firms were reeling after the September 11th terrorist attack, Fuld seized the opportunity to grow the investment banking side of the business. For 2001, a year when a global recession and financial crisis led other chief executives to reduce their pay packages, Fuld received a $105 million compensation package, making him the fourth-highest-paid CEO in the United States. His reputation for lavish compensation became part of a reputation that stuck with and later hurt him.

Perhaps his greatest downfall was that he was unwilling or unable to recognize how serious the problems were that were plaguing Lehman and was reluctant to make changes even when he had the chance. For example, Fuld passed up an opportunity to sell 25 percent of the business to the Korean Development Bank, a move that might have provided the cash infusion Lehman needed to survive, because he thought the price was too low. He also reportedly balked at an offer to sell up to half of Lehman's shares to China's CITIC Securities because of a dispute over price. "Dick Fuld blew it," declared William Smith of New York–based Smith Asset Management. "How many opportunities did he have to sell Lehman?" According to Dartmouth professor Sydney Finkelstein, who studies the biases that cause CEOs to make bad decisions, Fuld "was unable to break out of his own experience and history by seeing the risks that Lehman had." "Nobody was more convinced [than Fuld] that Lehman was too big to fail," reported *BusinessWeek*.

Disbelief about the company's situation may have also led Fuld to act unethically. In testimony to the U.S. Congress about the financial collapse, he was questioned about making overly positive statements to analysts about Lehman's balance sheet just five days before it declared bankruptcy. Maryland Representative John Sarbanes called Fuld's statements to analysts "simply implausible," but Fuld did not admit to any wrongdoing. "Fuld went wrong in not taking seriously enough the impairment of his balance sheet. He had the typical hubris that any long-term CEO has: 'I built this thing, and it's got more value than the marketplace understands,'" said Charles Peabody, an analyst at Portales Partners, an independent research firm. Weeks after the Lehman bankruptcy, Fuld's questionable ethics made the news again when he sold his Florida mansion valued at $13.75 million to his wife for $100, a move considered by most to be an effort to prevent the home from being confiscated to pay creditors.

Fuld's failure to accept blame angered many and took its toll on his reputation. On the day Lehman declared bankruptcy, an irate employee punched Fuld in the face while he was on the treadmill at the bank's gym and knocked him out cold. Protesters gathered at the congressional hearing the day Fuld testified, to express outrage over his excessive pay and call for him to be jailed. Upon reviewing the Lehman bankruptcy filing, New York State Controller Thomas DiNapoli filed a motion in the U.S. Bankruptcy Court demanding Fuld's ouster. "Mr. Fuld's decisions drove the company toward ruin," wrote DiNapoli. "Without question, Mr. Fuld's stewardship of the company was a large factor in its demise." With that, Lehman's board of directors had little choice but to dismiss Fuld as CEO. In retrospect, regardless of who is to blame, it was Fuld's responsibility as Lehman's chairman and CEO to lead the company through the crisis. His failure to do so led to one of Wall Street's biggest failures ever.

Clearly, many of the decisions and actions of Richard Fuld were not in the best interests of the firm and its shareholders. In contrast, effective leaders play an important and often pivotal role in creating and implementing strategies.

This chapter provides insights into the role of strategic leadership in managing, adapting, and coping in the face of increased environmental complexity and uncertainty. First, we define leadership and its components. Then, we identify three elements of leadership that contribute to success—integrative thinking, overcoming barriers to change, and the effective use of power. The third section focuses on emotional intelligence, a trait that is increasingly acknowledged to be critical to successful leadership. Next, we emphasize the importance of developing a learning organization and how leaders can help their firms learn and proactively adapt in the face of accelerating change. Here, we focus on empowerment wherein employees and managers throughout an organization develop a sense of self-determination, competence, meaning, and impact that is centrally important to learning. Finally, we address the leader's role in building an ethical organization and the elements of an ethical culture that contribute to firm effectiveness.

Leadership: Three Interdependent Activities

In today's chaotic world, few would argue against the need for leadership, but how do we go about encouraging it? Is it enough to merely keep an organization afloat, or is it essential to make steady progress toward some well-defined objective? We believe custodial management is not leadership. Leadership is proactive, goal-oriented, and focused on the creation and implementation of a creative vision. **Leadership** is the process of transforming organizations from what they are to what the leader would have them become. This definition implies a lot: *dissatisfaction* with the status quo, a *vision* of what should be, and a *process* for bringing about change. An insurance company executive shared the following insight: "I lead by the Noah Principle: It's all right to know when it's going to rain, but, by God, you had better build the ark."

Doing the right thing is becoming increasingly important. Many industries are declining; the global village is becoming increasingly complex, interconnected, and unpredictable; and product and market life cycles are becoming increasingly compressed. When asked to describe the life cycle of his company's products, the CEO of a supplier of computer components replied, "Seven months from cradle to grave—and that includes three months to design the product and get it into production!" Richard D'Aveni, author of *Hypercompetition,* argued that in a world where all dimensions of competition appear to be compressed in time and heightened in complexity, *sustainable* competitive advantages are no longer possible.

> **leadership** the process of transforming organizations from what they are to what the leader would have them become.

Despite the importance of doing the "right thing," leaders must also be concerned about "doing things right." Charan and Colvin strongly believe that execution, that is, the implementation of strategy, is also essential to success.

> Mastering execution turns out to be the odds-on best way for a CEO to keep his job. So what's the right way to think about that sexier obsession, strategy? It's vitally important—obviously. The problem is that our age's fascination feeds the mistaken belief that developing exactly the right strategy will enable a company to rocket past competitors. In reality, that's less than half the battle.[2]

Thus, leaders are change agents whose success is measured by how effectively they formulate *and* implement a strategic vision and mission.[3]

Many authors contend that successful leaders must recognize three interdependent activities that must be continually reassessed for organizations to succeed. As shown in Exhibit 11.1, these are: (1) setting a direction, (2) designing the organization, and (3) nurturing a culture dedicated to excellence and ethical behavior.[4] Strategy Spotlight 11.1 describes how three successful leaders have exhibited these attributes in their organizations.

The interdependent nature of these three activities is self-evident. Consider an organization with a great mission and a superb organizational structure, but a culture that implicitly encourages shirking and unethical behavior. Or one with a sound direction and strong culture, but counterproductive teams and a "zero-sum" reward system that leads to the dysfunctional situation in which one party's gain is viewed as another party's loss, and collaboration and sharing are severely hampered. Clearly, such combinations would be ineffective.

Often, failure of today's organizations can be attributed to a lack of equal consideration of these three activities. The imagery of a three-legged stool is instructive: It will collapse if one leg is missing or broken. Let's briefly look at each of these activities.

Setting a Direction

A holistic understanding of an organization's stakeholders requires an ability to scan the environment to develop a knowledge of all of the company's stakeholders and other salient environmental trends and events. Managers must integrate this knowledge into a vision of what the organization could become.[5] It necessitates the capacity to solve increasingly complex problems, become proactive in approach, and develop viable strategic options. A strategic vision provides many benefits: a clear future direction; a framework for the organization's mission and goals; and enhanced employee communication, participation, and commitment.

At times the creative process involves what the CEO of Yokogawa, GE's Japanese partner in the Medical Systems business, called "bullet train" thinking.[6] That is, if you

>LO1

The three key interdependent activities in which all successful leaders must be continually engaged.

setting a direction
a strategic leadership activity of strategy analysis and strategy formulation.

Exhibit 11.1 **Three Interdependent Activities of Leadership**

How Leaders Lead in Tough Times

As companies failed and billions of dollars of shareholder wealth was lost during the financial crisis that began in 2008, new demands were placed on company executives to exhibit strong leadership. In the face of challenges, the leaders below displayed the three aspects of leadership that are the mark of successful organizations—setting a direction, designing the organization, and nurturing a culture dedicated to excellence and ethical behavior.

Dave Yost—Setting a Clear Direction

AmerisourceBergen is a $66 billion drug distribution company headquartered in Valley Forge, Pennsylvania. Because it's in an industry that operates on razor-thin margins—just one percent on average—holding down expenses is a companywide priority. As a result, Amerisource CEO Dave Yost is a model of frugality. He answers his own phone, keeps plastic plants in the lobby to save on watering, and flies economy class. Sitting in a 1970s-style plaid chair that looks like a yard sale item, Yost says, "The leader is very important in controlling business costs." He considers the familiar adage "stick to the knitting" outdated and says instead, "We're focused on knitting faster, better, and more creatively than anyone else." Although his tactics sound extreme, there are important payoffs: Amerisource profits increased 30 percent in a recent quarter compared to 8 percent at McKesson and 13 percent at Cardinal Health, its closest rivals. Company cost cutting also provided $500 million for recent investments to improve customer service technology and upgrade operations at key distribution centers.

Chad Holliday—Designing the Organization in the Face of a Crisis

DuPont is a $32 billion Delaware-based company with 60,000 employees. Its CEO, Chad Holliday, was meeting with a major customer in Japan in 2008 when the seriousness of the emerging financial crisis first struck him. The Japanese CEO said concern over a financial contagion was making him conserve cash for fear of not being able to raise capital. Upon returning home, Holliday received more bad news: Because DuPont provides paint for more than 30 percent of U.S. cars on a just-in-time basis, the automakers share their production schedules. Faced with collapsing auto sales, production scheduling had been temporarily halted. Based on such grim reports, Holliday reluctantly invoked the company's Corporate Crisis Management plan to identify a new set of mechanisms to integrate activities across all parts of the organization. Within hours, executive teams gathered to formulate a plan; within 10 days of creating the plan, every DuPont employee met face-to-face with a manager who explained their new responsibilities. Even though the initial response went smoothly, Holliday realized that some managers were not responding fast enough. "They were talking about things that would be implemented by January or February [2009], but there were things we needed implemented in October," explained Holliday. More meetings were held to heighten accountability and implement control systems that targeted costs, scheduled shutdowns, and revised working capital projections. Over 20,000 outside contractors were cut back, and employees whose operations were slowing were used to do the work instead. Within six weeks, Holliday's reality check led to a major redesign of DuPont's priorities and helped position it more securely for an uncertain future.

Herb Kelleher—Nurturing a Culture by Setting an Ethical Example

In Chapter 9, we discussed the executive pay dilemma: offering appealing pay packages to attract top talent versus providing over-the-top compensation for underperforming executives. For Herb Kelleher, Southwest Airlines' legendary former chairman and CEO, there is no dilemma for executives willing to do the right thing. From the start, Southwest took steps to maintain its unique culture—what Kelleher calls "this joie de vivre, this effervescence, in our company." Fairness and a willingness to share the pain during difficult times has been an important part of its corporate philosophy. When pilots were asked to freeze pay for five years, Kelleher also voluntarily took a five-year pay freeze "to honor what they had done. And I have turned down many, many millions of dollars in salary and options because it didn't set a good example." Corporate officers follow a similar practice. According to Kelleher, "Our officers have never received a salary increase that is larger on average than our noncontract employees have gotten. In other words, if they get a 3.5 percent increase, our officers get a 3.5 percent increase." Such policies have no doubt contributed to Southwest's remarkable success: As of 2008, the Dallas, Texas–based company has been profitable for 35 consecutive years and now carries more passengers per year than any other airline.

Sources: Charam, R. 2009 *Leadership in the Era of Economic Uncertainty.* New York: McGraw-Hill; McConnon, A. 2008. Lessons from a Skinflint CEO. *BusinessWeek*, October 6: 54–55; Smith, E. 2008. Herb Kelleher. *Texas Monthly*, June: 78–85; and, www.wikipedia.org.

want to increase the speed by 10 miles per hour, you look for incremental advances. However, if you want to double the speed, you've got to think "out of the box" (e.g., widen the track, change the overall suspension system). Leaders need more creative solutions than just keeping the same train with a few minor tweaks. Instead, they must come up with more revolutionary visions.

Robert Tillman, CEO of Lowe's, dramatically revitalized his firm by setting a clear and compelling direction:

> He made Lowe's into a formidable competitor to Home Depot, Inc.[7] In his six years as CEO, Tillman has transformed the $43 billion chain, based in Wilkesboro, North Carolina. Its shares have more than doubled over the past four years, while Home Depot's have fallen about 20 percent.
>
> Tillman has redirected Lowe's strategy by responding effectively to research showing that women initiate 80 percent of home projects. While Home Depot has focused on the professionals and male customers, Tillman has redesigned Lowe's stores to give them a brighter appearance, stocked them with more appliances, and focused on higher-margin goods (including everything from Laura Ashley paints to high-end bathroom fixtures). Like Wal-Mart, Lowe's has one of the best inventory systems in retailing. As a result, Lowe's profits are expected to continue to rise faster than Home Depot's.

Designing the Organization

designing the organization a strategic leadership activity of building structures, teams, systems, and organizational processes that facilitate the implementation of the leader's vision and strategies.

At times, almost all leaders have difficulty implementing their vision and strategies. Such problems may stem from a variety of sources:

- Lack of understanding of responsibility and accountability among managers.
- Reward systems that do not motivate individuals (or collectives such as groups and divisions) toward desired organizational goals.
- Inadequate or inappropriate budgeting and control systems.
- Insufficient mechanisms to integrate activities across the organization.

Successful leaders are actively involved in building structures, teams, systems, and organizational processes that facilitate the implementation of their vision and strategies. We discussed the necessity for consistency between business-level and corporate-level strategies and organizational control in Chapter 9. Without appropriately structuring organizational activities, a firm would generally be unable to attain an overall low-cost advantage by closely monitoring its costs through detailed and formalized cost and financial control procedures. With regard to corporate-level strategy, a related diversification strategy would necessitate reward systems that emphasize behavioral measures, whereas an unrelated strategy should rely more on financial (or objective) indicators of performance.

These examples illustrate the important role of leadership in creating systems and structures to achieve desired ends. As Jim Collins says about the importance of designing the organization, "Along with figuring out what the company stands for and pushing it to understand what it's really good at, building mechanisms is the CEO's role—the leader as architect."[8]

Nurturing an Excellent and Ethical Culture

excellent and ethical organizational culture an organizational culture focused on core competencies and high ethical standards.

Organizational culture can be an effective means of organizational control. Leaders play a key role in changing, developing, and sustaining an organization's culture. After he became CEO of AMD, a $6 billion microprocessor producer, Hector Ruiz dramatically improved his firm's competitive position vis-à-vis Intel—a firm six times as large. He says:[9]

> We have gotten larger and more complex. By definition that means we're going to make some mistakes. I'm much more comfortable in an environment when I know that's going to happen. That means we're learning. An aura of confidence begins to develop around people who can make mistakes and learn and go forward. At employee meetings I say, "Please, go get speeding tickets. I don't want you to get parking tickets."

strategy spotlight

Whirlpool: Becoming a Leader in Innovation

David R. Whitwam realized he had a major problem. The chairman and CEO had helped build Whirlpool into the world's number one maker of big-ticket appliances, attaining unmatched economies of scale. He had also repeatedly cut costs by hundreds of millions of dollars. However, in 1999, everything—the stock price, profit margins, market share—had been about where it was a decade earlier. At the time, housing and sales of Whirlpool appliances were booming. Despite the strong demand, prices were falling by an average of 3.4 percent a year. The underlying problem was that its machines had been reduced to commodities. The solution was straightforward: Whirlpool had to come up with exciting new products that could command premium prices.

Whitman's goal of "innovation from everyone, everywhere" required major changes in the firm's management processes and culture, which had been designed to drive operational efficiency. He appointed Nancy Snyder, a corporate vice president to be Whirlpool's first "innovation czar." She rallied her colleagues around what was to become a five-year quest to reinvent the company's management processes. Key changes included:

- Making innovation a central topic in Whirlpool's leadership development programs.

- Setting aside $45 million from the capital budget for innovation in 2000 and doubling it in 2001 for projects that met a stringent standard of innovativeness.

- Requiring every product development plan to contain a sizable component of new-to-market innovation.

Sources: Arndt, M. 2006. Creativity Overflowing. www.businessweek.com, May 8; Hamel, G. 2006. The Why, What, and How of Management Innovation. *Harvard Business Review*, 84(2): 72–87; and Salter, C. 2005. Whirlpool Finds Its Cool. *Fast Company*, June: 73.

- Training more than 600 innovation mentors charged with encouraging a culture of innovation throughout the company.

- Setting up an intranet site that offered a do-it-yourself course on innovation and listing every project in the pipeline.

- Establishing innovation as a significant component of senior management's compensation program. If they failed to meet annual revenue and pipeline targets, they could lose 30 percent of their annual bonus.

- Setting aside time in quarterly business review meetings for an in-depth discussion of each unit's innovation performance.

Whirlpool's innovation efforts are paying off. The Duet, a matching washer and dryer introduced in 2001, has become a must-have appliance that seems to be selling like iPods. At $2,000, it is the company's most expensive washer-dryer set. With its stylish lines, portholelike door, and eye-catching colors, the Duet, says Chuck Jones, Whirlpool's Design Chief, "is like a Ferrari in your laundry room." That same year, Paris's Louvre Museum displayed Whirlpool's next generation concept products. And, in 2002, the Smithsonian Institution named Whirlpool the winner of its annual National Design Award in corporate achievement.

The bottom line results of Snyder's initiatives have been impressive. Since 2001, revenues from products that fit the company's definition of innovation have soared from $10 million to $760 million by 2005, or over five percent of the firm's record $14.3 billion revenue. Whirlpool's shares as of early 2007 were around $90—nearly double what they were five years earlier. And prices were no longer eroding. Over the previous three years, the average price of Whirlpool's appliances had risen five percent annually.

In sharp contrast, leaders can also have a very detrimental effect on a firm's culture and ethics. Imagine the negative impact that Todd Berman's illegal activities have had on a firm that he cofounded—New York's private equity firm Chartwell Investments.[10] He stole more than $3.6 million from the firm and its investors. Berman pleaded guilty to fraud charges brought by the Justice Department. For 18 months he misled Chartwell's investors concerning the financial condition of one of the firm's portfolio companies by falsely claiming it needed to borrow funds to meet operating expenses. Instead, Berman transferred the money to his personal bank account, along with fees paid by portfolio companies.

Clearly, a leader's ethical behavior can make a strong impact on an organization—for good or for bad. Strategy Spotlight 11.2 provides a positive example. It discusses how Nancy Snyder was effective in instilling a culture of innovation at Whirlpool Corporation.

Managers and top executives must accept personal responsibility for developing and strengthening ethical behavior throughout the organization. They must consistently demonstrate that such behavior is central to the vision and mission of the organization. Several elements must be present and reinforced for a firm to become highly ethical, including role models, corporate credos and codes of conduct, reward and evaluation systems, and policies and procedures. Given the importance of these elements, we address them in detail in the last section of this chapter.

Elements of Effective Leadership

The demands on leaders in today's business environment require them to perform a variety of functions. The success of their organizations often depends on how they as individuals meet challenges and deliver on promises. What practices and skills are needed to get the job done effectively? In this section, we focus on three capabilities that are marks of successful leadership—integrative thinking, overcoming barriers to change, and the effective use of power. Then, in the next section, we will examine an important human trait that helps leaders be more effective—emotional intelligence.

Integrative Thinking

integrative thinking a process of reconciling opposing thoughts by generating new alternatives and creative solutions rather than rejecting one thought in favor of another.

The challenges facing today's leaders require them to confront a host of opposing forces. As the previous section indicated, maintaining consistency across a company's culture, vision, and organizational design can be difficult, especially if the three activities are out of alignment.

How does a leader make good strategic decisions in the face of multiple contingencies and diverse opportunities? A recent study by Roger L. Martin reveals that executives who have a capability known as "integrative thinking" are among the most effective leaders. In his book *The Opposable Mind,* Martin contends that people who can consider two conflicting ideas simultaneously, without dismissing one of the ideas or becoming discouraged about reconciling them, often make the best problem solvers because of their ability to creatively synthesize the opposing thoughts. In explaining the source of his title, Martin quotes F. Scott Fitzgerald, who observed, "The test of a first-rate intelligence is the ability to hold two opposing ideas in mind at the same time and still retain the ability to function. One should, for example, be able to see that things are hopeless yet be determined to make them otherwise."[11]

In contrast to conventional thinking, which tends to focus on making choices between competing ideas from a limited set of alternatives, integrative thinking is the process by which people reconcile opposing thoughts to identify creative solutions that provide them with more options and new alternatives. Exhibit 11.2 outlines the four stages of the integrative thinking and deciding process. Martin uses the admittedly simple example of deciding where to go on vacation to illustrate the stages:

- *Salience*—Take stock of what features of the decision you consider relevant and important. For example: Where will you go? What will you see? Where will you stay? What will it cost? Is it safe? Other features may be less important, but try to think of everything that may matter.
- *Causality*—Make a mental map of the causal relationships between the features, that is, how the various features are related to one another. For example, is it worth it to invite friends to share expenses? Will an exotic destination be less safe?
- *Architecture*—Use the mental map to arrange a sequence of decisions that will lead to a specific outcome. For example, will you make the hotel and flight arrangements

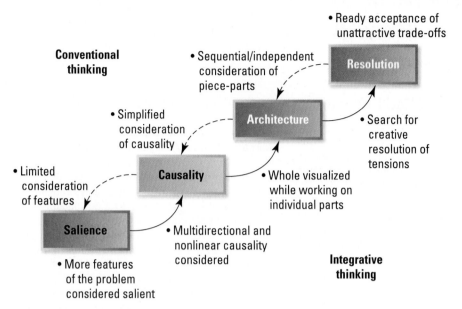

Conventional thinking

- Ready acceptance of unattractive trade-offs

Resolution

- Sequential/independent consideration of piece-parts

- Search for creative resolution of tensions

Architecture

- Simplified consideration of causality

- Whole visualized while working on individual parts

Causality

- Limited consideration of features

- Multidirectional and nonlinear causality considered

Salience

- More features of the problem considered salient

Integrative thinking

Source: Martin, R. L. 2007. *The Opposable Mind.* Boston: Harvard Business School Press.

Exhibit 11.2 Integrative Thinking: The Process of Thinking and Deciding

first, or focus on which sightseeing tours are available? No particular decision path is right or wrong, but considering multiple options simultaneously may lead to a better decision.

- **_Resolution_**—Make your selection. For example, choose which destination, which flight, and so forth. You final resolution is linked to how you evaluated the first three stages; if you are dissatisfied with your choices, the dotted arrows in the diagram (Exhibit 11.2) suggest you can go back through the process and revisit your assumptions.

Applied to business, an integrative thinking approach enables decision makers to consider situations not as forced trade-offs—either decrease costs or invest more; either satisfy shareholders or please the community—but as a method for synthesizing opposing ideas into a creative solution. The key is to think in terms of "both-and" rather than "either-or." "Integrative thinking," says Martin, "shows us that there's a way to integrate the advantages of one solution without canceling out the advantages of an alternative solution."

Although Martin found that integrative thinking comes naturally to some people, he also believes it can be taught. But it may be difficult to learn, in part because it requires people to *un*learn old patterns and become aware of how they think. For executives willing to take a deep look at their habits of thought, integrative thinking can be developed into a valuable skill. Strategy Spotlight 11.3 tells how Red Hat, Inc. cofounder Bob Young made his company a market leader by using integrative thinking to resolve a major problem in the domain of open-source software.

Overcoming Barriers to Change

What are the **barriers to change** that leaders often encounter, and how can they best bring about organizational change? After all, people generally have some level of choice about how strongly they support or resist a leader's change initiatives. Why is there often so much

barriers to change characteristics of individuals and organizations that prevent a leader from transforming an organization.

>LO2

Three elements of effective leadership: integrative thinking, overcoming barriers to change, and the effective use of power.

Integrative Thinking at Red Hat, Inc.

How can a software developer make money giving away free software? That was the dilemma Red Hat founder Bob Young was facing during the early days of the open-source software movement. A Finnish developer named Linus Torvalds, using freely available UNIX software, had developed an operating system dubbed "Linux" that was being widely circulated in the freeware community. The software was intended specifically as an alternative to the pricey proprietary systems sold by Microsoft and Oracle. To use proprietary software, corporations had to pay hefty installation fees and were required to call Microsoft or Oracle engineers to fix it when anything went wrong. In Young's view it was a flawed and unsustainable business model.

But the free model was flawed as well. Although several companies had sprung up to help companies use Linux, there were few opportunities to profit from using it. As Young said, "You couldn't make any money selling [the Linux] operating system because all this stuff was free, and if you started to charge money for it, someone else would come in and price it lower. It was a commodity in the truest sense of the word." To complicate matters, hundreds of developers were part of the software community that was constantly modifying and debugging Linux—at a rate equivalent to three updates per day. As a result, systems administrators at corporations that tried to adopt the software spent so much time keeping track of updates that they didn't enjoy the savings they expected from using free software.

Young saw the appeal of both approaches but also realized a new model was needed. While contemplating the dilemma, he realized a salient feature that others had overlooked—because most major corporations have to live with software decisions for at least ten years, they will nearly always choose to do business with the industry leader. Young realized he had to position Red Hat as the top provider of Linux software. To do that, he proposed a radical solution: provide the authoritative version of Linux and deliver it in a new way—as a download rather than on CD. He hired programmers to create a downloadable version—still free—and promised, in essence, to maintain its quality (for a fee, of course) by dealing with all the open-source programmers who were continually suggesting changes. In the process, he created a product companies could trust and then profited by establishing ongoing service relationships with customers. Red Hat's version of Linux became the de facto standard. By 2000, Linux was installed in 25 percent of server operating systems worldwide and Red Hat had captured over 50 percent of the global market for Linux systems.

By recognizing that a synthesis of two flawed business models could provide the best of both worlds, Young exhibited the traits of integrative thinking. He pinpointed the causal relationships between the salient features of the marketplace and Red Hat's path to prosperity. He then crafted an approach that integrated aspects of the two existing approaches into a new alternative. By resolving to provide a free downloadable version, Young also took responsibility for creating his own path to success. The pay-off was substantial: when Red Hat went public in 1999, Young became a billionaire on the first day of trading. And, by 2008 Red Hat had over $.5 billion in annual revenues and a market capitalization of over $3 billion.

Source: Martin, R. L. 2007. *The Opposable Mind.* Boston: Harvard Business School Press.

resistance? Organizations at all levels are prone to inertia and are slow to learn, adapt, and change because:

systemic barriers barriers to change that stem from an organizational design that impedes the proper flow and evaluation of information.

1. Many people have **vested interests in the status quo.** People tend to be risk averse and resistant to change. There is a broad stream of research on "escalation," wherein certain individuals continue to throw "good money at bad decisions" despite negative performance feedback.[12]

2. There are **systemic barriers.** The design of the organization's structure, information processing, reporting relationships, and so forth impede the proper flow and evaluation of information. A bureaucratic structure with multiple layers, onerous requirements for documentation, and rigid rules and procedures will often "inoculate" the organization against change.

3. **Behavioral barriers** cause managers to look at issues from a biased or limited perspective due to their education, training, work experiences, and so forth. Consider an incident shared by David Lieberman, marketing director at GVO, an innovation consulting firm:

> A company's creative type had come up with a great idea for a new product. Nearly everybody loved it. However, it was shot down by a high-ranking manufacturing representative who exploded: "A new color? Do you have any idea of the spare-parts problem that it will create?" This was not a dimwit exasperated at having to build a few storage racks at the warehouse. He'd been hearing for years about cost cutting, lean inventories, and "focus." Lieberman's comment: "Good concepts, but not always good for innovation."

4. **Political barriers** refer to conflicts arising from power relationships. This can be the outcome of a myriad of symptoms such as vested interests, refusal to share information, conflicts over resources, conflicts between departments and divisions, and petty interpersonal differences.

5. **Personal time constraints** bring to mind the old saying about "not having enough time to drain the swamp when you are up to your neck in alligators." Gresham's law of planning states that operational decisions will drive out the time necessary for strategic thinking and reflection. This tendency is accentuated in organizations experiencing severe price competition or retrenchment wherein managers and employees are spread rather thin.

Leaders must draw on a range of personal skills as well as organizational mechanisms to move their organizations forward in the face of such barriers. Integrative thinking provides one avenue by equipping leaders with an ability to consider creative alternatives to the kind of resistance and doubt that cause many barriers. Two factors mentioned earlier—building a learning organization and ethical organization—provide the kind of climate within which a leader can advance the organization's aims and make progress toward its goals. One of the most important tools a leader has for overcoming barriers to change is their personal and organizational power. On the one hand, good leaders must be on guard not to abuse power. On the other hand, successful leadership requires the measured exercise of power. We turn to that topic next.

The Effective Use of Power

Successful leadership requires effective use of power in overcoming barriers to change.[13] As humorously noted by Mark Twain, "I'm all for progress. It's change I object to." **Power** refers to a leader's ability to get things done in a way he or she wants them to be done. It is the ability to influence other people's behavior, to persuade them to do things that they otherwise would not do, and to overcome resistance and opposition to changing direction. Effective exercise of power is essential for successful leadership.[14]

A leader derives his or her power from several sources or bases. The simplest way to understand the bases of power is by classifying them as organizational and personal, as shown in Exhibit 11.3.

Organizational bases of power refer to the power that a person wields because of holding a formal management position. These include legitimate power, reward power, coercive power, and information power. *Legitimate power* is derived from organizationally conferred decision-making authority and is exercised by virtue of a manager's position in the organization. *Reward power* depends on the ability of the leader or manager to confer rewards for positive behaviors or outcomes. *Coercive power* is the power a manager exercises over employees using fear of punishment for errors of omission or commission. *Information power* arises from a manager's access, control, and distribution of information that is not freely available to everyone in an organization.

behavioral barriers barriers to change associated with the tendency for managers to look at issues from a biased or limited perspective based on their prior education and experience.

political barriers barriers to change related to conflicts arising from power relationships.

power a leader's ability to get things done in a way he or she wants them to be done.

organizational bases of power a formal management position that is the basis of a leader's power.

Exhibit 11.3 A Leader's Bases of Power

personal bases of power a leader's personality characteristics and behavior that are the basis of the leader's power.

A leader might also be able to influence subordinates because of his or her personality characteristics and behavior. These would be considered the **personal bases of power,** including referent power and expert power. The source of *referent power* is a subordinate's identification with the leader. A leader's personal attributes or charisma might influence subordinates and make them devoted to that leader. The source of *expert power* is the leader's expertise and knowledge in a particular field. The leader is the expert on whom subordinates depend for information that they need to do their jobs successfully.

Successful leaders use the different bases of power, and often a combination of them, as appropriate to meet the demands of a situation, such as the nature of the task, the personality characteristics of the subordinates, the urgency of the issue, and other factors. Leaders must recognize that persuasion and developing consensus are often essential, but so is pressing for action. At some point stragglers must be prodded into line.[15] Peter Georgescu, who recently retired as CEO of Young & Rubicam (an advertising and media subsidiary of the UK-based WPP Group), summarized a leader's dilemma brilliantly (and humorously), "I have knee pads and a .45. I get down and beg a lot, but I shoot people too."[16]

Strategy Spotlight 11.4 addresses some of the subtleties of power. It focuses on William Bratton, Chief of the Los Angeles Police Department, who has enjoyed a very successful career in law enforcement.

Emotional Intelligence: A Key Leadership Trait

>LO3

The crucial role of emotional intelligence (EI) in successful leadership as well as its potential drawbacks.

In the previous sections, we discussed skills and activities of strategic leadership. The focus was on "what leaders do and how they do it." Now, the issue becomes "who leaders *are,*" that is, what leadership traits are the most important. Clearly, these two issues are related, because successful leaders possess the valuable traits that enable them to perform effectively in order to create value for their organization.[17]

There has been a vast amount of literature on the successful traits of leaders.[18] These traits include integrity, maturity, energy, judgment, motivation, intelligence, expertise, and so on. For simplicity, these traits may be grouped into three broad sets of capabilities:

- Purely technical skills (like accounting or operations research).
- Cognitive abilities (like analytical reasoning or quantitative analysis).
- Emotional intelligence (like self-management and managing relationships).

William Bratton: Using Multiple Bases of Power

William Bratton, Chief of the Los Angeles Police Department has an enviable track record in turning around police departments in crime-ridden cities. First, while running the police division of Massachusetts Bay Transit Authority (MBTA) in Boston, then as police commissioner of New York in the mid-1990s, and now in Los Angeles since 2002, Chief Bratton is credited with reducing crime and improving police morale in record time. An analysis of his success at each of these organizations reveals similar patterns both in terms of the problems he faced and the many ways in which he used the different bases of power to engineer a rapid turnaround.

In Boston, New York, and Los Angeles, Chief Bratton faced similar hurdles: organizations wedded to the status quo, limited resources, demotivated staffs, and opposition from powerful vested interests. But he does not give up in the face of these seemingly insurmountable problems. He is persuasive in calls for change, capable of mobilizing the commitment of key players, silencing vocal naysayers, and building rapport with superiors and subordinates while building bridges with external constituencies.

Chief Bratton's persuasion tactics are unconventional, yet effective. When he was running the MBTA police, the Transit Authority decided to buy small squad cars, which are cheaper to buy and to run, but inadequate for the police officer's task. Instead of arguing, Bratton invited the general manager for a tour of the city. He rode with the general manager in exactly the same type of car

that was ordered for ordinary officers, and drove over every pothole on the road. He moved the seats forward so that the general manager could feel how little leg room was there. And he put on his belt, cuffs, and gun so that the general manager could understand how limited the space was. After two hours in the cramped car, the general manager was ready to change the order and get more suitable cars for the officers!

Another tactic Bratton used effectively was insisting on community meetings between police officers and citizens. This went against the long-standing practice of detachment between police and community to decrease the chances of corruption. The result was that his department had a better understanding of public concerns and rearranged their priorities, which in turn led to better community relations. For internal communications, he relied mainly on professionally produced videos instead of long, boring memos.

Chief Bratton also shows a remarkable talent for building political bridges and silencing naysayers. As he was introducing his zero-tolerance policing approach that aggressively targets "quality of life" crimes such as panhandling, drunkenness, and prostitution, opposition came from the city's courts, which feared being inundated by a large number of small-crimes cases. Bratton enlisted the support of Rudolph Giuliani, the mayor of New York, who had considerable influence over the district attorneys, the courts, and the city jail. He also took the case to the *New York Times* and managed to get the issue of zero-tolerance on the front pages of the newspaper. The courts were left with no alternative but to cooperate.

To a great extent, Bratton's success can be attributed to his understanding of the subtleties of power, including persuasion, motivation, coalition building, empathy for subordinates, and a focus on goals.

Sources: Chan Kim, W. & Renee Mauborgne, R. 2003. Tipping Point Leadership. *Harvard Business Review,* 81(4): 60–69; and McCarthy, T. 2004. The Gang Buster. *Time,* January 19: 56–58.

"Emotional intelligence (EI)" has become popular in both the literature and management practice in recent years.[19] *Harvard Business Review* articles published in 1998 and 2000 by psychologist/journalist Daniel Goleman, who is most closely associated with the concept, have become *HBR*'s most highly requested reprint articles. And two of Goleman's recent books, *Emotional Intelligence* and *Working with Emotional Intelligence,* were both on the *New York Times*'s best-seller lists. Goleman defines **emotional intelligence** as the capacity for recognizing one's own emotions and those of others.[20]

Recent studies of successful managers have found that effective leaders consistently have a high level of EI.[21] Findings indicate that EI is a better predictor of life success (economic well-being, satisfaction with life, friendship, family life), including occupational attainments, than IQ. Such evidence has been extrapolated to the catchy phrase: "IQ gets you hired, but EQ (Emotional Quotient) gets you promoted." Human resource managers believe this statement to be true, even for highly technical jobs such as those of scientists and engineers.

emotional intelligence (EI) an individual's capacity for recognizing his or her own emotions and those of others, including the five components of self awareness, self regulation, motivation, empathy, and social skills.

Exhibit 11.4   The Five Components of Emotional Intelligence at Work

	Definition	Hallmarks
Self-management skills:		
Self-awareness	• The ability to recognize and understand your moods, emotions, and drives, as well as their effect on others.	• Self-confidence • Realistic self-assessment • Self-deprecating sense of humor
Self-regulation	• The ability to control or redirect disruptive impulses and moods. • The propensity to suspend judgment—to think before acting.	• Trustworthiness and integrity • Comfort with ambiguity • Openness to change
Motivation	• A passion to work for reasons that go beyond money or status. • A propensity to pursue goals with energy and persistence.	• Strong drive to achieve • Optimism, even in the face of failure • Organizational commitment
Managing relationships:		
Empathy	• The ability to understand the emotional makeup of other people. • Skill in treating people according to their emotional reactions.	• Expertise in building and retaining talent • Cross-cultural sensitivity • Service to clients and customers
Social skill	• Proficiency in managing relationships and building networks. • An ability to find common ground and build rapport.	• Effectiveness in leading change • Persuasiveness • Expertise in building and leading teams

Source: Adapted and reprinted by permission of *Harvard Business Review.* Exhibit from "What Makes a Leader," by D. Goleman, January 2004. Copyright © 2004 by the Harvard Business School Publishing Corporation; all rights reserved.

This is not to say that IQ and technical skills are irrelevant, but they become "threshold capabilities." They are the necessary requirements for attaining higher-level managerial positions. EI, on the other hand, is essential for leadership success. Without it, Goleman claims, a manager can have excellent training, an incisive analytical mind, and many smart ideas but will still not be a great leader.

Exhibit 11.4 identifies the five components of EI: self-awareness, self-regulation, motivation, empathy, and social skill.

Self-Awareness

Self-awareness is the first component of EI and brings to mind that Delphic oracle who gave the advice "know thyself" thousands of years ago. Self-awareness involves a person having a deep understanding of his or her emotions, strengths, weaknesses, and drives. People with strong self-awareness are neither overly critical nor unrealistically optimistic. Instead, they are honest with themselves and others.

People generally admire and respect candor. Leaders are constantly required to make judgment calls that require a candid assessment of capabilities—their own and those of others. People who assess themselves honestly (i.e., self-aware people) are well suited to do the same for the organizations they run.[22]

Self-Regulation

Biological impulses drive our emotions. Although we cannot do away with them, we can strive to manage them. Self-regulation, which is akin to an ongoing inner conversation, frees us from being prisoners of our feelings.[23] People engaged in such conversation feel bad moods and emotional impulses just as everyone else does. However, they find ways to control them and even channel them in useful ways.

Self-regulated people are able to create an environment of trust and fairness where, political behavior and infighting are sharply reduced and productivity tends to be high. People who have mastered their emotions are better able to bring about and implement change in an organization. When a new initiative is announced, they are less likely to panic; they are able to suspend judgment, seek out information, and listen to executives explain the new program.

Motivation

Successful executives are driven to achieve beyond expectations—their own and everyone else's. Although many people are driven by external factors, such as money and prestige, those with leadership potential are driven by a deeply embedded desire to achieve for the sake of achievement.

Motivated people show a passion for the work itself, such as seeking out creative challenges, a love of learning, and taking pride in a job well done. They also have a high level of energy to do things better as well as a restlessness with the status quo. They are eager to explore new approaches to their work.

Empathy

Empathy is probably the most easily recognized component of EI. Empathy means thoughtfully considering an employee's feelings, along with other factors, in the process of making intelligent decisions. Empathy is particularly important in today's business environment for at least three reasons: the increasing use of teams, the rapid pace of globalization, and the growing need to retain talent.[24]

When leading a team, a manager is often charged with arriving at a consensus—often in the face of a high level of emotions. Empathy enables a manager to sense and understand the viewpoints of everyone around the table.

Globalization typically involves cross-cultural dialogue that can easily lead to miscues. Empathetic people are attuned to the subtleties of body language; they can hear the message beneath the words being spoken. They have a deep understanding of the existence and importance of cultural and ethnic differences.

Empathy also plays a key role in retaining talent. Human capital is particularly important to a firm in the knowledge economy when it comes to creating advantages that are sustainable. Leaders need empathy to develop and keep top talent, because when high performers leave, they take their tacit knowledge with them.

Empathetic leaders recognize that work is often demanding and employees can sometimes get worn down or stressed out. Strategy Spotlight 11.5 discusses steps some business owners are taking to create a healthy work environment and support workers' efforts to stay fit.

Social Skill

While the first three components of EI are all self-management skills, the last two—empathy and social skill—concern a person's ability to manage relationships with others. Social skill may be viewed as friendliness with a purpose: moving people in the direction you desire, whether that's agreement on a new marketing strategy or enthusiasm about a new product.

strategy spotlight

11.5

Creating a Healthy Workplace

Demanding jobs and professional challenges often make the workplace a stressful environment. And studies show that stress is a major contributor to health problems such as heart disease and musculoskeletal disorders. To counter the pressures of work, empathetic leaders have introduced wellness programs designed to make work a more pleasant and healthy experience. "With the expenditure of modest resources," says Jay Vandergriff, founder of workplace wellness provider Wellness Coaches USA, "a company can build a culture and work environment that is committed to wellness values."

Jon S. Wheeler, CEO of Virginia Beach, Virginia, real estate firm Wheeler Interests, has made corporate wellness a central part of the workplace culture. The company offers its 34 employees various perks, including midday kayaking breaks, an onsite gym, and access to a personal trainer. Rather than enforce a vacation policy, Wheeler allows his employees to take vacation time whenever they like as long as get their work done. "Employees are appreciative and supportive of the concept," says Wheeler, whose company generates over $13 million in annual revenues.

Some leaders go a step farther by providing incentives to participate in wellness programs. Scott Rosenberg, CEO of New Jersey–based Miro Consulting, a $25 million software licensing company, ran his own version of *The Biggest Loser*. After the three-month contest, members of the winning team received $500 each. John Roberson, CEO of Nashville, Tennessee–based marketing firm Advent, customizes incentives to match employees' interests. To motivate his 32 employees, he has given them everything from cowboy boots and guitar lessons to yoga classes and time off to help build orphanages in Central America.

"We define wellness more liberally than others might," says Roberson, whose sales were expected to reach $7 million in 2008. "It's about more than the physical; it's the whole person. So we encourage those things that that will help not only [employees'] physical health, but their emotional well-being, too."

Sources: Spaeder, K. E. 2008. All Well and Good. *Entrepreneur,* November: 24; Spaeder, K. E. 2008. Shape Up. *Entrepreneur,* September: 26; and, www.wikipedia.org.

Socially skilled people tend to have a wide circle of acquaintances as well as a knack for finding common ground and building rapport. They recognize that nothing gets done alone, and they have a network in place when the time for action comes.

Social skill can be viewed as the culmination of the other dimensions of EI. People will be effective at managing relationships when they can understand and control their own emotions and empathize with others' feelings. Motivation also contributes to social skill. People who are driven to achieve tend to be optimistic, even when confronted with setbacks. And when people are upbeat, their "glow" is cast upon conversations and other social encounters. They are popular, and for good reason.

Strategy Spotlight 11.6 provides John Chambers's personal reflection on how he goes about his job as CEO of Cisco Systems, the $39 billion networking giant. This empathetic leader has become one of America's most respected high-tech executives.

Emotional Intelligence: Some Potential Drawbacks and Cautionary Notes

Many great leaders have great reserves of empathy, interpersonal astuteness, awareness of their own feelings, and an awareness of their impact on others.[25] More importantly, they know how to apply these capabilities judiciously as best benefits the situation. Having some minimum level of EI will help a person be effective as a leader as long as it is channeled appropriately. However, if a person has a high level of these capabilities it may become "too much of a good thing" if he or she is allowed to drive inappropriate behaviors. Some additional potential drawbacks of EI can be gleaned by considering the flip side of its benefits.

Emotional Intelligence: Cisco Systems' CEO John Chambers's

John Chambers's recently shared his insights on how he goes about performing his responsibilities as CEO of Cisco Systems. He exemplifies many of the concepts of emotional intelligence and, in his 15 years at Cisco Systems, has become one of the most respected high-tech executives in the world. Chambers's brief essay is one of a series in *Fortune* magazine on the topic of "How I Work."

> I started with the classic communications methods when I got here 15 years ago. I'd walk around and talk to small groups and larger groups. I'd see whose car is out in the parking lot. Then e-mail became very effective, because it gave me the ability to send a message to the whole group. But I'm a voice person. I communicate with emotion that way. I like to listen to emotion too. It's a lot easier to listen to a key customer if I hear how they're describing a problem to me. I'll leave 40 or 50 voicemails a day.

Sources: Chambers's, J. 2006. Lights! Camera! Cue From CEO! *Fortune*, August 21: 27. (Interviewed by Adam Lashinsky.) Copyright © 2006 Time, Inc. All rights reserved; McGirt, E. 2008/2009. Revolution in San Jose. *Fast Company*, December/January: 89–136; and www.wikipedia.org.

> As far as how I hear from employees, I host a monthly birthday breakfast. Anybody who has a birthday in that month gets to come and quiz me for an hour and 15 minutes. No directors or VPs in the room. It's how I keep my finger on the pulse of what's working and what's not. It's brutal, but it's my most enjoyable session.
>
> To be informed, I like summaries. Because of my dyslexia, I do very little novel reading or that type of activity. I love quick articles. Before every meeting and every panel I study briefing binders with all the information I need: What we're doing in a presentation, who we're meeting with, backgrounds on them, etc. It's two or three pages on each topic, and that is how I like to learn.

As his essay indicates, Chambers's seems like a down-to earth guy—remarkable for the CEO and chairman of a $39 billion *Fortune* 100 company. When asked recently his counsel for making it through the difficult financial times, Chambers's said folks must, "focus on what we can influence, and not over- or underreact to things we cannot. It's a question of living in the world as it is, not the way we want it to be." That sounds like advice from someone who is emotionally balanced.

Effective Leaders Have Empathy for Others However, they also must be able to make the "tough decisions." Leaders must be able to appeal to logic and reason and acknowledge others' feelings so that people feel the decisions are correct. However, it is easy to overidentify with others or confuse empathy with sympathy. This can make it more difficult to make the tough decisions.

Effective Leaders Are Astute Judges of People A danger is that leaders may become judgmental and overly critical about the shortcomings they perceive in others. They are likely to dismiss other people's insights, making them feel undervalued.

Effective Leaders Are Passionate about What They Do, and They Show It This doesn't mean that they are always cheerleaders. Rather, they may express their passion as persistence in pursuing an objective or a relentless focus on a valued principle. However, there is a fine line between being excited about something and letting your passion close your mind to other possibilities or cause you to ignore realities that others may see.

Effective Leaders Create Personal Connections with Their People Most effective leaders take time to engage employees individually and in groups, listening to their ideas, suggestions and concerns, and responding in ways that make people feel that their ideas are respected and appreciated. However, if the leader makes too many unannounced visits, it may create a culture of fear and micromanagement. Clearly, striking a correct balance is essential.

From a moral standpoint, emotional leadership is neither good nor bad. On the one hand, emotional leaders can be altruistic, focused on the general welfare of the company and its employees, and highly principled. On the other hand, they can be manipulative, self-ish, and dishonest. For example, if a person is using leadership solely to gain power, that is not leadership at all.[26] Rather, they are using their EI to grasp what people want and pander to those desires in order to gain authority and influence. After all, easy answers sell.

Next, we turn to guidelines for developing a "learning organization." In today's competitive environment, the old saying that "a chain is only as strong as the weakest link" applies more than ever before. To learn and adapt proactively, firms need "eyes, ears, and brains" throughout all parts of the organization. One person, or a small group of individuals, can no longer think and learn for the entire entity.

Developing a Learning Organization

>LO4

The value of creating and maintaining a learning organization in today's global marketplace.

Charles Handy, author of *The Age of Unreason* and *The Age of Paradox* and one of today's most respected business visionaries, shared an amusing story:

> The other day, a courier could not find my family's remote cottage. He called his base on his radio, and the base called us to ask directions. He was just around the corner, but his base managed to omit a vital part of the directions. So he called them again, and they called us again. Then the courier repeated the cycle a third time to ask whether we had a dangerous dog. When he eventually arrived, we asked whether it would not have been simpler and less aggravating to everyone if he had called us directly from the roadside telephone booth where he had been parked. "I can't do that," he said, "because they won't refund any money I spend." "But it's only pennies!" I exclaimed. "I know," he said, "but that only shows how little they trust us!"[27]

At first glance, it would appear that the story epitomizes the lack of empowerment and trust granted to the hapless courier: Don't ask questions, Do as you're told![28] However, implicit in this scenario is also the message that learning, information sharing, adaptation, decision making, and so on are *not* shared throughout the organization. In contrast, leading-edge organizations recognize the importance of having everyone involved in the process of actively learning and adapting. As noted by today's leading expert on learning organizations, MIT's Peter Senge, the days when Henry Ford, Alfred Sloan, and Tom Watson *"learned **for** the organization"* are gone.

> In an increasingly dynamic, interdependent, and unpredictable world, it is simply no longer possible for anyone to "figure it all out at the top." The old model, "the top thinks and the local acts," must now give way to integrating thinking and acting at all levels. While the challenge is great, so is the potential payoff. "The person who figures out how to harness the collective genius of the people in his or her organization," according to former Citibank CEO Walter Wriston, "is going to blow the competition away."[29]

Learning and change typically involve the ongoing questioning of an organization's status quo or method of procedure. This means that all individuals throughout the organization must be reflective. Many organizations get so caught up in carrying out their day-to-day work that they rarely, if ever, stop to think objectively about themselves and their businesses. They often fail to ask the probing questions that might lead them to call into question their basic assumptions, to refresh their strategies, or to reengineer their work processes. According to Michael Hammer and Steven Stanton, the pioneer consultants who touched off the reengineering movement:

> Reflection entails awareness of self, of competitors, of customers. It means thinking without preconception. It means questioning cherished assumptions and replacing them with new approaches. It is the only way in which a winning company can maintain its leadership position, by which a company with great assets can ensure that they continue to be well deployed.[30]

To adapt to change, foster creativity, and remain competitive, leaders must build learning organizations. Exhibit 11.5 lists the five elements of a learning organization.

Exhibit 11.5
Key Elements of a
Learning Organization

These are the five key elements of a learning organization. Each of these items should be viewed as *necessary, but not sufficient.* That is, successful learning organizations need all five elements.

1. Inspiring and motivating people with a mission or purpose.
2. Empowering employees at all levels.
3. Accumulating and sharing internal knowledge.
4. Gathering and integrating external information.
5. Challenging the status quo and enabling creativity.

Inspiring and Motivating People with a Mission or Purpose

Successful **learning organizations** create a proactive, creative approach to the unknown, actively solicit the involvement of employees at all levels, and enable all employees to use their intelligence and apply their imagination. Higher-level skills are required of everyone, not just those at the top.[31] A learning environment involves organizationwide commitment to change, an action orientation, and applicable tools and methods.[32] It must be viewed by everyone as a guiding philosophy and not simply as another change program.

A critical requirement of all learning organizations is that everyone feels and supports a compelling purpose. In the words of William O'Brien, CEO of Hanover Insurance, "Before there can be meaningful participation, people must share certain values and pictures about where we are trying to go. We discovered that people have a real need to feel that they're part of an enabling mission."[33] Such a perspective is consistent with an intensive study by Kouzes and Posner, authors of *The Leadership Challenge.*[34] They recently analyzed data from nearly one million respondents who were leaders at various levels in many organizations throughout the world. A major finding was that what leaders struggle with most is communicating an image of the future that draws others in, that is, it speaks to what others see and feel. To illustrate:

> Buddy Blanton, a principal program manager at Rockwell Collins, learned this lesson firsthand. He asked his team for feedback on his leadership, and the vast majority of it was positive. However, he got some strong advice from his team about how he could be more effective in inspiring a shared vision. "You would benefit by helping us, as a team, to understand how you go to your vision. We want to walk with you while you create the goals and vision, so we all get to the end of the vision together."[35]

Inspiring and motivating people with a mission or purpose is a necessary but not sufficient condition for developing an organization that can learn and adapt to a rapidly changing, complex, and interconnected environment.

Empowering Employees at All Levels

"The great leader is a great servant," asserted Ken Melrose, CEO of Toro Company and author of *Making the Grass Greener on Your Side.*[36] A manager's role becomes one of creating an environment where employees can achieve their potential as they help move the organization toward its goals. Instead of viewing themselves as resource controllers and power brokers, leaders must envision themselves as flexible resources willing to assume numerous roles as coaches, information providers, teachers, decision makers, facilitators, supporters, or listeners, depending on the needs of their employees.[37]

The central key to empowerment is effective leadership. Empowerment can't occur in a leadership vacuum. According to Melrose, "You best lead by serving the needs of your people. You don't do their jobs for them; you enable them to learn and progress on the job." Robert Quinn and Gretchen Spreitzer made an interesting point about two diametrically opposite perspectives on empowerment—top-down and bottom-up.[38]

learning organizations
organizations that create a proactive, creative approach to the unknown, characterized by (1) inspiring and motivating people with a mission and purpose, (2) empowering employees at all levels, (3) accumulating and sharing internal knowledge, (4) gathering and integrating external information, and (5) challenging the status quo and enabling creativity.

In the top-down perspective, empowerment is about delegation and accountability—senior management has developed a clear vision and has communicated specific plans to the rest of the organization.[39] This strategy for empowerment encompasses the following:

- Start at the top.
- Clarify the organization's mission, vision, and values.
- Clearly specify the tasks, roles, and rewards for employees.
- Delegate responsibility.
- Hold people accountable for results.

By contrast, the bottom-up view looks at empowerment as concerned with risk taking, growth, and change. It involves trusting people to "do the right thing" and having a tolerance for failure. It encourages employees to act with a sense of ownership and typically "ask for forgiveness rather than permission." Here the salient elements of empowerment are:

- Start at the bottom by understanding the needs of employees.
- Teach employees self-management skills and model desired behavior.
- Build teams to encourage cooperative behavior.
- Encourage intelligent risk taking.
- Trust people to perform.

These two perspectives draw a sharp contrast in assumptions that people make about trust and control. Quinn and Spreitzer recently shared these contrasting views of empowerment with a senior management team. After an initial heavy silence, someone from the first group voiced a concern about the second group's perspective, "We can't afford loose cannons around here." A person in the second group retorted, "When was the last time you saw a cannon of any kind around here?"

Many leading-edge organizations are moving in the direction of the second perspective—recognizing the need for trust, cultural control, and expertise at all levels instead of the extensive and cumbersome rules and regulations inherent in hierarchical control.[40] Some have argued that too often organizations fall prey to the "heroes-and-drones syndrome," wherein the value of those in powerful positions is exalted and the value of those who fail to achieve top rank is diminished. Such an attitude is implicit in phrases such as "Lead, follow, or get out of the way" or, even less appealing, "Unless you're the lead horse, the view never changes." Few will ever reach the top hierarchical positions in organizations, but in the information economy, the strongest organizations are those that effectively use the talents of all the players on the team. In fact, General Electric has learned that the best method of empowering whole teams is to train them together. Strategy Spotlight 11.7 illustrates how team training can enhance organizational learning.

Accumulating and Sharing Internal Knowledge

Effective organizations must also *redistribute information, knowledge* (skills to act on the information), and *rewards*.[41] A company might give frontline employees the power to act as "customer advocates," doing whatever is necessary to satisfy customers. The company needs to disseminate information by sharing customer expectations and feedback as well as financial information. The employees must know about the goals of the business as well as how key value-creating activities in the organization are related to each other. Finally, organizations should allocate rewards on how effectively employees use information, knowledge, and power to improve customer service quality and the company's overall performance.[42]

Jack Stack is the president and CEO of Springfield ReManufacturing Corporation (SRC) in Springfield, Missouri, and author of *The Great Game of Business*. He is generally considered the pioneer of "open book" management—an innovative way to gather and disseminate internal information. Implementing this system involves three core activities.[43]

Accelerating Learning by Teaching Teams

General Electric has a long-standing tradition of using training to empower its managers to improve performance. Recently, a Leadership, Innovation, and Growth (LIG) program launched by GE in 2006 learned some important lessons: when whole teams are trained rather than individual managers, the shared learning has a more profound effect. In the past, when individual managers took the lessons learned from a program at GE's famed management development center back to their offices, they often had trouble persuading others to go along with what they had learned. By training all team members at once, LIG has accelerated the speed with which new learning is implemented as well as its long-term effectiveness. As Jon Katzenbach and Douglas Smith reported in *The Wisdom of Teams,* "by translating longer-term purposes into definable performance goals and then developing the skills needed to meet those goals, learning not only occurs in teams but endures."

The accelerated learning experience is enhanced when a few key principles are followed:

- *Reach consensus about the barriers to change and how to address them.* By having all team members together, the team can articulate both hard barriers (structural impediments, capabilities, and resource constraints) and soft barriers (team dynamics and competing priorities) that might affect proposed solutions.

- *Develop a common language.* Team members often need a new vocabulary of change—actual words that become part of the daily conversation when teams return to work. Referring to his company's new goals, GE CEO Jeffrey Immelt said the aim of the LIG program was "to embed growth into the DNA of our company." Learning a common language can help team members make the shift.

- *Create an action plan and a commitment to follow-through.* Although an initial draft is all that is typically developed in most four-day training sessions, the focused work on an actual plan forms the basis for continued effort and ongoing learning. It also builds commitment.

By making learning team-based, GE has accelerated the kinds of change processes that are needed to remain effective in a new business environment. The LIG program was developed specifically to enact Immelt's vision of a new GE—one in which expanding existing businesses and creating new ones takes priority over making acquisitions. Recognizing that such a change requires a lot of new learning, Immelt said, "A major change-management effort like this is a 10-year process. It takes a decade to build the talent, culture, and tools, and to learn from our mistakes." Clearly, creating a learning organization is a central aspect of Immelt's new plan for GE.

Sources: Katzenbach, J. R. & Smith, D. K. 2003. *The Wisdom of Teams.* New York: Collins Business; Prokesch, S. 2009. How GE Teaches Teams to Lead Change. *Harvard Business Review,* 87(1): 99–106; and www.ge.com.

First, numbers are generated daily for each of the company's employees, reflecting his or her work performance and production costs. Second, this information is aggregated once a week and shared with all of the company's people from secretaries to top management. Third, employees receive extensive training in how to use and interpret the numbers—how to understand balance sheets as well as cash flows and income statements.

In explaining why SRC embraces open book management, Stack provided an insightful counterperspective to the old adage "Information is power."

> We are building a company in which everyone tells the truth every day—not because everyone is honest but because everyone has access to the same information: operating metrics, financial data, valuation estimates. The more people understand what's really going on in their company, the more eager they are to help solve its problems. Information isn't power. It's a burden. Share information, and you share the burdens of leadership as well.

Let's take a look at Whole Foods Market, Inc., the largest natural foods grocer in the United States.[44] An important benefit of the sharing of internal information at Whole Foods becomes the active process of *internal benchmarking.* Competition is intense at Whole Foods.

Teams compete against their own goals for sales, growth, and productivity; they compete against different teams in their stores; and they compete against similar teams at different stores and regions. There is an elaborate system of peer reviews through which teams benchmark each other. The "Store Tour" is the most intense. On a periodic schedule, each Whole Foods store is toured by a group of as many as 40 visitors from another region. Lateral learning—discovering what your colleagues are doing right and carrying those practices into your organization—has become a driving force at Whole Foods.

● Whole Foods Market is well-known for sharing company information with its employees and practicing internal benchmarking.

In addition to enhancing the sharing of company information both up and down as well as across the organization, leaders also have to develop means to tap into some of the more informal sources of internal information. In a recent survey of presidents, CEOs, board members, and top executives in a variety of nonprofit organizations, respondents were asked what differentiated the successful candidates for promotion. The consensus: The executive was seen as a person who listens. According to Peter Meyer, the author of the study, "The value of listening is clear: You cannot succeed in running a company if you do not hear what your people, customers, and suppliers are telling you. . . . Listening and understanding well are key to making good decisions."[45]

Strategy Spotlight 11.8 addresses a critical aspect of obtaining information from internal sources—listening skills. General Peter Pace, former chairman of the Joint Chiefs of Staff, the highest-ranking military officer in the United States, shares his perspective on this topic.

Gathering and Integrating External Information

Recognizing opportunities, as well as threats, in the external environment is vital to a firm's success. As organizations *and* environments become more complex and evolve rapidly, it is far more critical for employees and managers to become more aware of environmental trends and events—both general and industry-specific—and more knowledgeable about their firm's competitors and customers. Next, we will discuss some ideas on how to do it.

First, the Internet has dramatically accelerated the speed with which anyone can track down useful information or locate people who might have useful information. Prior to the Net, locating someone who used to work at a company—always a good source of information—was quite a challenge. However, today people post their résumés on the Web; they participate in discussion groups and talk openly about where they work.

Marc Friedman, manager of market research at $1 billion Andrew Corporation, a fast-growing manufacturer of wireless communications products provides an example of effective Internet use.[46] One of Friedman's preferred sites to visit is Corptech's website, which provides information on 45,000 high-tech companies and more than 170,000 executives. One of his firm's product lines consisted of antennae for air-traffic control systems. He got a request to provide a country-by-country breakdown of upgrade plans for various airports. He knew nothing about air-traffic control at the time. However, he found a site on the Internet for the International Civil Aviation Organization.

strategy spotlight

Listening Skills: A Key to Obtaining Valuable Internal Information

"I don't want any yes-men around me," movie mogul Samuel Goldwyn once said. "I want them to tell me the truth, even if it costs them their jobs." We may laugh because it is often true. Organizations are usually not in the habit of rewarding people who speak uncomfortable truths—or, in the vernacular, "going against the company line." However, we need to hear from them.

According to General Peter Pace, "If you walk into a room as a senior person and innocently say, 'Here's what I'm thinking about this,' you have already skewed people's thinking. His approach: "Start out with a question and don't voice an opinion."

Why? People can't support your position if they do not know where you stand on the issue. After all, supporting the boss is usually the politically expedient thing to do! Further, if you present subordinates with an intellectual challenge, they feel freer to offer their opinions without fear of offending somebody ranking higher in the organization. "If you are looking for answers, ask the question," suggests Pace, and "if you are looking for an honest critique, you ought to be the first person to self-critique." This is different from generals' metaphorically taking off their stars to ask for honest feedback. People know the stars will be back!

Source: Useem, M. & Useem, J. 2005. Great Escapes. *Fortune,* June 27: 98, 100.

Fortunately, it had a great deal of useful data, including several research companies working in his area of interest.

Second, company employees at all levels can use "garden variety" traditional sources to acquire external information. Much can be gleaned by reading trade and professional journals, books, and popular business magazines. Other venues for gathering external information include membership in professional or trade organizations, attendance at meetings and conventions, and networking among colleagues inside and outside of your industry. Intel's Andy Grove gathers information from people like DreamWorks SKG's Steven Spielberg and Tele-Communications Inc.'s John Malone.[47] He believes that such interaction provides insights into how to make personal computers more entertaining and better at communicating. Internally, Grove spends time with the young engineers who run Intel Architecture labs, an Oregon-based facility that Grove hopes will become the de facto R&D lab for the entire PC industry.

Third, benchmarking can be a useful means of employing external information. Here managers seek out the best examples of a particular practice as part of an ongoing effort to improve the corresponding practice in their own organization.[48] There are two primary types of benchmarking. *Competitive benchmarking* restricts the search for best practices to competitors, while *functional benchmarking* endeavors to determine best practices regardless of industry. Industry-specific standards (e.g., response times required to repair power outages in the electric utility industry) are typically best handled through competitive benchmarking, whereas more generic processes (e.g., answering 1-800 calls) lend themselves to functional benchmarking because the function is essentially the same in any industry.

Ford Motor Company used benchmarking to study Mazda's accounts payable operations.[49] Its initial goal of a 20 percent cut in its 500-employee accounts payable staff was ratcheted up to 75 percent—and met. Ford found that staff spent most of their time trying to match conflicting data in a mass of paper, including purchase orders, invoices, and receipts. Following Mazda's example, Ford created an "invoiceless system" in which invoices no longer trigger payments to suppliers. The receipt does the job.

Fourth, focus directly on customers for information. For example, William McKnight, head of 3M's Chicago sales office, required that salesmen of abrasives products talk directly to the workers in the shop to find out what they needed, instead of calling on only front-office executives.[50] This was very innovative at the time—1909! But it illustrates the need to get to the end user of a product or service. (McKnight went on to become 3M's president from 1929 to 1949 and chairman from 1949 to 1969.) More recently, James Taylor, senior vice president for global marketing at Gateway 2000, discussed the value of customer input in reducing response time, a critical success factor in the PC industry.

> We talk to 100,000 people a day—people calling to order a computer, shopping around, looking for tech support. Our website gets 1.1 million hits per day. The time it takes for an idea to enter this organization, get processed, and then go to customers for feedback is down to minutes. We've designed the company around speed and feedback.[51]

Challenging the Status Quo and Enabling Creativity

Earlier in this chapter we discussed some of the barriers that leaders face when trying to bring about change in an organization: vested interests in the status quo, systemic barriers, behavioral barriers, political barriers, and personal time constraints. For a firm to become a learning organization, it must overcome such barriers in order to foster creativity and enable it to permeate the firm. This becomes quite a challenge if the firm is entrenched in a status quo mentality.

Perhaps the best way to challenge the status quo is for the leader to forcefully create a sense of urgency. For example, when Tom Kasten was vice president of Levi Strauss, he had a direct approach to initiating change.

> You create a compelling picture of the risks of *not* changing. We let our people hear directly from customers. We videotaped interviews with customers and played excerpts. One big customer said, "We trust many of your competitors implicitly. We sample their deliveries. We open *all* Levi's deliveries." Another said, "Your lead times are the worst. If you weren't Levi's, you'd be gone." It was powerful. I wish we had done more of it.[52]

Such initiative, if sincere and credible, establishes a shared mission and the need for major transformations. It can channel energies to bring about both change and creative endeavors.

Establishing a "culture of dissent" can be another effective means of questioning the status quo and serving as a spur toward creativity. Here norms are established whereby dissenters can openly question a superior's perspective without fear of retaliation or retribution. Consider the perspective of Steven Balmer, Microsoft's CEO.

> Bill [Gates] brings to the company the idea that conflict can be a good thing. . . . Bill knows it's important to avoid that gentle civility that keeps you from getting to the heart of an issue quickly. He likes it when anyone, even a junior employee, challenges him, and you know he respects you when he starts shouting back.[53]

Motorola has gone a step further and institutionalized its culture of dissent.[54] By filing a "minority report," an employee can go above his or her immediate supervisor's head and officially lodge a different point of view on a business decision. According to former CEO George Fisher, "I'd call it a healthy spirit of discontent and a freedom by and large to express your discontent around here or to disagree with whoever it is in the company, me or anybody else."

Closely related to the culture of dissent is the fostering of a culture that encourages risk taking. "If you're not making mistakes, you're not taking risks, and that means you're not going anywhere," claimed John Holt, coauthor of *Celebrate Your Mistakes.*[55] "The key is to make errors faster than the competition, so you have more chances to learn and win."

Companies that cultivate cultures of experimentation and curiosity make sure that *failure* is not, in essence, an obscene word. They encourage mistakes as a key part of their competitive advantage. This philosophy was shared by Stan Shih, CEO of Acer, a Taiwan-based computer company. If a manager at Acer took an intelligent risk and made a

ethics a system of right and wrong that assists individuals in deciding when an act is moral or immoral and/or socially desirable or not.

Exhibit 11.6   **Best Practices: Learning from Failures**

It's innovation's great paradox: Success—that is, true breakthroughs—usually comes through failure. Here are some ideas on how to help your team get comfortable with taking risks and learning from mistakes:

- **Formalize Forums for Failure**
  To keep failures and the valuable lessons they offer from getting swept under the rug, *carve out time for reflection.* GE recently began sharing lessons from failures by bringing together managers whose "Imagination Breakthrough" efforts are put on the shelf.

- **Move the Goalposts**
  Innovation requires flexibility in meeting goals, since early predictions are often little more than educated guesses. Intuit's Scott Cook even suggests that teams developing new products ignore forecasts in the early days. "For every one of our failures, we had spreadsheets that looked awesome," he says.

- **Share Personal Stories**
  If employees hear leaders discussing their own failures, *they'll feel more comfortable talking about their own.* But it's not just the CEO's job. Front-line leaders are even more important, says Harvard Business School professor Amy Edmondson. "That person needs to be inviting, curious, and the first to say: 'I made a mistake'."

- **Bring in Outsiders**
  Outsiders can *help neutralize the emotions and biases that prop up a flop.* Customers can be the most valuable. After its DNA chip failed, Corning brought pharmaceutical companies in early to test its new drug-discovery technology, Epic.

- **Prove Yourself Wrong, Not Right**
  Development teams tend to look for supporting, rather than countervailing, evidence. "You have to reframe what you're seeking in the early days," says Innosight's Scott Anthony. *"You're not really seeking proof that you have the right answer. It's more about testing to prove yourself wrong."*

- **Celebrate Smart Failures**
  Managers should design performance-management systems that reward risk taking and foster a long-term view. But they should also *celebrate failures that teach something new,* energizing people to try again and offering them closure.

Source: McGregor, J. 2006. How Failure Breeds Success. *BusinessWeek.* July 10: 42–52.

mistake—even a costly one—Shih wrote off the loss as tuition payment for the manager's education. Such a culture must permeate the entire organization. As a high-tech executive told us during an interview: "Every person has a freedom to fail."

Exhibit 11.6 has insights on how organizations can both embrace risk and learn from failure.

>LO5
The leader's role in establishing an ethical organization.

Creating an Ethical Organization

Ethics may be defined as a system of right and wrong.[56] Ethics assists individuals in deciding when an act is moral or immoral, socially desirable or not. The sources for an individual's ethics include religious beliefs, national and ethnic heritage, family practices, community standards, educational experiences, and friends and neighbors. Business ethics is the application of ethical standards to commercial enterprise.

organizational ethics the values, attitudes, and behavioral patterns that define an organization's operating culture and that determine what an organization holds as acceptable behavior.

Individual Ethics versus Organizational Ethics

Many leaders think of ethics as a question of personal scruples, a confidential matter between employees and their consciences. Such leaders are quick to describe any wrongdoing as an isolated incident, the work of a rogue employee. They assume the company should not bear any responsibility for individual misdeeds. In their view, ethics has nothing to do with leadership.

Ethics has everything to do with leadership. Seldom does the character flaw of a lone actor completely explain corporate misconduct. Instead, unethical business practices typically involve the tacit, if not explicit, cooperation of others and reflect the values, attitudes, and behavior patterns that define an organization's operating culture. Ethics is as much an organizational as a personal issue. Leaders who fail to provide proper leadership to institute proper systems and controls that facilitate ethical conduct share responsibility with those who conceive, execute, and knowingly benefit from corporate misdeeds.[57]

ethical orientation
the practices that firms use to promote an ethical business culture, including ethical role models, corporate credos and codes of conduct, ethically-based reward and evaluation systems, and consistently enforced ethical policies and procedures.

The **ethical orientation** of a leader is a key factor in promoting ethical behavior. Ethical leaders must take personal, ethical responsibility for their actions and decision making. Leaders who exhibit high ethical standards become role models for others and raise an organization's overall level of ethical behavior. Ethical behavior must start with the leader before the employees can be expected to perform accordingly.

There has been a growing interest in corporate ethical performance. Some reasons for this trend may be the increasing lack of confidence regarding corporate activities, the growing emphasis on quality of life issues, and a spate of recent corporate scandals. Without a strong ethical culture, the chance of ethical crises occurring is enhanced. Ethical crises can be very expensive—both in terms of financial costs and in the erosion of human capital and overall firm reputation. Merely adhering to the minimum regulatory standards may not be enough to remain competitive in a world that is becoming more socially conscious. Strategy Spotlight 11.9 highlights potential ethical problems at utility companies that are trying to capitalize on consumers' desire to participate in efforts to curb global warming.

The past several years have been characterized by numerous examples of unethical and illegal behavior by many top-level corporate executives. These include executives of firms such as Enron, Tyco, WorldCom, Inc., Adelphia, and Healthsouth Corp., who were all forced to resign and are facing (or have been convicted of) criminal charges. Perhaps the most glaring example is Bernie Madoff, whose Ponzi scheme, which unraveled in 2008, defrauded investors of $50 billion in assets they had set aside for retirement and charitable donations.

The ethical organization is characterized by a conception of ethical values and integrity as a driving force of the enterprise.[58] Ethical values shape the search for opportunities, the design of organizational systems, and the decision-making process used by individuals and groups. They provide a common frame of reference that serves as a unifying force across different functions, lines of business, and employee groups. Organizational ethics helps to define what a company is and what it stands for.

There are many potential benefits of an ethical organization, but they are often indirect. Research has found somewhat inconsistent results concerning the overall relationship between ethical performance and measures of financial performance.[59] However, positive relationships have generally been found between ethical performance and strong organizational culture, increased employee efforts, lower turnover, higher organizational commitment, and enhanced social responsibility.

The advantages of a strong ethical orientation can have a positive effect on employee commitment and motivation to excel. This is particularly important in today's knowledge-intensive organizations, where human capital is critical in creating value and competitive advantages. Positive, constructive relationships among individuals (i.e., social capital) are vital in leveraging human capital and other resources in an organization. Drawing on the concept of stakeholder management, an ethically sound organization can also strengthen its bonds among its suppliers, customers, and governmental agencies.

Green Energy: Real or Just a Marketing Ploy?

Many consumers want to "go green" and are looking for opportunities to do so. Utility companies that provide heat and electricity are one of the most obvious places to turn, because they often use fossil fuels that could be saved through energy conservation or replaced by using alternative energy sources. In fact, some consumers are willing to pay a premium to contribute to environmental sustainability efforts if paying a little more will help curb global warming. Knowing this, many power companies in the United States have developed alternative energy programs and appealed to customers to help pay for them.

Unfortunately, many of the power companies that are offering eco-friendly options are falling short on delivering on them. Some utilities have simply gotten off to a slow start or found it difficult to profitably offer alternative power. Others, however, are suspected of committing a new type of fraud—"greenwashing." This refers to companies that make unsubstantiated claims about how environmentally friendly their products or services really are. In the case of many power companies, their claims of "green power" are empty promises. Instead of actually generating additional renewable energy, most of the premiums are going for marketing costs. "They are preying on people's goodwill," says Stephen Smith, executive director of the Southern Alliance for Clean Energy, an advocacy group in Knoxville, Tennessee.

Exhibit 11.7 shows what three power companies offered and how the money was actually spent. Unfortunately, utilities that spend only a fraction of voluntary energy premiums on renewable energy are becoming more rather than less common. It will likely be up to consumers or Public Service Commissions to hold the utilities to a higher ethical standard—either by making power companies' advertising more truthful or, better still, by insisting that they deliver on their renewable energy promises. Either way, the idea of defrauding customers who are trying to "do the right thing" makes the utilities' unethical decision even more dishonorable.

Sources: Elgin, B. & Holden, D. 2008. Green Power: Buyers Beware. *Business-Week*, September 29: 68–70; and www.cleanenergy.org.

environmental sustainability

Exhibit 11.7 How "Green" Utilities Actually Used Customer Payments

Company/Program	What Customers Were Told	What Really Happened
Duke Energy of Indiana GoGreen Power	Pay a green energy premium and a specified amount of electricity will be obtained from renewable sources.	Less than 18 percent of voluntary customer contributions in a recent year went to renewable energy development.
Alliant Energy of Iowa Second Nature ™	"Support the growth of earth-friendly 'green power' created by wind and biomass."	More than 56 percent of expenditures went to marketing and administrative costs, not green energy development.
Georgia Power Green Energy®	Paying the premium "is equivalent to planting 125 trees or not driving 2,000 miles" and will "help bring more renewable power to Georgia."	Customers pay an annual $54 premium, but green energy is actually cheaper to provide than electricity from conventional sources.

Sources: Elgin, B. & Holden, D. 2008. Green Power: Buyers Beware. *BusinessWeek*, September 29: 68–70; www.alliantenergy.com; www.duke-energy.com; and www.georgiapower.com.

>LO6
The difference
between integrity-
based and
compliance-based
approaches to
organizational ethics.

Integrity-Based versus Compliance-Based Approaches to Organizational Ethics

Before discussing the key elements of an ethical organization, one must understand the links between organizational integrity and the personal integrity of an organization's members.[60] There cannot be high-integrity organizations without high-integrity individuals. However, individual integrity is rarely self-sustaining. Even good people can lose their bearings when faced with pressures, temptations, and heightened performance expectations in the absence of organizational support systems and ethical boundaries. Organizational integrity rests on a concept of purpose, responsibility, and ideals for an organization as a whole. An important responsibility of leadership is to create this ethical framework and develop the organizational capabilities to make it operational.[61]

Lynn Paine, an ethics scholar at Harvard, identifies two approaches: the compliance-based approach and the integrity-based approach. (See Exhibit 11.8 for a comparison of compliance-based and integrity-based strategies.) Faced with the prospect of litigation, several organizations reactively implement **compliance-based ethics programs.** Such programs are typically designed by a corporate counsel with the goal of preventing, detecting, and punishing legal violations. But being ethical is much more than being legal, and an integrity-based approach addresses the issue of ethics in a more comprehensive manner.

Integrity-based ethics programs combine a concern for law with an emphasis on managerial responsibility for ethical behavior. It is broader, deeper, and more demanding than a legal compliance initiative. It is broader in that it seeks to enable responsible conduct. It is deeper in that it cuts to the ethos and operating systems of an organization and its members, their core guiding values, thoughts, and actions. It is more demanding because it requires an active effort to define the responsibilities that constitute an organization's ethical compass. Most importantly, organizational ethics is seen as the responsibility of management.

A corporate counsel may play a role in designing and implementing integrity strategies, but it is managers at all levels and across all functions that are involved in the process. Once integrated into the day-to-day operations, such strategies can prevent damaging ethical lapses, while tapping into powerful human impulses for moral thought and action.

compliance-based ethics programs
programs for building ethical organizations that have the goal of preventing, detecting, and punishing legal violations.

integrity-based ethics programs
programs for building ethical organizations that combine a concern for law with an emphasis on managerial responsibility for ethical behavior, including (1) enabling ethical conduct; (2) examining the organization's and members' core guiding values, thoughts, and actions; and (3) defining the responsibilities and aspirations that constitute an organization's ethical compass.

Exhibit 11.8 Approaches to Ethics Management

Characteristics	Compliance-Based Approach	Integrity-Based Approach
Ethos	Conformity with externally imposed standards	Self-governance according to chosen standards
Objective	Prevent criminal misconduct	Enable responsible conduct
Leadership	Lawyer-driven	Management-driven with aid of lawyers, HR, and others
Methods	Education, reduced discretion, auditing and controls, penalties	Education, leadership, accountability, organizational systems and decision processes, auditing and controls, penalties
Behavioral Assumptions	Autonomous beings guided by material self-interest	Social beings guided by material self-interest, values, ideals, peers

Source: Reprinted by permission of *Harvard Business Review*. Exhibit from "Managing Organizational Integrity," by L. S. Paine. Copyright © 1994 by the Harvard Business School Publishing Corporation; all rights reserved.

Ethics becomes the governing ethos of an organization and not burdensome constraints. Here is an example of an organization that goes beyond mere compliance to laws in building an ethical organization:

> In teaching ethics to its employees, Texas Instruments, the $14 billion chip and electronics manufacturer, asks them to run an issue through the following steps: Is it legal? Is it consistent with the company's stated values? Will the employee feel bad doing it? What will the public think if the action is reported in the press? Does the employee think it is wrong? If the employees are not sure of the ethicality of the issue, they are encouraged to ask someone until they are clear about it. In the process, employees can approach high-level personnel and even the company's lawyers. At TI, the question of ethics goes much beyond merely being legal. It is no surprise, that this company is a benchmark for corporate ethics and has been a recipient of three ethics awards: the David C. Lincoln Award for Ethics and Excellence in Business, American Business Ethics Award, and Bentley College Center for Business Ethics Award.[62]

Compliance-based approaches are externally motivated—that is, based on the fear of punishment for doing something unlawful. On the other hand, integrity-based approaches are driven by a personal and organizational commitment to ethical behavior.

A firm must have several key elements to become a highly ethical organization:

>LO7
Several key elements that organizations must have to become an ethical organization.

- Role models.
- Corporate credos and codes of conduct.
- Reward and evaluation systems.
- Policies and procedures.

These elements are highly interrelated. Reward structures and policies will be useless if leaders are not sound role models. That is, leaders who implicitly say, "Do as I say, not as I do," will quickly have their credibility eroded and such actions will sabotage other elements that are essential to building an ethical organization.

Role Models

For good or for bad, leaders are role models in their organizations. Leaders must "walk the talk"; they must be consistent in their words and deeds. The values as well as the character of leaders become transparent to an organization's employees through their behaviors. When leaders do not believe in the ethical standards that they are trying to inspire, they will not be effective as good role models. Being an effective leader often includes taking responsibility for ethical lapses within the organization—even though the executives themselves are not directly involved. Consider the perspective of Dennis Bakke, CEO of AES, the $13 billion global electricity company based in Arlington, Virginia.

> There was a major breach (in 1992) of the AES values. Nine members of the water treatment team in Oklahoma lied to the EPA about water quality at the plant. There was no environmental damage, but they lied about the test results. A new, young chemist at the plant discovered it, told a team leader, and we then were notified. Now, you could argue that the people who lied were responsible and were accountable, but the senior management team also took responsibility by taking pay cuts. My reduction was about 30 percent.[63]

Such action enhances the loyalty and commitment of employees throughout the organization. Many would believe that it would have been much easier (and personally less expensive!) for Bakke and his management team to merely take strong punitive action against the nine individuals who were acting contrary to the behavior expected in AES's ethical culture. However, by taking responsibility for the misdeeds, the top executives—through their highly

Elements of a Corporate Code

Corporate codes are not simply useful for conveying organizational norms and policies, but they also serve to legitimize an organization in the eyes of others. In the United States, federal guidelines advise judges, when determining how to sentence a company convicted of a crime, to consider whether it had a written code and was out of compliance with its own ethical guidelines. The United Nations and countries around the world have endorsed codes as a way to promote corporate social responsibility. As such, a code provides an increasingly important corporate social contract that signals a company's willingness to act ethically.

For employees, codes of conduct serve four key purposes:

Sources: Paine, L., Deshpande, R., Margolis, J. D., & Bettcher, K. E. 2005. Up to code: Does Your Company's Conduct Meet World Class Standards? *Harvard Business Review,* 82(12): 122–126; and Stone, A. 2004. Putting Teeth in Corporate Ethics Codes. www.businessweek.com, February 19.

1. Help employees from diverse backgrounds work more effectively across cultural backgrounds.

2. Provide a reference point for decision making.

3. Help attract individuals who want to work for a business that embraces high standards.

4. Help a company to manage risk by reducing the likelihood of damaging misconduct.

With recent scandals on Wall Street, many corporations are trying to put more teeth into their codes of conduct. Nasdaq now requires that listed companies distribute a code to all employees. German software giant SAP's code informs employees that violations of the code "can result in consequences that affect employment, and could possibly lead to external investigation, civil law proceedings, or criminal charges." Clearly, codes of conduct are an important part of maintaining an ethical organization.

● Johnson & Johnson is well known for its credo, which stresses honesty, integrity, superior products, and putting people before profits. Above is one of its many products.

visible action—made it clear that responsibility and penalties for ethical lapses go well beyond the "guilty" parties. Such courageous behavior by leaders helps to strengthen an organization's ethical environment.

Corporate Credos and Codes of Conduct

Corporate credos and codes of conduct are mechanisms that provide statements of norms and beliefs as well as guidelines for decision making. They provide employees with a clear understanding of the organization's policies and ethical position. Such guidelines also provide the basis for employees to refuse to commit unethical acts and help to make them aware of issues before they are faced with the situation. For such codes to be truly effective, organization members must be aware of them and what behavioral guidelines they contain.[64] Strategy Spotlight 11.10 identifies four key reasons why codes of conduct support organizational efforts to maintain a safe and ethical workplace.

Large corporations are not the only ones to develop and use codes of conduct. Consider the example of Wetherill Associates (WAI), a small, privately held supplier of electrical parts to the automotive market.

Exhibit 11.9
Johnson & Johnson's
Credo

We believe our first responsibility is to the doctors, nurses and patients, to mothers and fathers and all others who use our products and services. In meeting their needs everything we do must be of high quality. We must constantly strive to reduce our costs in order to maintain reasonable prices. Customers' orders must be serviced promptly and accurately. Our suppliers and distributors must have an opportunity to make a fair profit.

We are responsible to our employees, the men and women who work with us throughout the world. Everyone must be considered as an individual. We must respect their dignity and recognize their merit. They must have a sense of security in their jobs. Compensation must be fair and adequate, and working conditions clean, orderly, and safe. We must be mindful of ways to help our employees fulfill their family responsibilities. Employees must feel free to make suggestions and complaints. There must be equal opportunity for employment, development, and advancement for those qualified. We must provide competent management, and their actions must be just and ethical.

We are responsible to the communities in which we live and work and to the world community as well. We must be good citizens—support good works and charities and bear our fair share of taxes. We must encourage civic improvements and better health and education. We must maintain in good order the property we are privileged to use, protecting the environment and natural resources

Our final responsibility is to our stockholders. Business must make a sound profit. We must experiment with new ideas. Research must be carried on, innovative programs developed, and mistakes paid for. New equipment must be purchased, new facilities provided, and new products launched. Reserves must be created to provide for adverse times. When we operate according to these principles, the stockholders should realize a fair return.

Source: Reprinted with permission of Johnson & Johnson Co.

Rather than a conventional code of conduct, WAI has a Quality Assurance Manual—a combination of philosophy text, conduct guide, technical manual, and company profile—that describes the company's commitment to honesty, ethical action, and integrity. WAI doesn't have a corporate ethics officer, because the company's corporate ethics officer is Marie Bothe, WAI's CEO. She sees her main function as keeping the 350-employee company on the path of ethical behavior and looking for opportunities to help the community. She delegates the "technical" aspects of the business—marketing, finance, personnel, and operations—to other members of the organization.[65]

Perhaps the best-known credo is that of Johnson & Johnson (J&J). It is reprinted in Exhibit 11.9. The credo stresses honesty, integrity, superior products, and putting people before profits. What distinguishes the J&J credo from others is the amount of energy the company's top managers devote to ensuring that employees live by its precepts:

Over a recent three-year period, Johnson & Johnson undertook a massive effort to assure that its original credo, already decades old, was still valid. More than 1,200 managers attended two-day seminars in groups of 25, with explicit instructions to challenge the credo. The president or CEO of the firm presided over each session. The company came out of the process believing that its original document was still valid. However, the questioning process continues. Such "challenge meetings" are still replicated every other year for all new managers. These efforts force J&J to question, internalize, and then implement its credo. Such investments have paid off handsomely many times—most notably in 1982, when eight people died from swallowing capsules of Tylenol, one of its flagship products, that someone had laced with cyanide. Leaders such as James Burke, who without hesitation made an across-the-board recall of the product even though it affected only a limited number of untraceable units, send a strong message throughout the firm.

Reward and Evaluation Systems

It is entirely possible for a highly ethical leader to preside over an organization that commits several unethical acts. How? A flaw in the organization's reward structure may inadvertently cause individuals to act in an inappropriate manner if rewards are seen as being distributed on the basis of outcomes rather than the means by which goals and objectives are achieved.[66]

Consider the example of Sears, Roebuck & Co.'s automotive operations. Here, unethical behavior, rooted in a faulty reward system, took place primarily at the operations level: its automobile repair facilities.[67]

> In 1992 Sears was flooded with complaints about its automotive service business. Consumers and attorneys general in more than 40 states accused the firm of misleading customers and selling them unnecessary parts and services, from brake jobs to front-end alignments.
>
> In the face of declining revenues and eroding market share, Sears's management had attempted to spur the performance of its auto centers by introducing new goals and incentives for mechanics. Automotive service advisers were given product-specific quotas for a variety of parts and repairs. Failure to meet the quotas could lead to transfers and reduced hours. Many employees spoke of "pressure, pressure, pressure" to bring in sales.
>
> Not too surprisingly, the judgment of many employees suffered. In essence, employees were left to chart their own course, given the lack of management guidance and customer ignorance. The bottom line: In settling the spate of lawsuits, Sears offered coupons to customers who had purchased certain auto services over the most recent two-year period. The total cost of the settlement, including potential customer refunds, was estimated to be $60 million. The cost in terms of damaged reputation? Difficult to assess, but certainly not trivial.

This example makes two points. First, inappropriate reward systems may cause individuals at all levels throughout an organization to commit unethical acts that they might not otherwise commit. Second, the penalties in terms of damage to reputations, human capital erosion, and financial loss—in the short run and long run—are typically much higher than any gains that could be obtained through such unethical behavior.

Many companies have developed reward and evaluation systems that evaluate whether a manager is acting in an ethical manner. For example, Raytheon, a $20 billion defense contractor, incorporates the following items in its "Leadership Assessment Instrument":[68]

- Maintains unequivocal commitment to honesty, truth, and ethics in every facet of behavior.
- Conforms with the letter and intent of company policies while working to affect any necessary policy changes.
- Actions are consistent with words; follows through on commitments; readily admits mistakes.
- Is trusted and inspires others to be trusted.

As noted by Dan Burnham, Raytheon's former CEO: "What do we look for in a leadership candidate with respect to integrity? What we're really looking for are people who have developed an inner gyroscope of ethical principles. We look for people for whom ethical thinking is part of what they do—no different from 'strategic thinking' or 'tactical thinking.'"

No More Whistleblowing Woes!

The landmark Sarbanes-Oxley Act of 2002 gives those who expose corporate misconduct strong legal protection. Henceforth, an executive who retaliates against the corporate whistleblower can be held criminally liable and imprisoned for up to 10 years. That's the same sentence a mafia don gets for threatening a witness. The Labor Department can order a company to rehire an employee without going to court. If the fired workers feel their case is moving too slowly, they can request a federal jury after six months.

Companies need to revisit their current policies, including nondisclosure pacts. They may no longer be able to enforce rules requiring employees to get permission to speak to the media or lawyers. Even layoffs should be planned in advance, lest they seem retaliatory.

Sources: www.sarbanes-oxley.com/pcaob.php/level=2&pub_id=Sarbanes-Oxley&chap_id=PCAOB11; Dwyer, P., Carney, D., Borrus, A., Woellert, L., & Palmeri, C. 2002. Year of the Whistle Blower. *BusinessWeek*, December 16: 107–109; and www.buchalter.com/FSL5CS/articles/articles204.asp.

Employees of publicly traded companies are now the most protected whistleblowers. Provisions coauthored by Senator Grassley in the Sarbanes-Oxley corporate-reform law:

- Make it unlawful to "discharge, demote, suspend or threaten, harass, or in any manner discriminate against" a whistleblower.

- Establish criminal penalties of up to 10 years in jail for executives who retaliate against whistleblowers.

- Require board audit committees to establish procedures for hearing whistleblower complaints.

- Allow the secretary of labor to order a company to rehire a terminated whistleblower with no court hearings whatsoever.

- Give a whistleblower a right to jury trial, bypassing months or years of cumbersome administrative hearings.

Policies and Procedures

Many situations that a firm faces have regular, identifiable patterns. Leaders tend to handle such routine by establishing a policy or procedure to be followed that can be applied uniformly to each occurrence. Such guidelines can be useful in specifying the proper relationships with a firm's customers and suppliers. For example, Levi Strauss has developed stringent global sourcing guidelines and Chemical Bank (part of J. P. Morgan Chase Bank) has a policy of forbidding any review that would determine if suppliers are Chemical customers when the bank awards contracts.

Carefully developed policies and procedures guide behavior so that all employees will be encouraged to behave in an ethical manner. However, they must be reinforced with effective communication, enforcement, and monitoring, as well as sound corporate governance practices. Strategy Spotlight 11.11 describes how the recently enacted Sarbanes-Oxley Act provides considerable legal protection to employees of publicly traded companies who report unethical or illegal practices.

We close our chapter on strategic leadership with a brief discussion of the Goolsby Leadership Model. It is addressed in Strategy Spotlight 11.12 and includes three dimensions: integrity, courage, and impact. The Goolsby Model synthesizes many of the ideas that we have addressed in this chapter and has important implications for career success.

strategy spotlight

11.12

The Goolsby Leadership Model: Integrity, Courage, and Impact

For many years there has been a focus in leadership research on inspirational styles that emphasize such traits as vision, charisma, and transformation. Some have criticized such approaches and have suggested that they may lead to unethical behavior. Why? They are taught to appeal to emotion rather than reason, lack checks and balances, and exploit followers to their detriment and to the benefit of the leader(s). Thus, some writers have begun to distinguish between authentic and inauthentic leaders. The Goolsby Leadership Model grows from the transformational leadership tradition and is anchored in the concept of authentic leadership.

Clearly, most would agree that a healthy leader is at the heart of a healthy organization. Consider the alternative: The unhealthy leader has drawn attention to the damaging and debilitating effects—on both individuals and organizations—that result from such behaviors as excessive narcissism and toxic micromanagement. Also, recall the unethical and illegal activities in which some leaders participate that we addressed earlier in this chapter and in our discussion on corporate governance in Chapter 9. The Goolsby Leadership Model, in contrast, sets forth a healthy, positive model based on three core concepts: integrity, courage, and impact. This model is shown in Exhibit 11.10.

Integrity

Integrity, a concept at the heart of good business practice, can be defined as consistency between word and deed as well as sound moral character. The four core questions of the Rotary Four-Way Test aim to test personal integrity.

1. Is it the truth?
2. Is it fair to all concerned?
3. Will it build goodwill and better friendships?
4. Will it be beneficial to all concerned?

In building on these questions, two key attributes of integrity in the healthy leader emerge: authenticity and emotional competence. These two attributes, in part, draw on the concept of emotional intelligence (EI) that we addressed earlier in the chapter. Authenticity includes self-awareness, transparency, positive psychological states, and personal integrity. An authentic leader possesses good self-awareness, is transparent to others while being consistent, engenders positive psychological states within himself and his followers, and is widely known for having personal integrity. The opposite of authenticity is duplicity, which is a type of Jekyll-and-Hyde personality.

The second dimension of integrity is emotional competence, which involves the integration of thought and emotion and is defined by its four dimensions: awareness of self, management of self, awareness of others, and management of others. Emotionally competent *(continued)*

Exhibit 11.10 **The Goolsby Leadership Model**

Source: Quick, J. C., Macik-Frey, M., & Cooper, C. L. 2007. *Journal of Management Studies,* 44(2):195. Reprinted with permission of Wiley-Blackwell Publishing Ltd.

(continued) leaders are aware of their own feelings and emotions and aware of the feelings and emotions in other people. In addition, the emotionally competent leader is able to act in ways that appropriately manage his own emotions while accommodating the emotions of others. Emotional competence helps the healthy leader to be hopeful, positive, and compassionate in his actions and behaviors.

Courage

Courage is defined as the capacity to act, even in the presence of adversity, fear, and danger. Courage involves purpose, energy, and character. Purpose is the heart of great leadership and the heart of character. After conducting in-depth interviews with 28 senior executives, researchers recently found a wide variety of attributes and characteristics of great leaders. However, there was no variance along the dimension of purpose.

Energy and energy management are essential for healthy productivity and achievement. Consider, for example, the personal leadership track at PepsiCo's corporate leadership program in Purchase, New York. Here, consultants found that energy expenditure through full engagement is what leads to productive achievement and

Source: This Strategy Spotlight draws upon Quick, J. C., Macik-Frey, M., & Cooper, C. L. 2007. Managerial Dimensions of Organizational Health: The Healthy Leader at Work. *Journal of Management Studies*, 44(2): 189–295.

meaningful work accomplishment. PepsiCo has enjoyed an impressive 12 percent annual growth in market valuation in a recent period, twice the growth of its long-time rival Coca-Cola. Interestingly, to be most effective, the power of full engagement must be balanced with strategic disengagement through which leaders are able to achieve renewal based on the process of energy recovery.

A third dimension of courage is character, and it can be defined as who you are when no one is looking. Character is important because it leads to consistency in actions and behaviors based on core values and principles. Character is a powerful force that enables leaders to act with courage in the midst of business crises or disasters.

Impact

Strategic leadership is neither a philosophical nor contemplative activity. Great leaders have a strong impact on their followers and on the businesses they lead. Consider, for example, the impacts of such well-known leaders as Andy Grove at Intel, Richard Branson at Virgin, Inc., and Lou Gerstner at IBM. The Goolsby Leadership Model suggests that integrity and courage affect individuals and organizational health by affecting their vitality, productivity, and flexibility. When individuals and organizations function in a healthy manner, they get results and make a positive impact for a wide range of organizational stakeholders.

Reflecting on Career Implications . . .

- *Strategic Leadership:* Do managers in your firm effectively set the direction; design the organization; and, instill a culture committed to excellence and ethical behavior? If you are in a position of leadership, do you practice all of these three elements effectively?
- *Power:* What sources of power do managers in your organization use? For example, if there is an overemphasis on organizational sources of power (e.g., position power); there could be negative implications for creativity, morale and turnover among professionals. How much power do you have? What is the basis of it? How might it be used to both advance your career goals and benefit the firm?
- *Emotional Intelligence:* Do leaders of your firm have sufficient levels of EI? Alternatively, are there excessive levels of EI present that have negative implications for your organization? Is your level of EI sufficient to allow you to have effective interpersonal and judgment skills in order to enhance your career success?
- *Learning Organization:* Does your firm effectively practice all five elements of the learning organization? If one or more elements are absent, adaptability and change will be compromised. What can you do to enhance any of the elements that might be lacking?
- *Ethics:* Does your organization practice a compliance-based or integrity-based ethical culture? Integrity-based cultures can enhance your personal growth. In addition, such cultures foster greater loyalty and commitment among all employees.

Summary

Strategic leadership is vital in ensuring that strategies are formulated and implemented in an effective manner. Leaders must play a central role in performing three critical and interdependent activities: setting the direction, designing the organization, and nurturing a culture committed to excellence and ethical behavior. If leaders ignore or are ineffective at performing any one of the three, the organization will not be very successful. We also identified three elements of leadership that contribute to success—integrative thinking, overcoming barriers to change, and the effective use of power.

For leaders to effectively fulfill their activities, emotional intelligence (EI) is very important. Five elements that contribute to EI are self-awareness, self-regulation, motivation, empathy, and social skill. The first three elements pertain to self-management skills, whereas the last two are associated with a person's ability to manage relationships with others. We also addressed some of the potential drawbacks from the ineffective use of EI. These include the dysfunctional use of power as well as a tendency to become overly empathetic, which may result in unreasonably lowered performance expectations.

Leaders must also play a central role in creating a learning organization. Gone are the days when the top-level managers "think" and everyone else in the organization "does." With the rapidly changing, unpredictable, and complex competitive environments that characterize most industries, leaders must engage everyone in the ideas and energies of people throughout the organization. Great ideas can come from anywhere in the organization—from the executive suite to the factory floor. The five elements that we discussed as central to a learning organization are inspiring and motivating people with a mission or purpose, empowering people at all levels throughout the organization, accumulating and sharing internal knowledge, gathering external information, and challenging the status quo to stimulate creativity.

In the final section of the chapter, we addressed a leader's central role in instilling ethical behavior in the organization. We discussed the enormous costs that firms face when ethical crises arise—costs in terms of financial and reputational loss as well as the erosion of human capital and relationships with suppliers, customers, society at large, and governmental agencies. And, as we would expect, the benefits of having a strong ethical organization are also numerous. We contrasted compliance-based and integrity-based approaches to organizational ethics. Compliance-based approaches are largely externally motivated; that is, they are motivated by the fear of punishment for doing something that is unlawful. Integrity-based approaches, on the other hand, are driven by a personal and organizational commitment to ethical behavior. We also addressed the four key elements of an ethical organization: role models, corporate credos and codes of conduct, reward and evaluation systems, and policies and procedures.

Summary Review Questions

1. Three key activities—setting a direction, designing the organization, and nurturing a culture and ethics—are all part of what effective leaders do on a regular basis. Explain how these three activities are interrelated.

2. Define emotional intelligence (EI). What are the key elements of EI? Why is EI so important to successful strategic leadership? Address potential "downsides."

3. The knowledge a firm possesses can be a source of competitive advantage. Describe ways that a firm can continuously learn to maintain its competitive position.

4. How can the five central elements of "learning organizations" be incorporated into global companies?

5. What are the benefits to firms and their shareholders of conducting business in an ethical manner?

6. Firms that fail to behave in an ethical manner can incur high costs. What are these costs and what is their source?

7. What are the most important differences between an "integrity organization" and a "compliance organization" in a firm's approach to organizational ethics?

8. What are some of the important mechanisms for promoting ethics in a firm?

Key Terms

leadership, 385
setting a direction 386
designing the organization 388
excellent and ethical organizational culture 388
integrative thinking 390
barriers to change, 391
systemic barriers, 392
behavioral barriers, 393
political barriers, 393
power, 393

organizational bases of power, 393
personal bases of power, 394
emotional intelligence (EI), 395
learning organizations, 401
ethics, 406
organizational ethics 407
ethical orientation 408
compliance-based ethics programs, 410
integrity-based ethics programs, 410

Experiential Exercise

Select two well-known business leaders—one you admire and one you do not. Evaluate each of them on the five characteristics of emotional intelligence.

Emotional Intelligence Characteristics	Admired Leader	Leader Not Admired
Self-awareness		
Self-regulation		
Motivation		
Empathy		
Social skills		

Application Questions Exercises

1. Identify two CEOs whose leadership you admire. What is it about their skills, attributes, and effective use of power that causes you to admire them?

2. Founders have an important role in developing their organization's culture and values. At times, their influence persists for many years. Identify and describe two organizations in which the cultures and values established by the founder(s) continue to flourish. You may find research on the Internet helpful in answering these questions.

3. Some leaders place a great emphasis on developing superior human capital. In what ways does this help a firm to develop and sustain competitive advantages?

4. In this chapter we discussed the five elements of a "learning organization." Select a firm with which you are familiar and discuss whether or not it epitomizes some (or all) of these elements.

Ethics Questions

1. Sometimes organizations must go outside the firm to hire talent, thus bypassing employees already working for the firm. Are there conditions under which this might raise ethical considerations?

2. Ethical crises can occur in virtually any organization. Describe some of the systems, procedures, and processes that can help to prevent such crises.

References

1. The Richard Fuld example is based on Auletta, K. 1987. *Greed and glory on Wall Street: The fall of the house of Lehman.* New York: Warner Books; Becker, B. & White, B. 2008. Lehman managers portrayed as irresponsible. wwwnytimes.com, October 6; Boyle, M. 2008. Bad management: Why managers make poor decisions. www.businessweek.com, November 14; Feiden, D. 2008. Disgraced Lehman Brothers CEO Richard Fuld calling it quits. www.nydailynews.com, November 5; Goldstein, M. 2008. Lehman's Fuld goes begging. www.businessweek.com, September 10; Plumb, C. & Wilchins, D. 2008. Lehman CEO Fuld's hubris contributed to meltdown. www.reuters.com, September 14; Shin, A. 2008. Capitol grilling for Lehman CEO. www.washingtonpost.com, October 7; Worst managers of 2009. *BusinessWeek,* January 19: 42; and, www.answers.com.

2. Charan, R. & Colvin, G. 1999. Why CEOs fail. *Fortune,* June 21: 68–78.

3. Yukl, G. 2008. How leaders influence organizational effectiveness. *Leadership Quarterly,* 19(6): 708–722.

4. These three activities and our discussion draw from Kotter, J. P. 1990. What leaders really do. *Harvard Business Review,* 68(3): 103–111; Pearson, A. E. 1990. Six basics for general managers. *Harvard Business Review,* 67(4): 94–101; and Covey, S. R. 1996. Three roles of the leader in the new paradigm. In *The leader of the future:* 149–160. Hesselbein, F., Goldsmith, M., & Beckhard, R. (Eds.). San Francisco: Jossey-Bass. Some of the discussion of each of the three leadership activity concepts draws on Dess, G. G. & Miller, A. 1993. *Strategic management:* 320–325. New York: McGraw-Hill.

5. García-Morales, V. J., Lloréns-Montes, F. J., & Verdú-Jover, A. J. 2008. The effects of transformational leadership on organizational performance through knowledge and innovation. *British Journal of Management,* 19(4): 299–319.

6. Day, C., Jr. & LaBarre, P. 1994. GE: Just your average everyday $60 billion family grocery store. *Industry Week,* May 2: 13–18.

7. The best (& worst) managers of the year. 2003. *BusinessWeek,* January 13: 63.

8. Collins, J. 1997. What comes next? *Inc. Magazine.* October: 34–45.

9. Kirkpatrick, D. 2006. Use humility as a weapon. *Fortune.* October 30: 118.

10. Anonymous. 2006. Looking out for number one. *BusinessWeek,* October 30: 66.

11. Evans, R. 2007. The either/or dilemma. www.ft.com, December 19; and Martin, R. L. 2007. *The opposable mind.* Boston: Harvard Business School Press.

12. For insightful perspectives on escalation, refer to Brockner, J. 1992. The escalation of commitment to a failing course of action. *Academy of Management Review,* 17(1): 39–61; and Staw, B. M. 1976. Knee-deep in the big muddy: A study of commitment to a chosen course of action. *Organizational Behavior and Human Decision Processes,* 16: 27–44. The discussion of systemic, behavioral, and political barriers draws on Lorange, P. & Murphy, D. 1984. Considerations in implementing strategic control. *Journal of Business Strategy,* 5: 27–35. In a similar vein, Noel M. Tichy has addressed three types of resistance to change in the context of General Electric: technical resistance, political resistance, and cultural resistance. See Tichy, N. M. 1993. Revolutionize your company. *Fortune,* December 13: 114–118. Examples draw from O'Reilly, B. 1997. The secrets of America's most admired corporations: New ideas and new products. *Fortune,* March 3: 60–64.

13. This section draws on Champoux, J. E. 2000. *Organizational behavior: Essential tenets for a new millennium.* London: South-Western; and The mature use of power in organizations. 2003. *RHR International-Executive Insights,* May 29, 12.19.168.197/execinsights/8-3.htm.

14. An insightful perspective on the role of power and politics in organizations is provided in Ciampa, K. 2005. Almost ready: How leaders move up. *Harvard Business Review,* 83(1): 46–53.

15. A discussion of the importance of persuasion in bringing about change can be found in Garvin, D. A. & Roberto, M. A. 2005. Change through persuasion. *Harvard Business Review,* 83(4): 104–113.

16. Lorsch, J. W. & Tierney, T. J. 2002. *Aligning the stars: How to succeed when professionals drive results.* Boston: Harvard Business School Press.

17. Some consider EI to be a "trait," that is, an attribute that is stable over time. However, many authors, including Daniel Goleman, have argued that it can be developed through motivation, extended practice, and feedback. For example, in D. Goleman, 1998, What makes a leader? *Harvard Business Review,* 76(5): 97, Goleman addresses this issue in a sidebar: "Can emotional intelligence be learned?"

18. For a review of this literature, see Daft, R. 1999. *Leadership: Theory and practice.* Fort Worth, TX: Dryden Press.

19. This section draws on Luthans, F. 2002. Positive organizational behavior: Developing and managing psychological strengths. *Academy of Management Executive,* 16(1): 57–72; and Goleman, D. 1998. What makes a leader? *Harvard Business Review,* 76(6): 92–105.

20. EI has its roots in the concept of "social intelligence" that was first identified by E. L. Thorndike in 1920 (Intelligence and its uses. *Harper's Magazine,* 140: 227–235). Psychologists have been uncovering other intelligences for some time now and have grouped them into such clusters as abstract intelligence (the ability to understand and manipulate verbal and mathematical symbols), concrete

intelligence (the ability to understand and manipulate objects), and social intelligence (the ability to understand and relate to people). See Ruisel, I. 1992. Social intelligence: Conception and methodological problems. *Studia Psychologica,* 34(4–5): 281–296. Refer to trochim.human.cornell.edu/gallery.

21. See, for example, Luthans, op. cit.; Mayer, J. D., Salvoney, P., & Caruso, D. 2000. Models of emotional intelligence. In Sternberg, R. J. (Ed.). *Handbook of intelligence.* Cambridge, UK: Cambridge University Press; and Cameron, K. 1999. Developing emotional intelligence at the Weatherhead School of Management. *Strategy: The Magazine of the Weatherhead School of Management,* Winter: 2–3.

22. Tate, B. 2008. A longitudinal study of the relationships among self-monitoring, authentic leadership, and perceptions of leadership. *Journal of Leadership & Organizational Studies,* 15(1): 16–29.

23. Moss, S. A., Dowling, N., & Callanan, J. 2009. Towards an integrated model of leadership and self-regulation. *Leadership Quarterly,* 20(2): 162–176.

24. An insightful perspective on leadership, which involves discovering, developing and celebrating what is unique about each individual, is found in Buckingham, M. 2005. What great managers do. *Harvard Business Review,* 83(3): 70–79.

25. This section draws upon Klemp. G. 2005. *Emotional intelligence and leadership: What really matters.* Cambria Consulting, Inc., www.cambriaconsulting.com.

26. Heifetz, R. 2004. Question authority. *Harvard Business Review,* 82(1): 37.

27. Handy, C. 1995. Trust and the virtual organization. *Harvard Business Review,* 73(3): 40–50.

28. This section draws upon Dess, G. G. & Picken, J. C. 1999. *Beyond productivity.* New York: AMACOM. The elements of the learning organization in this section are consistent with the work of Dorothy Leonard-Barton. See, for example, Leonard-Barton, D. 1992. The factory as a learning laboratory. *Sloan Management Review,* 11: 23–38.

29. Senge, P. M. 1990. The leader's new work: Building learning organizations. *Sloan Management Review,* 32(1): 7–23.

30. Hammer, M. & Stanton, S. A. 1997. The power of reflection. *Fortune,* November 24: 291–296.

31. Hannah, S. T. & Lester, P. B. 2009. A multilevel approach to building and leading learning organizations. *Leadership Quarterly,* 20(1): 34–48.

32. For some guidance on how to effectively bring about change in organizations, refer to Wall, S. J. 2005. The protean organization: Learning to love change. *Organizational Dynamics,* 34(1): 37–46.

33. Covey, S. R. 1989. *The seven habits of highly effective people: Powerful lessons in personal change.* New York: Simon & Schuster.

34. Kouzes, J. M. & Posner, B. Z. 2009. To lead, create a shared vision. *Harvard Business Review,* 87(1): 20–21.

35. Kouzes and Posner, op. cit.

36. Melrose, K. 1995. *Making the grass greener on your side: A CEO's journey to leading by servicing.* San Francisco: Barrett-Koehler.

37. Tekleab, A. G., Sims Jr., H. P., Yun, S., Tesluk, P. E., & Cox, J. 2008. Are we on the same page? Effects of self-awareness of empowering and transformational

leadership. *Journal of Leadership & Organizational Studies,* 14(3): 185–201.

38. Quinn, R. C. & Spreitzer, G. M. 1997. The road to empowerment: Seven questions every leader should consider. *Organizational Dynamics,* 25: 37–49.

39. For an interesting perspective on top-down approaches to leadership, see Pellegrini, E. K. & Scandura, T. A. 2008. Paternalistic leadership: A review and agenda for future research. *Journal of Management,* 34(3): 566–593.

40. Helgesen, S. 1996. Leading from the grass roots. In *Leader of the future:* 19–24 Hesselbein et al.

41. Bowen, D. E. & Lawler, E. E., III. 1995. Empowering service employees. *Sloan Management Review,* 37: 73–84.

42. Easterby-Smith, M. & Prieto, I. M. 2008. Dynamic capabilities and knowledge management: An integrative role for learning? *British Journal of Management,* 19(3): 235–249.

43. Stack, J. 1992. *The great game of business.* New York: Doubleday/Currency.

44. Schafer, S. 1997. Battling a labor shortage? It's all in your imagination. *Inc.,* August: 24.

45. Meyer, P. 1998. So you want the president's job . . . *Business Horizons,* January–February: 2–8.

46. Imperato, G. 1998. Competitive intelligence: Get smart! *Fast Company,* May: 268–279.

47. Novicki, C. 1998. The best brains in business. *Fast Company,* April: 125.

48. The introductory discussion of benchmarking draws on Miller, A. 1998. *Strategic management:* 142–143. New York: McGraw-Hill.

49. Port, O. & Smith, G. 1992. Beg, borrow—and benchmark. *BusinessWeek,* November 30: 74–75.

50. Main, J. 1992. How to steal the best ideas around. *Fortune,* October 19: 102–106.

51. Taylor, J. T. 1997. What happens after what comes next? *Fast Company,* December–January: 84–85.

52. Sheff, D. 1996. Levi's changes everything. *Fast Company,* June–July: 65–74.

53. Isaacson, W. 1997. In search of the real Bill Gates. *Time,* January 13: 44–57.

54. Baatz, E. B. 1993. Motorola's secret weapon. *Electronic Business,* April: 51–53.

55. Holt, J. W. 1996. *Celebrate your mistakes.* New York: McGraw-Hill.

56. This opening discussion draws upon Conley, J. H. 2000. Ethics in business. In Helms, M. M. (Ed.). *Encyclopedia of management* (4th ed.): 281–285; Farmington Hills, MI: Gale Group; Paine, L. S. 1994. Managing for organizational integrity. *Harvard Business Review,* 72(2): 106–117; and Carlson, D. S. & Perrewe, P. L. 1995. Institutionalization of organizational ethics through transformational leadership. *Journal of Business Ethics,* 14: 829–838.

57. Pinto, J., Leana, C. R., & Pil, F. K. 2008. Corrupt organizations or organizations of corrupt individuals? Two types of organization-level corruption. *Academy of Management Review,* 33(3): 685–709.

58. Soule, E. 2002. Managerial moral strategies—in search of a few good principles. *Academy of Management Review,* 27(1): 114–124.

59. Carlson & Perrewe, op. cit.

60. This discussion is based upon Paine. Managing for organizational integrity; Paine, L. S. 1997. *Cases in leadership, ethics, and organizational integrity: A Strategic approach.* Burr Ridge, IL: Irwin; and Fontrodona, J. 2002. Business ethics across the Atlantic. Business Ethics Direct, www.ethicsa.org/BED_art_fontrodone.html.

61. For more on operationalizing capabilities to sustain an ethical framework, see Largay III, J. A. & Zhang, R. 2008. Do CEOs worry about being fired when making investment decisions. *Academy of Management Perspectives,* 22(1): 60–61.

62. See www.ti.com/corp/docs/company/citizen/ethics/benchmark.shtml; and www.ti.com/corp/docs/company/citizen/ethics/quicktest.shtml.

63. Wetlaufer, S. 1999. Organizing for empowerment: An interview with AES's Roger Sant and Dennis Bakke. *Harvard Business Review,* 77(1): 110–126.

64. For an insightful, academic perspective on the impact of ethics codes on executive decision making, refer to Stevens, J. M., Steensma, H. K., Harrison, D. A., & Cochran, P. S. 2005. Symbolic or substantive document? The influence of ethics code on financial executives' decisions. *Strategic Management Journal,* 26(2): 181–195.

65. Paine. Managing for organizational integrity.

66. For a recent study on the effects of goal setting on unethical behavior, read Schweitzer, M. E., Ordonez, L., & Douma, B. 2004. Goal setting as a motivator of unethical behavior. *Academy of Management Journal,* 47(3): 422–432.

67. Paine. Managing for organizational integrity.

68. Fulmer, R. M. 2004. The challenge of ethical leadership. *Organizational Dynamics,* 33 (3): 307–317.

Managing Innovation and Fostering Corporate Entrepreneurship

After reading this chapter, you should have a good understanding of:

LO1 The importance of implementing strategies and practices that foster innovation.

LO2 The challenges and pitfalls of managing corporate innovation processes.

LO3 How corporations use new venture teams, business incubators, and product champions to create an internal environment and culture that promote entrepreneurial development.

LO4 How corporate entrepreneurship achieves both financial goals and strategic goals.

LO5 The benefits and potential drawbacks of real options analysis in making resource deployment decisions in corporate entrepreneurship contexts.

LO6 How an entrepreneurial orientation can enhance a firm's efforts to develop promising corporate venture initiatives.

To remain competitive, established firms must continually seek out opportunities for growth and new methods for strategically renewing their performance. Changes in customer needs, new technologies, and shifts in the competitive landscape require that companies continually innovate and initiate corporate ventures in order to compete effectively. This chapter addresses how entrepreneurial activities can be an avenue for achieving competitive advantages.

In the first section, we address the importance of innovation in identifying venture opportunities and strategic renewal. Innovations can take many forms, including radical breakthroughs, incremental improvements, and disruptive innovations. Innovations often create new markets, update products or services, and help renew organizational processes. We discuss how firms can successfully manage the innovation process. Impediments and challenges to effective innovation are discussed, and examples of good innovation practices are presented.

We discuss the unique role of corporate entrepreneurship in the strategic management process in the second section. Here we highlight two types of activities corporations use to remain competitive—focused and dispersed. New venture groups and business incubators are often used to focus a firm's entrepreneurial activities. In other corporations, the entrepreneurial spirit is dispersed throughout the organization and gives rise to product champions and other autonomous strategic behaviors that organizational members engage in to foster internal corporate venturing. We also discuss the benefits and potential drawbacks of real options analysis in making decisions about which venture activities merit additional investment and which should be abandoned.

In the final section we describe how a firm's entrepreneurial orientation can contribute to its growth and renewal as well as enhance the methods and processes strategic managers use to recognize opportunities and develop initiatives for internal growth and development. The chapter also evaluates the pitfalls that firms may encounter when implementing entrepreneurial strategies.

Learning from Mistakes

Companies often grow by commercializing new technologies. This is one of the most important paths to corporate entrepreneurship. But the most successful technologies are quickly imitated, and new entrants are often able to undermine the efforts of early leaders. Consider the case of Nortel Networks Corp., once a leading telecommunications industry innovator and darling of the Toronto Stock Exchange.[1]

Soon after Nortel Networks celebrated its 100-year anniversary in 1995, it became one of the leading players in the emerging digital technology revolution in the telecommunications industry. Nortel built much of the fiber optic equipment that is used today to carry data on the Internet. It pioneered the development of equipment and software that made wireless phone networks possible. It grew to be the largest employer in Ottawa, Canada, and at its peak in July 2000, Nortel's stock sold for $124.50 Canadian dollars on the Toronto Stock Exchange. When it filed for bankruptcy in January 2009, the stock closed at a market price of 12 Canadian cents.

What went wrong? What took this highly successful company from being Ottawa's "bastion of innovation" to the brink of failure? Clearly, the recent economic downturn and some bad luck contributed to its troubles. But stiff global competition, misguided innovation efforts, and a poorly managed portfolio of businesses conspired to weaken Nortel and eventually topple it. Even its tough CEO, Mike Zafirovski, brought in after leading turnaround successes at GE and Motorola, could not overcome the tidal wave of events that brought Nortel down.

An accounting scandal that led to criminal charges, though it did not occur on his watch, demanded a lot of Zafirovski's attention during his first year as CEO. It also required him to invest heavily in regaining shareholder confidence. "The stock became almost tainted merchandise," says Michel R. Sprung, president of Sprung & Co. Investment Counsel. "The investment community certainly had doubts about his ability and the board's to turn the company around."

Meanwhile, Nortel's portfolio of businesses had spread the company's efforts in a lot of directions. Some of the divisions had questionable prospects; others required that Nortel collaborate with strategic partners to be successful. Zafirovski took stock of these problems, but the speed and decisiveness with which he tried to solve them left some thinking he was not acting aggressively enough and possibly even taking the company in the wrong direction. As it grew, Nortel had extended its reach into many businesses—optical networks, wireless infrastructure, enterprise systems, and government. But it was not a leader in any of these arenas. A consensus was emerging that Nortel needed to exit some these businesses. Instead, "Nortel tried to hold on to all of its pieces," says Ronald Gruia, a telecom analyst for consulting firm Frost & Sullivan. Rather than create a manageable program of innovation and growth, Nortel seemed to be coasting.

To make matters worse, when Nortel finally did decide to exit a business, many believe it picked the wrong one. It jettisoned a promising next-generation 3G technology called UMTS because it only had a 5–6 percent market share and opted instead for a technology where it had a 22 percent share and an agreement with Verizon Wireless to keep using it. Other leading wireless providers, however, favored the more advanced UMTS, prompting analyst Gruia to declare, "Getting out of UMTS was a mistake." Zafirovski disagreed: "We looked at how do we redirect R&D spending." In hockey terms, he said Nortel "wanted to go where the puck [was being hit] rather than where the person is."

In the end, Nortel's entire enterprise became unsustainable. Although Chapter 11 bankruptcy will provide it time to reorganize, several analysts believe it is headed for liquidation. Ping Zhao, of investment research firm CreditSights gave Nortel little hope. "They were already out of favor due to their weak finances, but for any of the new projects, they are definitely out of the picture" because of the filing. "I don't think it's going to exist," commented Mark Sue, an analyst with RBC Capital Markets (a unit of the Royal Bank of Canada).

Nortel failed largely because it lost its ability to effectively manage its innovation activities. As large corporations use their early successes to expand into new areas, they often lose focus on the elements of the business that provide them with strategic advantages.

In attractive industries such as telecommunications, there are incentives for competitors to take market share through proactive and aggressive innovation efforts that often topple market leaders. When this happens, whole communities suffer. "Nortel is why Ottawa grew with new, disruptive products," says Brian Hurley, a former Nortel executive who left to found Liquid Computing. If "Nortel has to carve up its parts and sell them off, Ottawa will be a very different place. There won't be the same level of entrepreneurial activity."

In short, Nortel Networks stopped thinking and acting like an entrepreneurial firm. As a result, what had once been a leading innovator and top financial performer lost its focus and fizzled out.

Managing change is one of the most important functions performed by strategic leaders. There are two major avenues through which companies can expand or improve their business—innovation and corporate entrepreneurship. These two activities go hand-in-hand because they both have similar aims. The first is strategic renewal. Innovations help an organization stay fresh and reinvent itself as conditions in the business environment change. This is why managing innovation is such an important strategic implementation issue. The second is the pursuit of venture opportunities. Innovative breakthroughs, as well as new product concepts, evolving technologies, and shifting demand, create opportunities for corporate venturing. In this chapter we will explore these topics—how change and innovation can stimulate strategic renewal and foster corporate entrepreneurship.

> **>LO1**
> The importance of implementing strategies and practices that foster innovation.

Managing Innovation

One of the most important sources of growth opportunities is innovation. **Innovation** involves using new knowledge to transform organizational processes or create commercially viable products and services. The sources of new knowledge may include the latest technology, the results of experiments, creative insights, or competitive information. However it comes about, innovation occurs when new combinations of ideas and information bring about positive change.

> **innovation** the use of new knowledge to transform organizational processes or create commercially viable products and services.

The emphasis on newness is a key point. For example, for a patent application to have any chance of success, one of the most important attributes it must possess is novelty. You can't patent an idea that has been copied. This is a central idea. In fact, the root of the word *innovation* is the Latin *novus,* which means new. Innovation involves introducing or changing to something new.[2]

Among the most important sources of new ideas is new technology. Technology creates new possibilities. Technology provides the raw material that firms use to make innovative products and services. But technology is not the only source of innovations. There can be innovations in human resources, firm infrastructure, marketing, service, or in many other value-adding areas that have little to do with anything "high-tech." Strategy Spotlight 12.1 highlights a simple but effective innovation implemented by Target stores. As the Target example suggests, innovation can take many forms.

Types of Innovation

Although innovations are not always high-tech, changes in technology can be an important source of change and growth. When an innovation is based on a sweeping new technology, it often has a more far-reaching impact. Sometimes even a small innovation can add

strategy spotlight

Target's Low-Tech, High-Value Design Innovation

Sometimes a simple change can make a vast improvement. That's what Target discovered when it adopted a new design for the traditional amber-colored prescription pill bottle. The new design literally flips the old bottle on its head. The base of the bottle is a large cap that uses color-coded rings to help family members distinguish between different containers. The upper part includes a flat surface

that holds wider and easier-to-read labels. "They're much easier to use, and it's a lot easier to read," says Target customer Pat Howell.

Design student Deborah Adler came up with the new bottle after her grandmother Helen accidentally took her grandfather Herman's prescription. She noticed that the small lettering on the curved label of a traditional pill bottle was hard to read. Target, which commissioned a study that found that nearly 60 percent of prescription drugs are taken improperly, welcomed the design innovation. The new bottle, called the ClearRX, has won several design awards and improved Target's prescription drug sales by 14 percent—from $1.4 billion to $1.6 billion in a recent year.

Sources: Target Turns Old Pill Bottle Design on Its Head. 2005. MSNBC.com, www.msnbc.com, April 26; Finn, B. 2006. Target ClearRX Bottle. *Business 2.0*, April: 120; and www.target.com.

value and create competitive advantages. Innovation can and should occur throughout an organization—in every department and all aspects of the value chain.

One distinction that is often used when discussing innovation is between process innovation and product innovation.[3] *Product innovation* refers to efforts to create product designs and applications of technology to develop new products for end users. Recall from Chapter 5 how generic strategies were typically different depending on the stage of the industry life cycle. Product innovations tend to be more common during the earlier stages of an industry's life cycle. Product innovations are also commonly associated with a differentiation strategy. Firms that differentiate by providing customers with new products or services that offer unique features or quality enhancements often engage in product innovation.

Process innovation, by contrast, is typically associated with improving the efficiency of an organizational process, especially manufacturing systems and operations. By drawing on new technologies and an organization's accumulated experience (Chapter 5), firms can often improve materials utilization, shorten cycle time, and increase quality. Process innovations are more likely to occur in the later stages of an industry's life cycle as companies seek ways to remain viable in markets where demand has flattened out and competition is more intense. As a result, process innovations are often associated with overall cost leader strategies, because the aim of many process improvements is to lower the costs of operations.

Another way to view the impact of an innovation is in terms of its degree of innovativeness, which falls somewhere on a continuum that extends from incremental to radical.[4]

radical innovation
an innovation that fundamentally changes existing practices.

- *Radical innovations* produce fundamental changes by evoking major departures from existing practices. These breakthrough innovations usually occur because of technological change. They tend to be highly disruptive and can transform a company or even revolutionize a whole industry. They may lead to products or processes that can be patented, giving a firm a strong competitive advantage. Examples include electricity, the telephone, the transistor, desktop computers, fiber optics, artificial intelligence, and genetically engineered drugs.

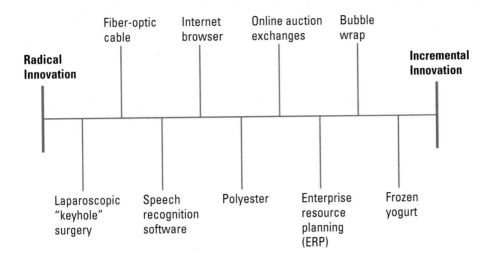

Exhibit 12.1 Continuum of Radical and Incremental Innovations

- *Incremental innovations* enhance existing practices or make small improvements in products and processes. They may represent evolutionary applications within existing paradigms of earlier, more radical innovations. Because they often sustain a company by extending or expanding its product line or manufacturing skills, incremental innovations can be a source of competitive advantage by providing new capabilities that minimize expenses or speed productivity. Examples include frozen food, sports drinks, steel-belted radial tires, electronic bookkeeping, shatterproof glass, and digital telephones.

incremental innovation an innovation that enhances existing practices or makes small improvements in products and processes.

Some innovations are highly radical; others are only slightly incremental. But most innovations fall somewhere between these two extremes (see Exhibit 12.1).

Recently, Harvard Business School Professor Clayton M. Christensen introduced another useful approach to characterize types of innovations.[5] Christensen draws a distinction between sustaining and disruptive innovations. *Sustaining innovations* are those that extend sales in an existing market, usually by enabling new products or services to be sold at higher margins. Such innovations may include either incremental or radical innovations. For example, the Internet was a breakthrough technology that transformed retail selling. But rather than disrupting the activities of catalog companies such as Lands' End and L.L. Bean, the Internet energized their existing business by extending their reach and making their operations more efficient.

By contrast, *disruptive innovations* are those that overturn markets by providing an altogether new approach to meeting customer needs. The features of a disruptive innovation make it somewhat counterintuitive. Disruptive innovations:

- Are technologically simpler and less sophisticated than currently available products or services.
- Appeal to less demanding customers who are seeking more convenient, less expensive solutions.
- Take time to take effect and only become disruptive once they have taken root in a new market or low-end part of an existing market.

Christensen cites Wal-Mart and Southwest Airlines as two disruptive examples. Wal-Mart started with a single store, Southwest with a few flights. But because they both represented major departures from existing practices and tapped into unmet needs, they steadily grew into ventures that appealed to a new category of customers and eventually overturned the status quo. "Instead of sustaining the trajectory of improvement that has been established in a market," says Christensen, a disruptive innovation "disrupts it and redefines it by bringing to the market something that is simpler."[6]

strategy spotlight

Portable Kidney Dialysis Technology: A Disruptive Innovation

In 2001, software engineer Colin Mackay got a rare auto-immune disease that destroyed his kidneys. At age 32, Mackay was faced with spending the rest of his life getting kidney dialysis. The treatment, which involves using a machine to clean the blood when normal kidney functioning has failed, is needed by over 300,000 Americans who suffer from renal failure caused by diseases such as diabetes. Patients who need the treatments check into a dialysis center for a four-hour procedure three times a week. The treatment is exhausting and between treatments, toxins build up, leading to headaches, bloating, and difficulty sleeping. One reason patients have to take treatments in a dialysis center is because the equipment is expensive and bulky—the size of a large refrigerator.

A few years later, Mackay's wife heard about a home dialysis treatment using a portable machine from NxStage Medical in Lawrence, Massachusetts. Just a few months after starting home treatments, his energy returned and the fluid build-up subsided. He was able to play soccer again with his 5- and 7-year-old children. Vanessa Evans, a 36-year-old home treatment patient who also began using the home machine used to get pounding headaches from conventional treatments in a dialysis center. "I never want to go back," declares Evans.

Sources: Christensen, C. M., Grossman, J. H., & Hwang, J. 2008. *The Innovator's Prescription.* New York: McGraw-Hill; Langreth, R. 2008. The Home Cure. *Forbes,* November, 17: 84–85; and, Templeton, D. 2008. Patients Can Learn to Do Time Consuming Dialysis at Home. www.post-gazette.com, January 9.

The NxStage machine, which is the size of a microwave and costs around $21,000, is simple to use. A key improvement over traditional models is that the filtration system uses disposable cartridges. "You slide the cartridge in, close the door, and away you go," says Mackay. Treatments can either occur more frequently for a shorter duration, or overnight while the patient sleeps. Either way, patients who have used it feel better and enjoy a healthier lifestyle.

Even so, the simple and effective home treatment is being used by only 1 percent of dialysis patients. One reason is that Medicare reimbursement rules apply only to dialysis received in dialysis centers. Some centers have bought or leased the NxStage machines so they can run home programs. Also, some doctors, including Stanford University nephrologist Glenn Chertow, have legitimate concerns whether home treatments have been sufficiently tested to claim they are as effective as treatment in dialysis centers. Such resistance has bogged down the process of making the move to a simpler, cheaper, and more convenient approach to dialysis. Yet with rising obesity rates, as many as a million people in the United States are projected to require dialysis in coming years.

In *The Innovator's Prescription,* Clayton Christensen and colleagues contend that "industry leaders have repeatedly lobbied for legislation and regulation that block disruptive approaches from being used anywhere until they are certifiably good enough to be used everywhere. This traps the industry where it began, in the world of ever higher costs. The health care industry needs to be disrupted." According to Christensen, home dialysis systems like the one produced by NxStage, are an example of the type of disruptive innovation that can begin to transform health care in the United States.

The Linux operating system provides a more recent example. When it first became available, few systems administrators used the open-source operating system even though it was free. However, problems with more expensive proprietary operating systems, such as Microsoft Windows, have made Linux increasingly popular. By 2008, the majority of Internet hosting companies and supercomputer operating systems were Linux-based. Today, in addition to being relatively more convenient to use, it is supported by a community of developers. Desktop computers preloaded with the Linux operating system have become increasingly popular.[7]

In the book *The Innovator's Prescription,* Christensen and his co-authors argue that the U.S. health care system is poised for the kind of creative disruption that is needed to stimulate badly needed improvements in health care practices. Strategy Spotlight 12.2 describes a technology that is threatening to disrupt the status quo at Medicare-supported dialysis centers—an easy to use, low-cost kidney dialysis machine that patients can use at home.[8]

Innovation is a force in both the external environment (technology, competition) and also a factor affecting a firm's internal choices (generic strategy, value-adding activities).[9] Nevertheless, innovation can be quite difficult for some firms to manage, especially those that have become comfortable with the status quo.

Challenges of Innovation

Innovation is essential to sustaining competitive advantages. Recall from Chapter 3 that one of the four elements of the Balanced Scorecard is the innovation and learning perspective. The extent and success of a company's innovation efforts are indicators of its overall performance. As management guru Peter Drucker warned, "An established company which, in an age demanding innovation, is not capable of innovation is doomed to decline and extinction."[10] In today's competitive environment, most firms have only one choice: "Innovate or die."

>LO2

The challenges and pitfalls of managing corporate innovation processes.

As with change, however, firms are often resistant to innovation. Only those companies that actively pursue innovation, even though it is often difficult and uncertain, will get a payoff from their innovation efforts. But managing innovation is challenging.[11] As former Pfizer chairman and CEO William Steere puts it: "In some ways, managing innovation is analogous to breaking in a spirited horse. You are never sure of success until you achieve your goal. In the meantime, everyone takes a few lumps."[12]

What is it that makes innovation so difficult? The uncertainty about outcomes is one factor. Companies are often reluctant to invest time and resources into activities with an unknown future. Another factor is that the innovation process involves so many choices. These choices present five dilemmas that companies must wrestle with when pursuing innovation.[13]

- *Seeds versus Weeds.* Most companies have an abundance of innovative ideas. They must decide which of these is most likely to bear fruit—the "Seeds"—and which should be cast aside—the "Weeds." This is complicated by the fact that some innovation projects require a considerable level of investment before a firm can fully evaluate whether they are worth pursuing. Firms need a mechanism with which they can choose among various innovation projects.
- *Experience versus Initiative.* Companies must decide who will lead an innovation project. Senior managers may have experience and credibility but tend to be more risk averse. Midlevel employees, who may be the innovators themselves, may have more enthusiasm because they can see firsthand how an innovation would address specific problems. Firms need to support and reward organizational members who bring new ideas to light.
- *Internal versus External Staffing.* Innovation projects need competent staffs to succeed. People drawn from inside the company may have greater social capital and know the organization's culture and routines. But this knowledge may actually inhibit them from thinking outside the box. Staffing innovation projects with external personnel requires that project managers justify the hiring and spend time recruiting, training, and relationship building. Firms need to streamline and support the process of staffing innovation efforts.
- *Building Capabilities versus Collaborating.* Innovation projects often require new sets of skills. Firms can seek help from other departments and/or partner with other companies that bring resources and experience as well as share costs of development. However, such arrangements can create dependencies and inhibit internal skills development. Further, struggles over who contributed the most or how the benefits of the project are to be allocated may arise. Firms need a mechanism for forging links with outside parties to the innovation process.

- ***Incremental versus Preemptive Launch.*** Companies must manage the timing and scale of new innovation projects. An incremental launch is less risky because it requires fewer resources and serves as a market test. But a launch that is too tentative can undermine the project's credibility. It also opens the door for a competitive response. A large-scale launch requires more resources, but it can effectively preempt a competitive response. Firms need to make funding and management arrangements that allow for projects to hit the ground running and be responsive to market feedback.

These dilemmas highlight why the innovation process can be daunting even for highly successful firms. Next, we consider four steps that firms can take to manage the innovation process.[14]

Defining the Scope of Innovation

Firms must have a means to focus their innovation efforts. By defining the "strategic envelope"—the scope of a firm's innovation efforts—firms ensure that their innovation efforts are not wasted on projects that are outside the firm's domain of interest. Strategic enveloping defines the range of acceptable projects. As Alistair Corbett, an innovation expert with the global consulting firm Bain & Company, recently said, "One man's radical innovation is another man's incremental innovation."[15] A strategic envelope creates a firm-specific view of innovation that defines how a firm can create new knowledge and learn from an innovation initiative even if the project fails. It also gives direction to a firm's innovation efforts, which helps separate seeds from weeds and builds internal capabilities.

One way to determine which projects to work on is to focus on a common technology. Then, innovation efforts across the firm can aim at developing skills and expertise in a given technical area. Another potential focus is on a market theme. Consider how DuPont responded to a growing concern for environmentally sensitive products:

> In the early 1990s, DuPont sought to use its knowledge of plastics to identify products to meet a growing market demand for biodegradable products. It conducted numerous experiments with a biodegradable polyester resin it named Biomax. By trying different applications and formulations demanded by potential customers, the company was finally able to create a product that could be produced economically and had market appeal. Recently, Biomax was certified biodegradable and compostable by the Biodegradable Products Institute, an endorsement that should further boost sales.[16]

Companies must be clear not only about the kinds of innovation they are looking for but also the expected results. Each company needs to develop a set of questions to ask itself about its innovation efforts:

- How much will the innovation initiative cost?
- How likely is it to actually become commercially viable?
- How much value will it add; that is, what will it be worth if it works?
- What will be learned if it does not pan out?

However a firm envisions its innovation goals, it needs to develop a systematic approach to evaluating its results and learning from its innovation initiatives. Viewing innovation from this perspective helps firms manage the process.[17]

Managing the Pace of Innovation

Along with clarifying the scope of an innovation by defining a strategic envelope, firms also need to regulate the pace of innovation. How long will it take for an innovation initiative to realistically come to fruition? The project time line of an incremental innovation may be 6 months to 2 years, whereas a more radical innovation is typically long term—10 years or more.[18] Radical innovations often begin with a long period of exploration in which experimentation makes strict timelines unrealistic. In contrast, firms that are innovating incrementally in order to exploit a window of opportunity may use a milestone approach that is more stringently driven by goals and deadlines. This kind of sensitivity to realistic time frames helps companies separate dilemmas temporally so they are easier to manage.

Time pacing can also be a source of competitive advantage because it helps a company manage transitions and develop an internal rhythm.[19] Time pacing does not mean the company ignores the demands of market timing; instead, companies have a sense of their own internal clock in a way that allows them to thwart competitors by controlling the innovation process.

Not all innovation lends itself to speedy development, however. Radical innovation often involves open-ended experimentation and time-consuming mistakes. The creative aspects of innovation are often difficult to time. When software maker Intuit's new CEO, Steve Bennett, began to turn around that troubled business, he required every department to implement Six Sigma, a quality control management technique that focuses on being responsive to customer needs. Everybody, that is, but the techies.

> "We're not GE, we're not a company where Jack says 'Do it,' and everyone salutes," says Bill Hensler, Intuit's vice president for process excellence. That's because software development, according to many, is more of an art than a science. At the Six Sigma Academy, president of operations Phil Samuel says even companies that have embraced Six Sigma across every other aspect of their organization usually maintain a hands-off policy when it comes to software developers. Techies, it turns out, like to go at their own pace.[20]

Some projects can't be rushed. Companies that hurry up their research efforts or go to market before they are ready can damage their ability to innovate—and their reputation. Thus, managing the pace of innovation can be an important factor in long-term success.

Staffing to Capture Value from Innovation

People are central to the processes of identifying, developing, and commercializing innovations effectively. They need broad sets of skills as well as experience—experience working with teams and experience working on successful innovation projects. To capture value from innovation activities, companies must provide strategic decision makers with staff members who make it possible.

This insight led strategy experts Rita Gunther McGrath and Thomas Keil to research the types of human resource management practices that effective firms use to capture value from their innovation efforts.[21] Four practices are especially important:

- Create innovation teams with experienced players who know what it is like to deal with uncertainty and can help new staff members learn venture management skills.
- Require that employees seeking to advance their career with the organization serve in the new venture group as part of their career climb.
- Once people have experience with the new venture group, transfer them to mainstream management positions where they can use their skills and knowledge to revitalize the company's core business.
- Separate the performance of individuals from the performance of the innovation. Otherwise, strong players may feel stigmatized if the innovation effort they worked on fails.

There are other staffing practices that may sound as if they would benefit a firm's innovation activities but may, in fact, be counterproductive:

- Creating a staff that consists only of strong players whose primary experience is related to the company's core business. This provides too few people to deal with the uncertainty of innovation projects and may cause good ideas to be dismissed because they do not appear to fit with the core business.

Staffing for Innovation Success at Air Products

When it comes to implementing its innovation efforts, Air Products and Chemicals, Inc. (APCI) recognizes the importance of staffing for achieving success. Air Products is a global manufacturer of industrial gases, chemicals, and related equipment. Headquartered in Allentown, Pennsylvania, Air Products has annual sales of $10 billion, manufacturing facilities in over 30 countries, and 22,000 employees worldwide. The company has a strong reputation for effectively embedding innovation into its culture through its unique employee engagement processes.

Ron Pierantozzi, a 30-year veteran of the company and its director of innovation and new product development, says "Innovation is about discipline. . . . It requires

a different type of training, different tools and new approaches to experimentation." To enact this philosophy, Pierantozzi begins with his people. He recruits people with diverse backgrounds and a wide range of expertise including engineers, entrepreneurs, and government officials. It is made clear to those on his innovation teams that they will return to mainstream operations after four years—a fact that most consider a plus since working in the innovation unit usually provides a career boost. He also assures players that there is no stigma associated with a failed venture because experimentation is highly valued.

Innovation teams are created to manage the company's intellectual assets and determine which technologies have the most potential value. A key benefit of this approach has been to more effectively leverage its human resources to achieve innovative outcomes without increasing its R&D expenses. These efforts resulted in an innovation award from APQC (formerly known as the American Productivity and Quality Center) which recognizes companies for exemplary practices that increase productivity.

Sources: Chesbrough, H. 2007. Why Bad Things Happen to Good Technology. *The Wall Street Journal:* April 28–29, R11; Leavitt, P. 2005. Delivering the Difference: Business Process Management at APCI. *APQC,* www.apqc.com; McGrath, R. G. & Keil, T. 2007. The value captor's process: Getting the Most out of Your New Business Ventures. *Harvard Business Review,* May: 128–136; and www.apci.com.

- Creating a staff that consists only of volunteers who want to work on projects they find interesting. Such players are often overzealous about new technologies or overly attached to product concepts, which can lead to poor decisions about which projects to pursue or drop.
- Creating a climate where innovation team members are considered second-class citizens. In companies where achievements are rewarded, the brightest and most ambitious players may avoid innovation projects with uncertain outcomes.

Unless an organization can align its key players into effective new venture teams, it is unlikely to create any differentiating advantages from its innovation efforts.[22] An enlightened approach to staffing a company's innovation efforts provides one of the best ways to ensure that the challenges of innovation will be effectively met. Strategy Spotlight 12.3 describes the approach Air Products and Chemicals, Inc. is using to enhance its innovation efforts.

Collaborating with Innovation Partners

It is rare for any one organization to have all the information it needs to carry an innovation from concept to commercialization. Even a company that is highly competent with its current operations usually needs new capabilities to achieve new results. Innovation partners provide the skills and insights that are needed to make innovation projects succeed.[23]

Innovation partners may come from many sources, including research universities and the federal government. Each year the federal government issues requests for proposals (RFPs) asking private companies for assistance in improving services or finding solutions to public problems. Universities are another type of innovation partner. Chip-maker Intel, for example, has benefited from underwriting substantial amounts of university research.

Rather than hand universities a blank check, Intel bargains for rights to patents that emerge from Intel-sponsored research. The university retains ownership of the patent, but Intel gets royalty-free use of it.[24]

Strategic partnering requires firms to identify their strengths and weaknesses and make choices about which capabilities to leverage, which need further development, and which are outside the firm's current or projected scope of operations.

To choose partners, firms need to ask what competencies they are looking for and what the innovation partner will contribute.[25] These might include knowledge of markets, technology expertise, or contacts with key players in an industry. Innovation partnerships also typically need to specify how the rewards of the innovation will be shared and who will own the intellectual property that is developed.[26]

Innovation efforts that involve multiple partners and the speed and ease with which partners can network and collaborate are changing the way innovation is conducted.[27] Strategy Spotlight 12.4 outlines the efforts of three major corporations that are using crowdsourcing technologies to collaborate with customers to enhance their innovation efforts.

Successful innovation involves a companywide commitment because the results of innovation affect every part of the organization. Innovation also requires an entrepreneurial spirit and skill set to be effective. Few companies have a more exemplary reputation than W. L. Gore. Exhibit 12.2 highlights the policies that help make Gore an innovation leader. One of the most important ways that companies improve and grow is when innovation is put to the task of creating new corporate ventures.

Corporate Entrepreneurship

Corporate entrepreneurship (CE) has two primary aims: the pursuit of new venture opportunities and strategic renewal.[28] The innovation process keeps firms alert by exposing them to new technologies, making them aware of marketplace trends, and helping them evaluate new possibilities. CE uses the fruits of the innovation process to help firms build new sources of competitive advantage and renew their value propositions. Just as the innovation process helps firms to make positive improvements, corporate entrepreneurship helps firms identify opportunities and launch new ventures. Strategy Spotlight 12.5 addresses how Danish toymaker Lego effectively used entrepreneurial initiatives to strategically renew its aging business.

Corporate new venture creation was labeled "intrapreneuring" by Gifford Pinchot because it refers to building entrepreneurial businesses within existing corporations.[29] However, to engage in corporate entrepreneurship that yields above-average returns and contributes to sustainable advantages, it must be done effectively. In this section we will examine the sources of entrepreneurial activity within established firms and the methods large corporations use to stimulate entrepreneurial behavior.

In a typical corporation, what determines how entrepreneurial projects will be pursued? That depends on many factors, including:

- Corporate culture.
- Leadership.
- Structural features that guide and constrain action.
- Organizational systems that foster learning and manage rewards.

All of the factors that influence the strategy implementation process will also shape how corporations engage in internal venturing.

Other factors will also affect how entrepreneurial ventures will be pursued.

- The use of teams in strategic decision making.
- Whether the company is product or service oriented.

corporate entrepreneurship
the creation of new value for a corporation, through investments that create either new sources of competitive advantage or renewal of the value proposition.

Web 2.0 Collaboration: Using Social Networking to Enhance Innovation

Throughout this text, we have shared examples of companies that are using crowdsourcing techniques to connect with customers and other stakeholders. One of the key reasons to use Web 2.0 capabilities, that is, technologies that make online collaboration and social networking possible, is to gather innovative insights from people outside the company. "The idea that the users of products are often best equipped to innovate is something many entrepreneurs know intuitively," says Max Chafkin, author of *The Customer Is the Company*. Each of the major corporations below, which are known for their innovative activities, are beginning to using crowdsourcing to enhance their entrepreneurial efforts.

Dell's IdeaStorm

One of the first social networking sites launched by a major corporation, IdeaStorm now plays an important role in driving business innovation at Dell. A key aim of the website is to help Dell learn about the latest innovations and spot business opportunities before they go mainstream. The company has implemented several of the 8,000 suggestions it has received since its launch in 2007, including offering a line of computers preloaded with Linux software. Users of the site can see the status of suggestions—"under review," "partially implemented," and so forth. Dell anticipates an even larger role for IdeaStorm in the future. Founder Michael Dell envisions it as a beginning step in "co-creation of products.... a company this size is not going to be about a couple of people coming with ideas. It's going to be about millions of people and harnessing the power of those ideas." Currently, Dell is considering using the IdeaStorm concept and technology to help it build a partner network consisting of IT consultants, service providers, and value-added resellers to help it reinvigorate sales and provide support in underserved markets.

General Electric's SupportCentral

GE has focused its networking efforts on internal customers. Created entirely by GE engineers, SupportCentral is a highly sophisticated enterprise collaboration system that allows GE workers to connect with one another using the network model that best suits how they work—some focused on people, others on documents, discussion groups, and so on. The searchable system offers a variety of features, such as applications, data, directories, and expert networks, designed to help workers communicate more broadly and get answers faster. Because it has replaced hundreds of separate websites and attracts 5 to 10 innovative suggestions a day, it has cut costs and saved GE "millions" according to SupportCentral manager Dr. Sukh Grewal. The system has 400,000 global users in 6,000 locations around the world, supports over 20 languages, and gets 25 million Web hits a day. Users have created 50,000 communities and over 100,000 experts are available to answer questions and manage information. According to Chief Information Officer Gary Reiner, GE has "gone out of our way to call it professional networking rather than social networking." Whatever it's called, SupportCentral is an innovation that "is becoming sort of a heartbeat of the company," Reiner admits, and is increasingly vital to GE's success.

Starbucks' MyStarbucksIdea.com

At its 2008 annual meeting, Starbucks CEO Howard Schultz stated, "We somehow evolved from a culture of entrepreneurship, creativity, and innovation to a culture of, in a way, mediocrity and bureaucracy." Schultz returned to the helm of Starbucks after an eight-year absence to help lead it out of a financial slump. He then announced a series of initiatives designed to counter that trend and renew the spirit of innovation at Starbucks. One of these was its new online community, MyStarbucksIdea.com, a website that encourages Starbucks customers to make suggestions and interact with employees. Within about four months of its launch, the site had received over 130,000 separate suggestions. One of the most frequent requests was healthier food options, and the protein-enriched Vivanno drinks launched in mid-2008 are seen as a response to that request—Starbucks' first innovative drink product since the Cinnamon Dolce Latte in 2006. Other ideas, ranging from how to have shorter lines (by, for one thing, encoding credit cards with standing orders that could be scanned as soon as a customer walks in) to suggestions for how to more aggressively participate in recycling efforts, are being seriously evaluated.

Even though these initiatives have been well-received, they are new and it is not clear what the payoff will be. For example, IdeaStorm has been criticized for being little more than an effort to make Dell look good to a small group of users rather than a serious attempt to drive innovation. Others, however, disagree, including MIT professor Eric von Hippel, an expert in innovation management. In his view, crowdsourcing approaches *(continued)*

(continued) to innovation are becoming a viable substitute for in-house R&D. "This is really the biggest paradigm shift in innovation since the Industrial Revolution," says von Hippel. "For a couple hundred years or so, manufacturers have been really imperfect at understanding people's needs. Now people get to decide what they want for themselves."

Sources: Colvin, G. 2008. Information Worth Billions. www.cnnmoney.com, July 21; Jarvis, J. 2008. One Shot of Coffee and Two Shots at Changing the Way Starbucks Is Run. www.guardian.co.uk, April 21; Kaufman, W. 2008. Crowd-sourcing Turns Business on Its Head. www.npr.com, August 20; Marks, O. 2008. GE's Enterprise Collaboration Backbone. www.zdnet.com, July 18, np.; Panettieri, J. 2008. Dell's IdeaStorm: Social Networking Driving Business Innovation. www.seekingalpha.com, April 1; Stone, B. 2008. Starbucks Plans Return to Its Roots. www.nytimes.com, March 20; and www.wikipedia.org.

crowdsourcing

Exhibit 12.2
W. L. Gore's New Rules for Fostering Innovation

Rule	Implications
The power of small teams	Gore believes that small teams promote familiarity and autonomy. Even its manufacturing plants are capped at just 200 people. That way everyone can get to know one another on a first-name basis and work together with minimal rules. This also helps to cultivate "an environment where creativity can flourish," according to CEO Chuck Carroll.
No ranks, no titles, no bosses	Because Gore believes in maximizing individual potential, employees, dubbed "associates," decide for themselves what new commitments to take on. Associates have "sponsors," rather than bosses, and there are no standardized job descriptions or categories. Everyone is supposed to take on a unique role. Committees of co-workers evaluate each team member's contribution and decide on compensation.
Take the long view	Although impatient about the status quo, Gore exhibits great patience with the time—often years, sometimes decades—it takes to nurture and develop breakthrough products and bring them to market.
Make time for face time	Gore avoids the traditional hierarchical chain of command, opting instead for a team-based environment that fosters personal initiative. Gore also discourages memos and e-mail and promotes direct, person-to-person communication among all associates—anyone in the company can talk to anyone else.
Lead by leading	Associates are encouraged to spend about 10 percent of their time pursuing speculative new ideas. Anyone is free to champion products, as long as they have the passion and ideas to attract followers. Many of Gore's breakthroughs started with one person acting on his or her own initiative and developed as colleagues helped in their spare time.
Celebrate failure	When a project doesn't work out and the team decides to kill it, they celebrate just as they would if it had been a success—with some beer and maybe a glass of champagne. Rather than condemning failure, Gore figures that celebrating it encourages experimentation and risk taking.

Source: Deutschman, A. 2004. The Fabric of Creativity. *Fast Company,* 89: 54–62; Levering, R. & Moskowitz, M. 2006. The 100 Best Companies to Work For. *Fortune,* www.fortune.com, January; and www.gore.com.

Entrepreneurial Initiatives Help Reinvent the Lego Group

"Toy of the Century" is the lofty label given to Lego's iconic plastic bricks by *Fortune* magazine in 1999. With such impressive statistics as "seven boxes of Lego are sold every second" and "19 billion components are produced every year," the Denmark-based Lego Group would appear to be a huge success by any standards.

But 1999 was followed by a dark period for Lego, as electronic games and digital products increasingly captured children's attention. Lego took several steps to try to bolster its sinking business, including offering branded products such as books and watches and launching a Lego theme park. But for six years, the company continued to report heavy losses, including a $300 million loss in 2004. The founding family heir, CEO Kjeld Kirk Kristiansen, injected millions of his own money into the company to prevent bankruptcy and eventually resigned.

He was replaced by 35-year old Jorgen Vig Knudstrop, who made drastic changes at the company, including outsourcing manufacturing of the bricks to the Czech Republic and cutting nearly 2,000 jobs. The cost savings were matched with entrepreneurial initiatives that challenged the core of the company's business culture. It launched a series of interactive games, including a highly successful *Star Wars* computer game. But the traditional company, whose mission had always included "nurturing the child," found it difficult to depart from its image as a producer of playful, constructive toys. Referring to *Star Wars* creator George Lucas, play expert and 22-year Lego veteran Niels Sandal Jakobsen recalls, "getting the license from Lucas was nothing compared to the internal struggles over having the word *war* appear under the Lego brand." Nevertheless, Knudstrop persisted and more interactive games

were introduced, including a *Star Wars* game for the Wii and an online *Mars Mission* game.

Crowdsourcing contributed to one of Lego's digital product successes: Mindstorms, a set of programmable bricks with electronic motors, sensors, and Lego Technic pieces (such as gears, axles, and beams). Within weeks of Mindstorms' release, user groups had started reverse engineering the software to make improvements. At first, Lego threatened to sue the tinkerers, but quickly realized that might be a mistake. The company changed course, even including a "right to hack" as part of the Mindstorms software licensing agreement. The community of users expanded, and many of them now participate in the annual Lego World convention in the Netherlands. One of them showed up at a recent convention with a fully operational pinball machine made from 20,000 Lego bricks and 13 programmable microchips. And when Lego began design on the next version of Mindstorms, it took on a group of the most dedicated enthusiasts as de facto employees during the 11-month development cycle. Such innovations are indicative of the Lego Group's new entrepreneurial perspective.

The fusion of mass customization and peer production has extended beyond the Mindstorms project. Its new Lego Factory system gives customers access to a virtual warehouse where they can design their own custom Lego sets. According to Mark Hansen, director of Lego Interactive Experiences, "With Lego Factory we can expand beyond our one hundred in-house product designers to marvel at the creativity of more than three hundred thousand designers worldwide."

The entrepreneurial spirit that animates the revitalized Lego Group has paid off. Despite a downturn in toy sales worldwide, Lego reported a 32 percent increase in profits in 2008. Included in *Fast Company*'s 2009 list of the world's 50 most innovative companies, Lego has made a remarkable rebound. The reason, according to CEO Knudstrop, is because, "We're about many more things than just a set of bricks and a box. It's about everyday people getting incremental new ideas."

Sources: At 50, Lego Still Going Strong. 2008. www.abc.net.au, January 29; 2009. *Fast Company* Staff. #41 Lego. *Fast Company,* March: 93; Schwartz, N. D. 2006. One Brick at a Time. www.cnnmoney.com, June 8; Tapscott, D. & Williams, A. D. 2006. *Wikinomics.* New York: Penguin; and www.wikipedia.org.

- Whether its innovation efforts are aimed at product or process improvements.
- The extent to which it is high-tech or low-tech.

Because these factors are different in every organization, some companies may be more involved than others in identifying and developing new venture opportunities.[30] These factors will also influence the nature of the CE process.

Successful CE typically requires firms to reach beyond their current operations and markets in the pursuit of new opportunities. It is often the breakthrough opportunities that provide the greatest returns. Such strategies are not without risks, however. In the sections that follow, we will address some of the strategic choice and implementation issues that influence the success or failure of CE activities.

Two distinct approaches to corporate venturing are found among firms that pursue entrepreneurial aims. The first is *focused* corporate venturing, in which CE activities are isolated from a firm's existing operations and worked on by independent work units. The second approach is *dispersed,* in which all parts of the organization and every organization member are engaged in intrapreneurial activities.

Focused Approaches to Corporate Entrepreneurship

>LO3
How corporations use new venture teams, business incubators, and product champions to create an internal environment and culture that promote entrepreneurial development.

Firms using a focused approach typically separate the corporate venturing activity from the other ongoing operations of the firm. CE is usually the domain of autonomous work groups that pursue entrepreneurial aims independent of the rest of the firm. The advantage of this approach is that it frees entrepreneurial team members to think and act without the constraints imposed by existing organizational norms and routines. This independence is often necessary for the kind of open-minded creativity that leads to strategic breakthroughs. The disadvantage is that, because of their isolation from the corporate mainstream, the work groups that concentrate on internal ventures may fail to obtain the resources or support needed to carry an entrepreneurial project through to completion. Two forms—new venture groups (NVGs) and business incubators—are among the most common types of focused approaches.

New Venture Groups (NVGs) Corporations often form NVGs whose goal is to identify, evaluate, and cultivate venture opportunities. These groups typically function as semi-autonomous units with little formal structure. The **new venture group** may simply be a committee that reports to the president on potential new ventures. Or it may be organized as a corporate division with its own staff and budget. The aims of the NVG may be open-ended in terms of what ventures it may consider. Alternatively, some corporations use them to promote concentrated effort on a specific problem. In both cases, they usually have a substantial amount of freedom to take risks and a supply of resources to do it with.[31]

new venture group a group of individuals, or a division within a corporation, that identifies, evaluates, and cultivates venture opportunities.

NVGs usually have a larger mandate than a typical R&D department. Their involvement extends beyond innovation and experimentation to coordinating with other corporate divisions, identifying potential venture partners, gathering resources, and actually launching the venture.

Business Incubators The term *incubator* was originally used to describe a device in which eggs are hatched. **Business incubators** are designed to "hatch" new businesses. They are a type of corporate NVG with a somewhat more specialized purpose—to support and nurture fledgling entrepreneurial ventures until they can thrive on their own as stand-alone businesses. Corporations use incubators as a way to grow businesses identified by the NVG. Although they often receive support from many parts of the corporation, they still operate independently until they are strong enough to go it alone. Depending on the type of business, they are either integrated into an existing corporate division or continue to operate as a subsidiary of the parent firm.

business incubator a corporate new venture group that supports and nurtures fledgling entrepreneurial ventures until they can thrive on their own as stand-alone businesses.

Incubators typically provide some or all of the following five functions.[32]

- *Funding.* Includes capital investments as well as in-kind investments and loans.
- *Physical space.* Incubators in which several start-ups share space often provide fertile ground for new ideas and collaboration.

- **Business services.** Along with office space, young ventures need basic services and infrastructure; may include anything from phone systems and computer networks to public relations and personnel management.
- **Mentoring.** Senior executives and skilled technical personnel often provide coaching and experience-based advice.
- **Networking.** Contact with other parts of the firm and external resources such as suppliers, industry experts, and potential customers facilitates problem solving and knowledge sharing.

The risks associated with incubating ventures should not be overlooked. Companies have at times spent millions on new ideas with very little to show for it. Major corporations such as Lucent, British Airways, and Hewlett-Packard deactivated their incubators and scaled back new venture portfolios after experiencing major declines in value during recent financial downturns.[33]

To encourage entrepreneurship, corporations sometimes need to do more than create independent work groups or venture incubators to generate new enterprises. In some firms, the entrepreneurial spirit is spread throughout the organization.

Dispersed Approaches to Corporate Entrepreneurship

The second type of CE is dispersed. For some companies, a dedication to the principles and practices of entrepreneurship is spread throughout the organization. One advantage of this approach is that organizational members don't have to be reminded to think entrepreneurially or be willing to change. The ability to change is considered to be a core capability. This leads to a second advantage: Because of the firm's entrepreneurial reputation, stakeholders such as vendors, customers, or alliance partners can bring new ideas or venture opportunities to anyone in the organization and expect them to be well-received. Such opportunities make it possible for the firm to stay ahead of the competition. However, there are disadvantages as well. Firms that are overzealous about CE sometimes feel they must change for the sake of change, causing them to lose vital competencies or spend heavily on R&D and innovation to the detriment of the bottom line. Two related aspects of dispersed entrepreneurship include entrepreneurial cultures that have an overarching commitment to CE activities and the use of product champions in promoting entrepreneurial behaviors.

Entrepreneurial Culture   In some large corporations, the corporate culture embodies the spirit of entrepreneurship. A culture of entrepreneurship is one in which the search for venture opportunities permeates every part of the organization. The key to creating value successfully is viewing every value-chain activity as a source of competitive advantage. The effect of CE on a firm's strategic success is strongest when it animates all parts of an organization. It is found in companies where the strategic leaders and the culture together generate a strong impetus to innovate, take risks, and seek out new venture opportunities.[34]

In companies with an entrepreneurial culture, everyone in the organization is attuned to opportunities to help create new businesses. Many such firms use a top-down approach to stimulate entrepreneurial activity. The top leaders of the organization support programs and incentives that foster a climate of entrepreneurship. Many of the best ideas for new corporate ventures, however, come from the bottom up. Here's what Martin Sorrell, CEO of the WPP Group, a London-based global communication services group, says about drawing on the talents of lower-level employees:

> The people at the so-called bottom of an organization know more about what's going on than the people at the top. The people in the trenches are the ones in the best position to make critical decisions. It's up to the leaders to give those people the freedom and the resources they need.[35]

Best Buy's Spirit of Innovation

Best Buy remains the number one electronics retailer despite intense competition from competitors such as rival Wal-Mart (see Strategy Spotlight 8.11). A major key to its success is the climate of innovation that permeates the company. According to Shari Ballard, Best Buy's vice president for human resources, "If you're going to turn on an innovation engine, a lot depends on whether managers listen for the brilliance in their employees' ideas." Here are a couple of Best Buy's recent innovation successes:

- Project manager Nate Omann noticed that a high number of flat-panel TVs were being damaged during home delivery. It was making customers angry and running up replacement costs. So Nate came up with the "TV taco"—a reusable device that fits around TVs to better protect them during transit. It is expected to save the company millions of dollars.

- *Sound and Vision Magazine* awarded Best Buy the Retail Innovation Award in 2005 for its Magnolia Home Theatre store-within-a-store concept. This innovation offers the kind of services usually found only at small specialty stores—quiet demo rooms, comfortable seating, a highly knowledgeable staff, and top quality brands.

● Best Buy is well-known as an innovative electronics retailer.

More radical than its store innovations, Best Buy is also winning kudos for innovative human resources management. It implemented a program, called ROWE for "results-only work environment," designed to dramatically increase employee autonomy by focusing on output instead of hours worked. The program has been so successful, in fact, that Best Buy formed a subsidiary named CultureRx to implement similar programs at other compa-

nies. What it implements, however, is not the usual flextime, telecommuting program. ROWE co-founders Jody Thompson and Cali Ressler consider those programs, which still focus on hours worked, to be overly bureaucratic. ROWE employees, by contrast, are required to put in only as much time as it actually takes to do their work.

Is it working? In 2006, Best Buy's procurement department increased savings by 50 percent over the previous year after it entered the ROWE program. In the online ordering division, orders processed by people not working in the office were as much as 18 percent higher than those working in the office. Across the company, voluntary turnover has decreased significantly and ROWE participants report that they feel 35 percent more productive. As a result, Workforce Management gave Best Buy and CultureRx its 2007 Optimas Award for innovation.

Sources: Anonymous. 2006. 2005 Editor's Choice Awards: Best Buy. *Sound and Vision Magazine,* www.soundandvision.mag, February; Ballard, S. 2006. Fast Talk: Best Brains, *Fast Company,* November: 66; Conlin, M. 2006. Smashing the Clock. *BusinessWeek,* www.businessweek.com, December 11; and Frauenheim, E. 2007. Best Buy & CultureRx: Optimas Award Winner for Innovation, *Workforce Management,* www.workforce.com, March 26.

An entrepreneurial culture is one in which change and renewal are on everybody's mind. Sony, 3M, Intel, and Cisco are among the corporations best known for their corporate venturing activities. Many fast-growing young corporations also attribute much of their success to an entrepreneurial culture. Best Buy's CEO Brad Anderson considers an entrepreneurial spirit to be essential for success in retailing. Strategy Spotlight 12.6 describes the kinds of activities that promote an entrepreneurial culture at Best Buy.

Product Champions   CE does not always involve making large investments in start-ups or establishing incubators to spawn new divisions. Often, innovative ideas emerge in the normal course of business and are brought forth and become part of the way of doing business. Entrepreneurial champions are often needed to take charge of internally generated ventures. **Product** (or project) **champions** are those individuals working within a corporation who bring entrepreneurial ideas forward, identify what kind of market exists for the product or service, find resources to support the venture, and promote the venture concept to upper management.[36]

product champion
an individual working within a corporation who brings entrepreneurial ideas forward, identifies what kind of market exists for the product or service, finds resources to support the venture, and promotes the venture concept to upper management.

When lower-level employees identify a product idea or novel solution, they will take it to their supervisor or someone in authority. A new idea that is generated in a technology lab may be introduced to others by its inventor. If the idea has merit, it gains support and builds momentum across the organization.[37] Even though the corporation may not be looking for new ideas or have a program for cultivating internal ventures, the independent behaviors of a few organizational members can have important strategic consequences.

No matter how an entrepreneurial idea comes to light, however, a new venture concept must pass through two critical stages or it may never get off the ground:

1. *Project definition.* An opportunity has to be justified in terms of its attractiveness in the marketplace and how well it fits with the corporation's other strategic objectives.
2. *Project impetus.* For a project to gain impetus, its strategic and economic impact must be supported by senior managers who have experience with similar projects. It then becomes an embryonic business with its own organization and budget.

For a project to advance through these stages of definition and impetus, a product champion is often needed to generate support and encouragement. Champions are especially important during the time after a new project has been defined but before it gains momentum. They form a link between the definition and impetus stages of internal development, which they do by procuring resources and stimulating interest for the product among potential customers.[38] Often, they must work quietly and alone. Consider the example of Ken Kutaragi, the Sony engineer who championed the PlayStation.

> Even though Sony had made the processor that powered the first Nintendo video games, no one at Sony in the mid-1980s saw any future in such products. "It was a kind of snobbery," Kutaragi recalled. "For Sony people, the Nintendo product would have been very embarrassing to make because it was only a toy." But Kutaragi was convinced he could make a better product. He began working secretly on a video game. Kutaragi said, "I realized that if it was visible, it would be killed." He quietly began enlisting the support of senior executives, such as the head of R&D. He made a case that Sony could use his project to develop capabilities in digital technologies that would be important in the future. It was not until 1994, after years of "underground" development and quiet building of support, that Sony introduced the PlayStation. By the year 2000, Sony had sold 55 million of them, and Kutaragi became CEO of Sony Computer Entertainment. By 2005, Kutagari was Sony's Chief Operating Officer, and was supervising efforts to launch PS3, the next generation version of the market-leading PlayStation video game console.[39]

Product champions play an important entrepreneurial role in a corporate setting by encouraging others to take a chance on promising new ideas.[40]

Measuring the Success of Corporate Entrepreneurship Activities

At this point in the discussion, it is reasonable to ask whether CE is successful. Corporate venturing, like the innovation process, usually requires a tremendous effort. Is it worth it? We consider factors that corporations need to take into consideration when evaluating the success of CE programs. We also examine techniques that companies can use to limit the expense of venturing or to cut their losses when CE initiatives appear doomed.

Comparing Strategic and Financial CE Goals   Not all corporate venturing efforts are financially rewarding. In terms of financial performance, slightly more than 50 percent of corporate venturing efforts reach profitability (measured by ROI) within six years of their launch.[41] If this were the only criterion for success, it would seem to be a rather poor return. On the one hand, these results should be expected, because CE is riskier than other investments such as expanding ongoing operations. On the other hand, corporations expect a higher return from corporate venturing projects than from normal operations. Thus, in terms of the risk–return trade-off, it seems that CE often falls short of expectations.[42]

>LO4
How corporate entrepreneurship achieves both financial goals and strategic goals.

There are several other important criteria, however, for judging the success of a corporate venture initiative. Most CE programs have strategic goals. The strategic reasons for undertaking a corporate venture include strengthening competitive position, entering into new markets, expanding capabilities by learning and acquiring new knowledge, and building the corporation's base of resources and experience. Three questions should be used to assess the effectiveness of a corporation's venturing initiatives:[43]

1. *Are the products or services offered by the venture accepted in the marketplace?* Is the venture considered to be a market success? If so, the financial returns are likely to be satisfactory. The venture may also open doors into other markets and suggest avenues for other venture projects.
2. *Are the contributions of the venture to the corporation's internal competencies and experience valuable?* Does the venture add to the worth of the firm internally? If so, strategic goals such as leveraging existing assets, building new knowledge, and enhancing firm capabilities are likely to be met.
3. *Is the venture able to sustain its basis of competitive advantage?* Does the value proposition offered by the venture insulate it from competitive attack? If so, it is likely to place the corporation in a stronger position relative to competitors and provide a base from which to build other advantages.

These criteria include both strategic and financial goals of CE. Another way to evaluate a corporate venture is in terms of the four criteria from the Balanced Scorecard (Chapter 3). In a successful venture, not only are financial and market acceptance (customer) goals met but so are the internal business and innovation and learning goals. Thus, when assessing the success of corporate venturing, it is important to look beyond simple financial returns and consider a well-rounded set of criteria.[44]

Exit Champions   Although a culture of championing venture projects is advantageous for stimulating an ongoing stream of entrepreneurial initiatives, many—in fact, most—of the ideas will not work out. At some point in the process, a majority of initiatives will be abandoned. Sometimes, however, companies wait too long to terminate a new venture and do so only after large sums of resources are used up or, worse, result in a marketplace failure. Motorola's costly global satellite telecom project known as Iridium provides a useful illustration. Even though problems with the project existed during the lengthy development process, Motorola refused to pull the plug. Only after investing $5 billion and years of effort was the project abandoned.[45]

One way to avoid these costly and discouraging defeats is to support a key role in the CE process: **exit champions.** In contrast to product champions and other entrepreneurial enthusiasts within the corporation, exit champions are willing to question the viability of a venture project.[46] By demanding hard evidence and challenging the belief system that is carrying an idea forward, exit champions hold the line on ventures that appear shaky.

Both product champions and exit champions must be willing to energetically stand up for what they believe. Both put their reputations on the line. But they also differ in important

exit champion an individual working within a corporation who is willing to question the viability of a venture project by demanding hard evidence of venture success and challenging the belief system that carries a venture forward.

ways.[47] Product champions deal in uncertainty and ambiguity. Exit champions reduce ambiguity by gathering hard data and developing a strong case for why a project should be killed. Product champions are often thought to be willing to violate procedures and operate outside normal channels. Exit champions often have to reinstate procedures and re-assert the decision-making criteria that are supposed to guide venture decisions. Whereas product champions often emerge as heroes, exit champions run the risk of losing status by opposing popular projects.

The role of exit champion may seem unappealing. But it is one that could save a corporation both financially and in terms of its reputation in the marketplace. It is especially important because one measure of the success of a firm's CE efforts is the extent to which it knows when to cut its losses and move on.

Real Options Analysis: A Useful Tool

>LO5
The benefits and potential drawbacks of real options analysis in making resource deployment decisions in corporate entrepreneurship contexts.

One way firms can minimize failure and avoid losses from pursuing faulty ideas is to apply the logic of real options. **Real options analysis** (ROA) is an investment analysis tool from the field of finance. It has been slowly, but increasingly, adopted by consultants and executives to support strategic decision making in firms. What does ROA consist of and how can it be appropriately applied to the investments required to initiate strategic decisions? To understand *real* options it is first necessary to have a basic understanding of what *options* are.

Options exist when the owner of the option has the right but not the obligation to engage in certain types of transactions. The most common are stock options. A stock option grants the holder the right to buy (call option) or sell (put option) shares of the stock at a fixed price (strike price) at some time in the future.[48] The investment to be made immediately is small, whereas the investment to be made in the future is generally larger. An option to buy a rapidly rising stock currently priced at $50 might cost as little as $.50.[49] Owners of such a stock option have limited their losses to $.50 per share, while the upside potential is unlimited. This aspect of options is attractive, because options offer the prospect of high gains with relatively small up-front investments that represent limited losses.

real options analysis an investment analysis tool that looks at an investment or activity as a series of sequential steps, and for each step the investor has the option of (a) investing additional funds to grow or accelerate, (b) delaying, (c) shrinking the scale of, or (d) abandoning the activity.

The phrase "real options" applies to situations where options theory and valuation techniques are applied to real assets or physical things as opposed to financial assets. Applied to entrepreneurship, real options suggest a path that companies can use to manage the uncertainty associated with launching new ventures. Some of the most common applications of real options are with property and insurance. A real estate option grants the holder the right to buy or sell a piece of property at an established price some time in the future. The actual market price of the property may rise above the established (or strike) price—or the market value may sink below the strike price. If the price of the property goes up, the owner of the option is likely to buy it. If the market value of the property drops below the strike price, the option holder is unlikely to execute the purchase. In the latter circumstance, the option holder has limited his or her loss to the cost of the option, but during the life of the option retains the right to participate in whatever the upside potential might be.

Applications of Real Options Analysis to Strategic Decisions

The concept of options can also be applied to strategic decisions where management has flexibility. Situations arise where management must decide whether to invest additional funds to grow or accelerate the activity, perhaps delay in order to learn more, shrink the scale of the activity, or even abandon it. Decisions to invest in new ventures or other business activities such as R&D, motion pictures, exploration and production of oil wells, and the opening and closing of copper mines often have this flexibility.[50] Important issues to note are:

- ROA is appropriate to use when investments can be staged; a smaller investment up front can be followed by subsequent investments. Real options can be applied to an investment decision that gives the company the right, but not the obligation, to make follow-on investments.
- Strategic decision makers have "tollgates," or key points at which they can decide whether to continue, delay, or abandon the project. Executives have flexibility. There are opportunities to make other go or no-go decisions associated with each phase.
- It is expected that there will be increased knowledge about outcomes at the time of the next investment and that additional knowledge will help inform the decision makers about whether to make additional investments (i.e., whether the option is in the money or out of the money).

Many strategic decisions have the characteristic of containing a series of options. The phenomenon is called "embedded options," a series of investments in which at each stage of the investment there is a go/no–go decision. Consider the real options logic that Johnson Controls, a maker of car seats, instrument panels, and interior control systems uses to advance or eliminate entrepreneurial ideas.[51] Johnson options each new innovative idea by making a small investment in it. To decide whether to exercise an option, the idea must continue to prove itself at each stage of development. Here's how Jim Geschke, vice president and general manager of electronics integration at Johnson, describes the process:

> Think of Johnson as an innovation machine. The front end has a robust series of gates that each idea must pass through. Early on, we'll have many ideas and spend a little money on each of them. As they get more fleshed out, the ideas go through a gate where a go or no-go decision is made. A lot of ideas get filtered out, so there are far fewer items, and the spending on each goes up. . . . Several months later each idea will face another gate. If it passes, that means it's a serious idea that we are going to develop. Then the spending goes way up, and the number of ideas goes way down. By the time you reach the final gate, you need to have a credible business case in order to be accepted. At a certain point in the development process, we take our idea to customers and ask them what they think. Sometimes they say, "That's a terrible idea. Forget it." Other times they say, "That's fabulous. I want a million of them."

This process of evaluating ideas by separating winning ideas from losing ones in a way that keeps investments low has helped Johnson Controls grow its revenues to over $34 billion a year. Using real options logic to advance the development process is a key way that firms reduce uncertainty and minimize innovation-related failures.[52] Strategy Spotlight 12.7 provides an example of a pharmaceutical company that used ROA to guide its decision-making process.

Potential Pitfalls of Real Options Analysis

Despite the many benefits that can be gained from using ROA, managers must be aware of its potential limitations or pitfalls. Below we will address three major issues.[53]

Agency Theory and the Back-Solver Dilemma Let's assume that companies adopting a real-options perspective invest heavily in training and that their people understand how to effectively estimate variance—the amount of dispersion or range that is estimated for potential outcomes. Such training can help them use ROA. However, it does not solve another inherent problem: managers may have an incentive and the know-how to "game the system." Most electronic spreadsheets permit users to simply back-solve any

Using Real Options Analysis to Evaluate a Pharmaceutical Venture

Pharmaceutical companies often use real options analysis in evaluating decisions about whether to invest in new R&D ventures. Developing new pharmaceutical products requires at least four stages of investments: basic research to yield new compounds and three FDA-mandated phases of clinical trials. Generally, each phase is more expensive to undertake than the previous phase. However, as each phase unfolds, management knows more about the underlying drug and its many sources of uncertainty, including the technical difficulties it faces and external market conditions that could affect sales. With this information, management can make the decision to invest more, speed up the process, delay the start of the next phase, or even abandon the R&D project.

Consider, for example, a privately held biotechnology firm that used real options analysis to evaluate whether to invest in a veterinary pharmaceutical product. The firm had developed a unique technology for introducing the coat protein of a particular virus into animal feedstocks. Ingesting the coat protein generated an immune response, thus protecting the animal from the virus. The firm was at

Sources: Janney, J. J. & Dess, G. G. 2004. Can Real-Options Analysis Improve Decision Making? Promises and Pitfalls. *Academy of Management Executive*, 18(4): 60–75; Stockley, R. L., Jr., Curtis, S., Jafari, J., & Tibbs, K. 2003. The Options Value of an Early-Stage Biotechnology Investment. *Journal of Applied Finance*, 15(2): 44–55; and Triantis, A., et al. 2003. University of Maryland Roundtable on Real Options and Corporate Practice. *Journal of Applied Corporate Finance*, 15(2): 8–23.

the beginning of the preclinical trials stage, the first of a series of tests required by FDA regulation and conducted through the FDA subagency called the Center for Veterinary Medicine.

The company expected the stage to take 18 months and cost $2 million. Long-standing experience indicated that 95 percent of new drug investigations are abandoned during this phase. Abandonment rates in subsequent stages would decrease somewhat, but costs would rise, with a total outflow from 2002 through its anticipated launch in 2007 of at least $18.5 million. The company's best estimate of the market from 2007 through 2017 was about $85 million per year. Still, there was a possibility the product would gain as much as a 50 percent market share. In short, there was huge potential, but in the interim there was a tremendous chance of failure (i.e., high risk), significant early outflows, and delayed inflows of revenue.

A traditional net present value (NPV) analysis (which sums revenues and costs for the life of the project and then discounts them using current interest rates) yielded a negative $2 million with an 11 percent risk-adjusted discount rate. However, viewing the investment as a multistage option and incorporating management's flexibility to alter its decision at least four times between 2002 and 2007 changes the valuation markedly. That is, a real options analysis demonstrated a present value of about $22 million. The question, then, was not whether to risk $18.5 million, but whether to invest $2 million today for the opportunity to earn $22 million at a future date.

formula; that is, you can type in the answer you want and ask what values are needed in a formula to get that answer. If managers know that a certain option value must be met in order for the proposal to get approved, they can back-solve the model to find a variance estimate needed to arrive at the answer that upper management desires.

Agency problems are typically inherent in investment decisions. They may occur when the managers of a firm are separated from its owners—when managers act as "agents" rather than "principals" (owners). A manager may have something to gain by not acting in the owner's best interests, or the interests of managers and owners are not co-aligned. Agency theory suggests that as managerial and owner interests diverge, managers will follow the path of their own self-interests. Sometimes this is to secure better compensation: Managers who propose projects may believe that if their projects are approved, they stand a much better chance of getting promoted. So while managers have an incentive to propose projects that *should* be successful, they also have an incentive to propose projects that *might* be successful. And because of the subjectivity involved in formally modeling a real option, managers may have an incentive to choose variance values that increase the likelihood of approval.

Managerial Conceit: Overconfidence and the Illusion of Control   Often, poor decisions are the result of such traps as biases, blind spots, and other human frailties. Much of this literature falls under the concept of **managerial conceit.**[54]

managerial conceit
biases, blind spots, and other human frailties that lead to poor managerial decisions.

First, managerial conceit occurs when decision makers who have made successful choices in the past come to believe that they possess superior expertise for managing uncertainty. They believe that their abilities can reduce the risks inherent in decision making to a much greater extent than they actually can. Such managers are more likely to shift away from analysis to trusting their own judgment. In the case of real options, they can simply declare that any given decision is a real option and proceed as before. If asked to formally model their decision, they are more likely to employ variance estimates that support their viewpoint.

Second, employing the real-options perspective can encourage decision makers toward a bias for action. Such a bias may lead to carelessness. Managerial conceit is as much a problem (if not more so) for small decisions as for big ones. Why? The cost to write the first stage of an option is much smaller than the cost of full commitment, and managers pay less attention to small decisions than to large ones. Because real options are designed to minimize potential losses while preserving potential gains, any problems that arise are likely to be smaller at first, causing less concern for the manager. Managerial conceit could suggest that managers will assume that those problems are the easiest to solve and control—a concern referred to as the illusion of control. Managers may fail to respond appropriately because they overlook the problem or believe that since it is small, they can easily resolve it. Thus, managers may approach each real-option decision with less care and diligence than if they had made a full commitment to a larger investment.

Managerial Conceit: Irrational Escalation of Commitment   A strength of a real options perspective is also one of its Achilles heels. Both real options and decisions involving escalation of commitment require specific environments with sequential decisions.[55] As the escalation-of-commitment literature indicates, simply separating a decision into multiple parts does not guarantee that decisions made will turn out well. This condition is potentially present whenever the exercise decision retains some uncertainty, which most still do. The decision to abandon also has strong psychological factors associated with it that affect the ability of managers to make correct exercise decisions.[56]

An option to exit requires reversing an initial decision made by someone in the organization (such as an exit champion). Organizations typically encourage managers to "own their decisions" in order to motivate them. As managers invest themselves in their decision, it proves harder for them to lose face by reversing course. For managers making the decision, it feels as if they made the wrong decision in the first place, even if it was initially a good decision. The more specific the manager's human capital becomes, the harder it is to transfer it to other organizations. Hence, there is a greater likelihood that managers will stick around and try to make an existing decision work. They are more likely to continue an existing project even if it should perhaps be ended.[57]

Despite the potential pitfalls of a real options approach, many of the strategic decisions that product champions and top managers must make are enhanced when decision makers have an entrepreneurial mind-set.

Entrepreneurial Orientation

>LO6
How an entrepreneurial orientation can enhance a firm's efforts to develop promising corporate venture initiatives.

Firms that want to engage in successful CE need to have an entrepreneurial orientation (EO).[58] EO refers to the strategy-making practices that businesses use in identifying and launching corporate ventures. It represents a frame of mind and a perspective toward entrepreneurship that is reflected in a firm's ongoing processes and corporate culture.[59]

Exhibit 12.3
Dimensions of Entrepreneurial Orientation

Dimension	Definition
Autonomy	Independent action by an individual or team aimed at bringing forth a business concept or vision and carrying it through to completion.
Innovativeness	A willingness to introduce novelty through experimentation and creative processes aimed at developing new products and services as well as new processes.
Proactiveness	A forward-looking perspective characteristic of a market-place leader that has the foresight to seize opportunities in anticipation of future demand.
Competitive aggressiveness	An intense effort to outperform industry rivals characterized by a combative posture or an aggressive response aimed at improving position or overcoming a threat in a competitive marketplace.
Risk taking	Making decisions and taking action without certain knowledge of probable outcomes; some undertakings may also involve making substantial resource commitments in the process of venturing forward.

Sources: Dess, G. G. & Lumpkin, G. T. 2005. The Role of Entrepreneurial Orientation in Stimulating Effective Corporate Entrepreneurship. *Academy of Management Executive,* 19(1): 147–156; Covin, J. G. & Slevin, D. P. 1991. A Conceptual Model of Entrepreneurship as Firm Behavior. *Entrepreneurship Theory & Practice,* Fall: 7–25; Lumpkin, G. T. and Dess, G. G. 1996. Clarifying the Entrepreneurial Orientation Construct and Linking It to Performance. *Academy of Management Review,* 21: 135–172; Miller, D. 1983. The Correlates of Entrepreneurship in Three Types of Firms. *Management Science,* 29: 770–791.

An EO has five dimensions that permeate the decision-making styles and practices of the firm's members: autonomy, innovativeness, proactiveness, competitive aggressiveness, and risk taking. These factors work together to enhance a firm's entrepreneurial performance. But even those firms that are strong in only a few aspects of EO can be very successful.[60] Exhibit 12.3 summarizes the dimensions of **entrepreneurial orientation.** Below, we discuss the five dimensions of EO and how they have been used to enhance internal venture development.

Autonomy

Autonomy refers to a willingness to act independently in order to carry forward an entrepreneurial vision or opportunity. It applies to both individuals and teams that operate outside an organization's existing norms and strategies. In the context of corporate entrepreneurship, autonomous work units are often used to leverage existing strengths in new arenas, identify opportunities that are beyond the organization's current capabilities, and encourage development of new ventures or improved business practices.[61]

The need for autonomy may apply to either dispersed or focused entrepreneurial efforts. Because of the emphasis on venture projects that are being developed outside of the normal flow of business, a focused approach suggests a working environment that is relatively autonomous. But autonomy may also be important in an organization where entrepreneurship is part of the corporate culture. Everything from the methods of group interaction to the firm's reward system must make organizational members feel as if they can think freely about venture opportunities, take time to investigate them, and act without

entrepreneurial orientation the strategy-making practices that businesses use in identifying and launching new ventures, consisting of autonomy, innovativeness, proactiveness, competitive aggressiveness, and risk taking.

autonomy independent action by an individual or team aimed at bringing forth a business concept or vision and carrying it through to completion.

Exhibit 12.4   Autonomy Techniques

Autonomy		
Technique	**Description/Purpose**	**Example**
Use skunkworks to foster entrepreneurial thinking	Skunkworks are independent work units, often physically separate from corporate headquarters. They allow employees to get out from under the pressures of their daily routines to engage in creative problem solving.	Overstock.com created a skunkworks to address the problem of returned merchandise. The solution was a business within-a-business: Overstock auctions. The unit has grown by selling products returned to Overstock and offers fees 30 percent lower than eBay's auction service.
Design organizational structures that support independent action	Established companies with traditional structures often need to break out of such old forms to compete more effectively.	Deloitte Consulting, a division of Deloitte Touche Tohmatsu, found it difficult to compete against young agile firms. So it broke the firm into small autonomous units called "chip-aways" that operate with the flexibility of a start-up. In its first year, revenues were $40 million—10 percent higher than its projections.

Sources: Conlin, M. 2006. Square Feet. Oh How Square! *BusinessWeek,* www.businessweek.com, July 3; Cross, K. 2001. Bang the Drum Quickly. *Business 2.0,* May: 28–30; Sweeney, J. 2004. A Firm for All Reasons. *Consulting Magazine,* www.consultingmag.com; and Wagner, M. 2005. Out of the Skunkworks. *Internet Retailer,* January, www.internetretailer.com.

fear of condemnation. This implies a respect for the autonomy of each individual and an openness to the independent thinking that goes into championing a corporate venture idea. Thus, autonomy represents a type of empowerment (see Chapter 11) that is directed at identifying and leveraging entrepreneurial opportunities. Exhibit 12.4 identifies two techniques that organizations often use to promote autonomy.

Creating autonomous work units and encouraging independent action may have pitfalls that can jeopardize their effectiveness. Autonomous teams often lack coordination. Excessive decentralization has a strong potential to create inefficiencies, such as duplication of effort and wasting resources on projects with questionable feasibility. For example, Chris Galvin, former CEO of Motorola, scrapped the skunkworks approach the company had been using to develop new wireless phones. Fifteen teams had created 128 different phones, which led to spiraling costs and overly complex operations.[62]

For autonomous work units and independent projects to be effective, such efforts have to be measured and monitored. This requires a delicate balance: companies must have the patience and budget to tolerate the explorations of autonomous groups and the strength to cut back efforts that are not bearing fruit. It must be undertaken with a clear sense of purpose—namely, to generate new sources of competitive advantage.

Innovativeness

Innovativeness refers to a firm's efforts to find new opportunities and novel solutions. In the beginning of this chapter we discussed innovation; here the focus is on innovativeness—a firm's attitude toward innovation and willingness to innovate. It involves creativity and experimentation that result in new products, new services, or improved technological processes.[63] Innovativeness is one of the major components of an entrepreneurial strategy. As indicated at the beginning of the chapter, however, the job of managing innovativeness can be very challenging.

innovativeness
a willingness to introduce novelty through experimentation and creative processes aimed at developing new products and services as well as new processes.

Innovativeness requires that firms depart from existing technologies and practices and venture beyond the current state of the art. Inventions and new ideas need to be nurtured even when their benefits are unclear. However, in today's climate of rapid change, effectively producing, assimilating, and exploiting innovations can be an important avenue for achieving competitive advantages. Interest in global warming and other ecological concerns has led many corporations to focus their innovativeness efforts on solving environmental problems. Strategy Spotlight 12.8 describes three organizations that are using entrepreneurial thinking and innovative practices to identify socially responsible solutions.

As our earlier discussion of CE indicated, many corporations owe their success to an active program of innovation-based corporate venturing.[64] Exhibit 12.5 highlights two of the methods companies can use to enhance their competitive position through innovativeness.

Innovativeness can be a source of great progress and strong corporate growth, but there are also major pitfalls for firms that invest in innovation. Expenditures on R&D aimed at identifying new products or processes can be a waste of resources if the effort does not yield results. Another danger is related to the competitive climate. Even if a company innovates a new capability or successfully applies a technological breakthrough, another company may develop a similar innovation or find a use for it that is more profitable. Finally R&D and other innovation efforts are among the first to be cut back during an economic downturn.

Even though innovativeness is an important means of internal corporate venturing, it also involves major risks, because investments in innovations may not pay off. For strategic managers of entrepreneurial firms, successfully developing and adopting innovations can generate competitive advantages and provide a major source of growth for the firm.

Exhibit 12.5   Innovativeness Techniques

Innovativeness		
Technique	**Description/Purpose**	**Example**
Foster creativity and experimentation	Companies that support idea exploration and allow employees to express themselves creatively enhance innovation outcomes.	To tap into its reserves of innovative talent, Royal Dutch/Shell created "GameChanger" to help employees develop promising ideas. The process provides funding up to $600,000 for would-be entrepreneurs to pursue innovative projects and conduct experiments.
Invest in new technology, R&D, and continuous improvement	The latest technologies often provide sources of new competitive advantages. To extract value from a new technology, companies must invest in it.	Dell Computer Corporation's new OptiPlex manufacturing system revolutionized the traditional assembly line. Hundreds of custom-built computers can be made in an eight-hour shift using state of the art automation techniques that have increased productivity per person by 160 percent.

Sources: Breen, B. 2004. Living in Dell Time. *Fast Company,* November: 88–92: Hammonds, K. H. 2002. Size Is Not a Strategy. *Fast Company,* August: 78–83; Perman, S. 2001. Automate or Die. eCompanyNow.com, July; Dell, M. 1999. *Direct from Dell.* New York: HarperBusiness; and Watson, R. 2006. Expand Your Innovation Horizons. *Fast Company,* www.fastcompany.com, May.

Socially Responsible Corporate Entrepreneurship

One of the most important trends in U.S. business today is corporate social responsibility (CSR). Proactively oriented firms are seizing opportunities to take a leading role in issues such as the environment, product safety, and fair trade. Among the most interesting examples of this, as suggested in the Chapter 1 section on social innovation, are those firms that are taking an entrepreneurial approach to CSR. That is, they are using new technologies, environmentally friendly ventures, and entrepreneurial practices to advance their social responsibility goals. Following is a sample of three corporations that are taking a very entrepreneurial approach to corporate social responsibility.

Whirlpool Corporation—From efficiency to advocacy

Whirlpool is perhaps best known for its "white boxes"—the refrigerators, freezers, and laundry appliances that account for over 60 percent of its $13 billion in annual sales. To explore what creates customer loyalty, Whirlpool conducted a global survey of its customers. "We discovered there is a strong correlation between a company's performance in appliance markets and their social response to issues such as energy efficiency and pollution," said Steve Willis, director of Whirlpool's global environment, health, and safety programs. One result has been its innovative Duet Series of washers and dryers that significantly reduces energy consumption. Recently, Whirlpool decided to take its environmental efforts a step farther: It joined The Natural Step, an entrepreneurial organization that is advancing the movement toward environmental sustainability by advocating the development of innovative products that meet high standards of ecological sustainability.

Timberland—Green labeling its shoes

Timberland has been recognized as one of the most socially conscious companies because of its culture dedicated to environmental awareness. For example, the company sponsored the planting of a million trees and sponsored Earth Day events in countries around the world. Its "Path of Service" program allows employees to use 40 hours of paid time to volunteer for community projects. More

recently, the Stratham, New Hampshire, maker of footwear and apparel initiated a program to put a label on its products, similar to a food label, that tells consumers where the product was produced, how it was made, and its impact on local communities and the environment. "We thought about how closely consumers read nutritional labels on food products and thought, why doesn't this happen in our space?" says Dave Aznavorian, a senior global brand manager at Timberland. It is another move that reflects the ethics of CEO Jeff Swartz, an outspoken advocate of corporate responsibility who sees the role of Timberland as more than just manufacturing. "We are not a boot company, we are a brand," says Swartz, "and our brand is about confidently striding through life's challenges."

Green Mountain Coffee Roasters—Empowering local entrepreneurs

As the name suggests, this NASDAQ-listed corporation (GMCR) is located in the Green Mountains of Vermont. But its reach is global. As a roaster and distributor of specialty coffees, GMCR has become a leading advocate for fair trade practices and providing financial support for local coffee growers. "Our president and CEO Robert Stiller visited places where coffee is grown and was struck by the levels of poverty. He wanted to do something about it," said Rick Peyser, director of public relations. As a result, GMCR now purchases coffee beans from small farm cooperatives in Peru, Mexico, and Sumatra. It also provides micro-loans to underwrite family businesses that are trying to create more diverse agricultural economies. Back home in its Waterbury, Vermont, roasting facility, GMCR uses a 95-kilowatt cogeneration system that captures waste heat from its propane-fired generator and recycles it for both coffee roasting and space heating.

Each of these companies has recently been named one of the 100 Best Corporate Citizens by *Business Ethics* magazine. However, major corporations still have their critics. In fact, companies that claim to be making progress in advancing CSR are often the most loudly criticized. For example, British Petroleum, which has endeavored to be an oil industry leader in supporting environmentally sensitive energy development, is often attacked by environmental groups despite initiatives such as investing $48 million to develop the world's largest solar energy project. Despite such criticism, it is encouraging to note that entrepreneurial activities can help companies achieve their social responsibility goals as well as their innovation and growth goals.

Sources: Asmus, P. 2005. 100 Best Corporate Citizens for 2005. *Business Ethics,* www.business-ethics.com; Asmus, P. 2003. 100 Best Corporate Citizens for 2003. *Business Ethics,* www.business-ethics.com; Baker, M. 2001. BP Announces World's Largest Solar Project. *Business Respect,* 1: April 6; Hawken, P., Lovins, A., & Lovins, H. 2000. *Natural Capitalism.* Boston: Back Bay Books; see also www.bp.com; www.domini.com; www.hoovers.com; www.ifsia.com; and Borden, M. & Kamenetz, A. 2008. The prophet CEO. *Fast Company,* September: 126–129.

environmental sustainability

Proactiveness

proactiveness a forward-looking perspective characteristic of a marketplace leader that has the foresight to seize opportunities in anticipation of future demand.

Proactiveness refers to a firm's efforts to seize new opportunities. Proactive organizations monitor trends, identify the future needs of existing customers, and anticipate changes in demand or emerging problems that can lead to new venture opportunities. Proactiveness involves not only recognizing changes but also being willing to act on those insights ahead of the competition. Strategic managers who practice proactiveness have their eye on the future in a search for new possibilities for growth and development. Such a forward-looking perspective is important for companies that seek to be industry leaders. Many proactive firms seek out ways not only to be future oriented but also to change the very nature of competition in their industry.

Proactiveness puts competitors in the position of having to respond to successful initiatives. The benefit gained by firms that are the first to enter new markets, establish brand identity, implement administrative techniques, or adopt new operating technologies in an industry is called first mover advantage.[65]

First movers usually have several advantages. First, industry pioneers, especially in new industries, often capture unusually high profits because there are no competitors to drive prices down. Second, first movers that establish brand recognition are usually able to retain their image and hold on to the market share gains they earned by being first. Sometimes these benefits also accrue to other early movers in an industry, but, generally speaking,

Exhibit 12.6   **Proactiveness Techniques**

Proactiveness		
Technique	**Description/Purpose**	**Example**
Introduce new products or technological capabilities ahead of the competition.	Being a first mover provides companies with an ability to shape the playing field and shift competitive advantages in their favor.	Sony's mission states, "We should always be the pioneers with our products—out front leading the market." This philosophy has made Sony technologically strong with industry-leading products such as the PlayStation and Vaio laptop computers.
Continuously seek out new product or service offerings.	Firms that provide new resources or sources of supply can benefit from a proactive stance.	Costco seized a chance to leverage its success as a warehouse club that sells premium brands when it introduced Costco Home Stores. The home stores are usually located near its warehouse stores and its rapid inventory turnover gives it a cost advantage of 15 to 25 percent over close competitors such as Bassett Furniture and the Bombay Company.

Sources: Bryce, D. J. & Dyer, J. H. 2007. Strategies to Crack Well-Guarded Markets. *Harvard Business Review,* May: 84–92; Collins, J. C. & Porras, J. I. 1997. *Built to Last.* New York: HarperBusiness; Robinson, D. 2005. Sony Pushes Reliability in Vaio Laptops. *IT Week,* www.itweek .co.uk, October 12; and www.sony.com

first movers have an advantage that can be sustained until firms enter the maturity phase of an industry's life cycle.[66]

First movers are not always successful. The customers of companies that introduce novel products or embrace breakthrough technologies may be reluctant to commit to a new way of doing things. In his book *Crossing the Chasm,* Geoffrey A. Moore noted that most firms seek evolution, not revolution, in their operations. This makes it difficult for a first mover to sell promising new technologies.[67]

Even with these caveats, however, companies that are first movers can enhance their competitive position. Exhibit 12.6 illustrates two methods firms can use to act proactively.

Being an industry leader does not always lead to competitive advantages. Some firms that have launched pioneering new products or staked their reputation on new brands have failed to get the hoped-for payoff. Coca-Cola and PepsiCo invested $75 million to launch sodas that would capitalize on the low-carb diet trend. But with half the carbohydrates taken out, neither *C2,* Coke's entry, nor *Pepsi Edge* tasted very good. The two new brands combined never achieved more than one percent market share. PepsiCo halted production in 2005 and Coca-Cola followed suit in 2007.[68] Such missteps are indicative of the dangers of trying to proactively anticipate demand. Another danger for opportunity-seeking companies is that they will take their proactiveness efforts too far. Strategy Spotlight 12.9 discusses a pair of proactive marketing practices that may backfire with consumers.

● Coca-Cola has many successful products on supermarket shelves. C2—its low carb diet drink—isn't one of them.

Careful monitoring and scanning of the environment, as well as extensive feasibility research, are needed for a proactive strategy to lead to competitive advantages. Firms that do it well usually have substantial growth and internal development to show for it. Many of them have been able to sustain the advantages of proactiveness for years.

Competitive Aggressiveness

Competitive aggressiveness refers to a firm's efforts to outperform its industry rivals. Companies with an aggressive orientation are willing to "do battle" with competitors. They might slash prices and sacrifice profitability to gain market share or spend aggressively to obtain manufacturing capacity. As an avenue of firm development and growth, competitive aggressiveness may involve being very assertive in leveraging the results of other entrepreneurial activities such as innovativeness or proactiveness.

Competitive aggressiveness is directed toward competitors. The SWOT analysis discussed in Chapters 2 and 3 provides a useful way to distinguish between these different approaches to CE. Proactiveness, as we saw in the last section, is a response to opportunities—the O in SWOT. Competitive aggressiveness, by contrast, is a response to threats—the T in SWOT. A competitively aggressive posture is important for firms that seek to enter new markets in the face of intense rivalry.

Strategic managers can use competitive aggressiveness to combat industry trends that threaten their survival or market position. Sometimes firms need to be forceful in

competitive aggressiveness
an intense effort to outperform industry rivals characterized by a combative posture or an aggressive response aimed at improving position or overcoming a threat in a competitive marketplace.

strategy spotlight

Over-the-Top Marketing Pitches: Proactiveness Gone Wild?

Research indicates that proactiveness is the EO dimension that is most likely to contribute to strong performance. Given that, can a company ever be too proactive? Definitely, according to consumers of some of the world's top brands. In the case of two popular forms of marketing—product placements and brand extensions—some well-respected name brands have taken their proactiveness beyond the limit.

Consider the hit television series *American Idol.* Viewers have started to notice how often the judges lift up their Coca-Cola cups or explain why the Apple iPhone is the perfect device for casting a vote for your favorite contestant. "I know they want to make some money," says 18-year-old Michigan viewer Caitlin Knott. "But no one wants to see Ryan Seacrest selling stuff." That sentiment

has not stopped *Idol* from rapidly increasing its placement activity: in the first 38 episodes of 2008, the show featured 4,151 product placements, according to Nielsen Media Research. That amounts to a total of 545 minutes, a 19 percent increase in screen time in one year.

The brand extensions trend is another practice that has consumers asking, "What were they thinking?" For example, famed leather-goods maker Salvatore Ferragamo recently started selling wristwatches at its Fifth Avenue store in New York City. The watches, made by Timex, will no doubt keep time just fine. But are customers going to pay $7,300, albeit for the 18-karat gold version, just because they like Ferragamo's handbags and shoes? Other luxury designers are making the same bet as Ferragamo: Prada is offering cellphones, Versace is decorating airplanes, and Giorgio Armani recently made an agreement with Samsung to produce luxury LCD televisions. The trend does not just apply to designers. Michael Stone, CEO of the Beanstalk Group, a licensing and branding unit of Omnicom Group, tells how a pizza brand recently approached him about launching a line of fashion apparel. "I thought, 'How fast can I get out of here?'" says Stone. Clearly, there is a limit to how proactively a company can extend its good name.

Sources: Binkley, C. 2007. Like Our Sunglasses? Try Our Vodka! *Wall Street Journal,* November 8: D1; Grover, R. 2008. *American Idol*'s Ads Infinitum. *BusinessWeek,* June 2: 38–39; and Rauch, A., Wiklund, J., Lumpkin, G. T., & Frese, M. 2009. Entrepreneurial Orientation and Business Performance: An Assessment of Past Research and Suggestions for the Future. *Entrepreneurship Theory and Practice,* 33(3): 49–62.

defending the competitive position that has made them an industry leader. Firms often need to be aggressive to ensure their advantage by capitalizing on new technologies or serving new market needs. Exhibit 12.7 suggests two of the ways competitively aggressive firms enhance their entrepreneurial position.

Another practice companies use to overcome the competition is to make preannouncements of new products or technologies. This type of signaling is aimed not only at potential customers but also at competitors to see how they will react or to discourage them from launching similar initiatives. Sometimes the preannouncements are made just to scare off competitors, an action that has potential ethical implications.

Competitive aggressiveness may not always lead to competitive advantages. Some companies (or their CEOs) have severely damaged their reputations by being overly aggressive. Although it continues to be a dominant player, Microsoft's highly aggressive profile makes it the subject of scorn by some businesses and individuals. Efforts to find viable replacements for the Microsoft products have helped fuel the open source software movement that threatens to erode Microsoft's leading role as a software provider.[69]

Competitive aggressiveness is a strategy that is best used in moderation. Companies that aggressively establish their competitive position and vigorously exploit opportunities

Exhibit 12.7   Competitive Aggressiveness Techniques

Competitive Aggressiveness		
Technique	**Description/Purpose**	**Example**
Enter markets with drastically lower prices.	Narrow operating margins make companies vulnerable to extended price competition.	Using open source software, California-based Zimbra, Inc. has become a leader in messaging and collaboration software. Its product costs about one-third less than its direct competitor Microsoft Exchange. Zimbra now has over 4 million users including 12,000 H&R Block tax preparers.
Find successful business models and copy them.	As long as a practice is not protected by intellectual property laws, it's probably okay to imitate it. Finding solutions to existing problems is generally quicker and cheaper than inventing them.	Best Practices, LLC is a North Carolina consulting group that seeks out best practices and then repackages and resells them. With annual revenues in excess of $8 million, Best Practices has become a leader in continuous improvement and benchmarking strategies.

Sources: Guth, R. A. 2006. Trolling the Web for Free Labor, Software Upstarts Are New Force. *The Wall Street Journal,* November 12: 1; Mochari, I. 2001. Steal This Strategy. *Inc.,* July: 62–67; www.best-in-class.com; and www.zimbra.com.

to achieve profitability may, over the long run, be better able to sustain their competitive advantages if their goal is to defeat, rather than decimate, their competitors.

Risk Taking

Risk taking refers to a firm's willingness to seize a venture opportunity even though it does not know whether the venture will be successful—to act boldly without knowing the consequences. To be successful through corporate entrepreneurship, firms usually have to take on riskier alternatives, even if it means forgoing the methods or products that have worked in the past. To obtain high financial returns, firms take such risks as assuming high levels of debt, committing large amounts of firm resources, introducing new products into new markets, and investing in unexplored technologies.

All of the approaches to internal development that we have discussed are potentially risky. Whether they are being aggressive, proactive, or innovative, firms on the path of CE must act without knowing how their actions will turn out. Before launching their strategies, corporate entrepreneurs must know their firm's appetite for risk.[70]

Three types of risk that organizations and their executives face are business risk, financial risk, and personal risk:

- *Business risk taking* involves venturing into the unknown without knowing the probability of success. This is the risk associated with entering untested markets or committing to unproven technologies.
- *Financial risk taking* requires that a company borrow heavily or commit a large portion of its resources in order to grow. In this context, risk is used to refer to the risk/return trade-off that is familiar in financial analysis.

risk taking making decisions and taking action without certain knowledge of probable outcomes. Some undertakings may also involve making substantial resource commitments in the process of venturing forward.

Exhibit 12.8   **Risk Taking Techniques**

Risk Taking		
Technique	**Description/Purpose**	**Example**
Research and assess risk factors to minimize uncertainty	Companies that "do their homework"—that is, carefully evaluate the implications of bold actions—reduce the likelihood of failure.	Graybar Electric Co. took a risk when it invested $144 million to revamp its distribution system. It consolidated 231 small centers into 16 supply warehouses and installed the latest communications network. Graybar is now considered a leader in facility redesign and its sales have increased steadily since the consolidation, topping $4 billion in sales in a recent year.
Use techniques that have worked in other domains	Risky methods that other companies have tried may provide an avenue for advancing company goals.	Autobytel.com, one of the first companies to sell cars online, decided on an approach that worked well for others—advertising during the Super Bowl. It was the first dot–com ever to do so and its $1.2 million 30-second ad paid off well by generating weeks of free publicity and favorable business press.

Sources: Anonymous. 2006. Graybar Offers Data Center Redesign Seminars. *Cabling Installation and Maintenance,* www.cim.pennnet.com, September 1; Keenan, F. & Mullaney, T. J. 2001. Clicking at Graybar. *BusinessWeek,* June 18: 132–34; Weintraub, A. 2001. Make or break for Autobytel. *BusinessWeek e.biz,* July 9: EB30-EB32; www.autobytel.com; and www.graybar.com.

- *Personal risk taking* refers to the risks that an executive assumes in taking a stand in favor of a strategic course of action. Executives who take such risks stand to influence the course of their whole company, and their decisions also can have significant implications for their careers.

Even though risk taking involves taking chances, it is not gambling. The best-run companies investigate the consequences of various opportunities and create scenarios of likely outcomes. A key to managing entrepreneurial risks is to evaluate new venture opportunities thoroughly enough to reduce the uncertainty surrounding them. Exhibit 12.8 indicates two methods companies can use to strengthen their competitive position through risk taking.

Risk taking, by its nature, involves potential dangers and pitfalls. Only carefully managed risk is likely to lead to competitive advantages. Actions that are taken without sufficient forethought, research, and planning may prove to be very costly. Therefore, strategic managers must always remain mindful of potential risks. In his book *Innovation and Entrepreneurship,* Peter Drucker argued that successful entrepreneurs are typically not risk takers. Instead, they take steps to minimize risks by carefully understanding them. That is how they avoid focusing on risk and remain focused on opportunity.[71] Risk taking is a good place to close this chapter on corporate entrepreneurship. Companies that choose to grow through internal corporate venturing must remember that entrepreneurship always involves embracing what is new and uncertain.

Reflecting on Career Implications . . .

- *Innovation:* Look around at the types of innovations being pursued by your company. Do they tend to be incremental or radical? Product-related or process-related? What new types of innovations might benefit your organization? How can you add value to such innovations?
- *Managing Innovation:* How might your organization's chances of a successful innovation increase through collaboration with innovation partners? Your ability to collaborate with individuals from other departments and firms will make you more receptive to and capable of innovation initiatives and enhance your career opportunities.
- *Corporate Entrepreneurship:* Do you consider the company you work for to be entrepreneurial? If not, what actions might you take to enhance its entrepreneurial spirit? If so, what have been the keys to its entrepreneurial success? Can these practices be repeated to achieve future successes?
- *Entrepreneurial Orientation:* Consider the five dimensions of entrepreneurial orientation. Is your organization especially strong at any of these? Especially weak? What are the career implications of your company's entrepreneurial strengths or weaknesses?

Summary

To remain competitive in today's economy, established firms must find new avenues for development and growth. This chapter has addressed how innovation and corporate entrepreneurship can be a means of internal venture creation and strategic renewal, and how an entrepreneurial orientation can help corporations enhance their competitive position.

Innovation is one of the primary means by which corporations grow and strengthen their strategic position. Innovations can take several forms, ranging from radical breakthrough innovations to incremental improvement innovations. Innovations are often used to update products and services or for improving organizational processes. Managing the innovation process is often challenging, because it involves a great deal of uncertainty and there are many choices to be made about the extent and type of innovations to pursue. By defining the scope of innovation, managing the pace of innovation, staffing to capture value from innovation, and collaborating with innovation partners, firms can more effectively manage the innovation process.

We also discussed the role of corporate entrepreneurship in venture development and strategic renewal. Corporations usually take either a focused or dispersed approach to corporate venturing. Firms with a focused approach usually separate the corporate venturing activity from the ongoing operations of the firm in order to foster independent thinking and encourage entrepreneurial team members to think and act without the constraints imposed by the corporation. In corporations where venturing activities are dispersed, a culture of entrepreneurship permeates all parts of the company in order to induce strategic behaviors by all organizational members. In measuring the success of corporate venturing activities, both financial and strategic objectives should be considered. Real options analysis is often used to make better quality decisions in uncertain entrepreneurial situations. However, a real options approach has potential drawbacks.

Most entrepreneurial firms need to have an entrepreneurial orientation: the methods, practices, and decision-making styles that strategic managers use to act entrepreneurially. Five dimensions of entrepreneurial orientation are found in firms that pursue corporate venture strategies. Autonomy, innovativeness, proactiveness, competitive aggressiveness, and risk taking each make a unique contribution to the pursuit of new opportunities. When deployed effectively, the methods and practices of an entrepreneurial orientation can be used to engage successfully in corporate entrepreneurship and new venture creation. However, strategic managers must remain mindful of the pitfalls associated with each of these approaches.

Summary Review Questions

1. What is meant by the concept of a continuum of radical and incremental innovations?

2. What are the dilemmas that organizations face when deciding what innovation projects to pursue? What steps can organizations take to effectively manage the innovation process?

3. What is the difference between focused and dispersed approaches to corporate entrepreneurship?

4. How are business incubators used to foster internal corporate venturing?

5. What is the role of the product champion in bringing a new product or service into existence in a corporation? How can companies use product champions to enhance their venture development efforts?

6. Explain the difference between proactiveness and competitive aggressiveness in terms of achieving and sustaining competitive advantage.

7. Describe how the entrepreneurial orientation (EO) dimensions of innovativeness, proactiveness, and risk taking can be combined to create competitive advantages for entrepreneurial firms.

Key Terms

innovation, 427
radical innovation, 428
incremental
  innovation, 429
corporate
  entrepreneurship, 435
new venture group, 439
business incubator, 439
product champion, 442
exit champion, 443
real options analysis, 444
managerial conceit 447
entrepreneurial
  orientation, 448
autonomy, 448
innovativeness, 449
proactiveness, 452
competitive
  aggressiveness, 453
risk taking, 455

Experiential Exercise

Select two different major corporations from two different industries (you might use Fortune 500 companies to make your selection). Compare and contrast these organizations in terms of their entrepreneurial orientation.

Entrepreneurial Orientation	Company A	Company B
Autonomy		
Innovativeness		
Proactiveness		
Competitive Aggressiveness		
Risk Taking		

Based on Your Comparison:

1. How is the corporation's entrepreneurial orientation reflected in its strategy?

2. Which corporation would you say has the stronger entrepreneurial orientation?

3. Is the corporation with the stronger entrepreneurial orientation also stronger in terms of financial performance?

Application Questions Exercises

1. Select a firm known for its corporate entrepreneurship activities. Research the company and discuss how it has positioned itself relative to its close competitors. Does it have a unique strategic advantage? Disadvantage? Explain.

2. Explain the difference between product innovations and process innovations. Provide examples of firms

that have recently introduced each type of innovation. What are the types of innovations related to the strategies of each firm?

3. Using the Internet, select a company that is listed on the NASDAQ or New York Stock Exchange. Research the extent to which the company has an entrepreneurial culture. Does the company use product champions? Does it have a corporate venture capital fund? Do you believe its entrepreneurial efforts are sufficient to generate sustainable advantages?

4. How can an established firm use an entrepreneurial orientation to enhance its overall strategic position? Provide examples.

Ethics Questions

1. Innovation activities are often aimed at making a discovery or commercializing a technology ahead of the competition. What are some of the unethical practices that companies could engage in during the innovation process? What are the potential long-term consequences of such actions?

2. Discuss the ethical implications of using entrepreneurial policies and practices to pursue corporate social responsibility goals. Are these efforts authentic and genuine or just an attempt to attract more customers?

References

1. The Nortel Networks example is based on Austen, I. 2009. Nortel seeks bankruptcy protection. www.nytimes.com, January 15; Crockett, R. O. 2009. Nortel's road to bankruptcy. www.businessweek.com, January 15; Kerner, S. M. 2009. Nortel bankruptcy a Canadian tragedy. www.internetnews.com, January 16; *Ottawa Business Journal* Staff. 2009. Nortel news leaves tech community reeling. www.ottawabusinessjournal.com, January 15; and Silver, S. & Lublin. J. S. 2009. Nortel Networks files for Chapter 11. www.wsj.com, January 15.

2. For an interesting discussion, see Johannessen, J. A., Olsen, B., & Lumpkin, G. T. 2001. Innovation as newness: What is new, how new, and new to whom? *European Journal of Innovation Management,* 4(1): 20–31.

3. The discussion of product and process innovation is based on Roberts, E. B. (Ed.). 2002. *Innovation: Driving product, process, and market change.* San Francisco: Jossey-Bass; Hayes, R. & Wheelwright, S. 1985. Competing through manufacturing. *Harvard Business Review,* 63(1): 99–109; and Hayes, R. & Wheelwright, S. 1979. Dynamics of product–process life cycles. *Harvard Business Review,* 57(2): 127–136.

4. The discussion of radical and incremental innovations draws from Leifer, R., McDermott, C. M., Colarelli, G.,

O'Connor, G. C., Peters, L. S., Rice, M. P., & Veryzer, R. W. 2000. *Radical innovation: How mature companies can outsmart upstarts.* Boston: Harvard Business School Press; Damanpour, F. 1996. Organizational complexity and innovation: Developing and testing multiple contingency models. *Management Science,* 42(5): 693–716; and Hage, J. 1980. *Theories of organizations.* New York: Wiley.

5. Christensen, C. M. & Raynor, M. E. 2003. *The innovator's solution.* Boston: Harvard Business School Press.

6. Dressner, H. 2004. The Gartner Fellows interview: Clayton M. Christensen. www.gartner.com, April 26.

7. Christensen et al., op. cit.; and www.wikipedia.org.

8. Christensen, C. M., Grossman, J. H., & Hwang, J. 2008. *The innovator's prescription.* New York: McGraw-Hill; Christensen, C. M. & Raynor, M. E. 2003. *The innovator's solution.* Boston: Harvard Business School Press.

9. For another perspective on how different types of innovation affect organizational choices, see Wolter, C. & Veloso, F. M. 2008. The effects of innovation on vertical structure: Perspectives on transactions costs and competences. *Academy of Management Review,* 33(3): 586–605.

10. Drucker, P. F. 1985. *Innovation and entrepreneurship: 2000* New York: Harper & Row.

11. Birkinshaw, J., Hamel, G., & Mol, M. J. 2008. Management innovation. *Academy of Management Review,* 33(4): 825–845.

12. Steere, W. C., Jr. & Niblack, J. 1997. Pfizer, Inc. In Kanter, R. M., Kao, J., & Wiersema, F. (Eds.), *Innovation: Breakthrough thinking at 3M, DuPont, GE, Pfizer, and Rubbermaid:* 123–145. New York: HarperCollins.

13. Morrissey, C. A. 2000. Managing innovation through corporate venturing. *Graziadio Business Report,* Spring, gbr.pepperdine.edu; and Sharma, A. 1999. Central dilemmas of managing innovation in large firms. *California Management Review,* 41(3): 147–164.

14. Sharma, op. cit.

15. Canabou, C. 2003. Fast ideas for slow times. *Fast Company,* May: 52.

16. Biodegradable Products Institute. 2003. "Compostable Logo" of the Biodegradable Products Institute gains momentum with approval of DuPont™ Biomax® resin, www.bpiworld.org, June 12; Leifer et al., op. cit.

17. For more on defining the scope of innovation, see Valikangas, L. & Gibbert, M. 2005. Boundary-setting strategies for escaping innovation traps. *MIT Sloan Management Review,* 46(3): 58–65.

18. Leifer et al., op. cit.

19. Bhide, A. V. 2000. *The origin and evolution of new businesses.* New York: Oxford University Press; Brown, S. L. & Eisenhardt, K. M.

1998. *Competing on the edge: Strategy as structured chaos.* Cambridge, MA: Harvard Business School Press.

20. Caulfield, B. 2003. Why techies don't get Six Sigma. *Business 2.0,* June: 90.

21. McGrath, R. G. & Keil, T. 2007. The value captor's process: Getting the most out of your new business ventures. *Harvard Business Review,* May: 128–136.

22. For an interesting discussion of how sharing technology knowledge with different divisions in an organization can contribute to innovation processes, see Miller, D. J., Fern, M. J., & Cardinal, L. B. 2007. The use of knowledge for technological innovation within diversified firms. *Academy of Management Journal,* 50(2): 308–326.

23. Ketchen Jr., D. J., Ireland, R. D., & Snow, C. C. 2007 Strategic entrepreneurship, collaborative innovation, and wealth creation. *Strategic Entrepreneurship Journal,* 1(3–4): 371–385.

24. Chesbrough, H. 2003. *Open innovation: The new imperative for creating and profiting from technology.* Boston: Harvard Business School Press.

25. For a recent study of what makes alliance partnerships successful, see Sampson, R. C. 2007. R&D alliances and firm performance: The impact of technological diversity and alliance organization on innovation. *Academy of Management Journal,* 50(2): 364–386.

26. For an interesting perspective on the role of collaboration among multinational corporations see Hansen, M. T. & Nohria, N. 2004. How to build collaborative advantage. *MIT Sloan Management Review,* 46(1): 22–30.

27. Wells, R. M. J. 2008. The product innovation process: Are managing information flows and cross-functional collaboration key? *Academy of Management Perspectives,* 22(1): 58–60.

28. Guth, W. D. & Ginsberg, A. 1990. Guest editor's introduction: Corporate entrepreneurship. *Strategic Management Journal,* 11: 5–15.

29. Pinchot, G. 1985. *Intrapreneuring.* New York: Harper & Row.

30. For an interesting perspective on the role of context on the discovery and creation of opportunities, see Zahra, S. A. 2008. The virtuous cycle of discovery and creation of entrepreneurial opportunities. *Strategic Entrepreneurship Journal,* 2(3): 243–257.

31. Birkinshaw, J. 1997. Entrepreneurship in multinational corporations: The characteristics of subsidiary initiatives. *Strategic Management Journal,* 18(3): 207–229; and Kanter, R. M. 1985. *The change masters.* New York: Simon & Schuster.

32. Hansen, M. T., Chesbrough, H. W., Nohria, N., & Sull, D. 2000. Networked incubators: Hothouses of the new economy. *Harvard Business Review,* 78(5): 74–84.

33. Stein, T. 2002. Corporate venture investors are bailing out. *Red Herring,* December: 74–75.

34. For more on the importance of leadership in fostering a climate of entrepreneurship, see Ling, Y., Simsek, Z., Lubatkin, M. H., & Veiga, J. F. 2008. Transformational leadership's role in promoting corporate entrepreneurship: Examining the CEO-TMT interface. *Academy of Management Journal,* 51(3): 557–576.

35. Is your company up to speed? 2003. *Fast Company,* June: 86.

36. For an interesting discussion, see Davenport, T. H., Prusak, L., & Wilson, H. J. 2003. Who's bringing you hot ideas and how are you responding? *Harvard Business Review,* 80(1): 58–64.

37. Howell, J. M. 2005. The right stuff. Identifying and developing effective champions of innovation. *Academy of Management Executive,* 19(2): 108–119. See also Greene, P., Brush, C., & Hart, M. 1999. The corporate venture champion: A resource-based approach to role and process. *Entrepreneurship Theory & Practice,* 23(3): 103–122; and Markham, S. K. & Aiman-Smith, L. 2001. Product champions: Truths, myths and management. *Research Technology Management,* May–June: 44–50.

38. Burgelman, R. A. 1983. A process model of internal corporate venturing in the diversified major firm.

Administrative Science Quarterly, 28: 223–244.

39. Hamel, G. 2000. *Leading the revolution.* Boston: Harvard Business School Press.

40. Greene, Brush, & Hart, op. cit.; and Shane, S. 1994. Are champions different from non-champions? *Journal of Business Venturing,* 9(5): 397–421.

41. Block, Z. & MacMillan, I. C. 1993. *Corporate venturing—Creating new businesses with the firm.* Cambridge, MA: Harvard Business School Press.

42. For an interesting discussion of these trade-offs, see Stringer, R. 2000. How to manage radical innovation. *California Management Review,* 42(4): 70–88; and Gompers, P. A. & Lerner, J. 1999. *The venture capital cycle.* Cambridge, MA: MIT Press.

43. Albrinck, J., Hornery, J., Kletter, D., & Neilson, G. 2001. Adventures in corporate venturing. *Strategy + Business,* 22: 119–129; and McGrath, R. G. & MacMillan, I. C. 2000. *The entrepreneurial mind-set.* Cambridge, MA: Harvard Business School Press.

44. For an interesting discussion of how different outcome goals affect organizational learning and employee motivation, see Seijts, G. H. & Latham, G. P. 2005. Learning versus performance goals: When should each be used? *Academy of Management Executive,* 19(1): 124–131.

45. Crockett, R. O. 2001. Motorola. *BusinessWeek,* July 15: 72–78.

46. The ideas in this section are drawn from Royer, I. 2003. Why bad projects are so hard to kill. *Harvard Business Review,* 80(1): 48–56.

47. For an interesting perspective on the different roles that individuals play in the entrepreneurial process, see Baron, R. A. 2008. The role of affect in the entrepreneurial process. *Academy of Management Review,* 33(2): 328–340.

48. Hoskin, R. E. 1994. *Financial accounting.* New York: Wiley.

49. We know stock options as derivative assets—that is, "an asset whose value depends on or is derived from the value of another, the underlying asset": Amram, M. & Kulatilaka, N. 1999. *Real options: Managing strategic*

investment in an uncertain world: 34. Boston: Harvard Business School Press.

50. For an interesting discussion on why it is difficult to "kill options," refer to Royer, I. 2003. Why bad projects are so hard to kill. *Harvard Business Review,* 81(2): 48–57.

51. Slywotzky, A. & Wise, R. 2003. Double-digit growth in no-growth times. *Fast Company,* April: 66–72; www.hoovers.com; and www.johnsoncontrols.com.

52. For more on the role of real options in entrepreneurial decision making, see Folta, T. B. & O'Brien, J. P. 2004. Entry in the presence of dueling options. *Strategic Management Journal,* 25: 121–138.

53. This section draws on Janney, J. J. & Dess, G. G. 2004. Can real options analysis improve decision-making? Promises and pitfalls. *Academy of Management Executive,* 18(4): 60–75. For additional insights on pitfalls of real options, consider McGrath, R. G. 1997. A real options logic for initiating technology positioning investment. *Academy of Management Review,* 22(4): 974–994; Coff, R. W. & Laverty, K. J. 2001. Real options on knowledge assets: Panacea or Pandora's box. *Business Horizons,* 73: 79, McGrath, R. G. 1999. Falling forward: Real options reasoning and entrepreneurial failure. *Academy of Management Review,* 24(1): 13–30; and, Zardkoohi, A. 2004.

54. For an understanding of the differences between how managers say they approach decisions and how they actually do, March and Shapira's discussion is perhaps the best. March, J. G. & Shapira, Z. 1987. Managerial perspectives on risk and risk-taking. *Management Science,* 33(11): 1404–1418.

55. A discussion of some factors that may lead to escalation in decision making is included in Choo, C. W. 2005. Information failures and organizational disasters. *MIT Sloan Management Review,* 46(3): 8–10.

56. For an interesting discussion of the use of real options analysis in the application of wireless communications, which helped to lower the potential for escalation, refer to McGrath, R. G., Ferrier, W. J., & Mendelow, A. L. 2004. Real options as engines of choice and heterogeneity. *Academy of Management Review,* 29(1): 86–101.

57. One very useful solution for reducing the effects of managerial conceit is to incorporate an "exit champion" into the decision process. Exit champions provide arguments for killing off the firm's commitment to a decision. For a very insightful discussion on exit champions, refer to Royer, I. 2003. Why bad projects are so hard to kill. *Harvard Business Review,* 81(2): 49–56.

58. For more on how entrepreneurial orientation influences organizational performance, see Wang, L. 2008. Entrepreneurial orientation, learning orientation, and firm performance. *Entrepreneurship Theory & Practice,* 32(4): 635–657; and Runyan, R., Droge, C., & Swinney, J. 2008. Entrepreneurial orientation versus small business orientation: What are their relationships to firm performance? *Journal of Small Business Management,* 46(4): 567–588.

59. Covin, J. G. & Slevin, D. P. 1991. A conceptual model of entrepreneurship as firm behavior. *Entrepreneurship Theory and Practice,* 16(1): 7–24; Lumpkin, G. T. & Dess, G. G. 1996. Clarifying the entrepreneurial orientation construct and linking it to performance. *Academy of Management Review,* 21(1): 135–172; and McGrath, R. G. & MacMillan, I. C. 2000. *The entrepreneurial mind-set.* Cambridge, MA: Harvard Business School Press.

60. Lumpkin, G. T. & Dess, G. G. 2001. Linking two dimensions of entrepreneurial orientation to firm performance: The moderating role of environment and life cycle. *Journal of Business Venturing,* 16: 429–451.

61. For an interesting discussion, see Day, J. D., Mang, P. Y., Richter, A., & Roberts, J. 2001. The innovative organization: Why new ventures need more than a room of their own, *McKinsey Quarterly,* 2: 21–31.

62. Crockett, R. O. 2001. Chris Galvin shakes things up—again. *Business-Week,* May 28: 38–39.

63. For insights into the role of information technology in innovativeness, see Dibrell, C., Davis, P. S., & Craig, J. 2008. Fueling innovation through information technology in SMEs. *Journal of Small Business Management,* 46(2): 203–218.

64. For an interesting discussion of the impact of innovativeness on organizational outcomes see Cho, H. J. & Pucik, V. 2005. Relationship between innovativeness, quality, growth, profitability, and market value. *Strategic Management Journal,* 26(6): 555–575.

65. Lieberman, M. B. & Montgomery, D. B. 1988. First mover advantages. *Strategic Management Journal,* 9 (Special Issue): 41–58.

66. The discussion of first mover advantages is based on several articles, including Lambkin, M. 1988. Order of entry and performance in new markets. *Strategic Management Journal,* 9: 127–140; Lieberman & Montgomery, op. cit.: 41–58; and Miller, A. & Camp, B. 1985. Exploring determinants of success in corporate ventures. *Journal of Business Venturing,* 1(2): 87–105.

67. Moore, G. A. 1999. *Crossing the chasm* (2nd ed.). New York: HarperBusiness.

68. Mallas, S. 2005. PepsiCo loses its Edge. *Motley Fool,* June 1, www.fool.com.

69. Lyons, D. 2006. The cheap revolution. *Forbes,* September 18: 102–111.

70. Miller, K. D. 2007. Risk and rationality in entrepreneurial processes. *Strategic Entrepreneurship Journal,* 1(1–2): 57–74.

71. Drucker, op. cit., pp. 109–110.

Analyzing Strategic Management Cases

>learning objectives

After reading this chapter, you should have a good understanding of:

LO1 How strategic case analysis is used to simulate real-world experiences.

LO2 How analyzing strategic management cases can help develop the ability to differentiate, speculate, and integrate when evaluating complex business problems.

LO3 The steps involved in conducting a strategic management case analysis.

LO4 How to get the most out of case analysis.

LO5 How conflict-inducing discussion techniques can lead to better decisions.

LO6 How to use the strategic insights and material from each of the 12 previous chapters in the text to analyze issues posed by strategic management cases.

Case analysis is one of the most effective ways to learn strategic management. It provides a complement to other methods of instruction by asking you to use the tools and techniques of strategic management to deal with an actual business situation. Strategy cases include detailed descriptions of management challenges faced by executives and business owners. By studying the background and analyzing the strategic predicaments posed by a case, you first see that the circumstances businesses confront are often difficult and complex. Then you are asked what decisions you would make to address the situation in the case and how the actions you recommend will affect the company. Thus, the processes of analysis, formulation, and implementation that have been addressed by this textbook can be applied in a real-life situation.

In this chapter we will discuss the role of case analysis as a learning tool in both the classroom and the real world. One of the benefits of strategic case analysis is to develop the ability to differentiate, speculate, and integrate. We will also describe how to conduct a case analysis and address techniques for deriving the greatest benefit from the process, including the effective use of conflict-inducing decision techniques. Finally, we will discuss how case analysis in a classroom setting can enhance the process of analyzing, making decisions, and taking action in real-world strategic situations.

Why Analyze Strategic Management Cases?

>LO1

How strategic case analysis is used to simulate real-world experiences.

It is often said that the key to finding good answers is to ask good questions. Strategic managers and business leaders are required to evaluate options, make choices, and find solutions to the challenges they face every day. To do so, they must learn to ask the right questions. The study of strategic management poses the same challenge. The process of analyzing, decision making, and implementing strategic actions raises many good questions.

- Why do some firms succeed and others fail?
- Why are some companies higher performers than others?
- What information is needed in the strategic planning process?
- How do competing values and beliefs affect strategic decision making?
- What skills and capabilities are needed to implement a strategy effectively?

case analysis a method of learning complex strategic management concepts such as environmental analysis, the process of decision making, and implementing strategic actions through placing students in the middle of an actual situation and challenging them to figure out what to do.

How does a student of strategic management answer these questions? By strategic case analysis. **Case analysis** simulates the real-world experience that strategic managers and company leaders face as they try to determine how best to run their companies. It places students in the middle of an actual situation and challenges them to figure out what to do.[1]

Asking the right questions is just the beginning of case analysis. In the previous chapters we have discussed issues and challenges that managers face and provided analytical frameworks for understanding the situation. But once the analysis is complete, decisions have to be made. Case analysis forces you to choose among different options and set forth a plan of action based on your choices. But even then the job is not done. Strategic case analysis also requires that you address how you will implement the plan and the implications of choosing one course of action over another.

A strategic management case is a detailed description of a challenging situation faced by an organization.[2] It usually includes a chronology of events and extensive support materials, such as financial statements, product lists, and transcripts of interviews with employees. Although names or locations are sometimes changed to provide anonymity, cases usually report the facts of a situation as authentically as possible.

One of the main reasons to analyze strategic management cases is to develop an ability to evaluate business situations critically. In case analysis, memorizing key terms and conceptual frameworks is not enough. To analyze a case, it is important that you go beyond textbook prescriptions and quick answers. It requires you to look deeply into the information that is provided and root out the essential issues and causes of a company's problems.

>LO2

How analyzing strategic management cases can help develop the ability to differentiate, speculate, and integrate when evaluating complex business problems.

The types of skills that are required to prepare an effective strategic case analysis can benefit you in actual business situations. Case analysis adds to the overall learning experience by helping you acquire or improve skills that may not be taught in a typical lecture course. Three capabilities that can be learned by conducting case analysis are especially useful to strategic managers—the ability to differentiate, speculate, and integrate.[3] Here's how case analysis can enhance those skills.

1. **Differentiate.** Effective strategic management requires that many different elements of a situation be evaluated at once. This is also true in case analysis. When analyzing cases, it is important to isolate critical facts, evaluate whether assumptions are useful or faulty, and distinguish between good and bad information. Differentiating between the factors that are influencing the situation presented by a case is necessary for making a good analysis. Strategic management also involves understanding that problems are often complex and multilayered. This applies to case analysis as well. Ask whether the case deals with operational, business-level, or corporate issues. Do the problems stem from weaknesses in the internal value chain or threats in the external environment? Dig deep. Being too quick to accept the easiest or least controversial answer will usually fail to get to the heart of the problem.

2. **Speculate.** Strategic managers need to be able to use their imagination to envision an explanation or solution that might not readily be apparent. The same is true with case analysis. Being able to imagine different scenarios or contemplate the outcome of a decision can aid the analysis. Managers also have to deal with uncertainty since most decisions are made without complete knowledge of the circumstances. This is also true in case analysis. Case materials often seem to be missing data or the information provided is contradictory. The ability to speculate about details that are unknown or the consequences of an action can be helpful.

3. **Integrate.** Strategy involves looking at the big picture and having an organization-wide perspective. Strategic case analysis is no different. Even though the chapters in this textbook divide the material into various topics that may apply to different parts of an organization, all of this information must be integrated into one set of recommendations that will affect the whole company. A strategic manager needs to comprehend how all the factors that influence the organization will interact. This also applies to case analysis. Changes made in one part of the organization affect other parts. Thus, a holistic perspective that integrates the impact of various decisions and environmental influences on all parts of the organization is needed.

In business, these three activities sometimes "compete" with each other for your attention. For example, some decision makers may have a natural ability to differentiate among elements of a problem but are not able to integrate them very well. Others have enough innate creativity to imagine solutions or fill in the blanks when information is missing. But they may have a difficult time when faced with hard numbers or cold facts. Even so, each of these skills is important. The mark of a good strategic manager is the ability to simultaneously make distinctions and envision the whole, and to imagine a future scenario while staying focused on the present. Thus, another reason to conduct case analysis is to help you develop and exercise your ability to differentiate, speculate, and integrate.

Case analysis takes the student through the whole cycle of activity that a manager would face. Beyond the textbook descriptions of concepts and examples, case analysis asks you to "walk a mile in the shoes" of the strategic decision maker and learn to evaluate situations critically. Executives and owners must make decisions every day with limited information and a swirl of business activity going on around them. Consider the example of Sapient Health Networks, an Internet start-up that had to undergo some analysis and problem solving just to survive. Strategy Spotlight 13.1 describes how this company transformed itself after a serious self-examination during a time of crisis.

As you can see from the experience of Sapient Health Networks, businesses are often faced with immediate challenges that threaten their lives. The Sapient case illustrates how the strategic management process helped it survive. First, the company realistically assessed the environment, evaluated the marketplace, and analyzed its resources. Then it made tough decisions, which included shifting its market focus, hiring and firing, and redeploying its assets. Finally, it took action. The result was not only firm survival, but also a quick turnaround leading to rapid success.

How to Conduct a Case Analysis

>LO3
The steps involved in conducting a strategic management case analysis.

The process of analyzing strategic management cases involves several steps. In this section we will review the mechanics of preparing a case analysis. Before beginning, there are two things to keep in mind that will clarify your understanding of the process and make the results of the process more meaningful.

First, unless you prepare for a case discussion, there is little you can gain from the discussion and even less that you can offer. Effective strategic managers don't enter into problem-solving situations without doing some homework—investigating the situation,

Analysis, Decision Making, and Change at Sapient Health Network

Sapient Health Network (SHN) had gotten off to a good start. CEO Jim Kean and his two cofounders had raised $5 million in investor capital to launch their vision: an Internet-based health care information subscription service. The idea was to create an Internet community for people suffering from chronic diseases. It would provide members with expert information, resources, a message board, and chat rooms so that people suffering from the same ailments could provide each other with information and support. "Who would be more voracious consumers of information than people who are faced with life-changing, life-threatening illnesses?" thought Bill Kelly, one of SHN's cofounders. Initial market research and beta tests had supported that view.

During the beta tests, however, the service had been offered for free. The troubles began when SHN tried to convert its trial subscribers into paying ones. Fewer than 5 percent signed on, far less than the 15 percent the company had projected. Sapient hired a vice president of marketing who launched an aggressive promotion, but after three months of campaigning SHN still had only 500 members. SHN was now burning through $400,000 per month, with little revenue to show for it.

At that point, according to SHN board member Susan Clymer, "there was a lot of scrambling around trying to figure out how we could wring value out of what we'd

Sources: Ferguson, S. 2007. Health Care Gets a Better IT Prescription. *Baseline*, www.baselinemag.com, May 24. Brenneman, K. 2000. Healtheon/WebMD's Local Office Is Thriving. *Business Journal of Portland*, June 2; Raths, D. 1998. Reversal of Fortune. *Inc. Technology*, 2: 52–62.

already accomplished." One thing SHN had created was an expert software system which had two components: an "intelligent profile engine" (IPE) and an "intelligent query engine" (IQE). SHN used this system to collect detailed information from its subscribers.

SHN was sure that the expert system was its biggest selling point. But how could they use it? Then the founders remembered that the original business plan had suggested there might be a market for aggregate data about patient populations gathered from the website. Could they turn the business around by selling patient data? To analyze the possibility, Kean tried out the idea on the market research arm of a huge East Coast health care conglomerate. The officials were intrigued. SHN realized that its expert system could become a market research tool.

Once the analysis was completed, the founders made the decision: They would still create Internet communities for chronically ill patients, but the service would be free. And they would transform SHN from a company that processed subscriptions to one that sold market research.

Finally, they enacted the changes. Some of it was painful, including laying off 18 employees. Instead, SHN needed more health care industry expertise. It even hired an interim CEO, Craig Davenport, a 25-year veteran of the industry, to steer the company in its new direction. Finally, SHN had to communicate a new message to its members. It began by reimbursing the $10,000 of subscription fees they had paid.

All of this paid off dramatically in a matter of just two years. Revenues jumped to $1.9 million and early in the third year, SHN was purchased by WebMD. Less than a year after that, WebMD merged with Healtheon. The combined company still operates a thriving office out of SHN's original location in Portland, Oregon.

---

analyzing and researching possible solutions, and sometimes gathering the advice of others. Good problem solving often requires that decision makers be immersed in the facts, options, and implications surrounding the problem. In case analysis, this means reading and thoroughly comprehending the case materials before trying to make an analysis.

The second point is related to the first. To get the most out of a case analysis you must place yourself "inside" the case—that is, think like an actual participant in the case situation. However, there are several positions you can take. These are discussed in the following paragraphs:

- **Strategic decision maker.** This is the position of the senior executive responsible for resolving the situation described in the case. It may be the CEO, the business owner, or a strategic manager in a key executive position.
- **Board of directors.** Since the board of directors represents the owners of a corporation, it has a responsibility to step in when a management crisis threatens the company. As a board member, you may be in a unique position to solve problems.

- **Outside consultant.** Either the board or top management may decide to bring in outsiders. Consultants often have an advantage because they can look at a situation objectively. But they also may be at a disadvantage since they have no power to enforce changes.

Before beginning the analysis, it may be helpful to envision yourself assuming one of these roles. Then, as you study and analyze the case materials, you can make a diagnosis and recommend solutions in a way that is consistent with your position. Try different perspectives. You may find that your view of the situation changes depending on the role you play. As an outside consultant, for example, it may be easy for you to conclude that certain individuals should be replaced in order to solve a problem presented in the case. However, if you take the role of the CEO who knows the individuals and the challenges they have been facing, you may be reluctant to fire them and will seek another solution instead.

The idea of assuming a particular role is similar to the real world in various ways. In your career, you may work in an organization where outside accountants, bankers, lawyers, or other professionals are advising you about how to resolve business situations or improve your practices. Their perspective will be different from yours but it is useful to understand things from their point of view. Conversely, you may work as a member of the audit team of an accounting firm or the loan committee of a bank. In those situations, it would be helpful if you understood the situation from the perspective of the business leader who must weigh your views against all the other advice that he or she receives. Case analysis can help develop an ability to appreciate such multiple perspectives.

One of the most challenging roles to play in business is as a business founder or owner. For small businesses or entrepreneurial start-ups, the founder may wear all hats at once—key decision maker, primary stockholder, and CEO. Hiring an outside consultant may not be an option. However, the issues faced by young firms and established firms are often not that different, especially when it comes to formulating a plan of action. Business plans that entrepreneurial firms use to raise money or propose a business expansion typically revolve around a few key issues that must be addressed no matter what the size or age of the business. Strategy Spotlight 13.2 reviews business planning issues that are most important to consider when evaluating any case, especially from the perspective of the business founder or owner.

Next we will review five steps to follow when conducting a strategic management case analysis: becoming familiar with the material, identifying the problems, analyzing the strategic issues using the tools and insights of strategic management, proposing alternative solutions, and making recommendations.[4]

Become Familiar with the Material

Written cases often include a lot of material. They may be complex and include detailed financials or long passages. Even so, to understand a case and its implications, you must become familiar with its content. Sometimes key information is not immediately apparent. It may be contained in the footnotes to an exhibit or an interview with a lower-level employee. In other cases the important points may be difficult to grasp because the subject matter is so unfamiliar. When you approach a strategic case try the following technique to enhance comprehension:

- Read quickly through the case one time to get an overall sense of the material.
- Use the initial read-through to assess possible links to strategic concepts.
- Read through the case again, in depth. Make written notes as you read.
- Evaluate how strategic concepts might inform key decisions or suggest alternative solutions.
- After formulating an initial recommendation, thumb through the case again quickly to help assess the consequences of the actions you propose.

strategy spotlight

Using a Business Plan Framework to Analyze Strategic Cases

Established businesses often have to change what they are doing in order to improve their competitive position or sometimes simply to survive. To make the changes effectively, businesses usually need a plan. Business plans are no longer just for entrepreneurs. The kind of market analysis, decision making, and action planning that is considered standard practice among new ventures can also benefit going concerns that want to make changes, seize an opportunity, or head in a new direction.

The best business plans, however, are not those loaded with decades of month-by-month financial projections or that depend on rigid adherence to a schedule of events that is impossible to predict. The good ones are focused on four factors that are critical to new-venture success. These same factors are important in case analysis as well because they get to the heart of many of the problems found in strategic cases.

1. *The People.* "When I receive a business plan, I always read the résumé section first," says Harvard Professor William Sahlman. The people questions that are critically important to investors include: What are their skills? How much experience do they have? What is their reputation? Have they worked together as a team? These same questions also may be used in case analysis to evaluate the role of individuals in the strategic case.

2. *The Opportunity.* Business opportunities come in many forms. They are not limited to new ventures.

Sources: Wasserman, E. 2003. A Simple Plan. *MBA Jungle,* February: 50–55; DeKluyver, C. A. 2000. *Strategic Thinking: An Executive Perspective.* Upper Saddle River, NJ: Prentice Hall; and Sahlman, W. A. 1997. How to Write a Great Business Plan. *Harvard Business Review,* 75(4): 98–108.

The chance to enter new markets, introduce new products, or merge with a competitor provides many of the challenges that are found in strategic management cases. What are the consequences of such actions? Will the proposed changes affect the firm's business concept? What factors might stand in the way of success? The same issues are also present in most strategic cases.

3. *The Context.* Things happen in contexts that cannot be controlled by a firm's managers. This is particularly true of the general environment where social trends, economic changes, or events such as the September 11, 2001, terrorist attacks can change business overnight. When evaluating strategic cases, ask: Is the company aware of the impact of context on the business? What will it do if the context changes? Can it influence the context in a way that favors the company?

4. *Risk and Reward.* With a new venture, the entrepreneurs and investors take the risks and get the rewards. In strategic cases, the risks and rewards often extend to many other stakeholders, such as employees, customers, and suppliers. When analyzing a case, ask: Are the managers making choices that will pay off in the future? Are the rewards evenly distributed? Will some stakeholders be put at risk if the situation in the case changes? What if the situation remains the same? Could that be even riskier?

Whether a business is growing or shrinking, large or small, industrial or service oriented, the issues of people, opportunities, context, and risks and rewards will have a large impact on its performance. Therefore, you should always consider these four factors when evaluating strategic management cases.

Identify Problems

When conducting case analysis, one of your most important tasks is to identify the problem. Earlier we noted that one of the main reasons to conduct case analysis was to find solutions. But you cannot find a solution unless you know the problem. Another saying you may have heard is, "A good diagnosis is half the cure." In other words, once you have determined what the problem is, you are well on your way to identifying a reasonable solution.

Some cases have more than one problem. But the problems are usually related. For a hypothetical example, consider the following: Company A was losing customers to a new competitor. Upon analysis, it was determined that the competitor had a 50 percent faster delivery time even though its product was of lower quality. The managers of company A could not understand why customers would settle for an inferior product. It turns out that no one was marketing to company A's customers that its product was superior. A second problem was that falling sales resulted in cuts in company A's sales force. Thus, there were two related problems: inferior delivery technology and insufficient sales effort.

When trying to determine the problem, avoid getting hung up on symptoms. Zero in on the problem. For example, in the company A example above, the symptom was losing customers. But the problems were an underfunded, understaffed sales force combined with an outdated delivery technology. Try to see beyond the immediate symptoms to the more fundamental problems.

Another tip when preparing a case analysis is to articulate the problem.[5] Writing down a problem statement gives you a reference point to turn to as you proceed through the case analysis. This is important because the process of formulating strategies or evaluating implementation methods may lead you away from the initial problem. Make sure your recommendation actually addresses the problems you have identified.

One more thing about identifying problems: Sometimes problems are not apparent until *after* you do the analysis. In some cases the problem will be presented plainly, perhaps in the opening paragraph or on the last page of the case. But in other cases the problem does not emerge until after the issues in the case have been analyzed. We turn next to the subject of strategic case analysis.

Conduct Strategic Analyses

This textbook has presented numerous analytical tools (e.g., five-forces analysis and value-chain analysis), contingency frameworks (e.g., when to use related rather than unrelated diversification strategies), and other techniques that can be used to evaluate strategic situations. The previous 12 chapters have addressed practices that are common in strategic management, but only so much can be learned by studying the practices and concepts. The best way to understand these methods is to apply them by conducting analyses of specific cases.

The first step is to determine which strategic issues are involved. Is there a problem in the company's competitive environment? Or is it an internal problem? If it is internal, does it have to do with organizational structure? Strategic controls? Uses of technology? Or perhaps the company has overworked its employees or underutilized its intellectual capital. Has the company mishandled a merger? Chosen the wrong diversification strategy? Botched a new product introduction? Each of these issues is linked to one or more of the concepts discussed earlier in the text. Determine what strategic issues are associated with the problems you have identified. Remember also that most real-life case situations involve issues that are highly interrelated. Even in cases where there is only one major problem, the strategic processes required to solve it may involve several parts of the organization.

Once you have identified the issues that apply to the case, conduct the analysis. For example, you may need to conduct a five-forces analysis or dissect the company's competitive strategy. Perhaps you need to evaluate whether its resources are rare, valuable, difficult to imitate, or difficult to substitute. Financial analysis may be needed to assess the company's economic prospects. Perhaps the international entry mode needs to be reevaluated because of changing conditions in the host country. Employee empowerment techniques may need to be improved to enhance organizational learning. Whatever the case, all the strategic concepts introduced in the text include insights for assessing their effectiveness. Determining how well a company is doing these things is central to the case analysis process.

Financial ratio analysis is one of the primary tools used to conduct case analysis. Appendix 1 to Chapter 13 includes a discussion and examples of the financial ratios that are often used to evaluate a company's performance and financial well-being. Exhibit 13.1 provides a summary of the financial ratios presented in Appendix 1 to this chapter.

In this part of the overall strategic analysis process, it is also important to test your own assumptions about the case.[6] First, what assumptions are you making about the case

financial ratio analysis a method of evaluating a company's performance and financial well-being through ratios of accounting values, including short-term solvency, long-term solvency, asset utilization, profitability, and market value ratios.

Exhibit 13.1 **Summary of Financial Ratio Analysis Techniques**

Ratio	What It Measures
Short-term solvency, or liquidity, ratios:	
Current ratio	Ability to use assets to pay off liabilities.
Quick ratio	Ability to use liquid assets to pay off liabilities quickly.
Cash ratio	Ability to pay off liabilities with cash on hand.
Long-term solvency, or financial leverage, ratios:	
Total debt ratio	How much of a company's total assets are financed by debt.
Debt-equity ratio	Compares how much a company is financed by debt with how much it is financed by equity.
Equity multiplier	How much debt is being used to finance assets.
Times interest earned ratio	How well a company has its interest obligations covered.
Cash coverage ratio	A company's ability to generate cash from operations.
Asset utilization, or turnover, ratios:	
Inventory turnover	How many times each year a company sells its entire inventory.
Days' sales in inventory	How many days on average inventory is on hand before it is sold.
Receivables turnover	How frequently each year a company collects on its credit sales.
Days' sales in receivables	How many days on average it takes to collect on credit sales (average collection period).
Total asset turnover	How much of sales is generated for every dollar in assets.
Capital intensity	The dollar investment in assets needed to generate $1 in sales.
Profitability ratios:	
Profit margin	How much profit is generated by every dollar of sales.
Return on assets (ROA)	How effectively assets are being used to generate a return.
Return on equity (ROE)	How effectively amounts invested in the business by its owners are being used to generate a return.
Market value ratios:	
Price–earnings ratio	How much investors are willing to pay per dollar of current earnings.
Market-to-book ratio	Compares market value of the company's investments to the cost of those investments.

materials? It may be that you have interpreted the case content differently than your team members or classmates. Being clear about these assumptions will be important in determining how to analyze the case. Second, what assumptions have you made about the best way to resolve the problems? Ask yourself why you have chosen one type of analysis over another. This process of assumption checking can also help determine if you have gotten to the heart of the problem or are still just dealing with symptoms.

As mentioned earlier, sometimes the critical diagnosis in a case can only be made after the analysis is conducted. However, by the end of this stage in the process, you should know the problems and have completed a thorough analysis of them. You can now move to the next step: finding solutions.

Propose Alternative Solutions

It is important to remember that in strategic management case analysis, there is rarely one right answer or one best way. Even when members of a class or a team agree on what the problem is, they may not agree upon how to solve the problem. Therefore, it is helpful to consider several different solutions.

After conducting strategic analysis and identifying the problem, develop a list of options. What are the possible solutions? What are the alternatives? First, generate a list of all the options you can think of without prejudging any one of them. Remember that not all cases call for dramatic decisions or sweeping changes. Some companies just need to make small adjustments. In fact, "Do nothing" may be a reasonable alternative in some cases. Although that is rare, it might be useful to consider what will happen if the company does nothing. This point illustrates the purpose of developing alternatives: to evaluate what will happen if a company chooses one solution over another.

Thus, during this step of a case analysis, you will evaluate choices and the implications of those choices. One aspect of any business that is likely to be highlighted in this part of the analysis is strategy implementation. Ask how the choices made will be implemented. It may be that what seems like an obvious choice for solving a problem creates an even bigger problem when implemented. But remember also that no strategy or strategic "fix" is going to work if it cannot be implemented. Once a list of alternatives is generated, ask:

- Can the company afford it? How will it affect the bottom line?
- Is the solution likely to evoke a competitive response?
- Will employees throughout the company accept the changes? What impact will the solution have on morale?
- How will the decision affect other stakeholders? Will customers, suppliers, and others buy into it?
- How does this solution fit with the company's vision, mission, and objectives?
- Will the culture or values of the company be changed by the solution? Is it a positive change?

The point of this step in the case analysis process is to find a solution that both solves the problem and is realistic. A consideration of the implications of various alternative solutions will generally lead you to a final recommendation that is more thoughtful and complete.

Make Recommendations

The basic aim of case analysis is to find solutions. Your analysis is not complete until you have recommended a course of action. In this step the task is to make a set of recommendations that your analysis supports. Describe exactly what needs to be done. Explain why this course of action will solve the problem. The recommendation should also include suggestions for how best to implement the proposed solution because the recommended actions and their implications for the performance and future of the firm are interrelated.

Recall that the solution you propose must solve the problem you identified. This point cannot be overemphasized; too often students make recommendations that treat only symptoms or fail to tackle the central problems in the case. Make a logical argument that shows how the problem led to the analysis and the analysis led to the recommendations you are proposing. Remember, an analysis is not an end in itself; it is useful only if it leads to a solution.

The actions you propose should describe the very next steps that the company needs to take. Don't say, for example, "If the company does more market research, then I would recommend the following course of action. . . ." Instead, make conducting the research part of your recommendation. Taking the example a step further, if you also want to suggest subsequent actions that may be different *depending* on the outcome of the market research, that's OK. But don't make your initial recommendation conditional on actions the company may or may not take.

In summary, case analysis can be a very rewarding process but, as you might imagine, it can also be frustrating and challenging. If you will follow the steps described above, you will address the different elements of a thorough analysis. This approach can give your analysis a solid footing. Then, even if there are differences of opinion about how to interpret the facts, analyze the situation, or solve the problems, you can feel confident that you have not missed any important steps in finding the best course of action.

Students are often asked to prepare oral presentations of the information in a case and their analysis of the best remedies. This is frequently assigned as a group project. Or you may be called upon in class to present your ideas about the circumstances or solutions for a case the class is discussing. Exhibit 13.2 provides some tips for preparing an oral case presentation.

Exhibit 13.2 **Preparing an Oral Case Presentation**

Rule	Description
Organize your thoughts.	Begin by becoming familiar with the material. If you are working with a team, compare notes about the key points of the case and share insights that other team members may have gleaned from tables and exhibits. Then make an outline. This is one of the best ways to organize the flow and content of the presentation.
Emphasize strategic analysis.	The purpose of case analysis is to diagnose problems and find solutions. In the process, you may need to unravel the case material as presented and reconfigure it in a fashion that can be more effectively analyzed. Present the material in a way that lends itself to analysis—don't simply restate what is in the case. This involves three major categories with the following emphasis: Background/Problem Statement 10–20% Strategic Analysis/Options 60–75% Recommendations/Action Plan 10–20% As you can see, the emphasis of your presentation should be on analysis. This will probably require you to reorganize the material so that the tools of strategic analysis can be applied.
Be logical and consistent.	A presentation that is rambling and hard to follow may confuse the listener and fail to evoke a good discussion. Present your arguments and explanations in a logical sequence. Support your claims with facts. Include financial analysis where appropriate. Be sure that the solutions you recommend address the problems you have identified.
Defend your position.	Usually an oral presentation is followed by a class discussion. Anticipate what others might disagree with and be prepared to defend your views. This means being aware of the choices you made and the implications of your recommendations. Be clear about your assumptions. Be able to expand on your analysis.
Share presentation responsibilities.	Strategic management case analyses are often conducted by teams. Each member of the team should have a clear role in the oral presentation, preferably a speaking role. It's also important to coordinate the different parts of the presentation into a logical, smooth-flowing whole. How well a team works together is usually very apparent during an oral presentation.

How to Get the Most from Case Analysis

One of the reasons case analysis is so enriching as a learning tool is that it draws on many resources and skills besides just what is in the textbook. This is especially true in the study of strategy. Why? Because strategic management itself is a highly integrative task that draws on many areas of specialization at several levels, from the individual to the whole of society. Therefore, to get the most out of case analysis, expand your horizons beyond the concepts in this text and seek insights from your own reservoir of knowledge. Here are some tips for how to do that.[7]

>LO4
How to get the most out of case analysis.

- *Keep an open mind.* Like any good discussion, a case analysis discussion often evokes strong opinions and high emotions. But it's the variety of perspectives that makes case analysis so valuable: Many viewpoints usually lead to a more complete analysis. Therefore, avoid letting an emotional response to another person's style or opinion keep you from hearing what he or she has to say. Once you evaluate what is said, you may disagree with it or dismiss it as faulty. But unless you keep an open mind in the first place, you may miss the importance of the other person's contribution. Also, people often place a higher value on the opinions of those they consider to be good listeners.

- *Take a stand for what you believe.* Although it is vital to keep an open mind, it is also important to state your views proactively. Don't try to figure out what your friends or the instructor wants to hear. Analyze the case from the perspective of your own background and belief system. For example, perhaps you feel that a decision is unethical or that the managers in a case have misinterpreted the facts. Don't be afraid to assert that in the discussion. For one thing, when a person takes a strong stand, it often encourages others to evaluate the issues more closely. This can lead to a more thorough investigation and a more meaningful class discussion.

- *Draw on your personal experience.* You may have experiences from work or as a customer that shed light on some of the issues in a case. Even though one of the purposes of case analysis is to apply the analytical tools from this text, you may be able to add to the discussion by drawing on your outside experiences and background. Of course, you need to guard against carrying that to extremes. In other words, don't think that your perspective is the only viewpoint that matters! Simply recognize that firsthand experience usually represents a welcome contribution to the overall quality of case discussions.

- *Participate and persuade.* Have you heard the phrase, "Vote early . . . and often"? Among loyal members of certain political parties, it has become rather a joke. Why? Because a democratic system is built on the concept of one person, one vote. Even though some voters may want to vote often enough to get their candidate elected, it is against the law. Not so in a case discussion. People who are persuasive and speak their mind can often influence the views of others. But to do so, you have to be prepared and convincing. Being persuasive is more than being loud or long-winded. It involves understanding all sides of an argument and being able to overcome objections to your own point of view. These efforts can make a case discussion more lively. And they parallel what happens in the real world; in business, people frequently share their opinions and attempt to persuade others to see things their way.

- *Be concise and to the point.* In the previous point, we encouraged you to speak up and "sell" your ideas to others in a case discussion. But you must be clear about what you are selling. Make your arguments in a way that is explicit and direct. Zero in on the most important points. Be brief. Don't try to make a lot of points at once by jumping around between topics. Avoid trying to explain the whole case situation at once. Remember, other students usually resent classmates who go on and on, take up a lot of "airtime," or repeat themselves unnecessarily. The best way to avoid this is to stay focused and be specific.

- **Think out of the box.** It's OK to be a little provocative; sometimes that is the consequence of taking a stand on issues. But it may be equally important to be imaginative and creative when making a recommendation or determining how to implement a solution. Albert Einstein once stated, "Imagination is more important than knowledge." The reason is that managing strategically requires more than memorizing concepts. Strategic management insights must be applied to each case differently—just knowing the principles is not enough. Imagination and out-of-the-box thinking help to apply strategic knowledge in novel and unique ways.

- **Learn from the insights of others.** Before you make up your mind about a case, hear what other students have to say. Get a second opinion, and a third, and so forth. Of course, in a situation where you have to put your analysis in writing, you may not be able to learn from others ahead of time. But in a case discussion, observe how various students attack the issues and engage in problem solving. Such observation skills also may be a key to finding answers within the case. For example, people tend to believe authority figures, so they would place a higher value on what a company president says. In some cases, however, the statements of middle managers may represent a point of view that is even more helpful for finding a solution to the problems presented by the case.

- **Apply insights from other case analyses.** Throughout the text, we have used examples of actual businesses to illustrate strategy concepts. The aim has been to show you how firms think about and deal with business problems. During the course, you may be asked to conduct several case analyses as part of the learning experience. Once you have performed a few case analyses, you will see how the concepts from the text apply in real-life business situations. Incorporate the insights learned from the text examples and your own previous case discussions into each new case that you analyze.

- **Critically analyze your own performance.** Performance appraisals are a standard part of many workplace situations. They are used to determine promotions, raises, and work assignments. In some organizations, everyone from the top executive down is subject to such reviews. Even in situations where the owner or CEO is not evaluated by others, they often find it useful to ask themselves regularly, Am I being effective? The same can be applied to your performance in a case analysis situation. Ask yourself, Were my comments insightful? Did I make a good contribution? How might I improve next time? Use the same criteria on yourself that you use to evaluate others. What grade would you give yourself? This technique will not only make you more fair in your assessment of others but also will indicate how your own performance can improve.

- **Conduct outside research.** Many times, you can enhance your understanding of a case situation by investigating sources outside the case materials. For example, you may want to study an industry more closely or research a company's close competitors. Recent moves such as mergers and acquisitions or product introductions may be reported in the business press. The company itself may provide useful information on its website or in its annual reports. Such information can usually spur additional discussion and enrich the case analysis. (*Caution:* It is best to check with your instructor in advance to be sure this kind of additional research is encouraged. Bringing in outside research may conflict with the instructor's learning objectives.)

Several of the points suggested above for how to get the most out of case analysis apply only to an open discussion of a case, like that in a classroom setting. Exhibit 13.3 provides some additional guidelines for preparing a written case analysis.

Exhibit 13.3   Preparing a Written Case Analysis

Rule	Description
Be thorough.	Many of the ideas presented in Exhibit 13.2 about oral presentations also apply to written case analysis. However, a written analysis typically has to be more complete. This means writing out the problem statement and articulating assumptions. It is also important to provide support for your arguments and reference case materials or other facts more specifically.
Coordinate team efforts.	Written cases are often prepared by small groups. Within a group, just as in a class discussion, you may disagree about the diagnosis or the recommended plan of action. This can be healthy if it leads to a richer understanding of the case material. But before committing your ideas to writing, make sure you have coordinated your responses. Don't prepare a written analysis that appears contradictory or looks like a patchwork of disconnected thoughts.
Avoid restating the obvious.	There is no reason to restate material that everyone is familiar with already, namely, the case content. It is too easy for students to use up space in a written analysis with a recapitulation of the details of the case—this accomplishes very little. Stay focused on the key points. Only restate the information that is most central to your analysis.
Present information graphically.	Tables, graphs, and other exhibits are usually one of the best ways to present factual material that supports your arguments. For example, financial calculations such as break-even analysis, sensitivity analysis, or return on investment are best presented graphically. Even qualitative information such as product lists or rosters of employees can be summarized effectively and viewed quickly by using a table or graph.
Exercise quality control.	When presenting a case analysis in writing, it is especially important to use good grammar, avoid misspelling words, and eliminate typos and other visual distractions. Mistakes that can be glossed over in an oral presentation or class discussion are often highlighted when they appear in writing. Make your written presentation appear as professional as possible. Don't let the appearance of your written case keep the reader from recognizing the importance and quality of your analysis.

Using Conflict-Inducing Decision-Making Techniques in Case Analysis

Next we address some techniques often used to improve case analyses that involve the constructive use of conflict. In the classroom—as well as in the business world—you will frequently be analyzing cases or solving problems in groups. While the word *conflict* often has a negative connotation (e.g., rude behavior, personal affronts), it can be very helpful in arriving at better solutions to cases. It can provide an effective means for new insights as well as for rigorously questioning and analyzing assumptions and strategic alternatives. In fact, if you don't have constructive conflict, you may only get consensus. When this happens, decisions tend to be based on compromise rather than collaboration.

In your organizational behavior classes, you probably learned the concept of "group-think."[8] Groupthink, a term coined by Irving Janis after he conducted numerous studies on executive decision making, is a condition in which group members strive to reach agreement or consensus without realistically considering other viable

>LO5
How conflict-inducing discussion techniques can lead to better decisions.

strategy spotlight

Relying on "Rivals" to Stimulate Debate

When Barack Obama was elected U.S. President, he had to move quickly to select a group of reliable advisors and form a cabinet. During the presidential campaign, Obama let it be known that he was a student of Abraham Lincoln, one of his favorite former presidents. He also reported he had been reading Doris Kearns Goodwin's 2005 book *Team of Rivals,* which described Lincoln's decision to surround himself in part with politicians who were known to hold sharply different political views than his own.

Obama, who had fought a difficult primary battle with Senator Hillary Clinton of New York, created mild shock waves when he announced he would nominate her to be secretary of state. His decision, he said, was based in part on his team-of-rivals perspective—that independent and well-informed voices are needed to make the best decisions. At the press conference announcing his national security team, including Clinton, here is how Obama answered questions from the press:

REPORTER: You've selected a number of high profile people for your national security team. How can you ensure that the staff that you are assembling is going to be a smoothly functioning team of rivals and not a clash of rivals?

OBAMA: I assembled this team because I'm a strong believer in strong personalities and strong opinions. I think that's how the best decisions are made. One of the dangers in the White House, based on my reading of history, is that you get wrapped up in groupthink and everybody agrees with everything and there's no discussion and there are no dissenting views. So I'm going to be welcoming vigorous debate inside the White House.

But understand I will be setting policy as president. I will be responsible for the vision that this team carries out, and I expect them to implement the vision once decisions are made. . . You know, most of the people who are standing here are people who I've worked with, and on the broad core vision of where America needs to go, we are in almost complete agreement. There are going to be differences in tactics and different assessments and judgments made. That's what I expect. That's what I welcome. That's why I asked them to join the team.

Good decision making often requires dissenting voices and the expression of strong opinions. While conflict in discussion groups may be momentarily unpleasant, if it leads to high-quality decisions, everyone usually benefits in the long run.

alternatives. In effect, group norms bolster morale at the expense of critical thinking and decision making is impaired.[9] Strategy Spotlight 13.3 discusses a recent highly publicized decision to avoid groupthink by giving voice to thought leaders who were known to disagree.

Many of us have probably been "victims" of groupthink at one time or another in our life. We may be confronted with situations when social pressure, politics, or "not wanting to stand out" may prevent us from voicing our concerns about a chosen course of action. Nevertheless, decision making in groups is a common practice in the management of many businesses. Most companies, especially large ones, rely on input from various top managers to provide valuable information and experience from their specialty area as well as their unique perspectives. Chapter 11 emphasized the importance of empowering individuals at all levels to participate in decision-making processes. In terms of this course, case analysis involves a type of decision making that is often conducted in groups. Strategy Spotlight 13.4 provides guidelines for making team-based approaches to case analysis more effective.

476 Part 4:: Case Analysis

Making Case Analysis Teams More Effective

Working in teams can be very challenging. Not all team members have the same skills, interests, or motivations. Some team members just want to get the work done. Others see teams as an opportunity to socialize. Occasionally, there are team members who think they should be in charge and make all the decisions; other teams have freeloaders—team members who don't want to do anything except get credit for the team's work.

One consequence of these various styles is that team meetings can become time wasters. Disagreements about how to proceed, how to share the work, or what to do at the next meeting tend to slow down teams and impede progress toward the goal. While the dynamics of case analysis teams are likely to always be challenging depending on the personalities involved, one thing nearly all members realize is that, ultimately, the team's work must be completed. Most team members also aim to do the highest quality work possible. The following guidelines provide some useful insights about how to get the work of a team done more effectively.

Spend More Time Together

One of the factors that prevents teams from doing a good job with case analysis is their failure to put in the necessary time. Unless teams really tackle the issues surrounding case analysis—both the issues in the case itself and organizing how the work is to be conducted—the end result will probably be lacking because decisions that are made too quickly are unlikely to get to the heart of the problem(s) in the case. "Meetings should be a precious resource, but they're treated like a necessary evil," says Kenneth Sole, a consultant who specializes in organizational behavior. As a result, teams that care more about finishing the analysis than getting the analysis right often make poor decisions.

Therefore, expect to have a few meetings that run long, especially at the beginning of the project when the work is being organized and the issues in the case are being sorted out, and again at the end when the team must coordinate the components of the case analysis that will be presented. Without spending this kind of time together, it is doubtful that the analysis will be comprehensive and the presentation is likely to be choppy and incomplete.

Make a Focused and Disciplined Agenda

To complete tasks and avoid wasting time, meetings need to have a clear purpose. To accomplish this at Roche, the Swiss drug and diagnostic product maker, CEO Franz Humer implemented a "decision agenda." The agenda focuses only on Roche's highest value issues and discussions are limited to these major topics. In terms of case analysis, the major topics include sorting out the issues of the case, linking elements of the case to the strategic issues presented in class or the text, and assigning roles to various team members. Such objectives help keep team members on track.

Agendas also can be used to address issues such as the time line for accomplishing work. Otherwise the purpose of meetings may only be to manage the "crisis" of getting the case analysis finished on time. One solution is to assign a team member to manage the agenda. That person could make sure the team stays focused on the tasks at hand and remains mindful of time constraints. Another role could be to link the team's efforts to the steps presented in Exhibits 13.2 and Exhibit 13.3 on how to prepare a case analysis.

Pay More Attention to Strategy

Teams often waste time by focusing on unimportant aspects of a case. These may include details that are interesting but irrelevant or operational issues rather than strategic issues. It is true that useful clues to the issues in the case are sometimes embedded in the conversations of key managers or the trends evident in a financial statement. But once such insights are discovered, teams need to focus on the underlying strategic problems in the case. To solve such problems, major corporations such as Cadbury Schweppes and Boeing hold meetings just to generate strategic alternatives for solving their problems. This gives managers time to consider the implications of various courses of action. Separate meetings are held to evaluate alternatives, make strategic decisions, and approve an action plan.

Once the strategic solutions or "course corrections" are identified—as is common in most cases assigned—the operational implications and details of implementation will flow from the strategic decisions that companies make. Therefore, focusing primarily on strategic issues will provide teams with insights for making recommendations that are based on a deeper understanding of the issues in the case.

Produce Real Decisions

Too often, meetings are about discussing rather than deciding. Teams often spend a lot of time talking without reaching any conclusions. As Raymond Sanchez, *(continued)*

(continued) CEO of Florida-based Security Mortgage Group, says, meetings are often used to "rehash the hash that's already been hashed." To be efficient and productive, team meetings need to be about more than just information sharing and group input. For example, an initial meeting may result in the team realizing that it needs to study the case in greater depth and examine links to strategic issues more carefully. Once more analysis is conducted, the team needs to reach a consensus so that the decisions that are made will last once the meeting is over. Lasting decisions are more actionable because it frees team members to take the next steps.

One technique for making progress in this way is recapping each meeting with a five-minute synthesis report.

Sources: Mankins, M. C. 2004. Stop Wasting Valuable Time. *Harvard Business Review,* September: 58–65; and Sauer, P. J. 2004. Escape from Meeting Hell. *Inc. Magazine,* May, www.inc.com.

According to Pamela Schindler, director of the Center for Applied Management at Wittenberg University, it's important to think through the implications of the meeting before ending it. "The real joy of synthesis," says Schindler, "is realizing how many meetings you won't need."

Not only are these guidelines useful for helping teams finish their work, but they can also help resolve some of the difficulties that teams often face. By involving every team member, using a meeting agenda, and focusing on the strategic issues that are critical to nearly every case, the discussion is limited and the criteria for making decisions become clearer. This allows the task to dominate rather than any one personality. And if the team finishes its work faster, this frees up time to focus on other projects or put the finishing touches on a case analysis presentation.

● Effectively working in teams is a critical skill—both in the classroom and in business organizations.

Clearly, understanding how to work in groups and the potential problems associated with group decision processes can benefit the case analysis process. Therefore, let's first look at some of the symptoms of groupthink and suggest ways of preventing it. Then, we will suggest some conflict-inducing decision-making techniques—devil's advocacy and dialectical inquiry—that can help to prevent groupthink and lead to better decisions.

Symptoms of Groupthink and How to Prevent It

Irving Janis identified several symptoms of groupthink, including:

- *An illusion of invulnerability.* This reassures people about possible dangers and leads to overoptimism and failure to heed warnings of danger.
- *A belief in the inherent morality of the group.* Because individuals think that what they are doing is right, they tend to ignore ethical or moral consequences of their decisions.
- *Stereotyped views of members of opposing groups.* Members of other groups are viewed as weak or not intelligent.
- *The application of pressure to members who express doubts about the group's shared illusions or question the validity of arguments proposed.*
- *The practice of self-censorship.* Members keep silent about their opposing views and downplay to themselves the value of their perspectives.
- *An illusion of unanimity.* People assume that judgments expressed by members are shared by all.
- *The appointment of mindguards.* People sometimes appoint themselves as mindguards to protect the group from adverse information that might break the climate of consensus (or agreement).

Clearly, groupthink is an undesirable and negative phenomenon that can lead to poor decisions. Irving Janis considers it to be a key contributor to such faulty decisions as the failure to prepare for the attack on Pearl Harbor, the escalation of the Vietnam conflict, and the failure to prepare for the consequences of the Iraqi invasion. Many of the same sorts of flawed decision making occur in business organizations—as we discussed above with the EDS example. Janis has provided several suggestions for preventing groupthink that can be used as valuable guides in decision making and problem solving:

- Leaders must encourage group members to address their concerns and objectives.
- When higher-level managers assign a problem for a group to solve, they should adopt an impartial stance and not mention their preferences.
- Before a group reaches its final decision, the leader should encourage members to discuss their deliberations with trusted associates and then report the perspectives back to the group.
- The group should invite outside experts and encourage them to challenge the group's viewpoints and positions.
- The group should divide into subgroups, meet at various times under different chairpersons, and then get together to resolve differences.
- After reaching a preliminary agreement, the group should hold a "second chance" meeting which provides members a forum to express any remaining concerns and rethink the issue prior to making a final decision.

devil's advocacy
a method of introducing conflict into a decision-making process by having specific individuals or groups act as a critic to an analysis or planned solution.

Using Conflict to Improve Decision Making

In addition to the above suggestions, the effective use of conflict can be a means of improving decision making. Although conflict can have negative outcomes, such as ill will, anger, tension, and lowered motivation, both leaders and group members must strive to assure that it is managed properly and used in a constructive manner.

Two conflict-inducing decision-making approaches that have become quite popular are *devil's advocacy* and *dialectical inquiry*. Both approaches incorporate conflict into the decision-making process through formalized debate. A group charged with making a decision or solving a problem is divided into two subgroups and each will be involved in the analysis and solution.

● Conflict-inducing decision-making techniques, such as devil's advocacy, can be very effective.

Devil's Advocacy   With the devil's advocate approach, one of the groups (or individuals) acts as a critic to the plan. The devil's advocate tries to come up with problems with the proposed alternative and suggest reasons why it should not be adopted. The role of the devil's advocate is to create dissonance. This ensures that the group will take a hard look at its original proposal or alternative. By having a group (or individual) assigned the role of devil's advocate, it becomes clear that such an adversarial stance is legitimized. It brings out criticisms that might otherwise not be made.

Some authors have suggested that the use of a devil's advocate can be very helpful in helping boards of directors to ensure that decisions are addressed comprehensively and to avoid groupthink.[10] And Charles Elson, a director of Sunbeam Corporation, has argued that:

> Devil's advocates are terrific in any situation because they help you to figure a decision's numerous implications. . . . The better you think out the implications prior to making the decision, the better the decision ultimately turns out to be. That's why a devil's advocate is always a great person, irritating sometimes, but a great person.

As one might expect, there can be some potential problems with using the devil's advocate approach. If one's views are constantly criticized, one may become demoralized. Thus, that person may come up with "safe solutions" in order to minimize embarrassment or personal risk and become less subject to criticism. Additionally, even if the devil's advocate is successful with finding problems with the proposed course of action, there may be no new ideas or counterproposals to take its place. Thus, the approach sometimes may simply focus on what is wrong without suggesting other ideas.

Dialectical Inquiry   Dialectical inquiry attempts to accomplish the goals of the devil's advocate in a more constructive manner. It is a technique whereby a problem is approached from two alternative points of view. The idea is that out of a critique of the opposing perspectives—a thesis and an antithesis—a creative synthesis will occur. Dialectical inquiry involves the following steps:

dialectical inquiry
a method of introducing conflict into a decision-making process by devising different proposals that are feasible, politically viable, and credible, but rely on different assumptions; and debating the merits of each.

1.   Identify a proposal and the information that was used to derive it.
2.   State the underlying assumptions of the proposal.
3.   Identify a counterplan (antithesis) that is believed to be feasible, politically viable, and generally credible. However, it rests on assumptions that are opposite to the original proposal.
4.   Engage in a debate in which individuals favoring each plan provide their arguments and support.
5.   Identify a synthesis which, hopefully, includes the best components of each alternative.

There are some potential downsides associated with dialectical inquiry. It can be quite time consuming and involve a good deal of training. Further, it may result in a series of compromises between the initial proposal and the counterplan. In cases where the original proposal was the best approach, this would be unfortunate.

Despite some possible limitations associated with these conflict-inducing decision-making techniques, they have many benefits. Both techniques force debate about underlying assumptions, data, and recommendations between subgroups. Such debate tends to prevent the uncritical acceptance of a plan that may seem to be satisfactory after a cursory analysis. The approach serves to tap the knowledge and perspectives of group members and continues until group members agree on both assumptions and recommended actions. Given that both approaches serve to use, rather than minimize or suppress, conflict, higher quality decisions should result. Exhibit 13.4 briefly summarizes these techniques.

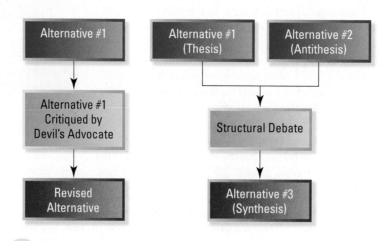

Exhibit 13.4 Two Conflict-Inducing Decision-Making Processes

Following the Analysis-Decision-Action Cycle in Case Analysis

In Chapter 1 we defined strategic management as the analysis, decisions, and actions that organizations undertake to create and sustain competitive advantages. It is no accident that we chose that sequence of words because it corresponds to the sequence of events that typically occurs in the strategic management process. In case analysis, as in the real world, this cycle of events can provide a useful framework. First, an analysis of the case in terms of the business environment and current events is needed. To make such an analysis, the case background must be considered. Next, based on that analysis, decisions must be made. This may involve formulating a strategy, choosing between difficult options, moving forward aggressively, or retreating from a bad situation. There are many possible decisions, depending on the case situation. Finally, action is required. Once decisions are made and plans are set, the action begins. The recommended action steps and the consequences of implementing these actions are the final stage.

Each of the previous 12 chapters of this book includes techniques and information that may be useful in a case analysis. However, not all of the issues presented will be important in every case. As noted earlier, one of the challenges of case analysis is to identify the most critical points and sort through material that may be ambiguous or unimportant.

In this section we draw on the material presented in each of the 12 chapters to show how it informs the case analysis process. The ideas are linked sequentially and in terms of an overarching strategic perspective. One of your jobs when conducting case analysis is to see how the parts of a case fit together and how the insights from the study of strategy can help you understand the case situation.

>LO6

How to use the strategic insights and material from each of the 12 previous chapters in the text to analyze issues posed by strategic management cases.

1. ***Analyzing organizational goals and objectives.*** A company's vision, mission, and objectives keep organization members focused on a common purpose. They also influence how an organization deploys its resources, relates to its stakeholders, and matches its short-term objectives with its long-term goals. The goals may even impact how a company formulates and implements strategies. When exploring issues of goals and objectives, you might ask:
   - Has the company developed short-term objectives that are inconsistent with its long-term mission? If so, how can management realign its vision, mission, and objectives?
   - Has the company considered all of its stakeholders equally in making critical decisions? If not, should the views of all stakeholders be treated the same or are some stakeholders more important than others?
   - Is the company being faced with an issue that conflicts with one of its long-standing policies? If so, how should it compare its existing policies to the potential new situation?

2. ***Analyzing the external environment.*** The business environment has two components. The general environment consists of demographic, sociocultural, political/legal, technological, economic, and global conditions. The competitive environment includes rivals, suppliers, customers, and other factors that may directly affect a company's success. Strategic managers must monitor the environment to identify opportunities and threats that may have an impact on performance. When investigating a firm's external environment, you might ask:
   - Does the company follow trends and events in the general environment? If not, how can these influences be made part of the company's strategic analysis process?
   - Is the company effectively scanning and monitoring the competitive environment? If so, how is it using the competitive intelligence it is gathering to enhance its competitive advantage?

- Has the company correctly analyzed the impact of the competitive forces in its industry on profitability? If so, how can it improve its competitive position relative to these forces?

3. ***Analyzing the internal environment.*** A firm's internal environment consists of its resources and other value-adding capabilities. Value-chain analysis and a resource-based approach to analysis can be used to identify a company's strengths and weaknesses and determine how they are contributing to its competitive advantages. Evaluating firm performance can also help make meaningful comparisons with competitors. When researching a company's internal analysis, you might ask:

- Does the company know how the various components of its value chain are adding value to the firm? If not, what internal analysis is needed to determine its strengths and weakness?
- Has the company accurately analyzed the source and vitality of its resources? If so, is it deploying its resources in a way that contributes to competitive advantages?
- Is the company's financial performance as good as or better than that of its close competitors? If so, has it balanced its financial success with the performance criteria of other stakeholders such as customers and employees?

4. ***Assessing a firm's intellectual assets.*** Human capital is a major resource in today's knowledge economy. As a result, attracting, developing, and retaining talented workers is a key strategic challenge. Other assets such as patents and trademarks are also critical. How companies leverage their intellectual assets through social networks and strategic alliances, and how technology is used to manage knowledge may be a major influence on a firm's competitive advantage. When analyzing a firm's intellectual assets, you might ask:

- Does the company have underutilized human capital? If so, what steps are needed to develop and leverage its intellectual assets?
- Is the company missing opportunities to forge strategic alliances? If so, how can it use its social capital to network more effectively?
- Has the company developed knowledge-management systems that capture what it learns? If not, what technologies can it employ to retain new knowledge?

5. ***Formulating business-level strategies.*** Firms use the competitive strategies of differentiation, focus, and overall cost leadership as a basis for overcoming the five competitive forces and developing sustainable competitive advantages. Combinations of these strategies may work best in some competitive environments. Additionally, an industry's life cycle is an important contingency that may affect a company's choice of business-level strategies. When assessing business-level strategies, you might ask:

- Has the company chosen the correct competitive strategy given its industry environment and competitive situation? If not, how should it use its strengths and resources to improve its performance?
- Does the company use combination strategies effectively? If so, what capabilities can it cultivate to further enhance profitability?
- Is the company using a strategy that is appropriate for the industry life cycle in which it is competing? If not, how can it realign itself to match its efforts to the current stage of industry growth?

6. ***Formulating corporate-level strategies.*** Large firms often own and manage portfolios of businesses. Corporate strategies address methods for achieving synergies among these businesses. Related and unrelated diversification techniques are alternative approaches to deciding which business should be added to or removed from a portfolio. Companies can diversify by means of mergers, acquisitions, joint ventures,

strategic alliances, and internal development. When analyzing corporate-level strategies, you might ask:

- Is the company competing in the right businesses given the opportunities and threats that are present in the environment? If not, how can it realign its diversification strategy to achieve competitive advantages?
- Is the corporation managing its portfolio of businesses in a way that creates synergies among the businesses? If so, what additional business should it consider adding to its portfolio?
- Are the motives of the top corporate executives who are pushing diversification strategies appropriate? If not, what action can be taken to curb their activities or align them with the best interests of all stakeholders?

7. *Formulating international-level strategies.* Foreign markets provide both opportunities and potential dangers for companies that want to expand globally. To decide which entry strategy is most appropriate, companies have to evaluate the trade-offs between two factors that firms face when entering foreign markets: cost reduction and local adaptation. To achieve competitive advantages, firms will typically choose one of three strategies: global, multidomestic, or transnational. When evaluating international-level strategies, you might ask:

- Is the company's entry into an international marketplace threatened by the actions of local competitors? If so, how can cultural differences be minimized to give the firm a better chance of succeeding?
- Has the company made the appropriate choices between cost reduction and local adaptation to foreign markets? If not, how can it adjust its strategy to achieve competitive advantages?
- Can the company improve its effectiveness by embracing one international strategy over another? If so, how should it choose between a global, multidomestic, or transnational strategy?

8. *Formulating entrepreneurial strategies.* New ventures add jobs and create new wealth. To do so, they must identify opportunities that will be viable in the marketplace as well as gather resources and assemble an entrepreneurial team to enact the opportunity. New entrants often evoke a strong competitive response from incumbent firms in a given marketplace. When examining the role of strategic thinking on the success of entrepreneurial ventures and the role of competitive dynamics, you might ask:

- Is the company engaged in an ongoing process of opportunity recognition? If not, how can it enhance its ability to recognize opportunities?
- Do the entrepreneurs who are launching new ventures have vision, dedication and drive, and a commitment to excellence? If so, how have these affected the performance and dedication of other employees involved in the venture?
- Have strategic principles been used in the process of developing strategies to pursue the entrepreneurial opportunity? If not, how can the venture apply tools such as five-forces analysis and value-chain analysis to improve its competitive position and performance?

9. *Achieving effective strategic control.* Strategic controls enable a firm to implement strategies effectively. Informational controls involve comparing performance to stated goals and scanning, monitoring, and being responsive to the environment. Behavioral controls emerge from a company's culture, reward systems, and organizational boundaries. When assessing the impact of strategic controls on implementation, you might ask:

- Is the company employing the appropriate informational control systems? If not, how can it implement a more interactive approach to enhance learning and minimize response times?

- Does the company have a strong and effective culture? If not, what steps can it take to align its values and rewards system with its goals and objectives?
- Has the company implemented control systems that match its strategies? If so, what additional steps can be taken to improve performance?

10. **Creating effective organizational designs.** Organizational designs that align with competitive strategies can enhance performance. As companies grow and change, their structures must also evolve to meet new demands. In today's economy, firm boundaries must be flexible and permeable to facilitate smoother interactions with external parties such as customers, suppliers, and alliance partners. New forms of organizing are becoming more common. When evaluating the role of organizational structure on strategy implementation, you might ask:
    - Has the company implemented organizational structures that are suited to the type of business it is in? If not, how can it alter the design in ways that enhance its competitiveness?
    - Is the company employing boundaryless organizational designs where appropriate? If so, how are senior managers maintaining control of lower-level employees?
    - Does the company use outsourcing to achieve the best possible results? If not, what criteria should it use to decide which functions can be outsourced?

11. **Creating a learning organization and an ethical organization.** Strong leadership is essential for achieving competitive advantages. Two leadership roles are especially important. The first is creating a learning organization by harnessing talent and encouraging the development of new knowledge. Second, leaders play a vital role in motivating employees to excellence and inspiring ethical behavior. When exploring the impact of effective strategic leadership, you might ask:
    - Do company leaders promote excellence as part of the overall culture? If so, how has this influenced the performance of the firm and the individuals in it?
    - Is the company committed to being a learning organization? If not, what can it do to capitalize on the individual and collective talents of organizational members?
    - Have company leaders exhibited an ethical attitude in their own behavior? If not, how has their behavior influenced the actions of other employees?

12. **Fostering corporate entrepreneurship.** Many firms continually seek new growth opportunities and avenues for strategic renewal. In some corporations, autonomous work units such as business incubators and new-venture groups are used to focus corporate venturing activities. In other corporate settings, product champions and other firm members provide companies with the impetus to expand into new areas. When investigating the impact of entrepreneurship on strategic effectiveness, you might ask:
    - Has the company resolved the dilemmas associated with managing innovation? If so, is it effectively defining and pacing its innovation efforts?
    - Has the company developed autonomous work units that have the freedom to bring forth new product ideas? If so, has it used product champions to implement new venture initiatives?
    - Does the company have an entrepreneurial orientation? If not, what can it do to encourage entrepreneurial attitudes in the strategic behavior of its organizational members?

Summary

Strategic management case analysis provides an effective method of learning how companies analyze problems, make decisions, and resolve challenges. Strategic cases include detailed accounts of actual business situations. The purpose of analyzing such cases is to gain exposure to a wide variety of organizational and managerial situations. By putting yourself in the place of a strategic decision maker, you can gain an appreciation of the difficulty and complexity of many strategic situations. In the process you can learn how to ask good strategic questions and enhance your analytical skills. Presenting case analyses can also help develop oral and written communication skills.

In this chapter we have discussed the importance of strategic case analysis and described the five steps involved in conducting a case analysis: becoming familiar with the material, identifying problems, analyzing strategic issues, proposing alternative solutions, and making recommendations. We have also discussed how to get the most from case analysis. Finally, we have described how the case analysis process follows the analysis-decision-action cycle of strategic management and outlined issues and questions that are associated with each of the previous 12 chapters of the text.

Key Terms

case analysis, 464

financial ratio analysis, 469

devil's advocacy 479

dialectical inquiry 480

References

1. The material in this chapter is based on several sources, including Barnes, L. A., Nelson, A. J., & Christensen, C. R. 1994. *Teaching and the case method: Text, cases and readings.* Boston: Harvard Business School Press: Guth, W. D. 1985. Central concepts of business unit and corporate strategy. In W. D. Guth (Ed.). *Handbook of business strategy:* 1–9. Boston: Warren, Gorham & Lamont; Lundberg, C. C., & Enz, C. 1993. A framework for student case preparation. *Case Research Journal,* 13 (Summer): 129–140; and Ronstadt, R. 1980. *The art of case analysis: A guide to the diagnosis of business situations.* Dover, MA: Lord Publishing.

2. Edge, A. G. & Coleman, D. R. 1986. *The guide to case analysis and reporting* (3rd ed.). Honolulu, HI: System Logistics.

3. Morris, E. 1987. Vision and strategy: A focus for the future. *Journal of Business Strategy* 8: 51–58.

4. This section is based on Lundberg & Enz, op. cit., and Ronstadt, op. cit.

5. The importance of problem definition was emphasized in Mintzberg, H., Raisinghani, D. & Theoret, A. 1976. The structure of "unstructured" decision processes. *Administrative Science Quarterly,* 21(2): 246–275.

6. Drucker, P. F. 1994. The theory of the business. *Harvard Business Review,* 72(5): 95–104.

7. This section draws on Edge & Coleman, op. cit.

8. Irving Janis is credited with coining the term *groupthink,* and he applied it primarily to fiascos in government (such as the Bay of Pigs incident in 1961). Refer to Janis, I. L. 1982. *Victims of groupthink* (2nd ed.). Boston: Houghton Mifflin.

9. Much of our discussion is based upon Finkelstein, S. & Mooney, A. C. 2003. Not the usual suspects: How to use board process to make boards better. *Academy of Management Executive,* 17(2): 101–113; Schweiger, D. M., Sandberg, W. R., & Rechner, P. L. 1989. Experiential effects of dialectical inquiry, devil's advocacy, and consensus approaches to strategic decision making. *Academy of Management Journal,* 32(4): 745–772; and Aldag, R. J. & Stearns, T. M. 1987. *Management.* Cincinnati: South-Western Publishing.

10. Finkelstein and Mooney, op. cit.

Financial Ratio Analysis

Standard Financial Statements

One obvious thing we might want to do with a company's financial statements is to compare them to those of other, similar companies. We would immediately have a problem, however. It's almost impossible to directly compare the financial statements for two companies because of differences in size.

For example, Oracle and IBM are obviously serious rivals in the computer software market, but IBM is much larger (in terms of assets), so it is difficult to compare them directly. For that matter, it's difficult to even compare financial statements from different points in time for the same company if the company's size has changed. The size problem is compounded if we try to compare IBM and, say, SAP (of Germany). If SAP's financial statements are denominated in German marks, then we have a size *and* a currency difference.

To start making comparisons, one obvious thing we might try to do is to somehow standardize the financial statements. One very common and useful way of doing this is to work with percentages instead of total dollars. The resulting financial statements are called *common-size statements*. We consider these next.

Common-Size Balance Sheets

For easy reference, Prufrock Corporation's 2008 and 2009 balance sheets are provided in Exhibit 13A.1. Using these, we construct common-size balance sheets by expressing each item as a percentage of total assets. Prufrock's 2008 and 2009 common-size balance sheets are shown in Exhibit 13A.2.

Exhibit 13A.1

Prufrock Corporation

Balance Sheets as of December 31, 2008 and 2009 ($ in millions)

	2008	2009
Assets		
Current assets		
Cash	$ 84	$ 98
Accounts receivable	165	188
Inventory	393	422
Total	$ 642	$ 708
Fixed assets		
Net plant and equipment	$2,731	$2,880
Total assets	$3,373	$3,588
Liabilities and Owners' Equity		
Current liabilities		
Accounts payable	$ 312	$ 344
Notes payable	231	196
Total	$ 543	$ 540
Long-term debt	$ 531	$ 457
Owners' equity		
Common stock and paid-in surplus	$ 500	$ 550
Retained earnings	1,799	2,041
Total	$2,299	$2,591
Total liabilities and owners' equity	$3,373	$3,588

Source: Adapted from Rows, S. A., Westerfield, R. W., & Jordan, B. D. 1999. *Essentials of Corporate Finance* (2nd ed.). chap. 3. New York: McGraw-Hill, 1999.

Exhibit 13A.2

Prufrock Corporation

Common-Size
Balance Sheets as
of December 31,
2008 and 2009 (%)

	2008	2009	Change
Assets			
Current assets			
Cash	2.5%	2.7%	+ .2%
Accounts receivable	4.9	5.2	+ .3
Inventory	11.7	11.8	+ .1
Total	19.1	19.7	+ .6
Fixed assets			
Net plant and equipment	80.9	80.3	− .6
Total assets	100.0%	100.0%	.0%
Liabilities and Owners' Equity			
Current liabilities			
Accounts payable	9.2%	9.6%	+ .4%
Notes payable	6.8	5.5	−1.3
Total	16.0	15.1	− .9
Long-term debt	15.7	12.7	−3.0
Owners' equity			
Common stock and paid-in surplus	14.8	15.3	+ .5
Retained earnings	53.3	56.9	+3.6
Total	68.1	72.2	+4.1
Total liabilities and owners' equities	100.0%	100.0%	.0%

Note: Numbers may not add up to 100.0% due to rounding.

Notice that some of the totals don't check exactly because of rounding errors. Also notice that the total change has to be zero since the beginning and ending numbers must add up to 100 percent.

In this form, financial statements are relatively easy to read and compare. For example, just looking at the two balance sheets for Prufrock, we see that current assets were 19.7 percent of total assets in 2009, up from 19.1 percent in 2008. Current liabilities declined from 16.0 percent to 15.1 percent of total liabilities and equity over that same time. Similarly, total equity rose from 68.1 percent of total liabilities and equity to 72.2 percent.

Overall, Prufrock's liquidity, as measured by current assets compared to current liabilities, increased over the year. Simultaneously, Prufrock's indebtedness diminished as a percentage of total assets. We might be tempted to conclude that the balance sheet has grown "stronger."

Common-Size Income Statements

A useful way of standardizing the income statement, shown in Exhibit 13A.3, is to express each item as a percentage of total sales, as illustrated for Prufrock in Exhibit 13A.4.

This income statement tells us what happens to each dollar in sales. For Prufrock, interest expense eats up $.061 out of every sales dollar and taxes take another $.081. When all is said and done, $.157 of each dollar flows through to the bottom line (net income), and that amount is split into $.105 retained in the business and $.052 paid out in dividends.

These percentages are very useful in comparisons. For example, a relevant figure is the cost percentage. For Prufrock, $.582 of each $1.00 in sales goes to pay for goods sold. It would be interesting to compute the same percentage for Prufrock's main competitors to see how Prufrock stacks up in terms of cost control.

Sales		$2,311
Cost of goods sold		1,344
Depreciation		276
Earnings before interest and taxes		$ 691
Interest paid		141
Taxable income		$ 550
Taxes (34%)		187
Net income		$ 363
Dividends	$121	
Addition to retained earnings	242	

Exhibit 13A.4

Prufrock Corporation

2009 Common-Size
Income Statement (%)

Sales		100.0%
Cost of goods sold		58.2
Depreciation		11.9
Earnings before interest and taxes		29.9
Interest paid		6.1
Taxable income		23.8
Taxes (34%)		8.1
Net income		15.7%
Dividends	5.2%	
Addition to retained earnings	10.5	

Ratio Analysis

Another way of avoiding the problems involved in comparing companies of different sizes is to calculate and compare *financial ratios*. Such ratios are ways of comparing and investigating the relationships between different pieces of financial information. We cover some of the more common ratios next, but there are many others that we don't touch on.

One problem with ratios is that different people and different sources frequently don't compute them in exactly the same way, and this leads to much confusion. The specific definitions we use here may or may not be the same as others you have seen or will see elsewhere. If you ever use ratios as a tool for analysis, you should be careful to document how you calculate each one, and, if you are comparing your numbers to those of another source, be sure you know how its numbers are computed.

For each of the ratios we discuss, several questions come to mind:

1. How is it computed?
2. What is it intended to measure, and why might we be interested?
3. What is the unit of measurement?
4. What might a high or low value be telling us? How might such values be misleading?
5. How could this measure be improved?

Financial ratios are traditionally grouped into the following categories:

1. Short-term solvency, or liquidity, ratios.
2. Long-term solvency, or financial leverage, ratios.
3. Asset management, or turnover, ratios.
4. Profitability ratios.
5. Market value ratios.

We will consider each of these in turn. In calculating these numbers for Prufrock, we will use the ending balance sheet (2009) figures unless we explicitly say otherwise. The numbers for the various ratios come from the income statement and the balance sheet.

Short-Term Solvency, or Liquidity, Measures

As the name suggests, short-term solvency ratios as a group are intended to provide information about a firm's liquidity, and these ratios are sometimes called *liquidity measures.* The primary concern is the firm's ability to pay its bills over the short run without undue stress. Consequently, these ratios focus on current assets and current liabilities.

For obvious reasons, liquidity ratios are particularly interesting to short-term creditors. Since financial managers are constantly working with banks and other short-term lenders, an understanding of these ratios is essential.

One advantage of looking at current assets and liabilities is that their book values and market values are likely to be similar. Often (though not always), these assets and liabilities just don't live long enough for the two to get seriously out of step. On the other hand, like any type of near cash, current assets and liabilities can and do change fairly rapidly, so today's amounts may not be a reliable guide to the future.

Current Ratio   One of the best-known and most widely used ratios is the *current ratio.* As you might guess, the current ratio is defined as:

$$\text{Current ratio} = \frac{\text{Current assets}}{\text{Current liabilities}}$$

For Prufrock, the 2009 current ratio is:

$$\text{Current ratio} = \frac{\$708}{\$540} = 1.31 \text{ times}$$

Because current assets and liabilities are, in principle, converted to cash over the following 12 months, the current ratio is a measure of short-term liquidity. The unit of measurement is either dollars or times. So, we could say Prufrock has $1.31 in current assets for every $1 in current liabilities, or we could say Prufrock has its current liabilities covered 1.31 times over.

To a creditor, particularly a short-term creditor such as a supplier, the higher the current ratio, the better. To the firm, a high current ratio indicates liquidity, but it also may indicate an inefficient use of cash and other short-term assets. Absent some extraordinary circumstances, we would expect to see a current ratio of at least 1, because a current ratio of less than 1 would mean that net working capital (current assets less current liabilities) is negative. This would be unusual in a healthy firm, at least for most types of businesses.

The current ratio, like any ratio, is affected by various types of transactions. For example, suppose the firm borrows over the long term to raise money. The short-run effect would be an increase in cash from the issue proceeds and an increase in long-term debt. Current liabilities would not be affected, so the current ratio would rise.

Finally, note that an apparently low current ratio may not be a bad sign for a company with a large reserve of untapped borrowing power.

Quick (or Acid-Test) Ratio   Inventory is often the least liquid current asset. It's also the one for which the book values are least reliable as measures of market value, since the quality of the inventory isn't considered. Some of the inventory may later turn out to be damaged, obsolete, or lost.

More to the point, relatively large inventories are often a sign of short-term trouble. The firm may have overestimated sales and overbought or overproduced as a result. In this case, the firm may have a substantial portion of its liquidity tied up in slow-moving inventory.

To further evaluate liquidity, the *quick,* or *acid-test, ratio* is computed just like the current ratio, except inventory is omitted:

$$\text{Quick ratio} = \frac{\text{Current assets} - \text{Inventory}}{\text{Current liabilities}}$$

Notice that using cash to buy inventory does not affect the current ratio, but it reduces the quick ratio. Again, the idea is that inventory is relatively illiquid compared to cash.

For Prufrock, this ratio in 2009 was:

$$\text{Quick ratio} = \frac{\$708 - 422}{\$540} = .53 \text{ times}$$

The quick ratio here tells a somewhat different story than the current ratio, because inventory accounts for more than half of Prufrock's current assets. To exaggerate the point, if this inventory consisted of, say, unsold nuclear power plants, then this would be a cause for concern.

Cash Ratio A very short-term creditor might be interested in the *cash ratio:*

$$\text{Cash ratio} = \frac{\text{Cash}}{\text{Current liabilities}}$$

You can verify that this works out to be .18 times for Prufrock.

Long-Term Solvency Measures

Long-term solvency ratios are intended to address the firm's long-run ability to meet its obligations, or, more generally, its financial leverage. These ratios are sometimes called *financial leverage ratios* or just *leverage ratios*. We consider three commonly used measures and some variations.

Total Debt Ratio The *total debt ratio* takes into account all debts of all maturities to all creditors. It can be defined in several ways, the easiest of which is:

$$\text{Total debt ratio} = \frac{\text{Total assets} - \text{Total equity}}{\text{Total assets}}$$

$$= \frac{\$3,588 - 2,591}{\$3,588} = .28 \text{ times}$$

In this case, an analyst might say that Prufrock uses 28 percent debt.[1] Whether this is high or low or whether it even makes any difference depends on whether or not capital structure matters.

Prufrock has $.28 in debt for every $1 in assets. Therefore, there is $.72 in equity ($1 − .28) for every $.28 in debt. With this in mind, we can define two useful variations on the total debt ratio, the *debt-equity ratio* and the *equity multiplier:*

$$\text{Debt-equity ratio} = \text{Total debt/Total equity}$$
$$= \$.28/\$.72 = .39 \text{ times}$$
$$\text{Equity multiplier} = \text{Total assets/Total equity}$$
$$= \$1/\$.72 = 1.39 \text{ times}$$

The fact that the equity multiplier is 1 plus the debt-equity ratio is not a coincidence:

$$\text{Equity multiplier} = \text{Total assets/Total equity} = \$1/\$.72 = 1.39$$
$$= (\text{Total equity} + \text{Total debt})/\text{Total equity}$$
$$= 1 + \text{Debt-equity ratio} = 1.39 \text{ times}$$

The thing to notice here is that given any one of these three ratios, you can immediately calculate the other two, so they all say exactly the same thing.

Times Interest Earned Another common measure of long-term solvency is the *times interest earned* (TIE) *ratio*. Once again, there are several possible (and common) definitions, but we'll stick with the most traditional:

$$\text{Times interest earned ratio} = \frac{\text{EBIT}}{\text{Interest}}$$

$$= \frac{\$691}{\$141} = 4.9 \text{ times}$$

[1]Total equity here includes preferred stock, if there is any. An equivalent numerator in this ratio would be (Current liabilities + Long-term debt).

As the name suggests, this ratio measures how well a company has its interest obligations covered, and it is often called the interest coverage ratio. For Prufrock, the interest bill is covered 4.9 times over.

Cash Coverage A problem with the TIE ratio is that it is based on earnings before interest and taxes (EBIT), which is not really a measure of cash available to pay interest. The reason is that depreciation, a noncash expense, has been deducted. Since interest is most definitely a cash outflow (to creditors), one way to define the *cash coverage ratio* is:

$$\text{Cash coverage ratio} = \frac{\text{EBIT} + \text{Depreciation}}{\text{Interest}}$$

$$= \frac{\$691 + 276}{\$141} = \frac{\$967}{\$141} = 6.9 \text{ times}$$

The numerator here, EBIT plus depreciation, is often abbreviated EBDIT (earnings before depreciation, interest, and taxes). It is a basic measure of the firm's ability to generate cash from operations, and it is frequently used as a measure of cash flow available to meet financial obligations.

Asset Management, or Turnover, Measures

We next turn our attention to the efficiency with which Prufrock uses its assets. The measures in this section are sometimes called *asset utilization ratios.* The specific ratios we discuss can all be interpreted as measures of turnover. What they are intended to describe is how efficiently, or intensively, a firm uses its assets to generate sales. We first look at two important current assets: inventory and receivables.

Inventory Turnover and Days' Sales in Inventory During the year, Prufrock had a cost of goods sold of $1,344. Inventory at the end of the year was $422. With these numbers, *inventory turnover* can be calculated as:

$$\text{Inventory turnover} = \frac{\text{Cost of goods sold}}{\text{Inventory}}$$

$$= \frac{\$1,344}{\$422} = 3.2 \text{ times}$$

In a sense, we sold off, or turned over, the entire inventory 3.2 times. As long as we are not running out of stock and thereby forgoing sales, the higher this ratio is, the more efficiently we are managing inventory.

If we know that we turned our inventory over 3.2 times during the year, then we can immediately figure out how long it took us to turn it over on average. The result is the average *days' sales in inventory:*

$$\text{Days' sales in inventory} = \frac{365 \text{ days}}{\text{Inventory turnover}}$$

$$= \frac{365}{3.2} = 114 \text{ days}$$

This tells us that, on average, inventory sits 114 days before it is sold. Alternatively, assuming we used the most recent inventory and cost figures, it will take about 114 days to work off our current inventory.

For example, we frequently hear things like "Majestic Motors has a 60 days' supply of cars." This means that, at current daily sales, it would take 60 days to deplete the available inventory. We could also say that Majestic has 60 days of sales in inventory.

Receivables Turnover and Days' Sales in Receivables Our inventory measures give some indication of how fast we can sell products. We now look at how fast we collect on those sales. The *receivables turnover* is defined in the same way as inventory turnover:

$$\text{Receivables turnover} = \frac{\text{Sales}}{\text{Accounts receivable}}$$

$$= \frac{\$2,311}{\$188} = 12.3 \text{ times}$$

Loosely speaking, we collected our outstanding credit accounts and reloaned the money 12.3 times during the year.[2]

This ratio makes more sense if we convert it to days, so the *days' sales in receivables* is:

$$\text{Days' sales in receivables} = \frac{365 \text{ days}}{\text{Receivables turnover}}$$

$$= \frac{365}{12.3} = 30 \text{ days}$$

Therefore, on average, we collect on our credit sales in 30 days. For obvious reasons, this ratio is very frequently called the *average collection period* (ACP).

Also note that if we are using the most recent figures, we can also say that we have 30 days' worth of sales currently uncollected.

Total Asset Turnover   Moving away from specific accounts like inventory or receivables, we can consider an important "big picture" ratio, the *total asset turnover ratio.* As the name suggests, total asset turnover is:

$$\text{Total asset turnover} = \frac{\text{Sales}}{\text{Total assets}}$$

$$= \frac{\$2,311}{\$3,588} = .64 \text{ times}$$

In other words, for every dollar in assets, we generated $.64 in sales.

A closely related ratio, the *capital intensity ratio,* is simply the reciprocal of (i.e., 1 divided by) total asset turnover. It can be interpreted as the dollar investment in assets needed to generate $1 in sales. High values correspond to capital intensive industries (e.g., public utilities). For Prufrock, total asset turnover is.64, so, if we flip this over, we get that capital intensity is $1/.64 = $1.56. That is, it takes Prufrock $1.56 in assets to create $1 in sales.

Profitability Measures

The three measures we discuss in this section are probably the best known and most widely used of all financial ratios. In one form or another, they are intended to measure how efficiently the firm uses its assets and how efficiently the firm manages its operations. The focus in this group is on the bottom line, net income.

Profit Margin   Companies pay a great deal of attention to their *profit margin:*

$$\text{Profit margin} = \frac{\text{Net income}}{\text{Sales}}$$

$$= \frac{\$363}{\$2,311} = 15.7\%$$

This tells us that Prufrock, in an accounting sense, generates a little less than 16 cents in profit for every dollar in sales.

All other things being equal, a relatively high profit margin is obviously desirable. This situation corresponds to low expense ratios relative to sales. However, we hasten to add that other things are often not equal.

For example, lowering our sales price will usually increase unit volume, but will normally cause profit margins to shrink. Total profit (or, more importantly, operating cash flow) may go up or down; so the fact that margins are smaller isn't necessarily bad. After all, isn't it possible that, as the

---

[2]Here we have implicitly assumed that all sales are credit sales. If they were not, then we would simply use total credit sales in these calculations, not total sales.

saying goes, "Our prices are so low that we lose money on everything we sell, but we make it up in volume!"[3]

Return on Assets   *Return on assets* (ROA) is a measure of profit per dollar of assets. It can be defined several ways, but the most common is:

$$\text{Return on assets} = \frac{\text{Net income}}{\text{Total assets}}$$

$$= \frac{\$363}{\$3,588} = 10.12\%$$

Return on Equity   *Return on equity* (ROE) is a measure of how the stockholders fared during the year. Since benefiting shareholders is our goal, ROE is, in an accounting sense, the true bottom-line measure of performance. ROE is usually measured as:

$$\text{Return on equity} = \frac{\text{Net income}}{\text{Total equity}}$$

$$= \frac{\$363}{\$2,591} = 14\%$$

For every dollar in equity, therefore, Prufrock generated 14 cents in profit, but, again, this is only correct in accounting terms.

Because ROA and ROE are such commonly cited numbers, we stress that it is important to remember they are accounting rates of return. For this reason, these measures should properly be called *return on book assets* and *return on book equity*. In addition, ROE is sometimes called *return on net worth*. Whatever it's called, it would be inappropriate to compare the results to, for example, an interest rate observed in the financial markets.

The fact that ROE exceeds ROA reflects Prufrock's use of financial leverage. We will examine the relationship between these two measures in more detail below.

Market Value Measures

Our final group of measures is based, in part, on information not necessarily contained in financial statements—the market price per share of the stock. Obviously, these measures can only be calculated directly for publicly traded companies.

We assume that Prufrock has 33 million shares outstanding and the stock sold for $88 per share at the end of the year. If we recall that Prufrock's net income was $363 million, then we can calculate that its earnings per share were:

$$\text{EPS} = \frac{\text{Net income}}{\text{Shares outstanding}} = \frac{\$363}{33} = \$11$$

Price-Earnings Ratio   The first of our market value measures, the *price-earnings,* or *PE, ratio* (or multiple), is defined as:

$$\text{PE ratio} = \frac{\text{Price per share}}{\text{Earnings per share}}$$

$$= \frac{\$85}{\$11} = 8 \text{ times}$$

In the vernacular, we would say that Prufrock shares sell for eight times earnings, or we might say that Prufrock shares have, or "carry," a PE multiple of 8.

Since the PE ratio measures how much investors are willing to pay per dollar of current earnings, higher PEs are often taken to mean that the firm has significant prospects for future growth. Of course, if a firm had no or almost no earnings, its PE would probably be quite large; so, as always, be careful when interpreting this ratio.

---

[3]No, it's not; margins can be small, but they do need to be positive!

Market-to-Book Ratio A second commonly quoted measure is the *market-to-book ratio:*

$$\text{Market-to-book ratio} = \frac{\text{Market value per share}}{\text{Book value per share}}$$

$$= \frac{\$88}{(\$2{,}591/33)} = \frac{\$88}{\$78.5} = 1.12 \text{ times}$$

Notice that book value per share is total equity (not just common stock) divided by the number of shares outstanding.

Since book value per share is an accounting number, it reflects historical costs. In a loose sense, the market-to-book ratio therefore compares the market value of the firm's investments to their cost. A value less than 1 could mean that the firm has not been successful overall in creating value for its stockholders.

Conclusion

This completes our definition of some common ratios. Exhibit 13A.5 summarizes the ratios we've discussed.

I. Short-term solvency, or liquidity, ratios

$$\text{Current ratio} = \frac{\text{Current assets}}{\text{Current liabilities}}$$

$$\text{Quick ratio} = \frac{\text{Current assets} - \text{Inventory}}{\text{Current liabilities}}$$

$$\text{Cash ratio} = \frac{\text{Cash}}{\text{Current liabilities}}$$

II. Long-term solvency, or financial leverage, ratios

$$\text{Total debt ratio} = \frac{\text{Total assets} - \text{Total equity}}{\text{Total assets}}$$

$$\text{Debt-equity ratio} = \text{Total debt/Total equity}$$

$$\text{Equity multiplier} = \text{Total assets/Total equity}$$

$$\text{Times interest earned ratio} = \frac{\text{EBIT}}{\text{Interest}}$$

$$\text{Cash coverage ratio} = \frac{\text{EBIT} + \text{Depreciation}}{\text{Interest}}$$

III. Asset utilization, or turnover, ratios

$$\text{Inventory turnover} = \frac{\text{Cost of goods sold}}{\text{Inventory}}$$

$$\text{Days' sales in inventory} = \frac{365 \text{ days}}{\text{Inventory turnover}}$$

$$\text{Receivables turnover} = \frac{\text{Sales}}{\text{Accounts receivable}}$$

$$\text{Days' sales in receivables} = \frac{365 \text{ days}}{\text{Receivables turnover}}$$

$$\text{Total asset turnover} = \frac{\text{Sales}}{\text{Total assets}}$$

$$\text{Capital intensity} = \frac{\text{Total assets}}{\text{Sales}}$$

IV. Profitability ratios

$$\text{Profit margin} = \frac{\text{Net income}}{\text{Sales}}$$

$$\text{Return on assets (ROA)} = \frac{\text{Net income}}{\text{Total assets}}$$

$$\text{Return on equity (ROE)} = \frac{\text{Net income}}{\text{Total equity}}$$

$$\text{ROE} = \frac{\text{Net income}}{\text{Sales}} \times \frac{\text{Sales}}{\text{Assets}} \times \frac{\text{Assets}}{\text{Equity}}$$

V. Market value ratios

$$\text{Price-earnings ratio} = \frac{\text{Price per share}}{\text{Earnings per share}}$$

$$\text{Market-to-book ratio} = \frac{\text{Market value per share}}{\text{Book value per share}}$$

Exhibit 13A.5 A Summary of Five Types of Financial Ratios

Sources of Company and Industry Information*

In order for business executives to make the best decisions when developing corporate strategy, it is critical for them to be knowledgeable about their competitors and about the industries in which they compete. The process used by corporations to learn as much as possible about competitors is often called "competitive intelligence." This appendix provides an overview of important and widely available sources of information that may be useful in conducting basic competitive intelligence. Much information of this nature is available in libraries in article databases, business reference books, and on websites. This list will recommend a variety of them. Ask a librarian for assistance, because library collections and resources vary.

The information sources are organized into 10 categories:

Competitive Intelligence

Public or Private—Subsidiary or Division—U.S. or Foreign?

Annual Report Collections—Public Companies

Guides and Tutorials

SEC Filings/EDGAR—Company Disclosure Reports

Company Rankings

Business Websites

Strategic and Competitive Analysis—Information Sources

Sources for Industry Research and Analysis

Search Engines

Competitive Intelligence

Students and other researchers who want to learn more about the value and process of competitive intelligence should see four recent books on this subject.

> Norton Paley. "Prioritize Competitive Intelligence: The Underpinnings of Business Strategy." In *Mastering the Rules of Competitive Strategy*. New York: Auerbach Publications, 2008.

> Leonard M. Fuld. *The Secret Language of Competitive Intelligence*. New York: Crown Business, 2006.

> David L. Blenkhorn and Craig S. Fleisher, eds. *Competitive Intelligence and Global Business*. Westport, CT: Praeger Publishers, 2005.

> Benjamin Gilad. *Early Warning: Using Competitive Intelligence to Anticipate Market Shifts, Control Risk, and Create Powerful Strategies*. New York: American Management Association, 2004.

Public or Private—Subsidiary or Division—U.S. or Foreign?

Companies traded on stock exchanges in the United States are required to file a variety of reports that disclose information about the company. This begins the process that produces a wealth of data on public companies and at the same time distinguishes them from private companies, which often lack available data. Similarly, financial data of subsidiaries and divisions are typically filed in a consolidated financial statement by the parent company, rather than treated independently, thus limiting the kind of data available on them. On the other hand, foreign companies that trade on U.S. stock exchanges are required to file 20F reports, similar to the 10-K for U.S. companies, the most comprehensive of the required reports.

*This information was compiled by Ruthie Brock and Carol Byrne, Business Librarians at The University of Texas at Arlington. We greatly appreciate their valuable contribution.

Corporate Directory of U.S. Public Companies. San Mateo, CA: Walker's Research, LLC, 2009.

The *Corporate Directory* provides company profiles of more than 9,000 publicly traded companies in the United States, including foreign companies trading on the U.S. exchanges (ADRs). Some libraries may subscribe to an alternative online version at www.walkersresearch.com.

Corporate Affiliations. New Providence, NJ: LexisNexis, 2009.

This 8-volume directory features brief profiles of major U.S. and foreign corporations, both public and private, as well as their subsidiaries, divisions, and affiliates. The directory also indicates hierarchies of corporate relationships. An online version of the directory allows retrieval of a list of companies that meet specific criteria. Results can be downloaded to a spreadsheet. The online version requires a subscription, available in some libraries.

ReferenceUSA. Omaha, NE: infoUSA

ReferenceUSA is an online directory of more than 14 million businesses located in the United States. One of the unique features is that it includes public and private companies, both large and small. Custom and Guided search tabs are available. Also, results can be analyzed using the data summary feature, which allows for a snapshot of how the industry breaks down by size, geographic location, etc. Other subscription options are available using the ReferenceUSA interface and may be available in some libraries.

Ward's Business Directory of U.S. Private and Public Companies. Farmington Hills, MI: Gale CENGAGE Learning, 2008. 8 vols.

Ward's Business Directory lists brief profiles on more than 112,000 public and private companies and indicates whether they are public or private, a subsidiary or division. Two volumes of the set are arranged using the Standard Industrial Classifications (SIC) and the North American Industry Classification System (NAICS) and feature company rankings within industries. Some libraries may offer this business directory as part of a database called *Gale Directory Library.*

Annual Report Collections—Public Companies

Most companies have their annual report to shareholders and other financial reports available on their corporate website. Note that some companies use a variation of their company name in their Web address, such as Procter & Gamble: www.pg.com. A few "aggregators" have also conveniently provided an accumulation of links to many reports of U.S. and international corporations or include a PDF document as part of their database, although these generally do not attempt to be comprehensive.

AnnualReports.com. Weston, FL: IR Solutions

This website contains annual reports in HTML or PDF format. Reports can be retrieved by company name, ticker symbol, exchange, industry, or sector.
www.annualreports.com

Company Annual Reports Online (CAROL). London, UK: Carol Ltd.

This website is based in the United Kingdom; therefore, many reports are European. Links are also provided for companies in Asia and the United States. A pull-down menu allows selecting companies within an industry. Access is free, but registration is required.
www.carol.co.uk/

Public Register's Online Annual Report Service. Woodstock Valley, CT: Bay Tact Corp.

Visitors to this website may choose from company annual reports and 10-K filings to view online or order a paper copy. Access is free, but registration is required.
www.annualreportservice.com/

Mergent Online. New York, NY: Mergent, Inc.

Mergent Online provides company financial data for public companies headquartered in the United States, as well as those headquartered in other countries, including a large collection of corporate annual reports in PDF format. For industry ratios, Mergent Online offers an advanced search option. Industry Reports are available as one of several Mergent subscription add-ons and may not be available in all libraries.
www.mergentonline.com

Guides and Tutorials

Researching Companies Online. Debbie Flanagan. Fort Lauderdale, FL
This site provides a step-by-step process for finding free company and industry information on the Web.
www.learnwebskills.com/company/

Guide to Financial Statements and *How to Read Annual Reports.* Armonk, NY: IBM
These two educational guides, located on IBM's website, provide basic information on how to read and make sense of financial statements and other information in 10-K and shareholder annual reports for companies in general, not IBM specifically.
www.ibm.com/investor/help/guide/introduction.wss
www.ibm.com/investor/help/reports/introduction.wss

EDGAR Full-Text Search Frequently Asked Questions (FAQ). Washington DC: U.S. Securities and Exchange Commission
The capability to search full-text SEC filings (popularly known as EDGAR filings), was vastly improved when the SEC launched its new search form in late 2006. Features are explained at the FAQ page.
www.sec.gov/edgar/searchedgar/edgarfulltextfaq.htm

Locating Company Information. Tutorial. William and Joan Schreyer Business Library, Penn State University, University Park, PA
Created by librarians at Penn State, this outstanding tutorial provides suggestions for online and print resources for company information. Click on "how to" links for each item to view a brief instruction vignette.
www.libraries.psu.edu/instruction/business/information/companyi.htm

Locating Industry Information. Tutorial. William and Joan Schreyer Business Library, Penn State University, University Park, PA
Created by librarians at Penn State, this outstanding tutorial provides suggestions for online and print resources for industry information. Click on "how to" links for each item to view a brief instruction vignette.
www.libraries.psu.edu/instruction/business/information/industryi.htm

Ten Steps to Industry Intelligence. Industry Tutorial. George A. Smathers Libraries, University of Florida, Gainesville, FL
Provides a step-by-step approach for finding information about industries, with embedded links to recommended sources.
http://businesslibrary.uflib.ufl.edu/industryresearch

SEC Filings/EDGAR—Company Disclosure Reports

SEC Filings are the various reports that publicly traded companies must file with the Securities Exchange Commission to disclose information about their corporation. These are often referred to as "EDGAR" filings, an acronym for the Electronic Data Gathering, Analysis and Retrieval System. Some websites and commercial databases improve access to these reports by offering additional retrieval features not available on the official (www.sec.gov) website.

EDGAR Database Full-Text Search. U.S. Securities and Exchange Commission (SEC), Washington, DC
10-K reports and other required corporate documents are made available in the SEC'S EDGAR database within 24 hours after being filed. Annual reports, on the other hand, are typically sent directly to shareholders and are not required as part of EDGAR by the SEC, although some companies voluntarily include them. Both 10-Ks and shareholder's annual reports are considered basic sources of company research. The SEC offers a search interface for full-text searching of the content and exhibits of EDGAR SEC filings. The advanced search is recommended to locate "hard-to-find" information within documents filed by corporations and their competitors. Searches for specific types of reports or certain industries can also be performed.
http://searchwww.sec.gov/EDGARFSClient/jsp/EDGAR_MainAccess.jsp

LexisNexis Academic—SEC Filings & Reports. Bethesda, MD: LexisNexis.

Company Securities Exchange Commission filings and reports are available through the "Business" option of LexisNexis Academic. These reports and filings can be retrieved by company name, industry code, or ticker symbol for a particular time period or by a specific report. Proxy, prospectus, and registration filings are also available.

Mergent Online—EDGAR. New York, NY: Mergent, Inc.

From the "EDGAR Search" tab within *Mergent Online,* EDGAR SEC filings and reports can be searched by company name or ticker symbol, filing date range, and file type (10-K, 8-K, ARS). The reports are available in HTML, MS Word format, and PDFs. Using the "Find in Page" option from the browser provides the capability of jumping to specific sections of an SEC report.

Company Rankings

Fortune 500. New York, NY: Time Inc.

The *Fortune 500* list and other company rankings are published in the printed edition of *Fortune* magazine and are also available online.

http://money.cnn.com/magazines/fortune/fortune500/2008/full_list/index.html

Hoover's Handbook of American Business. Austin, TX: Hoover's Business Press, 2008.

This two-volume set gives a company overview, a list of competitors, and basic financial information for large American companies. A special feature is a section called "The List Lovers' Companion," which includes a variety of lists with company rankings, some that include companies listed in Hoover's Handbooks; others reprinted from *Fortune, Forbes,* and other publications. In addition to the American edition, Hoover's Handbooks are available for private companies, emerging companies, and companies headquartered outside of the United States.

Ward's Business Directory of U.S. Private and Public Companies. Farmington Hills, MI: Gale CENGAGE Learning, 2008, 8 vols.

Ward's Business Directory is one of the few directories to rank both public and private companies together by sales within an industry, using both the Standard Industrial Classification system (in vol. 5 only) and the North American Industry Classification System (in vol. 8 only). With this information, it is easy to spot who the big "players" are in a particular product or industry category. Market share within an industry group can be calculated by determining what percentage a company's sales figure is of the total given by Ward's for that industry group. Some libraries may offer this business directory as part of a database called *Gale Directory Library.*

Business Websites

Business.com. Santa Monica, CA: Business.com, Inc.

A business-focused search engine with 26 top-level industry categories and links to more than 25,000 categories and subcategories that include over 400,000 business-oriented websites that are especially useful for locating industry association information.

www.business.com/

Big Charts. San Francisco, CA: MarketWatch, Inc.

BigCharts is the world's most comprehensive and easy-to-use investment research website, providing access to professional-level research tools such as interactive charts, current and historical quotes, industry analysis, and intraday stock screeners, as well as market news and commentary.

http://bigcharts.marketwatch.com/

GlobalEdge. East Lansing, MI: Michigan State University

GlobalEdge is a Web portal providing a significant amount of information about international business, countries around the globe, the U.S. states, industries, and news.

http://globaledge.msu.edu/

Hoover's Online. Hoover's, Inc., Short Hills, NJ: Dun & Bradstreet Corp.

Hoover's includes a limited amount of free information on companies, industries, and executives. The subscribers' edition provides more in-depth information, especially for competitors and industries.

www.hoovers.com/free

Internet Intelligence Index. Cambridge, MA: Fuld & Co.

This website gathers information from a wide variety of public services. The site contains links to over 600 intelligence-related Internet sites, covering everything from macroeconomic data to individual company stock quote information. The Industry section links to a variety of industry websites, such as apparel, publishing/media, technology/telecommunications, and many more.

www.fuld.com/Tindex/I3.html

Yahoo Finance. Sunnyvale, CA: Yahoo! Inc.

This website links to information on U.S. markets, world markets, data sources, finance references, investment editorials, financial news, and other helpful websites.

http://finance.yahoo.com

Strategic and Competitive Analysis—Information Sources

Analyzing a company can take the form of examining its internal and external environment. In the process, it is useful to identify the company's strengths, weaknesses, opportunities and threats (SWOT). Sources for this kind of analysis are varied, but perhaps the best would be to locate articles from The *Wall Street Journal,* business magazines and industry trade publications. Publications such as these can be found in the following databases available at many public and academic libraries. When using a database that is structured to allow it, try searching the company name combined with one or more keywords, such as "IBM and competition" or "Microsoft and lawsuits" or "AMR and fuel costs" to retrieve articles relating to the external environment.

ABI/Inform Complete. Ann Arbor, MI: ProQuest LLC

ABI/Inform Complete provides abstracts and full-text articles covering management, law, taxation, human resources, and company and industry information from more than 4,000 business and management journals. *ABI/Inform* includes market condition reports, corporate strategies, case studies, executive profiles, and global industry conditions.

Business & Company Resource Center. Farmington Hills, MI. Gale CENGAGE Learning

Business & Company Resource Center provides company and industry intelligence for a selection of public and private companies. Company profiles include parent-subsidiary relationships, industry rankings, products and brands, investment reports, industry statistics, and financial ratios. A selection of full-text investment reports is also available.

Business Source Complete. Ipswich, MA. EBSCO Publishing

Business Source Complete is a full-text database with over 3,800 scholarly business journals covering management, economics, finance, accounting, international business, and more. The database also includes detailed company profiles for the world's 10,000 largest companies, as well as selected country economic reports provided by the Economist Intelligence Unit (EIU). The database includes case studies, investment and market research reports, SWOT analyses, and more. *Business Source Complete* contains over 1,100 peer-reviewed business journals.

Investext Research Reports. Detroit, MI: Thomson Reuters Corp.

Investext Research Reports offer full-text analytical reports on more than 30,000 companies worldwide. The research reports are excellent sources for strategic and financial profiles of a company and its competitors and of industry trends. Developed by a global roster of brokerage, investment banking, and research firms, these full-text investment reports include a wealth of current and historical information useful for evaluating a company or industry over time.

International Directory of Company Histories. Detroit, MI: St. James Press, 1988–present. 106 volumes to date.

This directory covers more than 8,500 multinational companies, and the series is still adding volumes. Each company history is approximately three to five pages in length and provides a summary of the company's mission, goals, and ideals, followed by company milestones, principal subsidiaries, and competitors. Strategic decisions made during the company's period of existence are usually noted. This series covers public and private companies and nonprofit entities. Entry information includes a company's legal name, headquarters information, URL, incorporation date, ticker symbol, stock exchange, sales figures, and the primary North American Industry Classification System (NAICS) code. Further reading selections complete the entry information. The complete collection, volume 1 to current date, is available electronically in the Gale Virtual Reference Library database from Gale CENCAGE Learning.

LexisNexis Academic. Bethesda, MD: LexisNexis

The "business" category in *LexisNexis Academic* provides access to timely business articles from newspapers, magazines, journals, wires, and broadcast transcripts. Other information available in this section includes detailed company financials, company comparisons, and industry and market information for over 25 industries. The Company Dossier research tool allows a researcher to compare up to five companies' financial statements at one time with download capabilities.

LexisNexis Statistical. Bethesda, MD: LexisNexis

LexisNexis Statistical provides access to a variety of statistical publications indexed in the American Statistics Index (ASI), Statistical Reference Index (SRI), and the Index to International Statistics (IIS). Use the PowerTables search to locate historical trends, future projections, and industry or demographic information. *LexisNexis Statistical* provides links to originating government websites when available.

The Wall Street Journal. New York: Dow Jones & Co.

This respected business newspaper is available in searchable full-text from 1984 to the present in the *Factiva* database. The "News Pages" link provides access to current articles and issues of *The Wall Street Journal.* Dow Jones, publisher of the print version of the *Wall Street Journal,* also has an online subscription available at wsj.com. Some libraries provide access to *The Wall Street Journal* through the ProQuest Newspapers database.

Sources for Industry Research and Analysis

Factiva. New York: Dow Jones & Co.

The *Factiva* database has several options for researching an industry. One would be to search the database for articles in the business magazines and industry trade publications. A second option in *Factiva* would be to search in the Companies/Markets category for company/industry comparison reports.

Mergent Online. New York: Mergent Inc.

Mergent Online is a searchable database of over 15,000 U.S. public companies and more than 20,000 international public companies. The database offers worldwide industry reports, U.S. and global competitors, and executive biographical information. *Mergent*'s Basic Search option features searching by primary industry codes (either SIC or NAICS). Once the search is executed, companies in that industry should be listed. A comparison or standard peer group analysis can be created to analyze companies in the same industry on various criteria. The Advanced Search allows the user to search a wider range of financial and textual information. Results, including ratios for a company and its competitors, can be downloaded to a spreadsheet.

North American Industry Classification System (NAICS)

The North American Industry Classification System has officially replaced the Standard Industrial Classification (SIC) as a numerical structure used to define and analyze industries, although some publications and databases offer both classification systems. The NAICS codes are used in Canada, the United States, and Mexico. In the United States, the NAICS codes are used to conduct an Economic Census every five years providing a snapshot of the U.S. economy at a given moment in time.

NAICS: www.census.gov/eos/www/naics/

Economic Census: www.census.gov/econ/census02/

NetAdvantage. New York: Standard & Poor's

The database includes company, financial, and investment information as well as the well-known publication called *Industry Surveys.* Each industry report includes information on the current environment, industry trends, key industry ratios and statistics, and comparative company financial analysis. Available in HTML, PDF, or Excel formats.

Search Engines

Google. Mountain View, CA: Google, Inc.
Recognized for its advanced technology, quality of results, and simplicity, the search engine Google is highly recommended by librarians and other expert Web surfers.
www.google.com

Clusty. Pittsburgh, PA: Vivisimo, Inc.
This search engine not only finds relevant results, but also organizes them in logical subcategories.
www.clusty.com

photo credits

Chapter 1: page 20, The McGraw-Hill Companies, Inc./John Flournoy, photographer; page 23, The McGraw-Hill Companies, Inc./Doug Sherman, photographer

Chapter 2: page 53, Royalty-Free/CORBIS; page 70, The McGraw-Hill Companies, Inc./John Flournoy, photographer

Chapter 3: page 86, The McGraw-Hill Companies, Inc./John Flournoy, photographer; page 99, Keith Eng 2007

Chapter 4: page 133, Corbis; page 148, The McGraw-Hill Companies, Inc./L.Niki

Chapter 5: page 171, Royalty-Free/CORBIS; page 184, The McGraw-Hill Companies, Inc./Andrew Resek, photographer

Chapter 6: page 201, The McGraw-Hill Companies, Inc./Christopher Kerrigan, photographer; page 219, The McGraw-Hill Companies, Inc./Andrew Resek, photographer

Chapter 7: page 252, Getty Images; page 260, Digital Vision/Getty Images

Chapter 8: page 278, The McGraw-Hill Companies, Inc./John Flournoy, photographer; page 288, JupiterImages

Chapter 9: page 318, Janis Christie/Getty Images; page 321, The McGraw-Hill Companies, Inc./John Flournoy, photographer

Chapter 10: page 366, Digital Vision/Getty Images; page 368, The McGraw-Hill Companies, Inc./Jill Braaten, photographer

Chapter 11: page 404, The McGraw-Hill Companies, Inc./Lars A. Niki, photographer; page 412, The McGraw-Hill Companies, Inc./Rick Brady, photographer

Chapter 12: page 441, The McGraw-Hill Companies, Inc./Andrew Resek, photographer; page 453, The McGraw-Hill Companies, Inc./Andrew Resek, photographer

Chapter 13: page 478, Digital Vision/Getty Images; page 479, PhotoDisc Imaging/Getty Images

company index

Page numbers followed by n refer to footnotes.

a

A. T. Kearney, 41, 165
Accenture, 127, 144, 240
Access Health, 144–145
Accessory Transit Company, 224
Ace Hardware, 172
Acer, 405–407
Actavis Pharmaceuticals, 360
Adam's Mark Hotels, 165
Adelphia Communications, 225, 328, 408
Adidas, 368
Adobe Systems, 127, 131
ADP Corporation, 315
Advanced Micro Devices, 297, 388
versus Intel, 298
Advent, 398
AES, 411
Airbus Industrie, 296
Aircraft Interior Products, Inc., action plans, 322
Air Products and Chemicals, Inc., staffing for innovation, 434
Alberto-Culver, 183
Alcan, 258
Allen Brothers, 53
Alliant Energy of Iowa, 409
Allied Signal, 88
Allstate Corporation, 128
Alstrom, 258
Amazon.com, 19, 22, 65, 97, 168, 291, 297
AMD; see Advanced Micro Devices
American Airlines, 9
American Business Information, 58
American International Group, 17
financial crisis, 313–314
American Pet Products Manufacturing Association, 293
American Productivity and Quality Center, 434
America Online, 21, 197
AmerisourceBergen, 387
Ameritrade, 4
Amgen, 11
Amoco, 19, 198
Amp'd Mobile, learning from mistakes, 272–273
AmTech, 196
AmTran Technology Company, 292
Analog Devices, 254
Anchor Yachts, 53
Andersen Consulting, 134–135, 144
Andersen Worldwide, 224
Anderson Windows, 173
Andrew Corporation, 404
Animal Planet, 255
AOL Time Warner, 228, 329
Apple Inc., 4, 5, 69, 130, 149, 168, 198n, 200–201, 299
complementors, 70
core competence, 202
Apple iPhone, 454
Aravind Eye Care, 236
Arcelor, 215
Arco, 198
Arcor, 339
Arquicor, 196

Arthur Andersen, 17, 334
Arthur D. Little, 91
Asea Brown Boveri, 256
ATI Technologies, 298
AT&T, 89, 168, 197, 215, 312
Autobytel.com, 456
AutoNation, 30
Aventis, 258
Avis Budget Group, Inc., 325

b

B. Dalton, 97
BAE, 258
Bain & Company, 127, 432
Bank of America, 197, 225
Barnes & Noble, 297
Barrons, 225
Bassett Furniture, 452
Basset-Walker, 203
Bayer AG, 258
BCG Group, 266
Beanstalk Group, 454
Beecham Group, 218
BellSouth, 50, 215
Beneficial, 217
Berkshire Hathaway, 84, 202, 207, 329
Bertelsmann, 204
Besen Group, 272
Besex, 262
Bessemer Trust, 171–172
Best Buy, 90–91, 91, 298, 299
spirit of innovation, 441
Best Practices, LLC, 455
Big Bowl restaurants, 354
Big Charts, 498
Big Toys Inc., 280
Biodegradable Products Institute, 432
BizRate, 66, 114
Blockbuster, 296
Blue Cross of California, 68
BMW, 70, 72, 165, 167
Body Shop, 290
Boeing Company, 252, 296, 366, 477
Bombay Company, 452
Book Industry Study Group, 65
Books-A-Million, 65
Booz Allen Hamilton, 329
Boston Consulting Group, 162, 211, 295
Boston Scientific, 215
Bowls: A Cereal Joint, 169
Boyd Group, 164
BP Amoco, 30, 52, 258
Brinker International, 8, 29, 359–360
divisional structure, 354
Bristol-Myers Squibb, 104
British Airways, 164, 301, 440
British Petroleum, 198, 451
British Sky Broadcasting, 337
Brocade, 325
BTR, 209
Buckman Laboratories, 142–143
Burdines, 85
Business.com, 498

c

Cabor Corporation, 213
Cadbury Schweppes, 321, 477
CalPers, 331
Campbell Soup, 21, 84, 89
divestiture of Godiva, 219
Cannondale, 165, 173
Canon, 27, 258
Carbon Trust, 89
Cardinal Health, 387
Cargill, 96
Carling O'Keefe Breweries, 221
Carlyle Group, 264
Carnival Cruise Line, 328
Carrefour, 216
Carrier Air Conditioning, 44, 365
Casas Bahias, 236
Casio, 200
Caterpillar, 165, 182, 263, 356
in China, 264
CBS, 367
Celanese Chemical Corporation, 246
Cemex, 339
Center for Automotive Research, 68
Center for Progress, 61
Cerberus Capital Management, 197
Cereal Bowl, 169
Cereal Cabinet, 169
Cereality, 169
Cessna, 322
Challenger Electrical Distribution, 367
Champion International, 209
Charles Schwab Corporation, 4, 217
Chartered Semiconductor, 298
Chartwell Investments, 389
Cheesecake Factory Incorporated, 331
Chemical Bank, 415
Chery Automobile Company, 72
Chevrolet, 71
Chili's, 8, 29, 354
Chrysler Corporation, 18, 187, 197, 203, 302
Ciba-Geigy, 199, 213
Circuit City, 8, 41, 298, 299
Cirque du Soleil, 290
Cisco Systems, 55, 149, 198, 216, 279, 398, 442
emotional intelligence, 300
Citibank, 25, 400
Citicorp, 252
CITIC Securities, 384
Citigroup, 5, 45, 50
Clayton, Dublilier & Rice, 209
ClearForest, 360
ClickA.com, 178
Clorox, learning from mistakes, 348
CNBC, 47, 335
CNET, 66, 114
Coach, 159–160
Coca-Cola Company, 182, 241, 245–246, 249, 258, 417, 453, 454
Columbia Pictures, 197
Comcast Cable, 94
Commerce Bank, reverse positioning, 185
CompUSA, 298, 299
Computer Associates, 321

c

ConAgra, 60, 96, 355
Cone Communications, 22
Conferenza, 66
Conseco, 197, 217
Consumers Union, 64
Continental Airlines, 96
Cookshack, 85
customer service, 87
Cooley Godward, 135
Cooper Industries, 198, 199, 209–210
Cooper Software, Inc., 125, 323
Corel, 41, 218
Corning, 407
Corporate Library, 328
Corptech, 404
Costco Home Stores, 452
Costco Wholesale Corporation, 20, 216, 292, 452
Countrywide Financial Corporation, 141
financial crisis, 142
County Crisp Catfish Strips, 60
CP Group, 355
CreditSights, 426
Crescott Real Estate Equities, 328
Crown Financial Ministries, 141
Crucell, 196
CultureRx, 441
Custom Research Inc., 167
CVS Pharmacies, 169
Cybercorp Inc., 217
Cypress Semiconductor, 27

d

Daigeo, 258
Daimler Benz, 197, 203
DaimlerChrysler, 244
Dart, 226
Dayton Hudson Corporation, 226
Deere & Company, in India, 242
Deja News, 44
Del Frisco's, 53
Dell Inc., 4, 95, 110, 172, 238, 241, 298, 356, 366, 450
eroded competitive advantage, 98–99
IdeaStorm, 436
Deloitte & Touche, 160
Deloitte Consulting, 449
Deloitte Touche Tohmatsu, 449
Delphi Corporation, 68
Delta Pride Catfish, supplier power, 60
Diamond Offshore Drilling, 210
Digital Directory Assistance, 58
Digital Equipment Corporation, 45, 140
Discovery Channel, 255
Disneyland, 27
Dove, 21
Dow Chemical, 360
DreamWorks SKG, 404
Duke Energy of Indiana, 409
Dun & Bradstreet, 139, 498
Du Pont Corporation, 387, 432
Duracell, 169, 202
Durkee Famous Foods, 211

e

EADS, 258
Eastman Kodak, 143, 258
eBay, 135, 168, 449
  founding of, 278
EcoAmerica, 124
Ecolab, 296
Electrolux, 258
Electronic Accounting Systems, 67
Electronic Arts, 328
Eleuria, 173
Eli Lilly & Company, 21, 62, 320
  Internet-based collaboration, 371
E-Loan, 305
Embraer, 339
EMC, 170–171, 172
Emerson Electric, 209, 214, 318, 319
Encyclopaedia Britannica, Inc., 41, 44–45, 81
Energizer, 169
Enron Corporation, 17, 224, 225, 328, 334, 335, 336, 408
Enterprise Rent-A-Car, 131
Environmental Defense Fund, 124
Epinions, 114
Ericsson, 258
Ernst & Young, 135
ESPN, 273
Estee Lauder, 290
E*Trade, 6, 8
  learning from mistakes, 4–5
Exodus Communications, 196
ExxonMobil, 50, 198

f

Facebook, 302
  founding of, 278
  versus MySpace, 303
Family Firm Institute, 275
Fannie Mae, 45
Farm Fresh, 60
Federal Bank, 18
Federal Express, 29, 30, 93, 167, 168, 318, 323
Ferragamo, 454
Ferrari, 71
Fidelity Investments, 330, 364
Financial News Network, 335
Firefox, 301
Flash Networks, 245
Fleet Mortgage, 85
Flextronics, 258
Food Lion, 81
Ford Motor Company, 24, 71, 72, 203, 243, 252, 256–257, 302, 332, 404
  learning from mistakes, 80, 234
Forest Laboratories, 332
Forrester Research, 182
Fortune Brands, 30
Fox Network, 204
Fox News, 303
Freddie Mac, 45
FreeMarkets Online, 58–59
Freeport-McMoran, 198
Fremantle Licensing Worldwide, 204
Fremantle Media, 203
  and American Idol, 204
Frost & Sullivan, 426
Fuld & Company, 43–44, 499
Future Solutions, Inc., 280
Fynanz, 281

g

Gaiam, Inc., 288
Gartner, 247, 273
Gateway 2000, 405
Genentech, 122
General Dynamics, 186
General Electric, 5, 88, 89, 125, 126, 129, 203, 224–225, 234, 239, 320, 336, 363, 386, 402, 407, 426, 456
  SupportCentral, 436
  teaching teams, 403
General Electric Aerospace, 186
General Electric Healthcare, 128
General Electric Lighting, 364
General Electric Medical Systems, 126
General Electric Wind Energy, 13
General Mills, 161, 163, 261, 319, 367
General Motors, 24, 68, 72, 80, 302, 335
  divisional structure, 353
Genzyme, 250
Georgia Power, 409
Gerber Products Company, 96
Gibson's guitars, 168–169
Gillette Company, 94, 169, 200, 202, 215, 216, 217
Giorgio Armani, 454
GlaxoSmithKline, 128, 258
Glaxo Wellcome, 217
Glidden paints, 211
Global Crossing, 224, 334
GlobalEdge, 498
GlobeFunder.com, 281
Godiva, 219
GoGreenSola.com, 61
Goldman Sachs, 8
Goodyear Aerospace, 186
Google, Inc., 4, 27, 44, 122, 125, 127, 128, 297, 302, 501
  interactive control system, 316
Google AdSense, 316
Google Lively, 316
Google News, 316
Google Print Ads, 316
Grameen Bank, 236
Graybar, 456
Green Careers, 124
Green Mountain Coffee Roasters, 451
Green Tree Financial, 197, 217
Greyhound, 30
Groupe Michelin, learning from mistakes, 158
Gucci, 169–170
Guidant, 215
Gulfstream, 322
GVO, 393

h

H. H. Cutler, 203
Hamilton Sunstrand, 365
Hanover Insurance, 401
Hanson Trust PLC, 209, 211, 355
  unrelated diversification, 362–363
HarperCollins, 22
HCI Direct, 85
Headhunter.com, 96
Healthsouth Corporation, 408
Hewitt Associates, 132

Hewlett-Packard, 6, 26, 130, 132, 140, 143, 172, 222, 238, 241, 263, 318, 325, 366, 440
Hilb Regal & Hobbs Company, 331
Hill & Knowlton/Harris Interactive, 22
Hindustan Lever, 236
Home Depot, Inc., 49, 172, 214, 319, 323, 324, 388
Honda Goldwing motorcycles, 165
Honda motorcycles, 253
Honda Motors, 71, 83, 208, 302
Honda Odyssey, 158
Honeywell, 88, 203
Honeywell ElectricOptics, 186
Hoover's Online, 498
Hotjobs.com, 96
Household International, 217
HyperRoll, 360
Hyundai, 53, 70, 71, 72

i

IBM, 24, 46, 60, 100, 132, 135, 186, 238, 240, 252, 258, 263, 281, 336, 371, 417, 486, 497
ICI, 202
Icos Corporation, 62
Ignition Corporation, 135
IHS Global Insight, 7, 72
IKEA, 10
ImClone Systems, 17
Indymac, 18
Infosys, 240
Ingram, 65
Institute of Radio Engineering, 370
Intel Architecture Labs, 404
Intel Capital, 198n
Intel Corporation, 5, 8, 17, 89, 247, 254, 258, 263, 295, 297, 302, 324, 329, 404, 434–435, 441
  versus AMD, 298
Interland, 55
International Franchise Association, 275
International Paper, 122
Internet Intelligence Index, 499
InterSecurities, 50
Intuit, 187, 407, 433
  customers as suppliers, 21
Invacare Corporation, 331
Investment Company Institute, 50
Iowa Beef Processors, 96
ITT, 355
ITT China, 89
iTunes Music Stores, 70
Izzo Consulting, 135

j

J. D. Power & Associates, 7, 167, 168, 175, 223, 312
J. P. Morgan Chase, 415
Jazz Semiconductor, 196
Jazz Technologies, 196
JCPenney, 71
JetBlue Airways, 88, 295, 302
Jitterbug, 273
Jobsearch.com, 96
Johnson & Johnson, 42, 150, 412
  credo, 413
Johnson Controls, 445
JPMorgan, 197
Juno Online Services, 85
Jupitermedia Corporation, 178

k

Kansas City Southern, 50
Kazaa, 70
Kellogg's, 250
Kentucky Fried Chicken, 205
Kia Motors, 71
Kidder Peabody, 224–225
Kiva.com, 281
Kmart, 70, 182
Kmart Holdings Corporation, 215
K'Netix, 142
Kohlberg, Kravis, Roberts & Company, 209
Korean Development Bank, 384
KPMG, 23, 127, 334
Kraft Foods
  alliance with bagel maker, 221
  in China's market, 86

l

L. L. Bean, 429
Lafarge, 258
Lamborghini, 71
Lands' End, 173, 429
LaPage's Inc., 205
La-Z-Boy, 331
Leading Hotels of the World, 53
Learning Channel, 255
Lego Group, 46, 435
  reinventing itself, 438
Lehman Brothers, 17, 127
  learning from mistakes, 384–385
Lending Club, 281
Lending Tree, 305
Levi Strauss & Company, 46, 405, 415
Lexus, 165, 167, 168, 318
LG (Lucky Goldstar), 40
Liberty Mutual Group, 179
  cost and differentiation advantages, 180
Linux, 301
LiveWorld, 21
Lockheed Martin, 11, 127, 131, 186, 208, 320, 370
Loews Corporation, 210
Logitech Inc., 358–359
Loral Corporation, 208
L'Oreal, 258, 290
Los Angeles Police Department, 394, 395
Lotus Corporation, 100, 263
Lowe's, 49, 172, 388
Lucent Technologies, 440
LVMH, 258

m

Maggiano's Italian Grill, 8
Mahindra & Mahindra, 242
Mail Boxes Etc., 288
Mandalay Entertainment, 26
Marantz stereo components, 165
MarketWatch, Inc., 498
Marriott Corporation, 160
Martin guitars, 165
Martin Marietta, 11
Marvel Studios, financial turnaround, 5–6
Massachusetts Bay Transit Authority, 395
Matsushita, 292
Mazda, 404

McCaw Cellular, 215
McDonald's Corporation, 27, 205, 209, 250, 258, 312, 321, 329, 340
McKesson, 387
McKinsey & Company, 23, 45, 135, 266
Medtronic, 27, 165
Me Inc., 135
MeKesson, 199
Menlo Worldwide, 30
Mercedes-Benz, 70, 71, 160, 203
Merck & Company, 104, 121, 129
Mergent Inc., 500
Merrill Lynch, 197, 225
Metorex, 8
Miami Heat, 328
Michelin, 258
Microsoft Corporation, 8, 41, 45, 85–86, 102, 121, 123, 135, 143, 198, 223, 239, 244, 247, 262, 301, 323, 336, 371, 392, 405, 454, 455
and H-1B visa restrictions, 51
Microsoft Encarta, 81
Microsoft Windows, 430
Microsoft Word, 125
Mini Cooper, 21
Mint.com, 289
Miro Consulting, 398
Misiu Systems, outsourcing experience, 248
Mittel Steel, 215
Molson Companies, 221
Mommy SWAT Teams, 283
Monsanto, 84–85, 311
Monster.com, 96, 124
MonsterTRAK.com, 124
Morgan Stanley, 165, 223
Motel 6, 42, 45
Motorola, Inc., 27, 126, 198n, 258, 426, 443, 449
learning from mistakes, 40
Mozilla Corporation, 301
MP3, 147
MSA Aircraft Interior Products, Inc., 322
MTV Networks, 272
diverse workforce, 134
My Docs Online Inc., 66
mySimon, 66
MySpace, 94, 302
versus Facebook, 303

n
Napster, 70, 147
NASCAR, 162
National Association of Home-Based Businesses, 275
National Association of Manufacturing, 49
National Association of Realtors, 45
National Basketball Association, 328
National Federation of Independent Business, 284
National Instruments, 131
National Wilderness Preservation System, 348
Nationjob.com, 96
Nature's Path, 184
Navistar, 80
NCR, 197
NEC, 22
Neiman Marcus, 71
Nestlé, 203–204, 249, 256
Netflix, 21, 167, 295, 296
differentiation, 168
Network Appliance, 170–171, 172

Newell Rubbermaid, 318
NewPage Corporation, 124
News Corporation, 22, 303
Nextel, 215, 312
NextJet, Inc., 29
mission change, 30
Nickelodeon, 134
Nielsen Media Research, 454
Nielsen Online, 65
Nike, Inc., 207, 247, 251, 288
outsourcing by, 368–369
Nikeid.com, 173
Nintendo, 69
Nissan Motors, 258, 302
Nokia, 40, 165, 222, 258
Nordstrom, 70, 85, 165
Nortel Networks Corporation, 326
learning from mistakes, 426–427
North Face, 165
Novartis, 199, 213
Novell, 41, 218, 302
NTP, 148
Nucor Corporation, 122, 318, 361
Nutmeg Industries, 203
NxStage Medical, 430
Nynex, 58

O
O. R. T. Technologies, 245
Omnicom Group, 454
On the Border, 8, 29
Oracle Corporation, 122, 226, 243, 392, 486
Otis Elevator, 44, 365
Outback Steakhouse, 19
Outboard Marine Corporation, 27
Overstock.com, 168, 449
Oxford ClycoSciences, 250

p
Paccar, focus strategy, 171
Pacific Gas and Electric, 335
Palm Pilot, 183
Panasonic, 292, 299
Paradise 4 Paws, 293
Paramount Studios, 6
Parkdale Mills, functional structure, 352
Parker Pen, 202
Paychex, 67
PBD Worldwide Fulfillment Services, 141
PeopleSoft, 226
PepsiCo, 127, 205, 238, 241, 417, 453
Pfizer, Inc., 62, 104, 196, 215, 244, 431
Phelps Dodge, 198
Philips Electronics, 258
Pier 1 Imports, 42
Pilates, 53
Pilgrim's Pride, 328
Pizza Hut, 205
PlanetFeedback, 114
Playboy Enterprises, 272
Plum Organics, 289
Polaroid, 140
Porsche, 71, 167
Portales Partners, 384–385
Potash Corporation of Saskatchewan, Inc., 165
PPG, 30
Prada, 454
Pratt & Whitney, 365

Priceline.com, 94, 95, 223
PriceSCAN, 66
PricewaterhouseCoopers, 133, 364, 367
Principal Financial Group, 127
ProCD, 58, 81
Procter & Gamble, 20, 22, 30, 104, 135, 183, 198, 215, 216, 217, 238, 254, 293, 371
Puritan-Bennett Corporation, 367

q
Quaker Oats, 197, 218
Quicken, 21

r
RAND Corporation, 61
Raytheon, 137–138, 414
RBC Capital Markets, 426
Recreational Equipment, 131
Recreational Vehicle Dealer Association, 206
Red Hat, Inc., 391
integrative thinking at, 392
Reebok International, 207, 288
outsourcing by, 368
Renault-Nissan alliance, 198
Research in Motion, 147
intellectual property lawsuit, 148
Ringling Brothers & Barnum and Bailey, 290
Ritz-Carlton Hotels, 222, 321
leadership center, 223
Roche, 258, 477
Rockwell Collins, 401
Rolls-Royce, 53
Royal Bank of Canada, 426
Royal Dutch/Shell, 450
Rubber Flooring, Inc., 280
Running Press, 292–293
Ryanair, 163, 301
cost leadership strategy, 164

S
Salesforce.com, founding of, 278–279
Samsung Auto, 28
Samsung Electronics, 40, 292, 454
Samsung Group, 28
SAP, 239, 412, 486
Sapient Health Networks, 465
analysis, decision making and change, 466
Satyam Computer Services, 325
SCM, 211
Sears, Roebuck & Company, 4, 71, 105–106, 165, 215, 413
Securities America, 50
Security Mortgage Group, 478
Sephora.com, 85
SG Cowen Securities, 217
Shandong SEM Machinery, 264
Sharp Corporation, 200–201
boundaryless design, 363–364
Shaw Industries, 19, 23, 84, 199, 202, 206
going green, 24
vertical integration, 207
Shell Oil Company, 22, 130
scenario planning, 46

Siebel Systems, 252
Sierra Club, 349
learning from mistakes, 348
Sikorsky helicopters, 44, 365
Sirius Satellite Radio, 304
Skanska, 258
Sky Tower Telecommunications, 286
pioneering technology, 287
Smith Asset Management, 384
Smith-Corona, 211
SmithKline, 218
SmithKlineBeecham, 217, 364
Snapple Beverage Company, 197, 218
Sodima, 261
Solar Ventures, 328
Solectron, 126
Solomon Smith Barney, 197
Solvay Pharmaceuticals, 371
Sonopia, 273
Sony Computer Entertainment America, 369, 442
Sony Corporation, 23, 197, 258, 292, 441, 442, 452
Sony Entertainment, 6
video game development, 369
Sony Ericsson, 40
Southern Alliance for Clean Energy, 409
Southwest Airlines, 5, 10, 89, 94, 96, 125, 163, 164, 295, 296, 301, 318, 319, 387, 429
Spanx, 289
Springfield ReManufacturing Corporation, 402–403
Sprint Corporation, 101, 215
Sprint Nextel, 43
learning from mistakes, 312
Sprung & Company Investment Counsel, 426
Standard Pacific Corporation, 331
Staples, 279
Starbucks Corporation, 223, 277
innovation at, 436
STMicroelectronics, 221
Sunbeam Corporation, 224, 479
Sun Microsystems, 143, 258
SunTrust Banks Inc., 336
Swatch Group, breakaway positioning, 185
Symantec, 319

t
T. Rowe Price, 330
Taco Bell, 205
Tandem Computers, 130–131
TangentWorks, 283
Target Stores, 4, 20, 182, 217, 226, 427
design innovation, 428
Tata Consulting Services, 262
Tata Motors, 72
TCS, 240
TCS China, 262
Technical Computer Graphics, boundaryless organization, 373
Tele-Communications Inc., 404
Texas Instruments, 254, 411
Textron, 31, 220
TGI Fridays, 254
Third Millennium, 135
Thomson Financial, 360
3M Corporation, 96, 149, 199, 222, 258, 318, 404–405, 441
knowledge base, 145
market power failure, 205

TIAA-CREF, 331, 333
  on executive compensation, 331
Tiffany, 8, 159–160
Timberland, 451
Times Mirror Company, 199
Time Warner Inc., 197, 220, 228
Timex, 454
T-Mobile, 272
Toro Company, 401
Tower Semiconductor, 196
Toyota Homes, 201
Toyota Motor Corporation, 71–72,
  83, 167, 200, 201, 208, 243, 258,
  302, 318
Toyota Production System, 201
Travel Channel, 255
Travelocity, 114–115
True Value, 172
Tweeter's, 299
Twitter, 94
Tyco International, 17, 329, 408

U

Ulker Group, 219
Under Armour, Inc., 289
Unilever, 183, 236, 258
Unilever Bestfoods, 244
Unilever Groups, 244
Union Pacific, 122
United Airlines, 96
United Parcel Service, 30
United Technologies Corporation
  boundaryless concept, 365
  competitive intelligence, 44
Unocal, 208

US Airways, 296
Usenet, 44
U.S. Trust Corporation, 217
UTC Fire & Security Systems,
  365

V

Values Technology, 130
Vanguard, 131
Verizon Wireless, 131, 272, 273,
  312, 426
VF Corporation, 203
Viacom, 133
Viewpoint DataLabs International,
  100
VIP Desk, 283
Virgin, Inc., 417
Virgin Atlantic, 280
Virgin Group, 25, 43, 280
Virgin Mobile USA, 21, 43
  environmental awareness, 42
Visteon Corporation, 336
Vivisimo, Inc., 501
Vizio, Inc., 291
  low-cost imitator, 292
Volkswagen, 234

W

W. L. Gore, 435
  rules for innovation, 437
Wachovia Corporation, 18, 197
Walgreen's Company, 30, 89

Wal-Mart, 10, 19, 70, 71, 174–175,
  182, 216, 217, 253, 296, 298,
  302, 319, 324, 388, 429
  cutthroat pricing schemes, 299
  profits from arbitrage, 241
  stakeholder issues, 20
Walnut Venture Associates, 282
Walt Disney Company, 203, 255,
  329
Warner Brothers, 6, 26
Warner Brothers Publications, 204
Washington Mutual, 17, 45, 197
Waste Management, 224
WD-40 Company, 291
WebMD, 466
Weisenbach Specialty Printing &
  Manufacturing, 280
Wellness Coaches USA, 398
WellPoint Health Network, 28,
  67–68, 160–161, 164
Wells Fargo, 27, 30, 127, 197
Wendy's, 263
Westinghouse, 367
Wetherill Associates, 412–413
Wheeler Interests, 398
Wheels of Zeus, 196
Whirlpool Corporation, 25, 451
  innovation leader, 389
Whole Foods Markets, Inc., 94, 289
  internal benchmarking, 403–404
Wildfire restaurants, 354
Wilshire Associates, 331
Winnebago, 206
Wipro, 240
Workforce Management, 441
World Bank, 235, 243
WorldCom, 17, 224, 225, 329, 334,
  336, 408
Worldwatch Institute, 61

Worn Again, 280
WPP Group PLC, 142, 394, 440
Wyeth, 196, 215

X

Xerox Corporation, 27, 334
XM Satellite Radio, 304
Xugong Group Construction
  Machinery, 264

Y

Yahoo!, 116, 283, 297, 302
Yahoo Finance, 499
Yellow Roadway Corporation, 336
Yokugawa, 386
Yoplait, 261
Young & Rubicam, 394
YouTube, 94
Yugo, 160
Yum! Brands, 205

Z

Zales, 8
Zappos, 94
Zhejiang Geely Holding Company,
  72
Zimbra, Inc., 455
Zopa, 281
Zurich Financial Services, 252

Page numbers followed by n refer to footnotes.

a

Aaker, David A., 190, 268
Abdullah, M., 325
Abraham, M., 111
Abuelsamid, S., 267
Adams, S., 152
Adler, Deborah, 428
Adler, P. S., 153
Afuah, A., 77, 116n, 117, 380
Agel, R., 113
Ahlstrom, D., 337, 338, 345
Aiman-Smith, L., 460
Ajakie, Zaina, 283
Albrinck, J., 460
Aldag, R. J., 485
Aldrich, H. E., 307
Alessandri, T. M., 344
Alexander, M., 229
Allard, M. J., 153
Allmond, K., 24
Allred, B., 373
Alvarez, S. A., 75
Alvin, Mike, 242
Amabile, T. M., 153
Amburgey, T. L., 379
Amelio, Gil, 196
Amit, E., 113
Amram, M., 460
Anard, B. N., 230
Anderson, Brad, 441
Anderson, E., 112
Anderson, J. C., 111
Anderson, P., 151
Anderson, Tom, 303
Angel, R., 107
Angevine, R., 180
Angwin, J. S., 231
Anslinger, P. A., 229
Ansoff, H. I., 75
Ante, S. E., 303, 341
Anthony, Scott, 407
Argawal, A., 343
Argyris, Chris, 313, 341
Arikan, A. M., 34
Arison, Micky M., 328
Armstrong, R. W., 190
Arndt, M., 190, 230, 344, 389
Arno, A., 230
Arnold, D., 269
Arnott, D. A., 342
Arregle, J. L., 154
Asaba, S., 307
Ashkenas, R., 364
Asmus, P., 451
Aston, A., 35, 52, 76
Augustine, Norman R., 8, 34, 192, 320, 342, 370
Aumann, Yonatan, 360
Austen, I., 459
Austin, R. D., 35, 190
Autio, E., 282
Aznavorian, Dave, 451

b

Baatz, E. B., 422
Bachman, J., 268
Bader, P., 154
Bahrami, H., 372
Baier, J., 152
Bailey, Daniel, Jr., 142
Baker, M., 451
Baker, S., 52, 76, 342
Bakke, Dennis, 411, 422
Balfour, F., 244
Ball, D., 343
Ballard, S., 441
Balmer, Steven, 406
Bamford, C. E., 76
Bandyk, M., 281
Bansal, P., 152
Barkema, H. P., 192, 230
Barnes, Christopher, 367, 380
Barnes, L. A., 485
Barnett, M. L., 77
Barnevik, Percy, 36, 153
Barney, J. B., 34, 75, 92, 98, 112, 152, 190
Baron, R. A., 152, 306, 460
Barr, A., 142
Barrett, A., 230
Barringer, B. R., 381
Bart, C. K., 37
Bartlett, C. A., 191, 267, 354, 379
Bartness, A., 381
Barwise, P., 153
Basker, E., 241
Baumgartner, P., 77, 190
Bayers, C., 115n
Baysinger, B. D., 343
Beamish, P. W., 267, 307
Bearden, W. O., 191
Becker, B., 419
Becker, G. S., 152
Beckhard, R., 34, 36, 420
Begley, T. M., 34, 254
Beller, P. C., 342
Belton, C., 267
Benioff, Marc, 278
Bennett, James, 168
Bennett, N., 343
Bennett, Stephen M., 187, 433
Bensaou, B. M., 111
Benz, M., 35
Bergen, M. A., 308
Bergen, M. E., 190
Berggren, E., 111
Bergstrom, B., 205
Berkowitz, E. N., 191, 268, 269
Berle, Adolf, 326
Berman, P., 352
Berman, Todd, 389
Bernanke, Ben, 45
Bernardino, Joseph, 224
Berner, R., 104, 113, 296, 299
Bernoff, J., 94
Berns, G., 151
Berns, Gregory, 120
Bernstein, A., 345
Berry, M. S., 36
Besen, Alex, 272
Besley, S., 231
Bettcher, K. E., 412
Bezos, Jeff, 291
Bhagat, R. S., 268
Bhatacharya, A. K., 268
Bhattacharya, C. B., 36
Bhide, A. V., 307, 345, 459
Bierce, Ambrose, 326
Bigley, G. A., 35
Birch, David, 274
Birkinshaw, J., 12, 35, 269, 381, 459, 460
Blake, Dennis, 36
Blake, S., 153
Blank, Arthur, 318
Blanton, Buddy, 401
Blenkhorn, David L., 495
Blinder, Alan S., 8
Block, Z., 460
Bloom, M., 344
Blyler, M., 113
Bodick, N., 190
Bodily, S., 67
Bodwell, C., 36
Bogle, 344
Bogner, W. C., 152
Bolton, L. E., 111
Bonnabeau, E., 190
Borden, G., 268
Borden, M., 451
Borrus, A., 415
Bothe, Marie, 413
Bowen, D. E., 421
Bowen, H. P., 229
Bower, J. L., 12
Bowie, N. E., 226
Bowles, J., 75
Boyd, D. P., 34, 254
Boyle, M., 53, 76, 299, 419
Brabeck, Peter, 256, 269
Brady, D., 154
Brandenburger, A., 68, 69, 77
Brandes, P., 344
Brandt, R., 342
Branson, Richard, 25, 36, 43, 153, 417
Bratton, William, 394, 395
Breen, B., 450
Brenneman, K., 466
Bresser, R. F., 113
Brigham, E. F., 231
Brinkley, C., 454
Broache, A., 76
Brock, Ruthie, 495n
Brockner, J., 420
Brockovich, Erin, 335
Brooker, K., 34, 191
Brouthers, L. E., 268
Brown, E., 336, 360, 380
Brown, R. H., 267
Brown, R. L., 76
Brown, S. L., 459
Brown, Shona, 316
Brown, T., 167
Brush, C., 460
Bruton, G. D., 337, 338, 345
Bryan, M., 289
Bryant, James, 58, 81
Bryce, D. J., 452
Buchanan, L., 308
Buckingham, M., 421
Buckley, M. R., 246
Buckman, R. C., 154
Buffett, Warren, 40, 329
Bunderson, J. S., 380
Burgelman, R. A., 308, 380, 460
Burke, D., 314
Burke, James, 413
Burnham, Dan, 414
Burns, E., 191
Burrows, P., 34, 113
Burt, Ronald S., 137–138, 154
Bush, D., 205
Bush, George W., 328
Bush, J., 229
Busyh, J., 78
Butz, H. E., 191
Buzzell, R. D., 230
Bygrave, W. D., 274, 276, 282, 306, 307
Byrne, Carol, 495n
Byrne, J. A., 343
Byrnes, N., 113, 314, 330, 344

c

Cadbury, Adrian, 321
Cadbury, S. A., 342
Caesar, G., 307
Caldwell, T., 371
Callanan, J., 421
Cameron, K., 421
Camillus, J., 20, 219
Camp, B., 461
Campbell, A., 229
Campbell, C., 205
Campbell, Lewis, 31
Canabou, C., 459
Cannella, A. A., Jr., 343
Capell, K., 164, 280
Caplan, J., 191
Caplan, Mitch, 4–5
Capozzi, M. M., 114n
Cappelli, P., 152, 153
Cardin, R., 152
Cardinal, L. B., 460
Carey, D., 230
Carey, J., 36, 77, 289
Cargile, D., 60
Carley, W. M., 153
Carlson, D. S., 422
Carney, D., 415
Carr, N. G., 77
Carroll, Chuck, 437
Carrott, G. T., 35
Carruba, Frank, 366
Caruso, D., 421
Cash, J. I., Jr., 112
Casico, W. F., 229
Cassidy, J. C., 191
Cassidy, John, 365
Cattani, K., 191
Caulfield, B., 460
Cehn, S.-F.-S., 380
Cendrowski, S., 190
Cerny, K., 381
Cescau, Patrick, 236
Chafkin, Max, 436
Chakrabarti, A., 268
Challenger, J., 76
Chambers, John, 398, 399
Chambers, Sara, 288
Champion, David, 169
Champoux, J. E., 420
Champy, James, 374, 381
Chan Kim, W., 395
Chan, P., 191
Chandler, A. D., 379
Chang, V., 152
Charan, R., 386, 387, 420
Charitou, C. D., 75
Charnock, Mark, 124

Charples, S. S., 75
Chatman, J., 152
Chatterjee, S., 37, 343
Chen Xin, 40
Chen, M. J., 294, 300, 308
Chen, Winston, 126
Chen, X.-P., 307
Cheng, R., 341
Chertow, Glenn, 430
Chesbrough, H., 434, 460
Cho, H. J., 461
Choi, T. Y., 380
Choo, C. W., 461
Chow, Dan, 244
Chowdhury, S. D., 344
Chrisman, J. J., 307
Christakis, N. A., 154
Christensen, Clayton M., 429, 430, 459
Christiansen, C. R., 485
Chung, J., 314
Chung, M., 138, 154
Ciampa, K., 420
Cisneros, Henry S., 142
Clayton, M., 61
Clifford, M. L., 267
Clinton, Hillary, 476
Clymer, Susan, 466
Cochran, P. L., 342
Cochran, P. S., 422
Coff, R. W., 113, 344, 461
Cohen, D., 154
Cohen, Tony, 204
Colarelli, G., 459
Cole, David E., 68
Coleman, D. R., 485
Coleman, J. S., 154
Colin, M., 449
Collier, P., 267
Collins, Jim C., 34, 285, 307, 317, 342, 388, 420, 452
Collis, D. J., 36, 112, 113, 229, 230, 380
Colvin, G., 76, 191, 386, 420, 437
Colvin, J., 268
Combs, J. G., 112
Conant, Doug, 219
Conaway, W., 268
Conley, J. G., 155
Conley, J. H., 422
Conlin, M., 132, 441
Conroy, Pat, 160
Conyon, M. J., 344
Cook, Scott, 407
Cooney, J., 204
Cooper, Alan, 125
Cooper, Alice, 196
Cooper, C. L., 416, 417
Cooper, S., 307
Copeland, M. V., 284, 360
Copeland, T. E., 229
Corbett, Alistair, 432
Corp, Katherine, 53
Cotte, J., 36
Coucke, K., 380
Courtney, H., 75
Coutu, D., 153
Covel, S., 221
Covey, S. R., 421
Covin, J. G., 448, 461
Covsey, S. R., 421
Cowell, Simon, 204
Cox, J., 421
Cox, T. H., 153
Cox, T. L., 153
Coy, P., 230
Coyle, M., 180
Craig, J., 461
Criag, S., 34
Crockett, R. O., 75, 459, 460, 461
Crook, T. R., 112
Cross, N., 449
Cross, R., 75, 152, 154, 365

Csere, C., 78
Cullen, J. B., 268
Curtis, S., 446
Cusack, M., 229

Dacin, M. T., 231
Dacin, T., 379
Daft, R., 420
Dahan, E., 191
Dahlvig, Anders, 342
Daily, C. M., 343
Damanpour, F., 459
Daneshkhu, S., 314
Daniel, J. D., 379
Das, T. K., 381
D'Aveni, Richard, 385
Davenport, Craig, 466
Davenport, T. H., 153, 191, 268, 316, 381, 460
David, P., 344
Davidson, A., 365
Davidsson, P., 308
Davies, A., 76
Davies, E. W., 381
Davies, M., 300
Davis, E., 342, 381
Davis, P. S., 191, 461
Davis, S., 190
Dawar, N., 267, 268
Dawn, K., 379
Day, C., Jr., 420
Day, G. S., 75, 112, 191
Day, J. D., 461
Dayton, Berry, 145
Deal, T. E., 342
Dean, B. V., 191
Dean, T. J., 76
Decio, Ben, 281
Deeds, D. L., 307
Deephouse, D. L., 112
Delgrosso, P., 190
De la Torre, J., 339
Dell, Michael, 98, 366, 379, 380, 436, 450
DeLong, T. J., 35
De Meuse, K. P., 192
Dennis, W. J., Jr., 284
Deogun, N., 228, 230
Der Hovanesian, M., 50
DeSanctis, G., 381
Deshpande, R., 412
DeSimone, L. D., 362
DeSio, Tony, 288
Dess, G. G., 34, 67, 81, 112, 146, 151, 153, 154, 190, 191, 229, 230, 269, 341, 342, 379, 380, 381, 420, 421, 446, 448, 461
De Tienne, D. R., 307
Deutsch, T., 343
Deutschman, A., 437
Dexter, Billy, 134
Dharwadkar, R., 344
Dholakia, Paul, 281
Dibrell, C., 461
Dickson, O., 284
Dickson, P. R., 191
DiFucci, John, 226
Dockter, Scott, 141
Doh, J. P., 36
Dolan, K. A., 268
Dolan, M., 267
Dolida, Roger J., 367
Domoto, H., 269
Donlon, J. P., 112
Douglas, S. P., 268
Douma, B., 422
Doving, E., 155
Dowell, G., 307

Dowling, G. R., 152
Dowling, N., 421
Downes, L., 55
Downey, Robert, Jr., 5
Doz, Yves L., 269, 381
Dranove, D., 77
Dressner, H., 459
Droege, Scott B., 67, 191
Droge, C., 461
Drucker, Peter F., 40, 44, 75, 307, 431, 456, 459, 461, 485
Dubini, P., 307
Duffield, David, 226
Duncan, James, 89
Duncan, R. E., 379
Duncan, Robert, 381
Dunlap, S., 154
Dunn, Patricia, 325
Dutta, S., 112
Dutton, G., 152
Dwyer, P., 113, 415
Dyer, J. H., 111, 152, 154, 269, 452

Earl, M., 111, 112
Easterby-Smith, M., 421
Ebbers, Bernard, 225, 329
Echikson, W., 267
Eden, L., 268
Edge, A. G., 485
Edmondson, Amy, 407
Edmondson, G., 231
Edvisson, Leif, 151–152
Edwards, C., 113, 298, 369
Ehrenfeld, J. R., 36
Eickhoff, Gerald, 134–135
Einhorn, B., 75
Einstein, Albert, 86, 474
Eisenberg, Melvin Aron, 326
Eisenhardt, K. M., 155, 307, 343, 459
Eisner, Michael, 329
Elenkov, D. S., 75
Elfenbein, H. A., 36
Elgin, B., 409
Eliason, Frank, 94
Ellison, Larry, 226
Ellstrand, A. E., 343
Elson, Charles, 479
Elstrom, P., 230
Emerson, Ralph Waldo, 45
Engardio, P., 244, 267, 380
Ensing, I. M., 381
Enz, C., 485
Epstein, J., 45
Erickson, T. J., 152, 153
Eselius, E. D., 230
Esperanca, J., 339
Esrey, William, 101
Ethiraj, S. K., 112
Ettenson, R., 111
Evans, P. B., 75
Evans, R., 420
Evans, Vanessa, 430
Ewing, J., 34

Faems, D., 269
Fahey, E., 191
Fahey, J., 229
Fahey, L., 75
Fahlander, A., 152
Fairclough, G., 78
Fama, Eugene, 343
Fan Gong, 238

Farr, David, 214
Farrel, A., 278
Feeny, D., 111
Feiden, D., 419
Felps, W., 35
Felsted, A., 314
Ferguson, G., 76
Ferguson, S., 466
Fern, M. J., 460
Ferragamo, Salvatore, 454
Ferrier, W. J., 294, 300, 308, 461
Fey, C. F., 344
Field, J. M., 111
Filatochev, I., 343
Finegold, D., 35
Finkelstein, Brian, 94
Finkelstein, Sydney, 151, 384, 485
Finn, B., 428
Fiorina, Carly, 6
Fisher, A., 127, 153, 202
Fisher, George, 406
Fisher, M. L., 111
Fishman, C., 20
Fishman, R., 268
Fitzgerald, F. Scott, 390
Fitzpatrick, Cynthia, 141
Fitzsimmons, J., 308
Fjelstad, O. D., 111, 113, 114
Flanagan, Debbie, 497
Fleisher, Craig S., 495
Flint, J., 191
Folta, T. B., 461
Fontrodona, J., 422
Forbath, T., 35, 269
Forbes, Walter, 325
Ford, Henry, 24, 326, 400
Forster, J., 380
Foust, D., 76, 77
Fowler, S. W., 112
Frank, Barney, 45
Frauenfelder, M., 287
Frauenheim, E., 441
Fredrickson, J. W., 380
Freeman, R. E., 34, 35, 153, 308, 324n, 343, 379
Frese, M., 454
Freston, Tom, 134
Frey, B. S., 35
Friedman, Marc, 404
Friedman, Stewart D., 132
Friesen, P. H., 379
Frohman, Jessica, 348
Fromartz, S., 306
Frost, T., 267, 268
Fry, Art, 318
Fryer, B., 76, 268, 342
Fuld, Leonard M., 43, 495
Fuld, Richard S., Jr., 17, 384–385, 419
Fuller, J., 75
Fulmer, R. M., 422
Furu, P., 344

Gaal, Stephen, 282
Gaba, V., 307
Gabarro, J. J., 35
Gadiesh, O., 174, 191
Gaglio, C. M., 306, 307
Galbraith, J. R., 350, 379
Gale, B. T., 230
Galin, Liam, 245
Galvin, Chris, 449
Gao, Y., 268
Garcia-Morales, V. J., 420
Garda, R. A., 300
Garnier, J. P., 111
Garten, J. E., 268
Garvin, D. A., 35, 379, 420

Gates, Bill, 51, 123, 406, 422
Gaudin, S., 298
Gauna, Lysette, 280
Gee, P., 308
Gelb, B. D., 205
Georgescu, Peter, 394
Gerdes, L., 127, 131, 343
Gerstner, Louis, 417
Geschke, Kim, 445
Ghemawat, Pankaj, 162, 239, 241, 255, 267, 269
Ghoshal, S., 75, 152, 191, 267, 268, 354, 379
Ghosn, Carlos, 198, 229
Gibbert, M., 459
Gibson, C. B., 12, 154, 155, 381
Gikkas, N. S., 268
Gilad, Benjamin, 495
Gilbert, J. L., 174, 191
Gilmartin, Ray, 129
Gilmore, J. H., 191
Gimbel, B., 190, 230, 267
Ginsberg, A., 460
Ginsburg, J., 76
Giuliani, Rudolph, 395
Glass, J. T., 381
Glatz, Hanns, 244
Goddard, J., 35
Goers, Steve, 221
Goff, John, 328
Goffee, R., 152
Gogoi, P., 299
Goldberg, Anne, 371
Goldman, Ron, 22
Goldsmith, M., 420
Goldsmith, Marshall, 34, 36, 142
Goldstein, A., 30
Goldstein, M., 419
Goldstein, N. J., 342
Goldstein, S., 142
Goldstine, J., 190
Goldwasser, Dan, 332
Goldwyn, Samuel, 405
Goleman, Daniel, 395–396, 420
Golisano, Tom, 67
Gompers, P. A., 460
Gonsalves, A., 298
Goode, Mary, 135
Gooderham, P. N., 155
Goodstein, L. D., 191
Goodwin, Doris Kearns, 476
Goold, M., 229, 341
Goranova, M., 344
Gottfredson, M., 380
Govindarajan, V., 267, 269
Graebner, M. E., 343
Graen, G. B., 342
Graham, Ben, 152
Grahan, A. B., 380
Grant, R. M., 92, 113
Grassley, Chuck, 415
Gratton, L., 153
Green, H., 55
Green, S., 112
Greenberg, Jack M., 329
Greene, J., 51
Greene, P., 460
Greenspan, R., 115n, 191
Greenwald, B., 76
Greenwood, R., 35
Gregg, F. M., 267
Greising, D., 342
Grenon, G., 90
Grewal, Sukh, 436
Grimm, C. M., 294, 300, 308
Grossman, J. H., 430, 459
Grossman, W., 344
Grove, Andrew S., 5, 55, 89, 295, 308, 324, 405, 417
Grover, R., 6, 343, 344, 369, 454
Grow, B., 76, 111, 230
Groysberg, Boris, 140
Gruber, Peter, 26

Gruia, Ronald, 426
Gulati, R., 308
Gull, N., 307
Gumbeel, P., 268
Guntner, T., 76
Gupta, A. K., 267, 269
Gupta, P., 198
Guterman, J., 76
Guth, R. A., 455
Guth, W. D., 191, 229, 460, 485

h

Haas, M. R., 152
Habib, M. M., 379
Haddad, C., 111
Hage, J., 459
Hagel, J., 268
Hagmeier, Katerine, 380
Halkias, M., 296
Hall, B. J., 342
Hall, Brian, 130
Hall, D. J., 380
Hall, R. H., 342, 379
Hall, S., 344
Hall, W. K., 191
Hambrick, D. C., 192, 229, 300, 308, 342, 343
Hamel, Gary, 36, 40, 75, 121, 151, 190, 229, 316, 381, 459, 460
Hamilton, A., 8
Hammer, Michael, 374, 381, 400, 421
Hammonds, K. H., 34, 450
Hancock, Ellen, 196
Handy, Charles, 35, 367, 380, 400, 421
Hannah, S. T., 421
Hansen, M. T., 152, 155, 460
Hansen, Mark, 438
Hanson, James, 362
Hardin, D., 230
Hardy, Q., 37, 114n
Hargreaves, D., 229
Harrar, G., 381
Harrigan, K., 229
Harrison, D. A., 422
Harrison, J. S., 34, 35, 153, 230, 308, 343, 379, 381
Hart, M., 460
Hart, S. L., 36
Hart, Stuart, 23
Hartley, S. W., 191
Harveston, P. D., 268
Harvey, C. P., 153
Harvey, M., 246
Hasan, F., 112
Haspelagh, P., 229
Hassan, A., 325
Hastings, Reed, 295
Hatch, N. W., 152
Haughton, K., 78
Haugland, S. A., 230
Hawken, P., 451
Hax, A. C., 229
Hayashi, A. M., 151
Hayes, R., 459
Healey, J. R., 78
Healy, M., 65
Hegge, Betty-Ann, 165
Heifetz, R., 421
Heine, K., 77
Heineman, B. W., Jr., 344
Heinzl, M., 343
Helft, M., 316
Helgesen, Sally, 25, 36, 421
Helm, B., 53
Helms, M. M., 36, 191, 267, 379, 422

Helper, S., 77
Hemp, P., 34
Henderson, Larry, 246
Hendricks, John, 255
Henke, John, Jr., 80
Henkel, J., 148
Henkoff, R., 112, 152
Henricks, M., 229
Henry, D., 336
Hensler, Bill, 433
Herzog, V. L., 373
Hesse, Daniel, 312
Hessedahl, A., 198n
Hessel, E., 35
Hesselbein, F., 34, 36, 420, 421
Hesseldahl, A., 70
Hill, A., 229
Hill, C. W., L., 380
Hill, S., 111
Hillman, A., 343, 344
Hills, G. E., 306
Hilmer, F. C., 380
Hindo, B., 229
Hitt, M. A., 34, 35, 92, 112, 113, 152, 153, 154, 192, 229, 230, 268, 308, 343, 344, 379
Hodgen, Todd, 248
Hoetker, G., 111
Hof, R. D., 59, 342
Hoffman, B. G., 111
Hofstede, Geert, 268
Holcomb, T. R., 192
Holden, D., 409
Hollender, J., 36
Holliday, Chad, 387
Holmes, S., 190
Holt, J. W., 422
Holt, John, 406
Hoover, V. L., 294, 308
Hope, B., 154
Hopkins, M. S., 77
Hornery, J., 460
Hoskin, R. E., 460
Hoskisson, R. E., 92, 229, 269, 343, 344, 379, 380
Hotard, D., 191
House, Andrew, 369
Hout, T., 267, 268
Howe, J., 204
Howe, Jeff, 19, 35
Howell, J. M., 460
Howell, Pat, 428
Howell, Robert A., 121
Hoynes, M., 65
Hrebiniak, L. G., 34, 229, 379
Huber, Peter, 268
Hudspeth, B., 30
Hult, T. M., 78
Humer, Franz, 477
Hurd, Mark, 26
Hurley, Brian, 427
Hutt, M. D., 230
Huy, Q. H., 36
Hymowitz, C., 128

i

Ibarra, H., 37
Icahn, Carl, 331, 344
Immelt, Jeffrey, 88, 112, 234, 403
Imperato, G., 111, 421
Ingram, T. N., 191
Inkpen, A. C., 269, 381
Ireland, R. D., 92, 112, 113, 152, 229, 230, 268, 269, 379, 460
Isaacson, W., 422
Isenberg, D. J., 360
Iverson, Ken, 361
Iyer, B., 191, 268, 381
Izzo, John, 135

j

Jackson, E. M., 343
Jackson, M., 111
Jackson, S. E., 35
Jacobson, Michael, 135
Jafari, J., 446
Jakobsen, Niels Sandal, 438
Janis, Irving L., 475, 478–479, 485
Jankowski, W., 223
Janney, J. J., 446, 461
Janssens, M., 269
Jap, S. D., 112
Jargon, J., 86
Jarvis, J., 380, 437
Jensen, C., 190
Jensen, Michael, 343
Jensen, Michael C., 344
Jeppersen, L., 371
Jermias, J., 325
Jespersen, F. F., 344
Jiang, G. D., 338
Jiang, Y., 345
Jindra, B., 343
Joachimsthaler, E., 268
Jobs, Steven, 5, 70, 130, 152, 196, 201, 202
Johannessen, J. A., 459
Johansson, P., 134
Johnson, Bob, 312
Johnson, G., 223
Johnson, J. L., 268, 343
Johnson, R. A., 344
Johnson, S., 76
Johnson, Warren, 328
Jomard, Thierry, 364
Jones, Chuck, 389
Jones, G., 152
Jones, J., 30
Jones, T. J., 35
Jordan, B. D., 486
Joshi, S., 230
Joyce, W. F., 34, 229, 379

k

Kahn, J., 76
Kaiser, R. B., 153
Kalathus, Raj, 242
Kale, P., 112
Kambil, A., 230
Kamenetz, A., 379, 451
Kamitschnig, M., 34
Kampur, D., 239
Kane, Y. I., 292
Kang, E., 343
Kanter, Rosabeth Moss, 459, 460
Kao, J., 459
Kaplan, R. E., 153
Kaplan, Robert S., 35, 101, 104, 106n, 113, 153
Kaplan, S. N., 344
Kaple, P., 269
Karr, R., 190
Kasten, Tom, 406
Katz, J. A., 306
Katz, J. H., 153
Katzenbach, Jon R., 381, 403
Kauffman, C., 153
Kaufman, W., 437
Kazanjian, R. K., 350, 379
Keats, B., 379
Kedia, B. L., 268
Keenan, F., 456
Keil, Thomas, 230, 343, 433, 434, 460
Kelleher, Herb, 5, 89, 96, 387
Kelly, Bill, 466

Kennedy, A. A., 342
Kenworthy, T. P., 379
Kerin, R. A., 191
Kerner, S. M., 459
Kerr, J., 342
Kerwin, K. R., 78
Ketchen, D. J., Jr., 78, 112, 294, 308, 460
Kets de Vries, M. F. R., 36, 153, 380
Keynes, John Maynard, 29
Khanna, T., 230, 308, 345
Kharif, O., 75, 306
Kidd, J. B., 269
Kidwell, R. E., Jr., 343
Kiley, D., 267
Killinger, Kerry, 17
Kilmann, R. H., 381
Kim, E., 191
Kim, H., 380
Kim, L., 191
Kim, P. H., 307
Kim, W. Chan, 289, 307, 308
Kimbrell, Duke, 352
King, A. A., 77
Kini, Mark, 114
Kirchhoff, B., 282
Kirkland, J., 75
Kirkman, B. L., 154, 155
Kirkpatrick, D., 303, 420
Kirn, S. P., 113
Klemp, G., 421
Kletter, D., 460
Kling, K., 342
Knauss, Donald, 348
Knott, Caitlin, 454
Knudstrop, Jorgen Vig, 438
Kochen, S., 152
Kocher, Joel, 55
Koerner, P., 201
Kogut, B., 269
Koogle, Tim, 283
Koppel, B., 379
Kor, Y. Y., 34
Koretz, G., 190
Kosnik, R. D., 344
Kotabe, M., 269
Kotha, S., 307
Kotter, John P., 420
Koudsi, S., 230
Kouzes, J. M., 401, 421
Koza, M. P., 269
Kozlowski, Dennis, 225, 231, 329
Kraus, C., 339
Kripalani, M., 239
Krishnan, H., 230
Krishnan, M. S., 112, 190
Krishnan, R. A., 230
Kristiansen, Kjeld Kirk, 438
Kroll, M., 191, 342
Kron, Steven, 8
Ku, G., 228
Kuermmerle, W., 379
Kulatilaka, N., 460
Kumar, A., 308
Kumar, N., 77
Kunii, I., 380
Kutaragi, Ken, 442
Kwak, M., 70, 77
Kwon, S. W., 153

l

Laamanen, T., 230, 343
LaBarre, P., 420
Labianca, G., 138, 154
Labianca, Joseph, 138, 154
Lachenauer, Rob, 295, 296, 308
Lacity, M., 111
Lacy, S., 303
Lafley, A. F., 216

LaForge, R. W., 191
Lakhani, K., 371
Lam, K., 112
La Monica, P. R., 226
Landes, D. S., 267
Langreth, R., 430
Laplume, A. O., 35
Largay, J. A., III, 422
Lash, J., 36
Lashinsky, Adam, 228, 399
Latham, G. P., 153, 342, 460
Lavelle, L., 113, 344
Lavelle, M., 35
Laverty, K. J., 461
Lawler, E. E., 35, 421
Lawrence, Joanne, 218
Lawrence, T. B., 112
Lawton, C., 292
Lazaridis, Mike, 148
Leahy, J., 262
Leana, C. R., 154, 422
Leavitt, P., 434
Lee, G. K., 112
Lee, J., 342
Lee, K. G., 155
Lee, Kun-Hee, 28
Lee-St. John, J., 281
Lees, R. J., 35
Lei, D., 154, 191, 268, 380
Leifer, 459
Leifer, R., 459
Lelii, S. R., 77
LeMay, Ronald T., 101
Lenzner, R., 153, 229
Leonard, Meredith, 216
Leonard-Barton, Dorothy A., 126, 140, 153, 154, 421
Lerner, J., 460
Lester, P. B., 421
Lester, R. H., 343
Letzing, J., 244
Levering, R., 152, 437
Levesque, L. C., 35, 379
Levin, Gerald M., 329
Levitt, Theodore, 248, 268
Lewin, A. Y., 268
Lewis, Ken, 225
Li, J. J., 112, 154
Li, J. T., 269
Libert, B., 21, 35, 43, 87, 168
Lichthental, John, 246
Lieberman, M. B., 307, 461
Lieberthal, K., 267, 268
Lieberzman, David, 393
Liedtka, J., 365
Light, D. A., 75, 154
Light, L., 190
Likert, B., 371
Lim. Y., 191
Linblad, C., 342
Lincoln, Abraham, 476
Ling, Y., 460
Lipin, S., 228, 230
Lipparini, A., 112
Lipton, M., 36, 37
Litan, Avivah, 281
Litz, R. A., 35
Liu, S. X. Y., 112
Lloréns-Montes, F. J., 420
Locke, Edwin A., 342
Loeb, M., 34
Lohr, S., 192
Long, W., 306
Loomis, C. J., 314
Lopez, José Ignacio, 153
Lorange, P., 75, 381, 420
Lorenzoni, G., 112
Lorsch, Jay W., 344, 420
Lovins, A., 451
Lovins, H., 451
Low, C. K., 325
Lowey, T., 190, 230
Lowry, T., 229
Lu, J. W., 267, 307

Lubatkin, M. H., 460
Lublin, J. S., 459
Lucas, George, 438
Luchs, K., 229
Luehrman, T. A., 113
Luhby, T., 124
Lumpkin, G. T., 67, 153, 306, 448, 454, 459, 461
Lundberg, C. C., 485
Lunnan, R., 230
Luthans, Fred, 420, 421
Lutz, Robert, 18
Lynton, Michael, 369
Lyons, D., 308, 461

m

Ma, H., 190
Mabey, C., 152
MacCormack, A., 35, 269
MacDonald, E., 328
MacDonald, I., 51
Macik-Frey, M., 416, 417
Mackay, Colin, 430
MacMillan, I. C., 190, 191, 267, 460, 461
Madhok, A., 269
Madoff, Bernard, 45, 408
Magretta, J., 380
Mahmood, I., 268
Maiello, M., 307, 344
Main, J., 422
Maisel, David, 5, 6
Majluf, N. S., 229
Makino, S., 267
Malhotra, D., 228
Malkin, E., 267
Mallas, S., 461
Malone, John, 405
Malone, Michael S., 151–152
Malone, Tom, 136
Maloney, Sean, 298
Mandel, M., 76, 267
Mandela, Nelson, 45
Mandelker, G., 343
Mandl, Alex, 215–216
Maney, K., 228
Mang, P. Y., 461
Mankins, M. C., 37, 230, 478
Manning, S., 268
March, J. G., 381, 461
Marcial, G., 77
Marcus, Bernard, 318
Margolis, J. D., 36
Markham, S. K., 460
Markides, C. C., 75, 190
Marks, M. S., 112, 192
Marks, O., 437
Marriott, J. W., Jr., 160, 190
Martha, J., 90
Martin, J., 152, 269
Martin, J. E., 155
Martin, K. D., 268
Martin, K. L., 35, 379
Martin, R., 45
Martin, Roger L., 390–391, 392, 420
Martin, X., 269
Martinez, Arthur, 4
Martinez, J., 339
Mass, N. J., 113
Massini, S., 268
Mathur, S. K., 76, 239
Matias, Yossi, 360
Matlack, C., 78, 190
Matthews, C. H., 307
Mauborgne, Renee, 289, 307, 308, 395
Maurer, H., 342, 343
May, R. C., 75
Mayer, J. D., 421
Mayes, Michelle Coleman, 128
Maynard, M., 111

McAfee, A., 112
McCarthy, D., 343
McCarthy, T., 395
McCartney, S., 296
McConnon, A., 299
McCune, J. C., 269
McDermott, C. M., 459
McDonald, D., 223
McDonald, M. L., 229, 343
McDonald, Mackey, 203
McDougall, P. P., 350, 379
McDougall, Ronald A., 354
McGahan, Anita M., 77
McGann, R., 55, 77
McGeehan, P., 343
McGirt, E., 399
McGrath, Rita Gunther, 190, 192, 267, 433, 434, 460, 461
McGrath, C., 154
McGrath, Judy, 134
McGregor, J., 20, 89, 224, 236, 407
McKnight, William, 405–406
McLaughlin, K. J., 380
McLean, B., 345
McLean, Bethany, 335
McMillan, W. E., 306, 307
McNamee, M., 113
McNicol, J. P., 268
McVae, J., 35
McVey, Henry, 165
Means, Gardiner C., 326
Meckling, W. H., 343, 344
Meehan, Sean, 153
Mehta, S. N., 191, 342
Meier, D., 228
Meiland, D., 112
Meindl, J. R., 34
Melcher, R. A., 343
Melrose, Ken, 401, 421
Mendelow, A. L., 461
Merchant, H., 269
Meredith, R., 267
Mero, J., 242
Merritt, Randy, 24
Meyer, A. D., 307
Meyer, K. E., 269
Meyer, Peter, 404, 421
Michael, D. C., 268
Michelangelo, 225
Michelin, Edouard, 158
Miles, R. E., 372, 373
Miller, A., 34, 190, 230, 342, 379, 420, 421, 461
Miller, C. C., 236
Miller, D., 342, 379, 380, 448
Miller, D. J., 229, 460
Miller, F., 153
Miller, K. D., 461
Miller, W., 380
Milner, Alex, 245
Minniti, M., 274
Minow, Neil, 16, 35, 324, 342, 343, 344
Mintzberg, Henry, 13, 34, 35, 313, 341, 485
Misangyi, V. F., 34
Mitchell, R., 342
Mittel, Lakshmi, 230
Mochari, I., 455
Mol, M. J., 459
Moldoveanu, M., 36
Monahan, J., 284
Monahan, Tom, 288
Monks, Robert, 16, 35, 324, 342, 343, 344
Monteiro, K. A., 230
Montgomery, C. A., 112, 113, 229, 380
Montgomery, D. B., 461
Moon, I., 369
Moon, Y., 185, 191
Mooney, A. C., 485
Moore, G. A., 461

Moore, Geoffrey A., 453
Moore, J. F., 381
Moore, Rob, 6
Moran, G., 42
Moran, P., 154
Morioka, Senta, 201
Morison, R., 112
Morita, Akio, 23
Moritz, S., 75
Morris, B., 152, 341
Morris, E., 485
Morrison, C. A., 459
Morrison, T., 268
Morrow, J. S., 192
Morse, E. A., 112
Morse, G., 230
Moskowitz, M., 152, 437
Moss, S. A., 421
Mouio, A., 230
Mowery, D. C., 381
Mozilo, Angelo, 142
Mudambi, R. A., 77, 269
Mui, C., 55
Muir, John, 348
Mulally, Alan, 332
Mullaney, T. J., 192, 456
Muller, J., 190
Munk, N., 113
Murdoch, James, 337
Murdoch, Rupert, 22, 303, 337
Murninghan, J. K., 228
Murphy, D., 420
Murphy, Kevin J., 344
Murphy, P., 268
Mussberg, W., 380

n

Nacher, T., 111
Nadeem, Saq, 293
Nader, Ralph, 335–336
Nahapiet, J., 152
Nalebuff, B. J., 68, 69, 77
Nam, D., 191
Nandiwada, Raj, 196
Narasimhan, O., 112
Narayanan, V. K., 75
Naylor, Mary, 283
Ndofor, H., 308
Nedham, Charles, 8
Neilson, G. L., 35, 342, 379, 460
Nelson, A. J., 485
Nelson, B., 44
Nelson, M. G., 30
Neuborne, E., 191
Neumann, Dan, 53
Newbert, S. L., 35, 112
Nexon, M., 153
Niblack, J., 459
Niven, P., 107, 113
Nmarus, J. A., 111
Nobel, R., 269
Nohria, N., 155, 308, 460
Nonaka, I., 152
Noorda, Raymond, 302
Noot, Walter, 100
Nordstrom, Dan, 85
Norton, David P., 35, 101, 104, 106n, 113
Norton, Edward, 6
Novicki, C., 421
Nutt, P. C., 35

o

Obama, Barack, 476
Obodaru, O., 37
O'Brien, Bob, 225

O'Brien, J. M., 131, 153
O'Brien, J. P., 461
O'Brien, S., 76
O'Brien, William, 401
O'Connor, G. C., 459
Odell, A. M., 124
Odlyzko, A., 76
O'Donnell, S. W., 269
Oh, H., 138, 154
Ohmae, Kenichi, 267, 381
Okie, Francis G., 318
O'Leary, Michael, 164
O'Leary-Kelly, A. M., 342
Oliver, C., 231
Olofson, C., 77
Olsen, B., 459
Olsen, Kenneth H., 45
Omann, Nate, 441
Omidyar, Pierre, 278
O'Neill, H. M., 379
Ordonez, L., 422
Oreck, Diane, 223
O'Reilly, B., 420
O'Reilly, C. A., 152, 381
O'Reilly, Charles, 375
Orey, M., 76
Osso, Steve, 60
Oster, S. M., 229
Oster, Sharon, 162
Ouchi, William, 342
Overholt, A., 236
Oviatt, B. M., 350, 379
Owens, Jim, 264
Oxley, J. E., 381
Ozzie, Raymond, 100

p

Pace, Peter, 404
Paine, L. S., 422
Paine, Lynn S., 410, 412
Palanjian, A., 289
Palazzo, G., 343
Paley, Norton, 495
Palmer, A. T., 190
Palmer, T. B., 78
Palmeri, C., 190, 415
Palmisano, Samuel, 60
Parboteeah, P., 268
Pare, T. P., 228, 229
Parise, S., 152
Parry, P., 90
Parsons, C., 476
Pascual, A. M., 190, 230
Pasternack, B. A., 342
Patel, Deep, 61
Patscot, Steven, 126
Pauleen, D. J., 268
Pauling, Linus, 139
Pawlowski, Janina, 282–283, 307
Peabody, Charles, 384
Pearce, J. A. H., 36, 191
Pearson, A. E., 420
Pearson, D. R., 322
Peck, S. I., 344
Pedroza, G. M., 307
Pellegrini, E. K., 421
Peng, Michael W., 258, 268, 337, 338, 345
Pentland, A., 154
Peridis, Theo, 155
Perkins, A. B., 152
Perman, S, 450
Perrewe, P. L., 422
Perry, Michael, 18
Peteraf, M. A., 77, 153, 308
Peters, L. S., 459
Peters, S., 230, 269
Peters, Thomas J., 342
Peyser, Rick, 451
Pfeffer, Jeffrey, 34, 124, 153, 366, 380

Pham, A., 316
Pham, V. H., 241
Phelan, Dan, 128
Phillips, C., 380
Picasso, Pablo, 120
Picken, Joseph C., 81, 112, 146, 151, 191, 229, 230, 322, 341, 342, 381, 421
Pickens, T. Boone, 45
Pierantozzi, Ron, 434
Pigorini, P., 339
Pil, F. K., 422
Pilgrim, Lonnie, 328
Pinchot, Gifford, 435, 460
Pine, B. J. H., 191
Ping Zhao, 426
Pinto, J., 422
Pistorio, Pasquale, 222
Pitchford, Mark, 135
Pitts, R. A., 154, 379, 380
Pizzo, V. G., 380
Plenge, Robert, 322
Plumb, C., 419
Poitier, Sidney, 329
Polanyi, M., 152
Polek, D., 231
Pollack, Lindsey, 124
Pondy, L. R., 381
Pope, B., 111
Pope, Carl, 348, 379
Poppo, L., 154
Porras, J. I., 317, 342, 452
Port, O., 421
Porter, Michael E., 34, 56, 57, 69, 76, 77, 82, 83, 87, 111, 113, 154, 157, 158–159, 160, 161, 162, 166, 171, 190, 191, 223, 229, 230, 233, 235–236, 238, 239–240, 267, 268, 380
Posner, R. Z., 401, 421
Pottruck, D. A., 380
Pound, J., 342
Powell, T. C., 190
Powers, E., 35, 379
Prahalad, C. K., 40, 75, 121, 151, 154, 190, 229, 236, 267, 268, 269
Pridor, Baradok, 360
Priem, R. L., 75, 380
Prieto, I. M., 421
Prince, C. J., 284
Prior, B., 75
Pritchard, David, 323
Prusak, L., 114n, 154, 460
Pucik, V., 461
Puffer, S. M., 343
Purda, L. D., 76
Puryear, R., 380
Putten, A. B., 267

q

Quick, J. C., 416, 417
Quigley, J. V., 37
Quinn, James Brian, 151, 313, 341, 380
Quinn, R. C., 421
Quinn, R. T., 113
Quinn, Robert, 401–402

r

Raisinghani, D., 485
Rajendra, Eric, 165
Rajiv, S., 112
Ramalinga, Raju, 325
Ramamurti, R., 239

Ramaswamy, V., 154
Ramos, A., 339
Rampersad, H., 107, 113
Ramstead, E., 380
Randall, D., 344
Randall, T., 173, 191
Rao, A. R., 190
Rappa, M., 17
Rappaport, A., 230
Rasheed, A. M. A., 76, 380
Raths, D., 466
Rauch, A., 454
Raynor, M. E., 459
Rayport, J. F., 111
Rechelbacher, H., 280
Rechner, P. L., 485
Reddy, C. N., 328
Reddy, N. Damodar, 328
Reebe, Michael, 134
Reed, A. H., 111
Reed, S., 230
Regan, Judith, 22
Reinartz, Werner, 113, 114, 191
Reiner, Gary, 436
Reinert, U., 267
Reingen, P. H., 230
Reinhardt, A., 231
Reitzig, M., 148
Resnick, B. G., 34
Ressler, Cali, 441
Reuer, J. J., 230, 269
Reyes, Gregory, 325
Reynolds, P. D., 282
Rhodes, D., 190
Rice, M. P., 459
Rich, L., 135
Richter, A., 461
Ricks, D., 269
Ridge, Garry, 291
Rigas family, 225
Rigby, D. K., 229
Ritzman, L. P., 111
Rivkin, Jan W., 113, 345
Roberson, John, 398
Roberto, M. A., 420
Roberts, D., 78, 264
Roberts, E. B., 459
Roberts, J., 461
Roberts, P. W., 152
Robins, J. A., 112
Robinson, D., 452
Robinson, Mark, 19
Robinson, R. B., 191
Robinson, S. L., 342
Robinson, Smokey, 196
Robinson-Jacobs, K., 8
Rockenwagner, P., 6
Rodengen, J. L., 380
Rodgers, T. J., 27
Rodriguez, P., 267
Rollag, K., 152
Rollins, Kevin B., 298, 356, 379
Romanelli, E., 307
Romero, Gayle R., 312
Rondinelli, D. A., 34, 36
Ronstadt, R., 485
Roos, J., 381
Root, Alan, 26
Rosen, B., 154, 155
Rosenberg, Scott, 398
Rosenblum, D., 77
Rosenfeld, Irene, 86
Rosenfeld, J., 190
Rosenthal, J., 306
Rossetti, C., 380
Roth, David, 169
Roth, K., 112
Rothaermel, F. T., 307
Rothenbuecher, J., 228
Rouse, T., 267
Rowley, I., 78, 201, 369
Rowley, T. J., 36
Rows, S. A., 486
Roy, J. P., 231

Royer, I., 460, 461
Rucci, A. J., 113
Rudden, E., 268
Rugman, Alan M., 257–258, 269
Ruisel, I., 421
Ruiz, Hector, 388
Rukstad, M. G., 36
Rumelt, R. P., 379
Runyan, R., 461
Ryan, L. V., 344

S

St. John, W., 308
Sacks, D., 20
Safferstone, T., 34
Safizadeh, M. H., 111
Sahlman, William A., 468
Saias, M. A., 380
Sakaibara, M., 381
Salancik, G. R., 34
Salman, W. A., 77
Salter, C., 389
Salvoney, P., 421
Sampson, R. C., 460
Samuel, Phil, 433
Samuelson, J., 34
Sanchez, Raymond, 477–478
Sandberg, Sheryl, 128
Sandberg, W. R., 485
Sandler, N., 245
Sanger, Stephen, 161–162
Sant, Roger, 36, 422
Sarbanes, John, 384
Sassen, J., 330, 344
Scandura, T. A., 421
Schaeffer, Leonard, 160
Schafer, S., 421
Schaper, M., 280
Schawlow, Arthur, 130
Scheck, J., 342
Schecter, S. M., 192
Schein, Edgar H., 352, 379
Schellenbarger, S., 283
Schendel, D., 269
Schenkel, M. T., 307
Scherer, A. G., 343
Schijven, M., 192
Schindler, Pamela, 478
Schiro, Jim, 133
Schmerken, I., 34
Schmidt, Eric, 76
Schmidt, G., 191
Schneider, M., 344
Schoemaker, J. H., 113
Schoemaker, P. J. H., 75
Schol, M., 35
Schoonhoven, C. B., 307
Schreyogg, G., 75
Schrottke, J., 228
Schultz, Howard, 277, 436
Schwartz, N. D., 268, 438
Schwartzberg, Gary, 221
Schweiger, D. M., 485
Schweitzer, M. E., 422
Schwert, G. William, 228
Scott, B. R., 379
Scott, F. S., 75
Scott, L., 77
Seacrest, Ryan, 454
Seeger, J., 230
Seglin, J. L., 307
Seijits, G. H., 153, 460
Sellers, P., 230, 267, 342
Sen, S., 36
Senge, Peter M., 11, 24, 34, 36, 400, 421
Server, A., 207
Sexton, D. A., 37

Seybold, P., 191
Shah, B., 76
Shah, R. H., 231
Shah, S., 325
Shanley, M., 77
Shapira, Z., 461
Shapiro, C., 76, 81
Sharer, Kevin, 11, 34
Shari, M., 268
Sharma, A., 269, 341, 459
Shaw, J. D., 154
Shaw, Peter, 202
Shaw, Robert, 207
Sheff, D., 422
Shepherd, D. A., 307
Shih, Stan, 406–407
Shin, A., 419
Shinal, J., 230
Shook, C., 153
Short, H. C., 78
Shrader, R. C., 306
Siebel, Tom, 252, 268, 342
Sieber, Tim, 164
Sigiura, H., 268
Siklos, R., 6
Silver, S., 459
Silverberg, Brad, 135
Silverman, B. S., 381
Simmons, Cal, 279
Simon, Anthony, 244
Simon, B., 244
Simons R., 341, 342
Simpson, Nicole Brown, 22
Simpson, O. J., 22
Sims, H. P., Jr., 421
Simsek, Z., 460
Singh, H., 154, 229, 269
Singh, J. V., 112
Singh, K., 268
Sirmon, D. G., 112, 154, 192, 230
Sirower, M. L., 230
Skula, V., 267
Slater, K., 129, 153
Slavin, D. P., 448
Sleuwaegen, L., 380
Slevin, D. P., 381, 461
Slick, Grace, 196
Sloan, Alfred P., 24, 400
Sloan, P., 204
Slocum, J. W., Jr., 154, 191, 342, 380
Sloviter, Dolores K., 205
Slowinski, G., 381
Slywotzky, A., 461
Smith, A. D., 113
Smith, B. R., 307
Smith, Douglas K., 153, 373, 381, 403
Smith, Fred, 167
Smith, G., 76, 268, 421
Smith, K. G., 294, 300, 308
Smith, Stephen, 409
Smith, William, 384
Smunt, T. L., 180
Smut, T. J., 34
Snoop Dogg, 272
Snow, C. C., 294, 308, 372, 373, 460
Snow, D. C., 192
Snyder, Nancy, 25, 389
Sole, Kenneth, 477
Solomon, Howard, 332
Sonpar, K., 35
Sorrell, Martin, 142, 440
Soule, E., 422
Souza, I., 339
Spaeder, K. E., 398
Spector, J., 21, 35, 43, 87, 168, 371
Spencer, J. W., 155
Spencer, James, 148
Spielberg, Steven, 405
Spiers, E., 8
Spinelli, S., 276, 306
Spraggins, Mike, 322

Spreitzer, Gretchen M., 401–402, 421
Sprung, Michel R., 426
Staats, B. R., 112
Stabell, C. B., 111, 113, 114
Stack, Jack, 402–403, 421
Stadter, G., 113
Stafford, E. R., 230
Stalk, George, Jr., 295, 296, 308
Stanton, Steven A., 400, 421
Staw, B. M., 420
Stead, D., 190
Stearns, T. M., 485
Stebbins, Theodore, 336
Stecklow, S., 342
Steele, R., 37
Steensma, H. K., 422
Steere, W. C., Jr., 459
Steere, William, 431
Steffens, P., 308
Stein, T., 460
Steiner, L. M., 283
Steinmann, H., 75
Stelter, B., 94
Stelter, D., 190
Stephan, J., 343
Sternberg, R. J., 421
Stewart, C., 352
Stewart, T. A., 151, 152, 153, 230, 307
Stewart, Thomas, 122–123
Stewart, W. H., 75
Stibel, J. M., 190
Stieglitz, N., 77
Stiller, Robert, 451
Stimpert, J. L., 191
Stockley, R. L., Jr., 446
Stone, A., 412
Stone, B., 437
Stone, Bill, 272–273
Stone, Michael, 454
Strack, R., 152
Stratton, Hal, 244
Straus, S., 154
Strickland, A. J., III, 342
Stringer, R., 460
Stross, R. E., 267
Stuckey, J., 381
Su, K. H., 308
Sue, Mark, 426
Sull, D. N., 37, 155, 460
Sullivan, C. T., 35
Sullivan, Martin, 17
Sun, J. J. M., 112
Sunwyn, Mark, 124
Sutcliffe, C. L., 180
Sutcliffe, K. M., 75, 380
Swaminathan, A., 307
Swaminathan, V., 231
Swap, W., 153
Swartz, Jeff, 451
Sweeney, J., 449
Swenson, Sue, 272
Sweo, R., 75
Swinney, J., 461
Symonds, W. C., 190, 191
Szobocsan, J., 155

†

Takeuchi, I., 152
Tallman, Joseph, 145
Tang, C., 244
Tanner, J., 191
Tapscott, Dan, 55, 438
Task, A., 231
Tate, B., 421
Taub, E. A., 292
Taylor, A., III, 78, 190
Taylor, J. T., 422

Taylor, James, 406
Taylor, W. C., 154
Taylor, William, 89
Teague, D., 65
Teece, David J., 147–148, 155
Teicher, C. M., 65
Teitelbaum, R., 342
Tekleab, A. G., 421
Templeton, D., 430
Teng, B. S., 381
Teramoto, Y., 269
Terwiesch, C., 173, 191
Tesluk, P. E., 154, 155, 421
Thain, John, 225, 231
Theirault, John, 244
Theoret, A., 485
Thiel, Peter, 303
Thilmany, J., 145
Thomas, J. G., 36
Thomas, R. J., 75, 154
Thompson, A. A., Jr., 342
Thompson, Jody, 441
Thompson, John, 318–319
Thompson, Kenneth, 18
Thorndike, E. L., 420
Thornton, E., 190, 230
Tibbs, K., 446
Tichy, Noel M., 420
Tierney, T., 155
Tierney, T. J., 420
Tilie, A., 284
Timmons, H., 344
Timmons, J. A., 276, 306, 307
Tischler, L., 77
Tiwana, A., 231
Todd, S. Y., 112
Toledo, Melissa, 84–85
Tome, Carol B., 323
Tomlinson, D., 77
Torres, N. L., 307
Torvalds, Linus, 392
Townshend, Lyn, 281
Tretter, M. J., 379
Trevino, L. K., 342
Triandis, H. C., 268
Triantis, A., 446
Trudel, R., 36
Tsai, W., 308
Tsao, A., 76
Tu, H., 191
Tucci, C. A., 116n, 117
Tully, S., 198, 342, 380
Turk, T. A., 344
Tushman, Michael, 375
Tushman, Michael L., 381
Twain, Mark, 393
Tyson, D., 111

U

Uhl-Bien, M., 342
Uhlenbruck, K., 268
Ulaga, W., 191
Ulrich, D., 112
Ulrich, K. T., 173, 191
Unruh, G. C., 24
Upton, D. M., 112
Useem, J., 405
Useem, Michael L., 329, 405
Usinier, J. C., 269
Uzzi, B., 154

V

Vagelos, P. Roy, 121
Valeant-Yenichek, Julie, 49
Valikangas, L., 459

Van Aukun, P. M., 37
Van Buren, H. J., 154
Van Buren, M. E., 34
Vance, A., 8
Van den Brul, Nick, 164
Vanderbilt, Cornelius, 224
Vandergriff, Jay, 398
Van Gogh, Vincent, 120
Van Looy, B., 269
Van Nuys, K. E., 342
Varian, H. R., 76
Veen, M., 343
Veiga, J. F., 460
Veloso, F. M., 459
Venkataraman, S., 67
Verbeke, Alain, 257–258, 269, 379
Verdú-Jover, A. H., 420
Vermeulen, F., 230
Very, P., 154
Veryzer, R. W., 459
Vesper, K. H., 306, 307
Vestring, T., 267
Victor, B., 379
Viguerie, P., 75
Vijungco, Jeff, 127
Vogel, C., 307
Vogel, D. J., 36
Volpi, Mike, 230
Von Hippel, Eric, 36, 436–437

Waddock, S., 36
Wagner, M., 449
Wahlgren, E., 248
Walker, B. A., 230
Wall, S. J., 421
Wallace, B., 308
Walsh, J. P., 344
Walters, B. A., 75, 230, 269, 342
Walton, Sam, 20, 318

Wan, W. P., 269
Wang, E. Z., 344
Wang, L., 461
Wang, William, 292
Ward, R. D., 344
Ward, S., 190
Warlick, Andy, 352
Warner, M., 76
Warnholz, J.-L., 267
Warren, Shawn, 86
Wasserman, E., 468
Waterman, Robert H., 342
Watkins, M. D., 76
Watson, R., 450
Watson, Tom, 24, 400
Weaver, G. R., 342
Weaver, K. M., 284
Webber, A. M., 152
Weber, J., 34, 342
Weber, K., 75
Weddigne, R.-M., 230
Weinberg, N., 344
Weintraub, A., 190, 456
Weiss, L., 365
Weiss, L. M., 114n
Welch, D., 77
Welch, Jack, 5, 89, 125, 224–225, 231, 320, 363
Wellington, F., 36
Wells, R. M. J., 460
Welsch, Harold L., 306
Werder, A. V., 342
Werhane, P. H., 226
Wernerfeldt, B., 153
Wessman, Robert, 360
Westerfield, R. W., 486
Weston, J. F., 231
Weston, John S., 315, 341
Westphal, J. D., 229, 343
Wetlaufer, S., 36, 269, 342, 422
Whalen, C. J., 190, 191, 230
Wheeler, Jon S., 398
Wheelwright, S., 459
Whelan, D., 76
White, B., 419

White, D., 381
White, Gordon, 362, 380
White, J., 207
Whitwam, David R., 389
Wiersema, F., 459
Wiersema, M. F., 112, 229
Wiggett, Jim, 85
Wiklund, J., 307, 454
Wilchins, D., 419
Wiley, R., 111
Willcocks, L. P., 111
Williams, A. D., 438
Williams, M., 153
Williams, S., 307
Williamson, Oliver E., 229
Willis, Steve, 451
Wilson, H. J., 460
Wilson, S., 292
Wind, Yoram, 268
Wingfield, N., 231
Winston, Andrew, 20
Wise, R., 77, 190, 461
Woellert, L., 415
Wojdyla, B., 78
Wolfenson, J., 75
Wolk, M., 148
Wolter, C., 459
Wood, J., 112
Woolley, S., 35
Worrell, D., 289
Wozniak, Steven, 196
Wright, P., 191, 342
Wriston, Walter, 25, 224, 400
Wurster, T. S., 75
Wysocki, Bernard, Jr., 134, 154

Yang, C., 55
Yang, Q., 269
Yao, X., 307
Yeoh, P. L., 112

Yoffie, D. B., 70, 77
Yosano, Kaora, 267
Yost, Dave, 387
Young, Beth, 328
Young, Bob, 391, 392
Young, Michael N., 337, 338, 345, 380
Yu, L., 325
Yu, R., 293
Yukl, Gary, 420
Yun, S., 421
Yunus, Muhammad, 236

Z

Zaccaro, S. J., 154
Zacharakis, A. L., 307
Zafirovski, Mike, 426
Zahra, S. A., 75, 269, 460
Zajac, E. J., 342
Zandkoohi, A., 343, 461
Zell, D., 154
Zelleke, A., 344
Zellner, Wendy, 342
Zeng, Ming, 113, 114
Zhang, R., 422
Zhou, J., 293
Zhou, K. Z., 154
Zhu, D. H., 112
Zimmerman, A., 343
Zollo, M., 228
Zrike, Stephen, 182
Zuckerberg, Mark, 278
Zuckerman, G., 34

subject index

Page numbers followed by n refer to footnotes.

a

ABI/Inform Complete, 499
Absolute cost advantage, 163
Accountability, 402
Accounting, 17
  impact of Sarbanes-Oxley Act, 50, 335, 336
Acid-test ratio, 489–490
Acquisitions; *see also* Mergers and acquisitions
  compared to mergers, 214–215
  definition, 215
  disappointing, 196–197
  expensive blunders, 197
  GE-Honeywell failure, 203
  Hanson PLC, 211
  pooled negotiating power, 205
  premiums paid, 198
  value destruction by, 196
Action plans, 320–321
  at Aircraft Interior Products, 322
  and strategy implementation, 320–321
Actions, 9
Adaptability, 375
Adaptation
  backfiring, 254
  and cost structure, 254
  degree of, 254–255
  versus standardization, 248–251
  in transnational strategy, 255–256
Adaptive new entry
  definition, 288
  differentiation in, 291
  examples, 289
  pitfalls, 288
Administration activities, 88–89
Administrative costs, 209
  and vertical integration, 209
Advertising, with cultural symbols, 245–246
Advertising-based models, 116, 117
Affiliate model, 116
Africa, 235
African Americans, 131
Agency theory, 326–327, 336
  and back-solver dilemma, 445–446
Agendas, 477
Agents, 326
Age of Paradox (Handy), 400
Age of Unreason (Handy), 367, 400
Aggregate demand, 182
Aging populations, 49, 50, 53
Airline industry
  disruptive innovation, 429
  frontal assaults, 301
  Ryanair fares, 164
Alignment, 375
Alliance-management knowledge, 263
Alumni programs, 135
Ambidexterity concept, 11, 13, 375
Ambidextrous organizational design
  and adaptability, 375
  alignment, 375
  breakthrough projects, 375
  definition, 375
  effective structure, 376
  performance results, 375–376
American Business Ethics Award, 411
American Idol, 204
Americans with Disabilities Act, 50
Analysis, 9

Analysis-decision-action cycle; *see* Case analysis
Angel investors, 279
Annual report collections, 496
Annual Reports.com, 496
Antitakeover laws, 226
Antitakeover tactics, 333–334
  benefits to stakeholders, 226
  golden parachutes, 225
  greenmail, 225
  poison pills, 225
Apparel industry, 368–369
Arbitrage
  international opportunities, 241
  Wal-Mart, 241
Architecture of decision making, 390–391
Artists, 120
Asia, emerging markets, 325
Asian Americans, 131
Asset management measures
  average collection period, 492
  capital intensity ratio, 492
  days' sales in inventory, 491
  days' sales in receivables, 491–492
  inventory turnover, 491
  receivables turnover, 491–492
  total asset turnover, 492
Asset restructuring, 210, 211
Asset sales/dissolution, 219n
Asset surgery, 187
Asset utilization ratios, 102, 470, 491–492
Association of Southeast Asian Nations, 258
Auditors
  and corporate governance, 334
  and Sarbanes-Oxley Act, 336
Automated manufacturing systems, 173
Automobile industry
  boom and bust cycles, 208
  in China, 72
  competitive analysis, 43
  effects of financial crisis, 7–8
  fate of Yugo, 160
  Ford model name, 234
  government bailout, 175
  impact of financial crisis, 53
  in India, 72
  legacy costs, 175
  price cutting, 302
  profit pool, 174, 208
  sales decline, 175
  Samsung's venture in, 28
  strategic group analysis, 71–72
  transaction-specific investments, 208–209
Autonomous work groups, 439
Autonomous work units, 449
Autonomy, 448–449
Average collection period, 492
Aviation Consumer Action, 335

b

Baby Boomers
  aging, 49, 50
  number of, 50
Back-solver dilemma, 445–446
Backward integration, 206, 349
  by buyers, 56
Bailout of auto companies, 175

Balanced scorecard, 79
  and challenge of innovation, 431
  definition, 104
  description and benefits
    customer perspective, 105
    financial perspective, 104–105
    internal business perspective, 105
    learning and innovation, 104
  limitations
    contrasting views, 106
    inappropriate links to compensation, 107
    insufficient commitment, 106–107
    lack of clear strategy, 107
    limited executive sponsorship, 107
    poor data, 107
    quick-fix view, 106
    terminology problems, 107
  and new venture success, 443
Balance sheet, 486–487, 488
Bangladesh, 236
Bank financing, 279
Banking business, 171
Bankruptcy, Lehman Brothers, 385
Banks
  competitive intelligence, 43
  and corporate governance, 334
  securitization of mortgages, 7
Bargaining power
  of buyers
    in book industry, 65
    conditions for, 58–59
    effect of digital technologies, 64
  of managers, 100–101
  of suppliers
    conditions for, 59–60
    Delta Pride Catfish, 60
    effect of digital technologies, 64–66
    and newly hired employees, 59
Barrier-free organizations
  definition, 364
  and external constituencies, 366–367
  permeable and internal boundaries, 365–366
  pros and cons, 367
  risks, challenges, and downsides, 367
  teams in, 366
Barriers to change
  behavioral, 393
  challenging, 406–407
  definition, 391
  overcoming, 391–393
  personal time constraints, 393
  political, 393
  systemic, 392
  vested interest in status quo, 392
Barriers to entry
  access to distribution channels, 57
  capital requirements, 57
  cost disadvantages, 57
  customer loyalty, 167
  dot.com firms, 172
  economies of scale, 57
  and entrepreneurial strategy, 286
  lowered by Internet, 62
  product differentiation, 57
  switching costs, 57
  and threat of new entrants, 56–58
Barriers to mobility, 71
Beachhead strategy, 260
Behavioral barriers to change, 393
Behavioral control, 16, 312, 315, 316–324

alternative approaches, 324
boundaries and constraints
  action plans, 321–323
  minimizing improper conduct, 321–323
  operational efficiency, 321
  rule-based controls, 321
  short-term objectives, 320–321
  strategic priorities, 320
in bureaucratic organizations, 323
and competitive environment, 316–317
  essential elements, 317
  focus of, 316
  incentive programs, 319
  internalizing rewards and culture, 323–324
  and key employees, 317
  organizational culture, 317–318
  regulations and sanctions, 323
  reward systems, 318–320
  situational factors, 323
Beliefs of society, 40
Benchmarking, 162
  competitive, 405
  external information, 405
  functional, 405
  internal, 403–404
Bentley College Center for Business Ethics Award, 411
Best practices
  for flextime, 132
  at General Electric, 363
  learning from failure, 407
Biregional companies, 257
Blogs, 94
Blue ocean strategy
  Cirque du Soleil, 290
  difficult to imitate, 290
  elements of, 289–290
  essence of, 290
Blue Ocean Strategy (Kim & Mauborgne), 289
Board of directors
  agency theory, 326–327
  best practices ideas, 330
  in case analysis, 466
  committed and involved, 327–329
  criticisms of, 17
  cronyism, 17
  director independence, 329
  duties, 327
  failure, 329
  fiduciary failure, 332
  functions, 17, 327
  at Intel, 329
  interlocking directorships, 329
  in Latin America, 339
  outside directors, 329
  and shareholders, 16–17
Body language, 397
Book per value share, 494
Book publishing industry, 65
Bottom of the pyramid, 236
Bottom-up empowerment, 402
Boundaries and constraints
  action plans, 320–321
  barrier-free types, 364
  evolving to rewards and culture from, 323–324
  external, 364
  focus on strategic priorities, 320
  geographic, 364

horizontal, 364
improving operational efficiency, 321
minimizing improper conduct, 321–323
in organizational design, 364
permeable, 365–366
personal time constraints, 393
setting, 320–321
short-term objectives, 320–321
vertical, 364
Boundaryless organizational design, 348
barrier-free, 364–367
definition and types, 363–364
effective implementation, 372–374
Eli Lilly, 371
factors to consider
common culture, 374
communication, 374
horizontal organizational structure, 374
horizontal systems and processes, 374
human resources practices, 374
information technology, 374
shared values, 374
integrating mechanism, 363
modular, 367–370
Technical Computer Graphics, 373
triangulation approach, 373
United Technologies, 365
virtual organization, 370–371
Boundary mindset, 364
Bozo filter, 125, 323
Brainstorming, 366
Brand identity
and differentiation, 291
diluted, 169–170
undermined by Internet, 177
Brand name prestige, 168
Breakaway positioning, 183, 184
example, 185
Breakthrough projects
carrying out, 375
performance evaluation, 375–376
Bribery, 254, 321
Bridging relationships, 137–139
Bureaucratic organizations, 323
barriers to change in, 392
Bureau of Statistics, 49
Business activities cycle, 465
Business environment, 3; *see also*
Competitive environment;
External environment; Internal
environment
analysis of, 15
global economy, 24–25
pace of change in, 9
rapidly changing, 450
unpredictable, 13
Business Ethics, 451
Business Format Franchise, 275
Business groups, 338
Business incubators
functions, 439–440
risks, 440
Business-level strategy, 156–187
in case analysis, 482
for competitive advantage, 15, 158–176
combination strategies, 172–176
differentiation strategy, 165–170
focus strategy, 170–172
overall cost leadership, 160–165
effects of digital technologies
combination strategies, 179
differentiation strategy, 177–178
focus strategy, 178–179
overall cost leadership, 176–177
experience curve, 160, 162, 163
formulating, 15
industry life cycle stages, 179–187
decline stage, 184–186
growth stage, 182–183

introduction stage, 182
maturity stage, 183–184
summary of, 181
turnaround strategies, 187
and leadership, 388
learning from mistakes, 158
reward and evaluation systems, 360–362
differentiation strategy, 361–362
overall cost leadership, 361
stuck in the middle, 159–160
Business models
Business Format Franchise, 275
on Internet
advertising-based, 116, 117
commission-based, 116, 117
fee-for-service-based, 117
markup-based, 116, 117
referral-based, 116, 117
subscription-based, 116–117
and peer-to-peer lending, 281
Business plan
focus on new ventures, 468
framework for case analysis, 468
Business processes, 374
Business risk-taking, 455
Business Roundtable, 327–328
Business services, 440
Business Source Complete, 499
Business-to-business e-commerce, 64–65
BusinessWeek, 5, 6, 43, 104, 158, 218, 335, 384
Buyer channel intermediaries, 64
Buyers
bargaining power, 63
channel intermediaries, 64
end users, 64
and low-cost position, 163
perception of differentiation, 170
price premium for, 168

C

Canada, view of balanced scorecard, 106
Capabilities vs. collaboration, 431
Capacity augmentation, 62
Capital intensity ratio, 102, 492
Capitalism, 235
Capital requirements, 57
Capital restructuring, 210, 211
Captain America, 6
Career implications
balanced scorecard, 107
business-level strategy, 188
of corporate entrepreneurship, 457
of corporate governance, 339
corporate-level strategy, 226
of external environment, 73
human capital, 149
of innovation, 457
of international strategy, 264
of leadership, 417
of learning organization, 417
new venture analysis, 304
of organizational ethics, 417
of organizational structure, 376
resource-based view of firm, 107
social capital, 149
of strategic control, 339
of strategic management, 31
technology, 149
value chain activities, 107
Case analysis
analysis-decision-action cycle
business-level strategy, 482
corporate entrepreneurship, 484
corporate-level strategy, 482–483
entrepreneurial strategies, 483
ethical organization, 484
external environment, 481–482

intellectual assets, 482
internal environment, 482
international-level strategy, 483
learning organization, 484
organizational design, 484
organizational goals and objectives, 481
strategic control, 483–484
benefits from
concise and focused, 473–474
critical analysis, 474
drawing on personal experience, 473
insights from other cases, 474
learning from others, 474
open mind, 473
outside research, 474
participation and persuasion, 473
taking a stand, 473
thinking out of the box, 474
business cycle activities, 465
company and industry information
annual reports, 496
business websites, 498–499
categories, 495
company data, 495–496
company rankings, 498
competitive intelligence, 495
guides and tutorials, 497
industry research analysis, 500
search engines, 501
SEC filings, 497–498
strategic and competitive analysis, 498–499
components of cases, 464
comprehension techniques, 467
conducting
business plan framework, 468
determining strategic issues, 469
familiarity with material, 466–467
with financial ratio analysis, 469–470, 488–494
financial statement analysis, 486–487
five-forces analysis, 469
identify problems, 468–469
making recommendations, 471–472
propose alternative solutions, 471
role playing, 467
strategic analysis, 469–470
strategy implementation choices, 466–467
testing assumptions, 469–470
thinking like a decision maker, 471
conflict-inducing decision making
devil's advocacy, 479–480
dialectical inquiry, 480
groupthink problem, 475–476
groupthink symptoms and prevention, 478–479
relying on rivals, 476
definition, 464
to evaluate business situation, 464
oral presentation, 472
questions for, 464
reasons for, 464–465
Sapient Health Network, 466
skills enhancement
differentiating, 464
integrating, 465
speculating, 465
written presentation, 475
Case analysis teams, 477–478
Cash coverage ratio, 102, 491
Cash cows, 212–213
Cash financing, 279
Cash ratio, 102, 490
Causal ambiguity, 96
Causality, 390
Celebrate Your Mistakes (Holt), 406
Center for Auto Safety, 336
Center for Study of Responsive Law, 336

CEO compensation
and corporate governance, 101
excessive, 329
pay for performance, 332
performance bonuses, 17–18
stock options, 332
TIAA-CREF principles, 332, 333
CEOs; *see also* Top-level executives
and boards of directors, 327–330
from controlling families, 337
departures for performance reasons, 329
external view of leadership, 6
romantic view of leadership, 5–6
and Sarbanes-Oxley Act, 335
Chaebols, 338
Change
current pace of, 9
predicting, 45
from sense of urgency, 406
Channel intermediaries, 64
Charisma, 285
Chief diversity officer, 133, 134
Chief financial officers, and Sarbanes-Oxley Act, 335
China
auto industry in, 72
counterfeiting in, 244
as economic power, 52
footwear production, 368
growing market, 238–240
Kraft Foods in, 86
middle class, 238
mobile phone market, 40
National Economy Research Institute, 238
population, 240
production for Wal-Mart, 20
software piracy, 147
Wal-Mart supplier, 241
Classical economics, 237
Closure relationships, 137
Code of Ethics on Competitive Intelligence, 44
Codes of conduct
elements of, 412
nature of, 412
Wetherhill Associates, 413
Coercive power, 393
Collaboration
versus capabilities, 431
by electronic teams, 143–144
with innovation partners, 434–435
using social networks, 436–437
Combination strategies, 172–176
automated manufacturing, 173
definition, 173
for e-business success, 179
effect of digital technologies, 179
exploiting profit pool concept, 173–174
extended value chain, 174–175
and five-forces model, 175
flexible manufacturing, 173
goal of, 172–173
at Liberty Mutual, 180
mass customization, 173
for new ventures, 293–294
potential pitfalls
getting stuck in the middle, 175
managerial time, 175–176
miscalculating profit pool sources, 175
miscalculating revenue sources, 175
underestimating value chain expenses, 175
primary benefits, 172–173
Commission-based models, 116, 117
Commitment
to excellence, 285
irrational escalation of, 447
Commoditized products, 66
Common-size balance sheet, 486–487, 488

Common-size income statement, 487–488
Common-size statements, 486
Communication
 in boundaryless organizations, 374
 by electronic teams, 143–144
 by e-mail, 141–142
 in functional structure, 352
 in global start-ups, 359
 by networks, 141–143
Communities, as stakeholders, 18
Company Annual Reports Online, 496
Company disclosure reports, 497–498
Company information sources
 annual reports, 496
 business websites, 498–499
 company data, 495–496
 company rankings, 498
 competitive intelligence, 495
 guides and tutorials, 497
 Securities and Exchange Commission filings, 497–498
 strategic and competitive analysis, 499–500
Company rankings, 498
Comparison shopping, 179
 online, 114
Compensation; *see also* CEO compensation; Reward systems
 manager-worker ratio, 332
 top-level executives, 100–101
Competencies, 92; *see also* Core competencies
Competing for the Future (Hamel & Prahalad), 40
Competition
 among divisions, 354
 and co-opetition, 302–304
 effect of organizational structure on, 359–360
 limited in introduction stage, 182
 made irrelevant, 289
 from new entrants, 172
Competitive actions
 new, 294–295
 tactical, 300–301
 types
  defensive actions, 301
  frontal assault, 301
  guerrilla offensive, 301
  selective attacks, 301
  strategic, 300–301
Competitive advantage
 business-level strategy, 15
  combination strategies, 172–176
  differentiation strategy, 165–170
  focus strategy, 170–172
  kinds of, 158–160
  overall cost leadership, 160–166
 and business performance, 159
 from core competencies, 200
 criteria for, 98
 definition, 9
 in dynamic capabilities, 147–149
 erosion at Dell, 98–99
 exploiting profit pool concept, 173–174
 from firm's resources, 94–98
 in general administration, 88–89
 in global markets
  global strategy, 251–252
  global vs. regional approach, 257–259
  international strategy approach, 250–251
  multidomestic strategy, 253–255
  standardization vs. adaptation, 248–240
  transnational strategy, 255–257
 for global start-ups, 359
 of industry leaders, 453
 in intellectual property, 147
 knowledge as source of, 235

 knowledge codified for, 144–145
 limitations of SWOT analysis, 81
 no longer possible, 385
 by preannouncements, 454
 from time pacing, 433
 from value-chain activities, 440
Competitive Advantage (Porter), 82
Competitive aggressiveness, 448, 453–455
Competitive analysis checklist, 63
Competitive benchmarking, 405
Competitive dynamics, 15
 choosing not to react
  co-opetition, 302–304
  forbearance, 302
 definition, 294
 Facebook vs. MySpace, 303
 hardball strategies, 294, 295
 knowledge of, 273
 likelihood of competitive reaction, 301–302
  actor's reputation, 302
  competitors' resources, 302
  market dependence, 302
 motivation and capability to respond
  firm's age and size, 299
  intent of response, 298
  launching an attack, 298
  resources for retaliation, 299
  seriousness of attack, 297
  Wal-Mart, 299
 new competitive actions, 294–295
 threat analysis
  awareness, 295–297
  market commonality, 297
  resource similarity, 297
 types of competitive actions
  defensive actions, 301
  frontal assault, 301
  guerrilla offensive, 301
  selective attacks, 301
  strategic, 300–301
  tactical, 300–301
Competitive environment
 and behavioral control, 316–317
 effect of digital technologies, 62–67
 factors relevant to firms, 56
 five-forces model, 56–67
 industry analysis, 67–70
 industry-related factors, 39
 strategic groups, 70–72
Competitive intelligence
 ethical guidelines, 44
 examples, 43
 failure to identify new competitors, 44–45
 information sources, 495
 purpose, 42
 using Internet, 43–44
Competitive Intelligence and Global Business (Blenkhorn & Fleisher, eds.), 495
Competitive parity, 160–161
 lack of, 165
Competitive position
 with combination strategies, 175
 enhanced by divestment, 220
 from financial ratios, 104
 identifying, 71
 stuck-in-the-middle, 175
Competitive reaction factors, 301–302
 actor's reputation, 302
 competitors' resources, 302
 market dependence, 302
Competitive rivalry, effect of digital technologies on, 66
Competitor intelligence, 39
Competitors
 actions in decline stage, 184
 close, for new ventures, 294
 and competitive aggressiveness, 453
 cooperative relationships, 366–367

 cost parity relative to, 167
 easily imitated differentiation, 169
 effects of pooled negotiating power, 203–205
 equally balanced, 61
 and experience curve, 162
 intensity of rivalry among
  contributing factors, 61–62
  effect of digital technologies, 66, 67
 likelihood of response, 301–302
 in mature industries, 292
 mistake of ignoring new, 44–45
 potential, 56
 reputation of, 302
 resources of, 302
 response to proactiveness, 452
 sharing inputs, 165
 versus too much differentiation, 169
Complementors
 Apple Inc., 70
 conflict among, 69
Complements, 69
Compliance-based ethics programs, 410–411
Compliance costs of Sarbanes-Oxley Act, 336
Computer-aided design, 51, 173
Computer-aided manufacturing, 51, 173
Computer industry, erosion of Dell's competitive advantage, 98–99
Conglomerate, 355
Consolidation strategy, defense industry, 186
Constraints; *see* Boundaries and constraints
Consumer demand; *see also* Demand
 in India, 240
 and international rivalry, 238
 national conditions, 237
Consumer groups, 335–336
Consumer price index, 52
Consumer Product Safety Commission, 244
Consumer Reports, 64, 169
Consumer spending, impact of women on, 49
Consumer websites, 66
Contemporary approaches to strategic control
 behavioral control, 315
 characteristics, 315
 components, 314
 informational control, 315
Continuous replenishment program, 84
Contract-based outcomes, 327
Contract costs, 208
Contracts
 franchising, 261
 government, 283
Control, 402; *see also* Corporate governance; Strategic control
 external mechanisms, 18
 in holding company structure, 355
 illusion of, 447
 strategic types, 16
Control mechanism, financial rewards as, 130
Control systems, 88
Conventional thinking, 390, 391
Co-opetition, 302–304
Coordination
 in functional structure, 352
 in global start-ups, 359
 to maximize human capital, 373–374
Core competencies, 350n
 at Apple Inc., 202
 definition, 200
 difficult to imitate, 200–201
 lack of substitutes for, 200–201
 leveraging, 200–201
 for modular organizations, 368
 value creation from, 200
 for vertical integration, 208

Corporate Affiliations, 496
Corporate Citizenship poll, 22
Corporate credo
 definition, 412
 Johnson & Johnson, 413
Corporate Culture (Deal & Kennedy), 317
Corporate Directory of U.S. Public Companies, 496
Corporate entrepreneurship, 16; *see also* Entrepreneurial orientation
 in case analysis, 484
 definition, 435
 determining factors, 435
 dispersed approaches
  entrepreneurial culture, 440–441
  product champions, 442
 focused approaches
  business incubators, 439–440
  new venture groups, 439
 for innovation, 435
 and intrapreneuring, 435
 learning from mistakes, 426–427
 at Lego Group, 438
 means of pursuing, 435–438
 measuring success of, 442–444
  exit champions, 443–444
  strategic vs. financial goals, 443
 primary issues, 435
 real options analysis
  application to strategic decisions, 444–445
  characteristics, 444
  potential pitfalls, 445–447
 requirements, 439
 risk-return trade-off, 443
 socially responsible, 451
Corporate ethical performance, 408
Corporate governance, 312, 324–339
 antitakeover tactics, 334
 board of directors, 17–18
 business groups, 338
 and CEO compensation, 101
 crony capitalism, 328
 definition, 16, 324
 and demands of stakeholders, 324n
 effectiveness mechanisms, 18
 emerging markets, 325
 examples of flaws, 325–326
 external control mechanisms, 18
 external mechanisms
  auditors, 334
  banks, 334
  definition, 332
  market for corporate control, 333–334
  media, 335–336
  public activists, 335–336
  regulatory bodies, 335
  stock analysts, 334
  takeover constraint, 333–334
 family control, 339
 financial performance, 325
 impact of Sarbanes-Oxley Act, 50, 336
 internal mechanisms
  boards of directors, 327–330
  manager rewards/incentives, 331–332
  shareholder activism, 330–331
 international perspective, 336–339
 and investment decisions, 325
 in Latin America, 339
 learning from mistakes, 312
 ownership-control separation
  agency theory, 326–327
  risk-sharing problem, 327
 participants, 3, 16–17
 poor performers, 331
 and price performance, 325
 primary participants, 324
 principal-agent conflicts, 337–338
 principal-principal conflicts, 337–338
 research evidence, 325

and return on capital employed, 325
stakeholder management
  crowdsourcing, 18–21
  environmental sustainability,
    22–24
  social responsibility, 21–22
  triple bottom line, 22–23
  zero-sum vs. symbiosis, 18–19
strategic control, 16
Corporate lawyers, and Sarbanes-
  Oxley Act, 335
Corporate-level strategy; see also
  Related diversification; Unrelated diversification
achieving diversification
  and divestments, 218–220
  internal development, 222–223
  joint ventures, 220–222
  mergers and acquisitions,
    215–220
  strategic alliances, 220–222
in case analysis, 482–483
disappointing acquisitions,
  196–197
diversification risk reduction, 214
expensive blunders, 197
formulating, 15
issues in, 15
and leadership, 388
learning from mistakes, 196
main issues in, 195
managerial motives
  antitakeover tactics, 225–226
  egotism, 224–225
  growth for growth's sake,
    223–224
reward and evaluation systems
  related diversification, 362
  unrelated diversification, 362–63
shareholder value and
  diversification, 198
successful diversification, 198–199
Corporate malfeasance, 17
Corporate parenting, 209–210
Corporate raiders, 333
Corporate reputation, 94
Corporate scandals, 224, 225
  and auditors, 334
  and Sarbanes-Oxley Act, 336
Corporate social responsibility, 3;
  see also Social responsibility
  and corporate entrepreneurship,
    451
  and customers, 22
  demands for, 22
  focus of critics, 22
Corporations; see also Corporate
  governance
agency theory, 325–326
and business groups, 338
concentrated ownership, 336–337
crony capitalism, 328
definition, 325
expropriation of minority shareholders, 338
family control, 336–337
patterns of growth, 349–350
principal-agent conflicts, 337–338
principal-principal conflicts,
  337–338
principals and agents, 326
proposed definitions, 325
regulatory requirements, 335
risk-sharing problem, 327
separation of ownership and
  management, 326–327
Cost(s)
  or terrorism, 53
  and workforce diversity, 132
Cost advantages, erosion of, 165,
  172
Cost disadvantages, derivation
  of, 57
Cost focus, 170–171
Cost management by Internet, 179

Cost parity, 167
Cost reductions
  in global markets, 248–251
  in global strategy, 251–252
  by International expansion,
    242–243
Cost saving
  in holding company structure,
    355
  from sharing activities, 202
Cost surgery, 187
Counterfeiting, 244
Counterproductive behavior, 320
Country Risk Rankings, 243
Courage, 417
Creative tension, 11
Creativity, 92
  enabling, 406–407
  and workforce diversity, 132
Credit crisis, 7–8
Credit market crisis, 5
Creditors as stakeholders, 18
Credit rating agencies, 314
Crony capitalism, 328
Cronyism, 17
Cross-cultural dialogue, 397
Cross-functional skills, 369
Cross-functional teams, 374, 375
Crossing the Chasm (Moore), 453
Crowdsourcing
  Cookshack, 87
  definition, 19
  for environmental analysis, 43
  and Intuit, 21
  Kraft Foods, 221
  at Lego Group, 438
  at Netflix, 168
  stakeholder roles, 19–21
Cultural differences, 397
  examples, 246
  and management risks, 245–246
  and mergers and acquisitions, 218
  in strategic alliances, 262
  in TV programs, 255
Cultural history, 259
Cultural symbols, 245–246
Culture of dissent, 406
Currency devaluation, 245
Currency risks, 244–245
Current ratio, 102, 489
Customer feedback, 115
Customer Is the Company (Chafkin),
  436
Customer loyalty, 57, 167
Customer needs
  and country preferences, 249
  homogenization of, 247–248
Customers
  and balanced scorecard, 105
  and corporate social responsibil-
    ity, 22
  end users, 64
  as information source, 405–406
  and mass customization, 177
  and pooled negotiating power,
    203–205
  price information available to, 165
  as stakeholders, 18
  using social technologies, 94
Customer service, 85
  at Cookshack, 87
Cyberstorage, 66

d

David C. Lincoln Award for Eth-
  ics, 411
Days' sales in inventory, 102, 491
Days' sales in receivables, 102,
  491–492
Debt-equity mix, 210, 211
Debt-equity ratio, 102, 490
Decision agenda, 477

Decision making
  conflict-inducing techniques
    devil's advocacy, 479–480
    dialectical inquiry, 480
    and groupthink problem,
      475–476
    preventing groupthink, 478–479
    relying on rivals, 476
  effect of manager credibility/ego,
    218
  in functional structure, 352
  heterogeneity, 133
  including stakeholders, 10
  integrative thinking, 390–391
  managerial conceit, 447
  in new ventures, 291
  requirements, 476
  in simple organizational structure,
    351
  strategic, 444–445
  for strategic management, 464–465
Decisions, 9
Decision to abandon, 447
Decline stage strategies
  and actions of rivals, 184
  consolidation, 186
  definition, 184
  exiting the market, 185–186
  harvesting, 185
  improving the old, 186
  maintaining, 184–185
  and new technologies, 186
  price-performance trade-offs, 186
  reasons for decline, 184
  retreating to defensible ground, 186
Dedication, 285
Defense industry, 186
Defensible ground, retreating to, 186
Defensive actions, 301
Delegating, 402
Deliberate strategies, 13
Delivery time, 83
Demand; see also Consumer demand
  aggregate, 182
  create and capture, 289
  level of stability, 208
  in mature industries, 292
  selective, 182
Demand conditions
  definition, 236
  in India, 239–240
  and national competitiveness, 237
Demographics, 53
  aging Baby Boomers, 50
  aging populations, 50
  in general environment, 49
  industries affected, 54
  key trends and events, 48
  workforce diversity trends, 131–133
Denmark, 237
Departmental isolation, 352
Department of Commerce, 275
Department of Defense, 186
Department of Energy, 71
Department of Justice, 389
Department of Labor, 415
Department store industry, 71
Derivatives, 314
Design, collaborative, 176
Developing human capital, 126–129
Devil's advocacy, 479–480
Devil's Dictionary (Bierce), 326
Dialectical inquiry, 480
Diamond of national advantage
  factors in, 236
  for India, 239–240
Differentiating skills, 464
Differentiation
  in adaptive new entry, 291
  and brand identity, 291
  competitive parity based on, 160
  country-to-country, 249
  diminished by Internet, 179
  lack of parity in, 165
  with low cost, 290

  in pioneering new entry, 291
  too much, 169
Differentiation focus, 170–171
Differentiation strategy
  in combination strategies,
    172–176
  cost parity, 167
  definition, 165
  effects of digital technologies, 177
  enhanced by sharing activities,
    202–203
  examples, 167
  and five-forces model, 167–168
  forms of, 165
  at Netflix, 168
  for new ventures, 291
  potential pitfalls
    dilution of brand identity,
      169–170
    easy imitation, 169
    Internet-related, 178
    perceptions of buyers and sell-
      ers, 160
    summary of, 170
    too high price premium, 169
    too much differentiation, 169
    uniqueness not valuable,
      168–169
  price premium, 167
  requirements, 158, 361
  reward and evaluation systems,
    361–362
  value-chain activities, 166
Digital technologies
  customer feedback, 115
  effect on competitive strategies
    combination strategies, 179
    differentiation strategy, 177–178
    focus strategy, 178–179
    overall cost leadership, 176–177
  effects on external environment, 55
  effects on five-forces model
    benefits and disadvantages, 67
    buyer bargaining power, 64
    intensity of rivalry, 66
    supplier bargaining power,
      64–66
    threat of new entrants, 62–64
    threat of substitutes, 66
  entertainment programming, 115
  evaluation activities, 114
  expertise, 115
  problem-solving activities, 114–115
  search activities, 113–114
  transaction activities, 115
  value added by, 79, 113–117
Digital technology revolution, 426
Direction, set by leadership, 386–388
Director independence, 329
Disclosure requirements, 334
Disintermediation, 65
  lowering transaction costs, 176
Disparities of wealth, 235
Dispersed approach to corporate
  entrepreneurship, 440
Disruptive innovation
  in airline industry, 429
  definition, 429
  Linux operating system, 430
  portable dialysis technology,
    430–431
Dissolution, 219n
Distribution agreement, 284
Distribution channels
  access to, 57, 64
  effects of vertical integration,
    206–208
  Netflix, 168
  new, 300
Diversification; see also Related
  diversification; Unrelated
  diversification
achieving
    internal development, 222–223
    joint ventures, 220–222

Diversification;—*Cont.*
  achieving—*Cont.*
    mergers and acquisitions, 215–220
    strategic alliances, 220–222
  and antitakeover tactics, 225–226
  disappointing acquisitions, 196–197
  excessive, 333
  expensive blunders, 197
  by Fremantle Media, 204
  hierarchical relationships, 198–199
  horizontal relationships, 198–199
  learning from mistakes, 196
  into several product lines, 349–350
  and shareholder value, 198–199, 327
  successful, 198–199
  for synergies, 198
  by Toyota, 204
  value creation by, 199
Diversity management guidelines, 132–133
Divestment
  by Campbell Soup, 219
  and competitive position, 220
  criteria for candidates, 220
  definition, 218
  examples, 218
  Hanson plc, 211
  means of, 219n
  objectives, 219–220
  percentage of acquisitions, 197
Divisional organizational structure
  advantages, 353–354, 358
  Brinker International, 354
  competition among divisions, 354
  definition, 353
  disadvantages, 354, 358
  General Motors, 353
  holding company, 355
  international market, 349
  into market niches, 360
  and related diversification, 349
  strategic business unit structure, 355
Dogs, 212
Dollar appreciation, 245
Dot.com firms, 172
Double-loop learning, 315
Dow Jones Industrial Average, 52
Downstream value-chain activities, 175, 208, 256
Drive, 285
DVD rentals, 168
Dynamic capabilities
  definition, 147
  examples, 149
  protecting, 147–149

e

Early Warning: Using Competitive Intelligence to Anticipate Market Shifts (Gilad), 495
East Asia, 235
  family control in, 337
Eastern Europe, 235
E-business
  combination strategies, 179
  differentiation strategy, 177–178
  focus strategies, 178–179
  overall cost leadership, 176–177
Echo Boom generation, 127
Eco-entrepreneurs, 280
E-commerce, erosion of profit, 94–95
Economic environment
  industries affected, 54
  key indicators, 52
  key trends and events, 48
Economic growth, national comparisons, 235
Economic integration
  European Union, 258
  regional, 259
Economic risk, 244

Economies of scale
  as barrier to entry, 57
  in China, 240
  global products and services, 249
  by international expansion, 240–241
  problems with, 252
  in transnational strategy, 256
Economies of scope
  core competencies, 200–201
  definition, 199
  in related diversification, 199–203
  from sharing activities, 201–203
Economist, 116–117
Economy, central role of knowledge in, 122–123
EDGAR Database Full-Text Search, 497
EDGAR Full-Text Search Frequently Asked Questions, 497
Education
  in China, 238
  of foreign professionals, 50–51
  of women, 49
Effectiveness-efficiency trade-off, 11
Efficiency, 11
  in functional structure, 349
Egotism, managerial, 224–225
Electronic invoices, 180
Electronic storage, 66
Electronic teams
  advantages, 143
  challenges, 144
  definition, 143
E-mail, 141–142
  Countrywide Financial, 142
Embedded options, 445
Emergent strategies, 13
Emerging markets, 325
Emission permits, 52
Emotional competence, 416–417
Emotional intelligence
  cautionary notes, 398–400
  at Cisco Systems, 399
  components, 396
  definition, 395
  empathy, 397
  and integrity, 416
  and IQ, 395–396
  for managing relationships, 396
  motivation, 397
  potential drawbacks, 398–400
  self-awareness, 396
  self-management skills, 396
  self-regulation, 397
  sets of capabilities, 394–396
  social skill, 397–398
Emotional support, 137
Empathy, 397
  and tough decisions, 399
Employees; *see also* Human capital
  backlash from, 59
  bargaining power, 100
  computerized training, 93
  counterproductive behavior, 320
  exit costs, 100
  flexible work arrangements, 132
  foreign professionals, 50–51
  key, 317
  lifetime employment, 362
  rationality, 319
  relationship-first values, 130
  replacement cost, 100
  in simple organizational structure, 351
  source of referrals, 126
  as stakeholders, 18
  star performers, 140
  task-first relationship, 130
  on teams, 366
  training, 125
  tribal loyalty, 130
  whistleblowers, 415
Employment contracts, 129–130

Empowering employees
  bottom-up strategy, 402
  enabling creativity, 406–407
  with external knowledge, 404–406
  with internal knowledge, 402–404
  leadership for, 401–402
  top-down strategy, 402
Empowerment, lack of, 400
End users, 64
Energy-efficient supply chain, 90
Enforcement costs, 208
Engineering, value-chain activities, 91
Entertainment programming, 115
Entrants; *see* Threat of new entrants
Entrepreneur, 279
Entrepreneurial culture
  at Best Buy, 441
  characteristics, 440–441
Entrepreneurial leadership
  commitment to excellence, 285
  dedication and drive, 285
  vision, 285
Entrepreneurial opportunities; *see also* New ventures
  discovery phase, 277
  evaluation of, 277
  Internet entrepreneurs, 278–279
  learning from mistakes, 272–273
  market potential, 277
  recognition, 276–277
  viability factors, 277
Entrepreneurial orientation, 447–456
  autonomy, 448–449
  competitive aggressiveness, 453–455
  definition, 448
  dimensions of, 448
  innovativeness, 449–450
  proactiveness, 452–453, 454
  risk taking, 455–456
Entrepreneurial resources
  financial
    angel investors, 279
    bank financing, 279
    cash, 279
    from family and friends, 280
    government contracts, 283
    informal investment vs. venture capital, 282
    peer-to-peer lending, 279, 281
    personal savings, 279
    and scale of venture, 279
    and stage of venture development, 279
    for start-ups, 279
    venture capital, 279
  government resources, 283
  human capital, 282
  manufacturing alliances, 284
  retail alliances, 284
  Small Business Administration loans, 283
  social capital, 282–283
  technology alliances, 284
Entrepreneurial strategies
  and barriers to entry, 286
  in case analysis, 483
  definition, 285
  determining factors, 276
  entry strategies
    adaptive new entry, 288–290
    blue ocean strategy, 289–290
    decision factors, 286
    imitative new entry, 287–288
    pioneering new entry, 286–287
  evolution of industry conditions, 286
  and five-forces model, 286
  formulating, 15
  generic
    combination strategies, 293–294
    differentiation strategy, 291
    focus strategy, 292–293
    overall cost leadership, 290–291
  and threat of retaliation, 286

Entrepreneurs
  commitment to excellence, 285
  competitive dynamics, 294–304
  dedication and drive, 285
  eco-entrepreneurs, 280
  on Internet, 278–279
  from microcredit, 236
  teams vs. lone wolf, 282
  vision, 285
Entrepreneurship
  corporate, 16
  definition, 273
  learning from mistakes, 272–273
  by small businesses, 274–275
Entry modes; *see* Market entry
Environmental analysis, 40
Environmental forecasting
  dangers, 45
  definition, 45
  purpose, 45
  scenario analysis, 45–46
  significant errors, 45
Environmental issues, going green, 124
Environmentally friendly manufacturing, 84
Environmental models, 95
Environmental monitoring, 39, 42
Environmental Protection Agency, 24, 283
  Affirmative Procurement Program, 282
Environmental revolution, 22–23
Environmental scanning, 39, 41–42
Environmental sustainability, 23–24
  energy-efficient supply chain, 90
  at Wal-Mart, 20
Equal Employment Opportunity Commission, 133
Equity carve-outs, 219n
Equity multiplier, 102, 490
Escalation research, 392
Ethical lapses, 224
Ethical organization, creating, 16
Ethical orientation, 408
Ethical values, 408
Ethics
  definition, 407
  individual vs. organizational, 407–408
  and leadership, 387, 388–390, 408
  sources, 407
Ethics management, 410–411
Euro, 245
Euromoney, 243
European Union, 52, 258
Evaluation
  of commitment, 447
  of human capital, 128–129
Evaluation activities, Internet, 114
Every Business Needs an Angel (Simmons), 279
Everyday low pricing strategy, 241
Excellence, 285
Excessive product-market diversification, 333
Exchange rate fluctuations, 244–245
Exchange rate swings, 244
Executive leaders, 25
Exit barriers, high, 62
Exit champions, 443–444
Exit cost of employees, 100
Exiting the market, 185–186
Experience curve
  comparing effects of, 163
  definition, 170
  questions to consider, 162
Experience vs. initiative, 431
Expertise, 115, 139
Expert power, 394
Explicit knowledge, 122, 144
Export/import agreement, 284
Exporting
  for market entry
    benefits, 260

definition, 260
  risks and limitations, 260
  by small businesses, 275
Expropriation
  of minority shareholders, 338
  by related transactions, 338
Extended value chain
  challenge of coordinating, 175
  by information technology, 174–175
External constituencies, 366–367
External environment
  analysis of, 15
  in case analysis, 481
  competitive environment
    components, 56
    effect of digital technologies, 55, 62–67
    five-forces model, 56–67
    using industry analysis, 67–72
  competitive intelligence, 41–45
  crowdsourcing, 43
  environmental forecasting, 45
  environmental scanning, 41
  gathering and integrating information from, 404–406
  general, 15
  general environment
    demographic segment, 49
    economic segment, 52
    global segment, 52–53
    industry analysis, 54
    key trends and events, 48
    political/legal segment, 50–51
    relationship among segments, 53–54
    sociocultural segment, 49
    technological segment, 51–52
  industry, 15
  informational control, 316
  narrow focus of SWOT analysis, 80
  recognizing threats and opportunities, 40
  scenario analysis, 45–46
  strategies
    learning from mistakes, 40
    responsive to, 39
  SWOT analysis, 47
  trend spotting, 52
  and turnaround strategies, 187
External governance control mechanisms
  auditors, 334
  banks, 334
  definition, 332
  market for corporate control, 333–334
  media, 335–336
  public activists, 335–336
  regulatory bodies, 335
  stock analysts, 334
  takeover constraint, 333–334
External knowledge, gathering and integrating, 404–406
External staffing, 431
External view of leadership, 6

f

Factiva, 500
Factor endowments
  definition, 236
  in India, 239–240
  and national competitiveness, 237
Factor prices in transnational strategy, 256
Factors of production for national competitiveness, 237
Failure. learning from, 407
Family business, 275
Family control, 336–337
  in East Asia, 337
  in Latin America, 339
Fast Company, 438

Feasibility analysis, 277
Federal Trade Commission, 85
Feedback loop, 313
Feedback systems, 128–129
Fee-for-service-based models, 117
Film industry, 6, 26
Financial crisis
  causes and effects on industries, 7–8
  errors in forecasting, 45
  impact on luxury goods, 53
  leadership during, 387
  Lehman Brothers collapse, 384–385
  mortgage-backed securities, 5
Financial fraud, 224, 225
  and auditors, 334
  related-party deals, 328
  and Sarbanes-Oxley Act, 335, 336
Financial goals vs. strategic goals, 443
Financial industry, performance bonuses, 17–18
Financial leverage ratios, 102, 470, 490–491
Financial performance
  and balanced scorecard, 105–106
  and ethics, 408
  financial ration analysis, 102–104
  monitoring
    by auditors, 334
    by banks, 334
    by stock analysts, 334
  real options analysis, 444–447
  regulatory requirements, 335
Financial press, 335
Financial ratio analysis; see also Ratio analysis
  and balanced scorecard, 104
  for case analysis, 469–470, 488–494
  changes over time, 101
  common-size balance sheet, 486–487, 488
  common-size income statement, 487–488
  comparison with key competitors, 104
  definition, 101
  historical comparisons, 102
  industry norms comparison, 102–103
  ratios for, 488–494
  standard financial statements, 486
  summary of techniques, 470
  types of ratios, 101, 102
  variation among industries, 103
Financial resources, 92
  angel investors, 279
  bank financing, 279
  cash, 279
  for new ventures, 278–282
  peer-to-peer lending, 279, 281
  personal savings, 279
  and scale of venture, 279
  Small Business Administration loans, 283
  stage of venture development, 279
  venture capital, 279
Financial resources, capital requirements, 57
Financial rewards, 130–131
Financial risk-taking, 455
Financial services industry
  crisis in, 7–8
  E*Trade, 4–5
  mortgage-backed securities, 5
  pressure for short-term performance, 11
Financial statements
  audits of, 334
  for performance evaluation, 486–488
  periodic, 105
  uselessness, 121
Financial strategic objectives, 30

Firm infrastructure
  in differentiation strategy, 166
  in overall cost leadership, 161
Firms; see also Learning from mistakes; Organizational structure; Organizations
  alumni programs, 135
  and balanced scorecard, 105
  best to work for, 127
  changes in Fortune 500, 4
  competitive advantage of resources
    availability of substitutes, 97–98
    inimitability, 95–97
    rarity, 95
    value, 95
  creating competitive advantage, 9
  dynamic capabilities, 147–149
  external environment, 15
  goals and objectives, 15
  going green, 124
  identifying with competitive advantage, 159
  intellectual assets, 15
    codifying knowledge, 144–145
    human capital, 123–133
    in knowledge economy, 120–123
    protecting, 147–149
    social capital, 133–141
    technology for leveraging, 141–144
  internal environment, 15
  levels of strategy, 15
  number of small businesses, 274
  performance evaluation
    balanced scorecard, 104–107
    financial ratio analysis, 101–104
  portfolio management, 211–214
  preventing information transfer, 129–130
  protecting human capital, 123
  regionalization, 258
  resource-based view, 91–101
    competitive advantage, 94–99
    generation and distribution of profits, 99–101
    types of resources, 92–94
  scope of innovation, 432
  strategic group analysis, 70–72
  structural holes, 137
  SWOT analysis, 47
Firm-specific factors of production, 237
Firm-specific knowledge, 237
Firm strategy, structure, and rivalry
  definition, 236
  in India, 239–240
  national competitiveness, 238
First-mover advantage, 182, 452–453
Five-forces model of industry competition, 56–67
  and barriers to entry, 57
  buyer bargaining power, 58–59
  and combination strategies, 175
  criticisms of
    static analysis, 69
    zero-sum game assumption, 68
  and differentiation strategy, 167–168
  effect of digital technologies
    benefits and disadvantages, 67
    on buyer bargaining power, 64
    on intensity of rivalry, 66
    on supplier bargaining power, 64–66
    on threat of new entrants, 62–64
    on threat of substitutes, 66
  and focus strategy, 172
  guidelines for conducting, 69
  illustrated, 57
  intensity of rivalry, 61–62
  and new ventures, 273
  and overall cost leadership, 163–164
  supplier bargaining power, 59–60

threat of new entrants, 56–58
  threat of substitutes, 60–61
Fixed costs, high, 62
Flat-panel television sets, 292
Flexible manufacturing system, 173, 177
Flexible work arrangements, 132
Focused approaches; see Corporate entrepreneurship
Focus strategy
  characteristics, 159
  cost focus, 170–171
  definition, 170
  differentiation focus, 170–171
  effects of digital technologies, 178
  examples, 170–171
  and five-forces model, 172
  market niche focus, 170
  for new ventures, 292–293
  at Paccar, 171
  at Paradise 4 Paws, 293
  potential pitfalls
    erosion of cost advantages, 172
    imitation, 172
    Internet-related, 178–179
    new entrants, 172
    too narrow a focus, 172
Food and Drug Administration, 160, 446
Footwear industry, 368–369
Forbearance, 302
Forbes, 5, 498
Forecasting, 39
Foreign Corrupt Practices Act, 254
Fortune, 5, 43, 53, 121, 125, 127, 197, 218, 335, 399, 438
Fortune 500, 4, 498
Forward integration, 206, 349
  threat by suppliers, 60
Fossil fuels, substitutes for, 61
401-k plans, 50
Franchise agreement, 284
Franchises, number and output of, 275
Franchising
  built on copying, 288
  by Fremantle Media, 204
  for market entry
    benefits, 261
    definition, 261
    risks and limitations, 261
Free riding, 137
Free software, 392
Frontal assaults, 301
Functional benchmarking, 405
Functional division, worldwide, 349
Functional organizational structure
  advantages, 352, 358
  for breakthrough projects, 374
  definition, 351
  departmental isolation, 351
  disadvantages, 352–353, 358
  kinds of businesses with, 351
  options available for, 349
  Parkdale Mills, 352
Funding function of business incubators, 439
Future of Work (Malone), 136

g

Gallup poll, 17
Game theory, 69
General administration
  summary of, 87
  in value-chain analysis, 88–89
General Agreement on Tariffs and Trade, 52
General environment, 15, 39
  components, 15
  definition and characteristics, 47

General environment—*Cont.*
demographic segment, 49
economic segment, 52
effect of digital technologies, 55
global segment, 52–53
impact on industries, 54
key trends and events, 48
political/legal segment, 50–51
relationship among segments, 53–54
sociocultural segment, 49–50
technological segment, 51–52
Generation Y, 127
Geographic area division, 349
Geographic area division structure, 357
Geographic concentration, effect on target markets, 252
Germany, population, 240
Getting from College to Career (Pollack), 124
Glass-Steagall Act repeal, 50
Global competition, effective leadership for, 383
Global economy, 24–25, 234–235
accessing worldwide talent, 234–235
achieving competitive advantage, 248–259
disparities of wealth, 235
and rise of market capitalism, 235
sustainable, 23
Global Entrepreneurship Monitor, 282
Global environment
and costs of terrorism, 53
elements of, 522
industries affected, 54
key trends and events, 48
Globalization
advantages to firms, 52
cross-cultural dialogue, 397
dimensions of distance, 258
dual trends in, 41
effect on organizational structure, 350n
increasing, 257
versus regionalization, 247–259
and rise of market capitalism, 235
trading blocs, 258
Global knowledge sharing network, 142–143
Global marketplace, 16, 233, 357
Global start-ups, 350n, 358–360
Global strategies, 357–358
Global strategy
definition, 251
economies of scale, 251–252
risks and challenges, 252
standard quality, 252
strengths and limitations, 253
weak pressure for adaptation, 251–252
Global vs.. regional strategy, 257–259
Go-green movement, 282
Going green, 124
marketing ploy, 409
Golden parachutes, 225, 334
Good to Great (Collins), 285, 317
Goolsby Leadership Model
courage, 417
impact, 417
integrity, 416–417
Gorillas in the Mist, 26
Government
requests for proposal, 434
as stakeholder, 18
support for new ventures, 283
Government contracts, 283
Government regulation, 335
Great Game of Business (Stack), 402
Greenhouse gases, 52
Green labeling, 451
Greenmail, 225, 334
Gresham's law of planning, 393
Gross domestic product
by family-owned businesses, 275
knowledge-based, 120–121
small business percentage, 274

Groups; *see also* Strategic groups
bridging relationships, 137–139
closure, 137
friendships outside of, 138
inducing decision making, 475–480
informal friendships in, 138
inherent morality of, 478
insular, 138
as social networks, 136–137
Groupthink
as decision-making obstacle, 475–476
and social capital, 140
symptoms and prevention, 478–479
Growth for growth's sake, 223–224
Growth share matrix, 211–213
limitations, 213
Growth stage strategies
repeat purchases, 183
revenue increase, 182–183
sales increase, 182
Guatemala, 235
Guernica (Picasso), 120
Guerrilla offensives, 301
Guide to Financial Statements, 497
Guitar makers, 158–169

h

Harvard Business Review, 12, 23, 123, 167
Harvesting strategy, 185
Headhunters, 126
Hedging strategies, 245
Heroes and drone syndrome, 402
Hierarchical control, 366
Hierarchical relationships, 198–199, 209
Hierarchy of goals, 3, 26, 27
High-tech firms
company-owned venture capital, 198n
Internet information sources on, 404–405
strategic control in, 323
uncontrolled growth, 223–224
visas for foreign professionals, 50–51
Hiring, 123
advice on, 127
for attitude, 125
bozo filter, 125, 323
poor practices, 124
referrals, 126
Hispanic Americans, 131
Holding company structure, 350, 355
Hollywood studios, 6
Home-based businesses, 275
H-1B visas
avoidance of restrictions on, 51
legislation, 50
Hong Kong, 235
Hoover's Handbook of American Business, 498
Horizontal organizational structure, 374
Horizontal relationships, 198–199, 209
Horizontal systems and processes, 374
Hostile takeovers
Oracle and PeopleSoft, 226
reasons for, 225
Housing bubble, 7
Housing prices, 7
How to Read Annual Reports, 497
Human capital
attracting
by going green, 124
hiring for attitude, 125

input control, 125
recruiting approaches and networking, 125–126
training for skill, 125
definition, 122
developing
evaluation systems, 128–129
monitoring, 128
tracking development, 128
transferring knowledge, 126–128
widespread involvement, 126
foundation of intellectual capital, 123–133
interdependent activities, 123–124
for knowledge economy, 397
maximizing, 373–374
for new ventures, 282
protecting, 123
retaining, 129–131
best practices, 127
challenging work environment, 130–131
identifying with mission and values, 130–131
rewards and incentives, 130–131
value creation issues, 146
workforce diversity, 131–132
Human Equation (Pfeffer), 366
Human resource management
and Best Buy, 441
in boundaryless organizations, 374
in differentiation strategy, 166
dysfunctional, 141
for innovation, 433
in overall cost leadership, 161
summary of, 87
in value-chain analysis, 87
Human resources, 92
for global start-ups, 359
Human resources professionals, 125
Hypercompetition (D'Aveni), 385

i

Iconoclast (Berns), 120
IdeaStorm, 436
Identification and coordination activities, 144
If I Did It (Simpson), 22
Illegal behavior, 408
Illusion of control, 447
Imitation
in cost leadership strategy, 165
danger for new entrants, 293
in differentiation strategy, 169
difficult in blue ocean strategy, 290
difficult with blue ocean strategy, 290
easy in differentiation, 169
low-cost, 292
as poor strategy, 288
of products and services, 172
of synergies from mergers, 218
threat to low-cost leaders, 177
of value creation, 165
Imitative new entry
definition, 287
franchising, 288
key to success, 287–288
Impact, 417
Improper conduct, minimizing, 321–323
Inbound logistics, 83
in differentiation strategy, 166
in overall cost leadership, 161
for service organizations, 90
Incentive compensation, 361
Incentive systems
creating effective programs, 319–320
example, 318–319
financial and nonfinancial, 130–131
for managers, 327, 331–332
at Nucor Corporation, 361

potential downsides, 319
promotions, 362
purpose, 318
Income disparities, national, 235
Income statement, 487–488
Incredible Hulk, 6
Incremental innovation, 429
Incremental management, 9
Incremental vs. preemptive launch, 432
India
auto industry in, 72
diamond of national advantage, 239–240
footwear production, 368
outsourcing into, 247
population, 240
research and development in, 247
Individual rationality, 10
Individual vs. organizational ethics, 407–408
Indonesia, 244
Industries
effects of financial crisis, 7–8
effects of nanotechnology, 52
low-profit, 67
market dependence, 302
mature, 292
redefining value chain, 174–175
slow-growth, 62
strategic groups concept, 70–72
wind energy, 13
Industry analysis, 41; *see also* Company information sources; Five-forces model of industry competition
for auto industry, 43
benefits of Internet, 67
caveats on, 67–70
concept of complementors, 69–70
disadvantages of Internet, 67
effect of demographics, 54, 59
environmental forecasting, 45–46
game theory use, 69
guidelines for, 69
information sources, 500
merit of low-profit industries, 67–68
search engines, 501
static analysis, 69
strategic industry groups, 70–72
SWOT analysis, 47
value net, 68–69
zero-sum game assumption, 68
Industry consolidation
for market power, 204–205
from mergers and acquisitions, 217
Industry environment, 15
components, 15
Industry leaders, 453
Industry life cycle
caveat on, 182
decline stage strategies, 184–186
definition, 181
growth stage strategies, 182–183
introduction stage strategies, 182
key functional areas, 181–182
maturity stage strategies, 183–184
significance of, 179–181
stages and factors in, 181
turnaround strategies, 187
Industry norms, comparison with, 102–103
Industry-specific factors of production, 237
Industry Surveys, 500
Industry trends, 71
Inexperience, value of, 26
Infomediaries, 66
Informal friendships, 138
Information
available on Internet, 64
from customers, 405–406
external, 402–404

garden variety services, 405
internal, 402–404
Internet sources, 404–405
network to share, 141–143
private, 139
redistributing, 402–404
Informational control, 16, 315
by Google, Inc., 316
key issues, 315
ongoing process, 315
Information power, 393
Information systems, 89
Information technology, 53
in boundaryless organizations, 374
to extend value chain, 174–175
InformationWeek, 4
Inimitability of resources, 95–97
causal ambiguity, 96
path dependence, 96
physical uniqueness, 96
social complexity, 96–97
Initiative vs. experience, 431
Innovation, 16, 92
at Air Products and Chemicals, 434
and balanced scorecard, 105
at Best Buy, 441
challenges of
capabilities vs. collaboration, 431
experience vs. initiative, 431
incremental vs. preemptive launch, 432
internal vs. external staffing, 431
seeds vs. weeds, 431
collaborating for, 434–435, 436–437
corporate entrepreneurship for, 425
defining scope of, 432
definition, 427
IdeaStorm, 436
leadership for, 389
learning from mistakes, 426–427
managing, 427
managing pace of, 432–433
new rules for fostering
celebrate failures, 437
face time, 437
leadership, 437
long view, 437
no ranks or titles, 437
small teams, 437
questions about effects, 432
real options analysis, 444–447
staffing to capture value, 433–434
at Target Stores, 428
types
disruptive, 429–431
incremental, 429
process, 428
product, 428
radical, 428–429
sustaining, 429
at Whirlpool, 389
Innovation and Entrepreneurship (Drucker), 456
Innovation partners, 434–435
Innovation teams, 434
Innovativeness, 448, 449–450
Innovator's Prescription (Christiansen), 430
Inputs
procurement, 85–86
for related and supporting industries, 237–238
In Search of Excellence (Peters & Waterman), 317
Institutional investors, 331
Insurance business, 180
AIG failure, 314
Intangible resources
definition, 93
kinds of, 92
Integrating skills, 465
Integration, to maximize human capital, 373–374

Integrative thinking
versus conventional thinking, 391
and multiple contingencies, 390
to overcome barriers to change, 393
at Red Hat, Inc., 392
stages of, 390–391
Integrity, 416–417
Integrity-based ethics programs, 410–411
Intellectual assets, 118–150
analysis of, 15
in case analysis, 482
central role of in economy, 120–123
codifying knowledge, 144–145
human capital, 120–133
learning from mistakes, 120
protecting
dynamic capabilities, 147–149
intellectual property rights, 147
social capital, 133–141
technology for leveraging
electronic teams, 143–144
networks, 141–143
Intellectual capital
definition, 121–122
human capital as foundation of, 123–133
Intellectual property, financial losses, 244
Intellectual property rights
litigation over, 146
protecting, 147
Intended strategy, 13
Intensity of rivalry
effect of digital technologies, 66, 67
factors leading to, 61–62
high vs. low conditions, 63
Interactive control system, 316
Interdependence, in related diversification, 363
Interest rates, impact of increases, 52
Interlocking directorships, 329
Internal benchmarking, 403–404
Internal constituencies, 366–367
Internal development
disadvantages, 222
versus mergers and acquisitions, 222
Ritz Carlton Hotels, 223
Internal environment, 78–110
analysis of, 15
in case analysis, 482
comparisons across firms, 79
definition, 82
primary activities, 82, 83–85
support activities, 82, 85–89
environmentally friendly manufacturing, 84
informational control, 316
learning from mistakes, 80
limitations of SWOT analysis, 80–81
performance evaluation
balanced scorecard, 104–107
financial ratio analysis, 101–104
resource-based view of the firm, 79
competitive advantage, 94–99
definition, 92
generation and distribution of profits, 99–101
intangible resources, 92, 93
organizational capabilities, 92, 93–94
tangible resources, 92, 93
SWOT analysis for, 47
and turnaround strategies, 187
value-chain analysis, 79
within and across organizations, 89–90
for service organizations, 90–91
value-creating activities, 80
Internal information
and listening skills, 405
sources, 404

Internal knowledge, accumulating and sharing, 402–404
Internal networkers, 25
Internal vs. external staffing, 431
International Civil Aviation Organization, 404
International Directory of Company Histories, 499
International division, 349
International division structure, 357
International expansion
global start-ups, 358–360
patterns of organizational change, 357
International-level strategy
achieving competitive advantage
adapting to local markets, 248–250
global strategy, 251–253
global vs. regional approach, 257–259
international strategy approach, 250–251
multidomestic strategy, 253–255
reducing costs, 248–250
transnational strategy, 255–257
in case analysis, 483
Caterpillar in China, 264
Country Risk Rankings, 243
dealing with bribery, 254
Deere & Company, 242
disparities of wealth, 235
entry modes
degree of ownership and control, 259
exporting, 260
franchising, 261
joint ventures, 261–262
licensing, 261
strategic alliances, 261–262
wholly owned subsidiaries, 263–264
formulating, 15
global economy overview, 234–235
global value chain dispersion, 246–248
offshoring, 247
outsourcing, 247
Israel, 245
learning from mistakes, 234
and local customs, 246
marketing to the poor, 236
Misiu Systems, 248
motivation for expansion
arbitrage opportunities, 241
attain economies of scale, 240–241
cost reductions, 242–243
extending product life cycle, 241
increase market size, 238–240
optimizing value chain activities, 241–242
performance enhancement, 242
risk reduction, 243
national competitiveness factors
conclusions, 238
demand conditions, 237
diamond of national advantage, 236
factor endowments, 237
firm strategy, structure, and rivalry, 238
for India, 239–240
related and supporting industries, 237–238
piracy threat, 244
potential risks
Country Risk Ratings, 243
currency risks, 244–245
economic risk, 244
management risks, 245–246
political risk, 243–244
rise of globalization, 235
standardization vs. adaptation, 248–250

TV programming, 255
Wal-Mart, 241
International operations
contingencies, 357
geographic area divisions, 357
global start-ups, 358–360
international divisions, 357
and multidomestic strategy, 357
and organizational structure, 357
primary types, 357
worldwide functional structure, 357
worldwide matrix structure, 357
worldwide product division, 357
International strategy approach
basis of, 250
examples, 251
pharmaceutical industry, 250
risks and challenges, 251
International trade
exporting, 260
and globalization, 52
increase in, 234
Internet; *see also* Digital technologies
affiliate model, 116
business models, 116–117
comparison shopping, 179
for competitive intelligence, 43–44
for cost management, 179
and crowdsourcing, 19–21
customer feedback, 115
effect on competitive strategies, 176–179
effects on five-forces model, 62–67
electronic storage, 66
entertainment programming, 115
entrepreneurs, 278–279
evaluation activities, 114
expertise, 115
and external environment, 55
as information source, 64, 404–405
lowering transaction costs, 176
number of users worldwide, 55
peer-to-peer lending, 281
pricing information from, 165
problem-solving activities, 114–115
search activities, 113–114
transaction activities, 115
use by small and medium-sized businesses, 55
value added by, 113–117
Internet Intelligence Index, 499
Interrelationships in value-chain activities, 89–90
Intrapreneuring, 435
Introduction stage strategies
first-mover advantage, 182
late-mover advantage, 182
Inventions, 450
Inventories
inbound logistics, 83
outbound logistics, 84
Inventory turnover, 491
Inventory turnover ratio, 102
Investext Research Reports, 499
Investment
formal, vs. venture capital, 282
transaction-specific, 208–209
Investment banks, 334
Investment decision
and agency theory, 445–446
and corporate governance, 325
embedded option, 445
net present value analysis, 446
real options analysis, 444
Investors Business Daily, 335
Invulnerability illusion, 478
Iron Man, 5, 6
Iron Man 2, 6

Irrational escalation of
commitment, 447
Italian footwear industry, 237–238

j

Japan
factor endowments, 237
keiretsu, 338
lifetime employment, 362
population, 240
Joint ventures
Canadian view, 221
cost reductions, 221
definition, 220
develop new technologies, 221–222
to enter new markets, 220
for market entry
benefits, 261–262
risks and limitations, 262–263
partners for three countries, 262
potential downsides, 222
with related industries, 237
Time Warner, Inc., 220
and virtual organizations, 372
Just-in-time systems, 68
purpose of, 83

k

Keiretsu, 338
Key competitors, comparison of
financial ratios, 104
Key economic indicators, 52
Key employees, 317
Knowledge
central role in economy, 120–123
codified for competitive advantage, 144–145
creation of, 122
explicit, 122, 144
external, 404–406
firm-specific, 237
global sharing network, 142–143
for innovation, 427
intellectual capital, 121–122
internal, 402–404
source of competitive advantage, 235
tacit, 122, 144
technology for leveraging, 141–145
transferring, 126–128
using technology to leverage
electronic teams, 143–144
networks, 141–143
Knowledge economy
definition, 121
human capital, 122
human capital for, 397
intellectual capital, 121–122
social capital, 133
Knowledge management
human capital, 123–133
social capital, 136–140
Knowledge retention, 145
Knowledge transfer, 257
Knowledge workers, 15, 121, 123

l

Labor force, aging of, 49
Labor supply, projected shortage, 49
Late-mover advantage, 182
Lateral learning, 404
Latin America, 235
corporate governance, 339
emerging markets, 325
Leaders
altruistic vs. manipulative, 399–400

ethical orientation, 408
judgmental, 399
personal connections, 399–400
as role models, 411–412
for strategy implementation, 16
types needed by firms, 25
Leadership
cautionary notes, 398–400
at Cisco Systems, 399
definition, 385
dissatisfaction with status quo, 385
doing the right thing, 385
doing things right, 386
effective
integrative thinking, 390–391
overcoming barriers to change, 391–393
use of power, 393–394
emotional intelligence, 394–400
definition, 395
empathy, 397
motivation, 397
self-awareness, 396
self-regulation, 397
sets of capabilities, 394–396
social skill, 397–398
for empowering employees, 401–402
entrepreneurial, 285
and ethics, 408
ethics role, 387, 388–390
external view of, 6
failure of, 6
for global competition, 383
Goolsby Leadership Model, 416–417
in innovation, 389
for innovation projects, 431
interdependent activities, 385–390
nurturing ethical culture, 388–390
organizational design, 388
setting direction, 386–388
learning from mistakes, 384–385
potential drawbacks, 398–400
proactive, 9
process for change, 385
romantic view of, 5–6
for strategic management, 25
in tough times, 387
transformational, 285
vision, 385
Leadership assessment chart, 129
Leadership Challenge (Kouzes & Posner), 401
Leadership teams, 285
Learning
and balanced scorecard, 105
and change, 400
core competencies as, 200
double-loop, 315
experience curve, 160
lateral, 404
from teaching teams, 403
Learning from mistakes
Acquicor, 196
Amp'd Mobile, 272–273
E*Trade, 4–5
Ford Motor Company, 80, 234
Groupe Michelin, 158
Lehman Brothers, 384–385
Motorola, Inc., 40
at Nortel Networks, 426–427
Sierra Club and Clorox, 348
Sprint Nextel, 312
Van Gogh vs. Picasso, 120
Learning organizations
accumulating and sharing internal knowledge, 402–404
best practices, 407
in case analysis, 484

changing status quo, 406–407
creating, 16
definition, 401
developing, 406–407
empowering employees, 401–402
enabling creativity, 406–407
gathering and integrating external information, 404–405
inspiring and motivating, 401
key elements, 401
learning from failure, 407
reflection, 401
support for, 401
teaching teams, 403
Legacy costs, 175
Legal environment, 50–51, 53–54
Legitimate power, 393
Leverage ratios, 490–491
Leveraging core competencies
by mergers and acquisitions, 216
in related diversification, 200–201
Lexis/Nexis Academic, 500
Lexis/Nexis Statistical, 500
Licensing
agreements, 284
for market entry
benefits, 261
definition, 261
risks and limitations, 261
Lifestyles, 40
Lifetime employment, 362
Linux operating system, 19, 392, 430
Liquidity measures, 102, 470
cash ratio, 490
current ratio, 489
quick (acid-test) ratio, 489–490
Listening skills, 405
Litigation, and compliance-based ethics, 410
Local adaptation, 249–250
Local line leaders, 25
Local pressures, 249
Locating Company Information, 497
Locating Industry Information, 497
Location decisions
in global strategy, 252
in international expansion, 242
in transnational strategy, 255–256
Logistics
inbound, 83
outbound, 84
Long-term performance, 11
Long-term solvency measures, 102, 470
cash coverage ratio, 491
debt-equity ratio, 490
equity multiplier, 490
times interest earned ratio, 490–491
total debt ratio, 490
Louvre Museum, 389
Low cost
with differentiation, 290
in global startups, 359
Low-cost leader strategy, Internet-enabled, 176
Low-cost position, 163
advantages, 163
in focus strategy, 172
Low-cost-position, avoiding need for, 167
Low-cost sourcing, Wal-Mart, 20
Luxury goods, impact of recession, 53

m

Machine age, 121
Maintaining strategy, 184–185
Making the Grass Greener on Your Side (Melrose), 401
Malcolm Baldrige National Quality Award, 222, 223

Management
agency theory, 326–327
of global start-ups, 359
incremental, 9
in Latin America, 339
reinvented at Whirlpool, 389
takeover constraint, 333–334
view of stakeholders, 18–21
women in, 49
Management innovations, 9–10
Management restructuring, 210, 211
Management risks, 245–246
Managerial conceit
illusion of control, 447
irrational escalation of commitment, 447
overconfidence, 447
Managerial time, 175–176
Managers
adaptability, 375
antitakeover tactics, 334
and balanced scorecard, 105
bargaining power, 100–101
biases and assumptions, 40
biases of, 175
credibility and ego, 218
in divisional structure, 353–354
of employees, 100
erosion of value creation
antitakeover tactics, 225–226
egotism, 224–225
growth for growth's sake, 223–224
in global marketplace, 357
golden parachutes, 225
informal friendships, 138
local pressures, 249
motivated by reward systems, 360
need for alignment, 375
for new ventures, 282
opportunistic behavior, 333
participation in orientation, 126
participative style, 373–374
pressure to lower costs, 249
rating of, 129
reward and compensation agreements, 327
rewards and incentives for, 331–332
and stakeholders, 10
teleconferencing by, 60
trade-offs by, 11
understanding stakeholders, 386
of virtual organizations, 372
Managing relationships, 396
Manufacturing
environmentally friendly, 84
value-chain analysis, 82–90
Manufacturing alliance, 285
Maquiladoras, 242
Market, created by blue ocean strategy, 290
Market capitalism, 235
Market dependence, 302
Market entry
diversification for
joint ventures, 220–222
strategic alliances, 220–222
for international expansion
beachhead strategy, 260
Caterpillar in China, 264
degree of ownership and control, 259
exporting, 260
franchising, 261
joint ventures, 261–263
licensing, 261
strategic alliances, 261–263
wholly owned subsidiaries, 263–264
pre-emption, 359
as strategic action, 300
Market for corporate control, 333–334

Marketing
  to bottom of the pyramid, 235, 236
  in differentiation strategy, 166
  effect of mass customization, 177
  going green, 409
  illegal and unethical, 85
  increased efforts, 300
  at Monsanto, 84–85
  in overall cost leadership, 161
  summary of, 83
  in value-chain analysis, 84–85
  and workforce diversity, 132
Marketing agreement, 284
Marketing research
  by Google, Inc., 316
  Kraft Foods in China, 86
Market niche, 360
  for new ventures, 292–293
Market niche focus, 170
Market potential evaluation, 277
Market power
  combating differences in, 302
  definition, 203
  failure at 3M Corporation, 205
  at Fremantle Media, 204
  from industry consolidation,
    204–205
  from mergers and acquisitions, 216
  pooled negotiating power, 203–205
  related diversification for, 203–209,
    299
  from vertical integration
    benefits and risks, 206–208
    key issues, 207–208
    transaction cost perspective,
      208–209
Market pruning, 187
Market segments
  entered by mergers, 217
  in focus strategy, 170–171
  in introduction stage, 182
Market share
  loss for hardware stores, 172
  Wal-Mart, 20
Market space, uncontested, 289
Market-to-book ratio, 102, 494
Market-to-book value ratio
  examples, 121–122
Market value, 121n
Market value measures, 470
  market-to-book value, 494
  price-earnings ratio, 493
Market value ratio, 102
Markup-based models, 116, 117
Mass customization, 177, 438
Mass production, 90
*Mastering the Rules of Competitive
  Strategy,* 495
Matrix organizational structure, 350
Matrix structure
  advantages, 357, 358
  definition, 356
  at Dell Inc., 356
  disadvantages, 357, 358
  in multinational corporations, 356
  worldwide, 349
Maturity stage strategies
  breakaway positioning, 183, 184
  exit of competitors, 183
  intense rivalry, 183
  reverse positioning, 183–184
  softening demand, 183
Maven knowledge base, 145
Media, and corporate governance,
  335–336
Men, and social capital, 140
Mentoring, 128
  function of business incubators, 440
Mercosur, 258
Mergent Online, 496, 498, 500
Mergers; *see also* Acquisitions
  antitakeover tactics, 223–224,
    225–226
  blunders, 197
  Cisco Systems, 216

compared to acquisitions, 214–215
definition, 215
and divestments, 218–220
global value 1997–2008, 215, 216
growth for growth's sake, 223–224
hostile takeovers, 225
versus internal development, 222
motives and benefits
  achieving synergies, 216
  entering new market segments,
    216
  expanded product lines, 216
  forcing industry consolidation,
    216
  leveraging core competencies, 215
  market power, 215
  obtaining valuable resources, 216
  sharing activities, 215
potential limitations
  cultural differences, 218
  imitation by competitors, 218
  manager credibility, 218
  takeover premium, 217
Procter & Gamble, 216–217
reasons for increase in, 215
recent, 215
Shaw Industries, 207
Sprint and Nextel, 312
as strategic action, 300
successful, 198–199
Mergers and acquisitions failures, 197
Mexico, *maquiladoras,* 242
Microcredit, 236
Middle class, in China, 238
Middle East violence, 244
Millennials, 124, 127
Mindguards, 478
Mindset, 141
  boundary, 364
Minority report, 406
Minority shareholders, 338
Mission
  employee identification with, 130
  motivating with, 401
Mission statement
  Aircraft Interior Products, 332
  compared to vision, 28
  definition, 28
  effective, 28–29
  examples, 28–29
  and financial performance, 29
  NextJet, 30
  strategic objectives, 29–31
  strategic priorities, 29
Mobile phone market, 40, 43
Mobile virtual network operators, 273
Mobile workplace, 60
Mobility barriers, 71
Modular organizations
  advantages, 368
  in apparel industry, 368–369
  compared to virtual organiza-
    tions, 371
  cross-functional skills, 369
  definition, 367–368
  outsourcing by, 367–368
  preconditions, 368
  pros and cons, 370
  strategic risks in outsourcing,
    368–369
Monitoring, 128
  continuous, 315
Monitoring costs, 208
Mortgage-backed securities, 5, 7
Mortgages, securitization of, 7
Motivation
  with mission or purpose, 401
  and social skill, 398
Multidivisional organizations, 366
Multidivisional structure, 353
Multidomestic strategy
  backfiring adaptation, 254
  cost structure and adaptation, 254
  cultural differences, 253
  dealing with bribery, 254

definition, 253
degree of local adaptation, 254–255
differentiating strategy, 253
in international operations,
  357–358
limitations, 255
packaging decisions, 253
personnel practices, 253
risks and challenges, 254–255
strengths, 255
TV programming, 255
Multilatinas, 339
Multinational companies
  dealing with bribery, 254
  environmental sustainability, 23–24
  exporting for market entry, 260
  international strategy, 250–251
  wholly owned subsidiaries, 263–264
Multiple reward systems, 319

n

Nanotechnology, 51–53
National Aeronautics and Space
  Administration, 186
National competitiveness factors
  conclusions, 238
  demand conditions, 237
  diamond of national advantage,
    235–238, 236
  factor endowments, 237
  firm strategy, structure, and rivalry,
    238
  India, 239
  related and supporting industries,
    237–238
National Design Award, 389
Negotiating costs, 208
NetAdvantage, 500
Net present value analysis, 446
Networking
  function of business incubators, 440
  and recruiting, 125–126
Networks
  brokers, 139
  Pied Piper effect, 134–135
  to share information, 141–143
New Economy, 235
New entrants, 273
  adaptive new entry, 288–289
  blue ocean strategy, 289–290
  competition from, 172
  danger of imitation, 293
  pioneering new entry, 286–287
New product introduction, 300
New venture creation, 435
New venture groups, 439
New venture opportunities, 435
New ventures
  business incubators, 440
  business plan, 468
  close competitors, 294
  competitive dynamics
    choosing not to react, 302–304
    defensive actions, 301
    definition, 294
    Facebook vs. MySpace, 202
    guerrilla offensive, 301
    hardball tactics, 296
    likelihood of competitive
      reaction, 301–302
    motivation and capability to
      respond, 297–300
    new competitive actions,
      294–295
    selective attacks, 301
    strategic actions, 300–301
    tactical actions, 300–301
    threat analysis, 295–297
  contexts for creation of, 273–276
  deciding factors, 435
  decision making, 291
  development costs, 279

eco-entrepreneurs, 280
effective leadership, 285
and entrepreneurial culture,
  440–441
entrepreneurship, 273
entry strategies
  adaptive, 288–290
  blue ocean strategy, 289–290
  decision factors, 286
  imitative, 287–288
  pioneering, 286–287
exit champions, 443–444
feasibility analysis, 277
financial resources, 279–282
and five-forces model, 273
generic strategies
  combination strategies, 293–294
  differentiation strategy, 391
  focus strategy, 292–293
  overall cost leadership, 290–292
government resources, 283
human capital, 282
informal investment vs. venture
  capital, 282
Internet pioneers, 278–279
learning from mistakes, 272–273
low-budget start-ups, 279
market niche for, 292–293
market potential evaluation, 277
Mommy SWAT teams, 283
opportunities for, 271
opportunity discovery, 277
opportunity evaluation, 277
opportunity recognition, 276
product champions, 442
questions for effectiveness, 443
real options analysis, 444–447
risk-return trade-off, 443
risks in, 440
risk-taking, 455–456
small businesses, 274–275
social capital, 282–283
strategic alliances, 284
strategic vs. financial goals, 443
venture capital, 279
viable opportunities, 277
New York State Controller, 385
New York Times, 116, 158
Niche business, 178
  overextended, 179
No-frills products, 163
Noncompete clause, 129–130
Nonfinancial rewards, 130–131
Nonfinancial strategic objectives, 30
Nonprofit organizations, boundaries, 320
North American Free Trade Agreement, 52, 258
North American Industry Classifica-
  tion System, 500

o

Offshoring, 246–248
  definition, 247
  reasons for increase in, 247
Oil embargo of 1973, 46
Oil prices, effect of embargo, 46
Old Guitarist (Picasso), 120
One-Click purchasing technology, 65
100 Best Corporate Citizens, 451
Online bidding, 176
Online brokers, 165
Online comparative shopping, 114
Online invoicing, 180
Online order processing, 176
Online procurement systems, 64–66
Online purchase orders, 176
On the job consumption, 333
Open source model of talent, 130
Open-source operating system, 430
Open source software movement, 301

Open sourcing, 19
Operating control, 353–354
Operational effectiveness, 9–10
Operational efficiency and effectiveness, 321
Operations, 84
  in differentiation strategy, 166
  in functional structure, 349
  in overall cost leadership, 161
  in service organizations, 90
  summary of, 83
Opportunistic managers, 333
Opportunities; see also SWOT analysis
  and changes in external environment, 276
  discovery phase, 277
  evaluation of, 277
  market potential evaluation, 277
  recognizing, 40
  sources of, 276
  viability factors, 277
Opposable Mind (Martin), 390
Options, 444
Option to exit, 447
Oral case presentation preparation, 472
Organizational bases of power, 393
Organizational boundaries, 16
Organizational capabilities
  definition, 93–94
  kinds of, 92
Organizational conflict, 319
Organizational culture
  in boundaryless organizations, 374
  to challenge status quo, 406–407
  and counterproductive behavior, 320
  definition, 317
  effective reward programs, 319–320
  entrepreneurial, 440–441
  evolving from boundaries to, 323–324
  examples, 317
  excellent and ethical, 388–389
  leadership for, 387, 388–390
  and leadership teams, 285
  at Lehman Brothers, 384
  pep talks, 318
  role of, 317–318
  setting boundaries, 317–318
  at Sharp Corporation, 362
  storytelling, 318
  sustaining, 318
  Technical Computer Graphics, 373
  at United Technologies, 365
Organizational design
  in case analysis, 484
  components, 347
  effective, 16
  leadership for, 387, 388
Organizational ethics
  benefits, 408
  in case analysis, 484
  compliance-based programs, 410–411
  definition, 407
  ethical orientation, 408
  ethical values, 408
  examples of failure, 408
  and going-green campaign, 409
  Goolsby Leadership Model, 416–417
  growing interest in, 408
  versus individual ethics, 407–408
  integrity-based programs, 410–411
  management approaches, 410–413
    codes of conduct, 412–413
    corporate credos, 412–413
    role models, 411–412
  policies and procedures, 415
  reward and evaluation systems, 414
  whistleblowing, 415

Organizational flexibility with workforce diversity, 133
Organizational goals
  and objectives, 10, 15, 481
  and reward systems, 324
Organizational learning, 315
Organizational rationality, 10
Organizational resources, 92
Organizational structure
  ambidextrous design, 375–376
  boundaryless designs, 348, 363–374
  components, 347
  effective, 16
  effect of globalization, 350n
  effect of transaction costs, 350n
  global start-ups, 358–360
  horizontal, 374
  influence on strategy formulation, 359–360
  international implications, 357–358
  leadership for, 388
  learning from mistakes, 348
  managerial activities, 349
  modular, 367–370
  traditional forms
    choices available, 349
    divisional, 349, 353–355
    functional, 349
    functional structure, 351–353
    holding company, 355
    matrix, 356–357
    patterns of growth, 349–350
    simple structure, 349, 351
    strategic business units structure, 355
  virtual organization, 370–372
Organizational vision; see Vision
Organizations; see also Corporations; Learning organizations
  core competencies, 200–202
  environmentally aware, 40–42
  environmental sustainability, 22–24
  flatter, 139–140
  heroes and drone syndrome, 402
  hierarchy of goals, 3, 26, 27
  informal friendships in, 138
  key stakeholders, 18
  multidivisional, 366
  multiple reward systems, 319
  redistributing knowledge, 402
  social responsibility, 21–22
  strategy-structure relationships, 349–350
  subcultures in, 319
  triple bottom line, 22–23
  types of leaders needed, 25
  types of risks in, 455–456
Orphan Drug Act of 1983, 250
Outbound logistics, 84
  in differentiation strategy, 166
  in overall cost leadership, 161
  for service organizations, 90
  summary of, 83
Output, and experience curve, 162
Outside consultants, in case analysis, 467
Outside contracting agreement, 284
Outside directors, 329
Outsourcing, 246–248
  advantages for noncore functions, 368
  definition, 247
  to keep costs low, 247–248
  manufacturing sector, 247
  at Mitsiu Systems, 248
  by modular organizations, 367–368
  at Netflix, 248
  reasons for increase in, 247
  in service sector, 247
  strategic risks in, 368–369
  for talent, 369
  and vertical integration, 208

Outward Bound activities, 138
Overall cost leadership
  absolute cost advantage, 162
  basis of, 158
  in combination strategies, 172–176
  competitive parity, 160
  effects of digital technologies, 176
  examples, 160–162
  experience curve, 160, 162, 163
  and five-forces model, 162
  for new ventures, 290–291, 292
  potential pitfalls
    easy imitation, 165
    erosion of cost advantages, 165
    focus on few value-chain activities, 164
    Internet-related, 177
    lack of parity on differentiation, 165
    rivals' share inputs, 165
    summary of, 170
  requirements, 361
  reward and evaluation systems, 361
  at Ryanair, 164
  tactics required, 160
  value-chain activities, 161, 164
  at Vizio, Inc., 292
Overconfidence, 447
Overengineering, 10
Owner-managers
  in functional structure, 351
  in simple organizational structure, 351
Ownership-control separation, 326

P

Parenting advantage, 209–210
Patents, 261
  held by small businesses, 275
Path dependency, 96
Pay for performance, 332
Peer-based control, 366
Peer production, 438
Peer-to-peer lending, 279, 281
Pension Rights Center, 336
Pep talks, 318
Performance bonuses, 17–18
Performance enhancement, by international expansion, 242
Performance evaluation
  balanced scorecard, 104–107
  for breakthrough projects, 375–376
  in business-level strategy
    differentiation strategy, 361–362
    overall cost leadership, 361
  in case analysis, 482
  for corporate governance, 331
  in corporate-level strategy
    related diversification, 362
    unrelated diversification, 362–363
  financial ratio analysis, 101–104, 469–470, 488–494
  removing individual metrics, 89
  self-analysis, 474
Performance materials, 88
Personal bases of power, 394
Personal risk-taking, 456
Personal savings, 279
Personal time constraints, 393
Pharmaceutical industry, 250
  real options analysis, 446
Physical resources, 92
Physical space of business incubators, 439
Physical uniqueness, 96
Piecemeal improvements, 187
Pied Piper effect, 134–135
Pioneering new entry
  definition, 286
  differentiation in, 291

pitfalls, 287
  SkyTower Telecommunications, 287
Piracy risk, 244
Poison pills, 225, 334
Political barriers to change, 393
Political/legal environment, 53–54
  characteristics, 50–51
  industries affected, 54
  key trends and events, 48
Political risk, 243–244
Pollution control, emission permits, 52
Ponzi scheme, 45
Pooled negotiating power, 203–205
Poor, marketing to, 235, 236
Population
  China, 240
  Germany, 240
  India, 240
  United States, 240
  world total, 240
Portable kidney dialysis technology, 430
Portfolio management
  definition, 211
  description and potential benefits, 211–214
  divestments, 218–220
  growth share matrix, 211–213
  key purpose, 211
  limitations, 213–214
  mergers and acquisitions, 215–218
  at Nortel Networks, 426
  and shareholder value, 212–213
Portfolio of businesses, 15
Positioning strategies
  breakaway positioning, 183, 184
  reverse positioning, 183–184
Potential markets, size of, 238–240
Power
  coercive, 393
  definition, 393
  expert, 394
  information, 393
  and leadership, 393–394
  legitimate, 393
  multiple bases of, 395
  organizational bases, 393
  personal bases, 394
  referent, 394
  reward, 393
  in social networks, 139–140
Power relationships, 393
Preannouncements, 454
Preemptive launch, 432
Presidential Green Chemistry Challenge Award, 24
Prestige pricing, undermined by Internet, 177
Price(s)
  and experience curve, 162
  information from Internet, 165
Price cutting, 300
  by auto makers, 302
Price-earnings ratio, 102, 493
Price increases, vulnerability of firms, 165
Price performance, 325
Price-performance trade-offs, 186
Price premium
  for buyers, 168
  in differentiation strategy, 167
  set too high, 169
Primary value-chain activities; see Value-chain analysis
Prime Time Live, 335
Principal-agent conflicts, 336–338
Principal-principal conflicts, 337–338
Principals, 326
Private information, 139
Proactive leadership, 9
Proactiveness, 452–453

Problem identification, 468–469
Problem solving, 133
Problem-solving activities, Internet, 114–115
Process innovation, 428
Process losses, 144
Process research and development agreement, 284
Procurement
    in differentiation strategy, 166
    in overall cost leadership, 161
    in service organizations, 91
    summary of, 87
Product(s); *see also* Industry life cycle
    adaptation or standardization, 248–250
    commoditized, 66
    complements, 69–70
    counterfeiting, 244
    effects of changing lifestyles, 49
    environmentally sensitive, 432
    incremental vs. preemptive launch, 432
    Internet advantages, 114–117
    no-frills, 163
    preannouncements, 454
    stability of demand for, 208
    undifferentiated, 56
Product champions
    compared to exit champions, 443–444
    definition, 442
    and project definition, 442
    and project impetus, 442
    at Sony, 442
    uncertainty and ambiguity, 444
Product development cycles, 41
Product differentiation
    as barrier to entry, 57
    and intensity of rivalry, 66
    lack of, 62
Product division, worldwide, 349
Product enhancements, 300
Product innovation, 428
Production
    capacity changes, 300
    economies of scale, 57
Production costs, and experience curve, 162
Productivity, piecemeal improvements, 187
Product life cycle
    and experience curve, 162
    extended by international expansion, 241
Product line
    auto industry, 72
    discontinuing, 187
    diversification into several, 349–350
    expanded by mergers and acquisitions, 216
Product line extensions, and dilution of brand identity, 169–170
Product-market, excessive diversification, 333
Product markets, price-sensitive segment, 249
Product pruning, 187
Product research and development agreement, 284
Profit
    and buyer bargaining power, 56
    in decline stage, 184
    diverted to top management, 101
    generation and distribution of, 99–101
Profitability measures
    profit margin, 492–493
    return on assets, 493
    return on equity, 493
Profitability ratios, 102, 470
Profit margin, 492–493
Profit margin ratio, 102

Profit pool
    auto industry, 174, 208
    and competitive advantage, 173–174
    definition, 173
    miscalculating sources of, 175
Project definition at Sony, 442
Project impetus at Sony, 442
Promotion incentive, 362
Public activists, and corporate governance, 335–336
Public Register's Online Annual Report Service, 496
Public Service Commissions, 409
Purchaser/supplier agreement, 284

q

Quality standardization, 252
Question marks, 212
Quick ratio, 102, 489–490

r

Radical innovation
    nature of, 428–429
    time-consuming mistakes, 434
    timeline, 432–433
Rarity of resources, 95
Ratio analysis; *see also* Financial ratio analysis
    asset management measures, 491–492
    categories of ratios, 488
    liquidity measures, 489–490
    long-term solvency measures, 490–491
    market value measures, 493–494
    problems with, 488
    profitability measures, 492–493
    summary of, 494
Rationality
    individual vs. organizational, 319
    organizational vs. individual, 10
Real estate option, 444
Real estate prices, 7
Realized strategy, 13
Real options analysis
    application to strategic decisions, 444–445
    definition, 444
    existence of options, 444
    at Johnson Controls, 445
    in pharmaceutical industry, 446
    potential pitfalls
        agency theory and back-solver dilemma, 445–446
        managerial conceit, 448
    valuation techniques, 444
Receivables turnover, 102, 491–492
Recession
    impact on luxury goods, 53
    in United States after 2007, 7–8
Recommenders, 168
Recruitment
    attracting human capital, 125–126
    GreenCareers, 124
    at JetBlue Airways, 88
Recycled products, 282
Reengineering the Corporation (Hammer & Champy), 374
Reference USA, 496
Referent power, 394
Referral-based models, 116, 117
Referrals, 126
Reflection, 400
Regional companies, 258–259
Regional economic integration, 259
Regionalization, 258–259
Regional trading blocs, 258
Regulatory bodies, 335
Reintermediation, 65–66

Related and supporting industries
    definition, 236
    in India, 239–240
    and national competitiveness, 237–238
Related diversification
    definition, 199
    economies of scope, 199–203
    by Fremantle Media, 204
    horizontal relationships, 198–199
    leading to divisional structure, 349
    leveraging core competencies, 200–202
    market power from, 203–209, 199
    need for interdependence, 363
    pooled negotiating power, 203–205
    by Procter & Gamble, 198
    revenue enhancement, 202–203
    reward and evaluation systems, 362
    selecting candidates for, 320
    sharing activities, 201–203
        cost savings, 202
        differentiation, 202–203
        revenue enhancement, 202–203
    by Toyota, 201
    vertical integration
        benefits and risks, 206–208
        key issues, 207–208
        at Shaw Industries, 207
        transaction cost perspective, 208–209
Related-party deals, 328
Related transactions, 338
Renewable energy sources, 60–61
Rents, 99–100
Repeat purchases, 183
Replacement cost of employees, 100
Reputation, 92
    of competitors, 302
    corporate, 94
    erosion of, 224
Requests for proposal, 434
Research and development, 180
    expenditures, 450
    in India, 247
Researching Companies Online (Flanagan), 497
Resolution, 391
Resource acquisition, and workforce diversity, 132
Resource allocation rules, 213, 214
Resource-based view of the firm
    competitive advantage
        attributes needed, 95
        availability of substitutes, 97–98
        erosion at Dell, 98–99
        of resources, 95–97
        summary of, 98
    perspectives on, 91–93
    and social capital, 134
    types of resources, 92
        external analysis, 91
        generation and distribution of profits, 99–101
        intangible, 92, 93
        internal analysis, 91
        organizational capabilities, 93–94
        tangible, 92, 93
Resources
    competitive advantage from
        attributes needed, 94–99
        availability of substitutes, 97–98
        of competitors, 302
        inimitable, 95–97
        obtained by mergers and acquisitions, 216
        rarity, 95
        types of, 92–94
        value of, 95
Restatement of earnings, 334
Restaurant industry, effects of financial crisis, 8

Restructuring
    asset, 210, 211
    capital, 210, 211
    definition, 210
    Hanson plc, 21
    Loews Corporation, 210
    management, 210, 211
    management insight, 210
Results-only work environment, 441
Retail alliance, 285
Retailers/Retailing
    customer service, 85
    effects of financial crisis, 8
    market share losses, 172
    recommenders, 168
    value-chain activities, 91
    Wal-Mart, 20
Retaining human capital, 129–131
Retaliation
    resources for, 299
    threat to new ventures, 292
Return on assets, 493
Return on assets ratio, 102
Return on book assets, 493
Return on book equity, 493
Return on capital employed, 325
Return on equity, 493
Return on equity ratio, 102
Return on investment, 443
Return on sales, 102, 103
Revenue
    of Fremantle Media, 204
    in growth stage, 182–183
    miscalculating sources of, 175
Revenue enhancement
    at Fremantle Media, 204
    from sharing activities, 202
Reverse positioning, 183–184
    example, 185
Reward and compensation agreements, 327
Reward and evaluation systems
    in business-level strategy
        differentiation strategy, 361–362
        overall cost leadership, 361
    in corporate-level strategy
        related diversification, 362
        unrelated diversification, 362–363
    and organizational ethics, 414
Reward power, 393
Rewards, financial and nonfinancial, 130–131
Reward systems
    aligned for all employees, 332
    and business unit results, 319
    creating effective programs, 319–320
    definition, 318
    evolving to culture, 323–324
    example, 318–319
    and focus on growth, 319
    for managers, 331–332
    for motivating managers, 360
    multiple, 319
    and organizational goals, 324
    and performance, 323
    potential downsides, 319
    purpose, 323
Risk reduction
    goal of diversification, 214
    in international expansion, 243
Risk-return trade-off, 443
Risks
    of business incubators, 440
    in international expansion
        Country Risk Rankings, 243
        currency risks, 244–245
        economic risk, 244
        management risks, 245–246
        piracy, 244
        political risk, 243–244
    international-level strategy
        global strategy, 252
        international strategy, 251
        multidomestic strategy, 254–255
        transnational strategy, 256–258

Risks—*Cont.*
  international-level strategy—*Cont.*
    market entry modes
      exporting, 260
      franchising, 261
      joint ventures, 262–263
      licensing, 261
      of strategic alliances, 262–263
      wholly owned subsidiaries, 263
    organizational types, 455–456
    of vertical integration, 206–207
Risk-sharing problem, 327
Risk-taking, 402, 448, 455–456
Rivalry
  effect of digital technologies, 66, 67
  factors leading to, 61–62
  international, 238
Robots, 66
Role models, 411–412
Role playing, in case analysis, 466–467
Romantic view of leadership, 5–6
Rotary Four-Way Test, 416
Rule-based controls, 321
Russia, devaluation of ruble, 245

S

Sales
  decline in auto industry, 7–8, 72
  in decline stage, 184
  in differentiation strategy, 166
  in growth stage, 182
  illegal and unethical, 85
  at Monsanto, 84–85
  in overall cost leadership, 161
  summary of, 83
  in value-chain analysis, 84–85
Salience, 390
Sarbanes-Oxley Act, 50
  backlash against, 336
  and crony capitalism, 328
  protecting whistleblowers, 415
  provisions, 335
  and unethical behavior, 323
Scenario analysis
  definition and purpose, 45–46
  at Shell Oil, 46
Scent of a Mystery, 287
Search activities, Internet, 113–114
Search costs, 208
Search engines, 501
  Google, 114
Secret Language of Competitive Intelligence (Fuld), 495
Securities and Exchange Commission
  filings, 497–498
  penalties for banks, 334
  suit against KPMG, 334
Securities industry fraud, 50
Securitization, 7
Seeds vs. weeds, 431
Selective attacks, 301
Selective demand, 182
Self-censorship, 478
Self-management skills, 396
Self-Portrait (Van Gogh), 120
Sellers, perception of differentiation, 170
Sell-offs, 219n
Service; *see also* Customer service
  adaptation or standardization, 248–250
  at Cookshack, 87
  in differentiation strategy, 166
  Internet advantages, 114–117
  in overall cost leadership, 161
  of third parties, 58–59
  in value-chain analysis, 83, 85
Service-based view of the firm, 79
Service enhancements, 300
Service organizations, value-chain analysis, 90–91

Service sector, outsourcing in, 247–248
Shareholder activism, 327, 330–331
Shareholder rights, 326, 330
  and CalPERS, 331
  in Latin America, 339
  power of, 330–331
Shareholders
  and boards of directors, 16–17, 327–330
  and diversification, 198
  expropriation of, 338
  institutional investors, 331
  and market for corporate control, 333
Shareholder value, 18, 332
  and diversification, 327
  in portfolio management, 212–213
Sharing activities
  cost savings from, 202
  definition, 201
  differentiation from, 202–203
  from mergers and acquisitions, 216
  negative effects on differentiation, 203
  revenue enhancement, 202–203
Shawshank Redemption, 312
Shirking, 333
Shopping robots, 66
Short-term objectives, 320–321
Short-term performance, 11
Short-term solvency measures, 490
Short-term solvency ratios, 102, 470
Signaling, by preannouncements, 454
Silos, 352
Simple organizational structure
  advantages, 351
  definition, 351
  disadvantages, 351
  options for, 349
Singapore, 235
Six Sigma quality control, 433
Skill levels
  in barrier-free organizations, 365
  in modular organizations, 368–369
Skills, 92
  cross-functional, 369
Skill sets, 139
Small and medium-sized businesses; *see* Small businesses
Small Business Administration loan guarantee programs, 283
Small Business Development Centers, 283
Small businesses
  aided by Internet, 178
  alliances and long-term agreements, 284
  burden of Sarbanes-Oxley Act, 336
  contribution to economy, 274–275
  exporting by, 274
  family businesses, 275
  focus strategy, 292–293
  franchises, 275
  government contracts, 283
  home-based, 275
  job creation by, 274
  from microcredit, 236
  number of, 274
  number of employees, 274
  patents of, 275
  percentage of GDP, 274
  recycling initiatives, 282
  reliance on Internet, 55
  statistics on types of, 274
  tactical actions by, 302
Small Office/Home Office, 275
Smell-O-Vision, 287
Social capital
  alumni programs, 135
  to attract and retain talent, 133–135
  bridging relationships, 137–139
  closure relationships, 137
  definition, 122

  development of, 133
  electronic teams, 143–144
  emigration to start-ups, 135
  men vs. women, 140
  for new ventures, 282–283
  Pied Piper effect, 34–135
  potential downsides
    costs of socialization, 141
    groupthink, 140
    mindsets, 141
    pursuit of self-interest, 141
  relation to human capital, 133–134
  social networks, 136–140, 141–143
  summary of, 146
  value creation issues, 146
Social complexity, 96–97
Socialization process, 141
Social network analysis
  bridging relationships, 137–139
  career implications
    access to skill sets, 139
    power, 139–140
    private information, 139
  closure relationships, 137
  communication patterns, 136
  and competitive environment, 138–139
  definition and purpose, 136
  informal friendships, 138
  key ideas, 136–137
  and strategy of firms, 139
  structural holes, 137
Social networking, 93, 94
  for collaboration, 436–437
    Dell Inc., 436
    General Electric, 436
    Starbucks, 436
Social pressure, 137
Social responsibility, 451; *see also* Corporate social responsibility
  definition, 21
  and stakeholder management, 21–22
Social skill, 397–398
Sociocultural environment
  composition of, 49
  industries affected, 54
  key trends and events, 48
Software, free, 392
Software piracy, 147
South Korea, 235
  chaebols, 338
Speculating skills, 465
Spin-offs, 219n
Split-ups, 219n
Staffing
  at Air Products and Chemicals, 434
  to capture value from innovation, 433–434
  internal vs. external, 431
Stakeholder management, 3
  alternative perspectives
    crowdsourcing, 19–21
    zero-sum vs. symbiosis, 18–19
  and corporate governance, 16–24
  and environmental sustainability, 22–24
  at Intuit, 21
  social responsibility, 21–22
  and triple bottom line, 22–23
  at Wal-Mart, 20
Stakeholders
  and balanced scorecard, 106
  benefits of antitakeover measures, 226
  in decision making, 10
  definition, 18
  impact of vertical integration, 208
  key, 18
  manager understanding of, 386
Stakeholder symbiosis, 3, 19
Standard & Poor's Index, 331, 332
Standard financial statements, 486
Standardization

  versus adaptation, 248–251
  in global strategy, 251
Starry Night (Van Gogh), 120
Stars, 212
Start-ups; *see also* New ventures
  financing of, 279–282
  global, 358–360
  low-budget, 279
  in mature industries, 292
  migration of talent to, 135
  Mommy SWAT teams, 283
Star Wars, 438
State antitakeover laws, 226
Static analysis, 69
Status quo
  challenging, 406–407
  dissatisfaction with, 385
  questioning, 400
  vested interest in, 392
Stock, undervalued, 225
Stock analysts, 140
  and corporate governance, 334
Stock market indexes, 52
Stock options, 332, 444
Stock price, and mergers and acquisitions, 217, 218
Storage costs, high, 62
Storytelling, 318
Stove pipes, 352
Strategic actions
  definition, 301
  types, 300
Strategic alliances, 16
  alliance-management knowledge, 263
  for cost reductions, 221
  definition, 220
  to develop new technologies, 221–222
  to enter new markets, 220
  Kraft Foods, 221
  for market entry
    benefits, 261–262
    risks and limitations, 262–263
  for new ventures
    manufacturing, 284
    pitfalls, 284
    retail, 284
    technology, 284
  potential downsides, 222
  STMicroelectronics, 221–222
  triangulation approach, 373
  virtual organizations, 370–372
Strategic analyses, 469–470
Strategic business units
  categories of, 212–213
  limitation of portfolio models, 212–213
Strategic business unit structure, 350, 355
Strategic control, 311–324; *see also* Corporate governance
  behavioral control, 316–324
  in bureaucratic organizations, 323
  in case analysis, 483–484
  central aspects of, 312
  contemporary approaches, 314–315
  definition, 312
  failure at AIG, 314
  hierarchical, 366
  in holding company structure, 355
  informational control, 313–316
  interactive system, 316
  learning from mistakes, 312
  peer-based, 366
  rule-based, 321
  separate from operating control, 353–354
  for strategy implementation, 311
  traditional approaches, 313–314
Strategic decision making
  in case analysis, 466
  embedded option, 445
  real options analysis, 444–445

Strategic direction, coherence in, 25–31
  hierarchy of goals, 26, 27
  mission statement, 28–29
  strategic objectives, 29–31
  vision, 26–28
Strategic envelope, 432
Strategic goals, 9
  versus financial goals, 443
Strategic groups, 39
  as analytical tool, 70–71
  auto industry, 71–72
  charting future directions, 71
  definition, 70
  financial and competitive position, 104
  greater rivalry within, 70
  identifying competitive position, 71
  identifying mobility barriers, 71
  implications of industry trends, 71
Strategic management
  ambidexterity concept, 11
  career implications, 31
  coherence in direction
    hierarchy of goals, 26, 27
    mission statement, 28–29
    strategic objectives, 29–31
    vision, 26–28
  components, 3
  concepts, 10
  definition and functions, 9–10
  essence of, 9
  external view of leadership, 6
  during financial crisis, 7–8
  in global economy, 24–25
  key attributes, 3
    effectiveness-efficiency trade-off, 12
    goals and objectives, 13
    short- vs. long-term perspective, 11
    stakeholders and decision making, 13
  leadership for, 25
  learning from mistakes, 4–5
  management role, 24–25
  romantic view of leadership, 5–6
  skills required for, 464–465
  throughout organizations, 24–25
Strategic management cases; see Case analysis
Strategic management process, 3, 12–16
  intended vs. realized strategies, 13
  strategy analysis, 13–15
    external environment, 15
    goals and objectives, 15
    intellectual assets, 15
    internal environment, 15
  strategy formulation
    business-level, 15
    competitive dynamics, 15
    corporate-level, 15
    entrepreneurial, 15
    international, 15
  strategy implementation
    control and corporate governance, 16
    effective organizational design, 16
    fostering entrepreneurship, 16
    learning and ethical organization, 16
Strategic objectives, 3
  consistency in implementation, 31
  criteria for, 29
  definition, 29
  financial, 30
  and mission statements, 29–31
  nonfinancial, 30
  of virtual organizations, 372
Strategic plan, 373
Strategic planning at Shell Oil, 46
Strategic priorities, 320

Strategic vision, 386
Strategies/Strategy
  charting future directions, 71
  definition, 9
  deliberate, 13
  easily imitated, 165
  emergent, 13
  global, 357–358
  global vs. regional, 257–259
  intended vs. realized, 13
  limitations of SWOT analysis, 81
  and mix of resources, 95
  versus new realities, 40
  responsive to external environment, 39
  unrealized, 13
  value of inexperience, 26
Strategy analysis
  as advance work, 13–15
  external environment, 15
  intellectual assets, 15
  internal environment, 15
  organizational goals and objectives, 15
Strategy formulation
  business-level strategy, 15
  competitive dynamics, 15
  corporate-level strategy, 15
  entrepreneurial strategy, 15
  with flexibility, 313
  influenced by organizational structure, 359–360
  international strategy, 15
  and strategic control, 313
Strategy implementation
  control and corporate governance, 16
  corporate entrepreneurship, 16
  effective organizational design, 16
  ethical organization, 16
  learning organization, 16
  problems, 388
  strategic control for, 311
Strategy-structure relationships, 349–350, 359–360
Strengths; see also SWOT analysis
  not leading to advantage, 80
Structural holes, 137
Structure of Corporation Law (Eisenberg), 326
Stuck-in-the-middle, 159–160, 175
Subcultures, 319
Subprime mortgage crisis, 7–8
Subscription-based models, 116–117
Subsidiaries
  data information sources, 495–496
  of Hanson PLC, 362–363
  parenting advantage, 209–210
  pooled negotiating power, 203–205
  and restructuring, 210–211
  wholly owned, 263–264
Substitutability, 97
Substitutes
  identifying, 60
  lacking for core competencies, 200–201
  lacking for resources, 97–98
  low-cost, 66
  and low-cost position, 163
  threat of
    conditions for, 60
    effect of digital technologies, 66, 67
    for fossil fuels, 61
    high vs. low conditions, 63
Supplier power
  and overall cost leadership, 163
  reduced by differentiation, 167–168
Suppliers
  bargaining power
    conditions for, 59–60
    Delta Pride Catfish, 60
    effect of digital technologies, 64–66
    high vs. low conditions, 63

  beneficial relationships with, 68
  business-to-business, 64–65
  complementors, 69–70
  effects of vertical integration, 206–208
  Ford's relationships with, 80
  formal review of, 85–86
  for General Motors, 68
  holding manufacturers hostage, 369
  and low-cost position, 163
  to modular organizations, 368
  and pooled negotiating power, 203–205
  as stakeholders, 18
Supply chain, energy-efficient, 90
Supply-chain intermediaries, 65
Support value chain activities; see Value-chain analysis
Sustainable competitive advantage, 385
  achieving, 9–10
Sustainable global economy, 23
Sustaining innovation, 429
Swaps, 314
Switching costs
  as barrier to entry, 57
  of buyers, 56
  and intensity of rivalry, 66
  lack of, 62
SWOT analysis, 39, 95
  and competitive aggressiveness, 453
  definition and functions, 47
  limitations, 80–81
  versus resource-based view of the firm, 91
Symbiosis among stakeholders, 3, 19
Symbiosis view of stakeholder management, 18–19
Synergy, 15
  Canadian view, 221
  from corporate parenting, 209–210
  from diversification, 198
  imitation by competitors, 218
  from mergers and acquisitions, 216
  from restructuring, 210–211
  from sharing activities, 201–202
  in strategic alliances, 222
  in strategic business unit structure, 355
  at Toyota, 200, 201
Systemic barriers to change, 392

T

Tacit knowledge, 122, 144
Tactical actions
  definition, 301
  by small businesses, 302
  types, 300
Taiwan, 235
Takeover constraint, 333–334
Takeover premium, 217
Talent
  attracted and retained by social capital, 134–135
  emigration to start-ups, 135
  open source model, 130
  outsourcing for, 369
  retaining, 397
Tangible resources
  definition, 93
  kinds of, 92
Target markets
  isolated in global strategy, 252
  misreading, 178
Teaching teams, 403
Team of Rivals (Goodwin), 476
Teams
  autonomous, 449
  autonomous work groups, 439

  in barrier-free organizations, 366
  for case analysis, 477–478
  cross-functional, 374, 375
  good vs. mediocre, 366
  for innovation, 434
  for teaching, 403
  unsupported, 375
  varying styles of, 477
  at Whole Foods Markets, 404
Technological change, and decline stage, 186
Technological environment
  challenges in, 55
  digital technologies, 55, 62–67
  industries affected, 54
  Internet, 55
  key trends and events, 48
  nanotechnology, 51–52
  number of Internet users, 55
  recent innovations, 51–52
Technological resources, 92
Technology
  downsides to, 52
  last-gasp, 186
  to leverage human capital, 141–147
    codifying knowledge, 141–146
    electronic teams, 143–144
    networks, 141–143
  source of new ideas, 427
  for training, 125
  value creation issues, 146
  value engineering, 162
Technology alliance, 285
Technology development
  in differentiation strategy, 166
  in overall cost leadership, 161
  summary of, 87
Telecommunications industry, 426–427
Teleconferencing, 60
Television programming, 204
  international, 255
Tender offer, 225
Ten Steps to Industry Intelligence, 497
Terrorism, costs of, 53
Terrorist attack of 2001, 22
Thailand, currency devaluation, 245
Theory of the business, 40
Theory Z (Ouchi), 317
Third-party services, 58–59
Thor, 6
Threat of new entrants
  and barriers to entry, 57
  conditions for, 56–58
  effect of digital technologies, 62–74
  high vs. low conditions, 63
  to new ventures, 273
Threat of substitutes
  conditions for, 60
  effect of digital technologies, 66, 67
  for fossil fuels, 61
  high vs. low conditions, 63
Threats; see also SWOT analysis
  recognizing, 40
360-degree leadership assessment, 128–129
Time constraints, 393
Timeline for innovation, 432–433
Time pacing, 433
Times interest earned ratio, 102, 490–491
Time to market, 41
Tire industry, 158
Top-down empowerment, 402
Top-level executives; see also CEO *entries;* Managers
  compensation for, 100–101
  erosion of value creation, 223–226
  during financial crisis, 387
  illegal behavior, 408

Top-level executives—*Cont.*
and organizational success, 89
and restructuring, 210, 211
risk preferences, 327
and Sarbanes-Oxley Act, 335
Total asset turnover, 102
Total-debt ratio, 102, 490
Total performance indicators,
105–106
Trademarks, 261
Trade-offs by managers, 11
Trading blocs, 258
Traditional strategic control
critique of, 313
failure of, 313–314
sequence, 313
Training
computerized, 93
mentoring, 128
monitoring, 128
as obligation to employees, 126
and reward systems, 323
for skill, 125
with teaching teams, 403
Transaction cost perspective,
208–209
Transaction costs
effect on organizational structure,
350n
lowered, 176
types of, 208–209
Transactions, Internet, 115
Transaction-specific investments,
208–209
Transformational leadership, 285
Transnational strategy
adaptation for competitive situations, 256
adaptation in, 255–256
at Asea Brown Boveri, 256
factor prices and quality, 256–257
integration of worldwide operations, 256
knowledge transfer, 257
limitations, 257
location decisions, 255–256
at Nestlé, 256
purpose, 255
risks and challenges, 256–257
strengths, 257
value-chain activities, 256
Trends, monitoring, 41–42
Tribal loyalty, 130
Triple bottom line, 22–23
Truck makers, 171
Trust, 402
in strategic alliances, 262
Turnaround strategies
asset and cost surgery, 187
definition, 187
at Intuit, 187
piecemeal improvements, 187
product and market pruning, 187
Turnaround strategy, 4–5
Turnover measures, 102, 470,
491–492

U

Unanimity illusion, 478
Unethical business practices, 408
Unethical conduct, minimizing,
321–323
Uniqueness, not valuable, 158–169
Unit costs, lower, 249
United States
aging labor force, 49
contribution of small businesses
to, 274–275

intellectual assets, 120–121
New Economy, 235
number of Baby Boomers, 50
population, 240
projected labor shortage, 49
recession after 2007, 7–8
United States Bankruptcy Court, 385
University research, 434–435
UNIX software, 19, 392
Unrealized strategy, 13
Unrelated diversification
benefits for vertical relationships,
209
corporate parenting, 209–210
definition, 209
hierarchical relationships, 198–199
holding company structure, 355
portfolio management, 211–214
restructuring, 210–211
reward and evaluation systems,
362–363
and risk reduction, 214
Unsupported teams, 375
Upstream value-chain activities,
256
Utility companies, 409

V

Value
captured from innovation, 433–434
definition, 82
of mergers and acquisitions, 215,
216
of resources, 95
Value added
by digital technologies, 113–117
in service organizations, 90–91
Value chain, 15
applied to service organizations,
90–91
and arbitrage, 241
components, 82
context, 82
extended by information technology, 174–175
global dispersion
offshoring, 246–248
outsourcing, 246–248
integration at multiple points, 167
redefining, 174–175
Value-chain activities
challenge of coordinating, 175
downstream, 175, 208, 256
in engineering, 91
in harvesting strategy, 185
interrelationships in, 89–90
in modular organizations, 368
optimizing location of, 241–242
primary, 82, 83–85
in differentiation strategy, 166
in overall cost leadership, 161
in retailing, 91
source of competitive advantage,
440
support, 82, 85–89
in differentiation strategy, 166
in overall cost leadership, 161
too narrow a focus on, 164
in transnational strategy, 256
upstream, 256
and vertical integration, 208
Value-chain analysis, 79
in case analysis, 482
definition, 82
interrelationships, 89–90
primary activities
definition, 82
factors to consider, 83

inbound logistics, 83
marketing and sales, 84–85
operations, 84
outbound logistics, 84
service, 85
summary, 83
for service organizations, 90–91
support activities
definition, 82
factors to consider, 87
general administration, 88–89
human resource management,
88
procurement, 85–86
summary, 87
technology development, 88
Value/cost trade-off, breaking, 290
Value-creating activities, 80, 93
Value creation, 15, 82
from core competencies, 200
by diversification, 198
easily imitated, 165
eroded by managers
antitakeover tactics, 225–226
egotism, 224–225
growth for growth's sake, 223–224
by human capital, 146
by new ventures, 276
by sharing activities, 201–203
by social capital, 146
by technology, 146
Value destruction, 196
Value engineering, 162
Value net, 68–69
Value of the firm, enhanced by business groups, 338
Values
in boundaryless organizations, 374
employee identification with, 130
of ethical organizations, 408
of society, 40
Venture capital, 279
amount of funding, 280
company-owned aims, 198n
versus formal investment, 282
Venture capitalists, and global
start-ups, 359
Vertical integration, 349
and administrative costs, 209
benefits, 206–207
bypassing, 350n
definition, 206
effects on suppliers/distribution,
206–208
key issues, 207–208
risks, 206–207
at Shaw Industries, 206, 207
transaction cost perspective,
208–209
Vertical relationships, 209
Vested interest in status quo, 392
Video game industry, 369
Nintendo, 69
Virtual organizations
in biotechnology, 371
challenges and risks, 371–372
compared to modular
organization, 371
definition, 370
impermanence, 370–371
Lockheed Martin, 370
pros and cons, 372
Vision
anchored in reality, 28
created in a vacuum, 28
definition, 26
development of, 26–27
of entrepreneurs, 285
examples, 27
functions, 27
grandiose, 28

holy grail of management, 28
idealistic, 27
implementation problems, 388
irrelevance, 28
and lack of confidence, 27
of leadership, 385
sloganeering campaign, 27
Vision statements, 27–28
Voice Over Internet Protocol, 64

W

Wall Street Journal, 43, 134, 218,
335, 500
*Ward's Business Directory of Private
and Public Companies,* 496
*Ward's Business Directory of U.S.
Private and Public Companies,*
498
Weaknesses; *see also* SWOT analysis
Weak teams, 316
Wealth disparities worldwide, 235
Web of Inclusion (Helgesen), 25
Whistleblowing, 415
Wholly owned subsidiaries
benefits, 263
Caterpillar in China, 264
definition, 263
risks and limitations, 263
Wikipedia, 21
Wind energy industry, 13
Window manufacturing, 173
Windows, 19
Wired magazine, 19
Wireless communication systems,
287
Wireless technologies, 64
Wisdom of Teams (Katzenbach &
Smith), 403
Wisdom of Teams (Smith), 373
Women
educational attainments, 49
in management, 49
and social capital, 140
Workforce diversity
benefits of, 132–133
demographics of, 131–132
at MTV Networks, 134
Workplace
healthy, 398
mobile, 60
stimulating, 130, 131
World Customs Organization, 244
World Health Organization, 244
World population total, 240
World Trade Organization, on
outsourcing, 246–247
Worldwide functional division, 349
Worldwide functional structure, 357
Worldwide matrix division, 349
Worldwide matrix structure, 357
Worldwide product division, 349, 357
Written case analysis, 475

Y

Yahoo Finance, 499

Z

Zero-sum game assumption, 68
Zero-sum game sense, 354
Zero-sum view of stakeholder
management, 18–19